HANDBOOK OF ECONOMIC GROWTH
VOLUME 1B

HANDBOOKS
IN
ECONOMICS

22

Series Editors

KENNETH J. ARROW
MICHAEL D. INTRILIGATOR

ELSEVIER
NORTH-HOLLAND

AMSTERDAM · BOSTON · HEIDELBERG · LONDON · NEW YORK · OXFORD
PARIS · SAN DIEGO · SAN FRANCISCO · SINGAPORE · SYDNEY · TOKYO

HANDBOOK OF ECONOMIC GROWTH

VOLUME 1B

Edited by

PHILIPPE AGHION
Harvard University

and

STEVEN N. DURLAUF
University of Wisconsin at Madison

ELSEVIER
NORTH-HOLLAND

2005

AMSTERDAM · BOSTON · HEIDELBERG · LONDON · NEW YORK · OXFORD
PARIS · SAN DIEGO · SAN FRANCISCO · SINGAPORE · SYDNEY · TOKYO

ELSEVIER B.V.	ELSEVIER Inc.	ELSEVIER Ltd	ELSEVIER Ltd
Radarweg 29	525 B Street, Suite 1900	The Boulevard	84 Theobalds Road
P.O. Box 211	San Diego	Langford Lane, Kidlington	London
1000 AE Amsterdam	CA 92101-4495	Oxford OX5 1GB	WC1X 8RR
The Netherlands	USA	UK	UK

First edition 2005

Library of Congress Cataloging in Publication Data
A catalog record is available from the Library of Congress.

British Library Cataloguing in Publication Data
A catalogue record is available from the British Library.

ISBN-10: 0-444-50837-6 (set, comprising vols. 1A & 1B)
ISBN-13: 978-0-444-50837-9

ISBN-10: 0-444-52041-4 (vol. 1A)
ISBN-13: 978-0-444-52041-8

ISBN-10: 0-444-52043-0 (vol. 1B)
ISBN-13: 978-0-444-52043-2

ISSN: 0169-7218 (Handbooks in Economics series)
ISSN: 1574-0684 (Handbooks of Economic Growth series)

∞ The paper used in this publication meets the requirements of ANSI/NISO Z39.48-1992 (Permanence of Paper).

Printed in The Netherlands.

INTRODUCTION TO THE SERIES

The aim of the *Handbooks in Economics* series is to produce Handbooks for various branches of economics, each of which is a definitive source, reference, and teaching supplement for use by professional researchers and advanced graduate students. Each Handbook provides self-contained surveys of the current state of a branch of economics in the form of chapters prepared by leading specialists on various aspects of this branch of economics. These surveys summarize not only received results but also newer developments, from recent journal articles and discussion papers. Some original material is also included, but the main goal is to provide comprehensive and accessible surveys. The Handbooks are intended to provide not only useful reference volumes for professional collections but also possible supplementary readings for advanced courses for graduate students in economics.

KENNETH J. ARROW and MICHAEL D. INTRILIGATOR

PUBLISHER'S NOTE

For a complete overview of the Handbooks in Economics Series, please refer to the listing at the end of this volume.

CONTENTS OF THE HANDBOOK

VOLUME 1A

INTRODUCTION: GROWTH IN RETROSPECT AND PROSPECT

Reflections on Growth Theory
ROBERT M. SOLOW

PART I: THEORIES OF ECONOMIC GROWTH

Chapter 1
Neoclassical Models of Endogenous Growth: The Effects of Fiscal Policy,
Innovation and Fluctuations
LARRY E. JONES and RODOLFO E. MANUELLI

Chapter 2
Growth with Quality-Improving Innovations: An Integrated Framework
PHILIPPE AGHION and PETER HOWITT

Chapter 3
Horizontal Innovation in the Theory of Growth and Development
GINO GANCIA and FABRIZIO ZILIBOTTI

Chapter 4
From Stagnation to Growth: Unified Growth Theory
ODED GALOR

Chapter 5
Poverty Traps
COSTAS AZARIADIS and JOHN STACHURSKI

Chapter 6
Institutions as a Fundamental Cause of Long-Run Growth
DARON ACEMOGLU, SIMON JOHNSON and JAMES A. ROBINSON

Chapter 7
Growth Theory through the Lens of Development Economics
ABHIJIT V. BANERJEE and ESTHER DUFLO

PART II: EMPIRICS OF ECONOMIC GROWTH

Chapter 8
Growth Econometrics
STEVEN N. DURLAUF, PAUL A. JOHNSON and JONATHAN R.W. TEMPLE

Chapter 9
Accounting for Cross-Country Income Differences
FRANCESCO CASELLI

Chapter 10
Accounting for Growth in the Information Age
DALE W. JORGENSON

Chapter 11
Externalities and Growth
PETER J. KLENOW and ANDRÉS RODRÍGUEZ-CLARE

PART III: GROWTH POLICIES AND MECHANISMS

Chapter 12
Finance and Growth: Theory and Evidence
ROSS LEVINE

Chapter 13
Human Capital and Technology Diffusion
JESS BENHABIB and MARK M. SPIEGEL

Chapter 14
Growth Strategies
DANI RODRIK

Chapter 15
National Policies and Economic Growth: A Reappraisal
WILLIAM EASTERLY

VOLUME 1B

PART IV: TECHNOLOGY

Chapter 16
Growth and Ideas
CHARLES I. JONES

Chapter 17
Long-Term Economic Growth and the History of Technology
JOEL MOKYR

Chapter 18
General Purpose Technologies
BOYAN JOVANOVIC and PETER L. ROUSSEAU

Chapter 19
Technological Progress and Economic Transformation
JEREMY GREENWOOD and ANANTH SESHADRI

Chapter 20
The Effects of Technical Change on Labor Market Inequalities
ANDREAS HORNSTEIN, PER KRUSELL and GIOVANNI L. VIOLANTE

Chapter 21
A Unified Theory of the Evolution of International Income Levels
STEPHEN L. PARENTE and EDWARD C. PRESCOTT

PART V: TRADE AND GEOGRAPHY

Chapter 22
A Global View of Economic Growth
JAUME VENTURA

Chapter 23
Trade, Growth and the Size of Countries
ALBERTO ALESINA, ENRICO SPOLAORE and ROMAIN WACZIARG

Chapter 24
Urbanization and Growth
J. VERNON HENDERSON

PART VI: GROWTH IN BROADER CONTEXTS

Chapter 25
Inequality, Technology and the Social Contract
ROLAND BÉNABOU

Chapter 26
Social Capital
STEVEN N. DURLAUF and MARCEL FAFCHAMPS

Chapter 27
The Effect of Economic Growth on Social Structures
FRANÇOIS BOURGUIGNON

Chapter 28
Economic Growth and the Environment: A Review of Theory and Empirics
WILLIAM A. BROCK and M. SCOTT TAYLOR

PREFACE TO THE HANDBOOK OF ECONOMIC GROWTH

The progress which is to be expected in the physical sciences and arts, combined with the greater security of property, and greater security in disposing of it, which are obvious features in the civilization of modern nations, and with the more extensive and skillful employment of the joint-stock principle, afford space and scope for an indefinite increase of capital and production, and for the increase of population that is its ordinary accompaniment.

John Stuart Mill, *Principles of Political Economy*, 1848

Interest is economic growth has been an integral part of economics since its inception as a scholarly discipline. Remarkably, this ancient lineage is consistent with growth economics representing one of the most active areas of research in economics in the last two decades. Perhaps more surprising, this activity followed a relatively long period of calm in the aftermath of the seminal theoretical and empirical work by Robert Solow on the neoclassical growth model [Solow (1956, 1957)]. Solow's research set the growth research agenda for over 25 years. In terms of economic theory, much of the work of the 1960's consisted of translating the Solow framework into an explicit intertemporal optimizing framework; this translation, enshrined in economics as the Cass–Koopmans model [David Cass (1965), Tjalling Koopmans (1965)] has been of great importance in much of the new growth theory as well. In terms of empirical work, Solow's accounting framework stimulated many studies [a style of work well summarized in Edward Denison (1974)] which attempted more elaborate decompositions of growth patterns into components due to human and physical capital accumulation and a technology residual. Indeed, from the perspective of 1980, growth economics might have itself appeared to have achieved a steady state.

This apparent steady state was shattered on both the theoretical and empirical levels in the late 1980's and the 1990's. In terms of theory, new models of endogenous growth[1] questioned the neoclassical emphasis on capital accumulation as the main engine of growth, focusing instead on the Schumpeterian idea that growth is primarily driven by innovations that are themselves the result of profit-motivated research activities and create a conflict between the old and the new by making old technologies become obsolete. On the empirical side, Robert Barro (1991) and N. Gregory Mankiw,

---

[1] Also based on capital accumulation are the so-called AK models of endogenous growth [Frankel (1962), Romer (1986), Lucas (1988)], in which capital accumulation generates knowledge accumulation. See the books by Grossman and Helpman (1991), Jones (2002), Barro and Sala-i-Martin (2003) or Aghion and Howitt (1998), for other references.

David Romer, and David Weil (1992) launched the use of cross-country growth regressions to explore growth differences across countries; a cross-section that is far more extensive and covers much more of the world than occurred in earlier growth studies. These two parallel developments themselves gave birth to a whole range of new theoretical and empirical explorations of the determinants of growth and convergence – in particular the economic organizations and policies and the political institutions that are growth-enhancing at different stages of development. At the same time, new empirical methods were developed to reexamine issues of growth accounting on one end and which have begun to employ sophisticated statistical methods to uncover heterogeneities and nonlinearities on the other.

This renaissance of growth economics reflects several factors. On the theory side, much of the work has been stimulated by modeling techniques imported in the 1970s from the new theory of international trade[2] or the new theory of industrial organization,[3] which made it possible to introduce imperfect competition and innovations in simple general equilibrium settings. Empirical work has been facilitated by the construction of new data sets, of which Alan Heston and Robert Summers [see Heston, Summers and Aten (2002) for the latest incarnation] has been especially influential. More recent work has made increasing use of new micro data, whether cross-industry, or cross-firm, or plant level. The availability of these new data sets, in turn has initiated a new phase in growth economics in which theory and empirics go hand in hand as the development of new growth theories generates or is itself prompted by the introduction of new statistical tools and empirical exercises. This phase is particularly exciting as one can more directly analyze the impact of specific institutional reforms or macroeconomic policies on economic growth across different types of countries.

The *Handbook of Economic Growth* is designed to communicate the state of modern growth research. However, in contrast to other handbook volumes, we looked for chapters by active growth researchers. We then asked these authors to primarily convey the frontier ideas they are currently working on, anticipating that in order to put the reader up to speed with their current research agendas, the authors would also have to provide introductory surveys of contributions in their fields. As our readers will see, some chapters contain overlaps with other chapters and in a number of cases they partly disagree with one another. This only shows that growth economics is a lively field, with professional disagreements, alternative perspectives and outstanding controversies, but at the same time there exists a common eagerness to better understand the mechanics of economic development.

The Handbook consists of 28 chapters and is divided into six parts.

Part I lays out the theoretical foundations. The first chapter surveys the neo-classical and AK models of growth. The second chapter develops the Schumpeterian growth

---

[2] See the product variety models of Romer (1990) and Grossman and Helpman (1990) and the whole literature that builds upon this approach, surveyed in Chapter 3 below.

[3] The Schumpeterian models with quality-improving innovations, starting with Segerstrom, Anant and Dinopoulos (1990) and Aghion and Howitt (1992), belong to this second category.

model with quality-improving innovations and confronts it with new empirical evidence. The third chapter surveys the literature that built upon Paul Romer's product-variety model. The fourth chapter looks at growth in the very long run and analyzes the interplay between technical change and demographic transitions, and explores the issue of transitions between different growth regimes. The next chapter analyzes the central role of economic and political institutions, and describes the mechanisms whereby the dynamics of political institutions interacts with the dynamics of economic institutions and that of income inequality. The following chapter focuses on the emergence and existence of poverty traps, a question of particular importance in development contexts. The final chapter further explores the interplay of growth economics and development economics, with particular attention to how factors such as credit market constraints and intersectoral heterogeneity can explain outstanding puzzles concerning capital flows and interest rates, which are major elements of the growth process.

Part II examines the empirics of growth. An important aspect of these chapters is the diversity of approaches that have been taken to link growth theory to data. Growth accounting continues to play an important role in growth economics, both in terms of organizing facts and in terms of identifying the domain in which new growth theories can supplement neoclassical explanations. Growth economics has at the same time stimulated the development of new econometrics tools to address the specific data implications of various growth theories, implications in some cases challenge the assumptions that underlie conventional econometric tools. One theme of the work in this Part of the Handbook is that there exist limits to what may be learned about the structural elements of the growth process from formal statistical models. At the same time, empirical growth work plays a key role in identifying the stylized facts that growth theories need to address.

Part III of the Handbook examines a range of growth mechanisms. Some of these mechanisms have to do with the microeconomics of technology and education. Other mechanisms lie outside the domain of the neoclassical model and have to do with issues of political and economic institutions and social structure. Another theme that is developed here concerns the links between inequality and growth, which naturally raises issues of equity/efficiency tradeoffs. Finally, the role of government policy in affecting long run growth is studied. Much of the exciting work on growth has consisted of efforts to understand how factors beyond capital accumulation and technological change can affect growth; this very broad conception of the growth process is reflected in this section.

Part IV explores a range of aspects concerning technology. The discussion starts with a chapter that reviews the history of technology from a growth perspective. This discussion is a valuable complement to the formal statistical analyses studied in Part II. The analysis then turns to alternative theories by which technology evolves and diffuses in an economy. General purpose technologies are studied as an engine of growth. The consequences of technological diffusion for economic transformations are described and the inequality consequences of technological change are considered. Finally, the role of technology barriers in producing persistent international inequality is examined.

Part V considers the relationship between trade and geography. The discussion explores how trade and geographic agglomeration can affect growth trajectories as well as how growth interacts with geography to produce national boundaries.

Further, some of the consequences of economic growth for a range of macroeconomic phenomena are explored in Part VI. Different chapters explore how growth affects inequality, sociological outcomes, and the environment.

Finally, we are honored that Robert Solow has contributed a set of reflections on the state of growth economics to complete the Handbook. While growth economics has made immense strides in the last two decades, it is of course the case that the field "stands on the shoulders of giants". And in this regard, Solow's contributions are not alone. One can see the intertemporal optimization methodology that underlies the current theoretical analyses in the work of Frank Ramsey [Ramsey (1928)] and the ideas of social increasing returns in an early paper by Kenneth Arrow (1962). Such observations do not diminish the new growth economics, but rather speak well to the nature of progress in economics.

We would like to thank Kenneth Arrow and Michael Intriligator for their support in initiating this project as well as in providing invaluable guidance throughout the process. Valerie Teng of North-Holland, Lauren LaRosa at Harvard and Alisenne Sumwalt at Wisconsin have provided terrific administrative assistance at various stages of this project. And of course, we are deeply grateful to the authors for their work. If nothing else, their contributions reinforce our view that the human capital contribution to production takes pride of place, at least when the growth of knowledge is concerned.

Philippe Aghion and Steven Durlauf

References

Aghion, P., Howitt, P. (1992). "A model of growth through creative destruction". Econometrica 60, 323–351.

Aghion, P., Howitt, P. (1998). Endogenous Growth Theory. MIT Press.

Arrow, K. (1962). "The economic implications of learning by doing". Review of Economic Studies 29, 155–173.

Barro, R. (1991). "Economic growth in a cross section of countries". Quarterly Journal of Economics 106 (2), 407–443.

Barro, R., Sala-i-Martin, X. (2003). Economic Growth. MIT Press.

Cass, D. (1965). "Optimum growth in an aggregative model of capital accumulation". Review of Economic Studies 32 (3), 233–240.

Denison, E. (1974). Accounting for United States Economic Growth, 1929–1969. Brookings Institution Press, Washington, DC.

Frankel, M. (1962). "The production function in allocation and growth: A synthesis". American Economic Review 52, 995–1022.

Grossman, G., Helpman, E. (1990). "Comparative advantage and long-run growth". American Economic Review 80, 796–815.

Grossman, G., Helpman, E. (1991). Innovations and Growth in the Global Economy. MIT Press.

Heston, A., Summers, R., Aten, B. (2002). "Penn World Table Version 6.1". Center for International Comparisons at the University of Pennsylvania (CICUP).

Jones, C. (2002). Introduction to Economic Growth, second ed. W.W. Norton, New York.

Koopmans, T. (1965). "On the concept of optimal growth". In: The Econometric Approach to Development Planning. Rand-McNally, Chicago.

Lucas, R. (1988). "On the mechanics of economic development". Journal of Monetary Economics 22, 3–42.

Mankiw, N.G., Romer, D., Weil, D. (1992). "A contribution to the empirics of economic growth". Quarterly Journal of Economics 107 (2), 407–437.

Ramsey, F. (1928). "A mathematical theory of savings". Economic Journal 38, 543–559.

Romer, P. (1986). "Increasing returns and long-run growth". Journal of Political Economy 94, 1002–1037.

Romer, P. (1990). "Endogenous technical change". Journal of Political Economy 98, 71–102.

Segerstrom, P., Anant, T., Dinopoulos, E. (1990). "A Schumpeterian model of the life cycle". American Economic Review 80, 1077–1092.

Solow, R. (1956). "A contribution to the theory of economic growth". Quarterly Journal of Economics 70, 65–94.

Solow, R. (1957). "Technical change and the aggregate production function". Review of Economics and Statistics 39 (3), 312–320.

CONTENTS OF VOLUME 1B

Introduction to the Series   v

Contents of the Handbook   vii

Preface   xi

PART IV: TECHNOLOGY

Chapter 16
Growth and Ideas
CHARLES I. JONES   1063
Abstract   1064
Keywords   1064
1. Introduction   1065
2. Intellectual history of this idea   1069
3. A simple idea-based growth model   1070
   3.1. The model   1070
   3.2. Solving for growth   1072
   3.3. Discussion   1073
4. A richer model and the allocation of resources   1074
   4.1. The economic environment   1074
   4.2. Allocating resources with a rule of thumb 1076
   4.3. The optimal allocation of resources   1079
   4.4. A Romer-style equilibrium with imperfect competition 1082
   4.5. Discussion   1086
5. Scale effects   1088
   5.1. Strong and weak scale effects   1090
   5.2. Growth effects and policy invariance   1093
   5.3. Cross-country evidence on scale effects 1095
   5.4. Growth over the very long run   1097
   5.5. Summary: scale effects   1101
6. Growth accounting, the linearity critique, and other contributions 1101
   6.1. Growth accounting in idea-based models 1101
   6.2. The linearity critique   1103
   6.3. Other contributions   1105
7. Conclusions   1106
Acknowledgements   1108
References   1108

Chapter 17
Long-Term Economic Growth and the History of Technology
JOEL MOKYR   1113
Abstract   1114
Keywords   1114
 1. Introduction   1115
 2. Technology and economic growth   1116
 3. A historical theory of technology   1119
 4. The significance of the Industrial Revolution   1126
 5. The intellectual roots of the Industrial Revolution   1131
 6. The dynamic of technological modernity   1144
 7. Human capital and modern economic growth   1155
 8. Institutions and technological progress   1161
 9. Conclusions: Technology, growth, and the rise of the occident   1169
Acknowledgements   1173
References   1174

Chapter 18
General Purpose Technologies
BOYAN JOVANOVIC AND PETER L. ROUSSEAU   1181
Abstract   1182
Keywords   1183
 1. Introduction   1184
   1.1. What is a GPT?   1185
   1.2. Summary of findings   1186
 2. Measuring the three characteristics of a GPT   1187
   2.1. Pervasiveness of the GPT   1187
   2.2. Improvement of the GPT   1195
   2.3. Ability of the GPT to spawn innovation   1198
 3. Other symptoms of a GPT   1203
   3.1. Productivity slowdown   1204
   3.2. The skill premium   1205
   3.3. Entry, exit, and mergers should rise   1206
   3.4. Stock prices should fall   1207
   3.5. Young firms should do better   1208
   3.6. Consumption, interest rates, and the trade deficit   1217
 4. Conclusion   1221
Acknowledgements   1221
References   1221

Chapter 19
Technological Progress and Economic Transformation
JEREMY GREENWOOD AND ANANTH SESHADRI   1225
Abstract   1226
Keywords   1226
  1. Introduction   1227
      1.1. Technological progress in the market   1227
      1.2. Technological progress in the home   1229
      1.3. The goal   1230
  2. The baby bust and baby boom   1231
      2.1. The environment   1231
      2.2. Analysis   1233
  3. The U.S. demographic transition   1238
      3.1. The environment   1238
      3.2. Analysis   1242
  4. The demise of child labor   1246
      4.1. The environment   1247
      4.2. Analysis   1248
  5. Engines of liberation   1250
      5.1. The environment   1252
      5.2. Analysis   1254
      5.3. Analysis with nondurable household products and services   1258
  6. Conclusion   1260
  7. Literature review   1261
      7.1. Fertility   1261
      7.2. The economics of household production   1262
      7.3. Structural change   1263
      7.4. Child labor   1264
      7.5. Female labor-force participation   1266
Acknowledgements   1268
Appendix: 1268
      A.1. Supporting calculations for Lemmas 2 and 4   1268
      A.2. Supporting calculations for Lemmas 5 and 6   1270
References   1271

Chapter 20
The Effects of Technical Change on Labor Market Inequalities
ANDREAS HORNSTEIN, PER KRUSELL AND GIOVANNI L. VIOLANTE   1275
Abstract   1278
Keywords   1278
  1. Introduction   1279
  2. A look at the facts   1281
      2.1. Labor market inequalities   1281
      2.2. Technological change   1289

3. Skill-biased technical change: Inside the black box   1298

   3.1. Capital-skill complementarity   1298

   3.2. Innate skills and the Nelson–Phelps hypothesis   1301

   3.3. Endogenous skill-biased technical change   1304

   3.4. A historical perspective on the skill premium   1308

   3.5. Technology and the gender gap   1311

4. Technical change and the returns to experience   1313

   4.1. Experience with general purpose technologies   1313

   4.2. Vintage-specificity of experience   1315

   4.3. Technology-experience complementarity in adoption   1316

   4.4. On-the-job training with skill-biased technological change   1317

5. Inside the firm: The organization of work   1319

   5.1. The Milgrom–Roberts hypothesis: IT-driven organizational change   1320

   5.2. Directed organizational change   1323

   5.3. Discussion   1325

6. Technical progress as a source of change in labor market institutions   1325

   6.1. Skill-biased technology and the fall in union density   1327

   6.2. Skill-biased technology and the fall in centralized bargaining   1328

   6.3. Discussion   1329

7. Technological change in frictional labor markets   1331

   7.1. Technological progress and frictional unemployment   1332

   7.2. Technological heterogeneity and the returns to luck   1333

   7.3. Vintage human capital with frictions   1334

   7.4. Random matching vs. directed search as source of luck   1338

8. Technology-policy complementarity: United States vs. Europe   1339

   8.1. The Krugman hypothesis   1340

   8.2. Rise in microeconomic turbulence   1342

   8.3. Slowdown in total factor productivity   1346

   8.4. Acceleration in capital-embodied technical change   1346

   8.5. Skill-biased technical change   1349

   8.6. Endogenous technology adoption   1350

   8.7. Sectoral transformation   1352

   8.8. Discussion   1353

9. Welfare and policy implications   1353

   9.1. Lifetime earnings inequality   1354

   9.2. Consumption inequality   1355

   9.3. Welfare implications   1356

   9.4. Brief directions for policy   1359

10. Concluding remarks   1360

Acknowledgements   1361

References   1362

Chapter 21
A Unified Theory of the Evolution of International Income Levels
STEPHEN L. PARENTE AND EDWARD C. PRESCOTT   1371
Abstract   1372
Keywords   1372
  1. Introduction   1373
  2. A theory of economic development   1376
    2.1. Classical theory: the pre-1700 era   1377
    2.2. Modern growth theory: the post-1900 era   1382
    2.3. The combined theory   1383
  3. A theory of relative efficiencies   1389
    3.1. The aggregate production function   1391
    3.2. Consequences of constraints for aggregate efficiency   1392
    3.3. Estimates of aggregate relative efficiency   1394
    3.4. Reasons for constraints   1395
  4. A unified theory of the evolution of international incomes   1396
    4.1. Delays in starting dates   1397
    4.2. No catch-up after the transition in many countries   1400
    4.3. Catch-up and growth miracles   1403
    4.4. Unmeasured investment   1406
  5. Catching up   1407
    5.1. Catch-up facts   1407
    5.2. Reasons for catching up or not catching up   1408
  6. Concluding remarks   1413
Acknowledgements   1414
References   1414

PART V: TRADE AND GEOGRAPHY

Chapter 22
A Global View of Economic Growth
JAUME VENTURA   1419
Abstract   1420
Keywords   1420
  0. Introduction   1421
  1. The integrated economy   1426
    1.1. A workhorse model   1426
    1.2. Diminishing returns, market size and economic growth   1430
    1.3. The effects of economic integration   1436
  2. Specialization, trade and diminishing returns   1442
    2.1. Economic growth in autarky   1444
    2.2. Factor price equalization   1446
    2.3. Formal aspects of the model   1454

2.4. Limits to structural transformation (I): factor proportions   1456
2.5. Limits to structural transformation (II): industry productivities   1464
3. Transport costs and market size   1472
  3.1. Nontraded goods and the cost of living   1473
  3.2. Agglomeration effects   1481
  3.3. The role of local markets   1487
4. Final remarks   1490
Acknowledgements   1492
References   1492

Chapter 23
Trade, Growth and the Size of Countries
ALBERTO ALESINA, ENRICO SPOLAORE AND ROMAIN WACZIARG   1499
Abstract   1500
1. Introduction   1501
2. Size, openness and growth: Theory   1502
  2.1. The costs and benefits of size   1502
  2.2. A model of size, trade and growth   1506
  2.3. The equilibrium size of countries   1510
  2.4. Summing up   1513
3. Size, openness and growth: Empirical evidence   1514
  3.1. Trade and growth: a review of the evidence   1514
  3.2. Country size and growth: a review of the evidence   1516
  3.3. Summing up   1518
  3.4. Trade, size and growth in a cross-section of countries   1518
  3.5. Endogeneity of openness: 3SLS estimates   1525
4. Country size and trade in history   1530
  4.1. The city-states   1530
  4.2. The absolutist period   1531
  4.3. The birth of the modern nation-state   1531
  4.4. The colonial empires   1532
  4.5. Borders in the interwar period   1533
  4.6. Borders in the post–Second World War period   1534
  4.7. The European Union   1536
5. Conclusion   1538
Acknowledgements   1539
References   1539

Chapter 24
Urbanization and Growth
J. VERNON HENDERSON   1543
Abstract   1544
Keywords   1544

1. Facts and empirical evidence   1547

    1.1. The size distribution of cities and its evolution   1548

    1.2. Geographic concentration and urban specialization   1554

    1.3. Urbanization in developing countries   1558

2. Cities and growth   1564

    2.1. The systems of cities at a point in time   1565

    2.2. Growth in a system of cities   1571

    2.3. Extensions   1573

3. Urbanization and growth   1577

    3.1. Two sector approaches, without cities   1577

    3.2. Urbanization with cities   1579

    3.3. Extensions and policy issues   1582

4. Some issues for a research agenda   1586

Acknowledgement   1587

References   1587

PART VI: GROWTH IN BROADER CONTEXTS

Chapter 25
Inequality, Technology and the Social Contract
ROLAND BÉNABOU

ROLAND BÉNABOU   1595

Abstract   1596

Keywords   1596

Introduction   1597

1. Inequality, redistribution and growth   1600

    1.1. Production, preferences and policy   1601

    1.2. Distributional dynamics and aggregate growth   1603

    1.3. Voter preferences, political power and equilibrium policy   1606

2. Sustainable social contracts   1609

    2.1. Dynamics and steady states   1609

    2.2. Which societies grow faster?   1611

3. Technology and the social contract   1612

    3.1. Exogenous technical change and the viability of the welfare state   1613

    3.2. Skills, technology and income inequality   1618

    3.3. Technological choice and endogenous flexibility   1619

4. Endogenous institutions and endogenous technology   1623

5. Exporting inequality: Spillovers between social contracts   1627

    5.1. A shift in one country's technological frontier   1628

    5.2. A shift in one country's political institutions   1629

6. Conclusion   1629

Acknowledgements   1630

Appendix: Proofs   1630

References   1635

Chapter 26
Social Capital
STEVEN N. DURLAUF AND MARCEL FAFCHAMPS   1639
Abstract   1640
Keywords   1640
  1. Introduction   1641
  2. Social capital: Basic concepts   1642
    2.1. Defining social capital   1642
    2.2. The efficiency of social exchange 1645
    2.3. Social capital and development   1648
    2.4. Social capital and equity   1650
  3. When does social capital matter?   1651
    3.1. Sources of inefficiency   1651
    3.2. Channels   1652
    3.3. Formal theory   1658
  4. From theory to empirics: Econometrics and social capital 1660
    4.1. Externalities and individual vs. aggregate effects 1661
    4.2. Model specification   1663
    4.3. Identification   1667
    4.4. Additional issues   1671
  5. Empirical studies of the effects of social capital 1672
    5.1. Individual-level studies   1672
    5.2. Aggregate studies   1680
  6. Empirical studies of the level and determinants of social capital 1685
  7. Suggestions for future research   1688
  8. Conclusions   1692
Acknowledgements   1693
References   1693

Chapter 27
The Effect of Economic Growth on Social Structures
FRANÇOIS BOURGUIGNON   1701
Abstract   1702
Keywords   1702
Introduction   1703
  1. Statistical relationships between growth and social structures 1705
  2. The effect of economic growth on social structures:
    Theoretical considerations   1711
    2.1. The sectoral shift view   1713
    2.2. General equilibrium models of the distributional effects of growth 1715
    2.3. Nonlinear savings behavior   1719
    2.4. The role of technical progress   1720
    2.5. Conclusion   1722

  3. The effect of economic growth on social structures: Empirical evidence   1723
     3.1. The sectoral shift effect of growth on social structures   1723
     3.2. Effect of growth on inequality between socio-economic groups   1726
     3.3. Effects of growth on inequality among individuals   1731
  4. Conclusions   1739
     4.1. The foremost importance of sectoral shift phenomena   1739
     4.2. The role of market integration   1739
     4.3. Social costs of transitory adjustment   1740
     4.4. Effect of growth on social structures through social institutions   1740
Acknowledgements   1742
References   1742

Chapter 28
Economic Growth and the Environment: A Review of Theory and Empirics
WILLIAM A. BROCK AND M. SCOTT TAYLOR   1749
Abstract   1750
Keywords   1750
  1. Introduction   1751
  2. Preliminaries   1757
     2.1. Scale, composition and technique   1757
  3. Stylized facts on sources and sinks   1761
  4. Some illustrative theory   1772
     4.1. The Green Solow benchmark   1772
     4.2. Intensifying abatement: the Stokey alternative   1778
     4.3. Composition shifts: the source and sink model   1787
  5. Induced innovation and learning by doing   1798
     5.1. Induced innovation and the Kindergarten Rule model   1799
     5.2. Empirical implications   1810
     5.3. Balanced growth path predictions   1810
     5.4. The Environmental Catch-up Hypothesis   1811
     5.5. The ECH and the EKC   1813
     5.6. Pollution characteristics   1814
  6. Conclusion and suggestions for future research   1816
References   1819

Author Index   I-1

Subject Index   I-37

PART IV

TECHNOLOGY

Chapter 16

GROWTH AND IDEAS

CHARLES I. JONES

Department of Economics, University of California, Berkeley
and
NBER

Contents

Abstract	1064
Keywords	1064
1. Introduction	1065
2. Intellectual history of this idea	1069
3. A simple idea-based growth model	1070
3.1. The model	1070
3.2. Solving for growth	1072
3.3. Discussion	1073
4. A richer model and the allocation of resources	1074
4.1. The economic environment	1074
4.2. Allocating resources with a rule of thumb	1076
4.3. The optimal allocation of resources	1079
4.4. A Romer-style equilibrium with imperfect competition	1082
4.5. Discussion	1086
5. Scale effects	1088
5.1. Strong and weak scale effects	1090
5.2. Growth effects and policy invariance	1093
5.3. Cross-country evidence on scale effects	1095
5.4. Growth over the very long run	1097
5.5. Summary: scale effects	1101
6. Growth accounting, the linearity critique, and other contributions	1101
6.1. Growth accounting in idea-based models	1101
6.2. The linearity critique	1103
6.3. Other contributions	1105
7. Conclusions	1106
Acknowledgements	1108
References	1108

Handbook of Economic Growth, Volume 1B. Edited by Philippe Aghion and Steven N. Durlauf
DOI: 10.1016/S1574-0684(05)01016-6

Abstract

Ideas are different from nearly all other economic goods in that they are nonrivalrous. This nonrivalry implies that production possibilities are likely to be characterized by increasing returns to scale, an insight that has profound implications for economic growth. The purpose of this chapter is to explore these implications.

Keywords

economic growth, ideas, scale effects, survey

JEL classification: O40, E10

1. Introduction

People in countries like the United States are richer by a factor of about 10 or 20 than people a century or two ago. Whereas U.S. per capita income today is $33,000, conventional estimates put it at $1800 in 1850. Yet even this difference likely understates the enormous increase in standards of living over this period. Consider the quality of life of the typical American in the year 1850. Life expectancy at birth was a scant 40 years, just over half of what it is today. Refrigeration, electric lights, telephones, antibiotics, automobiles, skyscrapers, and air conditioning did not exist, much less the more sophisticated technologies that impact our lives daily in the 21st century.[1]

Perhaps the central question of the literature on economic growth is "Why is there growth at all?" What caused the enormous increase in standards of living during the last two centuries? And why were living standards nearly stagnant for the thousands and thousands of years that preceded this recent era of explosive growth?

The models developed as part of the renaissance of research on economic growth in the last two decades attempt to answer these questions. While other chapters discuss alternative explanations, this chapter will explore theories in which the economics of ideas takes center stage. The discoveries of electricity, the incandescent lightbulb, the internal combustion engine, the airplane, penicillin, the transistor, the integrated circuit, just-in-time inventory methods, Wal–Mart's business model, and the polymerase chain reaction for replicating strands of DNA all represent new ideas that have been, in part, responsible for economic growth over the last two centuries.

The insights that arise when ideas are placed at the center of a theory of economic growth can be summarized in the following Idea Diagram:

$$\text{Ideas} \Rightarrow \text{Nonrivalry} \Rightarrow \text{IRS} \Rightarrow \text{Problems with CE.}$$

To understand this diagram, first consider what we mean by "ideas". Romer (1993) divides goods into two categories: ideas and objects. Ideas can be thought of as instructions or recipes, things that can be codified in a bitstring as a sequence of ones and zeros. Objects are all the rivalrous goods we are familiar with: capital, labor, output, computers, automobiles, and most fundamentally the elemental atoms that make up these goods. At some level, ideas are instructions for arranging the atoms and for using the arrangements to produce utility. For thousands of years, silicon dioxide provided utility mainly as sand on the beach, but now it delivers utility through the myriad of goods that depend on computer chips. Viewed this way, economic growth can be sustained even in the presence of a finite collection of raw materials as we discover better ways to arrange atoms and better ways to use the arrangements. One then naturally wonders about possible limits to the ways in which these atoms can be arranged, but

---

[1] Ideally, the calculations of GDP should take the changing basket of goods and changes in life expectancy into account, but the standard price indices used to construct these comparisons are inadequate. See, for example, DeLong (2000) and Nordhaus (2003).

the combinatorial calculations of Romer (1993) and Weitzman (1998) quickly put such concerns to rest. Consider, for example, the number of unique ways of ordering twenty objects (these could be steps in assembling a computer chip or ingredients in a chemical formula). The answer is 20!, which is on the order of 10^{18}. To put this number in perspective, if we tried one different combination every second since the universe began, we would have exhausted less than twenty percent of the possibilities.[2]

The first arrow in the Idea Diagram links ideas with the concept of nonrivalry. Recall from public economics that a good is nonrivalrous if one person's use of the good does not diminish another's use. Most economic goods – objects – are rivalrous: one person's use of a car, a computer, or an atom of carbon dimishes the ability of someone else to use that object. Ideas, by contrast, are nonrivalrous. As examples, consider public key cryptography and the famous introductory bars to Beethoven's Fifth Symphony. Audrey's use of a particular cryptographic method does not inhibit my simultaneous use of that method. Nor does Benji's playing of the Fifth Symphony limit my (in)ability to perform it simultaneously. For an example closer to our growth models, consider the production of computer chips. Once the design of the latest computer chip has been invented, it can be applied in one factory or two factories or ten factories. The design does not have to be reinvented every time a new computer chip gets produced – the same idea can be applied over and over again. More generally, the set of instructions for combining and using atoms can be used at any scale of production without being diminished.

The next link between nonrivalry and increasing returns to scale (IRS) is the first indication that nonrivalry has important implications for economic growth. As discussed in Romer (1990), consider a production function of the form

$$Y = F(A, X), \tag{1}$$

where Y is output, A is an index of the amount of knowledge that has been discovered, and X is a vector of the remaining inputs into production (e.g. capital and labor). Our standard justification for constant returns to scale comes from a replication argument. Suppose we'd like to double the production of computer chips. One way to do this is to replicate all of the standard inputs: we build another factory identical to the first and populate it with the same material inputs and with identical workers. Crucially, however, we do not need to double the stock of knowledge because of its nonrivalry: the existing design for computer chips can be used in the new factory by the new workers.

One might, of course, require additional copies of the blueprint, and these blueprints may be costly to produce on the copying machine down the hall. The blueprints are not ideas; the copies of the blueprints might be thought of as one of the rivalrous inputs included in the vector X. The bits of information encoded in the blueprint – the design for the computer chip – constitute the idea.

---

[2] Of course, one also must consider the fraction of combinations that are useful. Responding to one such combinatorial calculation, George Akerlof is said to have wondered, "Yes, but how many of them are like chicken ice cream?".

Mathematically, we can summarize these insights in the following two equations. For some number $\lambda > 1$,

$$F(A, \lambda X) = \lambda Y, \tag{2}$$

and as long as more knowledge is useful,

$$F(\lambda A, \lambda X) > \lambda Y. \tag{3}$$

That is, there are constant returns to scale to the standard rivalrous inputs X and, therefore, increasing returns to scale to these inputs and A taken together. If we double the number of factories, workers, and materials *and* double the stock of knowledge, then we will more than double the production of computer chips. Including ideas as an input into production naturally leads one to models in which increasing returns to scale plays an important role. Notice that a "standard" production function in macroeconomics of the form $Y = K^{\alpha}(AL)^{1-\alpha}$ builds in this property.

Introducing human capital into this framework adds an important wrinkle but does not change the basic insight. Suppose that the design for a computer chip must be learned by a team of scientists overseeing production before it can be used, thus translating the idea into human capital. To double production, one can double the number of factories, workers, and scientists. If one incorporates a better-designed computer chip as well, production more than doubles. Notice that the human capital is rivalrous: a scientist can work on my project or your project, but not on both at the same time. In contrast, the idea is nonrivalrous: two scientists can both implement a new design for a computer chip simultaneously.

Confusion can arise in thinking about human capital if one is not careful. For example, consider a production function that is constant returns in physical and human capital, the two rivalrous inputs: $Y = K^{\alpha}H^{1-\alpha}$. Now, suppose that $H = hL$, where h is human capital per person. Then, this production function is $Y = K^{\alpha}(hL)^{1-\alpha}$. There were constant returns to K and H in our first specification, but one is tempted conclude that there are increasing returns to K, L, and h together in the rewritten form. Which is it? Does the introduction of human capital involve increasing returns, just like the consideration of ideas?

The answer is no. To see why, consider a different example, this time omitting human capital altogether. Suppose $Y = K^{\alpha}L^{1-\alpha}$. This is perhaps our most familiar Cobb–Douglas production function and it exhibits constant returns to scale in K and L. Now, rewrite this production function as $Y = k^{\alpha}L$, where $k \equiv K/L$ is physical capital per person. Would we characterize this production function as possessing increasing returns? Of course not! Obviously a simple change of variables cannot change the underlying convexity of a production function.

This example suggests the following principle. In considering the degree of homogeneity of a production function, one must focus on the function that involves total quantities, so that nothing is "per worker". Intuitively, this makes sense: if one is determining returns to scale, the presence of "per worker" variables will of course lead to confusion. The application of this principle correctly identifies the production function based on human capital $Y = K^\alpha H^{1-\alpha}$ as possessing constant returns. Introducing ideas into the production function leads to increasing returns because of nonrivalry.

Finally, the last link in our diagram connects increasing returns to scale to "Problems with CE", by which we mean problems with the standard decentralization of the optimal allocation of resources using a perfectly competitive equilibrium. A central requirement of a competitive equilibrium is that factors get paid their marginal products. But with increasing returns to scale, as is well known, this is not possible. Continuing with the production function in Equation (1), the property of constant returns in X guarantees that[3]

$$F_X X = Y. \tag{4}$$

That is, paying each rivalrous factor its marginal product exhausts output, so that nothing would be left over to compensate the idea inputs

$$F_X X + F_A A > Y. \tag{5}$$

If the stock of knowledge is also paid its marginal product, then the firm would make negative profits. This means that the standard competitive equilibrium will run into problems in a model that includes ideas.

These two implications of incorporating ideas into our growth models – increasing returns and the failure of perfect competition to deliver optimal allocations – are the basis for many of the insights and results that follow in the remainder of this chapter. This chain of reasoning provides the key foundation for idea-based growth theory.

The purpose of this chapter is to outline the contribution of idea-based growth models to our understanding of economic growth. The next section begins by providing a brief overview of the intellectual history of idea-based growth theory, paying special attention to developments that preceded the advent of new growth theory in the mid-1980s. Section 3 presents the simplest possible model of growth and ideas in order to illustrate how these theories explain long-run growth. Section 4 turns to a richer model. This framework is used to compare the allocation of resources in equilibrium with the optimal allocation. The richer model also serves as the basis for several applications that follow in Sections 5 and 6. Section 5 provides a discussion of the scale effects that naturally emerge in models in which ideas play an important role and reviews a number of related contributions. Section 6 summarizes what we have learned from growth accounting in idea-based growth models, considers a somewhat controversial criticism of endogenous growth models called the "linearity critique", and briefly summarizes some of the additional literature on growth and ideas. Finally, Section 7 of this chapter concludes by discussing several of the most important open questions related to growth and ideas.

---

[3] Since X is a vector, the notation in this equation should be interpreted as the dot product between the vector of derivatives and the vector of inputs.

It is worth mentioning briefly as well what this chapter omits. The most significant omission is a careful presentation of the Schumpeterian growth models of Aghion and Howitt (1992) and Grossman and Helpman (1991) and the very interesting directions in which these models have been pushed. This omission, however, is remedied in another chapter of this Handbook by Aghion and Howitt. Probably the next most important omission is a serious discussion of the empirical work in what is known as the productivity literature on the links between R&D, growth, and social rates of return. An excellent overview of this literature can be found in Griliches (1998).

2. Intellectual history of this idea

The fundamental insight conveyed by the Idea Diagram is an idea itself. And like many ideas, it is one that has been discovered, at least in part, several times in the past, at times being appreciated as a deep insight and at times being forgotten. A brief intellectual history of this idea follows, in part because it is useful to document this history but also in part because it helps to illuminate the idea itself.

William Petty, an early expert on the economics of taxation, identified in 1682 one of the key benefits of a larger population:

> As for the Arts of Delight and Ornament, they are best promoted by the greatest number of emulators. And it is more likely that one ingenious curious man may rather be found among 4 million than 400 persons. [Quoted by Simon (1998), p. 372.]

More than a century later, Thomas Jefferson came closer to characterizing the nonrivalrous nature of an idea:[4]

> Its peculiar character ...is that no one possesses the less, because every other possesses the whole of it. He who receives an idea from me, receives instruction himself without lessening mine; as he who lights his taper at mine, receives light without darkening me. That ideas should freely spread from one to another over the globe, for the moral and mutual instruction of man, and improvement of his condition, seems to have been peculiarly and benevolently designed by nature, when she made them, like fire, expansible over all space, without lessening their density at any point ... [Letter from Thomas Jefferson to Isaac McPherson, August 13, 1813, collected in Lipscomb and Bergh (1905), pp. 333–335.]

But it was not until the 1960s that economists systematically explored the economics of ideas. Kuznets (1960) intuits a link between population, ideas, and economic growth, and Boserup (1965) emphasizes how population pressure can lead to the adoption of

---

[4] David (1993) cites this passage in emphasizing that ideas are "infinitely expansible", a phrase picked up by Quah (1996).

new technologies. Arrow (1962b) and Shell (1966) clearly recognize the failure of models of perfect competition to deliver optimal resource allocation in the presence of ideas. Phelps (1966) and Nordhaus (1969) present explicit models in which the nonrivalry of knowledge leads to increasing returns and derive the result, discussed in detail below, that long-run growth in per capita income is driven by population growth.[5] Still, neither of these papers knows quite how seriously to take this prediction, with Nordhaus calling it a "peculiar result" (p. 23). Within two years, however, Phelps (1968) is convinced:

> One can hardly imagine, I think, how poor we would be today were it not for the rapid population growth of the past to which we owe the enormous number of technological advances enjoyed today... If I could re-do the history of the world, halving population size each year from the beginning of time on some random basis, I would not do it for fear of losing Mozart in the process. [Pp. 511–512.]

This implication then becomes central to the popular writings of Julian Simon in the debates over the merits and drawbacks of population growth, as in Simon (1986, 1998).

The formal literature on idea-based growth falters considerably in the 1970s and early 1980s. Much of the work that is carried out involves applications of the basic Solow (1956) model and the growth accounting calculations that subsequently followed. By the mid-1980s, many of the insights gleaned during the 1960s were no longer being taught in graduate programs. In part, this period of neglect seems to have stemmed from a lack of adequate techniques for modeling the departures from perfect competition that are implied by the economics of ideas [e.g. see Romer (1994b)]. This theoretical gap gets filled through the work on imperfect competition by Spence (1976) and Dixit and Stiglitz (1977).

Idea-based growth models are thrust to center stage in the profession with the publication of a series of papers by Romer (1986, 1987, 1990). These papers – most especially the last one – lay out with startling clarity the link between economic growth and ideas.[6] Shortly thereafter, the models of Aghion and Howitt (1992) and Grossman and Helpman (1991) introduce the Schumpeterian notions of creative destruction and business stealing, pushing idea-based growth theory further.[7]

3. A simple idea-based growth model

3.1. The model

It is useful to begin with the simplest possible idea-based growth model in order to see clearly how the key ingredients fit together to provide an explanation of long-run

---

[5] The learning-by-doing models of Arrow (1962a) and Sheshinski (1967) contain a similar result.

[6] This brief review obviously ignores many fundamental contributions to growth theory in order to focus on the history of idea-based growth models. Other chapters in this Handbook will lay out the roles played by neoclassical growth models, AK models, and models of growth driven by human capital accumulation.

[7] Other important contributions around this time include Judd (1985) and Segerstrom, Anant and Dinopoulos (1990).

growth. To strip the model to its essence, we ignore physical capital and human capital; these will be introduced in the richer framework of Section 4.

Suppose that in our toy economy the only rivalrous input in production (the X variable in the Introduction) is labor. The economy contains a single consumption good that is produced according to

$$Y_t = A_t^\sigma L_{Yt}, \quad \sigma > 0, \tag{6}$$

where Y is the quantity of output of the good, A is the stock of knowledge or ideas, and L_Y is the amount of labor used to produce the good. Notice that there are constant returns to scale to the rivalrous inputs, here just labor, and increasing returns to labor and ideas taken together. To double the production of output, it is sufficient to double the amount of labor using the same stock of knowledge. If we also double the stock of knowledge, we would more than double output.

The other good that gets produced in this economy is knowledge itself. Just as more workers can produce more output in Equation (6), more researchers can produce more new ideas:

$$\dot{A}_t = v(A_t) L_{At} = v L_{At} A_t^\phi, \quad v > 0. \tag{7}$$

If A is the stock of knowledge, then $\dot{A}$ is the amount of new knowledge produced at time t. L_A denotes the number of researchers, and each researcher can produce $v(A)$ new ideas at a point in time. To simplify further, we assume that $v(A)$ is a power function.

Notice the similarity between Equations (6) and (7). Both equations involve constant returns to scale to the rivalrous labor input, and both allow departures from constant returns because of the nonrivalry of ideas. Ideas are simply another good in this economy that labor can produce.

If $\phi > 0$, then the number of new ideas a researcher invents over a given interval of time is an increasing function of the existing stock of knowledge. We might label this the *standing on shoulders effect*: the discovery of ideas in the past makes us more effective researchers today. Alternatively, though, one might consider the case where $\phi < 0$, i.e. where the productivity of research declines as new ideas are discovered. A useful analogy in this case is a fishing pond. If the pond is stocked with only 100 fish, then it may be increasingly difficult to catch each new fish. Similarly, perhaps the most obvious new ideas are discovered first and it gets increasingly difficult to find the next new idea.

With these production functions given, we now specify a resource constraint and a method for allocating resources. The number of workers and the number of researchers sum to the total amount of labor in the economy, L,

$$L_{Yt} + L_{At} = L_t. \tag{8}$$

The amount of labor, in turn, is assumed to be given exogenously and to grow at a constant exponential rate n,

$$L_t = L_0 e^{nt}, \quad n > 0. \tag{9}$$

Finally, the only allocative decision that needs to be made in this simple economy is how to allocate labor. We make a Solow-like assumption that a constant fraction s of the labor force works as researchers, leaving $1 - s$ to produce goods.

3.2. Solving for growth

The specification of this economy is now complete, and it is straightforward to solve for growth in per capita output, $y \equiv Y/L$. First, notice the important result that $y_t = (1 - s)A_t^\sigma$, i.e. per capita output is proportional to the stock of ideas (raised to some power). Because of the nonrivalry of ideas, per capita output depends on the *total* stock of ideas, not on the stock of ideas per capita.

Taking logs and time derivatives, we have the corresponding relation in growth rates

$$\frac{\dot{y}_t}{y_t} = \sigma \frac{\dot{A}_t}{A_t}. \tag{10}$$

Growth of per capita output is proportional to the growth rate of the stock of knowledge, where the factor of proportionality measures the degree of increasing returns in the goods sector.

The growth rate of the stock of ideas, in turn is given by

$$\frac{\dot{A}_t}{A_t} = \nu \frac{L_{At}}{A_t^{1-\phi}}. \tag{11}$$

Under the assumption that $\phi < 1$, it is straightforward to show that the dynamics of this economy lead to a stable balanced growth path (defined as a situation in which all variables grow at constant rates, possibly zero). For the growth rate of A to be constant in Equation (11), the numerator and denominator of the right-hand side of that equation must grow at the same rate. Letting g_x denote the growth rate of some variable x along the balanced growth path, we then have

$$g_A = \frac{n}{1 - \phi}. \tag{12}$$

The growth rate of the stock of ideas, in the long-run, is proportional to the rate of population growth, where the factor of proportionality depends on the degree of returns to scale in the production function for ideas.

Finally, this equation can be substituted into Equation (10) to get the growth rate of output per worker in steady state,

$$g_y = \sigma g_A = \frac{\sigma n}{1 - \phi}. \tag{13}$$

The growth rate of per capita output is proportional to the rate of population growth, where the factor of proportionality depends on the degree of increasing returns in the two sectors.

3.3. Discussion

Why is this the case? There are two basic elements of the toy economy that lead to the result. First, just as the total output of any good depends on the total number of workers producing the good, more researchers produce more new ideas. A larger population means more Mozarts and Newtons, and more Wright brothers, Sam Waltons, and William Shockleys. Second, the nonrivalry of knowledge means that per capita output depends on the total stock of ideas, not on ideas per person.[8] Each person in the economy benefits from the new ideas created by the Isaac Newtons and William Shockleys of the world, and this benefit is not degraded by the presence of a larger population.

Together, these steps imply that output per capita is an increasing function, in the long run, of the number of researchers in the economy, which in turn depends on the size of the population. Log-differencing this relation, the growth rate of output per capita depends on the growth rate of the number of researchers, which in turn is tied to the rate of population growth in the long run.

At some basic level, these results should not be surprising at all. Once one grants that the nonrivalry of ideas implies increasing returns to scale, it is nearly inevitable that the size of the population affects the level of per capita income. After all, that is virtually the definition of increasing returns.

In moving from this toy model to the real world, one must obviously be careful. Probably the most important qualification is that our toy model consists of a single country. Without thinking more carefully about the flows of ideas across countries in the real world, it is more accurate to compare the predictions of this toy economy to the world as a whole rather than to any single economy. Taiwan and China both benefit from ideas created throughout the world, so it is not the Taiwanese or Chinese population that is especially relevant to those countries' growth experiences.

Another qualification relates to the absence of physical and human capital from the model. At least as far as long-run growth is concerned, this absence is not particularly harmful: recall the intuition from the Solow growth model that capital accumulation is not, by itself, a source of long-run growth. Still, because of transition dynamics these factors are surely important in explaining growth over any given time period, and they will be incorporated into the model in the next section.

Finally, it is worth mentioning briefly how this result differs from the original results in the models of Romer (1990), Aghion and Howitt (1992), and Grossman and Helpman (1991). Those models essentially make the assumption that $\phi = 1$ in the production function for new ideas. That is, the growth rate of the stock of knowledge depends on the number of researchers. This change serves to strengthen the importance of increasing returns to scale in the economy, so much so that a growing number of researchers causes the growth rate of the economy to grow exponentially. We will discuss this result in more detail in later sections.

---

[8] Contrast this to the case in which "capital" replaces the word "ideas" in this phrase. Because capital is rivalrous, output per capita depends on capital per person.

4. A richer model and the allocation of resources

The simple model given in the previous section provides several of the key insights of idea-based growth models, but it is too simple to provide others. In particular, the final implication in the basic Idea Diagram related to the problems a competitive equilibrium has in allocating resources has not been discussed. In this section, we remedy this shortcoming and discuss explicitly several mechanisms for allocating resources in an economy in which ideas play a crucial role. In addition, we augment the simple model with the addition of physical capital, human capital, and the Dixit–Stiglitz love of variety approach that has proven to be quite useful in modeling growth.

The model presented in this section is developed in a way that has become a de facto standard in macroeconomics. First, the economic environment – the collection of production technologies, resource constraints, and utility functions – is laid out. Any method of allocating resources is constrained by the economic environment. Next, we present several different ways in which resources can be allocated in this economy and derive results for each allocation. The first allocation is the simplest: a rule-of-thumb allocation analogous to the constant saving rate assumption of Solow (1956). The second allocation is the optimal one, i.e. the allocation that maximizes utility subject to the constraints imposed by the economic environment. These first two are very natural allocations to consider. One then immediately is led to ask the question of whether a decentralized equilibrium allocation, that is one in which markets allocate resources rather than a planner, can replicate the optimal allocation. In general, the answer to this question is that it depends on the nature of the institutions that govern the equilibrium. We will solve explicitly for one of these equilibrium allocations in Section 4.4 and then discuss several alternative institutions that might be used to allocate resources in this model.

4.1. The economic environment

The economic environment for this new model consists of a set of production functions, a set of resource constraints, and preferences. These will be described in turn.

First, the basic production functions are these:

$$Y_t = \left(\int_0^{A_t} x_{it}^\theta \, di \right)^{\alpha/\theta} H_{Yt}^{1-\alpha}, \quad 0 < \alpha < 1, \; 0 < \theta < 1, \tag{14}$$

$$\dot{K}_t = Y_t - C_t - \delta K_t, \quad K_0 > 0, \; \delta > 0, \tag{15}$$

$$\dot{A}_t = \nu H_{At}^\lambda A_t^\phi, \quad A_0 > 0, \; \nu > 0, \lambda > 0, \; \phi < 1. \tag{16}$$

Equation (14) is the production function for the final output good. Final output Y is produced using human capital H_Y and a collection of intermediate capital goods x_i. A represents the measure of these intermediate goods that are available at any point in time. These intermediate goods enter the production function through a CES aggregator function, and the elasticity of substitution between intermediate goods is $1/(1-\theta) > 1$.

Notice that there are constant returns to scale in H_Y and these intermediate goods in producing output for a given A. However, there are increasing returns to scale once A is treated as a variable. The sense in which this is true will be made precise below.

Equation (15) is a standard accumulation equation for physical capital.

Equation (16) is the production function for new ideas. In this economy, ideas have a very precise meaning – they represent new varieties of intermediate goods that can be used in the production of final output. New ideas are produced with a Cobb–Douglas function of human capital and the existing stock of knowledge.[9] As in the simple model, the parameter ϕ measures the way in which the current stock of knowledge affects the production of new ideas. It nets out the standing on shoulders effect and the fishing out effect. The parameter λ represents the elasticity of new idea production with respect to the number of researchers. A value of $\lambda = 1$ implies that doubling the number of researchers doubles the production of new ideas at a point in time for a given stock of knowledge. On the other hand, one imagines that doubling the number of researchers might less than double the number of new ideas because of duplication, suggesting $\lambda < 1$.

Next, the resource constraints for the economy are given by

$$\int_0^{A_t} x_{it}\, di = K_t, \tag{17}$$

$$H_{At} + H_{Yt} = H_t, \tag{18}$$

$$H_t = h_t L_t, \tag{19}$$

$$h_t = e^{\psi \ell_{ht}}, \quad \psi > 1, \tag{20}$$

$$L_t = (1 - \ell_{ht}) N_t, \tag{21}$$

$$N_t = N_0 e^{nt}, \quad N_0 > 0, \ n > 0. \tag{22}$$

Breaking slightly from my taxonomy, Equation (17) involves a production function as well as a resource constraint. In particular, one unit of raw capital can be transformed instantaneously into one unit of any intermediate good for which a design has been discovered. Equation (17) then is the resource constraint that says that the total quantity of intermediate goods produced cannot exceed the amount of raw capital in the economy.

Equation (18) says that the amount of human capital used in the production of goods and ideas equals the total amount of human capital available in the economy. Equation (19) states the identity that this total quantity of human capital is equal to human capital per person h times the total labor force L (all labor is identical). An individual's

---

[9] Physical capital is not used in the production of new ideas in order to simplify the model. A useful alternative to this approach is the "lab equipment" approach suggested by Rivera-Batiz and Romer (1991) where units of the final output good are used to produce ideas, i.e. capital and labor combine in the same way to produce ideas as to produce final output. Apart from some technicalities, all of the results given below have exact analogues in a lab-equipment approach.

human capital is related by the Mincerian exponential to the amount of time spent accumulating human capital, ℓ_h, in Equation (20). We simplify the model by assuming there are no dynamics associated with human capital accumulation.[10] Equation (21) defines the labor force to be the population multiplied by the amount of time that people are not accumulating human capital, and Equation (22) describes exogenous population growth at rate n.

Finally, preferences in this economy take the usual form:[11]

$$U_t = \int_t^\infty N_s u(c_s) e^{-\rho(s-t)} \, ds, \quad \rho > n, \tag{23}$$

$$c_t \equiv \frac{C_t}{N_t}, \tag{24}$$

$$u(c) = \frac{c^{1-\zeta} - 1}{1 - \zeta}, \quad \zeta > 0. \tag{25}$$

4.2. Allocating resources with a rule of thumb

Given this economic environment, we can now consider various ways in which resources may be allocated. The primary allocative decisions that need to be made are relatively few. At each point in time, we need to determine the amount of time spent gaining human capital ℓ_h, the amount of consumption c, the amount of human capital allocated to research H_A, and the split of the raw capital into the various varieties $\{x_i\}$. Once these allocative decisions have been made, the twelve equations in (14) to (25) above, combined with these four allocations pin down all of the quantities in the model.[12]

The simplest way to begin allocating resources in just about any model is with a "rule of thumb". That is, the modeler specifies some simple, exogenous rules for allocating resources. This is useful for a number of reasons. First, it forces us to be clear from

---

[10] This approach can be justified by a simple dynamic system of the form $\dot{h} = \mu e^{\psi \ell_h} - \delta h$, where human capital depreciates at rate δ. It is readily seen that in the steady state, this equation implies that h is proportional to $e^{\psi \ell_h}$, as we have assumed. More generally, of course, richer equations for human capital can be imagined.

[11] To keep utility finite, we require a technical condition on the parameters of the model. The appropriate condition can be determined by looking at the utility function and takes the form

$$\rho > n + \frac{\lambda}{1 - \phi} \frac{\sigma}{1 - \alpha} (1 - \zeta) n.$$

[12] The counting goes as follows. At a point in time we have the four allocation rules and the twelve equations given above. The four rules pin down the allocations ℓ_h, C, H_A, $\{x_i\}$ and then twelve equations deliver Y, K, A, H_Y, H, h, L, N, U, c and u. The careful counter will notice I have mentioned 15 objects but 16 equations. The subtlety is that we should think of the allocation rule as determining $\{x_i\}$ subject to the resource constraint in (17). (For comparison, notice that we choose H_A and the resource constraint pins down H_Y. Similarly, but loosely speaking, we choose "all but one" of the x_i and the resource constraint pins down the last one.)

the beginning about exactly what allocation decisions need to be made. Second, it reveals how key endogenous variables depend on the allocations themselves. This is nice because the subsequent results will hold along a balanced growth path even if other mechanisms are used to allocated resources.

DEFINITION 4.1. A *rule of thumb allocation* in this economy consists of the following set of equations:

$$\ell_{ht} = \bar{\ell}_h \in (0, 1), \tag{26}$$

$$1 - \frac{C_t}{Y_t} = \bar{s}_K \in (0, 1), \tag{27}$$

$$\frac{H_{At}}{H_t} = \bar{s}_A \in (0, 1), \tag{28}$$

$$x_{it} = \bar{x}_t \equiv \frac{K_t}{A_t} \quad \text{for all } i \in [0, A_t]. \tag{29}$$

As is obvious from the definition, our rule of thumb allocation involves agents in the economy allocating a constant fraction of time to the accumulation of human capital, a constant fraction of output for investment in physical capital, a constant division of human capital into research, and allocating the raw capital symmetrically in the production of the intermediate capital goods.

With this allocation chosen, one can now in principle solve the model for all of the endogenous variables at each point in time. For our purposes, it will be enough to solve for a few key results along the balanced growth path of the economy, which is defined as follows:

DEFINITION 4.2. A *balanced growth path* in this economy is a situation in which all variables grow at constant exponential rates (possibly zero) and in which this constant growth could continue forever.

The following notation will also prove useful in what follows. Let $y \equiv Y/N$ denote final output per capita and let $k \equiv K/N$ represent capital per person. We will use an asterisk superscript to denote variables along a balanced growth path. And finally, g_x will be used to denote the exponential growth rate of some variable x along a balanced growth path.

With this notation, we can now provide a number of useful results for this model.

RESULT 1. With constant allocations of the form given above, this model yields the following results:

    (a) Because of the symmetric use of intermediate capital goods, the production function for final output can be written as

$$Y_t = A_t^\sigma K_t^\alpha H_{Yt}^{1-\alpha}, \quad \sigma \equiv \alpha\left(\frac{1}{\theta} - 1\right). \tag{30}$$

(b) Along a balanced growth path, output per capita y depends on the total stock of ideas, as in

$$y_t^* = \left(\frac{\bar{s}_K}{n + g_k + \delta} \right)^{\alpha/(1-\alpha)} h^*(1 - \bar{s}_A)(1 - \bar{\ell}_h)A_t^{*\sigma/(1-\alpha)}. \tag{31}$$

(c) Along a balanced growth path, the stock of ideas is increasing in the number of researchers, adjusted for their human capital,

$$A_t^* = \left(\frac{\nu}{g_A} \right)^{1/(1-\phi)} H_{At}^{*\lambda/(1-\phi)}. \tag{32}$$

(d) Combining these last two results, output per capita along the balanced growth path is an increasing function of research, which in turn is proportional to the labor force,

$$y_t^* \propto H_{At}^{*\gamma} = (h\bar{s}_A L_t)^\gamma, \quad \gamma \equiv \frac{\sigma}{1-\alpha}\frac{\lambda}{1-\phi}. \tag{33}$$

(e) Finally, taking logs and derivatives of these relationships, one gets the growth rates along the balanced growth path,

$$g_y = g_k = \frac{\sigma}{1-\alpha}g_A = \gamma g_{H_A} = g \equiv \gamma n. \tag{34}$$

In general, these results show how the simple model given in the previous section extends when a much richer framework is considered. Result 1(a) shows that this Dixit–Stiglitz technology reduces to a familiar-looking production function when the various capital goods are used symmetrically. Result 1(b) derives the level of output per capita along a balanced growth path, obtaining a solution that is closely related to what one would find in a Solow model. The first term on the right-hand side is simply the capital–output ratio in steady state, the second term adjusts for human capital, the third term adjusts for the fraction of the labor force working to produce goods, and the fourth term adjusts for labor force participation. The final term shows, as in the simple model, that per capita output along a balanced growth path is proportional to the total stock of knowledge (raised to some power).

Result 1(c) provides the analogous expression for the other main production function in the model, the production of ideas. The stock of ideas along a balanced growth path is proportional to the level of the research input (labor adjusted for human capital), again raised to some power. More researchers ultimately mean more ideas in the economy.

Result 1(d) combines these last two expressions to show that per capita output is proportional to the level of research input, which, since human capital per worker is ultimately constant, means that per capita output is proportional to the size of the labor force.[13] The exponent γ essentially measures the total degree of increasing returns to

---

[13] From now on we will leave the "raised to some power" phrase implicit.

scale in this economy. Notice that it depends on the parameters of both the goods production function and the idea production function, both of which may involve increasing returns.

Finally, Result 1(e) takes logs and derivatives of the relevant "levels" solutions to derive the growth rates of several variables. Output per worker and capital per worker both grow at the same rate. This rate is proportional to the growth rate of the stock of knowledge, which in turn is proportional to the growth rate of the effective level of research. The growth rate of research is ultimately pinned down by the growth rate of population. This last equality parallels the result in the simple model: the fundamental growth rate in the economy is a product of the degree of increasing returns and the rate of population growth. An interesting feature of this result is that the long-run growth rate does not depend on the allocations in this model. Notice that $\bar{s}_A$, for example, does not enter the expression for the long-run growth rate. Changes in the allocation of human capital to research have "level effects", as shown in Result 1(b), but they do not affect the long-run growth rate. This aspect of the model will turn out to be a relatively robust prediction of a class of idea-based growth models.[14]

Pausing to consider the key equations that make up Result 1, the reader might naturally wonder about the restrictive link between the growth rate of human capital and the growth rate of the labor force that has been assumed. For example, in considering Result 1(d), one might accept that per capita output is proportional to research labor adjusted for its human capital, but wonder whether one can get more "action" on the growth side by letting human capital per researcher grow endogenously (in contrast, it is constant in this model).

The answer is that it depends on how one models human capital accumulation. There are many richer specifications of human capital accumulation that deliver results that ultimately resemble those in Result 1. One example is given in footnote 10. Another is given in Chapter 6 of Jones (2002a). In this latter example, an individual's human capital represents the measure of ideas that the individual knows how to work with, which grows over time along a balanced growth path paralleling the growth in knowledge.

An example in which one gets endogenous growth in human capital per worker occurs when one specifies an accumulation equation that is linear in the stock of human capital itself $\dot{h} = \beta e^{\psi \ell_h} h$, reminiscent of Lucas (1988). For reasons discussed in Section 6.2, this approach is unsatisfactory, at least in my view.

4.3. The optimal allocation of resources

The next allocation we will consider is the optimal allocation. That is, we seek to solve for the allocation of resources that maximizes welfare. Because this model is based on a representative agent, this is a straightforward objective, and the optimal allocation is relatively easy to solve for.

---

[14] This invariance result can be overturned in models in which the population growth rate is an endogenous variable, but the direction of the effects are sometimes odd. See Jones (2003).

DEFINITION 4.3. The *optimal allocation* of resources in this economy consists of time paths $\{c_t, \ell_{ht}, s_{At}, \{x_{it}\}\}_{t=0}^{\infty}$ that maximize utility U_t at each point in time given the economic environment, i.e. given Equations (14)–(25), where $s_{At} \equiv H_{At}/H_t$.

In solving for the optimal allocation of resources, it is convenient to work with the following current-value Hamiltonian

$$\mathcal{H}_t = u(c_t) + \mu_{1t}\left(y_t - c_t - (n+\delta)k_t\right) + \mu_{2t} v s_{At}^{\lambda} h_t^{\lambda}(1 - \ell_{ht})^{\lambda} N_t^{\lambda} A_t^{\phi}, \tag{35}$$

where

$$y_t = A_t^{\sigma} k_t^{\alpha}\left[(1 - s_{At})h_t(1 - \ell_{ht})\right]^{1-\alpha}. \tag{36}$$

This last equation incorporates the fact that because of symmetry, the optimal allocation of resources requires the capital goods to be employed in equal quantities.

The current-value Hamiltonian $\mathcal{H}_t$ reflects the utility value of what gets produced at time t: the consumption, the net investment, and the new ideas. As suggested by Weitzman (1976), it is the utility equivalent of net domestic product. The necessary first-order conditions for an optimal allocation can then be written as a set of three control conditions $\partial\mathcal{H}_t/\partial m_t = 0$, where m is a placeholder for c, s_A and ℓ_h and two arbitrage-like equations

$$\bar{\rho} = \frac{\partial\mathcal{H}_t/\partial z_t}{\mu_{it}} + \frac{\dot{\mu}_{it}}{\mu_{it}}, \tag{37}$$

with their corresponding transversality conditions $\lim_{t\to\infty}\mu_{it}e^{-\bar{\rho}t}z_t = 0$. In these expressions, z is a placeholder for k and A, with $i = 1, 2$, respectively, and $\bar{\rho} = \rho - n$ is the effective rate of time preference. The arbitrage interpretation equates the effective rate of time preference to the "dividend" and "capital gain" associated with owning either capital or ideas, where the dividend is the additional flow of utility, $\partial\mathcal{H}_t/\partial z_t$.

RESULT 2. In this economy with the optimal allocation of resources, we have the following results:

(a) All of the results in Result 1 continue to hold, provided the allocations are interpreted as the optimal allocations rather than the rule-of-thumb allocations. For example, output per person along the balanced growth path is proportional to the stock of ideas (raised to some power), which in turn is proportional to the effective amount of research and therefore to the size of the population. As another example, the key growth rates of the economy are determined as in Equation (34), i.e. they are ultimately proportional to the rate of population growth where the factor of proportionality measures the degree of increasing returns in the economy.

(b) The optimal allocation of consumption satisfies the standard Euler equation

$$\frac{\dot{c}_t}{c_t} = \frac{1}{\zeta}\left(\frac{\partial y_t}{\partial k_t} - \delta - \rho\right). \tag{38}$$

(c) The optimal allocation of labor to research equates the value of the marginal product of labor in producing goods to the value of the marginal product of labor in producing new ideas. One way of writing this equation is

$$\frac{s_{At}^{op}}{1 - s_{At}^{op}} = \frac{(\mu_{2t}/\mu_{1t})\lambda \dot{A}_t}{(1 - \alpha)y_t}, \tag{39}$$

where the "op" superscript denotes the optimal allocation. This equation says that the ratio of labor working to produce ideas to labor working to produce goods is equal to labor's contribution to the value of the new ideas that get produced divided by labor's contribution to the value of output per person that gets produced. Notice that μ_2/μ_1 is essentially the relative price of a new idea in units of output per person.

Along a balanced growth path, we can rewrite this expression as

$$\frac{s_A^{op}}{1 - s_A^{op}} = \frac{\frac{\sigma Y_t/A_t}{r^* - (g_Y - g_A) - \phi g_A}\lambda \dot{A}_t}{(1 - \alpha)Y_t}, \tag{40}$$

where $r^* \equiv \rho + \zeta g_c$ functions as the effective interest rate for discounting future output to the present. The relative price of a new idea is given by the presented discounted value of the marginal product of the new idea in the goods production function. This marginal product at one point in time is $\sigma Y/A$, and the equation divides by $r^* - (g_Y - g_A) - \phi g_A$ to adjust for time discounting, growth in this marginal product over time at rate $g_Y - g_A$, and an adjustment for the fact that each new idea helps to produce additional ideas according to the spillover parameter ϕ. Finally, one can cancel the Y's from the numerator and denominator and replace $\dot{A}/A$ by g_A to get a closed-form solution for the allocation of labor to research along a balanced growth path.

(d) The optimal saving rate in this economy along a balanced growth path can be solved for from the Euler equation and the capital accumulation equation. It is given by

$$s_K^{op} = \frac{\alpha(n + g + \delta)}{\rho + \delta + \zeta g}, \tag{41}$$

where g is the underlying growth rate of the economy, given in Result 1(e). Notice that the optimal investment rate is proportional to the ratio of the marginal product of capital evaluated at the golden rule, $n + g + \delta$, to the marginal product of capital evaluated at the modified golden rule, $\rho + \delta + \zeta g$.

(e) The optimal allocation of time to human capital accumulation is straightforward in this model, and essentially comes down to picking ℓ_h to maximize $e^{\psi \ell_h} \times (1 - \ell_h)$. The solution is to set $\ell_{ht}^{op} = 1 - 1/\psi$ for all t. As mentioned before, this model introduces human capital in a simple fashion, so the optimal allocation is correspondingly simple.

4.4. A Romer-style equilibrium with imperfect competition

A natural question to ask at this point is whether some kind of market equilibrium can reproduce the optimal allocation of resources. The discussion at the beginning of this chapter made clear the kind of problems that an equilibrium allocation will have to face: the economy is characterized by increasing returns and therefore a standard competitive equilibrium will generally not exist and will certainly not generate the optimal allocation of resources. We are forced to depart from a perfectly competitive economy with no externalities, and therefore one will not be surprised to learn in this section that the equilibrium economy, in the absence of some kind of policy intervention, does not generally reproduce the optimal allocation of resources.

In this section, we study the equilibrium with imperfect competition first described for a model like this by Romer (1990). Romer built on the analysis by Ethier (1982), who extended the consumer variety approach to imperfect competition of Spence (1976) and Dixit and Stiglitz (1977) to the production side of the economy. The economic environment (potentially) involves departures from constant returns in two places, the production function for the consumption–output good and the production function for ideas. We deal with these departures by introducing imperfect competition for the former and externalities for the latter.

Briefly, the economy consists of three sectors. A final goods sector produces the consumption–capital–output good using labor and a collection of capital goods. The capital goods sector produces a variety of different capital goods using ideas and raw capital. Finally, the research sector employs human capital in order to produce new ideas, which in this model are represented by new kinds of capital goods. The final goods sector and the research sector are perfectly competitive and characterized by free entry, while the capital goods sector is the place where imperfect competition is introduced. When a new design for a capital good is discovered, the design is awarded an infinitely-lived patent. The owner of the patent has the exclusive right to produce and sell the particular capital good and therefore acts as a monopolist in competition with the producers of other kinds of capital goods. The monopoly profits that flow to this producer ultimately constitute the compensation to the researchers who discovered the new design in the first place.

As is usually the case, defining the equilibrium allocation of resources in a growth model is more complicated than defining the optimal allocation of resources (if for no other reason than that we have to specify markets and prices). We will begin by stating the key decision problems that have to be solved by the various agents in the economy and then we will put these together in our formal definition of equilibrium.

PROBLEM (HH). Households solve a standard optimization problem, choosing a time path of consumption and an allocation of time. That is, taking the time path of $\{w_t, r_t\}$ as given, they solve

$$\max_{\{c_t, \ell_{ht}, \ell_t\}} \int_0^\infty N_t u(c_t) e^{-\rho t} \, dt \tag{42}$$

subject to

$$\dot{v}_t = (r_t - n)v_t + w_t h_t \ell_t - c_t, \quad v_0 \text{ given}, \tag{43}$$

$$h_t = e^{\psi \ell_{ht}}, \tag{44}$$

$$\ell_{ht} + \ell_t = 1, \tag{45}$$

$$N_t = N_0 e^{nt}, \tag{46}$$

$$\lim_{t \to \infty} v_t \exp\left\{ -\int_0^t (r_s - n)\, ds \right\} \geq 0, \tag{47}$$

where v_t is the financial wealth of an individual, w_t is the wage rate per unit of human capital, and r_t is the interest rate.

PROBLEM (FG). A perfectly competitive final goods sector takes the variety of capital goods in existence as given and uses the production technology in Equation (14) to produce output. That is, at each point in time t, taking the wage rate w_t, the measure of capital goods A_t, and the prices of the capital goods p_{it} as given, the representative firm solves

$$\max_{\{x_{it}\}, H_{Yt}} \left(\int_0^{A_t} x_{it}^\theta \, di \right)^{\alpha/\theta} H_{Yt}^{1-\alpha} - w_t H_{Yt} - \int_0^{A_t} p_{it} x_{it} \, di. \tag{48}$$

PROBLEM (CG). Each variety of capital good is produced by a monopolist who owns a patent for the good, purchased at a one-time price P_{At}. As discussed in describing the economic environment, one unit of the capital good can be produced with one unit of raw capital. The monopolist sees a downward-sloping demand curve for her product from the final goods sector and chooses a price to maximize profits. That is, at each point in time and for each capital good i, a monopolist solves

$$\max_{p_{it}} \pi_{it} \equiv (p_{it} - r_t - \delta)x(p_{it}), \tag{49}$$

where $x(p_{it})$ is the demand from the final goods sector for intermediate good i if the price is p_{it}. This demand curve comes from a first-order condition in Problem (FG). The monopoly profits are the revenue from sales of the capital goods less the cost of the capital need to produce the capital goods (including depreciation). The monopolist is small relative to the economy and therefore takes aggregate variables and the interest rate r_t as given.[15]

---

[15] To be more specific, the demand curve $x(p_i)$ is given by

$$x(p_{it}) = \left(\alpha \frac{Y}{\int_0^{A_t} x_{it}^\theta \, di} \frac{1}{p_{it}} \right)^{1/(1-\theta)}.$$

We assume the monopolist is small relative to the aggregate so that it takes the price elasticity to be $-1/(1-\theta)$.

PROBLEM (R&D). The research sector produces ideas according to the production function in Equation (16). However, each individual researcher is small and takes the productivity of the idea production function as given. In particular, each researcher assumes that the idea production function is

$$\dot{A}_t = \bar{v}_t H_{At}. \tag{50}$$

That is, the duplication effects associated with λ and the knowledge spillovers associated with ϕ in Equation (16) are assumed to be external to the individual researcher. In this perfectly competitive research sector, the representative research firm solves

$$\max_{H_{At}} P_{At} \bar{v}_t H_{At} - w_t H_{At}, \tag{51}$$

taking the price of ideas P_{At}, research productivity $\bar{v}_t$, and the wage rate w_t as given.

Now that these decision problems have been described, we are ready to define an equilibrium with imperfect competition for this economy.

DEFINITION 4.4. An *equilibrium with imperfect competition* in this economy consists of time paths for the allocations $\{c_t, \ell_{ht}, \ell_t, \{x_{it}\}, Y_t, K_t, v_t, \{\pi_{it}\}, H_{Yt}, H_{At}, H_t, h_t, L_t, N_t, A_t, \bar{v}_t\}_{t=0}^{\infty}$ and prices $\{w_t, r_t, \{p_{it}\}, P_{At}\}_{t=0}^{\infty}$ such that for all t:

1. c_t, v_t, h_t, ℓ_{ht} and ℓ_t solve Problem (HH).
2. $\{x_{it}\}$ and H_{Yt} solve Problem (FG).
3. p_{it} and π_{it} solve Problem (CG) for all $i \in [0, A_t]$.
4. H_{At} solves Problem (R&D).
5. (r_t) The capital market clears: $V_t \equiv v_t N_t = K_t + P_{At} A_t$.
6. (w_t) The labor market clears: $H_{Yt} + H_{At} = H_t$.
7. $(\bar{v}_t)$ The idea production function is satisfied: $\bar{v}_t = v H_{At}^{\lambda-1} A_t^{\phi}$.
8. (K_t) The capital resource constraint is satisfied: $\int_0^{A_t} x_{it}\, di = K_t$.
9. (P_{At}) Assets have equal returns: $r_t = \frac{\pi_{it}}{P_{At}} + \frac{\dot{P}_{At}}{P_{At}}$.
10. Y_t is given by the production function in (14).
11. A_t is given by the production function in (16).
12. $H_t = h_t L_t$.
13. $L_t = \ell_t N_t$ and $N_t = N_0 e^{nt}$.

Notice that, roughly speaking, there are twenty equilibrium objects that are part of the definition of equilibrium and there are twenty equations described in the conditions for equilibrium that determine these objects at each point in time.[16] Not surprisingly, one cannot solve in general for the equilibrium outside of the balanced growth path, but along a balanced growth path the solution is relatively straightforward, and we have the following results.

---

[16] The condition omitted from this definition of equilibrium is the law of motion for the capital stock, given in the economic environment in Equation (15). That this equation holds in equilibrium is an implication of Walras' law. It can be derived in equilibrium by differentiating the capital market clearing condition that $V = K + P_A A$ with respect to time and making the natural substitutions.

RESULT 3. In the equilibrium with imperfect competition:
(a) All of the results in Result 1 continue to hold along the balanced growth path, provided the allocations are interpreted as the equilibrium allocations rather than the rule-of-thumb allocations. For example, output per person along the balanced growth path is proportional to the stock of ideas (raised to some power), which in turn is proportional to the effective amount of research and therefore to the size of the population. As another example, the key growth rates of the economy are determined as in Equation (34), i.e. they are ultimately proportional to the rate of population growth where the factor of proportionality measures the degree of increasing returns in the economy.
(b) The Euler equation for consumption and the allocation of time to human capital accumulation are undistorted in this equilibrium. That is, the equations that apply are identical to the equations describing the optimal allocation of resources:

$$\frac{\dot{c}_t}{c_t} = \frac{1}{\zeta}\left(r_t^{eq} - \rho\right),$$ (52)

$$\ell_{ht}^{eq} = 1 - \frac{1}{\psi}.$$ (53)

(c) The solution to Problem (CG) involves a monopoly markup over marginal cost that depends on the CES parameter in the usual way,

$$p_{it}^{eq} = p_t^{eq} \equiv \frac{1}{\theta}\left(r_t^{eq} + \delta\right).$$ (54)

Because of this monopoly markup, however, capital is paid less than its marginal product, and the equilibrium interest rate is given by

$$r_t^{eq} = \alpha\theta\frac{Y_t}{K_t} - \delta.$$ (55)

Because the equilibrium economy grows at the same rate as the economy with optimal allocations, the steady-state interest rate determined from the Euler equation is the same in the two economies. Therefore, the fact that capital is paid less than its marginal product translates into a suboptimally low capital–output ratio in the equilibrium economy. Similarly, the equilibrium investment rate along a balanced growth path is given by

$$s_K^{eq} = \frac{\alpha\theta(n + g + \delta)}{\rho + \delta + \zeta g} = \theta s_K^{op}.$$ (56)

(d) The equilibrium allocation of human capital to research equates the wage of human capital in producing goods to its wage in producing ideas. This result can be written in an equation analogous to (39) as

$$\frac{s_{At}^{eq}}{1 - s_{At}^{eq}} = \frac{P_{At}\dot{A}_t}{(1 - \alpha)Y_t}.$$ (57)

The ratio of the share of human capital working to produce ideas to that working to produce goods is equal to the value of the output of new ideas divided by labor's share of the value of final goods.

Along the balanced growth path, we can rewrite this expression as

$$\frac{s_A^{eq}}{1 - s_A^{eq}} = \frac{\frac{\sigma\theta Y_t/A_t}{r^{eq}-(g_Y-g_A)}\dot{A}_t}{(1-\alpha)Y_t}, \tag{58}$$

which is directly comparable to the optimal allocation in Equation (40). In comparing these two equations, we see three differences. The first two differences reflect the externalities in the idea production function. The true marginal product of human capital in research is lower by a factor of $\lambda < 1$ than the equilibrium economy recognizes because of the congestion/duplication externality, which tends to lead the equilibrium to overinvest in research. On the other hand, the equilibrium allocation ignores the fact that the discovery of new ideas may raise the future productivity of research if $\phi > 0$. This changes the effective rate at which the flow of future ideas is discounted, potentially causing the equilibrium to underinvest in research. Finally, the third difference reflects the appropriability of returns. A new idea raises the current level of output in the final goods sector according to the marginal product $\sigma Y/A$. However, the research sector appropriates only the fraction $\theta < 1$ of this marginal product. The reason is familiar from the standard monopoly diagram in undergraduate classes: the profits appropriated by a monopolist are strictly lower than the consumer surplus created by that monopolist. This appropriability effect works to cause the equilibrium allocation of human capital to research to be too low. Overall, these three distortions do not all work in the same direction, so that theory cannot tell us whether the equilibrium allocation to research is too high or too low.

4.5. Discussion

Let us step back for a moment to take stock of what we learn from the developments in this section. The most important finding is Result 1, together with the fact that it carries over into the other allocations as Result 2(a) and Result 3(a). This result is simply a confirmation of the basic results from the simple model in Section 3. Because of the nonrivalrous nature of ideas, output per person depends on the total stock of ideas in the economy instead of the per capita stock of ideas. This is a direct implication of the fact that nonrivalry leads to increasing returns to scale. In turn, it implies that output per capita, in the long run, is an increasing function of the total amount of research, which in turn is an increasing function of the scale of the economy, measured by the size of its total population. Log-differencing this statement, we see that the growth rate of output per worker ultimately depends on the growth rate of the number of researchers and therefore on the growth rate of population. This has been analyzed and discussed extensively in a number of recent papers; these will be reviewed in detail in Section 5.

The second main finding from models like this is that the equilibrium allocation of resources is not generally optimal, at least not in the absence of some kind of policy intervention. Here, the allocation of resources to the production of new ideas can be either too high or too low, as discussed above.[17] In addition, investment rates are too low in equilibrium, reflecting the fact that capital is paid less than its marginal product so that some resources are available to compensate inventive effort.

In this equilibrium, the suboptimal allocation of resources is easily remedied. A subsidy to capital accumulation and a subsidy or tax on research can be financed with lump sum taxes in order to generate the optimal allocation of resources. A useful exercise is to solve for the equilibrium in the presence of such taxes in order to determine the optimal tax rates along a balanced growth path.

Given the simplicity of this economic environment, there exist alternative institutions that are equally effective in getting optimal allocations. For example, consider a perfectly competitive economy in which all research is publicly-funded. The government raises revenue with lump-sum taxes and uses these taxes to hire researchers that produce new ideas. These new ideas are then released into the public domain where anyone can use them to produce capital goods in perfect competition.[18]

In practice of course, one suspects that obtaining the optimal allocation of resources is more difficult than either the world of imperfect competition with taxes and subsidies or the perfectly-competitive world with public funding of research suggest. There are many different directions for research, many different kinds of labor (different skill levels and talents), and individual effort choices that are unobserved by the government. Indeed, the available evidence suggests that the allocation of resources to research falls short of the optimal level. Jones and Williams (1998) take advantage of a large body of empirical work in the productivity literature to conclude that the social rate of return to research substantially exceeds the private rate of return, suggesting that research effort falls short of the optimum.

The implication of this is that there is no reason to think that we have found the best institutions for generating the optimal allocation of resources to research. Institutions like the patent system or the Small Business Innovative Research (SBIR) grants program are themselves ideas. These institutions have evolved over time to promote an efficient

---

[17] This conclusion also holds true in the Schumpeterian growth models of Aghion and Howitt (1992) and Grossman and Helpman (1991) discussed in Chapter 2 of this Handbook, but for a different reason. In these quality-ladder models, a firm discovers a better version of an existing product, displacing the incumbent producer. Some of the rents earned by the innovator are the result of past discoveries, and some of the rents earned by future innovators will be due to the discovery of the current innovator. This business stealing creates another distortion in the allocation of resources to research. Because an innovator essentially steals first and gets expropriated later, the effect of this business stealing distortion is to promote excessive research. Because the model also features appropriability problems and knowledge spillovers, the equilibrium amount of research can be either too high or too low in these models.

[18] A useful exercise here is to define the competitive equilibrium with public funding of research and to solve for optimal taxes and public expenditure.

allocation of resources, but it is almost surely the case that better institutions – better ideas – are out there to be discovered.

Interestingly, this result can be illustrated within the model itself. Notice how much easier it is to define the optimal allocation than it is to define the equilibrium allocation. The equilibrium with imperfect competition requires the modeler to be "clever" and to come up with the right institutions (e.g., a patent system, monopolistic competition, and the appropriate taxes and subsidies) to make everything work out. In reality, society must invent and implement these institutions.

Three recent papers deserve mention in this context. Romer (2000) argues that subsidizing the key input into the production of ideas – human capital in the form of college graduates with degrees in engineering and the natural sciences – is preferable to government subsidies downstream like the SBIR program. Kremer (1998) notes the large ex-post monopoly distortions associated with patents in the pharmaceutical industry and elsewhere and proposes a new mechanism for encouraging innovation. In particular, he suggests that the government (or other altruistic organizations such as charitable foundations) should consider purchasing the patents for particular innovations and releasing them into the public domain to eliminate the monopoly distortion. Boldrin and Levine (2002), in a controversial paper, are even more critical of existing patent and copyright systems and propose restricting them severely or even eliminating them altogether.[19] They argue that first-mover advantages, secrecy, and imitation delays provide ample protection for innovators and that an economy without patent and copyright systems would have a better allocation of resources than the current regime in which copyright protection is essentially indefinite and patents are used as a weapon to discourage innovation. Each of these papers makes a useful contribution by attempting to create new institutions that might improve the allocation of resources.

5. Scale effects

Idea-based growth models are linked tightly to increasing returns to scale, as was noted earlier in the Idea Diagram. The mechanism at the heart of this link is nonrivalry: the fact that knowledge can be used by an arbitrarily large number of people simultaneously without degradation means that there is something special about the first instantiation of an idea. There is a cost to creating an idea in the first place that does not have to be re-incurred as the idea gets used by more and more people. This fixed cost implies that production is, at least in the absence of some other fixed factor like land, characterized by increasing returns to scale.

Notice that nothing in this argument relies on a low marginal cost of production or on the absence of learning and human capital. Consider the design of a new drug for treating high blood pressure. Discovering the precise chemical formulation for the drug

---

[19] See also the important elaborations and clarifications in Quah (2002).

may require hundreds of millions of dollars of research effort. This idea is then simply a chemical formula. Producing copies of the drug – pills – may be expensive, for example if the drug involves the use of a rare chemical compound. It may also be such that only the best-trained biochemists have the knowledge to understand the chemical formula and manufacture the drug. Nevertheless, an accurate characterization of the production technology for producing the drug is as a fixed research cost followed by a constant marginal cost. Once the chemical formula is discovered, to double the production of pills we simply double the number of highly-trained biochemists, build a new (identical) factory, and purchase twice as much of the rare chemical compound used as an input.

Because the link between idea-based growth theory and increasing returns is so strong, the role of "scale effects" in growth models has been the focus of a series of theoretical and empirical papers. In discussing these papers, it is helpful to consider two forms of scale effects. In models that exhibit "strong" scale effects, the growth rate of the economy is an increasing function of scale (which typically means overall population or the population of educated workers). Examples of such models include the first-generation models of Romer (1990), Aghion and Howitt (1992) and Grossman and Helpman (1991). On the other hand, in models that exhibit "weak" scale effects, the level of per capita income in the long run is an increasing function of the size of the economy. This is true in the "semi-endogenous" growth models of Jones (1995a), Kortum (1997) and Segerstrom (1998) that were written at least partially in response to the strong scale effects in the first generation models. The models examined formally in the previous sections of this chapter fit into this category as well.

To use an analogy from the computer software industry, are scale effects a bug or a feature? I believe the correct answer is slightly complicated. I will argue that overall they are a feature, i.e. a useful prediction of the model that helps us to understand the world. However, in some papers, most notably in the first generation of idea-based growth models, these scale effects appeared in an especially potent way, producing predictions in these models that are easily falsified. This strong form of scale effects – in which the long-run growth rate of the economy depends on its scale – is a bug. Subsequent research has remedied this problem, maintaining everything that is important about idea-based growth models but eliminating the strong form of the scale effects prediction. This still leaves us, as discussed above, with a weak form of scale effects: the size of the economy affects, in some sense, the level of per capita income. This, of course, is nothing more than a statement that the economy is characterized by increasing returns to scale. The weak form of scale effects has its critics as well, but I will argue two things. First, these criticisms are generally misplaced. And second, it's fortunate that this is the case: the weak form of scale effects is so inextricably tied to idea-based growth models that rejecting one is largely equivalent to rejecting the other.

The remainder of this section consists of two basic parts. Section 5.1 returns to the simple growth model presented in Section 3 to formalize the strong and weak versions of scale effects. The remaining sections then discuss a range of applications in the literature related to scale effects.

5.1. Strong and weak scale effects

The simple model in Section 3 revealed that the growth rate of per capita income is proportional to the growth rate of the stock of ideas. Consider that same model, but replace the idea production function in Equation (7) with

$$\dot{A}_t = \nu L_{At}^{\lambda} A_t^{\phi}. \tag{59}$$

We could go further and incorporate human capital, as we did in the richer model of Section 4, but this will not change the basic result, so we will leave out this complication.

Now consider two cases. In the first, we impose the condition that $\phi < 1$. In the second, we will instead assume that $\phi = 1$. In the case of $\phi < 1$, the analysis goes through exactly as in the models developed earlier, and the growth rate of the stock of ideas along a balanced growth path is given by

$$g_A = \frac{\lambda n}{1 - \phi}, \tag{60}$$

which pins down all the key growth rates in the model. Notice that, as before, the growth rate is proportional to the rate of population growth. It is straightforward to show, as we did earlier, that the level of per capita income in such an economy is an increasing function of the size of the population. That is, this model exhibits weak scale effects. Finally, notice that this equation cannot apply if $\phi = 1$; in that case, the denominator would explode.

To see more clearly the source of the problem, rewrite the idea production function when we assume $\phi = 1$ as

$$\frac{\dot{A}_t}{A_t} = \nu L_{At}^{\lambda}. \tag{61}$$

In this case, the growth rate of knowledge is proportional to the number of researchers raised to some power λ. If the number of researchers is itself growing over time, the simple model will not exhibit a balanced growth path. Rather, the growth rate itself will be growing! With $\phi = 1$, the simple model exhibits strong scale effects.

The first generation idea-based growth models of Romer (1990), Aghion and Howitt (1992) and Grossman and Helpman (1991) all include idea production functions that essentially make the assumption of $\phi = 1$, and all exhibit the strong form of scale effects.[20] The problem with the strong form of scale effects is easy to document and understand. Because the growth rate of the economy is an increasing function of research effort, these models require research effort to be constant over time to match the relative

---

[20] This is easily seen in the Romer expanding variety model, as that model is the building block for the models developed in this chapter. It is slightly trickier to see this in the quality ladder models of Aghion and Howitt (1992) and Grossman and Helpman (1991). In those models, each researcher produces a constant number of ideas, but ideas get bigger over time. In particular, each new idea generates a *proportional* improvement in productivity.

stability of growth rates in the United States and some other advanced economies. However, research effort is itself growing over time (for example, if for no other reason than
simply because the population is growing). These facts are now documented in more
detail.

A useful stylized fact that any growth model must come to terms with is the relative
stability of growth rates in the United States over more than a century. This stability can
be easily seen by plotting per capita GDP for the United States on a logarithmic scale,
as shown in Figure 1. A straight line with a growth rate of 1.8 percent per year provides
a very accurate description of average growth rates in the United States dating back to
1870. There are departures from this line, of course, most clearly corresponding to the
Great Depression and the recovery following World War II. But what is truly remarkable
about this figure is how well a straight line describes the trend.

Jones (1995b) made this point in the following way. Suppose one drew a trend line
using data from 1870 to 1929 and then extrapolated that line forward to predict per
capita GDP today. It turns out that such a prediction matches up very well with the
current level of per capita GDP, confirming the hypothesis that growth rates have been
relatively stable on average.[21]

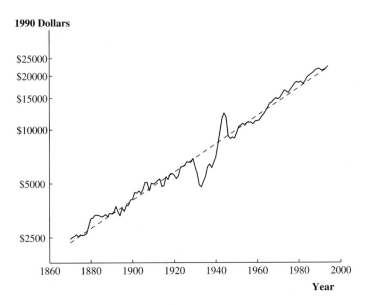

Figure 1. U.S. GDP per capita log scale. *Source*: Maddison (1995).

---

[21] Of course this is only an approximation. The growth rate from 1950 to 1994 averaged 1.95 percent, while
the growth rate from 1870 to 1929 averaged 1.75 percent [see, e.g., Ben-David and Papell (1995) on this
increase]. On the other hand, the 2.20 percent growth rate in the 1950s and 1960s is slightly higher than the
1.74 percent growth rate after 1970, reflecting the productivity slowdown. Similar results can be obtained
with GDP per worker and GDP per hour worked, see Williams (1995).

This stylized fact represents an important benchmark that any growth model must match. Whatever the engine driving long run growth, it must (a) be able to produce relatively stable growth rates for a century or more, and (b) must not predict that growth rates in the United States over this period of time should depart from such a pattern. To see this force of this argument, consider first a theory like Lucas (1988) that predicts that investment in human capital is the key to growth. In this model, the growth rate of the economy is proportional to the investment rate in human capital. But if investment rates in human capital have risen significantly in the 20th century in the United States, as data on educational attainment suggests, this is a problem for the theory. It could be rescued if investment rates in human capital in the form of on-the-job training have fallen to offset the rise in formal education, but there is little evidence suggesting that this is the case.

This stylized fact is even more problematic for the first-generation idea-based growth models of Romer (1990), Aghion and Howitt (1992) and Grossman and Helpman (1991) (R/AH/GH). These models predict that growth is an increasing function of research effort, but research effort has apparently grown tremendously over time. As one example of this fact, consider Figure 2. This figure plots an index of the number of scientists and engineers engaged in research in the G-5 countries. Between 1950 and 1993, this index of research effort rose by more than a factor of eight. In part this is because of the general growth in employment in these countries, but as the figure shows, it also reflects a large increase in the fraction of employment devoted to research. A similar fact can be

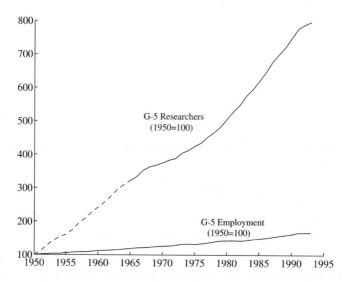

Figure 2. Researchers and employment in the G-5 countries (index). *Note.* From calculations in Jones (2002b). Data on researchers before 1950 in countries other than the United States is backcasted using the 1965 research share of employment. The G-5 countries are France, Germany, Japan, the United Kingdom and the United States.

documented using just the data for the United States, or by looking at spending on R&D rather than employment.[22] The bottom line is that resources devoted to research have exhibited a tremendous amount of growth in the post-war period, while growth rates in the United States have been relatively stable. The implication is that models that exhibit strong scale effects are inconsistent with the basic trends in aggregate data. Evidence like this is one of the main arguments in favor of models that exhibit weak scale effects instead.[23]

5.2. Growth effects and policy invariance

At some level, the rejection of models with strong scale effects in favor of models with weak scale effects should not be especially interesting. The only difference between the two models, as discussed above, is essentially the strength of the knowledge spillover parameter. In expanding variety models, is $\phi = 1$ or is $\phi < 1$? Nothing in the evidence necessarily rules out $\phi = 0.95$, and continuity arguments suggest that the economics of $\phi = 0.95$ and $\phi = 1$ cannot be that different.

The main difference in the economic results that one obtains in the two models pertains to the ability of changes in policy to alter the long-run growth rate of the economy. In the models that exhibit strong scale effects, the long-run growth rate is an increasing function of the number of researchers. Hence, a policy that increases the number of researchers, such as an R&D expenditure subsidy, will increase the long-run growth rate. In contrast, if $\phi < 1$, then the long-run growth rate depends on elasticities of production functions and on the rate of population growth. To the extent that these parameters are unaffected by policy – as one might naturally take to be the case, at least to a first approximation – policy changes such as a subsidy to R&D or a tax on capital will have no affect on the long-run growth rate. They will of course affect the long-run level of income and will affect the growth rate along a transition path, but the long-run growth rate is invariant to standard policy changes.

This statement can be qualified in a couple of ways. First, the population growth rate is really an endogenous variable determined by fertility choices of individuals. Policy changes can affect this choice and hence can affect long-run growth even in a model with weak scale effects, as shown in Jones (2003). However, the effects can often be counter to the usual direction. For example, a subsidy to R&D can lead people to perform more research and have fewer kids, reducing fertility. Hence a subsidy to research

---

[22] There are several ways to look at the R&D spending share of GDP. For total R&D expenditures as a share of GDP in the United States, most of the increase in the R&D share occurs before 1960. However, if one substracts out R&D expenditures on defense and space (which might be a reasonable thing to do since government output is valued at cost), or if one focuses on non-federally-financed research, the trend in the U.S. share emerges clearly; see Chapter 4 of the NSF's *Science and Engineering Indicators, 2004*. Alternatively, there are substantial trends in the R&D shares for most of the other G-7 countries; in addition to the 2004 edition, see also the 1993 edition of the NSF's *Science and Engineering Indicators* to get data on the research shares back to 1970.

[23] The other main argument is the "linearity critique" discussed further in Section 6.2.

can reduce the long-run growth rate. This can be true even if it is optimal to subsidize research – this kind of model makes clear that long-run growth and welfare are two very different concepts. The second qualification is that one can imagine subsidies that affect the direction of research and that can possibly affect long-run growth. For example, Cozzi (1997) constructs a model in which research can proceed in different directions that may involve different knowledge spillover elasticities. By shifting research to the directions with high spillovers, it is possible to change the long-run growth rate.

Despite these qualifications, it remains true that in the semi-endogenous growth models written to address the problem of strong scale effects, straightforward policies do not affect the long-run growth rate. This has led a number of researchers to seek alternative means of eliminating the strong scale effects prediction while maintaining the potency of policy to alter the long-run growth rate. Key papers in this line of research include Young (1998), Peretto (1998), Dinopoulos and Thompson (1998) and Howitt (1999) (Y/P/DT/H).

These papers all work in a similar way.[24] In particular, each adds a second dimension to the model, so that research can improve productivity for a particular product or can add to the variety of products. To do this in the simplest way, suppose that aggregate consumption (or output) is a CES composite of a variety of different products

$$C_t = \left(\int_0^{B_t} Y_{it}^{1/\theta} \, di \right)^{\theta}, \quad \theta > 1, \tag{62}$$

where B_t represents the variety of goods that are available at date t and Y_{it} is the output of variety i. Assume that each variety Y_i is produced using the Romer-style technology with $\phi = 1$ in the simple model given earlier in Section 3.

The key to the model is the way in which the number of different varieties B changes over time. To keep the model as simple as possible, assume

$$B_t = L_t^{\beta}. \tag{63}$$

That is, the number of varieties is proportional to the population raised to some power β. Notice that this relationship could be given microfoundations with an idea production function analogous to that in Equation (16).[25]

Finally, let us assume each intermediate variety is used in the same quantity so that $Y_{it} = Y_t$, implying $C_t = B_t^{\theta} Y_t$. Per capita consumption is then $c_t = B_t^{\theta} y_t$, and per capita consumption growth along a balanced growth path is

$$g_c = \theta g_B + \sigma g_A = \theta \beta n + \sigma g_A. \tag{64}$$

Assuming an idea production function with $\phi = 1$, like that in R/AH/GH, the growth rate of the stock of ideas is proportional to research effort per variety, $L_{At}/B_t = sL_t/B_t$,

$$g_A = \frac{vsL_t}{B_t} = vsL_t^{1-\beta}. \tag{65}$$

---

[24] This section draws heavily on Jones (1999).

[25] For example, if $\dot{B} = LB^{\gamma}$, then Equation (63) holds along a balanced growth path with $\beta = 1/(1 - \gamma)$.

Substituting this equation back into (64) gives the growth rate of per capita output as a function of exogenous variables and parameters

$$g_c = \theta \beta n + \sigma v s L_t^{1-\beta}. \tag{66}$$

With $\beta = 1$ so that $B_t = L_t$, the strong scale effect is eliminated from the model, while the effect of policy on long-run growth is preserved. That is, a permanent increase in the fraction of the labor force working in research, s, will permanently raise the growth rate. This is the key result sought by the Y/P/DT/H models.

However, there are two important things to note about this result. First, it is very fragile. In particular, to the extent that $\beta \neq 1$, problems reemerge. If $\beta < 1$, then the model once again exhibits strong scale effects. Alternatively, if $\beta > 1$, then changes in s no longer permanently affect the long-run growth rate. Thus, the Y/P/DT/H result depends crucially on a knife-edge case for this parameter value, in addition to the Romer-like knife-edge assumption of $\phi = 1$. Second, as the first term in Equation (66) indicates, the model still exhibits the weak form of scale effects. This result is not surprising given that these are idea-based growth models, but it is useful to recognize since many of the papers in this literature have titles that include the phrase "growth without scale effects". What these titles really mean is that the papers attempt to eliminate strong scale effects; all of them still possess weak scale effects. These points are discussed in more detail in Jones (1999) and Li (2000, 2002).

5.3. Cross-country evidence on scale effects

One source of evidence on the empirical relevance of scale effects comes from looking across countries or regions at a point in time. Consider first the ideal cross-sectional evidence. One would observe two regions, one larger than the other, that are otherwise identical. The two regions would not interact in any way and the only source of new ideas in the two regions would be the regions' own populations. In such an ideal experiment, one could search for scale effects by looking at the stock of ideas and at per capita income in each region over time. In the long-run, one would expect that the larger region would end up being richer.

In practice, of course, this ideal experiment is never observed. Instead, we have data on different countries and regions in the world, but these regions almost certainly share ideas and they almost certainly are not equal in other dimensions. It falls to clever econometricians to use this data to approximate the ideal experiment. No individual piece of evidence is especially compelling, but the collection taken together does indeed suggest that the cross-sectional evidence on scale effects supports the basic model.

Certainly the most creative approximation to date is found in Kremer (1993) and later appears in the Pulitzer Prize-winning book *Guns, Germs, and Steel* by Diamond (1997). The most recent ice age ended about 10,000 B.C. Before that time, ocean levels were lower, allowing humans to migrate around the world – for example across the Bering Strait and into the Americas. In this sense, ideas could diffuse across regions. However, with the end of the ice age, sea levels rose, and various regions of the world were effectively isolated from each other, at least until the advent of large sailing ships sometime around the year 1000 or 1500. In particular, for approximately 12,000 years, five regions were mutually isolated from one another: the Eurasian/African continents, the Americas, Australia, Tasmania (an island off the coast of Australia), and the Flinders Island (a very small island off the coast of Tasmania). These regions are also nicely ranked in terms of population sizes, from the relatively highly-populated Eurasian/African continent down to the small Flinders Island, with a population that likely numbered fewer than 500.

It is plausible that 12,000 years ago these regions all had similar technologies: all were relatively primitive hunter-gatherer cultures. Now fast-forward to the year 1500 when a wave of European exploration reintegrates the world. First, the populous Old World has the highest level of technological sophistication; they are the ones doing the exploring. The Americas follow next, with cities, agriculture, and the Aztec and Mayan civilizations. Australia is in the intermediate position, having developed the boomerang, the atlatl, fire-making, and sophisticated stone tools, but still consisting of a hunter-gatherer culture. Tasmania is relatively unchanged, and the population of Flinders Island had died out completely. The technological rank of these regions more than 10,000 years later matches up exactly with their initial population ranks at the end of the last ice age.

Turning to more standard evidence from the second-half of the 20th century, one is first struck by the apparent lack of support for the hypothesis of weak scale effects. The most populous countries of the world, China and India, are among the poorest, while some of the smallest countries like Hong Kong and Luxembourg are among the richest. And the countries with the most rapid rates of population growth – many in Africa – are among the countries with the slowest rates of per capita income growth. However, a moment's thought suggests that one must be careful in interpreting this evidence. It is clearly not the case that Hong Kong and Luxembourg are isolated countries that grow solely based on the ideas created by their own populations. These countries benefit tremendously from ideas created around the world. And in the case of the poor countries of the world, "other things" are clearly not equal. These countries have very different levels of human capital and different policies, institutions, and property rights that contribute to their poverty. Hence, we must turn to econometric evidence that seeks to neutralize these differences.

The clearest cross-country evidence in favor of weak scale effects comes from papers that explicitly control for differences in international trade. Intuitively, openness to international trade is likely related to openness to idea flows, and the flow of ideas from other countries is one of the key factors that needs to be neutralized. Backus, Kehoe and Kehoe (1992), Frankel and Romer (1999) and Alcala and Ciccone (2002) are the main examples of this line of work, and all find an important role for scale. Alcala and Ciccone (2002) provide what is probably the best specification, controlling for both trade and institutional quality (and instrumenting for these endogenous variables), but the results in Frankel and Romer (1999) are similar. Alcala and Ciccone find a long-run elasticity of GDP per worker with respect to the size of the workforce that is equal to 0.20.[26] That is, holding other things equal, a 10 percent increase in the size of the workforce in the long run is associated with a 2 percent higher GDP per worker.[27]

Other cross-country studies, of course, have not been able to precisely estimate this elasticity. Hall and Jones (1999), for example, found a point estimate of about 0.05, but with a standard error of 0.06. Sala-i-Martin (1997) does not find the size of the population to be a robust variable in his four million permutations of cross-country growth regressions. Finally, it should be recognized that this cross-country estimate of the scale elasticity is not necessarily an estimate of the structural parameter γ in the idea models presented earlier in Section 4. One needs a theory of technology adoption and idea flows in order to make sense of the estimates. For example, in a world where ideas flow to all places instantaneously, there would be no reason to find a scale effect in the cross-section evidence.

A final piece of evidence that is often misinterpreted as providing evidence against the weak scale effects prediction is the negative coefficient on population growth in a cross-country growth regression, such as in Mankiw, Romer and Weil (1992). Recall that the standard interpretation of these regressions is that they are estimating transition dynamics. The negative coefficient on population growth is interpreted as capturing the dilution of the investment rate associated with the Solow model. Consider two countries that are identical but for different population growth rates. The country with the faster population growth rate must equip a larger number of new workers with the existing capital–labor ratio, effectively diluting the investment rate. The result is that such an economy has a lower capital–output ratio in steady state, reducing output per worker along the balanced growth path. But this same force is also at work in any growth model, including idea-based models, as was apparent above in Result 1(b). The implication is that this cross-country evidence is not inconsistent with models in which weak scale effects play a role.

5.4. Growth over the very long run

Additional evidence on the potential relevance of scale effects to economic growth comes from what at first might seem an unlikely place: the history of growth from thousands of years ago to the present.

One of the important applications of models of economic growth in recent years has been to understand economic growth over this very long time period. Many of our workhorse models of growth were constructed with an eye toward 20th-century growth. Asking how well they explain growth over a much longer period of time therefore provides a nice test of our models.

---

[26] The standard error of this particular point estimate is about 0.10. Across different specifications, the elasticity ranges from a low of about 0.10 to a high of about 0.40.

[27] Of course in the model with trade, other things would not be equal: a change in population would almost surely affect the trade-GDP ratios that measure openness in the regression.

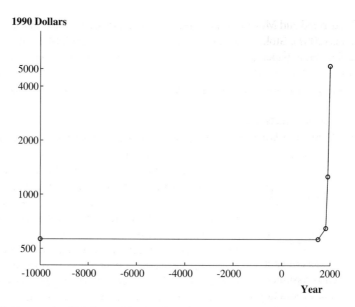

Figure 3. World per capita GDP (log scale). *Note*. Data from Maddison (1995) for years after 1500. Before 1500, we assume a zero growth rate, as suggested by Maddison and others.

The key fact that must be explained over this period is quite stunning and is displayed in Figure 3. For thousands and thousands of years prior to the Industrial Revolution, standards of living were relatively low. In particular, the evidence suggests that there was no sustained growth in per capita incomes before the Industrial Revolution.[28] Then, quite suddenly from the standpoint of the sweep of world history, growth rates accelerated and standards of living began rising with increasing rapidity. At the world level, per capita income today is probably about 10 times higher than it was in the year 1800 or 1500 or even 10,000 years ago. A profound question in economic history – and one that growth economists have begun delving into – is this: How do we understand this entire time path? Why were standards of living relatively low and stagnant for so long, why have they risen so dramatically in the last 150 years, and what changed?[29]

The recent growth literature on this question is quite large, and a thorough review is beyond the scope of the present chapter (additional discussion can be found in Chapter 4 of this Handbook, by Oded Galor). Representative papers include Lee (1988), Kremer

---

[28] See Lucas (1998), Galor and Weil (2000), Jones (2001) and Clark (2001) for a discussion of this evidence.

[29] A cottage industry (!) in recent years has sprung up in which macroeconomists bring their modeling tools to bear on major questions in economic history. In addition to growth over the very long run, macroeconomists have studied the Great Depression [Ohanian and Cole (2001)], the Second Industrial Revolution [Atkeson and Kehoe (2002)], and the rise in female labor force participation over the course of the 20th century [Greenwood, Seshadri and Yorukoglu (2001)] among other topics.

(1993), Goodfriend and McDermott (1995), Lucas (1998), Galor and Weil (2000), Clark (2001), Jones (2001), Stokey (2001), Hansen and Prescott (2002) and Tamura (2002).

In several of these papers, scale effects play a crucial role. Scale is at the heart of the models of Lee (1988), Kremer (1993) and Jones (2001), and it also plays an important role in getting growth started in the model based on human capital in Galor and Weil (2000).

The role of scale effects in these models can be illustrated most effectively by looking at the elegant model of Lee (1988). The three key equations of that model are:

$$Y_t = A_t L_t^{1-\beta} T_t^{\beta}, \quad T_t = 1, \tag{67}$$

$$\frac{\dot{A}_t}{A_t} = \gamma \log L_t, \quad A_0 \text{ given}, \tag{68}$$

$$\frac{\dot{L}_t}{L_t} = \alpha \left(\log \frac{Y_t}{L_t} - \log \bar{y} \right), \quad L_0 \text{ given}. \tag{69}$$

Equation (67) describes a production function that depends on ideas A, labor L, and land T, which is assumed to be in fixed supply and normalized to one. Equation (68) is a Romer-like production function for new ideas. Notice that we have assumed the $\phi = 1$ case so that we can get an analytic solution below, but the nature of the results does not depend on this assumption. Notice also that we assume all labor can produce ideas, and we assume a log form. This makes the model log-linear, which is the second key assumption needed to get a closed-form solution. Finally, Equation (69) is a Malthusian equation describing population growth. If output per person is greater than the subsistence parameter $\bar{y}$, then population grows; if less then population declines.

The model can be solved as follows. First, choose the units of output such that the subsistence term gets normalized to zero, $\log \bar{y} = 0$. Next, let $a \equiv \log A$ and $\ell \equiv \log L$. Then the model reduces to a linear homogeneous system of differential equations:

$$\dot{a}_t = \gamma \ell_t, \tag{70}$$

$$\dot{\ell}_t = \alpha a_t - \alpha \beta \ell_t. \tag{71}$$

It is straightforward to solve this system to find

$$\log \frac{Y_t}{L_t} = \omega_1 e^{\theta_1 t} + \omega_2 e^{\theta_2 t}, \tag{72}$$

where $\theta_1 > 0$ and $\theta_2 < 0$ are the eigenvalues associated with this system, and $\omega_1 > 0$.[30] That is, the solution involves a double exponential: the natural log of output per worker

---

[30] The differential system can be solved using linear algebra, as in Barro and Sala-i-Martin (1995, p. 480) or, even more intuitively, by writing it as a single second-order differential equation, as in Boyce and DiPrima (1997, pp. 123–125). The values for the constants in Equation (72) are $\theta_1 = (-\alpha\beta + \sqrt{(\alpha\beta)^2 + 4\alpha\gamma})/2$, $\theta_2 = (-\alpha\beta - \sqrt{(\alpha\beta)^2 + 4\alpha\gamma})/2$, $\omega_1 = (\theta_1/\alpha)(\alpha(a_0 - \beta\ell_0) - \theta_2\ell_0)/(\theta_1 - \theta_2)$, $\omega_2 = (\theta_2/\alpha)(\theta_1\ell_0 - \alpha(a_0 - \beta\ell_0))/(\theta_1 - \theta_2)$.

grows exponentially, so that the growth rate of output per worker, $y \equiv Y/L$, itself grows exponentially,

$$\frac{\dot{y}_t}{y_t} = \omega_1 \theta_1 e^{\theta_1 t} + \omega_2 \theta_2 e^{\theta_2 t}. \tag{73}$$

Mathematically, it is this double exponential growth that allows the model to deliver a graph that looks approximately like that in Figure 3.

Analytically, Lee's result is extremely nice. However, the analytic results are obtained only by simplifying the model considerably – perhaps too much. For example, the model generates double exponential growth in population as well. As shown in Kremer (1993), this pattern fits the broad sweep of world history, but it sharply contradicts the demographic transition that has set in over the last century, where population growth rates level off and decline. In addition, the analytic results require the strong assumption that $\phi = 1$.

If one wishes to depart from the log-linear structure of Lee's model, the analysis must be conducted numerically. This is done in Jones (2001), with a more realistic demographic setup and with an idea production function that incorporates $\phi < 1$. The basic insights from Lee (1988) apply over the broad course of history, but the model also predicts a demographic transition and a leveling off of per capita income growth in the 20th century. The model with weak scale effects, then, is able to match the basic facts of income and population growth over both the very long run and the 20th century.

The economic intuition for these results is straightforward. Thousands and thousands of years ago, the population was relatively small and the productivity of the population at producing ideas was relatively low. Per capita consumption, then, stayed around the Malthusian level that kept population constant ($\bar{y}$ in the Lee model above). Suppose it took 1000 years for this population to discover a new idea. With the arrival of the new idea, per capita income and fertility rose, producing a larger population. Diminishing returns associated with a fixed supply of land drove consumption back to its subsistence level, but now the population was larger. Instead of requiring 1000 years to produce a new idea, this larger population produced a new idea sooner, say in 800 years. Continuing along this virtuous circle, growth gradually accelerated. Provided the economic environment is characterized by a sufficiently large degree of increasing returns (to offset the diminishing returns associated with limited land), the acceleration in population growth produces a scale effect that leads to the acceleration of per capita income growth. Eventually, the economy becomes sufficiently rich that a demographic transition sets in, leading population growth and per capita income growth to level out.[31]

---

[31] It is even possible for the demographic transition to drive population growth rates down to zero, in which cases per capita income growth rates decline as well. There is always growth in this world – even a constant population produces new ideas – but the growth rate is no longer exponential. See Jones (2001).

5.5. Summary: scale effects

Virtually all idea-based growth models involve some kind of scale effect, for the basic reason laid out earlier in the presentation of the Idea Diagram. The strong scale effects of many first-generation idea-based growth models – in which the growth rate of the economy is an increasing function of its size – are inconsistent with the relative stability of growth rates in the United States in the 20th century. Subsequent idea-based growth models replaced this strong scale effect with a weak scale effect, where the long-run level of per capita income is an increasing function of the size of the economy. The long-run growth rate in these models is generally an increasing function of the rate of growth of research effort, which in turn depends on the population growth rate of the countries contributing to world research. However, this growth rate is typically taken to be exogenous, producing the policy-invariance results common in these models.

Simple correlations (say of income per person with population, or growth rates of per capita income with population growth rates) on first glance appear to be inconsistent with weak scale effects. However, the ceteris paribus assumption is not valid for such comparisons. Attempts to render other things equal using careful econometrics certainly reveal no inconsistency with the weak scale effects prediction, although they also do not necessarily provide precise estimates of the magnitude of the key scale elasticity.

More broadly, the very long-run history of economic growth appears consistent with weak scale effects. Models in which scale plays an important role have proven capable of explaining the very long-run dynamics of population and per capita income, including the extraordinarily slow growth over much of history and the transition to modern economic growth since the Industrial Revolution.

6. Growth accounting, the linearity critique, and other contributions

This section summarizes a variety of additional insights related to idea-based growth models. Section 6.1 discusses growth accounting in such models, showing that scale effects have accounted for only about 20 percent of U.S. growth in the post-war period. Increases in educational attainment and increases in R&D intensity account for the remaining 80 percent. Section 6.2 considers a somewhat controversial "linearity critique" of endogenous growth models that first appeared in the 1960s. Finally, Section 6.3 will discuss briefly several other important contributions to the literature on growth and ideas that have not yet been mentioned.

6.1. Growth accounting in idea-based models

Growth accounting in a neoclassical framework has a long, illustrious tradition, beginning with Solow (1957). As is well known, such accounting typically finds a residual, which is labeled "total factor productivity growth" (TFP growth). In some ways, endogenous growth models can be understood as trying to find ways to endogenize TFP growth, i.e. to make it something that is determined within the model rather than assumed to be completely exogenous. Having such a model in hand, then, it is quite natural to ask how the model decomposes growth into its sources. That is, quantitatively, how does a particular model account for growth?

Jones (2002b) conducts one of these growth accounting exercises in an economic environment that is basically identical to that analyzed in Section 4. In the long run in that model, per capita growth is proportional to the rate of population growth of the idea-producing regions. Off a balanced growth path, of course, growth can come from transition dynamics, for example, due to capital deepening or to rapid growth in the stock of ideas. Given the stylized fact that U.S. growth rates have been relatively stable over a long period of time, one might be tempted to think that the U.S. is close to its balanced growth path so that growth due to transition dynamics is negligible. On the contrary, however, Jones shows that just the opposite is true. Approximately 80 percent of U.S. growth in the post-war period is due to transition dynamics associated in roughly equal parts with increases in educational attainment and with increases in world R&D intensity. Only about 20 percent of U.S. growth is attributed to the scale effect associated with population growth in the idea-generating countries.[32]

This finding raises a couple of important questions. First, how it is that growth rates can be relatively stable in the United States if transition dynamics are so important? The answer proposed by Jones (2002b) can be seen in a simple analogy. Consider a standard Solow (1956) model that begins in steady state. Now suppose the investment rate increases permanently by 1 percentage point. We know that growth rates rise temporarily and then decline. Now suppose the investment rate, rather than staying constant, grows exponentially. We know that this cannot happen forever since the investment rate is bounded below one. However, it could happen for awhile. In such a world, it is possible for the continued increases in the investment rate to sustain a constant growth rate that is higher than the long-run growth rate. In the idea-based growth model analyzed by Jones (2002b), it is not the investment rate in physical capital that is driving the transition dynamics. Instead, educational attainment and research intensity (the fraction of the labor force working to produce ideas in advanced countries) appear to be rising smoothly in a way that can generate stable growth, at least as an approximation.

The second natural question raised by this accounting concerns the future of U.S. growth. If 80 percent of U.S. growth is due to transition dynamics, then a straightforward implication of the result is that growth rates could slow substantially at some point in the future when the U.S. transits to its balanced growth path. To the extent that population growth rates in the idea-producing countries are declining, this finding is reinforced. Still, there are many other qualifications that must be made concerning this result. Most importantly, it is not clear when the transition dynamics will "run out", particularly since the fraction of the labor force engaged in research seems to be relatively

---

[32] Comin (2002) suggests that the contribution of R&D to growth could be even smaller. The key assumptions he needs to get this result are that R&D as a share of GDP is truly small, as measured, and that the elasticity of output with respect to ideas is small.

small. In addition, the increased development of countries like China and India means that the pool of potential idea creators could rise for a long time.

6.2. The linearity critique

This section considers the somewhat controversial "linearity critique" of endogenous growth models that first appeared in the 1960s. A coarse version of the criticism is that such models rely on a knife-edge assumption that a particular differential equation is linear in some sense. If the linearity is relaxed slightly, the model either does not generate long-run growth or exhibits growth rates that explode. This section first presents the basic issue and then attempts to show how it can be used productively to make progress in our understanding of economic growth.[33]

Growth models that are capable of producing steady-state growth require strong assumptions. For example, it is well known that steady-state growth is possible only if technological change is labor-augmenting or if the production function is Cobb–Douglas.[34] Another requirement is that the model must possess a differential equation that is linear. That is, all growth models that exhibit steady-state growth ultimately rest on an assumption that some differential equation takes the form

$$\dot{X} = \underline{\quad} X. \tag{74}$$

Growth models differ primarily according to the way in which they label the X variable and the way in which they fill in the blank in this differential equation.[35]

For example, in the Solow (1956) model without technological progress, the differential equation for capital accumulation is less than linear, and the model cannot produce sustained exponential growth. On the other hand, when one adds exogenous technological change in the form of a linear differential equation $\dot{A}_t = gA_t$, one obtains a model with steady-state growth. In the AK growth models of Frankel (1962) and Rebelo (1991), the law of motion for physical capital is assumed to be linear. In the human capital model of Lucas (1988), it is the law of motion for human capital accumulation that is assumed to be linear. Finally, in the first-generation idea-based growth models of Romer (1990), Aghion and Howitt (1992) and Grossman and Helpman (1991), it is the idea production function itself that is assumed to be a linear differential equation.

This kind of knife-edge requirement has made economists uncomfortable for some time. Stiglitz (1990) and Cannon (2000) note that this is one reason endogenous growth models did not catch on in the 1960s even though several were developed.[36] Solow (1994) resurrects this criticism in arguing against recent models of endogenous growth.

---

[33] This section draws heavily on Jones (2003).

[34] See, for example, the Appendix to Chapter 2 in Barro and Sala-i-Martin (1995).

[35] This approach to characterizing growth models is taken from Romer (1995). Two qualifications apply. First, this linearity can be hidden in models with multiple state variables, as discussed in Mulligan and Sala-i-Martin (1993). Second, linearity is an asymptotic requirement, not a condition that needs to hold at every point in time, as noted by Jones and Manuelli (1990).

[36] The very nice AK model of Frankel (1962) is perhaps the clearest example.

What is not sufficiently well appreciated, however, is that *any* model of sustained exponential growth requires such a knife-edge condition. Neoclassical growth models are not immune to this criticism; they just assume the linearity to be completely unmotivated. One can then proceed in two possible directions. First, one can give up on the desire that a model exhibit steady-state growth. It is not clear where this direction leads, however. One still wants a model to be able to match the steady exponential growth exhibited in the United States for the last 125 years, and it seems likely that a model that produces this kind of behavior will require a differential equation that is nearly linear. Alternatively, one can see the linearity critique as an opportunity for helping us improve our growth models. That is, if a growth model requires a linear differential equation, one can look for an economic explanation for why linearity should hold and/or seek empirical evidence supporting the linearity.

To see how this might work, consider briefly the main types of endogenous growth models and the key differential equations of those models:

1. AK model, $\dot{K} = sK^{\phi}$.
2. Lucas model, $\dot{h} = uh^{\phi}$.
3. R/AH/GH model, $\dot{A} = H_A A^{\phi}$.
4. Fertility model, $\dot{N} = (b - d)N^{\phi}$.

In each case, we can ask the question: "Why should we believe that $\phi \approx 1$ is valid in this model?". In particular, we consider the following experiment. Suppose we hold constant the individual decision variables (e.g. the investment rate in physical capital or time spent accumulating human capital). Suppose we then double the state variable. Do we double the change in the state variable?

In the AK model, ϕ is the elasticity of output with respect to capital. In the absence of externalities, this elasticity is the share of capital in income. Narrowly interpreting the model as applying to physical capital, one gets a benchmark value of about $1/3$. Some people prefer to include human capital as well, which can get the share a little higher.[37] But then one must appeal to large externalities, and these externalities must be exactly the right size in order to get $\phi \approx 1$.

Now turn to the human capital model of Lucas (1988). Consider a representative agent who lives forever and spends 10 hours per week studying to obtain skills. Are the skills that are added by one period of this studying doubled if the individual's stock of human capital is doubled? A natural benchmark might be that studying for 10 hours a week adds the same amount, whether one is highly skilled or has little skill. It is far from obvious that the 10 hours of studying increases skills proportionately over time.[38]

---

[37] I personally think this is a mistake. Human capital is different from physical capital in many ways and gets treated differently in models that are careful about the distinction, e.g. Bils and Klenow (2000).

[38] A subtlety in thinking through the human capital model comes from the Mincerian wage regression evidence. Each year of schooling appears to raise a worker's wage – and hence productivity – by a constant percentage. One might be tempted to use this to argue that $\phi = 1$ in the human capital case. Bils and Klenow (2000) suggest instead that a human capital accumulation equation of the form $\dot{h} = e^{\theta u} h^{\phi}$ is the right way to capture this evidence.

This chapter has already discussed the Romer/AH/GH assumption of $\phi = 1$. Recall that one can make a case for $\phi < 0$ if it gets harder over time to find new ideas or $\phi > 0$ if knowledge spillovers increase research productivity, or even $\phi = 0$ if researchers produce a constant number of ideas with each unit of effort. The case of $\phi = 1$ appears to have little in the way of intuition or evidence to recommend it.

Finally, the last case above suggests placing the linearity in the equation for population growth, as was done implicitly in the models discussed earlier in the chapter. It can be thought of in this way: Let b and d denote the birth rate and the mortality rate for an individual, respectively. Hold constant an individual's fertility behavior, and suppose we double the number of people in the population. A natural benchmark assumption is that we double the number of offspring. This is the intuition for why a linear differential equation makes sense as a benchmark for the population growth equation.

More generally, I would make the claim that population growth is the least objectionable place to locate a linear differential equation in a growth model, for two reasons. First, if we take population as exogenous and feed in the observed population growth rates into an idea-based growth model, we can explain sustained exponential growth. No additional linearity is needed. Second, the intuition above suggests that it is not crazy to think this differential equation might be close to linear: people reproduce in proportion to their number.[39]

This is one example of how the linearity critique can be used productively. Proponents of particular endogenous growth models can seek evidence and economic insights supporting the hypothesis that the particular engine of growth in a model does indeed involve a differential equation that is close to linear.

6.3. Other contributions

There are a number of other very interesting papers that I have not had time to discuss. These should be given more attention than simply the brief mention that follows, but this chapter is already too long.

Kortum (1997) and Segerstrom (1998) are two important papers that present growth models that exhibit weak scale effects. Both are motivated in part by the stylized fact that total U.S. patents granted to U.S. inventors does not show a large time trend for nearly a century, from roughly 1910 until 1990. If patents are a measure of useful ideas, this fact suggests that the number of new ideas per year might have been relatively stable during a time when per capita income was growing at a relatively constant rate. How can this be? In the models provided above, the stock of ideas grows at a constant rate, just like output. Kortum (1997) and Segerstrom (1998) solve this puzzle by supposing that ideas, at least on average, represent *proportional* improvements in productivity. The

---

[39] This does not mean that fertility behavior, b, will ensure a positive rate of population growth forever. That is a different question. Indeed, Jones (2001) supposes that a demographic transition ultimately leads to zero population growth in attempting to explain growth over the very long run.

papers also assume that new ideas are increasingly difficult to obtain, so that in steady state, a growing number of researchers produce a constant number of new ideas, which in turn leads to a constant rate of exponential growth.

Romer (1994a) makes an interesting point that appears (at least based on citations) to have been under appreciated in the literature. The paper considers the welfare cost of trade restrictions from the standpoint of models in which ideas play an important role. In neoclassical models, trade restrictions, like other taxes, typically have small effects associated with Harberger triangles that depend on the square of the tax rate. In contrast, Romer shows that if trade restrictions reduce the range of goods (ideas) available within a country, the welfare affect is proportional to the level of the tax rate rather than its square. As a result, distortions that affect the use of ideas can have much larger welfare effects than those same distortions in neoclassical models.

Acemoglu (2002) surveys a number of important results that come from thinking about the direction of technological change. In this general framework, researchers can choose to search for ideas that augment different factors. For example, they may search for ideas that augment capital or skilled labor or unskilled labor. Other things equal, a market size effect suggests that research will be targeted toward augmenting factors that are in greater supply, especially when these factors can be easily substituted for other factors of production.

Greenwood, Hercowitz and Krusell (1997) and Whelan (2001) focus on the rapid technological change that is associated with the declines in the relative prices of consumer and producer durables (driven in large part by the rapid declines in the quality-adjusted price of semiconductors). Greenwood, Hercowitz and Krusell (1997) show that investment-specific technological change can account for roughly half of per capita income growth in the United States in recent decades. Whelan (2001) extends this analysis by tying it to the introduction of chained indexes in the national income and product accounts.

Finally, it is worth mentioning again that this chapter has largely omitted a very important part of the literature on growth and ideas, that associated with the Schumpeterian models of Aghion and Howitt (1992) and Grossman and Helpman (1991). These models were applied in detail to international trade in Grossman and Helpman (1991). Aghion and Howitt (1998) contain a rich analysis of an even wider range of applications, to such topics as unemployment, the effects of increases in competition, patent races, and leader-follower effects in R&D. In addition to these excellent treatments, a separate Handbook chapter by Aghion and Howitt surveys some of these important topics.

7. Conclusions

Thinking carefully about the way in which ideas are different from other economic goods leads to a profound change in the way we understand economic growth. The nonrivalry of ideas implies that increasing returns to scale is likely to characterize production possibilities. This leads to a world in which scale itself can serve as a source of long run growth. The more inventors we have, the more ideas we discover, and the richer we all are. This also leads to a world where the first fundamental welfare theorem no long necessarily holds. Perfectly competitive markets may not lead to the optimal allocation of resources. This means that other institutions may be needed to improve welfare. The patent system and research universities are examples of such institutions, but there is little reason to think we have found the best institutions – after all these institutions are themselves ideas.

While we have made much progress in understanding economic growth in a world where ideas are important, there remain many open, interesting research questions. The first is "What is the shape of the idea production function?" How do ideas get produced? The combinatorial calculations of Romer (1993) and Weitzman (1998) are fascinating and suggestive. The current research practice of modeling the idea production function as a stable Cobb–Douglas combination of research and the existing stock of ideas is elegant, but at this point we have little reason to believe that it is correct. One insight that illustrates the incompleteness of our knowledge is that there is no reason why research productivity in the idea production function should be a smooth, monotonic function of the stock of ideas. One can easily imagine that some ideas lead to a domino-like unraveling of phenomena that were previously mysterious, much like the general purpose technologies of Helpman (1998). Indeed, perhaps the decoding of the human genome or the continued boom in information technology will lead to a large upward shift in the production function for ideas.[40] On the other hand, one can equally imagine situations where research productivity unexpectedly stagnates, if not forever then at least for a long time. Progress in the time it takes to travel from New York to San Francisco represents a good example of this.

A second unresolved research question is "What is the long-run elasticity of output per worker with respect to population?". That is, how large are increasing returns to scale. This parameter (labeled γ in the main models of this chapter) is crucially related to the long-run rate of growth of the economy. Estimating it precisely would not only provide confirmation of idea-based growth theory but would also help us in accounting for the sources of economic growth.

Finally, a policy-related question: "What are better institutions and policies for encouraging the efficient amount of research?". There is a large, suggestive literature on social rates of return to research and on the extent to which firms might underinvest in research. Still, none of these individual studies is especially compelling, and more accurate estimates of these gaps would be valuable. To the extent that the returns to research do not reflect the marginal benefit to society, better institutions might improve allocations.

---

[40] Dale Jorgenson, in his Handbook chapter, suggests that the information technology revolution may do just this.

Acknowledgements

I am grateful to Philippe Aghion and Paul Romer for helpful comments, and to the National Science Foundation for research support.

References

Acemoglu, D. (2002). "Directed technical change". Review of Economic Studies 69 (4), 781–810.
Aghion, P., Howitt, P. (1992). "A model of growth through creative destruction". Econometrica 60 (2), 323–351.
Aghion, P., Howitt, P. (1998). Endogenous Growth Theory. MIT Press, Cambridge, MA.
Alcala, F., Ciccone, A. (2002). "Trade and productivity". Mimeo. Universitat Pompeu Fabra.
Arrow, K.J. (1962a). "The economic implications of learning by doing". Review of Economic Studies 29 (June), 153–173.
Arrow, K.J. (1962b). "Economic welfare and the allocation of resources for invention". In: Nelson, R.R. (Ed.), The Rate and Direction of Inventive Activity. Princeton University Press (NBER), Princeton, NJ, pp. 609–625.
Atkeson, A.A., Kehoe, P.J. (2002). "The transition to a new economy following the second industrial revolution". NBER Working Paper 8676.
Backus, D.K., Kehoe, P.J., Kehoe, T.J. (1992). "In search of scale effects in trade and growth". Journal of Economic Theory 58 (August), 377–409.
Barro, R.J., Sala-i-Martin, X. (1995). Economic Growth. McGraw-Hill, New York.
Ben-David, D., Papell, D.H. (1995). "The great wars, the great crash, and steady-state growth: Some new evidence about an old stylized fact". Journal of Monetary Economics 36 (December), 453–475.
Bils, M., Klenow, P. (2000). "Does schooling cause growth?". American Economic Review 90 (December), 1160–1183.
Boldrin, M., Levine, D.K. (2002). "Perfectly competitive innovation". FRB of Minneapolis Staff Report 303.
Boserup, E. (1965). The Conditions of Agricultural Progress. Aldine Publishing Company, Chicago, IL.
Boyce, W.E., DiPrima, R.C. (1997). Elementary Differential Equations and Boundary Value Problems. Wiley, New York.
Cannon, E. (2000). "Economies of scale and constant returns to capital: A neglected early contribution to the theory of economic growth". American Economic Review 90 (1), 292–295.
Clark, G. (2001). "The secret history of the industrial revolution". Mimeo. University of California, Davis.
Comin, D. (2002). "R&D? A small contribution to productivity growth". Mimeo. New York University.
Cozzi, G. (1997). "Exploring growth trajectories". Journal of Economic Growth 2 (4), 385–399.
David, P.A. (1993). "Knowledge, property, and the system dynamics of technological change". Proceedings of the World Bank Annual Conference on Development Economics, 1992, 215–248.
DeLong, J.B. (2000). "Slouching Toward Utopia". University of California, Berkeley. Online at: http://econ161.berkeley.edu/TCEH/Slouch_Old.html.
Diamond, J. (1997). Guns, Germs, and Steel. W.W. Norton and Co., New York.
Dinopoulos, E., Thompson, P. (1998). "Schumpeterian growth without scale effects". Journal of Economic Growth 3 (4), 313–335.
Dixit, A.K., Stiglitz, J.E. (1977). "Monopolistic competition and optimum product diversity". American Economic Review 67 (June), 297–308.
Ethier, W.J. (1982). "National and international returns to scale in the modern theory of international trade". American Economic Review 72 (June), 389–405.
Frankel, J.A., Romer, D. (1999). "Does trade cause growth?". American Economic Review 89 (3), 379–399.
Frankel, M. (1962). "The production function in allocation and growth: A synthesis". American Economic Review 52 (December), 995–1022.

Galor, O., Weil, D. (2000). "Population, technology, and growth: From the Malthusian regime to the demographic transition". American Economic Review 90 (September), 806–828.

Goodfriend, M., McDermott, J. (1995). "Early development". American Economic Review 85 (1), 116–133.

Greenwood, J., Hercowitz, Z., Krusell, P. (1997). "Long-run implications of investment-specific technological change". American Economic Review 87 (3), 342–362.

Greenwood, J., Seshadri, A., Yorukoglu, M. (2001). "Engines of liberation". Mimeo. University of Rochester.

Griliches, Z. (1998). R&D and Productivity: The Econometric Evidence. University of Chicago Press.

Grossman, G.M., Helpman, E. (1991). Innovation and Growth in the Global Economy. MIT Press, Cambridge, MA.

Hall, R.E., Jones, C.I. (1999). "Why do some countries produce so much more output per worker than others?". Quarterly Journal of Economics 114 (1), 83–116.

Hansen, G.D., Prescott, E.C. (2002). "Malthus to Solow". American Economic Review 92 (4), 1205–1217.

Helpman, E. (Ed.) (1998). General Purpose Technologies and Economic Growth. MIT Press, Cambridge, MA.

Howitt, P. (1999). "Steady endogenous growth with population and R&D inputs growing". Journal of Political Economy 107 (4), 715–730.

Jones, C.I. (1995a). "R&D-based models of economic growth". Journal of Political Economy 103 (4), 759–784.

Jones, C.I. (1995b). "Time series tests of endogenous growth models". Quarterly Journal of Economics 110 (441), 495–525.

Jones, C.I. (1999). "Growth: With or without scale effects?". American Economic Association Papers and Proceedings 89 (May), 139–144.

Jones, C.I. (2001). "Was an Industrial Revolution inevitable? Economic growth over the very long run". Advances in Macroeconomics 1 (2). Article 1. http://www.bepress.com/bejm/advances/voll/iss2/artl.

Jones, C.I. (2002a). Introduction to Economic Growth, second ed. W.W. Norton and Co., New York.

Jones, C.I. (2002b). "Sources of U.S. economic growth in a world of ideas". American Economic Review 92 (1), 220–239.

Jones, C.I. (2003). "Population and ideas: A theory of endogenous growth". In: Aghion, P., Frydman, R., Stiglitz, J., Woodford, M. (Eds.), Knowledge Information and Expectations in Modern Macroeconomics: In Honor of Edmund S. Phelps. Princeton University Press, Princeton, NJ, pp. 498–521.

Jones, C.I., Williams, J.C. (1998). "Measuring the social return to R&D". Quarterly Journal of Economics 113 (4), 1119–1135.

Jones, L.E., Manuelli, R. (1990). "A convex model of economic growth: Theory and policy implications". Journal of Political Economy 98 (October), 1008–1038.

Judd, K.L. (1985). "On the performance of patents". Econometrica 53 (3), 567–585.

Kortum, S.S. (1997). "Research, patenting, and technological change". Econometrica 65 (6), 1389–1419.

Kremer, M. (1993). "Population growth and technological change: One million B.C. to 1990". Quarterly Journal of Economics 108 (4), 681–716.

Kremer, M. (1998). "Patent buyouts: A mechanism for encouraging innovation". Quarterly Journal of Economics 113 (November), 1137–1167.

Kuznets, S. (1960). "Population change and aggregate output". In: Demographic and Economic Change in Developed Countries. Princeton University Press, Princeton, NJ.

Lee, R.D. (1988). "Induced population growth and induced technological progress: Their interaction in the accelerating stage". Mathematical Population Studies 1 (3), 265–288.

Li, C.-W. (2000). "Endogenous vs. semi-endogenous growth in a two-R&D-sector model". Economic Journal 110 (462), C109–C122.

Li, C.-W. (2002). "Growth and scale effects: The role of knowledge spillovers". Economics Letters 74 (2), 177–185.

Lipscomb, A.A., Bergh, A.E. (1905). The Writings of Thomas Jefferson, vol. 13. Thomas Jefferson Memorial Association, Washington. Online at http://press-pubs.uchicago.edu/founders/documents/al_8_8sl2.html.

Lucas, R.E. (1988). "On the mechanics of economic development". Journal of Monetary Economics 22 (1), 3–42.

Lucas, R.E. (1998). "The Industrial Revolution: Past and Future". Mimeo. University of Chicago.

Maddison, A. (1995). Monitoring the World Economy 1820–1992. Organization for Economic Cooperation and Development, Paris.

Mankiw, N.G., Romer, D., Weil, D. (1992). "A contribution to the empirics of economic growth". Quarterly Journal of Economics 107 (2), 407–438.

Mulligan, C.B., Sala-i-Martin, X. (1993). "Transitional dynamics in two-sector models of endogenous growth". Quarterly Journal of Economics 108 (3), 739–774.

Nordhaus, W.D. (1969). "An economic theory of technological change". American Economic Association Papers and Proceedings 59 (May), 18–28.

Nordhaus, W.D. (2003). "The health of nations: The contribution of improved health to living standards". In: Murphy, K.M., Topel, R. (Eds.), Measuring the Gains from Medical Research: An Economic Approach. University of Chicago Press, Chicago, IL, pp. 9–40.

Ohanian, L., Cole, H. (2001). "Re-examining the contribution of money and banking shocks to the U.S. great depression". NBER Macroeconomics Annual 16, 183–227.

Peretto, P. (1998). "Technological change and population growth". Journal of Economic Growth 3 (4), 283–311.

Phelps, E.S. (1966). "Models of technical progress and the golden rule of research". Review of Economic Studies 33 (2), 133–145.

Phelps, E.S. (1968). "Population increase". Canadian Journal of Economics 1 (3), 497–518.

Quah, D.T. (1996). "The Invisible Hand and the Weightless Economy". Mimeo. LSE Economics Department. April.

Quah, D. (2002). "Almost efficient innovation by pricing ideas". Mimeo. LSE. June.

Rebelo, S. (1991). "Long-run policy analysis and long-run growth". Journal of Political Economy 99 (June), 500–521.

Rivera-Batiz, L.A., Romer, P.M. (1991). "Economic integration and endogenous growth". Quarterly Journal of Economics 106 (May), 531–555.

Romer, P.M. (1986). "Increasing returns and long-run growth". Journal of Political Economy 94 (October), 1002–1037.

Romer, P.M. (1987). "Growth based on increasing returns to specialization". American Economic Review Papers and Proceedings 77 (May), 56–62.

Romer, P.M. (1990). "Endogenous technological change". Journal of Political Economy 98 (5), S71–S102.

Romer, P.M. (1993). "Two strategies for economic development: Using ideas and producing ideas". Proceedings of the World Bank Annual Conference on Development Economics 1992, 63–115.

Romer, P.M. (1994a). "New goods, old theory, and the welfare costs of trade restrictions". Journal of Development Economics 43, 5–38.

Romer, P.M. (1994b). "The origins of endogenous growth". Journal of Economic Perspectives 8, 3–22.

Romer, P.M. (1995). "Comment on a paper by T.N. Srinivasan". In: Growth Theories in Light of the East Asian Experience. University of Chicago Press, Chicago, IL.

Romer, P.M. (2000). "Should the government subsidize supply or demand in the market for scientists and engineers?". NBER Working Paper 7723, June.

Sala-i-Martin, X. (1997). "I just ran four million regressions". NBER Working Paper 6252.

Segerstrom, P. (1998). "Endogenous growth without scale effects". American Economic Review 88 (5), 1290–1310.

Segerstrom, P.S., Anant, T.C.A., Dinopoulos, E. (1990). "A Schumpeterian model of the product life cycle". American Economic Review 80 (5), 1077–1091.

Shell, K. (1966). "Toward a theory of inventive activity and capital accumulation". American Economic Association Papers and Proceedings 56, 62–68.

Sheshinski, E. (1967). "Optimal accumulation with learning by doing". In: Shell, K. (Ed.), Essays on the Theory of Economic Growth. MIT Press, Cambridge, MA, pp. 31–52.

Simon, J.L. (1986). Theory of Population and Economic Growth. Blackwell, New York.

Simon, J.L. (1998). The Ultimate Resource 2. Princeton University Press, Princeton, NJ.

Solow, R.M. (1956). "A contribution to the theory of economic growth". Quarterly Journal of Economics 70 (1), 65–94.

Solow, R.M. (1957). "Technical change and the aggregate production function". Review of Economics and Statistics 39 (3), 312–320.

Solow, R.M. (1994). "Perspectives on growth theory". Journal of Economic Perspectives 8 (1), 45–54.

Spence, M. (1976). "Product selection, fixed costs, and monopolistic competition". Review of Economic Studies 43 (2), 217–235.

Stiglitz, J.E. (1990). "Comments: Some retrospective views on growth theory". In: Diamond, P. (Ed.), Growth/Productivity/Unemployment: Essays to Celebrate Robert Solow's Birthday. MIT Press, Cambridge, MA, pp. 50–69.

Stokey, N.L. (2001). "A quantitative model of the British industrial revolution, 1780–1850". Carnegie Rochester Conference Series on Public Policy 55, 55–109.

Tamura, R. (2002). "Human capital and the switch from agriculture to industry". Journal of Economic Dynamics and Control 27, 207–242.

Weitzman, M.L. (1976). "On the welfare significance of national product in a dynamic economy". Quarterly Journal of Economics 90 (1), 156–162.

Weitzman, M.L. (1998). "Recombinant growth". Quarterly Journal of Economics 113 (May), 331–360.

Whelan, K. (2001). "Balance growth revisited: A two-sector model of economic growth". Mimeo. Federal Reserve Board of Governors.

Williams, J.C. (1995). "Tax and Technology Policy in an Endogenous Growth Model". Ph.D. Dissertation. Stanford University.

Young, A. (1998). "Growth without scale effects". Journal of Political Economy 106 (1), 41–63.

Chapter 17

LONG-TERM ECONOMIC GROWTH AND THE HISTORY OF TECHNOLOGY

JOEL MOKYR

Departments of Economics and History, Northwestern University

Contents

Abstract	1114
Keywords	1114
1. Introduction	1115
2. Technology and economic growth	1116
3. A historical theory of technology	1119
4. The significance of the Industrial Revolution	1126
5. The intellectual roots of the Industrial Revolution	1131
6. The dynamic of technological modernity	1144
7. Human capital and modern economic growth	1155
8. Institutions and technological progress	1161
9. Conclusions: Technology, growth, and the rise of the occident	1169
Acknowledgements	1173
References	1174

Handbook of Economic Growth, Volume 1B. Edited by Philippe Aghion and Steven N. Durlauf
© 2005 Elsevier B.V. All rights reserved
DOI: 10.1016/S1574-0684(05)01017-8

Abstract

Modern economic growth started in the West in the early nineteenth century. This survey discusses the precise connection between the Industrial Revolution and the beginnings of growth, and connects it to the intellectual and economic factors underlying the growth of useful knowledge. The connections between science, technology and human capital are re-examined, and the role of the eighteenth century Enlightenment in bringing about modern growth is highlighted. Specifically, the paper argues that the Enlightenment changed the agenda of scientific research and deepened the connections between theory and practice.

Keywords

Industrial Revolution, economic growth, technological progress, access costs, useful knowledge

JEL classification: N13, O31, O41

Some of the material in this chapter is adapted from my books *The Lever of Riches: Technological Creativity and Economic Change*, Oxford University Press, New York, 1990; *The Gifts of Athena: Historical Origins of the Knowledge Economy*, Princeton University Press, Princeton, 2002 and *The Enlightened Economy: An Economic History of Britain, 1700–1850*, Penguin Press, Harmondsworth, forthcomming, as well as from a number of more detailed papers available upon request.

1. Introduction

As every economist knows, the modern era is the era of economic growth. In the past two centuries, measures of output per capita have increased dramatically and in a sustained manner, in a way they had never done before. It seems by now a consensus to term the start of this phenomenon "the Industrial Revolution", although it is somewhat in dispute what precisely is meant by that term [Mokyr (1998b)]. In the past two decades an enormous literature has emerged to explain this phenomenon. A large number of "deep" questions have been raised, which this literature has tried to answer. Below I list the most pertinent of these questions and in the subsequent pages, I shall make an attempt to answer them.

1. What explains the *location* of the Industrial Revolution (in Europe as opposed to the rest of the world, in Britain as opposed to the rest of Europe, in certain regions of Britain as opposed to others). What role did geography play in determining the main parameters of the Industrial Revolution?
2. What explains the *timing* of the Industrial Revolution in the last third of the eighteenth century (though the full swing of economic growth did not really start until after 1815)? Could it have started in the middle ages or in classical antiquity?
3. Is sustained economic growth and continuous change the "normal" state of the economy, unless it is blocked by specific "barriers to riches", or is the stationary state the normal condition, and the experience of the past 200 years is truly a revolutionary regime change?
4. What was the role of technology in the origins of the Industrial Revolution and the subsequent evolution of the more dynamic economies in which rapid growth became the norm?
5. What was the relation between demographic behavior (and specifically the fall in mortality after 1750 and the subsequent decline in fertility and shift toward fewer but higher-quality children) in bringing about and sustaining modern economic growth?
6. What was the role of institutions (in the widest sense of the word) in bringing about modern economic growth, and to what extent can we separate it from other factors such as technology and factor accumulation?
7. To what extent is modern growth due to "culture", that is, intellectual factors regarding beliefs, attitudes, and preferences? Does culture normally adapt to the

economic environment, or can one discern autonomous cultural changes that shaped the economy?

8. Did the "Great Divergence" really start only in the eighteenth century, and until then the economic performance and potential of occident and the orient were comparable, or can signs of the divergence be dated to the renaissance or even the middle ages?

9. Was the Industrial Revolution "inevitable" in the sense that the economies a thousand years earlier already contained the seeds of modern economic growth that inexorably had to sprout and bring it about?

10. What was the exact role of human capital, through formal education or other forms, in bringing about modern economic growth?

2. Technology and economic growth

Economists have become accustomed to associating long-term economic growth with technological progress; it is deeply embedded in the main message of the Solow-inspired growth models, which treated technological change as exogenous, and even more so in the endogenous growth models.[1] An earlier growth literature regarded technology as a deus ex machina that somehow made productivity grow miraculously a little each year. The more modern literature views it as being produced within the system by the rational and purposeful application of research and development and the growth of complementary human and physical capital. The historical reality inevitably finds itself somewhere in between those two poles, and what is interesting above all is the shift of the economies of the West in that continuum. Whatever the case may be, technology is central to the dynamic of the economy in the past two centuries. Many scholars believe that people are inherently innovative and that if only the circumstances are right (the exact nature of these conditions differs from scholar to scholar), technological progress is almost guaranteed. This somewhat heroic assumption is shared by scholars as diverse as Robert Lucas and Eric L. Jones, yet it seems at variance with the historical record before the Industrial Revolution. That record is that despite many significant, even path-breaking innovations in many societies since the start of written history, it has not really been a major factor in economic growth, such as it was, before the Industrial Revolution.

Instead, economic historians studying earlier periods have come to realize that technology was less important than institutional change in explaining pre-modern episodes of economic growth. It is an easy exercise to point to the many virtues of "Smithian Growth", the increase in economic output due to commercial progress (as opposed to technological progress). Better markets, in which agents could specialize according to

---

[1] The opening line of the standard textbook in the area states that the "most basic proposition of growth theory is that in order to sustain a positive growth rate of output per capita in the long run, there must be continual advances in technological knowledge" [Aghion and Howitt (1997, p. 11)].

their comparative advantage and take full advantage of economies of scale, and in which enhanced competition would stimulate allocative efficiency and the adoption of best-practice technology could generate growth sustainable for decades and even centuries. Even with no changes whatsoever in technology, economies can grow in the presence of peace, law and order, improved communications and trust, the introduction of money and credit, enforceable and secure property rights, and similar institutional improvements [Greif (2005)]. Similarly, better institutions can lead to improved allocation of resources: law and order and improved security can and will encourage productive investment, reduce the waste of talent on rent-seeking and the manipulation of power for the purposes of redistribution [North (1990), Shleifer and Vishny (1998) and Baumol (2002)]. Tolerance for productive "service minorities" who lubricated the wheels of commerce (Syrians, Jews and many others) played important roles in the emergence of commerce and credit. Economic history before 1750 is primarily about this kind of growth. The wealth of Imperial Rome and the flourishing of the medieval Italian and Flemish cities, to pick just a few examples, were based above all on commercial progress, sometimes referred to as "Smithian Growth".[2]

It is usually assumed by economists that sustained economic growth is a recent phenomenon simply because if modern rates of growth had been sustained, a simple backward projection suggests that income in 1500 or in 1000 would have been absurdly low.[3] Clearly, growth at the rates we have gotten used to in the twentieth century are unthinkable in the long run. Yet it is equally implausible to think that just because growth was slower, there was *none* of it – after all, there is a lot of time in the long run. One does not have to fully subscribe to Graeme Snooks' use of Domesday book and Gregory King's numbers 600 years later to accept his view that by 1688 the British economy was very different indeed from what it had been at the time of William the Conqueror. Adam Smith had no doubt that "the annual produce of the land and labour of England . . . is certainly much greater than it was a little more than century ago at the restoration of Charles II (1660) . . . and [it] was certainly much greater at the restoration than we can suppose it to have been a hundred years before" [Smith (1976 [1776], pp. 365–366)].[4] On the eve of the Industrial Revolution, large parts of Europe and some

---

[2] To be sure, much of this commerce was closely related to the manufacturing bases of the surrounding area, such as woolen cloth production in Flanders or the production of glass in Venice.

[3] For instance, income per capita in the UK in 1890 was about $4100 in 1990 international dollars. It grew in the subsequent years by an average of 1.4% per year. Had it been growing at that same rate in the previous 300 years, income per capita in 1590 would have been $61, which clearly seems absurdly low.

[4] Snooks (1994) belief in pre-modern growth is based essentially on his comparison between the income per capita he has calculated from the Domesday book (1086) and the numbers provided by Gregory King for 1688. While such computations are of course always somewhat worrisome (what, exactly, does it mean to estimate the nominal income of 1086 in the prices of 1688 given the many changes in consumption items?), the order of magnitude provided by Snooks (an increase of real income by 580 percent) may survive such concerns. Maddison (2001, p. 265) estimates that GDP per capita in constant prices increased at a rate of 0.13 percent in Western Europe between 1000 and 1500 and 0.15% between 1500 and 1820. In the UK and the Netherlands growth between 1500 and 1820 was about 0.28 percent per year. Medievalists tend to agree with the

parts of Asia were enjoying a standard of living that had not been experienced ever before, in terms of the quantity, quality, and variety of consumption.[5] Pre-1750 growth was primarily based on Smithian and Northian effects: gains from trade and more efficient allocations due to institutional changes. The Industrial Revolution, then, can be regarded not as the beginnings of growth altogether but as the time at which technology began to assume an ever-increasing weight in the generation of growth and when economic growth accelerated dramatically. An average growth rate of 0.15–0.20% per annum, with high year-to-year variation and frequent setbacks was replaced by a much more steady growth rate of 1.5% per annum or better. Big differences in degree here are tantamount to differences in quality. This transition should not be confused with the demographic transition, which came later and whose relationship with technological progress is complex and poorly understood.[6]

This is not to say that before the Industrial Revolution technology was altogether unimportant in its impact on growth. Medieval Europe was an innovative society which invented many important things (including the mechanical clock, movable type, gunpowder, spectacles, iron-casting) and adopted many more inventions from other societies (paper, navigational instruments, Arabic numerals, the lateen sail, wind power). Yet, when all is said and done, it is hard to argue that the impact of these inventions on the growth of GDP or some other measure of aggregate output were all that large. The majority of the labor force was still employed in agriculture where progress was exceedingly slow (even if over the long centuries between 800 and 1300 the three-field system and the growing efficiency at which livestock was employed did produce considerable productivity gains).

Moreover, it is true for the pre-1750 era – as it was a fortiori after 1750 – that technology itself interacted with Smithian growth because on balance improved technology made the expansion of trade possible – above all maritime technology in all its many facets, but also better transport over land and rivers, better military technology to defeat

---

occurrence of economic growth in Britain, though their figures indicate a much slower rate of growth, about a 111 percent growth rate between 1086 and 1470 [Britnell (1996, p. 229)], which would require more economic growth in the sixteenth and seventeenth centuries than can be justified to square with Snooks' numbers. Engerman (1994, p. 116) assesses that most observers will agree with Snooks' view that by 1700 England had a high level of per capita income and was in a good position to "seek the next stage of economic growth". Yet clearly he is correct in judging that "modern" economic growth (prolonged, continuous, rapid) did not begin until the early nineteenth century.

[5] Indeed, many historians speak of a "consumer revolution" *prior to* the Industrial Revolution, which would be inexplicable without rising income before 1750. Lorna Weatherill (1988) suggests that if there was a Consumer Revolution at all, it peaked in the period 1680–1720. Moreover, consumer revolutions were taking place elsewhere in Europe. Seventeenth century Holland was, of course, the most obvious example thereof, but Cissie Fairchilds (1992) has employed probate records to show that France, like England, experienced a consumer revolution, albeit fifty years later.

[6] It is in that sense that the view of modern economists [e.g. Galor and Weil (2000, p. 809)] that "the key event that separates Malthusian and post-Malthusian regimes is the acceleration of the pace of technological progress" is a bit misleading, since it draws a link between technological progress and demographic change that thus far has not been closely examined.

pirates, better knowledge of remote lands, and the growing ability to communicate with strangers. A decomposition of growth into a technology component and a trade-and-institutions component must take into account such interactions.

All the same, the main reason why technological progress was at best an also-ran in the explanation of economic growth before 1750 is that even the best and brightest mechanics, farmers, and chemists – to pick three examples – knew relatively little about the fields of knowledge they sought to apply. The pre-1750 world produced, and produced well. It made many pathbreaking inventions. But it was a world of engineering without mechanics, iron-making without metallurgy, farming without soil science, mining without geology, water-power without hydraulics, dye-making without organic chemistry, and medical practice without microbiology and immunology. Not enough was known to generate sustained economic growth based on technological change.[7] Such statements are of course to some extent provocative and perhaps even irresponsible: how can we define "relatively little" in any meaningful sense? Who knew "that which was known" and how did they use it? In what follows I shall propose a simple framework to understand how and why new technology emerged and how it was limited before the eighteenth century and subsequently liberated from its constraints. I will then argue that "technological modernity" means an economy in which *sustained* technological progress is the primary engine of growth and that it depended on the persistence of technological progress. What is needed is a good theory of the kind of factors that make for sustained technological progress.

Such a theory needs to stress the basic complementarity between the creation and diffusion of new technology and the institutional factors that allowed this knowledge to be applied, become profitable, and lead to economic expansion. These institutional factors – such as the establishment of intellectual property rights, the supply of venture capital, the operation of well-functioning commodity and labor markets, and the protection of innovators and entrepreneurs against a technological reaction – are of central importance but they have been discussed elsewhere [Mokyr (1998b, 2005a)] and in what follows the focus will be on the growth of knowledge itself. All the same, it should be kept in mind that growth cannot result from a growth of knowledge *alone*. It needs to occur in an environment in which knowledge can be put to work.

3. A historical theory of technology

Technology is knowledge. Knowledge, as is well known, has always been a difficult concept for standard economics to handle. It is at the core of modern economic growth,

---

[7] The great agronomist Arthur Young sighed hopefully in 1772 that while in his day the farmers were largely ignorant of the "peculiar biasses" of individual soils, perhaps "one day the nature of all soils and the vegetables they particularly affect will be known experimentally . . . a desideratum in natural philosophy worthy of another Bacon" [Young (1772, p. 168)].

but many characteristics make it slippery to handle. Knowledge is above all a non-rivalrous good, that is, sharing it with another person does not diminish the knowledge of the original owner. It is not quite non-excludable, but clearly excludability is costly and for many types of knowledge exclusion costs are infinite. It is produced in the system, but the motivation of its producers are rarely purely economic. Indeed, the producers of scientific knowledge almost never collect but a tiny fraction of the surplus they produce for society. It is the mother of all spillover effects. A more fruitful approach than to view knowledge as an odd sort of good, pioneered by Olsson (2000, 2003), is to model knowledge as a set, and to analyze its growth in terms of the properties of existing knowledge rather than looking at the motivations of individual agents.

The basic unit of analysis of technology is the "technique". A technique is a set of instructions, much like a cookbook recipe, on how to produce goods and services. As such, it is better defined than the concept of a stock of "ideas" that some scholars prefer [e.g., Charles Jones (2001)]. The entire set of feasible techniques that each society has at its disposal is bound by the isoquant. Each point on or above the isoquant in principle represents a set of instructions on how to combine various ingredients in some way to produce a good or service that society wants. While technology often depends on artifacts, the artifacts are not the same as the technique and what defines the technique is the content of the instructions. Thus, a piano is an artifact, but what is done with it depends on the technique used by the pianist, the tuner, or the movers. Society's production possibilities are bound by what society knows. This knowledge includes both designing and building artefacts and using them.

But who is "society"? The only sensible way of defining knowledge at a social level is as the *union* of all the sets of individual knowledge. This definition is consistent with our intuitive notion of the concept of an invention or a discovery – at first only *one* person has it, but once that happens, society as a whole feels it has acquired it. Knowledge can be stored in external storage devices such as books, drawings, and artifacts but such knowledge is meaningless unless it can be transferred to an actual person. Such a definition immediately requires a further elaboration: if one person possesses a certain knowledge, how costly is it for others to acquire it? This question indeed is at the heart of the idea of a "technological society". Knowledge is shared and distributed, and its transmission through learning is essential for such a society to make effective use of it. Between the two extreme models of a society in which all knowledge acquired by one member is "episodic" and not communicated to any other member, and the other one in which all knowledge is shared instantaneously to all members through some monstrous network, there was a reality of partial and costly sharing and access. But these costs were not historically invariant, and the changes in them are one of the keys to technological change.

Progress in exploiting the existing stock of knowledge will depend first and foremost on the efficiency and cost of access to knowledge. Although knowledge is a public good in the sense that the consumption of one does not reduce that of others, the private costs of acquiring it are not negligible, in terms of time, effort, and often other real resources as well [Reiter (1992, p. 3)]. Access costs include the costs of finding out whether an answer to a question actually exists, if so, where it can be found, then paying the cost of acquiring it, and finally verifying the correctness of the knowledge. When the access costs become very high, it could be said in the limit that social knowledge has disappeared.[8] Language, mathematical symbols, diagrams, and physical models are all means of reducing access costs. Shared symbols may not always correspond precisely with the things they signify, as postmodern critics believe, but as long as they are shared they reduce the costs of accessing knowledge held by another person or storage device. The other component of access cost, tightness, is largely determined by the way society deal with authority and trust. It is clear that propositional knowledge is always and everywhere far larger that any single individual can know. The concepts of trust and authority are therefore central to the role that propositional knowledge can play in society, and how it is organized is central to the economic impact of useful knowledge. In the scientific world of the late seventeenth and eighteenth centuries, a network of trust and verification emerged in the West that seems to have stood the test of time. It is well described by Polanyi (1962, pp. 216–222): the space of useful knowledge is divided in small neighboring units. If individual B is surrounded by neighbors A and C who can verify his work, and C is similarly surrounded by B and D and so on, the world of useful knowledge reaches an equilibrium in which science, as a whole, can be trusted even by those who are not themselves part of it.

The determinants of these access costs are both institutional and technological: "open knowledge" societies, in which new discoveries are published as soon as they are made and in which new inventions are placed in the public domain through the patenting system (even if their application may be legally restricted), are societies in which access costs will be lower than in societies in which the knowledge is kept secret or confined to a small and closed group of insiders whether they are priests, philosophers, or mandarins. Economies that enjoyed a high level of commerce and mobility were subject to knowledge through the migration of skilled workmen and the opportunities to imitate and reverse-engineer new techniques. As access costs fell in the early modern period, it became more difficult to maintain intellectual property rights through high access costs, and new institutions that provided incentives for innovators became necessary, above all the patent system, which emerged in the late fifteenth and sixteenth centuries. The printing press clearly was one of the most significant access-cost-reducing inventions of

---

[8] This cost function determines how costly it is for an individual to access information from a storage device or from another individual. The *average* access cost would be the average cost paid by all individuals who wish to acquire the knowledge. More relevant for most useful questions is the *marginal* access cost, that is, the *minimum* cost for an individual who does not yet have this information. A moment reflection will make clear why this is so: it is very expensive for the average member of a society to have access to the Schrödinger wave equations, yet it is "accessible" at low cost for advanced students of quantum mechanics. If someone "needs" to know something, he or she will go to an expert for whom this cost is as low as possible to find out. Much of the way knowledge has been used in recent times has relied on such experts. The cost of finding experts and retrieving knowledge thus determines marginal access costs. Equally important, as we shall see, is the technology that provides access to storage devices.

the historical past.[9] The nature of the books printed, such as topic, language, and accessibility, played an equally central role in the reduction of access costs. People normally acquired knowledge and skills vertically, but also from one another through imitation. Postdoctoral students in laboratory settings full-well realize the differences between the acquisition of codifiable knowledge and the acquisition of tacit knowledge through imitation and a certain *je ne sais quoi* we call experience.[10] Improvements in transport and communication technology, that made people more mobile and sped up the movement of mail and newspapers also reduced access costs in the second half of the eighteenth century, a movement that continued through the nineteenth century and has not stopped since.

Techniques constitute what I have called *prescriptive* knowledge – like any recipe they essentially comprise instructions that allow people to "produce", that is, to exploit natural phenomena and regularities in order to improve human material welfare.[11] The fundamental unit of the set of prescriptive knowledge has the form of a list of do-loops (often of great complexity, with many if–then statements), describing the "hows" of what we call production.

There are two preliminary observations we need to point out in this context. One is that it is impossible to specify explicitly the entire content of a set of instructions. Even a simple cooking recipe contains a great deal of assumptions that the person executing the technique is supposed to know: how much a cup is, when water is boiling, and so on. For that reason, the person executing a technique is supposed to have certain knowledge that I shall call *competence* to distinguish it from the knowledge involved in writing the instructions for the first time (that is, actually making the invention). Competence consists of the knowledge of how to read, interpret, and execute the instructions in the technique and the supplemental tacit knowledge that cannot be fully written down in the technique's codified instructions. There is a continuum between the implicit understandings and clever tricks that make a technique work we call tacit knowledge, and

---

[9] Elizabeth Eisenstein (1979) has argued that the advent of printing created the background on which the progress of science and technology rests. In her view, printing created a "bridge over the gap between town and gown" as early as the sixteenth century, and while she concedes that "the effect of early printed technical literature on science and technology is open to question" she still contends that print made it possible to publicize "socially useful techniques" (pp. 558, 559).

[10] It should be obvious that in order to read such a set of instructions, readers need a "codebook" that explains the terms used in the technique [Cowan and Foray (1997)]. Even when the techniques are explicit, the codebook may not be, and the codebook needed to decipher the first codebook and the next, and so on, eventually must be tacit. Sometimes instructions are "tacit" even when they could be made explicit but it is not cost-effective to do so.

[11] These instructions are similar to the concept of "routines" proposed by Nelson and Winter (1982). When these instructions are carried out in practice, we call it production, and then they are no longer knowledge but action. "Production" here should be taken to include household activities such as cooking, cleaning, childcare, and so forth, which equally require the manipulation of natural phenomena and regularities. The execution of instructions is comparable to DNA instructions being "expressed". Much like instructions in DNA, the lines in the technique can be either "obligate" (do X) or "facultative" (if Y, do X). For more complex techniques, nested instructions are the rule.

the minor improvements and refinements introduced subsequent to invention that involve actual adjustments in the explicit instructions. The latter would be more properly thought off as microinventions, but a sharp distinction between them would be arbitrary. All the same, "competence" and "knowledge" are no less different than the differences in skills needed to play the Hammerklavier sonata and those needed to compose it. One of the most interesting variables to observe is the ratio between the knowledge that goes into the first formulation of the technique in question (invention) and the competence needed to actually carry out the technique. As we shall see, it is this ratio around which the importance of human capital in economic growth will pivot.

The second observation is the notion that every technique, because it involves the manipulation and harnessing of natural regularities, requires an *epistemic base,* that is, a knowledge of nature on which it is based. I will call this type of knowledge *propositional* knowledge, since it contains a set of propositions about the physical world. The distinction between propositional and prescriptive knowledge seems obvious: the planet Neptune and the structure of DNA were not "invented"; they were already there prior to discovery, whether we knew it or not. The same cannot be said about diesel engines or aspartame. Polanyi (1962) notes that the distinction is recognized by patent law, which permits the patenting of inventions (additions to prescriptive knowledge) but not of discoveries (additions to propositional knowledge). He points out that the difference boils down to observing that prescriptive knowledge can be "right or wrong" whereas "action can only be successful or unsuccessful" (p. 175). Purists will object that "right" and "wrong" are judgments based on socially constructed criteria, and that "successful" needs to be defined in a context, depending on the objective function that is being maximized.

The two sets of propositional and prescriptive knowledge together form the set of useful knowledge in society. These sets satisfy the conditions set out by Olsson (2000) for his "idea space". Specifically, the sets are infinite, closed, and bounded. They also are subsets of much larger sets, the sets of knowable knowledge. At each point of time, the actual sets describe what a society knows and consequently what it can do. There also is a more complex set of characteristics that connect the knowledge at time t with that in the next period. Knowledge is mostly cumulative and evolutionary. The "mostly" is added because it is not wholly cumulative (knowledge *can* be lost, though this has become increasingly rare) and its evolutionary features are more complex than can be dealt with here [Mokyr (2005b)].

The actual relation between propositional and prescriptive knowledge can be summarized in the following 10 generalizations:

1. Every technique has a minimum epistemic base, which contains the least knowledge that society needs to possess for this technique to be invented. The epistemic base contains at the very least the trivial statement that technique i works.[12]

---

[12] This statement is true because the set of propositional knowledge contains as a subset the list (or catalog) of the techniques that work – since a statement such as "technique i works" can itself be interpreted as a natural regularity.

There are and have been some techniques, invented accidentally or through trial and error, about whose modus operandi next to nothing was known except that they worked. We can call these techniques *singleton* techniques (since their domain is a singleton).

2. Some techniques require a minimum epistemic base larger than a singleton for a working technique to emerge. It is hard to imagine the emergence of such techniques as nuclear resonance imaging or computer assisted design software in any society from serendipitous finds or trial-and-error methods, without the designers having a clue of why and how they worked.

3. The actual epistemic base is equal to or larger than the minimum epistemic base. It is never bound from above in the sense that the amount that can be known about the natural phenomena that govern a technique is infinite. In a certain sense, we can view the epistemic base at any given time much like a fixed factor in a production function. As long as it does not change, it imposes concavity and possibly even an upper bound on innovation and improvement. On the other hand, beyond a certain point, the incremental effect of widening the actual epistemic base on the productivity growth of a given technique will run into diminishing returns and eventually be limited.

4. There is no requirement that the epistemic base be "true" or "correct" in any sense. In any event, the only significance of such a statement would be that it conforms to contemporary beliefs about nature (which may well be refuted by future generations). Thus the humoral theory of disease, now generally rejected, formed the epistemic base of medical techniques for many centuries. At the same time, some epistemic bases can be more effective than others in the sense that techniques based on them perform "better" by some agree-upon criterion. "Effective knowledge" does not mean "true knowledge" – many effective techniques were based on knowledge we no longer accept and yet were deployed for long periods with considerable success.[13]

5. The wider the actual epistemic base supporting a technique relative to the minimum one, the more likely an invention is to occur, ceteris paribus. A wider epistemic base means that it is less likely for a researcher to enter a blind alley and to spend resources in trying to create something that cannot work.[14] Thus, a wider epistemic base reduces the costs of research and development and increases the likelihood of success.

---

[13] Here one can cite many examples. Two such examples are the eighteenth century metallurgical writings and inventions of René Réaumur and Tobern Bergman, firmly based on phlogiston physics, and the draining of swamps based on the belief that the "bad air" they produced caused malaria.

[14] Alchemy – the attempt to turn base metals into gold by chemical means – was still a major occupation of the best minds of the scientific revolution above all Isaac Newton. By 1780 Alchemy was in sharp decline and in the nineteenth century chemists knew enough to realize that it was a misallocation of human capital to search for the stone of the wise or the fountain of youth. The survival of astrology in our time demonstrates that the prediction of the future – always a technique based on a very narrow epistemic base – has not benefited in a similar way from a widening of the prescriptive knowledge on which it was based.

6. The wider the epistemic base, the more likely an existing technique is to be improved, adapted, and refined through subsequent microinventions. The more that is known about the principles of a technique, the lower will be the costs of development and improvement. This is above all because as more is known about *why* something works, the better the inventor can tweak its parameters to optimize and debug the technique. Furthermore, because invention so often consists of analogy with or the recombination of existing techniques, lower access cost to the catalog of existing techniques (which is part of propositional knowledge) stimulates and streamlines successful invention.

7. Historically, the epistemic bases in existence during the early stages of an invention are usually quite narrow at first, but in the last two centuries have often been enlarged following the appearance of the invention, and sometimes directly on account of the invention.

8. Both propositional and prescriptive knowledge can be "tight" or "untight". Tightness measures the degree of confidence and consensualness of a piece of knowledge: how sure are people that the knowledge is "true" or that the technique "works". The tighter a piece of propositional knowledge, the lower are the costs of verification and the more likely a technique based on it is to be adopted. Of course, tightness is correlated with effectiveness: a laser printer works better than a dot matrix, and there can be little dispute about the characteristics here. If two techniques are based on incompatible epistemic bases, the one that works better will be chosen and the knowledge on which it is based will be judged to be more effective. But for much of history, effectiveness turned out to be difficult to measure and propositional knowledge was more often selected on the basis of authority and tradition that effectiveness. Even today, for many medical and farming techniques it is often difficult to observe which technique works better without careful statistical analysis or experimentation.

9. It is not essential that the person writing the instructions actually knows himself everything that is in the epistemic base. Even if very few individuals in a society know quantum mechanics, the practical fruits of the insights of this knowledge to technology may still be available just as if everyone had been taught advanced physics. It is a fortiori true that the people carrying out a set of instructions do not have to know how and why these instructions work, and what the support for them is in propositional knowledge. No doctor prescribing nor any patient taking an aspirin will need to study the biochemical properties of prostaglandins, though such knowledge may be essential for those scientists working on a design of an analgesic with, say, fewer side effects. What counts is collective knowledge and the cost of access as discussed above. It is even less necessary for the people actually carrying out the technique to possess the knowledge on which it is based, and normally this is not the case.

10. The existence of a minimum epistemic base is a necessary but insufficient condition for a technique to emerge. A society may well accumulate a great deal of propositional knowledge that is never translated into new and improved tech-

niques. Knowledge opens doors, but it does not force society to walk through them.

4. The significance of the Industrial Revolution

Historians in the 1990s have tended to belittle the significance of the Industrial Revolution as a historical phenomenon, referring to it as the so-called Industrial Revolution, and pointing to the slowness and gradualness of economic change, as well as the many continuities that post 1760 Britain had with earlier times [for a critical survey, see Mokyr (1998b)].

Before I get to the heart of the argument, two points need to be cleared away. The first is the myth that the Industrial Revolution was a purely British affair, and that without Britain's leadership Europe today would still be largely a subsistence economy. The historical reality was that many if not most of the technological elements of the Industrial Revolution were the result of a joint international effort in which French, German, Scandinavian, Italian, American and other "western" innovators collaborated, swapped knowledge, corresponded, met one another, and read each others' work.

It is of course commonplace that in most cases the first successful economic *applications* of the new technology appeared in Britain. By 1790 Britain had acquired an advantage in the execution of new techniques. Yet an overwhelming British advantage in *inventing* – especially in generating the crucial macroinventions that opened the doors to a sustained trajectory of continuing technological change – is much more doubtful, and a British advantage in expanding the propositional knowledge that was eventually to widen the epistemic bases of the new techniques is even more questionable. Britain's technological precociousness in the era of the Industrial Revolution was a function of three factors.

First, by the middle of the eighteenth century Britain had developed an institutional strength and agility that provided it with a considerable if temporary advantage over its Continental competitors: it had a healthier public finance system, weaker guilds, no internal tariff barriers, a superior internal transportation system, fairly well-defined and enforceable property rights on land (enhanced and modified by Parliamentary acts when necessary), and a power structure that favored the rich and the propertied classes. Moreover, it had that most elusive yet decisive institutional feature that makes for economic success: the flexibility to adapt its economic and legal institutions without political violence and disruptions. Britain's great asset was not so much that she had "better" government but rather that its political institutions were nimbler, and that they could be changed at low social cost by a body assigned to changing the rules and laws by which the economic game was played. Many of the rules still on the books in the eighteenth century were not enforced, and rent-seeking arrangements, by comparison, were costly to attain and uncertain in their yield. British mercantilist policy was already in decline on the eve of the Industrial Revolution. Yet as the Industrial Revolution unfolded, it required further change in the institutional basis of business. The Hanoverian governments in Britain were venal and nepotist, and much of the business of government was intended to enrich politicians. On the Continent matters were no better. But with the growing notion that rent seeking was harmful, this kind of corruption weakened [Mokyr (2005a)]. As Porter (1990, p. 119) put it, with the rise of the laissez faire lobby, Westminster abandoned its long-standing mercantilist paternalism, repealing one regulation after another. Abuses may have been deeply rooted, and entrenched rent-seekers resisted all they could, but from the last third of the eighteenth century on rent-seeking was on the defensive, and by 1835 many of the old institutions had vanished, and the British state, for a few decades, gave up on redistributing income as a main policy objective. Following North (1990, p. 80) we might call this adaptive efficiency, meaning not only the adaptation of the allocation of resources but of the institutions themselves. To bring this about, what was needed was a meta-institution with a high degree of legitimacy, such as parliament, that was authorized to change the rules in a consensual manner.

Second, Britain's entrepreneurs proved uncannily willing and able to adopt new inventions regardless of where they were made, free from the "not made here" mentality of other societies. Some of the most remarkable inventions made on the Continent were first applied on a wide scale in Britain. Among those, the most remarkable were gaslighting, chlorine bleaching, the Jacquard loom, the Robert continuous paper-making machine, and the Leblanc soda making process. In smaller industries, too, the debt of the British Industrial Revolution to Continental technology demonstrates that in no sense did Britain monopolize the inventive process.[15] The British advantage in application must be chalked up largely to its comparative advantage in microinventions and in the supply of the human capital that could carry out the new techniques.[16] To employ the terminology proposed earlier: Britain may not have had more propositional

---

[15] The great breakthrough in plate glass was made in France by a Company founded in the 1680s, which cast a far superior product by pouring it over a perfectly smooth metallic table, a concept as simple in principle as it was hard to carry out in practice, perfected by the St. Gobain company. The British tried for many decades to copy the process, but never matched the French for quality Harris (1992b, p. 38). The most important subsequent breakthrough in the glass industry was made in 1798 by Pierre Louis Guinand, a Swiss, who invented the stirring process in which he stirred the molten glass in the crucible using a hollow cylinder of burnt fireclay, dispersing the air bubbles in the glass more evenly. The technique produced optical glass of unprecedented quality. Guinand kept his process secret, but his son sold the technique to a French manufacturer in 1827, who in turn sold it to the Chance Brothers Glass Company in Birmingham, which soon became one of the premier glassmakers in Europe. The idea of preserving food by cooking followed by vacuum sealing was hit upon by the Frenchman Nicolas Appert in 1795. Appert originally used glassware to store preserved foods, but in 1812 an Englishman named Peter Durand suggested using tin-plated cans, which were soon found to be superior. By 1814, Bryan Donkin was supplying canned soups and meats to the Royal Navy.

[16] This was already pointed by Daniel Defoe, who pointed out in 1726 that "the English ... are justly fam'd for improving Arts rather than inventing" and elsewhere in his Plan of English Commerce that "our great Advances in Arts, in Trade, in Government and in almost all the great Things we are now Masters of and in which we so much exceed all our Neighbouring Nations, are really founded upon the inventions of others". The great engineer John Farey, who wrote an important treatise on steam power, testified a century later that "the prevailing talent of English and Scotch people is to apply new ideas to use, and to bring such applications to perfection, but they do not imagine as much as foreigners".

knowledge available for its invention and innovation process, but if its workers possessed higher levels of competence, then the new techniques that emerged were more likely to find their first applications there. Its successful system of informal technical training, through master-apprentice relationships, created workers of uncommon skill and mechanical ability [Humphries (2003)]. Britain also was lucky to have a number of successful industries that generated significant technical spillovers to other industries.[17] This system produced, of course, inventors: the most famous of these such as the clockmakers John Harrison and Benjamin Huntsman, the engineer John Smeaton, the instrument maker Jesse Ramsden, the wondrously versatile inventor Richard Roberts, the chemists James Keir and Joseph Black, and of course Watt himself were only the first row of a veritable army of people, who in addition to possessing formal knowledge, were blessed by a technical intuition and dexterity we identify as the very essence of tacit knowledge.

Third, Britain was at peace in a period when the Continent was engulfed in political and military upheaval. Not only that there was no fighting and political chaos on British soil; the French revolution and the Napoleonic era was a massive distraction of talent and initiative that would otherwise have been available to technology and industry.[18] The attention of both decision makers and inventors was directed elsewhere.[19] During the stormy years of the Revolution, French machine breakers found an opportunity to mount an effective campaign against British machines, thus delaying their adoption [Horn (2003)].

Compared to Britain, the Continental countries had to make a greater effort to cleanse their economic institutions from medieval debris and the fiscal ravages of absolutism,

---

[17] A number of high-skill sectors that had developed in Britain since 1650 played important roles in subsequent technological development. Among those instrument- and clock-making, mining, and ship yards were of central importance. Cardwell (1972, p. 74) points out that a number of basic technologies converge on mining (chemistry, civil engineering, metallurgy) and that mining sets the hard, "man-sized" problems, controlling powerful forces of nature and transforming materials on a large scale. In addition, however, British millwrights were technologically sophisticated: the engineer John Fairbairn, a millwright himself, noted that eighteenth century British millwrights were "men of superior attainments and intellectual power", and that the typical millwright would have been "a fair arithmetician, knew something of geometry, levelling and mensuration and possessed a very competent knowledge of practical mechanics" [cited in Musson and Robinson (1969, p. 73)].

[18] The chemists Claude Berthollet and Jean-Antoine Chaptal, for instance, directed their abilities toward administration during the Empire. Their illustrious teacher, the great Lavoisier himself, was executed as a tax farmer. Another example is Nicolas de Barneville, who was active in introducing British spinning equipment into France. De Barneville repeatedly was called upon to serve in military positions and was "one of those unfortunate individuals whose lives have been marred by war and revolution ... clearly a victim of the troubled times" [McCloy (1952, pp. 92–94)].

[19] The Frenchman Philippe LeBon, co-inventor of gas-lighting in the 1790s, lost out in his race for priority with William Murdoch, the ingenious Boulton and Watt engineer whose work in the end led the introduction of this revolutionary technique in the illumination of the Soho works in 1802. As one French historian sighs, "during the terrors of the Revolution ... no one thought of street lights. When the mob dreamed of lanterns, it was with a rather different object in view" [cited by Griffiths (1992, p. 242)].

undo a more complex and pervasive system of rent-seeking and regulation, and while extensive reforms were carried out in France, Germany, and the Low Countries after the French Revolution, by 1815 the work was still far from complete and had already incurred enormous social costs. It took another full generation for the Continent to pull even. All the same, none of the British advantages was particularly deep or permanent. They explain Britain's position as the lead car in the Occident Express that gathered steam in the nineteenth century and drove away from the rest of the world, but it does not tell us much about the source of power. Was Britain the engine that pulled the other European cars behind it, or was Western Europe like an electric train deriving its motive power from a shared source of energy?

One useful mental experiment is to ask whether there would have been an Industrial Revolution in the absence of Britain. A counterfactual industrial revolution led by Continental economies would have been delayed by a few decades and differed in some important details. It might have relied less on "British" steam and more on "French" water power and "Dutch" wind power technology, less on cotton and more on wool and linen. It would probably have had more of an *étatist* and less of a free-market flavor, with a bigger emphasis on military engineering and public projects. Civil servants and government engineers might have made some decisions that were made by entrepreneurs. But in view of the capabilities of French engineers and German chemists, the entrepreneurial instincts of Swiss and Belgian industrialists, and the removal of many institutions that had hampered the effective deployment of talents and resources on the Continent before 1789, a technological revolution would have happened not all that different from what actually transpired. Even without Britain, by the twentieth century the gap in GDP per capita between Europe and the rest of the world would have existed [Mokyr (2000)].

The second point to note is that the pivotal element of the Industrial Revolution took place later than is usually thought. The difference between the Industrial Revolution of the eighteenth century and other episodes of a clustering of macroinventions was not just in the celebrated inventions in the period 1765–1790. While the impact of the technological breakthroughs of these years of *sturm und drang* on a number of critical industries stands undiminished, the critical difference between this Industrial Revolution and previous clusters of macroinventions is not that these breakthroughs occurred at all, but that their momentum did not level off and peter out after 1800 or so. In other words, what made the Industrial Revolution into the "great divergence" was the *persistence* of technological change after the first wave. We might well imagine a counterfactual technological steady state of throstles, wrought iron, and stationary steam engines, in which there was a one-off shift from wool to cotton, from animate power to stationary engines, and from expensive to plentiful wrought iron. It is easy to envisage the economies of the West settling into these techniques without taking them much further, as had happened in the wave of inventions of the fifteenth century.

But this is not what happened. The "first wave" of innovations was followed after 1820 by a secondary ripple of inventions that may have been less spectacular, but included the microinventions that provided the muscle to the downward trend in production costs. The second stage of the Industrial Revolution adapted ideas and techniques to be applied in new and more industries, improved and refined earlier inventions, extended and deepened their deployment, and eventually these efforts showed up in the productivity statistics. Among the remarkable later advances we may list the perfection of mechanical weaving after 1820; the invention of Roberts' self-acting mule in spinning (1825); the extension and adaptation of the techniques first used in cotton and worsted to carded wool and linen; the improvement in the iron industry through Neilson's hot blast (1829) and related inventions; the continuous improvement in crucible steelmaking through coordinated crucibles (as practiced for example by Krupp in Essen); the pre-Bessemer improvements in steel thanks to the work of Scottish steelmakers such as David Mushet (father of Robert Mushet, celebrated in one of Samuel Smiles' *Industrial Biographies*), and the addition of manganese to crucible steel known as Heath's process (1839); the continuing improvement in steampower, raising the efficiency and capabilities of the low pressure stationary engines, while perfecting the high pressure engines of Trevithick, Woolf and Stephenson and adapting them to transportation; the advances in chemicals before the advent of organic chemistry (such as the breakthroughs in candle-making and soap manufacturing thanks to the work of Eugène-Michel Chevreul on fatty acids); the introduction and perfection of gas-lighting; the breakthroughs in high-precision engineering and the development of better machine-tools by Maudslay, Whitworth, Nasmyth, Rennie, the Brunels, the Stephensons, and the other great engineers of the "second generation"; the growing interest in electrical phenomena leading to electroplating and the work by Hans Oersted and Joseph Henry establishing the connection between electricity and magnetism, leading to the telegraph in the late 1830s.

The second wave of inventions was the critical period in the sense that it shows up clearly in the total income statistics. Income per capita growth after 1830 accelerates to around 1.1 percent, even though recent calculations confirm that only about a third of that growth was due to total factor productivity growth [Antrás and Voth (2003, p. 63) and Mokyr (2004)]. Income per capita growth in Britain during the "classical" Industrial Revolution was modest. This fact is less difficult to explain than some scholars make it out to be, and any dismissal of the Industrial Revolution as a historical watershed for that reason seems unwarranted. After all, the disruptions of international commerce during the quarter century of the French Wars coincided with bad harvests and unprecedented population growth. Yet the main reason is simply that in the early decades the segment of the British economy affected by technological progress and that can be regarded as a "modern sector" was simply small, even if its exact dimensions remain in dispute. After 1830 this sector expanded rapidly as the new technology was applied more broadly (especially to transportation), growth accelerates, and by the mid-1840s there is clear-cut evidence that the standard of living in Britain was rising even for the working class. The second wave also serves as a bridge between the first Industrial Revolution and the more intense and equally dramatic changes of the second Industrial Revolution.

The success of the Industrial Revolution in generating sustainable economic growth, then, must be found in the developments in the area of useful knowledge that occurred in Europe before and around 1750. What mattered was not so much scientific knowledge itself but rather the method and culture involving the generation and diffusion of propositional knowledge. The Industrial Revolution and its aftermath were based on a set of propositional knowledge that was not only increasing in size, but which was also becoming increasingly accessible, and in which segments that were more effective were becoming tighter. The effectiveness of propositional knowledge was increasingly tested by whether the techniques that were based on it actually worked satisfactorily either by experiment or by virtue of economic efficiency.

To sum up, then, the period 1760–1830 Western Europe witnessed a growing relative importance of improving technology in economic growth. The emergence and continuous improvement of new techniques in the long run were to have an enormous impact on productivity and growth. People started to know more about how and why the techniques they used worked, and this knowledge was widespread. Without belittling the other elements that made the Industrial Revolution possible, the technological breakthroughs of the period prepared the ground for the economic transformation that made the difference between the West and the Rest, between technological modernity and the much slower and often-reversed economic growth episodes of the previous millennia. In order to come up with a reasonable explanation of the technological roots of economic growth in this period, we must turn to the intellectual foundations of the explosion of technical knowledge.

5. The intellectual roots of the Industrial Revolution

Economic historians like to explain economic phenomena with other economic phenomena. The Industrial Revolution, it was felt for many decades, should be explained by economic factors. Relative prices, better property rights, endowments, changes in fiscal and monetary institutions, investment, savings, exports, and changes in labor supply have all been put forward as possible explanations [for a full survey, see Mokyr (1998a)]. Yet the essence of the Industrial Revolution was technological, and technology is knowledge. How, then, can we explain not only the famous inventions of the Industrial Revolution but also the equally portentous fact that these inventions did not peter out fairly quickly after they emerged, as had happened so often in the past?

The answer has to be sought in the intellectual changes that occurred in Europe *before* the Industrial Revolution. These changes affected the sphere of propositional knowledge, and its interaction with the world of technology. As economic historians have known for many years, it is difficult to argue that the scientific revolution of the seventeenth century that we associate with Galileo, Descartes, Newton, and the like had a direct impact on the Industrial Revolution [McKendrick (1973) and Hall (1974)]. Few important inventions, both before and after 1800, can be directly attributed to great scientific discoveries or were dependent in any direct way on scientific expertise. The advances in physics, chemistry, biology, medicine, and other areas occurred too late to have an effect on the industrial changes of the last third of the eighteenth century.[20] The scientific advances of the seventeenth century, crucial as they were to the understanding of nature, had more to do with the movement of heavenly bodies, optics, magnetism, and the classification of plants than with the motions of machines. To say that therefore they had no economic significance is an exaggeration: many of the great scientists and mathematicians of the eighteenth century wrote about mechanics and the properties of materials. After 1800 the connection becomes gradually tighter, yet the influence of science proper on some branches of production (and by no means all at that) does not become decisive until after 1870.[21] The marginal product of scientific knowledge proper on technology varied from industry to industry and over time. Examples of useful applications of pure scientific insights in the eighteenth century can be provided [Musson and Robinson (1969)], but tend to be specific to a few industries.[22]

All the same, the scientific revolution was in many ways the prelude to the intellectual developments at the base of the Industrial Revolution. The culture of science that evolved in the seventeenth century meant that observation and experience were placed in the public domain. Betty Jo Dobbs (1990), William Eamon (1990, 1994), and more recently Paul David (2004) have pointed to the scientific revolution of the seventeenth century as the period in which "open science" emerged, when knowledge about the natural world became increasingly nonproprietary and scientific advances and discoveries were freely shared with the public at large. Thus scientific knowledge became a public good, communicated freely rather than confined to a secretive exclusive few as had been the custom in medieval Europe. The sharing of knowledge within "open science" required systematic reporting of methods and materials using a common vocabulary and consensus standards, and should be regarded as an exogenous decline in access costs, which made the propositional knowledge, such as it was, available to those who might find a use for it. Those who added to useful knowledge would be rewarded by honor, peer recognition, and fame – not a monetary reward that was in any fashion proportional to their contribution. Even those who discovered matters of significant insight to

[20] Unlike the technologies that developed in Europe and the United States in the second half of the nineteenth century, science, in this view, had little direct guidance to offer to the Industrial Revolution [Hall (1974, p. 151)]. Shapin (1996) notes that "it appears unlikely that the 'high theory' of the Scientific Revolution had any substantial direct effect on *economically useful* technology either in the seventeenth century or in the eighteenth ... historians have had great difficulty in establishing that any of these spheres of technologically or economically inspired science bore substantial fruits" (pp. 140–141, emphasis added).

[21] As Charles Gillispie has remarked in the eighteenth century, whatever the interplay between science and production may have been, "it did *not* consist in the application if up-to-date theory to techniques for growing and making things" [Gillispie (1980, p. 336)]. True enough, but had progress consisted only of analyzing existing procedures, identify the best of them, try to make them work as well as possible, and then standardize them, the process would eventually have run into diminishing returns and fizzled out.

[22] Thus the most spectacular insight in metallurgical knowledge, the celebrated 1786 paper by Monge, Berthollet and Vandermonde that established the chemical properties of steel had no immediate technological spin-offs and was "incomprehensible except to those who already knew how to make steel" [Harris (1998, p. 220)]. Harris adds that there may have been real penalties for French steelmaking in its heavy reliance on scientists or technologists with scientific pretensions.

industry, such as Claude Berthollet, Joseph Priestley, and Humphry Davy, often wanted credit, not profit.

The rhetorical conventions in scientific discourse changed in the seventeenth century, with the rules of persuasions continuously shifting away from "authority" toward empirics. It increasingly demanded that empirical knowledge be tested so that useful knowledge could be both accessible and trusted.[23] Verification meant that a deliberate effort was made to make useful knowledge tighter and thus more likely to be used. It meant a willingness, rarely observed before, to discard old and venerable interpretations and theories when they could be shown to be in conflict with the evidence. Scientific method meant that in the age of Enlightenment a class of experts evolved who would often decide which technique worked best.[24]

The other crucial transformation that the Industrial Revolution inherited from the seventeenth century was the growing change in the very purpose and objective of propositional knowledge. Rather than proving some religious point, such as illustrating the wisdom of the creator, or the satisfaction of that most creative of human characteristics, curiosity, natural philosophers in the eighteenth century came increasingly under the influence of the idea that the main purpose of knowledge was to improve mankind's material condition – that is, find to technological applications. Bacon in 1620 had famously defined technology by declaring that the control of humans over things depended on the accumulated knowledge about how nature works, since "she was only to be commanded by obeying her". This idea was of course not entirely new, and traces of it can be found in medieval thought and even in Plato's *Timaeus*, which proposed a rationalist view of the Universe and was widely read by twelfth-century intellectuals. In the seventeenth century, however, the practice of science became increasingly permeated by the Baconian motive of material progress and constant improvement, attained by the accumulation of knowledge.[25] The founding members of the Royal Society justified their activities by their putative usefulness to the realm. There was a self-serving element in this, of

---

[23] Shapin (1994) has outlined the changes in trust and expertise in Britain during the seventeenth century associating expertise, for better or worse, with social class and locality. While the approach to science was ostensibly based on a "question authority" principle (the Royal Society's motto was *nullius in verba* – on no one's word), in fact no system of useful (or for that matter any kind of) knowledge can exist without some mechanism that generates trust. The apparent skepticism with which scientists treated the knowledge created by their colleagues increased the trust that outsiders could have in the findings, because they could then assume – as is still true today – that these findings had been scrutinized and checked by other "experts".

[24] As Hilaire-Pérez (2000, p. 60) put it, "the value of inventions was too important an economic stake to be left to be dissipated among the many forms of recognition and amateurs: the establishment of truth became the professional responsibility of academic science".

[25] Robert K. Merton (1970 [1938], pp. ix, 87) asked rhetorically how "a cultural emphasis upon social utility as a prime, let alone an exclusive criterion for scientific work affects the rate and direction of advance in science" and noted that "science was to be fostered and nurtured as leading to the improvement of man's lot by facilitating technological invention". He might have added that non-epistemic goals for useful knowledge and science, that is to say, goals that transcend knowledge for its own sake and look for some application, affected not only the rate of growth of the knowledge set but even more the chances that existing knowledge will be translated into techniques that actually increase economic capabilities and welfare.

course, much as with National Science Foundation grant proposals today. Practical objectives in the seventeenth century were rarely the primary objective of the growth of formal science. But the changing cultural beliefs implied a gradual change in the agenda of research.

And yet, the central intellectual change in Europe before the Industrial Revolution has been oddly neglected by economic historians: the Enlightenment. Historically it bridges the Scientific and the Industrial Revolutions. Definitions of this amorphous and often contradictory historical phenomenon are many, but for the purposes of explaining the Industrial Revolution we only to examine a slice of it, which I have termed the *Industrial Enlightenment*. To be sure, some historians have noted the importance of the Enlightenment as a culture of rationality, progress, and growth through knowledge.[26] Perhaps the most widely diffused Enlightenment view involved the notion that long-term social improvement was possible although not all Enlightenment philosophers believed that progress was either desirable or inevitable. Above all was the pervasive cultural belief in the Baconian notion that we can attain material progress (that is, economic growth) through controlling nature and that we can only harness nature by understanding her. Francis Bacon, indeed, is a pivotal figure in understanding the Industrial Enlightenment and its impact. His influence helped create the attitudes, institutions, and mechanisms by which new useful knowledge was generated, spread, and put to good use. Modern scholars seem agreed: Bacon was the first to regard knowledge as subject to constant growth, an entity that continuously expands and adds to itself rather than concerned with retrieving, preserving and interpreting old knowledge [Farrington (1979) and Vickers (1992, esp. pp. 496–497)].[27] The understanding of nature was a social project in which the division of knowledge was similar to Adam Smith's idea of the division of labor, another enlightenment notion.[28] Bacon's idea of bringing this about was through what he called a "House of Salomon" – a research academy in which teams of specialists collect data and experiment, and a higher level of scientists try to distill these into general regularities and laws. Such an institution was – at least in theory, if not always

---

[26] One of the most cogent statements is in McNeil (1987, pp. 24–25) who notes the importance of a "faith in science that brought the legacy of the Scientific Revolution to bear on industrial society ... it is imperative to look at the interaction between culture *and* industry, between the Enlightenment and the Industrial Revolution".

[27] Bacon was pivotal in inspiring the Industrial Enlightenment. His influence on the Industrial Enlightenment can be readily ascertained by the deep admiration the encyclopédistes felt toward him, including a long article on Baconisme written by the Abbé Pestre and the credit given him by Diderot himself in his entries on *Art* and *Encyclopédie*. The *Journal Encyclopédique* wrote in 1756 "If this society owes everything to Chancellor Bacon, the philosopher doe not owe less to the authors of the *Encyclopédie*" [cited by Kronick (1962, p. 42)]. The great Scottish Enlightenment philosophers Dugald Stewart and Francis Jeffrey agreed on Baconian method and goals, even if they differed on some of the interpretation [Chitnis (1976, pp. 214–215)].

[28] A typical passage in this spirit was written by the British chemist and philosopher Joseph Priestley (1768, p. 7): "If, by this means, one art or science should grow too large for an easy comprehension in a moderate space of time, a commodious subdivision will be made. Thus all knowledge will be subdivided and extended, and *knowledge* as Lord Bacon observes, being *power*, the human powers will be increased ... men will make their situation in this world abundantly more easy and comfortable".

in practice – the Royal Society, whose initial objectives were inspired by Lord Bacon. Bacon was cited approvingly by many of the leading lights of the Industrial Enlightenment, including Lavoisier, Davy, and the astronomer John Herschel [Sargent (1999, pp. xxvii–xxviii)].[29]

Nothing of the sort, I submit, can be detected in the Ottoman Empire, India, Africa, or China. It touched only ever so lightly (and with a substantial delay) upon Iberia, Russia, and South America but in many of these areas it encountered powerful resistance and retreated. Invention, as many scholars have rightly stressed, had never been a European monopoly, and much of its technological creativity started with adopting ideas and techniques the Europeans had observed elsewhere [Mokyr (1990)]. The Enlightenment, however, provided the ideological foundation of invention, namely a belief that the understanding of nature was the key to growing control of the physical environment. Moreover, it laid out an agenda on how to achieve this control by demanding that this understanding take the form of general and widely applicable principles. With the success of this program came rising living standards, comfort and wealth. The historical result, then, was that eighteenth century Europe created the ability to break out of the ineluctable concavity and negative feedback that the limitations of knowledge and institutions had set hitherto on practically all economies. The stationary state was replaced by the steady state. It is this phenomenon rather than coal or the ghost acreage of colonies that answers Pomeranz's (2000, p. 48) query why Chinese science and technology – which did not "stagnate" – "did not revolutionize the Chinese economy".

The Industrial Enlightenment can be viewed in part as a movement that insisted on asking not just "*which* techniques work" but also "*why* techniques work" – realizing that such questions held the key to continuing progress. In the terminology introduced above, the intellectuals at its center felt intuitively that constructing and widening an epistemic base for the techniques in use would lead to continuing technological progress. Scientists, engineers, chemists, medical doctors, and agricultural improvers made sincere efforts to generalize from the observations they made, to connect observed facts and regularities (including successful techniques) to the formal propositional knowledge of the time, and thus provide the techniques with wider epistemic bases. The bewildering complexity and diversity of the world of techniques in use was to be reduced to a finite set of general principles governing them. If that proved too difficult, at least catalog and classify them in such ways as to make the knowledge more organized and thus easier to access.[30] These insights would lead to extensions, refinements, and improvements,

---

[29] McClellan (1985, p. 52). It should be added that strictu sensu the Royal Society soon allowed in amateurs and dilettantes and thus became less of a pure "Baconian" institution than the French Académie Royale. Dear (1985, p. 147) notes that the Royal Society was "more of a club than a college".

[30] One thinks, of course, above all of the work of Carl Linnaeus. The lack of theory to explain living things similar to physics was acutely felt. Thus Erasmus Darwin, grandfather of the biologist and himself a charter member of the Lunar Society and an archtypical member of the British Industrial Enlightenment, complained in 1800 that Agriculture and Gardening had remained only Arts without a true theory to connect them [Porter (2000, p. 428)]. For details about Darwin, see especially McNeil (1987) and Uglow (2002).

as well as speed up and streamline the process of invention.[31] Asking such questions was of course much easier than answering them. In the longer term, however, raising the questions and developing the tools to get to the answers were essential if technical progress was not to fizzle out.[32] The typical enlightenment inventor did more than tinkering and trial-and-error fiddling with existing techniques: he tried to relate puzzles and challenges to whatever *general* principles could be found, and if necessary to formulate such principles anew. To do so, each inventor needed some mode of communication that would allow him to tap the knowledge of others. The paradigmatic example of such an inventor remains the great James Watt, whose knowledge of mathematics and physics were matched by his tight connections to the best scientific minds of his time, above all Joseph Black and Joseph Priestley. The list of slightly less famous pioneers of technology who cultivated personal connections with scientists can be made arbitrarily long.

The other side of the Industrial Enlightenment had to do with the diffusion of and access to *existing* knowledge. The *philosophes* realized that, in terms of the framework outlined above, access costs were crucial and that useful knowledge should not be confined to a select few but should be disseminated as widely as possible.[33] Diffusion needed help, however, and much of the Industrial Enlightenment was dedicated to making access to useful knowledge easier and cheaper.[34] From the widely-felt need to rationalize and standardize weights and measures, the insistence on writing in vernacular language, to the launching of scientific societies and academies (functioning as de facto clearing houses of useful knowledge), to that most paradigmatic Enlightenment triumph, the *Grande Encyclopédie*, the notion of diffusion found itself at the center of attention among intellectuals.[35] Precisely because the Industrial Enlightenment was not a national or local phenomenon, it became increasingly felt that differences in language and standards became an impediment and increased access costs. Watt, James Keir,

---

[31] Somewhat similar views have been expressed recently by other scholars such as John Graham Smith (2001) and Picon (2001).

[32] George Campbell, an important representative of the Scottish Enlightenment noted that "All art [including mechanical art or technology] is founded in science and practical skills lack complete beauty and utility when they do not originate in knowledge" [cited by Spadafora (1990, p. 31)].

[33] Some Enlightenment thinkers believed that this was already happening in their time: the philosopher and psychologist David Hartley believed that "the diffusion of knowledge to all ranks and orders of men, to all nations, kindred and tongues and peoples ... cannot be stopped but proceeds with an ever accelerating velocity" [cited by Porter (2000, p. 426)].

[34] The best summary of this aspect of the Industrial Enlightenment was given by Diderot in his widely-quoted article on "Arts" in the *Encyclopédie*: "We need a man to rise in the academies and go down to the workshops and gather material about the [mechanical] arts to be set out in a book that will persuade the artisans to read, philosophers to think along useful lines, and the great to make at least some worthwhile use of their authority and wealth".

[35] Roche (1998, pp. 574–575) notes that "if the *Encyclopédie* was able to reach nearly all of society (although ... peasants and most of the urban poor had access to the work only indirectly), it was because the project was broadly conceived as a work of popularization, of useful diffusion of knowledge". The cheaper versions of the Diderot–d'Alembert masterpiece, printed in Switzerland, sold extremely well: the Geneva (quarto) editions sold around 8000 copies and the Lausanne (octavo) editions as many as 6000.

and the Derby clockmaker John Whitehurst, worked on a system of universal terms and standards, that would make French and British experiments "speak the same language" [Uglow (2002, p. 357)]. Books on science and technology were translated rather quickly, even when ostensibly Britain and France were at war with one another.

Access costs depended in great measure on knowing what was known, and for that search engines were needed. The ultimate search engine of the eighteenth century was the encyclopedia. Diderot and d'Alembert's *Encyclopédie* did not augur the Industrial Revolution, it did not predict factories, and had nothing to say about mechanical cotton spinning equipment or steam engines. It catered primarily to the landowning elite and the bourgeoisie of the *ancien régime* (notaries, lawyers, local officials) rather than specifically to an innovative industrial bourgeoisie, such as it was. It was, in many ways, a conservative document [Darnton (1979, p. 286)]. But the Industrial Enlightenment, as embodied in the *Encyclopédie* and similar works that were published in the eighteenth century implied a very different way of looking at technological knowledge: instead of intuition came systematic analysis; instead of mere dexterity, an attempt to attain an understanding of the principles at work; instead of secrets learned from a master, an open and accessible system of training and learning. It was also a comparatively user-friendly compilation, arranged in an accessible way, and while its subscribers may not have been mostly artisans and small manufacturers, the knowledge contained in it dripped down through a variety of leaks to those who could make use of it.[36] Encyclopedias and "dictionaries" were supplemented by a variety of textbooks, manuals, and compilations of techniques and devices that were somewhere in use. The biggest one was probably the massive *Descriptions des arts et métiers* produced by the French Académie Royale des Sciences.[37] Many other specialist compilations of technical and engineering data appeared.[38] In agriculture, meticulously compiled data collections looking at such topics as yields, crops, and cultivation methods were common.[39]

---

[36] Pannabecker points out that the plates in the *Encyclopédie* were designed by the highly skilled Louis-Jacques Goussier who eventually became a machine designer at the Conservatoire des arts et métiers in Paris [Pannabecker (1996)]. They were meant to popularize the rational systematization of the mechanical arts to facilitate technological progress. The parish priest in St. Hubert (in Flanders) traveled to Brussels to purchase a copy, since he had heard of its emphasis on technology and was eager to learn of new ways to extract the coal resources of his land [Jacob (2001, p. 55)].

[37] The set included 13,500 pages of text and over 1,800 plates describing virtually every handicraft practiced in France at the time, and every effort was made to render the descriptions "realistic and practical" [Cole and Watts (1952, p. 3)].

[38] An example is the detailed description of windmills (*Groot Volkomen Moolenboek*) published in the Netherlands as early as 1734. A copy was purchased by Thomas Jefferson and brought to North America [Davids (2001)]. Jacques-François Demachy's *l'Art du distillateur d'eaux fortes* (1773) (published as a volume in the *Descriptions*) is a "recipe book full of detailed descriptions of the construction of furnaces and the conduct of distillation" [John Graham Smith (2001, p. 6)].

[39] William Ellis' *Modern Husbandman or Practice of Farming* published in 1731 gave a month-by-month set of suggestions, much like Arthur Young's most successful book, *The Farmer's Kalendar* (1770). Most of these writings were empirical or instructional in nature, but a few actually tried to provide the readers with

The Industrial Enlightenment realized instinctively that one of the great sources of technological stagnation was a social divide between those who knew things ("*savants*") and those who made things ("*fabricants*"). To construct pipelines through which those two groups could communicate was at the very heart of the movement.[40] The relationship between those who possessed useful knowledge and those who might find a productive use for it was changing in eighteenth-century Europe and points to a reduction in access costs. They also served as a mechanism through which practical people with specific technical problems to solve could air their needs and thus influence the research agenda of the scientists, while at the same time absorbing what best-practice knowledge had to offer. The movement of knowledge was thus bi-directional, as seems natural to us in the twenty-first century. In early eighteenth-century Europe, however, such exchanges were still quite novel.

An interesting illustration can be found in the chemical industry. Pre-Lavoisier chemistry, despite its limitations, is an excellent example of how *some* knowledge, no matter how partial or erroneous, was believed to be of use in mapping into new techniques.[41] The pre-eminent figure in this field was probably William Cullen, a Scottish physician and chemist. His work "exemplifies all the virtues that eighteenth-century chemists believed would flow from the marriage of philosophy and practice" [Donovan (1975, p. 84)]. Ironically, this marriage remained barren for many decades. In chemistry the expansion of the epistemic base and the flurry of new techniques it generated did not occur fully until the mid-nineteenth century [Fox (1998)]. Cullen's prediction that chemical theory would yield the principles that would direct innovations in the practical arts remained, in the words of the leading expert on eighteenth-century chemistry, "more in the nature of a promissory note than a cashed-in achievement" [Golinski (1992, p. 29)]. Manufacturers needed to know why colors faded, why certain fabrics took dyes more

---

some systematic analysis of the principles at work. One of those was Francis Home's *Principles of Agriculture and Vegetation* (1757). One of the great private data collection projects of the time were Arthur Young's famed *Tours* of various parts of England and William Marshall's series on *Rural Economy* [Goddard (1989)]. They collected hundreds of observations on farm practice in Britain and the continent. However, at times Young's conclusions were contrary to what his own data indicated [see Allen and Ó Gráda (1988)].

[40] This point was first made by Zilsel (1942) who placed the beginning of this movement in the middle of the sixteenth century. While this may be too early for the movement to have much economic effect, the insight that technological progress occurs when intellectuals communicate with producers is central to its historical explanation.

[41] Cullen lectured (in English) to his medical students, but many outsiders connected with the chemical industry audited his lectures. Cullen believed that as a philosophical chemist he had the knowledge needed to rationalize the processes of production [Donovan (1975, p. 78)]. He argued that pharmacy, agriculture, and metallurgy were all "illuminated by the principles of philosophical chemistry" and added that "wherever any art [that is, technology] requires a matter endued with any peculiar physical properties, it is chemical philosophy which informs us of the natural bodies possessed of these bodies" [cited by Brock (1992, pp. 272–273)]. He and his colleagues worked, among others, on the problem of purifying salt (needed for the Scottish fish-preservation industry), and that of bleaching with lime, a common if problematic technique in the days before chlorine.

readily than others, and so on, but as late as 1790 best-practice chemistry was incapable of helping them much [Keyser (1990, p. 222)]. Before the Lavoisier revolution in chemistry, it just could not be done, no matter how suitable the social climate: the minimum epistemic base simply did not exist. All the same, Cullen personifies a social demand for propositional knowledge for economic purposes. Whether or not the supply was there, his patrons and audience in the culture of the Scottish Enlightenment believed that there was a chance he could [Golinski (1988)] and put their money behind their beliefs. At times, clever and ingenious people, especially could contribute to the solution of problems. The greatest British mathematician of the eighteenth century, Colin MacLaurin, was reputed to be at hand to resolve "whatever difficulty occurred concerning the construction or perfection of machines, the working of mines, the improvement of manufactures, or the conveying of water" [Murdoch (1750, p. xxiv)]. The great French physicist René Réaumur (1683–1757) studied in great detail the properties of Chinese porcelain and the physics of iron and steel, and produced over 200 copper plates depicting the operation of workshops, machines, and tools of a range of trades [Gillispie (1980, pp. 346–347)]. But most of this promise was not realized till after 1800.

To dwell on one more example, consider the development of steam power. The ambiguities of the relations between James Watt and his mentor, the Scottish scientist Joseph Black are well known. Whether or not Watt's crucial insight of the separate condenser was due to Black's theory of latent heat, there can be little doubt that the give-and-take between the scientific community in Glasgow and the creativity of men like Watt was essential in smoothing the path of technological progress.[42] The same was true in the South of Britain. Richard Trevithick, the Cornish inventor of the high pressure engine, posed sharp questions to his scientist acquaintance Davies Gilbert (later President of the Royal Society), and received answers that supported and encouraged his work [Burton (2000, pp. 59–60)].

The physics of energy remains one of the most striking illustrations of the interactions between propositional and prescriptive knowledge. Only in the decades after 1824 did the understanding that steam was a heat engine and not a device run by pressure break through. The work of Mancunians Joule and Rankine on thermodynamics led to the development of the two cylinder compound marine steam engine and the re-introduction of steam-jacketing. It led to a different way of looking at thermal efficiency that drove home the insight that no matter how one improved a steam engine, its efficiency would always be low – thus pointing the way to internal combustion engines as a solution. Most

---

[42] Hills (1989, p. 53) explains that Black's theory of latent heat helped Watt compute the optimal amount of water to be injected without cooling the cylinder too much. More interesting, however, was his reliance on William Cullen's finding that in a vacuum water would boil at much lower, even tepid, temperatures, releasing steam that would ruin the vacuum in a cylinder. In some sense that piece of propositional knowledge was essential to his realization that he needed a separate condenser. In other areas, too, the discourse between those who had access to propositional knowledge and those who built new techniques was fruitful. Henry Cort, whose invention of the puddling and rolling process was no less central than Watt's separate consenser, also consulted Joseph Black during his work.

important, the widening of the epistemic base pointed to what could *not* be done, and thus prevented inventors and engineers from walking into blind alleys and working on projects that were infeasible. John Ericsson's "regenerative" engine of 1853 was still an attempt to "recycle" heat over and over again, before the ineluctable energy-accounting truths of thermodynamics had fully sunk in [Bryant (1973)]. Such advances were slow and not always monotonic. At times a little knowledge could be a dangerous thing, such as theory of latent heat which made many engineers experiment with alternative fluids whose physical properties were thought to contain less latent heat.[43]

Some of the most interesting enlightenment figures made a career out of specializing in building bridges between propositional and prescriptive knowledge. Among these facilitators was William Nicholson, the founder and editor of the first truly scientific journal, namely *Journal of Natural Philosophy, Chemistry, and the Arts* (more generally known at the time as *Nicholson's Journal*), which commenced publication in 1797. It published the works of most of the leading scientists of the time, and played the role of today's *Nature* or *Science*, that is, to announce important discoveries in short communications. In it, leading scientists including John Dalton, Berzelius, Davy, Rumford, and George Cayley communicated their findings and opinions.[44] Another was John Coakley Lettsom, famous for being one of London's most successful and prosperous physicians and for liberating his family's slaves in the Caribbean. He corresponded with many other Enlightenment figures including Benjamin Franklin, Erasmus Darwin and the noted Swiss physiologist Albrecht von Haller. He wrote about the Natural History of Tea and was a tireless advocate of the introduction of mangel wurzel into British agriculture [Porter (2000, pp. 145–147)]. A third Briton who fits this description as a mediator between the world of propositional knowledge and that of technology was Joseph Banks, one of the most distinguished and respected botanists of his time. Banks, a co-founder (with Rumford) of the Royal Institution in 1799, was a friend to George III and president of the Royal Society for 42 years, every inch an enlightenment figure, devoting his time and wealth to advance learning and to use the learning to create wealth, "an awfully English *philosophe*" in Roy Porter's (2000, p. 149) memorable phrase.

As might be expected, in some cases the bridge between propositional and prescriptive knowledge occurred within the same mind: the very same people who also were

---

[43] The example also points to the importance of tightness as a concept. In the early days of thermodynamics, there was still a lot of confusion about what was and was not feasible. Bryant (1973, p. 161) notes that "it seems strange that inventors [such as Ericsson] operating on what seems to us a pretty shaky theory were able to get financial support". The answer is that at that early stage of the theory, an authority on heat engines could be perfectly sound on thermodynamics yet still be uncertain when faced by a complicated engine supported by "data".

[44] Nicholson also was a patent agent, representing other inventors, and around 1800 ran a "scientific establishment for pupils" on London's Soho square. The school's advertisement ran that "this institution affords a degree of practical knowledge of the sciences which is seldom acquired in the early part of life" delivering weekly lectures on natural philosophy and chemistry "illustrated by frequent exhibition and explanations of the tools, processes and operations of the useful arts and common operations of society".

contributing to science also made some critical inventions (even if the exact connection between their science and their ingenuity is not always clear). The importance of such dual or "hybrid" careers, as Eda Kranakis (1992) has termed them, is that access to the propositional knowledge that could underlie an invention is immediate, as is the feedback from technological advances to propositional knowledge. In most cases the technology shaped the propositional research as much as the other way around. The idea that those contributing to propositional knowledge should specialize in research and leave its "mapping" into technology to others had not yet ripened. Among the inventions made by people whose main fame rests on their scientific accomplishments were the chlorine bleaching process invented by the chemist Claude Berthollet, the invention of carbonated (sparkling) water and rubber erasers by Joseph Priestley, and the mining safety lamp invented by the leading scientist of his age, Humphry Davy (who also, incidentally, wrote a textbook on agricultural chemistry and discovered that a tropical plant named *catechu* was a useful additive to tanning).[45]

Typical of the "dual career" phenomenon was Benjamin Thompson (later Count Rumford, 1753–1814), an American-born mechanical genius who was on the loyalist side during the War of Independence and later lived in exile in Bavaria, London, and Paris; he is most famous for the scientific proof that heat is not a liquid (known at the time as *caloric*) that flows in and out of substances. Yet Rumford was deeply interested in technology, helped establish the first steam engines in Bavaria, and invented (among other things) the drip percolator coffeemaker, a smokeless-chimney stove, and an improved oil lamp. He developed a photometer designed to measure light intensity and wrote about science's ability to improve cooking and nutrition [Brown (1999, pp. 95–110)]. Rumford is as good a personification of the Industrial Enlightenment as one can find. Indifferent to national identity and culture, Rumford was a "Westerner" whose world spanned the entire northern Atlantic area (despite being an exile from the United States, he left much of his estate to establish a professorship at Harvard). In that respect he resembled his older compatriot inventor Benjamin Franklin, who was as celebrated in Britain and France as he was in his native Philadelphia. Rumford could map from his knowledge of natural phenomena and regularities to create things he deemed useful for mankind [Sparrow (1964, p. 162)].[46] Like Franklin and Davy, he refused to take out a patent on any of his inventions – as a true child of the Enlightenment he was committed to the concept of open and free knowledge.[47] Instead, he

---

[45] It is unclear how much of the best-practice science was required for the safety lamp, and how much was already implied by the empirical propositional knowledge accumulated in the decades before 1815. It is significant that George Stephenson, of railway fame, designed a similar device at about the same time.

[46] It is telling that Rumford helped found the London Royal Institute in 1799. This institute was explicitly aimed at the diffusion of useful knowledge to wider audiences through lectures. In it the great Humphry Davy and his illustrious pupil Michael Faraday gave public lectures and did their research.

[47] The most extreme case of a scientist insisting on open and free access to the propositional knowledge he discovered was Claude Berthollet, who readily shared his knowledge with James Watt, and declined an offer by Watt to secure a patent in Britain for the exploitation of the bleaching process [J.G. Smith (1979, p. 119)].

felt that honor and prestige were often a sufficient incentive for people to contribute to useful knowledge. He established the Rumford medal, to be awarded by the Royal Society "in recognition of an outstandingly important recent discovery in the field of thermal or optical properties of matter made by a scientist working in Europe, noting that Rumford was concerned to see recognised discoveries that tended to promote the good of mankind". Not all scientists eschewed such profits: the brilliant Scottish aristocrat Archibald Cochrane (Earl of Dundonald) made a huge effort to render the coal tar process he patented profitable, but failed and ended up losing his fortune. Incentives were, as always, central to the actions of the figures of the Industrial Enlightenment, but we should not assume that these incentives were homogeneous and the same for all.

The other institutional mechanism emerging during the Industrial Enlightenment to connect between those who possessed prescriptive knowledge and those who wanted to apply it was the emergence of meeting places where men of industry interacted with natural philosophers. So-called scientific societies, often known confusingly as literary and philosophical societies, sprung up everywhere in Europe. They organized lectures, symposia, public experiments, and discussion groups, in which the topics of choice were the best pumps to drain mines, or the advantages of growing clover and grass.[48] Most of them published some form of "proceedings", as often meant to popularize and diffuse existing knowledge as it was to display new discoveries. Before 1780 most of these societies were informal and ad hoc, but they eventually became more formal. The British Society of Arts, founded in 1754, was a classic example of an organization that embodied many of the ideals of the Industrial Enlightenment. Its purpose was "to embolden enterprise, to enlarge science, to refine art, to improve manufacture and to extend our commerce". Its activities included an active program of awards and prizes for successful inventors: over 6,200 prizes were granted between 1754 and 1784.[49] The society took the view that patents were a monopoly, and that no one should be excluded from useful knowledge. It therefore ruled out (until 1845) all persons who had taken out a patent from being considered for a prize and even toyed with the idea of requiring every prize-winner to commit to never take out a patent.[50] It served as a communications network and clearing house for technological information, reflecting the feverish growth of supply and demand for useful knowledge.

What was true for Britain was equally true for Continental countries affected by the Enlightenment. In the Netherlands, rich but increasingly technologically backward, heroic efforts were made to set up organizations that could infuse the economy with

---

[48] The most famous of these societies were the Manchester Literary and Philosophical Society (founded in 1781) and the Birmingham Lunar Society, where some of the great entrepreneurs and engineers of the time mingled with leading chemists, physicists, and medical doctors. But in many provincial cities such as Liverpool, Hull and Bradford, a great deal of similar activity took place.

[49] For details see Wood (1913) and Hudson and Luckhurst (1954).

[50] Hilaire-Pérez (2000, p. 197), Wood (1913, pp. 243–245).

more innovativeness.[51] In Germany, provincial academies to promote industrial, agricultural, and political progress through science were founded in all the significant German states in the eighteenth century. The Berlin Academy was founded in 1700 by the great Leibniz, and among its achievements was the discovery that sugar could be extracted from beets (1747). Around 200 societies appeared during the half-century spanning from the Seven-Years War to the climax of the Napoleonic occupation of Germany, such as the Patriotic Society founded at Hamburg in 1765 [Lowood (1991, pp. 26–27)]. These societies, too, emphasized the welfare of the population at large and the country over private profit. Local societies supplemented and expanded the work of learned national academies.[52] Publishing played an important role in the work of societies bent on the encouragement of invention, innovation and improvement. This reflected the emergence of open knowledge, a recognition that knowledge was a non-rivalrous good, the diffusion of which was constrained by access costs.

In France, great institutions were created under royal patronage, above all the *Académie Royale des Sciences*, created by Colbert and Louis XIV in 1666 to disseminate information and resources.[53] Yet the phenomenon was nationwide: 33 official learned societies were functioning in the French provinces during the eighteenth century counting over 6,400 members. Overall, McClellan (1981, p. 547) estimates that during

---

[51] The first of these was established in Haarlem in 1752, and within a few decades the phenomenon spread (much like in England) to the provincial towns. The Scientific Society of Rotterdam known oddly as the *Batavic Association for Experimental Philosophy* was the most applied of all, and advocated the use of steam engines (which were purchased in the 1770s but without success). The Amsterdam Society was known as *Felix Meritis* and carried out experiments in physics and chemistry. These societies stimulated interest in physical and experimental sciences in the Netherlands, and they organized prize-essay contests on useful applications of natural philosophy. For decades a physicist named Benjamin Bosma gave lectures on mathematics, geography, and applied physics in Amsterdam. A Dutch Society of Chemistry founded in the early 1790s helped to convert the Dutch to the new chemistry proposed by Lavoisier [Snelders (1992)]. The Dutch high schools, known as *Athenea* taught mathematics, physics, astronomy, and at times counted distinguished scientists among their staff.

[52] The German local societies were private institutions, unlike state-controlled academies, which enabled them to be more open, with few conditions of entry, unlike the selective, elitist academies. They broke down social barriers, for the established structures of Old Regime society might impede useful work requiring a mixed contribution from the membership of practical experience, scientific knowledge, and political power. Unlike the more scientifically-inclined academies, they invited anyone to join, such as farmers, peasants, artisans, craftsmen, foresters, and gardeners, and attempted to improve the productivity of these occupations and solve the economic problems of all classes. Prizes rewarded tangible accomplishments, primarily in the agricultural or technical spheres. Their goal was not to advance learning like earlier academies, but to apply useful results of human knowledge, discovery and invention to practical and civic life [Lowood (1991)].

[53] It was one of the oldest and financially best supported scientific societies of the eighteenth century, with a membership which included d'Alembert, Buffon, Clairaut, Condorcet, Fontenelle, Laplace, Lavoisier and Reaumur. It published the most prestigious and substantive scientific series of the century in its annual proceedings *Histoire et Mémoires* and sponsored scientific prize contests such as the Meslay prizes. It recognized achievement and rewarded success for individual discoveries and enhanced the social status of scientists, granting salaries and pensions. A broad range of scientific disciplines were covered, with mathematics and astronomy particularly well represented, as well as botany and medicine.

the century perhaps between 10,000 and 12,000 men belonged to learned societies that dealt at least in part with science. The *Académie Royale* exercised a fair amount of control over the direction of French scientific development and acted as technical advisor to the monarchy. By determining what was published and exercising control over patents, the *Académie* became a powerful administrative body, providing scientific and technical advice to government bureaus. France, of course, had a somewhat different objective than Britain: it is often argued that the *Académie* linked the aspirations of the scientific community to the utilitarian concerns of the government thus creating not a Baconian society open to all comers and all disciplines but a closed academy limited primarily to Parisian scholars [McClellan (1981)]. Yet the difference between France and Britain was one of emphasis and nuance, not of essence: they shared a utilitarian optimism of mankind's ability to create wealth through knowledge. In other parts of Europe, such as Italy, scientific societies were active in the eighteenth century [Inkster (1991, p. 35) and Cochrane (1961)]. At the level of the creation of propositional knowledge, at least, there is little evidence that the *ancien régime* was incapable of generating sustained progress.

To summarize, then, the Industrial Revolution had intellectual preconditions that needed to be met if sustained economic growth could take place just as it had to satisfy economic and social conditions. The importance of property rights, incentives, factor markets, natural resources, law and order, market integration, and many other economic elements is not in question. But we need to realize that without understanding the changes in attitudes and beliefs of the key players in the growth of useful knowledge, the technological elements will remain inside a black box.

6. The dynamic of technological modernity

The essence of technological modernity is non-stationarity: many scholars have observed that technological change has become self-propelled and autocatalytic, in which change feeds on change. Unlike other forms of growth, spiraling technological progress does not appear to be bounded from above. Predictions in the vein of "everything that can be invented already has been" have been falsified time and again. The period that followed the Industrial Revolution was one in which innovation intensified, and while we can discern a certain ebb and flow, in which major breakthroughs and a cluster of macroinventions were followed by waves of microinventions and secondary extensions and applications, the dynamic has become non-ergodic, that is to say, the present and the future are nothing like the past. In the premodern past, whether in Europe or elsewhere in the world, invention had remained the exception, if perhaps not an uncommon one. In the second half of the nineteenth century and even more so in the twentieth century, change has become the norm, and even in areas previously untouched by technological innovation, mechanization, automation, and novelty have become inevitable. There is no evidence to date that technology in its widest sense converges to anything.

To oversimplify, the Industrial Revolution could be reinterpreted in light of the changes in the characteristics and structure of propositional knowledge in the eighteenth century and the techniques that rested on it. Before 1750 the human race, as a collective, did not know enough to generate the kind of sustained technological progress that could account for the growth rates we observe. In the absence of such knowledge, no set of institutions, no matter how benevolent, could have substituted for useful knowledge. Pre-modern society had always been limited by its epistemic base and suppressed by economic and social factors. The dynamics of knowledge itself were critical to the historical process. The Industrial Revolution can be seen as what physicists call a "phase transition".[54] Useful knowledge in the decades that followed increased by feeding on itself, spinning out of control as it were.

How do we explain this change in technological dynamic? In economics, phase transitions can be said to occur when a dynamic system has multiple steady states such as an economy that has a "poverty trap" (low-income equilibrium) and a high income (or rapid growth steady state). A phase transition occurs when the system switches from one equilibrium or regime to another. A simple model in which this can be illustrated is one in which capital and skills are highly complementary. In such models one equilibrium is characterized by rapid investment, which raises the demand for skills; the positive feedback occurs because the increase in the rate of return to human capital induces parents to invest more in their children and have fewer children (since they become more expensive), which raises the rate of return on physical capital even more and encourages investment. A second equilibrium is one of low investment, low skills, and high birth rates. A regime change may occur when an exogenous shock is violent enough to bump the system off one basin of attraction and move it to another one. The difficulty with this model for explaining the emergence of modern growth is to identify a historical shock that was sufficiently powerful to "bump" the system to a rapid growth trajectory.

Recent work in growth theory have produced a class of models that reproduce this feature in one form or another. Cervellati and Sunde (2005) for example assume that human capital comes in two forms, a "theoretical" form and a "practical" form, corresponding roughly to "scientific" and "artisanal" knowledge or the categories of useful knowledge proposed above. They assume that human abilities are heterogeneous but that there is a threshold at which people start to invest in "theoretical" knowledge as opposed to "crafts", determined endogenously by life expectancy. This threshold level depends on the costs of acquiring the two types of human capital, their respective rates of return, and the life expectancy over which they are amortized. Further, they model the relationship between mortality and human capital investment. This is a little explored aspect of modernization, but one that must have been of some importance. All other things equal, longer life expectancy would encourage investment in human capital, although it is important to emphasize that a reduction in infant mortality would not directly bring this about, because decisions about human capital are made later in life. Increases in life expectancy at age 10 or so are more relevant here. Given their assumptions, the locus of points in the life-expectancy-ability space that define an intra-generational equilibrium

---

[54] For a definition of phase transitions, see for instance Ruelle (1991, pp. 122–123).

is S-shaped. A second relationship in this model is that life expectancy itself depends on the level of education of the previous generation: better educated parents will be better situated to help their children survive. The model is closed by postulating a relationship between high-quality human capital and total productivity. The neat aspect of the Cervellati–Sunde model is that if for some reason the productivity of the high-quality human capital rises, it produces the kind of observed phase transition when the old poverty trap is no longer an equilibrium and the system abruptly starts to move to a new "high-level" equilibrium. An exogenous disturbance that raises the marginal productivity of "scientific activity" will have the same effect, including an exogenous increase in the stock of propositional knowledge and an ideologically-induced change in the research agenda. Clearly, then, the Industrial Enlightenment, much like an endogenous growth in productivity, can produce an "Industrial Revolution" of this type. While under the assumptions of their paper an Industrial Revolution is "inevitable", the authors recognize that if technological progress has stochastic elements, this could imply a different prediction (p. 23). Either way, however, the emergence of technologically-based "modern growth" can be understood without the need for a sudden violent shock.

The alternative is to presume that historical processes cause the underlying parameters to change slowly but cumulatively, until one day what was a slow-growth steady state is no longer an equilibrium at all and the system, without a discernible shock, moves rather suddenly into a very different steady state. These models, pioneered by Galor and Weil (2000), move from comparative statics with respect to a parameter determining the dynamic structure, to a dynamical system in which this parameter is a latent state variable that evolves and can ultimately generate a phase transition.[55] In the Galor–Weil model, the economic *ancien régime* is not really a steady state but a "pseudo steady state" despite its long history: within a seeming stability the seeds for the phase transition are germinating invisibly.

A similar model, in which technology plays a "behind the scenes" role, is the highly original and provocative model by Galor and Moav (2002). In that model, the phase transition is generated by evolutionary forces and natural selection. The idea is that there are two classes of people, those who have many children (r-strategists) and others (K-strategists) who have relatively few but "high-quality" offspring and who invest more in education. When "quality types" are selected for, more smart and creative people are added and technology advances. Technological progress increases the rate of return to human capital, induces more people to have more "high quality" (educated) children which provides the positive feedback loop. Moreover, as income advances,

---

[55] Another example of this type of "phase transition" has been proposed recently by David (1998). He envisages the community of "scientists" to consist of local networks or "invisible colleges" in the business of communicating with each other. Such transmission between connected units can be modeled using percolation models in which information is diffused through a network with a certain level of connectivity. David notes that these models imply that there is a minimum level of persistently communicative behavior that a network must maintain for knowledge to diffuse through and that once this level is achieved the system becomes self-sustaining.

households have more resources to spend on education, which add to further expansion. Again, technology in this model is wholly endogenous to education and investment in human capital, and an autonomous development in the social factors governing human knowledge and the interplay between propositional and prescriptive knowledge is not really modeled. Despite the somewhat limiting assumptions of this model (the "type" is purely inherited and not a choice variable), this paper presents an innovative way of looking at the problem of human capital formation and economic growth in the historical context of the Industrial Revolution.

In one sense Galor and Moav's reliance on evolutionary logic to explain technological progress is ironic. In recent years it has been realized increasingly that knowledge *itself* is subject to evolutionary dynamics, in that new ideas and knowledge emerge much like evolutionary innovations (through mutations or recombinations) and are selected for (or not). Knowledge systems follow a highly path-dependent trajectory governed by Darwinian forces [Ziman (2000) and Mokyr (2005b)]. Yet this important insight still awaits to be incorporated in the "take-off" models of growth theorists. Evolutionary models predict that sudden accelerations or "explosions" of evolutionary change (known oddly as "adaptive radiation") occur when conditions are ripe, such as the so-called Cambrian explosion which has been compared to the Industrial Revolution [Kauffman (1995, p. 205)]. Another example of rapid evolutionary innovation is the spectacular proliferation of mammals at the beginning of the Cenozoic following the disappearance of the giant reptiles. The idea that evolution proceeds in the highly nonlinear rhythm known as "punctuated equilibrium" has been suggested as a possible insight that economic historians can adapt from evolutionary biology [Mokyr (1990)].

Some of these (and other, similar) models may be more realistic than others, and economic historians may have to help to sort them out. A phase transition model without reliance on the quality of children and human capital is proposed by Charles Jones (2001) relying on earlier work by Michael Kremer (1993). In Jones' model, what matters is the size rather than the quality of the labor force. In very small populations, the few new technological ideas lead in straightforward Malthusian fashion to higher populations and not to higher income per capita. As the population gets larger and larger and the number of creative individuals increases, however, new ideas become more and more frequent, and productivity pulls ahead. The model assumes increasing returns in population and thus generates a classic multiple equilibria kind of story. The positive feedback thus works through fertility behavior responding to higher productivity, and through an increasing returns to population model. As per capita consumption increases, parents substitute away from children to consume other goods, and fertility eventually declines. In this fashion these models succeed in generating both a sudden and discontinuous growth of income per capita or consumption and the fertility transition. Jones shows that for reasonable parameter values he can simulate a world economy that reproduces the broad outlines of modern economic history (including an initial rise in fertility in the early stages of the Industrial Revolution, followed by a decline).

Yet the exact connection between demographic changes and the economic changes in the post 1750 period are far from understood, and much of the new growth literature pays scant attention to many variables that surely must have affected the demand for children and fertility behavior. These include technological changes in contraceptive technology, a decline in infant and child mortality, and changing demand for children in the household economy due to technological changes in agriculture and manufacturing. It is also open to question whether and to what extent "numbers matter", that is, whether the more people are around, the more likely – all other things equal – new technological ideas are to emerge.[56] The real question is whether the ideas that count are really a monotonic function of population size (Jones assumes a positive elasticity of 0.75 to generate his results), or whether they are generated by a negligible minority and that small changes in the fraction of creative people matters more than a rise in the raw size of population.[57] The historical record on that is subject to serious debate. It might be added that population growth in Britain was almost nil in the first half of the eighteenth century, and while it took off during the post-1750 era, the same was true for Ireland, where no comparable Industrial Revolution can be detected.

Most endogenous growth historical models, however, depend on the notion that the variable critical to the process of "take-off" or phase transition is investment in human capital.[58] Historically, however, such a view is not unproblematic either. The idea that the fertility reduction was a consequence of changing rates of return on human capital, especially advanced by Lucas (2002), runs into what may be called the European Fertility Paradox: the first nation to clearly reduce its fertility rate through a decline in marital fertility (that is, intentional and conscious behavior) was *not* the country in which advanced technological techniques were adopted in manufacturing, but France. In Britain fertility rates came down eventually, but the decline did not start until the mid-1870s, a century after the beginning of the Industrial Revolution [e.g., Tranter (1985, chapter 4)]. Imperial Germany, which became the technological leader in many of the cutting-edge industries of the second Industrial Revolution, maintained a fertility rate far above France's and Britain's.[59] To argue, therefore, that technological progress was rooted in demographic behavior (through smaller families) seems at variance with the facts. It may well be that this nexus held in the twentieth century, but given the decline in wage premia it is hard to see the rate of return on human capital to be the driving factor. Beyond Europe, of course, population-driven theories of the "the-more-the-merrier" variety must confront the difficult fact that China not only had a population vastly larger

---

[56] The pedigree of this idea clearly goes back to the work of Julian Simon (1977, 2000).

[57] This sensitivity is reflected in Jones' simulations: the proportion inventors in the population in 1700 in his computations (set to match the demographic data) is 0.875%, but it *declines* in 1800 to less than half that number. By constraining the twentieth century data to stay at that level, Jones shows that the Industrial Revolution would be delayed by 300 years.

[58] For a similar view advanced by an economic historian before the new growth economics, see Easterlin (1981).

[59] In 1900, the total fertility rate (average number of children per woman) in Germany was 4.77, contrasting with 3.40 and 2.79 in England and France respectively. By that time, to be sure, German fertility rates were falling rapidly as they were elsewhere in the industrialized world. See e.g. Livi Bacci (2000, p. 136).

than any European economy but that its population grew at a rapid rate in the very century that Europe experienced its Enlightenment: from a low point of about 100 million in 1685, it exceeded 300 million in 1790, thus experiencing a per annum population growth of 1.05 percent, though admittedly from an unusually low base.

To understand the "phase transition" within the dynamic of useful knowledge, we need to look again at the relationship between propositional and prescriptive knowledge. As the two forms of knowledge co-evolved, they enriched one another increasingly, eventually tipping the balance of the feedback mechanism from negative to positive and creating the phase transition. During the early stages of the Industrial Revolution, propositional knowledge mapped into new techniques, creating what we call "inventions". This mapping should not be confused with the linear models of science and technology that were popular in the mid-twentieth century, which depicted a neat flow from theory to applied science to engineering and from there to technology. Much of the propositional knowledge that led to invention in the eighteenth century was artisanal and mechanical, pragmatic, informal, intuitive, and empirical. Only very gradually did the kind of formal and consensual knowledge we think of today as "science" become a large component of it. It was, in all cases, a small fraction of what is known today. What matters is that it was subject to endogenous expansion: prescriptive knowledge in its turn enhanced propositional knowledge, and thus provided positive feedback between the two types of knowledge, leading to continuous mutual reinforcement. When powerful enough, this mechanism can account for the loss of stability of the entire system and for continuous unpredictable change.

The positive feedback from prescriptive to propositional knowledge took a variety of forms. One of those forms is what Rosenberg has called "focusing devices": technology posed certain riddles that science was unable to solve, such as "why (and how) does this technique work". It has been suggested, for instance that the sophisticated waterworks that supplied power to the famous Derby silk mills established by the Lombe brothers in the 1710s stimulated local scientists interested in hydraulics and mechanics [Elliott (2000, p. 98)]. The most celebrated example of such a loop is the connection between steam power and thermodynamics, exemplified in the well-known tale of Sadi Carnot's early formulation, in 1824, of the Second Law of Thermodynamics by watching the difference in fuel economy between a high pressure (Woolf) steam engine and a low pressure one of the Watt type.[60] The next big step was made by an Englishman, James P. Joule, who showed the conversion rates from work to heat and back.[61] Joule's work

---

[60] It is interesting to note that Carnot's now famous *Reflexions sur la puissance motrice du feu* (1824) was initially ignored in France. Eventually it found its way second hand and through translation into Britain, where there was considerably more interest in his work because of the growing demand by builders of gigantic steam engines such as William Fairbairn in Manchester and Robert Napier in Glasgow for theoretical insights that would help in making better engines.

[61] The ways in which the growth of practical knowledge can influence the emergence of propositional knowledge are well illustrated by Joule's career: he was a child of industrial Lancashire (his father owned a brewery) and in the words of one historian, "with his hard-headed upbringing in industrial Manchester, was unambigu-

and that of Carnot were then reconciled by a German, R.J.E. Clausius (the discoverer of entropy), and by 1850 a new branch of science dubbed "thermodynamics" by William Thomson (later Lord Kelvin) had emerged [Cardwell (1971, 1994)].[62] Power technology and classical energy physics subsequently developed cheek by jowl, culminating in the career of the Scottish physicist and engineer William Rankine, whose *Manual of the Steam Engine* (1859) made thermodynamics accessible to engineers and led to a host of improvements in actual engines. In steam power, then, the positive feedback can be clearly traced: the first engines had emerged in the practical world of skilled blacksmiths, millwrights, and instrument makers with only a minimum of theoretical understanding. These machines then inspired theorists to come to grips with the natural regularities at work and to widen the epistemic base. The insights generated were in turn fed back to engineers to construct more efficient engines. This kind of mutually reinforcing process can be identified, in a growing number of activities, throughout the nineteenth century. They required the kind of intellectual environment that the Industrial Enlightenment had created: a world in which technical knowledge was accessible and communicable in an international elite community, a technological invisible college that encompassed much of the Western world.

A less well-known example of this feedback mechanism, but equally important to economic welfare, is the interaction between the techniques of food-canning and the evolution of bacteriology. As noted earlier, the canning of food was invented in 1795 by Nicolas Appert.[63] He discovered that when he placed food in champagne bottles, corked them loosely, immersed them in boiling water, and then hammered the corks tight, the food was preserved for extended periods. Neither Appert nor his English emulators who perfected the preservation of food in tin-plated canisters in 1810 really understood why and how this technique worked, because the definitive demonstration of the notion that microorganisms were responsible for putrefaction of food was still in the future. It is therefore a typical example of a working technique with a narrow epistemic base. The canning of food led to a prolonged scientific debate about what caused food to spoil. The debate was not put to rest until Pasteur's work in the early 1860s. Pasteur claimed ignorance of Appert's experimental work, but eventually admitted that his own work on the preservation of wine was only a new application of Appert's method. Be that

---

ously concerned with the *economic* efficiency of electromagnetic engines ... he quite explicitly adopted the language and concerns of the economist and the engineer" [Morus (1998, p. 187), emphasis in original]. As Ziman (1976, p. 26) remarks, the first law of thermodynamics could easily have been derived from Newton's dynamics by mathematicians such as Laplace or Lagrange, but it took the cost accountancy of engineers to bring it to light.

[62] Research combining experiment and theory in thermodynamics continued for many decades after that, especially in Scotland and in Mulhouse, France, where Gustave Adolphe Hirn, a textile manufacturer, led a group of scientists in tests on the steam engines in his factory and was able to demonstrate the law of conservation of energy.

[63] Experimental work by, among others, the Italian naturalist Lazaro Spallanzani, had earlier indicated that heating organic materials and subsequent airtight flashing would prevent putrefaction. It is unclear whether Appert and his British imitators knew of this work. See Clow and Clow (1952, p. 571).

as it may, his work on the impossibility of spontaneous generation clearly settled the question of why the technique worked and provided the epistemic base for the technique in use. When the epistemic base of food-canning became wider, techniques improved: the optimal temperatures for the preservation of various foods with minimal damage to flavor and texture were worked out by two MIT scientists, Samuel Prescott and William Underwood.[64]

A different feedback mechanism from prescriptive to propositional knowledge was described by Derek Price as "Artificial Revelation". The idea is fairly simple: our senses limit us to a fairly narrow slice of the universe that has been called a "mesocosm": we cannot see things that are too far away, too small, or not in the visible light spectrum [Wuketits (1990, pp. 92, 105)]. The same is true for our other senses, for the ability to make very accurate measurements, for overcoming optical and other sensory illusions, and – perhaps most important in our own time – the computational ability of our brains. Technology consists in part in helping us overcome these limitations that evolution has placed on us and learn of natural phenomena we were not meant to see or hear.[65] The period of the Industrial Revolution witnessed a great deal of improvement in techniques whose purpose it was to enhance propositional knowledge. The great potter Josiah Wedgwood maintained a close relationship with the chemist James Keir: while Keir supplied Wedgwood with counsel, Wedgwood's factory provided Keir with the tubes and retorts he used in his laboratory near Birmingham [Stewart (2004, p. 18)]. The accuracy of instruments that measured time, distance, weight, pressure, temperature and so on increased by orders of magnitude in the eighteenth century.[66] Pumps and electrical machines allowed the study of vacuums and electrical phenomena. Lavoisier and his circle were especially good in designing and utilizing better laboratory equipment that allowed them to carry out more sophisticated experiments.[67] Alessandro Volta invented a pile of alternating silver and zinc disks that could generate an electric current in 1800. Volta's battery was soon produced in industrial quantities by William Cruickshank.

---

[64] A University of Wisconsin scientist, H.L. Russell, proposed to increase the temperature of processing peas from 232°F to 242°F, thus reducing the percentage spoiled can from 5 percent to 0.07 percent Thorne (1986, p. 145).

[65] Derek Price (1984b, p. 54) notes that Galileo's discovery of the moons of Jupiter was the first time in history that somebody made a discovery by a process that did not involve a deep and clever thought and instead relied on the application of a novel technology.

[66] See Heilbron (1990, pp. 5–9). Interestingly, Heilbron believes that the main motives for these improvements were raisons d'etat and sheer curiosity, without allowing for the possibility that industrial and commercial application might have contributed something. But in the same volume Lundgren (1990, p. 250) points out that in Sweden the analytical quantification of assaying was a consequence of the expanding production of minerals and ores.

[67] The famous mathematician Pierre-Simon de Laplace was also a skilled designer of equipment and helped to build the calorimeter that resulted in the celebrated "Memoir on Heat" jointly written by Laplace and Lavoisier (in 1783), in which respiration was identified as analogous to burning. Much of the late eighteenth-century chemical revolution was made possible by new instruments such as Volta's eudiometer, a glass container with two electrodes intended to measure the content of air, used by Cavendish to show the nature of water as a compound.

Through the new tool of electrolysis, pioneered by William Nicholson and Humphry Davy, chemists were able to isolate element after element and fill in much of the detail in the maps whose rough contours had been sketched by Lavoisier and Dalton. Volta's pile, as Davy put it, acted as an "alarm bell to experimenters in every part of Europe" [cited by Brock (1992, p. 147)]. The development of the technique of in vitro culture of micro-organisms had similar effects (the Petri dish was invented in 1887 by R.J. Petri, an assistant of Koch's). Price feels that many such advances in knowledge are "adventitious" (1984a, p. 112). Travis (1989) has documented in detail the connection between the tools developed in the organic chemical industry and advances in cell biology. These connections between prescriptive and propositional knowledge are just a few examples of advances in scientific techniques that can be seen as adaptations of ideas originally meant to serve an entirely different purpose, and they reinforce the contingent and accidental nature of much technological progress [Rosenberg (1994, pp. 251–252)].

The invention of the modern compound microscope in 1830 attributed to Joseph J. Lister (father of the famous surgeon) serves as another good example. Lister was an amateur optician, whose revolutionary method of grinding lenses greatly improved image resolution by eliminating spherical aberrations.[68] His invention and the work of others changed microscopy from an amusing diversion to a serious scientific endeavor and eventually allowed Pasteur, Koch, and their disciples to refute spontaneous generation and to establish the germ theory, a topic I return to below. The germ theory was one of the most revolutionary changes in useful knowledge in human history and mapped into a large number of new techniques in medicine, both preventive and clinical. Indeed, the widespread use of glass in lenses and instruments in the West was itself something coincidental, a "giant accident", possibly a by-product of demand for wine and different construction technology [Macfarlane and Martin (2002)]. It seems plausible that without access to this rather unique material, the development of propositional knowledge in the West would have taken a different course.[69]

A third mechanism of technology feeding back into prescriptive knowledge is through what might be called the "rhetoric of knowledge". This harks back to the idea of "tightness" introduced earlier. Techniques are not "true" or "false". Either they work according to certain predetermined criteria or they do not, and thus they can be interpreted to confirm or refute the propositional knowledge that serves as their epistemic base. Propositional knowledge has varying degrees of tightness, depending on the degree to which the available evidence squares with the rhetorical conventions for acceptance. Laboratory technology transforms conjecture and hypothesis into an accepted fact, ready to go into textbooks and to be utilized by engineers, physicians, or farmers.

---

[68] The invention was based on a mathematical optimization for combining lenses to minimize spherical aberration and reduced average image distortion by a huge proportion, from 19 to 3 percent. Lister is reputed to have been the first human being ever to see a red blood cell.

[69] Macfarlane and Martin (2002, pp. 81–82) note that glass lenses not only made specific discoveries possible but led to a growing confidence in a world of deeper truths to be discovered, destabilizing conventional views. "The obvious was no longer true. Hidden connections and buried forces could be analyzed".

But in the past a piece of propositional knowledge was often tested simply by verifying that the techniques based on it actually worked. The earthenware manufacturer Josiah Wedgwood felt that his experiments in pottery actually tested the theories of his friend Joseph Priestley, and professional chemists, including Lavoisier, asked him for advice. Similarly, once biologists discovered that insects could be the vectors of pathogenic microparasites, insect-fighting techniques gained wide acceptance. The success of these techniques in eradicating yellow fever and malaria was the best confirmation of the hypotheses about the transmission mechanisms of the disease and helped earn them wide support.

Or consider the matter of heavier-than-air flight. Much of the knowledge in aeronautics in the early days was experimental rather than theoretical, such as attempts to tabulate coefficients of lift and drag for each wing shape at each angle. It might be added that the epistemic base supporting the first experiments of the Wright brothers was quite untight: in 1901 the eminent astronomer and mathematician Simon Newcomb (the first American since Benjamin Franklin to be elected to the Institute of France) opined that flight carrying anything more than "an insect" would be impossible.[70] The success at Kitty Hawk persuaded all but the most stubborn doubting Thomases that human flight in heavier-than-air fixed wing machines was possible. Clearly their success subsequently inspired a great deal of subsequent research on aerodynamics. In 1918 Ludwig Prandtl published his magisterial work on how wings could be scientifically rather than empirically designed and the lift and drag precisely calculated [Constant (1980, p. 105) and Vincenti (1990, pp. 120–125)]. Even after Prandtl, not all advances in airplane design were neatly derived from first principles in an epistemic base in aerodynamic theory, and the ancient method of trial and error was still widely used in the search for the best use of flush riveting in holding together the body of the plane or the best way to design landing gear [Vincenti (1990, pp. 170–199; 2000)].

It is important not to exaggerate the speed and abruptness of the transition. Thomas Edison, a paradigmatic inventor of the 2nd Industrial Revolution, barely knew any science, and in many ways should be regarded an old-fashioned inventor who relied mostly on trial-and-error through intuition, dexterity and luck. Yet he knew enough to know what he did not know, and that there were others who knew what he needed. Among those who supplied him with the propositional knowledge necessary for his research were the mathematical physicist Francis Upton, the trained electrical engineer Hermann Claudius, the inventor and engineer Nikola Tesla, the physicist Arthur E. Kennelly (later professor of electrical engineering at Harvard), and the chemist Jonas W. Aylsworth. Yet by that time access costs had declined enough so that he could learn for instance of the work of the great German physicist Hermann von Helmholtz through a translated copy of the latter's work on acoustics.

---

[70] He was joined in that verdict by the Navy's chief engineer, Admiral George Melville [Kelly (1943, pp. 116–117) and Crouch (1989, p. 137)]. Nor were the inventors themselves all that certain: in a widely quoted remark, Wilbur Wright remarked to his brother in a despondent mood that "not within a thousand years would men ever fly" [Kelly (1943, p. 72)].

The positive feedback from technology to prescriptive knowledge entered a new era with development of the computer. In the past, the practical difficulty of solving differential equations limited the application of theoretical models to engineering. A clever physicist, it has been said, is somebody who can rearrange the parameters of an insoluble equation so that it does not have to be solved. Computer simulation can evade that difficulty and help us see relations in the absence of exact closed-form solutions and may represent the ultimate example of Bacon's "vexing" of nature. In recent years simulation models have been extended to include the effects of chemical compounds on human bodies. Combinatorial chemistry and molecular biology are both equally unimaginable without fast computers. It is easy to see how the mutual reinforcement of computers and their epistemic base can produce a virtuous circle that spirals uncontrollably away from its basin of attraction. Such instability is the hallmark of Kuznets' vision of the role of "useful knowledge" in economic growth.

In addition to the positive feedback within the two types of knowledge, one might add the obvious observation that *access costs* were themselves a function of improving techniques, through better communications, storage, and travel techniques. In this fashion, expansions in prescriptive knowledge not only expanded the underlying supporting knowledge but made it more accessible and thus more likely to be used. As already noted, this is particularly important because so much technological progress consists of combinations and applications of existing techniques in novel ways, or parallels from other techniques in use. Precisely for this reason, cheap and reliable access to the monster catalog of all feasible techniques is an important element in technological progress. As the total body of useful knowledge is expanding dramatically in our own time, it is only with the help of increasingly sophisticated search engines that needles of useful knowledge can be retrieved from a haystack of cosmic magnitude.

Technological modernity is created when the positive feedback from the two types of knowledge becomes self-reinforcing and autocatalytic. We could think of this as a phase transition in economic history, in which the old parameters no longer hold, and in which the system's dynamics have been unalterably changed. There is no necessity for this to be true even in the presence of positive feedback; but for certain levels of the parameters, the system as a whole becomes unstable. It may well that this instability in the knowledge-producing system are what is behind what we think of as "technological modernity". Kuznets, of course, felt that the essence of modern growth was the increasing reliance of technology on modern science. This view, as I have argued above, needs clarification and amplification. Inside the black box of technology is a smaller black box called "research and development" which translates inputs into the output of knowledge. This black box itself contains an even smaller black box which models the available knowledge in society, and it is this last box I have tried to pry open. Yet all this is only part of the story: knowledge creates opportunities, but it does not guarantee action. Knowledge is an abstract concept, it glosses over the human agents who possess it and decide to act upon it. What motivates them, and why did some societies seem to be so much more inclined to generate new knowledge and to exploit the knowledge it had? To understand why during the past two centuries the "West" has been able to take advantage of these opportunities we need to examine the institutional context of innovation.

7. Human capital and modern economic growth

The role of education and human capital in the Industrial Revolution is more ambiguous than much of the New Growth literature would suggest. Britain, the most advanced industrial nation in 1850, was far from being the best educated, the most literate, or in some other way the best-endowed in traditional human capital. Increases in male literacy in Britain during the Industrial Revolution were in fact comparatively modest and its educational system as a whole lagging behind [Mitch (1998)]. The Lutheran nations of the Continent – Germany and the Scandinavian nations – were far more literate and, in one formulation, "impoverished sophisticates".[71] Jewish minorities throughout European history were unusually well-endowed in human capital [Botticini and Eckstein (2003)], yet contributed little or nothing to the Industrial Revolution before 1850. Clearly human capital is indispensable as a concept, but we need to be far more specific as to what *kind* of human capital was produced, for and by whom, what was the source of the demand for it, and how it was distributed over the population. In his recent survey, the social historian Peter Kirby (2003, p. 118) concludes that the idea that nineteenth century education and literacy emerged as a response to a need for a trained labor force is misleading. There was a significant gap between formal 'education' and 'occupational training', the latter remaining embedded in the workplace in the form of apprenticeships and trainee positions. Before 1870, at least, the rate of return on formal education in his view was so low that its benefits did not outweigh the costs. That is not to say that being literate did not convey advantages in terms of social and occupational mobility [Long (2003)], but many of the skills that we associate with formal schooling could be attained informally.

The historical role of human capital in economic growth must then be re-examined with some care. In terms of the framework delineated here its primary importance was in reducing access costs: literate and educated innovators could and did read articles, books and personal letters from scientist, as well as familiarize themselves with techniques used elsewhere. They could understand mathematical and chemical notation, interpret figures, read blueprints, and follow computations and mechanical arguments. Moreover, by knowing more, the cost of *verification* fell: some obviously bogus and ineffective pieces of propositional knowledge could be rejected offhand. Secondly, a more literate and better educated labor force is assumed to be more competent, that is, be able to execute instructions contained in more and more complex techniques. Yet because the total set of useful knowledge could be divided up more and more thanks to better access, the actual amount of such knowledge that a *single* worker had to control may not

---

[71] This is a term used by Lars Sandberg in a pathbreaking paper [Sandberg (1979)].

have increased, it may have just changed, becoming more specialized, a smaller slice of a bigger whole. Human capital may have been more important in learning *new* instructions than in executing more complex and difficult techniques: as technology changed more rapidly, technical tricks had to be learned and unlearned at more rapid rates.

Above all, investment in human capital is supposed to have created the conditions for faster innovation. It made for the prepared minds that, as Pasteur famously said, are favored by Fortune. Much technological progress consisted of fumbling and stumbling into some lucky find – but only systematic training allowed inventors to recognize what they found and how to apply it most fruitfully. Yet it is a fair question to ask of all economists who draw links between demographic change and human capital on the one hand and technological progress on the other – whether through the quality-quantity trade-off or otherwise – how many inventors and technically competent people were needed to generate sustained technological progress.

The answer, of course, depends, on what we mean by "competent". Eighteenth century Britain did have a cadre of highly skilled technicians and mechanics, almost all of whom were trained in the apprenticeship system rather than in formal academies, and these contributed materially to its technological development. The Continent, too, had its share of skilled and well-trained craftsmen, although if we are to judge from the net migration flow of talent, Britain may have had an edge, especially in coal-using industries.[72] But the process of training apprentices did not always correspond to the neoclassical depiction of human capital formation. In addition to imparting skills, it was a selection process in which naturally gifted mechanics taught themselves from whatever source was available as much as they learned from their masters. Such sources multiplied as a direct result of the Industrial Enlightenment. In the eighteenth century the publishing industry supplied a large flow of popular science books, encyclopedias, technical dictionaries and similar "teach-yourself" kind of books.[73] These mechanics and technicians were the ones that made the Industrial Revolution possible. They generated a stream of microinventions that accounted for the actual productivity gains when the great breakthroughs or macroinventions created the opportunities to do so. They were also the people who provided the competence to carry out the new instructions, that is, to build and operate the new devices according to specifications.[74]

---

[72] Britain received as much as she gave in terms of skilled artisans and applied scientists: among the foreigners who settled in Britain during the Industrial Revolution were the French inventor Aimé Argand, the Portuguese applied scientist, instrument maker and merchant Jean-Hyacinthe de Magellan, the Italian physicist Tiberius Cavallo, the German inventors Friedrich Koenig and Frederic Winsor (né Winzer), the Swiss engineer J.G. Bodmer, and the great French engineer and machine builder, Marc I. Brunel.

[73] Among the many eminent self-educated scientists was Michael Faraday, whose interests in electricity were first stimulated by reading an article in the *Encyclopedia Britannica*.

[74] An apt description of the importance of competence is provided by the early nineteenth-century steel industry: "controlling the pace at which coal was fed to the furnace and its placing on the hearth [the skilled worker] had to cope with variations in the quality of the fuel and adjust his stoking accordingly and sometimes add coal of various sizes and grades ... all this was a matter of judgement, but in many instances this judgement governed the efficiency or even the practicability of the process. This sort of judgment was not the kind of thing one learned from books" [Harris (1992a, p. 26)].

How many such people were necessary? Better not teach the peasants how to read, Voltaire reputedly said, for someone has to plow the fields.[75] Technological change in the era of the Industrial Revolution, based on invention, innovation, and implementation, did not necessarily require that the entire labor force, or even most of it (much less the population at large), be highly educated; the effects of education depended on whether the relation between innovation and the growth of competence was strong and positive. An economy that is growing technologically more sophisticated and more productive may end up using techniques that are more difficult to invent and artefacts that are more complex in design and construction, but may actually be easier to use and run on the shop floor. Production techniques became more modular and standardized, meaning that labor might become more specialized and that each worker had to know less rather than more. If much of the new technology introduced after 1825 was like the self-actor – simpler to use if more complex to build – it may well be that the best models to explain technological progress (in the sense of inventing new techniques rather than implementing existing ones) should focus not on the *mean* level of human capital (or, as model-builders have it, the level of human capital of a representative agent), but just on the *density in the upper tail* of the distribution. In other words, what mattered above all was the level of education and sophistication of a small and pivotal elite of engineers, mechanics, and chemists. Dexterous, motivated, well-trained technically, and imaginative, with some understanding of the science involved, these workers turned the ideas of the "Great Men" into a more productive technology. The new technological system depended on the increased skills of low-level technicians, supervisors, foremen, and skilled artisans who introduced and operated new techniques on the shop floor and made the necessary adjustments to specific tasks and usages. What knowledge the firms could not supply from its own workforce, it purchased from the outside in the form of consulting engineers.[76]

Technical education for the masses might have been beneficial because among the working classes there might have been "diamonds in the rough", technically gifted lads who, with the proper training, could become part of the creative elite. The sample of 316 industrialists assembled by Crouzet (1985) – admittedly only the tip of a largely

---

[75] This is the way Darnton (2003, p. 5) phrases it. Actually, Voltaire view was a bit more involved. In his *Dictionaire Philosophique* he noted that even in the most enlightened villages at most two peasants could read and write, but that this in no way affected their ability to build, plant and harvest. Adam Smith expressed the same idea in his "Early Draft" for the *Wealth of Nations* when he noted that "to think or to reason comes to be, like every other employment, a particular business, which is carried on by very few people who furnish the public with all the thought and reason possessed by the vast multitudes that labour". The benefits of the "speculations of the philosopher ... may evidently descend to the meanest of people" if they led to improvements in the mechanical arts [Smith (1978, pp. 569–572)].

[76] Such outside professional consultants included the famous British "coal-viewers" who advised coal mine owners not only on the optimal location and structure of coal mines but also on the use of the Newcomen steam pumps employed in mines in the eighteenth century [Pollard (1968, pp. 152–153)]. "Civil engineers" was a term coined by the great engineer John Smeaton (1724–1792), who spent much of his life "consulting" to a large number of customers in need of technical advice.

unknown pyramid – contained only 31 persons whose occupations were "unskilled workmen" and only 16 fathers out of 226 "founders of large industrial undertakings" were working class. The bulk of the labor force consisted of rank-and-file workers whose ex post technical skills may have mattered but little, and thus any model that relates human capital to demographic behavior runs into a serious dilemma. Technological progress and competence had a complex relation with one another because ingenuity and detailed propositional knowledge could be frontloaded in the instructions or artefacts, thus reducing the competence needed to carry out the actual production.[77]

It stands to reason that the ratio of competence to knowledge was higher in agriculture than in manufacturing and in services, since a great deal of competence involved uncodified knowledge about very local and time-specific conditions of soil and weather. The share of agriculture in the labor force and total output declined, and this may be one reason why the relative importance of this form of human capital has declined in the twentieth century. It has also been suggested [Harris (1992a)] that the importance of tacit skills was especially prominent in coal-using industries such as glass and iron, which explains Britain's initial advantage in these industries and the need for Continental Europe to import British skilled workers after 1800 during the years of "catching-up".

The human capital argument can be tested, at a rudimentary level, by looking at the ratio between skilled and unskilled wages (or "wage premium"). The problem is of course that without estimating a complete model of the market for skills, the historical course of that ratio cannot be assigned to demand or supply factors. If, however, we assume that technology is the prime mover in this market and we keep in mind that the supply of skills will lag considerably behind a rise in wages (since the acquisition of skills takes time), it would stand to reason that if the Industrial Revolution led to a net increase in the demand for skilled labor, we should observe some increase in the skill premium during the Industrial Revolution. No such change can be observed. Indeed, recent research into the wage premium has established that it changed little between 1450 and 1900, yet it was much lower in Western Europe than in either Southern and Eastern Europe or Asia, indicating perhaps that Europe was more capable of generating the kind of skills and abilities we associate with human capital in an age in which literacy mattered less [Van Zanden (2004)]. It is even more surprising that this skill ratio declined precipitously in the twentieth century [Knowles and Robertson (1951)]. This could be caused by an (otherwise unexplained) increase in supply, but it is at least consistent with a story that stresses the ability of unskilled labor to operate effectively in a sophisticated technological environment.

---

[77] An interesting example of such a technique is the construction of the *Nautical Almanacs*, detailed tables that allowed sailors to calculate their longitude before Harrison's clocks were cheap enough to be made widely available, a technique pioneered by the German Astronomer Tobias Mayer in 1755. Nevil Maskelyne, the Astronomer Royal, designed tables put together by highly numerate "computers" that would allow seamen to compute with accuracy their location at sea in 30 minutes as opposed to the four hours required by Mayer's original technique [Croarken (2002)].

The argument I propose, that technological progress is driven by a relatively small number of pivotal people, is not a call for a return to the long-defunct "heroic inventor" interpretation of the Industrial Revolution. The great British inventors stood on the shoulders of those who provided them with the wherewithal of tools and workmanship. John Wilkinson, it is often remarked, was indispensable for the success of James Watt, because his Bradley works had the skilled workers and equipment to bore the cylinders exactly according to specification. Mechanics and instrument makers such as Jesse Ramsden, Edward Nairn, Joseph Bramah, and Henry Maudslay; clock-makers such as Henry Hindley, Benjamin Huntsman (the inventor of the crucible technique in making high-quality steel), John Whitehurst (a member of the Lunar Society), and John Kay of Warrington (not to be confused with his namesake, the inventor of the flying shuttle, who was trained as a reed- and comb-maker), engineers such as John Smeaton, Richard Roberts, and Marc I. Brunel; ironmasters such as the Darbys, the Crowleys, and the Crawshays; steam engine specialists such as William Murdoch and Richard Trevithick; chemists such as John Roebuck, Alexander Chisholm, and James Keir were as much part of the story as the "textbook superstars" Arkwright, Cort, Crompton, Hargreaves, Cartwright, Trevithick, and Watt.[78] These were obviously men who could squeeze a great deal out of a narrow epistemic base and who could recognize more effective useful knowledge and base better techniques on them. Eventually, however, there was no escaping a more formal and analytical approach, in which a widening reliance on physics and mathematics was inevitable. Oddly enough, this approach originated in France more than in Britain.[79] Over the nineteenth century, the importance of advantages in competence (tacit skills and dexterity) declined, and that of formal codified useful knowledge increased, thus eroding the advantages Britain may have had in its skilled craftsmen that other nations envied and coveted in the years before 1815.

Below the great engineers came a much larger contingent of skilled artisans and mechanics, upon whose dexterity and adroitness the top inventors and thus Britain's technological success relied. These were the craftsmen, highly skilled clock- and instrument-makers, woodworkers, toymakers, glasscutters, and similar specialists, who could accurately produce the parts, using the correct dimensions and materials, who could read blueprints and compute velocities, understood tolerance, resistance, friction, and the interdependence of mechanical parts. These were the applied chemists who could manipulate laboratory equipment and acids, the doctors whose advice sometimes saved lives even if nobody yet quite understood why, agricultural specialists who experimented with new breeds of animals, fertilizers, drainage systems, and fodder crops.

---

[78] A good description of this class of people is provided by Griffiths' judgment of William Murdoch (the gifted and ingenious Watt and Boulton employee, credited with the invention of the famous Sun-and-Planets gear): "his inventiveness was instinctive, not analytical. He had an innate sense of mechanical propriety, of the chose juste, which led him to simple, robust and highly original solutions" [Griffiths (1992, p. 209)].

[79] The "Big Three *polytechnicien*" engineers of the early nineteenth century, Gustave-Gaspard Coriolis, Jean-Victor Poncelet, and Louis Navier, placed mechanical and civil engineering on a formal base, and supported practical ideas with more mathematical analysis than their more pragmatic British colleagues.

These anonymous but capable workers produced a cumulative torrent of small, incremental, but cumulatively indispensable microinventions, without which Britain would not have become the "workshop of world". They were artisans, but they were the skilled aristocracy of trained craftsmen, not the average man in his workshop. It is perhaps premature to speak of an "invention industry" by this period, but technical knowledge at a level beyond the reach of the run-of-the-mill artisan became increasingly essential to creating the inventions associated with the Industrial Revolution.

The average "quality" of the majority of the labor force – in terms of their technical training – may thus be less relevant to the development and adoption of the new techniques than is commonly believed. The distribution of knowledge within society was highly skewed, but as long as access costs were sufficiently low, such a skewedness would not impede further technological progress. Rosenberg has pointed out that in Adam Smith's view, though the *modal* level of knowledge may be low, the highest levels of scientific attainment were remarkable and the *collective* intelligence of a civilized society is great and presents unprecedented opportunities for further technological progress [Rosenberg (1965, p. 137)]. A venerable tradition in economic history, in fact, has argued that technological progress in the first stages of the Industrial Revolution was "deskilling", requiring workers who were able to carry out repetitive routine actions instead of the skilled labor of skilled craftsmen.[80] The "factory system" required workers to be supervised and assisted by skilled mechanics, and hence the variance of the skill level may have increased even if we cannot be sure what happened to *average* skills. Much innovation, both historically and in our time, has been deliberately aimed to be *competence-reducing*, that is made more user-friendly and requiring less skill and experience to use even if it took far more knowledge to design.[81] Human capital was instrumental in creating competence rather than useful knowledge itself, in teaching how to carry out instructions rather than writing them. Yet given that much of what I termed above competence consisted of tacit knowledge and experience, and given that much of the competence could be front-loaded into the equipment by a small number of brilliant designers, the role of the size of the population and its "mean" level of human capital should be questioned. It seems plausible that the degree of networking and the level of access costs *within* the relatively small community of highly trained engineers and scientists may have been of greater importance.

Furthermore, the term "skill" may be too confining. Human capital was in part produced in schools, but what future workers were taught in schools may have had as much

---

[80] Deskilling probably commenced already in the century before the Industrial Revolution, when much of the manufacturing in Europe was carried out in the homes of unskilled rural workers. Yet the cottage industries of Europe were certainly capable of technological change even if their limited size in the end imposed a binding constraint. See especially Berg (1994).

[81] An earlier example of such competence-reducing innovation was the introduction of fire-arms in Europe in the fifteenth century. Early fire-arms were not as effective as the longbow, but the latter took an inordinate amount of skill and strength to operate, whereas the use of fire-arms could be taught in a few weeks. In that regard, there is an interesting parallel between the "military revolution" of the fifteenth century and the Industrial Revolution.

to do with behavior as with competence. Docility and punctuality were important characteristics that factory owners expected from their workers. "The concept of industrial discipline was new, and called for as much innovation as the technical inventions of the age", writes Pollard (1968, p. 217). Early factories designed incentives to bring about the discipline, but they also preferred to hire women and children, who were believed to be more docile. Skill may have mattered less than drill. Some of the literature by economists on human capital acquisition may have to be reinterpreted in this fashion.

8. Institutions and technological progress

Beyond the interaction of different kinds of knowledge was the further level of interaction and feedback between human knowledge and the institutional environment in which it operates. Before 1750, economic progress of any kind had tended to run into what could best be called negative institutional feedback. One of the few reliable regularities of the pre-modern world was that whenever a society managed, through thrift, enterprise, or ingenuity to raise its standard of living, a variety of opportunistic parasites and predators were always ready to use power, influence, and violence to appropriate this wealth. Such rent-seekers, who redistributed wealth rather than created it, came either from within the economy in the form of tax-collectors, exclusive coalitions, and thugs, or from outside as alien pillagers, mercenaries, and plunderers. Before 1815 the most obvious and costly form of negative institutional feedback was, of course, war. Rent-seeking and war often went in hand-in-hand. Britain, France, the United Provinces, and most other Continental powers fought one another constantly in hugely costly attempts to redistribute taxable real estate, citizens, and activities from one to the other – a typical "mercantilist" kind of policy.[82] Economic growth indirectly helped instigate these conflicts. Wealth accumulation, precisely because it was mostly the result of "Smithian Growth", was usually confined to a region or city and thus created an incentive to greedy and well-armed neighbors to engage in armed rent-seeking. It was surely no accident that the only areas that had been able to thwart off such marauders with some success were those with natural defenses such as Britain and the Netherlands. Yet the Dutch United Provinces were weakened by the relentless aggressive mercantilist policies of powerful neighbors.[83] The riches of the Southern Netherlands – unfortunately easier

---

[82] O'Brien (2003, p. 5) notes that between the Nine-Years War (starting in 1688) and the Congress of Vienna in 1815, Britain and France were at or on the brink of war for more than half the period, justifying the term "Second Hundred-Years War".

[83] The standard argument is that national defense was so costly that high indirect taxes led to high nominal wages, which rendered much of Dutch manufacturing uncompetitive. See for example Charles Wilson (1969). De Vries and Van Der Woude (1997, p. 680) point out that in 1688 the Dutch committed huge resources to an invasion of England because the future economic well-being on the Republic depended on the destruction of French mercantilism and the establishment of an international order in which the Dutch economy could prosper, yet it "proved to be a profitless investment". More recently, Ormrod (2003) has confirmed the view that the decline of the Dutch Republic was a direct consequence of the mercantilist policies of its neighbors, especially Britain.

to invade – were repeatedly laid to waste by invading mercenary soldiers after 1570. More subtle forms of rent-seeking came from local monopolists (whose claims to a right to exclude others were often purchased from strongmen), guilds with exclusionary rights, or nobles with traditional rights such as *banalités*. A particularly harmful form of rent-seeking took the form of price controls on grain that redistributed resources from the countryside to the city by keeping grain prices at below equilibrium levels [Root (1994)].

Had institutional feedback remained negative, as it had been before 1750, the economic benefits of technological progress would have remained limited. Mercantilism, as Ekelund and Tollison (1981, 1997) have emphasized, was largely a system of rent-seeking, in which powerful political institutions redistributed wealth from foreigners to themselves as well as between different groups and individuals within the society. The political economy associated with the Enlightenment increasingly viewed the old rent-seeking traditions of exclusionary privileges as both unfair and inefficient. Mercantilism had been a game of international competition between rival political entities. To defeat an opponent, a nation had to outcompete it, which it often did by subsidizing exports and raw materials imports, and imposing a tariff on finished goods. As it dawned upon people that higher productivity could equally outcompete other producers, they switched to a different policy regime, one that economists would certainly recognize as more enlightened.[84] In the decades around 1750, mercantilism had begun to decline in certain key regions in Western Europe, above all in Britain, where many redistributive arrangements such as guilds, monopolies, and grain price regulations were gradually weakening, though their formal disappearance was still largely in the future. The Age of Enlightenment led to a few pre-1789 reforms on the Continent thanks to the enlightened despots, but it was the French Revolution and the ensuing political turmoil that did more than anything else to transform Enlightenment ideas into genuine institutional changes that paved the road for economic growth [Mokyr (2005a)]. The Enlightenment also advocated more harmonious and cosmopolitan attitudes in international relations, which may have contributed to the relative calm that settled upon Europe after the Congress of Vienna. Political reforms that weakened privileges and permitted the emergence of freer and more competitive markets had an important effect on economic performance. The institutional changes in the years between 1770 and 1815 saw to it that the Industrial Revolution was not followed by a surge in rent-seeking and violence that could eventually have reversed the process [Mokyr (2005a)].

The positive feedback between technological and institutional change is central to the process of historical change. The co-evolution of technological knowledge and institutions during the second Industrial Revolution has been noticed before.[85] Above all, three

---

[84] In 1773, the steam engine manufacturer Matthew Boulton told Lord Harwich that mechanization and specialization made it possible for Birmingham manufacturers to defeat their Continental competitors [cited by Uglow (2002, p. 212)].

[85] Nelson (1994) has pointed to a classic example, namely the growth of the large American business corporation in the closing decades of the nineteenth century, which evolved jointly with the high-throughput

kinds of institutions were important in facilitating the sustained technological progress central to economic growth: (1) those that provided for connections between the people concerned mostly with propositional knowledge and those on the production side; (2) those that set the agenda of research to generate new propositional knowledge that could be mapped into new techniques; and (3) those institutions that created and safeguarded *incentives* for innovative people to actually spend efforts and resources in order to map this knowledge into techniques and weakened the effective social and political resistance against new techniques. As noted above, even some of the formal endogenous growth models require a growing proportion of labor in the "invention sector", a condition that clearly demands that their profits not be expropriated altogether.

The formal institutions that created the bridges between prescriptive and propositional knowledge in late eighteenth and nineteenth century Europe are well understood: scientific societies, universities, polytechnic schools, publicly funded research institutes, museums, agricultural research stations, research departments in large financial institutions. Improved access to useful knowledge took many forms. Cheap and widely diffused publications disseminated it. All over the Western world, textbooks of applied science (or "experimental philosophy" in the odd terminology of the time), professional journals, technical encyclopedias, and engineering manuals appeared in every field and made it easier to "look things up". Technical subjects penetrated school curricula in every country in the West (although Britain, the leader in the first Industrial Revolution, lost its momentum in the Victorian era). The professionalization of expertise meant that anyone who needed some piece of useful knowledge could find with increasing ease someone who knew, or who knew someone who knew. Learned technical journals first appeared in the 1660s and by the late eighteenth century had become one of the main vehicles by which prescriptive knowledge was diffused. In the eighteenth century, most scientific journals were in fact deliberately written in an accessible style, because they more often than not catered to a lay audience and were thus media of education and dissemination rather than repositories of original contributions [Kronick (1962, p. 104)]. Review articles and book reviews that summarized and abstracted books and learned papers (especially those published overseas and were less accessible), another obvious example of an access-cost reduction, were popular.[86] In the nineteenth century, specialized scientific journals became increasingly common and further reduced access costs,

---

technology of mass production and continuous flow. In their pathbreaking book, Fox and Guagnini (1999) point to the growth of practically-minded research laboratories in academic communities, which increasingly cooperated and interacted successfully with industrial establishments to create an ever-growing stream of technological adaptations and microinventions. Many other examples can be cited, such as the miraculous expansion of the British capital market which emerged jointly with the capital-hungry early railroads and the changes in municipal management resulting from the growing realization of the impact of sanitation on public health [Cain and Rotella (2001)].

[86] This aspect of the Industrial Enlightenment was personified by the Scottish writer and mathematician John Playfair (1748–1819) whose textbooks and review essays in the *Edinburgh Review* made a special effort to incorporate the work of Continental mathematicians, as witnessed by his 1807 essays on the work of Mechain and Delambre on the Earth's meridian, and his 1808 review of Laplace's *Traité de Mécanique Celeste* [Chitnis (1976, pp. 176–177, 222)].

at the cost of requiring more and more the intermediation of experts who could decode the jargon.

To be sure, co-evolution did not always produce the desired results quickly. The British engineering profession found it difficult to train engineers using best-practice knowledge, and the connections between science and engineering remained looser and weaker than elsewhere. In 1870 a panel appointed by the Institute of Civil Engineers concluded that "the education of an Engineer [in Britain] is effected by ... a simple course of apprenticeship to a practicing engineer ... it is not the custom in England to consider *theoretical* knowledge as absolutely essential" [cited by Buchanan (1985, p. 225)]. A few individuals, above all William Rankine at Glasgow, argued forcefully for more bridges between theory and practice, but significantly he dropped his membership in the Institute of Civil Engineers. Only in the late nineteenth century did engineering become a respected discipline in British universities.

Elsewhere in Europe, the emergence of universities and technical colleges that combined research and teaching in the nineteenth century simultaneously expanded propositional knowledge and reducing access costs. An especially good and persuasive example is provided by Murmann (2003), who describes the co-evolution of technology and institutions in the chemical industry in imperial Germany, where the new technology of dyes, explosives, and fertilizers emerged in constant interaction with the growth of research and development facilities, institutes of higher education, and large industrial corporations with a knack for industrial research.[87] Institutions remained a major determinant of access costs. To understand the evolution of knowledge, we need to ask who talked to whom and who read what. Yet the German example illustrates that progress in this area was halting and complex; it needs to be treated with caution as a causal factor in explaining systematic differences between nations. The famed *technische Hochschulen*, in some ways the German equivalent of the French *polytechniques*, had lower social prestige than the universities and were not allowed to award engineering diplomas and doctorates till 1899. The same is true for the practical, technically oriented *Realschulen*, which had lower standing than the more classically inclined *Gymnasien*. Universities conducted a great deal of research, but it goes too far to state that what they did was a *deliberate* application of science to business problems.[88] Universities and businesses co-evolved, collaborating through personal communications, overlapping personnel, and revolving doors. The second Industrial Revolution rested as much

---

[87] Most famous, perhaps, was the invention of alizarin in 1869, a result of the collaboration between the research director at BASF, Caro, with the two academics Graebe and Liebermann.

[88] James (1990, p. 111) argues that Germany's "staggering supremacy" was not due to scientists looking for applicable results but came about "because her scientists experimented widely without any end in mind and then discovered that they could apply their new information". This seems a little overstated, but all the same we should be cautious in attributing too much intent and directionality in the growth of knowledge. Much of it was partly random or the unintended consequence of a different activity – it was the selection process that gave it its technological significance. In that respect, the evolutionary nature of the growth in useful knowledge is reaffirmed.

on industry-based science as on the more common concept of science-based industry [König (1996)].

Designing institutions that create the correct ex ante motivations to encourage invention is not an easy task. Economists believe that agents respond to economic incentives. A system of relatively secure property rights, such as emerged in Britain in the seventeenth century, is widely regarded as a prerequisite. Without it, even if useful knowledge would expand, the investment and entrepreneurship required for a large scale implementation of the new knowledge would not have been forthcoming. On a more specific level, the question of the role of intellectual property rights and rewards for those who add to the stock of useful knowledge in generating economic growth is paramount. Some of the best recent work in the economic history of technological change focuses on the working of the patent system as a way of preserving property rights for inventors. In a series of ingenious papers, Kenneth Sokoloff and Zorina Khan have shown how the American patent system exhibited many of the characteristics of a market system: inventors responded to demand conditions, did all they could to secure the gains from their invention and bought and sold licenses in what appears to be a rational fashion. It was far more accessible, more open, and cheaper to use than the British system, and attracted ordinary artisans and farmer as much as professional inventors and eccentrics [Khan and Sokoloff (1993, 1998, 2001) and Khan (2005)].

Whether this difference demonstrates that a well-functioning system of intellectual property rights was essential to the growth of useful knowledge remains an open question. For one thing, the American patent system was far more user-friendly than the British system prior to its reform in 1852. Yet despite the obvious superiority of the U.S. system and the consequent higher propensity of Americans to patent, there can be little doubt that the period between 1791 and 1850 coincides roughly with the apex of British superiority in invention. The period of growing American technological leadership, after 1900, witnessed a stagnation and then a decline in the American per capita patenting rate. Other means of appropriating the returns on R&D became relatively more attractive. In Britain, MacLeod (1988) has shown that the patent system during the Industrial Revolution provided only weak and erratic protection to inventors and that large areas of innovation were not patentable. Patenting was associated with commercialization and the rise of a profit-oriented spirit, but its exact relation to technological progress is still obscure.[89]

What is sometimes overlooked is that patents placed technical information in the public realm and thus reduced access costs. Inventors, by observing what had been

---

[89] In fact, economists have argued that for countries that are relatively technologically backward, strict patent systems may be on balance detrimental to economic welfare [for a summary, see Lerner (2000)]. In a different context, Hilaire-Pérez (2000) has shown how different systems of invention encouragement in eighteenth-century Europe were consistent with inventive activity. Whereas in France the state played an active role of awarding "privileges" and pensions to inventors deemed worthy by the French Academy, in Britain the state was more passive and allowed the market to determine the rewards of a successful inventor. These systems were not consistently enforced (some British inventors whose patents for one reason or another failed to pay off were compensated by special dispensation) and, as Hilaire-Pérez shows, influenced one another.

done, saw what was possible and were inspired to apply the knowledge thus acquired to other areas not covered by the patent. In the United States, *Scientific American* published lists of new patents starting in 1845, and these lists were widely consulted. Despite the limitations that patents imposed on applications, these lists reduced access costs to the knowledge embodied in them. The full specification of patents was meant to inform the public. In Britain this was laid out in a decision by chief justice Lord Mansfield, who decreed in 1778 that the specifications should be sufficiently precise and detailed so as to fully explain it to a technically educated person. In the Netherlands, where patenting had existed from the 1580s, the practice of specification was abandoned in the mid-1630s but revived in the 1770s [Davids (2000, p. 267)].

In at least two countries, the Netherlands and Switzerland, the complete absence of a patent system in the second half of the nineteenth century does not seem to have affected the rate of technological advance [Schiff (1971)]. Of course, being small, such countries could and did free-ride on technological advances made elsewhere, and it would be a fallacy to infer from the Dutch and Swiss experience that patents did not matter. It also seems plausible that reverse causation explains part of what association there was between the propensity to patent and the generation of new techniques: countries in which there were strong and accessible bridges between the *savants* and the *fabricants* would feel relatively more need to protect the offspring of these contacts. Lerner (2000) has shown that rich and democratic economies, on the whole, provided more extensive patent protection. The causal chain could thus run from technological success to income and from there to institutional change rather than from the institutions to technological success, as Khan and Sokoloff believe. It may well be true, as Abraham Lincoln said, that what the patent system did was "to add the fuel of interest to the fire of genius" [cited by Khan and Sokoloff (2001, p. 12)], but that reinforces the idea that we need to be able to say something about how the fire got started in the first place.

Other institutions have been widely recognized as aiding in the generation of new techniques. Among those are relatively easy entry and exit from industries, the availability of venture capital in some form, the reduction of uncertainty by a large source of assured demand for a new product or technique (such as military procurement or captive colonial markets), the existence of agencies that coordinated and standardized the networked components of new techniques, and revolving doors between industry and organizations that specialize in the generation of propositional knowledge such as universities and research institutes.

There is a fundamental complementarity between knowledge growth and institutional change in the economic growth of the West. Augmenting and diffusing knowledge produced the seeds that germinated in the fertile soils that economic incentives and functional markets created. Without these seeds, improved incentives for innovation would have been useless. Commercial, entrepreneurial, and even sophisticated capitalist societies have existed that made few important technical advances, simply because the techniques they employed rested on narrow epistemic bases and the propositional knowledge from which these bases were drawn was not expanding. The reasons for this could be many: the agendas of intellectual activity may not have placed a high priority on *useful* knowledge, or a dominant conservative religious philosophy might have stifled a critical attitude toward existing propositional knowledge. Above all, there has to be a belief that such knowledge may eventually be socially useful even if the gains are likely to be reaped mostly by persons others than those generating the novel propositional knowledge. Given that increasing this knowledge was costly and often regarded as socially disruptive, the political will by agents who controlled resources to support this endeavor, whether they were rich aristocratic patrons or middle-class taxpayers, was not invariably there. The amounts of resources expended on R&D, however, are not the only variable that matters. Equally important is how they were spent, on what, and what kind of access potential users had to this knowledge.

One specific example of an area in which technological innovation and institutional change interacted in this fashion was in the resistance of vested interests to new technology [Mokyr (1994, 2002)]. Here institutions are particularly important, because by definition such resistance has to operate outside the market mechanism. If left to markets to decide, it seems likely that superior techniques and products will inexorably drive out existing ones. For the technological status quo to fight back against innovation thus meant to use non-market mechanisms. These could be legal, through the manipulation of the existing power structure, or extralegal, through machine-breaking, riots, and the use of personal violence against inventors and the entrepreneurs who tried to adopt their inventions.

At one level, eighteenth-century Enlightenment thinking viewed technological change as "progress" and implicitly felt that social resistance to it was socially undesirable. Yet there was a contrary strand of thought, associated with Rousseau and with later elements of romanticism such as Cobbett and Carlyle continuing with the Frankfurt school in the twentieth century, that sincerely viewed industrialization and modern technology and the Enlightenment that spawned them as evil and destructive. Such ideological qualms often found themselves allied with those whose human and physical capital was jeopardized by new techniques. Mercantilist thought, with its underlying assumptions of a zero-sum society, was hugely concerned with the employment-reducing effects of technological progress. The ensuing conflict came to a crashing crescendo during the Industrial Revolution. The Luddite rebellion – a complex set of events that involved a variety of grievances, not all of which were related to rent-seeking – was mercilessly suppressed. It would be a stretch to associate the harsh actions of the British army in the midlands in 1812 with anything like the Enlightenment. All the same, it appears that rent-seeking inspired resistance against new technology had been driven into a corner by that time by people who believed that "freedom" included the freedom to innovate and that higher labor productivity did not necessarily entail unemployment.

The British example is quite telling.[90] In the textile industries, by far the most resistance occurred in the woolen industries. Cotton was a relatively small industry on the eve of the Industrial Revolution and had only weakly entrenched power groups. There

---

[90] Some of the following is based on Mokyr (1994).

were riots in Lancashire in 1779 and 1792, and a Manchester firm that pioneered a pow-
erloom was burnt down. Yet cotton was unstoppable and must have seemed that way
to contemporaries. Wool, however, was initially far larger and had an ancient tradition
of professional organization and regulation. Laborers in the wool trades tried to use the
political establishment for the purposes of stopping the new machines. In 1776 workers
petitioned the House of Commons to suppress the jennies that threatened the livelihood
of the industrious poor, as they put it. After 1789, Parliament passed sets of repressive
laws (most famously the Combination Act of 1799), which in Horn's (2003) view were
intended not only to save the regime from French-inspired revolutionary turmoil, but
also to protect the Industrial Revolution from resistance "from below". Time and again,
groups and lobbies turned to Parliament requesting the enforcement of old regulations or
the introduction of new legislation that would hinder the machinery. Parliament refused.
The old laws regulating the employment practices in the woolen industry were repealed
in 1809, and the 250 year old Statute of Artificers was repealed in 1814. Lacking political support in London, the woolworkers tried extralegal means. As Randall has shown,
in the West of England the new machines were met in most places by violent crowds,
protesting against jennies, flying shuttles, gig mills, and scribbling machines [Randall
(1986, 1989)]. Moreover, in these areas magistrates were persuaded by fear or propaganda that the machine breakers were in the right. The tradition of violence in the West
of England, writes Randall, deterred all but the most determined innovators. Worker
resistance was responsible for the slow growth and depression of the industry rather
than the reverse [Randall (1989)]. The West of England, as a result, lost its supremacy
to Yorkshire. Resistance in Yorkshire was not negligible either, but there it was unable to stop mechanization. Violent protests, such as the Luddite riots, were forcefully
suppressed by soldiers. As Paul Mantoux put it well many years ago, "Whether [the]
resistance was instinctive or considered, peaceful or violent, it obviously had no chance
of success" [Mantoux (1961 [1928], p. 408)]. Had that not been the case, sustained
progress in Britain would have been severely hampered and possibly brought to an end.

In other industries as well resistance appeared, sometimes from unexpected corners.
When Samuel Clegg and Frederick Windsor proposed a central gas distribution plan for
London, they were attacked by a coalition that included the eminent scientist Humphry
Davy, the novelist Walter Scott, the cartoonist George Cruickshank, insurance companies, and the aging James Watt [Stern (1937)]. The steam engine was resisted in urban
areas by fear of "smoky nuisances", and resistance to railroads was rampant in the first
years of their incipience. Mechanical sawmills, widely used on the Continent, were virtually absent from Britain until the nineteenth century.[91] Even in medical technology,
where the social benefits were most widely diffused, the status quo tried to resist. When

---

[91] The resistance against sawmills is a good example of attempts to use both legal and illegal means. It
was widely believed in the eighteenth century that sawmills, like gigmills, were illegal although there is no
evidence to demonstrate this. When a wind-powered sawmill was constructed at Limehouse (on the Thames,
near London) in 1768, it was damaged by a mob of sawyers "on the pretence that it deprived many workmen
of employment" [Cooney (1991)].

Edward Jenner applied to the Royal Society to present his findings, he was told "not to risk his reputation by presenting to this learned body anything which appeared so much at variance with established knowledge and withal so incredible" [Keele (1961, p. 94)].[92] In medical technology, in general, resistance tended to be particularly fierce because many of the breakthroughs after 1750 were inconsistent with accepted doctrine, and rendered everything that medical professionals had laboriously learned null and void. It also tended, more than most other techniques, to incur the wrath of ethical purists who felt that some techniques in some way contradicted religious principles, not unlike the resistance to cloning and stem-cell research in our own time. Even such a seemingly enormously beneficial and harmless invention as anesthesia was objected to on a host of philosophical grounds [Youngson (1979, pp. 95–105; 190–198)].

With the rise of the factory and the strengthening of the bargaining power of capitalists, authority and discipline might have reduced, the ability of labor to resist technological progress at least for a while. The factory, however, did not solve the problem of resistance altogether; unions eventually tried to undermine the ability of the capitalist to exploit the most advanced techniques. Collective action by workers imposed an effective limit on the "authority" exercised by capitalists. Workers' associations tried to ban some new techniques altogether or tried to appropriate the entire productivity gains in terms of higher piece wages, thus weakening the incentive to innovate. On the other hand, laborers' industrial actions often led to technological advances aimed specifically at crippling strikes [Bruland (1982) and Rosenberg (1976, pp. 118–119)].[93]

9. Conclusions: Technology, growth, and the rise of the occident

In economic history, more so perhaps than in other disciplines, everything is a matter of degree, and there are no absolutes. The arguments made in this survey represent an interpretation that is by no means generally accepted. Many scholars have argued eloquently and persuasively for continuity rather than radical and abrupt change in western society between 1760 and 1830. Almost every element we associate with the Industrial Revolution can be seen to have precedent and precursor. Some of these are quite valid (episodes of growth and "modernity" can be found in earlier periods; the use of coal and non-animate energy was expanding already in the centuries before the Industrial

---

[92] Jenner's famous discovery of the smallpox vaccine ran into the opposition of inoculators concerned about losing their lucrative trade [Hopkins (1983, p. 83)]. The source of the vaccine, infected animals, was a novelty and led to resistance in and of itself: Clergy objected to the technique because of the "iniquity of transferring disease from the beasts of the field to Man" [Cartwright (1977, p. 86)]. Cartoonists depicted people acquiring bovine traits, and one woman complained that after he daughter was vaccinated she coughed like a cow and grew hairy [Hopkins (1983, p. 84)]. Despite all this, of course, the smallpox vaccine was one of the most successful macroinventions of the Industrial Revolution and its inventor became an international celebrity.

[93] The most famous example of an invention triggered by a strike was that of the self-acting mule, invented in 1825 by Richard Roberts at the prompting of Manchester manufacturers plagued by a strike of mule operators.

Revolution; agricultural productivity may have been as high in 1290 as it was in 1700; factory-like settings can be found in earlier periods). Others are based on misapprehensions (the aeolipiles built by Hero of Alexandria were *not* atmospheric steam engines). In the end, the debate on continuity can only be settled if we accept a criterion by which to judge the degree of continuity. If the criterion is economic growth, the continuity faction in the end will have to concede defeat, even if the victory is one in overtime. The era of the Industrial Revolution *itself* was not a period of rapid economic growth, but it is clear beyond question that it set into motion an economic process that by the middle of the nineteenth century created a material world that followed a dynamic not hitherto experienced.

Not only was growth faster and more geographically dispersed (covering by 1914 most of Europe, North America, other European offshoots, and Japan) than had been experienced by any economy before, it was sustainable. Unlike previous episodes, it kept rolling through the twentieth century. A moment of reflection will underline the enormity of this achievement. The twentieth century was in many ways a very bad century for the Western world: two horrid World Wars, a hugely costly depression, the collapse of international trade after 1914, the disastrous collectivist experiment in Russia extended to all of Eastern Europe in 1945, and the loss of its Colonial Empires – all of these should have pointed to catastrophe, misery, and a return to economic barbarism for the *Abendland*. Something similar may have happened in the fourteenth century, the disasters of which in some views set Europe's economy back for a century or more. Yet by the early years of the twenty-first century, the gap between rich and poor nations is bigger than ever and Danny Quah's "twin peaks" are getting further and further apart. Despite the huge setbacks, the engine that drove the Occident express had become so immensely powerful that it easily overwhelmed the twentieth century roadblocks that bad luck and human stupidity placed on its tracks. The Great Divergence train stormed on, undaunted.

Social scientists and historians discussing this issue are often accused of "triumphalism" and "teleologies", which are paired with "Eurocentricity" or "Western-centricity". Whether the scholars who make such accusations actually mean to argue that the gap in income and living standards is imaginary (or ephemeral), or whether they just feel that it is unjust and unfair, is sometimes hard to tell.[94] Yet it seems otiose to gainsay the importance of the topic. Whether or not the rest of the world is to eventually enjoy the material comforts available to most people in the West or not, we should not give up on our attempt to understand "how the West did it".

If we want to understand *why* the West did what it did we should ask questions about the *when*. The consensus is that by 1750, the gap between the twin peaks was much smaller than it is today. If Europe was richer than the rest of the world, it was so by a margin that looks thin by comparision. The so-called "California School" has been arguing indeed that living standards and measurable indicators of economic performance

---

[94] Such confusions mark especially the literature associated with Frank (1998) and Blaut (1993).

between China and Europe were not all that different by 1750.[95] If this is accepted, and if we are willing to take the Yang-Zhi delta as indicative of economic conditions of the non-European world, the current gap between rich and poor is largely the result of the Industrial Revolution and the events that followed it. Be that as it may, underneath its surface the European soil in 1500 already contained the seeds of the future divergence in 1750. There was, however, nothing inexorable about what happened after: the seeds need not have sprouted, they could have been washed away by the flood of wars, or the young sprouts of future growth might have been pulled out by rapacious tax collectors or burned by intolerant religious authorities. There could have been a Great *Convergence* after 1800 instead of what actually took place, in which Europe would have reverted back to the kind of economic performance prevalent in 1500. In the end, the economic history of technology – like all evolutionary sequences – contains a deep and irreducible element of contingency. Not all that was had to be.

The question of "when" is important because it makes geographical explanations that explain Europe's success by its milder climate or conveniently located coal reserves less powerful, because these differences are time-invariant. Something had changed in Europe before the Industrial Revolution that destabilized the economic dynamic in the West, but not elsewhere. The question of "where" is also important. Britain was not "Europe", and even today there are some European regions that clearly are not part of the Western economic development pattern or else are very recent arrivals. On the other hand, a number of non-European nations have been able to join the "convergence club".

There are two alternative scenarios of the emergence of the gap. One is that, regardless of living standards and income in 1750, Europe at that time was already deeply different from the rest of the world in many respects. In their different ways, David Landes (1998), Eric Jones (1981, 1988), Avner Greif (2005) and Angus Maddison (1998) subscribe to this view. By 1750 Europe had already had Calvin and Newton, Spinoza and Galileo, Bacon and Descartes. It had a commercial capitalism thriving especially in Atlantic Ports, an institutional structure that supported long-distance trade, a well-functioning monetary system, and the ability of rulers to tax their subjects and suppress nonconformists and heretics had been constrained in complex but comparatively effective ways. It had universities, representative parliamentary bodies, embryonic financial institutions, powerful navies and armies, microscopes and printing presses. Its agriculture was gradually switching to more productive rotations, adopting new crops, and experimenting with animal breeding. Its manufacturing system was market-oriented and competitive. It had established the beginning of a public health system that had conquered the plague (still rampant elsewhere) and was making inroads against smallpox. Its ships, aided by sophisticated navigational instruments and maps, had already subjugated and colonized some parts of the non-European world, and neither the Mongols nor the Ottoman Turks were a threat anymore. It drank tea, ate sugar, smoked tobacco, wore silk and cotton, and ate from better plates in coal- or peat-heated homes. Its income per capita, as well as we can measure it, may have been little different from what

---

[95] See especially Wong (1997), Pomeranz (2000) and Goldstone (2002).

it had been in the late Middle Ages (though Adam Smith disagreed), yet Europe was already ahead.

The alternative school emphasizes that many of these European features could be found in other societies, especially in China and Japan, and that when Europe and the Orient differed, the difference was not always necessarily conducive to economic growth. Ch'ing China may not have been an open economy, but it had law and order, a meritocratic bureaucracy, peace, effective property rights, and a great deal of medium- and long-distance trade within its borders. We need to be wary of the logical fallacy that all initial differences between Europe and China contributed to the outcome. Some of the initial difference may have actually worked the other way; the Great Divergence took place despite them. Others were ambiguous in their effect.[96] In order to understand what triggered Europe's economic miracle, we need to identify an event that happened before the Industrial Revolution, happened in the right areas, and which can be logically connected to subsequent growth.

I have identified this event as "the Industrial Enlightenment" and have attempted to show how it affected the two central elements of the Industrial Revolution, technology and institutions, and further how these two elements then affected one another. Not everything that is normally included in the historians' idea of the Enlightenment mattered, and not everything that mattered could be attributed to the Industrial Enlightenment. John Stuart Mill's reflection that "the great danger in the study of history is not so much mistaking falsehood for truth, as to mistake a part for the whole" is pertinent here.

The emphasis on the Enlightenment illustrates how economists should think about culture and cultural beliefs as discussed in great length by Greif (2005). Culture mattered to economic development – how could it not? But we have to show the exact ways in which it mattered and through which channels it operated. I have argued that cultural beliefs changed in the eighteenth century. Beyond Greif's notion of beliefs about other people's behavior, I would include the metaphysical beliefs that people held about their environment and the natural world, and their attitudes toward the relationship between production and useful knowledge. It should also include their cultural beliefs about the possibility and desirability of progress and their notions of economic freedom, property, and novelty.

In that sense, at least, the Enlightenment may constitute the missing link that economic historians have hitherto missed. Greif (2005, Chapter 13) points out that many of the institutional elements of modern Europe were already in place in the late Middle Ages: individualism, man-made formal law, corporatism, self governance, and rules that were determined through a legislative process in which those who were subject

---

[96] An example is the European States System, often hailed as the element of competition that constrained and disciplined European governments into a more rational behavior, lest they weaken their military power. Yet the costs of wars may well have exceeded the gains, and the mercantilist policies that the States System triggered in the seventeenth century had deleterious effects on economic performance.

to them could be heard and had an input. Yet these elements did not trigger modern growth at that time, and it bears reflecting why not. The technological constraints were too confining, and the negative feedbacks too strong.

The story of the growth of the West is the story of the dissolution of these constraints. The Baconian belief that the universe is logical and understandable, that the understanding of nature leads to its control, and that control of nature is the surest route to increased wealth, was the background of a movement that, although it affected but a minute percentage of Europe's population, played a pivotal role in the emergence of modern growth. If culture mattered, it did so because the prevailing ideology of knowledge among those who mattered started to change in a way it did not elsewhere. The eighteenth century Enlightenment, moreover, brought back many of the institutional elements of an orderly and civil society, together with the growing realization, most eloquently expressed by Adam Smith, that economic activity was not a zero-sum game and that redistributive institutions and rent-seeking are costly to society.

All the same, ideological changes and cultural developments are not the entire story. A desire for improvement and even the "right" kind of institutions by themselves do not produce *sustained* growth unless society produces new useful knowledge, and unless the growth of knowledge can be sustained over time. Useful knowledge grows because in each society there are people who are creative and original, and are motivated by some combination of greed, ambition, curiosity, and altruism. All four of those motives can be seen to be operating among the people who helped make the Industrial Revolution, often in the same people. Given that the generation of innovations was not yet dominated by large corporations, the relative weight of "greed" may have been smaller than in the twentieth-first century, and that of curiosity and altruism correspondingly higher, though these motives are hard to gauge. Yet in order to be translated from personal predilections to facts on the ground, and from there to economic growth, an environment that produced the correct incentives and the proper access to knowledge had to exist. The uniqueness of the European Enlightenment was that it created that kind of environment in addition to the useful knowledge that revolutionized production.

The experience of the past two centuries in the western world supports the view that useful knowledge and its application to production went through a phase transition, in which it entered a critical region where equilibrium concepts may no longer apply. This means that as far as future technological progress and economic growth are concerned, not even the sky is the limit. Science Fiction writers have known this all along.

Acknowledgements

I am indebted to Philippe Aghion, Ken Alder, Margaret C. Jacob, Margaret Shabas, and Richard Unger for helpful comments. Fabio Braggion, Chip Dickerson, Hillary King, and Michael Silver provided essential research assistance.

References

Aghion, P., Howitt, P. (1997). Endogenous Growth Theory. MIT Press, Cambridge, MA.

Allen, R.C., Ó Gráda, C. (1988). "On the road again with Arthur Young: English, Irish, and French agriculture during the Industrial Revolution". Journal of Economic History 48 (1), 93–116.

Antrás, P., Voth, J. (2003). "Factor prices and productivity growth during the British Industrial Revolution". Explorations in Economic History 40, 52–77.

Baumol, W.J. (2002). The Free-Market Innovation Machine: Analyzing the Growth Miracle of Capitalism. Princeton University Press, Princeton, NJ.

Berg, M. (1994). The Age of Manufactures, second rev. ed. Routledge, London.

Blaut, , J.M. (1993). The Colonizer: Model of the World. Guilford Press, New York.

Botticini, M., Eckstein, Z. (2003). "From farmers to merchants: A human capital interpretation of Jewish Economic history". Unpublished Manuscript. Boston University.

Britnell, R.H. (1996). The Commercialization of English Society, 1000–1500. Manchester University Press, Manchester.

Brock, W.H. (1992). The Norton History of Chemistry. W.W. Norton, New York.

Brown, G.I. (1999). Scientist, Soldier, Statesman, Spy: Count Rumford. Sutton Publishing, Gloucestershire, U.K.

Bruland, T. (1982). "Industrial conflict as a source of technical innovation: Three cases". Economy and Society 11, 91–121.

Bryant, L. (1973). "The role of thermodynamics: The evolution of the heat engine". Technology and Culture 14, 152–165.

Buchanan, R.A. (1985). "The rise of scientific engineering in Britain". British Journal for the History of Science 18 (59), 218–233.

Burton, A. (2000). Richard Trevithick: Giant of Steam. Aurum Press, London.

Cain, L., Rotella, E. (2001). "Death and spending: Did urban mortality shocks lead to municipal expenditure increases?". Annales de Démographie Historique 1, 139–154.

Cardwell, D.S.L. (1971). From Watt to Clausius: The Rise of Thermodynamics in the Early Industrial Age. Cornell University Press, Ithaca, NY.

Cardwell, D.S.L. (1972). Turning Points in Western Technology. Neale Watson, Science History Publications, New York.

Cardwell, D.S.L. (1994). The Fontana History of Technology. Fontana Press, London.

Cartwright, F.F. (1977). A Social History of Medicine. Longman, London.

Cervellati, M., Sunde, U. (2005). "Human capital formation, life expectancy, and the process of economic development". American Economic Review, in press.

Chitnis, A. (1976). The Scottish Enlightenment. Croom Helm, London.

Clow, A., Clow, N.L. (1952). The Chemical Revolution: A Contribution to Social Technology. Batchworth, London. Reprinted Gordon and Breach, New York, 1992.

Cochrane, E.W. (1961). Tradition and Enlightenment in the Tuscan Academies, 1690–1800. University of Chicago Press, Chicago.

Cole, A.H., Watts, G.W. (1952). The Handicrafts of France as Recorded in the Descriptions des Arts et Métiers 1761–1788. Baker Library, Boston.

Constant, E.W. (1980). The Origins of the Turbojet Revolution. Johns Hopkins University Press, Baltimore.

Cooney, E.W. (1991). "Eighteenth century Britain's missing sawmills: A blessing in disguise?". Construction History 7, 29–46.

Cowan, R., Foray, D. (1997). "The economics of codification and the diffusion of knowledge". Industrial and Corporate Change 6 (3), 595–622.

Croarken, M. (2002). "Providing longitude for all: The eighteenth century computers of the Nautical Almanac". Journal of Maritime Research 9, 1–22.

Crouch, T. (1989). The Bishop's Boys: A Life of Wilbur and Orville Wright. W.W. Norton, New York.

Crouzet, F. (1985). The First Industrialists: The Problems of Origins. Cambridge University Press, Cambridge.

Darnton, R. (1979). The Business of Enlightenment. Harvard University Press, Cambridge, MA.

Darnton, R. (2003). George Washington's False Teeth. W.W. Norton, New York.

David, P.A. (1998). "The collective cognitive performance of 'invisible colleges'". Presented to the Santa Fe Institute Workshop "The Evolution of Science".

David, P.A. (2004). "Patronage, reputation and common agency contracting in the Scientific Revolution". Unpublished Manuscript. Oxford University.

Davids, K. (2000). "Patents and patentees in the Dutch Republic between c. 1580 and 1720". History and Technology 16, 263–283.

Davids, K. (2001). "Windmills and the openness of knowledge: Technological innovation in a Dutch industrial district, the Zaanstreek, c. 1600–1800". Unpublished Paper, Presented to the Annual Meeting of the Society for the History of Technology, San Jose, CA.

Dear, P. (1985). "Totius in verba: Rhetoric and authority in the early Royal Society". Isis 76 (2), 144–161.

De Vries, J., Van Der Woude, A.M. (1997). The First Modern Economy: Success, Failure, and Perseverance of the Dutch Economy, 1500–1815. Cambridge University Press, Cambridge.

Dobbs, B.J.T. (1990). "From the secrecy of alchemy to the openness of chemistry". In: Frängsmyr, T. (Ed.), Solomon's House Revisited: The Organization and Institutionalization of Science. Science History Publishing, Canton, MA, pp. 75–94.

Donovan, A.L. (1975). Philosophical Chemistry in the Scottish Enlightenment. Edinburgh University Press, Edinburgh.

Eamon, W. (1990). "From the secrets of nature to public knowledge". In: Lindberg, D.C., Westman, R.S. (Eds.), Reappraisals of the Scientific Revolution. Cambridge University Press, Cambridge, pp. 333–365.

Eamon, W. (1994). Science and the Secrets of Nature. Princeton University Press, Princeton, NJ.

Easterlin, R. (1981). "Why isn't the whole world developed?". Journal of Economic History 41 (1), 1–19.

Eisenstein, E. (1979). The Printing Press as an Agent of Change. Cambridge University Press, Cambridge.

Ekelund Jr., R.B., Tollison, R.D. (1981). Mercantilism as a Rent-Seeking Society. Texas A&M University Press, College Station.

Ekelund Jr., R.B., Tollison, R.D. (1997). Politicized Economies: Monarchy, Monopoly, and Mercantilism. Texas A&M University Press, College Station.

Elliott, P. (2000). "The birth of public science in the English provinces: Natural philosophy in Derby, c. 1690–1760". Annals of Science 57, 61–100.

Engerman, C. (1994). "The Industrial Revolution revisited". In: Snooks, G.D. (Ed.), Was the Industrial Revolution Necessary? Routledge, London.

Fairchilds, C. (1992). "A comparison of the 'Consumer Revolutions' in eighteenth-century England and France". Unpublished Paper. Submitted to the Economic History Association Annual Meeting, Boston.

Farrington, B. (1979). Francis Bacon: Philosopher of Industrial Science. Farrar, Straus and Giroux, New York.

Fox, R. (1998). "Science, practice and innovation in the Age of Natural Dyes, 1750–1860". In: Berg, M., Bruland, K. (Eds.), Technological Revolutions in Europe. Edward Elgar, Cheltenham, U.K., pp. 86–95.

Fox, R., Guagnini, A. (1999). Laboratories, Workshops, and Sites: Concepts and Practices of Research in Industrial Europe, 1800–1914. Office for History of Science and Technology, University of California, Berkeley.

Frank, A.G. (1998). Re-Orient: Global Economy in the Asian Age. University of California Press, Berkeley, CA.

Galor, O., Moav, O. (2002). "Natural selection and the origins of economic growth". Quarterly Journal of Economics 117 (4), 1133–1191.

Galor, O., Weil, D. (2000). "Population, technology, and growth". American Economic Review 90 (4), 806–828.

Gillispie, C.C. (1980). Science and Polity in France at the End of the Old Regime. Princeton University Press, Princeton.

Goddard, N. (1989). "Agricultural literature and societies". In: Mingay, G.E. (Ed.), The Agrarian History of England and Wales, vol. 6: 1750–1850. Cambridge University Press, Cambridge, pp. 361–383.

Goldstone, J.A. (2002). "Efflorescences and economic growth in world history: Rethinking the 'Rise of the West' and the Industrial Revolution". Journal of World History 13 (2), 323–389.

Golinski, J. (1988). "Utility and audience in eighteenth century chemistry: Case studies of William Cullen and Joseph Priestley". British Journal for the History of Science 21 (68), 1–31.

Golinski, J. (1992). Science as Public Culture: Chemistry and Enlightenment in Britain, 1760–1820. Cambridge University Press, Cambridge.

Greif, A. (2005). Institutions and the Path to the Modern Economy. Cambridge, University Press, Cambridge. in press.

Griffiths, J. (1992). The Third Man: The Life and Times of William Murdoch, Inventor of Gaslight. André Deutsch, London.

Hall, A.R. (1974). "What did the Industrial Revolution in Britain owe to science?". In: McKendrick, N. (Ed.), Historical Perspectives: Studies in English Thought and Society. Europa Publications, London.

Harris, J.R. (1992a). "Skills, coal and British industry in the eighteenth century". In: Essays in Industry and Technology in the Eighteenth Century: England and France. Ashgate, Aldershot, U.K., pp. 18–33.

Harris, J.R. (1992b). "Saint Gobain and Ravenhea". In: Essays in Industry and Technology in the Eighteenth Century: England and France. Ashgate, Aldershot, U.K., pp. 34–77.

Harris, J.R. (1998). Industrial Espionage and Technology Transfer. Ashgate, Aldershot, U.K.

Heilbron, J.L. (1990). "Introductory essay". In: Frängsmyr, T., Heilbron, J.L., Rider, R.E. (Eds.), The Quantifying Spirit in the 18th Century. University of California Press, Berkeley, pp. 1–23.

Hilaire-Pérez, L. (2000). L'invention technique au siècle des lumières. Albin Michel, Paris.

Hills, R.L. (1989). Power from Steam: A History of the Stationary Steam Engine. Cambridge University Press, Cambridge.

Hopkins, D.R. (1983). Princes and Peasants: Smallpox in History. University of Chicago Press, Chicago.

Horn, J. (2003). "Machine breaking in England and France during the age of revolution". Unpublished Manuscript. Manhattan College.

Hudson, D., Luckhurst, K.W. (1954). The Royal Society of Arts, 1754–1954. John Murray, London.

Humphries, J. (2003). "English apprenticeship: A neglected factor in the First Industrial Revolution". In: David, P., Thomas, M. (Eds.), The Economic Future in Historical Perspective. Oxford University Press, Oxford, pp. 73–102.

Inkster, I. (1991). Science and Technology in History: An Approach to Industrial Development. Rutgers University Press, New Brunswick, NJ.

Jacob, M.C. (2001). The Enlightenment. Bedford/St. Martin's, Boston.

James, H. (1990). "The German experience and the myth of British cultural exceptionalism". In: Collins, B., Robbins, K. (Eds.), British Culture and Economic Decline. St. Martin's Press, New York, pp. 91–128.

Jones, C.I. (2001). "Was an Industrial Revolution inevitable? Economic growth over the very long run". Advances in Macroeconomics 1 (2), 1–43. Berkeley Electronic Press.

Jones, E.L. (1981). The European Miracle: Environments, Economies and Geopolitics in the History of Europe and Asia, second ed. Cambridge University Press, Cambridge.

Jones, E.L. (1988). Growth Recurring. Oxford University Press, Oxford.

Kauffman, S.A. (1995). At Home in the Universe: The Search for the Laws of Self-Organization and Complexity. Oxford University Press, New York.

Keele, K.D. (1961). "The influence of clinical research on the evolution of medical practice in Britain". In: Poynter, F.N.L. (Ed.), The Evolution of Medical Practice in Britain. Pitman Medical Publishing, London, pp. 81–96.

Kelly, F.C. (1943). The Wright Brothers. Harcourt, Brace & Co., New York.

Keyser, B.W. (1990). "Between science and craft: The case of Berthollet and Dyeing". Annals of Science 47 (3), 213–260.

Khan, B.Z. (2005). The Democratization of Inventions: Patents and Copyrights in American Economic Development, 1790–1920. Cambridge University Press, Cambridge.

Khan, B.Z., Sokoloff, K.L. (1993). "'Schemes of practical utility': Entrepreneurship and innovation among 'Great Inventors' in the United States, 1790–1865". Journal of Economic History 53 (2), 289–307.

Khan, B.Z., Sokoloff, K.L. (1998). "Patent institutions, industrial organization, and early technological change: Britain and the United States, 1790–1850". In: Berg, M., Bruland, K. (Eds.), Technological Revolutions in Europe. Edward Elgar, Cheltenham, U.K., pp. 292–313.

Khan, B.Z., Sokoloff, K.L. (2001). "The early development of intellectual property institutions in the United States". Journal of Economic Perspectives 15 (2), 1–15.

Kirby, P. (2003). Child Labor in Britain, 1750–1870. Palgrave–MacMillan, Basingstoke.

Knowles, K., Robertson, D. (1951). "Differences between the wages of skilled and unskilled workers, 1880–1950". Bulletin of the Oxford University Institute of Statistics (April), 109–127.

König, W. (1996). "Science-based industry or industry-based science? Electrical engineering in Germany before World War I". Technology and Culture 37 (1), 70–101.

Kranakis, E. (1992). "Hybrid careers and the interaction of science and technology". In: Kroes, P., Bakker, M. (Eds.), Technological Development and Science in the Industrial Age. Kluwer, Dordrecht, pp. 177–204.

Kremer, M. (1993). "Population growth and technological change: One million BC to 1990". Quarterly Journal of Economics 108 (4), 681–716.

Kronick, D.A. (1962). A History of Scientific and Technical Periodicals. Scarecrow Press, New York.

Landes, D.S. (1998). The Wealth and Poverty of Nations: Why Some Are So Rich and Some So Poor. W.W. Norton, New York.

Lerner, J. (2000). "150 years of Patent Protection". Working Paper 7477. National Bureau of Economic Research, Cambridge, MA.

Livi Bacci, M. (2000). The Population of Europe. Blackwell, Oxford.

Long, J. (2003). "The economic return to primary schooling in Victorian England". Unpublished Manuscript. Colby College.

Lowood, H. (1991). Patriotism, Profit, and the Promotion of Science in the German Enlightenment: The Economic and Scientific Societies, 1760–1815. Garland Publ., New York.

Lucas, R.E. (2002). Lectures on Economic Growth. Harvard University Press, Cambridge, MA.

Lundgren, A. (1990). "The Changing Role of Numbers in 18th Century Chemistry". In: Frängsmyr, T., Heilbron, J.L., Rider, R.E. (Eds.), The Quantifying Spirit in the 18th Century. University of California Press, Berkeley, pp. 245–266.

Macfarlane, A., Martin, G. (2002). Glass: A World History. University of Chicago Press, Chicago.

MacLeod, C. (1988). Inventing the Industrial Revolution: The English Patent System, 1660–1880. Cambridge University Press, Cambridge.

Maddison, A. (1998). Chinese Economic Performance in the Long-Run. OECD, Paris.

Maddison, A. (2001). The World Economy: A Millennial Perspective. OECD, Paris.

Mantoux, P. (1961 [1928]). The Industrial Revolution in the Eighteenth Century. Harper Torchbooks, New York.

McClellan III, J.E. (1981). "The Academie Royale des Sciences, 1699–1793: A statistical portrait". Isis 72 (4), 541–567.

McClellan III, J.E. (1985). Science Reorganized: Scientific Societies in the Eighteenth Century. Columbia University Press, New York.

McCloy, S.T. (1952). French Inventions of the Eighteenth Century. University of Kentucky Press, Lexington.

McKendrick, N. (1973). "The role of science in the Industrial Revolution". In: Teich, M., Young, R. (Eds.), Changing Perspectives in the History of Science. Heinemann, London, pp. 274–319.

McNeil, M. (1987). Under the Banner of Science: Erasmus Darwin and His Age. Manchester University Press, Manchester.

Merton, R.K. (1970 [1938]). Science, Technology, and Society in Seventeenth Century England, second ed. Fertig, New York.

Mitch, D. (1998). "The role of education and skill in the British Industrial Revolution". In: Mokyr, J. (Ed.), The British Industrial Revolution: An Economic Perspective, second ed. Westview Press, Boulder, CO, pp. 241–279.

Mokyr, J. (1990). The Lever of Riches: Technological Creativity and Economic Progress. Oxford University Press, New York.

Mokyr, J. (1994). "Progress and inertia in technological change". In: James, J., Thomas, M. (Eds.), Capitalism in Context: Essays in Honor of R.M. Hartwell. University of Chicago Press, Chicago, pp. 230–254.

Mokyr, J. (1998a). "The political economy of technological change: Resistance and innovation in economic history". In: Berg, M., Bruland, K. (Eds.), Technological Revolutions in Europe. Edward Elgar, Cheltenham, pp. 39–64.

Mokyr, J. (1998b). "Editor's introduction: The new economic history and the Industrial Revolution". In: Mokyr, J. (Ed.), The British Industrial Revolution: An Economic Perspective. Westview Press, Boulder, pp. 1–127.

Mokyr, J. (2000). "The Industrial Revolution and the Netherlands: Why did it not happen?". De Economist 148 (4), 503–520. Amsterdam.

Mokyr, J. (2002). The Gifts of Athena: Historical Origins of the Knowledge Economy. Princeton University Press, Princeton.

Mokyr, J. (2004). "Accounting for the Industrial Revolution". In: Johnson, P., Floud, R. (Eds.), The Cambridge Economic History of Modern Britain, vol. 1: Industrialisation, 1700–1860. Cambridge University Press, Cambridge, pp. 1–27.

Mokyr, J. (2005a). "Mercantilism, the Enlightenment, and the Industrial Revolution". Presented to the Conference in Honor of Eli F. Hechscher, Stockholm, May 2003. In: Findlay, R., Henriksoon, R., Lindgren, H., Lundahl, M. (Eds.), Eli F. Heckscher (1979–1952): A Celebratory Simposium. MIT Press, Cambridge, MA, in press.

Mokyr, J. (2005b). "Useful knowledge as an evolving system: The view from economic history". In: Blume, L.E., Durlauf, S.N. (Eds.), The Economy as an Evolving Complex System, III. Oxford University Press, New York, in press.

Morus, I.R. (1998). Frankenstein's Children: Electricity, Exhibition, and Experiment in Early-Nineteenth-Century London. Princeton University Press, Princeton, NJ.

Murdoch, P. (1750). "An account of the life and writing of the author". In: MacLaurin, C. (Ed.), An Account of Sir Isaac Newton's Philosophical Discoveries. Printed for A. Millar, London.

Murmann, J.P. (2003). Knowledge and Competitive Advantage: The Coevolution of Firms, Technology, and National Institutions. Cambridge University Press, Cambridge.

Musson, A.E., Robinson, E. (1969). Science and Technology in the Industrial Revolution. Manchester University Press, Manchester.

Nelson, R.R. (1994). "Economic growth through the co-evolution of technology and institutions". In: Leydesdorff, L., Van Den Besselaar, P. (Eds.), Evolutionary Economics and Chaos Theory: New Directions in Technology Studies. St. Martin's Press, New York, pp. 21–32.

Nelson, R.R., Winter, S. (1982). An Evolutionary Theory of Economic Change. The Belknap Press, Cambridge, MA.

North, D.C. (1990). Institutions, Institutional Change, and Economic Performance. Cambridge University Press, Cambridge.

O'Brien, P. (2003). "The Hanoverian state and the defeat of the continental state". Presented to the Conference in honor of Eli F. Heckscher, Stockholm, May.

Olsson, O. (2000). "Knowledge as a set in idea space: An epistemological view on growth". Journal of Economic Growth 5 (3), 253–276.

Olsson, O. (2003). "Technological opportunity and growth". Unpublished Manuscript, Göteborg University.

Ormrod, D. (2003). The Rise of Commercial Empires: England and the Netherlands in the Age of Mercantilism, 1650–1770. Cambridge University Press, Cambridge.

Pannabecker, J.R. (1996). "Diderot, Rousseau, and the mechanical arts: Disciplines, systems, and social context". Journal of Industrial Teacher Education 33 (4), 6–22.

Picon, A. (2001). "Technology". In: Delon, M. (Ed.), Encyclopedia of the Enlightenment. Fitzroy Dearborn, Chicago, pp. 1317–1323.

Polanyi, M. (1962). Personal Knowledge: Towards a Post-Critical Philosophy. Chicago University Press, Chicago.

Pollard, S. (1968). The Genesis of Modern Management. Penguin Books, London.

Pomeranz, K. (2000). The Great Divergence: China, Europe, and the Making of the Modern World Economy. Princeton University Press, Princeton, NJ.

Porter, R. (1990). English Society in the 18th Century, second ed. Penguin Books, London.

Porter, R. (2000). The Creation of the Modern World: The Untold Story of the British Enlightenment. W.W. Norton, New York.

Price, D.J.D. (1984a). "Notes towards a philosophy of the Science/Technology interaction". In: Laudan, R. (Ed.), The Nature of Knowledge: Are Models of Scientific Change Relevant? Kluwer, Dordrecht, pp. 105–114.

Price, D.J.D. (1984b). "Of sealing wax and string". Natural History 1, 49–56.

Priestley, J. (1768). An Essay on the First Principles of Government and on the Nature of Political, Civil and Religious Liberty. J. Doosley, London.

Randall, A.J. (1986). "The philosophy of Luddism: The case of the West of England workers, ca. 1790–1809". Technology and Culture 27 (1), 1–17.

Randall, A.J. (1989). "Work, culture and resistance to machinery in the West of England woollen industry". In: Hudson, P. (Ed.), Regions and Industries: A Perspective on the Industrial Revolution in Britain. Cambridge University Press, Cambridge, pp. 175–198.

Reiter, S. (1992). "Knowledge, discovery and growth". Discussion Paper 1011. Northwestern University Center for Mathematical Studies in Economics and Management Sciences.

Roche, D. (1998). France in the Enlightenment. Harvard University Press, Cambridge, MA.

Root, H. (1994). The Fountain of Privilege: Political Foundations of Markets in Old Regime France and England. University of California Press, Berkeley and Los Angeles.

Rosenberg, N. (1965). "Adam Smith on the division of labour: Two views or one?". Economica 32 (126), 127–139.

Rosenberg, N. (1976). Perspectives on Technology. Cambridge University Press, Cambridge.

Rosenberg, N. (1994). Exploring the Black Box. Cambridge University Press, New York.

Ruelle, D. (1991). Change and Chaos. Penguin Books, London.

Sandberg, L.G. (1979). "The case of the impoverished sophisticate: Human capital and Swedish economic growth before World War I". The Journal of Economic History 39 (1), 225–241.

Sargent, R.-M. (Ed.) (1999). Francis Bacon: Selected Philosophical Works. Hackett Publishing Co., Indianapolis.

Schiff, E. (1971). Industrialization without National Patent. Princeton University Press, Princeton, NJ.

Shapin, S. (1994). The Social History of Truth. University of Chicago Press, Chicago.

Shapin, S. (1996). The Scientific Revolution. University of Chicago Press, Chicago.

Shleifer, A., Vishny, R. (1998). The Grabbing Hand: Government Pathologies and Their Cures. Harvard University Press, Cambridge, MA.

Simon, J.L. (1977). The Economics of Population Growth. Princeton University Press, Princeton, NJ.

Simon, J.L. (2000). The Great Breakthrough and Its Cause. Edited by Timur Kuran. The University of Michigan Press, Ann Arbor.

Smith, A. (1976 [1776]). Cannan, E. (Ed.), The Wealth of Nations. University of Chicago Press, Chicago.

Smith, A. (1978). Lectures on Jurisprudence. Clarendon Press, Oxford.

Smith, J.G. (1979). The Origins and Early Development of the Heavy Chemical Industry in France. Clarendon Press, Oxford.

Smith, J.G. (2001). "Science and technology in the early French chemical industry". Unpublished Paper. Presented to the Colloquium on "Science, techniques, et sociétés", Paris.

Snelders, H.A.M. (1992). "Professors, amateurs, and learned societies". In: Jacob, M., Mijnhardt, W.W. (Eds.), The Dutch Republic in the Eighteenth Century: Decline, Enlightenment, and Revolution. Cornell University Press, Ithaca, pp. 308–323.

Snooks, G. (1994). "New perspectives on the Industrial Revolution". In: Snooks, G.D. (Ed.), Was the Industrial Revolution Necessary? Routledge, London.

Spadafora, D. (1990). The Idea of Progress in Eighteenth-Century Britain. Yale University Press, New Haven.

Sparrow, W.J. (1964). Knight of the White Eagle. Hutchinson and Co., London.

Stern, B.J. (1937). "Resistances to the adoption of technological innovations". In: Technological Trends and National Policy. United States Government Printing Office, Washington, DC.

Stewart, L. (2004). "The laboratory and the manufacture of the enlightenment". Unpublished Manuscript. University of Saskatchewan.

Thorne, S. (1986). The History of Food Preservation. Barnes and Noble Books, Totowa, NJ.

Tranter, N.L. (1985). Population and Society, 1750–1940. Longman, Burnt Mill.

Travis, A. (1989). "Science as receptor of technology: Paul Ehrlich and the synthetic dyestuff industry". Science in Context 3 (2), 383–408.

Uglow, J. (2002). The Lunar Men: Five Friends Whose Curiosity Changed the World. Farrar, Strauss and Giroux, New York.

Van Zanden, J.L. (2004). "Common workmen, philosophers, and the birth of the European knowledge economy". Prepared for the GEHN Conference on Useful Knowledge Leiden, September.

Vickers, B. (1992). "Francis Bacon and the progress of knowledge". Journal of the History of Ideas 53 (2), 493–518.

Vincenti, W. (1990). What Engineers Know and How They Know It. Johns Hopkins University Press, Baltimore.

Vincenti, W. (2000). "Real-world variation–selection in the evolution of technological form: Historical examples". In: Ziman, J. (Ed.), Technological Innovation as an Evolutionary Process. Cambridge University Press, Cambridge, pp. 174–198.

Weatherill, L. (1988). Consumer Behaviour and Material Culture in Britain, 1660–1760. Routledge, New York.

Wilson, C. (1969). "Taxation and the decline of empires: An unfashionable theme". In: Economic History and the Historians. Weidenfeld and Nicolson, London, pp. 117–127.

Wong, R.B. (1997). China Transformed: Historical Change and the Limits of European Experience. Cornell University Press, Ithaca.

Wood, H.T. (1913). A History of the Royal Society of Arts. John Murray, London.

Wuketits, F. (1990). Evolutionary Epistemology and Its Implications for Humankind. SUNY Press, Albany.

Young, A. (1772). Political Essays Concerning the Present State of the British Empire. W. Strahan and T. Cadell, London.

Youngson, A.J. (1979). The Scientific Revolution in Victorian Medicine. Holmes and Meier Publishers, New York.

Zilsel, E. (1942). "The sociological roots of science". American Journal of Sociology 47 (4), 544–560.

Ziman, J. (1976). The Force of Knowledge. Cambridge University Press, Cambridge.

Ziman, J. (Ed.) (2000). Technological Innovation as an Evolutionary Process. Cambridge University Press, Cambridge.

Chapter 18

GENERAL PURPOSE TECHNOLOGIES

BOYAN JOVANOVIC

New York University
and
NBER

PETER L. ROUSSEAU

Vanderbilt University
and
NBER

Contents

Abstract	1182
Keywords	1183
1. Introduction	1184
1.1. What is a GPT?	1185
1.2. Summary of findings	1186
1.2.1. Similarities between the Electrification and IT eras	1186
1.2.2. Differences between the Electrification and IT eras	1186
2. Measuring the three characteristics of a GPT	1187
2.1. Pervasiveness of the GPT	1187
2.1.1. Pervasiveness in the aggregate	1187
2.1.2. Pervasiveness among sectors	1189
2.1.3. Adoption by households	1193
2.1.4. On dating the endpoints of a GPT era	1194
2.2. Improvement of the GPT	1195
2.3. Ability of the GPT to spawn innovation	1198
2.3.1. Patenting	1198
2.3.2. Investment by new firms vs. investment by incumbents	1200
3. Other symptoms of a GPT	1203
3.1. Productivity slowdown	1204
3.2. The skill premium	1205
3.3. Entry, exit, and mergers should rise	1206
3.4. Stock prices should fall	1207

Handbook of Economic Growth, Volume 1B. Edited by Philippe Aghion and Steven N. Durlauf
© 2005 Elsevier B.V. All rights reserved
DOI: 10.1016/S1574-0684(05)01018-X

3.5. Young firms should do better	1208
3.5.1. The age of the leadership	1208
3.5.2. The age of firms at their IPO	1210
3.5.3. The stock market performance of the young vs. old after entry	1215
3.6. Consumption, interest rates, and the trade deficit	1217
3.6.1. The trade deficit	1218
3.6.2. The consumption–income ratio	1218
3.6.3. Interest rates	1220
4. Conclusion	1221
Acknowledgements	1221
References	1221

Abstract

A general purpose technology or GPT is a term coined to describe a new method of producing and inventing that is important enough to have a protracted aggregate impact. Electricity and information technology (IT) probably are the two most important GPTs so far. We analyze how the U.S. economy reacted to them. We date the Electrification era from 1894 until 1930, and the IT era from 1971 until the present. While we document some differences between the two technologies, we follow David [In: *Technology and Productivity: The Challenge for Economic Policy* (1991) 315–347] and emphasize their similarities. Our main findings are:

1. Productivity growth in the two GPT eras tended to be lower than it was in other periods, with productivity slowdowns taking place at the start of the two eras and the IT era slowdown stronger than that seen during Electrification.
2. Both GPTs were widely adopted, but electricity's adoption was faster and more uniform over sectors.
3. Both improved as they were adopted, but measured by its relative price decline, IT has shown a much faster improvement than Electricity did.
4. Both have spawned innovation, but here, too, IT dominates Electricity in terms of the number of patents and trademarks issued.
5. Both were accompanied by a rise in "creative destruction" and turbulence as measured by the entry and exit of firms, by mergers and takeovers, and by changing valuations on the stock exchange.

In sum, Electrification spread faster than IT has been spreading, and it did so more evenly and broadly over sectors. Also, IT comprises a smaller fraction of the physical capital stock than electrified machinery did at its corresponding stage. On the other hand, IT seems to be technologically more dynamic; the ongoing spread of IT and its continuing precipitous price decline are reasons for optimism about productivity growth in the 21st century.

Keywords

electricity, information technology, IT revolution, productivity slowdowns, technology improvement, creative destruction

JEL classification: O3, N2

1. Introduction

The term "general-purpose technology", or GPT, has seen extensive use in recent treatments of the role of technology in economic growth, and is usually reserved for changes that transform both household life and the ways in which firms conduct business. Steam, electricity, internal combustion, and information technology (IT) are often classified as GPTs for this reason. They affected the whole economy.

As David (1991) has pointed out, however, a GPT does not deliver productivity gains immediately upon arrival. Figure 1 shows the evolution of the growth in output per man-hour in the U.S. economy over the past 130 years, with periods of rapid diffusion of the two major GPTs shaded and the dashed line representing long-term trends as generated with the Hodrick–Prescott (HP) filter.[1] Productivity growth was apparently quite rapid during the heyday of steam power (c. 1870), but fell as Electrification arrived in the 1890s, with the defining moment in the transition probably being the startup of the first hydro-electric facility at Niagara Falls in 1894. It was only in the period after 1915, which saw the diffusion of machines operated by stand-alone secondary motors and the widespread establishment of centralized power grids, that Electricity finally pervaded businesses and households more generally and measures of productivity began to rise.

Figure 1 also shows that the arrival of IT, which we date with Intel's invention in 1971 of the "4004" microprocessor (the key component of the personal computer or "PC"), did not reverse the decline in productivity growth that had begun more than a decade earlier. It seems only now that we are finally seeing computers show up in the productivity figures.

But it is not obvious that the startup of the Niagara Falls dam and the invention of the 4004 chip should define the birth of the two GPTs. After all, Thomas Edison invented the incandescent bulb in 1879 and by 1882 the world's first large central power station had been installed at Pearl Street in New York City, twelve years before we mark Electricity's "arrival". And large mainframe computers predicted the winner of the 1952 U.S. Presidential election, nearly two decades prior to the advent of the microprocessor. An objective measure is needed, though, and we shall define the start of a GPT era as the point in time when the GPT achieves a one-percent diffusion in the median sector. This is another way to arrive at 1894 and 1971 as the starting points where the shading begins in Figure 1. Similarly, we would say that the era is over when the diffusion curve flattens out. For Electrification, it takes until about 1929 for net adoption to reach a plateau, whereas new adoption of IT is still rising today so that, on that criterion, the IT epoch continues.

Each shaded area in Figure 1 contains a productivity-growth slowdown in its initial phases. Will the growth slowdown of the current IT era be followed by a rise in growth

---

[1] Output per man-hour in the business, non-farm sector is from John Kendrick's series as published in U.S. Bureau of the Census (1975, Series D684, p. 162) for 1889–1947 and from the Bureau of Labor Statistics for 1948–2003. For 1874–1889, we use Kendrick's decadal averages for 1869–1879 and 1879–1889 and interpolate between these benchmarks assuming a constant growth rate from 1874–1884 and 1885–1889.

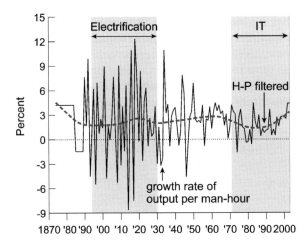

Figure 1. Annual growth in output per man-hour, 1874–2004.

in the first half of the 21st century? If the second shaded area in Figure 1 is in some fundamental respects like the first shaded area, then we can expect growth to pick up over the next several decades. In Jovanovic and Rousseau (2002a) we have argued that the first half of the 21st century will have higher growth than, say, the 1950s and 1960s. Gordon (2000), on the other hand, is pessimistic, arguing that IT does not measure up to Electricity and that it will not have such positive results. This chapter, while documenting key differences between the diffusion paths of the two technologies, will in the end conclude that the two GPT eras are strikingly similar in a number of respects. If anything, our finding that IT is the more "revolutionary" of the two GPTs suggests that its full impact is yet to be seen.

This chapter is organized around the presentation of a collection of facts. The facts are described mainly through graphs and tables which provide evidence on a set of models that we shall mention as we go along. A primarily analytic survey is Greenwood and Jovanovic (2001).

1.1. What is a GPT?

So, what are these "fundamental" features of GPTs that would allow us to compare one to another? And more generally, what criteria can one use to distinguish a GPT from other technologies? Bresnahan and Trajtenberg (1996) argue that a GPT should have the following three characteristics:

1. *Pervasiveness* – The GPT should spread to most sectors.
2. *Improvement* – The GPT should get better over time and, hence, should keep lowering the costs of its users.
3. *Innovation spawning* – The GPT should make it easier to invent and produce new products or processes.

Most technologies possess each of these characteristics to some degree, and thus a GPT cannot differ qualitatively from these other technologies. Note, too, that the third property is, in a sense, a version of the first property if we phrase the latter to say that the GPT should also spread to the innovation sector. Moreover, this list can be expanded to include more subtle features of GPTs, a subject that we consider in Section 3. Yet we find these three basic characteristics to be a useful starting point for evaluating and comparing the impact of various technologies through history. Investigating how Electricity and IT measure up on these three dimensions is the focus of Section 2. But first, we summarize our overall findings.

1.2. Summary of findings

The evidence shows similarities and differences between the Electrification and the IT eras. Electrification was more pervasive (#1), whereas IT has a clear lead in terms of improvement (#2) and innovation spawning (#3). Let us list the similarities and differences in more detail.

1.2.1. Similarities between the Electrification and IT eras

1. In both eras productivity growth rates are below those attained in the decades immediately preceding the GPT's arrival.
2. Measures of reallocation and invention – the entry and exit of firms to the stock market, investment by new firms relative to incumbents, and grants of patents and trademarks – are all higher during the GPT eras.
3. Private consumption rises gradually during each GPT era.
4. Real interest rates are about the same during the two GPT eras, and about three percentage points higher than from 1930 to 1970 – the period between the rapid adoptions of Electricity and IT.

1.2.2. Differences between the Electrification and IT eras

1. Innovation measures are growing much faster for IT than for Electrification – patents and trademarks surge much more strongly during the IT era, and the price of IT is falling 100 times faster, at least, than did the price of electricity.
2. IT is spreading more slowly than did Electrification, and it comprises a smaller part of the capital stock. Its net adoption continues to rise in the United States.
3. The productivity slowdown is stronger in the IT era.
4. No comparable sudden collapse of the stock market occurred early on in the Electrification era.
5. The Electrification era saw a surplus in the U.S. trade balance, in part because Europe had to finance a string of wars, whereas the IT era finds the United States with consistent trade deficits.

The differences seem to be quite important. But overall the evidence clearly supports the view that technological progress is uneven, that it does entail the episodic arrival of GPTs, and that these GPTs bring on turbulence and lower growth early on and higher growth and prosperity later. The bottom line is that with a wider body of data and fifteen more years of it than David (1991) had at his disposal, we confirm his hypothesis that Electrification and IT adoption are manifestations of the same force at work, namely the introduction of a GPT.

2. Measuring the three characteristics of a GPT

As suggested in Figure 1, we shall choose Electricity and IT as our candidate GPTs, and the measures that we construct will pertain mostly to these two technologies. In passing, we shall also touch upon steam and internal combustion. The three subsections below report, in turn, various measures of each characteristic – pervasiveness, improvement, and innovation – for the two GPTs at hand.

2.1. Pervasiveness of the GPT

The first characteristic is the technology's pervasiveness. We begin by looking at aggregates and proceed to consider individual industrial sectors in more detail.

2.1.1. Pervasiveness in the aggregate

Ideally we would like to track the evolution of various candidate GPTs using continuous time series from about 1850 to the present, but we do not have data that consistently cover this entire stretch of time, and thus will need to work with two overlapping segments: 1869–1954 and 1947–2003.

Figure 2 shows the shares of total horsepower in manufacturing by power source from 1869 to 1954.[2] The period covers the decline in usage of water wheels and turbines, the rise and fall of steam engines and turbines, the rise and gradual flattening out of the internal combustion engine's use in industrial applications, and the sharp rise in the use of primary and secondary electric motors. The symmetry of the plot is striking in that, with the exception of internal combustion, power-generating technologies seem to have led for the most part sequential existences. The relative brevity of the entire steam cycle, which rises and falls within a period of 50–60 years, suggests that the technology

---

[2] We construct the shares of total horsepower in manufacturing as ratios of each power source from DuBoff (1964, table 14, p. 59) to the total (table 13, p. 58). DuBoff estimates these quantities in 1869, 1879, 1889, 1899, 1904, 1909, 1914, 1919, 1923, 1925, 1927, 1929, 1939 and 1954, and we linearly interpolate between these years in Figure 2. This source does not include a breakdown of non-electrical capacity (i.e., water, internal combustion, and steam) after 1939, and so we mark the more broadly-defined "non-electrical" share for 1954 with an asterisk.

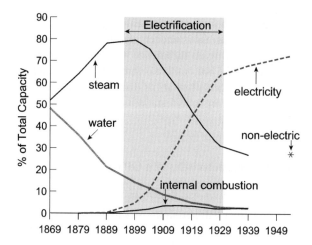

Figure 2. Shares of total horsepower generated by the main sources in U.S. manufacturing, 1869–1954.

which replaced it, Electricity, was important enough to force a rapid transition among manufacturers. In contrast, the decline of water power was more gradual.

If we could continue Figure 2 to the present, Electricity would surely still command a very high share of manufacturing power as the next new source (e.g., solar power?) has not yet emerged to replace it. The persistence of Electricity as the primary power source, even though its diffusion throughout the manufacturing sector was complete decades ago, helps to identify it as one of the breakthrough technologies of the modern era.

Figure 3 shows the diffusion of computers in the U.S. industrial sector as measured by the share of IT equipment and software in the aggregate capital stock.[3] Computer and software purchases appear to have reached the first inflection point in their "S-curve" more slowly than Electrification in the early years of its adoption, but it is striking how much faster the IT share has risen over the past few years. Moreover, while the diffusion of Electricity had slowed down by 1930, the year which we mark as the end of the Electrification era, computer and software sales continue their rapid rise to this day.

The vertical axes in Figures 2 and 3 are scaled differently. In Figure 2 the vertical axis measures the share of total horsepower in manufacturing, whereas in Figure 3 it is the share of IT equipment and software in the aggregate capital stock. But scaling aside, a comparison of the shape of the diffusions in the two figures suggests that the

---

[3] We build the ratio plotted in Figure 3 for 1961–2001 by summing the capital stocks of 62 SIC industrial sectors from the detailed nonresidential fixed asset tables in constant 1996 dollars made available by the U.S. Bureau of Economic Analysis (2002, 2004). IT capital includes mainframe and personal computers, storage devices, printers, terminals, integrated systems, and pre-packaged, custom, and own-account software. The total capital stock is the sum of all fixed asset types.

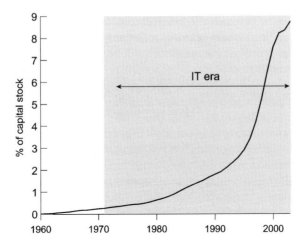

Figure 3. Shares of computer equipment and software in the aggregate capital stock, 1960–2003.

IT-adoption era will last longer than the 35 years of Electrification. Indeed, the acceleration in adoption, which was over by about 1905 for Electrification, did not end until about 1997 for IT. It also appears that IT forms a smaller part of the physical capital stock than did electric-powered machinery at the corresponding stages.

Why did Electricity spread faster than IT seems to be doing? Both technologies are subject to a network externality; Electricity because the connecting of cables and wires to a neighborhood was more profitable when the number of users was larger, and IT especially so after the Internet was invented. Perhaps electrical technologies were more profitable, or perhaps the rapid price decline of computers and peripherals makes it optimal to wait and adopt later as Jovanovic and Rousseau (2002a) emphasize.

2.1.2. Pervasiveness among sectors

Cummins and Violante (2002, p. 245) classify a technology as a GPT when the share of new capital associated with it reaches a critical level, and if adoption is widespread across industries. Electrification seems to fit this description. Figure 4 shows the shares of total horsepower electrified in manufacturing sectors at ten-year intervals from 1889 to 1954.[4] Electrical adoption was very rapid between 1899 and 1919 but slowed considerably thereafter, with the dispersion in the adoption rates largest around 1919.

The striking feature of Figure 4 is how *uniformly* electrical technology affected individual manufacturing sectors. Table 1, which shows the rank correlations of Electricity shares across sectors and time, indicates that there was little change in the relative ordering of the sectors. This means that the sectors that were the heaviest users of Electricity

---

[4] The shares of electrified horsepower include primary and secondary electric motors, and are computed using data from DuBoff (1964, tables E-11 and E-12a–E-12e, pp. 228–235).

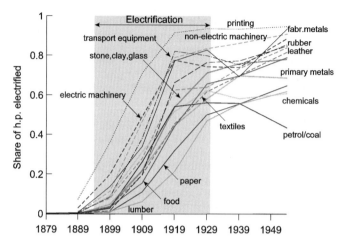

Figure 4. Shares of electrified horsepower by manufacturing sector, 1890–1954.

Table 1
Rank correlations of Electricity shares in total horsepower by manufacturing sector, 1889–1954

	1889	1899	1909	1919	1929	1939	1954
1889	1.000						
1899	0.707	1.000					
1909	0.643	0.918	1.000				
1919	0.686	0.746	0.893	1.000			
1929	0.639	0.718	0.739	0.871	1.000		
1939	0.486	0.507	0.571	0.750	0.807	1.000	
1954	0.804	0.696	0.650	0.789	0.893	0.729	1.000

in 1890 remained among the leaders as adoption slowed down in the 1930s. In sum, the adoption of Electricity was sweeping and widespread.

Why did that adoption take as long as it did? One answer is that it was costly to set up the wiring required to electrify households early on. This is apparent from the peculiar two-stage adoption process that many factories chose in adopting Electricity. Located to a large extent in New England factory towns, textile firms around the start of the 20th century readily adapted the new technology by using an electric motor rather than steam to drive the shafts which powered looms, spinning machines and other equipment [see Devine (1983)]. Moreover, delays in the distribution of electricity made it more costly to electrify a new industrial plant fully.

Figure 5 shows the same data as Figure 4, but now in percentile form. We build it by sorting the Electricity shares in each year and, given that only 15 sectors are represented, plotting the 2nd, 5th, 8th, 11th and 14th largest shares in each year. The percentile diffusion curves will be useful when drawing comparisons with the IT era. They also

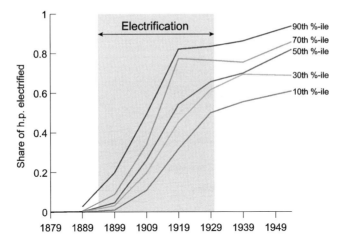

Figure 5. Shares of electrified horsepower by manufacturing sector in percentiles, 1890–1954.

help us in dating Electricity as a GPT. Linear extrapolation between the years 1890 and 1900 suggests that in 1894, about one percent of horsepower in the median industry was provided by Electricity. Whether or not this is actually the "right" percentage for dating the start of the Electrification era, we shall use a one percent share for the median industry to date the beginning of the IT era as well. This provides a common standard for choosing the left-end points of the two shaded areas.

In the century before the Electricity revolution, the technology that primarily drove manufacturing was steam. Figure 6 shows just how slowly steam was replaced between 1899 and 1939.[5] It is natural that industries such as rubber, primary metals, non-electric machinery, and stone, clay, and glass, which saw such rapid increases in electricity use over the same period, would withdraw from steam most rapidly. Indeed, most of the industries that quickly switched over to electricity had been heavy users of steam. This is clear from Figures 4 and 6, taken together, and from the rank correlations of steam shares in total horsepower in Table 2, which decay quickly and suggest a non-uniformity in the destruction of steam technology across the manufacturing sectors.

The spread of IT was also rapid, but does not appear to have been as widespread as Electricity. Figure 7 shows the share of IT equipment and software in the net capital stocks of 62 sectors from 1960 to 2001 plotted as annual percentiles.[6] Some sectors

---

[5] The sectoral shares of manufacturing horsepower driven by steam were computed from DuBoff (1964, tables E-12a–E-12e, pp. 229–233), and include steam engines and turbines. These shares are available on a decade basis from 1899 until 1939 only, which is why the time coverage in Figure 6 is shorter than that in Figure 4.

[6] The sectoral capital stocks are from the detailed non-residential fixed asset tables in constant 1996 dollars made available by the U.S. Bureau of Economic Analysis (2002). We present the sectoral shares for the IT era in percentile form because the number of sectors covered is much larger than was possible for electrification

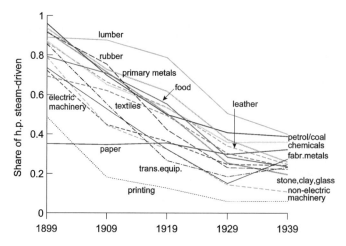

Figure 6. Shares of steam-driven horsepower by manufacturing sector, 1899–1939.

Table 2
Rank correlations of steam shares in total horsepower by manufacturing sector, 1889–1939

	1899	1909	1919	1929	1939
1899	1.000				
1909	0.825	1.000			
1919	0.604	0.800	1.000		
1929	0.525	0.604	0.832	1.000	
1939	0.261	0.282	0.496	0.775	1.000

adopted IT very rapidly, and by 1975 six of them (the 90th percentile) had already achieved IT equipment and software shares of more than 5 percent. Other sectors lagged behind, and some did not adopt IT in a substantive way until after 1985.

On the other hand, the rank correlations of the IT shares across sectors, shown in Table 3, are even higher than those obtained for Electrification. On the face of it then, Electrification would appear to have been the more sweeping GPT-type event because it diffused more rapidly in the U.S. economy and all sectors adopted it pretty much at the same time, whereas IT diffused rapidly in some sectors and not-so-rapidly in others. Nonetheless, the recent gains in IT shares show that the diffusion of this GPT has yet to slow down in the way that Electrification did after 1929.

So far we have discussed adoption by firms, and have used this concept to determine the dating of the two GPT-epochs. We turn to households next.

and steam. Changes in the industrial classifications and the level of detail provided in the BEA's publicly-available fixed asset tables require us to end the series in 2001.

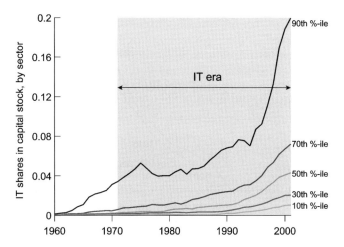

Figure 7. Shares of IT equipment and software in the capital stock by sector in percentiles, 1960–2001.

Table 3
Rank correlations of IT shares in capital stocks by sector, 1961–2001

	1961	1971	1981	1991	2001
1961	1.000				
1971	0.650	1.000			
1981	0.531	0.806	1.000		
1991	0.576	0.746	0.847	1.000	
2001	0.559	0.682	0.734	0.909	1.000

2.1.3. Adoption by households

Households also underwent Electrification and the purchase of PCs for home use during the respective GPT eras. Figure 8 shows the cumulative percentage of households that had obtained electric service and that owned a PC in each year following the arrival of the GPT.[7] If we continue to date Electricity as arriving in 1894 and the PC in 1971, Figure 8 shows that households adopted Electricity about as rapidly as they are adopting the PC. By the time the technology was officially 35 years old (in 1929), nearly 70 percent of households had electrical connections. A comparison with Figure 5 shows that this is just a little higher than the 1929 penetration of electrified horsepower

---

[7] Data on the spread of electricity use by consumers are approximations derived from U.S. Bureau of the Census (1975) *Historical Statistics of the United States* (series S108 and S120). Statistics on computer ownership for 1975–1998 are from Gates (1999, p. 118), and from the U.S. Bureau of the Census (2000–2004) *Current Population Survey* thereafter.

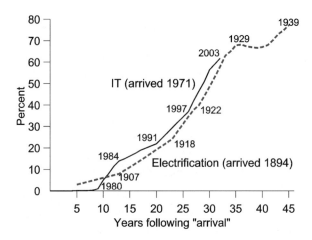

Figure 8. Percent of households with electric service and PCs during the two GPT eras.

as measured by its share in the median manufacturing sector. As in the case of firms, the Electrification of households reaches a plateau in 1929, although it resumed its rise a few years later. On the other hand, there is no sign yet that the diffusion of the computer among either households or firms is slowing down.

With households, as with firms, diffusion lags seem to arise for different reasons for the two technologies. Rural areas were difficult for Electricity to reach, but this is not the case for the PC, where the main barrier is probably the cost of learning how to use it. This barrier seems to have more to do with human capital than was the case with Electricity.

In some ways it is puzzling that the diffusion of the PC has not been much faster than that of Electricity. The price of computing capacity is falling much faster than the price of Electricity did. Affordable PCs came out in the 1980s, when the technology was some 15 years old. On the other hand, households had to wait longer for affordable electrical appliances. Only after 1915, when secondary motors began to diffuse widely and electrical appliances began to be invented, did the benefits of Electrification outweigh the costs for a majority of households. Greenwood, Seshadri and Yorukoglu (2002) document the spread of electrically-powered household appliances and argue that their diffusion helped to raise female labor-force participation by freeing up their time from housework.

2.1.4. On dating the endpoints of a GPT era

Our dating procedure reflects net adoption rates by firms, but the dates would not change much if we had instead used net adoption by households. The shaded areas in our figures are periods when the S-shaped adoption curves are, for the most part, rising. Whether or not they start to fall later should not affect the designated adoption eras. For instance,

Electricity has not yet been replaced in the same way that steam was phased out in the first half of the 20th century, but the Electrification era still ends in 1930 because adoption as measured in Figures 2, 4, and 5 flattens out. Figures 2 and 6 show that the steam era must have ended sometime around 1899 because net adoption had already become negative.

Net adoption is endogenous and should reflect the profitability of the technology at hand compared to that of other technologies. The Niagara Falls dam in 1894 and the development of alternating current made it possible to produce and distribute electricity more cheaply at greater distances. Figures 4 and 5 show that at the outset, some sectors (like printing) raced ahead of others in terms of how quickly they adopted. Later on, as the technology matures, its adoption becomes more universal. Eventually, the lagging sectors tend to catch up a bit, in relative terms, but not completely. Inequality of adoption is highest in the middle of the adoption era. We also see such a temporary rise in inequality among the declining steam shares (Figure 6) at about the same time that inequality was greatest in Electricity adoption.

2.2. Improvement of the GPT

The second characteristic that Bresnahan and Trajtenberg suggested is improvement in the efficiency of the GPT as it ages. Presumably this would show up in a decline in prices, an increase in quality, or both. How much a GPT improves can therefore be measured by how much cheaper a unit of quality gets over time. If technology is embodied in capital, then presumably capital as a whole should be getting cheaper faster during a GPT era, but especially capital that is tied to the new technology.

To investigate these implications, we first look at the price of capital goods generally and then at the prices of capital's components. Figure 9 is a quality-adjusted series

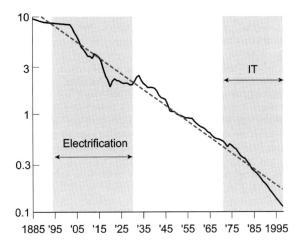

Figure 9. The price of equipment relative to consumption goods.

for the relative price of equipment as a whole, p_k/p_c (i.e., relative to the consumption price index) since 1885, constructed from a number of sources with a linear time trend included.[8] The figure shows that equipment prices declined most sharply between 1905 and 1920, and again after 1975. The 1905–1920 period is also the one that showed the most rapid growth of Electricity in manufacturing (see Figure 4) and in the home (see Figure 8). The post-1975 period follows the introduction of the PC.

Figure 10 considers the prices of components of the capital stock that are tied to our candidate GPTs (as well as to internal combustion), with all prices relative to the aggregate CPI. We use the price of electricity itself because deflators for electrically-powered capital are not available for the first half of the 20th century.[9] Declines in motor vehicle prices should capture the improvement in internal combustion as a possible GPT.[10] The use of the left-hand scale for electricity and motor vehicles and the right-hand scale for computers underscores the extraordinary decline in computer prices since 1960 compared to the earlier technologies.[11] While the relative prices of electricity and motor vehicles fall by a factor of 10, the index of relative computer prices falls by a factor of 10,000.

---

[8] Krusell et al. (2000) build such a series from 1963 using the consumer price index to deflate quality-adjusted estimates of producer equipment prices from Gordon (1990, table 12.4, col. 2, p. 541). Since Gordon's series ends in 1983, they use VAR forecasts to extend it through 1992. We start with Krusell et al. and work backward, deflating Gordon's remaining estimates (1947–1962) with an index for non-durable consumption goods prices that we derive from the National Income Accounts. Since we are not aware of a quality-adjusted series for equipment prices prior to 1947, we use the average price of electricity as a proxy for 1902–1946, and an average of Brady's (1966) deflators for the main classes of equipment for 1885–1902. We deflate the pre-1947 composite using the Bureau of Labor Statistics (BLS) consumer price index of all items [U.S. Bureau of the Census (1975, series E135)] for 1913–1946 and the Burgess cost of living index [U.S. Bureau of the Census (1975, series E184)] for 1885–1912.

[9] Electricity prices are averages of all electric services in cents per kilowatt hour from U.S. Bureau of the Census (1975, series S119, p. 827) for 1903, 1907, 1917, 1922 and 1926–1970, and from various issues of the *Statistical Abstract of the United States* for 1971–1989. We interpolate under a constant growth assumption between the missing years in the early part of the sample. For 1990–2000, prices are U.S. city averages (June figures) from the Bureau of Labor Statistics (*http://www.bls.gov*). We then set the index to equal 1000 in the first year of the sample (i.e., 1903).

[10] Motor vehicle prices for 1913–1940 are annual averages of monthly wholesale prices of passenger vehicles from the National Bureau of Economic Research (Macrohistory Database, series m04180a for 1913–1927, series m04180b for 1928–1940, *http://www.nber.org*). From 1941–1947, they are wholesale prices of motor vehicles and equipment from U.S. Bureau of the Census (1975, series E38, p. 199), and from 1948–2000 they are producer prices of motor vehicles from the Bureau of Labor Statistics (*http://www.bls.gov*). To approximate prices from 1901–1913, we extrapolate backward assuming constant growth and the average annual growth rate observed from 1913–1924. We then join the various components to form an overall price index and set it to equal 1000 in the first year of the sample (i.e., 1901).

[11] To construct a quality-adjusted price index, we join the "final" price index for computer systems from Gordon (1990, table 6.10, col. 5, p. 226) for 1960–1978 with the pooled index developed for desktop and mobile PCs by Berndt, Dulberger and Rappaport (2000, table 2, col. 1, p. 22) for 1979–1999. Since Gordon's index includes mainframe computers, minicomputers, and PCs while the Berndt et al. index includes only PCs, the two segments used to build our price measure are themselves not directly comparable, but a joining of them should still reflect quality-adjusted price trends in the computer industry reasonably well. We set the index to 1000 in the first year of the sample (i.e., 1960).

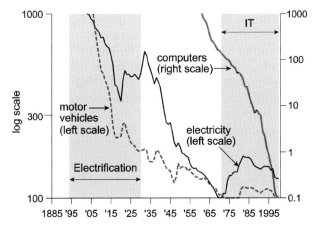

Figure 10. Price indices for products of the two GPT eras.

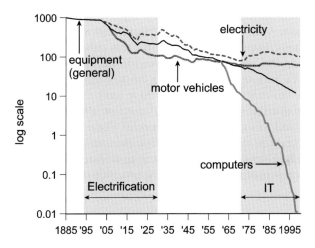

Figure 11. Comparison of the decline in general and GPT-specific equipment prices.

The more interesting question, however, is how the general decline in equipment prices relates to the declines associated more directly with the GPTs of each epoch. Figure 11 makes this comparison by plotting the relative prices of all three GPTs along with the general equipment price index on the same logarithmic scale, with the starting point for each of the GPTs normalized to the level of the general equipment index in that year. By this measure, it is clear that electricity and motor vehicle prices declined at about the same pace as that of equipment generally until the start of the IT price data, though it is also interesting that motor vehicle prices appear to have declined faster than electricity prices. After 1960, declining computer prices and rising shares of computers in equipment stocks seem to have drawn the general index downward, while computing prices fell thousands of times faster than the general index.

It can be said that the Electricity index, being the price of a kilowatt-hour, understates the accompanying technological change because it does not account for improvements in electrical equipment, and especially improvements in the efficiency of electrical motors. Such improvements may be contained in the price series for capital generally. But based on the price evidence in Figures 10 and 11, electricity, motor vehicles, and computers might all qualify as GPTs. Computers, however, are clearly the most revolutionary of the three.

2.3. Ability of the GPT to spawn innovation

The third characteristic that Bresnahan and Trajtenberg suggested was the technology's ability to generate innovation. Any GPT will affect all sorts of production processes, including those for invention and innovation. Some GPTs will be biased towards helping to produce existing products, others towards inventing and implementing new ones. An example of a more specific technology that was heavily skewed towards future products was hybrid corn. Griliches (1957, p. 502) explains why hybrid corn was not an invention immediately adaptable everywhere, but was rather an invention of a method of inventing, a method of breeding superior corn for specific localities.

Electricity and IT have both helped reduce costs of making existing products, and they both spawn innovation, but IT seems to have more of a skew towards the latter. There is no doubt that the 1920s, especially, also saw a wave a new products powered by electricity, but as the patenting evidence will bear out, the IT era has seen an unprecedented increase in inventive activity. For example, the role of the computer in simulation should be known to many of us writing research papers. Feder (1988) describes how computers play a similar role in the invention of new drugs.

2.3.1. Patenting

Patenting should be more intense after a GPT arrives and while it is spreading due to the introduction of related new products. Figure 12, which shows the numbers of patents issued per capita on inventions annually from 1790 to 2002 and trademarks registered from 1870 to 2002, shows two surges in activity – between 1900 and 1930, and again after 1977.[12] Is it mere chance that patenting activity was most intense during our

---

[12] We use the total number "utility" (i.e., invention) patents from the U.S. Patent and Trademark Office for 1963–2002, and from the U.S. Bureau of the Census (1975, series W-96, pp. 957–959) for 1790–1962. The number of registered trademarks are from the U.S. Bureau of the Census (1975, series W-107, p. 959) for 1870–1969, and from the *Statistical Abstract of the United States* [U.S. Bureau of the Census (1980, 1992, 2003)] for later years. Population figures, which are for the total resident population and measured at mid-year, are from U.S. Bureau of the Census (1975, series A-7, p. 8) for 1790–1970, and from the Census Bureau's web site thereafter.

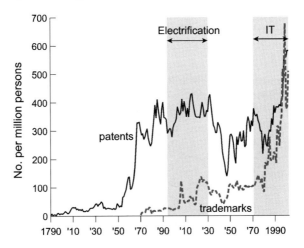

Figure 12. Patents issued on inventions and trademarks registered in the United States per million persons, 1790–2002.

GPT eras? Moreover, it appears that patenting activity picks up after the end of the U.S. Civil War in 1865, and again at the conclusion of World War II in 1945. The slowdown in patenting during the wars and the acceleration immediately thereafter suggest that there may be some degree of intertemporal substitution in the release of new ideas away from times when it might be more difficult to popularize them and towards times better suited for the entry of new products.

Does the surge in patenting reflect a rise in the number of actual inventions, or was the surge prompted by changes in the law that raised the propensity to patent? This question is important because, over longer periods of time, patents may reflect policy rather than invention. Figure 13 analyzes data described in Lerner (2000) and shows that worldwide, changes in patent policy are correlated with the patent series in Figure 12. It is possible, therefore, that the U.S. series reflects the stance of the courts regarding enforcement. Kortum and Lerner (1998) analyze this question and found that the surge of the 1990s was worldwide, but not systematically related to country-specific policy changes. They conclude that technology was the cause for the surge.

Further support for this view comes from the behavior of trademarks per capita, which we also plot in Figure 12. Trademarks behave more or less the same as patents do, except for their more sharply rising trend. Trademarks are easier to obtain than patents and are not governed by legal developments concerning patents. But with trademarks we have a different concern: Do trademarks proxy for the number of products, or do they just measure duplicative activity and the amount of competition? The answer may depend on what market one looks at. In the market for bananas, for example, Wiggins and Raboy (1996) find that brand names are correlated with measures of quality that do explain price variation, suggesting that brand names do signify product differentiation.

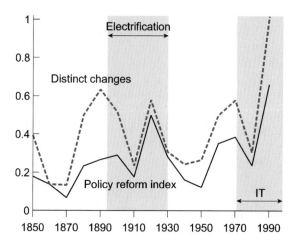

Figure 13. Indices of worldwide changes in patent laws.

2.3.2. Investment by new firms vs. investment by incumbents

New firms do not have costs sunk in old technologies and they are more flexible organizationally than existing firms. One should therefore expect to see job-reallocation waves and waves of entry and exit during the GPT eras. One measure of entry is the extent of new listings on the stock exchange. Figure 14 shows the value of firms entering the New York Stock Exchange (NYSE), the American Stock Exchange (AMEX), and NASDAQ in each year from 1885 through 2003 as percentages of total stock market value.[13] As predicted by Helpman and Trajtenberg (1998a, 1998b), initial public offerings (IPOs) surge between 1895 and 1929, and then after 1977, which again closely matches the dating of our two GPT eras.

The dashed line in Figure 14 is private investment since 1870 as a percent of the net stock of private capital in the U.S. economy as a whole, and as such is the aggregate analog of the solid line that covers only the stock market.[14] The solid line in Figure 15

---

[13] The data used to construct Figure 14 and others in this chapter that use stock market valuations are from the University of Chicago's Center for Research in Securities Prices (2004) (CRSP) files for 1925–2003. NYSE firms are available in CRSP continuously, AMEX firms after 1961, and NASDAQ firms after 1971. We extended the CRSP stock files backward from their 1925 starting year by collecting year-end observations from 1885 to 1925 for all common stocks traded on the NYSE. Prices and par values are from the *The Commercial and Financial Chronicle* (1885–1925), which is also the source of firm-level data for the price indices reported in the influential study by Cowles and Associates (1939). We obtained firm-level book capitalizations from *Bradstreet's* [Bradstreet Co. (1885–1925)], *The New York Times* and *The Annalist* [The New York Times Co. (1897–1928 and 1913–1925)]. The resulting dataset, which includes 25,319 firms, complements others that have begun to build a more complete view of securities prices for the pre-CRSP period [see, for example, Rousseau (1999) on Boston's 19th century equity market].

[14] To build the investment rate series, we start with gross private domestic investment in current dollars from the U.S. Bureau of Economic Analysis (2004) for 1929–2003 and then join it with the gross capital formation

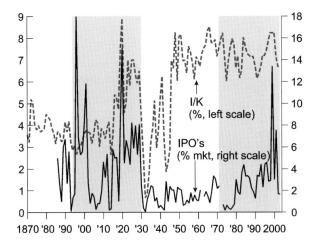

Figure 14. IPOs as a percent of stock market value, and private domestic investment as a percent of the net capital stock, 1870–2003.

shows the ratio of the solid and dashed lines in Figure 14. In both figures it is clear that, during the Electrification epoch, investment by stock market entrants accounted for a larger portion of stock market value than overall new investment in the U.S. economy contributed to the aggregate capital stock. This is consistent with the adoption of Electricity favoring the unencumbered entrant over the incumbent, who may have incurred substantial adjustment costs in using the new technology. We say this because aggregate investment, while indeed including new firms, has an even larger component attributable to incumbents. Moreover, the solid line in Figure 15 was highest in the early years of the Electrification period, which is when these adjustment costs would have been greatest.

Although the solid line in Figure 15 has so far stayed below unity for most of the IT era, it has rapidly risen to a higher level in recent years. This could be because IT adoption involved very large adjustment costs for both incumbents and entrants in the early years until the price of equipment and software fell enough to generate a wave of adoptions by new firms.

series in current dollars, excluding military expenditures, from Kuznets (1961b, Tables T-8 and T-8a) for 1870–1929. We construct the net capital stock using the private fixed assets tables of the U.S. Bureau of Economic Analysis (2004) for 1925–2003. Then, using the estimates of the net stock of nonmilitary capital from Kuznets (1961a, Table 3, pp. 64–65) in 1869, 1879, 1889, 1909, 1919 and 1929 as benchmarks, we use the percent changes in a synthetic series for the capital stock formed by starting with the 1869 Kuznets (1961a) estimate of $27 billion and adding net capital formation in each year through 1929 from Kuznets (1961b) to create an annual series that runs through the benchmark points. Finally, we join the resulting series for 1870–1925 to the later BEA series. The investment rate that appears in Figure 14 is the ratio of our final investment series to the capital stock series, expressed as a percentage.

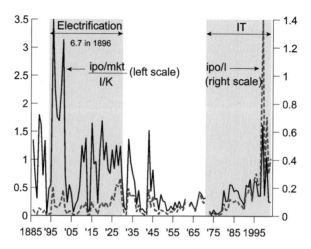

Figure 15. Other investment ratios, 1885–2003.

The solid line in Figure 15 shows a downward trend mainly because the stock market became more important as a vehicle for corporate financing among industrial firms in the early part of the 20th century. IPOs are normalized by total stock market value, which was small early on, and has since become larger. The dotted line in Figure 15 shows the ratio of the dollar values of IPOs and aggregate investment. It is upward sloping for the same reason: IPOs were not that important early on because the stock market was small. After 1970, IPOs capture a much larger share of investment by new entrants than they did before World War I, for example, and even a larger fraction than in the 1920s. When we consider both lines together, we do get the impression that new firms invest more during the GPT eras than at other times.

Does the distribution of entries across sectors shed light on the role of technological factors in the entry waves? Perhaps so. Figure 16 is a scatterplot of the share of IPOs in the market capitalizations of 15 manufacturing sectors between 1890 and 1930 vs. their respective shares of horsepower driven by electricity in 1929.[15] In other words, we ask whether sectors with more IPOs ended up adopting the new technology more vigorously than sectors with less entry. The regression line plotted in Figure 16 has a positive slope coefficient, though with only 15 observations it is not statistically significant.

In Figure 17, we regress IPOs over the 1971–2001 period on shares of computers and peripherals in equipment investment in 2000, and once again obtain a sectoral scatter with a positive slope coefficient, though like our result for the Electrification era, it is not statistically significant.

---

[15] We compute the IPO shares by summing year-end IPO values by sector for 1890–1930, converting the annual totals for each sector into real terms using the implicit price deflator for GDP, and then summing across years. We do the same for all listed firms by sector, and use the ratio of sectoral IPO values to total sector capitalization to compute the shares shown in Figure 16.

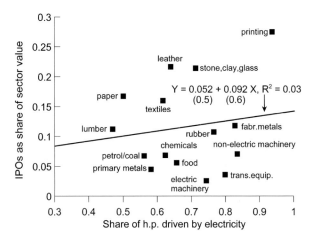

Figure 16. Scatterplot of IPOs as shares of sectoral market values, 1890–1930 vs. shares of horsepower electrified in 1929.

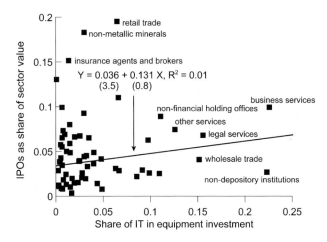

Figure 17. Scatterplot of IPOs as shares of sectoral market values, 1971–2001 vs. shares of IT in equipment investment in 2000.

3. Other symptoms of a GPT

So far we have provided some measures of the three qualities of a GPT – its pervasiveness, its rate of improvement, and its innovation-spawning tendency. Now we turn to less direct measures as suggested by various theoretical models that deal with GPTs. These models predict the following symptoms:

1. *Productivity should slow down* – The new technology may not be user-friendly at first, and output may fall for a while as the economy adjusts.

2. *The skill premium should rise* – If the GPT is not user-friendly at first, skilled people will be in greater demand when the new technology arrives and their earnings should rise compared to those of the unskilled.
3. *Entry, exit and mergers should rise* – These are alternative modes for the reallocation of assets.
4. *Stock prices should initially fall* – The value of old capital should fall. How fast it falls depends on the way that the market learns of the GPT's arrival.
5. *Young and small firms should do better* – The ideas and products associated with the GPT will often be brought to market by new firms. The market share and market value of young firms should therefore rise relative to old firms.
6. *Interest rates and the trade deficit* – The rise in desired consumption relative to output should cause interest rates to rise or the trade balance to worsen.

These, roughly speaking, are the hypotheses that emerge from the theoretical work on GPTs. Now we examine each empirically in turn, and as we go through the facts, we shall mention some of the relevant theories.

3.1. Productivity slowdown

As Bahk and Gort (1993) show, even in routine activities, learning seems to cause delays of several years before plant productivity peaks. It is far from settled, however, whether IT is the reason for the productivity slowdown – Bessen (2002) finds that IT did cause a big part of the slowdown, whereas Comin (2002) argues the opposite. It is also not yet definitely known from the work of Caballero and Hammour (1994) and others whether recessions at business-cycle frequencies are episodes of heightened reallocation. At any rate, the theoretical models of Atkeson and Kehoe (1993), Hornstein and Krusell (1996), Jovanovic and Nyarko (1996), Greenwood and Yorukoglu (1997) and Jovanovic and Rousseau (2002a) emphasize various adjustment costs and learning delays that may cause output to fall at first when a GPT arrives. David (1991) argues that the speed with which a new technology diffuses depends on the pool of investment opportunities that are available when it arrives, and remarks that the quality of this pool in the late 1960s was low because a large backlog from the post-war period had just and finally been eliminated. He also points out that there can often be "slippage" between the technological frontier and implementation due to high input costs and the slow introduction of complementary products.

Figure 1 shows that productivity did not rise quickly in the early phases of the two GPTs, though there is some evidence of greater productivity between 1918 and 1929 and after 1997 or so. Productivity was high in the early years of the Electrification period but fell rapidly as the technology matured. It stayed low through the Depression and 1940s, and then rose rapidly before the IT-age arrived. This pattern is consistent with David's view of exhausted investment opportunities. And while it is interesting to consider the productivity slowdown after 1971, it is also important to recognize that productivity is considerably higher today than it was before IT's arrival.

3.2. The skill premium

As Nelson and Phelps (1966) and Griliches (1969) argued, and Bartel and Lichtenberg (1987) and Krusell et al. (2000) have confirmed, new technology should raise the relative earnings of the skilled. Figure 18 presents a series for the earnings of skilled relative to unskilled labor. We construct the series by combining estimates of the wage ratio for urban skilled and unskilled workers for 1870–1894 from Williamson and Lindert (1980, p. 307) with estimates of the ratio of clerical to manufacturing production wages for 1895–1938 and the returns to 16 versus 12 years of schooling for men for 1939–1995 from Goldin and Katz (1999b).[16]

Although interpreting time series patterns in a continuous series formed from such disparate sources must be done with caution, we note that the series does have a U-shape, with the skill premium high in the early stages of Electrification (i.e., 1890 to 1918) and then rising rapidly during the post-1978 part of the IT epoch. We suspect that the decline in the skill premium from 1918–1924 would have been less deep, and thus the overall U-shape of Figure 18 more apparent, had it not been for the rapid rise of the public higher-education system after the end of World War I [see Goldin and Katz (1999a, p. 10)].

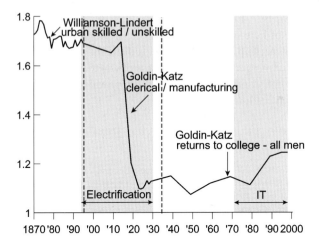

Figure 18. The skill premium.

[16] Combining several very different series into a continuous "skill premium" is necessary due to sectoral shifts in the skilled and unskilled labor forces that render some measures of skill more applicable to certain periods than others. For example, a college education appears to have become a more important determinant of income in the postwar period than it was in earlier years. Since the observations from Goldin and Katz (1999b) are generally decadal, we interpolate between them to obtain an annual series for 1895–1995. The vertical dotted lines in Figure 18 mark the points where we need to change data sources.

3.3. Entry, exit, and mergers should rise

Gort (1969) argued that technological change will generate merger waves. Evidence since then has shown that mergers and takeovers play a re-allocative role for an economy's stock of human and physical capital. Lichtenberg and Siegel (1987), McGuckin and Ngyen (1995) and Schoar (2002) find that the productivity of a target firm rises following a takeover. Jovanovic and Rousseau (2002b, 2002c) study the trade-off between exits and acquisitions at the margin for an economy that needs to update its capital stock. This last pair of papers shows that, at times when the value of organization capital is high, firms are more likely to place themselves on the merger market than to disassemble and sell their assets. Further, reallocation of assets among firms in general (i.e., by merger, consolidation, or purchases of unbundled used capital) is more likely to occur than purchases of new capital when firms need to make large adjustments to their capital stocks because of fixed costs associated with entering the merger market. We believe that both of these conditions are likely to hold during times of sweeping technological change.

The U-shaped top line of Figure 19 is our estimate of the total amount of capital that has been reallocated on the U.S. stock market from 1890 to 2003. Its components are the stock market capitalization of entering and exiting firms divided by two, and the value of merger targets.[17] Entries and exits divided by two, given by the center line, is a rough measure of how much capital exits from the stock market and comes back in under different ownership, or at least under a different name.[18] The lower line is the stock-market value of merger targets. Regardless of whether reallocation occurs through mergers or through entry and exit, it is much more prevalent during the periods that we associate with Electrification and IT.

---

[17] We identify targets for 1926–2003 using the CRSP stock files and various supplementary sources. CRSP itself identifies 9,758 firms that exited the database by merger between 1926 and 2003. We collected information on all mergers for 1895–1930 in the manufacturing and mining sectors from the original worksheets underlying Nelson (1959), and identified mergers from 1885 to 1894 from the financial news section of weekly issues of *The Commercial and Financial Chronicle* (1885–1925). The resulting target series includes the market values of 10,788 exchange-listed firms in the year prior to their acquisition. Stock market capitalizations are from our extension of CRSP backward to 1885 (see footnote 13). Before assigning a firm that no longer carries a price in our database as an "exit", we check the list of hostile takeovers from Schwert (2000) for 1975–1996 and individual issues of the *Wall Street Journal* [Dow Jones and Company, Inc. (1997–2004)] from 1997–2003 to ensure that we record firms taken private under a hostile tender offers as mergers.

[18] For this to be exactly true, of course, would require that the assets of all firms exiting the stock market be purchased by new firms that ended up listing on one of the major exchanges, and that the capital stocks of these new firms consist of only these used assets, assumptions that we know to be violated in practice. If the quantity of assets that do not return to the stock market through entry is roughly the same as the quantity of assets brought into the stock market by new entrants that are not associated with exiting firms, however, our measure would be roughly correct.

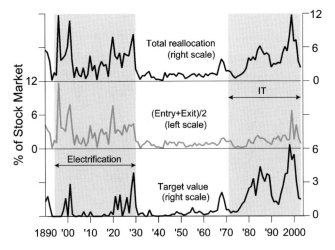

Figure 19. Reallocated capital and its components as percentages of stock market value, 1890–2003.

3.4. Stock prices should fall

The value of old capital should fall suddenly if the arrival of the GPT is a surprise, as in Greenwood and Jovanovic (1999), Hobijn and Jovanovic (2001), Jovanovic and Rousseau (2002a) and Laitner and Stolyarov (2003), or more gradually as in Helpman and Trajtenberg (1998a, 1998b). Figure 20 shows that the stock market declined in 1973–1974.[19] No such sudden drop is visible for stock prices in the early 1890s. Why not? Maybe because the market was thin and unrepresentative in those days, with railway stocks absorbing a large share of market capitalization. More likely, the realization that the new technology would work well was more gradual and not prompted by any single event such as the activation of the Pearl Street power station in 1882 or the completion of the Niagara Falls dam in 1894.

In other words, perhaps a decline in the stock market did not occur early in the Electrification period because the events of the early 1890s were foreseen, as would be the case in Helpman and Trajtenberg (1998a, 1998b). It also could be, as in Boldrin and Levine (2001), that old capital is essential to the production of new capital and that its value may not fall in quite the way that it would when capital can be produced from consumption goods alone, as is the case in many growth models including Jovanovic and Rousseau (2002a).

If stock price declines were caused by the threat of IT to incumbents, this should relate especially to those sectors that later invested heavily in IT. Hobijn and Jovanovic (2001, p. 1218) confirm this using regression analysis.

---

[19] We obtain the composite stock price index at the end of each year from Wilson and Jones (2002), updating through November 2004 using various issues of the *Wall Street Journal*. We deflate using the CPI.

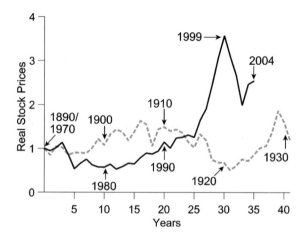

Figure 20. The real Cowles/S&P stock price index across the two GPT eras.

3.5. Young firms should do better

If new technologies are brought to market most effectively by new firms, we would expect younger firms in general to perform better than older firms during the eras of GPT adoption. The evidence on this hypothesis turns out to be mixed, but positive overall.

3.5.1. The age of the leadership

As a GPT takes hold, we should not only expect to see firms coming to market more quickly, but the market leaders getting younger as well. In other words, every stage in the lifetime of the firm should be shorter. This stands in contrast to Hopenhayn (1992), in which the age distribution of an industry's leadership is invariant when an industry is in a long-run stochastic equilibrium. That is, the average age of, say, the top 5 percent or top 10 percent of firms is fixed. Some leaders hold on to their positions and this tends to make the leading group older, but others are replaced by younger firms, and this has the opposite effect. In equilibrium the two forces offset one another and the age of the leadership stays the same. Keeping the age of the leaders flat requires, in other words, constant replacement.

Figures 21 and 22 plot the value-weighted average age of the largest firms whose market values sum to 5 and 10 percent of GDP, respectively. A firm's "age" is measured as the number of years since incorporation and since being listed on a major stock exchange. We label some important entries and exits from this group in Figure 21 (with exits denoted by "X"). The two figures show that, overall, the age of the leaders is anything *but* flat. It sometimes rises faster than the 45° line, indicating that the age of the leaders is rising faster than the passage of time. At other times it is flat or falling, indicating replacement.

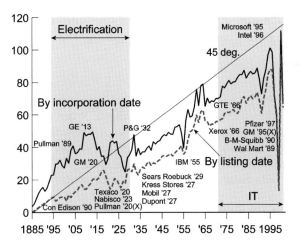

Figure 21. Average age (in years) of the largest firms whose market values sum to 5 percent of GDP, 1885–2001.

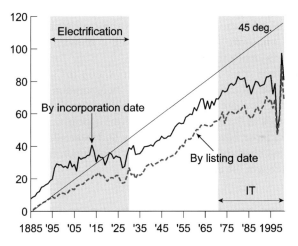

Figure 22. Average age (in years) of the largest firms whose market values sum to 10 percent of GDP, 1885–2001.

Based upon years from incorporation, for example, the leading firms were being re-placed by *older* firms over the first 30 years of our sample, because the solid line is then steeper than the 45° line. In the two decades after the Great Depression the leaders held their relative positions as the 45° slopes of the average age lines show. The leaders got younger in the 1990s, and their average ages now lie well below the 45° line.[20]

[20] The volatility in these series derives not from aggregate stock-market volatility, but from the volatility of individual firm valuations. The large dip and subsequent recovery in both series in 1999–2001, for example,

Both figures show, however, that the lines are flat or falling during the Electricity and IT periods, so that replacement at these times was high. This is best seen in Figure 22.

3.5.2. The age of firms at their IPO

According to the third "innovation-spawning" characteristic, when a GPT arrives it gives rise to new projects that are unusually profitable. When such projects arrive, firms will be more impatient to implement them. When it is new firms that come upon such projects (rather than incumbents), they will feel the pressure to list sooner. This argument is developed and tested in Jovanovic and Rousseau (2001). We argue there that the Electricity- and IT-era firms entered the stock market sooner because the technologies that they brought in were too productive to be kept out of the market for very long.

Figure 23 shows HP-filtered average waiting times from founding, first product or process innovation, and incorporation to exchange listing based upon individual company histories and our backward extension of the CRSP database.[21] The vertical distance between the solid and dotted lines shows that firms often have their first innovation soon after founding, but that it then takes years, even decades, to list on a stock exchange.[22] We interpret this delay as a period during which the firm and possibly its lenders learn about what the firm's optimal investment should be. But when the technology is highly innovative, the incentive to wait is reduced and the firm lists earlier, which is what the evidence shows.

Table 4 lists the first product or process innovation for some of the better-known companies, along with their dates of founding, incorporation, and stock exchange listing. It also includes the share of total market capitalization that can be attributed to each firm's common stock at the end of 2003. The firms appearing in the table separate into roughly 3 groups: those based upon electricity and internal combustion, those based upon chemicals and pharmaceuticals, and those based upon the computer and Internet. Let us consider a few of the entries more closely:

comes from Microsoft's enormous price appreciation in 1999, when it was worth more than 5 percent of GDP on its own, and its rapid decline in 2000, which transferred the full 5 percent share to GE. The two firms split the 5 percent share in 2001.

[21] Listing years after 1925 are those for which firms enter CRSP. For 1890–1924, they are years in which prices first appear in the NYSE listings of *The Annalist, Bradstreet's, The Commercial and Financial Chronicle* or *The New York Times*. The 6,632 incorporation dates used to construct Figure 23 are from *Moody's Industrial Manual* [Moody's Investors Service (1920, 1928, 1955, 1980)], Standard and Poor's *Stock Market Encyclopedia* [Standard and Poor's Corporation (1981, 1988, 2000)] and various editions of Standard and Poor's *Stock Reports* [Standard and Poor's Corporation (1971–2003)]. The 4,221 foundings are from Dun and Bradstreet's *Million Dollar Directory* [Dun and Bradstreet, Inc. (2003)], Moody's, Kelley (1954), and individual company web sites. The 482 first innovations were obtained by reading company histories in *Hoover's Online* [Hoover's, Inc. (2000)] and company web sites. We linearly interpolate the series between missing points before applying the HP-filter to get the time series in Figure 23.

[22] Figure 23 includes several years in the 1970s and early 1980s for which it appears that the average time from first innovation to listing exceeds that from founding to listing. This is a result of differences in the sample sizes used to construct each line.

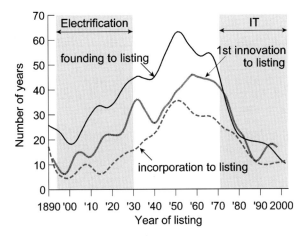

Figure 23. Waiting times to exchange listing, 1890–2003.

- *Electricity/Internal Combustion Engine* – Two of largest companies in the United States today are General Electric (GE) and AT&T. Founded in 1878, GE accounted for 2.1 percent of total stock market value at the end of 2003, and had already established a share of over 2 percent by 1910. AT&T, founded in 1885, contributed 4.6 percent to total market value by 1928, and more than 8.5 percent at the time of its forced breakup in 1984. Both were early entrants of the Electricity era. GE's founding was based upon the invention of the incandescent light bulb in 1879, while AT&T established a long-distance telephone line from New York to Chicago in 1892 to make use of Bell's 1876 invention of the telephone. Both technologies represented quantum leaps in the modernization of industry and communications, and both firms brought these technologies to the NYSE about 15 years after founding. General Motors (GM) was an early entrant to the automobile industry, listing on the NYSE in 1917 – nine years after its founding. By 1931 it accounted for more than 4 percent of stock market value, and its share would hover between 4 and 6.5 percent until 1965, when it began to decline gradually to its share in 2003 of only 0.2 percent. These examples suggest that many of the leading entrants at the turn of the 20th century created lasting market value. Further, the ideas that sparked their emergence were brought to market relatively quickly.
- *Chemicals/Pharmaceuticals* – Procter and Gamble (P&G), Bristol–Myers Squibb and Pfizer are both leaders in their respective industries, but took much longer to list on the NYSE than the Electrification-era firms. In fact, P&G and Pfizer were established before 1850, and thus predate all of them. Despite P&G's early start and the creation of the Ivory soap brand in 1879, it was not until 1932 that the company took its place among the largest U.S. firms by exploiting advances in radio transmission to sponsor the first "soap opera". Pfizer's defining moment came when it developed a process for mass-producing the breakthrough drug penicillin

Table 4
Key dates in selected company histories

Company name	Founding date	1st major product or process innovation	Incorporation date	Listing date	% of stock market in 2003
General Electric	1878	1880	1892	1892	2.09
AT&T	1885	1892	1885	1901	0.11
Detroit Edison	1886	1904	1903	1909	0.04
General Motors	1908	1912	1908	1917	0.20
Coca Cola	1886	1893	1919	1919	0.83
Pacific Gas & Electic	1879	1879	1905	1919	0.08
Burroughs/Unisys	1886	1886	1886	1924	0.03
Caterpillar	1869	1904	1925	1929	0.19
Kimberly–Clark	1872	1914	1880	1929	0.20
Procter & Gamble	1837	1879	1890	1929	0.87
Bristol–Myers Squibb	1887	1903	1887	1933	0.37
Boeing	1916	1917	1916	1934	0.23
Pfizer	1849	1944	1900	1944	1.81
Merck	1891	1944	1934	1946	0.69
Disney	1923	1929	1940	1957	0.32
Hewlett–Packard	1938	1938	1947	1961	0.47
McDonalds	1948	1955	1965	1966	0.21
Intel	1968	1971	1969	1972	1.40
Microsoft	1975	1980	1981	1986	1.99
America Online	1985	1988	1985	1992	0.52
Amazon	1994	1995	1994	1997	0.14
E-Bay	1995	1995	1996	1998	0.28

Source: Data from *Hoover's Online*, Kelley (1954), and company web sites.
Note. The first major products or innovations for the firms listed in the table are: GE 1880, Edison patents incandescent light bulb; AT&T 1892, completes phone line from New York to Chicago; DTE 1904, increases Detroit's electric capacity six-fold with new facilities; GM 1912, electric self-starter; Coca Cola 1893, patents soft-drink formula; PG&E 1879, first electric utility; Burroughs/Unisys 1886, first adding machine; CAT 1904, gas driven tractor; Kimberly–Clark 1914, celu-cotton, a cotton substitute used in WWI; P&G 1879, Ivory soap; Bristol–Myers Squibb 1903, Sal Hepatica, a laxative mineral salt; Boeing 1917, designs Model C seaplane; Pfizer 1944, deep tank fermentation to mass produce penicillin; Merck 1944, cortisone (first steroid); Disney 1929, cartoon with soundtrack; HP 1938, audio oscillator; McDonalds 1955, fast food franchising begins; Intel 1971, 4004 microprocessor (8088 microprocessor in 1978); Microsoft 1980, develops DOS; AOL 1988, "PC-Link"; Amazon 1995, first online bookstore; E-Bay 1995, first online auction house.

during World War II, and the good reputation that the firm earned at that time later helped it to become the main producer of the Salk and Sabin polio vaccines. In Pfizer's case, like that of P&G, the company's management and culture had been in place for some time when a new technology (in Pfizer's case antibiotics) presented a great opportunity.

- *Computer/IT* – Firms at the core of the recent IT revolution, such as Intel, Microsoft and Amazon, came to market shortly after founding. Intel listed in 1972, only four years after starting up, and accounted for 1.4 percent of total stock market value at the end of 2003. Microsoft took eleven years to go public. Conceived in an Albuquerque hotel room by Bill Gates in 1975, the company, with its new disk operating system (MS-DOS), was perhaps ahead of its time, but later joined the ranks of today's corporate giants with the proliferation of the PC. In 1998, Microsoft accounted for more than 2.5 percent of the stock market, but this share fell to 1.5 percent over the next two years in the midst of antitrust action. By the end of 2003 its share had recovered somewhat to nearly 2 percent of the stock market. Amazon caught the Internet wave from the outset to become the world's first on-line bookstore, going public in 1997 – only three years after its founding. As the complexities of integrating goods distribution with an Internet front-end came into sharper focus over the ensuing years, however, and as competition among Internet retailers continued to grow, Amazon's market capitalization by 2003 had fallen to 0.14 percent of total stock market value.

These firms, as well as the others listed in Table 4, are ones that brought new technologies into the stock market and accounted for more than 13 percent of its value at the close of 2003. The firms themselves also seem to have entered the stock market sooner during the Electricity and IT eras, at opposite ends of the 20th century, than firms based on mid-century technologies.

When firms gather less information before investing, the investments that they undertake will be riskier. One may conjecture that if new entrants waited less before investing during the GPT eras, then incumbents also undertook projects earlier than they would have normally. In these cases, the resulting investments would be riskier than if more time were allowed to plan them. Moreover, the newness of the GPT would add further risk. On all these grounds, we would expect interest rate differentials on the average investment to be higher in the GPT eras.

Figure 24, which shows the spread between interest rates on riskier and safe investments since 1885, shows that this has been for the most part the case.[23] It is important to note that we formed the series in Figure 24 by joining three different spreads together, and that the "safe" asset is a long-term U.S. government bond before 1920 and a short-term U.S. Treasury bill thereafter, yet the fluctuations in this series should still reflect risk perceptions reasonably well, at least to the extent that term premia rather than riskiness are the main factors that lead to yield differentials among the various government securities.

---

[23] In Figure 24, we use the spread between the interest rates on Baa-rated corporate bonds (from Moody's Investors Service) and three-month T-bills [from the FRED database of Federal Reserve Bank of St. Louis (2004) for 1934–2003 and the Board of Governors of the Federal Reserve System (1976) for 1920–1934] for the period from 1920 to the present. For 1900–1920, we join the spread between the interest rate on prime commercial paper with 60–90 days until maturity [Homer and Sylla (1991, table 49, p. 358)] and the redemption yields on the U.S. government consol 2s of 1930 [Homer and Sylla (1991, table 46, p. 343)] with the Baa – T-bill spread. Finally, for 1885–1899, we join the spread between the commercial paper rate [Homer and Sylla (1991, table 44, p. 320)] and the redemption yields on U.S. government refunding 4s of 1907 [Homer and Sylla (1991, table 43, p. 316)] with the previous result.

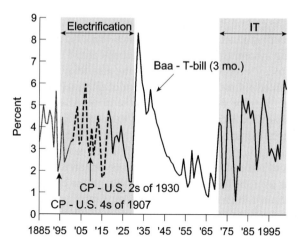

Figure 24. Nominal interest rate spreads between riskier and safer bonds, 1885–2003.

During the Electrification period, spreads rose between 1894 and 1907, which is when uncertainty about the usefulness and possibilities for adoption of the new technology was greatest. Spreads fell after that as the future of Electricity became clearer. In the IT era, spreads have a generally-upward trend throughout, though they did fall for a while in the late 1990s. This may well reflect the lag in the widespread adoption of IT. The spread's sharp rise in 1930 and very slow decline over the next 15 years probably has to do with the macroeconomic instability induced by events prior to and during the Great Depression, and then the heavy borrowing by the U.S. government to finance World War II, which raised rates on T-bills.

Another measure of risk perceptions can be obtained from the distribution of ratings for issues of new corporate bonds. Figure 25 uses data from Hickman (1958, pp. 153–154) and Atkinson (1967, p. 97) for the period from 1908–1965 to show four-year averages, starting at the dates shown on the horizontal axis, of the percent of the total par value of rated new corporate bond issues that received a Moody's rating of single-A or lower and Ba or lower. In other words, the solid line excludes the highest rated bonds (i.e., classes Aaa and Aa), but includes some investment grade bonds (i.e., A and Baa) along with the sub-investment grades (i.e., Ba and lower). The dashed line includes only the sub-investment grades.

The dashed line in Figure 25 indicates that subinvestment grade bonds made up a larger part of the value of total rated new issues during the Electrification era than after the start of the Great Depression, and though these data end in 1965, we note that subinvestment grade issues began to rise again only on the eve of the IT revolution in the mid-1960s. The solid line shows that issues of bonds not receiving the highest Moody's ratings actually rose during the latter part of the Electrification era, peaking in the 1924–1927 period, which was when a host of Electricity-related innovations and appliances were being brought to market. This does not imply an increase in junk-bond

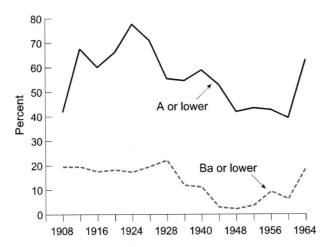

Figure 25. Percent of rated corporate bond offerings with Moody's ratings of A or lower and Ba or lower, four-year averages, 1908–1965.

issuance at this time, but rather is consistent with the view that investors recognized the risks involved with large-scale use of the new technology and were a bit more cautious about overpaying for debt securities associated with it.

3.5.3. The stock market performance of the young vs. old after entry

Young firms are smaller. If "creative destruction" does indeed mean that old firms give way to young firms, then we should see signs of it in Figure 26, which depicts the relative appreciation of the *total* market value of small versus large firms since 1885.[24] We define "small" firms as those in the lower quintile of CRSP, and "large" firms as those in the upper quintile. The regression line in Figure 26 (with *t*-statistics in parentheses) shows small firms outperforming large ones in the long run and an annual growth premium of about 7.5 percent. But the two GPT eras do not show a faster rise in relative appreciations than other times, and this is puzzling. Surprisingly, recessions do not seem to hurt the long-term prospects of small firms: The relative index rises in 10 of the 23 NBER recessions.

The two periods that we wish to focus on are 1929–1931 and the early 1970s. In both periods, the small-capitalization firms lost out relative to the large-capitalization ones. The first period comes at the end of the Electrification era and the relative decline of smaller firms is what one would have expected. But the early 1970s come at the beginning of a new GPT, and small firms should have outperformed the large firms at

---

[24] Being a total value index, this differs from the relative stock price index that is plotted in Figure 8 of Hobijn and Jovanovic (2001). For the post-1925 period, in which they overlap, the qualitative behavior of the two series is essentially the same.

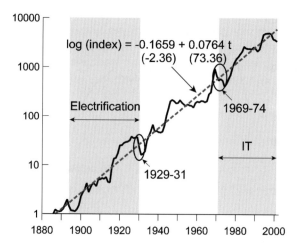

Figure 26. The relative capital appreciations of small vs. large firms, 1885–2001.

that time. Yet the opposite happened. It is only after 1974 that the small-capitalization firms start to perform better.

Regression evidence on age and stock market performance. If the GPT is brought in by young firms, then the capital loss imposed by the GPT's arrival should fall more heavily on old firms. To test this using data on individual firms, let

A_i = age since listing of firm i in 1970;

S_i = share (in firm i's sector) of IT capital in the capital stock in 2001.

This measures a firm's exposure to the impact of the new technology within its sector. We use the change in a firm's stock price over intervals that start in 1971 and end in 1975, 1980, 1985, 1990 and 1995 as measures of expected performance. These should reflect the market's assessment of how well the firm will handle the consequences of the GPT. The regressions take the form

$$\ln\left(\frac{P_{i,1975}}{P_{i,1970}}\right) = c_0 + c_1 A_i + c_2 S_i - c_3 A_i S_i.$$

We summarize the firm-level results in Table 5.

The interaction between the firm's age (A) and its exposure to the new technology (S) is negative and significant only when the period during which we measure price appreciation extends to 1990 and 1995. We would have expected this coefficient to be negative always, since older firms in sectors where IT would become important would be less able to adjust to the new technology than newer firms. The interaction term has a positive coefficient for the 1971–1975, 1971–1980 and 1971–1985 periods, but it is

Table 5
Age and stock market performance

	Dependent variable: $\ln(P_{t+i}/P_t)$				
	1971–1975	1971–1980	1971–1985	1971–1990	1971–1995
constant	−0.737	−0.143	0.152	−0.057	0.577
	(−24.3)	(−2.96)	(2.58)	(−0.59)	(6.06)
A	0.007	−0.001	−0.001	0.003	−0.002
	(6.40)	(−0.46)	(−0.55)	(0.97)	(−0.51)
S	−3.497	−2.266	−1.035	−0.602	2.719
	(−7.60)	(−3.37)	(−1.20)	(−0.46)	(1.88)
A ∗ S	0.047	0.043	−0.016	−0.122	−0.106
	(2.22)	(1.14)	(−0.39)	(−2.09)	(−1.76)
R^2	0.089	0.009	0.003	0.006	0.012
N	2218	1814	1367	981	843

Note. The table presents coefficient estimates for the subperiods included in the column headings with t-statistics in parentheses. The R^2 and number of observations (N) for each regression appear in the final two rows.

statistically significant only for the 1971–1975 period. It thus seems that IT firms took a long time to realize gains in the market after the technology's arrival. There are not very many firms with continuous price data prior to 1900, but we have enough observations to attempt the same regression for the Electrification era. In this case, we got

$$\ln \left(\frac{P_{i,1899}}{P_{i,1894}} \right) = \underset{(1.09)}{2.111} - \underset{(-0.46)}{0.129} \, A_i - \underset{(-0.88)}{2.307} \, S_i + \underset{(0.55)}{0.213} \, A_i S_i,$$

with t-statistics in parentheses and $R^2 = 0.015$, $N = 56$. In this very small sample, we do not see a direct effect of age on capital depreciation as Electrification got underway, and the interaction term is not statistically significant.

3.6. Consumption, interest rates, and the trade deficit

If it is unanticipated, the arrival of a GPT is good news for the consumer because it brings about an increase in wealth. How quickly wealth is perceived to rise depends on how quickly the public realizes the GPT's potential for raising output. The rise in wealth would raise desired consumption. But to implement the GPT firms would also need to increase their investment. Therefore aggregate demand would rise, and in a small open economy this would lead to a trade deficit. In a closed economy, on the other hand, since income does not immediately rise, the rise in aggregate demand would cause the rate of interest to rise so that the rise in aggregate demand would be postponed.

How much consumption rises depends on two factors. The first is the GPT's pervasiveness worldwide – if the entire world is equally affected then consumption could not rise right away and the main effects would be transmitted though the rate of interest. The second is the openness of the U.S. economy. Even if, say, the United States were the only country affected by the GPT, the rise in consumption would be related to how easily capital could flow in.

In these respects, the IT episode differs from the Electrification episode in several important respects. Capital inflows into the United States simply were not in the cards during a large part of the Electrification episode. World War I exhausted the European nations and the United States could not borrow from the rest of the world to finance its electrification-led expansion – it was instead a creditor during this period. Moreover, even if the war had not taken place, it is not clear whether the United States could have borrowed much from the rest of the world because Britain, Germany, France, and several other countries were undergoing the same process – Electrification was more synchronized across the developed world than IT has so far been.

In sum, we would expect the United States to have behaved more like a closed economy during the Electrification era and more like a small open economy during the IT era. Specifically, we would expect to see

(1) a larger rise in the trade deficit during the IT era than during the Electrification era,

(2) a smaller rise in consumption during the Electrification era then during the IT era,

(3) a larger rise in the rate of interest during the Electrification era.

3.6.1. The trade deficit

Figure 27, which plots the trade deficit as a percentage of GNP since 1790 along with an HP trend, shows sharply-rising trade deficits at the start of the IT revolution, though not in the early years of Electrification.[25] The trade deficit indeed opens up fairly dramatically during the IT era, whereas during the Electrification era we see a surplus. As we mentioned, this surplus was driven by the various Colonial wars that took place at the turn of the century and, of course, by World War I.

3.6.2. The consumption–income ratio

We expected to see a smaller rise in consumption during the Electrification era than during the IT era, and after we adjust for the downward long-run trend, this is indeed what has happened. Private consumption rises gradually during each GPT era, and this is set against a long-run secular trend for private consumption that is negative. Figure 28 shows the ratio of consumption to GDP since 1790.[26] As our GPT hypotheses would

---

[25] GDP and total imports and exports of goods and services are from the U.S. Bureau of Economic Analysis (2004) for 1929–2003. For 1790–1920, imports and exports are from U.S. Bureau of the Census (1975, series U-8 and U-1, p. 864, respectively), and the GDP series are from Kendrick (1961) and Berry (1988).

[26] The series for consumption and GDP are from the U.S. Bureau of Economic Analysis (2004) for 1929–2003, Kendrick (1961, table A-IIb, cols. 4 and 11, pp. 296–297) for 1889–1929, and Berry (1988,

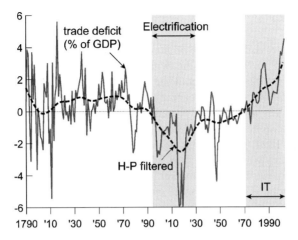

Figure 27. The trade deficit as a percent of GDP, 1790–2003.

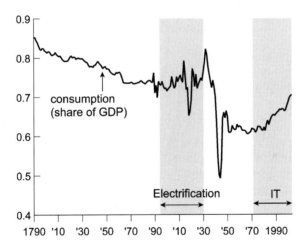

Figure 28. The ratio of consumption to income, 1790–2003.

suggest, the arrival of Electricity in 1890 seems to mark the end of a long-term decline in the ratio that been underway for a century. And though the level of the series falls during the Great Depression and World War II, never to return to its pre-1930 levels, consumption takes another sharp upward turn near the start of the IT revolution and continues to rise.

table 9, pp. 25–26) for 1790–1889. The BEA figures are for personal consumption, but the Kendrick and Berry figures include the government sector as well. Since consumption in the government sector was much smaller prior to World War I, we suspect that the downward trend in the 19th century is a result of changing private consumption patterns rather than a reduction in the government sector's consumption.

3.6.3. Interest rates

We expected a larger rise in the rate of interest during the Electrification era than during the IT era. Relative to HP trends, the evidence is not favorable. Figure 29 shows that ex-post real interest rates were about the same during the two GPT eras, and much lower in the middle 40 unshaded years of the 20th century.[27] The dashed line is the HP detrended series. The averages are presented in Table 6. We note that the ex-post rate is quite high in the first era, before 1894. If the arrival of electricity and its impact was foreseen prior to 1894, interest rates would have risen earlier, but this probably does not explain why they were so high then. More likely, the pre-1894 era reflects a lack of financial development: The stock market was small then, and the financial market not as deep. This may have given rise to an overall negative trend in interest rates over the 134-year period as a whole.

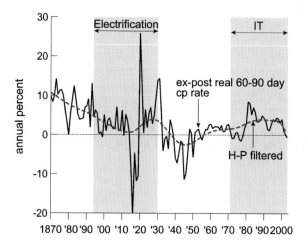

Figure 29. The ex-post real interest rate on commercial paper, 1870–2003.

Table 6

Era	Ex-post real interest rate
1870–1893	7.78
1894–1930	2.61
1931–1970	−0.16
1971–2003	2.75

[27] Commercial paper rates are annual averages from the FRED database for 1934–2003 and from Homer and Sylla (1991) for earlier years. We compute the ex-post return by subtracting inflation as computed by the growth of the implicit price deflator for GNP from the U.S. Bureau of Economic Analysis (2004) for 1929–2003 and Berry (1988) for earlier years.

4. Conclusion

Technological invention is uneven, and comes in bursts; that much has for a long time been clear to students of growth. Electricity and IT are, to most observers, the two most important GPTs to date, or at least they seem so according to the three criteria that Bresnahan and Trajtenberg proposed. In this chapter we have analyzed how the U.S. economy reacted to the creation of these two GPTs. Having discussed in detail GPTs with reference to the Electrification and IT eras, we believe that we have shown that the concept is a good way to organize how we think of technological change and its effects.

The Electricity and IT eras differ in some important ways. Electrification was more broadly adopted, whereas IT seems to be technologically more revolutionary. The productivity slowdown is stronger in the IT era but the ongoing spread of IT and its continuing precipitous price decline are reasons for optimism about growth in the coming decades relative to what happened in the middle of the 20th century following the spread of Electricity. But it is the similarities between the two epochs that are the most instructive and that will guide our expectations about how the next GPT will affect economic life when it comes along.

Acknowledgements

We thank Jason Cummins, Bart Hobijn, Josh Lerner and Gianluca Violante for providing us with some of the data used here. This research was supported in part by National Science Foundation Grant No. 30-3207-00-0079-286.

References

Atkeson, A., Kehoe, P.J. (1993). "Industry evolution and transition: The role of information capital". Staff Report No. 162. Federal Reserve Bank of Minneapolis, Minneapolis, MN.

Atkinson, T.R. (1967). Trends in Corporate Bond Quality. With the assistance of E.T. Simpson. Columbia University Press, New York, for National Bureau of Economic Research.

Bahk, B.H., Gort, M. (1993). "Decomposing learning by doing in plants". Journal of Political Economy 101, 561–583.

Bartel, A., Lichtenberg, F. (1987). "The comparative advantage of educated workers in implementing new technology". Review of Economics and Statistics 69, 1–11.

Berndt, E.R., Dulberger, E.R., Rappaport, N.J. (2000). "Price and quality of desktop and mobile personal computers: A quarter century of history". Working paper. MIT Sloan School, Cambridge, MA.

Berry, T.S. (1988). "Production and population since 1789: Revised GNP series in constant dollars". Bostwick Paper No. 6. The Bostwick Press, Richmond, VA.

Bessen, J. (2002). "Technology adoption costs and productivity growth: The 70's as a technology transition". Review of Economic Dynamics 5, 443–469.

Board of Governors of the Federal Reserve System (1976). Banking and Monetary Statistics 1914–1941. Board of Governors of the Federal Reserve System, Washington, DC.

Boldrin, M., Levine, D.K. (2001). "Growth cycles and market crashes". Journal of Economic Theory 96, 13–39.

Bradstreet Co. (1885–1925). Bradstreet's. Bradstreet Co., New York.

Brady, D.S. (1966). "Price deflators for final product estimates". In: Brady, D.S. (Ed.), Output, Employment, and Productivity in the United States After 1800. Columbia University Press, New York, pp. 91–116.

Bresnahan, T.F., Trajtenberg, M. (1996). "General purpose technologies: 'engines of growth'?". Journal of Econometrics, Annals of Econometrics 65, 83–108.

Caballero, R.J., Hammour, M.L. (1994). "The cleansing effect of recessions". American Economic Review 84, 1350–1368.

Comin, D. (2002). "Comments on James Bessen's 'Technology adoption costs and productivity growth: The 70's as a technology transition'". Review of Economic Dynamics 5, 470–476.

The Commercial and Financial Chronicle (1885–1925).

Cowles, A., Associates (1939). Common Stock Price Indexes. Cowles Commission for Research in Economics, Monograph No. 3, second ed. Principia Press, Bloomington, IN.

Cummins, J.G., Violante, G.L. (2002). "Investment specific technical change in the United States (1947–2000): Measurement and macroeconomic consequences". Review of Economic Dynamics 5, 243–284.

David, P. (1991). "Computer and dynamo: The modern productivity paradox in a not-too-distant mirror". In: Technology and Productivity: The Challenge for Economic Policy. OECD, Paris, pp. 315–347.

Devine, W.D. (1983). "From shafts to wires: Historical perspectives on electrification". Journal of Economic History 43, 347–372.

Dow Jones and Company, Inc. (1997–2004). The Wall Street Journal. Dow Jones, New York.

DuBoff, R.B. (1964). "Electric power in American manufacturing, 1889–1958". Ph.D. Dissertation. University of Pennsylvania.

Dun and Bradstreet, Inc. (2003). D&B Million Dollar Directory. Dun and Bradstreet, Inc., Bethlehem, PA.

Feder, B. (1988). "Advances in drugs, courtesy of computers". New York Times (August 3), 5.

Federal Reserve Bank of St. Louis (2004). FRED Database. Federal Reserve Bank of St. Louis, St. Louis, MO.

Gates, B. (1999). Business @ the Speed of Thought. Warner Books, New York.

Goldin, C., Katz, L.F. (1999a). "The shaping of higher education: The formative years in the United States, 1890 to 1940". Journal of Economic Perspectives 13, 37–62.

Goldin, C., Katz, L.F. (1999b). "The returns to skill in the United States across the twentieth century". Working Paper No. 7126. National Bureau of Economic Research, Cambridge, MA.

Gordon, R.J. (1990). The Measurement of Durable Goods Prices. University of Chicago Press, Chicago, IL.

Gordon, R.J. (2000). "Does the 'new economy' measure up to the great inventions of the past?". Journal of Economic Perspectives 14, 49–74.

Gort, M. (1969). "An economic disturbance theory of mergers". Quarterly Journal of Economics 94, 624–642.

Greenwood, J., Jovanovic, B. (1999). "The information-technology revolution and the stock market". American Economic Review Papers and Proceedings 89, 116–122.

Greenwood, J., Jovanovic, B. (2001). "Accounting for growth". In: Hulten, C.R., Dean, E.R., Harper, M.J. (Eds.), New Developments in Productivity Analysis. University of Chicago Press, Chicago, IL, for National Bureau of Economic Research, pp. 179–222.

Greenwood, J., Seshadri, A., Yorukoglu, M. (2002). "Engines of liberation". Economie d'Avant Guarde 2.

Greenwood, J., Yorukoglu, M. (1997). "1974". Carnegie–Rochester Conference Series on Public Policy 46, 49–95.

Griliches, Z. (1957). "Hybrid corn: An exploration in the economics of technological change". Econometrica 25, 501–522.

Griliches, Z. (1969). "Capital-skill complementarity". Review of Economics and Statistics 51, 465–468.

Helpman, E., Trajtenberg, M. (1998a). "A time to sow and a time to reap: Growth based on general purpose technologies". In: Helpman, E. (Ed.), General Purpose Technologies and Economic Growth. MIT Press, Cambridge, MA, pp. 55–83.

Helpman, E., Trajtenberg, M. (1998b). "The diffusion of general purpose technologies". In: Helpman, E. (Ed.), General Purpose Technologies and Economic Growth. MIT Press, Cambridge, MA, pp. 85–119.

Hickman, W.B. (1958). Corporate Bond Quality and Investor Experience. Princeton University Press, Princeton, NJ, for National Bureau of Economic Research.

Hobijn, B., Jovanovic, B. (2001). "The IT revolution and the stock market: Evidence". American Economic Review 91, 1203–1220.

Homer, S., Sylla, R. (1991). A History of Interest Rates, third ed. Rutgers University Press, New Brunswick, NJ.

Hoover's, Inc. (2000). Hoover's Online: The Business Network. Hoover's, Inc., Austin, TX.

Hopenhayn, H.A. (1992). "Entry, exit, and firm dynamics in long run equilibrium". Econometrica 60, 1127–1150.

Hornstein, A., Krusell, P. (1996). "Can technology improvements cause productivity slowdowns?". NBER Macroeconomics Annual 1996, 209–259.

Jovanovic, B., Nyarko, Y. (1996). "Learning by doing and the choice of technology". Econometrica 64, 1299–1310.

Jovanovic, B., Rousseau, P.L. (2001). "Why wait? A century of life before IPO". American Economic Review Papers and Proceedings 91, 336–341.

Jovanovic, B., Rousseau, P.L. (2002a). "Moore's law and learning-by-doing". Review of Economic Dynamics 4, 346–375.

Jovanovic, B., Rousseau, P.L. (2002b). "The Q-theory of mergers". American Economic Review Papers and Proceedings 92, 198–204.

Jovanovic, B., Rousseau, P.L. (2002c). "Mergers as reallocation". Working Paper No. 9277. National Bureau of Economic Research, Cambridge, MA.

Kelley, E.M. (1954). The Business Founding Date Directory. Morgan and Morgan, Scarsdale, NY.

Kendrick, J. (1961). Productivity Trends in the United States. Princeton University Press, Princeton, NJ.

Kortum, S., Lerner, J. (1998). "Stronger protection or technological revolution: What is behind the recent surge in patenting?". Carnegie–Rochester Conference Series on Public Policy 48, 247–304.

Krusell, P., Ohanian, L.E., Rios-Rull, J.V., Violante, G.L. (2000). "Capital-skill complementarity and inequality: A macroeconomic analysis". Econometrica 68, 1029–1053.

Kuznets, S. (1961a). Capital in the American Economy: Its Formation and Financing. Princeton University Press, Princeton, NJ.

Kuznets, S. (1961b). "Annual estimates, 1869–1955". Manuscript. Johns Hopkins University, Baltimore, MD.

Laitner, J., Stolyarov, D. (2003). "Technological change and the stock market". American Economic Review 93, 1240–1267.

Lerner, J. (2000). "150 years of patent protection". Working Paper. National Bureau of Economic Research, Cambridge, MA.

Lichtenberg, F., Siegel, D. (1987). "Productivity and changes in ownership of manufacturing plants". Brookings Papers on Economic Activity 3, 643–673. Special Issue on Microeconomics.

McGuckin, R., Ngyen, S. (1995). "On productivity and plant ownership change: New evidence form the longitudinal research database". RAND Journal of Economics 26, 257–276.

Moody's Investors Service (1920, 1928, 1955, 1980). Moody's Industrial Manual. Moody's Investors Service, New York.

Nelson, R.L. (1959). Merger Movements in American Industry, 1895–1956. Princeton University Press, Princeton, NJ, for National Bureau of Economic Research.

Nelson, R., Phelps, E. (1966). "Investment in humans, technological diffusion, and economic growth". American Economic Review 56, 69–79.

The New York Times Co. (1897–1928). The New York Times. The New York Times Co., New York.

The New York Times Co. (1913–1925). The Annalist: A Magazine of Finance, Commerce, and Economics. The New York Times Co., New York.

Rousseau, P.L. (1999). "Share liquidity and industrial growth in an emerging market: The case of New England, 1854–1897". Historical Working Paper No. 103. National Bureau of Economic Research, Cambridge, MA.

Schoar, A. (2002). "Effects of corporate diversification on productivity". Journal of Finance 57, 2379–2403.

Schwert, G.W. (2000). "Hostility in takeovers: In the eyes of the beholder?". Journal of Finance 55, 2599–2640.

Standard and Poor's Corporation (1981, 1988, 2000). Stock Market Encyclopedia. Standard and Poor's Corporation, New York.

Standard and Poor's Corporation (1971–2003). Stock Reports. Standard and Poor's Corporation, New York.

United States Bureau of the Census, Department of Commerce (1975). Historical Statistics of the United States, Colonial Times to 1970. Government Printing Office, Washington, DC.

United States Bureau of the Census, Department of Commerce (1980, 1992, 2003). Statistical Abstract of the United States. Government Printing Office, Washington, DC.

United States Bureau of the Census, Department of Commerce (2000–2004). Current Population Survey. Government Printing Office, Washington, DC.

United States Bureau of Economic Analysis (2002). Survey of Current Business. Government Printing Office, Washington, DC.

United States Bureau of Economic Analysis (2004). Survey of Current Business. Government Printing Office, Washington, DC.

University of Chicago Center for Research on Securities Prices (2004). CRSP Database. University of Chicago Center for Research on Securities Prices, Chicago, IL.

Wiggins, S.N., Raboy, D.G. (1996). "Price premia to name brands: An empirical analysis". Journal of Industrial Economics 44, 377–388.

Williamson, J.G., Lindert, P.H. (1980). American Inequality: A Macroeconomic History. Academic Press, New York.

Wilson, J.W., Jones, C.P. (2002). "An analysis of the S&P 500 index and Cowles's extensions: Price indexes and stock returns, 1870–1999". Journal of Business 75, 505–533.

Chapter 19

TECHNOLOGICAL PROGRESS AND ECONOMIC TRANSFORMATION

JEREMY GREENWOOD

University of Rochester

ANANTH SESHADRI

University of Wisconsin

Contents

Abstract	1226
Keywords	1226
1. Introduction	1227
1.1. Technological progress in the market	1227
1.2. Technological progress in the home	1229
1.3. The goal	1230
2. The baby bust and baby boom	1231
2.1. The environment	1231
2.2. Analysis	1233
3. The U.S. demographic transition	1238
3.1. The environment	1238
3.2. Analysis	1242
4. The demise of child labor	1246
4.1. The environment	1247
4.2. Analysis	1248
5. Engines of liberation	1250
5.1. The environment	1252
5.2. Analysis	1254
5.3. Analysis with nondurable household products and services	1258
6. Conclusion	1260
7. Literature review	1261
7.1. Fertility	1261
7.2. The economics of household production	1262
7.3. Structural change	1263

Handbook of Economic Growth, Volume 1B. Edited by Philippe Aghion and Steven N. Durlauf
© 2005 Elsevier B.V. All rights reserved
DOI: 10.1016/S1574-0684(05)01019-1

7.4. Child labor   1264
7.5. Female labor-force participation   1266
Acknowledgements   1268
Appendix: 1268
A.1. Supporting calculations for Lemmas 2 and 4   1268
A.2. Supporting calculations for Lemmas 5 and 6   1270
References   1271

Abstract

Growth theory can go a long way toward accounting for phenomena linked with U.S. economic development. Some examples are:

(i)   the secular decline in fertility between 1800 and 1980,
(ii) the decline in agricultural employment and the rise in skill since 1800,
(iii) the demise of child labor starting around 1900,
(iv) the increase in female labor-force participation from 1900 to 1980,
(v)   the baby boom from 1936 to 1972.

Growth theory models are presented to address all of these facts. The analysis emphasizes the role of technological progress as a catalyst for economic transformation.

Keywords

child labor, economic growth, educational attainment, female labor-force participation, fertility, household production theory, technological progress

JEL classification: D1, E1, J1, O3

1. Introduction

Life in the 1800s. Imagine living as a typical American child in the nineteenth century. You have six brothers and/or sisters. You live in a house, outside of an urban area, with no running water, no central heating, and no electricity. Your father labors 70 hours a week in the agricultural economy. Your mother probably puts in about the same amount of time doing work at home. Less than half of your years between the ages of 5 and 20 will be devoted to school. So, perhaps you are playing in the family kitchen that contains a cast iron range, a table, and a dresser. But, more likely you are helping your parents by doing one of a litany of chores: carrying wood or water into the house, washing clothes on a scrub board or ironing them with a flat iron, looking after younger siblings, preparing meals, cleaning the house, making clothes, tending crops or animals, etc. In this era, household production is an incredibly labor-intensive process. What changed this situation? The catalyst for the ensuing economic transformation to modern day life was technological progress, both in the market and at home, or so it will be argued here.

1.1. Technological progress in the market

Fertility. Over the period from 1830 to 1990 real wages increased by a factor of 9 – see Figure 1.[1] This rise was propelled by a near 7-fold increase in market-sector total factor productivity (TFP) between 1800 and 1990. Such tremendous technological advance had a dramatic impact on everyday life. As an example, consider the effect that economic progress could have had on fertility. Raising children takes time. A secular increase in real wages implies that the opportunity cost of having a child, when measured in terms of market goods, will rise. The utility value of an extra unit of market consumption relative to an extra child should fall, however, as market goods become more abundant with economic development. So long as the marginal utility of market goods falls by less than the increase in real wages fertility should decline. And so fertility did decline, from 7 kids per woman in 1800 to 2 today.

Industrialization and skilled labor. At the start of the 1800s America was largely a rural economy. Over seventy percent of workers were employed in agriculture – see Figure 2.[2] Less than 50 percent of children between the ages of 5 and 20 went to school. From 1800 to 1940 technological advance in the nonagricultural sector of the U.S. economy was twice as fast as in the agricultural sector. Furthermore, agricultural goods had a lower income elasticity than nonagricultural ones. These two facts together implied that the demand for labor in the nonagricultural sector of the economy rose relative to the demand for labor in the agricultural sector. Since the nonagricultural sector required

---

[1] The data sources used in Figure 1 are given in Greenwood, Seshadri and Vandenbroucke (2005).

[2] The enrollment rate figures come from "Historical Statistics of the United States: Colonial Times to 1970" [U.S. Bureau of the Census (1975, Series H 433)]. See Greenwood and Seshadri (2002) for the sources of the other data plotted in Figure 2.

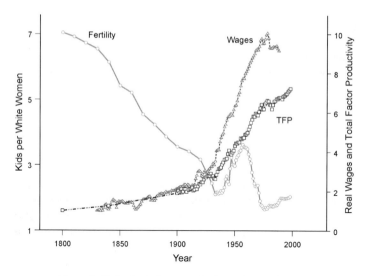

Figure 1. Technological progress in the market and fertility.

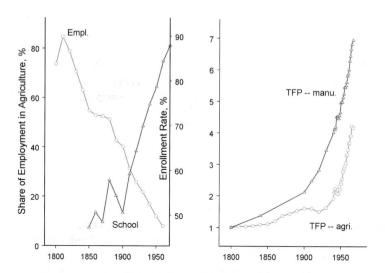

Figure 2. The decline in agriculture and the rise in skilled labor.

a more skill-intensive labor force than did the agricultural sector, the demand for skilled labor rose too.

Child labor. Children formed an important part of the labor force in the nineteenth century. Exact numbers are hard to come by, though. First, the data before 1870 is scarce. Lebergott (1964, p. 50) reports that 43 percent of textile workers in Massa-

Table 1
Children aged 10–15 as percentage of the gainfully employed

Year	All occupations	Agriculture	Manufacturing	Mining
1870	13.2	9.3	5.6	7.1
1880	16.8	11.6	6.7	
1890	18.1	11.5	2.8	
1900	18.2	11.4	3.2	2.1
1910	15.0	9.8	2.4	0.8
1920	11.3	8.0	1.3	<1.0
1930	4.7	3.3	<1.0	<1.0

Source: Lebergott (1964, p. 53).

chusetts around 1820 were children, as were 47 and 55 percent in Connecticut and Rhode Island. Second, the available figures pertain to paid labor. These statistics omit the labors of children on family farms and businesses, or around the home – the same is true for housewives of the era. The incidence of child labor rose until 1900, as Table 1 shows. At that time children made up about 20 percent of the paid labor force. It then began to decline. By 1930 child labor had vanished.

A reasonable hypothesis is that technological progress reduced the need for unskilled labor in agriculture and manufacturing. Take agriculture, for example, where the late nineteenth and early twentieth centuries saw massive improvements in agricultural technology. Two of the most important inventions were the horse-drawn harvester in the mid-nineteenth century and the tractor that began to diffuse into American farms in the early twentieth century. Mechanization of farms virtually eliminated the need for raw labor: In 1830, it would take a farmer 250–300 hours to produce 100 bushels of wheat; in 1890, 40–50 hours with the help of a horse-drawn machine; in 1930, 15–20 hours with a tractor; and in 1975, 3–4 hours with large tractors and combines.[3]

1.2. Technological progress in the home

Female labor-force participation. Just as the last 200 years have witnessed technological progress in the market sector, they have witnessed tremendous technological advance in the home sector. Since productivity numbers are not computed for the home sector, given the elusive nature of output and inputs, the evidence on technological progress is circumstantial. The household sector in the American economy was basically a cottage industry until the dawning of the Second Industrial Revolution. With the onset of the electric age a host of new appliances were ushered in: washing machines, refrigerators, etc. It took time for these new capital goods to diffuse through the econ-

---

[3] *Source*: U.S. Department of Agriculture.

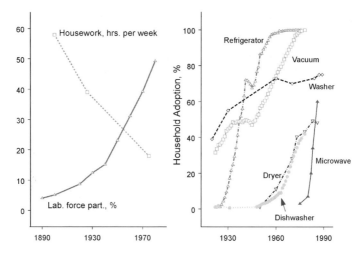

Figure 3. Technological progress in the home and female labor-force participation.

omy, as Figure 3 shows.[4] At the same time, the principles of scientific management were being applied to everyday household tasks. The large table and isolated dresser that characterized a kitchen of the 1800s were replaced by continuous countertops and built-in cabinets. This wave of technological progress in the home freed up tremendous amounts of labor – see Figure 3. The time spent on housework fell from 58 hours per week in 1900 to just 18 in 1975. Married women could now enter the labor force, and they did in droves.

Fertility.   Technological progress in the household sector could also have had implications for fertility. Labor-saving household goods that ease the burden of housework will lower the cost of raising children. Fertility should rise. In fact it did; between 1936 and 1957 fertility increased by 53 percent – see Figure 1.

1.3. The goal

The goal here is to persuade you that standard Solow (1956)–Ramsey (1928) growth theory can be fruitfully employed to explain these phenomena. Specifically, all of these facts can be accounted for by modifying the standard growth paradigm to incorporate fertility decisions, household production, human capital investment in children, labor-force participation, and multiple sectors. It will be argued that technological progress is the engine driving economic transformation. A selective review of the literature is provided in Section 7.

---

[4] The data sources for the Figure 3 are provided in Greenwood, Seshadri and Yorukoglu (2005).

2. The baby bust and baby boom

Two facts stand out about the fertility of American women. First, it has dropped drastically over the last two hundred years. This decline is called the demographic transition, but will be labeled here the baby bust. Second, the secular decline in fertility has had only one interruption, the baby boom. These two facts can easily be accounted for within the context of the neoclassical growth model. Just two modifications to the standard model are required: a fertility decision needs to be added, and household production incorporated.

2.1. The environment

Imagine a small open economy populated by overlapping generations.[5] People live for three periods, one period as children and two as adults. Young adults are endowed with one unit of time. They can use this time for either working or raising kids. An individual is fecund only in the first period of adulthood. Old agents are retired.

Tastes. The lifetime utility function for a young adult is given by

$$\phi \ln(c^y + \mathfrak{c}) + \beta\phi \ln(c^{o\prime}) + (1 + \beta)(1 - \phi) \ln n^y, \tag{1}$$

where c^y and $c^{o\prime}$ denote the adult's consumption when young and old, and n^y represents the number of kids that he would like to have when young. The constant $\mathfrak{c}$ proxies for the household production of market goods. As will be seen, it plays an important role in the analysis.

Income. Young agents work for the market wage w. They save for old age at the internationally determined time-invariant *gross* interest rate r.

Cost of children. Children are expensive. The production function for children is given by

$$n^y = x(l^y)^{1-\gamma}, \tag{2}$$

where l^y is the time a young adult devotes to raising children and x is the level of productivity in the home sector. The consumption cost, k, of raising n^y kids is therefore given by

$$k = w\left(\frac{n^y}{x}\right)^{1/(1-\gamma)}.$$

The cost of raising children is directly proportional to the wage rate.

---

[5] The model presented here is based on Greenwood, Seshadri and Vandenbroucke (2005).

The young agent's choice problem. The decision problem facing a young adult is

$$\max_{c^y,c^{o\prime},n^y} \left\{ \phi \ln\left(c^y + \mathfrak{c}\right) + \beta\phi \ln\left(c^{o\prime}\right) + (1 + \beta)(1 - \phi) \ln n^y \right\}$$

subject to

$$c^y + \frac{c^{o\prime}}{r} = w - w\left(\frac{n^y}{x}\right)^{1/(1-\gamma)}.$$

The Euler equation for consumption is

$$\frac{1}{c^y + \mathfrak{c}} = \beta r \frac{1}{c^{o\prime}}$$

which can be rewritten as

$$c^{o\prime} = \beta r\left(c^y + \mathfrak{c}\right). \tag{3}$$

This equation simply states that consumption of market goods over the household's lifetime will grow at the (gross) rate βr. If the gross rate of interest, r, exceeds the gross rate of time preference, $1/\beta$, consumption increases over the household's lifetime, and likewise will decline when $r < 1/\beta$.

The above optimization problem can be reformulated using (3) to appear as

$$\max_{c^y,n^y}\left\{(1 + \beta)\left[\phi \ln\left(c^y + \mathfrak{c}\right) + (1 - \phi) \ln n^y\right] + \beta\phi \ln(\beta r)\right\} \tag{4}$$

subject to

$$c^y + \mathfrak{c} = \frac{1}{1 + \beta}\left[w - w\left(\frac{n^y}{x}\right)^{1/(1-\gamma)} + \mathfrak{c}\right]. \tag{5}$$

The first-order condition to this problem is

$$\frac{\phi}{c^y + \mathfrak{c}}\frac{1}{1 + \beta}\frac{1}{1 - \gamma}wx^{-1/(1-\gamma)}\left(n^y\right)^{\gamma/(1-\gamma)} = \frac{1 - \phi}{n^y}. \tag{6}$$

The right-hand side of this equation gives the marginal benefit from having an extra kid. The left-hand side represents the marginal cost. This is the product of two components. Having an extra child necessitates working less in the market. This will lead to a sacrifice in terms of market consumption in the amount $[(1 + \beta) \times (1 - \gamma)]^{-1}wx^{-1/(1-\gamma)}(n^y)^{\gamma/(1-\gamma)}$. The marginal utility derived from an extra unit of consumption is $\phi/(c^y + \mathfrak{c})$.

The firm's problem. Let market output, o, be produced in line with the following production function:

$$o = zk^\alpha l^{1-\alpha},$$

where k and l are the inputs of capital and labor used in production and z is the level of productivity in the market sector. Now, suppose that capital depreciates fully after use in production. The rental rate on capital will then be r, since it must yield the same return as a bond. The problem facing the firm is therefore given by

$$\max_{k,l}\{zk^\alpha l^{1-\alpha} - rk - wl\}.$$

The first-order conditions connected to this problem are

$$\alpha zk^{\alpha-1}l^{1-\alpha} = r \tag{7}$$

and

$$(1-\alpha)zk^\alpha l^{-\alpha} = w. \tag{8}$$

These first-order conditions simply state that each factor gets paid its marginal product. By substituting Equation (7) into (8), it is easy to see that

$$w = (1-\alpha)\alpha^{\alpha/(1-\alpha)}z^{1/(1-\alpha)}r^{-\alpha/(1-\alpha)}. \tag{9}$$

Hence, the wage rate, w, is determined by the level of market productivity z and the international rate of return on capital r.

Population growth. Let s^y and s^o stand for the current sizes of the young and old adult populations, respectively. Since today's young generation will be tomorrow's old generation it must transpire that

$$s^{o\prime} = s^y, \tag{10}$$

where a prime affixed to a variable denotes its value next period. Now, each young adult has n^y kids so the size of next period's young generation is given by

$$s^{y\prime} = n^y s^y. \tag{11}$$

2.2. Analysis

LEMMA 1. *Fertility, n^y, decreases with market wages w and increases with the state of technology in the home sector, x.*

PROOF. Take the first-order condition for n^y, or (6), and rewrite it as

$$n^y = A^{1-\gamma}x\left[\frac{c^y + \mathfrak{c}}{w}\right]^{1-\gamma}, \tag{12}$$

where

$$A \equiv \frac{(1+\beta)(1-\gamma)(1-\phi)}{\phi}.$$

Plugging the above equation into the budget constraint (5) yields

$$c^y + \mathfrak{c} = \frac{1}{1+\beta+A}(w+\mathfrak{c}).$$

Last, using the solution for $c^y + c$ in (12) generates

$$n^y = \left[\frac{A}{1+\beta+A}\right]^{1-\gamma} x\left(1+\frac{c}{w}\right)^{1-\gamma}. \tag{13}$$

The proof is now complete since it is trivial to see that n^y is decreasing in w and increasing in x. □

Intuition. With the aid of some diagrams, it is easy to ferret out the intuition underlying the above lemma. First, observe that (5) specifies the consumption possibilities frontier facing the household. The slope of the frontier is

$$\frac{d(c^y + c)}{dn^y} = -w\left(\frac{1}{x}\right)^{1/(1-\gamma)} \frac{(n^y)^{\gamma/(1-\gamma)}}{(1+\beta)(1-\gamma)} \leqslant 0. \tag{14}$$

This is shown in Figure 4 by the concave consumption possibilities frontier, labeled PP. The frontier hits the vertical axis at the point $c^y + c = [w+c]/(1+\beta)$, and the horizontal one at $n^y = x(1+c/w)^{1-\gamma}$.

The objective function (4) defines indifference curves over the various $(n^y, c^y + c)$ combinations. The slope of an indifference curve is given by

$$\left.\frac{d(c^y + c)}{dn^y}\right|_{\text{utility constant}} = -\frac{(1-\phi)}{\phi}\frac{c^y + c}{n^y} \leqslant 0. \tag{15}$$

The equilibrium level of fertility and market consumption are shown in standard fashion by the point $(n^{y*}, c^{y*} + c)$ where the indifference curve is tangent to the consumption possibilities frontier – see Figure 4.

Let wages increase by a factor of λ and assume that $c = 0$. In response, the consumption possibilities frontier will rotate upwards from the curve PP, by a factor of λ, to the

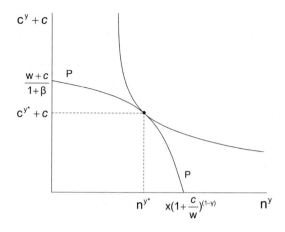

Figure 4. The determination of fertility.

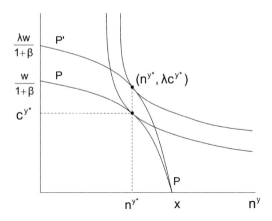

Figure 5. The effect of an increase in wages on fertility when $\mathfrak{c} = 0$.

position shown by the curve $P'P$ – see Figure 5. Thus, there is a positive income effect associated with an increase in wages. The slope of the consumption possibilities curve will increase by a factor of λ at any n^y point, too, as is evident from (14). That is, the marginal cost of an extra child rises. This effect should operate to reduce fertility. It is easy to deduce that consumption, c^y, will move up by a factor of λ and that fertility, n^y, will remain constant. This transpires because the substitution and income effects on fertility from an increase in wages exactly cancel out, an artifice of the logarithmic form of preferences adopted in (1). To see this, note that along any vertical line the slopes of the indifference curves increase in proportion with the increases in c^y, as is clear from (15). The slope of the indifference curve at the point $(n^{y*}, \lambda c^{y*})$ is higher by a factor of exactly λ relative to the slope of the curve at the point (n^{y*}, c^{y*}).

Now suppose that wages jump up by a factor of λ and assume that $\mathfrak{c} > 0$. The consumption possibilities frontier no longer shifts upwards in a proportional manner. The horizontal intercept now shifts in – see Figure 6. A higher wage rate implies that the household production of market goods, $\mathfrak{c}$, now frees up less time for kids. As can be seen, fertility must unambiguously fall from n^{y*} to $n^{y*'}$. Why? Suppose that fertility remains fixed at its old level n^{y*} and that consumption once again rises by a factor of λ, say from c^{y*} to λc^{y*}. (Note that c^{y*} and λc^{y*} are not labeled on the diagram.) The slope of the consumption possibilities frontier will once again increase by a factor of λ, in line with (14). The slope of the indifference curve through the point $(n^{y*}, \lambda c^{y*} + \mathfrak{c})$ will increase by less, though, due to the presence of the $\mathfrak{c}$ term in preferences – see (15) and the dashed indifference curve in Figure 6. Hence, a point of tangency cannot occur. At the margin a parent is willing to give up a child for $[(1 - \phi)/\phi](\lambda c^{y*} + \mathfrak{c})/n^{y*}$ units of consumption. According to his production possibilities he can get $\lambda w(1/x)^{1/(1-\gamma)}(n^{y*})^{\gamma/(1-\gamma)}/[(1 + \beta)(1 - \gamma)]$ units of consumption for an incremental cut in fertility. Now, $[(1 - \phi)/\phi](\lambda c^{y*} + \mathfrak{c})/n^{y*} < \lambda w(1/x)^{1/(1-\gamma)}(n^{y*})^{\gamma/(1-\gamma)}/[(1 + \beta)(1 - \gamma)]$, since $[(1 - \phi)/\phi](c^{y*} + \mathfrak{c})/n^{y*} =$

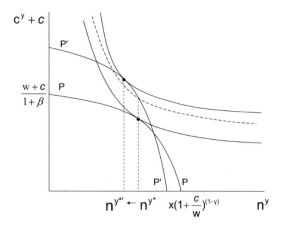

Figure 6. The effect of wages on fertility when $c \neq 0$.

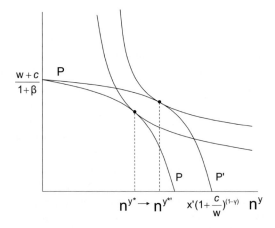

Figure 7. The effect of an improvement in household technology on fertility.

$w(1/x)^{1/(1-\gamma)}(n^{y*})^{\gamma/(1-\gamma)}/[(1+\beta)(1-\gamma)]$. Therefore, he should cut his level of fertility. In other words, when $c > 0$ the substitution effect from an increase in w outweighs the income effect.

Last, consider the effect of technological progress in the household sector. An increase in x shifts the consumption possibilities frontier outwards in the manner shown by Figure 7 (from PP to PP'). At any n^y point the consumption possibilities curve becomes less steep since the consumption cost of an extra kid falls. As a result, both the income and substitution effects operate to increase fertility. (Since kids are a normal good, as one moves upwards along any vertical line the slopes of the indifference curves increase. This implies that the new consumption point must lie to right of n^y.)

COROLLARY. *Fertility, n^y, is decreasing in the level of market productivity z. (Fertility is increasing in the international rate of return r.)*

PROOF. Substitute Equation (9) into (13) to get

$$n^y = \left[\frac{A}{1 + \beta + A} \right]^{1-\gamma} x \left[\frac{1 + c\alpha^{-\alpha/(1-\alpha)} z^{-1/(1-\alpha)} r^{\alpha/(1-\alpha)}}{1 - \alpha} \right]^{1-\gamma}. \tag{16}$$

The desired result is now immediate.[6]   □

The baby bust.   Now, suppose that market productivity is advancing over time at the constant rate $z'/z = \zeta > 1$. Wages must be growing at the constant rate $\zeta^{1/(1-\alpha)} > 1$, a fact evident from (9). Assume that there is no technological progress in the home sector. Fertility declines monotonically over time, as is immediate from (13). Since w is growing at a constant rate it must transpire that $c/w \to 0$ over time. Therefore, fertility converges from above to

$$n^y = \left[\frac{A}{1 + \beta + A} \right]^{1-\gamma} x.$$

Observe that

$$n^y \gtrless 1 \quad \text{as} \quad x \gtrless \left[\frac{1 + \beta + A}{A} \right]^{1-\gamma}.$$

Using (10) and (11) it is easy to see that the long-run growth rate of the population can be expressed as

$$\frac{s^{y\prime} + s^{o\prime}}{s^y + s^o} = \frac{n^y s^y + s^y}{s^y + s^y/n^y} = \frac{n^y + 1}{1 + 1/n^y} = n^y.$$

Hence, in the long-run the population may grow or shrink depending on the value of x.

EXAMPLE 1 (Fertility, 1800 and 1940). Assign the following parameter values to the model.
  (i) Tastes: $\beta = 0.94^{20}$, $\phi = 0.47$, $c = 2.97$.
  (ii) Technology: $\alpha = 0.33$, $\gamma = 0.33$, $r = 1/\beta$.
Normalize the level of market and home productivity for the year 1800 to be unity. That is, set $x = z = 1.0$ for 1800. With this configuration of parameter values, Equation (16) predicts that the level of fertility per adult should be 3.5, exactly the value observed in the U.S. in 1800 – at that time a married couple experienced 7 births on average. Now, between 1800 and 1940 market productivity grew by a factor of 3.5. So, reset z to equal 3.5 for 1940. The model predicts that fertility should fall to 1.2. It actually fell to 1.1.

---

[6] The intuition is obvious since w, the wage rate, is increasing in z and decreasing in r.

The baby boom. Once again presume that market productivity is growing over time at the constant rate $z'/z = \zeta > 1$. Now imagine that a once-and-for-all jump in household productivity happens. According to (13), fertility will jump up on this account. After this innovation fertility will revert back to its old time path of monotonic decline.

EXAMPLE 2 (Fertility, 1960 and 2000). Keep the parameter values from the previous example. U.S. fertility per prime-age adult (males plus females) rose from 1.1 to 1.8 between 1940 and 1960. This was the baby boom. By 1960 market-sector TFP had risen to 4.9, so now reset $z = 4.9$ for 1960. Using (16) it is easy to deduce that a fertility rate of 1.8 can be obtained by letting $x = 1.8$. That is, the baby boom can be generated by assuming that household-sector productivity grew by a factor 1.8 between 1940 and 1960. Finally, U.S. TFP had risen to 7.4 by the year 2000. The model predicts that the fertility rate should be 1.5, as opposed to the observed rate of 1.0.

3. The U.S. demographic transition

At the start of the nineteenth century most adult males worked in the agricultural sector and children got very little in the way of a formal education. By the end of the twentieth century almost no adult worked in agriculture, at least relative to nonagriculture. The average child received about 13 years of formal education. To address these facts, a two-sector version of the standard neoclassical growth model will be employed. One sector will represent agriculture, the other manufacturing. Agriculture hires unskilled workers while manufacturing employs skilled ones. In the framework developed, parents will decide upon both the number of children to have and the level of education for their offspring. The idea is that as manufacturing expands relative to agriculture, the demand for skilled labor rises. This entices parents to provide more education for their children. Since education is costly, they choose to have less kids too.

3.1. The environment

Take the setup of the previous section with two slight modifications.[7] First, assume that parents now care about the quality of their children in addition to the quantity of them. Second, suppose that there are two production sectors in the economy. One sector uses solely skilled labor, the other only unskilled workers. A unit of skilled labor earns the wage v, while a unit of unskilled labor gets w. A parent must choose the skill level to endow his offspring with (or the quality of his children).

---

[7] The model presented below is a simplified version of Greenwood and Seshadri (2002). Some aspects of the framework also bear a resemblance to Hansen and Prescott (2002) and Fernandez-Villaverde (2001).

Tastes. A young adult's preferences are described by

$$\psi \ln(c^y) + \beta \psi \ln(c^{o'}) + (1+\beta)\chi \ln n^y + (1+\beta)\chi \ln\left[w'(1-h') + v'h'\right], \quad (17)$$

with $0 \leqslant h' \leqslant 1$. This utility function is identical to (1), with two modifications. First, the children's skill level, h', now enters into the utility function. Other things equal, a parent would prefer to have skilled children because they will earn a higher wage when they grow up than unskilled children; i.e., $v' > w'$. In particular, a child's labor earnings are a weighted average of next period's skilled and unskilled wage rates, $w'(1-h') + v'h'$, where the weight on the skilled wage rate is the child's skill level. Second, the constant term c in (1) is now deleted. This term is responsible for getting fertility to fall as wages rise in the previous model – see (13). The current setup will rely instead on a quantity–quality trade-off in raising children to generate the decline in fertility.

Output. Suppose that consumption goods can be made using one of two production functions, a primitive technology, say agriculture, that converts unskilled labor into output

$$o^u = \frac{xu^\sigma}{\sigma},$$

and a modern technology, read manufacturing, that transforms skilled labor into output

$$o^s = \frac{zs^\sigma}{\sigma}.$$

In the above expressions o^u and o^s are the levels of output produced by the primitive and modern technologies, and s and u are the inputs of skilled and unskilled labor. Both technologies exhibit decreasing returns to scale. For simplicity, assume that each young adult owns a firm that can operate both of these technologies – hence the number of firms in the economy is the same as the number of young adults.

Budget constraint. The budget constraint for a young adult is

$$c^y + \frac{c^{o'}}{r} = \left(1 - \tau n^y - \phi n^y h'\right)\left[(1-h)w + hv + \pi\right]. \quad (18)$$

There are two types of costs associated with having children, connected with birth τ and education ϕ. These costs of having kids are expressed as fractions of family income. The young adult's skill level is represented by h (versus h' for his children). Since each *young* adult owns one of each type of production function he earns the profits, π, associated with operating them. Family income is $(1-h)w + hv + \pi$. The cost of having n^y children, plus providing each of them with the human capital level h', is $(\tau n^y + \phi n^y h')[(1-h)w + hv + \pi]$.

The young adult's choice problem.   The decision problem facing a young adult is

$$\max_{c^y,c^{o\prime},h',n^y} \{\psi \ln(c^y) + \beta\psi \ln(c^{o\prime}) + (1+\beta)\chi \ln n^y$$
$$+ (1+\beta)\chi \ln[w'(1-h') + v'h']\}$$

subject to (18). The Euler equation for consumption is given by

$$c^{o\prime} = r\beta c^y \tag{19}$$

which has the same intuition as (3). This allows the above problem to be restated as

$$\max_{c^y,h',n^y} \{\psi \ln(c^y) + \chi \ln n^y + \chi \ln[w'(1-h') + v'h']\} \tag{20}$$

subject to

$$c^y = (1 - \tau n^y - \phi n^y h')\frac{(1-h)w + hv + \pi}{1+\beta}.$$

The first-order conditions with respect to n^y and h' (after solving out for c^y) are

$$\frac{\psi(\tau + \phi h')}{(1 - \tau n^y - \phi n^y h')} = \frac{\chi}{n^y} \tag{21}$$

and

$$\frac{\psi \phi n^y}{(1 - \tau n^y - \phi n^y h')} = \frac{\chi(v' - w')}{w'(1-h') + v'h'}. \tag{22}$$

Dividing Equation (21) by Equation (22) yields

$$\frac{\tau + \phi h'}{\phi} = \frac{w'(1-h') + v'h'}{v' - w'},$$

which implies that

$$\frac{w'}{v'} = \frac{\tau}{\tau + \phi}. \tag{23}$$

In other words, tomorrow's skill premium is a constant, pinned down by the proportional costs for birth and education. Note that this follows directly from the assumption that quantity and quality have same weight χ in the utility function.

The firms' problems.   The firms in the agricultural and manufacturing sectors will solve the problems

$$\pi^u \equiv \max_u \left\{\frac{\chi u^\sigma}{\sigma} - wu\right\}$$

and

$$\pi^s \equiv \max_s \left\{\frac{z s^\sigma}{\sigma} - vs\right\}.$$

The first-order conditions associated with these problems are

$$w = xu^{\sigma-1} \tag{24}$$

and

$$v = zs^{\sigma-1}. \tag{25}$$

The profits earned by a young agent from operating these firms will be $\pi = \pi^u + \pi^s$.

Population growth.   Let s^y and s^o stand for the current sizes of the young and old adult populations, respectively. The manner in which these populations evolve is exactly the same as that in Section 2 and is given by Equations (10) and (11) – from here on out n^y will be replaced by n.

Labor market clearing conditions.   The markets for unskilled labor and skilled labor must clear each period. Consequently, the equations

$$u = (1 - h)$$

and

$$s = h \tag{26}$$

hold. (Recall that each young adult owns, and supplies labor, to his own firms.)

Equilibrium.   Using these two market clearing conditions in the firms' first-order conditions (24) and (25) yields

$$w = x\big[(1 - h)\big]^{\sigma-1} \tag{27}$$

and

$$v = z(h)^{\sigma-1}. \tag{28}$$

Substituting Equations (27) and (28) into (23) gives a single equation determining the human capital for a child, h',

$$x'(1 - h')^{\sigma-1} = \left(\frac{\tau}{\tau + \phi}\right)z'h'^{\sigma-1}. \tag{29}$$

The right-hand side implicitly represents the demand for skilled labor in the manufacturing sector.[8] The left-hand side specifies the supply of skilled labor available by

---

[8] It comes from (28), which implies that

$$h' = (z'/v')^{1/(1-\sigma)}.$$

As can be seen, the demand for skilled labor, h', is decreasing in the skilled wage v'.

freeing up workers from agriculture.[9] This equation can be solved to get a closed-form expression for the level of human capital that reads

$$h' = \frac{1}{1 + \omega(z'/x')^{1/(\sigma-1)}},$$ (30)

where $\omega \equiv [\tau/(\tau + \phi)]^{1/(\sigma-1)} > 1$.

3.2. Analysis

Now, imagine that the economy is resting in a steady state where z' and x' are constant. It is then easy to see from (30) that h' will be constant. Notice that if z' and x' were to increase at the same rate, h' would also remain unchanged. This result follows because identical increases in total factor productivity in both sectors leave unchanged the demand for each type of labor, given the constancy of the skill premium. This leaves unchanged the fraction of total labor allocated to each sector. So, when will human capital rise?

LEMMA 2. *As TFP in manufacturing, z, rises relative to agriculture x, human capital, h, increases and fertility, n, falls.*

PROOF. Using a backdated version of (30), it is easy to calculate that the derivative of h with respect to z/x is given by

$$\frac{\partial h}{\partial(z/x)} = \frac{1}{[1 + \omega(z/x)^{1/(\sigma-1)}]^2} \frac{\omega}{1-\sigma}(z/x)^{1/(\sigma-1)-1} > 0,$$ (31)

since $\sigma < 1$. Now, using (30), Equation (21) may be rewritten as

$$n = \frac{\chi}{(\psi + \chi)[\tau + \phi/(1 + \omega(z/x)^{1/(\sigma-1)})]}$$

$$= \frac{\chi}{\psi + \chi} \frac{1 + \omega(z/x)^{1/(\sigma-1)}}{[\tau + \phi + \tau\omega(z/x)^{1/(\sigma-1)}]}.$$

Hence,

$$\frac{\partial n}{\partial(z/x)} = -\frac{\chi}{\psi + \chi} \frac{1}{[\tau + \phi + \tau\omega(z/x)^{1/(\sigma-1)}]^2} \frac{\phi\omega}{1-\sigma}(z/x)^{1/(\sigma-1)-1} < 0.$$ (32)

□

---

[9] The left-hand side is based on (27). Equation (27) can be rewritten as

$$h' = 1 - (x'/w')^{1/(1-\sigma)}.$$

Hence, h' is increasing in the unskilled wage, or equivalently the skilled wage using (23).

The above lemma suggests that faster technological progress in the manufacturing sector, relative to the agricultural sector, increases the demand for skilled labor and this triggers a demographic transition and a rise in educational attainment. This accords well with U.S. historical experience.

What happens in the very long run?

LEMMA 3. *As* $z/x \to \infty$, *the agricultural sector vanishes or* $h \to 1$ *and fertility declines to its lower bound,* $n^* = \chi/[(\psi + \chi)(\tau + \phi)]$.

PROOF. From Equation (30), backdated, it is easy to see that $h \to 1$ as $z/x \to \infty$. Further, Equation (21) implies that $n \to n^* = \chi/[(\psi + \chi)(\tau + \phi)]$. □

Asymptotically, agriculture's share of GDP goes to zero as everyone in the economy becomes skilled. The economy eventually converges to a steady state where population grows at the constant rate n^*. One objection might be that, in reality, the ratio of manufacturing TFP to agricultural TFP has only grown two-fold or so during the last 200 years, thereby calling into question the importance of the above lemma. This is certainly true. A more realistic setup would have agricultural and manufacturing goods entering the utility function separately, with agricultural goods having a lower income elasticity of demand. As incomes rise, identical increases in z and x will reduce the demand for agricultural goods relative to manufacturing goods, at least in a closed economy. This creates an additional channel for structural transformation. Now, what can be said about the dynamics of human capital and fertility as z rises relative to x? Lemma 4 and its corollary provide a characterization.

LEMMA 4. *Human capital* h *is convex in* z/x *when* $z/x < [\omega\sigma/(2-\sigma)]^{1-\sigma} = (z/x)^*$, *and is concave otherwise.*

PROOF. Using Equation (31), it can be deduced that

$$\frac{\partial^2 h}{\partial (z/x)^2} = \frac{\omega}{1-\sigma} \frac{1}{[1+(z/x)^{1/(\sigma-1)}]^3} \frac{1}{1-\sigma}$$
$$\times (z/x)^{1/(\sigma-1)-2} [\sigma + \omega\sigma (z/x)^{1/(\sigma-1)} - 2].$$

Now,

$$\frac{\partial^2 h}{\partial (z/x)^2} \gtrless 0 \quad \text{as} \quad \sigma + \omega\sigma (z/x)^{1/(\sigma-1)} \gtrless 2,$$

or as

$$\frac{z}{x} \lessgtr \left(\frac{\omega\sigma}{2-\sigma}\right)^{1-\sigma}. \qquad\qquad □$$

The above lemma indicates that when incomes are low, human capital will increase at an increasing rate when z/x rises. After a certain point, the rate of increase in human capital will slow down, and human capital will increase at a decreasing rate as z/x rises. Thus, the convergence of h from a society where every individual is unskilled ($h = 0$) to one in which every one is skilled ($h = 1$) will have an S shape that is characteristic of the diffusion of many innovations. Now, recall that fertility is inversely related to human capital. Consequently, fertility will initially fall at a increasing rate, and then will eventually decline at an decreasing rate as it converges to n^*. The following corollary characterizes the dynamics of fertility.

COROLLARY. *Fertility* n *is convex in* z/x *when* $z/x > (\tau\omega\sigma/((\tau + \phi)(2 - \sigma)))^{1-\sigma} = (z/x)^{**}$ *and is concave otherwise.*

PROOF. Using Equation (32), it is easy to see that

$$\frac{\partial^2 n}{\partial(z/x)^2} = \frac{\chi}{\psi + \chi} \frac{\phi\omega}{1 - \sigma} \frac{1}{1 - \sigma} (z/x)^{1/(\sigma-1)-2} \frac{1}{[\tau + \phi + \tau\omega(z/x)^{1/(\sigma-1)}]^3}$$
$$\times \left\{ (\tau + \phi)(2 - \sigma) - \tau\omega\sigma(z/x)^{1/(\sigma-1)} \right\}.$$

Now,

$$\frac{\partial^2 n}{\partial(z/x)^2} \gtrless 0 \quad \text{as} \quad \frac{(\tau + \phi)(2 - \sigma)}{\tau\omega\sigma} \gtrless (z/x)^{1/(\sigma-1)},$$

or as

$$\frac{z}{x} \gtrless \left(\frac{\tau\omega\sigma}{(\tau + \phi)(2 - \sigma)} \right)^{1-\sigma}. \qquad \square$$

Figure 8 illustrates the dynamics of the transition path. One interesting aspect of the figure, as is evident from the above lemma and corollary, is that the point of inflection associated with the dynamics of fertility occurs at a lower value of z/x than does the corresponding number for human capital; i.e., $(z/x)^{**} < (z/x)^*$. This implies that the decline in fertility begins to slow down before the increase in human capital does. This is in accord with the evidence in the United States. What creates this asymmetry between the fall in fertility and the rise in human capital? The answer is the skill premium. Note that when the skill premium is zero, which transpires when $\phi = 0$, $(z/x)^{**} = (z/x)^*$. The analysis thus implies that economies with a higher skill premium will experience a longer delay between the slowdowns in the decline in fertility and the rise in human capital.

A numerical example will help clarify the ability of the model to match the historical facts.

EXAMPLE 3 (The U.S. demographic transition). Assume the parameter values given below.

(i) Tastes: $\beta = 0.94^{20}$, $\chi = 0.5$, $\psi = 1 - 0.5$.

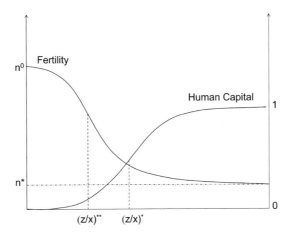

Figure 8. The dynamics of fertility and human capital.

(ii) Technology: $\sigma = 0.8$.

(iii) Child care: $\tau = 0.123, \phi = 0.4$.

The time is 1800. Assume that $(z/x)_{1800} = 2.36$. Then, Equation (30) implies that $h_{1800} = 0.05$; i.e., about 5 percent of the population are skilled. The rest of the population, 95 percent, live in the rural sector. Further, Equation (21) implies that $n_{1800} = \chi/[(\psi + \chi)(\tau + \phi h_{1800})] = 3.5$, which is exactly the number of kids per adult (male plus female) in 1800. An average married couple in 1800 had 7 kids. Now, move ahead to 1940. TFP in agriculture grew by a factor of 1.95, while TFP in manufacturing grew by a factor of 4.11. Consequently, $(z/x)_{1940} = (4.11/1.95) \times (z/x)_{1800} = 4.97$. Now, Equation (30) implies that $h_{1940} = 0.69$, or that about 31 percent of the population live in the rural sector. Further, $n_{1940} = \chi/[(\psi + \chi)(\tau + \phi h_{1940})] = 1.26$, so that an average family has 2.52 children (as opposed to 2.23 in the data). Finally, the long-run value of fertility is $n^* = 0.96$. In the long run an average family will give birth to 1.92 children.

Notice that even without employing any differences in curvature between manufacturing or agricultural goods, or differences in the skill intensities associated with the production of these goods, technological advance can account for most of the decline in fertility between 1800 and 1940.[10]

---

[10] Greenwood and Seshadri (2002) allow for agricultural and manufacturing goods to enter the utility function separately. The assumed form of their utility function ensures that agricultural goods have a lower income elasticity than do manufacturing goods. They show that a two-fold increase in z/x, together with a lower income elasticity of demand for agricultural goods relative to skill-intensive manufactured goods, can account for the demographic transition and the structural transformation that the United States experienced over the nineteenth and twentieth centuries.

4. The demise of child labor

Economically valuable and emotionally worthless to economically worthless and emotionally valuable. In 1896 the Southern Railroad Company of Georgia was sued for the wrongful death of a two-year-old boy.[11] The parents claimed that their son performed valuable services worth $2 per month, "going upon errands to neighbors ... watching and amusing ... younger child". The court's judgement allowed just for minimum burial expenses to be recovered. The ruling stated that the youngster was "of such tender years as to be unable to have any earning capacity, and hence the defendant could not be held liable in damages". The problem was that the boy was too young to do productive work. And the court attached no value to the pain and suffering connected with the loss of a child. An older child could earn money, but it was still a fraction of what an adult would get. For example, a ten-year-old in 1798 could earn the equivalent of $22 a year working as a farm laborer, as compared with $96 for an adult – Lebergott (1964, pp. 49–50).

Now move forward in time to January 1979. The New York State Supreme Court jury awarded $750,000 to the parents of three-year-old William Kennerly. He had been given a lethal dose of fluoride in a city dental clinic. The twentieth century has witnessed a profound transformation in the value of children. Along with the Second Industrial Revolution emerged the "economically worthless" and the "emotionally priceless" child. For in strict economic terms, today's children are worthless to their parents. They are expensive. The direct cost to a two-parent median income family of raising a child born in 1995 through to the age of 17 was estimated to be $145,320.[12] And this does not include college costs, time costs, and foregone earnings. In return they provide no labor.

What caused this dramatic change in society's valuation of children over such a relatively short period of time? And what accounts for the apparent paradox that the value in the twentieth century that society placed on an economically useless child far surpassed the one in the nineteenth century that society placed on an economically useful child? A case can be made that technological progress resulted in the liberation of children from work. Increased mechanization of agriculture and manufacturing in the late nineteenth and early twentieth centuries resulted in a decline in the demand for unskilled labor and a rise in the demand for skilled labor. Thus, the return to skill rose. This created an incentive for parents both to educate their offspring more, and to have less of them; i.e., to substitute away from quantity toward quality of children. The death of child labor was natural.

---

[11] This and the next case are taken from Zelizer (1994, pp. 138–139). This is the source for the quotations as well.

[12] *Source.* Expenditures on Children by Families, 1995 Annual Report, USDA Miscellaneous Publication Number 1528-1995.

4.1. The environment

The analysis here closely follows the setup of the previous section. Assume that an individual lives for three periods: the first as a child, and the second and third as an adult. In the first period of life a person undertakes no economic decisions; he simply accumulates the level of human capital dictated by his parents. He begins the second period of his life with a *fixed* number of children, η. In addition to being exogenous, childbearing is costless. Skilling a child, however, involves two costs. First, as before, there is the direct cost of educating the child. In particular, endowing a child with h' units of human capital involves a cost of $\phi h'$ units of unskilled time. Second, there is the opportunity cost of sending the child to school; that is, by going to school a child forgoes some labor earnings. Specifically, suppose that a child is as productive in the labor market as $\zeta < 1$ unskilled adults. Additionally, assume that in order for the child to acquire h' units of human capital he must go to school for h' units of time.

A young adult's decision problem. The economic environment is pretty much the same as that in the previous section, with the above notable exceptions. Another distinction is that a parent now cares about the leisure that his children will enjoy, in addition to his own consumption and the quality of his children. The purpose is to break the link between the time spent schooling and the time spent working by children. The analogue to choice problem (20) is

$$\max_{c^y, h', l} \left\{ \psi \ln(c^y) + \chi_1 \ln[w'(1 - h') + v'h'] + \chi_2 \ln l \right\}$$

subject to

$$c^y = \frac{[(1 - h)w + hv + \pi + w\zeta\eta(1 - h' - l) - w\phi\eta h']}{1 + \beta}, \tag{33}$$

where once again consumption when old, $c^{o'}$, has been substituted out using the Euler equation (19). In this maximization problem, h denotes the human capital of the parent, h' the human capital of the child, l the leisure time for the child, w the unskilled wage rate, v the skilled wage rate, and π is the flow of profits associated with the operation of firms in the agricultural and manufacturing sectors.

The first-order condition for h' is

$$\frac{\psi\eta}{1 + \beta} \frac{w\zeta + w\phi}{c^y} = \frac{\chi_1(v' - w')}{w'(1 - h') + v'h'}. \tag{34}$$

The right-hand side of this equation gives the value from extra human capital accumulation in children. It has the same form as (22). The left-hand side gives the cost of extra human capital accumulation. Observe that part of this cost is the forgone earnings $w\zeta$ that a child would realize by working instead of going to school. Also, the cost of educating kids is an increasing function of the number of kids η. Hence, one would expect that as η falls h' should rise. Note that an equiproportionate increase in v, v', w, w' and c^y will have no effect on h'. Consequently, along a balanced growth path h will be constant. Hence, in order to get some action it must transpire that v must rise relative to w, or equivalently that z must increase relative to x. Recall that this was exactly what was needed to account for the U.S. demographic transition in Section 3.

Finally, the first-order condition for leisure reads

$$\frac{\zeta \psi \eta}{1 + \beta} \frac{w}{c^y} = \frac{\chi_2}{l}. \tag{35}$$

The right-hand side of this equation gives the marginal benefit from providing an extra unit of leisure to each child while the left-hand side gives the marginal cost. Observe that for leisure, l, to increase, c^y must rise relative to $w\eta$. This will happen if either v rises relative to w, or if the level of human capital h increases, ceteris paribus. Note that a fall in fertility, η, plays an important role in increasing l. When fertility declines, the marginal cost to the parent of providing more leisure to each of his children falls, hence leisure rises.

4.2. Analysis

Imagine that the economy is resting in a steady state where z and x are constant.[13] Variables such as h, l, w/c^y and v/c^y will also be constant. Others such as the size of the young generation, s^y, will be changing at a constant rate dictated by the size of η. The market-clearing condition for skilled labor will again be described by (26). The one for unskilled labor will now appear as

$$u = \left[1 - h + (1 - h - l)\eta\zeta - \phi\eta h\right]. \tag{36}$$

The firms' problems are exactly the same as in Section 3.1. In a steady-state situation, wages will be given by

$$w = w' = x\left[1 - h + (1 - h - l)\eta\zeta - \phi\eta h\right]^{\sigma - 1}, \tag{37}$$

$$v = v' = z[h]^{\sigma - 1}, \tag{38}$$

which follow from Equations (24), (25), (26) and (36).

In principle one can solve the first-order conditions (34) and (35), in conjunction with (37) and (38), to obtain a solution for h and l.[14] General results are hard to obtain for

---

[13] For simplicity the analysis will be restricted to a study of comparative steady states.

[14] Additionally, it is easy to show that profits are

$$\pi = \left(\frac{1 - \sigma}{\sigma}\right)\{w[1 - h + (1 - h - l)\eta\zeta - \phi\eta h] + vh\},$$

so that consumption is given by

$$c^y = \frac{\{w[1 - h + (1 - h - l)\eta\zeta - \phi\eta h] + vh + \pi\}}{1 + \beta}$$

$$= \frac{1}{(1 + \beta)\sigma}\{w[1 - h + (1 - h - l)\eta\zeta - \phi\eta h] + vh\}.$$

this economy, however, so a numerical example will be used to highlight the effect of changes in z/x and η on h.[15] The goal of this example is to show that the above setup is capable of generating a large decline in child labor. Little attention has been paid to its realism.

EXAMPLE 4 (The natural death of child labor). Assume the parameter values listed below.
    (i) Tastes: $\beta = 0.94^{20}$, $\chi_1 = 0.14$, $\chi_2 = 0.03$, $\psi = 1 - \chi_1 - \chi_2$.
    (ii) Technology: $\sigma = 0.7$.
    (iii) Child care: $\phi = 0.1$.
    (iv) Child productivity: $\zeta = 0.15$.
Again, start off in 1800. Set $\eta_{1800} = 3.5$, since an average family gave birth to 7 children. Observe that in work a child has the productivity of 0.15 adults.[16] Assume that $z_{1800} = x_{1800} = 1$. Then Equations (34) and (35) imply that $h_{1800} = 0.025$ and $l_{1800} = 0.16$; i.e., about $(1 - h_{1800} - l_{1800}) \times 100 = 81.5$ percent of children are gainfully employed. Now, move ahead to 1940. TFP in agriculture grew by a factor of 1.95 while TFP in manufacturing grew by a factor of 4.11. Consequently, $(z/x)_{1940} = (4.11/1.95) \times (z/x)_{1800} = 2.1$. Also, let $\eta_{1940} = 1.1$. Now, $h_{1940} = 0.49$ and $l_{1940} = 0.51$ so that no child works in 1940!

Child labor laws and compulsory schooling laws. Child labor laws are often cited as a reason for the decline in child labor. While the National Child Labor Committee was formed as early as 1904, it was not until 1938, when the Fair Labor Standards Act was passed, that children were freed from the bondage of dangerous work. The data suggests that the process of the withdrawal of children from the workforce had been completed before child labor laws were firmly in place. The conventional wisdom among economic historians is that these laws had little impact on teen attendance early in the twentieth century because the laws were imperfectly enforced [Landes and Solmon (1972) and Eisenberg (1988)]. More recent work by Margo and Finegan (1996) finds significant positive effects on school attendance when compulsory schooling laws were coupled with child labor laws. There is still the possibility that the enactment of these laws was a reaction to the greater demand for skilled labor, and the lower demand for unskilled labor, caused by industrialization. Nardinelli (1990) echoes this sentiment and provides evidence that those areas that industrialized first were also among the first to adopt these laws. Hence the enactment of these laws in more industrialized states is consistent with

---

[15] Analytical solutions can be obtained in Section 3 due to the fact that the costs of raising kids are expressed as a fraction of family income. With child labor the convenience of this formulation disappears so a more traditional one is adopted – compare (18) with (33).
[16] Recall that according to Lebergott (1964), a child in agriculture could earn $22 in a year, while an adult would receive $8 \times 12 = \$96$. Assuming that the child would work from the age of 7, and given that a period in the model is 20 years, the child equivalent of a man is $(22/96) \times (13/20) = 0.149$.

the notion that technological progress increased the demand for skilled labor vis à vis unskilled labor and consequently reduced the demand for child labor.

The above example suggests that sector-specific technological progress alone can account for all of the decline in child labor. There are three effects at play. First, the demand for skilled labor rises relative to unskilled labor. This increases the skill premium, and promotes investment in skill via a substitution effect. Second, technological advance makes parents wealthier. This income effect makes parents more likely to invest in the well-being of their children. Third, fertility drops also, which reduces the cost of educating a family. Consequently, h and l both rise. A more serious treatment of the issue of child labor would endogenize fertility and incorporate the quantity–quality trade-off that parents face. There is one aspect of the data that make a technology-based explanation appealing. The period from 1900 to 1930 saw a dramatic decline in child labor. These three decades saw an enormous increase in manufacturing productivity relative to agricultural productivity z/x. The United States experience accords well with this implication. Last, observe that the utility flow that a parent realizes from a child increases with technological progress. This transpires because both the child's level of human capital (or quality) and leisure rise.

5. Engines of liberation

Is it, then, consistent to hold the developed woman of this day within the same narrow political limits as the dame with the spinning wheel and knitting needle occupied in the past? No, no! Machinery has taken the labors of woman as well as man on its tireless shoulders; the loom and the spinning wheel are but dreams of the past; the pen, the brush, the easel, the chisel, have taken their places, while the hopes and ambitions of women are essentially changed.

[Elizabeth Cady Stanton, "Solitude of Self", an address before United States Congressional Committee on the Judiciary, January 18, 1892.]

For ages woman was man's chattel, and in such condition progress for her was impossible; now she is emerging into real sex independence, and the resulting outlook is a dazzling one. This must be credited very largely to progression in mechanics; more especially to progression in electrical mechanics.
Under these new influences woman's brain will change and achieve new capabilities, both of effort and accomplishment.

[Thomas Alva Edison, as interviewed in *Good Housekeeping Magazine*, LV, no. 4 (October 1912, p. 440).]

The twentieth century witnessed a dramatic rise in labor-force participation by married women.[17] It will be argued here that technological advance in the household sector

[17] Labor-force participation also increased for single women, but not as dramatically. For instance, 38.4 percent of single white women worked in 1890 – Goldin (1990, Table 2.1, p. 17). By 1988 this had risen to 68.6 percent.

liberated women from the home, in particular from the oppressive burden of housework. The standard Solow (1956)–Ramsey (1928) growth model will be extended along two dimensions. First, household production will be included in the framework. Second, a technology adoption decision will be incorporated into the analysis.

Time savings. As a backdrop to the subsequent analysis, a quick detour will be taken to consider some evidence on the reduction of time spent on housework. At the start of Second Industrial Revolution women's magazines were filled with articles extolling the virtues of appliances, the new domestic servants. For example, in 1920 an article in the *Ladies' Home Journal* entitled "Making Housekeeping Automatic" claimed that appliances could save a 4-person family 18.5 hours a week in housework – see Table 2. Some more scientific evidence comes from the sociology literature – see Table 3. In 1924 a pair of famous sociologists, Robert and Helen Lynd, studied a small town in Indiana, Middletown. They found that 87 percent of married women in 1924 spent 4 or more hours doing housework each day. Zero percent spent less than 1 hour a day. The town

Table 2
Estimated weekly hours saved by appliances

Task	With appliances	Without appliances	Time savings
Breakfast	7	10	3
Luncheons	10.5	14	3.5
Dinners	10	12	2
Dishwashing and clearing	10.5	15.75	5.25
Washing and ironing	6.5	9	2.5
Marketing and errands	6	6	0
Sewing and mending	3.5	4	0.5
Bed making	2.75	3.5	0.75
Cleaning and dusting	2	3	1
Cleaning kitchen and refrigerator	2	2	0
Total	60.75	79.25	18.5

Source: Ladies' Home Journal (1920).

Table 3
Daily housework in Middletown (percentage of married housewives in each category)

Year	⩾4 hours	2–3 hours	⩽1 hour
1924	87	13	0
1977	43	45	12
1999	14	53	33

Source: Caplow, Hicks and Wattenberg (2001, p. 37).

was restudied by sociologists at two later dates. By 1999 only 14 percent of married women spent more than 4 hours a day on housework, and 33 percent spent less than 1 hour a day.

5.1. The environment

Consider a small open economy populated by overlapping generations.[18] Individuals live for two periods, they work in the first period and retire in the second. They are endowed with one unit of time for either working in the market or at home.

Tastes.   The lifetime utility function for a young adult is given by

$$\mu \ln c^y + (1 - \mu) \ln n^y + \beta \mu \ln c^{o'} + \beta (1 - \mu) \ln n^{o'}, \tag{39}$$

where c^y and $c^{o'}$ denote the individual's consumption when young and old, and (with a change in notation from the previous sections) n^y and $n^{o'}$ now stand for young and old household production.

Income.   Young adults work for the market wage, w. They save for old age at the internationally determined time-invariant gross interest rate r.

Household production technology.   Let the production of home goods, n, be governed by

$$n = \left[\theta \delta^\kappa + (1 - \theta) h^\kappa \right]^{1/\kappa} \quad \text{for } \kappa \leqslant 1,$$

where δ is the stock of household capital and (with another change in notation) h now represents the amount of time spent on housework. When $\kappa > 0$ ($\kappa < 0$), capital and labor are Edgeworth–Pareto substitutes (complements) in producing utility.[19] Finally, assume that household capital is lumpy or indivisible. A person acquires this capital when young and keeps it for his entire life, whereupon it fully depreciates. Let the *time* cost of purchasing δ units of household capital be q.

---

[18] The framework developed below is a stripped-down version of Greenwood, Seshadri and Yorukoglu (2005).

[19] Let

$$U(\delta, h) \equiv (1 - \mu) \ln\{ \left[\theta \delta^\kappa + (1 - \theta) h^\kappa \right]^{1/\kappa} \}.$$

It is easy to see that

$$U_{12}(\delta, h) \lesseqgtr 0 \quad \text{as } \kappa \gtreqless 0.$$

The young household's choice problem. Since the agent spends the entire one unit of his time endowment during retirement on household production, $h^{o'} = 1$. Consequently, $n^{o'} = [\theta \delta^\kappa + (1 - \theta)]^{1/\kappa}$, a constant. The decision problem facing a young adult is

$$U(w, r, \delta, q) = \max_{c^y, h^y, c^{o'}} \{\mu \ln c^y + (1 - \mu) \ln n^y + \beta \mu \ln c^{o'}\}$$

$$+ \beta(1 - \mu) \ln[\theta \delta^\kappa + (1 - \theta)]^{1/\kappa} \qquad (40)$$

subject to

$$c^y + \frac{c^{o'}}{r} = w(1 - h^y) - wq, \qquad (41)$$

and

$$n^y = [\theta \delta^\kappa + (1 - \theta)(h^y)^\kappa]^{1/\kappa}. \qquad (42)$$

Since there is only one h to worry about, let $h^y = h$ from here on out to save on notation. The function U is the household's indirect utility function. It gives the maximal level of utility that the household can attain given the prices w, r and q, and the level of household capital δ. Note the above problem presumes that the household purchases the household production technology represented by the pair (δ, q). This assumption will be relaxed later on.

The efficiency condition for housework reads

$$\frac{\mu w}{c^y} = \frac{1 - \mu}{n^y} [\theta \delta^\kappa + (1 - \theta)h^\kappa]^{1/\kappa - 1}(1 - \theta)h^{\kappa - 1}. \qquad (43)$$

This above equation can be derived by using (41) and (42) to substitute out for c^y and n^y in (40) and then differentiating with respect to h. The left-hand side gives the marginal cost of an extra unit of housework. An extra unit of time spent in housework comes at the expense of a forgone unit of market work that earns the wage rate, w. To convert this into utility terms multiply by the marginal utility of consumption when young, μ/c^y. The right-hand side represents the marginal benefit from an extra unit of housework. An additional unit of time spent at home increases household production by the marginal product of labor, $[\theta \delta^\kappa + (1 - \theta)h^\kappa]^{1/\kappa - 1}(1 - \theta)h^{\kappa - 1}$. To convert this to utility terms multiply by the marginal utility of home goods, $(1 - \mu)/n^y$. At the optimum, the marginal cost and benefit of housework must equal each other.

The Euler equation for consumption is exactly the same as Equation (19), which together with the budget constraint (41) gives

$$c^y = \frac{w[(1 - h) - q]}{1 + \beta} \quad \text{and} \quad c^{o'} = \frac{\beta r w[(1 - h) - q]}{1 + \beta}. \qquad (44)$$

Now, using (42) and (44) to substitute out for c^y and n^y in (43), while rearranging, yields a single equation determining the equilibrium level of housework, h,

$$1 = \frac{1 - \mu}{\mu(1 + \beta)} \frac{(1 - h) - q}{[\theta \delta^\kappa + (1 - \theta)h^\kappa]}(1 - \theta)h^{\kappa - 1}. \qquad (45)$$

The intuition underlying this equation will be presented later on.

The firm's problem. Once again let market output, o, be produced in line with the following production function:

$$o = zk^\alpha l^{1-\alpha},$$

where k and l are the inputs of capital and labor used in production and z is the level of productivity in the market sector. Now, suppose that capital depreciates fully after use in production. The rental rate on capital will therefore be r, since it must yield the same return as a bond. Given this production structure, once again wages will be given by (9).

5.2. Analysis

What is the effect of technological advance in the home sector on the amount of time devoted to housework? The answer will depend upon whether capital and labor in household production are Edgeworth–Pareto substitutes or complements in generating utility. Likewise, what impact will technological progress in the market sector have on the amount of time allocated to housework?

LEMMA 5. *An increase in the market wage rate, w, will have no effect on the amount of time spent in housework, h, while an increase in the stock of household capital, δ, will*

(a) *cause h to decline when capital and labor are Edgeworth–Pareto substitutes (or when $\kappa > 0$),*

(b) *cause h to increase when capital and labor are Edgeworth–Pareto complements (or when $\kappa < 0$),*

(c) *have no effect on h when capital and labor are neither Edgeworth–Pareto substitutes or complements (or when $\kappa = 0$).*

PROOF. The first part of the lemma is trivial since w does not enter Equation (45) and therefore cannot influence h. To establish the second part of the lemma, totally differentiate (45) with respect to h and δ to get

$$\frac{dh}{d\delta} = -\kappa \frac{[(1-h)-q]h\theta\delta^{\kappa-1}}{\{(1-q)[\theta\delta^\kappa + (1-\theta)h^\kappa] - \kappa(1-h-q)\theta\delta^\kappa\}}.$$

Now, the denominator of the above expression is unambiguously positive since $\kappa \leqslant 1$ and $(1-q) \geqslant (1-h-q)$. Therefore,

$$\mathrm{sign}\left(\frac{dh}{d\delta}\right) = -\mathrm{sign}(\kappa). \qquad \square$$

COROLLARY. *Technological progress in the market sector, or an increase in z, has no effect on time spent in housework h.*

PROOF. The proof is trivial since z does not enter (45), because w does not. $\qquad \square$

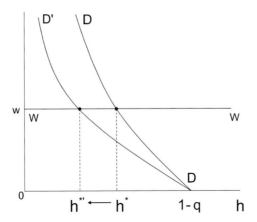

Figure 9. The effect of an improvement in household technology on time spent on housework.

Intuition. Observe that the first-order condition (43) can be expressed as

$$w = \frac{1-\mu}{\mu} \frac{c^y}{n^y} \left[\theta\delta^\kappa + (1-\theta)h^\kappa\right]^{1/\kappa - 1}(1-\theta)h^{\kappa-1}.$$

The left-hand side of this above equation is the marginal product of labor in the market sector, w. This is portrayed by the WW curve in Figure 9. The value of the marginal product of labor in the home sector is given by the right-hand side. This equals the marginal product of labor in the home sector, $\left[\theta\delta^\kappa + (1-\theta)h^\kappa\right]^{1/\kappa - 1}(1-\theta)h^{\kappa-1}$, multiplied by the (implicit) relative price of home goods, $[(1-\mu)/\mu]c^y/n^y$. Substituting out for c^y and n^y, using (44) and (42), gives

$$\begin{aligned} w &= \frac{1-\mu}{\mu(1+\beta)} \frac{w[(1-h)-q]}{[\theta\delta^\kappa + (1-\theta)h^\kappa]^{1/\kappa}} \left[\theta\delta^\kappa + (1-\theta)h^\kappa\right]^{1/\kappa - 1}(1-\theta)h^{\kappa-1} \\ &= \frac{1-\mu}{\mu(1+\beta)} \frac{w[(1-h)-q]}{[\theta\delta^\kappa + (1-\theta)h^\kappa]}(1-\theta)h^{\kappa-1} \\ &\equiv RHS(h; \delta, w). \end{aligned}$$

$\qquad\qquad\qquad\qquad\qquad\qquad\qquad\qquad\qquad\qquad\qquad\qquad\qquad (46)$

The right-hand side of the equation spells out the demand curve for housework, h. It is shown in Figure 9 by the DD curve. This curve is decreasing in h, a fact easily deduced by observing that both the price and marginal product terms are decreasing in h. Note that $RHS(h; \delta, w) \to \infty$ as $h \to 0$, and that $RHS(h; \delta, w) \to 0$ as $h \to 1-q$.

The equilibrium level of housework, h^*, is given by the point where the DD and WW curves intersect. So, how will technological advance in the home sector affect the equilibrium level of housework? It is clear from (46) that

$$\begin{aligned} \frac{\partial RHS(h; \delta, w)}{\partial\delta} &= -\kappa\frac{1-\mu}{\mu(1+\beta)} \frac{w[(1-h)-q]}{[\theta\delta^\kappa + (1-\theta)h^\kappa]^2} \\ &\times (1-\theta)h^{\kappa-1}\theta\delta^{\kappa-1} \lesseqgtr 0 \quad \text{as } \kappa \gtreqless 0. \end{aligned}$$

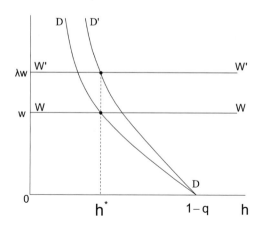

Figure 10. The effect of an increase in wages on time spent on housework.

Therefore, the demand curve for housework will shift down or up depending upon whether labor and capital are substitutes ($\kappa > 0$) or complements ($\kappa < 0$) in home production. Figure 9 portrays the case where labor and capital are substitutes.

Now, let wages jump up by a factor of λ. It is easy to deduce that the WW and DD curves will also shift up by a factor of λ to W'W' and D'D, as is shown in Figure 10. Hence, the equilibrium level of housework remains unaffected. With logarithmic preferences an increase in wages by a factor of λ will cause the consumption of market goods to increase by the same factor, which leads in turn to an equiproportionate rise in the relative price of home goods. Therefore, the value of marginal product curve shifts up by the factor λ.

EXAMPLE 5 (Female labor-force participation, 1900 and 1980). Assume the following parameter values.
  (i) Tastes: $\beta = 0.94^{20}$.
  (ii) Technology: $\theta = 0.33, \kappa = 0.5, q = 0$.
In 1900 about 5 percent of married white females worked. Assume that none did. There are about 224 nonsleeping hours available per couple in a week. If males worked a 40 hour week then $1 - h = 40/224 = 0.18$ in 1900. Now, suppose that the amount of household capital in 1900 is negligible; i.e., set $\delta = 0$. By using (45) it can be calculated that a value of $\mu = 0.145$ is need to generate $1 - h = 0.18$. Next, about 50 percent of white married women worked in 1980. Therefore, $1 - h = 60/224 = 0.27$. From (45) it can be deduced that this value for $1 - h$ can be obtained by setting $\delta = 1.41$. Thus, a rise in female labor-force participation from zero to 50 percent can be generated by letting δ increase from 0 to 1.41.

A technology adoption decision. Now suppose that the household faces a choice between two household production technologies, namely a new versus an old one. Represent the new technology by the pair (δ^1, q^1), and the old one by (δ^2, q^2). To make the problem interesting, assume that $\delta^1 > \delta^2$ and $q^1 > q^2$. The new technology offers more capital services but costs more. Characterizing the household's adoption decision is straightforward:

Adopt new technology   if $U(w, r, \delta^1, q^1) > U(w, r, \delta^2, q^2)$,

Adopt old technology   if $U(w, r, \delta^1, q^1) < U(w, r, \delta^2, q^2)$,

Adopt either technology   if $U(w, r, \delta^1, q^1) = U(w, r, \delta^2, q^2)$.

LEMMA 6. *When capital and labor are Edgeworth–Pareto substitutes in household production $(0 < \kappa \leqslant 1)$, the adoption of a new household technology will be associated with a decline in the amount of time spent on housework.*

PROOF. From Equation (45) it is easy to calculate that

$$\frac{dh}{dq} = -\frac{h[\theta\delta^\kappa + (1-\theta)h^\kappa]}{\{(1-q)[\theta\delta^\kappa + (1-\theta)h^\kappa] - \kappa(1-h-q)\theta\delta^\kappa\}} < 0,$$

where again the denominator is positive since $\kappa \leqslant 1$ and $(1-q) \geqslant (1-h-q)$. Second, it was already established in Lemma 5 that $\text{sign}(dh/d\delta) = -\text{sign}(\kappa)$. The result is now immediate since $q_1 > q_2$ and $\delta_1 > \delta_2$.   □

Often new technologies are prohibitively expensive when they are first introduced. Hence, they are not adopted initially. It is clear that there exists some threshold price, q^*, at which the household is indifferent between adopting the new technology or not. This price is defined by the equation

$$U(w, r, \delta^1, q^*) = U(w, r, \delta^2, q^2).$$

LEMMA 7. *The threshold price q^* exists and is unique. Above the price q^* the household will prefer to use the old technology while below it they will adopt the new one.*

PROOF. It is easy to deduce from (40) that

$$\frac{dU}{dq} = -\frac{\mu w}{c^y} < 0 \tag{47}$$

and

$$\frac{dU}{d\delta} = (1-\mu)\theta\delta^{\kappa-1}\left\{\frac{1}{\theta\delta^\kappa + (1-\theta)h^\kappa} + \frac{\beta}{\theta\delta^\kappa + (1-\theta)}\right\} > 0. \tag{48}$$

Equation (47) implies that the threshold price must be unique and that the household will use the new technology for any price $q^1 < q^*$ and the old one for any price $q^1 > q^*$. It is also easy to establish that the price q^* exits. Clearly when $q^1 = q^2$ the household will choose the new technology, since $U(w, r, \delta^1, q^2) > U(w, r, \delta^2, q^2)$ by (48). Likewise,

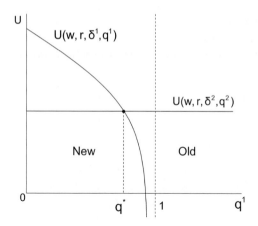

Figure 11. The determination of the threshold price, q^*.

$U(w, r, \delta^1, q^1 \simeq 1) < U(w, r, \delta^2, q^2)$ for q^1 sufficiently close to one, since at this high price there will be no resources left over for market consumption. Hence, by the Intermediate Value Theorem the threshold price q^* must exist. □

The situation described by the lemma is portrayed in Figure 11. So long as the price for the new technology declines over time to the point q^* households will eventually adopt it.

5.3. Analysis with nondurable household products and services

Over the last 100 years or so there has been a dramatic rise in the number of labor-saving nondurable household products and services. These goods and services economize on the need for housework. For example, in 1900 the bulk of baked goods, or 92 percent, was made at home.[20] The average housewife is said to have baked more than 1/2 ton of bread a year. She spent over 2 hours a week baking goods.[21] By 1965 this had dropped to 22 percent. Similarly, 96 percent of vegetables purchased were unprocessed in 1900, as opposed to 30 percent in 1965.[22] Per-capita consumption of canned fruits rose from 3.6 pounds in 1910 to 21.6 pounds in 1950.[23] Think of the time saved cleaning, pealing, canning, or otherwise preparing fruits and vegetables. There were about 2,100 packaged food products available in 1980, compared with 10,800 today.[24] Last, in 1900

---

[20] *Source*: Lebergott (1976, Table 1, p. 105).
[21] Lebergott (1993, p. 81).
[22] Again, see Lebergott (1976, Table 1, p. 105).
[23] *Source*: "Historical Statistics of the United States: Colonial Times to 1970" [U.S. Bureau of the Census (1975, Series G 893)].
[24] *Source*: Federal Reserve Bank of Dallas (1998, Exhibit 3, p. 6).

only 5 percent of food expenditure was on meals away from home. This had risen to 30 percent by 1987.[25] To explore how the introduction of new household products and services may promote female labor-force participation, a static model of the household will be presented.

Setup.   For tastes take a static version of (39), so that utility is given by

$$\mu \ln c + (1 - \mu) \ln n, \tag{49}$$

where c and n represent the individual's consumption of market and home goods, respectively. As before, the individual is endowed with one unit of time that he can use either for market work $1 - h$, or housework h. Market work is compensated at the wage rate w. Home goods are produced in line with the household production function given below

$$n = \left[\theta \sum_i^N (d_i)^\kappa + (1 - \theta) h^\kappa \right]^{1/\kappa} \quad \text{for } \kappa \leqslant 1, \tag{50}$$

where d_i denotes the agent's purchases of the ith household product. Let the ith household product sell at price p_i. There are N products available.

The household's choice problem.   The household's maximization problem is

$$\max_{c, \{d_i\}_{i=1}^N, h, n} \left[\mu \ln c + (1 - \mu) \ln n \right]$$

subject to (50) and

$$c + \sum_i^N p_i d_i = w(1 - h). \tag{51}$$

The first-order conditions for d_i and h can be written as

$$\frac{\mu p_i}{c} = (1 - \mu) \left[\theta \sum_i^N (d_i)^\kappa + (1 - \theta) h^\kappa \right]^{-1} \theta d_i^{\kappa - 1} \quad \text{for } i = 1, \ldots, N \tag{52}$$

and

$$\frac{\mu w}{c} = (1 - \mu) \left[\theta \sum_i^N (d_i)^\kappa + (1 - \theta) h^\kappa \right]^{-1} (1 - \theta) h^{\kappa - 1}. \tag{53}$$

It is immediate from (52) and (53) that

$$\frac{\theta}{1 - \theta} \left(\frac{d_i}{h} \right)^{\kappa - 1} = \frac{p_i}{w},$$

----

[25] Lebergott (1993, p. 77).

so that

$$d_i = \left[\frac{(1-\theta)p_i}{\theta w}\right]^{1/(\kappa-1)} h \equiv H_i h.$$

Using this in (53), in conjunction with (51), yields a closed-form solution for h,

$$h = \frac{(1-\mu)(1-\theta)}{\mu[\theta \sum_{i=1}^{N}(H_i)^{\kappa} + (1-\theta)] + (1-\mu)(1-\theta)(1+\sum_{i=1}^{N}(p_i/w)H_i)}. \tag{54}$$

Analysis.   The upshot of the above discussion is now within easy grasp.

LEMMA 8. *An expansion in the number of household products and services, N, will cause housework, h, to decrease and market work, $1 - h$, to increase.*

PROOF.   It is trivial to see that (54) is decreasing in N.   □

LEMMA 9. *A decline in the time price of the ith household product, p_i/w, will*
   (a) *cause housework, h, to decline when intermediates goods and labor are Edgeworth–Pareto substitutes (or when $\kappa > 0$),*
   (b) *cause housework, h, to increase when intermediates goods and labor are Edgeworth–Pareto complements (or when $\kappa < 0$),*
   (c) *have no effect on housework, h, when intermediates goods and labor are neither Edgeworth–Pareto substitutes or complements (or when $\kappa = 0$).*

PROOF.   Observe that H_i^{κ} and $(p_i/w)H_i$ are both decreasing or increasing in p_i/w depending on whether $\kappa > 0$ or $\kappa < 0$. The results follow.   □

Given the form of tastes (49) and the household production function (50), an increase in the number of household products reduces the marginal product of housework (measured in utility terms).[26] Hence, housework declines. Likewise, a decline in time price of household product i will lead to its increased use. When intermediates goods and housework are Edgeworth–Pareto substitutes (complements) in utility this causes a fall (rise) in the marginal product of housework (again denoted in utility terms). Housework again drops.

6. Conclusion

Technological progress has profoundly reshaped the economic landscape over the last 200 years. It is easy to understand how the emergence of Watt's steam engine, Crompton's cotton spinning mule, and Cort's puddling and rolling process for iron transformed

---

[26] I.e., the marginal product of housework multiplied by the marginal utility of home goods.

the industrial landscape during the 1800s. Likewise, it is easy to appreciate how the introduction of electricity, petrochemicals and the internal combustion engine changed manufacturing in the 1900s. Less well understood, however, is the impact that technological advance has had on the household sector. In 1800 the typical women labored in a rural home with 7, largely uneducated, kids. Today she is almost certain to live in an urban area, likely to work in the market sector, and have only two children who on average get 13 years of formal schooling. Times have changed, and a little growth theory can go a long way toward understanding this process.

7. Literature review

7.1. Fertility

The economics literature on fertility starts with Malthus (1798). He believed that an economy's population had a natural size. This size was limited by the economy's fixed factors, in particular land. A society's population would increase, until its standard of living fell down to a subsistence level, reigning in further expansion. When an economy's population exceeded its natural size either poverty stricken parents would voluntarily reduce their family size or their family size would involuntarily decline due to famine induced disease.

Two classic papers on fertility in modern macroeconomics are by Razin and Ben-Zion (1975) and Becker and Barro (1988). The Razin and Ben-Zion (1975) model is similar to the setup presented in Section 2. They develop a small-open-economy overlapping-generations model of fertility where kids simply enter their parents' utility function in the same way as other goods – say as in (1). The Becker and Barro (1988) model is more sophisticated, but harder to work with. It is an overlapping generations model, too, but now parents care about the utility of their children in addition to the number of kids. Since a parent cares about the happiness of his child who will in turn care about the happiness of his child (and so on, ad nauseam), the Becker and Barro (1988) model reformulates as an infinitely-lived representative agent model.

A milestone in the demographic transitions literature is a paper by Galor and Weil (2000). Over epochs of European history, fertility has followed a ∩-shaped pattern. Galor and Weil (2000) develop a model of this pattern by combining elements of Malthus (1798) and Razin and Ben-Zion (1975). They also allow for a human capital decision in the spirit of Becker and Tomes (1986). In addition they make two key assumptions: first, technological progress is an increasing function of population size, and second, the return on education rises with the rate of technological advance. In their framework, the world rests in a Malthusian equilibrium for a long time. Per-capita income remains more or less constant over time. All increases in aggregate income induced by technological progress are absorbed by expansions in the population. As the population slowly grows bigger, the pace of technological progress begins to pick up and the economy exits the Malthusian regime. At first parents use the extra income generated by technological advance to have more kids, since the return on education is still low. As the rate of technological progress accelerates the return to education rises, and parents choose to have fewer kids but invest more in them.[27]

A calibrated model that delivers a transition from Malthusian stagnation to growth, accompanied by a demographic transition from high to low fertility is presented in Doepke (2004). The engine in his analysis is a Becker and Barro (1988) style model modified to allow for parental human capital investment in children. He uses the model to study the role of social policies in shaping the demographic transition of a country – more on this later.

Fernandez-Villaverde (2001) examines the ability of technological advance to explain, quantitatively, the fall in British fertility. He uses a variant of the Becker and Barro (1988) and Becker and Tomes (1986) frameworks to do this. In his analysis capital and skilled labor are complements in production. As the capital stock rises with economic development, this creates an impetus for parents to substitute away from having a large number of uneducated children toward having a small number of educated ones.

Little work has been done on the underlying cause of the baby boom. The best known hypothesis is by Easterlin (1987). The generation that spawned the baby boom grew up during the hard times of the Great Depression and World War II. As a result, this generation had low material aspirations. They then entered the work force in the 1940s and 1950s, a good time economically speaking. Given their low material aspirations, they used family formation as an outlet for their earnings. This hypothesis is empirically flawed on several grounds.[28] First, there was no break in the trend for fertility during the Great Depression. Second, fertility in many OECD countries started to rise before the start of World War II. Third, at the peak of the baby boom (1960) the most fertile cohort of women (those in the 20 to 24 year old age group) were simply too young for either the Great Depression or World War II to have had much of an impact on them – they were not alive during the Great Depression and were less than 9 years old at the end of World War II.

7.2. The economics of household production

The economic importance of household production was probably first recognized in a classic book by Reid (1934). Reid (1934, p. v) felt that "the productive work of the household has been overlooked, even though more workers are engaged in it than any

---

[27] Often the drop in fertility is attributed to a decline in child mortality. In some countries, such as the France and the U.S., the decline in fertility proceeded the drop in child mortality. Doepke (2005) argues within the context of a sequential fertility model with uncertainty about child mortality that the impact of a decline in child mortality is likely to be small. That is, if the issue is child mortality, why would a woman who already has some surviving children give birth to yet more children as is observed in the data.

[28] The Easterlin hypothesis is critiqued in Greenwood, Seshadri and Vandenbroucke (2005).

other single industry". She carefully reported and analyzed the uses of time and capital by households of the era. The data was fragmentary then, and sadly still is. Reid (1934) knew in theory that labor-saving household capital could reduce the amount of time spent on housework, but the just emerging evidence at the time suggested that this effect was modest (see Table XIII, p. 91).

In a famous paper Becker (1965) develops the modern approach to household production: the treatment of the household as a small factory or plant using inputs, such as labor, capital and raw materials, to produce some sort of home goods. This is the notion underlying the household production functions (2) and (42) used in Sections 2 and 5. Benhabib, Rogerson and Wright (1991) introduce household production theory into a dynamic general equilibrium model in order to study the movement of labor over the business cycle. The idea is that in favorable economic times households may temporarily move labor out of the home sector to take advantage of good market opportunities, thereby increasing the elasticity of labor supply. Parente, Rogerson and Wright (2000) use a similar framework to investigate whether household production can explain cross-country income differentials. This is very much in the spirit of Reid (1934, pp. 165–166), who observed that the "(g)oods resulting from household production receive no market valuation. . .". She reports (p. 167) an estimate placing the value of housewives' services at \$15.3 billion in 1918 compared with a national income of \$61 billion. Last, Rios-Rull (1993) inserts household production into an overlapping generations model to examine its impact on the time allocations of skilled versus unskilled labor. In his framework, skilled labor (relative to unskilled labor) will tend to substitute market goods or services for labor in household production.

7.3. Structural change

Two well-known models of structural change have been developed by Echevarria (1997) and Laitner (2000). Laitner (2000) presents a closed-economy model with two sectors, viz agriculture and manufacturing. Two key features of the analysis are that the demand for agricultural goods has a zero income elasticity after a certain consumption level, and that production in the agricultural sector is subject to technological progress. As the state of technology advances in the agricultural sector less labor is required to satisfy the fixed demand for agricultural goods. Echevarria (1997) develops a more general three-sector model, which she solves numerically. Restrictions on tastes and technologies that allow for tractable solutions to models with structural change are developed in Kongsamut, Rebelo and Xie (2001). Caselli and Coleman (2001) study the process of regional convergence in the U.S. between the agricultural South and manufacturing North. They argue that declining costs of education, which allow the skills essential for manufacturing to be picked up more easily, play an important role in explaining the pattern of convergence in wages between the South and North. In particular, this latter feature allows convergence to obtain without a fall (in fact with a rise) in farm, relative to nonfarm, wages. Last, in Western economies there has been a secular shift in employment out of manufacturing into services. The growth of the service sector in several European countries, however, has been encumbered by institutional rigidities. These services have been provided by the household sector instead. This phenomena is analyzed by Rogerson (2002).

Now, the model presented in Section 3 has a single good that can be produced by one or both of two sectors, interpreted as agriculture and manufacturing. The pace of technological progress is assumed to be faster in the latter sector. This draws labor into manufacturing. A similar assumption is made in Hansen and Prescott (2002) who model the transition from the pre-industrial to the modern era. Grafted onto the model developed in Section 3 is a fertility decision à la Razin and Ben-Zion (1975). Also overlaid onto the framework is a human capital decision along the lines of Becker and Tomes (1986). Here parents care about the earnings that their kids will make, as in the Galor and Weil (2000) framework, as opposed to the level of their human capital – see (17).

It is easy to modify the framework developed in Section 3 to allow for two types of goods in tastes, agricultural and manufactured. By endowing agricultural goods with a lower income elasticity than manufactured ones an extra channel for structural change can be added.[29] In fact, a similar device is already employed in the model of the baby bust and baby boom in Section 2. Observe that the term $\mathfrak{c} > 0$ in (1) operates to lower the income elasticity of children relative to market goods. As income rises a parent switches resources away from children toward the consumption of market goods. [Interestingly, Jones (2001) sets $\mathfrak{c} < 0$. This raises the income elasticity of children relative to market goods. Hence, fertility will be low when a person is poor. Jones (2001) uses this to generate the left-hand side of the ∩-shaped pattern in fertility. The right-hand side obtains by assuming an isoelastic utility function in consumption, $(c + \mathfrak{c})^\rho/\rho$ (for $\rho \leqslant 1$), that is less curved than $\ln(c + \mathfrak{c})$ in $c + \mathfrak{c}$; i.e., by picking $\rho > 0$.[30] Therefore, at high levels of income, as income rises the marginal utility of consumption falls slower than the marginal utility of kids. This generates a decline in fertility.]

7.4. Child labor

Both demographers and economists have long stressed the economic value of children in societies. Adam Smith (1973, p. 173) said, when speaking of colonial America:

> Labour there is so well rewarded that a numerous family of children, instead of being a burden, is a source of opulence and prosperity to the parents. The labour of each child, before it can leave their house, is computed to be worth a hundred pounds clear gain to them.

Likewise Gary Becker (1960, p. 213) states:

---

[29] The interested reader can see Greenwood and Seshadri (2002).

[30] See also Greenwood and Seshadri (2002).

It is possible that in the mid-nineteenth century children were a net producer's good, providing rather than using income.

Noted demographer John Caldwell (1982) has argued that there are two types of societies: pre-transitional and post-transitional. The former are characterized by net flows from children to parents while the latter are characterized by net flows in the opposite direction – some of the flows from children to parents may be in the form old-age support for the latter. [For an application of the Caldwell hypothesis to the demographic transition literature, see Boldrin and Jones (2002).]

Now suppose that the net present value of a kid is positive and that the prime motivation for having children is wealth maximization. Then fertility rates should be close to their biological maximum. This does not seem to have been observed. While children undoubtedly made important contributions to the family income, as these quotes attest, most historical research suggests that it would have been very unlikely that the net present value of children could have been positive. Economic historian Nardinelli (1990) presents a comprehensive review of the literature on the cost of children and argues that it is extremely unlikely that children were capital goods. Economic demographer Mueller (1976) has shown that even under the most plausible assumptions, the net worth of children in peasant societies is negative and concludes "(i)n sum, the aggregate model and the life-cycle model agree in showing that children have negative economic value in peasant agriculture" (p. 145). The huge literature on slavery provides a clearer picture on the productivity of child labor in preindustrial societies. Fogel and Engerman (1974, p. 153) report that "prior to age twenty-six, the accumulated expenditures by planters on slaves were greater than the average accumulated income which they took from them". While critics have questioned their estimated rates of return, even higher estimates do not make children profitable in the short run. And surely if slave children had negative net worth, it seems likely that free children in agricultural societies would have had negative value. The basic problem is that children can earn very little for the first decade or so of their lives. Yet, they must be maintained. Discounting makes it difficult to overcome the front-end costs of raising children.[31]

Now, even if the net-present value of a child's earnings to his parents is negative the possibility of child labor may significantly defray the cost of bearing him or increase the cost of educating him – as is evident from the first-order condition (34). As such, it can still have a big influence on an adult's fertility decision, as well as on a parent's decision about educating his child. Doepke (2004) examines the impact that child labor laws and educational subsidies may have on fertility and growth – note that compulsory schooling laws can effectively limit child labor as well as subsidize schooling. Both policies operate to promote a higher level of human capital investment and faster fertility decline. Surprisingly, ruling out child labor turns out to be much more effective than subsidizing education in speeding up the demographic transition from high to low

---

[31] Still, if there is no good abode for savings in a society, then children may be better than nothing in providing for old age.

fertility. Hazan and Berdugo (2002) also argue that outlawing child labor expedites this transition process.

Last, in the model presented in Section 4 a rise in the demand for skilled labor leads to a decline in the use of child labor. If family size was variable, as in Section 3, then smaller families would result too. Doepke and Zilibotti (2003) use this mechanism to model the enactment of child labor laws as a country develops. Child labor substitutes in production for unskilled adult labor. Therefore, on this hand, unskilled adult labor gains from outlawing child labor. On the other hand, unskilled adults will earn income by letting their children work. At early stages of economic development most adults will be unskilled and families will be large. There will not be much support for child labor laws. Now, suppose that the return to skill rises over time due to economic development. As more and more unskilled families choose to have fewer children, and to educate them, the political equilibrium shifts to favoring a ban on child labor.

7.5. Female labor-force participation

The economic analysis of female labor-force participation began with the pioneering works of Mincer (1962) and Cain (1966). The massive rise in female labor-force participation over the course of the twentieth century has attracted a lot of notice from labor economists. Much attention has been devoted to examining the extent to which the rise in real wages and the narrowing of the gender gap can account for the rise in labor-force participation. The narrowing of the gender gap has been analyzed by Blau and Kahn (2000) and Goldin (1990). Galor and Weil (1996) provide an interesting general equilibrium model in which the increase in women's wages and labor-force participation is a by-product of the process of development where capital accumulation raises women's wages relative to men's wages. The underlying mechanism is that capital is more complementary to women's labor than it is to men's labor. Consequently capital accumulation will lead to greater increases in women's wages than men's wages. In a similar vein, Jones, Manuelli and McGrattan (2003) argue that decreases in the gender wage gap can account for increases in average hours worked by married females for the time period between 1950 and 1990.

It is easy to introduce the gender gap in the framework developed in Section 5. Recall that the model implies that a general increase in wages will have *no* effect on labor-force participation. This is proved in Lemma 5 and is easy to see from Equations (43) and (44). A rise in w will lead to an equiproportionate increase in c^y and hence will have no impact on h. Now suppose Equation (41) is changed to read

$$c^y + \frac{c^{o\prime}}{r} = 0.5w + \phi w(0.5 - h) - wq.$$

Here ϕ represents the gender gap, or the ratio of female to male wages. Males and females each have a time endowment of 0.5. Males are presumed always to work full time. Females can vary their market labor supply, $0.5 - h$. The efficiency condition for h will once again be given by (43), but now the left-hand side will be multiplied by ϕ. It is easy to deduce that an increase in ϕ will lead to an increase in h, since c^y will rise by less than ϕ.[32] Observe that unlike the Galor and Weil (1996) setup, but like the Jones, Manuelli and McGrattan (2003) one, the gender gap is taken to be exogenous.

Empirically speaking, the gender gap did not move much between 1930 and 1980. More specifically, data from Blau and Kahn (2000) suggest that between 1955 and 1980, the period associated with enormous increases in the labor force participation rate, the gap remained almost constant.[33] In 1969, the female-to-male weekly wage ratio was 0.56 and this number rose merely to 0.58 by 1979 [see Blau (1998, Table 4, p. 129)]. Unless labor supply elasticities for women are quite high, the narrowing down of the gender gap can only be a small part of the explanation. Additionally, the gender gap may have narrowed dramatically between 1820 and 1880 [Goldin (1987, Figure 3, p. 215)] with probably little rise in married female labor-force participation (given the very low rate in 1890). All of this suggests that something else was going on, in addition to the narrowing of the gender gap, which led women to enter the labor force, such as the introduction of labor-saving household goods. On this, perhaps the introduction of such goods increased the elasticity of female labor supply. Intriguingly, the data suggest that for the 1900–1930 period married women's uncompensated wage elasticities of labor-force participation were close to zero, while in the middle of the century women's uncompensated wage elasticities were quite high – as high as 1.5 in some studies.[34]

An interesting and related development fact is that female labor-force participation is U shaped over the course of economic development – see Goldin (1995). The U-shaped pattern is very prominent in the cross-section. She believes that the trough of the U for the U.S. was reached around 1920. A simple modification of the model introduced in Section 5 can be used to account for the U shape. Imagine adding a subsistence consumption constraint. When incomes are very low and consumption is below subsistence, women go out to work in order to achieve the subsistence level of consumption. As incomes rise with technological advance in the market sector, the income effect associated with easing the subsistence constraint dominates the substitution effect (holding fixed the household production function) and time spent in the paid labor force decreases. In other words, the declining portion of the U associated with the pre-1920 era can be accounted for. After 1920 the introduction of labor-saving appliances associated with technological progress in the home sector could have led to more women entering into the workforce. Thus, growth theory can go a long way toward accounting for the entire time path of married female labor-force participation over the course of economic development.

---

[32] Note that Equation (44) will change to

$$c^y = \frac{w[0.5 + \phi(0.5 - h) - q]}{1 + \beta}.$$

[33] In fact the gender pay gap *increased* between 1955 and 1968 [see Blau and Kahn (2000, Figure 1, p. 76)]. The gender gap did narrow considerably in the period after 1980.

[34] See Goldin (1990, Table 5.2, p. 132).

There are other explanations of the rise in female labor-force participation. The effect of World War II has received some attention, for instance. Goldin (1991) investigates the effects of World War II on women's labor-force participation and finds that a little over half of the women who entered the labor market during the war years exited by 1950. Another possibility is that attitudes toward working women might have changed considerably and this encouraged women to enter into the paid labor force. While this is hard to know, one can look at social surveys across time to gain a better understanding. After reviewing public opinion poll evidence, Oppenheimer (1970, p. 51) concludes "it seems unlikely that we can attribute much of the enormous postwar increases in married women's labor force participation to a change in attitudes about the propriety of their working". On this, Fernandez, Fogli and Olivetti (2004) present evidence suggesting that a man is more likely to have a working wife if his own mother worked than if she did not. In particular, men who had mothers who worked in World War II had a higher likelihood of marrying working women than those who did not. They develop a model where attitudes toward working women become more receptive over time. This idea complements those set out in Section 5. The famous sociologist William F. Ogburn hypothesized that culture and social institutions evolve, often with a lag, to technological progress in the economy (or presumably to other events such as wars). Ogburn (1965, p. 85) said:

> Unlike the natural environment, the technological environment is a huge mass in rapid motion. It is no wonder then that our society with its numerous institutions and organizations has an almost impossible task in adjusting to this whirling technological environment. It should be no surprise to sociologists that the various forms and shapes which our social institutions take and the many shifts in their function are the result of adjustments – not to a changing natural environment, not to a changing biological heritage – but to adaptations to a changing technology.

Acknowledgements

Matthias Doepke, Nezih Guner and Baris Kaymak are thanked for comments. Financial support from the NSF (award number 0136055) is gratefully acknowledged.

Appendix:

A.1: Supporting calculations for Lemmas 2 and 4

$$
\frac{\partial n}{\partial (z/x)} = \frac{\chi}{\psi + \chi} \left\{ -\frac{[1 + \omega(z/x)^{1/(\sigma-1)}](1/(\sigma-1))\tau\omega(z/x)^{1/(\sigma-1)-1}}{[\tau + \phi + \tau\omega(z/x)^{1/(\sigma-1)}]^2} \right.
$$
$$
\left. + \frac{\omega(z/x)^{1/(\sigma-1)-1}(1/(\sigma-1))}{[\tau + \phi + \tau\omega(z/x)^{1/(\sigma-1)}]} \right\}
$$

$$= \frac{\chi}{\psi + \chi} \frac{1}{[\tau + \phi + \tau\omega(z/x)^{1/(\sigma-1)}]^2} \frac{\omega}{\sigma - 1} (z/x)^{1/(\sigma-1)-1}$$
$$\times \left\{ -\left[1 + \omega(z/x)^{1/(\sigma-1)}\right]\tau + \left[\tau + \phi + \tau\omega(z/x)^{1/(\sigma-1)}\right]\right\}$$

$$= \frac{\chi}{\psi + \chi} \frac{1}{[\tau + \phi + \tau\omega(z/x)^{1/(\sigma-1)}]^2} \frac{\phi\omega}{\sigma - 1} (z/x)^{1/(\sigma-1)-1}.$$

$$\frac{\partial^2 n}{\partial (z/x)^2} = \frac{\chi}{\psi + \chi} \frac{\phi\omega}{\sigma - 1}$$
$$\times \left\{ -\frac{2}{\sigma - 1} \frac{1}{[\tau + \phi + \tau\omega(z/x)^{1/(\sigma-1)}]^3} \right.$$
$$\times (z/x)^{1/(\sigma-1)-1}\tau\omega(z/x)^{1/(\sigma-1)-1}$$
$$\left. + \left(\frac{1}{\sigma - 1} - 1\right) \frac{1}{[\tau + \phi + \tau\omega(z/x)^{1/(\sigma-1)}]^2} (z/x)^{1/(\sigma-1)-2} \right\}$$

$$= \frac{\chi}{\psi + \chi} \frac{\phi\omega}{\sigma - 1} \frac{1}{[\tau + \phi + \tau\omega(z/x)^{1/(\sigma-1)}]^3} (z/x)^{1/(\sigma-1)-2}$$
$$\times \left\{ -\frac{2}{(\sigma - 1)}\tau\omega(z/x)^{1/(\sigma-1)} + \frac{2 - \sigma}{\sigma - 1}\left[\tau + \phi + \tau\omega(z/x)^{1/(\sigma-1)}\right] \right\}$$

$$= \frac{\chi}{\psi + \chi} \frac{\phi\omega}{\sigma - 1} \frac{1}{\sigma - 1} \frac{1}{[\tau + \phi + \tau\omega(z/x)^{1/(\sigma-1)}]^3} (z/x)^{1/(\sigma-1)-2}$$
$$\times \left\{ (2 - \sigma)(\tau + \phi) - \sigma\tau\omega(z/x)^{1/(\sigma-1)} \right\}.$$

$$\frac{\partial h}{\partial (z/x)} = \frac{1}{[1 + \omega(z/x)^{1/(\sigma-1)}]^2} \frac{\omega}{1 - \sigma} (z/x)^{1/(\sigma-1)-1}.$$

$$\frac{\partial^2 h}{\partial (z/x)^2} = \frac{\omega}{1 - \sigma} \left\{ -\frac{2}{[1 + \omega(z/x)^{1/(\sigma-1)}]^3} (z/x)^{1/(\sigma-1)-1} \frac{1}{\sigma - 1}\omega(z/x)^{1/(\sigma-1)-1} \right.$$
$$\left. + \frac{1}{[1 + \omega(z/x)^{1/(\sigma-1)}]^2} \left(\frac{2 - \sigma}{\sigma - 1}\right)(z/x)^{1/(\sigma-1)-2} \right\}$$

$$= \frac{\omega}{1 - \sigma} \frac{1}{\sigma - 1} \frac{1}{[1 + \omega(z/x)^{1/(\sigma-1)}]^3} (z/x)^{1/(\sigma-1)-2}$$
$$\times \left\{ -2\omega(z/x)^{1/(\sigma-1)} + (2 - \sigma)\left[1 + \omega(z/x)^{1/(\sigma-1)}\right] \right\}$$

$$= \frac{\omega}{1 - \sigma} \frac{1}{\sigma - 1} \frac{1}{[1 + \omega(z/x)^{1/(\sigma-1)}]^3} (z/x)^{1/(\sigma-1)-2}$$
$$\times \left\{ 2 - \sigma - \sigma\omega(z/x)^{1/(\sigma-1)} \right\}.$$

A.2: Supporting calculations for Lemmas 5 and 6

Write Equation (45) as

$$1 = \Psi \frac{(1-h)-q}{[\theta\delta^\kappa + (1-\theta)h^\kappa]} h^{\kappa-1},$$

where

$$\Psi = \frac{(1-\theta)(1-\mu)}{\mu(1+\beta)}.$$

From this it is easy to compute that

$$\frac{dh}{d\delta} = -\kappa\Psi \frac{(1-h)-q}{[\theta\delta^\kappa + (1-\theta)h^\kappa]^2} h^{\kappa-1}\theta\delta^{\kappa-1}$$

$$\times \left\{ \Psi \frac{1}{[\theta\delta^\kappa + (1-\theta)h^\kappa]} h^{\kappa-1} + \Psi \frac{(1-h)-q}{[\theta\delta^\kappa + (1-\theta)h^\kappa]^2} \kappa h^{\kappa-1}(1-\theta)h^{\kappa-1} \right.$$

$$\left. - \Psi \frac{(1-h)-q}{[\theta\delta^\kappa + (1-\theta)h^\kappa]} (\kappa-1)h^{\kappa-2} \right\}^{-1}$$

$$= -\kappa[(1-h)-q]h^{\kappa-1}\theta\delta^{\kappa-1}$$

$$\times \left\{ [\theta\delta^\kappa + (1-\theta)h^\kappa]h^{\kappa-1} + [(1-h)-q]\kappa h^{\kappa-1}(1-\theta)h^{\kappa-1} \right.$$

$$\left. - [(1-h)-q][\theta\delta^\kappa + (1-\theta)h^\kappa](\kappa-1)h^{\kappa-2} \right\}^{-1}$$

$$= -\kappa[(1-h)-q]h^{\kappa-1}\theta\delta^{\kappa-1}$$

$$\times \left\{ [\theta\delta^\kappa + (1-\theta)h^\kappa]h^{\kappa-1} - [(1-h)-q]\theta\delta^\kappa(\kappa-1)h^{\kappa-2} \right.$$

$$\left. + [(1-h)-q](1-\theta)h^{2\kappa-2} \right\}^{-1}$$

$$= -\kappa[(1-h)-q]h\theta\delta^{\kappa-1}$$

$$\times \left\{ [\theta\delta^\kappa + (1-\theta)h^\kappa]h + [(1-h)-q]\theta\delta^\kappa(1-\kappa) \right.$$

$$\left. + [(1-h)-q](1-\theta)h^\kappa \right\}^{-1}$$

$$= -\kappa \frac{[(1-h)-q]h\theta\delta^{\kappa-1}}{\{(1-q)[\theta\delta^\kappa + (1-\theta)h^\kappa] - \kappa(1-h-q)\theta\delta^\kappa\}}.$$

Clearly, the denominator of the above expression is always positive, since $1 - q \geqslant 1 - h - q$ and $\kappa \leqslant 1$. Therefore

$$\operatorname{sign}\left(\frac{dh}{d\delta}\right) = -\operatorname{sign}(\kappa).$$

Likewise, it is easy to calculate that

$$\frac{dh}{dq} = -\frac{h[\theta\delta^\kappa + (1-\theta)h^\kappa]}{\{(1-q)[\theta\delta^\kappa + (1-\theta)h^\kappa] - \kappa(1-h-q)\theta\delta^\kappa\}} < 0,$$

where again the denominator of the above expression is always positive, since $1 - q \geqslant 1 - h - q$ and $\kappa \leqslant 1$.

References

Becker, G.S. (1960). "An economic analysis of fertility". In: A Report of the National Bureau of Economic Research, Demographic and Economic Change in Developed Countries: A Conference of the Universities–National Bureau Committee for Economic Research. Princeton University Press, Princeton, NJ, pp. 209–231.

Becker, G.S. (1965). "A theory of the allocation of time". Economic Journal 75 (299), 493–517.

Becker, G.S., Barro, R.J. (1988). "A reformulation of the economic theory of fertility". The Quarterly Journal of Economics 103 (1), 1–25.

Becker, G.S., Tomes, N. (1986). "Human capital and the rise and fall of families". Journal of Labor Economics 4 (3), part 2, S1–S39.

Benhabib, J., Rogerson, R., Wright, R. (1991). "Homework in macroeconomics: Household production and aggregate fluctuations". Journal of Political Economy 99 (6), 1166–1187.

Blau, F.D. (1998). "Trends in the well-being of American women, 1970–1995". Journal of Economic Literature 36 (1), 112–165.

Blau, F.D., Kahn, L.M. (2000). "Gender differences in pay". The Journal of Economic Perspectives 14 (4), 75–99.

Boldrin, M., Jones, L.E. (2002). "Mortality, fertility and savings in a Malthusian economy". Review of Economic Dynamics 5 (4), 775–814.

Cain, G.G. (1966). Married Women in the Labor Force: An Economic Analysis. University of Chicago Press, Chicago.

Caldwell, J.C. (1982). Theory of Fertility Decline. Academic Press, London.

Caplow, T., Hicks, L., Wattenberg, B.J. (2001). The First Measured Century: An Illustrated Guide to Trends in America, 1900–2000. The AEI Press, Washington, DC.

Caselli, F., Coleman II, W.J. (2001). "The U.S. structural transformation and regional convergence: A reinterpretation". Journal of Political Economy 109 (3), 585–616.

Doepke, M. (2004). "Accounting for fertility decline during the transition to growth". Journal of Economic Growth 9 (3), 347–383.

Doepke, M. (2005). "Child mortality and fertility decline: Does the Barro–Becker model fit the facts?". Journal of Population Economics 18 (2), in press.

Doepke, M., Zilibotti, F. (2003). "Macroeconomics of child labor regulation". Staff Report 354. Federal Reserve Bank of Minneapolis, submitted for publication in American Economic Review.

Easterlin, R.A. (1987). "Easterlin hypothesis". In: Eatwell, J., Milgate, M., Newman, P. (Eds.), The New Palgrave: A Dictionary of Economics, vol. 2. Macmillan Press Ltd, London, pp. 1–4.

Echevarria, C. (1997). "Changes in sectoral composition associated with economic growth". International Economic Review 38 (2), 431–452.

Eisenberg, M.J. (1988). "Compulsory attendance legislation in America, 1870–1915". Unpublished Ph.D. Dissertation. Department of Economics, University of Pennsylvania.

Federal Reserve Bank of Dallas (1998). The Right Stuff: America's Move to Mass Customization. 1998 Annual Report. Federal Reserve Bank of Dallas, Dallas, TX.

Fernandez-Villaverde, J. (2001). "Was Malthus right? Economic growth and population dynamics". Unpublished Paper. Department of Economics, University of Pennsylvania.

Fernandez, R., Fogli, A., Olivetti, C. (2004). "Mothers and sons: Preference formation and female labor force dynamics". The Quarterly Journal of Economics 119 (4), 1249–1299.

Fogel, R.W., Engerman, S.L. (1974). Time on the Cross: The Economics of American Negro Slavery. Little, Brown and Company, Boston.

Galor, O., Weil, D.N. (1996). "The gender gap, fertility, and growth". American Economic Review 86 (3), 374–387.

Galor, O., Weil, D.N. (2000). "Population, technology and growth: From Malthusian stagnation to the demographic transition and beyond". American Economic Review 90 (4), 806–828.

Goldin, C. (1987). "Women's Employment and Technological Change: A Historical Perspective". In: Hartmann, H. (Ed.), Computer Chips and Paper Clips: Technology and Women's Employment, vol. II. National Academy Press, Washington, DC, pp. 185–222.

Goldin, C. (1990). Understanding the Gender Gap: An Economic History of American Women. Oxford University Press, New York.

Goldin, C. (1991). "The role of World War II in the rise of women's employment". American Economic Review 81 (4), 741–756.

Goldin, C. (1995). "The U-shaped female labor force function in economic development and economic history". In: Schultz, T.P. (Ed.), Investment in Women's Human Capital and Economic Development. University of Chicago Press, Chicago, pp. 61–90.

Greenwood, J., Seshadri, A. (2002). "The U.S. demographic transition". American Economic Review (Papers and Proceedings) 92 (2), 153–159.

Greenwood, J., Seshadri, A., Vandenbroucke, G. (2005). "The baby boom and baby bust". American Economic Review 95 (1), 183–207.

Greenwood, J., Seshadri, A., Yorukoglu, M. (2005). "Engines of liberation". Review of Economic Studies 72 (1), 109–133.

Hansen, G., Prescott, E.C. (2002). "Malthus to Solow". American Economic Review 92 (4), 1205–1217.

Hazan, M., Berdugo, B. (2002). "Child labor, fertility, and economic growth". The Economic Journal 112 (482), 810–828.

Jones, C.I. (2001). "Was an industrial revolution inevitable? Economic growth over the very long run". Advances in Macroeconomics 1 (2), Article 1.

Jones, L., Manuelli, R.E., McGrattan, E. (2003). "Why are married women working so much?". Research Department Staff Report 317. Federal Reserve Bank of Minneapolis.

Kongsamut, P., Rebelo, S.T., Xie, D. (2001). "Beyond Balanced Growth". Review of Economic Studies 68 (4), 869–882.

Laitner, J. (2000). "Structural change and economic growth". Review of Economic Studies 67 (3), 545–561.

Landes, W., Solmon, L. (1972). "Compulsory schooling legislation: An economic analysis of law and social change in the nineteenth century". Journal of Economic History 32 (1), 54–91.

Lebergott, S. (1964). Manpower in Economic Growth: The American Record Since 1800. McGraw-Hill Book Company, New York.

Lebergott, S. (1976). The American Economy: Income, Wealth and Want. Princeton University Press, Princeton, NJ.

Lebergott, S. (1993). Pursuing Happiness: American Consumers in the Twentieth Century. Princeton University Press, Princeton, NJ.

Malthus, T.R. (1798). An Essay on the Principle of Population as It Affects the Future Improvement of Society with Remarks on the Speculations of Mr. Godwin, M. Condorcet, and Other Writers. J. Johnson, London.

Margo, R.A., Finegan, T.A. (1996). "Compulsory schooling legislation and school attendance in turn-of-the-century America: A "Natural Experiment" approach". Economic Letters 53 (1), 103–110.

Mincer, J. (1962). "Labor force participation of married women: A study of labor supply". In: Lewis, G.H. (Ed.), Aspects of Labor Economics: A conference of the Universities–National Bureau Committee for Economic Research. Princeton University Press, Princeton, NJ, pp. 63–105.

Mueller, E. (1976). "The Economic Value of Children in Peasant Agriculture". In: Ridker, R.G. (Ed.), Population and Development: The Search for Selective Interventions. Johns Hopkins University Press, Baltimore, pp. 98–153.

Nardinelli, C. (1990). Child Labor and the Industrial Revolution. Indiana University Press, Bloomington.

Ogburn, W.F. (1965). "Technology as Environment". In: Ogburn, W.F. (Ed.), On Cultural and Social Change: Selected Papers. The University of Chicago Press, Chicago, pp. 78–85.

Oppenheimer, V.K. (1970). The Female Labor Force in the United States: Demographic and Economic Factors Governing Its Growth and Changing Composition. Institute of International Studies University of California, Berkeley, CA.

Parente, S.L., Rogerson, R., Wright, R. (2000). "Homework in development economics: Household production and the Wealth of Nations". Journal of Political Economy 108 (4), 680–687.

Ramsey, F.P. (1928). "A mathematical theory of savings". Economic Journal 38 (152), 543–559.

Razin, A., Ben-Zion, U. (1975). "An intergenerational model of population growth". American Economic Review 65 (5), 923–933.

Reid, M.G. (1934). Economics of Household Production. John Wiley & Sons Inc., New York.

Rios-Rull, J.-V. (1993). "Working in the market, working at home, and the acquisition of skills: A general-equilibrium approach". American Economic Review 83 (4), 893–907.

Rogerson, R. (2002). "The evolution of OECD employment, 1960–2000: The role of structural transformation". Unpublished Paper. Department of Economics, Arizona State University.

Smith, A. (1973). The Wealth of Nations. Penguin Books Ltd, Harmondsworth.

Solow, R.M. (1956). "A contribution to the theory of economic growth". The Quarterly Journal of Economics 70 (1), 65–94.

U.S. Bureau of the Census (1975). Historical Statistics of the United States: Colonial Times to 1970. U.S. Bureau of the Census, Washington, DC.

Zelizer, V.A. (1994). Pricing the Priceless Child: The Changing Social Value of Children. Princeton University Press, New York.

Chapter 20

THE EFFECTS OF TECHNICAL CHANGE
ON LABOR MARKET INEQUALITIES

ANDREAS HORNSTEIN

Federal Reserve Bank of Richmond

PER KRUSELL

Princeton University,
Institute for International Economic Studies,
CAERP,
CEPR
and
NBER

GIOVANNI L. VIOLANTE

New York University
and
CEPR

Contents

Abstract	1278
Keywords	1278
1. Introduction	1279
2. A look at the facts	1281
2.1. Labor market inequalities	1281
2.2. Technological change	1289
2.2.1. Total factor productivity accounting	1290
2.2.2. Sector-specific productivity accounting	1291
2.2.3. Reconciling the acceleration in investment-specific productivity growth with the slowdown in TFP: general purpose technology and learning	1295
2.2.4. Factor-specific productivity accounting	1297
3. Skill-biased technical change: Inside the black box	1298
3.1. Capital-skill complementarity	1298
3.1.1. Further applications of the capital-skill complementarity hypothesis	1300
3.2. Innate skills and the Nelson–Phelps hypothesis	1301
3.2.1. Further applications of the Nelson–Phelps hypothesis	1303

Handbook of Economic Growth, Volume 1B. Edited by Philippe Aghion and Steven N. Durlauf
© 2005 Elsevier B.V. All rights reserved
DOI: 10.1016/S1574-0684(05)01020-8

    3.3. Endogenous skill-biased technical change   1304
          3.3.1. Sources of the skill-bias in recent times   1307
    3.4. A historical perspective on the skill premium   1308
          3.4.1. Capital-skill complementarity   1308
          3.4.2. Directed technical change   1311
    3.5. Technology and the gender gap   1311
          3.5.1. Technological change in the market   1312
          3.5.2. Technological change in the household   1312
4. Technical change and the returns to experience   1313
    4.1. Experience with general purpose technologies   1313
    4.2. Vintage-specificity of experience   1315
    4.3. Technology-experience complementarity in adoption   1316
    4.4. On-the-job training with skill-biased technological change   1317
5. Inside the firm: The organization of work   1319
    5.1. The Milgrom–Roberts hypothesis: IT-driven organizational change   1320
          5.1.1. Implications for the wage structure   1320
          5.1.2. Empirical evidence on the complementarity between technology, organizational
                change and human capital   1322
    5.2. Directed organizational change   1323
    5.3. Discussion   1325
6. Technical progress as a source of change in labor market institutions   1325
    6.1. Skill-biased technology and the fall in union density   1327
    6.2. Skill-biased technology and the fall in centralized bargaining   1328
    6.3. Discussion   1329
7. Technological change in frictional labor markets   1331
    7.1. Technological progress and frictional unemployment   1332
    7.2. Technological heterogeneity and the returns to luck   1333
    7.3. Vintage human capital with frictions   1334
          7.3.1. Occupation-specific human capital   1336
          7.3.2. A precautionary demand for general skills   1336
          7.3.3. Explaining the fall in real wages   1337
    7.4. Random matching vs. directed search as source of luck   1338
8. Technology-policy complementarity: United States vs. Europe   1339
    8.1. The Krugman hypothesis   1340
    8.2. Rise in microeconomic turbulence   1342
          8.2.1. The role of wage rigidity   1342
          8.2.2. The role of welfare benefits   1344
    8.3. Slowdown in total factor productivity   1346
    8.4. Acceleration in capital-embodied technical change   1346
    8.5. Skill-biased technical change   1349
    8.6. Endogenous technology adoption   1350
    8.7. Sectoral transformation   1352
    8.8. Discussion   1353

9. Welfare and policy implications   1353
   9.1. Lifetime earnings inequality   1354
   9.2. Consumption inequality   1355
   9.3. Welfare implications   1356
      9.3.1. Insurance and opportunities in the welfare analysis of wage inequality   1357
      9.3.2. Discussion   1358
   9.4. Brief directions for policy   1359
10. Concluding remarks   1360
Acknowledgements   1361
References   1362

Abstract

In this chapter we inspect economic mechanisms through which technological progress shapes the degree of inequality among workers in the labor market. A key focus is on the rise of U.S. wage inequality over the past 30 years. However, we also pay attention to how Europe did not experience changes in wage inequality but instead saw a sharp increase in unemployment and an increased labor share of income, variables that remained stable in the U.S. We hypothesize that these changes in labor market inequalities can be accounted for by the wave of capital-embodied technological change, which we also document. We propose a variety of mechanisms based on how technology increases the returns to education, ability, experience, and "luck" in the labor market. We also discuss how the wage distribution may have been indirectly influenced by technical change through changes in certain aspects of the organization of work, such as the hierarchical structure of firms, the extent of unionization, and the degree of centralization of bargaining. To account for the U.S.–Europe differences, we use a theory based on institutional differences between the United States and Europe, along with a common acceleration of technical change. Finally, we briefly comment on the implications of labor market inequalities for welfare and for economic policy.

Keywords

inequality, institutions, labor market, skills, technological change

JEL classification: D3, J3, O3

1. Introduction

In this chapter we discuss the recent three decades of data on technology, productivity, and labor market outcomes. In particular, we explore the hypothesis that technological change has affected the labor market in various ways. We argue that (i) there is ample evidence indicating significant capital-embodied and/or skill-biased technological change and that (ii) this kind of technological change would plausibly lead to many of the transformations in the labor markets that we have observed. On the one hand, we are interested in possible implications of non-neutral technological change – of the kind we think we have experienced – on variables like wage inequality, unemployment, labor share, and unionization. On the other hand, we explore the possibility that the labor market can be used as an additional source of evidence of non-neutral technological change, a testing ground of sorts.

The past 30 years are particularly informative because they have contained rather important trend changes in several variables. We have seen a productivity slowdown common to all industrialized countries and common to almost all industries, together with continuing structural change away from manufacturing and toward services. An exception to this widespread productivity slowdown was the fast and accelerating productivity growth of industries producing investment goods, in particular those producing equipment. Only very recently has there been a more widespread acceleration of productivity growth. Of course, in this context we are arguably in the midst of an "Information Technology Revolution". We also discuss evidence of changes in the workplace – in how production within firms is organized – possibly reflecting underlying changes in technology.

In the labor market, we have seen a sharp increase in wage inequality in the United States contrasting a roughly flat development in Europe, whereas we have witnessed a strong increase in European unemployment and no trend in U.S. unemployment.[1] The organization of labor markets seems to have changed too: for example, unions have lost prevalence during this period, and to the extent there have been unions, centralized bargaining has been replaced by decentralized bargaining in many sectors. Are all these developments consistent with basic economic theory and a short list of underlying technological driving forces? We argue that they are. To make our argument more convincing, we also put the past three decades in a historical perspective, going back as far as the early 20th century with data on technological change and the skill premium.

One distinctive feature of this literature is that the many different ideas have been presented in a wide variety of theoretical frameworks ranging from the neoclassical Ramsey–Cass–Koopmans growth model to the Schumpeterian endogenous growth model; from the traditional McCall search model to the Lucas–Prescott island economy; from the Mortensen–Pissarides matching model to the competitive directed search

---

[1] Although the word inequality literally would suggest a zero–one classification – either there is inequality or there is equality – we will use the term loosely to reflect some measure of dispersion. That is, we will attach quantifiers such as "more" or "less" to the word.

framework; and from the Bewley–Aiyagari incomplete-markets model to Arrow–Debreu economies with limited enforcement. We think two main reasons exist for the lack of a unified framework of analysis. First, this field of research is still relatively young; second, departing from the competitive model in studying labor markets is fairly natural, and many alternative frameworks exist that incorporate frictions. The main drawback of the lack of a unifying framework – we will repeat it often in the chapter – is that making structurally based quantitative comparisons between different mechanisms is difficult.

To us, these heterogeneous approaches pose a formidable challenge in the exposition. Our solution has been to give priority to presenting a range of ideas, using a variety of theoretical setups, rather than to discuss in great detail a few more specific frameworks. This approach has necessitated a summarization of some rather rich models in a few key equations, which misses some of the elegance and richness of the original frameworks. We hope, however, that our spanning a wide spectrum of ideas and macroeconomic effects of technological change helps paint a picture that is broader and that, at least in an impressionistic way, suggests that the main underlying hypothesis we are proposing is quite reasonable.

The presentation of the ideas in this chapter is organized into four parts. In the first part, Section 2, we review the main trends in the data on technological change and labor market inequalities. We then cover two kinds of theories that could account for the data.

In the second part of the chapter we cover "neoclassical" theory (i.e., models where wages directly reflect marginal productivity). We view the firm as hiring labor of different skill levels in a competitive and frictionless labor market. Wages, thus, will be influenced by technology in a very direct way. Similarly, the returns to education, ability, and experience, which we discuss in detail in Sections 3 and 4, respectively, will be directly tied to changes in technology. Therefore, within these kinds of theories, the shape of the production function of the firm is crucial. We then move beyond the production function of the firm or, rather, we attempt to go inside it. In particular, Section 5 explores the possibility that the organization of the workforce also has changed within firms. These transformations, of which there is some documentation, are arguably also a result of the kind of technological change we look at in this chapter. We point, in particular, to a recent literature that explores how firms are organized and how the IT revolution, by inducing organizational changes in the firm, had a substantial impact on wage inequality.

The second class of theories we cover, in the third part of the chapter, relies more on frictions in the labor market and deals more directly with how this market is organized. Here, technological change can still directly influence wages but there are new channels. For one, wages may not only reflect marginal productivity. Moreover, now unemployment is more in focus and is a function of technology, and since unemployment – through workers' outside option – may also feed back into wages, the picture becomes yet more complex. In the context of how wages are set, we furthermore argue in Section 6 that the importance of unions and their modus operandi are influenced by technology and, more generally, that labor income as a share of total income may respond to technological change in the presence of unions. An important point that we make in Section 7 is that "luck" can be a key part of wage outcomes for individuals active in a labor market with frictions, such as the search/matching frameworks, and that the "return to luck" can be greatly affected by technology as well. Finally, government participation in labor markets – labor-market "institutions", in the form of unemployment benefits, firing costs, and so on – likely interacts with technology in determining outcomes, and Section 8 completes the third part of this chapter by analyzing the interaction between technological shocks and labor market institutions in the context of the comparison between the United States and Europe.

The fourth and final part of the chapter asks the "So what?" question: given the significant transformations observed, is a government policy change called for? Our discussion here is very brief. It mainly points out that a basic element underlying any decisions on policy, namely, what the welfare outcomes of the changes in wages, unemployment, and so on, are for different groups in society, is studied only partially in the literature so far. Studies of changes in expected lifetime income of different groups exist, but it is reasonable to assume that risk matters too, especially with trend changes as large as those observed (at least to the extent they are hard to foresee and insure). In Section 9 we therefore cover some examples of more full-fledged attempts to look at the distribution of consumption and welfare outcomes of the changes in technology/labor market outcomes. Finally, Section 10 concludes the chapter.

2. A look at the facts

Before modeling the economic forces that connect changes in technology to labor market outcomes, it is useful to begin by summarizing how labor market inequalities and the aggregate technological environment evolved over the past three decades.

2.1. Labor market inequalities

In the late 1980s and early 1990s, an extensive body of empirical work has started to systematically document the changes in the U.S. wage structure over the past three decades. Levy and Murnane (1992) give the first overview of an already developed empirical literature. To date, Katz and Autor (1999) and, more recently, Eckstein and Nagypal (2004), offer the most exhaustive description of the facts. In between, numerous other papers have contributed significantly to our understanding of the data on wage inequality.[2]

The typical data source used in the empirical work on the subject is the sequence of yearly cross-sections in the March *Current Population Survey* (CPS). The other important data source is the longitudinal *Panel Study of Income Dynamics* (PSID). In this

---

[2] We refer the reader to the bibliographic lists in Levy and Murnane (1992), Katz and Autor (1999) and Eckstein and Nagypal (2004) for more details.

section, we limit ourselves to stating the main facts and briefly commenting on them, omitting the details on the data sets, the sample selection, and the calculations that can be found in the original references. Unless otherwise stated, the data refer to a sample of male workers with strong attachment to the labor force, i.e., full-time, full-year workers.[3]

OBSERVATION 1. Wage inequality in the United States is today at its historical peak over the post–World War II period. However, early in the century it was even larger. The returns to college and high school fell precipitously in the first half of the century and then rose again until now [Goldin and Katz (1999)].

In other words, the time series for inequality over the past 100 years is "U-shaped". Although the bulk of this chapter is devoted to interpreting the dynamics of the wage structure over the past three decades, it is useful to put the evidence in a historical perspective to appreciate that the high current level of inequality is not a unique episode in U.S. history. The rest of the facts characterize the evolution of inequality since the mid-1960s.[4]

OBSERVATION 2. Wage inequality increased steadily in the United States starting from the early 1970s. The 90–10 weekly wage ratio rose by 35 percent for both males and females in the period 1965–1995: from 1.20 to 1.55 for males, and from 1.05 to 1.40 for females. The increase in inequality took place everywhere in the wage distribution: both the 90–50 differential and the 50–10 differential rose by comparable amounts [Katz and Autor (1999)].

Qualitatively, the rise in inequality is present independently of the measure of dispersion and of the definition of labor income. For example, the standard deviation of log wages for males rose from 0.47 in 1965 to 0.62 in 1995, the Gini coefficient jumped from 0.25 to 0.34 [Katz and Autor (1999)], and the mean-median ratio rose from 1.00 to 1.18 over the same period [Eckstein and Nagypal (2004)]. Inequality of annual earnings increased even more.[5]

---

[3] Eckstein and Nagypal (2004) systematically document all the facts for males and females separately. Typically, measures of inequality in the literature refer to hourly or weekly wages, that is, they isolate the evolution of the "price" of certain labor market skills. The use of hourly or weekly wages then avoids the contamination of the data with endogenous labor supply decisions that, for example, is present in annual earnings.

[4] In Section 5 we return briefly to this historical pattern. In passing, we note that the data seems at odds with the so-called "Kuznets Hypothesis", i.e., the conjecture that income inequality first increases and then decreases as economies grow.

[5] The reason is, perhaps surprisingly, not a rise in the cross-sectional variance of hours worked, but rather a substantial increase in the wage-hours correlation over the past 30 years. See Heathcote, Storesletten and Violante (2003) for an account of these facts.

OBSERVATION 3. The average and median wage have remained constant in real terms since the mid-1970s. Real wages in the bottom of the wage distribution have fallen substantially. For example, the 10th wage percentile for males declined by 30 percent in real terms from 1970 to 1990 [Acemoglu (2002a)].[6] On the contrary, salaries in the very top of the wage distribution have grown rapidly. In 1970, the workers in the top 1 percent of the wage distribution held 5 percent of the U.S. wage bill, whereas in 1998 they received over 10 percent [Piketty and Saez (2003)].

A large part of the absolute increase of top range salaries is associated with the surge in CEO compensation. Piketty and Saez (2003) document that in 1970 the pay of the top 100 CEOs in the United States was about 40 times higher than the average salary. By 2000 those CEOs earned almost 1,000 times the average salary.

We now list a set of facts on the evolution of *between-group* inequality, i.e. inequality between groups of workers classified by observable characteristics (e.g., gender, race, education, experience, occupation). For this purpose, it is useful to write wages w_{it} using the Mincerian representation

$$\ln w_{it} = X'_{it} p_t + \omega_{it}, \tag{1}$$

where X_{it} is a vector measuring the set of observable features of individual i at time t, p_t can be interpreted as a vector of prices for each characteristic in X, and ω_{it} is the residual unobserved component.

OBSERVATION 4. The returns to education increased slightly from 1950 to 1970, fell in the 1970s, increased sharply in the 1980s, and continued to increase, although at a slower pace, in the 1990s. For example, the college wage premium – defined as the ratio between the average weekly wage of college graduates (at least 16 years of schooling) and that of workers with at most a high school diploma (at most 12 years of schooling) – was 1.45 in 1965, 1.35 in 1975, 1.50 in 1985, and 1.70 in 1995 [Eckstein and Nagypal (2004)]. If one estimates the coefficient on educational dummies in a standard Mincerian wage regression like (1), the finding is similar: the annual return to a college degree (relative to a high-school degree) was 33 percent in the 1980s and over 50 percent in the 1990s [Eckstein and Nagypal (2004)].

We plot the college wage premium over the period 1963–2002 in Figure 1 (top panel).[7] Interestingly, if one slices up the college-educated group more finely into workers with post-college degrees and workers with college degree only, the rise in the skill premium is still very apparent. The return to post-college education relative to college education doubled from 1970 to 1990 [Eckstein and Nagypal (2004)].

---

[6] Note, however, that the wages of the 10th wage percentile have started to increase again since the late 1990s [Eckstein and Nagypal (2004)].

[7] Authors differ in their treatment of workers who have attended college for some years, but did not obtain a college degree. In Figure 1 (top panel), we have followed the bulk of the literature and assigned half of them to the numerator and half of them to the denominator [e.g., Autor, Katz and Krueger (1998)].

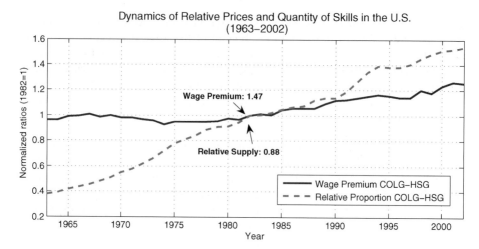

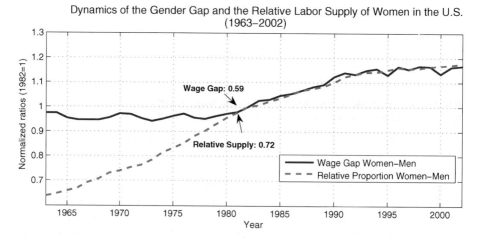

Figure 1. The top panel depicts the evolution of the skill premium (average wage of college graduates relative to the wage of high-school graduates) and of the relative quantity of skilled workers, from 1963–2002. The bottom panel depicts the evolution of the gender gap (average wage of female workers relative to the wage of male workers), over the same period of time.

OBSERVATION 5. The returns to professional and white-collar occupations relative to blue-collar occupations display dynamics and magnitudes similar to the data stratified by education. For example, the professional-blue collar premium rose by 20 percent from 1970 to 1995 [Eckstein and Nagypal (2004)].

Occupation is an interesting dimension of the wage structure that, until recently, received very little attention. For example, the "returns to occupation" appear large and significant, over and beyond returns to education. We discuss the theories of wage inequality that stress the changes in occupational structure in Section 7.

OBSERVATION 6. The returns to experience increased in the 1970s and the 1980s and leveled off in the 1990s. For example, the ratio of weekly wages between workers with 25 years of experience and workers with 5 years of experience rose from 1.3 in 1970 to 1.5 in 1995 [Katz and Autor (1999)]. An analysis by education group shows that the experience premium rose sharply for high-school graduates but remained roughly constant for college graduates [Weinberg (2003b)].

It is worth emphasizing, that although entry of the baby-boomers into the labor market in the early 1970s had a significant impact on the experience premium, the dynamics described above are robust to this and other demographic effects. See, for example, Juhn, Murphy and Pierce (1993).[8]

OBSERVATION 7. Inequality across race and gender declined since 1970. The black–white race differential, for workers of comparable experience, fell from 35 percent in 1965 to 20 percent in 1990 [Murphy and Welch (1992)]. The female–male wage gap fell from 45 percent in 1970 to 30 percent in 1995 [Katz and Autor (1999)].

We plot of the gender wage gap over the period 1963–2002 in Figure 1 (bottom panel). A unifying theory of the changes in the wage structure based on technological change should have something to say about gender as well as race. Admittedly, these two dimensions of inequality have been largely neglected by the literature. We return briefly to the gender gap in Section 4.

OBSERVATION 8. The composition of the working population changed dramatically over the past 40 years: in the period 1970–2000, women's labor force participation rate rose from 49 percent to 73 percent; college graduates rose from 15 to 30 percent of the male labor force and from 11 to 30 percent of the female labor force; professionals soared from 24 to 33 percent of the male labor force and from 8 to 28 percent of the female labor force [Eckstein and Nagypal (2004)].

We plot the relative supply of skilled workers and female workers over the time period 1963–2002 in Figure 1 (top and bottom panel, respectively).[9]
In terms of Equation (1), one can define the between-group component of wage inequality as the cross-sectional variance of $X'_{it} p_t$, and the within-group component as

---

[8] More recently, however, Card and Lemieux (2001) have argued in support of some "vintage effects" in the return to education. In particular, they argue that the college–high school premium is somewhat larger among the most recent cohorts of young workers entering the labor market.

[9] Skilled and unskilled labor are defined as in footnote 7.

the variance of the residual ω_{it}. The fraction accounted for by observable characteristics, in turn, can be decomposed into what is caused by a change in the dispersion in the quantities of observable characteristics (X_{it}), for given vector of prices, and what is due to a change in the prices associated to each observable characteristic (p_t), for a given distribution of quantities.

OBSERVATION 9. Overall, changes in quantities and prices of observable characteristics (gender, race, education, experience) explain about 40 percent of the increase in the variance of log wages from 1963 to 1995. The price component is by far larger than the quantity component. Increasing *within-group inequality*, i.e., wage dispersion within cells of "observationally equivalent" workers accounts for the residual 60 percent of the total increase. With respect to the timing, the rise in within-group inequality seems to anticipate that of the college premium by roughly a decade [Juhn, Murphy and Pierce (1993)].[10]

One can specify further the structure of the residual ω_{it} of Equation (1), for example as

$$\omega_{it} = \phi_t \alpha_i + \varepsilon_{it},$$

where α_i is the permanent part of unobservable skills (e.g., "innate ability"), ϕ_t is its time-varying price, and ε_{it} is the stochastic component due to earnings shocks whose variance is also allowed to change over time. If one is prepared to assume that the distribution of innate ability in the population is invariant, then with the help of panel data one can separate the rise in the return to ability from the increase in the volatility of transitory earnings shocks.

OBSERVATION 10. Around one-half of the rise in residual earnings inequality is explained by the permanent components (e.g., a higher return to ability), with the rest accounted for by transitory earnings shocks [Gottschalk and Moffitt (1994)].[11]

Interestingly, the rise in the transitory component is not due to higher job instability or labor mobility [Neumark (2000)], but rather to more volatile wage dynamics, in particular faster wage growth on the job and more severe wage losses upon displacement [Violante (2002)].

In Table 1 we report some key numbers on unemployment, wage inequality, and labor income shares for several OECD countries at five-year intervals from 1965 to 1995. We are particularly interested in the comparison between the United States and *continental*

---

[10] Notice that, typically, occupation is excluded from these regressions. Including occupation would reduce the fraction of unexplained wage variance.

[11] Note that a rise in the return on ability does generate an increase in cross-sectional variation of wages because it multiplies individual ability in the log-wage Mincerian equation.

Table 1

Data on the evolution of the labor share, the unemployment rate, and wage inequality across OECD countries from 1965–1995. Cross-country labor market data (1965–1995)

Country		1965	1970	1975	1980	1985	1990	1995	Change
Austria	Unemp. rate	0.018	0.011	0.017	0.029	0.045	0.054	0.061	0.043
	Labor share	0.698	0.679	0.717	0.694	0.665	0.646	0.645	−0.053
	Inequality				0.820	0.790	0.870	0.880	0.060
Belgium	Unemp. rate	0.023	0.022	0.064	0.114	0.111	0.110	0.142	0.120
	Labor share		0.667	0.729	0.730	0.682	0.685	0.676	0.009
	Inequality					0.660	0.650	0.640	−0.020
Denmark	Unemp. rate	0.014	0.016	0.061	0.093	0.085	0.112	0.103	0.089
	Labor share	0.736	0.723	0.732	0.706	0.677	0.635	0.605	−0.131
	Inequality				0.760	0.770	0.770		0.010
Finland	Unemp. rate	0.025	0.021	0.050	0.051	0.047	0.121	0.167	0.142
	Labor share	0.738	0.711	0.762	0.730	0.723	0.733	0.680	−0.058
	Inequality				0.890	0.920	0.940	0.930	0.040
France	Unemp. rate	0.020	0.027	0.049	0.079	0.101	0.105	0.115	0.095
	Labor share	0.688	0.674	0.707	0.710	0.645	0.618	0.603	−0.085
	Inequality				1.210	1.210	1.240	1.230	0.020
Germany	Unemp. rate	0.010	0.011	0.037	0.060	0.075	0.078	0.099	0.089
	Labor share	0.685	0.703	0.703	0.704	0.667	0.658	0.637	−0.048
	Inequality				0.870	0.830	0.830	0.810	−0.060
Ireland	Unemp. rate	0.047	0.055	0.078	0.112	0.164	0.146	0.120	0.073
	Labor share	0.828	0.842	0.835	0.833	0.763	0.715	0.645	−0.183
	Inequality								
Italy	Unemp. rate	0.041	0.043	0.051	0.070	0.099	0.096	0.120	0.079
	Labor share	0.669	0.687	0.711	0.690	0.656	0.653	0.606	−0.063
	Inequality				0.850	0.830	0.770	0.970	0.120
Netherlands	Unemp. rate	0.010	0.018	0.038	0.080	0.081	0.062	0.071	0.061
	Labor share	0.656	0.687	0.705	0.661	0.623	0.619	0.624	−0.032
	Inequality					0.920	0.960	0.950	0.030
Norway	Unemp. rate	0.016	0.015	0.018	0.026	0.030	0.056	0.049	0.034
	Labor share	0.750	0.771	0.782	0.757	0.739	0.713		−0.037
	Inequality				0.720	0.720	0.680		−0.040
Portugal	Unemp. rate	0.040	0.024	0.065	0.079	0.070	0.051	0.073	0.033
	Labor share	0.562	0.615	0.873	0.751	0.673	0.679	0.680	0.118
	Inequality								
Spain	Unemp. rate	0.028	0.030	0.059	0.161	0.200	0.196	0.230	0.202
	Labor share	0.763	0.780	0.788	0.756	0.679	0.669	0.616	−0.147
	Inequality								
Sweden	Unemp. rate	0.018	0.022	0.019	0.028	0.021	0.052	0.079	0.061
	Labor share	0.724	0.716	0.745	0.711	0.691	0.693	0.630	−0.095
	Inequality				0.750	0.760	0.730	0.790	0.040
U.K.	Unemp. rate	0.019	0.025	0.044	0.089	0.091	0.086	0.079	0.060
	Labor share	0.693	0.699	0.698	0.694	0.690	0.712	0.692	−0.002
	Inequality				0.920	1.050	1.150	1.200	0.280
Canada	Unemp. rate	0.040	0.058	0.076	0.099	0.089	0.103	0.096	0.056
	Labor share	0.716	0.660	0.652	0.634	0.630	0.666	0.659	−0.057
	Inequality				1.240	1.390	1.380	1.330	0.090

A. Hornstein et al.

Table 1
(Continued)

Country		1965	1970	1975	1980	1985	1990	1995	Change
USA	Unemp. rate	0.038	0.054	0.070	0.083	0.062	0.066	0.055	0.017
	Labor share	0.685	0.695	0.675	0.678	0.665	0.666	0.670	−0.015
	Inequality				1.180	1.350	1.380	1.470	0.290
Europe	Unemp. rate	0.024	0.024	0.047	0.076	0.087	0.095	0.110	0.086
(average)	Labor share	0.708	0.712	0.753	0.726	0.683	0.670	0.637	−0.062
	Inequality				0.859	0.841	0.844	0.900	0.040

Note. Data on unemployment rates are from Blanchard and Wolfers (2000). Data on labor shares are from Blanchard and Wolfers (2000) except the 1995 entry for Austria, Denmark, Ireland and Portugal which was computed directly from OECD data. Inequality is measured as the 90–10 log-wage differential for male workers. The data are taken from the OECD Employment Outlook (1996, Table 3.1). Austria: the measure is the 80–10 differential and data in the 1985 column are for 1987. Belgium: the measure is the 80–10 differential and data in the 1995 column are for 1993. Denmark: 1985 and 1990 columns are for 1983 and 1991 respectively. Finland: data in the 1985 column are for 1986. Germany: data in the 1985 and 1995 columns are for 1983 and 1993 respectively. Italy: data in the 1985, 1990 and 1995 columns are for 1984, 1991 and 1993 respectively. Netherlands: the measure of inequality is for males and females. Norway: data in the 1985 and 1990 columns are for 1983 and 1991 respectively. Moreover, the measure of inequality is for males and females. Portugal: data in the 1990 and 1995 columns are for 1989 and 1993 respectively. Canada: data in the 1980 and 1985 columns are for 1981 and 1986 respectively. For all countries, except USA and U.K., data in the 1995 column are for 1994. Europe average: unweighted mean of European countries, except U.K.

European countries (averaged in the row labeled Europe (average)). For completeness, we include data for the United Kingdom and Canada, whose behavior falls somewhere between that of the United States and continental Europe.

OBSERVATION 11. The time pattern of wage inequality over the past 30 years differs substantially across countries. The U.K. economy had a rise in wage inequality similar to that in the U.S. economy, except for the fact that the average real wage in the United Kingdom has kept growing [Machin (1996)]. Continental European countries had virtually no change in wage inequality, whereas over the same period they had large increases in their unemployment rates (roughly, all due to longer unemployment durations) and a sharp fall in the labor income share in GDP. On the contrary, in the United States both the unemployment rate and the labor share have remained relatively constant [Blanchard and Wolfers (2000)].

In 1965 the unemployment rate in virtually every European country was lower than in the United States. Thirty years later, the opposite was true: the U.S. unemployment rate rose only by 1.7 percent from 1965 to 1995, whereas the average unemployment rate increase of European countries was 8.4 percent.[12]

---

[12] Notice, however, that in the United States non-participation of the low-skilled males rose from 7 percent to 12 percent from the early 1970s to the late 1990s [Juhn (1992) and Murphy and Topel (1997)].

The labor income share has declined only marginally in the United States – by 1.5 percentage points from 1965 to 1995 – while on average it fell by almost 6 points in Europe. Wage inequality, measured by the percentage differential between the ninth and the first earnings deciles for male workers, rose only slightly in Europe by 4 percent in the period from 1980 to 1995, and it even declined in some countries (Belgium, Germany and Norway). Recall that, over the same period, earnings inequality surged in the United States: the OECD data show a rise of almost 30 percent, close to the numbers we reported earlier in this section.

Interestingly, the European averages hide much less cross-country variation than one would expect, given the raw nature of the comparison. For example, in 11 out of the 14 continental European countries, the increase in the unemployment rate has been larger than 6 percentage points, and in 9 countries the decline in the labor share has been greater than 5 percentage points.

Recently, Rogerson (2004) has argued that if one focuses on *employment* rate differences between the United States and Europe rather than on unemployment rate differences, a new set of insights emerges from the data. Employment rates in the United States start to increase relative to European employment rates twenty years before the divergence in unemployment rates. Moreover, the increase in European unemployment rates is correlated with the decline of European manufacturing employment.

2.2. Technological change

The standard measure of aggregate technological change, total factor productivity (TFP), does not distinguish between the different ways in which technology grows. First, technology growth may differ across final-output sectors and second, it may have different effects on the productivity of different input factors. The recent experience of developed countries, however, seems to suggest that in the past 30 years technological change has originated in particular sectors of the economy and has favored particular inputs of production.

Arguably, the advent of microelectronics (i.e., microchips and semiconductors) induced a sequence of innovations in information and communication technologies with two features. First, *sector-specific* productivity (SSP) growth substantially increased the productivity of the sector that produces new capital equipment, making the use of capital in production relatively less expensive. Second, *factor-specific* productivity (FSP) growth favored skilled and educated labor disproportionately. In other words, the recent technological revolution has affected the production structure in a rather asymmetric way.

Our assessment of the importance of SSP and FSP changes relies heavily on observed movements in relative prices. For SSP change, we rely on the substantial decline of the price of equipment capital relative to the price of consumption goods, a process that does not show any sign of slowing down. On the contrary, it shows an acceleration in recent years. For FSP change, we rely on the substantial increase in the wage of highly educated workers relative to less educated workers, the skill premium.

We first review the Solow growth accounting methodology for TFP within the context of the one-sector neoclassical growth model and then introduce SSP accounting and how it applies to the idea of capital-embodied technical change.[13] Next, we discuss how an acceleration of capital-embodied technical change might relate to the much-discussed TFP growth slowdown in the 1970s and 1980s; here, we discuss the possible relevance of the concept of General Purpose Technologies (GPTs). Finally, we explain the mapping between relative wages and FSP changes.

2.2.1. Total factor productivity accounting

Standard economic theory views production as a transformation of a collection of inputs into outputs. We are interested in how this production structure is changing over time. At an aggregate *National Income and Product Accounts* (NIPA) level we deal with some measure of aggregate output, y, and two measures of aggregate inputs: capital k and labor l. The production structure is represented by the production function F, $y = F(k, l, t)$. Since the production structure may change, the production function is indexed by time t. Aggregate total factor productivity changes when the production function shifts over time, i.e., when there is a change in output which we cannot attribute to changes in inputs. More formally, the marginal change in output is the sum of the marginal changes in inputs, weighted by their marginal contributions to output (marginal products), and the shift of the production function, $\dot{y} = F_k \dot{k} + F_l \dot{l} + F_t$.[14] This is usually expressed in terms of growth rates as

$$\hat{y} = \eta_k \hat{k} + \eta_l \hat{l} + \widehat{A}, \quad \text{with } \widehat{A} = \frac{F_t}{F}, \tag{2}$$

where hats denote percentage growth rates, and the weight on an input growth rate is the elasticity of output with respect to the input: $\eta_k = F_k k / F$ and $\eta_l = F_l l / F$. Alternatively, if we know the elasticities, we can derive productivity growth as output growth minus a weighted sum of input growth rates.

Solow's (1957) important insight was that, under two assumptions, we can replace an input's output elasticity – which we do not observe – with the input's share in total revenue, for which we have observations. First, we assume that production is constant returns to scale, i.e., that if we are to double all inputs, then output will double, implying that the output elasticities sum to one: $\eta_k + \eta_n = 1$. Second, we assume that producers act competitively in their output and input markets, i.e., that they take the prices of their

---

[13] Our presentation is instrumental to the discussion of the impact of technological change on labor markets, and hence it is kept to the bare minimum. Jorgenson's (2005) chapter of this Handbook provides an exhaustive treatment of traditional and modern growth accounting.

[14] The marginal change of a variable is its instantaneous rate of change over time; that is, if we write the value of a variable at a point in time as $x(t)$, then the marginal change is the time derivative, $\dot{x}(t) = \partial x(t)/\partial t$. Nothing is lost in the following if the reader interprets $\dot{x}(t)$ as the change of a variable from year to year; that is, $x(t) - x(t-1)$.

products and inputs as given. Profit maximization then implies that inputs are employed until the marginal revenue product of an input is equalized with the price of that input. In turn, this means that the output elasticity of an input is equal to the input's revenue share. For example, for the employment of labor, profit maximization implies that $p_y F_l = p_l$, which can be rewritten as $\eta_l = F_l l / F = p_l l / p_y y = \alpha_l$ (p_i stands for the price of good i). With these two assumptions, we can calculate aggregate productivity growth, also known as total factor productivity (TFP) growth, as

$$\widehat{A} = \hat{y} - (1 - \alpha_l)\hat{k} - \alpha_l \hat{l}. \tag{3}$$

The Solow growth accounting procedure has the advantage that its implementation does not require very stringent assumptions with respect to the production structure, except constant returns to scale, and it does not require any information beyond measures of aggregate output and input quantities and the real wage. This relatively low information requirement comes at a cost: this aggregate TFP measure does not provide any information on the specific sources or nature of technological change.

Given available data on quantities and prices for industry outputs and inputs, it is straightforward to apply the Solow growth accounting procedure and obtain measures of sector-specific technical change [see, for example, Jorgenson, Gollop and Fraumeni (1987)]. Recently Jorgenson and Stiroh (2000) have documented the substantial differences in output and TFP growth rates across U.S. industries over the period 1958–1996. In particular, they point out that TFP growth rates in high-tech industries producing equipment investment are about three to four times as high as a measure of aggregate TFP growth. Also based on industry data, Oliner and Sichel (2000) and Jorgenson (2001) attribute a substantial part of the increase of aggregate TFP growth over the second half of the 1990s to one industry: semiconductors.

2.2.2. Sector-specific productivity accounting

The convincing evidence for persistent differences of SSP growth raises the potential of serious aggregation problems for the analysis of aggregate outcomes. We now discuss SSP accounting in a simple two-sector growth model that focuses on the distinction between investment and consumption goods. This approach provides a straightforward measure of SSP growth, and it keeps the aggregation problems manageable. Based on this approach, we present evidence of substantial increases of the relative productivity in the equipment-investment goods producing industries and stagnant productivity in the consumption goods industries since the mid-1970s.

Greenwood, Hercowitz and Krusell (1997) use a two-sector model of the economy – where one sector produces consumption goods and the other new capital – to measure the relative importance of total-factor productivity changes in each of these sectors. Goods – consumption c and new capital x – are produced using capital and labor as inputs to constant-returns-to-scale technologies,

$$c = A_c F(k_c, l_c) \quad \text{and} \quad x = A_x F(k_x, l_x), \tag{4}$$

and total factor inputs can be freely allocated across sectors,

$$k_c + k_x = k \quad \text{and} \quad l_c + l_x = l. \tag{5}$$

Note that we have assumed that factor substitution properties are the same in the two sectors; that is, the functions relating inputs to outputs are the same. One can show that with identical factor substitution properties, the two-sector economy is equivalent to a one-sector economy with exogenous changes in the relative price of investment goods, $1/q$,

$$y = c + \frac{x}{q} = A_c F(k, l). \tag{6}$$

In particular, the relative price of investment goods is the inverse of the relative productivity advantage of producing new capital goods[15]

$$q = \frac{A_x}{A_c}. \tag{7}$$

The relative productivity of the investment goods sector is also called "capital-embodied" technical change, because q can be interpreted as the productivity level (quality) embodied in new vintages of capital.[16]

Accounting for quality improvements in new products is a basic problem of growth accounting.[17] This is especially true for our framework since we measure investment in terms of constant-quality capital goods. In a monumental study, Gordon (1990) constructed quality-adjusted price indexes for different types of producers' durable equipment. Building on Gordon's work, Hulten (1992), Greenwood, Hercowitz and Krusell (1997) and Cummins and Violante (2002) have derived aggregate time series for capital-embodied technical change in the U.S. economy.[18] They use the property just described: that the constant-quality price of investment relative to consumption (precisely, non-durable consumption and services) reveals the extent of productivity improvements. Their main finding is that:

---

[15] Jorgenson (2005), in this Handbook, labels this methodology, where *relative productivity* growth is measured off the decline in relative prices, the "price approach" to growth accounting.

[16] Define investments in consumption units as $i = x/q$. Then, the aggregate resource constraint reads

$$c + i = A_c F(k, l),$$

and the law of motion for capital in efficiency units is $k' = (1 - \delta)k + iq$.

[17] See this Handbook's chapter by Jorgenson (2005) for a comprehensive discussion on the different approaches to the measurement of quality changes.

[18] Hulten's series strictly uses Gordon's data and therefore spans until 1983. Greenwood et al. extend Gordon's index to 1992 by applying a constant adjustment factor to the National Income and Product Accounts (NIPA) official price index. Cummins and Violante update the series to 2000. Starting with Gordon's quality-adjusted price indexes for a variety of equipment goods from 1947 to 1983, they estimate the quality bias implicit in the NIPA price indexes for that period. Using the official NIPA series, they then extrapolate the quality bias from 1984 to 2000 for each equipment type and aggregate into an index for equipment and structure.

OBSERVATION 12. Productivity growth in the sector producing equipment investment has accelerated relative to the rest of the economy since the early to mid-1970s.

The solid line in Figure 2 shows the relative productivity of the equipment investment goods sector, q, for the period 1947–2000, normalized to 1 in the first year. This index grows at an annual rate of about 1.6 percent until 1975 and at an annual rate of 3.6 percent thereafter. In the 1990s, productivity growth embodied in capital has been spectacularly high, reaching an average annual rate just below 5 percent.

The measurement of SSP growth through changes in relative prices requires that the price measures used are appropriately adjusted for quality improvements, presenting a problem for the time period studied since, arguably, the IT revolution has caused large improvements in the quality of durable goods and has led to the introduction of a vast range of new items. Therefore, alternative ways of measuring capital-embodied productivity advancements have been proposed. Hobjin (2000) calculates the rate of embodied technical change by calibrating a vintage capital model. His findings are very similar to the price-based approach, both in terms of the average growth rate, and in terms of

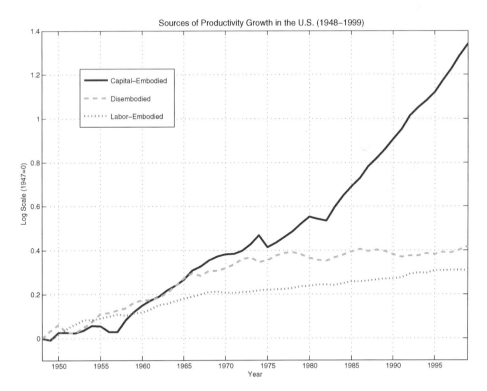

Figure 2. The dynamics of three sources of productivity growth in the postwar U.S. economy: disembodied, capital-embodied, and labor-embodied. *Source*: Cummins and Violante (2002).

the timing of the technological acceleration. Bahk and Gort (1993) and Sakellaris and Wilson (2004) use plant-level data to estimate production functions and assess the productivity effects of new investments. They estimate the growth rate of capital-embodied technical change to be between 12 and 18 percent per year, much higher than the rest of the literature.

We calculate the rate of SSP change in the consumption goods sector based on the standard Solow approach. It is well known that the U.S. labor income share in GDP has been remarkably stable for the time period considered. We therefore choose a Cobb–Douglas parametric representation of the production function,

$$y = A_c k^\alpha l^{1-\alpha}, \tag{8}$$

with labor income share, $1 - \alpha = 0.64$ [Cooley and Prescott (1995)]. Conditional on observations for real GDP (in terms of consumption goods), the real capital stock, and employment, we can use this expression to solve for the SSP of the consumption sector A_c.[19] The common finding from this computation, as evident from the dashed line in Figure 2, is the following observation.

OBSERVATION 13. Productivity in the sector producing consumption goods (precisely, non-durable and services) shows essentially no growth over the two decades 1975–1995.

The approach of Greenwood, Hercowitz and Krusell (1997) defines aggregate output in terms of consumption goods. This is rather non-standard. The usual approach, especially as applied to the study of SSP, defines aggregate output growth as a revenue-weighted sum of sectoral output growth rates: a Divisia index [see, e.g., Jorgenson (2001) or Oliner and Sichel (2000)]. For this more standard approach, one can write aggregate TFP growth as the revenue-weighted sum of sectoral TFP growth. While the Divisia-aggregator approach is a definition with some desirable properties, the Greenwood, Hercowitz and Krusell (1997) approach is based on a particular theory and requires certain identifying restrictions concerning the production structure. Hall (1973) shows that in multi-sector models a unique output aggregator, that is, a function that relates some measure of aggregate output to some measure of aggregate input, exists if certain separability conditions for the aggregate production possibility frontier are satisfied. The conditions for such an output aggregator to exist are, essentially, the ones

---

[19] It is important to adjust the capital and labor input measure for quality change. As pointed out above, quality adjustment of investment is useful so as to capture investment-specific technical change. The capital stock is then calculated as the cumulative sum of past undepreciated constant-quality investment. From our discussion of wage inequality it follows that the labor input needs to be adjusted for two reasons. First, the skill premium has been increasing since the mid-1970s, and thus the productivity of skilled labor, A_S, is increasing faster than the productivity of unskilled labor A_u. Second, at the same time, the relative supply of skilled labor has been increasing, inducing large changes in the composition of the stock of labor. To account for quality changes, we use the labor input index computed by Ho and Jorgenson (1999). The dotted line in Figure 2 plots this quality index for labor which grows at an average rate of 0.8% per year.

imposed by Greenwood, Hercowitz and Krusell (1997).[20] Given the definition of aggregate output in Equation (6), SSP for consumption, or A_c, is then sometimes interpreted as neutral, or disembodied, aggregate technological change.

2.2.3. *Reconciling the acceleration in investment-specific productivity growth with the slowdown in TFP: general purpose technology and learning*

The stagnation of aggregate TFP since the mid-1970s – evident from Figure 2 – accounts for the phenomenon often referred to as a "productivity slowdown" in the growth accounting literature.[21] How can we reconcile the acceleration of investment SSP with a slowdown of consumption SSP? One interpretation builds on learning-by-doing (LBD). New investment goods do not attain their full potential as soon as they are introduced but, rather, their productivity can stay temporarily below the productivity of older capital that was introduced same time ago. This feature is attributed to learning effects.[22]

These learning effects can be extremely important when the technological change is "drastic". Recent discussions suggest that the advent of microelectronics led to a radical shift in the technological paradigm, i.e., to a new "general purpose technology" (GPT). Bresnahan and Trajtenberg (1995) coined this term to describe certain major innovations that have the potential for pervasive use and application in a wide range of sectors of the economy. David (1990) and Lipsey, Bekar and Carlaw (1998) cite the microchip as the last example of such innovations that included, in ancient times, writing and printing and, in more recent times, the steam-engine and the electric dynamo.[23] Although it is hard to define the concept satisfactorily, given available data, we list as a "fact" the dominant view, which maintains that:

OBSERVATION 14. Technological change in the past 30 years displays a "general purpose" nature.

Though most of the evidence supporting this statement is anecdotal, there are some bits of hard evidence. Hornstein and Krusell (1996) document that the decline in TFP occurred roughly simultaneously across many developed countries. More recently, Cummins and Violante (2002) construct measures of productivity improvements for

---

[20] For further details on this issue, see Hornstein and Krusell (2000).

[21] Since non-equipment investment represents more than three-fourths of GDP, the slowdown of consumption SSP change accounts for most of the slowdown of aggregate TFP change.

[22] The literature on learning effects is large. Lucas (1993) discusses the classic example of LBD related to the construction of the liberty ships of World War II. Bahk and Gort (1993) measure substantial LBD effects at the plant level. Irwin and Klenow (1994) present evidence of LBD in the production of semiconductors. Jovanovic and Nyarko (1995) document learning curves in several professions. Huggett and Ospina (2001) find evidence that the effect of a large equipment purchase is initially to reduce plant-level total factor productivity growth.

[23] Gordon (2000) offers a dissenting view on the issue of whether or not information technologies measure up to the great inventions of the past. In his view, the aggregate productivity impact of computers and telecommunication equipment has been fairly small compared to, say, the telegraph, the railroad, or electricity.

26 different types of equipment goods. Using the sectoral input–output tables, they aggregate these indexes into 62 industry-level measures of equipment-embodied technical change, and document that their growth rate has accelerated by a similar amount in virtually every industry in the 1990s. Jovanovic and Rousseau (2005) draw an articulated parallel between the diffusion of electricity in the early 20th century and the diffusion of information technologies (IT) eighty years later based on a variety of data. Their evidence supports the view that both episodes marked a drastic discontinuity in the historical process of technological change. Taken together, all these observations suggest that, similar to other past GPTs, IT has affected productivity in a general way over the past three decades.

There are two versions of the argument that IT are responsible for the observed productivity slowdown. According to one, the slowdown is real: when learning-by-doing is important in improving the efficiency of a production technique, abandoning the older, but extensively used technology to embrace a new method of production involves a "step in the dark" that can lead to a temporary slowdown in labor productivity [Hornstein and Krusell (1996), Greenwood and Yorukoglu (1997) and Aghion and Howitt (1998, chapter 8)].

An alternative, complementary version maintains that the slowdown is a statistical artifact due to mismeasurement: if the phase of IT adoption coincides with associated investments in organizational or intangible capital, as our Section 5 will suggest, then insofar as these investments are not included in the official statistics, measured TFP growth will first underestimate and then overestimate "true" TFP growth [Hall (2001) and Basu et al. (2003)]. The reason is that initially, when large investments in organizational capital are made, the "output side" of the mismeasurement is severe. Later, when the economy has built a significant stock of organizational capital, the "input side" of mismeasurement becomes dominant.

This explanation of the TFP slowdown is appealing, but extremely difficult to evaluate quantitatively because of the lack of direct evidence on how organizations learn. Using some theory, Hornstein (1999) argues that one key parameter is the fraction of knowledge that firms can transfer from the old to the new technology but also shows that the model's predictions vary significantly across plausible parameterizations. Atkeson and Kehoe (2002) build an equilibrium model to measure the dynamics of organizational capital during the "electrification of America". They criticize the Bahk and Gort (1993) view that organizational learning is reflected into an increase in the productivity of labor at the plant level: in an equilibrium model where labor is mobile, productivity is equalized across plants. Instead, they argue that when organizations learn they expand in size. Thus, cross-sectional microdata on the size distribution of plants allows to identify the structural parameters of the stochastic process behind organizational learning.

Finally, Manuelli (2000) argues that, even in absence of learning effects, the anticipation of a future technological shock embodied in capital can result in a transitional phase of slowdown of economic activity. In the period between the announcement and the actual availability of the new technology, the existing firms prefer exercising the option of waiting to invest and the new firms prefer delay entering. Consequently, output falls temporarily until the arrival of the new technology.[24]

2.2.4. Factor-specific productivity accounting

In order to talk about changes in FSP, one possibility is to generalize the production function in Equation (8) by disaggregating the contributions to production of the two labor inputs – skilled (e.g., more educated) and unskilled (e.g., less educated) labor. Suppose the aggregate labor input, l, is a CES function of skilled and unskilled labor, l_s and l_u, with FSPs A_s and A_u,

$$l = \left[(A_s l_s)^\sigma + (A_u l_u)^\sigma\right]^{1/\sigma}, \quad \sigma \leqslant 1. \tag{9}$$

Relative wage data can then be employed to understand the nature and evolution of FSP in the economy. With competitive input markets, the relative wages are a function of the relative FSP and the relative labor supply

$$\ln\left(\frac{w_s}{w_u}\right) = \sigma \ln\left(\frac{A_s}{A_u}\right) - (1 - \sigma) \ln\left(\frac{l_s}{l_u}\right). \tag{10}$$

The elasticity of substitution between skilled and unskilled labor here is $1/(1 - \sigma)$. Katz and Murphy (1992) run a simple regression of relative wages on relative input quantities and a time trend to capture growth in the ratio A_s/A_u. They measure skilled labor input as total hours supplied to the market by workers with at least a college degree. Their estimate of the substitution elasticity – around 1.4 (or $\sigma = 0.29$) – indicates that a ten-percent increase in the relative supply of skilled labor implies a seven percent decline of the skill premium.[25] The estimated elasticity of substitution between factors, together with the growing skill premium, imply an increase in the relative FSP of skilled labor in excess of 11 percent per year. We conclude that the typical result of similar exercises on U.S. data is that:

OBSERVATION 15. Recent technological advancements have been favorable to the most skilled workers in the population. In other words, technical change has been *skill-biased*.

The "acceleration" in the rate of capital-embodied technical change, the "general purpose" nature of the new wave of technologies, and the "skill-biased" attribute of the recent productivity advancements are the three chief features of the new technological environment that seems to have emerged since the early to mid-1970s. The various economic theories that we are about to review in the rest of this chapter are built on various combinations of these features.

[24] We refer the reader to Hornstein and Krusell (1996) for a list of alternative explanations of the TFP slowdown that are not based on changes in technology.

[25] The estimated input elasticity of about 1.4 is consistent with a large empirical literature on factor substitution that uses a wide array of data sets (time series as well as cross-section) and methods; see, e.g., Hamermesh (1993).

3. Skill-biased technical change: Inside the black box

As we have just observed, the pattern of relative quantities of skills measured by education suggest that the behavior of the skill premium, that is, the increase in the wages of
highly educated workers relative to those of less educated workers, should be attributed
to a skill-biased labor demand shift, or to "skill-biased technical change". In the absence of a factor-bias in technological progress, the upward trend in the supply of skills
documented in Figure 1 (top panel) would have reduced the skill premium.

Katz and Murphy (1992) were the first to use a production framework with limited
substitution between skilled and unskilled labor to recover changes in relative FSP from
changes in the skill premium. One should note a substantial drawback of the pure skill-
biased technical change hypothesis: it is based on *unobservables* (relative FSP changes)
that are measured residually from Equation (10), so very much like TFP, it is a "black
box". In this section we review the attempts to give some specific economic content to
the notion of skill-biased technical change.

We start from the capital-skill complementarity conjecture advanced originally by
Krusell et al. (2000). Next, we analyze models based on the Nelson–Phelps hypothesis: the adoption phase of a new technology requires skilled and educated workers. If
one allows for an important role of FSP changes, then it is paramount to understand
what economic forces induce these changes endogenously. In this context, we review
the theory of "directed technical change" associated mainly to the work by Acemoglu
(2002b, 2003b): exogenous spurts in the relative supply of skilled labor can induce the
introduction of skill-biased technological advancements by affecting the incentives of
the innovators.

3.1. Capital-skill complementarity

Krusell et al. (2000; KORV henceforth) argue that the dynamics of SSP that induced
the substantial drop in the relative price of equipment capital is the force behind the
rise in the skill premium. The decline in the price of equipment due to productivity improvements, especially that embodied in information and communication technologies,
led to an increased use of equipment capital in production. KORV observe that, at least
since Griliches (1969), various empirical papers support the idea that skilled labor is
relatively more complementary to equipment capital than is unskilled labor. As a result,
the higher capital stock increased skilled wages relatively more than unskilled wages.
Consequently, the skill premium increased.

Thus, the key elements in KORV's analysis are: (1) separating the effect of equipment
capital from that of other capital, mainly structures, (2) allowing equipment to have
different degrees of complementarity with skilled and unskilled labor, (3) measuring
the efficiency units of capital, especially the new technologies, correctly.[26]

---

[26] The quality-adjusted equipment capital stock is again based on the work of Gordon (1990) and subsequent
updates, especially for IT technology.

KORV capture the differential complementarity between capital and skilled and unskilled labor using the following nested CES production function of four inputs: structures k_s, equipment k_e, skilled labor l_s, and unskilled labor l_u:

$$y = k_s^\alpha \left[\lambda \left[\mu (A_{k_e} k_e)^\rho + (1 - \mu)(A_s l_s)^\rho \right]^{\sigma/\rho} + (1 - \lambda)(A_u l_u)^\sigma \right]^{(1-\alpha)/\sigma}, \quad (11)$$

with $\rho, \sigma \leqslant 1$. Profit-maximizing behavior of a price-taking firm implies that the skill premium can be approximately written as

$$\ln \left(\frac{w_s}{w_u} \right) \simeq \sigma \ln \left(\frac{A_s}{A_u} \right) - (1 - \sigma) \ln \left(\frac{l_s}{l_u} \right) + \lambda \frac{\sigma - \rho}{\rho} \ln \left(\frac{k_e}{l_s} \right)^\rho. \quad (12)$$

KORV estimate $\sigma = 0.4$ and $\rho = -0.5$, and thus that the skill premium increases with the stock of equipment capital.[27] They find that the relative productivity of skilled labor grows at a modest 3 percent per year, a much more plausible number than the one estimated by Katz and Murphy (1992). Overall, KORV show that with their estimated parameters, the relative wage movements in the data can be quite closely tracked. This includes the decline of the wage premium in the 1970s, attributable to an acceleration in the growth of college enrollment due to the Vietnam war draft and the entry of the baby-boom cohorts.[28]

From Equation (12) it follows that the skill premium can increase, even if the relative productivity of skilled labor remains constant and the relative supply of skilled labor increases, provided the equipment-skilled labor ratio trends upward fast enough. From this perspective, the results of KORV complement Katz and Murphy's (1992) work: when capital and skills are complementary in production, capital accumulation can explain a large fraction of the residual trend in skill-biased productivity growth.[29]

---

[27] With this nested CES in 3 factors (equipment, skilled and unskilled labor) it is unclear how to define capital-skill complementarity. One possible, but slightly unorthodox, definition is that the skill premium rises with the stock of equipment. A more traditional definition involves comparing the Allen elasticities of substitution. The elasticity of substitution between equipment and unskilled labor is $1/(1 - \sigma)$, while the elasticity of substitution between equipment and skilled labor is

$$\frac{1}{1 - \sigma} + (\omega_e + \omega_s)^{-1} \left[\frac{1}{1 - \rho} - \frac{1}{1 - \sigma} \right],$$

where ω_e and ω_s are, respectively, the income shares of equipment and skilled labor. Thus, according to both definitions, the parameter estimates in KORV imply that equipment capital is more complementary with skilled labor compared to unskilled labor. See Ruiz-Arranz (2002) for a discussion of the various definitions of elasticity of substitution in production function with more than 2 inputs. Interestingly, Ruiz-Arranz divides equipment into finer categories and finds that IT capital (defined as computers, communication equipment and software) is the subgroup with the largest degree of capital-skill complementarity.

[28] Lee and Wolpin (2004) find evidence of capital-skill complementarity both in the goods-producing industries and services in the U.S. economy, and argue that it is an important ingredient to explain the pattern of relative wages and relative labor inputs across the two sectors, over the past 50 years.

[29] Acemoglu (2002a) argues that if the capital-skill complementarity hypothesis is valid, then in Equation (10) the relative price of equipment should proxy the shift in the demand for skills and perform better than

3.1.1. Further applications of the capital-skill complementarity hypothesis

In KORV, the production structure is "centralized" through an aggregate production function. Jovanovic (1998) models an economy with vintage capital where production is decentralized into machine–worker pairs. Newer machines are more productive than older machines, and workers differ in their innate skill level. The pair's output is a multiplicative function of these two inputs. Jovanovic assumes perfect information (no coordination frictions), and hence the labor market equilibrium assignment displays "positive sorting" between skills and machines' productivity [Becker (1973)], i.e., capital-skill complementarity emerges endogenously.[30] An acceleration in the growth rate of technology embodied in machines, that is, an increase of the relative productivity differences across vintages, has two effects: (1) for a given age range of machines, it widens the underlying distribution of job productivity differences and, since in equilibrium high-skilled workers are assigned to high-productivity machines, it magnifies the skill premium; (2) the faster rate of obsolescence shortens the optimal life of capital, that is, the range of operative vintages narrows, which tends to weaken inequality since the least productive workers are now matched with better machines. As we will see, these two counteracting forces will survive in the frictional economies of Section 7, in spite of the different nature of the equilibrium assignment of workers to machines.

The capital-skill complementarity hypothesis has proved to be helpful to interpret the dynamics of the skill premium in other countries. Perhaps the most interesting example is Sweden. Lindquist (2002) documents that the facts to be explained in Sweden are qualitatively similar to the U.S. facts: between 1983 and 1999 the college premium rose by over 20% and the supply of skilled workers increased substantially. Sweden represents an especially interesting test case for the KORV model because Swedish labor market institutions are commonly believed to play a crucial role in wage setting, arguably making market forces less critical in determining relative wage movements. The main result of Lindquist (2002) is that capital-skill complementarity explains close to half of the dynamics of the skill premium.[31]

How can one reconcile the traditional strength of labor market institutions, such as unions and collective bargaining, in the Swedish labor market with the finding that

---

a linear time trend. However, he finds the trend is always more significant. First, as Equation (12) shows, the right variable to add to the Katz–Murphy equation is not the relative price of equipment, but the equipment-skill labor ratio. Second, even using this latter variable one would be bound to find that the linear time trend is more significant because in an OLS regression the estimated coefficient on the time trend converges to its true value at a faster rate than the coefficient on the equipment-skill ratio. More importantly, the key insight of KORV is to give an economic content to the "skill-biased technical change" view, by replacing an unobservable trend with an observable variable.

[30] Holmes and Mitchell (2004) start from a more primitive level where production combines tasks of various complexity and the production factors can perform tasks at a given setup-cost per task. They show that under reasonable primitive assumptions on setup costs for capital, skilled labor and unskilled labor, the former two inputs display a form of complementarity.

[31] Lindquist uses the KORV specification for aggregate technology in Equation (11) and estimates $\rho = -0.92$ and $\sigma = 0.31$.

market forces account for a large part of relative wage dynamics? One possibility is that institutions set the aggregate share of income going to labor in any given period – possibly extracting rents from firms. The distribution of these rents among workers is then determined by their individual outside options, which differ across skill levels and are affected by technical change. In Section 8 we develop further this conjecture in the context of the decline in union membership in the United States, but the economic linkages between the dynamics of institutions and technological progress are far from being well understood.

More international evidence in favor of the capital-skill complementarity model is offered by Flug and Hercowitz (2000). They estimate a strong effect of equipment investment on relative wages and employment of skilled labor using a panel data set for a wide range of countries around the world.

Recently, the capital-skill complementarity idea has been imported into the study of inequality at the business-cycle frequency. The skill premium is found to be close to *acyclical* in the United States: its contemporaneous correlation with output is positive, but not statistically different from zero. Lindquist (2004) argues that, since unskilled labor is relatively more pro-cyclical than skilled labor, a Cobb–Douglas production function in three inputs (capital, skilled labor, and unskilled labor) would predict a strongly pro-cyclical skill premium. Inspection of Equation (12) suggests that introducing capital-skill complementarity in production can help matching the data since, at impact, skilled hours respond more than the stock of equipment: the capital-skill complementarity effect is countercyclical and offsets the change in relative supply.[32]

In sum, the studies discussed in this section indicate that capital-skill complementarity is a quantitatively important ingredient in competitive theories of relative wage determination, within centralized as well as decentralized production structures and at high as well as low frequencies.

3.2. Innate skills and the Nelson–Phelps hypothesis

Nelson and Phelps (1966) argued that the wage premium for more skilled workers is not just the result of their having higher "static productivity". Workers endowed with more skills, they contended, tend to deal better with technological change in the sense that their productivity is less adversely affected by the turmoil created by technological transformations of the workplace, or in that it is less costly for them to acquire the additional skills needed to use a new technology. Greenwood and Yorukoglu (1997) cite sources reporting that the skill premium also rose during the course of the first industrial revolution. In the context of the recent "IT revolution", Bartel and Lichtenberg (1987) provide evidence that more educated individuals have a comparative advantage at implementing the new technologies and Bartel and Sicherman (1998) argue that high-skilled workers sort themselves into industries with higher rates of technical change.

---

[32] Within a similar framework, Cohen-Pirani and Castro (2004) argue that capital-skill complementarity is important for understanding why the volatility of skilled labor (relative to GDP) has tripled after 1985.

The theory has been formalized in various formats. Lloyd-Ellis (1999) embeds a race between the innovation rate and the "technological absorption rate" of workers (the maximum numbers of innovations that can be adopted per unit of time) in a general equilibrium model: at times when the innovation rate exceeds the absorption rate, wage inequality increases due to the fierce competition for scarce, adaptable labor. Galor and Moav (2000) formalize this hypothesis differently and assume that technological change depreciates the human capital of the unskilled workers faster than that of skilled workers (the "erosion effect"). Krueger and Kumar (2004) distinguish between workers with general education and workers with vocational skill-specific education and postulate that only the former type remains productive when new technologies are incorporated into production.

It is important to remark that this hypothesis, in all its versions, applies to educational skills as well as dimensions of skills that are not necessarily observable or correlated with education. Hence, it can potentially account for the rise in within-group (or residual) inequality. Ingram and Neumann (1999) offer some evidence on the increase in the return to certain categories of skills not fully captured by education. They match individual data on wages and occupations from the CPS with the skill content of several occupations, obtained from the *Dictionary of Occupational Titles* (DOT). DOT data contain information on how much each occupation requires of each of a wide range of skills such as verbal aptitude, reasoning development, numerical ability, motor coordination, and so on. Using factor analysis they group over 50 type of skills into four factors (intelligence, clerical skills, motor skills, and physical strength) and estimate that the return to "intelligence" has almost doubled from 1971 to 1998. Moreover, adding the quantity of this factor to a standard Mincerian wage regression weakens the implied increase in the returns to college education significantly.[33]

The idea that the diffusion of IT may have raised the demand for adaptable skilled workers – thus, even within educational groups – has been formalized in various ways by Galor and Tsiddon (1997), Greenwood and Yorukoglu (1997), Caselli (1999), Galor and Moav (2000) and Aghion, Howitt and Violante (2002).

To illustrate the basic mechanism of such a theory, consider an economy where workers differ in their cost of learning the new technology.[34] Suppose that this economy starts in a steady-state equilibrium where production uses the "old" technology, $y_1 = A_1 k_1^\alpha l_1^{1-\alpha}$. The labor market is competitive; thus, in steady state, all workers are employed in the old sector and there is no wage inequality.

Suppose a new technology becomes available and the sector using this new technology can produce output with $y_0 = A_0 k_0^\alpha l_0^{1-\alpha}$ where $A_0 > A_1$. Because of the learning

---

[33] Autor, Levy and Murnane (2003) perform a similar exercise. By combining DOT and CPS data, they split job tasks requirements into "routine" and "non-routine" tasks and document that, starting from the 1970s, the labor input of non-routine analytic and interactive tasks increased sharply relative to routine cognitive and manual tasks. This shift was concentrated in rapidly computerizing industries and it was pervasive at all educational levels. They interpret these findings as evidence that the introduction of computers complemented labor endowed with generalized problem-solving, complex communication, and analytical skills.

[34] In the rest of this section, the exposition will be based mainly on the environment in Caselli (1999).

cost, labor is not perfectly mobile, and wages in the two sectors may differ. Capital, however, is free to move toward its more productive use, and factor-price equalization for capital yields

$$R_0 = R_1 \quad \Longrightarrow \quad \frac{l_1}{k_1} = \left(\frac{A_0}{A_1}\right)^{1/(1-\alpha)} \frac{l_0}{k_0}. \tag{13}$$

It is straightforward to show that

$$w_0 = \left(\frac{A_0}{A_1}\right)^{1/(1-\alpha)} w_1 > w_1.$$

Therefore, in equilibrium, a premium emerges for those workers with low learning cost (i.e., high ability) who can adapt quickly and move to the new sector.

The skill premium increases due to two effects. With full mobility of labor, inequality would disappear. With no labor mobility and no capital mobility, the skill premium would reflect the productivity difference A_0/A_1. In this class of models, labor mobility is limited by the distribution of ability in the economy, but capital moves freely. Full mobility of capital induces a general equilibrium feedback that amplifies inequality: factor-price equalization requires capital to flow to the sector operating the new technology to equate marginal productivities of capital.[35] Thus, workers on the new technologies are endowed with more capital, which boosts their relative wages further.

In its typical version, the Nelson–Phelps hypothesis implies that the rise in the skill premium will be transitory: it is only in the early adoption phase of a new technology that those who adapt more quickly can reap some benefits. Over time there will be enough workers who learn how to work with the new technology to offset the wage differential. Note the difference with the KORV hypothesis, where the effect on the skill premium is permanent. Are new technologies and skills complement in the whole production process or just in the adoption phase? Chun (2003) uses industry-level data for the U.S. to disentangle the impact of "adoption" and "use" of IT. He finds that the increase in the relative demand of educated workers from 1970 to 1996 in the U.S. is related significantly to both factors, but quantitatively the impact of use is twice as large.

3.2.1. Further applications of the Nelson–Phelps hypothesis

Aghion (2002) and Borghans and Weel (2003) emphasize that the Nelson–Phelps approach can explain why, in the 1970s, the college premium declined at the same time that the wage dispersion within college graduates increased. The idea is that in the early phase of IT diffusion in the 1970s only educated workers with high ability adopt.

---

[35] One implication of this mechanism, evident from Equation (13), is that a technological revolution should trigger a surge in the real rate of return on capital by a factor $(A_0/A_1)^{1/(1-\alpha)}$. Yearly U.S. long-term real interest rates were roughly 3 percent higher in the period 1980–1995 compared to the period 1965–1980. It is unclear whether this magnitude is quantitatively consistent with the observed increase in wage dispersion.

Naturally, this higher return to ability increases within-group inequality. The contemporaneous acceleration in the growth of the supply of educated labor, due to exogenous factors, explains the relative fall in the average wage of college graduates.

Beaudry and Green (2003) compare the United States and Germany, highlighting an apparently puzzling feature of the data: the relative supply of skilled labor in the United States grew faster than in Germany, and yet the skill premium rose in the United States, but not in Germany. They outline a model that combines elements of Caselli (1999) and Krusell et al. (2000). Consider an economy where there are two technologies in operation and the "new" technology displays more capital-skill complementarity than the old one. An exogenous rise in the supply of skills increases the relative return to capital in the new sector. Capital then flows from the old to the new sector and, ultimately, this higher capital intensity can raise the relative wage of skilled labor if labor is not perfectly mobile because, as in Caselli's model, only skilled workers can quickly adapt. Thus, in the long-run, the country with the initial spur in the supply of skilled labor (the United States) finds itself with a larger skill premium.

In their original paper, Nelson and Phelps (1966) developed the concept of "technological gap", defined as the percentage difference between the technology operated by the typical machine in the economy and the one embodied in the leading-edge machine. They conjectured that a rise in the technological gap should be associated with a large skill premium because of the surge in the demand for educated workers needed to adopt the new, more productive technologies. Cummins and Violante (2002) use data on the quality-adjusted relative prices and quantities of equipment investment to construct a measure of the technological gap for the U.S. economy.[36] Figure 3 shows that the technological gap and the skill premium have moved largely in tune over the past half century, confirming – at least in the time-series dimension – even the most literal version of the Nelson–Phelps hypothesis.

Put differently, the size of the technological gap can be thought of a proxy for shifts in the relative demand of skilled workers.

3.3. Endogenous skill-biased technical change

In the literature we discussed so far, the sector bias and the factor bias of technical change were assumed to be exogenous. Over the past 20 years a substantial body of work in the field of growth theory has formalized the idea that the efforts of innovators

---

[36] Precisely, if q_t is the level of productivity embodied in the new investment at time t, then the average unit of productive capital in the economy at time t embodies a technology with productivity Q_t, defined as

$$Q_t = \sum_{j=0}^{\infty} (1 - \delta)^j q_{t-j} \frac{i_{t-j}}{k_t},$$

where δ is the depreciation rate, i denotes investments and k the capital stock, both expressed in units of consumption. In other words, Q_t is the ratio between capital stock correctly measured in efficiency units (the numerator) and capital stock k not adjusted for quality. Then, the gap is defined as $(q_t - Q_t)/Q_t$.

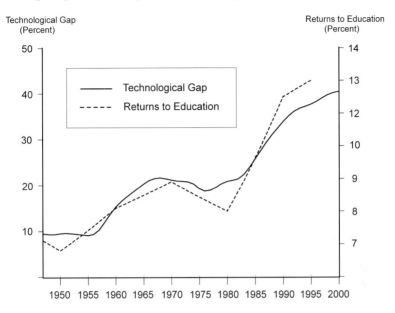

Figure 3. The joint dynamics of the returns to education and the technological gap (1947–2000) in the U.S. economy. The figure is reproduced from Cummins and Violante (2002).

are endogenous and respond to market incentives. The models belonging to the so-called "new growth theory" describe the endogenous determination of the *level* of innovative activity.

Recently, Acemoglu (1998, 2002b, 2003b) and Kiley (1999) have developed the idea that the composition, or *direction*, of innovations is also endogenous: if R&D activity can be purposefully directed toward productivity improvements of different inputs (capital, skilled labor, and unskilled labor), then it will be biased toward the factor that ensures the largest returns.

An important ingredient of this approach is that the returns to R&D targeted toward a given input are proportional to the total supply of that input, since "productivity" and "quantity" are complements in production. This creates a "market size" effect of R&D: productivity-improving resources are allocated to factor markets with large relative factor supplies.[37]

It is useful to see how this mechanism works within a simple model that represents a reduced form of the richer environments offered by Acemoglu and Kiley. Consider an economy with a given endowment of skilled and unskilled labor, l_s and l_u, and a production function (9) as in Section 2.2.4. Conditional on the FSPs, A_s and A_u, wages and

---

[37] It is useful here draw a parallel with certain traditional endogenous growth models, where the scale effect determines the level of the growth rate. See Jones (2005) for a survey of the models with scale effects.

employment are determined competitively, and the competitive equilibrium is Pareto-optimal. Now suppose that the Social Planner wants to maximize production subject to a given frontier of technological possibilities, that is, choices of A_s and A_u,

$$\max_{\{A_s, A_u\}} \left[(A_s l_s)^\sigma + (A_u l_u)^\sigma \right]^{1/\sigma}$$

$$\text{s.t.} \quad \left[\lambda A_s^\phi + (1-\lambda) A_u^\phi \right]^{1/\phi} = 1.$$

Assume that the technological frontier is convex, that is, that $\phi > 1$. Rearranging the first-order conditions, one arrives at

$$\frac{A_s}{A_u} = \frac{\lambda}{1-\lambda} \left(\frac{l_s}{l_u} \right)^{\sigma/(\phi-\sigma)}, \qquad (14)$$

which describes the optimal choice of skill-bias given the relative factor supply. The above equation shows that when skilled and unskilled labor are substitutes, $0 < \sigma \leqslant 1$, the skill bias is increasing in the relative supply of skills. This latter parametric condition implies that the marginal product of each innovation is increasing in its corresponding factor.

A surge in the relative endowment of skilled labor, like the one witnessed by the U.S. economy in the postwar period, induces the adoption of more skill-biased technologies in production. This force tends to counteract the direct relative supply effect on wage inequality. Can the endogenous skill bias be so strong in the long run as to overturn the initial supply effect?

To answer this question, we substitute the expression for the skill bias, (14), into the expression for the skill premium, (10), and obtain

$$\ln\left(\frac{w_s}{w_u} \right) \propto \frac{\sigma - \phi(1-\sigma)}{\phi - \sigma} \ln\left(\frac{l_s}{l_u} \right).$$

We see that the skill premium is increasing in the relative supply of skilled labor as long as $\phi \in (\sigma, \frac{\sigma}{1-\sigma})$. Thus, theoretically, it is possible to explain a positive long-run relationship between the relative supply of skilled labor and the skill premium as the one depicted in Figure 1 (top panel).

One limitation of existing models of directed technical change, and also of most of the literature surveyed in this section, is that arguments for the skill-premium focus on the response of a relative price to exogenous changes in relative factor supplies. Whereas one can reasonably assume that "ability" is largely pre-determined with respect to the point in the life-cycle when agents start making economic decisions, education is not. One would expect that changes in returns to education as large as the ones we observed in the past 30 years would significantly affect the incentives to acquire education. However, it is an open question to what extent the observed changes in returns were predicted by the cohorts affected by these returns when they made their education decisions.[38]

---

[38] See Abraham (2003) for a related analysis.

Models of directed technical change, augmented by an endogenous supply of skills, can give rise to multiple steady states. If the innovators expect the supply of educated workers to rise, they will invest in skill-biased R&D which, in turn, will augment the returns to college and induce households to acquire human capital, fulfilling the innovators' expectations.

3.3.1. Sources of the skill-bias in recent times

Equation (14) shows that the most natural candidate as engine of the recent skill-biased technical change was the rise in the relative supply of educated workers. The latter was, according to Acemoglu (2002a) largely exogenous, at least initially, and a result of the high college enrollment rates of the baby-boom cohort and of the Vietnam war draft. The crucial issue, still unresolved, is whether the necessary parametric restrictions discussed earlier are plausible, and whether the initial shock is large enough.[39] What other changes in the economic environment can be listed as potential sources of skill-biased innovations?

First, there are possible interactions between capital-skill complementarity and the direction of technical change. Hornstein and Krusell (2003) have taken a first step at incorporating the idea of factor-biased innovations into the KORV explanation of the skill premium. Intuitively, an acceleration in capital accumulation due, for example, to an exogenous fall in the price of capital increases the returns to skill-biased innovations if capital is more complementary with skilled labor. Hence, capital-embodied productivity improvements can be the source of factor-biased technical progress. For a calibrated version of their model, Hornstein and Krusell find that a persistent decline of the relative price of capital results in a temporary, but very persistent, increase of the skill premium. In their model the skill premium not only increases because of capital accumulation (as in KORV), but it also increases because of the endogenously induced spur of skill-biased technical change.

Second, the increased openness to trade can play a role. Using a Schumpeterian growth model, Dinopoulos and Segerstrom (1999) argue that if trade liberalization boosts the profitability for monopolistic suppliers by increasing the size of their markets, then resources shift from manufacturing to R&D activities. If, in turn, R&D is a skill-intensive sector, the skill premium rises. This model determines endogenously the level of R&D, but does not display endogenous factor bias in the equilibrium innovation rate. In Acemoglu (2003c), the direction of technical change is related to international trade. A natural assumption about factor endowments is that in the United States the ratio of skilled to unskilled labor is higher than in the rest of the world. After the U.S. economy opens to trade, the world prices are determined by the aggregate relative factor endowment, and thus skill-intensive goods become relatively more expensive. In the

---

[39] In the richer model developed by Acemoglu (2002b), this parametric restriction requires that the elasticity of substitution between skilled and unskilled labor be larger than 2. Most of the empirical literature on factor substitutability, however, points at values around 1.5 [Hamermesh (1993)].

class of models with an endogenous factor bias, factors which produce goods with the highest relative price – and the highest expected profits – will be the target of the largest amount of innovative activity (the "relative price" effect). Thus trade opening induces skill-biased technical change. This mechanism can, under some conditions, explain also the increase in the skill premium in less-developed countries documented, for example, by Robbins (1996).

Third, Cozzi and Impullitti (2004) argue that government policy may also have contributed to the bias in technical change. In the 1980s, U.S. technology policy rapidly shifted its priority from security and defense to economic competitiveness in order to counteract the emerging dominance of Japan in the sectors producing high-tech goods.[40] Within a Schumpeterian growth model, they show that when the government reallocates its expenditures toward the (high-tech) manufacturing goods with the highest potential quality improvement, it creates a market-size effect that can lead to a rise in the innovation rate in those sectors and a net increase in the demand for skilled R&D workers and their wages.[41]

Although we have learned from the above analyses about possible channels influencing the skill premium, there is little work that allows us to quantify each of the channels. A careful calibration and evaluation of a model which incorporates these various channels would be an important first step in this direction.

3.4. A historical perspective on the skill premium

In Section 2 we have observed that, over the last 100 years, wage inequality first declined and then increased, with the turning point somewhere around 1950. Can the theoretical models developed to interpret the increasing wage inequality for the second half of the 20th century also account for the declining wage inequality of the first half of the 20th century?

3.4.1. Capital-skill complementarity

Figure 4 plots the relative price of equipment together with the returns to one year of education (both college and high school) since 1929.[42] The pattern is rather striking and is broadly consistent with an explanation based on the capital-skill complementarity

---

[40] Japan's share of the high-tech goods markets rose from 7 percent to 16 percent during the period 1970–1990, while at the same time the U.S. share declined from 30 percent to 21 percent. In 1963 government spending on defense represented 1.37 percent of GDP. In 1980, it was down to 0.57 percent.

[41] Like the Dinopoulos and Segerstrom (1999) model, strictly speaking, this is not a model of directed-technical change, since skilled labor works only in the R&D sector, and each manufacturing sector employs unskilled labor. However, in a version of the model with endogenous factor-bias and a structure of manufacturing where high-tech goods are produced by skilled labor and low-tech goods by unskilled labor, the shift in technology policy would have the same qualitative effect.

[42] The relative price is computed from series available on the BEA website. In particular, compared to the series discussed previously in the chapter, there are no quality adjustments. As a result, the acceleration which

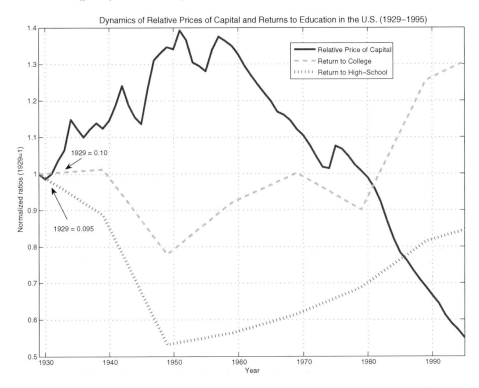

Figure 4. The dynamics of the relative price of capital and the returns to education from 1929–1995 in the U.S. economy. *Source*: Cummins and Violante (2002) and Goldin and Katz (1999).

hypothesis. During the first half of the century, the price of capital increased which slowed the demand for educated labor and the skill premium. Then around mid-century it started to decline, fostering a strong demand shift in favor of educated labor.

This extension of the KORV analysis to the whole 20th century is yet to be performed formally.[43] Thus, before one fully subscribes to this explanation, it is worth discussing the key assumption behind the model. Is it an accurate historical assessment that the introduction of new capital goods has systematically increased the productivity of skilled

occurred since the mid-1970s is less evident here. The series on the return to education for 1939, 1949, 1959, 1969, 1979, 1989 and 1995 are taken from Table 7 in Goldin and Katz (1999) and interpolated linearly for the missing years in between. The first datapoint for 1929 is obtained by linear interpolation from 1914.

[43] Admittedly, the evidence in Figure 4 is rather indirect. Looking directly at the stock of equipment (unadjusted for quality improvements), its average annual growth rate in the periods 1930–1950, 1950–1980, 1980–2000 is, respectively, 2.2%, 5.0% and 4.2%. However, when quality-adjusted, the growth rate of equipment from 1980–2000 is close to 8% [Cummins and Violante (2002)]. See also Hornstein (2004) for a discussion of historical trends of U.S. capital–output ratios.

labor relative to the productivity of unskilled labor? In other words, when can one date the birth of work organizations displaying capital-skill complementarity?

According to Goldin and Katz (1998), until the early 20th century there was no trace of skill-biased technical change; rather, the opposite bias was at work. The origins of capital-skill complementarity are associated with the introduction of electric motors, and a shift away from assembly lines and toward continuous and batch processes. This development started in the second and third decades of the 20th century. In particular, the declining relative price of electricity, and the consequent electrification of factories, made it possible to run equipment at a higher speed. This, in turn, increased the demand for skilled workers for maintenance purposes. Since then, the introduction of new equipment, such as numerically controlled machines, robotized assembly lines, and finally computers further increased the relative productivity of skilled labor. Thus, we conclude that based on anecdotal evidence, the period portrayed in Figure 4 is one where capital-skill complementarity became more important.

Mitchell (2001), in a related interpretation on the last century of data, emphasizes the technological aspects of optimal plant size. Mitchell documents a striking similarity between the historical path of wage inequality and the pattern of average plant size in manufacturing which rose over the 1900–1950 period and shrunk between 1950 and 2000, thus almost producing the mirror image of inequality at low frequencies. The time-path of plant size can be interpreted as an indicator of the magnitude of the fixed costs of capital and fits well with the evidence of Figure 4.

In Mitchell's model, production requires performing a large set of tasks with capital and two types of labor, skilled and unskilled. Entrepreneurs face a fixed cost to operate capital, skilled labor, and unskilled labor. Unskilled labor has a higher fixed cost and a lower variable cost than does skilled labor; e.g., unskilled labor is specialized and needs a certain amount of training to perform all the tasks, whereas skilled labor is naturally able in multi-tasking.[44]

The move from craft shops to assembly lines (1900–1950) induced a rise in the fixed cost: the optimal size of the plant rose and with a larger size, plants optimally employed more unskilled workers with large fixed cost, but low variable cost (wages). The demand for unskilled workers rose, weakening the skill premium. As an illustration of the importance of fixed costs for this type of production method, recall that all Ford plants had to be closed and redesigned when the "Model T" was discontinued [Milgrom and Roberts (1990)].

The shift toward more flexible, numerically controlled machines and IT capital (1950–2000) led firms to adopt a smaller scale of production and employ more highly skilled workers whose low fixed cost makes them preferable to unskilled workers in

---

[44] This idea is further developed in Holmes and Mitchell (2004). This paper develops a theory of the intrinsic difference between three key factors of production: capital, unskilled labor, and skilled labor. Based on this theory, the authors develop implications for: (1) how capital and skill intensity vary as a function of size of plants, (2) the micro-foundations of capital-skill complementarity, (3) the effect of trade on the skill premium and the historical relationship between the plant size-skill correlation and the skill premium.

small plants. The increased demand for skilled labor thus raised the skill premium. Based on a calibration exercise, the model can account for two thirds of the movements in the skill premium.[45]

3.4.2. Directed technical change

The theory of directed technical change maintains that a growth in the relative supply of a factor of production should induce technical change biased in favor of that factor. Historically, there are two important episodes of largely "exogenous" spurs in relative factor supply.

First, there was an increase in the supply of unskilled labor in urban areas of England during the 19th century. A careful look at the nature of technological progress over this period supports the theory. Goldin and Katz (1998) argue that in the 19th century the wave of technological innovations substituted physical capital and raw labor for skilled artisan workers [Braverman (1974) and Cain and Paterson (1986)]. For example, automobile production began in artisanal shops where the car was assembled from start to finish by a small group of "all-around mechanics". Only a few decades later, the Tayloristic model of manufacturing would bring together scores of unskilled workers in large-scale plants to assemble completely standardized parts in a fixed sequence of steps for mass production.

Second, there was a surge in skilled labor (i.e., workers with literacy and numerical skills) due to the "high-school movement" of 1910–1940. As pointed out by Aghion (2002), with respect to this episode, the theory finds weaker support. On the one hand, as we discussed earlier, it appears that the first part of the 20th century indeed marked the beginning of a transformation in production methods biased toward skilled labor (from assembly lines to continuous and batch production processes). On the other hand, there was a decline in the returns to high school and the returns to college were stable (see Figure 4). Why is it that this wave of skill-biased technical change, which was as strong as the one 50 years later, did not have a similar impact on the wage structure? This question remains unanswered to date.[46]

3.5. Technology and the gender gap

Here we explore briefly the interaction between the gender gap and the advancements of technological change, both in the market and in the household.

---

[45] Note that this model implies that the origin of capital-skill complementarity is to be located only around 1950, later than what was argued in Goldin and Katz (1998).

[46] Institutions might have played a role in the 1940s. Goldin and Margo (1992) argue that the National War Labor Board operated an explicit policy of wage compression during that period.

3.5.1. Technological change in the market

As evident from Figure 1 (bottom panel), since the mid-1970s the gender wage gap has closed substantially. Several studies have concluded that this is due to a rise in relative labor demand for women, as supply cannot have played a large role [Bertola, Blau and Kahn (1997)]. Was the recent technological revolution "gender-biased"?

Consider a simple model where jobs differ in their requirement of physical effort and all jobs are necessary for production of the final good. At the same time, men and women have two traits: physical ability and cognitive ability. The theory of comparative advantage then implies that men will be most efficiently assigned to jobs with high physical requirements and that women should work on jobs with a large fraction of cognitive tasks.

The arrival of a new technology, like computers, that increases productivity relatively more on jobs with high cognitive content therefore tends to raise the average wage of women more than it raises the average wage of men. Weinberg (2003a) tests this theory on microeconomic data for the United States and finds that the increase in computer use for women can explain up to 50 percent of the increase in the relative demand for female employment.

It is worth noting that the gender premium fell in spite of the fact that the female–male relative supply ratio grew almost by a factor of 2 between 1960 and 2000, i.e., by as much as the growth in the relative supply of college-educated labor. In the perspective of the directed technical change literature, one is left to ponder whether rising female participation was also a force that led innovators to spend resources on capital goods complementary with cognitive skills rather than with physical skills in order to exploit women's comparative advantage. This hypothesis remains to be analyzed in detail.

3.5.2. Technological change in the household

The postwar period witnessed another form of technological revolution: one that did not take place in factories and plants, but rather in the household. Greenwood, Seshadri and Yorukoglu (2005) argue that the decline in prices of household appliances (refrigerators, vacuum cleaners, washers, dishwashers, etc.) worked as "engines of liberations" for women: new and more productive capital in the households could free up potential hours to be supplied in the labor market. In particular, as household durables were introduced into the economy, the effective wage-elasticity of female labor supply increases, which, in turn, helps explaining the sharp rise in female market participation, even in the presence of not-so-large changes in the gender wage gap.[47]

---

[47] We refer the reader to Greenwood and Seshadri (2005) in this Handbook for a detailed analysis of this channel.

4. Technical change and the returns to experience

According to Card and DiNardo (2002), one of the most important challenges to the hypothesis that the recent changes in the wage structure are linked to technological progress is to explain the combination of the rise in the returns to labor market experience for the low-educated workers in the population and the flat, or declining, pattern of the experience premium for college graduates.

It turns out that the existing theoretical literature does not provide a unified answer to the question of how technological change affects the experience premium. Examples of the literature we review in this section include job-specific or technology-specific experience that, in principle, may be adversely affected by technological change, but that may also benefit from technological change if that change is of a 'general purpose' variety, that is, if it makes experience more widely applicable.[48] We also look at general labor-market experience as a vehicle to lower the cost of adapting to technological change.

4.1. Experience with general purpose technologies

An important feature of the recent technological developments that has not received much attention in the literature on inequality is its *general purpose nature*. Aghion, Howitt and Violante (2002) formalize the idea of "generality" of a technology and build a theoretical framework to understand how it affects various dimensions of wage inequality, such as the experience premium. They model generality in relation to human capital: a more general technology allows a larger degree of *transferability* of sector-specific experience across the different sectors of the economy. For example, the ability to use computers for word-processing or programming is useful in numerous sectors and jobs in the economy.[49] Given that actual technological change is uneven across sectors, transferability of experience then increases the value of experience, that is, the experience premium.

Consider a simple overlapping-generations (OLG) model with two-period lived agents, and two production sectors indexed by $i = 0, 1$. Each cohort of agents has measure one and works in both periods. Technological progress results in capital-embodied innovations that increase productivity by a factor $1 + \gamma$ occurring in each of the two

---

[48] We will return to the issue on how technological change interacts with the accumulation of job/technology-specific knowledge in the frictional models of Section 7.3.

[49] A survey conducted by the U.S. Bureau of Labor Statistics emphasizes that

...the technology, network systems, and software is similar across firms and industries. This is in contrast to technological innovations in the past, which often affected specific occupations and industries (for example, machine tool automation only involved production jobs in manufacturing). Computer technology is versatile and affects many unrelated industries and almost every job category [McConnell (1996, p. 5)].

sectors in alternation. Let "0" denote the new sector in the current period. Suppose, for simplicity, that production takes place with a fixed amount of capital, normalized to one: the production function in sector i (in the stationary transformation of the model) is $y_i = A_i^\alpha h_i^{1-\alpha}$, where A_i measures the efficiency of capital in sector i ($A_0/A_1 = 1+\gamma$), and h_{it} measures the effective labor input in sector $i = 0, 1$.

Young agents are always productive on the new technology, whereas old workers can productively move to the new sector only with probability σ. This captures the idea that young workers are more "adaptable" than old workers possibly because of vintage effects in their schooling, or because the ability to learn declines with age. Moreover, assume that this "adaptability constraint" is binding, in the sense that: (1) the equilibrium fraction σ^* of old workers who moves equals σ, and (2) there is not enough labor mobility (σ is sufficiently low) to offset the impact on wages of the sectoral productivity differential $1 + \gamma$.

Newborn agents start working in the new sector with initial knowledge normalized to 1.[50] Agents accumulate η additional units of experience through learning-by-doing in the first period of work. The generality of the technology determines the degree of skill transferability for the old workers τ_o, i.e., the fraction of accumulated knowledge η a worker can carry over if she moves to the leading-edge sector at the beginning of her second period of life. The entire knowledge η can be used if the worker stays in the old sector.

Aggregate human capital in the old sector h_1 is determined by old, non-adaptable workers, a fraction $1-\sigma$, who have accumulated $1+\eta$ units of experience. Human capital in the new sector is determined by the new cohorts that have one unit of experience, and old adaptable workers with transferable experience, that is, $h_0 = 1 + \sigma(1 + \tau_o\eta)$. With competitive labor markets, the ratio between the prices of efficiency units of labor in the old and the new sector therefore is

$$\frac{w_1}{w_0} = (1+\gamma)^{-\alpha}\left(\frac{h_0}{h_1}\right)^\alpha = (1+\gamma)^{-\alpha}\left[\frac{1+\sigma(1+\tau_o\eta)}{(1-\sigma)(1+\eta)}\right]^\alpha. \tag{15}$$

The steady-state experience premium, i.e., the average wage of old workers relative to the average wage of young workers, is therefore given by

$$x^* = \sigma(1 + \tau_o\eta) + (1-\sigma)(1+\eta)\frac{w_1}{w_0}, \tag{16}$$

where one can see immediately that x^* is increasing in τ_o. That is, an increase in the generality of technological knowledge raises skill transferability and amplifies the experience premium of adaptable workers, who are able to transfer more of their cumulated skills. It also indirectly raises the experience premium of non-adaptable old workers by making effective adaptable labor input relatively more abundant in the economy, hence depressing the wage of young workers.

---

[50] Aghion, Howitt and Violante (2002) show that this is indeed the optimal choice of young cohorts, for general conditions.

This result is particularly interesting in light of the fact that a version of this model that is based purely on the hypothesis that the rate of embodied technical change, γ, has accelerated would predict a decline in the experience premium. This is evident from the fact that the wage ratio w_1/w_0 is decreasing in γ: larger productivity differentials between the young and the old vintages represent a relative advantage to young workers who are more adaptable.

The more general model in Aghion, Howitt and Violante (2002) also features a flexible choice of capital. Another interpretation of generality of the technology offered in their paper is based on the *compatibility* of physical capital, i.e., the extent to which capital equipment embodying the old technology can be retooled – so as to embody the new leading-edge technology – and moved to the new sector. Under this interpretation, the arrival of a GPT, which increases the compatibility across vintages of capital, reduces the experience premium since it allows the transfer of more capital to the new sector where it benefits the young, inexperienced, but more adaptable workers.[51]

4.2. Vintage-specificity of experience

According to the GPT hypothesis, human capital becomes more transferable across sectors once the new technological platform has fully diffused throughout the economy. However, it is also reasonable to think that, at least in the transition phase, certain skills associated to the old way of producing quickly become obsolete. Or, put differently, human capital is vintage-specific. Thus, although in the final steady state skill transferability will be higher, it can undershoot during the transition.

To study the implications of vintage human capital for the experience premium, we can slightly modify the two-period OLG model in the previous section. To make this point starkly, consider the extreme case where old workers never find it profitable to move across sectors, so $\sigma^* = 0$, and suppose that when young workers join the new sector they lose a fraction $1 - \tau_y$ of their initial knowledge (as before, normalized to 1). Modifying appropriately the equilibrium wage ratio (15), Equation (16) for the experience premium becomes

$$x^* = \frac{(\tau_y + \eta)w_1}{\tau_y w_0} = \frac{1}{(1 + \gamma)^\alpha}\left[\frac{\tau_y + \eta}{\tau_y}\right]^{1-\alpha}, \tag{17}$$

which shows that x^* is decreasing in the skill transferability rate for young workers τ_y. The arrival of a new technology that makes the knowledge of its (young) users obsolete can widen the returns to experience.

In analyzing earlier Equation (16) we argued that a rise in γ would depress the experience premium, which is a problem for the pure "acceleration hypothesis". Vintage

---

[51] The model by Caselli (1999) outlined in Section 3.2 has exactly this feature of capital mobility from the old technology to the new and more productive technology; thus, a version of that model where the young workers are those with the lowest learning cost would have the same counterfactual prediction for the experience premium.

human capital can overturn this result. Suppose, as in Violante (2002), that the degree of skill transferability is decreasing in the speed of technological improvements, i.e., $\tau_y = (1 + \gamma)^{-\tau}$. Then, it is easy to see from (17) that as long as $\tau > \alpha/(1 - \alpha)$, the experience premium will rise after a technological acceleration, since the loss of vintage-specific human capital incurred by young workers is larger than the productivity improvement embodied in physical capital.[52] In Section 7.3 we return to the role of vintage human capital and discuss the plausibility of the assumption that the extent to which skills are transferable depends on γ.

4.3. Technology-experience complementarity in adoption

According to the standard technology adoption models, the adopters of the new technology are likely to be the young workers because they face a lower learning cost or a longer time horizon to recoup the adoption costs. Weinberg (2003b) challenges this view and argues that there is one other force that gives more experienced workers an advantage: complementarity between new technologies and skills, together with the fact that more experienced workers are more skilled, should lead to the prediction that older workers will adopt the new technology. What force dominates? And what are the implications for the experience premium?

Weinberg looks at the empirical pattern of computer usage (i.e., adoption of one of the new recent technologies) over the life-cycle and shows that it differs dramatically between high-school graduates and college graduates (see Figure 5).

Among uneducated individuals the profile is hump-shaped and peaks around 30 years of experience, while for educated individuals it is downward-sloping. As expected, the adoption rates for college graduates are higher at any given age.

These data suggest that the answer to the first question above depends on the level of schooling: for low-educated workers, experience is a substitute for general education, and the more experienced workers are also more productive in the new technology. Workers with high education levels are all equally adaptable to the new technology, so, for such workers, additional experience has a small marginal return in adoption. Since the learning cost increases with age, the youngest are more likely to adopt the new technology.

Adding to this mechanism the assumption that new technologies are more productive yields that the adopters gain a wage increase, which is consistent with the different pattern of the experience premium for low and high education groups that we described in Section 2.

---

[52] Note that this large skill loss for young workers does not necessarily imply that it is not optimal for them to begin working in the new sector. Indeed, by working with the new technology in the current period they improve *future* skill transferability.

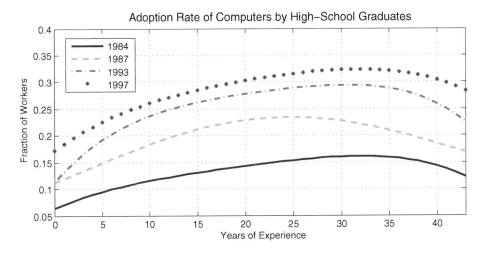

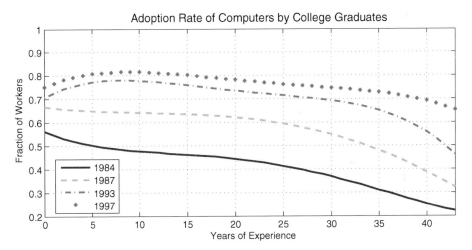

Figure 5. The top panel depicts the experience profile of the adoption rate of computers for U.S. high-school graduates for 1984, 1987, 1993 and 1997. The bottom panel plots similar experience profiles for college graduates. The figure is reproduced from Weinberg (2003b).

4.4. On-the-job training with skill-biased technological change

The models reviewed in this section treat the degree of skill transferability or adaptability of workers as exogenous. If old workers recognize that "new knowledge" is necessary for dealing with the transformed technological environment, then one should expect that they would be willing to forego some resources to acquire such skills through training.

Mincer and Higuchi (1991) advanced this hypothesis and found some supporting evidence from U.S. sectoral data: industries with faster productivity growth were also the ones with steeper experience profiles and lower job-separation rates. They interpreted these facts as reflecting the training channel in light of the findings of Lillard and Tan (1986) showing that the incidence of firm-specific on-the-job training is higher in sectors with high rates of productivity growth. Interestingly, Bartel and Sicherman (1998) document that the marginal impact of a rise in productivity growth on the likelihood of training (thus on the steepness of the wage profile) is stronger for low-educated workers, which is consistent with the pattern of the last 30 years mentioned in Section 2.

The model developed by Heckman, Lochner and Taber (1998) explains the recent dynamics of the experience premium based precisely on this mechanism. To simplify the exposition, consider again a two-period OLG model where risk-neutral workers are endowed with a unit of human capital, work in both periods, and choose how much time to devote to on-the-job training and production in the first period. Training increases human capital in the second and final period. The problem of a worker at time t is

$$\max_{\tau_t}\{w_t(1-\tau_t) + \beta w_{t+1} h_{t+1}\}$$

$$\text{s.t.} \quad h_{t+1} = \frac{A}{\theta}\tau_t^\theta,$$

where τ_t is the fraction of the unitary time endowment spent in training, β is the discount factor, w_t is the wage rate at time t, and h_t is human capital at time t. We assume that production of human capital has decreasing returns in the time input. It is easy to see that optimal training and human capital are functions of expected wage growth:

$$\tau_t = \left(A\beta\frac{w_{t+1}}{w_t}\right)^{1/(1-\theta)} \quad \text{and} \quad h_{t+1} = A^{1/(1-\theta)}\left(\beta\frac{w_{t+1}}{w_t}\right)^{\theta/(1-\theta)}.$$

The implied experience premium, that is, the wage of an experienced old worker relative to the wage of an inexperienced young worker at a given point in time, is then $x_t = h_t/(1-\tau_t)$.

In a stationary state where $w_t = w^*$ for any t, the optimal fraction of time spent in training is $\tau^* = (A\beta)^{1/(1-\theta)}$, and the corresponding steady-state experience premium is

$$x^* = \frac{1}{\theta}\left(\frac{A^{1/(1-\theta)}\beta^{\theta/(1-\theta)}}{1 - (A\beta)^{1/(1-\theta)}}\right).$$

The steady-state experience premium is increasing in the productivity of training A and in the discount factor β.

Suppose now that the economy undergoes a one-period transition toward a permanently higher level of skill-biased productivity. High-education (low-education) workers see their wage going up (down), i.e., $w_{t-1} = w_t = w^*$, $w_{t+n} = \bar{w}$ when $n > 1$, where for high-educated workers $\bar{w} > w^*$, and for low-educated workers $\bar{w} < w^*$. Since the two cases are perfectly symmetric, we solve for the transitional dynamics in the experience premium of the high-educated. Along the transition, in period t educated workers increase their investment in training since the anticipated rise in their wages increases the return to human capital accumulation, whereas in all future periods, i.e., $t + 1$ and higher, educated workers do not change their human capital investment decision since their anticipated wage change is not affected:

$$\tau_t = \left(A\beta \frac{\bar{w}}{w^*} \right)^{1/(1-\theta)} > \tau^*, \quad \tau_{t+n} = \tau^* \text{ for } n \geqslant 1.$$

The implied sequence of experience premia for educated workers is given by

$$x_t = \frac{h^*}{1 - \tau_t} > x_{t+1} = \frac{h_{t+1}}{1 - \tau^*} > x_{t+2} = x^*. \tag{18}$$

The experience premium first rises from x^* to x_t and then falls gradually toward the steady state. For low-educated workers, the opposite pattern will hold. If one thinks of time $t - 1$ as 1965, i.e., the moment before the rise in inequality started, time t as 1975, and so on, this stylized model can qualitatively explain the rise in the experience premium for the less educated workers and the decline in the experience premium for the more educated in the 1980s.

The key force is the intertemporal substitution between working and training that the expected changes in wages bring along.[53] Also, as emphasized by Heckman, Lochner and Taber (1998), it is important to recognize that movements in earnings, $w(1-\tau)$, can differ from movements in skill prices w when labor supply is endogenous. The major limit of the theory is probably that the mechanism depends crucially on the ability of agents to perfectly foresee changes in wage rates decades in advance.

5. Inside the firm: The organization of work

Hayek (1945) argued that a fundamental problem of societies is how to use optimally the knowledge that is available, but is dispersed across individuals. In frictionless markets, prices can solve this problem: they transmit knowledge about relative scarcity and relative productivity of resources. Since Coase (1937), it is well understood that frictions limit the efficiency of markets, and they divert certain transactions to occur within the boundaries of firms. Within the firm, the organization of work and production plays the role of the market as "information processor" to allow efficient use and transmission of knowledge.

It is therefore not surprising that the recent innovations that revolutionized the way in which information and communication takes place have affected the workplace organization within firms and the boundaries of firms. Their impact on the wage structure is

---

[53] Dooley and Gottschalk (1984) also explore a mechanism based on human capital investment in order to explain the rising inequality within cohorts of young workers in the United States. They attribute the changes in expected wages to aggregate fluctuations in labor force growth: the baby-boom and, subsequently, the baby-bust.

perhaps less clear. The maintained hypothesis in the literature is that the recent episodes of reorganization of production, especially in manufacturing, have favored adaptable workers who have general skills and who are more versed at multi-tasking activities. An alternative view, which we will develop later in this section, is that organizational change is not induced by technological change, but that the increased relative supply of skilled labor created the incentives to change the organization of production.

5.1. The Milgrom–Roberts hypothesis: IT-driven organizational change

Milgrom and Roberts (1990) were the first to emphasize the interaction between the diffusion of information technologies in the workplace and the reorganization of production. Their hypothesis builds on the idea that information technologies reduce a set of costs within the firm which triggers the shift toward a new organizational design. First, electronic data transmission through networks of computers reduces the cost of collecting and communicating data, and computer-aided design and manufacturing reduces the costs of product design and development. Second, there are complementarities among a wide group of strongly integrated activities within the firm (product design, marketing, and production), and pronounced non-convexities and indivisibilities in each activity.

As a result, as the marginal cost of IT declines, it is optimal to reorganize all activities to exploit this shock, and, due to non-convexities, organizational change can be sudden and drastic in nature. In particular, because of lower communication costs the layers in the hierarchical structure can be reduced, so that the organization of the firm becomes "flatter".[54] Workers no longer perform routinized, specialized tasks, but they are now responsible for a wide range of tasks within teams. These teams, in turn, communicate directly with managers. Because of the flexibility of IT capital, the scale of production decreases [recall the evidence in Mitchell (2001) on plant size], allowing greater production flexibility and product customization.

An elegant formalization of this hypothesis is contained in Bolton and Dewatripont (1994). They study the optimal hierarchical structure for an organization whose only objective is that of efficiently processing a continuous flow of information and show using their model that a reduction in communication costs leads to a flatter and smaller organization.

5.1.1. Implications for the wage structure

Although in their original papers neither Milgrom and Roberts nor Bolton and Dewatripont explore the implications of organizational change for the wage structure,

---

[54] Rajan and Wulf (2003) use detailed data on job descriptions in over 300 large U.S. companies to document that the number of layers between the lowest manager and the CEO has gone down over time, i.e., organizations have become "flatter".

a small but growing literature on IT-driven organizational change and inequality has developed since.

Lindbeck and Snower (1996) emphasize the "complementarity" aspect of the Milgrom–Roberts hypothesis. They consider a production function with two tasks and two types of workers. The Tayloristic model would assign one type of workers to each task, according to comparative advantages to exploit specialization. The alternative organization of production is the flexible model, where each type of worker performs both tasks. This more flexible organization is preferred when there are large informational complementarities across tasks. The introduction of IT capital amplifies these informational complementarities and makes the flexible organization more profitable. Moreover, firms increase the demand for skilled workers who are more adaptable and versed in multi-tasking, and the skill premium rises.

Möbius (2000) focuses on the "customization" aspect of organizational change. When products are standardized, demand is certain and production tasks perfectly predictable, inducing a high division of labor (the Tayloristic principle). New flexible capital allows firms to greatly expand the degree of product variety and customization in product markets. Larger variety implies a more uncertain demand mix because producers become subject to unpredictable "fad shocks" and producers therefore favor a flexible organization of production, with less division of labor. Once again, to the extent that the most skilled workers are also the most adaptable and versatile, the skill premium will increase.

The mechanism in Garicano and Rossi-Hansberg (2003) is based, instead, on the fall in the communication cost within the organization. Their paper has the particular merit of taking the literature on the internal organization of firms [e.g., Bolton and Dewatripont (1994)] one step further by recognizing that organizational hierarchies and labor market outcomes are determined simultaneously in equilibrium. Consider an organization where managers perform the most difficult and productive tasks and workers specialize in a set of simpler tasks. Managers also spend a fraction of their time "helping" workers unable to perform their task, and by so doing, they divert resources away from their most productive activities. The fall in the cost of communication allows workers to perform a wider range of tasks, using a smaller amount of the manager's time. The implications for wage inequality are stark. First of all, since workers are heterogeneous in ability, and ability is complementary to the number of tasks performed, inequality among workers within the firm increases. Second, the pay of the manager relative to that of the workers rises because the manager can concentrate on the tasks with high return.

The previous papers have studied how IT-based advances have affected the organizational structure within firms. Saint-Paul (2001) addresses the spectacular rise in the pay of CEOs and a few other professions (e.g., sportsmen and performers) documented in Section 2 using a model where IT-based advances affect the organization of markets with frictions. Saint-Paul combines a model with "superstar" or "winner-take-all" effects [Rosen (1981)] with the advent of information technology. In his model, human capital has two dimensions: productivity, i.e., the ability to produce units of output, and creativity, i.e., the ability to generate ideas that can spread (and generate return) over a segment of an economy, called a "network". The diffusion of information technology expands networks increasing the payoff to the most creative workers and widening the income distribution at the top. However, as networks become large enough, the probability that within the same network there will be somebody with another idea at least as good rises: superstars end up competing against each other, mitigating the inegalitarian effects of information technology. Under certain parametric assumptions, inequality first rises and then falls over time.

5.1.2. Empirical evidence on the complementarity between technology, organizational change and human capital

Bresnahan, Brynjolfsson and Hitt (2002) investigate the hypothesis that IT adoption, workplace reorganization, and product variety expansion (customization) are complementary at the firm level. Their view is that simply installing computers or communications equipment is not sufficient for achieving efficiency gains. Instead, firms must go through a process of organizational redesign. The combination of IT investments and reorganization represents a skill-biased force increasing the relative demand for more educated labor.

Their empirical analysis is based on a sample of over 300 large firms in the United States, and their definition of organizational change is a shift toward more decentralized decision making and more frequent teamwork. They find a significant correlation between IT, reorganization, and various measures of human capital.[55]

In a related paper, Caroli and Van Reenen (2001) argue that the existence of complementarities between organizational change and the demand for skilled labor leads to three predictions: (1) organizational change should be followed by a declining demand for less skilled workers; (2) in the vein of the directed technical change hypothesis (see next section), cheaper skilled labor should increase the occurrence of organizational change; and (3) organizational change should have a larger impact in workplaces with higher skill levels.

They test these predictions combining two data sets, one for the United Kingdom and one for France, with information on changes in work organization, working practices, and the skill level of the labor force. Interestingly, they also have information on the introduction of new IT capital, so they can distinguish the effect of organizational change from that of skill-biased technical progress. They find some supporting evidence for all three predictions.

Baker and Hubbard (2003) offer an example where technological change not only affects the organizational design of firms but also the boundary of firms. In particular, they study how IT may have reduced the moral hazard problem in the U.S. trucking industry. Drivers may simply operate the trucks as employees of the dispatching company,

---

[55] See Brynjolfsson and Hitt (2000) for a survey on the empirical work documenting the causal link from adoption of information technology and organizational transformation within the firm.

or they may actually own the trucks they operate. If the dispatcher owns the truck, there is only limited assurance that the driver will operate in a way that preserves the value of the asset, since the dispatcher cannot perfectly monitor the driving operations. When this moral hazard problem is severe, decentralized ownership will be the outcome, that is, the driver owns the truck. Using detailed truck-level data, Baker and Hubbard show that with the introduction of a new monitoring technology – on-board computers linked to the company servers – the share of driver-ownership decreased significantly.

5.2. Directed organizational change

An alternative hypothesis to that put forth by Milgrom and Roberts is contained in several papers discussing the parallel change in the organization and in the pay structure of work. This view maintains that the driving force of organizational shifts is not technology, but rather the secular rise in the supply of skilled workers that created incentives to modify the organization of production: directed organizational change of sorts.

Acemoglu (1999) models a frictional labor market where firms must choose the amount of capital, k, when they are vacant, before meeting the worker. Consider a simple static version of Acemoglu's model. There are two types of workers, skilled and unskilled, where ϕ is the fraction of skilled ones. Skilled workers have productivity h_s and unskilled workers h_u, which we normalize to $1 < h_s$. Output on each job is given by $y_i = h_i^\alpha k^{1-\alpha}$, where $i = s, u$. Wages and profits and are, respectively, a fraction ξ and $1 - \xi$ of output net of the cost of the capital installed k. The expected value of a firm choosing capacity k is

$$V(k) = (1 - \xi)\left[\phi I^s \left(h_s^\alpha k^{1-\alpha} - k\right) + (1 - \phi)I^u\left(k^{1-\alpha} - k\right)\right],$$

where I^i is an indicator variable that equals 1 if the firm accepts a match with a worker of type $i = s, u$ and 0 otherwise.[56] Suppose the firm chooses between two hiring strategies: a "pooling" strategy where it accepts all workers, $I^s = I^u = 1$, and a "separating" strategy where it only accepts skilled workers, $I^s = 1$, $I^u = 0$. Conditional on the hiring strategy, we can use the first-order condition to solve for the optimal choices of capacity, k^P and k^S. Substituting the capacity choice back into $V(k)$, the values of the two hiring strategies are

$$
\begin{aligned}
V^P &= \kappa(1 - \xi)\left[\phi h_s^\alpha + (1 - \phi)\right]^{1/\alpha}, \\
V^S &= \kappa(1 - \xi)\phi h_s,
\end{aligned}
\tag{19}
$$

where κ is a constant depending only on α. Comparing these two values, we conclude that the payoff to the "separating" strategy, V^S, dominates the payoff of the "pooling"

---

[56] Here, for simplicity we assume that workers accept passively each job offer. We do not consider equilibria where firms randomize, i.e., where $I^i \in (0, 1)$.

strategy, V^{P}, whenever

$$\left(\frac{1-\phi}{\phi^{\alpha}-\phi}\right)^{1/\alpha} < h_s. \tag{20}$$

Note that the left-hand side of this expression decreases in ϕ, the fraction of skilled workers. When the size of the skilled group is small, a "pooling" equilibrium arises where all firms invest the same amount of capital and search for both types of workers. As the relative size of the skilled group rises, the economy switches to a "separating" equilibrium where firms find it optimal to install more capital and accept exclusively skilled workers in their search process.[57] One can interpret the pooling and the separating equilibrium as different types of work organizations, displaying different degrees of segregation along the skill dimension within sectors. The switch from the low-segregation to the high-segregation organization stretches the wage structure and generates higher inequality.

In a related paper, Kremer and Maskin (1996) offer an alternative explanation for the rise in the degree of assortative matching in the workplace, using a frictionless assignment model. Their paper contains some suggestive evidence that the degree of sorting ("segregation") has risen within industries and plants. However, their model is based on an increase in the skill dispersion in the population, for which there is little evidence in the data.[58]

Thesmar and Thoenig (2000) embed a choice of organizational design into a Schumpeterian growth model. Firms can opt for a Tayloristic organization that has large product-specific set-up costs, with the benefit of a high level of productive efficiency. Alternatively, they can choose a new and more flexible organization that can be built with a lower initial fixed cost, but whose productivity level is lower.[59] As is common in this class of Schumpeterian models, there is an R&D sector, where product innovations are generated proportionately to the amount of skilled workers hired. The patent of each new product is then sold to a monopolistic producer who can choose optimally which organization of work to set up (Tayloristic or flexible) according to the volatility of the economic environment.

A rise in the supply of skilled workers will increase the innovation rate in the R&D sector: the higher the innovation rate, the shorter the product's life expectancy for a monopolistic producer, and the less profitable organizations with large fixed costs prove to be, compared to the more flexible production method. The model also produces a rise in segregation, since skilled workers tend to cluster into the R&D sector, as well as

[57] In the more general version of the model, which is dynamic with free entry of firms, there are other firms who install a small amount of capital (unskilled jobs) and search exclusively for unskilled workers.

[58] For example, Hoxby and Long (1998) report that the difference in the quality of education (measured by their wage) received by college students at more and less selective institutions has increased over time, but the increase is quantitatively small.

[59] This distinction between the Tayloristic firm and the new flexible firm is due to Piore and Sabel (1984).

a rise in inequality as unskilled workers lose from the abandonment of the Tayloristic model since the production phase becomes less efficient.[60]

5.3. Discussion

The case examined by Baker and Hubbard (2003) is one where IT improves firms' monitoring ability of workers' effort. However, it is plausible that the trend toward a "flatter" organizational design where single-task routinized work is replaced by multi-tasking team-work induces a *rise* in the cost of monitoring individual workers' effort. Firms would then, optimally, introduce incentive schemes (e.g., tournament contracts) with the result of increasing inequality in rewards. In other words, optimal contracts respond to technological and organizational changes that affect the extent of moral hazard within the firm. This line of research is largely unexplored at the moment.

All the models we surveyed in this section are qualitative in nature and, although they establish a logical link between organizational change and inequality, they do not provide any quantitative analysis. One of the main obstacles is that explicit models of organizations contain parameters and variables that are hard to observe, measure, and therefore calibrate (hierarchies, communication costs, number of tasks, etc.). Recently, several papers have started to measure, in various ways, "organizational capital" or "intangible capital" [see, e.g., Hall (2001), McGrattan and Prescott (2003) and Atkeson and Kehoe (2002)]. A promising avenue for research would try to incorporate this measurement into models that link reorganization with changes in the stock of organizational capital and that relate the latter to the wage structure in order to perform a more rigorous quantitative analysis.

6. Technical progress as a source of change in labor market institutions

Throughout the chapter, up to this point, we have maintained a "competitive" view of the labor market and argued that skills are priced at their marginal product, potentially explaining large parts of the observed dynamics of inequality. However, the labor market displays very peculiar features compared to many other markets in the economy: a sizeable fraction of labor may be considered as under-employed in any given period (unemployment), individual workers often organize themselves into coalitions (unions), and wages frequently seem to be set through some explicit negotiation between firms and workers (individual and collective bargaining). These attributes of the labor market are, arguably, better captured by non-competitive models. We begin our departure from the purely competitive framework by introducing unions and collective bargaining.

---

[60] Duranton (2004) provides yet another framework for formalizing the concept of "skill segregation" in production and analyzes the implied wage structure in the economy. In his model, a rise in the relative supply of skilled workers can lead to higher segregation and more inequality.

Historically, unions and centralized bargaining have been key institutions in the determination of wages and other important labor market outcomes. Over the past 30 years, the economies of the United States and the United Kingdom experienced rapid deunionization. In the United States, in the late 1970s, 30 percent of male non-agricultural private-sector workers were unionized. By 2000, only 14 percent were unionized [Farber and Western (2000)]. In the United Kingdom, union density among male workers was around 58 percent in the late 1970s and it has fallen uninterruptedly since to 30 percent today [Machin (2000, 2003)]. There is a variety of evidence that unions compress the structure of wages, even after controlling for workers' characteristics, and thus many economists suspect that their decline may have been an important factor in the increase in inequality in the Anglo-Saxon economies [see, e.g., Gosling and Machin (1995) and DiNardo, Fortin and Lemieux (1996)].

The existing literature has explored mainly two explanations for the decline in unions. The first generation of papers argued that an important force in the fall of unionization is the change in the composition of the economy away from industries, demographic groups, and occupations where union organization was comparatively cheaper and unions have been traditionally strong [Dickens and Leonard (1985)]. However, Farber and Krueger (1992) estimate that compositional shifts can account for at most 25 percent of the decline in the United States and have played virtually no role since the 1980s. Machin (2003) reports that only around 20 percent of the U.K. union decline of the last two decades can be attributed to compositional change.

The second hypothesis is that the legal and political framework supporting union membership deteriorated in the 1970s and 1980s.[61] To date, this explanation seems to have gained rather broad acceptance, even though this view has limits as well. For example, the fall in union organizing activity precedes two key political events: the air-traffic controller strike of 1981 and Reagan's Labor Board appointments in 1983 [Farber and Western (2002)]. U.K. data also show that the fall in union membership pre-dates the first Thatcher government. Overall, we think that the forces behind rapid deunionization are not yet well understood.

In most of continental Europe, unions are still strong, and there are no clear signs of decline in union coverage, but a marked change in union behavior has occurred over the past 30 years. Several indexes of coordination and centralization in unions' bargaining for Europe show a distinct trend toward more decentralized wage negotiations, especially in the Scandinavian countries, whose unionization rates are the highest [Iversen (1998)].

The standard explanation for the shift toward decentralized bargaining is based on the interaction between monetary policy and wage setting arrangements. With an independent national central bank, coordination in bargaining among unions is useful because it allows unions to internalize the implications of their wage claims on inflation. With

---

[61] Some authors emphasized anti-union management practices [Freeman (1988)]. Others focused on changes in the composition of the National Labor Relation Board [Levy (1985)].

the advent of the European monetary union and the institution of the European Central Bank within-country coordination proves less useful. However, the evidence in favor of this hypothesis is scant. First, monetary policy does not seem to Granger-cause centralization empirically [Bleaney (1996)]. Second, we did not observe a substantial trend toward cross-border coordination in unions' bargaining.

Recently, a new hypothesis for deunionization and decentralization in unions' wage setting, based on skill-biased technological change, has been advanced by Acemoglu, Aghion and Violante (2001) and Ortigueira (2002). Their arguments rest on the view that unions are coalitions of heterogeneous workers which extract rents from employers and only exist insofar as members have an incentive to stay in the coalition and continue bargaining in a centralized fashion. The conjecture of these authors is that skill-biased technical change can dramatically alter such incentives.

6.1. Skill-biased technology and the fall in union density

Here, we outline a reduced form model that conveys the basic trade-offs highlighted by Acemoglu, Aghion and Violante (2001). Suppose there are two kinds of workers l_s of which are skilled and $l_u = 1 - l_s$ of which are unskilled. If employed in the competitive sector, these workers will receive wages equal to their productivity, h_s and $h_u < h_s$, respectively. We will think of skill-biased technological change as a rise in h_s relative to h_u.

Workers can also be employed in unionized firms and receive wages, w_s and w_u. A main characteristic of unions is that they compress wages. In our setup, this means that the wage gap between the unionized skilled and unskilled workers is smaller than the productivity gap, or

$$w_s - w_u = \kappa (h_s - h_u),$$ (21)

where $\kappa < 1$ is the degree of wage compression. This equation may arise for a variety of reasons. Collective decision-making within a union may reflect the preferences of its median voter, and if this median voter is an unskilled worker, he will try to increase unskilled wages at the expense of skilled wages. It is also possible that union members choose to compress wages because of ideological reasons or for social cohesion purposes. Or, in presence of idiosyncratic uncertainty, unions could offer insurance to their members by setting a flatter income profile. The empirical literature is broadly consistent with the notion that unions compress wages, though it does not distinguish among the various possible reasons for it [see Booth (1995)].

Union wages (w_s, w_u) must also satisfy some participation constraint for firms (who would otherwise either shut down or open a non-unionized plant). Suppose that this takes the form of non-negative profits:

$$h_s l_s + h_u (1 - l_s) + \Omega (h_s, h_u) - \left[w_s l_s + w_u (1 - l_s) \right] \geqslant 0,$$ (22)

where $\Omega(h_s, h_u) > 0$ is the additional contribution of unions to output, as a function of both types of labor.[62] This could be because unions, ceteris paribus, increase productivity [for example, Freeman and Medoff (1984) and Freeman and Lazear (1995) argue this]. Or unions may encourage training [as in Acemoglu and Pischke (1999)].

Solving the wage compression and participation constraint Equations (21) and (22) as equalities, we obtain the maximum wage that a skilled worker can be paid as a union member:

$$\bar{w}_s = h_s - (1 - l_s)(1 - \kappa)(h_s - h_u) + \Omega(h_s, h_u).$$

Intuitively, as w_s rises, w_u must increase too in order to satisfy the wage compression constraint (21) but since profits fall with labor costs there is an upper bound to the wage of a skilled union member. Skilled workers will remain union members as long as what they are paid as union members exceeds their competitive salary,

$$\bar{w}_s \geqslant h_s. \tag{23}$$

From the no-quit condition (23) and the wage compression constraint (21), it follows that $\bar{w}_u \geqslant h_u$, so unskilled workers will always remain unionized. Observe that the slope of the maximum union skilled wage, $\bar{w}_s$, as a function of the productivity of skilled workers, h_s, is

$$\bar{w}_s'(h_s) = 1 - (1 - l_s)(1 - \kappa) + \Omega_1(h_s, h_u).$$

Since $\kappa < 1$, as long as the benefits of unionization, $\Omega(h_s, h_u)$, do not increase too rapidly in h_s (i.e., the benefits of unionization do not increase much with skill-biased technical change), we have $\bar{w}_s'(h_s) < 1$. Hence, there exists a cutoff level, h_s^*, such that $\bar{w}_s(h_s) < h_s$ for any $h_s > h_s^*$. This implies that once technical change takes h_s above h_s^*, the wage compression imposed by unions becomes unsustainable, and skilled workers will break away from unions.

Notice that skill-biased technical change is the cause of the deunionization and directly increases inequality. However, deunionization itself contributes to inequality as well. Before deunionization, the wage gap between skilled and unskilled workers is $w_s - w_u \leqslant \kappa(h_s - h_u)$, and widens smoothly with skill-biased technical change. It is only after deunionization that it jumps up discretely to $w_s - w_u = h_s - h_u$. Therefore, although deunionization is not the primary cause of the surge in wage inequality, it amplifies the original effect of these economic forces by removing the wage compression constraint imposed by unions.

6.2. Skill-biased technology and the fall in centralized bargaining

In many European countries – in particular among the Scandinavian countries – the so-called "Ghent system" creates a fiscal-policy link among unions. Under this system,

---

[62] As long as unions are sustainable, all workers, skilled and unskilled, will prefer to join the union.

unemployment benefits are administered by the individual unions, but they are funded by the government through aggregate labor income taxation. Hence, not only does the net income of unions' members depend on their negotiated wage, but, through the equilibrium tax rate, also on the wage claims of other unions. Ortigueira (2002) outlines a model economy with this institutional feature, where there are two types of workers, skilled and unskilled, and two unions that can choose to coordinate their wage determination. Unemployment is generated through a frictional labor market with a standard matching function.

Under decentralized bargaining, unions take the tax as given. Ortigueira (2002) shows that there are two possible steady states: in one, unions expect a low tax, thus making moderate wage claims which, in turn, keep equilibrium unemployment and tax rate low, fulfilling the initial expectation; in the other steady state, unions expect a high tax rate, thus making strong wage claims that produce high unemployment and a high tax rate. This second equilibrium yields lower income and lower welfare for union members. Centralized bargaining avoids the coordination failure and the associated welfare losses that can arise in this "bad equilibrium", and hence it can be preferred by unions. Note, however, that the "good equilibrium" under decentralized bargaining is still the best outcome. It is the ex-ante uncertainty that the bad equilibrium could arise that makes coordination attractive.

However, consider what happens with the advent of a skill-biased technology that increases the demand for skilled workers sharply, reducing their unemployment incidence. When unemployment benefits are proportional to wages, the fact that skilled workers are much less likely to be unemployed decreases the social expenditures of the government. As a result, under decentralized bargaining, the equilibrium with high taxes and low welfare does not survive the advent of a skill-biased technology. This justifies the shift in unions' wage setting policies toward decentralization.[63]

6.3. Discussion

The testable implications that can be identified above are that (1) among the experienced workers, the most skilled leave the unions in response to technological improvements and that (2) among the new entrant cohorts, the most educated workers opt for non-unionized jobs. However, these implications are derived from theories of technology-induced deunionization that are rather exploratory; more sophisticated and rigorous models of unions (with endogenous membership and endogenous wage-compression mechanisms) are yet to be developed.

---

[63] See also den Haan (2003) for a model with multiple steady states, one with low tax and unemployment rates and one with high tax and unemployment rates, applied to the U.S.–Europe comparison of labor market outcomes.

The recent empirical studies by Card (2001), for the United States, and Addison, Bailey and Siebert (2004), for the United Kingdom, compare the unionization rate across several skill groups before and after the collapse in union density in these two countries (1973 and 1993 for the United States, and 1983 and 1995 for the United Kingdom). The common finding of these two papers, is that unionization declined most for the low- and middle-skill groups.[64] Taken at face value, this preliminary evidence is not favorable to the hypothesis discussed in this section. However, one has to be cautious in interpreting these results because this work does not control for unobserved heterogeneity.[65] Suppose that – as documented by Card (1996) – unobserved ability is higher among unionized workers with low observable skills. Given that unionized firms offer a compressed wage schedule, such a contract would attract the highest ability workers with low education and the lowest ability workers with high education. Moreover, assume that technological change induces a rise in the market return for innate ability, as discussed in Section 3.2. Then, the theory suggests that one should observe exactly the cross-skill deunionization pattern documented from U.S. and U.K. data.

It should be mentioned that a technology-based theory of deunionization must also explain why union density did not fall (in fact, it expanded somewhat) in the public sector. Since the public sector is, by definition, sheltered from the international competition, it is reasonable to conjecture that the leap in competitive pressure faced by many manufacturing industries over the past 30 years eroded those rents that are, according to some researchers, at the heart of the existence of unions. A quantitative evaluation of the importance of this channel is yet to be performed.

Another avenue that so far has not been pursued is the analysis of deunionization in conjunction with the structural changes in workplace organization that occurred in the past 30 years. In Section 5, we argued that a distinct feature of the recent change in the production process, especially in manufacturing, is the switch from Tayloristic organizations, where workers repeatedly performed similar tasks around the conveyer belt, toward "flatter" organization built on teams where workers engage in multiple tasks and where the individual division of labor is much fuzzier. Union's wage setting arrangements, based on "equal pay for equal work", can be effective within a Tayloristic plant, but then become very inefficient in plants where production is organized through teams. There is no reason to assume that workers performing the same task will be equally productive, since they perform many other complementary operations simultaneously [see, e.g., Lindbeck and Snower (1996)].

---

[64] Note that wages in the union sector do not fully reflect skills. For this reason, these authors impute skill deciles to unionized workers based on what workers with similar observable characteristics (age, education, gender, race, etc.) would earn in the non-union sector.

[65] Card (2001) makes a rough adjustment for unobserved heterogeneity, based on Card (1996). A thorough analysis would require the use of longitudinal data, but both, Card (2001) and Addison, Bailey and Siebert (2004), are restricted to repeated cross-sections.

7. Technological change in frictional labor markets

Most of the models presented so far feature an aggregate production technology, i.e., the production structure is centralized, and competitive labor markets. Constructing a frictional model of the labor market requires departing from both attributes and moving toward a decentralized production structure and a labor market with imperfect coordination between workers and firms in the matching process. This class of models gives rise to frictional equilibrium unemployment and "frictional equilibrium inequality". By frictional inequality, we mean wage dispersion that is purely an artifact of frictions and that, without frictions, would disappear. A useful way to think about this phenomenon is to introduce the concept of "return to labor market luck".

Throughout this chapter, we have discussed several models where technological progress produces a rise in the return to observable and unobservable *permanent* components of individual skills, such as educational attainment, age, and innate ability. These permanent factors greatly determine inequality of earnings among the population, but they are not by any means exhaustive. Earnings display a large *stochastic* component (e.g., events related to the luck of individuals, firms, or industries) that is responsible for their fluctuations around the permanent component.[66]

Gottschalk and Moffitt (1994) were the first to ask how much of the observed increase in inequality is attributable to a rise in earnings volatility and instability around its permanent component. They used a simple statistical model where log wages, w_{it}, for an individual i at time t – net of their predictable age profile – are assumed to be the sum of two orthogonal components, a fixed individual effect α_i and a stochastic (i.i.d.) component ε_{it}. Using the covariance structure of wages within a panel of U.S. males (constructed from PSID data), they reached the conclusion that the fraction of the total increase in cross-sectional inequality attributable to a surge in earnings volatility is between one third and one half.[67] One can interpret this fact as a rise in frictional inequality, or in the "return to labor market luck". The argument set forth is that the rapid diffusion of a new technology leverages the importance of these stochastic factors, raising the premium to workers with no observable distinguishing characteristics other than their good fortune.

Most of the work we review uses the random matching model of the labor market [see, e.g., Mortensen and Pissarides (1998) or Pissarides (2000)]. In this framework the

---

[66] A large empirical literature documents wage dispersion among observationally equivalent workers that cannot be fully reconciled with unobserved heterogeneity in permanent components. Abowd, Kramarz and Margolis (1999) document that firm effects still play a role, after controlling exhaustively for individuals' effects. Krueger and Summers (1988) found that a worker moving from a high to a low wage industry is subject to a wage loss roughly equal to the inter-industry differential.

[67] The subsequent literature on the subject demonstrated the robustness of this result to richer statistical models for the stochastic component of wages. See Haider (2001), Heathcote, Storesletten and Violante (2003) and Meghir and Pistaferri (2004) for the United States and Blundell and Preston (1998) and Dickens (2000) for the United Kingdom.

existence of frictions creates a bilateral monopoly as a result of a meeting between a vacant firm and a worker. Wages are determined by bargaining over total output, so more productive firms tend to pay more, creating wage dispersion among ex-ante equal workers. We start by studying how technological change affects unemployment in this class of models. Next, we move to wage inequality. Random matching is a somewhat extreme characterization of frictions. In the last part of the section we contrast random search models to directed search models.

7.1. Technological progress and frictional unemployment

There is a sizeable literature trying to characterize how equilibrium unemployment reacts qualitatively to variations of the rate of technological change within a matching model à la Diamond–Mortensen–Pissarides (DMP) with vintage capital à la Solow (1960). Two distinct approaches emerge from the literature.

The first, that can be attributed to Aghion and Howitt (1994), argues that when new and more productive equipment enters the economy exclusively through the creation of new matches – because existing matches cannot be "upgraded" – it has a Schumpeterian "creative–destruction" effect: new capital competes with old capital by making it more obsolete and tends to destroy existing matches, because workers are better off separating from their old matches to search for the new firms endowed with the most productive technology. Thus, unemployment tends to go up as growth accelerates, due to a higher job-separation rate.

The second approach, due to Mortensen and Pissarides (1998), proposes an alternative view whereby the new technologies enter into existing firms through a costly "upgrading" process of old capital. In the extreme case where upgrading is free, we have the Solowian model of disembodied technological change, even though the carrier of technology is equipment. The separation rate is unaffected by faster growth and all the effects work through job creation. For small values of the upgrading cost, unemployment falls with faster growth, thanks to the familiar "capitalization effect": investors are encouraged to create more vacancies, knowing that they will be able to incorporate (and hence benefit from) future technological advances at low cost.[68]

Hornstein, Krusell and Violante (2003b) try to resolve the issue quantitatively. When they parameterize the model to match some salient features of the U.S. economy, they find that, in the vintage-matching model, the link between capital-embodied growth and unemployment does not importantly depend on to what parties – new matches or old ones – the benefits of the technological advancement accrue. The intuition for this "equivalence result" is that upgrading can be much better than creative destruction only

---

[68] An interesting qualification to this result is provided by King and Welling (1995): if, unlike what is customarily assumed in this family of models, workers bear the full fixed search cost, then the capitalization effect leads to an increase in the number of searchers and to longer unemployment durations. See Pissarides (2000, chapter 3) for a detailed discussion on growth and unemployment in matching models of the labor market.

if it is very costly for vacant firms to meet workers, but the data on the low average unemployment and vacancy durations imply that, in the model, this meeting friction is minor. That paper also shows that the same data on average unemployment duration impose severe restrictions on how much frictional wage inequality the model can generate. In the standard search model, high dispersion of wage opportunities makes workers very demanding and increases unemployment spells. Thus, a high wage dispersion could only coexist, in equilibrium, with long unemployment durations.

We now turn to the analysis of how technological progress impinges on frictional inequality in random matching models. In these models, however, the limits on the extent of wage inequality due to luck emphasized in Hornstein, Krusell and Violante (2003b) apply as well.

7.2. Technological heterogeneity and the returns to luck

In a frictional labor market populated by ex-ante equal workers, an increase in technological heterogeneity can increase the return to luck. We explain this mechanism within a simple framework based on Aghion, Howitt and Violante (2002).[69] Consider an economy populated by a measure one of infinitely lived, ex-ante equal, and risk-neutral workers as well as by the same measure of jobs. Jobs are machines embodying a given technology. The technological frontier advances every period at rate $\gamma > 0$. The machines have a productive life of two periods. An age $j \in \{0, 1\}$ machine that is matched with a worker produces output $y_j = (1 + \gamma)^{-j} h$ (normalized relative to the age 0 machine), where h represents the skill level of the workers.

The labor market is frictional, i.e., workers separated from their jobs are randomly re-matched with a vacant machine. To simplify, we assume that they always make contact with a machine. We postulate that, upon contact, the bilateral monopoly problem is solved by a rent sharing mechanism setting wages to be a constant fraction, ξ, of current output y_j, where ξ is a measure of the bargaining power of workers.

It is easy to see that in an equilibrium where all job offers are accepted, the lucky half of the workers will be employed on new machines and the unlucky half on old machines. The variance of log wages is simply given by $\text{var}(\log w) = \gamma^2/4$, which is increasing in the rate of embodied technological change. Intuitively, in this economy all the heterogeneity is generated by technological differentials across machines. A technological acceleration (rise in γ) amplifies the productivity gaps between jobs. Since in this non-competitive labor market individual wages are linked to individual output, this acceleration then also raises wage dispersion even among ex-ante equal workers, i.e., it raises the return to luck.[70] As in Jovanovic (1998), however, if the scrapping age of capital is endogenous, the model would display an offsetting force. This force is due to the

---

[69] See also Manuelli (2000) and Violante (2002).

[70] This increase in wage inequality is mirrored by a rise in wage instability along the lifetime of each worker: given a certain amount of labor turnover, larger cross-sectional productivity differences translate into more volatile individual wage profiles.

fact that, when the growth rate is higher, machines becomes obsolete faster, and firms scrap machines earlier. Therefore the equilibrium age range of machines in operation shrinks, compressing technological heterogeneity.

7.3. Vintage human capital with frictions

A technological acceleration not only affects transitory residual wage inequality through its impact on the underlying distribution of job productivity differences. The technological acceleration may also affect the distribution of worker productivity differences if it interacts with the accumulation of job/technology-specific knowledge.[71] Violante (2002) extends the above model to include vintage human capital. Employed workers accumulate, through learning-by-doing, knowledge about the technology they are matched with. We normalize the amount of specific skills cumulated after every employment period to 1, so that the learning curve of the workers is concave, i.e., learning is faster for workers with lower initial skills. To keep the model tractable, we also assume that skills fully depreciate after two periods.

A worker on a machine of age i who moves on to a machine of age j next period can transfer h_{ij} units of the accumulated skills to the new job

$$h_{ij} = \min\{(1+\gamma)^{\tau(j-i+1)}, 1\},\tag{24}$$

with $\tau > 0$ and $i, j \in \{0, 1\}$. The fraction of skills that can be transferred from an old to a newer machine is proportional to the *technological distance* between the two machines through a factor $\tau \geq 0$. The presence of the term γ in the transferability technology is crucial: the rate of quality improvement of capital-embodied technologies determines the degree by which new technology is different, more complex, and richer than the previous generation of machines. A higher γ reduces skill transferability in the economy.[72] Equation (24) and the depreciation assumption implies that we have three skill levels in the economy

$$h_{01} = 1, \qquad h_{00} = h_{11} = (1+\gamma)^{-\tau}, \qquad h_{10} = (1+\gamma)^{-2\tau},\tag{25}$$

and the corresponding wage rates (normalized relative to the wage on an age 0 machine) are $w_{ij} = \xi h_{ij}(1+\gamma)^{-j}$, $i, j \in \{0, 1\}$. Note that, given this simple expression

---

[71] The accumulation of job/technology-specific knowledge is also at the heart of the discussion of the experience premium in Section 4.

[72] The book by Gordon (1990) provides several examples of quality improvement in equipment requiring the performance of new tasks in the associated jobs. In the aircraft industry in the 1970s, new avionics were introduced that provided a safer but more complex navigation system. In the telephone industry, around the mid-1970s, electromechanical telephone switchboards were replaced by more sophisticated and flexible electronic equipment with larger programming possibilities. In the software industry, since the early 1980s, every new version of a software is equipped with new features. Those users who remain attached to an old version are often unfamiliar with many features of the new version.

for wages, the variance of log wages can be written as

$$\mathrm{var}(\tilde{w}) = \gamma^2 \, \mathrm{var}(j) + \mathrm{var}(\tilde{h}) - 2\gamma \, \mathrm{cov}(\tilde{h}, j), \tag{26}$$

which is the sum of technological heterogeneity (the force discussed earlier), ex-post skill heterogeneity among workers, and the degree of assortative matching between skills and technologies measured by their covariance.[73]

One can prove that, for large enough γ, workers separate from firms every period.[74] Under this optimal separation rule, the equilibrium level of wage dispersion is given by

$$\mathrm{var}(\tilde{w}) = \gamma^2 \left[\frac{1}{4} + \frac{1}{2}\tau(\tau - 1) \right], \tag{27}$$

so it is increasing in γ whenever the variance is well defined (positive). In particular, the equilibrium displays $\mathrm{var}(\tilde{h}) = \gamma^2\tau^2/2$, and $\mathrm{cov}(\tilde{h}, j) = \gamma\tau/4$. The variance of skills is increasing in γ since a higher γ reduces the skill transferability of the bottom-end workers (h_{10}), while not affecting the skill level of the top end workers (h_{01}). The covariance between skills and age of technology is also increasing in γ, a force that restrains inequality because it worsens equilibrium sorting in the economy. The reason is that a larger γ reduces the skills of workers moving to the new technology relatively more than the skills of workers moving to old technologies.

A common criticism of this class of models is that the degree of churning in the labor market (i.e., labor mobility or job reallocation) has to rise in order to generate more volatile earnings, whereas the empirical literature documents no significant rise in labor mobility [Neumark (2000)].[75] This is a misconception. One way to unravel this issue exploits the equivalence between cross-sectional wage dispersion and individual wage instability in a model with ex-ante equal and infinitely lived agents. A technological acceleration has two effects. First, it curtails skill transferability, thereby increasing wage losses upon separation. Second, it reduces the average skill level of workers who find themselves, on average, on the steeper portion of a concave learning curve, which in turn implies higher wage growth on the job. Both these forces tend to raise individual earnings volatility, for any given level of labor mobility. Violante (2002) offers some evidence of wage losses upon separation and wage growth on the job being larger in the 1980s than in the 1970s and shows that a calibrated full-scale version of this model can

---

[73] A rise in the degree of assortative assignment between workers' skill and machines' productivity is equivalent to a *fall* in the covariance component (recall that j is machine's age, which is inversely related to productivity) and a rise in the variance of wages.

[74] This result is related to the intertemporal trade-off intrinsic in the separation decision: choosing to remain on the old vintage improves the current wage (no vintage-specific skill is lost), but worsens future wages because in the next period the worker will have older knowledge, with low degree of transferability. As γ goes up, the expected future wage loss from holding old skills increases faster than the current wage gain, inducing the worker to optimally anticipate its separation decision.

[75] The empirical literature on labor mobility contains partly opposing results: whereas Jovanovic and Rousseau (2004) find a significant decline of labor mobility since the 1970s, Kambourov and Manovskii (2004) find that occupational mobility increased since the 1970s.

account up to 90 percent of the rise in wage instability in the U.S. economy, while at the same time implying only a very modest rise in equilibrium labor turnover.

7.3.1. Occupation-specific human capital

Occupation-specific experience may be one of the least transferable components of human capital, and a change in occupational mobility can have a big impact on the wage structure. Kambourov and Manovskii (2004) document an increase in occupational mobility in the United States from 16 percent in the early 1970s to 19 percent in the early 1990s.[76] Based on a calibration exercise Kambourov and Manovskii argue that 90 percent of the rise in residual inequality (i.e., in both the permanent and the stochastic component) is due to increased occupational mobility.

The authors build a model of occupation-specific human-capital accumulation based on the equilibrium search framework of Lucas and Prescott (1974). At any one time workers can work in one occupation only. Workers choose their occupation based on their occupation-specific experience. When working in an occupation, workers increase their specific experience, and they lose some of this experience when moving between occupations. A worker's wage in a given occupation depends on the specific experience and the occupation's productivity.

The productivity of occupations is subject to shocks, and increased variability of these shocks directly increases wage variability. However, the total impact of occupational productivity shocks on wage inequality depends on the occupational choice response of workers. Workers in an occupation whose productivity declines choose to move in search of better occupations and, by so doing, they dampen the effect of the shock on inequality. When the increased variance of productivity shocks is accompanied by decreased persistence – as conjectured by the authors – workers in occupations hit by moderately negative shocks may choose not to switch occupation because occupations which look profitable today may turn quickly into unproductive ones. This latter effect amplifies the direct effect of the initial shocks.[77]

7.3.2. A precautionary demand for general skills

Gottschalk and Moffitt (1994) found that the transitory component of inequality is larger (and increased more) for low-education workers. Gould, Moav and Weinberg (2001) model this phenomenon using a vintage human capital model where risk-averse workers choose their level of education. They study an economy where workers are ex-ante heterogeneous with respect to permanent innate ability, and the return to college education is increasing in ability. High-ability workers obtain a college education that provides

---

[76] Kambourov and Manovskii use occupational data from the PSID at the three-digit level, including almost 1000 occupational groups.

[77] The model of Bertola and Ichino (1995), discussed in Section 8, generates increased wage inequality through a similar mechanism.

them with general skills which do not depreciate as technology advances. Low-ability workers do not acquire general skills in college; rather, they acquire technology-specific experience through on-the-job learning. Here, we refer to workers with a college education as skilled and to workers without a college education as unskilled.

Gould, Moav and Weinberg (2001) consider a shock to the economy that simultaneously increases the rate of embodied technological change and the ex-ante variance of technological progress across jobs.[78] This shock increases the "precautionary" demand for college education, since holding technology-specific skills becomes more risky. The lowest ability threshold for college graduates falls, and thus permanent inequality increases within skilled workers and falls within the group of unskilled workers. At the same time, the rise in the variance of embodied technological change means that "skill erosion" has a bigger impact on the relative wages of unlucky and lucky unskilled workers, so the increase in their wage variance is mostly determined by transitory components.

This mechanism relies on the assumption that the variance of technical progress is heteroskedastic in the sense that it rises with its mean. We know very little about this property: Cummins and Violante (2002) analyze the whole cross-industry distribution of equipment-embodied technical change for 62 industries in the United States from 1947 to 2000 and find little evidence of changing variance, although the mean grows substantially over the period. However, they document a rise in the cross-sectoral variance of the "technological gap" between average capital and leading-edge machines.[79] According to the transferability technology (24), the technological gap closely measures the degree of skill erosion of an average worker displaced in a given industry.

7.3.3. Explaining the fall in real wages

Interestingly, in a set of model economies with vintage human capital [Helpman and Rangel (1999), Gould, Moav and Weinberg (2001), Violante (2002) or Kambourov and Manovskii (2004)], during the transition to the new steady state, and notwithstanding the technological acceleration, the fall in the average skill level of the workforce can generate a temporary slowdown in average wage growth and a fall in the real value of wages at the bottom of the distribution – two facts that have been documented extensively for the period of interest.

To illustrate this point, let us return to the model from Section 7.3. Note that in an equilibrium where workers separate every period – as assumed – each skill type represents one fourth of all workers. The four skills types are reported in expression (25). It is immediate to see that the normalized average log level of skills is $-\tau\gamma$, and thus it falls unambiguously when γ increases. This opens the interesting possibility that, in the

---

[78] This view of the past 30 years as being a period of high "turbulence" is also present in several models of the differential labor market performance between the United States and Europe, see Section 8.
[79] See Section 3.2.1 for a formal definition of the technological gap.

model, the average wage could decrease along the transition following a technological acceleration.

Suppose that at time t the economy is in steady state with $\gamma = \gamma_L$ (and with the productivity of the new machine normalized to 1). The average log wage is then $\tilde{w}_t = -\tau\gamma_L - \gamma_L/2$. Suppose now that γ rises to γ_H. Then, some simple algebra shows that in the next period, the average log wage is

$$\tilde{w}_{t+1} = \frac{\gamma_H}{2} - \frac{\tau}{2}(\gamma_L + \gamma_H) = \tilde{w}_t - \frac{\tau}{2}(\gamma_H - \gamma_L) + \frac{1}{2}(\gamma_L + \gamma_H).$$

Thus, despite the technological acceleration, the average wage decreases along the transition if $\tau > (\gamma_L + \gamma_H)/(\gamma_H - \gamma_L)$, that is, if τ or the increase in γ are large.

An alternative explanation for the fall in real wages – which does not depend on vintage human capital – is advanced by Manuelli (2000) within a frictional labor market model where workers have bargaining power and can seize a fraction of the firm's future stream of profits, through wage negotiations. Consider what happens when it is announced that: (1) a new technology will be available in the future; but (2) the incumbent firms will be able to adopt it only with some probability [as in Greenwood and Jovanovic (1999)]. Existing firms will anticipate a future increase in wages, driven by the new, more productive entrants. Hence, there will be a transitional phase before the arrival of the new technology, where the market value of the incumbent firms will fall and, with them, the wages they currently pay.

7.4. Random matching vs. directed search as source of luck

So far, we have analyzed economies where the friction is due to random matching. Wong (2003) argues that models with random matching can have counterfactual implications.[80] It is well known that in a matching model with two types of workers (skilled and unskilled) and two types of firms (high-tech and low-tech), there can be multiple equilibria (Sattinger, 1995). There are equilibria with perfect sorting where skilled (unskilled) workers are matched with high- (low-) tech firms and equilibria that display some degree of "mismatch". In the latter class of equilibria, luck plays a role as skilled workers, ex-ante equal, can end up in jobs with different productivities. Suppose output is the product between efficiency of capital z_i, where $i = l, h$ and $z_h > z_l$, and efficiency of labor h_j, where $j = s, u$ and $h_s > h_u$, i.e., $y_{ij} = z_i h_j$. A wave of skill-biased technical change (or a capital-embodied technological acceleration) that increases the relative productivity of high-tech jobs (i.e., the ratio z_h/z_l) makes high-tech firms more picky in their choice of workers, as now the same skill differences translate in larger output differences. The equilibrium with mismatch is less likely to survive. When the

---

[80] See also Albrecht and Vroman (2002) for a similar environment.

economy switches to the equilibrium with perfect sorting, luck-driven inequality among ex-ante equal workers falls to zero.[81]

One of the key reasons why the model has this counterfactual prediction is that, due to random matching, prices (wages) have no signaling value. Shi (2002) analyzes exactly the same framework (a two-worker, two-firm economy) but he replaces Nash bargaining and random matching with wage posting and directed search, following the alternative approach of "competitive search" [Moen (1997)]. His conclusion is that random matching is not essential for technical progress to leverage the effect of luck in the labor market: directed search works equally well.

In this environment, skilled workers only apply to high-tech jobs, while unskilled workers apply to both types of jobs. Ex ante, every unskilled worker is indifferent between jobs, but inequality is generated ex post. Since high-tech firms give always priority to skilled applicants, unskilled workers applying for high-tech jobs are less likely to become employed than are unskilled workers applying for low-tech jobs. Therefore unskilled workers applying for high-tech jobs have to be offered higher wages than in low-tech jobs.

With free entry, a rise in the relative productivity of high-tech jobs (skill-biased technical change) induces the creation of more high-tech vacancies. More unskilled workers become attracted to the high-tech sector and in equilibrium their job finding probability in the high-tech sector falls, so wages rise. In the meantime, fewer unskilled workers stay in the low-tech sector, so their wages fall. In sum, wage inequality among ex-ante equal workers rises with the degree of skill bias in technology.

Can one conclude that directed search models are more suitable than random search models for studying problems where heterogeneity is crucial, such as wage inequality? The answer depends on the dimension of inequality studied. Directed search seems a more reasonable assumption when the trait determining heterogeneity is observable (e.g., education, general experience), whereas random matching fits better in the analysis of wage inequality when the source of heterogeneity is not directly observable (e.g., ability or vintage-specific skills).

8. Technology-policy complementarity: United States vs. Europe

A large portion of this chapter has been dedicated to the analysis of a number of different economic models designed to decipher the dynamics of the U.S. wage distribution over the past three decades, in light of changes in technology.

In this section we expand our viewpoint to include other dimensions of labor market inequality, which allows us to contrast the U.S. experience with the European experience. In Section 2 we documented that while wage inequality soared in the United

---

[81] The argument in Wong (2003) regarding models with random matching is quite general; e.g., it applies in the model by Acemoglu (1999). From Equation (20) of Section 5, note that as h_s rises (skill-biased technical change), the pooling, or mismatch, equilibrium is less likely to survive, so within-group inequality falls.

States, both the labor share of income and the unemployment rate remained remarkably stable there. In sharp contrast, in most of the large continental European economies, the wage structure did not change much at all, while the labor share fell substantially and unemployment increased steadily. In particular, the increase in European unemployment largely reflects longer durations rather than higher unemployment incidence.

8.1. The Krugman hypothesis

Why have we observed such different outcomes for two regions of the world standing at a similar level of development and, therefore, being subject to very similar aggregate shocks? Are we witnessing a sort of *devil's bargain*, i.e., a trade-off between inequalities: low unemployment can only be achieved by paying the price of soaring wage inequality? And, if so, what determines the position of each country along this trade-off?

In Table 2 we report, for the set of countries from Table 1, some indexes of the rigidity of various labor market institutions reproduced from Nickell and Layard (1999). The conclusion is unambiguous: compared to the United States, continental Europe has stricter employment protection legislation, more generous and longer unemployment benefits, less decentralized wage bargaining, and more binding minimum wage law.

The large majority of papers in the literature have taken the data exhibited in Table 2 as uncontroversial evidence that the reason for the observed differences can be found in the differences in labor market institutions between United States and continental Europe. Krugman (1994) was probably the first to provide a simple formalized model of this hypothesis. Simply put, the interaction between a severe technological shock and rigid European institutions have induced an adjustment through equilibrium *quantities* of labor (i.e., the employment distribution), whereas in the flexible U.S. labor market, the adjustment occurred through *prices* (i.e., the wage distribution).

Several authors have tried to test the Krugman hypothesis econometrically. The typical analysis is based on a cross-country panel of institutions and shocks, i.e., it allows for changing institutions over time, beyond aggregate shocks. A statistical model linking shocks and institutions to the dynamics of unemployment and wage inequality is estimated to evaluate the role of shocks and institutions, first separately and then interacted. The shocks considered are usually of technological nature and are measured through changes in measured TFP and changes in the labor share of income, possibly capturing a form of capital-biased technical change. In all cases the shock is assumed to be common across countries.

Blanchard and Wolfers (2000) argue that changing institutions alone have little explanatory power. The performance of the statistical model in explaining cross-country patterns of unemployment rates improves once shocks and institutions are interacted: an equal-size technological shock has differential effects on unemployment when labor market institutions differ. Bertola, Blau and Kahn (2001) provide further evidence for this view. Bentolila and Saint-Paul (1999) also study the evolution of the labor share across OECD countries since 1970. Using panel data techniques, they find that in the

Table 2

Data on various labor market institutions across OECD countries. Averages for the period 1985–1995. Cross-country institutions data (1984–1995)

Country	Labor standards	Employment protection	Union density	Bargaining centralization	Ratio of min. to avg. wage	Benefit repl. rate	Benefit duration
Austria	5	16	46.2	17	0.62	0.50	2.0
Belgium	4	17	51.2	10	0.60	0.60	4.0
Denmark	2	5	71.4	14	0.54	0.90	2.5
Finland	5	10	72.0	13	0.52	0.63	2.0
France	6	14	9.8	7	0.50	0.57	3.0
Germany	6	15	32.9	12	0.55	0.63	4.0
Ireland	4	12	49.7	6	0.55	0.37	4.0
Italy	7	20	38.8	5	0.71	0.20	0.5
Netherlands	5	9	25.5	11	0.55	0.70	2.0
Norway	5	11	56.0	16	0.64	0.65	1.5
Portugal	4	18	31.8	7	0.45	0.65	0.8
Spain	7	19	11.0	7	0.32	0.70	3.5
Sweden	7	13	82.5	15	0.52	0.80	1.2
U.K.	0	7	39.1	6	0.40	0.38	4.0
Canada	2	3	35.8	1	0.35	0.59	1.0
USA	0	1	15.6	2	0.39	0.50	0.5
Europe average	5.15	13.77	44.52	10.77	0.54	0.61	2.38

Note. Data are taken from Nickell and Layard (1999, Tables 6, 7, 9, 10). Labor standards are summarized in an index whose max value is 10 and refers to labor market standards enforced by legislation. The employment protection index ranges from 1 to 10. Union density is measured as a percentage of all salary earners. Centralization is an index where 17 corresponds to the most centralized regime. Benefit duration is in years. Europe average: unweighted mean of European countries, except U.K.

presence of institutions that promote wage rigidity, shocks that reduce employment also significantly reduce the labor share of income. One common problem in this empirical literature is that the results are, in general, not robust to the chosen specification.[82]

Another problem of this methodology is that the economic mechanism behind the interaction between technology and policy is not explicit. Consistently with the approach we took in the chapter so far, we will devote more space to quantitative analyses based on "structural" equilibrium models. In the rest of this section, we present the various frameworks the literature has explored to understand the interactions between technological progress and labor market institutions in shaping the various dimensions of inequality. We have grouped these frameworks into six categories, according to the type of technological shock modeled: (1) a rise in microeconomic turbulence, linked to some fundamental change in technology, (2) a slowdown in total factor productivity,

---

[82] The recent results in Nickell and Nunziata (2002) seem to support an explanation of cross-country unemployment differentials largely based on changing institutions, with a common technological shock playing only a minor role.

(3) an acceleration in the rate of capital-embodied productivity improvements, (4) skill-biased technical change, (5) a technological innovation whose adoption is endogenous, and (6) the structural transformation from manufacturing to services.

8.2. Rise in microeconomic turbulence

In Section 2 we have documented that roughly one-half of the rise in cross-sectional wage differentials in the United States is not associated to a higher return to permanent skills. Rather, it is due to increased wage "instability" over the workers' life time. In other words, transitory idiosyncratic shocks to labor productivity and wages have become more important over time [Gottschalk and Moffitt (1994)]. These larger temporary wage movements constitute important evidence that there has been a rise in the degree of microeconomic turbulence in the U.S. economy.

More evidence comes from the firm side. Campbell et al. (2001) show that the cross-sectional variability of individual stock returns has trended upward from 1962 to 1997. Chaney, Gabaix and Philippon (2003) and Comin and Mulani (2003) use Compustat firm-level data to demonstrate that the firm-level volatility of real variables, such as investment and sales, has gone up from 1970–1975 to 1990–1995. Overall, these papers provide snapshots, from very different angles, of an economy where idiosyncratic turbulence and volatility have risen to a high level.

Bertola and Ichino (1995) and Ljungqvist and Sargent (1998, 2003) argue that a rise in microeconomic turbulence that interacted with more or less rigid institutions can explain the U.S.–Europe dichotomy. Interestingly, the former authors identify wage rigidity and strict employment protection laws as the culprits, while the latter emphasize the generosity of unemployment benefits. Note, though, that one key premise behind these theories is that the surge in turbulence is common to the United States and Europe. We are not aware of any empirical work documenting trends in microeconomic instability in continental Europe. Currently, this represents a limit for this class of explanations.

8.2.1. The role of wage rigidity

The framework proposed by Bertola and Ichino (1995) is inspired by the Lucas and Prescott (1974) island-model of equilibrium unemployment. The economy is populated with a measure, L, of risk-neutral workers and a measure one of firms, indexed by $i \in [0, 1]$. Each firm is subject to idiosyncratic productivity shocks that follow a two-state Markov chain taking values (A^G, A^B), with $A^G > A^B$, and with transition probability p, that the state (good G and bad B) changes. When labor mobility is perfect, employment adjusts across good and bad firms to equalize wage differentials, and a unique market-clearing wage rate arises in equilibrium, i.e., there is no wage inequality.

Consider now the case where wages are flexible, but where workers have to pay a fixed moving cost, $\kappa > 0$, to change firms (this is the U.S.-like economy). In any period, workers observe the productivity level in all firms, but moving takes one period.

Hence, when they start working, productivity might change. It is easy to see that the value functions of a worker in good- and bad-state firms, respectively, are

$$W^G = w^G + \frac{1}{1+r}\left[pW^B + (1-p)W^G\right],\tag{28}$$

$$W^B = \begin{cases} w^B + \frac{1}{1+r}\left[pW^G + (1-p)W^B\right] & \text{if staying,} \\ w^B - \kappa + \frac{1}{1+r}\left[pW^B + (1-p)W^G\right] & \text{if moving.} \end{cases}\tag{29}$$

If workers leave bad firms in equilibrium, the marginal worker has to be indifferent between staying in a B firm or moving, yielding

$$W^G - W^B = \frac{1+r}{1-2p}\kappa.$$

Using (28) and (29) together with this condition, one arrives at the expression for equilibrium wage inequality:

$$w^G - w^B = \frac{r+2p}{1-2p}\kappa.\tag{30}$$

On the one hand, the closer p is to 0, the more permanent are productivity changes. This justifies a large amount of wage-equalizing mobility, and hence there is smaller ex-post wage inequality across firms. On the other hand, the larger is the degree of volatility in the economy (the closer p is to $1/2$), the riskier it is to move for a worker, as the new firm can quickly turn into the B state, and the cost κ is wasted. In this case, mobility will be low and the ex-post wage differential will increase.

Now consider the same experiment in a Europe-like economy where wages are rigid, i.e., where $w^B = w^G = w$, and where firing costs are prohibitively high, so that employment at every firm is constant at $\bar{l}$. To analyze this situation, Bertola and Ichino assume that firm i has a linear marginal revenue product $\pi(l^i) = z^i - \alpha l^i$, so that the marginal values for a firm in the G and B state of a unit of labor, respectively, are

$$V^G = A^G - \alpha\bar{l} - w + \frac{1}{1+r}\left[pV^B + (1-p)V^G\right]$$

and

$$V^B = A^B - \alpha\bar{l} - w + \frac{1}{1+r}\left[pV^G + (1-p)V^B\right].$$

In an equilibrium with free-entry, the hiring firm in the G state will have $V^G = 0$. Hence, the system above can be easily solved for $\bar{l}$ to give

$$\bar{l} = \frac{A^G - w}{\alpha} - \left(\frac{p}{r+2p}\right)\left(\frac{A^G - A^B}{\alpha}\right),\tag{31}$$

which shows that a rise in p that increases the degree of turbulence in the rigid economy will reduce average employment, i.e., it will increase the unemployment rate, $L - \bar{l}$. The reason is straightforward: when firms are constrained in their ability to shed labor in the face of a negative shock, they will be very cautious in hiring new workers even in the high-productivity state. Note, in fact, that the larger is the productivity differential $A^G - A^B$ across states, the higher will average unemployment in the economy be.

In conclusion, a similar increase in economic uncertainty induces more caution in workers' mobility and larger wage differentials in an economy with flexible wages whereas it leads to more caution in firms' hiring and lower average employment in an economy with rigid wages and costly layoffs. This result remains qualitative, as the authors did not try an exploration of the quantitative importance of their mechanism. In particular, it would be of interest to study by how much labor turnover needs to decline in order to generate a rise in wage inequality of the magnitude observed in the U.S. economy. Interestingly, as mentioned earlier, Jovanovic and Rousseau (2004) document a substantial downward trend in labor mobility in the United States, from 50 percent in 1970 to 35 percent in 2000.

8.2.2. The role of welfare benefits

Ljungqvist and Sargent (1998, 2003) propose an alternative mechanism based on the standard search model of unemployment [McCall (1970)]. Here, we present a stripped-down version of their argument. Consider an unemployed worker with skill level h, who searches for a job, sampling wage offers every period from the stationary distribution $F(w)$, with finite support $[\underline{w}, \bar{w}]$. Her skill level, when unemployed, decays at the geometric rate δ, whereas, when employed, skills remain unchanged. Employment is an absorbing state (no exogenous breakup of jobs), and workers discount the future at rate r. Unemployment benefits are equal to b. The values of employment and unemployment for a worker of skills h are

$$W(w, h) = \frac{wh}{r} \quad \text{and}$$

$$U(h) = b + \frac{1}{1+r} \int_{\underline{w}}^{\bar{w}} \max\{U(h'), W(w, h')\} \, dF(w)$$

$$\text{s.t.} \quad h' = (1 - \delta)h,$$

respectively. The value of employment is simply the discounted present value of earnings, wh; the value of unemployment is given by the unemployment benefit plus the discounted future value of search with the lower skill levels $(1 - \delta)h$. At the reservation wage $w^*(h)$, the values of employment and unemployment are equalized, $U(h) = W(w^*(h), h)$. Standard algebra yields the following characterization of the reservation wage,

$$w^*\left(\frac{r+\delta}{1+r}\right) = r\frac{b}{h} + \frac{1-\delta}{1+r} \int_{w^*}^{\bar{w}} [1 - F(w)] \, dw. \tag{32}$$

Ljungqvist and Sargent model the increased turbulence in the economy as a rise in the "skill obsolescence" parameter δ. The introduction of a new technological paradigm, or an acceleration in the rate of technological change, can lead to a higher rate of obsolescence, insofar as skills are at least partly technology-specific (recall our discussion in Section 7).

It is straightforward to show, through simple comparative statics, that w^* falls with δ: a worker aware that her skills will become obsolete faster during unemployment chooses optimally to reduce her time spent searching and decreases her reservation wage. As a result, the unemployment duration falls.

However, an increase in δ has an equilibrium effect on the distribution of workers across skills: the average skill level in the population falls, and one can show that the reservation wage declines in the skill level, i.e., $dw^*/dh < 0$. The key behind this result is that the unemployment benefits, b, do not depend on the *current* skill level, h, of the unemployed workers, whereas wage offers are naturally linked to h. A fall in h worsens the value of the average wage offer relative to the value of remaining unemployed with benefits b. Thus, both the reservation wage and unemployment duration increase.[83] The net effect of these two forces is qualitatively ambiguous, and only a quantitative analysis can determine which force is paramount. Note that it is easy to show that the derivative, dw^*/dh, is increasing (in absolute value) in b. Thus, in Europe-like economies with more generous benefits, the second effect tends to be stronger.

Ljungqvist and Sargent embed this simple mechanism in a much richer and detailed model. They calibrate the increase in turbulence to reproduce average earnings losses upon separation of the size estimated in the labor economics literature and show that in economies with generous welfare state (high b), the rise in microeconomic uncertainty brings about a surge in unemployment comparable to the one observed in continental Europe, with all the increase explained by longer durations, as the data suggest. In a "laissez-faire" economy with low b, the faster rate of skill obsolescence barely has any effect.

A related explanation is set forth by Marimon and Zilibotti (1999). In their model, unemployment insurance has the standard result of reducing employment, but it also helps workers find a suitable job. They construct two artificial economies which only differ by the degree of unemployment insurance and assume that they are hit by a common technological shock which enhances the importance of "mismatch". This shock reduces the proportion of jobs which workers regard as acceptable in the economy with unemployment insurance, and unemployment doubles in the Europe-like economy.

In the Ljungqvist–Sargent and Marimon–Zilibotti frameworks, the shock-policy interaction operates entirely through the *labor supply* side. These authors essentially argue that unemployment in Europe went up because, for the jobless, it was more beneficial to collect unemployment insurance than to work at a low wage, given that technological change made their skills obsolete (or made it difficult to use them on the current jobs).

---

[83] One can easily generalize the model to allow b to depend on past earnings (thus, on *past* skills when employed) and the mechanism described would still be in place. This is what Ljungqvist and Sargent do.

8.3. Slowdown in total factor productivity

A decline of TFP growth rates, such as measured for the United States and Europe after the mid-1970s (see Section 2) can reduce employment in a matching framework through the standard "capitalization effect". Consider the decision of a firm to create a job: the firm will compare the set-up cost with the discounted present value of profits. In a growing economy, where technical change is disembodied and benefits all firms equally, a productivity slowdown increases the "effective rate" at which profits are discounted and discourages the creation of new jobs [Pissarides (2000)].

den Haan, Haefke and Ramey (2001) evaluate this explanation quantitatively within the context of a standard matching model, à la Mortensen and Pissarides (1998). They find that for this channel to have a significant effect on unemployment, one needs to put restrictions on the shape of the cross-sectional distribution of firms' productivities. Since useful data to test these restrictions are scant, the mechanism remains largely unexplored.

Interestingly, in the same paper the authors argue that once the Ljungqvist and Sargent mechanism is embedded into a model with endogenous job destruction, the comparative statics for increased turbulence are reversed, i.e., unemployment falls. The reason is that as the speed of skill obsolescence rises, workers become more reluctant to separate, and job destruction falls.[84] This force dominates the effect described in the previous section. Ljungqvist and Sargent (2003) counter-argue that such an economic mechanism would be relevant only if every worker who separates (including those who quit voluntarily) were hit by faster skill obsolescence. In their view, a more reasonable assumption is that only the workers who suffer an exogenous layoff see their skills decreasing, in which case the original result in Ljungqvist and Sargent (1998) remains intact.

8.4. Acceleration in capital-embodied technical change

Several measures of embodied technical change suggest that the rate of technical change accelerated around the mid-1970s in the U.S. economy (see Section 2, especially Figure 2). A recent OECD study [Colecchia and Schreyer (2002)] measures the decline in relative price for several high-tech equipment items across various countries in Europe from 1980 to 2000 and concludes that European countries experienced an acceleration quantitatively comparable to the United States. Jorgenson (2005, Table 3.5) measures the growth in the quality of the aggregate stock of capital across some OECD countries and finds that, even though the United States had the fastest average annual growth (1.5 percent from 1980 to 2001), Germany and Italy were quite close, with 1.3 percent and 1.1 percent annual growth rates, respectively.

---

[84] Recall that the original Ljungqvist and Sargent model is a standard search model where separations occur exogenously. Hence, workers are unable to respond to a negative shock hitting their job. In a matching model with wage bargaining, the workers can allow the firm to keep a larger fraction of output in order to avoid a separation in the face of a shock.

Hornstein, Krusell and Violante (2003a) study precisely whether the interaction between an acceleration in capital-embodied growth, common between the United States and Europe, and certain labor market institutions whose strength differs between the United States and Europe, can explain the simultaneous evolution of the three dimensions of labor market inequalities quantitatively: the unemployment rate, the labor share, and wage inequality.

Their environment builds on the matching model with vintage capital developed by Aghion and Howitt (1994).[85] Consider a continuous-time economy populated by a stationary measure one of ex-ante equal, infinitely lived workers who supply one unit of labor inelastically. Workers are risk-neutral and discount the future at rate r. Production requires one machine and one worker. Machines are characterized by their age, a, translating into match productivity $e^{-\gamma a}$, where γ is the rate of technological progress embodied in capital.[86]

At any time firms can freely enter the market and post a vacancy at a cost κ. Then they proceed to search for a worker in a frictional labor market governed by a standard constant-returns-to-scale matching function. Once matched, they produce and share output with the worker in a Nash fashion, with ξ denoting the bargaining power of the worker. At age $\bar{a}$ (determined endogenously), capital is scrapped and the job is destroyed.[87] Two key labor market policies are modeled explicitly: unemployment benefits b, and an employment protection system that combines a hiring subsidy T and an equal-size firing tax upon separation.

As is standard in this framework, it is possible to reduce the equilibrium of the model to two key equations – the job creation condition and the job destruction condition – in two unknowns, θ and $\bar{a}$. These equations, respectively, read

$$\kappa = q(\theta)(1 - \xi)S(0; \bar{a}),$$
$$e^{-\gamma \bar{a}} = b + p(\theta)\xi S(0; \bar{a}) - (r - \gamma)T. \tag{33}$$

Here, $q(\theta)$ and $p(\theta)$ are the meeting probabilities for firms and workers, respectively, expressed as a function of the vacancy–unemployment ratio θ. We denote by $S(0, \bar{a})$ the "surplus" of a match of age 0, conditional on destruction taking place at age $\bar{a}$: the surplus is the value of the relationship for the parties (the discounted present value of

---

[85] For expositional purposes, we simplify the framework in Hornstein, Krusell and Violante (2003a) substantially here. In particular, in the equilibrium of the original model, there are vacant firms with old vintages of machines, while here we make the standard assumption of matching models that all vacant firms embody the leading-edge technology.

[86] As usual, we normalize all variables concerning a vintage a machine relative to the corresponding variable of the newest machine.

[87] Productivity improvements enter the economy only through new capital. This is the typical Schumpeterian "creative–destruction" mechanism, which is at the heart of unemployment in this class of models. As mentioned in Section 7.1, Hornstein, Krusell and Violante (2003b) show that if one takes the view that technical progress can also benefit old machines, i.e., if old machines can be "upgraded" into new ones at a cost, then the model yields quantitatively similar results.

the output stream), net of their outside options. Clearly the surplus is increasing in $\bar{a}$, as a longer match yields a bigger surplus.

The job-creation curve states that vacancies are created (and $q(\theta)$ falls) until the expected return of the marginal vacancy equals its cost, κ. The job-destruction curve states that, at age $\bar{a}$, the pair is indifferent between continuing operating the machine, which gives output $e^{-\gamma\bar{a}}$, and separating, which yields the respective outside options for worker and firm (zero in equilibrium for the firm, because of free entry), net of the firing tax.

Figure 6 depicts the comparative statics of a rise in γ in a rigid economy (high b, high T) and in a flexible economy ($b = T = 0$) in the $(\theta, \bar{a})$ space.[88] Note that a low value for $\bar{a}$ corresponds to high separation rate and unemployment incidence, whereas a low value for θ corresponds to long unemployment durations. Thus, the two axes depict the two dimensions of equilibrium unemployment. To illustrate the result more sharply, we have chosen values for b and T in the rigid economy such that the initial equilibrium in the two economies is the same. This is possible since generous benefits and strict employment protection have offsetting effects on job destruction, while they are neutral on job creation, as evident from Equations (33). The model is therefore consistent with an initial situation where, originally, the labor markets of the United States and Europe looked alike, as the data for the 1960s show. Figure 6 illustrates that a rise in γ has a dramatically different impact across the two economies, especially regarding the amplitude of the shift in the job destruction curve.

To understand intuitively the economic forces at work, it is useful to think of the acceleration in equipment-embodied technology as an "obsolescence shock". As the rate of productivity growth of new capital accelerates, existing capital–worker matches – which have old vintages of capital – become obsolete faster. In the United States, this loss of economic value is to a higher extent borne by workers, whose wages fall in order to keep firms from scrapping capital and breaking up earlier to invest in better machines.

In Europe, however, labor payments are kept artificially high by generous unemployment benefits and by rents on firing costs, which make wages downwardly rigid. As a result, firms must bear the initial adjustment by destroying matches earlier and creating fewer jobs. The corresponding sharp increase in unemployment greatly improves the relative bargaining position of firms, which can now push workers closer to their outside option, thus reducing the labor share of output. Since the outside option is constant across all workers, this force also limits the rise in wage inequality that comes about with faster technical change because of larger productivity differentials across machines.[89] Thus, in response to a technological acceleration, an economy with rigid, European-like institutions would experience a higher unemployment rate, a more pronounced decline in the labor share, and a slower rise in wage inequality than would be observed in a more flexible economy.

---

[88] Once we recognize that $p'(\theta) > 0$, $q'(\theta) < 0$ and $S'(\cdot, \bar{a}) > 0$, understanding the slope of the two curves in (33) is immediate.

[89] This mechanism, which is based on technological heterogeneity and the existence of quasi-rents for workers, is the same as that analyzed in Section 7.2.

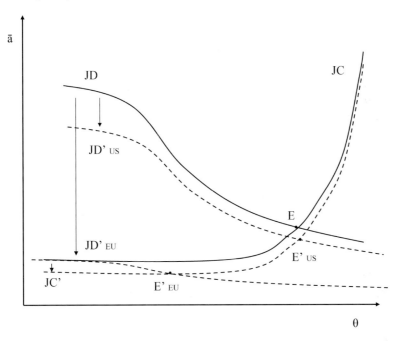

Figure 6. The equilibrium comparative statics of the model by Hornstein, Krusell and Violante (2003a). Following an acceleration in the rate of capital-embodied technical change, both the job-creation (JC) and the job-destruction (JD) curves shift. The amplitude of the shift is regulated by institutions, and hence it differs between the flexible economy (U.S.) and the rigid economy (EU).

Quantitatively, a permanent rise in the rate of capital-embodied productivity growth of the magnitude observed in the data can replicate a large fraction of the differential increase in the unemployment rate and of the capital share between the flexible U.S. economy and the rigid Europe-like economy (with the increase in unemployment taking place along the duration margin, as in the data). Wage inequality increases in the U.S.-like economy and declines in the rigid economy, but the changes generated by the model are rather small (recall our discussion of Section 7.1).

8.5. Skill-biased technical change

A number of explanations for the rise in wage inequality in the United States – many of which we have reviewed in Section 3 – build on the idea of skill-biased technical change. Could this type of technological advancement, interacted with more rigid institutions, also be at the origin of the rise in European unemployment?

Mortensen and Pissarides (1999) explore this question in a model where the economy is populated by a finite number of types of workers, ex-ante different in their skill (productivity level). Skill is observable (e.g., education), and all workers endowed with the same skill level are segmented in their own labor market, which is modeled as frictional with a standard matching function governing the meeting process.

In this model, unemployed workers receive welfare benefits which are partly proportional to their wage (and skill level), and partly lump-sum. The equilibrium unemployment is decreasing and convex in the skill level: low-skill markets have higher unemployment, as benefits represent a form of wage rigidity that is more binding at low levels of skills. As benefits become more generous, the convexity becomes more pronounced.

The skill-biased shock is introduced as a mean-preserving spread in the skill distribution, calibrated to match the rise in wage inequality in the economy with low benefits, like the United States. The model predicts a sharp surge in unemployment in the economy with generous benefits, due to the convex equilibrium relationship between unemployment and the skill level. A crucial ingredient of the Mortensen–Pissarides mechanism, which is present also in the Hornstein, Krusell and Violante (2003a) setup, is that welfare benefits are not fully proportional to wages and productivity; rather, they have a "flat", lump-sum component. If they were fully proportional, every skill market would just be a rescaled version of the highest-skill market, with the same unemployment rate. Hansen (1998) studies the institutional details of the welfare state in several European countries and argues that flat "social assistance" benefits are an important component of these welfare systems.[90]

Finally, the Mortensen and Pissarides model has the counterfactual implication that the rise in unemployment is concentrated among the low-skilled workers, whereas Nickell and Bell (1996) and Gottschalk and Smeeding (1997), among others, conclude that data from many European countries support the conclusion that unemployment rose proportionately across the entire skill spectrum.

8.6. Endogenous technology adoption

A careful look at Table 1 shows a non-monotonic evolution of the labor share in many European countries: the labor share rose between 1965 and 1980, only to decline sharply afterwards. In some countries this pattern is striking. In Portugal, for example, the labor share skyrocketed from 56 percent to 75 percent in the period 1965–1980, and then plunged to 68 percent by 1995. Blanchard (1997) and Caballero and Hammour (1998) proposed an explanation for these dynamics based on the idea that technological advancement responds to the relative cost of factor inputs.

The late 1960s and early 1970s witnessed a rapid evolution of capital–labor relationships in favor of labor in many European countries: "pro-labor" measures were

---

[90] Another key assumption is that markets are segregated across skills. This setup allows the model to avoid the criticism by Wong (2003) that skill-biased technical change can reduce the amount of mismatch and decrease within-group inequality. Mortensen and Pissarides describe their workers as differing in educational attainment. Given the observability of education, modeling firms as able to direct their search (and segregate the economy) seems appropriate.

introduced with the objective of consolidating unions' power, increasing the generosity and coverage of unemployment benefits, making economically motivated dismissals harder to justify.[91] The result was, in the language of Caballero and Hammour, an "appropriability shock" that shifted bargaining power away from capital.

In a model where the technological menu for capital–labor substitutability is fixed in the short run, but endogenous in the long run, one will observe an initial rise in the labor share as a result of such a shock. However, as time goes by, more and more firms respond to this institutional "pro-labor" push by introducing new technologies that substitute capital for labor. Therefore, in the long run the capital–labor ratio rises, and both the labor share and employment decline, as observed in the last two decades in Europe.

Why do the U.S. data not display the same pattern? According to Blanchard (1997), since the initial appropriability shock was much smaller, so was the response of capital. A natural question arises, if one follows this logic through: is it only a coincidence that the technological change away from unskilled labor was biased toward capital in Europe and toward skilled labor in the United States?

According to Acemoglu (2003a) the direction of the bias in technological innovations is endogenous (see also our discussion in Section 3) and institutional differences can be key in explaining different biases between the United States and Europe. Consider a flexible economy, like the United States, where firms can either produce with one unit of skilled labor with productivity h_s, or one unit of unskilled labor with productivity h_u, where $h_u < h_s$. Output is $y_i = h_i$, with $i = u, s$, and the wage paid to the worker is simply a fraction, ξ, of output. Firms can also choose to pay a fixed cost κ, and adopt a new technology that increases output by a factor $1 + A < h_s/h_u$. Consider first an equilibrium where

$$\kappa > (1 - \xi)Ah_s > (1 - \xi)Ah_u,$$

so that it is not profitable for firms to implement the new innovation, and wage inequality is simply given by $w_s/w_u = h_s/h_u$. Suppose now that, due to technological progress, the cost of capital decreases to a new value, $\kappa' < \kappa$, such that it is always profitable to adopt it for skilled workers, but not for unskilled workers, i.e.,

$$(1 - \xi)Ah_s > \kappa' > (1 - \xi)Ah_u.$$

As a result of this adoption decision, wage inequality jumps to the higher level $(1 + A)h_s/h_u$ in the U.S. economy.

Consider now an alternative economy, like Europe, where, because of some institutional constraint, wages cannot fall below a fixed level $\bar{w}$, where $\xi h_s > \bar{w} > \xi(1 + A)h_u$, so that the constraint is binding for the unskilled workers, even in the case of adoption, but never for the skilled workers.

---

[91] The "French May" in 1968 and the "Hot Italian Autumn" of 1969 are stark manifestations of the power of the labor movements in that period of European history.

Whenever the new cost level, κ', satisfies

$$Ah_u > \kappa' > (1 - \xi)Ah_u$$

in Europe, the new technology will be adopted also with unskilled workers; this is an effect of the minimum wage constraint. The intuition for this result is that, since firms in Europe pay a fixed wage $\bar{w}$ to the unskilled workers, whether or not they adopt the new technology, the institutional constraint makes the firm the residual claimant on output, once $\bar{w}$ is paid. The new technology increases output without changing the wage payment, and thus it may be optimal to adopt in an economy with wage rigidity and not to adopt in an economy with wage flexibility, with the obvious implication that inequality will not increase in Europe.[92]

Formalized models, where the direction of technical change is endogenous, are still in their infancy: in the case of this application to the U.S.–Europe comparison, one important extension would be verifying if this result survives when the "institutional wage rigidity" is endogenized so that it can respond to changes in the technological environment.

8.7. Sectoral transformation

The standard approach to the U.S.–Europe differentials is built on comparing the diverging dynamics in the *unemployment* rate. Rogerson (2004) argues that the analysis of relative unemployment rates is misleading, and if one focuses instead on *employment–population ratios*, new insights surface.

In particular, Rogerson shows two new features of the data: (1) the relative deterioration of European employment starts as early as in the 1950s, whereas unemployment rates start diverging in the mid-1970s; (2) the deterioration of European unemployment is largely explained by the differential in manufacturing employment growth.[93]

These facts lead Rogerson to focus on the importance of the structural transformation occurring in the economy, i.e., the secular pattern of reallocation of resources across broad sectors of the economy: first from agriculture to manufacturing, and then from manufacturing to services. Expressed in terms of the shocks-institutions paradigm that we have highlighted in this section, the relevant shock is the transformation of modern economies into service-driven economies, and the relevant institutions are those which hampered the full development of a service sector in Europe.

Although this new approach is still in its infancy, and as such it lacks a quantitative assessment within a rigorous equilibrium model, it appears to be quite promising.

---

[92] This hypothesis is also consistent with the fact that, at least until the impressive productivity surge of 1995–2000, labor productivity grew faster in Europe (e.g., in France, Germany, Italy and the United Kingdom) compared to the United States [Jorgenson (2005, Table 3.16)].

[93] The concept of "relative deterioration" refers to the difference between the U.S. variable (employment rate or unemployment rate) and its European counterpart.

8.8. Discussion

Nickell and Layard (1999), in a widely cited piece in the most recent edition of the *Handbook of Labor Economics*, carefully review the empirical literature and conclude that time spent worrying about the effects of several labor market institutions on cross-country unemployment differentials is largely wasted, given these effects seem small and are often even ambiguous in sign. From the perspective of the research surveyed in this section, however, it seems that when institutional differences are studied in conjunction with technological change, the results are more encouraging.

Of course, much is still far from being well understood. First, once we recognize that the interaction of shocks and institutions is important, what are the key common shocks and the crucial institutional differences that can account for the facts? One would, for example, like to see a unified structural equilibrium framework where several shocks and institutions are jointly analyzed in order to investigate which shock-policy interaction is quantitatively important and which is not.

Second, in answering this question, more "discipline" is needed in the quantitative analysis. Often, the approach in the literature is to calibrate the shock by matching either the rise in wage inequality or the fall in the labor share. We maintain the view that changes in employment/unemployment, wage inequality, and income shares are intimately related and must be explained jointly: they are dimensions along which the model should be evaluated rather than calibrated. Thus, the shock should be calibrated, as much as possible, using independent observations. The use of data on technological change such as that for the relative price of equipment goods is such an example.

Third, it is important to note that we are not aware of any quantitative model of a rigid Europe-like economy that can generate a rise in equilibrium unemployment which is similar across all skill levels, which is what the data suggest.

Fourth, the literature is split between labor-supply models (Ljungqvist and Sargent, Marimon and Zilibotti) and labor-demand models (Bertola and Ichino, Caballero and Hammour, Hornstein et al.). Obviously, interpreting the European and U.S. labor market outcomes in terms of "labor demand" or "labor supply" is not mutually exclusive. In a theoretical framework with elements of vintage human capital and vintage physical capital, an embodied technological acceleration will also worsen the rate of skill obsolescence – exactly as in Ljungqvist and Sargent's paper. The next generation of investigations of the European (un)employment puzzle should bring together supply and demand forces and allow a joint evaluation of their respective strength.

9. Welfare and policy implications

In traditional growth theory, technological progress is largely associated with productivity advancements, reflected in improvements in average wages, from which it would follow that there are welfare gains. While the first generation of growth models is based on the representative-agent assumption, the model economies we studied in these chapter are built on a heterogeneous-agents model. By raising the wage differential between more and less skilled workers (between-group inequality) and by amplifying the amount of labor market uncertainty faced by ex-ante equal households in the economy (residual inequality), in these economies technological change can lead to welfare costs, at least for certain groups of workers, and it has first-order implications for policy. In what follows we give an account of some early work on the subject.

9.1. Lifetime earnings inequality

The majority of the empirical investigations on rising inequality in the United States focus on the cross-sectional distribution of wages and earnings. Friedman (1982) argues that data on cross-sectional inequality at a point in time are difficult to interpret, as they provide no information on the degree of economic mobility: the same distribution can be generated either by a "dynamic society" or by a "status society".

A better measure of inequality, which incorporates some of Friedman's concerns, is provided by the distribution of lifetime earnings. A stark example of the pitfalls implicit in making welfare and policy statements simply based on distributions at a point in time is provided by Flinn (2002). Flinn compares Italy and the United States and documents that, although the dispersion in cross-sectional yearly earnings inequality in the United States is several times larger than in Italy, the distribution of lifetime earnings in the United States is more compressed due to larger individual variability of labor income and shorter duration of non-employment experiences. In other words, in Friedman's language, Italy somewhat surprisingly looks more like a "status society" than does the United States.[94]

Two papers, so far, have studied the change in the distribution of lifetime earnings in the United States in the past three decades through the lenses of a structural model.[95] Heckman, Lochner and Taber (1998) solve a deterministic competitive OLG model with endogenous human capital accumulation to study the implications of the widening educational premium for lifetime-earnings inequality across cohorts.[96] Their model implies that the low-educated cohorts entering in the mid-1980s are those suffering the largest drop in lifetime earnings from skill-biased technical change: roughly 11 percent. At the same time, they calculate a rise in lifetime earnings of 6 percent for the college graduates in the same cohort.

Similarly, Bowlus and Robin (2004) use a search model with risk-neutrality, estimated on matched CPS data from 1977 to 1997, to study how changes in wage and

---

[94] Cohen (1999) performs a similar exercise between the United States and France and finds that, using annual wages, inequality in the United States is 60 percent greater than in France, but based on lifetime earnings, the difference reduces to 15 percent.

[95] See Aaronson (2003) for a measurement of changes in lifetime earnings inequality not based on a structural model.

[96] We have discussed a simple version of this model in Section 4.

employment dynamics over the past thirty years have affected the evolution of lifetime labor income inequality in the U.S. labor market. They find that the median worker suffered only a small decline in present value lifetime earnings, but that there is large heterogeneity across educational groups with lifetime earnings declining by over 25 percent for high-school graduates and increasing by almost 20 percent for college graduates.

These numbers are over twice as large as those in Heckman, Lochner and Taber (1998). One reason is that Heckman et al. model the acquisition of education and the costs associated with schooling explicitly. A large fraction of the changes in lifetime earnings is attributable to the surge in the returns to education: since education in reality is the outcome of a costly investment choice, the difference in earnings alone likely overstates the true welfare differential between the two groups in the analysis of Bowlus and Robin.

9.2. Consumption inequality

There is a definite gain in moving from studying hourly wages to lifetime labor income, if one wants to make inference on welfare. However, one important limit of the studies above is that they effectively assume complete insurance against those transitory income fluctuations that cancel out in the long run and thus do not affect lifetime income. With imperfect insurance against labor market risk, consumption is not determined only by purely permanent shocks that translate one-for-one into permanent income, but the degree of earnings variability and its persistence become important, too. In this sense, consumption is an even better measure of welfare than lifetime earnings.

The evidence based on *Consumption and Expenditure Survey* (CEX) data suggests that consumption inequality rose slightly during the first half of the 1980s [Cutler and Katz (1992) and Johnson and Shipp (1997)] and has remained roughly stable thereafter [Krueger and Perri (2002)]. Interestingly, Blundell and Preston (1998) document that in Britain, where the increase in wage inequality followed a pattern similar to the United States, the rise in consumption inequality was also strong until the early 1980s, but weaker afterwards. This path of consumption inequality is, at first sight, puzzling, especially since wage inequality keeps increasing in the 1990s, albeit at a slower pace. Three explanations for this puzzle have been provided so far.

Krueger and Perri (2002) developed the first formal model to solve this apparent puzzle. They consider an Arrow–Debreu economy with limited enforcement of contracts [Kocherlakota (1996)]. In this economy, the degree of insurance market completeness is endogenous and responds to changes in income risk: as income shocks become larger and more persistent, the value of autarky declines, so agents are willing to enter more often into risk-sharing agreements. The central message of Krueger and Perri is that the rise of labor market inequality led to a development in financial markets – in particular the sharp expansion of consumer credit in the 1990s – and to a larger extent of risk sharing, limiting the rise in consumption inequality in this period.

Heathcote, Storesletten and Violante (2003) offer an alternative interpretation for this pattern of rising and then flattening consumption inequality. Through a statistical decomposition of the rise in wage dispersion into permanent and transitory components, they conclude that the relative importance of the two components changes substantially over the sample period. From the late 1970s to around 1990 the permanent component increases sharply, but in the 1990s it ceases to grow, whereas there is a substantial increase in the variance of transitory shocks. A standard overlapping-generations model with "exogenously" incomplete-markets [Huggett (1996)] predicts a trajectory for consumption inequality similar to the data: as the shocks become more transitory, they are easier to insure and tend to have a smaller impact on consumption. The finding that the first phase of the rise in inequality (1980s) had a more permanent nature than the second (1990s) is common to a number of empirical studies [Gottschalk and Moffitt (1994) for the United States, and Dickens (2000) and Blundell and Preston (1998) for the United Kingdom]. To our knowledge, there is no attempt to link this pattern of persistence with the nature of technical progress.

The third explanation is provided by Attanasio, Battistin and Ichimura (2003) who argue that once measurement error in the CEX data is properly taken into account, consumption inequality keeps rising also in the 1990s and, hence, that there is no puzzle.

9.3. Welfare implications

Studying consumption inequality is a further improvement toward the understanding of the welfare costs of rising inequality, but a complete welfare analysis cannot abstract from leisure.

One approach that has been taken in the literature makes minimal assumptions regarding the structure of the underlying economic model. Krueger and Perri (2003), in an exercise similar in spirit to that in Attanasio and Davis (1996), estimate a stochastic process directly on consumption and leisure data from the CEX and use standard intertemporal preferences to compute the welfare costs of rising inequality. The computation of welfare losses "under the veil of ignorance", i.e., before the worker finds out whether she will be high- or low-skilled, yields numbers between 1 percent and 2 percent, with a difference in the welfare losses between the 90th percentile (net winners) and the 10th percentile (net losers) of just over 10 percent. To put this number in perspective, the estimate of Bowlus and Robin (2004) is 50 percent.

This approach is based entirely on revealed preferences, and has the advantage that no restrictive assumptions have to be made on the degree and the nature of market completeness. However, without a structural model [like those of Bowlus and Robin (2004) and Heckman, Lochner and Taber (1998)], strong faith must be placed in the reliability of the consumption and hours data from the CEX. In particular, if there are large transitory measurement errors, then one would overestimate the extent of economic mobility and underestimate the welfare losses coming from the change in the wage structure. Moreover, all that can be assessed through this methodology is the welfare cost of changes in consumption and leisure inequality, without knowing exactly what fraction of these changes are attributable to rising wage inequality rather than, for example, tax reforms or changes in financial and insurance markets that occurred over the same period.

A second approach, developed by Heathcote, Storesletten and Violante (2003), builds on three steps: (1) an estimation of the dynamics of permanent and transitory components of individual wages over the period of interest, (2) a calibration of an OLG model with endogenous leisure and consumption choices and incomplete markets, (3) simulation of the model to compute the welfare costs of the changes in wage dynamics. This approach, thus, is fully structural and, as such, it does not rely heavily on survey data on consumption and hours worked. Rather, welfare calculations are based on the changes in the model-generated consumption and leisure paths due exclusively to observed and well-measured changes in the wage process over the period. At the same time, it incorporates a realistic range of insurance avenues (a saving technology, labor supply, and social security) without going as far as assuming complete markets.

According to the calculations of Heathcote, Storesletten and Violante (2003), welfare losses "under the veil of ignorance", although varied by cohort, average 2.5 percent across all cohorts, with a peak of 5 percent for the cohorts entered in the mid-1980s. The low-skill workers suffer a loss of 16 percent, and the high-skill workers enjoy a welfare gain of 13 percent. These numbers fall in between the estimates of Bowlus and Robin (2004) and those of Heckman, Lochner and Taber (1998).

Two main conclusions emerge. First, the welfare consequences of the observed rise in labor market risk are quite different across groups of workers: whereas the high-skill, high-educated workers are the winners, the low-skill, low-educated workers are the losers. Second, the ex-ante welfare loss from the rise in labor market risk in the United States is of the order of 2 percent of lifetime consumption, which is a rather large number.

9.3.1. Insurance and opportunities in the welfare analysis of wage inequality

The quantitative studies on the welfare consequences of the recent rise in inequality point to a sizeable welfare loss. But does the absence of full insurance always imply a welfare decrease when risk increases? The answer is no. We have already mentioned the case studied by Krueger and Perri (2002) where, with endogenous market incompleteness, a rise in uncertainty can lead to more risk sharing in society and increase welfare. The same result can arise for different reasons in models where the extent of risk-sharing is limited exogenously (Bewley–Aiyagari economies). Consider, as do Heathcote, Storesletten and Violante (2004), an economy populated by a measure one of infinitely-lived agents with preferences

$$U = E_0 \sum_{t=0}^{\infty} \beta^t \left[\frac{c_t^{1-\gamma} - 1}{1 - \gamma} - \varphi \frac{h_t^{1+\sigma}}{1 + \sigma} \right], \tag{34}$$

where $1/\gamma$ is the elasticity of intertemporal substitution and $1/\sigma$ is the Frisch elasticity of labor supply. Each agent i starts with zero wealth and faces log-normal productivity shocks to the efficiency units of labor ω_{it}. Shocks can be decomposed into two orthogonal components

$$\ln \omega_{it} = \alpha_i + \varepsilon_{it} \quad \text{with } \alpha_i \sim \text{N}\left(-\frac{v_\alpha}{2}, v_\alpha\right) \text{ and } \varepsilon_{it} \sim \text{N}\left(-\frac{v_\varepsilon}{2}, v_\varepsilon\right),$$

where α_i is the permanent-uninsurable component and ε_{it} is the transitory-insurable component. Note that the means have been normalized so that a rise in the variance of either component does not affect the average level of efficiency units.

After computing the allocations and substituting them into preferences (34), one can calculate the welfare gain of an increase in the two components of wage uncertainty – expressed as the equivalent consumption variation. The main finding is that one can obtain an (approximate) closed-form expression for the welfare gain $\mathcal{W}$,

$$\mathcal{W} = \frac{1}{\sigma}\Delta v_\varepsilon - \frac{(\gamma - 1) + \gamma(1 + \sigma)}{\gamma + \sigma}\Delta v_\alpha. \tag{35}$$

This expression only depends on two elasticity parameters (γ, σ) and on the change in the two variances $(\Delta v_\alpha, \Delta v_\varepsilon)$. The key feature to note, in the above equation, is that the welfare gain is not always negative. For example, as $\gamma \to 0$ (risk-neutrality), the welfare gain is positive and proportional to the rise in overall inequality $(\Delta v_\varepsilon + \Delta v_\alpha)$ through the Frisch elasticity.[97]

To understand this result, one has to keep in mind that there are two distinct effects of a rise in labor market uncertainty. On the one hand, "decreased insurance" induces a welfare loss. For example, as risk-aversion rises with γ or as the permanent-uninsurable component v_α expands, the second term becomes larger and the overall welfare gain tends to become negative. On the other hand, "improved production opportunities" induce a welfare gain. In presence of elastic labor supply (σ low), households supply more hours when they face a good productivity shock and enjoy leisure at times of low-productivity. When the variance of productivity shocks rises, this intertemporal behavior can improve households' welfare. The net effect depends on the parameterization of preferences and on the empirical assessment of what fraction of the rise in inequality is insurable.

9.3.2. Discussion

Economists have just started to tackle these issues, and many questions still lie ahead. One key area to explore is the role of the family in determining the welfare implications of the rise in wage inequality. Two offsetting forces are at work. First, there is positive assortative matching between spouses along the skill/education dimension. Second, shocks are imperfectly correlated between spouses [Hyslop (2001)]. While the first feature amplifies the surge in inequality and worsens welfare inequalities across families,

---

[97] This qualitative result can be reproduced also starting from Cobb–Douglas preferences, albeit the expression in (35) is different.

the second establishes a role for intra-family insurance in dampening the rise in labor market risk. Only a careful quantitative analysis can determine which force is dominant.

Finally, the current welfare studies abstract from some first-order "social" consequences of the rise in inequality and the fall in the wages of the unskilled, such as the decline in labor market participation for low-educated males [Murphy and Topel (1997)], the rise in the crime rate [Kelly (2000)], and the decline in the marriage rate [Gould and Paserman (2003)].[98]

9.4. Brief directions for policy

Welfare losses originating from the rise in U.S. inequality in the past three decades are almost one hundred times larger than the standard estimates of the costs of business cycles [Lucas (2003)]. In this sense, policies that act by reallocating risk across agents (like social insurance policies) are a macroeconomic priority compared to policies that reduce the impact of aggregate risk (like monetary or fiscal stabilization policies). But among the myriads of possible government interventions, what are the right redistributive policies?

In Sections 3.2 and 7 we discussed two complementary views of the link between technology and inequality. The first of these views is that technological progress in the past three decades has been complementary to certain permanent individual characteristics, such as ability or education (technology-skill complementarity). The second view is that labor market history is scattered with shocks and stochastic events related to the luck of individuals, firms or industries that determine the degree of fanning out of the skill and earnings distributions among ex-ante equal workers. The rapid diffusion of a new technology amplifies the importance of these stochastic factors, increasing overall earnings instability (technology-luck complementarity).

The emphasis we placed on these two approaches is not just for classification purposes, since they have profoundly different policy implications. Insofar as we are interested in designing policies that reduce inequalities among households, models of technology-ability complementarity suggest that the intervention should be targeted early in the life of an individual, possibly during childhood when the key components of learning ability are being formed. Models of technology-luck complementarity seem to call for interventions that allow the disadvantaged (or unlucky) workers to rebuild their skill level after a shock, such as displacement due to skill obsolescence, has hit.

Examples of both types of policies are abundant in the U.S. economy.[99] In general, the most recent evaluations of programs entailing expenditures and treatment at early

---

[98] Gould and Paserman argue that the higher male inequality in the United States increased the option value for single women to search longer for a husband.

[99] Programs like the Perry Pre-School program and the Syracuse Pre-School program provide intense family development support to disadvantaged children at very young ages (from birth to 5 years). The Harlem program ensures frequent individual teacher–child sessions for children of age 3–5. Several programs for adult retraining of displaced workers were initiated throughout the United States under the Job Training Partnership Act of 1982 and the Economic Dislocation and Worker Adjustment Assistance Act of 1988.

childhood report remarkable success. In contrast, the available evidence indicates that welfare-to-work and training programs directed toward adult workers are rather ineffi-cient, as they generate only modest increases in permanent earnings levels [LaLonde, Heckmen and Smith (1999)].

According to Heckman (2000), the reason for the divergence in outcomes across these two classes of policies is twofold. First, investments in human capital at old ages are less efficient, since the elderly worker has less time to recoup the investment; second, "learning begets learning", so human capital, skills, and abilities acquired at a young ages facilitate future learning.

In this sense, policymakers should have a life-cycle perspective: lifting the unskilled, displaced adults into skilled status is much easier and more efficient if the same workers have been developing their learning ability throughout childhood and youth, possibly with the help of government intervention. For the more mature low-skilled workers with limited learning ability who are subject to unavoidable wage losses due to biased technological change, targeted wage subsidies can be more effective than retraining programs.

10. Concluding remarks

This chapter argues that labor market inequalities are shaped by technological change through a variety of economic mechanisms. Within the technology-labor market nexus, however, which of the specific mechanisms we evaluate are most likely to survive the test of time?

Before answering this question, it is useful to put things in perspective and recall that most of the statements we have made in this chapter are not all meant to represent general insights; rather, they allude to a particular historical episode. Specifically, tech-nology has not always been skill-biased in the past: the transformation from artisanal workplaces to the factory in the 19th century had much the opposite effect [Goldin and Katz (1998)]. Moreover, not all the drastic productivity advancements in the past were embodied in equipment: electricity was to a large extent embodied in new structures, as the electrification of production required a whole new blueprint for the plant [Atkeson and Kehoe (2002)]. Even in reference to this particular historical episode, there are se-rious dissenting views on the overall impact of IT on the macroeconomy [e.g., Gordon (2000)] and on the role of technology in explaining the observed changes in the U.S. wage structure [e.g., Card and DiNardo (2002)].

In returning to the original question, we identify three rather general categories that we find particularly interesting and plausible.

The first idea is *factor-specificity* of the recent technological advancements. In par-ticular, the embodiment of productivity improvements in equipment capital goods, and the skill-bias of such productivity improvements. Whether in the Nelson–Phelps version of skills as a vehicle of adoption and innovation, or in the version of skills and capital as complementary in production, the skill-bias of the IT revolution is one of the most robust and pervasive in the literature. Skill-biased technical change and capital-skill complementarity are crucial to explain the climb of the skill premium, notwithstanding the continuous growth in the relative supply of skilled labor. A growing and promising avenue of research is on the endogenous determinants of the factor-bias in technological advancements [Acemoglu (2002b, 2003b)].

The second idea is *vintage human capital*. The technological specificity of knowledge appears to be an important idea to explain some of the most puzzling aspects of the data such as the rise in within-group or "residual" inequality, the fall of the real wages at the bottom of the skill distribution, the growth in the returns to experience, and the slowdown of output growth in the aftermath of a technological revolution.

The third idea is the *interaction between technology and the organization of labor markets*. Radical technological developments, like those we have witnessed in the past three decades, are bound to interact deeply with the various aspects of the structure of labor markets, like the organization of production within the firm, labor unions, and labor market policies. Through this interaction, the literature has successfully interpreted the move from the Tayloristic to the flatter multi-tasking organizational design of firms, the decline of unionization, and the upward trend in unemployment rate in Europe. In particular, the comparison of the U.S. and European experiences seems a fruitful way of studying this channel.

These ideas are the building blocks of the most successful and influential papers in the first generation of models that we have surveyed in this chapter. Where will the literature go next? We argued in various parts of the chapter that one major weakness of this literature is the scarcity of rigorous quantitative evaluations of the theories proposed. Most of the papers reviewed are qualitative in nature. This is not too surprising, given the young vintage of the literature (which developed only starting from the mid-1990s), and given that, in any field, it naturally takes a long time before a handful of theoretical frameworks emerge as successful and begin to be used for a systematic quantitative accounting of the facts (e.g., the search and matching model in the theory of unemployment, and the neoclassical and the endogenous growth model in the theory of cross-country income differences). In this chapter we have highlighted some features that seem important for a successful theory of the link between technological change and labor market outcomes. Quantitative theory should be a priority within this field of research over the years to come.

Acknowledgements

We are grateful to Philippe Aghion for his suggestions on how to improve an early draft. We thank Stephan Fahr, Giammario Impullitti, Matthew Lindquist, and John Weinberg for comments, Hubert Janicki for research assistance and Eva Nagypal and Bruce Weinberg for providing their data. Krusell thanks the NSF for research support. Violante thanks the CV Starr Center for research support. Any opinions expressed are those of the authors and do not necessarily reflect those of the Federal Reserve Bank of Richmond or the Federal Reserve System.

References

Aaronson, S. (2003). "The rise in lifetime earnings inequality among men". Mimeo. Federal Reserve Board.
Abowd, J.M., Kramarz, F., Margolis, D.N. (1999). "High wage workers and high wage firms". Econometrica 67, 251–334.
Abraham, A. (2003). "Wage inequality and education policy with skill-biased technological change in OG setting". Mimeo. Duke University.
Acemoglu, D. (1998). "Why do new technologies complement skills? Directed technical change and wage inequality". Quarterly Journal of Economics 113, 1055–1090.
Acemoglu, D. (1999). "Changes in unemployment and wage inequality: An alternative theory and some evidence". American Economic Review 89, 1259–1278.
Acemoglu, D. (2002a). "Technical change, inequality and the labor market". Journal of Economic Literature 40, 7–72.
Acemoglu, D. (2002b). "Directed technical change". Review of Economic Studies 69, 781–810.
Acemoglu, D. (2003a). "Cross-country inequality trends". Economic Journal 113, F121–F149.
Acemoglu, D. (2003b). "Labor- and capital-augmenting technical change". Journal of the European Economic Association 1, 1–37.
Acemoglu, D. (2003c). "Patterns of skill premia". Review of Economic Studies 70, 199–230.
Acemoglu, D., Aghion, P., Violante, G.L. (2001). "Deunionization, technical change, and inequality". Carnegie–Rochester Conference Series on Public Policy 55, 29–64.
Acemoglu, D., Pischke, J.-S. (1999). "The structure of wages and investment in general training". Journal of Political Economy 107, 539–572.
Addison, J.T., Bailey, R.W., Siebert, W.S. (2004). "The impact of deunionization on earnings dispersion revisited". Departmental Working Paper 14172. Department of Commerce, University of Birmingham.
Aghion, P. (2002). "Schumpeterian growth theory and the dynamics of income inequality". Econometrica 70, 855–882.
Aghion, P., Howitt, P. (1994). "Growth and unemployment". Review of Economic Studies 61, 477–494.
Aghion, P., Howitt, P. (1998). Endogenous Growth Theory. MIT Press, Cambridge and London.
Aghion, P., Howitt, P., Violante, G.L. (2002). "General purpose technology and within-group wage inequality". Journal of Economic Growth 7, 315–345.
Albrecht, J., Vroman, S. (2002). "A matching model with endogenous skill requirements". International Economic Review 43, 283–305.
Atkeson, A., Kehoe, P.J. (2002). "The transition to a new economy following the Second Industrial Revolution". NBER Working Paper 8676.
Attanasio, O., Battistin, E., Ichimura, H. (2003). "What really happened to consumption inequality in the US?". Mimeo. Institute of Fiscal Studies.
Attanasio, O., Davis, S.J. (1996). "Relative wage movements and the distribution of consumption". Journal of Political Economy 104, 1227–1262.
Autor, D., Katz, L., Krueger, A. (1998). "Computing inequality: Have computers changed the labor market?". Quarterly Journal of Economics 113, 1169–1213.
Autor, D., Levy, F., Murnane, R. (2003). "The skill content of recent technical change: An empirical exploration". Quarterly Journal of Economics 118, 1279–1334.
Bahk, B.H., Gort, M. (1993). "Decomposing learning by doing in new plants". Journal of Political Economy 101, 561–583.
Baker, G.P., Hubbard, T.N. (2003). "Contractibility and asset ownership: On-board computers and governance in U.S. trucking". American Economic Review 93, 1328–1353.

Bartel, A.P., Lichtenberg, F.R. (1987). "The comparative advantage of educated workers in implementing new technology". Review of Economics and Statistics 69, 1–11.

Bartel, A., Sicherman, N. (1998). "Technological change and the skill acquisition of young workers". Journal of Labor Economics 16, 718–755.

Basu, S., Fernald, J., Oulton, N., Srinivasan, S. (2003). "The case of the missing productivity growth: Or, does information technology explain why productivity accelerated in the United States and not in the United Kingdom?". In: Gertler, M., Rogoff, K. (Eds.), NBER Macroeconomics Annual, vol. 18. MIT Press, Cambridge and London, pp. 9–63.

Beaudry, P., Green, D.A. (2003). "Wages and employment in the United States and Germany: What explains the differences?". American Economic Review 93, 573–602.

Becker, G. (1973). "A theory of marriage". Journal of Political Economy 81, 813–846.

Bentolila, S., Saint-Paul, G. (1999). "Explaining movements in the labor share". Contributions to Macroeconomics 3 (1), 251–334.

Bertola, G., Ichino, A. (1995). "Wage inequality and unemployment: United States vs. Europe". In: Bernanke, B., Rotemberg, J. (Eds.), NBER Macroeconomics Annual, vol. 10. MIT Press, Cambridge and London, pp. 13–54.

Bertola, G., Blau, F.D., Kahn, L.M. (1997). "Swimming upstream: Trends in the gender wage differential in 1980s". Journal of Labor Economics 15, 1–42.

Bertola, G., Blau, F.D., Kahn, L.M. (2001). "Comparative analysis of labor market outcomes: Lessons for the United States from international long-run evidence". In: Krueger, A.B., Solow, R.M. (Eds.), The Roaring Nineties: Can Full Employment Be Sustained. Century Foundation Press, New York, pp. 159–218.

Blanchard, O. (1997). "The medium run". Brookings Papers of Economic Activity (Macroeconomics) 2, 89–141 .

Blanchard, O., Wolfers, J. (2000). "The role of shocks and institutions in the rise of European unemployment: The aggregate evidence". Economic Journal 110, C1–C33.

Bleaney, M. (1996). "Central Bank independence, bargaining structure, and macroeconomic performance in the OECD countries". Oxford Economic Papers 48, 20–38.

Blundell, R., Preston, I. (1998). "Consumption inequality and income uncertainty". Quarterly Journal of Economics 113, 603–640.

Bolton, P., Dewatripont, M. (1994). "The firm as a communication network". Quarterly Journal of Economics 109, 809–839.

Booth, A. (1995). The Economics of the Trade Union. Cambridge University Press, Cambridge, U.K.

Borghans, L., Weel, B. (2003). "The diffusion of computers and the distribution of wages". Mimeo. Maastricht University.

Bowlus, A.J., Robin, J.-M. (2004). "Twenty years of rising inequality in U.S. lifetime labor income values". Review of Economic Studies 71, 709–742.

Braverman, L. (1974). Labor and Monopoly Capital: The Degradation of Work in the Twentieth Century. Monthly Review Press, New York.

Bresnahan, T.F., Brynjolfsson, E., Hitt, L.M. (2002). "Information technology, workplace organization and the demand for skilled labor: Firm-level evidence". Quarterly Journal of Economics 117, 339–376.

Bresnahan, T.F., Trajtenberg, M. (1995). "General purpose technologies: 'Engines of growth'?". Journal of Econometrics 65, 83–108.

Brynjolfsson, E., Hitt, L.M. (2000). "Beyond computation: Information technology, organizational transformation and business performance". Journal of Economic Perspectives 14, 23–48.

Caballero, R.J., Hammour, M.L. (1998). "Jobless growth: Appropriability, factor substitution, and unemployment". Carnegie–Rochester Conference Series On Public Policy 48, 51–94.

Cain, L., Paterson, D. (1986). "Biased technical change, scale, and factor substitution in American industry, 1850–1919". Journal of Economic History 46, 153–164.

Campbell, J., Lettau, M., Malkiel, B., Xu, Y. (2001). "Have individual stocks become more volatile? An empirical exploration of idiosyncratic risk". Journal of Finance 56, 1–43.

Card, D. (1996). "The effects of unions on the structure of wages: A longitudinal analysis". Econometrica 64, 957–979.

Card, D. (2001). "The effects of unions on wage inequality in the US labor market". Industrial and Labor Relations Review 54, 296–315.

Card, D., DiNardo, J. (2002). "Skill biased technological change and rising wage inequality: Some problems and puzzles". NBER Working Paper 8769.

Card, D., Lemieux, T. (2001). "Can falling supply explain the rising return to college for younger men? A cohort-based analysis". Quarterly Journal of Economics 116, 705–746.

Caroli, E., Van Reenen, J. (2001). "Skill-biased organizational change? Evidence from a panel of British and French establishments". Quarterly Journal of Economics 116, 1449–1492.

Caselli, F. (1999). "Technological revolutions". American Economic Review 89, 78–102.

Chaney, T., Gabaix, X., Philippon, T. (2003). "The evolution of microeconomic and macroeconomic volatility". Mimeo. New York University, Stern School of Business.

Chun, H. (2003). "Information technology and the demand for educated workers: Disentangling the impacts of adoption versus use". Review of Economics and Statistics 85, 1–8.

Coase, R. (1937). "The nature of the firm". Economica 4, 386–405.

Cohen, D. (1999). "Welfare differentials across French and U.S. labor markets: A general equilibrium interpretation". CEPREMAP Working Paper 9904.

Cohen-Pirani, D., Castro, R. (2004). "Why has skilled employment become so procyclical after 1985?" Mimeo. Carnegie-Mellon University.

Colecchia, A., Schreyer, P. (2002). "ICT investment and economic growth in the 1990s: Is the United States a unique case? A comparative study of nine OECD countries". Review of Economic Dynamics 5, 408–442.

Comin, D., Mulani, D. (2003). "Diverging trends in macro and micro volatility: Facts". Mimeo. New York University.

Cooley, T.F., Prescott, E.C. (1995). "Economic growth and business cycles". In: Cooley, F. (Ed.), Frontiers of Business Cycle Research. Princeton University Press, Princeton, NJ, pp. 1–38.

Cozzi, G., Impullitti, G. (2004). "Technology policy and wage inequality". Mimeo. New York University.

Cummins, J., Violante, G.L. (2002). "Investment-specific technological change in the U.S. (1947–2000): Measurement and macroeconomic consequences". Review of Economic Dynamics 5, 243–284.

Cutler, D.M., Katz, L.M. (1992). "Rising inequality? Changes in the distribution of income and consumption in the 1980's". American Economic Review 82, 546–551.

David, P.A. (1990). "The dynamo and the computer: An historical perspective on the modern productivity paradox". American Economic Review 80, 355–361.

den Haan, W.J. (2003). "Temporary shocks and unavoidable transitions to a high-unemployment regime". Mimeo. London Business School.

den Haan, W., Haefke, C., Ramey, G. (2001). "Shocks and institutions in a job matching model". NBER Working Paper 8463.

Dickens, R. (2000). "The evolution of individual male earnings in Great Britain: 1975–1995". Economic Journal 110, 27–49.

Dickens, W.T., Leonard, J.S. (1985). "Accounting for the decline in union membership: 1950–1980". Industrial and Labor Relations Review 38, 323–334.

DiNardo, J., Fortin, N.M., Lemieux, T. (1996). "Labor market institutions and the distribution of wages, 1973–1992: A semiparametric approach". Econometrica 64, 1001–1044.

Dinopoulos, E., Segerstrom, P.S. (1999). "A Schumpeterian model of protection and relative wages". American Economic Review 89, 450–472.

Dooley, M., Gottschalk, P. (1984). "Earnings inequality among males in the United States: Trends and the effect of labor force growth". Journal of Political Economy 92, 59–89.

Duranton, G. (2004). "The economics of production systems: Segmentation and skill-biased change". European Economic Review 48, 307–336.

Eckstein, Z., Nagypal, E. (2004). "U.S. earnings and employment dynamics 1961–2002: Facts and interpretations". Mimeo. Northwestern University.

Farber, H., Krueger, A.B. (1992). "Union membership in the United States: The decline continues". NBER Working Paper 4216.

Farber, H.S., Western, B. (2000). "Round up the usual suspects: The decline of unions in the private sector, 1973–1998". Working Paper 437. Princeton University, Industrial Relations Sections.

Farber, H.S., Western, B. (2002). "Ronald Reagan and the politics of declining union organization". British Journal of Industrial Relations 40, 385–401.

Flinn, C. (2002). "Labour market structure and inequality: A comparison of Italy and the U.S.". Review of Economic Studies 69, 611–645.

Flug, K., Hercowitz, Z. (2000). "Equipment investment and the relative demand for skilled labor: International evidence". Review of Economic Dynamics 3, 461–485.

Freeman, R.B. (1988). "Contraction and expansion: The divergence of private sector and public sector unionism in the United States". Journal of Economic Perspectives 2, 63–88.

Freeman, R.B., Lazear, E.P. (1995). "An economic analysis of works councils". In: Rogers, J., Streeck, W. (Eds.), Works Councils: Consultation, Representation, and Cooperation in Industrial Relations, National Bureau of Economic Research Comparative Labor Markets Series. University of Chicago Press, Chicago and London, pp. 27–50.

Freeman, R.B., Medoff, J.L. (1984). "What unions do: Evidence, interpretation, and directions for research". Discussion Paper 1096. Harvard Institute of Economic Research.

Friedman, M. (1982). Capitalism and Freedom. Chicago University Press, Chicago, IL.

Galor, O., Moav, O. (2000). "Ability biased technological transition, wage inequality within and across groups, and economic growth". Quarterly Journal of Economics 115, 469–497.

Galor, O., Tsiddon, D. (1997). "Technological progress, mobility, and economic growth". American Economic Review 87, 362–382.

Garicano, L., Rossi-Hansberg, E. (2003). "Organization and inequality in a knowledge economy". NBER Working Paper 11458.

Goldin, C., Katz, L.M. (1998). "The origins of technology-skill complementarity". Quarterly Journal of Economics 113, 693–732.

Goldin, C., Katz, L.M. (1999). "The returns to skill in the United States across the twentieth century". NBER Working Paper 7126.

Goldin, C., Margo, R. (1992). "The great compression: The wage structure in the United States at mid-century". Quarterly Journal of Economics 107, 1–34.

Gordon, R.J. (1990). The Measurement of Durable Good Prices. University of Chicago Press, Chicago, IL.

Gordon, R.J. (2000). "Does the 'New Economy' measure up to the great inventions of the past?". Journal of Economic Perspectives 14, 49–74.

Gosling, A., Machin, S. (1995). "Trade unions and the dispersion of earnings in British establishments, 1980–1990". Oxford Bulletin of Economics and Statistics 57, 167–184.

Gottschalk, P., Moffitt, R. (1994). "The growth of earnings instability in the U.S. labor market". Brookings Papers of Economic Activity 2, 217–272.

Gottschalk, P., Smeeding, T.M. (1997). "Cross-national comparisons of earnings and income inequality". Journal of Economic Literature 35, 633–687.

Gould, E.D., Moav, O., Weinberg, B.A. (2001). "Precautionary demand for education, inequality and technological progress". Journal of Economic Growth 6, 285–315.

Gould, E.D., Paserman, M. (2003). "Waiting for Mr. Right: Rising inequality and declining marriage rates". Journal of Urban Economics 53, 257–281.

Greenwood, J., Hercowitz, Z., Krusell, P. (1997). "Long-run implications of investment-specific technological change". American Economic Review 87, 342–362.

Greenwood, J., Jovanovic, B. (1999). "The IT revolution and the stock market". American Economic Review 89, 116–122.

Greenwood, J., Seshadri, A. (2005). "Technological progress and economic transformation". In: Aghion, P., Durlauf, S. (Eds.), Handbook of Economic Growth. Elsevier, Amsterdam (Chapter 19).

Greenwood, J., Seshadri, A., Yorukoglu, M. (2005). "Engines of liberation". Review of Economic Studies 72, 109–133.

Greenwood, J., Yorukoglu, M. (1997). "1974". Carnegie–Rochester Conference Series on Public Policy 46, 49–96.

Griliches, Z. (1969). "Capital-skill complementarity". Review of Economics and Statistics 5, 465–468.

Haider, S. (2001). "Earnings instability and earnings inequality of males in the United States: 1967–1991". Journal of Labor Economics 19, 799–836.

Hall, R.E. (1973). "The specification of technology with several kinds of output". Journal of Political Economy 81, 878–892.

Hall, R.E. (2001). "The stock market and capital accumulation". American Economic Review 95, 1185–1202.

Hamermesh, D.S. (1993). Labor Demand. Princeton University Press, Princeton, NJ.

Hansen, H. (1998). "Transition from unemployment benefits to social assistance in seven European OECD countries". Empirical Economics 23, 5–30.

Hayek, F.A. (1945). "The use of knowledge in society". American Economic Review 35, 519–530.

Heathcote, J., Storesletten, K., Violante, G.L. (2003). "The macroeconomic implications of rising wage inequality in the U.S.". Mimeo. New York University.

Heathcote, J., Storesletten, K., Violante, G.L. (2004). "Insurance and opportunities: The welfare analysis of wage dispersion". Mimeo. New York University.

Heckman, J.J. (2000). "Policies to Foster human capital". Research in Economics 54, 3–56.

Heckman, J.J., Lochner, L., Taber, C. (1998). "Explaining rising wage inequality: Explorations with a dynamic general equilibrium model of labor earnings with heterogeneous agents". Review of Economic Dynamics 1, 1–58.

Helpman, E., Rangel, A. (1999). "Adjusting to a new technology: Experience and training". Journal of Economic Growth 4, 359–383.

Ho, M.S., Jorgenson, D.W. (1999). "The quality of the U.S. workforce". Mimeo. Harvard University.

Hobjin, B. (2000). "Identifying sources of growth". Mimeo. Federal Reserve Bank of New York.

Holmes, T., Mitchell, M.F. (2004). "A theory of factor allocation and plant size". NBER Working Paper 10079.

Hornstein, A. (1999). "Growth accounting with technological revolutions". Federal Reserve Bank of Richmond Economic Quarterly 85 (3), 1–24.

Hornstein, A. (2004). "(Un)balanced growth". Federal Reserve Bank of Richmond Economic Quarterly 90 (Fall), 25–45.

Hornstein, A., Krusell, P. (1996). "Can technology improvements cause productivity slowdowns?". In: NBER Macroeconomics Annual, vol. 11. MIT Press, Cambridge, MA, pp. 209–259.

Hornstein, A., Krusell, P. (2000). "The IT revolution: Is it evident in the productivity numbers?". Federal Reserve Bank of Richmond Economic Quarterly 86 (Fall), 49–78.

Hornstein, A., Krusell, P. (2003). "Implications of the capital-embodiment revolution for directed R&D and wage inequality". Federal Reserve Bank of Richmond Economic Quarterly 89 (Fall), 25–50.

Hornstein, A., Krusell, P., Violante, G.L. (2003a). "Vintage capital in frictional labor markets". Mimeo. New York University.

Hornstein, A., Krusell, P., Violante, G.L. (2003b). "A quantitative study of the replacement problem in frictional economies". Mimeo. New York University.

Hoxby, C.M., Long, B.T. (1998). "Explaining rising income and wage inequality among the college-educated". NBER Working Paper 6873.

Huggett, M. (1996). "Wealth distribution in life-cycle economies". Journal of Monetary Economics 38, 469–494.

Huggett, M., Ospina, S. (2001). "Does productivity growth fall after the adoption of new technology?". Journal of Monetary Economics 48, 173–195.

Hulten, C.R. (1992). "Growth accounting when technical change is embodied in capital". American Economic Review 82, 964–980.

Hyslop, D. (2001). "Rising U.S. earnings inequality and family labor supply: The covariance structure of intrafamily earnings". American Economic Review 91, 755–777.

Ingram, B., Neumann, G. (1999). "An analysis of the evolution of the skill premium". Mimeo. University of Iowa.

Irwin, D.A., Klenow, P.J. (1994). "Learning-by-doing spillovers in the semiconductor industry". Journal of Political Economy 102, 1200–1227.

Iversen, T. (1998). "Wage bargaining Central Bank independence and the real effects of money". International Organization 52, 469–504.

Johnson, D., Shipp, S. (1997). "Trends in inequality using consumption-expenditures in the U.S. from 1960 to 1993". Review of Income and Wealth 43, 133–152.

Jones, C. (2005). "Growth and ideas". In: Aghion, P., Durlauf, S. (Eds.), Handbook of Economic Growth. Elsevier, Amsterdam (Chapter 16).

Jorgenson, D.W. (2001). "Information technology and the U.S. economy". American Economic Review 91, 1–32.

Jorgenson, D.W. (2005). "Accounting for growth in the information age". In: Aghion, P., Durlauf, S. (Eds.), Handbook of Economic Growth. Elsevier, Amsterdam (Chapter 10).

Jorgenson, D.W., Gollop, F., Fraumeni, B. (1987). Productivity and U.S. Economic Growth. Harvard University Press, Cambridge, MA.

Jorgenson, D.W., Stiroh, K.J. (2000). "U.S. economic growth at the industry level". American Economic Review 90, 161–167.

Jovanovic, B. (1998). "Vintage capital and inequality". Review of Economic Dynamics 1, 497–530.

Jovanovic, B., Nyarko, Y. (1995). "A Bayesian learning model fitted to a variety of empirical learning curves". Brookings Papers on Economic Activity (Microeconomics) 1, 247–299.

Jovanovic, B., Rousseau, P. (2004). "Specific capital and the division of rents". Mimeo. New York University.

Jovanovic, B., Rousseau, P. (2005). "General purpose technologies". In: Aghion, P., Durlauf, S. (Eds.), Handbook of Economic Growth. Elsevier, Amsterdam (Chapter 18).

Juhn, C. (1992). "Decline of male labor market participation: The role of declining market opportunities". Quarterly Journal of Economics 107, 79–121.

Juhn, C., Murphy, K., Pierce, B. (1993). "Wage inequality and the rise in returns to skill". Journal of Political Economy 101, 410–442.

Kambourov, G., Manovskii, I. (2004). "Occupational mobility and wage inequality". Mimeo. University of Pennsylvania.

Katz, L., Autor, D. (1999). "Changes in the wage structure and earnings inequality". In: Ashenfelter, O., Card, D. (Eds.), Handbook of Labor Economics, vol. 3. North-Holland, Amsterdam, pp. 1463–1555.

Katz, L., Murphy, K. (1992). "Changes in relative wages, 1963–1987: Supply and demand factors". Quarterly Journal of Economics 107, 35–78.

Kelly, M. (2000). "Inequality and crime". The Review of Economics and Statistics 82, 530–539.

Kiley, M.T. (1999). "The supply of skilled labour and skill-biased technological progress". The Economic Journal 109, 708–724.

King, I., Welling, L. (1995). "Search, unemployment, and growth". Journal of Monetary Economics 3, 499–507.

Kocherlakota, N. (1996). "Implications of efficient risk sharing without commitment". Review of Economic Studies 63, 595–609.

Kremer, M., Maskin, E.S. (1996). "Wage inequality and segregation by skill". NBER Working Paper 5718.

Krueger, A.B., Summers, L.H. (1988). "Efficiency wages and the inter-industry wage structure". Econometrica 56, 259–293.

Krueger, D., Kumar, K. (2004). "Skill-specific rather than general education: A reason for US–Europe growth differences?". Journal of Economic Growth 9, 167–207.

Krueger, D., Perri, F. (2002). "Does income inequality lead to consumption inequality? Evidence and theory". Mimeo. Stanford University.

Krueger, D., Perri, F. (2003). "On the welfare consequences of the increase in inequality in the United States". In: Gertler, M., Rogoff, K. (Eds.), NBER Macroeconomics Annual, vol. 18. MIT Press, Cambridge, MA, pp. 1463–1555.

Krugman, P. (1994). "Past and prospective causes of high unemployment". Economic Review 79 (4), 23–43. (Federal Reserve Bank of Kansas City).

Krusell, P., Ohanian, L., Rios-Rull, J.-V., Violante, G.L. (2000). "Capital skill complementarity and inequality: A macroeconomic analysis". Econometrica 68, 1029–1053.

LaLonde, R.J., Heckman, J.J., Smith, J. (1999). "The economics and econometrics of active labor market programs". In: Ashenfelter, O., Card, D. (Eds.), Handbook of Labor Economics, vol. 3A. North-Holland, Amsterdam, pp. 1865–2097.

Lee, D., Wolpin, K. (2004). "Intersectoral labor mobility and the growth of the service sector". Mimeo. New York University.

Levy, P.A. (1985). "The unidimensional perspective of Reagan's labor board". Rutgers Law Journal 16, 269–390.

Levy, F., Murnane, R.J. (1992). "U.S. earnings levels and earnings inequality: A review of recent trends and proposed explanations". Journal of Economic Literature 30, 1333–1381.

Lillard, L.A., Tan, H.W. (1986). "Training: Who gets it and what are its effects on employment and earnings?". RAND Corporation Report R-3331-DOL/RC. Santa Monica.

Lindbeck, A., Snower, D.J. (1996). "Reorganization of firms and labor market inequality". American Economic Review, P&P 86, 315–321.

Lindquist, M.J. (2002). "Capital-skill complementarity and inequality in Sweden". Mimeo. University of Stockholm.

Lindquist, M.J. (2004). "Capital-skill complementarity and inequality over the business cycle". Review of Economic Dynamics 7, 519–540.

Lipsey, R.G., Bekar, C., Carlaw, K. (1998). "The consequences of changes in GPTs". In: Helpman, E. (Ed.), General Purpose Technologies and Economic Growth. MIT Press, Cambridge, MA, pp. 193–218.

Ljungqvist, L., Sargent, T.J. (1998). "The European unemployment dilemma". Journal of Political Economy 106, 514–550.

Ljungqvist, L., Sargent, T.J. (2003). "European unemployment and turbulence revisited in a matching model". Mimeo. New York University.

Lloyd-Ellis, H. (1999). "Endogenous technological change and wage inequality". American Economic Review 89, 47–77.

Lucas, R.E. Jr. (1993). "Making a miracle". Econometrica 61, 251–272.

Lucas, R.E. Jr. (2003). "Macroeconomic priorities". American Economic Review 93, 1–14.

Lucas, R.E. Jr., Prescott, E.C. (1974). "Equilibrium search and unemployment". Journal of Economic Theory 7, 188–209.

Machin, S. (1996). "Wage inequality in the UK". Oxford Review of Economic Policy 12, 47–64.

Machin, S. (2000). "Union decline in Britain". British Journal of Industrial Relations 38, 631–645.

Machin, S. (2003). "Trade union decline, new workplaces, new workers". In: Gospel, H., Wood, S. (Eds.), The Future of Unions, vol. 1. Routledge, London.

Manuelli, R. (2000). "Technological change, the labor market, and the stock market". NBER Working Paper 8022.

Marimon, R., Zilibotti, F. (1999). "Unemployment vs. mismatch of talents: Reconsidering unemployment benefits". Economic Journal 109, 266–291.

McCall, J.J. (1970). "Economics of information and job search". Quarterly Journal of Economics 84, 113–126.

McConnell, S. (1996). "The role of computers in reshaping the workforce". Monthly Labour Review 119 (August), 3–5.

McGrattan, E., Prescott, E.C. (2003). "Taxes, regulations, and the value of U.S. corporations: A general equilibrium analysis". Staff Report 309. Federal Reserve Bank of Minneapolis.

Meghir, C., Pistaferri, L. (2004). "Income variance dynamics and heterogeneity". Econometrica 72, 1–32.

Milgrom, P., Roberts, J. (1990). "The economics of modern manufacturing: Technology, strategy, and organization". American Economic Review 80, 511–528.

Mincer, J., Higuchi, Y. (1991). "Wage structures and labor turnover in the United States and Japan". Journal of the Japanese and International Economies 2, 97–133.

Mitchell, M.F. (2001). "Specialization and the skill premium in the, 20th century". Staff Report 290. Federal Reserve Bank of Minneapolis.

Möbius, M. (2000). "The evolution of work". Mimeo. Harvard University.

Moen, E.R. (1997). "Competitive search equilibrium". Journal of Political Economy 105, 385–411.

Mortensen, D.T., Pissarides, C.A. (1998). "Technological progress, job creation, and job destruction". Review of Economic Dynamics 1, 733–753.

Mortensen, D.T., Pissarides, C.A. (1999). "Unemployment responses to 'skill-biased' technology shocks: The role of labour market policy". Economic Journal 109, 242–265.

Murphy, K., Topel, R. (1997). "Unemployment and nonemployment". American Economic Review, P&P 87, 295–300.

Murphy, K., Welch, F. (1992). "The structure of wages". Quarterly Journal of Economics 107, 285–326.

Nelson, R.R., Phelps, E.S. (1966). "Investment in humans, technological diffusion, and economic growth". American Economic Review 56, 69–75.

Neumark, D. (2000). "Changes in job stability and job security: A collective effort to untangle, reconcile and interpret the evidence". In: Neumark, D. (Ed.), On the Job: Is Long-Term Employment a Thing of the Past. Russell Sage Foundation, New York, pp. 1–27.

Nickell, S., Bell, B. (1996). "Changes in the distribution of wages and unemployment in OECD countries". American Economic Review, P&P 86, 302–308.

Nickell, S., Layard, R. (1999). "Labor market institutions and economic performance". In: Ashenfelter, O., Card, D. (Eds.), Handbook of Labor Economics, vol. 3C. North-Holland, Amsterdam, pp. 3029–3084.

Nickell, S., Nunziata, L. (2002). "Unemployment in the OECD since the 1960s: What do we know?". Mimeo. Bank of England.

OECD Employment Outlook (1996). OECD, Paris.

Oliner, S.D., Sichel, D.E. (2000). "The resurgence of growth in the late, 1990s: Is information technology the story?". Journal of Economic Perspectives 14, 3–22.

Ortigueira, S. (2002). "The rise and fall of centralized wage bargaining". Mimeo. Cornell University.

Piketty, T., Saez, E. (2003). "Income inequality in the United States, 1913–1998". Quarterly Journal of Economics 118, 1–39.

Piore, M.J., Sabel, C.F. (1984). The Second Industrial Divide. Basic Books, New York.

Pissarides, C.A. (2000). Equilibrium Unemployment Theory. MIT Press, Cambridge, MA.

Rajan, R., Wulf, J. (2003). "The flattening firm: Evidence from panel data on the changing nature of corporate hierarchies". Mimeo. Chicago GSB.

Robbins, D. (1996). "Evidence on trade and wages in developing world". OECD Technical Paper 119.

Rogerson, R. (2004). "Two views on the deterioration of European labor market outcomes". Journal of the European Economic Association 2, 447–455.

Rosen, S. (1981). "The economics of superstars". American Economic Review 71, 845–858.

Ruiz-Arranz, M. (2002). "Wage inequality in the U.S.: Capital-skill complementarity vs. skill-biased technological change". Mimeo. Harvard University.

Saint-Paul, G. (2001). "On the distribution of income and worker assignment under intrafirm spillovers, with an application to ideas and networks". Journal of Political Economy 109, 1–37.

Sakellaris, P., Wilson, D.J. (2004). "Quantifying embodied technical change". Review of Economic Dynamics 7, 1–26.

Sattinger, M. (1995). "Search and the efficient assignment of workers to jobs". International Economic Review 36, 283–302.

Shi, S. (2002). "A directed search model of inequality with heterogeneous skills and skill-based technology". Review of Economic Studies 69, 467–491.

Solow, R. (1957). "Technical change and the aggregate production function". Review of Economics and Statistics 39, 312–320.

Solow, R. (1960). "Investment and technological progress". In: Arrow, K., Karlin, S., Suppes, S. (Eds.), Mathematical Methods in the Social Sciences. Stanford University Press, Stanford, CA, pp. 89–104.

Thesmar, D., Thoenig, M. (2000). "Creative destruction and firm organization choice". Quarterly Journal of Economics 115, 1201–1237.

Violante, G.L. (2002). "Technological acceleration, skill transferability and the rise in residual inequality". Quarterly Journal of Economics 117, 297–338.

Weinberg, B.A. (2003a). "Computer use and the demand for women workers". Industrial and Labor Relations Review 53, 290–308.

Weinberg, B.A. (2003b). "Experience and technology adoption". Working Paper. Ohio State University.

Wong, L.Y. (2003). "Can the Mortensen–Pissarides model with productivity changes explain U.S. wage inequality?". Journal of Labor Economics 21, 70–105.

Chapter 21

A UNIFIED THEORY OF THE EVOLUTION OF INTERNATIONAL INCOME LEVELS

STEPHEN L. PARENTE

University of Illinois at Urbana-Champaign

EDWARD C. PRESCOTT

Arizona State University
and
Federal Reserve Bank of Minneapolis

Contents

Abstract	1372
Keywords	1372
1. Introduction	1373
2. A theory of economic development	1376
2.1. Classical theory: the pre-1700 era	1377
2.1.1. Technology	1379
2.1.2. Preferences	1380
2.1.3. Endowments	1381
2.1.4. Population dynamics	1381
2.1.5. Equilibrium properties	1381
2.2. Modern growth theory: the post-1900 era	1382
2.3. The combined theory	1383
3. A theory of relative efficiencies	1389
3.1. The aggregate production function	1391
3.2. Consequences of constraints for aggregate efficiency	1392
3.3. Estimates of aggregate relative efficiency	1394
3.4. Reasons for constraints	1395
4. A unified theory of the evolution of international incomes	1396
4.1. Delays in starting dates	1397
4.2. No catch-up after the transition in many countries	1400
4.3. Catch-up and growth miracles	1403
4.4. Unmeasured investment	1406

Handbook of Economic Growth, Volume 1B. Edited by Philippe Aghion and Steven N. Durlauf
© 2005 Elsevier B.V.   All rights reserved
DOI: 10.1016/S1574-0684(05)01021-X

5. Catching up   1407
    5.1. Catch-up facts   1407
    5.2. Reasons for catching up or not catching up   1408
        5.2.1. The United States   1408
        5.2.2. Western Europe   1409
        5.2.3. Latin America   1411
        5.2.4. Southeast Asia   1412
        5.2.5. China   1412
        5.2.6. Russia   1412
6. Concluding remarks   1413
Acknowledgements   1414
References   1414

Abstract

This chapter develops a theory of the evolution of international income levels. In particular, it augments the Hansen–Prescott theory of economic development with the Parente–Prescott theory of relative efficiencies and shows that the unified theory accounts for the evolution of international income levels over the last millennium. The essence of this unified theory is that a country starts to experience sustained increases in its living standard when production efficiency reaches a critical point. Countries reach this critical level of efficiency at different dates not because they have access to different stocks of knowledge, but rather because they differ in the amount of society-imposed constraints on the technology choices of their citizenry.

Keywords

trading clubs, catch-up, transition to modern economic growth, aggregate economic efficiency, capital share

JEL classification: E0, F4, O11, O19

1. Introduction

Over the last decade, a fairly complete picture of the evolution of international income levels has emerged. Figure 1 plots the path of income per capita relative to the leader for four major regions of the world going back to 1700 using data from Maddison (1995). In 1700, the living standard of the richest country was less than three times the living standard of the poorest country.[1] This is the nature of the disparity prior to 1700 as well, as no single country experienced sustained increases in its living standard over the pre-1700 period. After 1700, huge differences in international incomes emerged, as some countries experienced large and sustained increases in their living standards well before others.

England was the first country to develop, that is, to realize sustained increases in per capita income. The exact date at which England began to develop is subject to debate. Some historians, such as Bairoch (1993), place this date at around 1700. Western European countries and countries that were ethnic offshoots of England began to develop shortly thereafter. At first, the increases in income experienced by these early developers were irregular and modest in size. For example, Bairoch (1993) reports that it took England nearly 100 years to double its income from its 1750 level. However, after the start of the twentieth century, these increases have been larger and relatively regular with income doubling every 35 years in these countries – a phenomenon Kuznets (1966) labels *modern economic growth*.

Countries located in other regions of the world started the development process later. For these countries, the gap in income with the leader continued to widen prior to the time they started modern economic growth. For Latin America, the beginning of the twentieth century is the approximate start of modern economic growth. For Asia, the middle of the twentieth century is the approximate start of modern economic growth. For Africa, modern economic growth has yet to start: although per capita income has increased in the majority of African countries since 1960, the increases have been modest and irregular in the period that has followed. As a result, Africa has continued to lose ground relative to the leader in the 1960–2000 period. Because of these later starting dates, the disparity in international income levels increased to their current levels.

Some countries and regions have dramatically reduced their income gap with the leader subsequent to starting modern economic growth. For example, in the post–World War II period, Western Europe has managed to eliminate much of its income gap with the United States, the leader since 1890. Asia is another region that has been catching up with the leader in this period. The catch-up in Asia, in fact, has been dramatic because of the growth miracle countries of Japan, South Korea, and Taiwan that doubled their income in a decade or less. Latin America, in contrast, is an example of a region that has not eliminated its gap with the leader since starting modern economic growth. Latin American per capita income has remained at roughly 25 percent of the leader for the last 100 years.

---

[1] Bairoch (1993) estimates this difference in 1700 to be smaller than a factor of two.

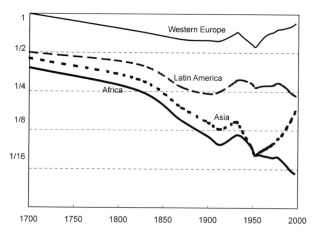

Figure 1. Evolution of international incomes: 1700–1990 (fraction of leader). *Source*: Maddison (1995).

A theory of the evolution of international income levels must account for these facts. The theory must generate an initial period with living standards at the pre-1700 level followed by a long transition period to modern economic growth. The theory must generate different starting dates for the transition to modern economic growth across countries. Namely, it must identify some factor or set of factors that differ across countries and that delay the start of the transition by as much as two centuries. The theory must also account for the sizable and persistent differences in living standards that characterize the experience of some countries that have been experiencing modern economic growth for as long as 100 years. Finally, the theory must be consistent with *growth miracles*, namely, the large increases in relative income experienced by some initially poor countries in a relatively short period after 1950.

There are well-tested theories of some of these phenomena, but not a comprehensive theory that accounts for all of them. This essay unifies these well-tested theories and examines whether the unified theory can account for all of these phenomena.[2] A well-tested theory of the first phenomenon, namely, the pattern of an initial period of stagnant living standards followed by a transition to modern economic growth, is provided by Hansen and Prescott (2002). The Hansen and Prescott theory is a combination of two long-standing and successful theories: the classical theory of the pre-1700 period and the neoclassical theory of the post-1900 period.

The classical economists, in particular, Malthus (1798) and Ricardo (1817), developed a theory that accounts well for the constant living standard that characterized the pre-1700 era. The main feature of this theory is an aggregate production function characterized by fixed factors, the most important of which is land. With this traditional

---

[2] Ngai (2004) provides a unification of these theories along the lines of this essay.

production function, increases in knowledge lead to increases in output that are completely offset by increases in population. As a result, living standards do not increase. Economists have also had for a long time a good theory of modern economic growth that has characterized the United States and much of Western Europe since 1900. Solow (1970) developed his growth model specifically to account for this post-1900 pattern of growth. The main feature of this theory is also an aggregate production function, but one with no fixed factor of production. With this modern production function, improvements in technology that lead to more output being produced with the same resources are not offset by increases in population. As a result, living standards rise.

Hansen and Prescott (2002) unify the classical and modern growth theories by allowing people to use both the traditional production function and the modern production function. They show that when total factor productivity (TFP) associated with the modern production function reaches a critical level, the economy moves resources out of the traditional sector and into the modern sector. This is the date at which the transition begins. The transition is found to last a long period, roughly a century. The model thus gives rise to a pattern of economic development characterized by a long initial period of economic stagnation, followed by a long transition, followed by modern economic growth, as observed in Western Europe and countries settled by Western Europeans.

The Hansen and Prescott theory is not a theory of the evolution of international income levels because it does not address the issues of different starting dates of the transition to modern economic growth, sizable income differences for countries experiencing modern economic growth, and growth miracles. Some factor that differs across countries must be added to the Hansen and Prescott theory to make it a theory of the evolution of international income levels.

Parente and Prescott (2000) develop a theory that accounts for the sizable differences in living standards for countries experiencing modern economic growth and that accounts for growth miracles. More specifically, they develop a theory of country-specific TFP and then introduce this factor into a model in which only the modern production function is available. Their theory of country-specific TFP, which they refer to as a *theory of relative efficiency*, is based on policy differences. More specifically, they show how various policies that constrain choices of technology and work practices at the level of the production unit determine the aggregate efficiency at which a country uses its resources in production. The development of a theory of relative efficiencies is essential. Despite the fact that there is ample empirical evidence that countries differ in relative efficiencies, a theory of international income levels that takes countries' TFPs as exogenous is sterile, because it offers no policy guidance.

In this chapter, we augment the Hansen and Prescott theory of economic development with the Parente and Prescott (2000) theory of relative efficiencies and show that the resulting unified theory is a theory of the evolution of international income levels. In this unified theory, a country begins its transition to modern economic growth when the efficiency with which it uses resources in the production of goods and services in the modern sector reaches a critical point. Countries reach this critical level of efficiency at different dates not because they have access to different stocks of knowledge, but rather because they differ in the amount of society-imposed constraints on the technology choices of their citizenry. After a country reaches this critical point it begins to grow, and its income gap with the leader eventually stops increasing. This gap only decreases if there is a subsequent increase in the efficiency at which the late starter uses resources in the modern production function. A large increase in a late starter's relative efficiency is the result of improvements in its policies and institutions.

We show that plausible differences in efficiencies delay the start of the transition to modern economic growth by more than two centuries, as observed in the data. We also show that sizable differences in living standards persist between countries that have been experiencing modern economic growth for as long as 100 years. Lastly, we show that a large increase in a late starter's relative efficiency can give rise to a growth miracle, as observed in Japan, South Korea, and Taiwan. Thus, the unified theory accounts for the way international income levels have evolved.

The chapter is organized as follows. Section 2 starts with a review of the classical theory of the pre-1700 income level followed by a review of the neoclassical growth theory of modern economic growth. It then concludes with a review of how Hansen and Prescott (2002) combine these two theories into a single theory of economic development. Section 3 deals with the second component of the theory, namely, differences in efficiencies. It reviews the Parente and Prescott (2000) theory of relative efficiencies. Section 4 presents the unified theory of international income levels. In Section 4 a model based on the unified theory is developed and calibrated to the U.K. and U.S. development experiences over the last three centuries. The calibrated model is used to examine the effect of differences in efficiencies across countries on the start of the transition to modern economic growth and the effect of an increase in a country's efficiency on the subsequent path of its per capita GDP. Section 5 examines the development experiences of individual countries and groups of countries over the last three centuries within the context of the theory. Section 6 concludes the chapter.

2. A theory of economic development

In this section, we present the theory of economic development put forth by Hansen and Prescott (2002). We do this in three stages. First, we describe the classical component of that theory and derive its equilibrium properties. Next, we describe the modern growth component of that theory, and also derive its equilibrium properties. The last stage merges these two components and, in doing so, presents the Hansen and Prescott model of economic development.

Figure 2 describes the general pattern of economic development. More specifically, Figure 2 reports per capita income of the leader country dating back to 2000 B.C. Up until 1700, the living standard in the leader country, or any other country for that matter, displayed no secular increase. These living standards were significantly above the subsistence level. In 1688, for example, the poorest quarter of the population in England – the paupers and the cottagers – survived on a consumption level that was roughly

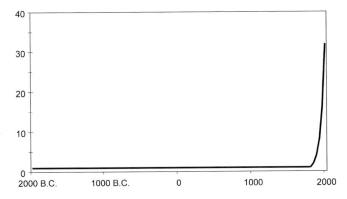

Figure 2. Income per capita of the leader relative to the pre-1800 level. *Source*: Bairoch (1993).

one-fourth the national average.[3] A few societies, such as the Roman Empire in the first century, the Arab Caliphates in the tenth century, China in the eleventh century, and India in the seventeenth century, realized some increases in their per capita income. However, these increases were not sustained. After 1700 per capita income in England started to increase. Over the next 150 years, these increases in the leader country were modest and irregular. However, since 1900, these increases have been larger and fairly regular, with per capita income doubling roughly every 35 years.

Technology was not stagnant over any part of this time period. Economic historians have documented a steady flow of technological innovations in this 2000 B.C. to A.D. 1700 period.[4] Yet these innovations prior to 1700 did not translate into increased living standards. Instead they translated into increased population: as total output increased, the population adjusted so as to maintain a constant level of per capita output. After 1700, these innovations did translate into increases in living standards.

2.1. Classical theory: the pre-1700 era

Classical economists, most notably Malthus and Ricardo, devised a theory that accounts well for the constant level of per capita income that characterized the pre-1700 era. The theory predicts a trade-off between living standards and population size. This trade-off exists because population growth is an increasing function of per capita consumption and because there is an important fixed factor of production, namely, land. A key implication of this theory is that there is a constant standard of living to which the economy adjusts. The theory predicts that increases in the stock of usable knowledge, which could translate into increases in living standards, instead translate into increases in population.

---

[3] See Maddison (1991, p. 10) and Bairoch (1993, pp. 101–108).
[4] See Mokyr (1990) for a review of this literature.

Malthus' theory of population is a biological one rather than an economic one. According to his theory, fertility rises and mortality falls as consumption increases. Being classical, the model has no utility theory and so agents have no decision over the number of children they have. Recently a number of authors, including Tamura (1988), Becker, Murphy and Tamura (1990), Doepke (2000), Galor and Weil (2000) and Lucas (2002), have generated Malthus-like population dynamics in a neoclassical model with household utility defined over consumption of goods and number of children. These models follow Becker (1960) by having a trade-off between quality and quantity of children.

We do not take their approach in this chapter. Instead the approach we take has society through its institutions and policies implicitly determine its population size. Although we similarly add household preferences to the classical theory of production, we do not define household preferences to be over the quantity of household children. Consequently, in this societal theory of population growth, the quantity of children is treated as exogenous from the standpoint of the household.

The reason we take this societal approach to population growth is twofold. First, there is no tested theory of population dynamics, and once modern economic growth begins, demographics play a secondary role in development. Second, and more important, the approach reflects the view that groups of individuals, namely, societies, have had a much larger say in deciding how many children a family has than the family itself. Societies have instituted and continue to institute policies that give them their desired population size. Often the policies of society are not what individual families want. In modern China, for example, a law effectively limits many households to one child. By contrast, Iran in the 1980s wanted a higher population and so implemented subsidies to encourage people to have more children. After achieving its objective, the government stopped these subsidies in the 1990s and began to subsidize contraceptives. India today, wanting a lower population growth rate, has set up family planning programs in many regions. In all these cases, the effects of policy upon demographics are dramatic. Even in poor and rural Indian villages, which did not experience any increase in human capital or income, policy has led to a dramatic decline in population growth rates in the late twentieth century.

Why did society choose population size prior to 1700 so as to maintain a constant living standard? The answer relates to the fact that land was an essential input to the production process in the pre-1700 era. In particular, as a valuable resource, land was subject to expropriation by outsiders. Prior to 1700, a small group of people with large amounts of quality-adjusted land and therefore a high living standard could not defend this land from outside expropriators. For this reason, there was a maximal sustainable living standard. Society set up social institutions that controlled population so as to maintain the highest possible living standard consistent with the ability to defend itself from outside expropriators. Once an economy switches to the modern production technology, land is no longer an important input, so its defense is not an issue. At the stage when the modern production technology dominates, society sets up its social institutions that it sees as maximizing living standards subject to a constraint that a society perpetuates itself.

For the purpose at hand, it is not essential that we model society's choices of institutions that affect fertility choices. Instead, it is sufficient to treat the growth rate of population in a simple mechanical way, namely, as a function of average consumption. In order to reflect society's choices, the function must display two properties. First, it must have a large positive slope, in the neighborhood of the pre-1700 consumption level. Second, for high levels of average consumption, the slope of the function must be near zero. The first property is only relevant for the theory of the pre-1700 era. The second property is only relevant for the theory of the post-1900 period. This is the approach that we take in this essay.

With this in mind, we proceed with a neoclassical formulation of the classical theory of constant living standards. There is a single good in the model that can be used for either consumption or investment purposes. The good is produced using a constant returns to scale technology that uses capital, labor, and land. An infinitely lived household owns the economy's land and capital and rents them to firms in the economy. Land is fixed and does not depreciate. The household is made up of many members, each of whom is endowed with one unit of time. The household uses its capital, labor, and land income for consumption and investment purposes. The growth rate of population is a function of average consumption of household members. A household member's utility in the period is defined over the member's consumption in the period. The household's objective is to maximize the sum of each member's utility. The details of the economy are described as follows.

2.1.1. Technology

The classical theory of production is given by a Cobb–Douglas technology,

$$Y_{Mt} = A_{Mt} K_{Mt}^{\phi} N_{Mt}^{\mu} L_{Mt}^{1-\phi-\mu}. \tag{2.1}$$

In Equation (2.1), Y_{Mt} is output, K_{Mt} is capital, N_{Mt} is labor, and L_{Mt} is land in period t. The parameter A_{Mt} is total factor productivity (TFP), parameter ϕ is capital share, and parameter μ is labor share. The Cobb–Douglas assumption implies unit elasticity of substitution.[5] We allow for exogenous growth in TFP. More specifically, we assume that technology grows at the exogenous rate of γ_M; that is, $A_{Mt} = A_{M0}(1+\gamma_M)^t$. This assumption reflects the fact that technological change was evident from 2000 B.C.[6]

Output can be used for either consumption or investment purposes. The resource constraint for the economy is given by

$$C_t + X_t = Y_{Mt}, \tag{2.2}$$

---

[5] The precise value of the elasticity of substitution between land and the other factors is not important provided that it is not greater than one. The evidence is that throughout most of history the substitution of these other factors for land was limited and, if anything, this elasticity of substitution was less than one. The unit elasticity assumption is made because it simplifies the analysis.

[6] We follow Hansen and Prescott's convention of using the letter M to index variables associated with the classical production function.

where C_t denotes total consumption and X_t denotes total investment.

2.1.2. Preferences

Household preferences are added to the classical theory of production as follows. Period utility of each household member is defined over the member's consumption of the final good. We assume a log utility function, because it is in the class of utility functions that is consistent with a constant-growth equilibrium and because empirically it is consistent with a wide variety of micro and macro observations. Household utility in each period is the sum of each individual member's utility in the period. Strict concavity of individual household members' preferences implies that the household's utility is maximized by giving equal consumption to each member. For this reason, the discounted stream of utility of the household is just

$$\sum_{t=0}^{\infty} \beta^t N_t \log(c_t), \tag{2.3}$$

where β is the time discount factor, c_t is consumption of a household member, and N_t is household size.

As is evident from Equation (2.3), we are using a dynastic construct. This is in contrast to Hansen and Prescott (2002), who use a two-period overlapping generations construct. We adopt an infinitely lived household framework rather than the two-period overlapping generations framework for two reasons. First and foremost, the empirical counterpart of a period is a year in the dynamic construct, while in the two-period overlapping generations construct the empirical counterpart of a period is 35 years. For the purpose of examining the model's ability to account for the large increases in output realized in a short period of time after 1950 by countries such as Japan and South Korea, 35 years is simply too long a period to study.

Second, the size of the effect on a country's steady state level of per capita output associated with policies that determine its savings rate is sensitive to the construct that is used. The tax rate system of a country is an example of such a policy. The level effects associated with this type of policy are in fact larger with the dynastic construct. This fact is important for judging whether differences in savings rates can account for the large differences in transition dates. If plausible differences in savings rates fail to give rise to 200-year delays in development in the dynastic construct, then they also fail to give rise to this delay in the overlapping generations framework, and we can conclude that some factor other than savings rates accounts for the pattern of development.[7] This is essentially the finding of the quantitative exercises undertaken by Parente and Prescott (2000). The choice of construct is irrelevant, however, in assessing the plausibility of other factors such as efficiency, as reflected in TFP differences: the size of the level effects is the same regardless of whether the dynastic or overlapping generations construct is employed.

---

[7] See Hendricks (2003) for a more detailed explanation of this phenomenon.

2.1.3. Endowments

Each member of the household is endowed with one unit of time, which the member can supply to firms in the economy to earn wage income. The household is also endowed with the economy's stock of land and capital, which the household rents to firms. Land in the economy is fixed in supply: it cannot be produced, and it does not depreciate. Without loss of generality, the total quantity of land in the economy is normalized to one. Since land has no alternative use aside from production, the input to production in each period is one. Capital is assumed to depreciate and evolves according to the following law of motion

$$K_{t+1} = (1 - \delta)K_t + X_t, \tag{2.4}$$

where δ is the depreciation rate.

2.1.4. Population dynamics

As mentioned earlier, because we take a societal approach to population size, we model population growth as a function of the average consumption level of household members. More specifically, we assume that the number of members born into a household in period $t + 1$ depends on the average consumption level of household members from period t. Let N_t denote the number of household members in period t, and let c_t denote their average consumption level. Then

$$N_{t+1} = g(c_t)N_t. \tag{2.5}$$

The function g is the growth factor of population from one period to the next. The classical prediction of a stable living standard at the pre-1700 level, c_M, requires that the function g have a sufficiently large and positive slope at c_M. This c_M is the maximal living standard consistent with a society being able to defend its land.

2.1.5. Equilibrium properties

For such a population growth function, there is a steady-state equilibrium with a constant living standard c_M and a population growth rate equal to $(1 + \gamma_M)^{1/(1-\phi-\mu)} - 1$. This constant living standard satisfies $g(c_M) = (1 + \gamma_M)^{1/(1-\phi-\mu)}$. Were the living standard to rise above c_M, say, because of plague or drought, population increase would exceed technological advances and the living standard would then fall until it returned to c_M. If for some reason c were below c_M, the population growth factor would be less than the one needed to maintain the living standard, and the living standard would increase until it was again c_M. Along the steady-state equilibrium path, aggregate output, capital, consumption, and the rental rate of land all grow at the rate of the population. Per capita variables as well as the rental price of labor and capital are all constant. Increases in technology in this model simply translate into a higher population rather than a higher living standard. This is precisely the pattern of development observed prior to 1700.

2.2. Modern growth theory: the post-1900 era

The classical theory accounts well for the pattern of economic development up to 1700. However, it does not account for the increase in living standards that occurred after 1900. Since about 1900, the growth rate of the early developers has been roughly constant, with a doubling of per capita output every 35 years. Modern growth theory, in contrast, does account for the increase. In addition to the roughly constant rate of growth achieved by developed countries over the last century and a half, other facts characterize modern economic growth. These facts are roughly that the consumption and investment shares of output are constant, the share of income paid to capital is constant, the capital-to-output ratio is constant, and the real return to capital is constant.

Modern growth theory accounts well for these modern growth facts. Quantitatively, the steady-state equilibrium of the economy mimics the long-run observations of the United Kingdom and the United States. This is no surprise: Solow (1970) developed the theory with these facts in mind. A key feature of that theory is a Cobb–Douglas production function that includes no fixed factor of production and that is subject to constant exogenous technological change. More specifically, the production technology for the composite good that can be used for either consumption or investment purposes is given by

$$Y_{St} = A_{St} K_{St}^{\theta} N_{St}^{1-\theta}. \tag{2.6}$$

In Equation (2.6), Y_{St} is output, K_{St} is capital, and N_{St} is labor in period t. The parameter θ is capital share, and the parameter A_{St} is TFP, which grows exogenously at the constant, geometric rate γ_S. As can be seen, the critical difference between the traditional and modern growth production functions is that the modern growth function does not include the fixed factor input, land.[8]

Because the final objective of this section is to merge the classical theory and the modern growth theory into a single model, we maintain the same assumptions regarding preferences, endowments, and population dynamics as in the preceding subsection. The household in the model rents capital to firms and supplies labor. It uses its capital and labor income to buy consumption for household members and to augment the household's stock of capital.

In contrast to the classical theory, population growth in the modern theory does not have any consequences for the growth rate of per capita variables in the long run. The choice of the population growth function is therefore unimportant in this respect. The standard procedure is to assume a population growth function $g(c)$ that is constant over the range of sufficiently high living standards associated with the modern growth era. Population thus grows at a constant exponential rate.

Clearly, population cannot grow at an exponential rate forever. At some population level, natural resources would become a constraining factor. If population were ever to

---

[8] Again, we follow Hansen and Prescott's convention of using S to index variables associated with the modern growth production function.

reach this level, it would be unreasonable to abstract from land as a factor of production. But societies control their population so that it never reaches this level. Indeed, reproduction rates have fallen dramatically in the last 50 years, so much in the rich countries, in fact, that these countries must increase their fertility rates to maintain their population size in the long run. This suggests a population growth function that asymptotically approaches one.

In the case where the population growth function is a constant, per capita output, consumption, and capital all increase at the rate $(1 + \gamma_S)^{1/(1-\theta)}$ along the equilibrium constant growth path. The rental price of labor also grows at this rate. The rental price of capital, in contrast, is constant. Consumption's share and investment's share of output are also constant as is capital's share which is equal to θ. As can be seen, the growth rate of the economy's living standard is independent of the economy's population growth rate: the only thing that matters is the exogenous growth rate of technological change. The population growth rate does have an effect on the level of per capita output along the constant growth path, but it is small. Thus, unlike in the model of the pre-1700 era, the population growth function in the model of the post-1900 era plays only a minor role.

2.3. The combined theory

The classical theory accounts well for the constant living standard that characterizes the pre-1700 era, and the modern growth theory accounts well for the doubling of living standards every 35 years that characterizes the post-1900 experience of most of the currently rich, large, industrialized countries. In the period in between, living standards increased in these countries, but at a slower and far more irregular rate compared to the post-1900 period.

We seek a theory of this development process, namely, a theory that generates a long period of stagnant living standards up to 1700, followed by a long transition, followed by modern economic growth. Given the success of the classical theory and the modern growth theory in accounting for the pre-1700 and post-1900 eras, the logical step, and the one taken by Hansen and Prescott (2002), is to merge the two theories by permitting both technologies to be used in both periods. We now present the combined theory of Hansen and Prescott, and use that theory to organize and interpret the development path of the leading industrialized country over the 1700–2000 period.

In the combined theory of Hansen and Prescott (2002), output in any period can be produced using the traditional or the modern growth production function or both. Both technologies, therefore, are available for firms to use in all periods.[9] Capital and labor are not specific to either production function. In light of these assumptions, the

---

[9] The maximum output that can be produced if both technologies are available is characterized by a standard aggregate production function $Y_t = A_t F(K_t, L_t, N_t)$. By *standard* we mean that it is weakly increasing and concave, homogeneous of degree one, and continuous. Even though both the Malthus and the Solow production functions are Cobb–Douglas technologies, the function F is not Cobb–Douglas.

aggregate resource constraint for the combined model economy is

$$N_t c_t + X_t \leqslant Y_{Mt} + Y_{St} = Y_t, \tag{2.7}$$

the capital rental market-clearing constraint is

$$K_t = K_{Mt} + K_{St}, \tag{2.8}$$

and the labor market-clearing condition is

$$N_t = N_{Mt} + N_{St}. \tag{2.9}$$

Household preferences continue to be given by Equation (2.3). Additionally, the population growth function continues to be given by Equation (2.5), and it displays the properties that the function has a large positive slope in the neighborhood of the pre-1700 consumption level and a slope near zero for large levels of consumption.

In their combined theory, Hansen and Prescott assume that the growth rate of TFP for the traditional production function and the growth rate of TFP for the modern economic growth production function are each constant over time. We deviate from Hansen and Prescott on this dimension. Although we maintain their assumption that the rate of TFP growth associated with the traditional technology is constant, we assume that the rate of TFP growth associated with the modern growth technology increases over time, converging asymptotically to the modern growth rate. We make this alternative assumption in light of the empirical counterparts of the two production functions and the historical evidence on technological change.

The empirical counterpart of the classical production function is a traditional technology for producing goods and services that is most commonly associated with the family farm. A key feature of this production technology is that it is based on the use of land in the production of hand tools and organic energy sources. For this technology, the historical record shows gradual improvements in these methods over the last 2,000 years at a roughly constant rate of change.[10] The empirical counterpart of the modern growth production function is a modern technology that is most commonly associated with the factory.[11] A key feature of this technology is that it uses machines driven by inanimate sources of energy. For this technology, the historical record suggests modest growth in the eighteenth century, followed by much higher growth in the nineteenth and twentieth centuries. Lighting, communication, and transportation were important areas where this accelerating pattern occurred. Consequently, a more plausible assumption is that the growth of TFP associated with the modern production function increased slowly

---

[10] The exception to this constant rate of growth might be the Green Revolution in the middle of the twentieth century, where the introduction of new seed varieties resulted in large increases in farm yields associated with traditional farming methods.

[11] The distinction between technologies is, thus, not along the lines of agriculture and manufactures. In this classification, modern agriculture with its use of synthetic fertilizers and tractors is associated with the modern growth production function.

after 1700 and converged to the rate associated with the modern growth era shortly after 1900.

We emphasize that the traditional sector should not be thought of as primarily the agricultural sector, though most outputs of this sector are agricultural products. What characterizes the traditional sector is that the household is the producing unit and typically consumes much of what it produces. Sugar plantations in the Caribbean and cotton plantations in the United States were not part of the traditional sector. There was little incentive for people working in the traditional sector to develop more efficient production methods. Rapid increases in agricultural productivity occurred only when goods developed in the industrial sector were introduced in farming. The reaper and the tractor dramatically increased productivity on farms. Insecticides and fertilizers also contributed to productivity, as did the development of hybrid corn and new seeds. This is all well documented by Johnson (2000).

An economy that starts out using only the traditional production function will eventually use the modern one. To see this, suppose that it were never profitable for firms to use the modern production function. Then the economy's equilibrium path would converge to the steady state of the pre-1700-only model. The steady state of that model is characterized by constant rental prices for capital and labor, r_M and w_M. Capital and labor are not specific to any one technology. Thus, a firm that first considers using the modern production function can hire any amount of capital and labor at the factor rental prices r_{Mt} and w_{Mt}. Profit maximization implies that a firm will not choose to operate the modern growth technology if

$$A_{St} < \left(\frac{r_{Mt}}{\theta}\right)^{\theta} \left(\frac{w_{Mt}}{1-\theta}\right)^{1-\theta}. \tag{2.10}$$

This inequality must be violated at some date. Asymptotically, the rental prices would approach constant values if only the traditional production function were operated, and so the right-hand side of (2.10) is bounded. The left-hand side is unbounded because TFP in the modern function grows forever at a rate bounded uniformly away from zero. The inequality given by (2.10), therefore, must eventually be violated.

At the date when TFP in the modern production function surpasses the critical level given by the right-hand side of (2.10), the economy will start using the modern growth production function. This marks the beginning of the Industrial Revolution. This result is independent of the size differences in the growth rates of TFP associated with the traditional and modern production functions. Over the transition, more and more capital and labor will be moved to the modern production sector. The traditional production function will, however, continue to be operated, though its share of output will decline to zero over time. This follows from the assumptions that land is used only in traditional production and that its supply is inelastic.

We now use the combined theory to organize and interpret the development path of the industrial leader over the 1700–2000 period. The empirical counterpart of a period is a year. The initial period of the model is identified with the year 1675.[12] We attribute the stagnation of the leader prior to 1700 to an insufficiently low level of TFP associated with the modern production function to warrant its use. We attribute the start of economic growth of the leader in 1700 to growth in TFP associated with the modern production function so that its level exceeds the critical value given by Equation (2.10). Lastly, we attribute the rising rate of growth of per capita output of the leader from 1700 to 1900 to greater use of the modern production function and the rising rate of growth of TFP.

We proceed to parameterize the model. The model is calibrated so that the economy starts to use the modern production function in 1700. Following Hansen and Prescott (2002), we calibrate the model so that the steady state of the classical-only model (Section 2.1) matches pre-1700 observations and the steady state of the modern growth-only model (Section 2.2) matches the post-1900 growth experience of the United States.

In the calibration, we deviate from Hansen and Prescott along two dimensions. First, we calibrate the population growth function so that it matches Maddison's (1995) estimates for U.K. population growth rates over subperiods of the 1675–1990 period.[13] Given our theory of population growth, it is more appropriate to use the time series data from a particular country to restrict the population growth function for that country rather than cross-section data as Hansen and Prescott do.[14] Second, we calibrate the annual growth rate of TFP for the modern production function so that it remains at the traditional rate up until 1700, increases linearly to reach one-half of its modern growth rate in 1825, and then increases linearly to reach its modern growth rate in 1925.

Following Hansen and Prescott, we pick the initial capital stock and the initial population so that if only the traditional production function were available, the equilibrium would correspond to the steady state of the pre-1700 model, and there would be no incentive to operate the modern production function if it were available. This ensures that in period 0 only the traditional production function is operated and that there is a period of constant living standards. Table 1 lists the values for each of the model parameters and provides comments where appropriate. The population growth rate function implied by the U.K. population growth data used in the computation is depicted in Figure 3.

For the parameterized model economy, it takes 150 years before 95 percent of the economy's output is produced in the modern sector. Figures 4–6 depict the model economy's development path along a number of dimensions. Figure 4 compares period t per capita output relative to 1700 per capita output for the model economy and the industrial leader as reported by Maddison (1995, Tables 1.1 and C.12). According to the model, an economy that begins the transition in 1700 will be approximately 28 times richer in

---

[12] There is nothing special about the choice of 1675. None of the results would change if the initial period were identified with some other year. Only the value of A_{S0} would change in the experiments.

[13] The calibration assumes constant population growth after 1973 equal to the average annual population growth of the United Kingdom from 1973 to 1994.

[14] We do not use the U.S. population growth rate data in the calibration. Doing so would not change any of the results because the population growth rate function is not important in the modern growth era.

Table 1
Restricted parameter values

Parameter	Value	Comment
γ_M – growth rate of TFP for traditional production	0.0009	Consistent with pre-1700 world population average annual growth rate of 0.003
ϕ – capital share in traditional production	0.10	Consistent with pre-1700 estimates of land's share reported by Clark (1998) and Hoffman (1996)
μ – labor share in traditional production	0.60	Chosen so that labor's share does not vary with the level of development as reported by Gollin (2002)
A_{M0} – initial TFP for traditional production	1.0	Normalization
δ – depreciation rate	0.06	Consistent with U.S. capital stock and investment rate since 1900
γ_S – asymptotic TFP growth rate for modern production	0.012	2 percent rate of growth of per capita GDP in modern growth era
θ – capital's share in modern production	0.40	U.S. physical capital's share of output
A_{S0} – initial TFP for modern production	0.53	1700 starting date given initial period for model is 1675
β – subjective time discount factor	0.97	Consistent with real rate of interest between 4 and 5 percent in modern growth era

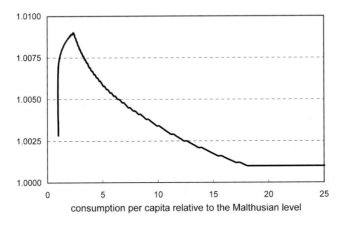

Figure 3. Population growth function $g(c)$ implied by U.K. data.

1990 than in 1700. Figure 5 depicts the growth rate of per capita output for the model economy over the 1700–2000 period. The growth rate of per capita output is slow at the onset of the transition, less than 1 percent per year on average before 1825. By 1900 the growth rate is near the modern growth rate of 2 percent per year. This pattern is

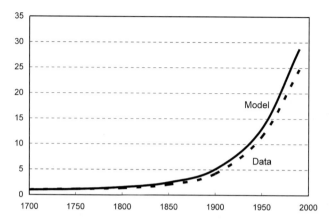

Figure 4. Income per capita relative to 1700. *Source*: Maddison (1995).

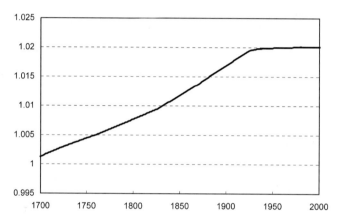

Figure 5. Predicted growth rate of per capita output, 1700–2000.

primarily a consequence of the assumption that TFP growth for the modern technology increases slowly over the 1700–1900 period. Figure 6 depicts the path of the rental prices of capital and labor over the 1700–2000 period. As can be seen, the real wage rate increases steadily once the transition begins. The real interest rate, in contrast, shows very little secular change over three centuries. These latter predictions conform well to the pattern of development associated with England, the United States, and other early developers.

The predictions of the model are not sensitive to the value of the capital share parameter in the modern growth production function. This is an important result, because the magnitude of the capital share with a broad definition of capital that includes intangible as well as tangible capital could well be greater than the 0.40 share value used in the above exercise. The paths of per capita GDP, its growth rate, and rental prices are

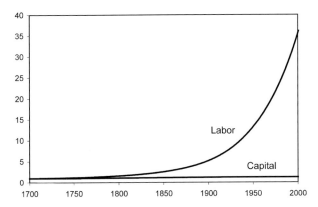

Figure 6. Predicted factor rental prices (1700 = 1), 1700–2000.

nearly identical to those shown in Figures 4–6 for alternative values of the capital share in the modern production function. The transition still takes a long time. For a capital share as high as 0.70, 140 years elapse before 95 percent of the economy's output is produced using the modern production function.

3. A theory of relative efficiencies

The Hansen and Prescott (2002) theory of economic development reviewed in Section 2 is not a theory of the evolution of international income levels. It does not address the issue of why modern economic growth started at different dates in different countries. India, for example, began modern economic growth nearly 200 years later than did the United Kingdom. As a result, India's income level relative to the leader fell from 50 percent in 1770 to only 5 percent in 1970. Neither does the theory address the issue of why some countries that have been experiencing modern economic growth for a century or more have failed to narrow the income gap with the industrial leader. In Latin American countries, for example, income levels have remained at roughly 25 percent the U.S. income level since the end of the nineteenth century when modern economic growth began there. The theory does not address the issue of why some countries in the 1950–2000 period have been able to substantially narrow the income gap with the industrial leader. These countries include Italy, Spain, Japan, Korea, and Taiwan, the latter three all of which experienced a growth miracle. Some factor that differs across countries must be added to the Hansen and Prescott theory to make it a theory of the evolution of international income levels.

One might be led to introduce differences in TFP associated with the modern production function to the model, because the Hansen and Prescott theory of development predicts that per capita income in a country starts to increase once TFP in the modern sector reaches a critical level. Moreover, there is ample evidence that countries (at least those experiencing modern economic growth) differ along this dimension.[15] Although it would be easy to introduce such differences into the Hansen and Prescott theory, it would not be useful, as long as country-specific TFP differences are treated exogenously. Absent a theory of country-specific TFP, the theory of the evolution of international income levels is sterile because it offers no policy guidance. What is needed is a policy-based theory of why TFP differs across countries at a point in time.

Parente and Prescott (2000) develop a theory of TFP that attributes differences in TFP to country-specific policies that both directly and indirectly constrain the choice of production units. Their theory of TFP is more appropriately called a *theory of relative efficiencies*. This is because Parente and Prescott (2000) decompose a country's TFP into the product of two components. The first component is a pure knowledge or technology component, denoted by A. The second is an efficiency component, denoted by E. In the context of the Hansen and Prescott model, the modern growth production function is

$$Y_{St} = E_S A_{St} K_{St}^{\theta} N_{St}^{1-\theta}. \tag{3.1}$$

The technology component of TFP, A_{St}, is common across countries. It is the same across countries because the stock of productive knowledge that is available for a country to use does not differ across countries.[16] The efficiency component differs across countries as the result of differences in economic policies and institutions. Here we consider the case in which a country's economic policies and institutions do not change over time, so E_S is not subscripted by t. The efficiency component is a number in the $(0, 1]$ interval. An efficiency level less than one implies that a country operates inside the production possibilities frontier, whereas an efficiency level equal to one implies that a country operates on the production possibilities frontier. Differences in efficiency, therefore, imply differences in TFP.

Relative efficiencies at a point in time, and not absolute efficiencies, can be determined using the production function and the data on quantities of the inputs and the output. Thus, it is not possible to determine if any country has an efficiency level equal to one, although we tend to doubt that this is the case. Changes in relative efficiencies of a given country can also be determined conditional on an assumption on the behavior of the technology component of TFP such as that it grows at some constant rate.

We now present the Parente and Prescott (2000) theory of relative efficiencies. To keep the analysis manageable, we present the theory of relative efficiencies in the context of an economy in which only the modern production function is available. The theory constitutes a theory of the aggregate production function when there are constraints at the production unit level.

In light of this, we first review the theory underlying the aggregate production function. We then show how policy constraints give rise to an aggregate production function

---

[15] See, for example, Klenow and Rodriguez-Clare (1997), Hall and Jones (1999) and Hendricks (2002).

[16] Much of the stock of productive knowledge is public information, and even proprietary information can be accessed by a country through licensing agreements or foreign direct investment.

with a different efficiency level. We follow this by providing estimates of cross-country relative efficiencies associated with the modern production function using the mapping from policy to aggregate efficiency derived in this section with estimates of the costs imposed by a country-specific policy. Finally, we conclude this section with a discussion of why constraints on the behavior of the production units exist.

3.1. The aggregate production function

Before developing the mapping from policy to aggregate efficiency, we briefly review the theory of the aggregate production function associated with modern growth. The theory underlying the aggregate production function is as follows. In each period, there is a set of plant technologies B. A plant technology $b \in B$ is a triplet that gives the plant's output y_b and its capital and labor inputs, k_b and n_b. A plan $\{\lambda_b\}$ specifies the measure of every type of plant operated. The aggregate production function, that is, the maximum Y that can be produced given aggregate inputs K and N is

$$Y = F(K, N) = \max_{\lambda \geqslant 0} \sum_b \lambda_b y_b \tag{3.2}$$

subject to the two resource constraints

$$\sum_b \lambda_b k_b \leqslant K \tag{3.3}$$

and

$$\sum_b \lambda_b n_b \leqslant N. \tag{3.4}$$

Assuming that this program has a solution, which it will under reasonable economic conditions, the aggregate production function will be weakly increasing, weakly concave, homogeneous of degree one, and continuous.

Empirically, the Cobb–Douglas aggregate production function is the one consistent with the post-1900 modern economic growth era. The question then is: What set of technologies B gives rise to the Cobb–Douglas aggregate production function? One such set is the set of plant technologies defined by

$$y \leqslant d(n)k^\theta. \tag{3.5}$$

The function $d(n)$ is an increasing and continuous function of the labor input. Assuming that $n^* = \arg \max d(n)n^{\theta-1}$ exists, the aggregate production function is

$$Y = AK^\theta N^{1-\theta}, \tag{3.6}$$

where $A = \max d(n)n^{\theta-1}$. A sketch of the proof is as follows. If any quantity of capital and labor is allocated to a single type plant in such a way that output is maximized, then the number of employees at each plant is n^*. Thus, all operated plants, for an optimum, must have n^* workers. Given $\theta < 1$, the capital stock must be allocated in equal quantity over every operated plant. Thus, the number of plants operated is N/n^*, capital per operated plant is $K/(N/n^*)$, the number of workers per operated plant is n^*, and maximal output is given by Equation (3.6). With the assumption that the function d increases over time, the expression A will increase over time.

3.2. Consequences of constraints for aggregate efficiency

Next, consider the plant production technology with constraints imposed on it. We consider two types of policy. The first type constrains how a particular plant technology can be operated. The second type constrains the choice of which plant technologies can be operated. Certainly, these are not the only types of constraints that will affect a country's TFP. A number of other types of policy have a similar effect.[17]

The first type of policy constrains how a given technology is operated. A policy that gives rise to this type of constraint is a work rule, which dictates the minimum number of workers or machines needed to operate a plant technology. In particular, suppose constraints are such that the input to a $b = (k, n, y)$ type plant must be $\phi_K k_b$ and $\phi_N n_b$ for all plant types where ϕ_K and ϕ_N each exceed one. This implies that a particular technology, if operated, must be operated with excessive capital and labor. With these constraints, the aggregate production function is

$$Y = E_S A K^\theta N^{1-\theta}, \tag{3.7}$$

where $E_S \equiv \phi_K^{-\theta} \phi_N^{\theta-1}$. This is the aggregate production function used in Section 2. If the nature of the constraints were to double the capital and labor requirements, then the efficiency measure would be one-half. If the nature of the constraints is to quadruple both the capital and labor requirements, then the efficiency measure would be one-fourth.

The second type of policy constrains the choice of which technology can be operated. This type of constraint maps into the efficiency parameter of an aggregate production function with a composite capital stock made up of both physical and intangible components. Any policy that serves to increase the amount of resources the production unit must spend in order to adopt a better technology is a constraint of this nature. Such policies and practices take the form of regulation, bribes, and even severance packages to factor suppliers whose services are eliminated or reduced when a switch to a more productive technology is made. In some instances, the policy is in the form of a law that specifically prohibits the use of a particular technology. The empirical evidence suggests that this second type of constraint is more prevalent than the first.[18]

Following Parente and Prescott (2000), let the output of a quality b plant be given by the following equation,

$$y_t = b k_{P_t}^{\theta_P} \left[\min(n_t, \bar{n})\right]^{\theta_n}, \quad \bar{n} > 0, \ \theta_P < 1. \tag{3.8}$$

---

[17] For example, Schmitz (2001) suggests a mapping from government subsidies directed at state-owned enterprises to aggregate efficiency.

[18] See Parente and Prescott (2000) for a survey of this evidence.

With this technology, a minimum number of workers, $\bar{n}$, is required to operate a plant. The variable k_P denotes the physical capital input. The subscript P is introduced in order to differentiate physical capital from intangible capital later in the analysis. There are no increasing returns to scale in the economy, because if the inputs of the economy are doubled, the number of plants doubles.[19]

A plant's quality is a choice variable. To improve its quality, resources are needed. This resource cost is the product of two components. The first component is technological in nature and reflects the cost in the absence of constraints. The second component, denoted by $\phi_I > 1$, reflects the constraint itself. The function that gives the required resources a plant must expend to advance its quality from b to b' is

$$x_{bb'} = \phi_I \int_b^{b'} \left(\frac{s}{W_t}\right)^\alpha ds. \tag{3.9}$$

Here W_t is the stock of pure knowledge in the world in period t. Its growth rate is exogenous and equal to γ_W. Thus

$$W_t = W_0(1 + \gamma_W)^t. \tag{3.10}$$

Integrating (3.9) and defining $x_{It} = x_{bb'}$ yields

$$x_{It} = \phi_I \frac{b_{t+1}^{\alpha+1} - b_t^{\alpha+1}}{W_0^\alpha (1 + \gamma_W)^{\alpha t}(1 + \alpha)}.$$

Let

$$k_{It} = \frac{\phi_I b_t^{\alpha+1}}{W_0^\alpha (1 + \gamma_W)^{\alpha(t-1)}(1 + \alpha)}.$$

The variable k_{It} has the interpretation of the plant's intangible capital stock; it is the value of the plant's past investments in quality improvements. The plant technology is specified by

$$y_t = \mu \phi_I^{-\theta_I}(1 + \gamma_W)^{\alpha \theta_I t} k_{It}^{\theta_I} k_{Pt}^{\theta_P}[\min(\bar{n}, n_t)]^{\theta_n}, \tag{3.11}$$

with

$$k_{It+1} = (1 - \delta_I)k_{It} + x_{It}, \tag{3.12}$$

where δ_I and μ are functions of α, γ_W and W_0, and $\theta_I \equiv 1/(1 + \alpha)$. The sum of θ_I and θ_P is strictly less than one, so there is an optimal plant size, with all operated plants having n^* workers and equal amounts of both capital stocks.

Aggregating over plants implies the following equilibrium aggregate production relation

$$Y_t = E_S A_0(1 + \gamma_S)^t K_{It}^{\theta_I} K_{Pt}^{\theta_P} N_t^{1-\theta_P-\theta_I}, \tag{3.13}$$

[19] See Hornstein and Prescott (1993) for a detailed coverage of this technology.

with $E_S \equiv \phi_I^{-\theta_I}$ and $(1 + \gamma_S) \equiv (1 + \gamma_W)^{\alpha\theta_I}$. The laws of motion for the aggregate capital stocks are

$$K_{I,t+1} = (1 - \delta_I)K_{It} + X_{It} \tag{3.14}$$

and

$$K_{P,t+1} = (1 - \delta_P)K_{Pt} + X_{Pt}, \tag{3.15}$$

where $(1 - \delta_I) \equiv 1/(1 + \gamma_W)^{\alpha}$.

Now if intangible capital has the same depreciation rate as physical capital, then the model with these two capital stocks is isomorphic to the model of Section 2.2 with a single capital stock. The single capital stock, K_t, is a composite of the intangible and physical capital stocks where

$$K_{It} = \frac{\theta_I}{\theta_I + \theta_P} K_t \tag{3.16}$$

and

$$K_{Pt} = \frac{\theta_P}{\theta_I + \theta_P} K_t. \tag{3.17}$$

The capital share in the single capital stock model, θ, is just the sum of θ_I and θ_P, and investment in the single capital stock model, X_t, is just the sum of the investments in physical and intangible capital, $X_{It} + X_{Pt}$.

For the sake of consistency and brevity, we continue to use the model economy with a single capital stock in our presentation of the unified theory of the evolution of international incomes. In those instances where we wish to consider the role of intangible capital, we proceed by assigning a value to the capital share parameter in the modern production function that exceeds 0.40, the share of physical capital's output in the national income accounts. We solve out the model economy with a single capital stock and then impute the intangible and physical capital components, as well as their investments. This can effectively be done using Equations (3.16) and (3.17) given a decomposition of the total capital share into its intangible and physical components.[20]

3.3. Estimates of aggregate relative efficiency

The mappings developed in the preceding subsection allow us to impute the aggregate relative efficiency associated with the modern production function for various constraints. In general, the size of the effect of the constraint on a country's aggregate

---

[20] We say *effectively* because there are two technical issues in the combined theory when capital is broadly defined. First, if intangible capital is not an input into the traditional production function, then the economy will need to make some investments specifically in intangible capital prior to switching to the modern production function. Second, after the transition, as new plants open, they will have a lower technology level compared to older plants.

efficiency depends on the factor input affected by the constraint and on that input's share in the production function. In the special case where the constraints affect all inputs equally, that is, $\phi = \phi_n = \phi_l = \phi_P$, the individual factor shares are unimportant and the efficiency level of a country is just $E_S = \phi^{-1}$. Hence, the implied difference in relative efficiencies is equal to the implied cost differences of policy. Thus, if the cost difference in policies between two countries is a factor of five, the implied factor difference in aggregate relative efficiency is also five.

Are factor differences in relative efficiency greater than five reasonable? Obviously, it is not possible to answer this question definitively without a comprehensive international study of the total costs of the constraints imposed by society. Some estimates of the cost differences associated with some country-specific policies do exist. Studies that estimate the costs of certain policies of individual countries that affect the technology and work practice choices of the production units located there do find that these costs vary systematically with income levels, with large differences existing between rich and poor countries. These studies suggest that factor differences in relative efficiencies could easily be as great as five.

For example, Djankov et al. (2002) calculate the costs associated with the legal requirements in 75 countries that an entrepreneur must meet in order to start a business. They find that the number of procedures required to start up a firm varies from a low of 2 in Canada to a high of 20 in Bolivia and that the minimum official time required to complete these procedures ranges from a low of 2 days in Canada to a high of 174 days in Mozambique. These costs do not reflect any unofficial costs involved with starting a firm, such as bribes or bureaucratic delays. Because these official cost measures are positively correlated with indexes that incorporate measures of bribes, the true difference in start-up costs between low-cost and high-cost countries is surely even larger than those reported in the study.

3.4. Reasons for constraints

The evidence strongly suggests that production units in poor countries are severely constrained in their choices, and the costs associated with these constraints are large. This prompts the question: Why does a society impose these constraints? A large number of studies, some of which are surveyed in Parente and Prescott (2000), suggest that constraints typically are imposed on firms in order to protect the interests of factor suppliers to the current production process. These groups stand to lose in the form of reduced earnings if new technology is introduced. These losses occur because either the input they supply is specialized with respect to the current production process or their industry's demand is price inelastic.[21]

---

[21] Parente and Prescott (1999) show in a model with no capital how a monopoly right granted to factor suppliers can significantly lower a country's efficiency. Herrendorf and Teixeira (2003) extend this model to include physical capital and show that these monopoly rights have even larger effects on a country's efficiency.

4. A unified theory of the evolution of international incomes

In this section we unify the Parente and Prescott (2000) theory of relative efficiencies and the Hansen and Prescott (2002) theory of development. The unified theory is then used to organize and interpret the evolution of international income levels. We unify the Parente and Prescott theory and the Hansen and Prescott theory as follows. We assume that technological level increases in both sectors result from growth in world knowledge. Consequently, the technology component of TFP in each production function is the same across countries at any point in time. The paths for the technology components of TFP are determined as in Section 2.3 by requiring that the leader country with an efficiency parameter in the modern sector set to one start its transition to modern economic growth in 1700. We then introduce differences in this efficiency parameter across countries. Given a country's relative efficiency parameter and the common path of the technology components of the TFPs, we compute the equilibrium path of the economy.

As mentioned in Section 3, we doubt than any country has or had an efficiency parameter equal to one. The assumption that efficiency in the leader is one in the unified theory is not important to any of the results because it is just a normalization. Again, only relative efficiencies matter and can be determined. This is the case for countries at a given time and across time in a given country.

We do not introduce cross-country differences in the efficiency parameter associated with traditional production. As mentioned in the Introduction, incomes did differ slightly prior to 1700, with the richest countries being no more than two or three times richer than the poorest. One possible explanation for these pre-1700 differences in income levels is that countries differed in policies that increased the inputs required for producing goods with the traditional production function. Because this technology corresponds to traditional farming and even manufactures produced within a home setting, we think the effect of policy differences for relative efficiencies associated with traditional production is small. For this reason, we favor the alternative explanation that some countries were better able to defend themselves from outside expropriations because of geography and thus were able to maintain a higher constant living standard during the pre-1700 era. Two countries that enjoyed such an advantage were England and Japan.

We interpret delays in the start of the transition to modern economic growth to late starters having a lower relative efficiency in the modern sector, at least up until the date their transitions began. We attribute the persistent percentage difference between such a country and the industrial leader to the continuation of its low relative efficiency. Finally, we attribute catch-up, including growth miracles, to large increases in relative efficiency in countries.

We begin by computing the relative efficiency of a late starter required to delay the start of its transition by a given length of time. The size of the required efficiency difference between the leader and the laggard that gives rise to any given delay is a function of the capital share parameter in the modern production function. *Our main finding is that differences in relative efficiency required to generate delays in starting dates of the lengths observed in the historical data are reasonable for all capital shares above 0.40.*

We then compute the entire equilibrium path of these late starters assuming that their efficiency levels relative to the leader never change. Large differences in incomes exist even after the late starters are in the modern economic growth phase. In fact, the gap between the leader and late starters increases for some time after the laggards have started the transition to modern economic growth. This is the case even though the transition period of late starters is shorter than that of early starters. *The main finding of these experiments is that the gap in incomes between early and late starters never narrows unless the laggard adopts polices that increase its productive efficiency.*

The final set of experiments allows for a one-time increase in a country's relative efficiency parameter. We assume that the change is unexpected from the standpoint of the late starter and viewed as permanent in nature. We then compute the equilibrium path and determine the country's output relative to that of the leader subsequent to the change. *We find that the late starter's path of output relative to the leader subsequent to the change in its efficiency parameter is consistent with the experience of growth miracle countries such as Japan, but only if the capital share is between one-half and two-thirds.*

We conclude from this analysis that capital's share must be large for the unified theory to be a successful theory of the evolution of international income levels. A large capital share implies an important role for intangible capital in the production of goods and services and large investment in intangible capital as a fraction of GDP. Investment in intangible capital goes unmeasured in the national income and product accounts. Thus, it is not possible to determine whether a large capital share is plausible by examining national account data. One must examine other evidence, in particular, micro evidence to determine the plausibility of a large capital share. Thus, we end this section by examining the micro evidence on the size of unmeasured investment in the economy. We conclude from this evidence that the size of unmeasured investment in the economy is as large as the size predicted by the unified theory.

4.1. Delays in starting dates

We first examine whether the unified theory predicts large delays in the start of the transition to modern economic growth that some countries have experienced. In particular, we determine the size of the difference in efficiency required to delay the start of the transition to modern economic growth by a certain number of years.

For the purpose at hand, it is important to provide a more thorough picture of the different starting dates for the transition corresponding to the experiences of individual countries. An issue is how to date the start of modern economic growth. Our definition of the *start* of modern economic growth is the earliest point in a country's history with the property that the trend growth rate is 1 percent or more for all subsequent time.[22] Fig-

---

[22] The concept of trend employed here is a highly smoothed path of per capita income.

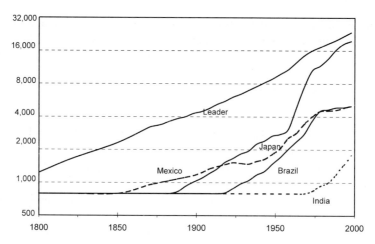

Figure 7. Different countries start at different dates, income per capita in 1990 $US. *Source*: Maddison (1995).

ure 7 shows the path of output in a number of countries relative to the industrial leader going back to 1800. As can be seen, starting dates vary substantially across countries. Mexico started its transition to modern economic growth sometime between 1800 and 1850; Japan started sometime between 1850 and 1900. Brazil started in the early twentieth century, and India started its transition sometime between 1950 and 1980. Each country's income gap with the leader increased prior to starting its transition to modern economic growth.

The key expression for determining the delay in the starting date associated with differences in relative efficiencies is Equation (3.12), which rewritten in relative efficiencies is

$$ E_S^i A_{St} < \left(\frac{r_{Mt}}{\theta} \right)^{\theta} \left(\frac{w_{Mt}}{1-\theta} \right)^{1-\theta}. \tag{4.1} $$

A country will not use the modern production function as long as the relation given by Equation (4.1) is satisfied. Once a country's efficiency, $E_S A_{St}$, exceeds the critical level given by the right-hand side of Equation (4.1), which it must, the country begins its transition to modern economic growth. Assuming as we do that relative efficiencies associated with the traditional production function do not differ across countries, the rental prices of land and labor will not differ much across countries over the periods when each country specializes in the traditional production function.[23] Consequently, this critical level of efficiency will not differ much across countries. It follows that

---

[23] They are roughly equal because the rental prices will not be constant in all periods that the economy specializes in the traditional production function. This is because agents will start to accumulate more capital per household member in anticipation of the modern production function being used.

the difference in starting dates between two countries i and j, with different relative efficiencies, is approximately given by the periods t_i and t_j for which

$$E_S^i A_{St_i} = \left(\frac{r_M}{\theta}\right)^\theta \left(\frac{w_M}{1-\theta}\right)^{1-\theta} = E_S^j A_{St_j}. \qquad (4.2)$$

It is not obvious looking at Equation (4.2), but the required relative efficiency E_S^i/E_S^j that gives rise to a particular delay in the start of the transition depends on the size of the capital share in the modern production function. The reason for this is that the required factor difference in relative efficiencies equals the factor difference in the stock of pure knowledge, A_S, between starting dates. It follows that the required relative efficiency difference is smaller for larger increases in the stock of pure knowledge between starting dates. The size of the increase in the stock of pure knowledge depends importantly on its asymptotic growth rate γ_S. The value of this parameter is calibrated so that the growth rate of per capita output associated with the constant growth path of the modern-growth-only model, given by $(1 + \gamma_S)^{1/(1-\theta)}$, equals 2 percent per year. Thus, the calibrated value of γ_S, and hence the implied size of the factor increase in pure knowledge between starting dates t_j and t_i, depends on capital's share in the modern growth production function.

We now compute the efficiency of the early starter relative to a late starter required to generate a given delay in the transition to modern economic growth. We do this for a range of values for the capital share parameter, since the value of capital's share is not well restricted. For each capital share value, we recalibrate the asymptotic growth rate of pure knowledge γ_S and the value of A_{S0} so that the country with $E_S = 1$ always starts its transition in 1700. These are the only parameters whose values are changed in the experiments.

We assume that late starters are endowed with an initial capital stock equal to the steady-state level associated with the classical model of Section 2.1. For the purpose of determining the date at which an economy starts to use the modern growth function, it is not necessary that we fully specify the population growth function of the late starters. In particular, it is not necessary to specify the population growth function for consumption levels sufficiently greater than the constant consumption level, c_m, associated with the pre-1700 period. For consumption levels below this, we use a population growth function with a sufficiently large and positive slope at c_M and for which $g(c_M) = (1+\gamma_M)^{1/(1-\phi-\mu)}$. These assumptions ensure that the living standard in a late starter is roughly constant prior to the period it begins its transition.

Table 2 reports the efficiency of the early starter relative to the late starter required to generate a 100-year, a 200-year, and a 250-year delay in the transition to modern economic growth. These delays roughly represent the difference in the start of the transition to modern economic growth between England and Mexico, England and Japan, and England and India. As Table 2 shows, the factor difference in efficiency needed for a given delay decreases as the capital share in the modern production function increases. The size of the required difference needed to delay the start of development for

Table 2
Required factor difference in relative efficiencies for delays

θ	1800 start	1900 start	1950 start
0.40	1.60	3.2	5.7
0.50	1.25	2.5	4.0
0.60	1.20	2.2	3.3
0.70	1.18	1.9	2.5

250 years is plausible for all values of θ in Table 2, with $\theta = 0.40$ probably at the lower bound of plausible values.

4.2. No catch-up after the transition in many countries

A number of countries, many of which are located in Latin America, began modern economic growth toward the end of the nineteenth century. By and large, these countries have failed to eliminate the gap with the leader over the twentieth century. We now examine whether the model can account for this feature of the data. In particular, we seek to determine if the model predicts a narrowing of the gap between a country's income level and the level of the leader once that country begins the transition to modern economic growth.

We address this question by examining whether the model absent any subsequent changes in relative efficiencies predicts a narrowing or widening of the gap between income levels between early and late starters. In particular, we compute the equilibrium paths of per capita output over the 1700 to 2050 period for the model economies associated with the required differences in relative efficiencies listed in Table 2. We also report their asymptotic income levels relative to the leader.

Before undertaking these experiments, it is necessary to address two issues. First, it is necessary to specify the population growth rate function for the late starters in these experiments because increases in population affect the size of the increases in per capita output over the transition. For this specification, we simply use the post-1800 population growth rates of Mexico for the model economy that starts its transition in 1800, the post-1900 population growth rates of Japan for the model economy that starts its transition in 1900, and the post-1950 population growth rates of India for the model economy that starts its transition in 1950. These population growth data are taken from Lucas (2002, Table 5.1). Second, for capital share values that reflect a broad concept of capital, it is necessary to adjust output by the amount of investment in intangible capital. This adjustment must be made in order to compare the predictions of the model with the national income and product accounts, because the latter fail to measure investments in intangible capital. Thus, GDP in the national accounts corresponds to $Y - X_I$ in the model economy.

A country's unmeasured investment as a fraction of its measured output can be determined given the decomposition of the capital share between its physical capital and intangible capital components. For a given total capital share, the physical capital component can be calibrated to the ratio of investment in physical capital to measured GDP in the leader countries of roughly 20 percent. In particular, the individual share parameter values can be calibrated to the steady state of the modern growth-only economy using this observation from the leader countries.

With values of the individual share parameters in the modern growth production function in hand, it is possible to compute the amount of unmeasured investment in any period along an economy's equilibrium path. Table 3 reports the size of the intangible capital share parameter and the asymptotic ratio of intangible capital investment to GDP for each of the total capital share values considered in Table 2. As the total capital share increases, both the intangible capital share and the intangible capital investment share of GDP increase. The sizes of the unmeasured investment shares range from 0.0 for $\theta = 0.40$ to 0.62 for $\theta = 0.70$.

Figure 8 plots the path of per capita GDP for late starters relative to the leader over the 1700–2050 period. The paths correspond to the case where $\theta = 0.40$. The paths are essentially the same for the other capital share values. For reasons of space, they are omitted in this chapter. Asymptotically, the model is just the steady state of the modern growth model of Section 2.2, and so income differences are just $(E_S^i/E_S^j)^{1/(1-\theta)}$. For the 1800 starter, the asymptotic relative income level is 50 percent of the leader, for the 1900 starter, it is 16 percent, and for the 1950 starter it is 6 percent.

Most of the difference in relative incomes in 2000 is the consequence of the poor country starting the development process later. However, even after starting to develop, a late starter's disparity with the leader increases, although at a much slower rate than before. There are two reasons for this. First, the disparity continues to increase because the traditional production function is still widely used at the start of the transition and the growth rate of TFP associated with the traditional production function is lower than the growth rate of TFP associated with the modern production function. Second, the population growth in these countries tends to be higher compared to the leader over the comparable period. The disparity with the leader stops increasing only after the modern production function starts being used on a large scale. For the 1800 starter, the disparity stops increasing around 1900. For the 1900 starter, the disparity stops increasing

Table 3
Implied intangible capital share and investments

θ	θ_I	$X_I/(Y - X_I)$
0.40	0.00	0.00
0.50	0.28	0.26
0.60	0.41	0.41
0.70	0.53	0.62

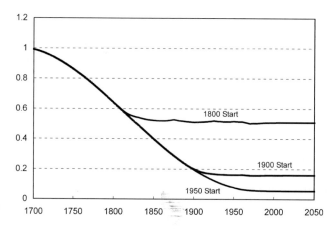

Figure 8. Predicted income per capita relative to the leader.

around 2000. And for the 1950 starter, the disparity stops increasing around 2050.[24]
The increase in disparity over the 1950–2000 period for the 1950 starter is consistent
with the fact that many sub-Saharan countries have fallen further behind the leader in
the 1950–2000 period despite experiencing absolute increases in living standards over
this period.

Laggards do experience larger increases in their income over their transition periods
compared to earlier starters. For example, the country that starts its transition in 1700
realizes a factor increase of 1.2 in its per capita income by 1750. In comparison, the
country that starts its transition in 1900 realizes a factor increase of 2 in its per capita
income over the next 50 years.[25] The reason for this difference is that the growth rate of
knowledge associated with the modern production function is initially low, but rises over
time. Thus, TFP growth in the modern production function over a late starter's transition
period is higher than an earlier starter's transition period. This gives late starters an
inherent advantage.

The data needed to verify whether this pattern exists are not readily available because
per capita income estimates going back to the eighteenth century exist for only a limited
number of countries. Thus, it is not possible to say whether transition periods have
become shorter over time. There is, however, strong evidence that late starters have
been able to double their incomes in far shorter time periods than earlier starters.

Figure 9 documents this general pattern. It plots the number of years a country took
to go from 10 percent to 20 percent of the 1985 U.S. per capita income level versus
the first year that country achieved the 10 percent level. The 1985 U.S. level was 2,000

---

[24] This is a key difference between our formulation and that of Ngai (2004). Ngai examines the effect of
policy on the starting date within Hansen and Prescott's overlapping generations model. In contrast, she finds
that some part of the income gap will be eliminated once poor countries start their transitions.
[25] This assumes the same population growth functions for both economies.

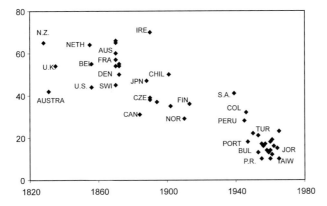

Figure 9. Years for income per capita to grow from 2,000 to 4,000 (1990 $US). *Source*: Maddison (1995) and Summers and Heston (1991).

in 1990 dollars. The set of countries considered had at least 1 million people in 1970 and had achieved and sustained per capita income of at least 10 percent of the 1985 U.S. level by 1965. There are 56 countries that fit these criteria and for which data are available. Of these 56 countries, all but four managed to double their per capita income by 1992. The four exceptions all had protracted armed insurgencies that disrupted their development.

The difference in the length of the doubling period between the sets of late and early starters is dramatic. For early starters, which are those achieving 10 percent of the 1985 U.S. level before 1950, the median length of the doubling period is 45 years. For late starters, defined as those achieving 10 percent of the 1985 U.S. level after 1950, the median length of the doubling period is 15 years. The choice of starting level is not important. A similar pattern emerges when the starting level is fixed at 5 percent and at 20 percent of the 1985 U.S. level.

Although the model absent changes in relative efficiency infers an advantage to late starters, quantitatively it is inconsistent with the number of years in which many late starters have been able to double their income. Many late starters that doubled their income in less than a 35-year period after 1950 did in fact narrow the gap with the leader over that period. The unified theory absent changes in relative efficiencies does not predict any catch-up for late starters. For the theory to account for this catch-up, it must consider changes in relative efficiency in a given country over time.

4.3. Catch-up and growth miracles

We now examine whether the theory can account for the record of catch-up. A key feature of the evolution of international income levels is that many countries have been able to narrow the gap with the leader, with some realizing large increases in output relative to the leader in a relatively short period of time. A number of countries, primarily located in Western Europe, caught up to the leader in the post–World War II period. A number of other countries primarily located in Southeast Asia eliminated a large fraction of their gap with the leader in this period. Some of these countries had miraculous growth experiences doubling their living standards in less than a decade in the post-1950 period. These growth miracles are a relatively recent phenomenon and are limited to countries that were relatively poor prior to undergoing their miracle. No country at the top of the income distribution has increased its per capita income by a factor of 4 in 25 years, and the leader has always taken at least 80 years to quadruple its income.

To account for the catch-up, including growth miracles, the theory requires an increase in the efficiency of a country relative to the leader.[26] In light of the Parente and Prescott (2000) theory, these changes in relative efficiency are easy to understand. Namely, they reflect policy changes. Following an improvement in policy that leads to a significant and persistent increase in efficiency, the theory predicts that the income of a late starter will go from its currently low level relative to the leader to a much higher level. As it does, its growth rate will exceed the rate of modern growth experienced by the leader, and the gap between its income and the leader's income will be narrowed.

We now consider an increase in a late starter's relative efficiency. In particular, we examine whether the unified theory can account for the growth miracle of Japan. Figure 10 depicts the path of per capita output for the Japanese and U.S. economies over the 1900–1995 period. There is really nothing special about Japan relative to other economies that similarly experienced growth miracles. It would have been just as easy to study the cases of other growth miracle countries such as China, South Korea, and Taiwan in this experiment. The precise time period of the Japanese growth miracle we consider in the analysis is the 1957–1969 period. We choose this period because by 1957 Japan had fully recovered from the wartime disruptions. Moreover, this period is one of the most dramatic in terms of Japan's catch-up. In this 12-year period, per capita GDP doubled from 25 percent of the leader to 50 percent of the leader. [See Summers and Heston (1991).] This catching-up was not the result of the leader's growth rate slowing down. Indeed, U.S. per capita GDP grew by 40 percent in this period. The Japanese economy in this period is a dramatic example of catching up.

The experiment assumes an unexpected increase in 1957 in the relative efficiency of the model economy, which started its transition in 1900, to the level of the leader. This assumption is made because the data suggest that Japan in the 1957–1969 period was converging to the U.S. balanced growth path. In calculating the equilibrium path of the model economy following this increase, we take the initial population to be the population corresponding to the equilibrium path of the model economy that starts the transition in 1900. The initial capital stock is assumed to be such that per capita GDP

---

[26] Additionally, an increase in efficiency can hasten the start of the transition to modern growth for countries that have not already begun this phase of development.

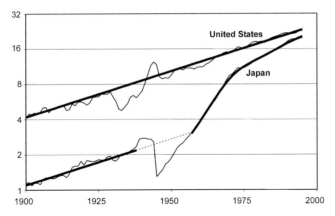

Figure 10. Income per capita 1900–1995 (1990 $US). *Source*: Maddison (1995) and Summers and Heston (1991).

relative to the leader equals 25 percent.[27] The population growth rate function for the model economy is the same as before and is based on Japanese population dynamics.

The important finding is that the total capital share must be large for an economy to take 12 years to move from 25 percent to 50 percent of the leader. Figure 11 plots the path of per capita GDP predicted by the model economy over this period for various values of θ. For a value of θ equal to 0.40, the predicted path shows too large an increase over the period. At the other end of the range, namely, $\theta = 0.70$, the predicted path shows too small an increase over this time period. This leads us to conclude that capital share values in the range from 0.55 to 0.65 are consistent with growth miracles.[28]

It is possible to introduce this increase in efficiency in the poor country at a much earlier date, say in 1800. The theory does not, however, predict that the poor country will experience a growth miracle. The theory, therefore, is consistent with the fact that growth miracles are a relatively recent phenomenon. Growth miracles are a relatively recent phenomenon because, as Figure 8 shows, differences in relative incomes between the low-efficiency and high-efficiency countries widen over time before leveling off. This widening is due to growth in the stock of pure knowledge associated with the modern production function, which the high-efficiency country uses from a very early date. Thus, as one goes back in time, the gap that a low-efficiency country could close by becoming a high-efficiency country becomes smaller and smaller. Obviously, if the gap is less than 50 percent, the low-efficiency country could never double its income in less than a decade. For the same reason, the unified theory is consistent with the fact

---

[27] In the case where capital is broadly defined, we assume the initial mix of physical and intangible capital is optimal in the sense that returns would be equal.

[28] There are a number of reasons capital's share may be somewhat less than 0.60. For one, we abstracted from leisure. For another, we abstracted from household durables. For an in-depth discussion of this issue, see Parente and Prescott (2000).

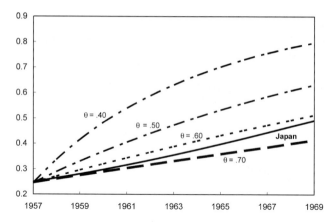

Figure 11. Growth miracles: income per capita as fraction of the leader. *Source*: Summers and Heston (1991).

that late starters have been able to double their incomes in far shorter times compared to early starters.

The theory is also consistent with the fact that growth miracles are limited to countries that were initially poor at the time their miracles began. Growth miracles are limited to this set of countries because a growth miracle in the theory requires a large increase in a country's relative efficiency. A large increase in efficiency can only occur in a poor country with a currently low efficiency parameter. This rules out a rich country, which by definition uses its resources efficiently, from having a growth miracle.

4.4. Unmeasured investment

For capital share values that are consistent with the evolution of international income levels, the implied size of unmeasured investment is between 35 and 55 percent of GDP. An important question is whether these intangible capital investment share numbers are plausible. This is not an easy question to answer. The difficulty in coming up with measures of the size of intangible capital investment is that the national income and product accounts (NIPA) treat investments in intangible capital as ordinary business expenses. Such investments, therefore, are not measured.

To better understand this, consider the case where a firm hires computer instructors for $100 to train its workers to use the latest software. This expenditure of $100 by the firm clearly represents an investment in the stock of intangible capital. It is not included in GDP in the national accounts. In terms of the national accounts, the $100 is the payment to the instructors, and so enters the income side of the national accounts under compensation to employees. However, since the expenditure is treated as an ordinary business expense, the firm's accounting profits are lowered by $100, and corporate profits in the national accounts are lowered by $100. These entries exactly offset each other so the transaction has no effect on either the income side or the output side of the national accounts. The investment in intangible capital, thus, goes unmeasured.

Parente and Prescott (2000) attempt to estimate the size of intangible capital investment in the U.S. economy by examining micro evidence of the size of the investments that firms and people make in intangible capital. In constructing their estimates, Parente and Prescott (2000) use the principle implied by theory that *investment* is any allocation of resources that is designed to increase future production possibilities. Using this principle, they identify such activities as starting up a new business, learning-on-the-job, training, education, research and development, and some forms of advertising as investments in intangible capital.[29] They conclude that the size of this investment may be as large as 50 percent of GDP. Such estimates are consistent with capital share values between one-half and two-thirds.

5. Catching up

The implication of the theory is that countries will be rich if they do not constrain production units as to which technologies can be operated and the manner in which a given technology can be operated. Currently poor countries will catch up to the industrial leader in terms of production efficiency if existing barriers to efficient production are eliminated and an arrangement is set up to ensure that barriers will not be re-erected in the future. The removal of such constraints is a necessary condition for catching up. As discussed in Section 3, there is strong evidence that suggests that these constraints exist to protect the interests of industry groups vested in the current production process. As such, their removal is likely to be contentious. For this reason, it is instructive to examine the record on catch-up in greater depth for the purpose of determining the circumstances under which barriers to efficient use of technology were reduced and catching up with the efficiency leader occurred.

5.1. Catch-up facts

Catching up is not uniform across regions, as can be seen in Figure 1. Latin American countries began modern economic growth in the late nineteenth century, and this set has not subsequently closed the living standard gap with the industrial leader; the per capita income of this set remained at roughly 25 percent of the industrial leader throughout the twentieth century. In comparison, Asian countries with the exception of Japan began modern economic growth later. This set of countries experienced significant catch-up in the last half of the twentieth century.

The large Western European countries, namely, Germany, Italy, and France, caught up to the industrial leader in the post–World War II period after trailing the leader for

---

[29] McGrattan and Prescott (2000) also noted that intangible investments are sizable. McGrattan and Prescott (2004) estimate a stock of intangible capital for the corporate sector equal to 0.65 times GDP. If rates of depreciation on tangible and intangible capital are comparable, then the size of intangible investment in the corporate sector is nearly 10 percent of GDP.

100 years. Modern economic growth in these countries began about 1840. At that time, their living standard was about 60 percent of the industrial leader, which at that time was the United Kingdom. For nearly 100 years, these countries maintained an income level that was about 60 percent that of the industrial leader. In the post–World War II period, output per hour worked in these countries, which is a good measure of living standards because it recognizes the value of nonmarket time, increased from 38 percent of the U.S. level in 1950 to 73 percent in 1973 and to 94 percent in 1992. Per capita output in Western Europe is still lower than the U.S. level, but this difference is accounted for by differences in the fraction of time that people work in the market, and not in the efficiency with which resources are used.

Another important example of catching up is the U.S. development experience in the 1865–1929 period. In 1870, U.K. per capita GDP was nearly a third higher than that of the United States. By 1929, the United Kingdom's per capita GDP was a third lower than that of the United States. The dramatic growth performance of the United States in this period is an important fact that needs to be explained.

5.2. Reasons for catching up or not catching up

5.2.1. The United States

We begin with the question of why the United States caught up with and surged past the United Kingdom in the 1865–1929 period. Our answer to this question is that the United Sates was and continues to be a free trade club, while the United Kingdom was not a member of a free trade club in this earlier period. Our definition of a *free trade club* is as follows. A set of states constitutes a free trade club if it meets two conditions. Member states cannot impose tariffs and other restrictions on the import of goods and services from other member states. In addition, member states must have a considerable degree of economic sovereignty from the collective entity. Just as no single state is able to block the movement of goods between states, the collective entity cannot block the adoption of a superior technology in one of its member states. Thus, a free trade club in our definition is far more than a set of countries with a free trade agreement.

The 50 United States certainly satisfy these two conditions, and thus, are a free trade club. The individual state governments have a considerable degree of sovereign power over the federal government. Additionally, the interstate commerce clause gives the federal government the right to regulate interstate commerce and prevent individual states from imposing tariffs and other restrictions on the import of goods and services. With the formation of the North American Free Trade Agreement and the recent approval of the free trade agreements with Chile and Singapore, the set of states constituting the free trade club to which the United States as a whole belongs may be getting larger.[30]

---

[30] The United States was probably more of a free trade club in the 1865–1929 period compared to the post-1929 period. This is because the interstate commerce clause was interpreted in the earlier period to mean that states could not interfere with interstate commerce. After 1929, the interpretation changed when the meaning of the clause was broadened to allow the federal government to regulate interstate commerce.

A free trade club, which prohibits individual states from discriminating against the goods produced in other member states and against producers from other member states operating within their borders, has the advantage that industry insiders in the various member states face elastic demand for what they supply. As a consequence, they are not hurt by the adoption of more efficient production methods as the increase in output leads to an increase in the employment of the factor they supply in that industry. If demand were inelastic, an increase in efficiency would lead to a fall in employment, something that industry insiders would strongly oppose.[31] Thus, a free trade club provides less incentive for groups of factor suppliers to form insider groups and block the adoption of more efficient technologies.

A free trade club need not be composed of individual democratic states, as is the case with the United States. However, in democratic states with legislatures representing districts, vested interests in other districts have a limited ability to block the adoption of technology in a given district if the citizens of the given district want that technology adopted. In the United States, for example, Toyota was able to locate an automobile plant with its just-in-time production in Kentucky in 1985. Those with vested interests in the less efficient technology in Michigan and other states with a large automotive industry were not able to prevent this from happening. The people in Kentucky wanted the large construction project and the high paying jobs in the automobile factory in their state. In 1995 political pressure mounted to block the import of luxury automobiles from Japan. Toyota responded by building plants in other states, including Indiana and West Virginia in 1998 and Alabama and Texas in 2003. These location decisions were as much politically motivated as economically motivated, and Toyota is close to being the third largest automobile producer in North America.

5.2.2. Western Europe

Western Europe caught up to the United States in terms of labor productivity in the 1957–1993 period for the same reason. With the creation of the European Union, Western Europe became an equally important free trade club. Its states enjoy even greater sovereignty than do U.S. member states. The German state cannot block the Toyota introduction of just-in-time production in Wales even though German politicians would if they could in response to domestic political pressure. If Toyota starts gaining market share, it will not be long before the auto industry throughout Europe adopts the superior technology, and productivity in the automobile industry increases. This is just competition at work.

The historical statistics lend strong empirical support to the theory that a trading club arrangement results in greater efficiency of production. Table 4 reports labor productivity defined as output per work hour for the original members of what became the

---

[31] Dowrick and Spencer (1994) review empirical literature that finds union resistance to the adoption of labor-saving innovations occurs within an industry when employment and wages will fall as the result of the adoption of the innovation. They go on to establish conditions under which this will and will not occur.

Table 4
Labor productivities of European Union members as a percentage
of U.S. productivity[a]

Year	Original members	Members joining in 1973
1870	62	
1913	53	
1929	52	
1938	57	
1957	53	57
1973	78	66
1983	94	76
1993	102	83
2002	101	85

[a]The prewar numbers are population weighted labor productivity numbers from Maddison (1995). The postwar numbers are also population weighted and were obtained from Maddison's Web page, http://www.eco.rug.nl/GGDC/index-series.html#top.

European Union and the labor productivity of members that joined in the 1970s and 1980s. Productivities are reported for an extended period before the EU was formed as well as for the period subsequent to its creation.

The Treaty of Rome was signed in 1957 by Belgium, France, Italy, Netherlands, Luxembourg, and West Germany to form the union. In 1973 Denmark, Ireland, and the United Kingdom joined. In 1981 Greece joined, followed by Portugal and Spain in 1986. They were followed by Austria, Finland, and Sweden in 1995. In 2004, the EU was expanded from 15 to 25 countires as Cyprus, the Czech Republic, Estonia, Hungary, Latvia, Lithuania, Malta, Poland, Slovakia and Slovenia joined.

One striking fact is that prior to forming the European Union, the original members had labor productivity that was only half that of the United States. This state of affairs persisted for over 60 years with no catching up. However, in the 36 years after forming what became the EU, the Treaty of Rome signers caught up with the United States in terms of labor productivity. The factor leading to this catch-up is an increase in the efficiency with which resources are used in production. Changes in capital/output ratios are of little significance in accounting for the change in labor productivity.[32] Productivity of the EU countries that joined in 1973 has also been catching up to the U.S. level since these countries joined the EU.

Another interesting comparison is between the productivity performance of the set of original EU members and the set of Western European countries that either joined in 1995 or still have not joined the EU. This latter set consists of Switzerland, Austria,

[32] See Prescott (2002).

Table 5
Labor productivity of other Western European countries as a percentage
of original EU members[a]

Year	Others/Original
1900	103
1913	99
1938	103
1957	106
1973	96
1983	85
1993	81

[a]The prewar figures are from Maddison (1995). For this period, GDP
per capita is used as a proxy for productivity. The postwar numbers are
also population weighted and were obtain from Maddison's Web page,
http://www.eco.rug.nl/GGDC/index-series.html#top.

Finland, and Sweden.[33] We label this set of four countries the *others*. Table 5 reports
labor productivities of the others to the original EU countries.

The important finding is that the original EU countries and the others are equally
productive in the pre–World War II period. In the 36 years from 1957 to 1993, the
others fell from 1.06 times as productive as the original EU countries to only 0.81 times
as productive in 1993. This constitutes strong empirical evidence that membership in
the EU fosters higher productivity.

If history is any guide, the 10 newest EU members will narrow the productivity gap
with the original EU members and the United States. Some of these countries such as the
Czech Republic, Hungary, Poland, and Slovakia, have a considerable amount of catching up to do. Maddison (2001, p. 337) estimates that their per employee GDP, which is
a good proxy for productivity, was about 40 percent of Western Europe in 1998. Others
do not. Cyprus, Malta, and Slovenia, already have relatively high GDP per capita and
have little catching up to do. They are all small countries that are highly economically
integrated with Western European states and have been de facto members of the Western
European trading club for a number of years. Countries that are economically integrated
with other sovereign states can be rich, even if no formal treaty exists.

5.2.3. Latin America

Latin American countries failed to catch up because they have failed to develop into a
free trade club. For this reason, Latin American per capita income has remained at the
same level relative to the leader for the last century. There is no free movement of goods

---

[33] Norway is not included in this set of countries because of the large size of its oil industry.

and people between the set of relatively sovereign states. A consequence of this is that often industry insiders in the sovereign states face inelastic demand for their products or services, and this leads them to block the adoption of more efficient production practices. If Latin American countries were to decentralize and restrict the authority of their central governments to be like the United States in the 1865–1929 period, then they too would quickly become as rich as Western Europe and the United States, or maybe richer.

5.2.4. Southeast Asia

The reasons for catch-up in Asia are slightly more involved. Countries such as South Korea, Taiwan, and Japan were forced to adopt policies that did not block efficient production as a condition for support from the United States. Further, the need to finance national defense made protecting those with vested interests in inefficient production too expensive to South Korea and Taiwan. These development miracles along with the Hong Kong and Singapore growth miracles made it clear to the people of the democratic states in the region that the policy that their elected representatives followed mattered for their living standard. Their elected representatives had no choice but to cut back on protecting industry insiders with vested interests in inefficient production or be voted out of office.

5.2.5. China

The recent catching up done by China is primarily a result of it becoming a free trade club. The rapid development of China began in 1978 when the Chinese government became more decentralized, with much of the centralized planning system dismantled. Although the central government gave more power to regional governments, it did not give the regional governments the right to restrict the flow of goods across regions. In fact, when individual regions attempted to erect trade barriers in the late 1980s and early 1990s, the central government immediately took steps to restore the free flow of goods and services.[34] The resulting competition between businesses in various provinces led to rapid growth in living standards.

5.2.6. Russia

While China's performance since its transition to capitalism has been spectacular, the same cannot be said for Russia's performance since its transition to capitalism. Whereas China has closed some of its income gap with the leader, Russia has fallen further behind the leader. Between 1985 and 1998, Russia's per capita GDP fell from 30 percent to 22 percent of the U.S. level. [See Heston, Summers and Aten (2002, p. 62).] Why has Russia failed to catch up to the leader following its switch to capitalism?

[34] See Young (2000).

Russia is not a free trade club and does not belong to a free trade club. It is not economically integrated with Western Europe. It is large enough both in terms of population and land that its regions could make up a free trade club. However, this is not the case. Local and regional governments in Russia have the power to discriminate against producers from other member states operating within their borders and to restrict the flow of goods and people into and out of their region. For example, in response to the financial crisis of August 1988, regional governments prohibited exports of food goods from their regions and put in place price ceilings for many of those items. Regional governments further have the discretion to use federal funds for purposes they see fit. Often, these funds are used to keep inefficient industries afloat. Local governments also have control over the use and privatization of land. There are essentially no land and real estate markets. In general, the purchase of land and the conversion of nonindustrial structures for new commercial activity are not possible. During the privatization phase, local governments refused to lease any property that had not been used commercially.[35]

6. Concluding remarks

Will the whole world be rich by the end of the twenty-first century? The implication of the theory reviewed in this essay is that a country will catch up to the leading industrial countries only if it eliminates the constraints relating to the use of technology. Although it is clear what a country must do to become rich, it is not clear whether a country will have either the political will or political power to make the necessary reforms. Removal of the constraints to the efficient use of resources is bound to be contentious, because such constraints typically exist to protect specialized groups of factor suppliers and corporate interests. As recent events in Argentina show, these groups can topple a government.

The historical record of catch-up suggests that joining a free trade club is an important way by which a society can eliminate barriers that were erected to protect specialized groups of factor suppliers and corporate interests and reduce the likelihood that such groups will seek similar protection in the future. The expansion of the European Union as well as the recent U.S. free trade agreements with Central American countries, Chile, Singapore, and Australia are encouraging events. These events show that more and more regions are gaining the political will to reduce these constraints. However, many other regions of the world, particularly Africa, the Indian subcontinent, and South America, still lack this will.

Why one country has this will and another does not is an important open question. As a first step toward answering it, it is imperative that economists better understand how it

---

[35] Parente and Ríos-Rull (2005) document the greater prevalence of specialized groups of factor suppliers in Russia compared to China, and the successful efforts by local governments in Russia to prevent the adoption of better technologies.

is that constraints to the efficient use of resources come to be imposed on a society in the first place. Some progress is being made in this area. Grossman and Helpman (1994), Holmes and Schmitz (1995, 2001), Krusell and Ríos-Rull (1996, 2002), McDermott (1999), Bridgman, Livshits and MacGee (2001), Kocherlakota (2001), Parente and Ríos-Rull (2005), Samaniego (2001), Teixeira (2001) and Parente and Zhao (2003) all deal with this issue to some degree. In our view, this will continue to be an important research area in the years to come.

Acknowledgements

The second author thanks the National Science Foundation and the University of Minnesota Foundation for research support. The views expressed herein are those of the authors and not necessarily those of the Federal Reserve Bank of Minneapolis or the Federal Reserve System.

References

Bairoch, P. (1993). Economics and World History: Myths and Paradoxes. University of Chicago Press, Chicago.
Becker, G.S. (1960). "An economic analysis of fertility". In: Easterlin, R. (Ed.), Demographic and Economic Change in Developed Countries, Universities–National Bureau Conference Series, vol. 11. Princeton University Press, Princeton, NJ, pp. 209–240.
Becker, G.S., Murphy, K.M., Tamura, R. (1990). "Human capital, fertility, and economic growth". Journal of Political Economy 98, S12–S37.
Bridgman, B., Livshits, I., MacGee, J. (2001). "For sale: Barriers to riches". Unpublished Manuscript. Federal Reserve Bank of Minneapolis.
Clark, G. (1998). "Nominal and real male agricultural wages in England, 1250–1850". Unpublished Manuscript. University of California, Davis.
Djankov, S., La Porta, R., Lopez-de-Silanes, F., Shleifer, A. (2002). "The regulation of entry". Quarterly Journal of Economics 117, 1–37.
Doepke, M. (2000). "Fertility, income distribution, and growth". Doctoral Dissertation. University of Chicago.
Dowrick, S., Spencer, B.J. (1994). "Union attitudes to labor-saving innovation: When are unions Luddites?". Journal of Labor Economics 12, 316–344.
Galor, O., Weil, D.N. (2000). "Population, technology, and growth: From Malthusian stagnation to the demographic transition and beyond". American Economic Review 90, 806–828.
Gollin, D. (2002). "Getting income shares right". Journal of Political Economy 110, 458–474.
Grossman, G.M., Helpman, E. (1994). "Protection for sale". American Economic Review 84, 833–850.
Hall, R.E., Jones, C.I. (1999). "Why do some countries produce so much more output per worker than others?". Quarterly Journal of Economics 114, 83–116.
Hansen, G.D., Prescott, E.C. (2002). "Malthus to Solow". American Economic Review 92, 1205–1217.
Hendricks, L. (2002). "How important is human capital for development? Evidence from immigrant earnings". American Economic Review 92, 198–219.
Hendricks, L. (2003). "Taxation and the intergenerational transmission of human capital". Journal of Economic Dynamics and Control 27, 1639–1662.
Herrendorf, B., Teixeira, A. (2003). "Monopoly rights can reduce income big time". Working Paper. University of Carlos III.

Heston, A., Summers, R., Aten, B. (2002). Penn World Table, version 6.1. Center for International Comparisons at the University of Pennsylvania (CICUP).

Hoffman, P.T. (1996). Growth in a Traditional Society: The French Countryside, 1450–1815. Princeton University Press, Princeton, NJ.

Holmes, T.J., Schmitz, J.A. Jr. (1995). "Resistance to new technology and trade between areas". Federal Reserve Bank of Minneapolis Quarterly Review 19, 2–17.

Holmes, T.J., Schmitz, J.A. Jr. (2001). "A gain from trade: From unproductive to productive entrepreneurship". Journal of Monetary Economics 47, 417–446.

Hornstein, A., Prescott, E.C. (1993). "The firm and the plant in general equilibrium theory". In: Becker, R., Boldrin, M., Jones, R., Thomson, W. (Eds.), General Equilibrium, Growth, and Trade II: The Legacy of Lionel McKenzie. Academic Press, San Diego, CA, pp. 393–410.

Johnson, D.G. (2000). "Population, food, and knowledge". American Economic Review 90, 1–14.

Klenow, P.J., Rodriguez-Clare, A. (1997). "Economic growth: A review essay". Journal of Monetary Economics 40, 597–617.

Kocherlakota, N.R. (2001). "Building blocks for barriers to riches". Staff Report 288. Federal Reserve Bank of Minneapolis.

Krusell, P., Ríos-Rull, J.-V. (1996). "Vested interests in a positive theory of stagnation and growth". Review of Economic Studies 63, 301–329.

Krusell, P., Ríos-Rull, J.-V. (2002). "Politico-economic transition". Review of Economic Design 7, 309–329.

Kuznets, S. (1966). Modern Economic Growth. Yale University Press, New Haven, CT.

Lucas, R.E. Jr. (2002). Lectures on Economic Growth. Harvard University Press, Cambridge, MA.

Maddison, A. (1991). Dynamic Forces in Capitalist Development: A Long-Run Comparative View. Oxford University Press, Oxford.

Maddison, A. (1995). Monitoring the World Economy: 1820–1992. Organisation for Economic Co-Operation and Development, Paris.

Maddison, A. (2001). The World Economy: A Millennial Perspective. Organisation for Economic Co-operation and Development, Paris.

Malthus, T.R. (1798). First Essays on Population. Macmillan, London. Republished in 1966.

McDermott, J. (1999). "Mercantilism and modern growth". Journal of Economic Growth 4, 55–80.

McGrattan, E.R., Prescott, E.C. (2000). "Is the stock market overvalued?". Federal Reserve Bank of Minneapolis Quarterly Review 24, 20–40.

McGrattan, E.R., Prescott, E.C. (2004). "Taxes, regulations, and the value of U.S. and U.K. corporations". Staff Report 309. Federal Reserve Bank of Minneapolis.

Mokyr, J. (1990). The Lever of Riches: Technological Creativity and Economic Progress. Oxford University Press, Oxford.

Ngai, L.R. (2004). "Barriers and the transition to modern economic growth". Journal of Monetary Economics 51, 1353–1383.

Parente, S.L., Prescott, E.C. (1999). "Monopoly rights: A barrier to riches". American Economic Review 89, 1216–1233.

Parente, S.L., Prescott, E.C. (2000). Barriers to Riches. MIT Press, Cambridge, MA.

Parente, S.L., Ríos-Rull, J.-V. (2005). "The success and failure of economic reforms in transition economies". Journal of Money, Credit and Banking 37, 23–42.

Parente, S.L., Zhao, R. (2003). "Slow development and special interests." Manuscript. University of Illinois, submitted for publication in International Economic Review.

Prescott, E.C. (2002). "Prosperity and depression". American Economic Review 92, 1–15.

Ricardo, D. (1817). On the Principals of Political Economy and Taxation. J. Murray, London.

Samaniego, R.M. (2001). "Does employment protection inhibit technology diffusion?". Unpublished Manuscript. University of Pennsylvania.

Schmitz, J.A. Jr. (2001). "Government production of investment goods and aggregate labor productivity". Journal of Monetary Economics 47, 163–187.

Solow, R.M. (1970). Growth Theory: An Exposition. Oxford University Press, Oxford.

Summers, R., Heston, A. (1991). "The Penn World Table (mark 5): An expanded set of international comparisons, 1950–1988". Quarterly Journal of Economics 106, 327–368.

Tamura, R.F. (1988). "Fertility, human capital, and the 'Wealth of Nations'". Doctoral Dissertation. University of Chicago.

Teixeira, A. (2001). "Effects of trade policy on technology adoption and investment". Unpublished Manuscript.

Young, A. (2000). "The razor's edge: Distortions and incremental reform in the People's Republic of China". Quarterly Journal of Economics 115, 1091–1135.

PART V

TRADE AND GEOGRAPHY

Chapter 22

A GLOBAL VIEW OF ECONOMIC GROWTH

JAUME VENTURA

CREI and Universitat Pompeu Fabra

Contents

Abstract   1420
Keywords   1420
0. Introduction   1421
1. The integrated economy   1426
    1.1. A workhorse model   1426
    1.2. Diminishing returns, market size and economic growth   1430
    1.3. The effects of economic integration   1436
2. Specialization, trade and diminishing returns   1442
    2.1. Economic growth in autarky   1444
    2.2. Factor price equalization   1446
    2.3. Formal aspects of the model   1454
    2.4. Limits to structural transformation (I): factor proportions   1456
    2.5. Limits to structural transformation (II): industry productivities   1464
3. Transport costs and market size   1472
    3.1. Nontraded goods and the cost of living   1473
    3.2. Agglomeration effects   1481
    3.3. The role of local markets   1487
4. Final remarks   1490
Acknowledgements   1492
References   1492

Handbook of Economic Growth, Volume 1B. Edited by Philippe Aghion and Steven N. Durlauf
DOI: 10.1016/S1574-0684(05)01022-1

Abstract

This paper integrates in a unified and tractable framework some of the key insights of the field of international trade and economic growth. It examines a sequence of theoretical models that share a common description of technology and preferences but differ on their assumptions about trade frictions. By comparing the predictions of these models against each other, it is possible to identify a variety of channels through which trade affects the evolution of world income and its geographical distribution. By comparing the predictions of these models against the data, it is also possible to construct coherent explanations of income differences and long-run trends in economic growth.

Keywords

economic growth, international trade, globalization

JEL classification: F10, F15, F40, F43, O11, O40, O41

All theory depends on assumptions that are not quite true. That is what makes it theory. The art of successful theorizing is to make the inevitable assumptions in such a way that the final results are not very sensitive. A "crucial" assumption is one on which the conclusions do depend sensitively, and it is important that crucial assumptions be reasonably realistic. When the results of a theory seem to flow specifically from a special crucial assumption, then if the assumption is dubious, the results are suspect.

Robert M. Solow (1956, p. 65)

0. Introduction

The world economy has experienced positive growth for an extended period of time. Figure 1 plots average world per capita income from 1500 to today, using data from Maddison's classic study of long run trends in the world economy. The most salient feature of the growth process is its nonlinear nature. For most of the past five hundred years, the world economy settled in a path of stagnation with little growth. But sometime around the early nineteenth century the world economy entered a path of sustained and even accelerating growth. While per capita income grew only by eighteen percent from 1500 to 1820, it has then grown by more than seven hundred and fifty percent from 1820 to today. And this growth has been far from steady. It averaged 0.53 percent from 1820 to 1870, and more than doubled to 1.30 from 1870 to 1913. Growth declined to 0.91 percent during the turbulent period that goes from 1913 to 1950, and then exploded to an unprecedented 2.93 percent from 1950 to 1973. Since then growth has markedly declined to 1.33 percent, even though this period still constitutes the second best growth performance in known human history.

This economic growth has not been distributed equally across the different regions of the world economy. Figure 2 shows per capita income growth for the different regions of the world economy in various time periods. Differences in regional growth experiences are quite remarkable.[1] Growth took off in Western Europe and its offshoots in the early nineteenth century and never stopped again. But other regions took longer to participate in the growth of the world economy. Perhaps the most dramatic case is that of Asia, which basically did not grow until 1950 just to become then the fastest growing region in the world. Another extreme case is that of Africa, which still today is unable to enjoy growth rates that would be considered modest in other regions. Another salient feature of the growth process is therefore its uneven geographical distribution: in each period there are some regions that have been able to grow and prosper, while others have been left behind.

---

[1] To get a sense of the magnitudes involved, remember that an annual growth rate of G leads per capita income to multiply itself by a factor $F \approx \exp\{GT\}$ in T years. For instance, in the last quarter of the twentieth century Asia has been able to increase its per capita income by a factor of 2.5, while Latin America has only managed to increase its per capita income by a factor of 1.2 and Africa has stagnated. Even a cursory look at the data shows that this disparity in growth performances constitutes the norm rather than the exception.

World per capita GDP

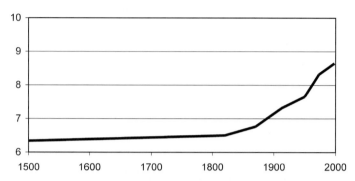

Figure 1. World per capita GDP. *Notes.* This figure shows the dynamics of world per capita GDP for the selected years 1500, 1820, 1870, 1913, 1950, 1973 and 1998 (in log of 1990 US$). Data are from Angus Maddison, "The World Economy – A Millennial Perspective", Table 3-1b, p. 126.

World economic growth has been accompanied by more than proportional growth in world trade. Figure 3 shows the evolution of world trade as a share of world production since 1870. The picture is quite clear: from 1870 to 1998 growth in world trade has quadrupled growth in world income. There also appears to be a strong positive correlation between growth in per capita income and growth in trade. Figure 4 plots the growth rates of these two variables against each other using pooled data from various regions and periods. The simple correlation between these variables is 0.64, and the regression results indicate that regions and periods with X percent higher than average trade growth tend to have per capita income growth which is $0.3X$ higher than average. It almost goes without saying that this statistical association between income and trade does not imply causation in any direction. But it strongly suggests that these variables are somehow related, and that there might be substantial payoffs to working with theories that jointly determine them.[2]

Despite this apparent relationship between income and trade, a substantial part of growth theory is built on the assumption that countries live in autarky and that there is no trade among them.[3] This is obviously a dubious assumption. But is it also a "crucial" one? And if so, what alternative assumptions would be reasonably realistic? At an abstract level, these are the questions that I attempt to answer here. A recurring theme throughout this chapter is that the growth experiences of the different world regions are

[2] For empirical work on the (causal) effect of trade on income levels and income growth see Sachs and Warner (1995), Frankel and Romer (1999), Ades and Glaeser (1999), Alesina, Spolaore and Wacziarg (2000) and their chapter in this Handbook, Rodriguez and Rodrik (2000), Alcalá and Ciccone (2003, 2004) and Dollar and Kraay (2003).

[3] A brief examination of the different chapters of this Handbook should quickly convince anyone doubting this statement.

Per capita GDP Growth

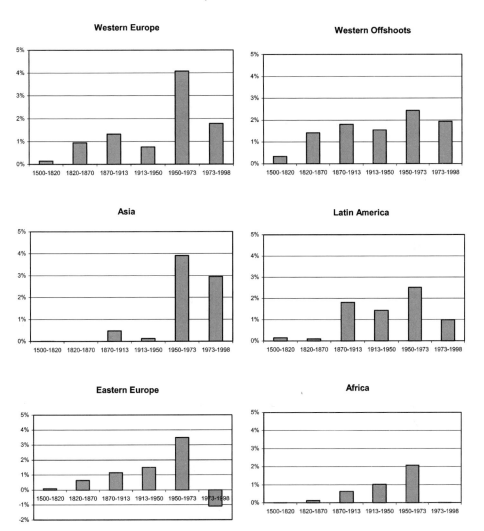

Figure 2. Per capita GDP growth. *Notes.* This figure shows average annual growth rates by major world regions for selected periods. Data are derived from Angus Maddison, "The World Economy – A Millennial Perspective", Table 3-1b, p. 126. (Western Europe contains Austria, Belgium, Denmark, Finland, France, Germany, Italy, Netherlands, Norway, Sweden, Switzerland, UK, Portugal, Spain, Greece and 13 small countries; Western Offshoots are United States, Canada, Australia and New Zealand; Asia is China, India, Japan, Korea, Indonesia, Indochina, Iran, Turkey and Other East and West Asian countries; Latin America includes Brazil, Mexico, Peru, and others; Eastern Europe contains Albania, Bulgaria, Hungary, Poland, Romania and territories of former Czechoslovakia and Yugoslavia; Africa is Egypt and others.)

World Exports as Share of World GDP

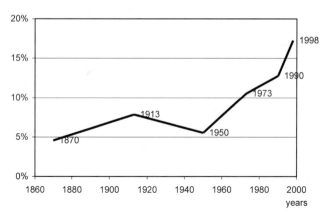

Figure 3. World exports as share of world GDP. *Notes.* The figure shows volume of world exports over world GDP (in constant US$) for selected dates. Data are from Tables 3-1b, A1-b, A2-b, A3-b, A4-b, pp. 126, 184, 194, 214 and 223 in Angus Maddison, "The World Economy – A Millennial Perspective".

Growth of Income and Trade

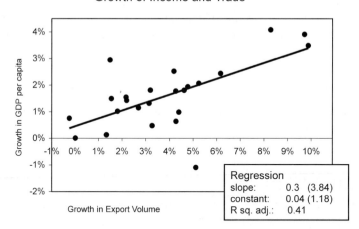

Figure 4. Growth of income and trade. *Notes.* This figure plots annualized rate of trade growth against annualized rate of per capita GDP growth for major world regions and selected periods. The regions are Western Europe, Western Offshoots, Eastern Europe and former USSR, Latin America, Asia and Africa. Periods are 1870–1913, 1913–1950, 1950–1973 and 1973–1998. Each data point stands for one region during one period. The solid line represents the prediction of a linear regression. The estimated regression are reported in the box, *t*-statistics are in brackets. Data are from Angus Maddison, "The World Economy – A Millennial Perspective". Data for GDP growth are obtained from Table 3-1b, p. 126, and Table B-10, p. 241 (to include Japan). Data for export growth are derived from Table F-3, p. 362, and Tables A1-b, A2-b, A3-b and A4-b, pp. 184, 194, 214 and 223, respectively.

intimately linked and cannot be analyzed in isolation. We therefore need a global view of economic growth that looks at the different regions of the world as parts of a single whole. Formally, this means that we should develop and systematically study world equilibrium models. These models and their predictions constitute the specific focus of this chapter.[4]

Rather than providing an all-encompassing survey of the field, my goal in writing this chapter has been to develop a unified and yet tractable framework to discuss key insights of the fields of international trade and economic growth. In particular, I examine a sequence of world equilibrium models that share a common description of technology and preferences but differ on their assumptions about trade frictions. By comparing the predictions of these models against each other, it is possible to identify a variety of channels through which trade affects the evolution of world income and its geographical distribution. By comparing their predictions against the data, it is also possible to construct coherent explanations of income differences and long run trends in economic growth. When viewed as a group, these models show that much is known about the relationship between income and trade. Despite this, I still feel we are only exploring the tip of the iceberg. The research program sketched here is ambitious, fun and it could eventually lead to a much deeper understanding of the forces that drive modern capitalist economies.

The rest of this chapter contains four sections. The first one describes growth in the integrated economy. This is an imaginary world where trade costs are negligible and geography does not matter. Section 2 introduces two trade frictions: the immobility of production factors and the absence of international financial markets. Section 3 adds

---

[4] Without doubt, the seminal book by Grossman and Helpman (1991c) is the single most influential contribution to the development and study of world equilibrium models of the growth process. It heavily influenced a whole generation of PhD students, like myself, that were searching for dissertation topics when the book first appeared. But there are, of course, many other important contributions. The bibliography at the end of this chapter is an (admittedly imperfect) attempt to list all published papers that use world equilibrium models to study the growth process. See Acemoglu (2003), Acemoglu and Zilibotti (2001), Aoki (1986), Arnold (2002), Backus, Kehoe and Kydland (1992), Baldwin (1992), Baldwin and Forslid (2000), Baldwin, Martin and Ottaviano (2001), Bardham (1965a, 1965b, 1966), Baxter (1992), Brems (1956, 1970), Buiter (1981), Chang (1990), Chui, Levine and Pearlman (2001), Cuñat and Mafezzoli (2004b), Devereux and Lapham (1994), Devereux and Saito (1997), Dinopoulos and Segerstrom (1999), Dinopoulos and Syropoulos (1997), Dollar (1986), Feenstra (1996), Findlay (1978, 1980), Findlay and Kierzkowski (1983), Fisher (1995), Flam and Helpman (1987), Francois (1996), Frenkel and Razin (1985, 1986), Gale (1971), Galor and Polemarchakis (1987), Gancia (2003), Glass and Saggi (1998, 2002), Greenwood and Williamson (1989), Grossman and Helpman (1989, 1990, 1991a, 1991b), Heathcote and Perri (2002), Helpman (1993), Jensen and Thursby (1987), Krugman (1979, 1981, 1991a), Lai (1995, 1998), Loayza, Knight and Villanueva (1993), Matsuyama (2004b), Modigliani and Ando (1963), Molana and Vines (1989), Mountford (1998), Myers (1970), Obstfeld (1989), Ono and Shibata (1991), Puga and Venables (1999), Rauch (1991), Rivera-Batiz and Romer (1991), Ruffin (1979), Sauré (2004a, 2004b), Segerstrom, Anant and Dinopoulos (1990), Şener (2001), Sibert (1985), Stokey (1991), Taylor (1993, 1994), van Elkan (1996), van de Klundert and Smulders (1996, 2001), Vanek (1971), Wang (1990), Yanagawa (1996), Yang and Maskus (2001) and Young (1991, 1995). I apologize to the authors of any relevant paper that has been overlooked.

a third trade friction: costs of transporting goods. The fourth and final section briefly concludes by taking stock what we have learned and pointing out potential avenues for further research.

1. The integrated economy

Imagine a world without borders, a world in which all goods and factors can be transported across different regions at negligible cost. Some industries spread their production process across many regions searching for the ideal environment for each specific phase of production. Other industries choose instead to concentrate production in a single region to exploit increasing returns to scale. Regardless of an industry's particular circumstances, its location choice maximizes productivity and is not affected by the local availability of production factors and/or final customers. If a region does not have the necessary production factors, these can be imported from abroad. If a region does not have enough customers, the goods produced can be exported abroad. In this world, global market forces arbitrage away regional differences in goods and factor prices and all the gains from trade are reaped. This imaginary world is the integrated economy, and is the subject of this section.

The integrated economy provides a natural benchmark for the study of economic growth in an interdependent world. Moreover, its simplicity and elegance encapsulates the essence of what growth theory is all about: deriving strong results using minimalist models. In the spirit of the so-called "new growth theory", I shall use a model that jointly determines the stock of capital and the level of technology. Admittedly, the model is somewhat lopsided. On the one hand, it contains a fairly sophisticated formulation of technology that includes various popular models as special cases. On the other hand, it uses a brutal simplification of the standard overlapping-generations model as a description of preferences. Despite this, I do not apologize for the imbalance. A robust theme in growth theory is that the interesting part of the story is nearly always on the technology side, and rarely on the side of preferences.

This section develops the basic framework that I use throughout the chapter. Section 1.1 describes the integrated economy, while Section 1.2 derives its main predictions for world growth. Section 1.3 goes back to a period in which all the regions of the world lived in autarky, and compares the growth process of this world with the integrated economy. This is just the first of various attacks to the question of globalization and its effects on the world economy.

1.1. A workhorse model

Consider a world economy inhabited by two overlapping generations: young and old. The young work and, if productive, they earn a wage. The old retire and live off their savings. All generations have size one. There are many final goods used for consumption and investment, indexed by $i \in I$. When this does not lead to confusion, I shall use I

to refer both to the set of final goods and also to the number of final goods. As we shall see later, the production of these final goods requires a continuum of intermediate inputs. There are two factors of production: labor and capital. For simplicity, I assume capital depreciates fully within one generation.[5] The world economy contains many regions. But geography has no economic consequences since goods and factors can be transported from one region to another at any time at negligible cost.

The citizens of this world differ in their preferences and access to education. S_t members of the generation born in date t are patient and maximize the expected utility of old age consumption, while the rest are impatient and maximize the expected utility of consumption when young. The utility function has consumption as its single argument, and it is homothetic, strictly concave and identical for all individuals. H_t members of the generation born in date t can access education and become productive, while the rest have no access to education and remain unproductive.[6] I refer to S_t and H_t as "savings" and "human capital", and I allow them to vary stochastically over time within the unit interval. Assuming that savings and human capital are uncorrelated within each generation, we obtain

$$K_{t+1} = S_t w_t H_t, \tag{1}$$

$$C_t = (1 - S_t)w_t H_t + r_t K_t, \tag{2}$$

where K_t and C_t are the average or aggregate capital stock and consumption, and w_t and r_t are the wage and rental rate of capital. Equation (1) states that the capital stock equals the savings of the young, which consist of the wage of those that are patient and productive. The assumption that capital depreciates fully in one generation implies that the capital stock is equal to investment. Equation (2) says that consumption equals the wage of the impatient and productive young plus the return to the savings of the old.[7]

Consumption and investment can be thought of as composites or aggregates of the different final goods. A very convenient assumption is that both composites take the same Cobb–Douglas form with spending shares that vary across industries, i.e. σ_i with $\sum_{i \in I} \sigma_i = 1$. Since there is a common ideal price index for consumption and investment, it makes sense to use it as the numeraire and this implies that aggregate spending

---

[5] The main role of this assumption is to ensure that investment is always strictly positive. This simplifies the presentation without substantially affecting the main results.

[6] The assumption that labor productivity is either one or zero is extreme, but inessential. We could also think of H_t as the average labor productivity of the world economy. The assumption that human capital is not industry specific is widespread, but not entirely innocent. See Basu and Weil (1998) and Brezis, Krugman and Tsiddon (1993) for interesting implications of relaxing this assumption.

[7] This representation of savings and consumption is nothing but a stripped-down version of Modigliani's life-cycle theory of savings. It abstracts from other motives for savings such as leaving bequests. These could be easily re-introduced in the theory through suitable and well-known modifications of the preferences of individuals. I shall not do this to keep the analysis as simple as possible. I conjecture that the bulk of the basic intuitions and results presented here would not be meaningfully affected by these extensions.

is given by $E_t \equiv C_t + K_{t+1}$. To sum up, we have that

$$E_{it} = \sigma_i E_t \quad \text{for all } i \in I, \tag{3}$$

$$1 = \prod_{i \in I} \left(\frac{P_{it}}{\sigma_i}\right)^{\sigma_i}, \tag{4}$$

where E_{it} and P_{it} are the total spending on and the price of the final good of industry i. Equation (3) states that spending shares are constant, while Equation (4) sets the common price of consumption and investment equal to one.

Production of final goods uses labor, capital and a continuum of different varieties of intermediate inputs, indexed by $m \in [0, M_{it}]$ for all $i \in I$. As usual, I interpret the measure of input varieties, M_{it} for all $i \in I$, as the degree of specialization or the technology of the industry. This measure will be determined endogenously as part of the equilibrium. The technology of industry i can be summarized by these total cost functions:

$$B_{it} = \left[\frac{1}{Z_{it}}\left(\frac{w_t}{1-\alpha_i}\right)^{1-\alpha_i}\left(\frac{r_t}{\alpha_i}\right)^{\alpha_i}\right]^{1-\beta_i}$$

$$\times \left[\int_0^{M_{it}} p_{it}(m)^{1-\varepsilon_i}\, dm\right]^{\beta_i/(1-\varepsilon_i)} Q_{it} \quad \text{for all } i \in I, \tag{5}$$

$$b_{it}(m) = \frac{1 + q_{it}(m)}{Z_{it}}$$

$$\times \left(\frac{w_t}{1-\alpha_i}\right)^{1-\alpha_i}\left(\frac{r_t}{\alpha_i}\right)^{\alpha_i} \quad \text{for all } m \in [0, M_{it}] \text{ and } i \in I, \tag{6}$$

where $0 \leqslant \beta_i \leqslant 1$, $\varepsilon_i > 1$ and $0 \leqslant \alpha_i \leqslant 1$, Q_{it} is total production of final good i, $q_{it}(m)$ and $p_{it}(m)$ are the quantity and price of the mth input variety of industry i, and the variables Z_{it} are meant to capture the influence on industry productivity of geography, institutions and other factors that are exogenous to the analysis.[8] I loosely refer to the Z_{it}'s as "industry productivities" and assume they vary stochastically over time within a support that is strictly positive and bounded above. Equation (5) states that the technology to produce the final good of industry i is a Cobb–Douglas function on human and physical capital, and intermediate inputs. The latter are aggregated with a standard CES function. Equation (6) states that the production of intermediates is also a Cobb–Douglas function on human and physical capital, and that there are fixed and variable costs.[9] I interpret the fixed costs as including both the costs of building a specialized production plant and the costs of inventing or developing a new variety

---

[8] Although popular, this is a quite simplistic view of the effects of geography and institutions. See Levchenko (2004) for an interesting discussion of alternative ways of modeling the effects of institutions.

[9] As usual, the fixed cost is paid if and only if there is strictly positive production.

of intermediate. An important simplifying assumption is that input varieties become obsolete in one generation and, as a result, all generations must incur these fixed costs.[10]

Since there are constant returns in the production of final goods, it is natural to assume that final good producers operate under perfect competition. Therefore, prices and intermediate input demands are given as follows:

$$P_{it} = \frac{\partial B_{it}}{\partial Q_{it}} \qquad \text{for all } i \in I, \tag{7}$$

$$q_{it}(m) = \frac{\partial B_{it}}{\partial p_{it}(m)} \qquad \text{for all } m \in [0, M_{it}] \text{ and } i \in I. \tag{8}$$

Equation (7) states that price equals marginal cost, while Equation (8) uses Shephard's lemma to describe the demand for intermediate inputs. Equations (5) and (8) imply that an increase in the price of a given input variety lowers its market share. But Equation (3) shows that the lost market share goes entirely to other input varieties of the same industry and does not affect the industry's overall market share.

Since the production of intermediate inputs exhibits increasing returns that are internal to the firm, input producers cannot operate under perfect competition. I assume instead they operate under monopolistic competition with free entry. This has the following implications:

$$p_{it}(m) = \frac{e_{it}(m)}{e_{it}(m) - 1} \frac{\partial b_{it}(m)}{\partial q_{it}(m)} \qquad \text{for all } m \in [0, M_{it}] \text{ and } i \in I, \tag{9}$$

$$p_{it}(m) q_{it}(m) = b_{it}(m) \qquad \text{for all } m \in [0, M_{it}] \text{ and } i \in I, \tag{10}$$

where $e_{it}(m)$ is the price-elasticity of input demand $e_{it}(m) = -\frac{p_{it}(m)}{q_{it}(m)} \frac{\partial q_{it}(m)}{\partial p_{it}(m)}$ with the derivative in this definition being applied to Equation (8). Equation (9) states that monopolistic firms charge a markup over marginal cost that is decreasing on the demand elasticity faced by the firm. As usual, the CES formulation implies that this demand elasticity is equal to the elasticity of substitution among inputs, i.e. $e_{it}(m) = \varepsilon_i$. Equation (10) states that profits must be zero and this is, of course, a direct implication of assuming free entry.

Finally, we must impose appropriate resource constraints or market-clearing conditions

$$P_{it} Q_{it} = E_{it} \qquad \text{for all } i \in I, \tag{11}$$

$$H_t = \sum_{i \in I} H_{it} \qquad \text{with } H_{it} = \frac{\partial B_{it}}{\partial w_t} + \int_0^{M_{it}} \frac{\partial b_{it}(m)}{\partial w_t} \, dm, \tag{12}$$

$$K_t = \sum_{i \in I} K_{it} \qquad \text{with } K_{it} = \frac{\partial B_{it}}{\partial r_t} + \int_0^{M_{it}} \frac{\partial b_{it}(m)}{\partial r_t} \, dm, \tag{13}$$

[10] This assumption is crucial for tractability, since it eliminates a potentially large set of state variables, i.e. M_{it} for all $i \in I$.

where H_{it} and K_{it} are the labor and capital demanded by industry i. Since the integrated economy is a closed economy, Equation (11) forces the aggregate supply of each good to match its demand, while Equations (12)–(13) state that the aggregate supply of labor and capital must equal their demands. The latter are the sum of their industry demands, and these are calculated using Shephard's lemma.

This completes the description of the model. For any admissible initial capital stock and sequences for S_t, H_t and Z_{it}, an equilibrium of the integrated economy consists of sequences of prices and quantities such that Equations (1)–(13) hold in all dates and states of nature. The assumptions made ensure that this equilibrium always exists and is unique. I shall show this by construction in the next section.

The reader might be wondering why I have not formally introduced financial markets. I have allowed individuals to construct their own capital and use it as a vehicle to carry on their savings into retirement (a world of family-owned firms?). But I have not allowed them to trade securities in organized financial markets. The reason is simply to save notation. The assumptions made ensure that asset trade does not matter in this world economy.[11] To see this, assume there exist sophisticated financial markets where all individuals can trade a wide array of state-contingent securities. Naturally, the old would not be able to trade these securities since they will not be back to settle claims one period later. But the young would not trade with each other either. Impatient young would not be willing to trade securities since they do not have income in their old age and are happy to consume all their income during their youth. Patient young are the only ones willing and able to trade these securities. But they all have identical preferences and face the same distribution of returns to capital, and therefore they find no motive to trade with each other. Thus, we can safely assume the integrated economy contains sophisticated financial markets that allow individuals to enter contracts that specify exchanges of various quantities of the different goods to be delivered at various dates and/or states of nature. It just happens that these financial markets do not make any difference for consumption and welfare.

1.2. Diminishing returns, market size and economic growth

To study the forces that determine economic growth in the integrated economy, it is useful to start with a familiar expression

$$\frac{K_{t+1}}{K_t} = s_t \frac{Q_t}{K_t}, \tag{14}$$

---

[11] This statement is not entirely correct. It applies to assets whose price reflects only fundamentals, but without additional assumptions it does not apply to securities whose price contains a bubble. I shall disregard the possibility of asset bubbles in this chapter, although this is far from an innocuous assumption. See Ventura (2002) for an example where asset bubbles have an important effect on the growth of the world economy and its geographical distribution.

where Q_t is the integrated economy's output or production, i.e. $Q_t \equiv \sum_{i \in I} P_{it} Q_{it}$ and s_t is the economy's (gross) savings rate, i.e. $s_t \equiv K_{t+1}/Q_t$. Equation (14) states that the (gross) growth rate of the capital stock is equal to the savings rate times the output–capital ratio or average product of capital. If this product stays above one asymptotically, the world economy exhibits sustained or long run growth. Otherwise, economic growth eventually ceases and the world economy stagnates. We shall study then the determinants of savings and the average product of capital.

To compute the savings rate, remember that industry i receives a share σ_i of aggregate spending of which a fraction $1 - \alpha_i$ goes to labor. Adding across industries, it follows that aggregate labor income is $w_t H_t = (1 - \alpha) Q_t$, where α is the aggregate or average share of capital, i.e. $\alpha \equiv \sum_{i \in I} \sigma_i \alpha_i$. Since only the patient young save, the savings rate consists of the fraction of labor income in the hands of patient consumers

$$s_t = (1 - \alpha) S_t. \tag{15}$$

Since the savings rate is less than one, sustained economic growth requires that the average product of capital remain above one as the economy grows. But what determines the aggregate output–capital ratio? I shall answer this question in a few steps, so as to develop intuition.

The first step consists of finding the output–capital ratio of a given industry as a function of its technology and factor proportions,[12]

$$\frac{Q_{it}}{K_{it}} = \left(\frac{\varepsilon_i}{\varepsilon_i - 1} \right)^{-\beta_i} M_{it}^{\beta_i / (\varepsilon_i - 1)} Z_{it} \left(\frac{K_{it}}{H_{it}} \right)^{\alpha_i - 1} \quad \text{for all } i \in I. \tag{16}$$

Equation (16) shows the effects of changes in factor proportions on the industry's output–capital ratio, *holding constant technology*. Since there are diminishing returns to physical and human capital in production, we find the standard result that increases in the physical to human capital ratio reduce the output–capital ratio. But technology is endogenously determined in this model, and it depends on the size of the industry,[13]

$$M_{it} = \frac{\beta_i}{\varepsilon_i} Z_{it} H_{it}^{1-\alpha_i} K_{it}^{\alpha_i} \quad \text{for all } i \in I. \tag{17}$$

Equation (17) shows that increases in factor usage or industry size raise the incentives to specialize and therefore improve technology. The larger is the size of the market, the easier it is to recoup the fixed costs of producing a new input variety and therefore the higher is the number of input varieties that can be sustained in equilibrium. We can now

---

[12] From Equations (7) and (11) find that $P_{it} Q_{it} = B_{it}$, and use this to eliminate B_{it} from Equation (5). Then, solve Equation (9) with Equation (6), substitute into Equation (5) and eliminate factor prices by noting that the industry factor shares, i.e. $w_t H_{it} / P_{it} Q_{it}$ and $r_t K_{it} / P_{it} Q_{it}$ are given by $1 - \alpha_i$ and α_i, respectively.

[13] Symmetry of intermediates and perfect competition in the final goods industry implies that $M_{it} p_{it} q_{it} = \beta_i P_{it} Q_{it}$, where p_{it} and q_{it} are the common price and quantity of all varieties of intermediates of industry i. Then, use Equations (6), (9) and (10) to eliminate p_{it} and q_{it} from this expression. Finally, eliminate factor prices once again by noting that the industry factor shares are $1 - \alpha_i$ and α_i.

put these two pieces together and write the output–capital ratio as follows,

$$\frac{Q_{it}}{K_{it}} = A_{it} H_{it}^{\mu_i(1-\alpha_i)} K_{it}^{\mu_i\alpha_i-1} \quad \text{for all } i \in I, \tag{18}$$

where μ_i is a measure of the importance of market size effects, i.e. $\mu_i = 1+\beta_i/(\varepsilon_i-1)$ and A_{it} is a measure of industry productivity, i.e. $A_{it} = (\frac{\varepsilon_i}{\varepsilon_i-1})^{-\beta_i}(\frac{\beta_i}{\varepsilon_i})^{\beta_i/(\varepsilon_i-1)}Z_{it}^{\mu_i}$. I shall refer to both Z_{it} and A_{it} as "industry productivities" when this is not a cause for confusion. Equation (18) summarizes the aggregate industry technology and shows direct and indirect effects of factor usage on the industry's output–capital ratio. Increases in human capital raise the output–capital ratio, as the direct positive effect of making physical capital scarce is reinforced by the indirect effect of increasing input variety. Increases in physical capital have an ambiguous effect on the output–capital ratio, as the direct negative effect of making physical capital abundant and the positive indirect effect of increasing input variety work in opposite directions. If diminishing returns are strong and market size effects are weak ($\mu_i\alpha_i < 1$) increases in physical capital reduce the industry's output–capital ratio. If instead diminishing returns are weak and market size effects are strong ($\mu_i\alpha_i \geqslant 1$) increases in physical capital raise the industry's output–capital ratio.

The next step is to aggregate these effects across industries. To do this, note first that factor allocations and aggregate output are determined as follows:[14]

$$H_{it} = \sigma_i \frac{1-\alpha_i}{1-\alpha} H_t \quad \text{for all } i \in I, \tag{19}$$

$$K_{it} = \sigma_i \frac{\alpha_i}{\alpha} K_t \quad \text{for all } i \in I, \tag{20}$$

$$Q_t = \prod_{i\in I} Q_{it}^{\sigma_i}. \tag{21}$$

Equations (19) and (20) show that the equilibrium allocations of human and physical capital to industry i depend on the corresponding factor share and the size of the industry. Equation (21) says that output is a Cobb–Douglas aggregate of industry outputs. This is, of course, the production function associated with the cost function in Equation (4). It is now immediate to substitute Equations (18), (19) and (20) into Equation (21) to find the aggregate output–capital ratio of the world economy

$$\frac{Q_t}{K_t} = A_t H_t^{\mu(1-\alpha)-\upsilon} K_t^{\mu\alpha+\upsilon-1}, \tag{22}$$

---

[14] Equations (19) and (20) are direct implications of the constant factor and spending shares. One way to think about Equation (21) is as the definition of the Cobb–Douglas aggregate that defines consumption and investment and therefore underlies Equations (3) and (4). Another way of thinking about Equation (21) is as an implication of Equations (3), (4) and (11).

where μ is the average value of μ_i, i.e. $\mu \equiv \sum_{i \in I} \sigma_i \mu_i$, υ is the covariance between μ_i and α_i, i.e. $\upsilon \equiv \sum_{i \in I} \sigma_i (\mu_i - \mu)(\alpha_i - \alpha)$ and A_t is an aggregate measure of productivity, i.e. $A_t \equiv \prod_{i \in I} [\sigma_i^{\mu_i} (\frac{1-\alpha_i}{1-\alpha})^{\mu_i(1-\alpha_i)} (\frac{\alpha_i}{\alpha})^{\mu_i \alpha_i} A_{it}]^{\sigma_i}$. Equation (22) is the aggregate production function and will play an important role in what follows. It shows that the industry intuitions on the effects of changes in factor usage carry on to the aggregate effects of changes in factor supplies. While increases in human capital unambiguously raise the output–capital ratio, increases in physical capital have ambiguous effects.[15] If the "representative" industry has strong diminishing returns and weak market-size effects ($\mu\alpha + \upsilon < 1$) physical capital accumulation reduces the aggregate output–capital ratio. If instead the "representative" industry has weak diminishing returns and strong market-size effects ($\mu\alpha + \upsilon \geqslant 1$) physical capital accumulation raises the output–capital ratio.

We are ready now to characterize the process of economic growth in the integrated economy. Substituting Equation (22) into Equation (14), we obtain the following law of motion for the capital stock

$$K_{t+1} = s_t A_t H_t^{\mu(1-\alpha)-\upsilon} K_t^{\mu\alpha+\upsilon}. \tag{23}$$

Equation (23) shows that the integrated economy behaves as if it were a Solow model with a Cobb–Douglas production function that exhibits increasing returns to scale, i.e. the sum of the share coefficients is $\mu \geqslant 1$. Figures 5 and 6 illustrate the dynamics of the stock of physical capital with the help of two simple examples. The first example is the "deterministic" world where savings, human capital and productivity are constant over time, i.e. $\{s_t, H_t, A_t\} = \{s, H, A\}$ for all t. The second example is the "stochastic" world where savings, human capital and productivity fluctuate between a "bad" state with $\{s_t, H_t, A_t\} = \{s_B, H_B, A_B\}$ and a "good" state with $\{s_t, H_t, A_t\} = \{s_G, H_G, A_G\}$, with $s_G A_G H_G^{\mu(1-\alpha)-\upsilon} > s_B A_B H_B^{\mu(1-\alpha)-\upsilon}$. The central point of these examples is to show that economic growth solves a tension between diminishing returns and market size effects.

Figure 5 shows the case in which diminishing returns are strong and market-size effects are weak, i.e. $\mu\alpha + \upsilon < 1$. The top panel depicts the evolution of the "deterministic" world. There is a unique steady state and the stock of physical capital converges monotonically towards it from any initial position. The steady state is stable because increases (decreases) in the stock of physical capital lower (raise) the output–capital ratio and lead to a lower (higher) growth rate. The bottom panel shows that the "stochastic" world exhibits similar dynamics, with the stock of physical capital monotonically converging to a steady state interval, rather than a steady state value. Once the stock of physical capital is trapped within this interval, its growth rate fluctuates between positive and negative values and averages zero in the long run. These examples illustrate why sustained growth is not possible if diminishing returns are strong and market size effects are weak.

---

[15] Note that $\mu(1 - \alpha) - \upsilon \geqslant 0$.

The "deterministic" case

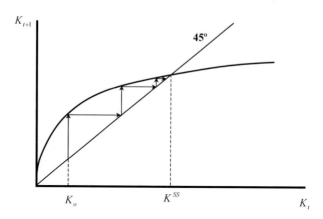

The "stochastic" case

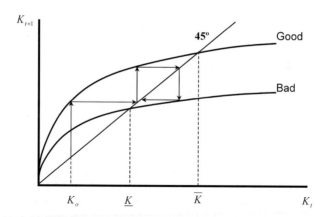

Figure 5. $\alpha\mu + \upsilon < 1$. *Notes.* This figure shows the case of strong diminishing returns and weak market size effects. In the top panel, the stock of physical capital converges monotonically to its unique steady state. The bottom panel shows the stochastic case, where the stock of physical capital converges to the steady state interval $[\underline{K}, \overline{K}]$ within which it fluctuates according to the states of the world.

Figure 6 shows the case in which diminishing returns are weak and market-size effects are strong, i.e. $\mu\alpha + \upsilon \geqslant 1$. The top panel shows the "deterministic" world again. There is unique steady state that is unstable. If the stock of physical capital starts above the steady state, it grows without bound at an accelerating rate. If it starts below, the stock of physical capital contracts over time also at an accelerating rate. The steady state is now unstable because increases (decreases) in the stock of physical capital raise

The "deterministic" case

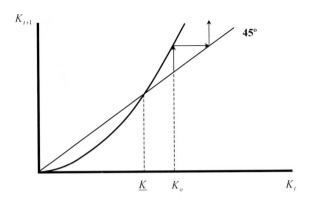

The "stochastic" case

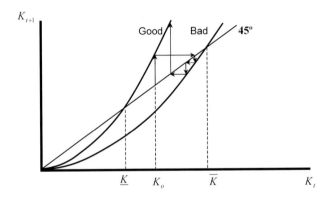

Figure 6. $\alpha\mu + \upsilon > 1$. *Notes.* This figure shows the case of weak diminishing returns and strong market size effects. In the top panel, the stock of physical capital grows at increasing rates since $K_o > \underline{K}$. In the bottom panel the stock of physical capital fluctuates between $\underline{K}$ and $\overline{K}$ according to the states of the world, until it eventually leaves this range.

(lower) the output–capital ratio and lead to a higher (lower) growth rate. The bottom panel shows that the "stochastic" world also exhibits similar dynamics. One difference however is that there is no steady state. Instead, there is a threshold interval. If the stock of physical capital is above (below) this interval, it grows (contracts) at an accelerating rate. If the stock of physical capital starts within the threshold interval, it fluctuates within it until it eventually exits. This happens with probability one, and only luck determines when this exit occurs and whether the world economy exits above and enters an expansionary path or, alternatively, it exits below and enters a contractionary path.

Therefore, sustained growth is possible (but not necessary) if diminishing returns are weak and market size effects are strong.

This model suggests a simple account of the history of the world economy since the 1500s. It is based on the "stochastic" world of Figure 6 and it goes as follows: for centuries, the size of the world economy was too small to generate sustained growth. Located within the threshold interval, the world economy was subject to periodic expansions and contractions with virtually zero average growth. This is consistent with Maddison's calculation that the world economy grew only about eighteen percent from 1500 to 1820. But this was an unstable situation in the very long run. The Industrial Revolution marks the moment in which, after a series of favorable shocks, the world economy reached enough size to exit the threshold interval and started traveling on the path of accelerating growth reported in Figure 1. As a result of this successful exit, the world economy grew more than seven hundred and fifty percent from 1820 to 1998.

Although suggestive, this account is far too sketchy and incomplete to be taken seriously. Moreover, I find highly improbable that the last five hundred years of the world economy can be understood in terms of a model that postulates negligible costs of transporting goods and factors and constant world population. Surely the demographic revolution and the process of globalization have both played central roles in shaping the growth process during this period. This chapter is not the place for a discussion of the growth effects of the demographic revolution.[16] But it is definitely the place to study the growth effects of globalization, and we turn to this topic next.

1.3. The effects of economic integration

Assume the world economy initially consisted of many regions or locations separated by geographical obstacles that made the costs of transporting goods and factors among them prohibitive. As a result, these regions were forced to live in autarky. I index these regions by $c \in C$, and let them differ on their savings, human capital, industry productivities and initial capital stock, i.e. on $S_{c,t}$, $H_{c,t}$, $Z_{c,it}$ and $K_{c,0}$. When this does not lead to confusion, I shall use C to refer to both the set of regions and also to the number of regions. Throughout, I denote world aggregates by omitting the region subindex. Typically, world aggregates refer to the sum of all corresponding regional variables. For instance, world aggregate savings, human and physical capital are $S_t = \sum_{c \in C} S_{c,t}$, $H_t = \sum_{c \in C} H_{c,t}$ and $K_t = \sum_{c \in C} K_{c,t}$. But there will be some exceptions. For instance, the relationship between $Z_{c,it}$ and the corresponding world aggregate Z_{it} is a bit more intricate and will be explained shortly.

---

[16] In this model, a sustained increase in population would generate sustained growth even if $\alpha\mu + \upsilon < 1$. The reason is that, holding constant both factor endowments and productivity, population growth increases the size of the market and this raises income. I have ruled out this possibility by simply assuming that the world population is constant. Given the purpose of this chapter, I think this is not a "crucial" assumption. But it might be so in other contexts. See Jones' chapter in this volume for a thorough and clear discussion of scale effects in growth models.

Although it is not really necessary to take a stand on the geographical distribution of population, I assume throughout that it is equally distributed across regions. This simplifies somewhat the presentation since absolute and per capita regional comparisons coincide. For instance, if $S_{c,t} > S_{c',t}$ then c also has higher savings per person than c'. Note also that, as the number of regions becomes arbitrarily large, the size of each of them becomes arbitrarily small and the effects of shocks to their characteristics on world aggregates become arbitrarily small. This limiting case is usually referred to as the small economy assumption.

The model of globalization considered here is embarrassingly simple: at date $t = 0$, all the geographical obstacles to trade suddenly disappear forever and the costs of transporting goods and factors fall from prohibitive to negligible. What are the effects of such a dramatic reduction in transport costs on world economic growth and its geographical distribution? To answer this question, we must characterize the growth process in the autarkic world economy and in the integrated world economy and compare them. Although this way of modeling globalization and its effects is almost a caricature, it turns out to be quite useful to develop intuitions that survive as we move to more sophisticated and realistic models.

In the world of autarky, each region constituted a smaller version of the integrated economy. Therefore, the world economy at $t < 0$ can be described by[17]

$$Y_{c,t} = A_{c,t} H_{c,t}^{\mu(1-\alpha)-\upsilon} K_{c,t}^{\mu\alpha+\upsilon} \qquad \text{for all } c \in C, \tag{24}$$

$$K_{c,t+1} = s_{c,t} A_{c,t} H_{c,t}^{\mu(1-\alpha)-\upsilon} K_{c,t}^{\mu\alpha+\upsilon} \qquad \text{for all } c \in C, \tag{25}$$

where $Y_{c,t}$ is the income of the region and, in autarky, it coincides with its production and spending, i.e. $Y_{c,t} = Q_{c,t} = E_{c,t}$ and $A_{c,t}$ is the corresponding measure of regional productivity, i.e. $A_{c,t} \equiv \prod_{i \in I} [\sigma_i^{\mu_i} (\frac{1-\alpha_i}{1-\alpha})^{\mu_i(1-\alpha_i)} (\frac{\alpha_i}{\alpha})^{\mu_i\alpha_i} A_{c,it}]^{\sigma_i}$ with $A_{c,it} = (\frac{\varepsilon_i}{\varepsilon_i-1})^{-\beta_i} (\frac{\beta_i}{\varepsilon_i})^{\beta_i/(\varepsilon_i-1)} Z_{c,it}^{\mu_i}$. Equations (24) and (25) have been discussed at length already and need no further comment.

In the integrated economy it is not possible in general to determine the production or spending located in a given region. Since goods and factors can move at negligible cost, any geographical distribution of production and factors that ensures all production takes place in the regions with the highest industry productivity is a possible equilibrium. Despite this indeterminacy, prices and aggregate quantities are uniquely determined as shown in Section 1.2. This means that it is possible to track the stock of physical capital owned by the original inhabitants of region c and their descendants as well as their

---

[17] Equation (25) is an analogue to Equation (23), while Equation (24) follows from the region counterparts to Equation (22) and the fact that $Y_{c,t} = Q_{c,t} = C_{c,t} + K_{c,t}$ in autarky.

income[18]

$$Y_{c,t} = \left[(1-\alpha)\frac{H_{c,t}}{H_t} + \alpha\frac{K_{c,t}}{K_t}\right] A_t H_t^{\mu(1-\alpha)-\upsilon} K_t^{\alpha\mu+\upsilon} \quad \text{for all } c \in C, \tag{26}$$

$$K_{c,t+1} = \frac{S_{c,t} H_{c,t}}{S_t H_t} s_t A_t H_t^{\mu(1-\alpha)-\upsilon} K_t^{\alpha\mu+\upsilon} \quad \text{for all } c \in C, \tag{27}$$

for all $c \in C$ and $t \geqslant 0$, and A_t is a measure of world productivity. Remember that we have now specified a set of industry productivities for each region, $Z_{c,it}$. But we only specified one set of industry productivities for the integrated economy in Section 1.1. The reason was that industries never locate in a region that offers less than the highest possible productivity. As a result, in the integrated world economy the only industry productivities that matter are the highest ones, i.e. $Z_{it} = \max_{c\in C}\{Z_{c,it}\}$. This implies that $A_t \geqslant A_{c,t}$ for all $c \in C$, and we can interpret aggregate productivity not as average productivity, but instead as the highest possible productivity or the world productivity frontier. With this in mind, Equation (27) traces the holdings of capital of the original inhabitants of region c and their descendants, while Equation (26) describes their income.

We are ready now to examine the growth effects of economic integration. Consider first the static or impact effects on the incomes of regions. A bit of straightforward algebra shows that[19]

$$\ln\left(\frac{Y_{c,0}^I}{Y_{c,0}^A}\right) = \underbrace{\ln\left(\frac{A_0}{A_{c,0}}\right)}_{\substack{\text{higher} \\ \text{productivity}}} + \underbrace{\ln\left(\frac{(1-\alpha)(H_{c,0}/H_0) + \alpha(K_{c,0}/K_0)}{(H_{c,0}/H_0)^{1-\alpha}(K_{c,0}/K_0)^\alpha}\right)}_{\substack{\text{improved factor} \\ \text{allocation}}}$$

$$+ \underbrace{\ln\left(\frac{H_0^{1-\alpha} K_0^\alpha}{H_{c,0}^{1-\alpha} K_{c,0}^\alpha}\right)^{\mu-1}}_{\substack{\text{increased} \\ \text{market size}}} \geqslant 0, \tag{28}$$

where $Y_{c,0}^I$ is the actual income of the inhabitants of region c at date $t = 0$, and $Y_{c,0}^A$ is the income they would have had at date $t = 0$ if globalization had not taken place. Since each of the terms in Equation (28) is nonnegative, the first result we obtain is that the overall impact or static gains from economic integration are nonnegative as well.

---

[18] Equation (26) follows from adding the income from human and physical capital of the inhabitants of the region, and noting that aggregate or world shares of human and physical capital are constant and equal to $1 - \alpha$ and α, respectively. Equation (27) follows from Equations (1) and (23), and the observation that wages are the same for all productive workers of the world. Without loss of generality, I keep assuming that there is no trade in securities.

[19] To derive this expression I have assumed a zero cross-industry correlation between α_i and μ_i, i.e. $\upsilon = 0$. This parameter restriction is useful because it allows us to unambiguously disentangle the "increased-market-size" and "improved-factor-allocation" effects.

These gains can be decomposed into three sources corresponding to each of the terms of Equation (28). The first one shows the growth of income that results from moving industries from low to high productivity locations. This term would vanish if region c had the highest productivity in all industries. The second term shows the growth of income that results from relocating factors away from those regions and/or industries in which they were abundant in autarky into those in which they were scarce. This term would vanish if region c had world average factor proportions. The third term shows the growth in income that is due to an increase in market size that allows industries to support a higher degree of specialization. This term would vanish if the size of region c were arbitrarily large with respect to the rest of the world. An implication of Equation (28) is that the static gains from economic integration are greater for regions with low productivity, extreme factor proportions and modest amounts of physical and human capital.

If coupled with an appropriate transfer scheme, globalization leads to a Pareto improvement in the world economy. Equation (28) shows that, with the same production factors, the integrated economy generates more output than the world of autarky. It is therefore possible to implement a transfer scheme that keeps constant the income of all current and future young and gives more income to all current and future old. Under this transfer scheme, investment and the stock of physical capital would be unaffected by economic integration. But the production and consumption of all generations born at date $t = 0$ or later would increase. Of course, there exist many alternative transfer schemes that ensure that globalization benefits all. Moreover, since each region gains from trade there exist Pareto-improving transfer schemes that can be implemented without the need for inter-regional transfers. That is, ensuring that globalization generates a Pareto improvement does not require compensation from one region to another.

How "large" the transfer scheme must be to ensure that economic integration leads to a Pareto improvement? The answer is "not much" if most of the gains from economic integration come from higher productivity and increased market size. The reason is that in this case all factors share in the gains from integration. The required transfer scheme could be "substantial" if the gains from integration come mostly from improved factor allocation. This is because within each region the owners of the abundant factor obtain more than proportional gains from integration while the owners of the region's scarce factor might have losses. In this case, implementing a Pareto improvement requires a transfer from the former to the latter.

Without a transfer scheme, it is relatively straightforward to trace the dynamic effects of economic integration. Assume for simplicity that the world contains many symmetric regions so that before integration all of them had the same law of motion. The top panel of Figure 7 shows the effects of economic integration in the "deterministic" world when diminishing returns are strong and market size effects are weak. Economic integration raises the steady state stock of physical capital and sets up a period of high growth that eventually ends. It is straightforward to see that the effects would be similar in the "stochastic" world, with economic integration permanently raising the steady state interval. Using the jargon of growth theory, if $\mu\alpha + \upsilon < 1$ economic integration has level effects

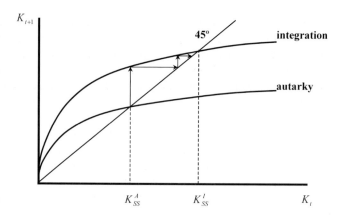

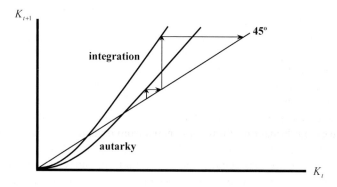

Figure 7. Effects of economic integration. *Notes.* This figure illustrates the effects of economic integration. The top panel shows that, if $\alpha\mu + \upsilon < 1$, economic integration has level effects on income. The bottom panel shows that, if $\alpha\mu + \upsilon > 1$, economic integration has growth effects on incomes.

on income. The bottom panel of Figure 7 shows the opposite case in which diminishing returns are weak and market size effects are strong. In this case, economic integration shifts down the steady state value, increasing the growth rate permanently. Once again, it is straightforward to see that the effects would be similar in the "stochastic" world, with trade shifting the threshold interval to the left. Using again the jargon of growth theory, if $\mu\alpha + \upsilon \geqslant 1$ integration has growth effects on income.

It is tempting now to revisit our earlier account of the history of the world economy since the 1500s, and propose an alternative version which is also based on the "stochastic" world with $\mu\alpha + \upsilon > 1$. It goes as follows: for centuries, the world economy consisted of a collection of autarkic regions that were too small to sustain economic growth. Located within the threshold interval, these regions were subject to periodic expansions and contractions with virtually zero average growth. Once again, this is consistent with Maddison's calculation that the world economy grew only about eighteen percent from 1500 to 1820. The Industrial Revolution occurs when a series of reductions in trade costs between some British regions raised their combined size above the threshold interval and set them on the path of accelerating growth. As time went on, more and more regions joined the initial core and the Industrial Revolution spread throughout Britain and moved into France, Germany and beyond. It is therefore a reduction of trade costs and the progressive extension of markets that made possible sustained growth and allowed the world economy to grow more than seven hundred and fifty percent from 1820 to 1998. This might also explain why this growth in world income was accompanied by an even higher growth in world trade.[20]

This view of the development process is also broadly consistent with the general observations about inequality between center and periphery discussed in the introduction. Regions that join the integrated economy (the "center") become rich and take off into steady growth. Regions that do not join the integrated economy (the "periphery") are left behind, technologically backward and capital poor. As more and more regions enter the integrated economy, those that are left behind become relatively poorer and world inequality increases. Eventually all regions will enter the integrated economy and world inequality will decline. Therefore, this model generates an inverted-U shape or Kuznets curve, with world inequality rising in the first stages of world development and declining later. Pritchett (1997), Bourguignon and Morrisson (2002) and others have shown that world inequality has increased from 1820 to now. It remains to be seen if this inequality will decline in the future.

This stylized model also illustrates some of the conflicts that globalization might create. It follows from Equation (28) that the gains from trade are large for regions whose factor proportions are far from the world average. Ceteris paribus, this means that regions in the center would like that new entrants into the integrated economy to move the world average factor proportions away from them. In fact, unless productivity and market size effects are substantial, the entry of a large region creates losses to other regions with similar factor proportions. This implies, for instance, that the Chinese process of economic integration should be seen with some concern in countries with similar factor proportions such as Mexico and Indonesia, but with hope in the European Union or the United States.

This view of globalization and growth leads to a powerful prescription for economic development: open up and integrate into the world economy. I believe this is a fundamentally sound policy prescription, and history is largely consistent with it. But there are a number of important qualifications that this stylized model cannot capture. Integrating into the world economy is not an "all-or-nothing" type of affair in which regions move overnight from autarky to complete integration. The process of economic integration is slow and full of treacherous steps. Obtaining general prescriptions for development in a world of imperfect integration has proved to be a much more challenging task. I shall

---

[20] The word "might" reflects the earlier observation that regional production and therefore trade is indeterminate in the integrated economy.

come back to this important point later, but we must first introduce trade frictions into the story.

2. Specialization, trade and diminishing returns

Let us revise our model of globalization. As in Section 1.3, assume that at date $t = 0$ the costs of transporting goods across regions suddenly fall from prohibitive to negligible. Unlike Section 1.3, assume now that the costs of transporting factors across regions remain prohibitive after date $t = 0$. An implication of this setup is that globalization equalizes goods prices across regions, but it does not necessarily equalize factor prices. This particular view of globalization has a longstanding tradition in trade theory and the goal of this section is to analyze it.

Assuming that human capital is immobile internationally is somewhat dubious, as there are some well-known examples of large contingents of people working overseas. But most of the results discussed here would go through with only minor changes under the weaker and reasonably realistic assumption that international flows of people are quantity constrained, although not necessarily at zero.[21] Assuming that physical capital is immobile is appropriate for buildings and structures and, probably, not too unreasonable for the most important types of machinery and equipment. Moreover, assuming that existing physical capital cannot be transported does not preclude physical capital to effectively "move" across regions over time, as it declines in some regions through depreciation and increases in others through investment.[22]

If physical capital is immobile, pieces of capital located in different regions might offer different return distributions. This opens up a role for financial markets. Although the old and the impatient young still have no incentive to trade securities, the patient young now have a motive. Those that are located in regions where physical capital offers an attractive distribution of returns want to sell securities and use the proceeds to finance additional purchases of domestic physical capital. Those patient young that are located in regions where physical capital offers an unattractive distribution of returns want to buy securities and reduce their holdings of domestic physical capital. And, regardless of their location, the patient young want to buy and sell securities in order to share regional risks. Thus, the immobility of physical capital creates a potentially important

---

[21] Of course, this becomes a weak or empty excuse if quantity constraints respond to economic incentives in a systematic way. See Lundborg and Segerstrom (2002) and Ortega (2004) for models in which this happens.

[22] Remember that we have assumed that physical capital depreciates in one generation. Therefore, assuming physical capital is immobile only means that it is not possible at date t to move around the stock of physical capital created and deployed at date $t - 1$, and that is being used for production at date t. But it is certainly possible to choose where to deploy the new stock of physical capital created at date t that will be used for production at date $t + 1$. The effects of physical capital immobility would be more severe quantitatively with a slower rate of depreciation. Note also that immobility matters only because physical capital is irreversible or putty-clay. In fact, it would be logically inconsistent to assume that physical capital is immobile if it could be converted back into mobile goods.

role for international financial markets: the geographical reallocation of investments and production risks.

Despite this, I will not let international financial markets play this role. This failure of financial markets could be due to technological motives or informational problems of various sorts. But I prefer instead to think of it as being caused by lack of incentives to enforce international contracts. In the integrated economy, individuals could enter into contracts that specify exchanges of various quantities of the different goods to be delivered at various dates and/or states of nature. It is standard convention to refer to the signing of contracts that involve only contemporaneous deliveries as "goods" trade, while the signing of contracts that involve future (and perhaps state contingent) deliveries is usually referred to as "asset" trade. Both types of trade require sufficiently low costs of transporting goods. But asset trade also requires that the signing parties credibly commit to fulfill their future contractual obligations. The domestic court system punishes those that violate contracts, thus creating the credibility or trust that serves as the foundation for domestic financial markets. But there is no international court system that endows sovereigns with the same sort of credibility, and this hampers international financial markets. I assume next this problem is so severe that it precludes all asset trade.

Unlike the integrated economy, in the world analyzed in this section each region's total production, spending and capital stock are always determined. Since trade balances and current accounts are zero, the income of each region equals the value of both its production and spending, i.e. $Y_{c,t} = Q_{c,t} = E_{c,t}$. Since the only vehicle for savings available to the young is physical capital, analogues to Equations (1)–(2) apply to each region. We can therefore write regional incomes and the laws of motion of regional capital stocks as follows:

$$Y_{c,t} = w_{c,t} H_{c,t} + r_{c,t} K_{c,t} \quad \text{for all } c \in C, \tag{29}$$

$$K_{c,t+1} = S_{c,t} w_{c,t} H_{c,t} \quad \text{for all } c \in C. \tag{30}$$

These equations apply to all the models of this section, including the world of autarky before globalization. Therefore, a complete analysis of the world income distribution and its evolution requires us to determine the cross-section of factor prices, i.e. $w_{c,t}$ and $r_{c,t}$ as a function of the state of the world economy. The latter consists of the savings, factor endowments and industry productivities of all regions of the world, i.e. $S_{c,t}$, $H_{c,t}$, $K_{c,t}$ and $Z_{c,it}$ for all $i \in I$ and all $c \in C$, plus the date, since trade in goods is only possible if $t \geqslant 0$.

The rest of this section is organized as follows. Section 2.1 studies further the world of autarky, while the rest of the section studies the world after globalization. In Section 2.2, we explore a world in which frictions to factor mobility and asset trade are not binding after globalization. Section 2.3 provides a formal description of the model. Sections 2.4 and 2.5 examine worlds where frictions to factor mobility and asset trade remain binding after globalization.

2.1. Economic growth in autarky

The analysis of the effects of globalization starts in the world of autarky. As explained
in Section 1.3, before globalization each region is a smaller and less efficient version of
the integrated economy and factor prices can be written as[23]

$$w_{c,t} = (1 - \alpha)A_{c,t} H_{c,t}^{\mu(1-\alpha)-\upsilon-1} K_{c,t}^{\mu\alpha+\upsilon} \quad \text{for all } c \in C, \tag{31}$$

$$r_{c,t} = \alpha A_{c,t} H_{c,t}^{\mu(1-\alpha)-\upsilon} K_{c,t}^{\mu\alpha+\upsilon-1} \quad \text{for all } c \in C. \tag{32}$$

Equations (31) and (32) describe the cross-section of factor prices. Holding constant
factor endowments, regions with higher than average industry productivities have higher
than average factor prices. Holding constant industry productivities, the relationship between factor prices and factor endowments depends on two familiar forces: diminishing
returns and market size. For a given set of industry technologies, an increase in one factor makes this factor relatively more abundant, lowering its price and raising the price of
the other factor. But an increase in one factor also raises income and demand in all industries, improving industry technologies and raising the prices of both factors. Equations
(31) and (32) put these two effects together. Hence, regions with higher-than-average
human capital have higher-than-average rental rates for all parameter values, and also
higher-than-average wages if $\mu(1 - \alpha) - \upsilon > 1$. Similarly, regions with higher-than-
average physical capital have higher-than-average wages for all parameter values, and
also higher-than-average rental rates if $\mu\alpha + \upsilon > 1$.

It follows from Equations (29)–(32) that, before globalization, we can write regional
incomes and capital stocks as follows:[24]

$$Y_{c,t} = A_{c,t} H_{c,t}^{\mu(1-\alpha)-\upsilon} K_{c,t}^{\mu\alpha+\upsilon} \quad \text{for all } c \in C, \tag{33}$$

$$K_{c,t+1} = s_{c,t} A_{c,t} H_{c,t}^{\mu(1-\alpha)-\upsilon} K_{c,t}^{\mu\alpha+\upsilon} \quad \text{for all } c \in C. \tag{34}$$

Equation (33) shows the income of regions, and it can be used to determine the relative contribution of factor endowments and productivity to income differences. For
instance, assume income is λ times higher than average in a given region. It could be
that in this region human capital is $\lambda^{1/(\mu(1-\alpha)-\upsilon)}$ higher than average or that physical
capital is $\lambda^{1/(\mu\alpha+\upsilon)}$ higher than average. It could also be that the region's productivity in industry i is $\lambda^{1/\sigma_i \mu_i}$ times higher than average.[25] Naturally, it could also be any
combination of these factors.

Equation (34) is the law of motion of the capital stocks and can be used to analyze the
dynamic response to a region-specific shock to savings, human capital and/or industry

---

[23] These equations follow from Equation (24) and the observation that the shares of human capital and physical capital are $1 - \alpha$ and α.

[24] These equations are identical to Equations (24) and (25) and have been reproduced here only for convenience.

[25] Here industry productivity means $Z_{c,it}$, and not $A_{c,it}$.

productivity. Positive (and permanent) shocks to any of these variables raise the region's capital stock and income. As Equation (34) shows, these shocks have growth effects if $\alpha\mu + \upsilon \geqslant 1$, but only have level effects if $\alpha\mu + \upsilon < 1$. Regardless of the case, the effects of these shocks never spill over to other regions.

Assume the joint distribution of savings, human capital and industry productivities is stationary. Then, Equations (33) and (34) imply a strong connection between the cross-sectional and time-series properties of the growth process. If diminishing returns are strong and market size effects are weak, i.e. if $\mu\alpha + \upsilon < 1$, world average income (Y_t) and its regional distribution $(Y_{c,t}/Y_t)$ are both stationary. If instead diminishing returns are weak and market size effects are strong, i.e. $\mu\alpha + \upsilon > 1$, world average income and its regional distribution are both nonstationary. This result provides a tight link between the long run properties of the growth process and the stability of the world income distribution. A weaker version of this result assumes that the world productivity frontier (A_t) is nonstationary but regional productivity gaps $(A_{c,t}/A_t)$ are stationary. Under this assumption, world average income is nonstationary even if diminishing returns are strong and market size effects are weak.

It is commonplace among growth theorists to interpret cross-country data from the vantage point of the autarky model.[26] One influential example is the work of Mankiw, Romer and Weil (1992). They combined Equations (33) and (34) to obtain an equation relating income to savings, human capital, country productivity, and lagged income; and estimated it using data for a large cross-section of countries. They interpreted the residuals of this regression as measuring differences in country productivities and measurement error, and concluded that differences in savings and human capital explain (in a statistical sense) about 80 percent of the cross-country variation in income. Their procedure imposed the restriction $\mu = 1$ (and therefore $\upsilon = 0$) and yielded an estimate of α of about two thirds. Hall and Jones (1999) and Klenow and Rodriguez-Clare (1997) interpreted this high estimate of α as a signal that the regression was miss-specified. Their argument was that savings, human capital and productivity were positively correlated and the omission of productivity from the regression biased upwards the estimate of α. These authors used Equations (33) and (34) to calibrate country productivities keeping the assumption that $\mu = 1$, but instead imposing a value of α of about one third.[27] With these productivities at hand, they found that about two thirds of the variation in incomes reflects variation in productivity, and only one third can be attributed to cross-country variation in savings and human capital.

Another influential example of the use of the autarky model to interpret available data is Barro (1991) who found that, after controlling for human capital and saving

[26] Unfortunately, the absence of direct and reliable measures of productivity precludes carrying out formal tests of the theory. The most popular empirical response to this problem has been to simply assume the theory is correct and use available data to make inferences about the determinants of the world income distribution and its evolution.

[27] This value corresponds to the share of capital in income in national accounts. This sort of calibration exercise is known as development accounting. Caselli's chapter in this volume is the definitive source on this topic.

rates, poor countries tend to grow faster than rich ones. This finding has been labeled "conditional convergence" since it implies that, if two countries have the same country characteristics, they converge to the same level of income.[28] If Equations (33) and (34) provide a good description of the real world, observing conditional convergence is akin to finding that $\mu\alpha + \upsilon < 1$.[29] Many have therefore interpreted the conditional convergence finding as evidence that diminishing returns are strong relative to market size effects.

These inferences about the nature of the growth process heavily rely on Equations (33) and (34), and these equations have been derived from a theoretical model that assumes that all regions of the world live in autarky. This assumption is obviously unrealistic. Is it also crucial? And if so, what alternative assumption would be reasonably realistic? I next turn to these questions. But the script should not be surprising. Globalization (as described at the beginning of this section) has profound effects on the world income distribution and its evolution. The newfound ability of regions to specialize and trade alters, sometimes quite dramatically, the effects of factor endowments and industry productivities on factor prices. This is most clearly illustrated in Section 2.2, which depicts a world in which goods trade allows the world economy to replicate the prices and allocations of the integrated economy. Of course, this is not a general feature of goods trade. Section 2.3 prepares the ground for the analysis of worlds where economic integration is imperfect and factor prices vary across regions. This analysis is then performed in Sections 2.4 and 2.5.

2.2. Factor price equalization

A good starting point for the analysis of the world economy after globalization is to ask whether restricting factor mobility matters at all. Somewhat surprisingly, the answer is "perhaps not". As Paul Samuelson (1948, 1949) showed more than half a century ago, goods trade might be all that is needed to ensure global efficiency. When this happens, we say that the equalization of goods prices leads to the equalization of factor prices. I shall describe Samuelson's result and its implications step by step, so as to develop intuition.[30]

Consider the set of all possible partitions of the world factor endowments at date t, H_t and K_t, among the different regions of the world or, for short, the set of all possible

---

[28] As Barro himself emphasized, this does not mean that per capita incomes tend to converge unconditionally since countries with high initial incomes also tend to have good country characteristics. There is a large number of papers that try to determine whether there is conditional convergence and measure how fast it takes place. See, for instance, Knight, Loayza and Villanueva (1993) and Caselli, Esquivel and Lefort (1996).

[29] An additional maintained assumption of this line of research is that savings, human capital and productivity are jointly stationary.

[30] The analysis here follows a long tradition in international trade. See Dixit and Norman (1989), Helpman and Krugman (1985) and Davis (1995).

factor distributions. This set is formally defined as follows:

$$D_t \equiv \left\{ (H_{c,t}, K_{c,t}) \text{ for all } c \in C \,\middle|\, H_{c,t} \geqslant 0, K_{c,t} \geqslant 0 \right.$$

$$\left. \text{s.t.} \sum_{c \in C} H_{c,t} = H_t \text{ and } \sum_{c \in C} K_{c,t} = K_t \right\}. \quad (35)$$

Define FPE_t as the subset of D_t for which the world economy replicates the prices and allocations of the integrated economy. To construct FPE_t, fix $d_t \in D_t$ and consider the integrated economy prices and quantities. At these prices, consumers are willing to purchase the integrated economy quantities of the different goods and also have enough income to do so. At these prices, producers located in regions with the highest industry productivities are willing to produce the integrated economy quantities of the different goods using the integrated economy quantities of factors. If these producers can find these quantities of factors in their regions, the integrated economy prices and quantities are in fact the equilibrium ones and we say that $d_t \in FPE_t$. Otherwise, the integrated economy prices and quantities cannot be the equilibrium ones and we say that $d_t \notin FPE_t$. Therefore, the set FPE_t can be formally defined as follows:

$$FPE_t \equiv \left\{ d_t \in D_t \,\middle|\, \exists x_{c,it}(m) \geqslant 0, x_{c,it}^{\mathrm{F}} \geqslant 0 \text{ with} \right.$$

$$\sum_{c \in C} x_{c,it}(m) = 1, \sum_{c \in C} x_{c,it}^{\mathrm{F}} = 1 \text{ and}$$

$$x_{c,it} = (1 - \beta_i) x_{c,it}^{\mathrm{F}} + \frac{\beta_i}{M_{it}} \int_0^{M_{it}} x_{c,it}(m) \, dm \text{ such that:}$$
$$\text{(R1) } x_{c,it} = 0 \text{ if } Z_{c,it} < \max_{c \in C}\{Z_{it}\}, \qquad\qquad\qquad (36)$$

$$\text{(R2) } H_{c,t} = \sum_{i \in I} x_{c,it} H_{it} \text{ and } K_{c,t} = \sum_{i \in I} x_{c,it} K_{it}, \text{ and}$$

$$\left. \text{(R3) } x_{c,it}(m) \in \{0, 1\} \text{ for all } m \in [0, M_{it}] \text{ and } i \in I \right\},$$

where M_{it}, H_{it} and K_{it} are defined in Equations (17), (19) and (20). To understand this definition, interpret $x_{c,it}$ as the share of the world production of industry i located in region c at date t, and note that this share includes the production of intermediate inputs, $x_{c,it}(m)$, and final goods, $x_{c,it}^{\mathrm{F}}$. Definition (36) then says that $d_t \in FPE_t$ if it is possible to achieve full employment of human and physical capital in all regions producing only in those regions with the highest productivity [requirement (R1)], using the same factor proportions as in the integrated economy [requirement (R2)], and without incurring the fixed cost of production more than once [requirement (R3)]. The set FPE_t is never empty since the factor distribution that applies in the integrated economy always belongs to it. In fact, the set FPE_t consists of all the factor distributions that are equilibria

of the integrated economy. The larger is the size of the indeterminacy in the geographical distribution of production and factors of the integrated economy, the larger is the
size of FPE_t.

The patterns of production and trade that support factor price equalization after globalization are easy to state and quite intuitive:

1. *In regions where human (physical) capital is relatively abundant, production shifts*
   towards industries that, on average, use human (physical) capital intensively. Ex-
   cess production in these industries is converted into exports that finance imports
   of industries that use physical (human) capital intensively.

EXAMPLE 2.1.1. Consider a world economy with H- and K-industries, such that
$I^H \cup I^K = I$ and $I^H \cap I^K = \emptyset$. Assume $\alpha_i = \alpha_H$ if $i \in I^H$ and $\alpha_i = \alpha_K$ if
$i \in I^K$, and $\alpha_H < \alpha_K$ and $\beta_i = 0$ for all $i \in I$. All regions have the same industry productivities, but A-regions have a higher ratio of human to physical capital than
B-regions. Factor price equalization is possible if the differences in factor proportions
between A- and B-regions are not too large relative to the differences in factor proportions between H- and K-industries. Figure 8 shows the geometry of this example. Since
all regions have the same factor costs, industries use the same factor proportions in all
regions. A-regions contain a more than proportional fraction of the integrated economy's H-industry, and a less than proportional fraction of the K-industry. The opposite
happens in B-regions. This is how specialization and trade ensure that in this world
economy factor endowments are used efficiently.

2. *In industries where a region's productivity is less than the world's highest, pro-*
   duction falls to zero and domestic spending shifts towards imports. To finance the
   latter, production expands in industries in which the region has the highest possi-
   ble productivity and the excess production is exported abroad.

EXAMPLE 2.1.2. Consider a world economy with H- and K-industries, such that
$I^H \cup I^K = I$ and $I^H \cap I^K = \emptyset$. Assume $\alpha_i = \alpha_H$ if $i \in I^H$ and $\alpha_i = \alpha_K$ if
$i \in I^K$, and $\alpha_H < \alpha_K$ and $\beta_i = 0$ for all $i \in I$. Within each type there are "advanced"
and "backward" industries. A-regions have the highest possible productivity in all industries, regardless of whether they are "advanced" or "backward". B-regions have the
highest possible productivity only in "backward" industries. Factor price equalization
is possible if the combined factor endowments of A-regions are large enough and the
subset of "advanced" industries is not too large. Figure 9 shows the geometry of this
example. Since all regions have the same factor costs, only producers located in regions
with the highest productivity can survive international competition. A-regions produce
the integrated economy quantities of "advanced" goods and a fraction of the integrated
economy quantities of "backward" goods. B-regions produce the remaining quantities

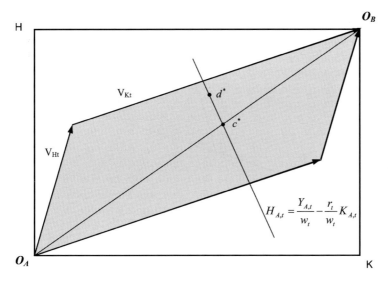

Figure 8. *Notes*. The box in this figure is a geometrical representation of the set D_t, as each element of this set is a point in the box and vice versa. For instance, d^* is a factor distribution such that A-regions have more human and physical capital than B-regions; but human capital is relatively more abundant in A-regions than in B-regions. The box also contains a set of vectors that represent the factor usage per industry that would apply in the integrated economy. For instance, the vector V_{it} has height H_{it} and width K_{it}. The set FPE_t is the gray area. Since all regions have the same industry productivities, production trivially takes place only in regions with the highest possible productivity [requirement (R1)]. Each of the points in the gray area can be generated as a convex combination of the integrated economy's vectors of factor usage per industry [requirement (R2)]. Since $\beta_i = 0$, trivially there are no fixed costs of production that are incurred twice [requirement (R3)]. Points outside of the shaded area do not have this property and therefore do not belong to FPE_t. The factor content of production is given by the regions' factor endowments, i.e. d^*. Since all regions have the same spending shares and use the same techniques to produce all goods, the factor content of consumption lies in the diagonal, i.e. c^*. In A-regions, the H-industry is a net exporter while the K-industry is a net importer. The opposite occurs in B-regions.

of "backward" goods. This is how specialization and trade ensure that in this world economy production takes place only where industry productivities are higher.

3. *Within each industry, only one region produces each input variety and exports it to all other regions. If an industry is split among various regions, there is likely to be two-way trade within the same industry.*[31]

EXAMPLE 2.1.3. Consider any of the world economies of the previous examples, but assume now that $\beta_i = 1$ for all $i \in I$. Assume $d_t \in FPE_t$. Since the fixed costs of

---

[31] I say "likely to be" because a region might produce the final good for domestic use, and import the necessary input varieties. It is usual in trade models to set $\beta_i = 1$ and then drop the "likely to be" from the statement.

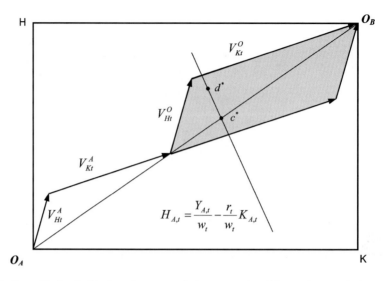

Figure 9. *Notes.* The box in this figure is a geometrical representation of the set D_t, as each element of this set is a point in the box and vice versa. For instance, d^* is a factor distribution such that A-regions have more human and physical capital than B-regions; but human capital is relatively more abundant in A-regions than in B-regions. There are four different industries, "advanced" physical (human) capital intensive and "backward" physical (human) capital intensive. The A-countries have a highest productivity in the "advanced" industries; technologies in the "backward" industries are equal in all countries. The vectors V_{it}^X have height H_{it}^X and width K_{it}^X and represent the factor content of the X-industries, where $X = A, B$ stands for "advanced" or "backward" industries. The set FPE_t is the shaded area. In this set, all "advanced" industries must be located in the A-countries [requirement (R1)]. Once this requirement is satisfied, each of the points in the shaded area can be generated as a convex combination of the integrated economy's vectors of factor usage of the "backward" industries [requirement (R2)]. Since $\beta_i = 0$, trivially there are no fixed costs of production that are incurred twice [requirement (R3)]. Points outside of the shaded area do not have both properties and therefore do not belong to FPE_t. The factor content of production is given by the regions' factor endowments, i.e. d^*. Since all regions have the same spending shares and use the same techniques to produce all goods, the factor content of consumption lies in the diagonal, i.e. c^*. In H-regions, the H-industry is a net exporter while the K-industry is a net importer. The opposite occurs in K-regions.

producing inputs contain the cost of building a specialized production plant, all input producers choose to concentrate their production in one region in order not to duplicate these costs. Therefore, each region produces a disjoint set of input varieties. This is how specialization and trade allow the world economy to exploit increasing returns to scale and therefore benefit from a larger market size.

By adopting these patterns of specialization and trade, the world economy is able to reap all the benefits of economic integration without any factor movements. Using the jargon of trade theory, goods trade is a "perfect substitute" for factor movements if $d_t \in FPE_t$. When this is the case, factor prices are given by

$$w_{c,t} = (1 - \alpha) A_t H_t^{\mu(1-\alpha)-\upsilon-1} K_t^{\mu\alpha+\upsilon} \quad \text{for all } c \in C, \tag{37}$$

$$r_{c,t} = \alpha A_t H_t^{\mu(1-\alpha)-\upsilon} K_t^{\mu\alpha+\upsilon-1} \qquad \text{for all } c \in C. \qquad (38)$$

The world economy is able to operate at the same level of efficiency as the integrated economy despite the immobility of factors. Equations (31) and (32) showed that, before globalization, cross-regional differences in factor proportions and industry productivities lead to differences in the way industries operate (i.e. their factor proportions and productivity) and also in the size of their markets. Regions with a high ratio of human to physical capital have high wage–rental ratios. Regions with high industry productivities and abundant human and physical capital have high factor prices. But Equations (37) and (38) show that, after globalization (and if $d_t \in FPE_t$), cross-regional differences in factor proportions and industry productivities neither change the way industries operate, nor do they affect the size of their markets. Goods trade allows regions to absorb their differences in factor endowments and industry productivities by specializing in those industries that use their abundant factors and have the highest possible productivity, without the need for having different factor prices. Goods trade also eliminates the effects of regional size on factor prices by creating global markets.

These observations have important implications for the world income distribution and, consequently, for any attempt to determine the relative contribution of factor endowments and productivity to income differences. Substituting Equations (37) and (38) into Equation (29), we find that

$$Y_t = A_t H_t^{\mu(1-\alpha)-\upsilon} K_t^{\mu\alpha+\upsilon}, \qquad (39)$$

$$\frac{Y_{c,t}}{Y_t} = (1-\alpha)\frac{H_{c,t}}{H_t} + \alpha\frac{K_{c,t}}{K_t} \qquad \text{for all } c \in C. \qquad (40)$$

A comparison between these equations and Equation (33) shows that the relative contribution of factor endowments and productivity to income differences is fundamentally affected by globalization. Equation (33) differs from Equations (39) and (40) in three important respects: the elasticity of substitution between domestic human and physical capital is one in Equation (33) but infinite in Equations (39) and (40); domestic productivity appears in Equation (34) but not in Equations (39) and (40); and income is homogeneous of degree μ on domestic factor endowments in Equation (34) but only of degree one in Equation (39) and (40). Each of these differences echoes a different aspect of globalization, and I shall discuss them in turn.

Globalization raises the elasticity of substitution between human and physical capital from one to infinity because structural transformation (a shift towards industries that use the locally abundant factor) replaces factor deepening (forcing industries to use more of the locally abundant factor) as a mechanism to absorb differences in factor proportions. Assume a region has a ratio of human to physical capital λ times higher than average. Before globalization, each of its industries is forced to operate with a ratio of human to physical capital that is λ times average, and this requires a wage–rental ratio that is λ^{-1} times average. After globalization, the region simply shifts its production towards industries that are human-capital intensive, keeping the ratio of human to physical capital of its industries constant. This does not require changes in the wage–rental ratio.

Globalization eliminates differences in industry productivities as a source of income differences because structural transformation (a shift towards industries that have high productivity) also replaces productivity deepening (forcing low-productivity industries to produce) as a mechanism to absorb differences in industry productivities. Assume now that a region has average factor endowments but higher than average industry productivities. For instance, the region's productivity is λ times higher than the rest of the world in a subset of industries of combined size σ, and equal to the rest of the world in the remaining ones. Before globalization, this productivity advantage allows the region to produce $\lambda^{\sigma\mu}$ output than average with the same factors, holding constant technology. After globalization, the region takes over all world production of those industries in which its productivity is higher and scales back the rest of its industries. This allows the rest of the world to take full advantage of the region's high productivity and catch up with it in terms of income (even though not in productivity).

Globalization reduces the effects of factor endowments on relative incomes because it converts regional markets into global ones. Assume now that a region has average industry productivities, but its human and physical capitals are both λ times above average. Before globalization, the region's higher factor endowments allow it to produce more output than the average region. This effect is further reinforced because the region's larger market size allows it to have a better technology than average. Therefore, in autarky the region's income is λ^μ times higher than the world's average. After globalization, this additional market size effect disappears since the relevant market is the world market and this is the same for all regions. Therefore, after globalization the region's income is only λ times higher than the world average income.

Globalization also influences the dynamics of the world economy. Assume $d_t \in FPE_t$ for all t, then it follows from Equations (30), (37) and (38) that

$$K_{t+1} = s_t A_t H_t^{\mu(1-\alpha)-\upsilon} K_t^{\mu\alpha+\upsilon}, \tag{41}$$

$$\frac{K_{c,t+1}}{K_{t+1}} = \frac{S_{c,t} H_{c,t}}{S_t H_t} \quad \text{for all } c \in C. \tag{42}$$

A comparison between these equations and Equation (34) shows how globalization affects the dynamic responses to region-specific shocks. After globalization, positive (and permanent) shocks to savings and human capital still raise a region's capital stock and income. But now the effects of these shocks spill over to other regions. Shocks to productivity can only affect a region's income if they push outward the world productivity frontier. And, in this case, all countries equally benefit.[32]

Another important implication of Equations (39)–(42) is that globalization breaks down the connection between the long run properties of the growth process and the stability of the world income distribution.[33] Assume again that the joint distribution of

---

[32] See Ventura (1997) and Atkeson and Kehoe (1998) for analyses of shocks to small open economies in the factor-price-equalization world.

[33] Ventura (1997) provides a dramatic example of this by constructing a world in which time-series convergence to a steady state is associated with cross-sectional divergence and vice versa.

savings, human capital and productivities is stationary. Then, Equation (41) shows that it still is the relative strength of diminishing returns and market size effects that determines whether world average income is stationary or not. But Equation (42) shows that now the world distribution of capital stocks is stationary regardless of parameter values. The same applies to the world income distribution [see Equation (40)]. Therefore, all regions share a common growth rate in the long run. The reason is simple: physical capital accumulation in high-savings and high-human capital regions is absorbed by increased production in industries that use physical capital intensively, and this lowers the prices of these industries and increases the prices of industries that use human capital intensively. This increases wages and savings in low-savings and low-human capital regions. In a nutshell, movements in goods prices positively transmit growth across regions and ensure the stability of the world income distribution.[34]

The main feature of the factor-price-equalization world is that diminishing returns and market size effects are global and not local. This observation has important implications for growth theory. Explanations for why the world grows faster today than in the past should feature diminishing returns and market size effects in the lead role, and relegate savings and human capital to a secondary one. But explanations of why some countries grow faster than others should do exactly the opposite, giving the lead role to savings and human capital and relegating diminishing returns and market size effects to a secondary role. A distinctive feature of the integrated economy is therefore a sharp disconnect between the determinants of average or long run growth and the determinants the dispersion or the cross-section of growth rates.[35]

The factor-price-equalization world neatly illustrates the potential effects of trade on the world income distribution and its dynamics, and it shows why and how goods trade can be a perfect substitute for factor movements. But the real world has not achieved yet the degree of economic integration that this model implies. One does not need sophisticated econometrics to conclude that wages vary substantially around the world. It is less obvious but probably true as well that rental rates also vary substantially around the world. These differences in factor prices indicate that regional differences in factor endowments and/or industry productivities are so large that goods trade cannot make up for factor immobility.

What trade always does is to create a global market in which only the most competitive producers of the world can survive. Trade forces high-cost industries to close down

---

[34] As a general proposition, it is not necessary that trade leads to the stability of the world income distribution. In fact, the study of the stability of world income distribution has received considerable attention recently. While Acemoglu and Ventura (2002) rely on specialization to generate a stable world income distribution, Deardorff (2001) presents a model in which mere differences in initial endowments create persistent difference in world income and "club convergence". Krugman (1987) and Howitt (2000) rely on endogenous technology change to generate such effects. See Brezis, Krugman and Tsiddon (1993) for a model of human capital accumulation that explains leapfrogging in the international income distribution.

[35] One implication of this is that Barro's conditional convergence finding cannot be used to determine whether diminishing returns are weak or strong relative to market size effects. See Ventura (1997).

and offers low-cost industries the opportunity to grow. If $d_t \in FPE_t$ all regions contain enough of these low-cost industries to employ all of their factors at common or equalized factor prices. But this need not be always the case. If $d_t \notin FPE_t$ regions with low industry productivities and sizable factor endowments are forced to offer cheap factors to compete, while regions with high industry productivities and small factor endowments are able to enjoy expensive factors. These price differences indicate that factors are not deployed where they should and the world economy does not operate efficiently. To study the origins and effects of these world inefficiencies, it is necessary first to review some formal aspects of the model after globalization.

2.3. Formal aspects of the model

As mentioned already, in the absence of asset trade analogues of Equations (1) and (2) apply now to each region of the world economy. A regional analogue to Equation (3) also applies since it is a direct implication of our Cobb–Douglas assumption for the consumption and investment composites. Since all regions share spending patterns and face the same goods prices, the price of consumption and investment is the same for all. We keep this common price as the numeraire and, as a result, Equation (4) also applies. Equations (5)–(6) describing technology apply to all regions, with the corresponding factor prices and industry productivities.

After globalization, Equations (7)–(10) describing pricing policies, input demands and the free-entry condition apply only to those regions that host the lowest-cost producers of the world. The rest cannot compete in global markets. To formalize this notion, define the following sets of industries:

$$I_{c,t} \equiv \left\{ i \in I \;\middle|\; c \in \underset{c' \in C}{\arg\min} \left\{ \frac{1}{Z_{c',it}} \left(\frac{w_{c',t}}{1 - \alpha_i} \right)^{1 - \alpha_i} \left(\frac{r_{c',t}}{\alpha_i} \right)^{\alpha_i} \right\} \right\} \quad \text{for all } c \in C. \tag{43}$$

An industry belongs to $I_{c,t}$ if and only if producers located in region c are capable of competing internationally in this industry at date t.[36] Note that a region can be competitive in a given industry because it offers high productivity or a cheap combination of factor prices. The main implication of goods trade is that industries do not locate in regions where they are not competitive,

$$Q_{c,it} = 0 \quad \text{if } i \notin I_{c,t} \text{ for all } i \in I \text{ and } c \in C. \tag{44}$$

Since goods markets are integrated, Equation (11) describing market clearing in global goods markets still applies. But now Equations (12) and (13) describing market clearing in global factor markets must be replaced by analogue conditions imposing

---

[36] This follows directly from the cost functions in Equations (5) and (6) and the observation that all producers in the world face the same world demand.

market clearing in each regional factor market:

$$H_{c,t} = \sum_{i \in I} H_{c,it}$$

$$\text{with } H_{c,it} = \frac{\partial B_{c,it}}{\partial w_{c,t}} + \int_0^{M_{it}} \frac{\partial b_{c,it}(m)}{\partial w_{c,t}} \, dm \quad \text{for all } c \in C, \tag{45}$$

$$K_{c,t} = \sum_{i \in I} K_{c,it}$$

$$\text{with } K_{c,it} = \frac{\partial B_{c,it}}{\partial r_{c,t}} + \int_0^{M_{it}} \frac{\partial b_{c,it}(m)}{\partial r_{c,t}} \, dm \quad \text{for all } c \in C. \tag{46}$$

Equations (45)–(46) state that the regional supplies of labor and capital must equal their regional demands. The latter are the sum of their industry demands, and these are calculated by applying Shephard's lemma to Equations (5) and (6).

This completes the formal description of the model. For any admissible set of capital stocks, i.e. $K_{c,0}$ for all $c \in C$, and sequences for the vectors of savings, human capital and industry productivities, i.e. $S_{c,t}$, $H_{c,t}$ and $A_{c,it}$ for all $c \in C$ and for all $i \in I$, an equilibrium of the world economy after globalization consists of sequences of prices and quantities such that the equations listed above hold at all dates and states of nature. Although there might be multiple geographical patterns of production and trade that are consistent with world equilibrium, the assumptions made ensure that prices and world aggregates are uniquely determined.[37]

We are ready now to re-examine the effects of globalization on factor prices and the world income distribution. We have already found that, if $d_t \in FPE_t$ globalization eliminates all regional differences in factor prices and permits the world economy to operate at the same level of efficiency as the integrated economy. In this case, global market forces are strong enough to ensure that diminishing returns and market size effects have a global rather than a regional scope. This is no longer the case if $d_t \notin FPE_t$ since globalization cannot eliminate all regional differences in factor prices. These factor price differences reflect inefficiencies of various sorts in the world economy.

Efficiency requires that factor usage within an industry be the same across regions. This is a direct implication of assuming diminishing returns to each factor in production. The problem, of course, is that regional factor proportions vary. Structural transformation allows regions to accommodate all or part of their differences in factor proportions without factor deepening. If there are enough industries that use different factor proportions, factor prices are equalized across regions. If there are not enough industries that use different factor proportions, regions must lower the price of their abundant factor and raise the price of their scarce one to attract enough firms to employ their factor endowments. In this case, industries in different regions use different factor proportions

---

[37] Despite the indeterminacy in trade patterns, the trade theorist will immediately recognize that, if $\beta_i = 1$ for all $i \in I$, the volume of trade is determined and the popular gravity equation applies to this world economy.

and the world economy is inefficient. Section 2.4 studies the properties of the growth process in this situation.

Efficiency also requires that industries locate in those regions that offer them the highest possible productivity. Structural transformation allows regions to accommodate all or part of their differences in industry productivities without productivity deepening. If all regions have enough industries with the highest productivity, factor prices are equalized across regions. If some regions do not have enough industries with the highest productivity, they are forced to produce in low productivity industries and must lower their factor prices to be able to compete internationally. Section 2.5 shows how this affects the properties of the growth process.

In the presence of these two types of inefficiency, diminishing returns retain a regional scope even after globalization. Regional differences in factor prices still reflect regional differences in factor abundance and industry productivities, although the mapping between these variables is much more subtle than in the world of autarky. However, even in the presence of these inefficiencies regional differences in factor prices cannot reflect regional differences in market size. For market size effects to retain a regional scope after globalization we need to introduce impediments to goods trade. And this task is left for Section 3.

2.4. Limits to structural transformation (I): factor proportions

It follows from Definition (36) that factor prices are equalized if and only if it is possible to achieve full employment of human and physical capital in all regions producing only with the highest productivity [requirement (R1)], with the factor proportions used in the integrated economy [requirement (R2)], and without incurring a fixed cost more than once [requirement (R3)]. Moving away from the factor-price-equalization world means that we must consider the violation of one or more of these requirements. Since the market for each input is "small", I assume that regions are large enough to ensure that requirement (R3) is always satisfied.[38] Therefore, in the remainder of this section I will focus on violations of requirements (R1) and (R2). In this subsection, we study the effects on the growth process of violations to requirement (R2), keeping the assumption that requirement (R1) is not binding. This assumption will be removed in Section 2.5.

To formalize the notion that requirement (R1) is not binding, define $I_{c,t}^*$ as the set of industries in which region c has the highest possible productivity $I_{c,t}^* \equiv \{i \in I \mid c \in \arg\max_{c' \in C}\{Z_{c',it}\}\}$ for all $c \in C$. To ensure that requirement (R1) is not binding in the models of this section, for each of them I first construct the set of "unrestricted" world equilibria by assuming that $I_{c,t}^* = I$ for all $c \in C$. As mentioned, all these equilibria share the same prices and world aggregates, but might exhibit different geographical patterns of production. In these "unrestricted" world equilibria, some industries might not operate in all regions. Naturally, prices and world aggregates would not be affected

---

[38] I shall explore the effects of violations to requirement (R3) in Sections 3.2 and 3.3.

if regions did not have the best possible technologies in some or all of the industries in which they do not produce. Therefore, we can trivially relax the assumption that $I_{c,t}^*$ contains all industries, and instead assume only that there exists an "unrestricted" equilibrium such that, for all $c \in C$, the industries not included in $I_{c,t}^*$ do not operate in the region. This defines the extent to which regional differences in industry productivities are allowed in this section. It follows that requirement (R1) is never binding and comparative advantage is determined solely by regional differences in factor proportions.

In the worlds we consider in this subsection it is not possible in general to employ all factors in all regions using the techniques of the integrated economy. Even if they concentrate all of their production in industries that use human capital intensively, regions with abundant human capital might lack enough physical capital to produce with the factor proportions that these industries would use in the integrated economy. These regions are therefore forced to use a higher proportion of human capital in their industries and this requires them to have a lower wage–rental ratio than in the integrated economy. Naturally, the exact opposite occurs in regions with abundant physical capital. This situation can be aptly described as a geographical mismatch between different factor endowments.

To study the causes and effects of this mismatch, I present two examples that help build intuitions that apply more generally. The first example is the two-industry case that is so popular in trade theory:

EXAMPLE 2.4.1. Consider a world economy with H- and K-industries, $I^H \cup I^K = I$ and $I^H \cap I^K = \emptyset$. Assume $\alpha_i = \alpha_H$, $\sigma_i = \sigma_H$ and $\max_{c \in C}\{Z_{c,it}\} = Z_{Ht}$ if $i \in I^H$, $\alpha_i = \alpha_K$, $\sigma_i = \sigma_K$ and $\max_{c \in C}\{Z_{c,it}\} = Z_{Kt}$ if $i \in I^K$, with $\alpha_H \leqslant \alpha_K$. (Note that $I^H \sigma_H + I^K \sigma_K = 1$.) For simplicity, assume also that $\varepsilon_i = \varepsilon$ and $\beta_i = \beta$ for all $i \in I$. The first step is to relate prices and world income to production,[39]

$$P_{it} = \sigma_i \prod_{i' \in I}\left(\sum_{c \in C} Q_{c,i't}\right)^{\sigma_i} \bigg/ \sum_{c \in C} Q_{c,it} \quad \text{for all } i \in I, \tag{47}$$

$$Y_t = \prod_{i \in I}\left(\sum_{c \in C} Q_{c,it}\right)^{\sigma_i}. \tag{48}$$

Equation (47) can be thought of as the "demand" side of the model, since it shows how prices depend negatively on quantities, while Equation (48) simply describes world income. The "supply" side of the model is given by the following set of equations:[40]

$$\frac{(1-\alpha_k)P_{Kt}}{w_{c,t}} \sum_{i \in I^K} Q_{c,it} + \frac{(1-\alpha_H)P_{Ht}}{w_{c,t}} \sum_{i \in I^H} Q_{c,it} = H_{c,t} \quad \text{for all } c \in C, \tag{49}$$

---

[39] These equations follow from Equations (3) and (4).
[40] Equations (49) and (50) follow from Equations (45) and (46), while Equations (51) and (52) follow from Equations (7) and (9) after using Equation (17) to eliminate the number of input varieties.

$$\frac{\alpha_k P_{Kt}}{r_{c,t}} \sum_{i \in I^K} Q_{c,it} + \frac{\alpha_H P_{Ht}}{r_{c,t}} \sum_{i \in I^H} Q_{c,it} = K_{c,t} \qquad \text{for all } c \in C, \quad (50)$$

$$\left(\frac{w_{c,t}}{1-\alpha_H}\right)^{1-\alpha_H} \left(\frac{r_{c,t}}{\alpha_H}\right)^{\alpha_H}$$

$$\geqslant \frac{\varepsilon - 1}{\varepsilon} Z_{Ht} p_{Ht}$$

$$= (A_{Ht} P_{Ht})^{1/\mu} (\sigma_H Y_t)^{(\mu-1)/\mu} = \phi_H f_{Ht} \qquad \text{for all } c \in C, \quad (51)$$

$$\left(\frac{w_{c,t}}{1-\alpha_K}\right)^{1-\alpha_K} \left(\frac{r_{c,t}}{\alpha_K}\right)^{\alpha_K}$$

$$\geqslant \frac{\varepsilon - 1}{\varepsilon} Z_{Kt} p_{Kt}$$

$$= (A_{Kt} P_{Kt})^{1/\mu} (\sigma_K Y_t)^{(\mu-1)/\mu} = \phi_K f_{Kt} \qquad \text{for all } c \in C, \quad (52)$$

where $\phi_i = (1-\alpha_i)^{\alpha_i-1} \alpha_i^{-\alpha_i}$ for all $i \in I$, and f_{Ht} and f_{Kt} are measures of the lowest factor costs in the world for the H- and K-industries since in equilibrium $f_{it} = \min_{c \in C} \{w_{c,t}^{1-\alpha_i} r_{c,t}^{\alpha_i}\}$ for all $i \in I$. Equations (49) and (50) are factor market clearing conditions, while Equations (51) and (52) are just a transformation of the pricing equations of each industry (for both final goods and intermediate inputs). Naturally, these pricing equations hold with strict equality if there is positive production in the corresponding industry. Equations (49)–(52) determine the production of each type of industry and the factor prices of region c, as a function of world prices and income.[41]

Equations (47)–(52) determine prices and quantities as a function of the distribution of factor endowments. Together with the regional analogues to Equation (1), the initial condition and the dynamics of the exogenous state variables, these equations provide a complete characterization of the world equilibrium. Next, I describe some its most salient features.

Regions with extreme factor proportions have specialized production structures, while regions with intermediate factor proportions have diversified production structures. Let C_{Kt} (C_{Ht}) be the set of regions where there is production only in K-industries (H-industries), and let C_{Mt} be the set of regions where there is production in both types of industries. In fact, it follows from Equations (49)–(52) that these sets of regions are

---

[41] If one is willing to take goods prices and factor endowments parametrically and further assume that the pricing equations hold with strict equality, it is possible to derive two popular results of trade theory from Equations (49)–(52). The Stolper–Samuelson effect says that an increase in the relative price of an industry leads to a more than proportional increase in the price of the factor that is used intensively in this industry and a decline in the price of the other factor. The Rybcynski effect says that an increase in a factor endowment leads to a more than proportional increase in the production of the industry that uses this factor intensively and a decline in the production of the other industry.

defined as follows:

$$C_{Kt} = \left\{ c \in C \;\middle|\; \frac{H_{c,t}}{K_{c,t}} \leqslant \frac{1 - \alpha_K}{\alpha_K} \left(\frac{f_{Kt}}{f_{Ht}} \right)^{1/(\alpha_K - \alpha_H)} \right\}, \tag{53}$$

$$C_{Ht} = \left\{ c \in C \;\middle|\; \frac{H_{c,t}}{K_{c,t}} \geqslant \frac{1 - \alpha_H}{\alpha_H} \left(\frac{f_{Kt}}{f_{Ht}} \right)^{1/(\alpha_K - \alpha_H)} \right\}, \tag{54}$$

$$C_{Mt} = \left\{ c \in C \;\middle|\; \frac{1 - \alpha_K}{\alpha_K} \left(\frac{f_{Kt}}{f_{Ht}} \right)^{1/(\alpha_K - \alpha_H)} < \frac{H_{c,t}}{K_{c,t}} < \frac{1 - \alpha_H}{\alpha_H} \left(\frac{f_{Kt}}{f_{Ht}} \right)^{1/(\alpha_K - \alpha_H)} \right\}. \tag{55}$$

It follows from Equations (51) and (52) that factor prices are the same for all $c \in C_M$. If the dispersion in regional factor proportions is not too large, and the dispersion in factor intensities is not too low, $C_{Kt} = C_{Ht} = \emptyset$ and there is factor price equalization. Otherwise, this world economy exhibits a limited version of the factor-price-equalization result since factor prices are still equalized for all $c \in C_{Mt}$. It is common in trade theory to refer to a group of regions that share the same factor prices as a "cone of diversification". In fact, we can write the wage and the rental as a function of f_{Ht} and f_{Kt} as follows:

$$w_{c,t} = \begin{cases} (1 - \alpha_K)\phi_K f_{Kt}\left(\frac{H_{c,t}}{K_{c,t}}\right)^{-\alpha_K} & \text{if } c \in C_{Kt}, \\ f_{Kt}^{-\alpha_H/(\alpha_K - \alpha_H)} f_{Ht}^{\alpha_K/(\alpha_K - \alpha_H)} & \text{if } c \in C_{Mt}, \\ (1 - \alpha_H)\phi_H f_{Ht}\left(\frac{H_{c,t}}{K_{c,t}}\right)^{-\alpha_H} & \text{if } c \in C_{Ht}, \end{cases} \tag{56}$$

$$r_{c,t} = \begin{cases} \alpha_K \phi_K f_{Kt}\left(\frac{H_{c,t}}{K_{c,t}}\right)^{1-\alpha_K} & \text{if } c \in C_{Kt}, \\ f_{Kt}^{(1-\alpha_H)/(\alpha_K - \alpha_H)} f_{Ht}^{(\alpha_K-1)/(\alpha_K - \alpha_H)} & \text{if } c \in C_{Mt}, \\ \alpha_H \phi_H f_{Ht}\left(\frac{H_{c,t}}{K_{c,t}}\right)^{1-\alpha_H} & \text{if } c \in C_{Ht}. \end{cases} \tag{57}$$

The wage is continuous and weakly declining on the human to physical capital ratio, while the rental is also continuous but increasing on this same ratio. The most noteworthy feature of these relationships is that they exhibit a "flat" for the set of human to physical capital ratios that define the cone of diversification. The top panel of Figure 10 shows how the wage–rental ratio varies with a region's ratio of human to physical capital. Regional differences in this ratio reflect factor abundance in the usual way. In regions with a high (low) ratio of human to physical capital the price of human capital is low (high) relative to physical capital. Factor prices do not reflect however regional differences in industry productivities and/or market size.

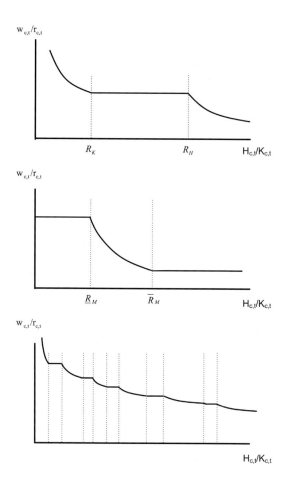

Figure 10. *Notes.* This figure shows how the wage–rental ratio varies with the factor proportions. The top panel represents a two-goods, one-cone world where countries with extreme factor proportions are outside the cone (Example 2.4.1). The middle panel represents a three-good, two-cone world where countries with intermediate factor proportions lie outside the cone (Example 2.4.2). The bottom panel shows a world with multiple goods and cones.

It is now straightforward to compute the world income distribution as a function of f_{Ht} and f_{Kt},

$$
Y_{c,t} = \begin{cases}
\phi_K f_{Kt} H_{c,t}^{1-\alpha_K} K_{c,t}^{\alpha_K} & \text{if } c \in C_{Kt}, \\
\begin{aligned}
& f_{Kt}^{-\alpha_H/(\alpha_K-\alpha_H)} f_{Ht}^{\alpha_K/(\alpha_K-\alpha_H)} H_{c,t} \\
& + f_{Kt}^{(1-\alpha_H)/(\alpha_K-\alpha_H)} f_{Ht}^{(\alpha_K-1)/(\alpha_K-\alpha_H)} K_{c,t}
\end{aligned} & \text{if } c \in C_{Mt}, \\
\phi_H f_{Ht} H_{c,t}^{1-\alpha_H} K_{c,t}^{\alpha_H} & \text{if } c \in C_{Ht}.
\end{cases}
\tag{58}
$$

We can use Equation (58) to re-evaluate earlier results about the relative contribution of factor endowments and industry productivities to income differences across regions. The first result is that the elasticity of substitution between human and physical capital is one outside the cone of diversification, but infinity within the cone. This elasticity reflects the relative importance of structural transformation and factor deepening as means to absorb regional differences in factor proportions. The second result is that regional differences in industry productivities continue not playing a role in determining regional income differences. This, of course, is not surprising given the assumption we have made about requirement (R1) not being binding. The third and final result is that relative incomes are homogeneous of degree one on factor endowments. This not surprising either since it simply confirms the absence of market size effects at the regional level.

We can also write the dynamics of the capital stock as a function of f_{Ht} and f_{Kt},

$$
K_{c,t+1} = \begin{cases} S_{c,t}(1-\alpha_K)\phi_K f_{Kt} H_{c,t}^{1-\alpha_K} K_{c,t}^{\alpha_K} & \text{if } c \in C_{Kt}, \\ S_{c,t} f_{Kt}^{-\alpha_H/(\alpha_K-\alpha_H)} f_{Ht}^{\alpha_K/(\alpha_K-\alpha_H)} H_{c,t} & \text{if } c \in C_{Mt}, \\ S_{c,t}(1-\alpha_H)\phi_H f_{Ht} H_{c,t}^{1-\alpha_H} K_{c,t}^{\alpha_H} & \text{if } c \in C_{Ht}. \end{cases}
\tag{59}
$$

The specific dynamics of this example are hard to determine, since f_{Ht} and f_{Kt} change from generation to generation. It is easy to construct examples in which the world economy moves towards factor-price equalization; examples in which the world economy moves away from factor-price equalization; or examples in which the world economy alternates between periods in which factor prices are equalized and periods in which they are not. These dynamics depend on all the parameters the model (including initial condition) and the evolution of the exogenous state variables, i.e. savings, human capital and industry productivities. Regardless of the specific dynamics, the world income distribution is stable if the joint distribution of these variables is stationary. Economic growth is positively transmitted across regions through changes in goods prices. This stabilizing role of trade is further reinforced by the fact that regions outside the cones cannot absorb capital accumulation through structural transformation and, consequently, experience diminishing returns in production.

Identifying cones of diversification is important because regional differences in factor proportions lead to structural transformation inside them, but to factor deepening outside them. In Example 2.4.1, there is one of such cones and contains regions with intermediate factor proportions. Regions with extreme factor proportions do not belong to any cone. This need not be always the case, as the next example shows.

EXAMPLE 2.4.2. Consider a world economy with H-, M- and K-industries, $I^H \cup I^M \cup I^K = I$, $I^H \cap I^M = \emptyset$, $I^H \cap I^K = \emptyset$ and $I^M \cap I^K = \emptyset$. Assume $\alpha_i = 0$ and $\max_{c \in C}\{Z_{c,it}\} = Z_{Ht}$ if $i \in I^H$; $\alpha_i = \alpha_M$ and $\max_{c \in C}\{Z_{c,it}\} = Z_{Mt}$ if $i \in I^M$; and $\alpha_i = 1$ and $\max_{c \in C}\{Z_{c,it}\} = Z_{Kt}$ if $i \in I^K$. For simplicity, assume also that $\varepsilon_i = \varepsilon$ and $\beta_i = \beta$ for all $i \in I$. The "demand" side of this model is still described by

Equations (47) and (48), but the "supply" side is now given by

$$\frac{(1 - \alpha_M) P_{Mt}}{w_{c,t}} \sum_{i \in I^M} Q_{c,it} + \frac{P_{Ht}}{w_{c,t}} \sum_{i \in I^H} Q_{c,it} = H_{c,t} \quad \text{for all } c \in C, \qquad (60)$$

$$\frac{P_{Kt}}{r_{c,t}} \sum_{i \in I^K} Q_{c,it} + \frac{\alpha_M P_{Mt}}{r_{c,t}} \sum_{i \in I^M} Q_{c,it} = K_{c,t} \quad \text{for all } c \in C, \qquad (61)$$

$$w_{c,t} \geqslant \frac{\varepsilon - 1}{\varepsilon} Z_{Ht} p_{Ht}$$
$$= (A_{Ht} P_{Ht})^{1/\mu} (\sigma_H Y_t)^{(\mu-1)/\mu} = f_{Ht} \quad \text{for all } c \in C, \qquad (62)$$

$$\left(\frac{w_{c,t}}{1 - \alpha_M} \right)^{1-\alpha_M} \left(\frac{r_{c,t}}{\alpha_M} \right)^{\alpha_M}$$
$$\geqslant \frac{\varepsilon - 1}{\varepsilon} Z_{Mt} p_{Mt}$$
$$= (A_{Mt} P_{Mt})^{1/\mu} (\sigma_M Y_t)^{(\mu-1)/\mu} = \phi_M f_{Mt} \quad \text{for all } c \in C, \qquad (63)$$

$$r_{c,t} \geqslant \frac{\varepsilon - 1}{\varepsilon} Z_{Kt} p_{Kt}$$
$$= (A_{Kt} P_{Kt})^{1/\mu} (\sigma_K Y_t)^{(\mu-1)/\mu} = f_{Kt} \quad \text{for all } c \in C. \qquad (64)$$

Unlike the previous example, we find now that regions with extreme factor proportions have diversified production structures, while regions with intermediate factor proportions have specialized production structures. These sets of regions are now given by[42]

$$C_{Kt} = \left\{ c \in C \,\Big|\, \frac{H_{c,t}}{K_{c,t}} \leqslant \frac{1 - \alpha_M}{\alpha_M} \left(\frac{f_{Kt}}{f_{Mt}} \right)^{1/(1-\alpha_M)} \right\}, \qquad (65)$$

$$C_{Ht} = \left\{ c \in C \,\Big|\, \frac{H_{c,t}}{K_{c,t}} \geqslant \frac{1 - \alpha_M}{\alpha_M} \left(\frac{f_{Mt}}{f_{Ht}} \right)^{1/\alpha_M} \right\}, \qquad (66)$$

$$C_{Mt} = \left\{ c \in C \,\Big|\, \frac{1 - \alpha_M}{\alpha_M} \left(\frac{f_{Kt}}{f_{Mt}} \right)^{1/(1-\alpha_M)} < \frac{H_{c,t}}{K_{c,t}} < \frac{1 - \alpha_M}{\alpha_M} \left(\frac{f_{Mt}}{f_{Ht}} \right)^{1/\alpha_M} \right\}. \qquad (67)$$

Regions in C_{Kt} (C_{Ht}) produce in the M-industries and the K-industries (H-industries), while regions in C_{Mt} produce only in M-industries. Factor prices are determined as follows:

$$w_{c,t} = \begin{cases} f_{Mt}^{1/(1-\alpha_M)} f_{Ht}^{-\alpha_M/(1-\alpha_M)} & \text{if } c \in C_{Kt}, \\ (1 - \alpha_M) \phi_M f_{Mt} \left(\frac{H_{c,t}}{K_{c,t}} \right)^{-\alpha_M} & \text{if } c \in C_{Mt}, \\ f_{Ht} & \text{if } c \in C_{Ht}, \end{cases} \qquad (68)$$

---

[42] Note that the sets C_{Kt} and C_{Ht} never intersect in world equilibrium. Assume the opposite, then it follows that equilibrium input prices must satisfy $f_{Mt} < (f_{Ht})^{1-\alpha_M} (f_{Kt})^{\alpha_M}$. But if this inequality held nobody would produce in M-industries and markets for the products of these industries would not clear.

$$
r_{c,t} = \begin{cases} f_{Kt} & \text{if } c \in C_{Kt}, \\ \alpha_M \phi_M f_{Mt} \left(\frac{H_{c,t}}{K_{c,t}} \right)^{1-\alpha_M} & \text{if } c \in C_{Mt}, \\ f_{Mt}^{1/\alpha_M} f_{Ht}^{(\alpha_M-1)/\alpha_M} & \text{if } c \in C_{Ht}. \end{cases} \tag{69}
$$

Once again, the wage is continuous and weakly declining on the human to physical capital ratio, while the rental is also continuous but increasing on this same ratio. But now these relationships exhibit at most two "flats", one for each set of human to physical capital ratios that defines a cone of diversification. Regional differences in factor prices reflect again factor abundance in the usual way. This world economy contains at most two cones of diversification.[43] Regions with extreme factor proportions belong to one of them, while regions with intermediate factor proportions do not. The middle panel of Figure 10 shows how the wage–rental varies with a region's ratio of human to physical capital.

It is straightforward to compute the analogues of Equations (58) and (59) for this example and check that the mapping from factor endowments to incomes and capital accumulation is also linear within the cones and takes the Cobb–Douglas form outside of them. The picture of the growth process that comes out of this example is therefore very similar to the on in Example 2.4.1.

Examples 2.4.1 and 2.4.2 can be generalized by introducing further industries with different factor intensities. As we do so, the potential number of cones increases. But the overall picture remains the same. The world economy sorts itself out in a series of cones of diversification. The bottom panel of Figure 10 depicts a case with multiple cones of diversification.[44] Small regional differences in factor proportions lead to structural transformation within cones, but to factor deepening outside them. Large regional differences in factor proportions might span one or more cones and therefore lead to a mix of structural transformation and factor deepening. Therefore, the world of diversification cones can be seen as being somewhere in between the world of factor-price equalization and the world of autarky.[45]

In the light of these results, we must slightly revise our earlier discussion of the effects of globalization on the source of income differences. As in the world of factor-price equalization, differences in domestic productivities cannot be a source of income differences and relative incomes are homogeneous of degree one with respect to factor

---

[43] I say "at most" because it is also possible that $\underline{R}_{Mt} = \overline{R}_{Mt}$, in which the case there would be a single cone. Cuñat and Mafezzoli (2004a) analyze a similar model under the assumption that none of the regions of the world have specialized production structures, i.e. $C_{Mt} = \emptyset$.

[44] Dornbusch, Fischer and Samuelson (1980) develop a similar model with a continuum of goods that vary in their factor intensity, although they do not specifically study the formation of cones.

[45] In pure Heckscher–Ohlin models, Deardorff (2001) and Cuñat and Mafezzoli (2004a) generate "club convergence". Stiglitz (1970) and Devereux and Shi (1991) are examples where cones of diversification establish due to inherently different time-preferences and incomes diverge. Oniki and Uzawa (1965) analyze conditions for diversification cones in two-sector model.

endowments. But unlike the world of factor-price equalization, the elasticity of substitution between domestic factors is no longer infinity but instead lies somewhere between one (outside cones) and infinity (within cones). As mentioned, this elasticity measures the relative importance of structural transformation and factor deepening as a means to accommodate regional differences in factor proportions. And this relative importance in turn depends on various factors, most notably how dispersed are factor intensities across industries. Two extreme examples make this point forcefully. If the dispersion in industry factor intensities is extreme, i.e. $\alpha_i \in \{0, 1\}$ for all $i \in I$, then regional differences in factor proportions always lead to structural transformation and the world income distribution is given by Equations (39) and (40).[46] If the dispersion in industry factor intensities is instead negligible, i.e. $\alpha_i = \alpha$ for all $i \in I$, then regional differences in factor proportions always lead to factor deepening and the world income distribution is given by[47]

$$Y_{c,t} = A_t H_{c,t}^{1-\alpha} K_{c,t}^{\alpha}. \tag{70}$$

As in the world of autarky, the elasticity of substitution across factors is one [see Equation (33)]. But unlike the world of autarky, regional differences in industry productivities and market size play no role in explaining regional income differences.

We do not need to revise however our earlier discussion of how globalization affects the dynamic responses to region-specific shocks. In this respect, the world with diversification cones offers the same insights as the world of factor-price equalization. Region-specific shocks to savings and human capital have positive effects that spill over to other regions, while shocks to industry productivities only have effects if they push outwards the world productivity frontier. Economic growth is positively transmitted across regions through changes in goods prices and this keeps the world income distribution stable. In fact, this force towards stability is further reinforced in regions that are outside a cone by the existence of diminishing returns in production.

We conclude therefore that violations to requirement (R2) do not alter much the picture came out of the factor-price-equalization world. Surely the geographical mismatch between different factor endowments implied by these violations might generate large inefficiencies that, in turn, might lead to sizable regional differences in factor prices. Therefore, there might be important quantitative differences between a world with many diversification cones and the world of factor-price-equalization. But the qualitative properties of the growth process of these two worlds remain relatively close to each other, and far away from those of the world of autarky.

2.5. Limits to structural transformation (II): industry productivities

Consider next worlds where requirement (R1) is either binding or fails. Regions with few high-productivity industries might find that even if they concentrate all of their

---

[46] This is the model used by Ventura (1997).

[47] One of many ways to find this result is as the appropriate limiting case of Examples 2.4.1 or 2.4.2.

production in those industries, they cannot employ all of their factors and produce the same quantities as the integrated economy. These regions are therefore forced to exceed the production of the integrated economy in those industries and/or move into low-productivity industries. Whatever the case, this requires these regions to offer low factor prices to employ all of their factors. This situation can be aptly described as a geographical mismatch between industry productivities and factor endowments.

To make further progress, it is necessary to be more explicit about why and how industry productivities differ across regions. The first example considers the case in which regional differences in productivities take the popular factor-augmenting form:

EXAMPLE 2.5.1. Consider a world where $Z_{c,it} = \pi_{c,Ht}^{1-\alpha_i} \pi_{c,Kt}^{\alpha_i}$ for all $i \in I$ and all $c \in C$, with $\sum_{c\in C} \pi_{c,Ht} \frac{H_{c,t}}{H_t} = 1$ and $\sum_{c\in C} \pi_{c,Kt} \frac{K_{c,t}}{K_t} = 1$. As usual, $\pi_{c,Ht}$ and $\pi_{c,Kt}$ are interpreted as labor- and capital-augmenting productivity differences. The world productivity frontier is given by $Z_{it} = \max_c \{\pi_{c,Ht}^{1-\alpha_i} \pi_{c,Kt}^{\alpha_i}\}$. In the integrated economy, industries would be located exclusively in the regions that are in this frontier. The set FPE_t is "small" and, except for a few very special or knife-edge cases, factor-price equalization is not possible and requirement (R1) fails.[48]

To understand the logic of this world, it is useful to follow the usual procedure of re-normalizing the model in terms of "efficiency" or "productivity-equivalent" factor units. That is, we can pretend that regional factor endowments are given by $\widehat{H}_{c,t} = \pi_{c,Ht} H_{c,t}$ and $\widehat{K}_{c,t} = \pi_{c,Kt} K_{c,t}$ for all $c \in C$; and that industry productivities are identical across regions, i.e. $\widehat{Z}_{c,it} = 1$ for all $i \in I$ and all $c \in C$. Then, productivity-adjusted factor prices are given by $\hat{w}_{c,t} = w_{c,t}/\pi_{c,Ht}$ and $\hat{r}_{c,t} = r_{c,t}/\pi_{c,Kt}$. The key observation is that the re-normalized model is formally equivalent to the model of the previous section.[49] Therefore, all the results we obtained in the previous sections regarding the cross-section of factor prices also apply here to productivity-adjusted factor prices, i.e. $\hat{w}_{c,t}$ and $\hat{r}_{c,t}$; but not to factor prices as usually measured, i.e. $w_{c,t}$ and $r_{c,t}$.[50]

As the worlds of the previous section, this world economy sorts itself out in a series of cones of diversification. All regions within a cone have the same productivity-adjusted

---

[48] Take, for instance, the case of two regions and two industries. If one region has the highest productivity in both industries the only factor distribution that leads to factor-price equalization is the one in which all factors are located in this region. If instead each region has the highest productivity in a different industry, the only factor distribution that leads to factor-price equalization is the one in which each region receives the exact quantity of factors that its high-productivity industry uses in the integrated economy.

[49] The re-normalized model is a bit less general than the model of the previous section since it does not display regional differences in industry productivities. We could (trivially) generalize this example to allow for regional differences in industry productivities, but keeping the assumption that requirement (R1) is not binding in the re-normalized model.

[50] For instance, Equations (56) and (57) describe the productivity-adjusted factor if we further assume that the world economy contains two types of industries as in Example 2.4.1. Similarly, Equations (68) and (69) describe productivity-adjusted factor prices if we instead assume that the world economy contains three types of industries as in Example 2.4.2.

factor prices, although possibly different factor prices as usually measured. Regional differences in productivity-adjusted factor proportions lead to structural transformation within cones, and to factor deepening across them. When all regions are located within a single cone, we have the conditional factor-price-equalization result emphasized by Trefler (1993). That is, regional differences in factor prices reflect only differences in factor-augmenting productivities and are not related to differences in productivity-adjusted factor proportions.

Although the presence of factor-augmenting productivity differences does not alter much the formal or mathematical structure of the model, it has important implications for the question of why some regions are richer than others. Unlike the worlds of Section 2.4, we now have that productivity differences become a source of income differences across countries. For instance, if all regions belong to a single cone of diversification we have the following counterpart to Equation (40),

$$\frac{Y_{c,t}}{Y_t} = (1-\alpha)\frac{\pi_{c,Ht}H_{c,t}}{H_t} + \alpha\frac{\pi_{c,Kt}K_{c,t}}{K_t} \quad \text{for all } c \in C. \tag{71}$$

Alternatively, if all the industries in the world have the same factor intensity we have the following counterpart of Equation (70),

$$Y_{c,t} = A_{c,t}H_{c,t}^{1-\alpha}K_{c,t}^{\alpha}, \tag{72}$$

where $A_{c,t} = \widehat{A}_t\pi_{c,Ht}^{1-\alpha}\pi_{c,Kt}^{\alpha}$.[51] The inability of the world economy to match best technologies with appropriate factors moves us a step closer to the world of autarky, since regional productivities now affect regional incomes. Moreover, since now the world operates below its productivity frontier shocks to regional factor productivities have effects even if they do not push this frontier. Note however that, as in the worlds of Section 2.4, the elasticity of substitution between domestic factors still lies somewhere between one (outside cones) and infinity (within cones); and relative incomes are homogeneous of degree one with factor endowments.

The rest of the picture of the growth process that comes out of this world remains close to the world of factor-price equalization. Region-specific shocks to savings and human capital have positive effects that spill over to other regions. Economic growth is positively transmitted across regions through goods prices and this keeps the world income distribution stable. If the conditional version of the factor-price-equalization theorem does not hold, regions outside the cones experience diminishing returns and this reinforces the effects of changes in product prices on the stability of the world income distribution.

Assuming that regional productivity differences take the factor-augmenting form discussed in Example 2.5.1 is popular because it yields tractable models. But the factor-augmenting view of productivity differences hides some interesting effects of trade on

---

[51] This model therefore provides an alternative theoretical foundation for the work of Mankiw, Romer and Weil (1992), Hall and Jones (1999) and Klenow and Rodriguez-Clare (1997).

the world income distribution and its stability. One reason is that, in the world of factor-augmenting productivity differences, comparative advantage is still determined solely by regional differences in factor proportions, albeit productivity-adjusted ones. The next example provides a dramatic illustration of how regional differences in industry productivities could determine comparative advantage, and how this brings about a new effect of trade on the world income distribution:

EXAMPLE 2.5.2. Consider a world with many industries and regions. Assume that $Z_{c,it} = 1$ if $i \in I_{c,t}^*$ and $Z_{c,it} = 0$ if $i \notin I_{c,t}^*$, where $I_{c,t}^*$ for all $c \in C$ constitutes a partition of I, $\bigcup_{c \in C} I_{c,t}^* = I$ and $I_{c,t}^* \cap I_{c',t}^* = \emptyset$ for all $c \in C$ and $c' \in C$. Assume also that $I_{c,t}^* \neq \emptyset$ for all $c \in C$. That is, each region knows how to produce a disjoint subset of goods. Since only one region knows how to produce each good, the corresponding industry is located in that region. That is, $I_{c,t} = I_{c,t}^*$ for all $c \in C$, regardless of the factor distribution. In this world, comparative advantage is driven solely by regional differences in industry productivities, and differences in factor proportions play no role. In this example, requirement (R1) does not fail but it is binding, except for a few very special and knife-edge cases.

A bit of straightforward algebra shows that production and factor allocations are given as follows:

$$Y_{c,t} = \sum_{i \in I_{c,t}^*} \phi_i f_{it} H_{c,it}^{1-\alpha_i} K_{c,it}^{\alpha_i} \quad \text{for all } c \in C, \tag{73}$$

$$H_{c,it} = \frac{\sigma_i}{\sum_{i' \in I_{c,t}^*} \sigma_{i'}} \frac{1-\alpha_i}{\sum_{i' \in I_{c,t}^*} \sigma_{i'}(1-\alpha_{i'})} H_{c,t} \quad \text{if } i \in I_{c,t}^* \quad \text{and}$$
$$H_{c,it} = 0 \quad \text{if } i \notin I_{c,t}^*, \tag{74}$$

$$K_{c,it} = \frac{\sigma_i}{\sum_{i' \in I_{c,t}^*} \sigma_{i'}} \frac{\alpha_i}{\sum_{i' \in I_{c,t}^*} \sigma_{i'}\alpha_{i'}} K_{c,t} \quad \text{if } i \in I_{c,t}^* \quad \text{and}$$
$$K_{c,it} = 0 \quad \text{if } i \notin I_{c,t}^*, \tag{75}$$

where, as usual by now, $\phi_i = (1 - \alpha_i)^{\alpha_i - 1} \alpha_i^{-\alpha_i}$ and $f_{it} = \min_{c \in C} \{ w_{c,t}^{1-\alpha_i} r_{c,t}^{\alpha_i} \}$ for all $i \in I$. Equation (73) describes the world income distribution as a function of factor allocations and goods prices, while Equations (74) and (75) provide the equilibrium factor allocations as a function of aggregate factor endowments. By substituting Equations (74) and (75) into Equation (73), we obtain the world income distribution as a function of factor endowments and input prices.[52] It is immediate to show that the elasticity of substitution between human and physical capital is between one and infinity; that re-

---

[52] This relationship is formally analogous, for instance, to Equation (58) in Example 2.4.1.

gional differences in industry productivities affect regional differences in income; and that the world income distribution is homogeneous of degree one with respect to factor endowments.

These results are obtained from a relationship between incomes, factor endowments and industry productivities that holds constant input prices. Once we substitute input prices into this relationship, we find that the world income distribution is given by

$$\frac{Y_{c,t}}{Y_t} = \sum_{i \in I_{c,t}^*} \sigma_i \quad \text{for all } c \in C. \tag{76}$$

Equation (76) states that the share of world income of each region equals that share of world spending on the industries located in the region, and it does not depend on domestic factor endowments. What is going on? Assume a region has a ratio of human to physical capital λ times higher than average. Since the region is producing a fixed set of goods, it is forced to operate with a ratio that is λ times higher than average, and this requires a wage–rental ratio that is λ^{-1} higher than average. Therefore the elasticity of substitution between human and physical capital in production is one. What is different here is that relative incomes are now homogeneous of degree zero with respect to factor endowments. Assume a region's human and physical capitals are both λ times average. Since production is homogeneous of degree one with factor endowments, its production of all industries is λ times average. But since the country faces a demand for its products with price-elasticity equal to one, the prices of its products are λ^{-1} times average. As a result, the income of the region is just average, despite its factor endowments being λ times average.

So what should we conclude about the degree of homogeneity of relative incomes with respect to factor endowments? As Equations (73)–(75) and (76) show, in empirical applications it will depend on whether we are holding goods prices constant or not. If we are holding these prices constant, then relative incomes are homogeneous of degree one in factor endowments. If we are not holding goods prices constant, then the degree of homogeneity of relative incomes with respect of factor endowments lies between zero and one. In this example, this degree of homogeneity is zero because regional differences in factor endowments are absorbed by regional variation in the quantities produced of each input. In Examples 2.4.1, 2.4.2 and 2.5.1, this degree of homogeneity was one because regional differences in factor endowments were absorbed by regional variation in the number of input varieties produced. The next example, inspired by Dornbusch, Fischer and Samuelson (1977), neatly clarifies this point by showing an intermediate world where both margins are at work.

EXAMPLE 2.5.3. Consider a world with two regions $C = \{N, S\}$, and a continuum of industries $I = [0, 1]$. Assume all industries have the same factor intensity, $\alpha_i = \alpha$ for all $i \in I$. For simplicity, let also $\varepsilon_i = \varepsilon$ and $\beta_i = \beta$ for all $i \in I$. It follows immediately that[53]

$$Y_{c,t} = \phi f_{c,t} H_{c,t}^{1-\alpha} K_{c,t}^{\alpha} \quad \text{for all } c \in C, \tag{77}$$

where $\phi = (1-\alpha)^{\alpha-1}\alpha^{-\alpha}$ and $f_{c,t}$ is a measure of factor costs of region c, i.e. $f_{c,t} = w_{c,t}^{1-\alpha} r_{c,t}^{\alpha}$ for all $c \in C$. To characterize the world income distribution in this world, we need to determine factor costs. Equation (77) is akin to Equation (58) or Equations (73)–(75) in the sense that it shows the world income distribution as a function of factor endowments and input prices. Not surprisingly, these relative incomes are homogeneous of degree one with respect to factor endowments. The next step is to determine input prices and substitute them into Equation (77).

Define $T_i \equiv Z_{N,it}/Z_{S,it}$ for all $i \in I$ as the industry productivity of North relative to South. Then, assign indices or order goods so that T_i is nonincreasing in i. Note that T_i might be neither continuous nor invertible.[54] It follows from this ordering that $I_{N,t} \equiv \{i \in I \mid f_{N,t}/f_{S,t} \leq T_i\}$ and $I_{S,t} \equiv \{i \in I \mid f_{N,t}/f_{S,t} \geq T_i\}$. That is, North (or N) specializes on low-index industries while South (or S) specializes in high-index industries. The cutoff industry, i^*, is determined as follows,[55]

$$\frac{f_{N,t}}{f_{S,t}} = T_{i^*}. \tag{78}$$

Let X_i be world share of spending on all industries with indices equal or lower than i, that is, $X_i \equiv \int_0^i \sigma_j \, dj$. Note that X_i is nondecreasing in i, and takes values zero and one for $i = 0$ and $i = 1$. It follows from this definition that $Y_{N,t} = X_{i^*}(Y_{N,t} + Y_{S,t})$ and, using Equation (78), this can be rewritten as follows,

$$\frac{f_{N,t}}{f_{S,t}} = \frac{X_{i^*}}{1 - X_{i^*}} \left(\frac{H_{S,t}}{H_{N,t}}\right)^{1-\alpha} \left(\frac{K_{S,t}}{K_{N,t}}\right)^{\alpha}. \tag{79}$$

Equations (78) and (79) jointly determine the pattern of production and trade (i^*) and relative factor costs ($f_{N,t}/f_{S,t}$) as a function of spending patterns, industry productivities and factor endowments. Finally, we can use the numeraire rule in Equation (4) to find that

$$
\begin{aligned}
Y_t &= \sum_{c \in \{N,S\}} \phi f_{c,t} H_{c,t}^{1-\alpha} K_{c,t}^{\alpha} \\
&= (\varepsilon - 1) \exp\left\{ \int_0^{i^*} Z_{N,it}\sigma_i \, di + \int_{i^*}^1 Z_{S,it}\sigma_i \, di \right\}.
\end{aligned}
\tag{80}
$$

---

[53] This follows directly from the observation that the share of human and physical capital in income are $1-\alpha$ and α, respectively.

[54] This ranking can vary over time, but this does not play any role here. Without loss of generality, the reader can focus on the case in which the ranking is time-invariant.

[55] If T_i is not invertible in the region of interest, this condition determines a set of candidate values for i^*.

Having already found the pattern of production and trade (i^*) and relative factor costs ($f_{N,t}/f_{S,t}$), Equation (80) can then be used to determine absolute factor costs.

This world is somewhat different form the ones we have seen so far in that we have only two regions. To think about the effects of factor endowments on relative incomes, I consider next a situation in which both regions have symmetric technologies and differ in that North's factor endowments are λ (> 1) times larger than South's.[56] Figure 11 depicts this world. The AA and BB lines represent Equations (78) and (79), respectively. The AA line is nonincreasing because T_i is nonincreasing in i, while the BB line is nondecreasing because X_i is nondecreasing in i. The existence of a unique crossing point follows since the BB line takes value zero at $i = 0$ and slopes upward towards infinity at $i = 1$.

The top panel of Figure 11 shows the case in which T_i is flat. This case corresponds to a world in which differences in industry productivities are minimal or irrelevant at the margin as in Examples 2.4.1, 2.4.2 and 2.5.1. This allows North to employ its larger factor endowments by producing a larger number of varieties than South. Factor costs are the same in both regions and, as a result, North's income is λ times South's. Relative incomes (after substituting in goods prices) are homogeneous of degree one on factor endowments.

The middle panel of Figure 11 shows the opposite case in which T_i is vertical. This case corresponds to a world in which differences in industry productivities are extreme as in Examples 2.5.2. North is forced to employ its larger factor endowments by producing a higher quantity of each of its varieties. Factor costs in North are λ^{-1} times those of South and, as a result, North's income equals that of South. Relative incomes (after substituting in goods prices) are homogeneous of degree zero on factor endowments.

The bottom panel shows the intermediate case in which T_i is neither flat nor vertical. Since the slope reflects how strong are differences in industry productivities, we are somewhere in between the two extreme examples considered up to now. North employs its larger factor endowments by producing a larger number of varieties and also a larger quantity of each of them. Factor costs in North are somewhere between λ^{-1} and one times those of South. The degree of homogeneity of relative incomes (after substituting in goods prices) on factor endowments is therefore somewhere between zero and one.

It is possible to generalize Example 2.5.3 in a variety of directions. For instance, one could allow for industry variation in factor intensities and many regions.[57] This is important in empirical applications, of course. But the central message remains. The effects of factor endowments on relative incomes depend on regional differences in industry productivities. If these differences are small, regions with larger factor endowments absorb them mostly through structural transformation: not changing much their

---

[56] By symmetric technologies, I mean that if there exists an industry i such that $T_i = \tau$ then there also exists another industry i' such that $T_{i'} = 1/\tau$ and $\alpha_i = \alpha_{i'}$, $\beta_i = \beta_{i'}$, $\varepsilon_i = \varepsilon_{i'}$ and $\sigma_i = \sigma_{i'}$.

[57] See Wilson (1980), Eaton and Kortum (2002), Matsuyama (2000) and Alvarez and Lucas (2004).

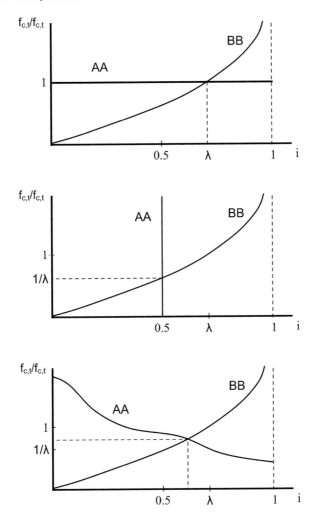

Figure 11. *Notes.* This figure shows how pattern of production and trade (i^*) and relative factor costs $(f_{N,t}/f_{S,t})$ are determined in Example 2.5.3. The top panel shows the case of arbitrarily small differences in industry productivities. The middle panel shows the case of arbitrarily large differences in industry productivities. The bottom panel shows the intermediate case.

production in existing industries and moving into new industries where the region's productivity relative to the rest of the world is similar to existing ones. If differences in industry productivities are large, regions with larger factor endowments absorb them by productivity deepening: substantially increasing their production in existing industries and/or moving into industries where the region's productivity relative to the rest of the world is substantially lower than in existing ones.

One can conclude from this discussion that differences in industry productivities create another force for diminishing returns to physical capital accumulation. As physical capital is accumulated, quantities produced increase and the terms of trade worsen. The result is a reduction in factor prices that lowers wages, savings and capital accumulation. This is a central aspect of the growth process in a world of interdependent regions generates a force towards the stability of the world income distribution.[58]

I argued at the end of Section 1 that, if globalization leads to the integrated economy, there is a powerful prescription for economic development: open up and integrate into the world economy. This allows regions to benefit from higher productivity, improved factor allocation and increased market size. Not much has changed here. Naturally, if factor prices are equalized the effects are literally the same as in Section 1 since then globalization leads to the integrated economy. If factor prices are not equalized, the world economy operates with a lower productivity and a worse factor allocation than the integrated economy. This also means that the size of the world economy will be smaller than that of the integrated economy. As a result, all the benefits from globalization are smaller in the worlds of Sections 2.4 and 2.5 than in the world of factor-price equalization. But it is still relatively straightforward to see that coupled with an appropriate transfer scheme globalization constitutes a Pareto improvement for the world economy. Moreover, since all regions gain from trade there exist Pareto-improving transfer schemes that do not require inter-regional transfers.[59] Therefore, the prescription for development remains the same: open up and integrate into the world economy.

We have traveled much already, and the global view of economic growth is starting to take shape. This view is more realistic and rich in details than the views that came out from either the world of autarky or the integrated economy. Despite this progress, we should not rest here yet. We have assumed so far that globalization eliminates all impediments to goods trade. This is obviously an unrealistic assumption. Is it also a crucial one?

3. Transport costs and market size

Despite the already large and growing importance of international trade, there are some important areas of economic activity where the degree of market integration is still relatively low. Surely the clearest case in point is the service sector.[60] As the textbook

---

[58] See Acemoglu and Ventura (2002) on this point.

[59] How do we know that all regions have nonnegative gains from globalization? Since regions have the choice of not trading, it is therefore possible to achieve the level of income and welfare of the world of autarky after globalization. Realizing these gains might require implementing an appropriate tax-subsidy scheme, though.

[60] In industrial economies, the service sector accounts for more than two thirds of production but only for about one fifth of exports and imports. Moreover, most trade in services is concentrated in activities related to transportation and travel even though these activities only constitute a small component of overall services production.

example of a haircut suggests, many services are inherently more difficult to transport than agricultural and manufacturing products. Services also tend to be more vulnerable to various governmental barriers to trade, such as professional licensing requirements that discriminate against foreigners, domestic content requirements in public procurement, or poor protection of intellectual property rights.[61] In addition, there are important examples of weak market integration that go beyond the service sector. Trade in some agricultural and manufacturing products is also severely restricted as a result of protectionist practices in industrial countries.

The goal of this section is to study the effects on the growth process of partial segmentation in goods markets. The new model of globalization that I shall adopt here is as follows: at date $t = 0$ the costs of transporting some (but not all) goods across regions suddenly fall from prohibitive to negligible. In particular, I partition the set of all industries into the sets of tradable and nontradable industries, i.e. T_t and N_t such that $T_t \cup N_t = I$ and $T_t \cap N_t = \emptyset$. The costs of transporting intermediate inputs and final goods fall from prohibitive to negligible at $t = 0$ if $i \in T_t$. But even after $t = 0$, the costs of transporting either the intermediate inputs, or the final goods, or both remain prohibitive if $i \in N_t$.[62] We keep assuming that the costs of transporting factors across regions remain prohibitive after $t = 0$, and that international trade in assets is not possible. Naturally, the model analyzed in Section 2 (and formally described in Section 2.3) obtains as the special case of this model in which $T_t = I$ and $N_t = \emptyset$ for $t \geqslant 0$.

A central aspect of the analysis turns out to be whether transport costs apply only to final goods, to intermediate inputs, or to both. Section 3.1 presents the case in which transport costs apply only to final goods. This model neatly generalizes the results obtained in the previous section. Section 3.2 studies the case in which transport costs apply only to intermediate inputs. This gives rise to agglomeration effects that can have a large and somewhat unexpected impact on the world income distribution. Section 3.3 analyzes the case in which transport costs apply to both final goods and intermediate inputs. The interaction between the two types of frictions brings about a new perspective on the role of local markets.

3.1. Nontraded goods and the cost of living

Consider next a world where some final goods are not tradable, although the intermediate inputs required to produce them are always tradable. In particular, the costs of

---

[61] There are also signs that this is changing rapidly. Advances in telecommunications technology, the appearance of e-commerce and the development of new and standardized software have all opened up the possibility of trading a wider range of services. Recent multilateral trade negotiations and the process of European integration have also led to the dismantling of various nontariff barriers to service trade.

[62] The most popular alternative to this model is the "iceberg" cost model whereby all goods are subject to the same proportional transport cost. In particular, a quantity τ (> 1) of a good must be shipped from source to ensure that one unit of it arrives to destination. The rest "melts" away in transit. See Matsuyama (2004a) for yet another model of transport costs.

trading intermediate inputs are negligible for all $i \in I$, and the costs of transporting final goods are negligible if $i \in T_t$ but prohibitive if $i \in N_t$. Since prices of final goods can differ across regions, a novel feature of this model is that regions will have different price levels.

I must now revise the formal description of the model. While regional analogues of Equations (1) and (2) continue to apply, one must now recognize that final goods prices in nontradable industries might differ across regions. As a result, the price of consumption and investment will vary across them even if Equation (3) describing spending patterns still applies to all regions. Therefore, we must write the analogues of Equations (1) and (2) as follows:

$$K_{c,t+1} = S_{c,t} \frac{w_{c,t}}{P_{c,t}} H_{c,t}, \tag{81}$$

$$C_{c,t} = (1 - S_{c,t}) \frac{w_{c,t}}{P_{c,t}} H_{c,t} + \frac{r_{c,t}}{P_{c,t}} K_{c,t}, \tag{82}$$

where $P_{c,t}$ is the price level (or cost of living) of region c, i.e. $P_{c,t} = \prod_{i \in I} (P_{c,it}/\sigma_i)^{\sigma_i}$ for all $c \in C$. A natural choice of numeraire now is the ideal price index for tradable industries,

$$1 = \prod_{i \in T_t} \left(\frac{P_{it}}{\sigma_i} \right)^{\sigma_i}. \tag{83}$$

Equation (83) replaces Equation (4). The latter obtains as the special case of the former in which all goods are tradable, i.e. $T_t = I$ and $N_t = \emptyset$. An implication of this choice of numeraire is that the price level of region c is equal to the ideal price index of its nontradable industries,

$$P_{c,t} = \prod_{i \in N_t} \left(\frac{P_{c,it}}{\sigma_i} \right)^{\sigma_i} \quad \text{for all } c \in C. \tag{84}$$

Since now price levels differ across regions it is necessary to distinguish between two concepts of income and factor prices: (1) market-based incomes and factor prices, i.e. $Y_{c,t}$, $w_{c,t}$ and $r_{c,t}$, and (2) real or PPP-adjusted incomes and factor prices, i.e. $Y_{c,t}/P_{c,t}$, $w_{c,t}/P_{c,t}$ and $r_{c,t}/P_{c,t}$. Whenever there is no risk of confusion, I shall refer to the former simply as income and factor prices, and to the latter as real income and real factor prices. As before, Equations (5) and (6) describing technology apply to all regions, with the corresponding factor prices and industry productivities.

After globalization, producers of intermediate inputs in all industries and producers of final goods in tradable industries face a global market and Equations (7)–(10) describing pricing policies, input demands and the free-entry condition therefore apply only to those regions where the lowest-cost producers are located. But even after globalization, producers of final goods in nontradable industries remain sheltered from foreign competition, and Equations (7) and (8) apply to all regions and not only to the lowest-cost ones. Thus, Equation (44) no longer applies to the producers of final goods in nontradable industries [Equation (43) still stands as a definition, though].

Market clearing conditions are also affected by the presence of transport costs. While Equations (45) and (46) describing market clearing in regional factor markets still apply, Equation (11) describing market clearing in global markets for final goods applies only to tradable industries. In nontradable industries, Equation (11) must be replaced by analogue conditions imposing market clearing in each regional market,

$$P_{c,it} Q_{c,it} = E_{c,it} \quad \text{for all } i \in N_t \text{ and } c \in C. \tag{85}$$

This completes the formal description of the model. For any admissible set of capital stocks, i.e. $K_{c,0}$ for all $c \in C$; sequences for the vectors of savings, human capital and industry productivities, i.e. $S_{c,t}$, $H_{c,t}$ and $A_{c,it}$ for all $c \in C$ and for all $i \in I$, and a sequence for the set N_t (or T_t), an equilibrium of the world economy after globalization consists of a sequence of prices and quantities such that the equations listed above hold at all dates and states of nature. Although there might be multiple geographical patterns of production that are consistent with world equilibrium, the assumptions made ensure that prices and world aggregates are uniquely determined.

The best way to start the analysis is by asking again whether the assumed trade restrictions matter at all. That is, to ask whether restricting factor mobility and now goods trade impede the world to achieve the level of efficiency of the integrated economy. Re-define the set FPE_t now as follows:

$$FPE_t \equiv \left\{ d_t \in D_t \,\middle|\, \exists x_{c,it}(m) \geqslant 0, x_{c,it}^F \geqslant 0 \right.$$

$$\text{with } \sum_{c \in C} x_{c,it}(m) = 1, \sum_{c \in C} x_{c,it}^F = 1 \text{ and}$$

$$x_{c,it} = (1 - \beta_i) x_{c,it}^F + \frac{\beta_i}{M_{it}} \int_0^{M_{it}} x_{c,it}(m) \, dm \text{ such that:}$$

$$\text{(R1) } x_{c,it} = 0 \text{ if } Z_{c,it} < \max_{c \in C} \{Z_{it}\}, \tag{86}$$

$$\text{(R2) } H_{c,t} = \sum_{i \in I} x_{c,it} H_{it} \text{ and } K_{c,t} = \sum_{i \in I} x_{c,it} K_{it},$$

$$\text{(R3) } x_{c,it}(m) \in \{0, 1\} \text{ for all } m \in [0, M_{it}] \text{ and } i \in I, \text{ and}$$

$$\left. \text{(R4) } x_{c,it}^F \geqslant (1 - \beta_i) \frac{Y_{c,t}^{IE}}{Y_t^{IE}} \text{ if } i \in N_t \right\}.$$

Comparing Definitions (36) and (86), we observe that the latter contains an additional requirement: each region should be able to produce all the final goods used for its own consumption and investment in nontradable industries. This additional restriction is a direct consequence of transport costs. The presence of this additional restriction reduces the size of FPE_t. In fact, it is now even possible that $FPE_t = \emptyset$. For instance, assume regional differences in industry productivities are such that there exists no region that has the highest possible productivity in all nontradable industries simultaneously. Then it is not possible to replicate the integrated economy.[63]

If $d_t \in FPE_t$, factor prices are equalized across regions and the world economy operates with the same efficiency as the integrated economy despite factor immobility and goods market segmentation. In this case, the world economy behaves exactly as the world of factor-price equalization of Section 2.2.[64] If $d_t \notin FPE_t$, the world economy cannot operate at the same level efficiency as the integrated economy. As a result, either market-based factor prices, or real factor prices, or both differ across regions. But even in this case the behavior of the world economy does not depart much from what we observed in the worlds of Section 2. To see this, define $H_{c,t}^{\mathrm{T}}$ and $K_{c,t}^{\mathrm{T}}$ as the factor endowments devoted to the production of tradable goods, i.e. all intermediate inputs and the final goods of tradable industries. Straightforward algebra shows that[65]

$$H_{c,t}^{\mathrm{T}} = \max\left\{ 0, H_{c,t}\left(1 - \sum_{i \in N_t}(1 - \beta_i)(1 - \alpha_i)\sigma_i \right) \right.$$

$$\left. - K_{c,t}\left(\frac{w_{c,t}}{r_{c,t}} \right)^{-1} \sum_{i \in N_t}(1 - \beta_i)(1 - \alpha_i)\sigma_i \right\} \quad \text{for all } c \in C, \quad (87)$$

$$K_{c,t}^{\mathrm{T}} = \max\left\{ 0, K_{c,t}\left(1 - \sum_{i \in N_t}(1 - \beta_i)\alpha_i\sigma_i \right) \right.$$

$$\left. - H_{c,t}\frac{w_{c,t}}{r_{c,t}} \sum_{i \in N_t}(1 - \beta_i)\alpha_i\sigma_i \right\} \quad \text{for all } c \in C. \quad (88)$$

Equations (87) and (88) show the factor supplies that are left after subtracting from aggregate factor supplies the factors used in the production of final goods in nontradable industries. In the special case in which $N_t = \emptyset$, these factor supplies equal the aggregate factor supplies and are independent of factor prices. But in the general case, these factor supplies depend on factor prices in the usual way. The higher is the wage–rental, the lower is the human to physical capital ratio used for the production of final goods in nontradable industries and, as a result, the higher is the relative supply of human to physical capital that is left after production of final goods in nontradable industries.

---

[63] That one or more regions with the highest possible productivity in all nontradable industries exist is a necessary but not sufficient condition for $FPE_t \neq \emptyset$. Since factor-price equalization requires that all factors be located in these regions, it is also necessary that at least one of these regions have the highest possible productivity for each tradable industry.

[64] Even the price levels would be equalized across regions, i.e. $P_{c,t} = 1$ for all $c \in C$. Note however that there is less indeterminacy regarding the patterns of production and trade, since nontradable final goods must now be produced in the same region where they are used for consumption or investment.

[65] To see this, note that the shares of human and physical capital devoted to producing the final good of the ith nontradable industry are $(1 - \beta_i)(1 - \alpha_i)$ and $(1 - \beta_i)\alpha_i$. Add over industries and note that the share of spending in the ith industry is $\sigma_i Y_{c,t}$.

With Equations (87) and (88) at hand, it is straightforward to see that all the results in Sections 2.4 and 2.5 regarding incomes and factor prices still go through in the presence of nontradable final goods. Take, for instance, Example 2.4.1. Equations (47)–(48) must be rewritten as follows:

$$P_{it} = \sigma_i \prod_{i' \in T_t} \left(\sum_{c \in C} Q_{c,i't} \right)^{\sigma_i / \sum_{i' \in T_t} \sigma_{i'}} \bigg/ \sum_{c \in C} Q_{c,it} \quad \text{for all } i \in T_t, \tag{89}$$

$$Y_t = \prod_{i \in T_t} \left(\sum_{c \in C} Q_{c,it} \right)^{\sigma_i / \sum_{i' \in T_t} \sigma_{i'}}, \tag{90}$$

while Equations (49)–(52) still apply provided that we write $H^{\mathrm{T}}_{c,t}$ and $K^{\mathrm{T}}_{c,t}$ instead of $H_{c,t}$ and $K_{c,t}$, in Equations (49) and (50). Factor prices and the pattern of trade are determined by these modified versions of Equations (47)–(52) together with Equations (87) and (88). Since factor supplies are well behaved, a brief analysis of this system reveals that all the discussion of the properties of the world income distribution and its dynamics after Equations (58) and (59) still goes through. In fact, all the results and intuitions developed in the examples of Sections 2.4 and 2.5 still apply after we remove the assumption that $N_t = \emptyset$.

The major difference between the world of this subsection and the one in Section 2 is that there is a discrepancy between market-based and real incomes and factor prices. To see this, we need to compute regional price levels. Equations (5)–(7) and (83) imply that

$$P_{c,t} = \prod_{i \in N_t} \left\{ \frac{1}{\sigma_i} \left[\frac{1}{Z_{c,it}} \left(\frac{w_{c,t}}{1 - \alpha_i} \right)^{1-\alpha_i} \left(\frac{r_{c,t}}{\alpha_i} \right)^{\alpha_i} \right]^{1-\beta_i} \right.$$
$$\left. \times \left[\int_0^{M_{it}} p_{it}(m)^{1-\varepsilon_i} \, dm \right]^{\beta_i/(1-\varepsilon_i)} \right\}^{\sigma_i}. \tag{91}$$

Since all regions face the same input prices, Equation (91) shows that, ceteris paribus, the price level is high in regions that have high factor prices and low productivity in non-tradable industries. This relationship is the first piece of a theory of the price level. The second piece is a relationship between factor prices, factor endowments and industry productivities. The following examples show how to obtain this additional relationship.

EXAMPLE 3.1.1. Consider a world economy with H- and K-industries, $I^H \cup I^K = I$ and $I^H \cap I^K = \emptyset$. Assume $\alpha_i = \alpha_H$ and $\max_{c \in C}\{Z_{c,it}\} = Z_{Ht}$ if $i \in I^H$, $\alpha_i = \alpha_K$ and $\max_{c \in C}\{Z_{c,it}\} = Z_{Kt}$ if $i \in I^K$, with $\alpha_H \leqslant \alpha_K$. For simplicity, assume also that $\varepsilon_i = \varepsilon$ and $\beta_i = \beta$ for all $i \in I$. As in Section 2.4, we assume that requirement (R1) is not binding.[66] The only difference between this world and the one in Example 2.4.1 is the presence of nontradable industries, i.e. $N_t \neq \emptyset$.

---

[66] Note that this implies that all regions have the same productivity in nontradable industries. That is, $Z_{c,it} = Z_{Ht}$ if $i \in N_t \cap I^H$ and $Z_{c,it} = Z_{Kt}$ if $i \in N_t \cap I^K$ for all $c \in C$.

Let P_{Ht} and P_{Kt} be the prices of final goods in tradable H- and K-industries. If a region is internationally competitive in tradable H-industries, then the price of final goods of its nontradable H-industries is also P_{Ht}.[67] If a region is not competitive internationally, then the price of final goods in its nontradable H-industries exceeds P_{Ht}. In fact, it follows from Equations (5) and (51)–(52) that the price of the final goods in nontradable H-industries is $\frac{w_{c,t}^{1-\alpha_H} r_{c,t}^{\alpha_H}}{f_{Ht}} P_{Ht} \geqslant 1$. A parallel argument shows that the price of the final goods in nontradable K-industries is $\frac{w_{c,t}^{1-\alpha_K} r_{c,t}^{\alpha_K}}{f_{Kt}} P_{Kt} \geqslant 1$. It then follows from Equations (83)–(84) that the price level of region c is given by

$$
\begin{aligned}
P_{c,t} =\ & \left[\frac{w_{c,t}^{1-\alpha_H} r_{c,t}^{\alpha_H}}{f_{Ht}} \frac{P_{Ht}}{\sigma_H} \right]^{\sum_{i \in N_t \cap I^H} \sigma_i} \\
& \times \left[\frac{w_{c,t}^{1-\alpha_K} r_{c,t}^{\alpha_K}}{f_{Kt}} \frac{P_{Kt}}{\sigma_K} \right]^{\sum_{i \in N_t \cap I^K} \sigma_i} \qquad \text{for all } c \in C.
\end{aligned} \tag{92}
$$

As in Example 2.4.1, regions with intermediate factor proportions have diversified production structures while regions with extreme factor proportions have specialized production structures. The sets C_{Mt}, C_{Kt} and C_{Ht} are still defined by Equations (53)–(55) provided we write $H_{c,t}^T$ and $K_{c,t}^T$ instead of $H_{c,t}$ and $K_{c,t}$. It follows from Equations (51), (52) and (92) that $P_{c,t} = (P_{Ht}/\sigma_H)^{\sum_{i \in N_t \cap I^H} \sigma_i} (P_{Kt}/\sigma_K)^{\sum_{i \in N_t \cap I^K} \sigma_i}$ if $c \in C_{Mt}$ and $P_{c,t} \geqslant (P_{Ht}/\sigma_H)^{\sum_{i \in N_t \cap I^H} \sigma_i} (P_{Kt}/\sigma_K)^{\sum_{i \in N_t \cap I^K} \sigma_i}$ if $c \in C_{Kt} \cup C_{Ht}$. All regions within the cone share the same price level, and this is the lowest in the world. The reason, of course, is that these regions are competitive both in H- and K-industries. Regions outside the cone have different price levels. Moreover, it is possible to show that these price levels increase the farther away the regions are from the cone. The reason is that the farther away from the cone, the less competitive a region is in one of the industry types and the more expensive it is to produce the final goods of the nontradable industries of this type.

Example 3.1.1 provides us with a simple theory of why and how the price level varies across regions. But it is difficult to reconcile this theory with the data. The later show that price levels are positively correlated with income, so that regional differences in real incomes are substantially smaller than regional differences in market-based incomes. To obtain this pattern in the world of Example 3.1.1 would require that poor regions be located inside the cone and rich regions outside of it. Although this is not impossible from a theoretical standpoint, it does not seem a promising starting point for the construction of an empirically successful theory of the price level.

---

[67] This follows because the technology to produce final goods is the same for all H-industries, and also because the number of input varieties of H-industries does not depend on whether the industry is tradable or nontradable.

A positive association between incomes and price levels could arise somewhat more naturally in the world of Example 2.4.2 once we remove the assumption that $N_t = \emptyset$. For instance, if nontradable industries tend to be more human-capital intensive than tradable industries the price level would be high in regions that belong to C_{Kt}, intermediate in regions that belong to C_{Mt}, and low in regions that belong to C_{Ht}. Assume then that most of the variation in income levels is due to differences in savings rates, so that rich regions are those that have low human to physical capital ratios. This does not seem implausible, since most nontradable industries tend to be in the service sector and this sector tends to use a higher human to physical capital ratio than other sectors.

More generally, in the worlds of Section 2.4 the correlation between income and price levels is positive or negative depending on how factor proportions vary with income and the factor intensities of nontradable industries relative to tradable ones. The central observation is that price levels should be high in regions that have factor proportions that are inadequate to produce nontradable goods. Building an empirically successful theory of the price level around this notion seems promising, although it remains to be done. Most of the existing research on the price level has focused instead on the role of regional differences in industry productivities. The next example presents a world where these differences generate a positive association between income and the price level.

EXAMPLE 3.1.2. Consider a world where $Z_{c,it} = \pi_{c,Ht}^{1-\alpha_i} \pi_{c,Kt}^{\alpha_i}$ for all $i \in T_t$ and $c \in C$, and $Z_{c,it} = 1$ for all $i \in N_t$, with $\sum_{c \in C} \pi_{c,Ht} \frac{H_{c,t}}{H_t} = 1$ and $\sum_{c \in C} \pi_{c,Kt} \frac{K_{c,t}}{K_t} = 1$. The crucial feature of this example is that productivity differences exist only in tradable industries.[68] This world economy is akin to that in Example 2.5.1. For instance, assume that there are H- and K-industries as in Examples 2.4.1 and 3.1.1. Then, we have that

$$
P_{c,t} = \left[\frac{(\pi_{c,Ht}\hat{w}_{c,t})^{1-\alpha_H}(\pi_{c,Kt}\hat{r}_{c,t})^{\alpha_H}}{\hat{f}_{Ht}} \frac{P_{Ht}}{\sigma_H} \right]^{\sum_{i \in N_t \cap IH} \sigma_i}
$$
$$
\times \left[\frac{(\pi_{c,Ht}\hat{w}_{c,t})^{1-\alpha_K}(\pi_{c,Kt}\hat{r}_{c,t})^{\alpha_K}}{\hat{f}_{Kt}} \frac{P_{Ht}}{\sigma_H} \right]^{\sum_{i \in N_t \cap IK} \sigma_i} \quad \text{for all } c \in C, \quad (93)
$$

where $\hat{f}_{it} = \min_{c \in C}\{\hat{w}_{c,t}^{1-\alpha_i}\hat{r}_{c,t}^{\alpha_i}\}$ for all $i \in I$. Since productivity differences in tradable industries are factor augmenting, regions with higher productivities have higher factor prices. Since there are no productivity differences in nontradable industries, regions with higher factor prices have a higher price level. Note that now a region inside the cone with high productivity in the tradable industries could have a higher price level than a region outside the cone with low productivity in the tradable industries.

---

[68] This assumption makes sense because nontradable industries consist mostly of services, and in the real world productivity differences in services seem small relative to productivity differences in agriculture or manufacturing.

In the world of this example, the price level is determined by a combination of two elements: how adequate are the region's factor proportions to produce in the nontradable industries; and how high is the region's productivity in the tradable industries relative to the nontradable ones. In the world of Example 3.1.1, this second force was not present and Equation (93) was reduced to Equation (92). We could also eliminate the first force by assuming that all regions belong to the cone, i.e. by assuming that there is conditional factor-price equalization. In this case, the price level is given by

$$
P_{c,t} = \left[\pi_{c,Ht}^{1-\alpha_H} \pi_{c,Kt}^{\alpha_H} \frac{P_{Ht}}{\sigma_H} \right]^{\sum_{i \in N_t \cap I^H} \sigma_i}
$$

$$
\times \left[\pi_{c,Ht}^{1-\alpha_K} \pi_{c,Kt}^{\alpha_K} \frac{P_{Kt}}{\sigma_K} \right]^{\sum_{i \in N_t \cap I^K} \sigma_i} \qquad \text{for all } c \in C. \qquad (94)
$$

In Equation (94) the only determinant of the price level is the level of productivity in the tradable industries. This special case is known as the Balassa–Samuelson hypothesis of why the price level is positively correlated with income. Higher productivity in the tradable industries is what makes regions both rich and expensive.

In addition to providing a theory of the price level, the world of this section is also useful because it allows us to study a smoother and more realistic version of the globalization process, i.e. a gradual reduction in the size of N_t. This is not only important for quantitative applications of the theory, but it also leads to new insights regarding the effects of globalization on welfare. The next example shows this.

EXAMPLE 3.1.3. Consider a world economy with H- and K-industries, such that $I^H \cup I^K = I$ and $I^H \cap I^K = \emptyset$. Assume $\alpha_i = 0$ if $i \in I^H$ and $\alpha_i = 1$ if $i \in I^K$, and $\beta_i = 0$ for all $i \in I$. Within each type there are "advanced" and "backward" industries. A-regions have the highest possible productivity in all industries, regardless of whether they are "advanced" or "backward". B-regions have the highest possible productivity only in "backward" industries. Up this point all the assumptions are as in Example 2.1.2, except that industry factor intensities are more extreme. Assume next that initially some industries are nontradable, i.e. $N_t = \emptyset$, and consider a small step in the globalization process: some "advanced" H-industries become tradable, i.e. some elements of the set $N_t \cap I^H$ move into the set $T_t \cap I^H$. What is the effect of this partial reduction in transport costs on regional incomes?

The reduction of transport costs leads to structural transformation: A-regions reduce their production in "backward" H-industries and increase their production in "advanced" H-industries, while B-regions do the opposite.[69] This increases efficiency and raises the combined world production of H-industries, lowering the price of their products and therefore wages all over the world. Therefore, a partial reduction of transport

---

[69] Given the extreme assumptions on industry factor intensities, we know that the distribution of production in K-industries will not be affected.

costs has two effects: an increase in efficiency that lowers prices and benefits all regions, and a change in relative prices that benefits some regions but hurts others. A-regions with a large enough ratio of human to physical capital are worse off as a result of this partial reduction in transport costs.[70] If coupled with an appropriate transfer scheme, partial globalization still constitutes a Pareto improvement for the world economy. But now this transfer scheme might require inter-regional transfers towards A-regions with large enough human to physical capital ratios.

The world of this subsection is a simple and yet very useful generalization of the world of Section 2. It allows us to study the sources of regional differences in price levels and also permits us to consider smoother versions of the globalization process. Despite this progress, the world of this subsection fails to capture a central aspect of transport costs because these only affect final goods. When transport costs affect intermediate inputs, they create incentives to agglomerate production in a single location. We study how this works next.

3.2. Agglomeration effects

Consider a world where transport costs apply only to intermediates, and not to final goods. In particular, assume that the costs of transporting inputs are negligible if $i \in T_t$ but prohibitive if $i \in N_t$, while the costs of trading final goods are negligible for all $i \in I$. An implication of this last assumption is that the price level is the same in all regions and market-based and PPP-adjusted incomes coincide. But this does not mean that we are back to the worlds of Section 2. The inability of trading intermediate inputs creates an incentive to concentrate all the production of an industry in a single region. Only in this way, production of final goods can fully take advantage from the benefits of specialization. This force towards the agglomeration of economic activity has profound effects on the world income distribution and its dynamics.

The formal description of the model is quite similar to that of Section 2.3. Regional analogues to Equations (1)–(3) apply. Since all regions share spending patterns and face the same final goods prices, the price of consumption and investment is the same for all, and we keep Equation (4) as the numeraire rule. Equations (5) and (6) describing technology apply to all regions, with the corresponding factor prices and industry productivities. The only difference with the model of Section 2.2 is that, even after globalization, producers of intermediate inputs in nontradable industries remain sheltered from foreign competition. As a result, in these industries Equations (9)–(10) apply to producers of intermediates in all regions and not only to the lowest-cost ones. Also Equation (8) applies to each region separately since only the demand from local producers of final goods matters for the producers of intermediate inputs. Thus, Equation (44)

---

[70] How is it possible that a region have negative gains from globalization? Since relative prices have changed, the region's trade opportunities have changed also and it might no longer be possible to achieve the level of income and welfare that the region enjoyed before the reduction of transport costs in the *H*-industries.

no longer applies to the producers of intermediate inputs in nontradable industries, and Equation (43) must be modified as follows:

$$I_{c,t} \equiv \left\{ i \in I \,\middle|\, c \in \underset{c' \in C}{\arg\min} \left\{ \left[\frac{1}{Z_{c,it}} \left(\frac{w_{c,t}}{1 - \alpha_i} \right)^{1-\alpha_i} \left(\frac{r_{c,t}}{\alpha_i} \right)^{\alpha_i} \right]^{1-\beta_i} \right. \right.$$

$$\left. \left. \times \left[\int_0^{M_{c,it}} p_{c,it}(m)^{1-\varepsilon_i} \, dm \right]^{\beta_i/(1-\varepsilon_i)} \right\} \right\} \quad \text{for all } c \in C.$$

$$(95)$$

Equation (95) simply recognizes that the number of intermediate inputs available and their prices can vary across regions.[71] Finally, the market clearing conditions in Equations (11), (45) and (46) apply.

This completes the formal description of the model. For any admissible set of capital stocks, i.e. $K_{c,0}$ for all $c \in C$, and sequences for the vectors of savings, human capital and industry productivities, i.e. $S_{c,t}$, $H_{c,t}$ and $A_{c,it}$ for all $c \in C$ and for all $i \in I$, and a sequence for the set N_t (or T_t); an equilibrium of the world economy after globalization consists of a sequence of prices and quantities such that the equations listed above hold at all dates and states of nature. Like the other worlds we have studied up to this point, there might be multiple geographical patterns of production that are consistent with world equilibrium. Unlike the worlds we have studied up to this point however, there might also be multiple prices and world aggregates that are consistent with world equilibrium. This is, in fact, the most prominent feature of this world.

As usual, we start the analysis by defining the set of factor distributions that allow the world economy to replicate the integrated economy. This set is now as follows:

$$FPE_t \equiv \left\{ d_t \in D_t \,\middle|\, \exists x_{c,it}(m) \geqslant 0, \, x^{F}_{c,it} \geqslant 0 \right.$$

$$\text{with } \sum_{c \in C} x_{c,it}(m) = 1, \sum_{c \in C} x^{F}_{c,it} = 1 \text{ and}$$

$$x_{c,it} = (1 - \beta_i) x^{F}_{c,it} + \frac{\beta_i}{M_{it}} \int_0^{M_{it}} x_{c,it}(m) \, dm \text{ such that:}$$

(R1) $x_{c,it} = 0$ if $Z_{c,it} < \max_{c \in C} \{Z_{it}\}$, (96)

(R2) $H_{c,t} = \sum_{i \in I} x_{c,it} H_{it}$ and $K_{c,t} = \sum_{i \in I} x_{c,it} K_{it}$, and

$$\left. (R3) \, x_{c,it} \in \{0, 1\}, \, i \in I \right\}.$$

When comparing this set to those in Definitions (36) and (86), we observe that requirement (R3) is much stronger now. While Definitions (36) and (86) only required

---

[71] Equation (95) assumes that regions always produce intermediates with the lowest indices. This simplifies notation a bit and carries no loss of generality.

that the entire production of each intermediate were located in a single region, Definition (96) requires that the entire production of each industry (i.e. all intermediates plus final goods) be located in a single region. This is a direct implication of the assumption that intermediate inputs are nontradable. Naturally, this strengthening of requirement (R3) reduces the size of FPE_t.[72] Therefore, this set is always smaller than the set in Definition (36). But it need not be smaller than the set in Definition (86), since requirement (R4) no longer applies when final goods are tradable.

Assume that industries are "small" and regions are "large" so that requirement (R3) is not binding. Then, it is straightforward to see that the equilibria studied in Section 2 still apply. If $d_t \in FPE_t$, there exists an equilibrium in which factor prices are equalized across regions and the world economy operates at the same level of efficiency as the integrated economy despite factor immobility and goods market segmentation. If $d_t \notin FPE_t$, the world economy cannot operate at the same level efficiency as the integrated economy and factor prices differ across regions. All the equilibria analyzed in Sections 2.4 and 2.5 are also equilibria for the world of this section, and all the results and intuitions we learned in these subsections remain valid without qualification.

There is however a major difference between this world and the ones we studied in Section 2. While the equilibria described in Section 2 were unique in the worlds analyzed there, they are only one among many in the world of this section. The next example makes this point very clear:

EXAMPLE 3.2.1. Consider a world where all industries are nontradable, i.e. $N_t = I$. Then, any collection of sets $I_{c,t}$ (with $I_{c,t} \neq \emptyset$ for all $c \in C$) that constitutes a partition of I is part of an equilibrium of the world economy.[73] This follows immediately from Equations (5) and (8), which now apply to each region, and Equation (95). Equation (5) shows that the cost of production of final good producers in a given region depends on the number of available inputs. But Equation (8) shows the number of inputs produced in a given region depends on the demand by local producers of final goods.

This world economy exhibits a very strong form of agglomeration effects, as a result of backward linkages in production.[74] If there are no input producers in a region, the cost of producing final goods is infinity and no final goods producer will choose to locate in the region. But if there are no final goods producers in a region, there is no demand for inputs and no input producer will choose to locate in the region. In this world economy, these forces for agglomeration are so strong that they dwarf comparative advantage.

---

[72] The set FPE_t is never empty, but it is smaller than the set of all the factor distributions that are equilibria of the integrated economy. The reason is that some of these equilibria split industries across regions.

[73] This world economy also has equilibria in which industries are split across regions. In these equilibria, all the regions that host a given industry have the same costs of producing the final goods but possibly different numbers and prices of inputs.

[74] Helpman and Krugman (1985) define a backward linkage as a situation in which a final good producer demands many inputs; and a forward linkage as a situation in which many final good producers demand the same input.

It is possible that a given industry locates in a region offering cheap factors and high productivity, but it is also possible that it ends up locating in region offering expensive factors and low productivity.

The world income distribution can be written as follows,

$$\frac{Y_{c,t}}{Y_t} = \sum_{i \in I_{c,t}} \sigma_i \quad \text{for all } c \in C. \tag{97}$$

Equation (97) is formally very similar to Equation (76). Remember that the latter described the world income distribution in Example 2.5.2 where differences in industry productivities were so strong so as to single-handedly determine comparative advantage. The formal similarity between these two worlds follows because both exhibit an extreme form of specialization. The difference, of course, is the underlying force that determines this specialization. While in Example 2.5.2 regions specialize in a given industry because of their high productivity, in Example 3.2.1 regions specialize in a given industry only because of luck. While in Example 2.5.2 the shape and evolution of the world income distribution reflects only the distribution of industry productivities, in Example 3.2.1 it reflects only randomness.[75]

Example 3.2.1 is extreme because it assumes all industries are nontradable. Assume instead that $T_t \neq \emptyset$, and let $I_{c,t}^{N_t} = N_t \cap I_{c,t}$. As a result of agglomeration effects, any collection of sets $I_{c,t}^{N_t}$ (with $I_{c,t}^{N_t} \neq \emptyset$ for all $c \in C$) that constitutes a partition of N_t is an equilibrium of the world economy. Let again $H_{c,t}^T$ and $K_{c,t}^T$ be the factor endowments used in the production of tradable goods, i.e. all final goods and the intermediate inputs of tradable industries. It follows that[76]

$$H_{c,t}^T = \max\left\{0, H_{c,t} - \sum_{i \in I_{c,t}^{N_t}} (1 - \alpha_i)\sigma_i \frac{Y_t}{w_{c,t}}\right\} \quad \text{for all } c \in C, \tag{98}$$

$$K_{c,t}^T = \max\left\{0, K_{c,t} - \sum_{i \in I_{c,t}^{N_t}} \alpha_i \sigma_i \frac{Y_t}{r_{c,t}}\right\} \quad \text{for all } c \in C. \tag{99}$$

Equations (98) and (99) show the factor supplies that are left after subtracting from aggregate factor supplies the factors used in nontradable industries. These equations are analogous to Equations (87) and (88) of Section 3.1. One can use Equations (98) and (99) and a given collection of sets $I_{c,t}^N$ to generalize the theory of Sections 2.4 and 2.5. For instance, in Example 2.4.1 Equations (47)–(52) still apply provided that we write $H_{c,t}^T$ and $K_{c,t}^T$ instead of $H_{c,t}$ and $K_{c,t}$.

---

[75] Given our assumption of full depreciation of inputs, nothing prevents the pattern of production to shift randomly from generation to generation. This model therefore is consistent with any dynamics for the world income distribution. If inputs depreciated slowly, initial randomness would persist for some time.

[76] Here, I am assuming that industries do not split across regions. As mentioned in an earlier footnote, this is possible too.

The effects of this generalization of the theory are hard to assess given the multiplicity of equilibria and the inherent difficulty of finding a "respectable" selection criteria.[77] It is always possible to find perverse equilibria in which regions specialize in the "wrong" industries, i.e. industries in which they do not have comparative advantage. Naturally, all the equilibria of Section 2 in which regions specialize in the industries in which they have comparative advantage still apply if requirement (R3) is not binding (as we have assumed so far). But there is no compelling reason to choose them over some of the alternatives. Moreover, if requirement (R3) is violated or is binding, the equilibria studied in Section 2 no longer apply to this world economy. The following example, inspired by Krugman and Venables (1995), relaxes the assumption that industries are "small" and clearly illustrates this point:

EXAMPLE 3.2.2. Consider a world with two industries $I = \{A, M\}$ and two regions $C = \{N, S\}$. Assume that both industries have the same factor intensities, i.e. $\alpha_i = \alpha$ for all $i \in I$, but different sizes $\sigma_A < 0.5 < \sigma_M$ (remember that $\sigma_A + \sigma_M = 1$). Also assume that both regions are identical, i.e. they have the same savings, human capital, industry productivities and initial condition. Assume next that the world starts in autarky and globalization proceeds in two stages: in the first one industry A becomes tradable, i.e. $N_t = \{M\}$ for $0 \leqslant t < T$; and in the second stage also industry M becomes tradable, i.e. $N_t = \emptyset$ for $t \geqslant T$. In the world of autarky, both regions have the same income and the question that I shall address here is: How does globalization affect the world income distribution?

At date $t = 0$, all transport costs disappear except for those that affect the intermediate inputs of industry M. There are two possible patterns of production and trade that can emerge as a result of this. The first one consists of both regions producing the same they did in autarky and not trading between them. Since both regions would have the same goods and factor prices, there would be no incentive for any producer to deviate from this equilibrium.[78] The second possible pattern of production and trade that can emerge consists of each region specializing in a different industry. For instance, assume N specializes in industry M. The absence of other local producers in industry M means that producers in S have no incentive to produce in industry M. Since spending on industry M is more than half of world spending, factor prices are higher in N and therefore producers in N cannot compete in industry A.[79]

It follows from this discussion that the first stage of globalization generates world inequality and world instability. In the world of autarky, both regions had the same income

---

[77] Matsuyama (1991), Krugman (1991b) and Fukao and Benabou (1993) study some interesting ways of resolving this indeterminacy.

[78] This is an example of an equilibirum in which $d_t \in FPE_t$ and factor prices are equalized and yet the world does not replicate the integrated economy.

[79] The assumption that industry M is large is crucial in reducing the number of equilibria to three. If there were many "small" M-industries there would also be additional equilibria that split these industries between regions in many different ways. Venables (1999) puts bounds on these equilibria.

level and income volatility was driven by volatility in fundamentals, i.e. savings, human capital and industry productivities. Globalization generates divergence in incomes because in the equilibrium with specialization the region that "captures" industry M has higher income than the region that is "stuck" producing in industry A. The world income distribution is determined by Equation (97). One effect of this inequality is faster physical capital accumulation in N than in S. Globalization also generates instability, since the pattern of specialization can now change capriciously just as a result of a change in expectations. At any time the specialization pattern can change to the detriment of N and to the advantage of S. This constitutes an additional source of income volatility that goes beyond fundamentals.

At date $t = T$, transport costs for the intermediate inputs of industry M vanish. Although the pattern of production and trade is not uniquely determined, we know that factor prices and incomes are uniquely determined.[80] Moreover, since we have assumed that both industries have the same factor intensities, the world income distribution is now given by Equation (70). It follows that the second stage of globalization starts a slow process of convergence in incomes that eventually restores equality across regions. Throughout this process, expectations no longer play any role and the only sources of income volatility are fluctuations in fundamentals.

This example features a combination of agglomeration effects and "large" industries that underlies most of the work known as economic geography.[81] This research has focused on explaining how income differences can arise among regions that initially have the same fundamentals. The view of globalization and development that arises from this literature is colorful and suggestive, although it has not been subjected yet to serious empirical analysis.

Not surprisingly, globalization might lead to a Pareto-inferior outcome in the world of this section. The following example, which is related to Examples 2.1.2 and 3.1.3, shows this:

EXAMPLE 3.2.3. Consider a world economy with H- and K-industries, such that $I^H \cup I^K = I$ and $I^H \cap I^K = \emptyset$. Assume $\alpha_i = 0$ if $i \in I^H$ and $\alpha_i = 1$ if $i \in I^K$, and β_i is small (but not zero) for all $i \in I$. Within each type there are "advanced" and "backward" industries. A-regions have the highest possible productivity in all industries, regardless of whether they are "advanced" or "backward". B-regions have the highest possible productivity only in "backward" industries. Assume next that after globalization all industries are nontradable. This world is just a special case of Example 3.2.1. We know therefore that there is an equilibrium in which A-regions specialize in "backwards" industries while B-regions specialize in "advanced" industries. This equilibrium can be easily shown to deliver equal or less income and welfare than autarky. Since β_i is small

---

[80] When $N_t = \emptyset$, we are back to the world of Section 2. The reason why the pattern of production is indeterminate is because I have assumed that industry A and M have the same factor intensities. Otherwise we would be in the case of Example 2.1.1.

[81] See Fujita, Krugman and Venables (1999) and Baldwin et al. (2003).

for all $i \in I$, the benefits from an increase in market size are negligible. Since the allocation of production worsens relative to autarky, production and income go down as a result of globalization. Therefore, it is not possible to find a transfer scheme that ensures that globalization benefits all.[82]

Although this is real a theoretical possibility, it is not clear yet how seriously should we take the possibility that globalization worsens the world allocation of production and reduces welfare. How important empirically are these agglomeration effects? What is the relative importance of randomness and comparative advantage in determining the pattern of production and trade? The answers to these questions are critical in determining whether the basic policy prescription that simply opening up to trade leads to development really applies or not. In the worlds of this section, opening up to trade can lead to miracles and disasters alike. A miracle is nothing but a lucky region that attracts a large number of industries exhibiting agglomeration effects. A disaster is an unlucky region that cannot do so. Opening up to trade is therefore a gamble. It opens the door for industries to come into the region and enrich it, but it also opens the door for industries to leave the region and impoverish it. Naturally, the temptation to change the odds of this gamble using industrial policies and protectionism might be overwhelming. The prescriptions for development are therefore easy to spot but not pleasant. This is a world characterized by negative international spillovers and strong temptations to use "beggar-thy-neighbor" policies.

What about market-size effects? In the world of Section 3.1, differences in regional market size played no role in determining the world income distribution. If intermediate inputs are tradable, all regions use the same specialized inputs and enjoy the same level of industry specialization or technology to produce final goods. In the world of this subsection, differences in regional market size can play a role in determining the world income distribution by allowing large regions to achieve a higher degree of industry specialization.[83] This is one possible mechanism through which market size matters. The next section depicts a world in which market size effects become central.

3.3. The role of local markets

We turn next to a world in which the costs of trading intermediate inputs and final goods are prohibitive if $i \in N_t$, but negligible if $i \in T_t$. As in all the worlds considered in this chapter, the benefits of developing specialized inputs depend on the size of the industry's market. For tradable industries, this market is the world economy. For nontradable industries, this market is the region. As a result, regional differences in market size will

---

[82] See Matsuyama and Takahashi (1998) for another suggestive example of welfare-reducing globalization.
[83] This would be the case if, for instance, in Example 3.2.2 we assumed that $0 = a_M < a_M < 1$. See Puga (1999).

be translated into regional differences in the degree of specialization or technology of nontradable industries.[84]

Formally, this model is very similar to the one in Section 3.1. Equations (81) and (82) describe investment and consumption, while Equations (83) and (84) still provide the numeraire rule and the price level. Naturally, Equation (3) describing spending patterns still applies to all regions, and Equations (5) and (6) describing technology apply to all regions, with the corresponding factor prices and industry productivities. The only difference with the model of Section 3.1 is when Equations (7)–(10) describing pricing policies, input demands and the free-entry condition apply. For tradable industries, these equations apply only to those regions where the lowest-cost producers are located. For nontradable industries, these equations apply to all regions and not only to the lowest-cost ones. Thus, Equation (44) no longer applies to producers in nontradable industries, and Equation (93) must be replaced by Equation (95). Market clearing conditions are also the same as in the model of Section 3.1, and consist of Equations (45) and (46) describing market clearing in regional factor markets, Equation (11) describing market clearing in global markets for tradable industries, and Equation (85) describing market clearing in regional markets for nontradable industries.

This completes the formal description of the model. For any admissible set of capital stocks, i.e. $K_{c,0}$ for all $c \in C$, sequences for the vectors of savings, human capital and industry productivities, i.e. $S_{c,t}$, $H_{c,t}$ and $A_{c,it}$ for all $c \in C$ and for all $i \in I$, and a sequence for the set N_t (or T_t); an equilibrium of the world economy after globalization consists of a sequence of prices and quantities such that the equations listed above hold in all dates and states of nature. Like other worlds we have studied up to now, there might be multiple geographical patterns of production that are consistent with world equilibrium. But unlike the world of the previous subsection (and like the worlds of Section 2 and Section 3.1), prices and world aggregates are uniquely determined.

In this world economy, the set FPE_t is empty. Since intermediate inputs that are produced in a region cannot be used in another region, the world economy cannot reach the level of efficiency of the integrated economy.[85] Despite this, it is relatively straightforward to analyze this world. Define again $H_{c,t}^{T}$ and $K_{c,t}^{T}$ as the factor endowments devoted to the production of tradable goods, i.e. all intermediate inputs and final goods

---

[84] There is little empirical evidence that regional differences in market size are an important determinant of income differences. When one interprets the data from the vantage point of the world of autarky, this observation implies that market size effects are weak and sustained growth is not possible. This has led many researchers to spend a substantial effort in developing autarky models where sustained growth is possible without market size effects. Somewhat ironically, once one takes a world equilibrium view of the growth process what requires a substantial effort is to develop models where regional differences in market size do affect the world income distribution.

[85] The set FPE_t might be nonempty in the limiting case where $\beta_i \rightarrow 0$ (or $\varepsilon_i \rightarrow \infty$) for all $i \in I$. But that limiting case brings us to the world of Section 3.1.

of tradable industries. Straightforward algebra shows that[86]

$$
H_{c,t}^{\mathrm{T}} = \max\left\{0, H_{c,t}\left(1 - \sum_{i \in N_t}(1 - \alpha_i)\sigma_i\right)\right.
$$

$$
\left. - K_{c,t}\left(\frac{w_{c,t}}{r_{c,t}}\right)^{-1}\sum_{i \in N_t}(1 - \alpha_i)\sigma_i\right\} \quad \text{for all } c \in C, \tag{100}
$$

$$
K_{c,t}^{\mathrm{T}} = \max\left\{0, K_{c,t}\left(1 - \sum_{i \in N_t}\alpha_i\sigma_i\right)\right.
$$

$$
\left. - H_{c,t}\frac{w_{c,t}}{r_{c,t}}\sum_{i \in N_t}\alpha_i\sigma_i\right\} \quad \text{for all } c \in C. \tag{101}
$$

Since factor supplies are well behaved, all the results in Sections 2.4 and 2.5 regarding market-based incomes and factor prices still go through in the presence of nontradable industries. As in Section 3.1, the only important difference between the world of this subsection and the one in Section 2 is that there is a discrepancy between market-based and real incomes and factor prices. In particular, we can write the price level of region c as follows,

$$
P_{c,t} = \prod_{i \in N_t}\left\{\frac{1}{\sigma_i}\left[\frac{1}{Z_{c,it}}\left(\frac{w_{c,t}}{1 - \alpha_i}\right)^{1-\alpha_i}\left(\frac{r_{c,t}}{\alpha_i}\right)^{\alpha_i}\right]^{1-\beta_i}\right.
$$

$$
\left. \times \left[\int_0^{M_{c,it}} p_{c,it}(m)^{1-\varepsilon_i}\,\mathrm{d}m\right]^{\beta_i/(1-\varepsilon_i)}\right\}^{\sigma_i} \quad \text{for all } c \in C. \tag{102}
$$

The only difference between this equation and Equation (91) is that the number and price of intermediate inputs varies across regions. Using Equations (6) and (10), we can transform Equation (103) into the following

$$
P_{c,t} = \prod_{i \in N_t}\left\{\frac{1}{\sigma_i^{\mu_i}A_{c,it}}\left(\frac{w_{c,t}}{1 - \alpha_i}\right)^{(1-\alpha_i)\mu_i}\left(\frac{r_{c,t}}{\alpha_i}\right)^{\alpha_i\mu_i}Y_{c,t}^{1-\mu_i}\right\}^{\sigma_i}. \tag{103}
$$

Basically, this model brings another element to the theory of the price level. To the extent that nontradable industries exhibit increasing returns, regions with larger markets have lower price levels and higher real incomes.

It is straightforward to re-do some of the previous examples in the context of this world. But I shall not do this. The picture that this world generates is clear and unappealing from an empirical standpoint: regional differences in market size are reflected in regional differences in price levels. Ceteris paribus, larger local markets do not lead to higher market-based incomes and factor prices. But they do lead to lower price levels and, as a result, to higher real incomes and factor prices. This is clearly counterfactual.

---

[86] To see this, note that the shares of human and physical capital devoted to producing the final good of the ith nontradable industry are now $(1 - \alpha_i)$ and α_i. Add over industries and note that the share of spending in the ith industry is $\sigma_i Y_{c,t}$.

4. Final remarks

This chapter has developed a unified and yet tractable framework that integrates many key insights of the fields of international trade and economic growth. Its distinguishing feature is that it provides a global view of the growth process, that is, a view that treats different regions of the world as parts of a single whole. This framework incorporates the standard idea that economic growth in the world economy is determined by a tension between diminishing returns and market size effects to capital accumulation. A substantial effort has been made to show how trade frictions of various sorts determine the shape of the world income distribution and its dynamics.

Despite the length of this chapter, some important topics have been left out. The first and most glaring omission is asset trade. This type of trade allows the world economy to redirect its investment towards regions that offer the highest risk-adjusted return.[87] To the extent that patterns of trade are determined by comparative advantage, these are the regions where capital is scarce and productive and this raises efficiency in the world economy. To the extent that patterns of trade are determined by luck, asset trade magnifies the effect of this randomness and this could either raise or lower the efficiency of the world economy. If this were all there is to asset trade, it would not be too difficult to add to this chapter a section on asset trade in which we endow the world economy with a complete set of asset markets. But asset trade does not seem to work as the standard theory of complete markets would suggest. Empirically asset trade seems both much smaller and much more volatile than it would be warranted by its fundamentals, i.e. savings, human capital and industry productivities. To understand these aspects of asset trade it seems necessary to incorporate to the theory features such as sovereign risk, asymmetric information and asset bubbles. Although this is a very important task, it would require another chapter of this magnitude and must therefore be left for future work.[88]

A second important omission of this chapter is government policy. A central aspect of globalization so far has been its imbalanced nature. While economic integration has proceeded at a relatively fast pace, political integration is advancing at a slower pace or not advancing at all. The world economy today features global (or semi-global) markets but local governments. In this context, globalization can lead to a decline in growth and income through a reduction in the quality of policies. International spillovers eliminate the incentives to adopt good but costly policies. Trade also "bails out" regions with bad policies since they can spare some of their costs by specializing in industries where bad

---

[87] Naturally, asset trade also allows for a better risk sharing and this raises welfare. Better risk sharing might also increase investment and growth. See Obstfeld (1994).

[88] Among the many papers that study the behavior of financial markets in world equilibrium models, see Gertler and Rogoff (1990), Acemoglu and Zilibotti (1997), Ventura (2002), Matsuyama (2004b), Martin and Rey (2002, 2004), Kraay et al. (2005) and Broner and Ventura (2005).

policies have little effects. As a result of these forces, globalization could create a "race to the bottom" in policies that lowers savings, human capital, and industry productivities. And this could potentially mitigate or even reverse the benefits from economic integration.[89] Understanding the circumstances under which this "race to the bottom" can happen and the appropriate policy corrections that are required to allow the world economy to take full advantage of globalization is another important task. But this task would also require another chapter of this magnitude and cannot be undertaken here.

At first sight, factor movements might seem a third important omission. But I think it is less so. As mentioned in Section 2, the notion that physical and human capital is geographically immobile seems a fair description of reality. Moreover, the benefits of factor mobility might be reaped without factors having to move at all. What is really important about factor movements is that they permit factors located in different regions to work together and produce. Advances in telecommunications technology and the standardization of software allow producers around the world to combine physical and human capital located in different regions in a single production process. We can always think of this situation as one in which the production process has been broken down into intermediate inputs. An increased ability to combine factors located in different regions could therefore be modeled as an increase in the tradability of intermediate inputs, or as an increase in the share of intermediate inputs, or as the development of additional inputs with more extreme factor intensities. All of these possibilities could be (and some have already been) analyzed within the framework developed in this chapter.[90]

The goal of this chapter has been to convey a global way of thinking about the growth process. To claim success, you should be persuaded by now that developing and systematically studying world equilibrium models is a necessary condition to gain a true understanding of the growth process. By "true", I mean the sort of understanding that allows us to frame clear and unambiguous hypotheses about why some countries are richer than others or what are the main forces that drive economic growth in the world economy. To claim success, you should also be convinced by now that much is already known about the structure of world equilibrium models. But you should also be aware that the global view of economic growth that these models reveal is still somewhat fuzzy and blurred. Sharpening this view is a major challenge for growth and trade theorists alike.

---

[89] See Levchenko (2004) for a situation in which globalization leads to a "race to the top" in government policies, though.

[90] An increase in the tradability of inputs corresponds to a gradual increase in T_t in the models of Sections 3.2 and 3.3. An increase in the share of intermediate inputs corresponds to a gradual increase in β_i, while the development of inputs with more extreme factor intensities corresponds to a gradual change in α_i. I have assumed throughout that industry characteristics are time-invariant only for simplicity. All the formulas in this chapter remain valid if we instead assume that industry characteristics vary, perhaps stochastically, over time.

Acknowledgements

I dedicate this research to the memory of Rudi Dornbusch, the best mentor, colleague and friend a young economist could have hoped for, and always capable of making others see things differently. I am thankful to Fernando Broner, Gino Gancia, Francesc Ortega and Diego Puga for their useful comments and to Matilde Bombardini, Philip Sauré and Rubén Segura-Cayuela for providing excellent research assistance. I am also grateful to the Fundación Ramón Areces for its generous financial support.

References

Acemoglu, D. (2003). "Patterns of skill premia". Review of Economic Studies 70, 199–230.

Acemoglu, D., Ventura, J. (2002). "The world income distribution". Quarterly Journal of Economics 107, 659–694.

Acemoglu, D., Zilibotti, F. (1997). "Was Prometheus unbound by chance? Risk, diversification and growth". Journal of Political Economy 105, 709–751.

Acemoglu, D., Zilibotti, F. (2001). "Productivity differences". Quarterly Journal of Economics 106, 563–605.

Ades, A., Glaeser, E.L. (1999). "Evidence on growth, increasing returns, and the extent of the market". Quarterly Journal of Economics 114 (3), 1025–1045.

Alcalá, F., Ciccone, A. (2003). "Trade, extent of the market, and economic growth 1960–1996". Mimeo. Universitat Pompeu Fabra.

Alcalá, F., Ciccone, A. (2004). "Trade and productivity". Quarterly Journal of Economics 119 (2), 613–646.

Alesina, A., Spolaore, E., Wacziarg, R. (2000). "Economic integration and political disintegration". American Economic Review 90 (5), 1276–1296.

Alvarez, F., Lucas, R. (2004). "General equilibrium analysis of the Eaton–Kourtum model of international trade". Manuscript. University of Chicago.

Aoki, M. (1986). "Dynamic adjustment behaviour to anticipated supply shocks in a two-country model". Economic Journal 96, 80–100.

Arnold, L.G. (2002). "On the growth effect of North–South trade: The role of labor market flexibility". Journal of International Economics 58, 451–466.

Atkeson, A., Kehoe, P. (1998). "Paths of development for early and late bloomers in a dynamic Hecksher–Ohlin model". Staff Report 256. Federal Reserve Bank of Minneapolis.

Backus, D., Kehoe, P., Kydland, F. (1992). "International real business cycle". Journal of Political Economy 100, 745–775.

Baldwin, R. (1992). "Measurable dynamic gains from trade". Journal of Political Economy 100, 162–174.

Baldwin, R., Forslid, R. (2000). "Trade liberalization and endogenous growth. A q-theory approach". Journal of International Economics 50, 497–517.

Baldwin, R., Martin, P., Ottaviano, G.I.P. (2001). "Global income divergence, trade, and industrialization: The geography of growth take-offs". Journal of Economic Growth 5, 5–37.

Baldwin, R., Forslid, R., Martin, P., Ottaviano, G., Robert-Nicaud, F. (2003). Economic Geography and Public Policy. Princeton University Press, Princeton, NJ, ISBN 0-691-10275-9.

Bardham, P. (1965a). "Equilibrium growth in the international economy". Quarterly Journal of Economics 79, 455–464.

Bardham, P. (1965b). "Optimal accumulation and international trade". Review of Economics Studies 32, 241–244.

Bardham, P. (1966). "On factor accumulation and the pattern of international specialization". Review of Economics Studies 33, 39–44.

Barro, R.J. (1991). "Economic growth in a cross section of countries". Quarterly Journal of Economics 106 (2), 407–443.

Basu, S., Weil, P. (1998). "Appropriate technology and growth". Quarterly Journal of Economics 113, 1025–1053.

Baxter, M. (1992). "Fiscal policy, specialization in the two-sector model: The return of Ricardo?". Journal of Political Economy 100, 713–744.

Bourguignon, F., Morrisson, C. (2002). "Inequality among world citizens: 1820–1992". American Economic Review 92 (4), 727–744.

Brems, H. (1956). "The foreign trade accelerator and the international transmission of growth". Econometrica 24, 223–238.

Brems, H. (1970). "A growth model of international direct investment". American Economic Review 60, 320–331.

Brezis, S.L., Krugman, P., Tsiddon, D. (1993). "Leapfrogging in international competition: A theory of cycles in national technological leadership". American Economic Review 83, 1211–1219.

Broner, F., Ventura, J. (2005). "Managing financial integration". Manuscript. CREI.

Buiter, W.H. (1981). "Time preference and international lending and borrowing in an overlapping-generations model". Journal of Political Economy 79, 769–797.

Caselli, F., Esquivel, G., Lefort, F. (1996). "Reopening the convergence debate: A new look at cross-country growth empirics". Journal of Economic Growth.

Chang, R. (1990). "International coordination of fiscal deficits". Journal of Monetary Economics 25, 347–366.

Chui, M., Levine, P., Pearlman, J. (2001). "Winners and losers in a North–South model of growth, innovation and product cycles". Journal of Development Economics 65, 333–365.

Cuñat, A., Mafezzoli, M. (2004a). "Neoclassical growth and commodity trade". Review of Economic Dynamics 7 (3), 707–736.

Cuñat, A., Mafezzoli, M. (2004b). "Heckscher–Ohlin business cycles". Review of Economic Dynamics 7 (3), 555–585.

Davis, D. (1995). "Intra-industry trade: A Heckscher–Ohlin–Ricardo approach". Journal of International Economics 39, 201–226.

Deardorff, A.V. (2001). "Rich and poor countries in neoclassical trade and growth". Economic Journal 61, 277–294.

Devereux, M., Lapham, B.J. (1994). "The stability of economic integration and endogenous growth". Quarterly Journal of Economics 59, 299–305.

Devereux, M.B., Saito, M. (1997). "Growth and risk-sharing with incomplete international assets markets". Journal of International Economics 42, 453–481.

Devereux, M.B., Shi, S. (1991). "Capital accumulation and the current account in a two-country model". Journal of International Economics 50, 1–25.

Dinopoulos, E., Segerstrom, P. (1999). "A Schumpeterian model of protection and relative wages". American Economic Review 89 (3), 450–472.

Dinopoulos, E., Syropoulos, C. (1997). "Tariffs and Schumpeterian growth". Journal of International Economics 42, 425–452.

Dixit, A.K., Norman, V. (1989). Theory of International Trade. Cambridge University Press, Cambridge, NY; Port Chester, Melbourne, Sydney, ISBN 0-521-23481-6, 1989.

Dollar, D. (1986). "Technological innovation, capital mobility, and the product cycle in North–South trade". American Economic Review 76, 177–190.

Dollar, D., Kraay, A. (2003). "Institutions, trade, and growth". Journal of Monetary Economics 50 (1), 133–162.

Dornbusch, R., Fischer, S., Samuelson, P.A. (1977). "Comparative advantage, trade, and payments in a Ricardian model with a continuum of goods". American Economic Review 67 (5), 823–839.

Dornbusch, R., Fischer, S., Samuelson, P.A. (1980). "Heckscher–Ohlin trade theory with a continuum of goods". Quarterly Journal of Economics 95 (2), 203–224.

Eaton, J., Kortum, S. (2002). "Technology, geography, and trade". Econometrica 70, 1741–1779.

Feenstra, R.C. (1996). "Trade and uneven growth". Journal of Development Economics 49, 229–256.

Findlay, R. (1978). "An 'Austrian' model of international trade and interest rate equalization". Journal of Political Economy 86, 989–1007.

Findlay, R. (1980). "The terms of trade and equilibrium growth in the world economy". American Economic Review 70, 291–299.

Findlay, R., Kierzkowski, H. (1983). "International trade and capital: A simple general equilibrium model". Journal of Political Economy 91, 957–978.

Fisher, O'N. (1995). "Growth, trade, and international transfers". Journal of International Economics 41, 143–158.

Flam, H., Helpman, E. (1987). "Vertical product differentiation and North–South trade". American Economic Review 77, 810–822.

Francois, J.F. (1996). "Trade, labour force growth and wages". Economic Journal 439, 1586–1609.

Frankel, J.A., Romer, D. (1999). "Does trade cause growth?". American Economic Review 89 (3), 379–399.

Frenkel, J., Razin, A. (1985). "Government spending, debt, and international economic interdependence". Economics Journal 95, 619–636.

Frenkel, J., Razin, A. (1986). "Fiscal policies in the world economy". Journal of Political Economy 94, 564–594.

Fujita, M.P., Krugman, P.R., Venables, A.J. (1999). The Spatial Economy. MIT Press, Cambridge, MA, ISBN 0-262-06204-6.

Fukao, K., Benabou, R. (1993). "History vs. expectations: A comment". Quarterly Journal of Economics 108, 535–542.

Gale, D. (1971). "General equilibrium with imbalance of trade". Journal of International Economics 1, 141–158.

Galor, O., Polemarchakis, H.M. (1987). "Intertemporal equilibrium and the transfer paradox". Review of Economic Studies 54, 147–156.

Gancia, G. (2003). "Globalization, divergence and stagnation". IIES Working Paper 720.

Gertler, M., Rogoff, K. (1990). "North–South lending and endogenous domestic capital market inefficiencies". Journal of Monetary Economics 26, 245–266.

Glass, A.J., Saggi, K. (1998). "International technology transfer and the technology gap". Journal of Development Economics 55, 369–398.

Glass, A.J., Saggi, K. (2002). "Intellectual property rights and foreign direct investment". Journal of International Economics 56, 387–410.

Greenwood, J., Williamson, S.D. (1989). "International financial intermediation and aggregate fluctuations under alternative exchange rate regimes". Journal of Monetary Economics 23, 401–431.

Grossman, G., Helpman, E. (1989). "Product development and international trade". Journal of Political Economy 97, 1261–1283.

Grossman, G.M., Helpman, E. (1990). "Comparative advantage and long-run growth". American Economic Review 53, 796–815.

Grossman, G., Helpman, E. (1991a). "Quality ladders in the theory of growth". Review of Economic Studies 58, 43–61.

Grossman, G.M., Helpman, E. (1991b). "Quality ladders and product cycles". Quarterly Journal of Economics 100, 557–586.

Grossman, G.M., Helpman, E. (1991c). Innovation and Growth in the Global Economy. MIT Press, Cambridge, MA, ISBN 0-262-07136-3.

Hall, R.E., Jones, C.I. (1999). "Why do some countries produces more output per worker than others?". Quarterly Journal of Economics.

Heathcote, J., Perri, F. (2002). "Financial autarky and international business cycles". Journal of Monetary Economics 49, 601–627.

Helpman, E. (1993). "Innovation, imitation, and intellectual property rights". Econometrica 61, 1247–1280.

Helpman, E., Krugman, P.R. (1985). Market Structure and Foreign Trade. MIT Press, Cambridge, MA; London, England, ISBN 0-262-08150-4.

Howitt, P. (2000). "Endogenous growth and cross-country income differences". American Economic Review 190, 829–846.

Jensen, R., Thursby, M. (1987). "A decision theoretic model of innovation, technology transfer and trade". Review of Economic Studies 54, 631–647.

Klenow, P.J., Rodriguez-Clare, A. (1997). "The neoclassical revival in growth economics: Has it gone too far?". NBER Macroeconomics Annual, 73–102.

Knight, M., Loayza, N., Villanueva, D. (1993). "Testing the neoclassical theory of economic growth". IMF Staff Papers 40, 512–541.

Kraay, A., Loayza, N., Servén, L., Ventura, J. (2005). "Country portfolios". Journal of the European Economic Association 3 (4), 914–945.

Krugman, P. (1979). "A model of innovation, technological transfer and the world distribution of income". Journal of Political Economy 87, 253–266.

Krugman, P. (1981). "Trade, accumulation, and uneven growth". Journal of International Economics 8, 149–161.

Krugman, P. (1987). "The narrow moving band, the Dutch disease, and the competitive consequences of Mrs. Thatcher". Journal of Development Economics 27, 41–55.

Krugman, P. (1991a). "Increasing returns and economic geography". Journal of Political Economy 99, 483–499.

Krugman, P. (1991b). "History vs. expectations". Quarterly Journal of Economics 107, 651–667.

Krugman, P., Venables, A. (1995). "Globalization and the inequality of nations". Quarterly Journal of Economics 109, 857–880.

Lai, E.L.-C. (1995). "The product cycle and the world distribution of income. A reformulation". Journal of International Economics 41, 369–382.

Lai, E.L.-C. (1998). "International intellectual property rights protection and the rate of product innovation". Journal of Development Economics 55, 133–153.

Levchenko, A. (2004). "Institutional quality and international trade". Manuscript. MIT.

Loayza, N.V., Knight, M., Villanueva, D. (1993). "Testing the neoclassical theory of economics growth: A panel data approach". IMF Staff Papers.

Lundborg, P., Segerstrom, P.S. (2002). "The growth and welfare effects of international mass migration". Journal of International Economics 56, 177–204.

Mankiw, N.G., Romer, D., Weil, D.N. (1992). "A contribution to the empirics of economic growth". Quarterly Journal of Economics 107 (2), 407–437.

Martin, P., Rey, H. (2002). "Globalization and emerging markets: With or without crash". CEPR Working Paper DP3378.

Martin, P., Rey, H. (2004). "Financial super-markets: Size matters for asset trade". Journal of International Economics 64, 335–661.

Matsuyama, K. (1991). "Increasing returns, industrialization and indeterminacy of equilibrium". Quarterly Journal of Economics 106, 617–650.

Matsuyama, K. (2000). "A Ricardian model with a continuum of goods under nonhomothetic preferences: Demand complementarities, income distribution, and North–South trade". Journal of Political Economy 108, 1093–1120.

Matsuyama, K. (2004a). "Beyond icebergs: Modeling globalization as biased technical change". Working Paper. Northwestern University.

Matsuyama, K. (2004b). "Financial market globalization, symmetry-breaking and endogenous inequality of nations". Econometrica 72 (3), 853–884.

Matsuyama, K., Takahashi, T. (1998). "Self-defeating regional concentration". Review of Economic Studies 65, 211–234.

Modigliani, F., Ando, A. (1963). "The life cycle hypothesis of saving". American Economic Review 53 (1), 55–84.

Molana, H., Vines, D. (1989). "North–South growth and the terms of trade: A model on Kaldorian lines". Economic Journal 99, 443–453.

Mountford, A. (1998). "Trade, convergence and overtaking". Journal of International Economics 46, 167–182.

Myers, M.G. (1970). "Equilibrium growth and capital movements between open economies". American Economic Review 60, 393–397.

Obstfeld, M. (1989). "Fiscal deficits and relative prices in a growing world economy". Journal of Monetary Economics 23, 461–484.

Obstfeld, M. (1994). "Risk-taking, global diversification, and growth". American Economic Review 84, 1310–1329.

Oniki, H., Uzawa, H. (1965). "Patterns of trade and investment in a dynamic model of international trade". Review of Economics Studies 32, 15–38.

Ono, Y., Shibata, A. (1991). "Spill-over effects of supply-side changes in a two-country economy with capital accumulation". Journal of International Economics 33, 127–146.

Ortega, F. (2004). "Immigration policy and the welfare state". Manuscript. Universitat Pompeu, Fabra.

Pritchett, L. (1997). "Divergence, big time". Journal of Economic Perspectives 11 (3), 3–17.

Puga, D. (1999). "The rise and fall of regional inequalities". European Economic Review 43, 303–334.

Puga, D., Venables, A.J. (1999). "Agglomeration and economic development: Import substitution vs. trade liberalisation". Economic Journal 109, 292–311.

Rauch, J.E. (1991). "Reconciling the pattern of trade with the pattern of migration". American Economic Review 81, 775–796.

Rivera-Batiz, L., Romer, P.M. (1991). "Economic integration and endogenous growth". Quarterly Journal of Economics 106, 531–555.

Rodriguez, F., Rodrik, D. (2000). "Trade policy and economic growth: A skeptic's guide to the cross-national evidence". NBER Macroeconomics Annual.

Ruffin, R.J. (1979). "Growth and the long-run theory of international capital movements". American Economic Review 69, 832–842.

Sachs, J., Warner, A. (1995). "Economic reform and the process of global integration". Brookings Papers on Economic Activity 1.

Samuelson, P.A. (1948). "International trade and the equalization of factor prices". Economic Journal 58, 163–184.

Samuelson, P.A. (1949). "International trade and the equalization of factor prices, again". Economic Journal 59, 181–197.

Sauré, P. (2004a). "Revisiting the infant industry argument". Manuscript. Universitat Pompeau, Fabra.

Sauré, P. (2004b). "How to use industrial policy to sustain trade agreements". Manuscript. Universitat Pompeau, Fabra.

Segerstrom, P.S., Anant, T.C.A., Dinopoulos, E. (1990). "A Schumpeterian model of the product life cycle". American Economic Review 80, 1077–1091.

Şener, F. (2001). "Schumpeterian unemployment, trade and wages". Journal of International Economics 56, 119–148.

Sibert, A. (1985). "Capital accumulation and foreign investment taxation". Review of Economic Studies 52, 331–345.

Solow, R.M. (1956). "A contribution to the theory of economic growth". Quarterly Journal of Economics 70 (1), 65–94.

Stiglitz, J.E. (1970). "Factor price equalization in a dynamic economy". Journal of Political Economy 78, 456–488.

Stokey, N.L. (1991). "The volume and composition of trade between rich and poor countries". Review of Economic Studies 58, 63–80.

Taylor, M.S. (1993). "Quality ladders and Ricardian trade". Journal of International Economics 34, 225–243.

Taylor, M.S. (1994). "Once-off and continuing gains from trade". Review of Economic Studies 61, 589–601.

Trefler, D. (1993). "International factor price differences: Leontief was right!". Journal of Political Economy 101 (6), 961–987.

van Elkan, R. (1996). "Catching up and slowing down: Learning and growth patterns in an open economy". Journal of International Economics 41, 95–111.

van de Klundert, T., Smulders, S. (1996). "North–South knowledge spillovers and competition: Convergence versus divergence". Journal of Development Economics 50, 213–232.

van de Klundert, T., Smulders, S. (2001). "Loss of technological leadership of rentier economies: A two-country endogenous growth model". Journal of International Economics 54, 211–231.

Vanek, J. (1971). "Economic growth and international trade in pure theory". Quarterly Journal of Economics 85, 377–390.

Venables, A. (1999). "The international division of industries: Clustering and comparative advantage in a multi-industry model". Scandinavian Journal of Economics 101 (4), 495–513.

Ventura, J. (1997). "Growth and interdependence". Quarterly Journal of Economics 112 (1), 57–84.

Ventura, J. (2002). "Bubbles and capital flows". NBER Working Paper No. 9304.

Wang, J.-Y. (1990). "Growth, technology transfer, and the long-run theory of international capital movements". Journal of International Economics 29, 255–271.

Wilson, C. (1980). "On the general structure of Ricardian models with a continuum of goods: Applications to growth, tariff theory, and technical change". Econometrica 48, 1675–1702.

Yanagawa, N. (1996). "Economic development in a world with many countries". Journal of Development Economics 49, 271–288.

Yang, G., Maskus, K.E. (2001). "Intellectual property rights, licensing, and innovation in an endogenous product-cycle model". Journal of International Economics 53, 169–387.

Young, A. (1991). "Learning by doing and the dynamic effects of international trade". Quarterly Journal of Economics 106 (2), 369–405.

Young, A. (1995). "The tyranny of numbers: Confronting the statistical realities of the East Asian growth experience". Quarterly Journal of Economics 110 (3), 641–680.

Chapter 23

TRADE, GROWTH AND THE SIZE OF COUNTRIES

ALBERTO ALESINA

Harvard University,
CEPR
and
NBER

ENRICO SPOLAORE

Tufts University

ROMAIN WACZIARG

Stanford University,
CEPR
and
NBER

Contents

Abstract	1500
1. Introduction	1501
2. Size, openness and growth: Theory	1502
2.1. The costs and benefits of size	1502
2.1.1. The benefits of size	1503
2.1.2. The costs of size	1505
2.2. A model of size, trade and growth	1506
2.2.1. Production and trade	1506
2.2.2. Capital accumulation and growth	1508
2.3. The equilibrium size of countries	1510
2.4. Summing up	1513
3. Size, openness and growth: Empirical evidence	1514
3.1. Trade and growth: a review of the evidence	1514
3.2. Country size and growth: a review of the evidence	1516
3.3. Summing up	1518
3.4. Trade, size and growth in a cross-section of countries	1518
3.4.1. Descriptive statistics	1519
3.4.2. Growth, openness and size: panel regressions	1522

Handbook of Economic Growth, Volume 1B. Edited by Philippe Aghion and Steven N. Durlauf
© 2005 Elsevier B.V.   All rights reserved
DOI: 10.1016/S1574-0684(05)01023-3

3.5. Endogeneity of openness: 3SLS estimates	1525
3.5.1. Magnitudes and summary	1527
4. Country size and trade in history	1530
4.1. The city-states	1530
4.2. The absolutist period	1531
4.3. The birth of the modern nation-state	1531
4.4. The colonial empires	1532
4.5. Borders in the interwar period	1533
4.6. Borders in the post–Second World War period	1534
4.7. The European Union	1536
5. Conclusion	1538
Acknowledgements	1539
References	1539

Abstract

Normally, economists take the size of countries as an exogenous variable. Nevertheless, the borders of countries and their size change, partially in response to economic factors such as the pattern of international trade. Conversely, the size of countries influences their economic performance and their preferences for international economic policies – for instance smaller countries have a greater stake in maintaining free trade. In this paper, we review the theory and evidence concerning a growing body of research that considers both the impact of market size on growth and the endogenous determination of country size. We argue that our understanding of economic performance and of the history of international economic integration can be greatly improved by bringing the issue of country size at the forefront of the analysis of growth.

1. Introduction

Does size matter for economic success? Of the five largest countries in the world in terms of population, China, India, the United States, Indonesia and Brazil, only the United States is a rich country.[1] In fact the richest country in the world in 2000, in terms of income per capita, was Luxembourg, with less than 500,000 inhabitants. Among the richest countries in the world, many have populations well below the world median, which was about 6 million people in 2000. And when we consider growth of income per capita rather than income levels, again we find small countries among the top performers. For example Singapore, with 3 million inhabitants, experienced the highest growth rate of per capita income of any country between 1960 and 1990.[2] These examples show that a country can be small and prosper, or, at the very least, that size alone is not enough to guarantee economic success.

In this chapter, we discuss the relationship between the scale of an economy and economic growth from two points of view. We first discuss the effects of an economy's size on its growth rate and we then examine how the size of countries evolves in response to economic factors.

The "new growth literature", with its emphasis on increasing returns to scale, has devoted much attention to the question of size of an economy.[3] It is therefore somewhat surprising that the question of the effect of border design and size of the polity as a determinant of economic growth has received limited attention. One reason is that, as we will see below, measures of country size (population or land area) used alone in growth regressions, generally do not have much explanatory power. Even less attention has been devoted to the endogenous determination of borders even by those researchers who have paid attention to the effect of geography on growth. Borders are not exogenous geographical features: they are a human-made institution. In fact, even the geographical characteristics of a country are in some sense endogenous: for instance whether a country is landlocked or not is the result of the design of its borders, which in turn depend upon domestic and international factors.

While economists have remain on the sidelines on this topic, philosophers devoted much energy thinking about country size. Plato, Aristotle and Montesquieu worried about the political costs of large states. Aristotle wrote in Politics that "experience has shown that it is difficult, if not impossible, for a populous state to be run by good laws".

---

[1] Throughout this paper we use the word "country", "nation" and "state" interchangeably, meaning a polity defined by borders and a national government and citizens. We are not dealing with the concept of a nation as a people not necessarily identified by borders and a government.

[2] Based on all measures of growth in per capita PPP income in constant prices constructed from the Penn World Tables, version 6.1.

[3] However, it is well known that increasing returns are not *necessary* for a positive relationship between market size and economic performance. As we will see in our analytical section, larger markets may entail larger gains from trade and higher income per capita even when the technology exhibits constant returns to scale.

Influenced by Montesquieu, the founding fathers of the United States were preoccupied with the potentially excessive size of the new Federal State. On the other hand, liberal thinkers who in the nineteenth century contributed to defining modern nation-states were concerned that in order to be economically, and therefore politically viable, countries should not be too small. Historians have studied the formation of states and their size and emphasized the role of wars and military technology as an important determinant. In fact, rulers, especially nondemocratic ones, have always seen size as a measure of power and tried to expand the size of the territory under their rule. So, while throughout history country size seemed to be a constant preoccupation of philosophers, political scientists and policymakers, economists have largely ignored this subject.

In recent decades the question of borders has risen to the center of attention in international politics. The collapse of the Soviet Union, decolonization, and the break-up of several countries have rapidly increased the number of independent polities. In 1946 there were 76 independent countries, in 2002 there were 193.[4] East Timor was the latest new independent country at the time of this writing.

In this chapter, we explore the relatively small recent economics literature dealing with the size of countries and its effect on economic growth. In particular we ask several questions: Does size matter for economic success, and if so why and through which channels? What forces lead to changes in the organization of borders, or to put it differently what determines the evolution of the size of countries? Obviously the second question is very broad. Here we focus specifically a narrower version of this question, namely how economic factors, especially the trade regime, influence size.[5]

This chapter is organized as follows. Section 2 discusses a general framework for thinking in economic terms about the optimal and the equilibrium size of countries, providing a formal model that focuses on the effect of size on income levels and growth, with special emphasis on the role of trade. Section 3 reviews the empirical evidence on these issues and provides updated and new results. Section 4 briefly explores how the relationship between country size, international trade and growth have played out historically. The last section highlights questions for future research.

2. Size, openness and growth: Theory

2.1. The costs and benefits of size

We think of the equilibrium size of countries as emerging from the trade-off between the benefit of size and the costs of preference heterogeneity in the population, an approach followed by Alesina and Spolaore (1997, 2003) and Alesina, Spolaore and Wacziarg (2000).

---

[4] These include the 191 member states of the United Nations, plus the Vatican and Taiwan.

[5] For a broader discussion see Alesina and Spolaore (2003) and Spolaore (2005).

2.1.1. The benefits of size

The main benefits from size in terms of population are the following:

(1) There are economies of scale in the production of public goods. The per capita cost of many public goods is lower in larger countries, where more taxpayers pay for them. Think, for instance, of defense, a monetary and financial system, a judicial system, infrastructure for communications, police and crime prevention, public health, embassies, national parks, etc. In many cases, part of the cost of public goods is independent of the number of users or taxpayers, or grows less than proportionally, so that the per capita costs of many public goods is declining with the number of taxpayers. Alesina and Wacziarg (1998) documented that the share of government spending over GDP is decreasing in population; that is, smaller countries have larger governments.

(2) A larger country (both in terms of population and national product) is less subject to foreign aggression. Thus, safety is a public good that increases with country size. Also, and related to the size of government argument above, smaller countries may have to spend proportionally more for defense than larger countries given economies of scale in defense spending. Empirically, the relationship between country size and share of spending of defense is affected by the fact that small countries can enter into military alliances, but in general, size brings about more safety. Note that if a small country enters into a military alliance with a larger one, the latter may provide defense, but it may extract some form of compensation, direct or indirect, from the smaller partner. In this sense, even allowing for military alliances, being large is an advantage.

(3) Larger countries can better internalize cross-regional externalities by centralizing the provision of those public goods that involve strong externalities.[6]

(4) Larger countries are better able to provide insurance to regions affected by imperfectly correlated shocks. Consider Catalonia, for instance. If this region experiences a recession worse than the Spanish average, it receives fiscal and other transfers, on net, from the rest of the country. Obviously, the reverse holds as well. When Catalonia does better than average, it becomes a net provider of transfers to other Spanish regions. If Catalonia, instead, were independent, it would have a more pronounced business cycle because it would not receive help during especially bad recessions, and would not have to provide for others in case of exceptional booms.[7]

---

[6] See Alesina and Wacziarg (1999) for a discussion of this point in the context of Europe. For example, fisheries policy has been centralized in Europe because if each country decided on its own fishing policy, the result would be overfishing and resource depletion. For some policies, such as policies to limit global warming, centralization at the world level might be justified.

[7] Obviously, this argument relies on an assumption that international capital markets are imperfect, so that independent countries cannot fully self-insure.

(5) Larger countries can build redistributive schemes from richer to poorer regions, therefore achieving distributions of after tax income which would not be available to individual regions acting independently. This is why poorer than average regions would want to form larger countries inclusive of richer regions, while the latter may prefer independence.[8]

(6) Finally, the role of market size is the issue on which we focus most in this article. Adam Smith (1776) already had the intuition that the extent of the market creates a limit on specialization. More recently, a well established literature from Romer (1986), Lucas (1988) to Grossman and Helpman (1991) has emphasized the benefits of scale in light of positive externalities in the accumulation of human capital and the transmission of knowledge, or in light of increasing returns to scale embedded in technology or knowledge creation.[9] Murphy, Shleifer and Vishny (1989) focused instead on the benefits of size in models of "take-off" or "big push" of industrialization, where the take-off phase is characterized by a transition from a slow growth, constant returns to scale technology to an endogenous growth, increasing returns to scale technology. Finally, several papers have stressed the pro-competitive effects of a larger market size: size enhances growth by raising the intensity of product market competition.[10] In these various models, size represents the stock of individuals, purchasing power and income that interact in the market. This market may or may not coincide with the political size of a country as defined by its borders. It does coincide with it if a country is completely autarkic, i.e. does not engage in exchanges of goods or factors of production with the rest of the world. On the contrary, market size and country size are uncorrelated in a world of complete free trade. So in models with increasing returns to scale, market size depends both on country size and on trade openness.

In theory, with no obstacle to the cross-border circulation of factors of productions, goods and ideas, country size should be, at least through the channel of market size, irrelevant for economic success. Thus, in a world of free trade, redrawing borders should have no effect on economic efficiency and productivity. However, a vast literature has convincingly shown that even in the absence of explicit trade policy barriers, crossing borders is indeed costly, so that economic interactions within a country are much easier and denser than across borders. This is true both for trade in goods and financial assets.[11] What explains this border effect, even in the absence of explicit policy barriers, is not

---

[8] See Bolton and Roland (1997) for a theoretical treatment of this point.

[9] A recent critique of some this class of models is due to Jones (1995b). Specifically, Jones pointed out that endogenous growth models generally imply that growth rates should increase with the stock of knowledge. Yet growth rates have been relatively stable or declining in advanced industrial economies, while the stock of knowledge has increased rapidly. In Section 3, we review and discuss this critique in much detail.

[10] See Aghion and Howitt (1998) and Aghion et al. (2002).

[11] On trade see McCallum (1995), Helliwell (1998). For the role of geographical factors in financial flows, see Portes and Rey (2000). For a theoretical discussion of transportation costs across borders and their effects on market integration, see Obstfeld and Rogoff (2000).

completely clear.[12] Whatever the source of the border effect, however, the correlation between the "political size" of a country and its market size does not totally disappear even in the absence of policy-induced trade barriers. Still, one would expect that the correlation between size and economic success is mediated by the trade regime. In a regime of free trade, small countries can prosper, while in a world of trade barriers, being large is much more important for economic prosperity, measured for instance by income per capita.

2.1.2. The costs of size

If size only had benefits, then the world should be organized as a single political entity. This is not the case. Why? As countries become larger and larger, administrative and congestion costs may overcome the benefits of size pointed out above. However, these types of costs become binding only for very large countries and they are not likely to be relevant determinants of the existing countries, many of which are quite small. As we noted above, the median country size is less than six million inhabitants.

A much more important constraint on the feasible size of countries lies in the heterogeneity of individuals' preferences. Being part of the same country implies sharing public goods and policies in ways that cannot satisfy everybody's preferences. It is true that certain policy prerogatives can be delegated to subnational levels of government through decentralization, but some policies have to be national.[13] Think for instance of defense and foreign policy, monetary policy, redistribution between regions, the legal system, etc.

The costs of heterogeneity in the population have been well documented, especially for the case in which ethnolinguistic fragmentation is used a as proxy for heterogeneity in preferences. Easterly and Levine (1997), La Porta et al. (1999) and Alesina et al. (2003) showed that ethnolinguistic fractionalization is inversely related to economic success and various measure of quality of government, economic freedom and democracy.[14] Easterly and Levine (1997), in particular, argued that ethnic fractionalization in Africa, partly induced by absurd borders left by colonizers, is largely responsible for the economic failures of this continent. There is indeed a sense in which African borders

---

[12] A recent literature prompted by Rose (2000) argues that not having the same currency creates large trade barriers. For a review of the evidence see Alesina, Barro and Tenreyro (2002). Other explanatory factors include different languages, different legal standards, difficulties in enforcing contracts across political borders, etc.

[13] In fact, the recent move towards regional decentralization in many countries can be partly viewed as a response of the political system to increasing pressures towards separatism. See Bardhan (2002) for an excellent discussion of this point, and De Figueiredo and Weingast (2002) for a formal treatment. Also, for an excellent review of the literature on federalism, see Oates (1999).

[14] A large literature provides results along the same lines for localities within the United States. For example, see Alesina, Baqir and Easterly (1999). Related to this, Alesina and La Ferrara (2000, 2002) show that measure related to social capital are lower in more heterogeneous communities in the U.S. Alesina, Baqir and Hoxby (2004) show how local political jurisdictions in the U.S. are smaller in more radially heterogeneous areas.

are "wrong", not so much because there are too many or too few countries in Africa, but because borders cut across ethnic lines in often inefficient ways.[15]

We can think of trade openness as shifting the trade-off between the costs and benefits of size. As international markets become more open, the benefits of size decline relative to the costs of heterogeneity, thus the optimal size of a country declines with trade openness. Or, to put it differently, small and relatively more homogeneous countries can prosper in a world of free trade. With trade restrictions, instead, heterogeneous individuals have to share a larger polity to be economically viable. Incidentally, above and beyond the income effect, this may reduce their utility if preference homogeneity is valued in a polity. While in this paper we focus on preference heterogeneity rather than income heterogeneity, the latter plays a key role as well, a point raised by Bolton and Roland (1997). Poor regions would like to join rich regions in order to maintain redistributive flows, while richer regions may prefer to be alone. There is a limit to how much poor regions can extract due to a nonsecession constraint, which is binding for the richer regions. Empirically, often more racially fragmented countries also have a more unequal distribution of income. That is, certain ethnic group are often much poorer than others and economic success and opportunities are associated with belonging to certain groups and not others. These are situations with the highest potential for political instability and violence.

2.2. A model of size, trade and growth

In this section we will present a simple model linking country size, international trade and economic growth. The model builds upon Alesina and Spolaore (1997, 2003), Alesina, Spolaore and Wacziarg (2000) and Spolaore and Wacziarg (2005).

2.2.1. Production and trade

Consider a world in which individuals are located on a segment [0, 1]. The world population is normalized to 1. Each individual living at location $i \in [0, 1]$ has the following utility function

$$\int_0^\infty \frac{C_{it}^{1-\sigma} - 1}{1 - \sigma} e^{-\rho t} \, dt,$$ (1)

where $C_i(t)$ denotes consumption at time t, with $\sigma > 0$ and $\rho > 0$. Let $K_i(t)$ and $L_i(t)$ denote aggregate capital and labor at location i at time t. Both inputs are supplied inelastically and are not mobile. At each location i a specific intermediate input $X_i(t)$ is produced using the location-specific capital according to the linear production function

$$X_i(t) = K_i(t).$$ (2)

[15] On this point see in particular Herbst (2000).

Each location i produces $Y_i(t)$ units of the same final good $Y(t)$, according to the production function

$$Y_i(t) = A\left(\int_0^1 X_{ij}^\alpha(t)\,dj\right)L_i^{1-\alpha}(t), \tag{3}$$

with $0 < \alpha < 1$. $X_{ij}(t)$ denotes the amount of intermediate input j used in location i at time t, and A captures total factor productivity. Intermediate inputs can be traded across different locations in perfectly competitive markets by profit-maximizing firms. Locations belong to N different countries. Country 1 includes all locations between 0 and S_1, country 2 includes all locations between S_1 and $S_1 + S_2, \ldots$, country N includes all locations between $\sum_{n=1}^{N-1} S_n$ and 1. Hence, we will say that country 1 has size S_1, country 2 has size $S_2, \ldots$, country $N-1$ has size S_{N-1}, and country N has size $S_N = 1 - \sum_{n=1}^{N-1} S_n$.

Political borders impose trading costs. In particular, we make the following two assumptions:

(A1) There are *no internal barriers* to trade: Intermediate inputs can be traded across locations that belong to the same country at no cost.

(A2) There are barriers to international trade: If one unit of an intermediate good produced at a location within country n' is shipped to a location i'' within a different country n'', only $(1 - \beta_{n'n''})$ units of the intermediate good will arrive, where $0 \leqslant \beta_{n'n''} \leqslant 1$.

Consider an intermediate good i produced in country n'. Let $D_{in'}(t)$ denote the units of intermediate input i used domestically (i.e., either at location i or at another location within country n'). Let $F_{in''}(t)$ denote the units of input i shipped to a location within a different country $n'' \neq n'$. By assumption, only $(1 - \beta_{n'n''})F_{in''}(t)$ units will be used for production. In equilibrium, as intermediate goods markets are assumed to be perfectly competitive, each unit of input i will be sold at a price equal to its marginal product both domestically and internationally. Therefore,

$$P_i(t) = \alpha A D_{in'}^{\alpha-1}(t) = \alpha A (1 - \beta_{n'n''})^\alpha F_{in''}^{\alpha-1}(t), \tag{4}$$

where $P_i(t)$ is the market price of input i at time t. From Equation (2) it follows that the resource constraint for each input i is

$$S_{n'} D_{in'}(t) + \sum_{n \neq n'} S_n F_{in}(t) = K_{in'}(t), \tag{5}$$

where $S_{n'}$ is the size of country n', while $K_{in'}(t)$ is the stock of capital in location i (belonging to country n') at time t.

By substituting (4) into (5) we obtain:

$$D_{in'}(t) = \frac{K_{in'}}{S_{n'} + \sum_{n \neq n'} S_n (1 - \beta_{n'n})^{\alpha/(1-\alpha)}} \tag{6}$$

and

$$F_{in''}(t) = \frac{(1 - \beta_{n'n''})^{\alpha/(1-\alpha)} K_{in'}}{S_{n'} + \sum_{n \neq n'} S_n (1 - \beta_{n'n})^{\alpha/(1-\alpha)}}. \tag{7}$$

As one would expect, barriers to trade tend to increase the domestic use of an intermediate output and to discourage international trade.

In the rest of this analysis, for simplicity, we will assume that the barriers to trade are uniform across countries, that is,

(A3) $\beta_{i'i''} = \beta$ for all i' and i'' belonging to different countries.[16]

We define

$$\omega \equiv (1 - \beta)^{\alpha/(1-\alpha)}. \tag{8}$$

This means that the lower the barriers to international trade are, the higher is ω. Hence ω can be interpreted as a measure of "international openness". ω takes on values between 0 and 1. When barriers are prohibitive ($\beta = 1$), $\omega = 0$, which means complete autarchy. By contrast, when there are no barriers to international trade ($\beta = 0$), we have $\omega = 1$, that is, complete openness.

Thus, Equations (6) and (7) simplify as follows:

$$D_{in'}(t) = \frac{K_{in'}(t)}{S_{n'} + (1 - S_{n'})\omega} \tag{9}$$

and

$$F_{in''}(t) = \frac{\omega K_{in'}(t)}{S_{n'} + (1 - S_{n'})\omega}. \tag{10}$$

2.2.2. Capital accumulation and growth

In each location i consumers' net household assets are identical to the stock of capital $K_{in'}(t)$. Since each unit of capital yields one unit of intermediate input i, the net return to capital is equal to the market price of intermediate input P_{it} (for simplicity, we assume no depreciation). From intertemporal optimization we have the following standard Euler equation

$$\frac{dC_{it}}{dt} \frac{1}{C_{it}} = \frac{1}{\sigma}\left[P_i(t) - \rho\right] = \frac{1}{\sigma}\left\{\alpha A\left[\omega + (1 - \omega)S_{n'}\right]^{1-\alpha} K_{in'}^{\alpha-1}(t) - \rho\right\}. \tag{11}$$

Hence, the steady-state level of capital at each location i of a country of size $S_{n'}$ will be

$$K_{in'}^{ss} = \left(\frac{\alpha A}{\rho}\right)^{\alpha/(1-\alpha)} \left[\omega + (1 - \omega)S_{n'}\right]. \tag{12}$$

By substituting (12) into (9) and (10), and using (3), we have the following proposition.

---

[16] For an analysis in which barriers are different across countries and are an endogenous function of size, see Spolaore and Wacziarg (2005).

PROPOSITION 1. *The steady-state level of output per capita in each location i of a country of size $S_{n'}$ is*

$$Y_i^{\text{ss}} = A^{1/(1-\alpha)} \left(\frac{\alpha}{\rho}\right)^{\alpha/(1-\alpha)} \left[\omega + (1-\omega)S_{n'}\right]. \tag{13}$$

Hence, it follows that:
(1) Output per capita in the steady-state is increasing in openness ω. That is,

$$\frac{\partial Y_i^{\text{ss}}}{\partial \omega} > 0. \tag{14}$$

(2) Output per capita is increasing in country size $S_{n'}$,

$$\frac{\partial Y_i^{\text{ss}}}{\partial S_{n'}} > 0. \tag{15}$$

(3) The effect of country size $S_{n'}$ is smaller the larger is ω, and the effect of openness is smaller the larger is country size $S_{n'}$. That is,

$$\frac{\partial^2 Y_i^{\text{ss}}}{\partial S_{n'} \partial \omega} < 0. \tag{16}$$

The above results show that openness and size have positive effects on economic performance, but (i) openness is less important for larger countries and (ii) size matters less in a more open world.[17] In fact, there were no barriers to trade ($\omega = 1$), output would be independent of country size.

Around the steady-state, the growth rate of output can be approximated by

$$\frac{dY}{dt}\frac{1}{Y} = \xi e^{-\xi} \left(\ln Y^{\text{ss}} - \ln Y(0)\right), \tag{17}$$

where $\xi \equiv \frac{\rho}{2}[(1 + 4(1-\alpha)/\alpha)^{1/2} - 1]$ and $Y(0)$ is initial income.[18] Hence, we will also have the proposition.

PROPOSITION 2. *The growth rate of income per capita around the steady-state is increasing in size, increasing in openness, and decreasing in size times openness.*

These results show how the economic benefits of size are decreasing in openness and the economic benefits from openness are decreasing in size. We will test the empirical implications of this model in Section 4.

---

[17] The result does not depend on the assumption that barriers to trade are uniform across countries. In particular, one can derive analogous results for the case of non uniform barriers. Moreover, analogous results can be obtained when "openness" is defined as trade over output rather than in terms of trade barriers. See Spolaore and Wacziarg (2005).

[18] For a derivation of this result, see Barro and Sala-i-Martin (1995, Chapter 2).

2.3. The equilibrium size of countries

So far we have taken the number and size of countries as given. However, in the long-run borders do change, and our model suggests that international openness may play a role in this process. As we have seen, country size affects output and growth when barriers to trade are high, while country size is less important in a world of international integration. Hence, the reduction of trade barriers should reduce the incentives to form larger countries. In what follows we will formalize this insight using the framework of country formation developed by Alesina and Spolaore (1997, 2003).[19]

If there were no costs associated with size, world welfare would be maximized by having only one country, which seems rather unrealistic. Following our previous discussion we model the costs of size as the result of heterogeneity of preferences over public policies and public goods, the collection of which we label "government". We assume that, for each location, there exists an "ideal" type of government. If individuals in location i belong to a country whose government is different from their ideal type (say $j \neq i$), their utility will be reduced by $h\Delta_{ij}$, where Δ_{ij} is the distance between j and i, and h is a parameter that measures "heterogeneity" costs – that is, the costs of being far from the median position in one's country. The distance from the government that give raise to these costs should be interpreted both as a distance in terms of preferences and in terms of location.[20]

On the other hand, in a country of size S_n the fixed costs of government can be spread through a larger population.[21] For example, if the fixed cost of government is G and it is shared equally by all citizens, each individual in a country of size S_n will have to pay G/S_n – which is obviously decreasing in S_n.

We consider the case in which borders are determined to maximize net income minus heterogeneity costs in steady-state.[22] That is, we assume that each individual at location i in a country n of size S_n is interested in maximizing the following steady-state welfare

$$W_{in} = Y_{in}^{ss} - t_{in} - h\Delta_{in}, \tag{18}$$

where Y_{in}^{ss} is steady-state income, given by $A^{1/(1-\alpha)}(\frac{\alpha}{\rho})^{\alpha/(1-\alpha)}[\omega + (1-\omega)S_{n'}]$, t_{in} denotes taxes of individual i in country n, Δ_{in} is individual i's "distance from the government".

---

[19] The economics literature on the endogenous formation of political borders, while still in its infancy, has been growing substantially in the past few years. An incomplete list of contributions, besides those cited in the text, includes Friedman (1977), Casella and Feinstein (2002), Findlay (1996) and Bolton and Roland (1997).

[20] This assumption is extreme but allows to have only one dimension. For more discussion see Alesina and Spolaore (2003).

[21] Obviously, not all the costs of government are fixed. Some depend positively on size, such as infrastructure spending or transfers. See Alesina and Wacziarg (1998) for an empirical examination of this point using cross-country data.

[22] The analysis could be extended in order to consider the more complex issue of border changes along the transitional dynamics, in which adjustment costs from changing borders would be explicitly modeled. Here we abstract from such issues and focus on borders in steady-state.

Country n's budget constraint is

$$\int_{S_{n-1}}^{S_n} t_{in}\, di = G. \tag{19}$$

How are borders going to be determined in equilibrium? First we consider how borders would be determined *efficiently*, that is, when the sum of everybody's welfare $\int_0^1 W_{in}\, di$ is maximized. First of all, one can immediately see that the efficient solution implies countries of equal size. This is due to the assumption that people are distributed uniformly in the segment $[0, 1]$.[23] Second, the government should be located "in the middle" of each country, since the median minimizes the sum of distances. When countries are all of equal size (call it $S = 1/N$, where N is the number of countries), and governments are located "in the middle", the average distance from the government is $S/4$. Hence, the sum of everybody's welfare becomes

$$\int_0^1 W_{in}\, di = A^{1/(1-\alpha)} \left(\frac{\alpha}{\rho}\right)^{\alpha/(1-\alpha)} \left[\omega + (1-\omega)S\right] - \frac{G}{S} - h\frac{S}{4} \tag{20}$$

which is maximized by the following "efficient size"[24]

$$S^* = \sqrt{\frac{4G}{h - 4(1-\omega)A^{1/(1-\alpha)}(\frac{\alpha}{\rho})^{\alpha/(1-\alpha)}}}. \tag{21}$$

Hence, we have that the "efficient size" of countries is:
  (1) increasing in the fixed cost of public goods provision (G),
  (2) decreasing in heterogeneity costs (h),
  (3) decreasing in the degree of international openness (ω),
  (4) increasing in total factor productivity (A).
  Therefore, in our model, if borders are set efficiently, increasing economic integration and globalization should be associated with a breakup of countries.
  Should we expect such a breakup to take place if borders are *not* set optimally? For example, what if, more realistically, borders are set by self-interested governments ("Leviathans") who want to maximize their net rents? We can model the equilibrium of those Leviathans by assuming that (a) they want to maximize their rents in steady-state, but (b) they are constrained in their rent maximization, since they must provide a minimum level of welfare to at least a fraction δ of their population (we can interpret this as a "no-insurrection constraint"). Hence, δ measures the degree to which Leviathans are constrained by their subjects' preferences.
  If we assume that each individual in a given country must pay the same taxes (that is, if we rule out inter-regional transfers), we can use t to denote taxes per person in a

---

[23] For a formal proof, see Alesina and Spolaore (1997, 2003).
[24] Equation (20) abstracts from the fact that the number of countries $N = 1/S$ must be an integer.

country of size S. Then, a Leviathan's total rents in a country of size N is given by

$$tS - G, \tag{22}$$

where t is chosen in order to satisfy the constraint

$$W_{in} = Y_i^{ss} - t - h\Delta_i \geqslant W_0 \tag{23}$$

for a mass of individuals of size δS.

The Leviathan will locate the government in the middle of his country, as the social planner would do, in order to minimize the costs of satisfying (23). Constraint (23) will be binding for the individual at a distance $\delta S/2$ from the government. Hence, we have

$$t = Y_i^{ss} - \frac{h\delta S}{2} - W_0. \tag{24}$$

By substituting (24) into (22) and maximizing with respect to S we have the following equilibrium size of countries in a world of Leviathans

$$S^e = \sqrt{\frac{2G}{h\delta - 2(1-\omega)A^{1/(1-\alpha)}(\frac{\alpha}{\rho})^{\alpha/(1-\alpha)}}}. \tag{25}$$

Again, the size of countries is increasing in the economies of scale in the provision of public goods (G) and in the level of total factor productivity (A), while decreasing in heterogeneity costs (h) and openness (ω).

We can note that $S^e = S^*$ when the Leviathans must provide minimum welfare to exactly half of their population, while countries are inefficiently large ($S^e > S^*$) when Leviathans are really dictatorial, that is, they can stay in power without the need to take into account the welfare of a majority of the population. But even in that case, more openness induces smaller countries.

The comparative statics predict that technological progress, in a world of barriers to trade, should be associated with larger countries. This result is intuitively appealing, since technological progress improves the gains from trade, and barriers to international trade increase the importance of domestic trade, and hence a larger domestic market. However, if technological progress is accompanied by a reduction in trade barriers, the result becomes ambiguous.[25] Moreover, a reduction in trade barriers (more openness) has a *bigger* impact (in absolute value) on the size of countries at *higher* levels of development – that is, the effect of globalization and economic integration on the size of countries is expected to be larger for more developed societies. Formally,

$$\frac{\partial^2 S^e}{\partial \omega \, \partial A} < 0. \tag{26}$$

---

[25] Another element of ambiguity would be introduced if one were to assume that the costs of government G are decreasing in A.

Of course, these comparative statics results are based on the highly simplifying assumption that technological progress is exogenous. An interesting extension of the model would be to consider endogenous links between political borders, the degree of international openness, and technological progress.[26]

Alesina and Spolaore (2003) also analyze the case in which borders are chosen by democratic rule (majority voting). They show that in this case one may or may not obtain the efficient solution depending on the availability of credible transfer programs. When the latter are not available, in a fully democratic equilibrium in which no one can prevent border changes decided by majority rule or prevent unilateral secessions, there would be more countries than the efficient number. A fortiori the democratically decided number of countries would be larger that the one chosen by a Leviathan for any value of $\delta < 1$. An implication of this analysis is that democratization should lead to secessions. For the purpose of this paper, even in the case of majority rule choice of borders, the comparative statics regarding trade, size and growth are the same as in the efficient case and in the Leviathan case.

2.4. Summing up

In this section we have provided a model in which the benefits of country size go down as international economic integration increases. Conversely, the benefits of trade openness and economic integration are larger, the smaller the size of a country. Secondly, we have argued that economic integration and political disintegration should go hand in hand. As the world economy becomes more integrated, one of the benefits of large countries (the size of markets) vanishes. As a result, the trade-off between size and heterogeneity shifts in favor of smaller and more homogeneous countries. This effect tends to be larger in more developed economies. By contrast, technological progress in a world of *high* barriers to trade should be associated with the formation of *larger* countries.

One can also think of the reverse source of causality: small countries have a particularly strong interest in maintaining free trade, since so much of their economy depends upon international markets. In fact, if openness were endogenized, one could extend our model to capture two possible worlds as equilibrium border configurations: a world of large and relatively closed economies, and one of many more smaller and more open economies. Spolaore (1995, 2002) provides explicit models with endogenous openness and multiple equilibria in the number of countries. Spolaore and Wacziarg (2005) also treat openness as an explicitly endogenous variable, and show empirically that larger countries tend to be more closed to trade. Empirically, both directions of causality between country size and trade openness, which are not mutually exclusive, likely coexist.

---

[26] For example, some authors have suggested that technological progress may be higher in a world with more Leviathans who compete with each other (such as Europe before and after the Industrial Revolution) than in a more centralized environment (such as China in the same period). For a recent formalization of these ideas, see Garner (2001).

Smaller countries do adopt more open trade policies (and are consequently more open when openness is measures using trade volumes), so that a world of small countries will tend to be more open to trade.[27] Conversely, changes in the average degree of openness in the world (brought forth for example by a reduction in trading costs) should be expected to lead to more secessions and smaller countries, as we will argue extensively below.

3. Size, openness and growth: Empirical evidence

In this section, we review the empirical evidence on trade openness and growth, as well as the empirical evidence on country size and growth. We then argue that the two are fundamentally linked, because both openness and country size determine the extent of the market. Thus, their impact on growth cannot be evaluated separately. Then we estimate a specification for the determination of growth as a function of market size (itself a function of both country size and trade openness), derived directly from the model presented in Section 2. Our estimates, which are consistent with a growing body of evidence on the role of scale for growth, also provide strong support for our specific model. In particular, we show that the costs of smallness can be avoided by being open. In other words, the impact of size on growth is decreasing in openness, or, conversely, the impact of openness on growth falls as the size of countries increases. This evidence suggests that the extent of the market is an important channel for the realization of the growth gains from trade.

3.1. Trade and growth: a review of the evidence

The literature on the empirical evidence of trade and growth is vast and a comprehensive survey is beyond the scope of this article. In this subsection, we simply summarize some of the salient results from recent studies in this literature, in order to set the stage for a discussion of the more specific issue of market size and growth.

The fact that openness to trade is associated with higher growth in post-1950 cross-country data was until recently subject to little disagreement.[28] Whether openness is measured by indicators of trade policy openness (tariffs, nontariff barriers, etc.) or by the volume of trade (the ratio of imports plus exports to GDP), numerous studies document this correlation. For example, Edwards (1998) showed that, out of nine indicators of trade policy openness, eight were positively and significantly related to TFP growth in a sample of 93 countries. Dollar (1992) argued that an indicator of openness based on price deviations was positively associated with growth. Ben-David (1993) demonstrated

---

[27] See Alesina and Wacziarg (1998) and Spolaore and Wacziarg (2005) for cross-country empirical evidence on this point.

[28] The pre-1990 literature was usefully surveyed in Edwards (1993). We will focus instead on salient papers in this literature since 1990.

that a sample of countries with open trade regimes displays absolute convergence in per capita income, while a sample of closed countries did not. Finally, in one of the most cited studies in this literature, Sachs and Warner (1995) classified countries using a simple dichotomous indicator of openness, and argued that "closed" countries experienced annual growth rates a full 2 percentage points below "open" countries in the period 1970–1989. They also confirmed Ben-David's result: open countries tend to converge, not closed ones.

These studies focused mostly on the correlation between openness and growth, conditional on other growth determinants. In other words, little attention was typically paid to issues of reverse causation. In contrast, a more recent study by Frankel and Romer (1999) focused on trade as a causal determinant of income levels. Using geographic variables as an instrument for openness, they estimated that a 1 percentage point increase in the trade to GDP ratio causes almost a 2 percent increase in the level of per capita income.[29] Wacziarg (2001) also addressed issues of endogeneity by estimating a simultaneous equations system where openness affects a series of channel variables which in turn affect growth. Results from this study suggest that a one standard deviation increase in the portion of the trade to GDP ratio attributable to formal trade policy barriers (tariffs, nontariff barriers, etc.) is associated with a 1 percentage point increase in annual growth across countries.

These six studies were recently scrutinized by Rodrik and Rodríguez (2000), who argued that their basic results were sensitive to small changes in specification, or that the measurement of trade policy openness captured other bad policies rather than trade impediments.[30] While it is true that cross-country empirical analysis is fraught with data pitfalls, specification problems and issues of endogeneity, these authors do recognize that it is difficult to find a specification where indicators of openness actually have a negative impact on growth.[31] In other words, they essentially conclude that the range of possible effects is bounded below by zero. One could argue that by the standards of the cross-country growth literature, this is already a huge achievement: it constitutes an important restriction on the range of possible estimates. Moreover, Rodrik and Rodríguez (2000) argue that one of the problems associated with estimating the impact of trade on growth is that protectionism is highly correlated with other growth-reducing policies, such as policies that perpetuate macroeconomic imbalances. This suggests that trade restrictions are one among a "basket" of growth-reducing policies. Since Rodrik and

---

[29] A crucial assumption is that the instrument (constructed as the sum of predicted bilateral trade shares, where only gravity/geographical variables are used as predictors of bilateral trade) be excludable from the growth regression, i.e. that it affects growth only through its impact on trade volumes.

[30] For another critical view of this literature, in particular of the Sachs and Warner (1995) study, see Harrison and Hanson (1999). Pritchett (1996) showed that various measures of policy openness were not highly correlated among themselves, suggesting that relying on any single measure was unlikely to capture the essence of trade policy.

[31] They state that "we know of no credible evidence – at least for the post-1945 period – that suggests that trade restrictions are systematically associated with higher growth rates" (p. 317).

Rodríguez (2000), the literature on trade and growth has proceeded apace. Using a new measure of the volume of trade, Alcalá and Ciccone (2004) revisit the issue of trade and growth, and argue that "in contrast to the marginally significant and non-robust effects of trade on productivity found previously, our estimates are highly significant and robust even when we include institutional quality and geographic factors in the empirical analysis". The difference stems for these authors' use of a measure of "real openness" defined as a U.S. dollar value of import plus export relative to GDP in PPP U.S. dollars, as further detailed below. The same authors argue that their results are robust to controlling for institutional quality, a point disputed by Rodrik, Subramanian and Trebbi (2004). In a within-country context, Wacziarg and Welch (2003) show that episodes of trade liberalization are followed by an average increase in growth on the order of 1–1.5 percentage points per annum.

An important drawback of the literature on trade and growth is that it does not generally focus on the channels through which trade openness affects economic performance.[32] This makes it difficult to assess whether the dynamic effects of trade openness are mediated by the extent of the market. There are many reasons that could explain a positive estimated coefficient in a regression of trade openness (however measured) on growth or income levels. Such effects could stem from better checks on domestic policies, an improved functioning of institutions, technological transmissions that are facilitated by openness to trade, increased foreign direct investment, scale effects of the type discussed in Section 2, traditional comparative advantage-induced static gains from trade, or all of the above. Few studies attempt to discriminate between these various hypotheses. Hence, while there is a general sense that trade openness increases growth and income levels, and while this creates a presumption that market size may be important, the accumulated evidence on trade and growth does not directly answer the question of whether it is market size that is good for growth, as opposed to some other aspect of openness.

3.2. Country size and growth: a review of the evidence

We now turn to the empirical evidence on the effects of country size on economic performance. There is a vast microeconometric literature on estimating the returns to scale in economic activities and how they relate to firm or industry productivity. This literature is beyond the scope of this paper, but a general sense is that, at least in some manufacturing sectors or industries, scale effects are present. It may therefore come as a surprise that the conventional wisdom seems to be that scale effects are not easily detected at the aggregate (country) level. The macroeconomic literature on country size and growth is much smaller than the microeconometric literature, but a common claim is that the size of countries does not matter for economic growth, either in a time-series context for individual economies, or in a cross-country context.

---

[32] An exception is Wacziarg (2001). Alcalá and Ciccone (2004) also examine whether the effect of openness works through labor productivity or capital accumulation (in its various forms).

In a time-series context, Jones (1995a, 1995b) made a simple point. Several endogenous growth models predict that the rate of long-run growth of an economy is directly proportional to the number of researchers, itself a function of population size.[33] Hence, as the population of the United States increased (and in particular the number of scientists and researchers), so should have growth. Yet while the number of researchers exploded, rates of growth in industrial countries have been roughly constant since the 1870s. This simple empirical fact created difficulties for first-generation endogenous growth models. In particular, it was taken as indicative of the absence of scale effects in long-run growth. However, while it contributed to the conventional wisdom that scale is unrelated to aggregate growth, this finding in no way precludes the existence of scale effects when it comes to income levels, which is the focus both of the theory presented in Section 2 and of our empirical estimates presented below.[34] Hence, Jones' objection applies neither to our theory nor to our evidence. Several recent theoretical papers have sought to extend and preserve the endogenous growth paradigm while eliminating scale effects on growth. See for instance Young (1998), Howitt (1999) and Ha and Howitt (2004).

In a cross-country context, some of the most systematic empirical tests of the scale implications of endogenous growth models appeared in Backus, Kehoe and Kehoe (1992). They showed empirically, in a specification where scale was defined as the size of total GDP, that scale and aggregate growth were largely unrelated. In their baseline regression of growth on the log of total GDP, the slope coefficient was positive but statistically insignificant.[35] Moreover, the number of scientists per countries was not found to be a significant predictor of growth, and the scale of inputs into the human accumulation process (meant to capture the extent of human capital spillovers) similarly did not help predict aggregate growth. The authors also showed that scale effects were present in the data when confining attention to the manufacturing sector (i.e. regressing manufacturing growth on total manufacturing output), and suggest that this is consistent with microeconometric studies, which typically focus on manufacturing. But the set of regressions relating to the aggregate economy is often cited as evidence that there are no effects of scale on growth at the country level.

---

[33] As suggested by Jones (1999), such models include Romer (1990), Grossman and Helpman (1991) and Aghion and Howitt (1992).

[34] Scale effects in our theory come purely from the border effect – namely the fact that it is more costly (in the iceberg cost sense) to conduct trade across borders than within. This allows us to combine scale effects with a neoclassical model of growth. Our theory has standard neoclassical implications as far as transitional growth is concerned. Thus, scale may affect growth in the transition to the steady-state, since it is a determinant of steady-state income *levels*. But scale has no impact on long-run growth, which is exogenous in our model.

[35] According to the authors, this univariate regression implies that "a hundredfold increase in total GDP is associated with an increase in per capita growth of 0.85". One could argue that this is a sizable effect, but the t-statistic on the slope coefficient is only 1.64 and the regression contains no other control variables. In a multivariate setting, the authors show that when "standard" growth regressors (but *not* trade openness) are controlled for, the coefficient estimate on total GDP remains essentially identical, but the t-statistic falls considerably.

A major problem with this approach is that variables defined at the national level may be poor proxies for the total scale of the economy, the extent of R&D activities or the importance of human capital externalities. Scale effects do not stop at the borders of countries. Since small countries adopt more open trade policies, and likely also import more technologies, a coefficient on size in a regression of growth on size that omits openness is going to be biased towards zero.[36] The authors do recognize (and show empirically) that imports of specialized inputs to production can lead to faster growth. They also mention that "by importing specialized inputs, a small country can grow as fast as a larger one". But they do not empirically examine variations in the degree of openness of an economy and how it might impact the effect of size on growth.[37] In other words, they examine separately whether country size on the one hand, and imports of specialized inputs on the other, affect growth. We propose instead to examine openness and country size jointly as determinants of market size and thus growth.

3.3. Summing up

The literature on trade and growth indicates that trade openness has favorable effects on growth and income levels, but for the most part does not inform us as to whether these effects are attributable to the extent of the market, or to other channels. The literature on scale and growth typically considers measures of scale that have to do with domestic market size (i.e. the size of a country or a national economy), and generally fails to consider that openness can substitute for a large domestic market. In what follows, we bring these literatures together to focus on the impact of market size on growth.

3.4. Trade, size and growth in a cross-section of countries

In this subsection, we bring Propositions 1 and 2 of Section 2 to the data. If small countries tend to be more open to trade, and if trade openness is positively related to growth, then a regression of growth on country size that excludes openness will understate the effect of scale. Moreover, our theory suggests that the effects of size become less important as an economy becomes more open, i.e. the coefficient on an interaction term between openness and country size is predicted to be negative. Ades and Glaeser (1999),

---

[36] See Alesina and Wacziarg (1998) and Spolaore and Wacziarg (2005) for empirical evidence that small countries tend to be more open to trade, when trade openness is measures by the trade to GDP ratio. Perhaps more surprisingly, such a relationship also holds when openness is measured by average weighted tariffs, i.e. by a direct measure of trade policy restrictiveness.

[37] Another shortcoming of the literature linking economic growth to country size is its failure to examine whether size might have different effects on growth at different levels of development. Growth may have different sources at different stages of development, and country size may affect these sources differently. For instance, scale effects may be more present in the increasing returns, endogenous growth phase that characterizes advanced industrialized countries, and have a smaller effect in the capital deepening phase that perhaps characterizes less advanced economies.

Alesina, Spolaore and Wacziarg (2000) and Spolaore and Wacziarg (2005) have examined how country size and openness interact in growth regressions, and have confirmed the pattern of coefficients on openness, country size and their interaction predicted by our theory. In this section, we update and expand upon these results. We focus on growth specifications of the form

$$\log \frac{y_{it}}{y_{it-\tau}} = \beta_0 + \beta_1 \log y_{it-\tau} + \beta_2 \log S_{it} + \beta_3 O_{it}$$
$$+ \beta_4 O_{it} \log S_{it} + \beta_5' Z_{it} + \varepsilon_{it}, \tag{27}$$

where y_{it} denotes per capita income in country i at time t, S_{it} is a measure of country size, O_{it} is a measure of openness, and Z_{it} is a vector of control variables. In this specification, the parameter estimates on openness, country size and their interaction will be our main focus. In the context of the theory presented in Section 2, these variables as well as the Z_{it} variables are to be interpreted as determinants of the steady-state *level* of per capita income.[38]

3.4.1. Descriptive statistics

Tables 1–3 display summary statistics for our main variables of interest, averaged over the period 1960–2000. The data on openness, investment rates, growth and income levels, government consumption, and population come from release 6.1 of the Penn World Tables [Heston, Summers and Aten (2002)], which updates their panel of PPP-comparable data to the year 2000. The rest of the data we use in this paper comes from Barro and Lee (1994, subsequently updated to 2000) or from the Central Intelligence Agency (2002). Country size is measured by the log of total GDP or by the log of total population, in order to capture both economic size and demographic size. Throughout, we define trade openness in two ways: as the ratio of imports plus exports in current prices to GDP in current prices, and as the ratio of imports plus exports in exchange rate $U.S. to GDP in PPP $U.S. We label the first variable "nominal openness" and the second one "real openness".

Recently, Alcalá and Ciccone (2003, 2004) have criticized the widespread use of the first measure, have advocated the use of the second, finding that the latter leads to more robust effects of openness on growth. The key difference between the two measure stems from the treatment of non tradable goods. Suppose that trade openness raises productivity, but does so more in the tradable than in the nontradable sector (a plausible assumption). This will lead to a rise in the relative price of nontradables, and a fall in conventionally measured openness under the assumptions that the demand for nontrad-

---

[38] Alesina, Spolaore and Wacziarg (2000) present direct evidence on the effects of market size based on levels regressions where initial income does not appear on the right-hand side. These regressions were consistent with the predictions of the theory presented in Section 2. We have repeated these levels regressions using the new cross-country data that extends to 1999, with little changes in the results.

Table 1
Descriptive statistics (1960–2000 averages)

	Number of observations	Mean	Standard deviation	Minimum	Maximum
Average annual growth	104	1.669	1.374	−1.259	5.515
Openness ratio (current)	114	64.098	41.871	14.373	322.128
Openness ratio (real)	114	37.363	35.376	4.350	244.631
Log of per capita GDP 1960	110	7.730	0.889	5.944	9.614
Log of total GDP	113	23.905	1.943	19.723	29.165
Log of population	114	15.763	1.678	11.019	20.670
Fertility rate	156	4.569	1.797	1.733	7.597
Female human capital	103	1.116	1.067	0.024	4.923
Male human capital	103	1.523	1.225	0.096	5.467
Investment rate (% GDP)	114	15.653	7.880	2.023	41.252
Government consumption (% GDP)	114	19.869	9.439	4.297	48.635

Table 2
Pairwise correlations for the main variables of interest (1960–2000 averages)

	Average annual growth	Log of total GDP	Log of per capita GDP 1960	Log of population	Openness ratio (current)
Average annual growth	1.000				
Log of total GDP	0.338	1.000			
Log of per capita GDP 1960	0.172	0.436	1.000		
Log of population	0.125	0.853	−0.058	1.000	
Openness ratio (current)	0.216	−0.334	0.135	−0.537	1.000
Openness ratio (real)	0.331	−0.042	0.382	−0.348	0.870

ables is relatively inelastic, as it may raise the denominator of the conventional measure of openness more than the numerator. So one may observe trade-induced productivity increases going hand in hand with a decline in conventional measures of openness. "Real openness" will address the problem, since the denominator now corrects for international differences in the price of nontradable goods. We show results based on both measures, in order to simultaneously address Alcalá and Ciccone's points and to allow comparability with past results.

Table 2 reveals that both measures of openness are closely related, with a correlation of 0.87. While high, this correlation justifies examining differences in results obtained using each measure. The correlation between our two measures of country size is also high, equal to 0.85. The correlation between openness and country size is negative, whatever the measures of openness and size, and in three out of four cases is of a magnitude between 0.33 and 0.54, confirming past results that small countries are more

Table 3
Conditional correlations (1960–2000)

Variable	Conditioning statement	Correlation with growth	Number of observations
Openness (current)	Log of population > median = 8.807	0.104	54
Openness (current)	Log of population ⩽ median = 8.807	0.511	50
Openness (current)	Log of GDP > median = 16.700	0.301	52
Openness (current)	Log of GDP ⩽ median = 16.700	0.462	52
Openness (real)	Log of population > median = 15.715	0.131	54
Openness (real)	Log of population ⩽ median = 15.715	0.579	50
Openness (real)	Log of GDP > median = 23.607	0.223	52
Openness (real)	Log of GDP ⩽ median = 23.607	0.474	52
Log of population	Openness (current) > median = 53.897	0.107	50
Log of population	Openness (current) ⩽ median = 53.897	0.426	54
Log of GDP	Openness (current) > median = 53.897	0.324	50
Log of GDP	Openness (current) ⩽ median = 53.897	0.563	54
Log of population	Openness (real) >median = 26.025	−0.089	51
Log of population	Openness (real) ⩽ median = 26.025	0.587	53
Log of GDP	Openness (real) > median = 26.025	0.137	51
Log of GDP	Openness (real) ⩽ median = 26.025	0.625	53

Notes. Medians computed from individual samples, while correlations are common sample correlations. Growth: average annual growth, 1960–2000.

open, and suggesting that an omission of openness in a regression of growth on country size would understate the effect of size. Finally, while the simple correlation between growth and size is 0.33 when size is measured by the log of total GDP, and the correlation between openness and growth is equal to 0.21 or 0.33 (when openness is measured in current or "real terms", respectively).

Preliminary evidence on Propositions 1 and 2 can be gleaned from conditional correlations displayed in Table 3. This table presents correlations of openness and growth conditional on country size being greater or lower than the sample median, and correlations of country size and growth conditional on openness being greater or lower than the sample median. For the sake of illustration, let us focus on the log of population as a measure of size and on current openness as a measure of openness (the results are qualitatively unchanged when using the other measures). The correlation between openness and growth is 0.51 for small countries (those smaller than 6.7 million inhabitants), and only 0.10 for large countries. Similarly, the correlation between country size and growth is 0.11 for open countries, and 0.43 for closed ones. This provides suggestive evidence that openness and country size are substitutes, and that the correlation between size and growth falls with the level of openness. To fully evaluate this claim, we now turn to panel data growth regressions.

3.4.2. *Growth, openness and size: panel regressions*

Tables 4–6 present Seemingly Unrelated Regression (SUR) estimates of regressions of growth on openness, country size and their interaction, as well as additional controls. The SUR estimator amounts to a flexible form of the random-effects panel estimator, which allows for different covariances of the error term across time periods.[39] Its use

Table 4
Constrained SUR estimates (size = log of population, openness = current openness)

	(1)	(2)	(3)	(4)
Size * Openness (current)	−0.006**	−0.006**	−0.007**	−0.005*
	(0.002)	(0.002)	(0.002)	(0.002)
Size	0.493**	0.481**	0.326*	0.412**
	(0.123)	(0.120)	(0.153)	(0.138)
Openness (current)	0.057**	0.055**	0.059**	0.054**
	(0.015)	(0.014)	(0.020)	(0.018)
Log of initial per capita income	–	0.185	−1.157**	−1.109**
		(0.112)	(0.248)	(0.230)
Fertility	–	–	−0.332**	−0.479**
			(0.118)	(0.110)
Male human capital	–	–	0.090	0.337
			(0.279)	(0.253)
Female human capital	–	–	−0.139	−0.260
			(0.327)	(0.299)
Government consumption (% GDP)	–	–	−0.052**	−0.035**
			(0.013)	(0.012)
Investment rate (% GDP)	–	–	0.133**	0.090**
			(0.016)	(0.016)
Intercept	−3.274**	−4.600**	8.530**	8.840**
	(1.175)	(1.355)	(3.085)	(2.84)
Intercept, 1970–1979	–	–	–	8.170**
				(2.87)
Intercept, 1980–1989	–	–	–	7.030*
				(2.86)
Intercept, 1990–2000	–	–	–	6.960*
				(2.81)
Number of countries (periods)	104 (4)	104 (4)	80 (4)	80 (4)
Adjusted *R*-squared	0.15 0.01	0.15 0.02	0.12 0.22	0.38 0.23
	0.11 0.03	0.10 0.05	0.35 0.14	0.47 0.23

Notes. Standard errors in parentheses.
*significant at 5% level;
**significant at 1% level.

[39] In contrast, the random-effects estimator imposes that the covariance between the error terms at time t and time $t+1$ be equal to the covariance between the error terms at time $t+1$ and time $t+2$.

Table 5
Constrained SUR estimates (size = log of GDP, openness = current openness)

	(1)	(2)	(3)	(4)
Size * Openness (current)	−0.005**	−0.005**	−0.003†	−0.003†
	(0.001)	(0.001)	(0.002)	(0.002)
Size	0.532**	0.592**	0.325*	0.438**
	(0.099)	(0.113)	(0.139)	(0.125)
Openness (current)	0.089**	0.093**	0.064*	0.063*
	(0.024)	(0.025)	(0.030)	(0.027)
Log of initial per capita income	–	−0.171	−1.252**	−1.342**
		(0.143)	(0.247)	(0.230)
Fertility	–	–	−0.317**	−0.466**
			(0.119)	(0.109)
Male human capital	–	–	−0.011	0.268
			(0.282)	(0.254)
Female human capital	–	–	−0.045	−0.184
			(0.331)	(0.300)
Government consumption (% GDP)	–	–	−0.050**	−0.034**
			(0.013)	(0.012)
Investment rate (% GDP)	–	–	0.126**	0.081**
			(0.017)	(0.016)
Intercept	−8.163**	−7.937**	6.358	6.740*
	(1.758)	(1.804)	(3.471)	(3.13)
Intercept, 1970–1979	–	–	–	6.010
				(3.16)
Intercept, 1980–1989	–	–	–	4.820
				(3.16)
Intercept, 1990–2000	–	–	–	4.680
				(3.12)
Number of countries (periods)	104 (4)	104 (4)	80 (4)	80 (4)
Adjusted R-squared	0.11 0.01	0.12 0.01	0.13 0.22	0.41 0.24
	0.09 0.02	0.07 0.02	0.35 0.06	0.47 0.19

Notes. Standard errors in parentheses.

†significant at 10% level;
*significant at 5% level;
**significant at 1% level.

in cross-country work is now widespread [see, for example, Barro and Sala-i-Martin (1995)]. The panel consists of four periods of 10 year-averages (1960–1969, 1970–1979, 1980–1989 and 1990–1999), and up to 113 countries. The estimation procedure is to formulate one equation per decade, constrain the coefficients to equality across periods, and run SUR on the resulting system of equations.[40]

[40] We use the term constrained SUR to refer to the fact that slope coefficients are constrained to equality across periods.

Table 6
Constrained SUR estimates (using real openness)

	Size = log of population		Size = log of GDP	
	(1)	(2)	(3)	(4)
Size * Real openness	−0.004*	−0.006[†]	−0.008**	−0.007*
	(0.002)	(0.003)	(0.002)	(0.003)
Size	0.250**	0.229[†]	0.496**	0.424**
	(0.093)	(0.129)	(0.096)	(0.126)
Real openness	0.075*	0.094[†]	0.198**	0.185**
	(0.031)	(0.052)	(0.050)	(0.068)
Log of per capita income, 1960	0.092	−1.295**	−0.244	−1.489**
	(0.135)	(0.235)	(0.160)	(0.238)
Fertility	–	−0.552**	–	−0.537**
		(0.111)		(0.110)
Male human capital	–	0.247	–	0.205
		(0.259)		(0.254)
Female human capital	–	−0.162	–	−0.130
		(0.298)		(0.292)
Government consumption (% GDP)	–	−0.033**	–	−0.033**
		(0.012)		(0.012)
Investment (% GDP)	–	0.090**	–	0.076**
		(0.016)		(0.017)
Intercept	−3.318	–	−8.823**	–
	(1.733)		(2.091)	
Number of countries (periods)	104 (4)	80 (4)	104 (4)	80 (4)
Adjusted R-squared	−0.18 −0.01	0.33 0.21	−0.14 0.03	0.35 0.19
	−0.07 0.02	0.47 0.22	−0.03 0.06	0.50 0.24

Notes. Standard errors in parentheses.

[†] significant at 10% level;

* significant at 5% level;

** significant at 1% level.

Columns (2) and (4) estimated with period specific intercepts (time effects not reported). Other specifications available upon request.

Table 4 present estimation results when the measure of country size is the log of population and the measure of openness involves variables in current prices. In all specifications, the parameter estimates on our three variables of interest (openness, country size and their interaction) are of the predicted sign and all are significant at the 5% level (and often at the 1% level). This holds whether we enter these variables alone [column (1)], whether we control for initial income [column (2)], whether we control for a long list of common growth regressors [column (3)] and whether we include time specific effects in addition to all the controls [column (4)]. Moreover, Table 5 shows that the results change little when size is measured by the log of total GDP, although the level of significance is reduced somewhat in the specifications that include many control variables. Finally, Table 6 shows that using "real openness" does not modify the overall pattern of coefficients. In fact our results are generally stronger (in the sense of the estimated coefficients being larger in magnitude) when using this measure of openness. Similar estimates in Alcalá and Ciccone (2003, written after first draft of this paper) lend further support to our results. They show how controlling for a host of additional variables including institutional quality does not change the nature of these results and that the use of "real openness" leads to coefficients that are larger and more robust than when using "nominal openness".

3.5. Endogeneity of openness: 3SLS estimates

Openness, especially when defined as the volume of trade divided by GDP (however deflated), may be an endogenous variable in growth regressions. As described above, in an important paper Frankel and Romer (1999) have developed a innovative instrument to deal with potential endogeneity bias in growth and income level regressions. We use our own set of geographic variables as well as Frankel and Romer's instrument to address potential endogeneity. Our panel data IV estimator relies on a three stage least squares (3SLS) procedure. This estimator achieves consistency through instrumentation, and efficiency through the estimation of cross-period error covariance terms. Table 7 presents parameter estimates of our basic specification when the list of instruments includes geographic variables, namely dummy variables for small countries, islands, small islands, landlocked countries and the interaction term between each of these measures and country size.[41] Again, the results are consistent with previous observations, namely the pattern of coefficients suggested by theory is maintained. In the specification with all the controls, the statistical significance of the coefficients of interest is reduced slightly when real openness is used instead of current openness (Table 8), though all remain significant at the 10% level. The signs of the main coefficients of interest are maintained and the magnitude of the openness coefficient is raised in all specifications, confirming the results of Alcalá and Ciccone (2003, 2004).[42]

Finally, Table 11 shows the same results using the geography-based instrument from Frankel and Romer (1999), as well as the interaction term between this variable and country size. In all specifications, the signs and basic magnitudes of the coefficients of interest are unchanged (although when openness is entered in "real" terms, the estimates cease to be statistically significant at the 5% level). Spolaore and Wacziarg (2005)

---

[41] This is the same list of instruments as was used in Alesina, Spolaore and Wacziarg (2000). Using Hausman tests, this paper showed that this set of instruments was statistically excludable from the growth regression, and first stage F-tests suggested that they were closely related to openness and the interaction term.

[42] Tables 9 and 10 present F-tests for the first stage of the 3SLS procedure. They test the joint significant of the instruments in regressions of the endogenous variables (openness and its interaction with country size) on all the exogenous variables in the system. These F-tests show that our instruments are closely related to the variables they are instrumenting for, limiting the potential for weak instruments, especially in the specifications with many controls.

Table 7
Constrained 3SLS estimates (current openness)

	Size = log of population			Size = log of GDP		
	(1)	(2)	(3)	(4)	(5)	(6)
Size * Openness (current)	−0.008**	−0.007**	−0.008**	−0.007**	−0.010**	−0.003†
	(0.002)	(0.002)	(0.003)	(0.002)	(0.002)	(0.002)
Size	0.507**	0.634**	0.375*	0.677**	1.070**	0.314*
	(0.157)	(0.144)	(0.176)	(0.143)	(0.167)	(0.158)
Openness (current)	0.068**	0.073**	0.069**	0.129**	0.193**	0.060†
	(0.020)	(0.018)	(0.024)	(0.038)	(0.039)	(0.036)
Log of initial per capita income	–	0.147	−1.157**	–	−0.525**	−1.257**
		(0.117)	(0.251)		(0.167)	(0.247)
Fertility	–	–	−0.330**	–	–	−0.319**
			(0.120)			(0.121)
Male human capital	–	–	0.125	–	–	−0.017
			(0.281)			(0.283)
Female human capital	–	–	−0.171	–	–	−0.039
			(0.329)			(0.332)
Government consumption (% GDP)	–	–	−0.052**	–	–	−0.050**
			(0.013)			(0.013)
Investment rate (% GDP)	–	–	0.134**	–	–	0.126**
			(0.016)			(0.017)
Intercept	−2.701	−5.945**	8.178*	−10.843**	−14.269**	6.596
	(1.537)	(1.513)	(3.299)	(2.604)	(2.561)	(3.813)
Number of countries (periods)	104 (4)	104 (4)	80 (4)	104 (4)	104 (4)	80 (4)
Adjusted R-squared	0.13 0.05	0.18 0.02	0.13 0.21	0.12 0.07	0.25 0.02	0.28 0.35
	0.19 0.01	0.11 0.03	0.34 0.15	0.13 0.01	0.16 0.24	0.14 0.18

Notes. Standard errors in parentheses.
† significant at 10% level;
* significant at 5% level;
** significant at 1% level.
Instruments used: dummies for small country, island, small island, landlocked country and the interaction of each of these measures with the log of country size.

present more evidence on this type of regression, by treating estimating a simultaneous equations system for the endogenous determination of openness and growth jointly. Their results are similar in spirit to those presented here.

Alcalá and Ciccone (2003) present further results along the same lines, and also explicitly consider institutional quality variables in addition to performing further sensitivity tests. Their empirical results are very consistent with ours, suggesting that predictions on the relationship between trade, country size and growth implied by our model are confirmed when the "real" measure of openness is used instead of nominal openness.

Table 8
Constrained 3SLS estimates (real openness)

	Size = log of population			Size = log of GDP		
	(1)	(2)	(3)	(4)	(5)	(6)
Size * Real openness	−0.006*	−0.006*	−0.007†	−0.014**	−0.014**	−0.007*
	(0.003)	(0.003)	(0.004)	(0.003)	(0.003)	(0.003)
Size	0.280**	0.317**	0.248†	0.630**	0.768**	0.440**
	(0.107)	(0.103)	(0.146)	(0.111)	(0.124)	(0.141)
Real openness	0.100*	0.098*	0.111†	0.350**	0.361**	0.195*
	(0.040)	(0.038)	(0.062)	(0.073)	(0.071)	(0.079)
Log of per capita income, 1960	−	0.017	−1.277**	−	−0.526**	−1.493**
		(0.157)	(0.237)		(0.187)	(0.239)
Fertility	−	−	−0.543**	−	−	−0.536**
			(0.112)			(0.110)
Male human capital	−	−	0.269	−	−	0.206
			(0.260)			(0.255)
Female human capital	−	−	−0.167	−	−	−0.13
			(0.299)			(0.292)
Government consumption (% GDP)	−	−	−0.033**	−	−	−0.033**
			(0.012)			(0.012)
Investment (% GDP)	−	−	0.092**	−	−	0.075**
			(0.017)			(0.017)
Intercept	−2.941	−3.922*	−	−13.883**	−13.503**	−
	(1.706)	(1.919)		(2.721)	(2.679)	
Number of countries (periods)	104 (4)	104 (4)	80 (4)	104 (4)	104 (4)	80 (4)
Adjusted R-squared	−0.17 −0.01	−0.20 −0.01	0.33 0.22	−0.10 0.02	−0.21 −0.01	0.35 0.19
	−0.09 0.01	−0.06 0.00	0.46 0.22	−0.15 −0.01	−0.08 −0.02	0.50 0.24

Notes. Standard errors in parentheses.

†significant at 10% level;

*significant at 5% level;

**significant at 1% level.

Instruments used: dummies for small country, island, small island, landlocked country, and the interaction of each of these measures with the log of population.

Columns (3) and (6) estimated with period specific intercepts (time effects not reported). Other specifications available upon request.

3.5.1. Magnitudes and summary

While the pattern of signs and the statistical significance of the estimates presented above is consistent with our theory, the effects could still be small in magnitude. However, they are not. To illustrate the extent of the substitutability between country size and openness, let us choose a baseline regression. Consider column (4) of Table 4 – this involves using the log of population as a measure of size, current openness as a

Table 9
First-stage F-tests for the instruments (current openness)

Specification	Endogenous variable	Openness (current)	Openness $*$ Size
	Size $=$ log of population		
1	F-statistics p value	4.83	3.92
		0.00	0.00
2	F-statistics p value	5.63	6.28
		0.00	0.00
3	F-statistics p value	4.22	4.49
		0.00	0.00
	Size $=$ log of GDP		
4	F-statistics p value	5.61	6.25
		0.00	0.00
5	F-statistics p value	10.38	11.23
		0.00	0.00
6	F-statistics p value	7.52	7.34
		0.00	0.00

Note. F-tests on the instruments from a regression of each endogenous variable on the list of instruments plus the exogenous regressors in each specification.

Table 10
First-stage F-tests for the instruments (real openness)

Specification	Endogenous variable	Openness (constant)	Openness $*$ Size
	Size $=$ log of GDP		
1	F-statistics p value	4.45	4.95
		0.00	0.00
2	F-statistics p value	9.09	9.92
		0.00	0.00
3	F-statistics p value	10.75	10.80
		0.00	0.00
	Size $=$ log of population		
4	F-statistics p value	4.55	3.52
		0.00	0.00
5	F-statistics p value	6.25	7.18
		0.00	0.00
6	F-statistics p value	5.67	7.20
		0.00	0.00

Note. F-tests on the instruments from a regression of each endogenous variable on the list of instruments plus the exogenous regressors in each specification.

measure of openness, and a wide range of controls in the growth regression. Consider a country with the median size. In our sample, when the data on log population are

Table 11
Constrained 3SLS estimates (using Frankel and Romer's instrument)

	Size = log of population		Size = log of GDP	
	Current openness (1)	Real openness (2)	Current openness (3)	Real openness (4)
Size * Openness	−0.008**	−0.010†	−0.003†	−0.009*
	(0.003)	(0.006)	(0.002)	(0.004)
Size	0.435*	0.273	0.399*	0.452**
	(0.180)	(0.197)	(0.166)	(0.173)
Openness	0.128**	0.163†	0.089†	0.242*
	(0.041)	(0.088)	(0.049)	(0.099)
Log of initial per capita income	−1.114**	−1.254**	−1.282**	−1.433**
	(0.251)	(0.252)	(0.245)	(0.255)
Fertility	−0.307*	−0.354**	−0.290*	−0.348**
	(0.122)	(0.120)	(0.125)	(0.118)
Male human capital	0.105	−0.011	−0.036	−0.086
	(0.280)	(0.291)	(0.283)	(0.284)
Female human capital	−0.164	−0.023	−0.043	0.031
	(0.321)	(0.327)	(0.325)	(0.320)
Government consumption (% GDP)	−0.053**	−0.052**	−0.051**	−0.052**
	(0.013)	(0.013)	(0.013)	(0.013)
Investment rate (% GDP)	0.131**	0.130**	0.122**	0.112**
	(0.017)	(0.017)	(0.017)	(0.019)
Intercept	3.959	7.991	2.219	2.694
	(4.408)	(4.296)	(4.948)	(4.547)
Number of countries (periods)	80 (4)	78 (4)	80 (4)	80 (4)
Adjusted *R*-squared	0.12 0.21	0.04 0.20	0.11 0.23	0.02 0.18
	0.36 0.14	0.37 0.10	0.37 0.02	0.40 0.12

Notes. Standard errors in parentheses.
†significant at 10% level;
*significant at 5% level;
**significant at 1% level.
Instruments used: Frankel–Romer instrument for openness and its interaction with the log of GDP.

averaged over the period 1960–2000, the median country turns out to be Mali (where the log of population is 8.802 – this corresponds to an average population of 6.6 million over the sample period). The effect of a one standard deviation change in openness (a change of 42 percentage points) on Mali's annual growth is estimated to be 0.419 percentage points. In contrast, in the smallest country in our sample (the Seychelles), the same change in openness would translate into an increase in growth of 1.40 percentage points. The effect of a marginal increase in openness on growth becomes zero when the log of population is equal to 10.8, which is the size of France (in our sample, only 13 countries are larger).

Conversely, the effect of size at the median level of openness, which is attained by South Korea (with a trade to GDP ratio of 54% on average between 1960 and 1999), the effect of multiplying the country's size by 10 would be to raise annual growth by 0.33 percentage points. In contrast, a relatively closed country such as Argentina (with a trade to GDP ratio of 15% on average between 1960 and 1998) would experience an increase in growth of 0.78 percentage points from decoupling its population. The effect of size on growth attains zero when openness reaches 82.4% (in our sample, 26 countries had a higher level of average openness over the 1960–1999 period). Using the results obtained with "real" measures of openness the magnitude of our results would typically be even larger.

Whether one "believes" these actual magnitudes or not, the signs and statistical significance of our variables of interest are very robust features of the data and independently confirmed and reinforced by Alcalá and Ciccone (2003). When evaluating the effects of scale on growth, it is essential to view scale as attainable either through a large domestic market, or through trade openness. Ignoring either would lead to underestimating scale effects in income. This section and the literature from which it is inspired has sought to bring together the research on the impact of trade on growth and the research on the impact of economic scale on growth, and in doing so has empirically established a substitutability between openness and country size.

4. Country size and trade in history

To what extent the size of countries respond to the economic "incentives" that we discussed above? Is there a sense that in the long-run the size of countries responds to economic forces? Our answer is yes, even though, of course, the determination of borders is driven by a highly complex web of politico-economic forces. The point of this section is simply to highlight the relationship between country size and trade in a brief historical excursion. We certainly we do not aim to discuss the entire history of state formation and their size. For a more extensive discussion we refer the reader to Alesina and Spolaore (2003), and to the voluminous literature cited therein.

4.1. The city-states

The city-states of Italy and the Low Countries of the Renaissance in Europe represent a clear example of a political entity that could prosper even if very small because they were taking advantage of world markets. Free trade was the key to prosperity of these small states. A contemporary observer described Amsterdam as a place were "commerce is absolutely free, absolutely nothing is forbidden to merchants, they have no rule to follow but their own interest. So when an individual seems to do in his own commercial interest something contrary to the state the state turns a blind eye and pretends not to notice".[43] The other reason why city-states could afford to be small is that the state

---

[43] From Braudel (1992, p. 206). Also cited in Alesina and Spolaore (2003).

did not provide many public goods, so that not much was lost in terms of tax burden from being small. Thus, the combination of a small states who provided very few public goods and complete freedom of trade allowed for the city state to reach unprecedented level of wealth based on trade.

4.2. The absolutist period

The emergence of centralized states from the consolidation of feudal manors was driven by three main forces. One is technological innovations in military technology that increased the benefits of scale in warfare. Secondly, there was a need to enforce property rights and to create markets above and beyond the maritime commerce of the city-states. Finally bellicose rulers needed vast populations in order to extract levies to finance wars and luxurious courts. Territorial expansion and fiscal pressure went hand in hand and city-states could not survive in this changed world. Italian city-states lost predominance. The Low Countries survived longer because of their role as Atlantic traders. While the small city-states blossomed on trade, as Wilson (1967) writes regarding France "by the second half of the sixteenth century primitive ideas about trade had already given rise to a corpus of legislation ... aimed at national self-sufficiency". Similarly, English policy turned quite protectionist in the early seventeenth century. From the small and open city-states with low taxation, the western world became organized in large countries, pursuing inward looking policies. So economic predominance switched from small open economies with cheap governments to large relatively closed economies with a heavier burden of taxation to service war.

Outside the core of Europe, absolutist regimes were based on heavy taxation raised without the parenthesis of city-states. This is the case, for instance of the Ottoman Empire, but also of India and China. The Ottoman Empire for instance, was largely based on extracting rents from its population. In India the level of taxation was extraordinarily high for that period. In the sixteenth century the estimated tax revenue of the central government was about 20% of GNP.

4.3. The birth of the modern nation-state

The nineteenth century marks the birth of the nation-state in modern forms, both in Europe and North America. It also marks the beginning of industrialization and the growth take-off, which likely transformed the relationship between country size and economic performance, raising the importance of scale effects. The liberal philosophers of these times viewed the "optimal size" of a nation-state as emerging from the trade-off between homogeneity of language and culture and the benefit of economic size. In fact, following the work of Adam Smith, they were well aware that with free trade a market economy can easily prosper even without a heavy central government. Nevertheless, the view was that there existed an minimum size that made an economy viable. For instance, certain regions, like Belgium, Ireland and Portugal were considered too small to prosper, but free trade was regarded as a way of allowing even relatively small countries to prosper. Giuseppe Mazzini, an architect of the Italian unification, suggested that the optimal number of states in Europe was 12. His argument was precisely based on the consideration of a trade-off between the economically viable size of country and nationalistic aspiration of various groups. A famous political economy treaty of the time argues that it was "ridiculous" that Belgium and Portugal should be independent because there economies were too small to be economically viable.[44]

The unification of Germany can in fact be viewed along similar lines. The German nation-state started as a customs union (the Zollverein) which was viewed as necessary to create a sufficiently large market. As Merriman (1996, p. 629) notes, before the customs union "German merchants and manufacturers began to object to the discouraging complexity of custom tariffs that created a series of costly hurdles ... many businessmen demanded an end to these unnatural impediments faced by neither of their French or British rivals". Clearly market size was a critical determinant of the birth of Germany. The external threat of a war with France was a second one, as emphasized by Riker (1964). The establishment of a common market free of trade barriers was also one of the motivating factor behind the creation of the United States.

4.4. The colonial empires

In the period between 1848 and early 1870's the share of international trade in GDP quadrupled in Europe.[45] From 1870 to the First World War trade grew much more slowly despite a drastic reduction of transportation costs, as documented in Estevadeordal, Frantz and Taylor (2003). In fact the extent of the reduction of trade amongst European powers in the half-century between 1870 and 1915 is a matter of dispute amongst historians. Bairoch (1989) has probably the most sanguine view on one side of the argument when he writes that the introduction of new large tariff by Germany in 1879 marks the "death" of free trade. While many historians may find this view a bit extreme, it is fairly noncontroversial that without the sharp reduction in trading costs international trade would have probably greatly suffered in this period, which was certainly associated with an increase in protectionism.

The last two decades of the nineteenth century witnessed the expansion of European (and North American) powers over much of the "less developed" world. One motivation of this expansionary policy was certainly the opening of new markets. As reported by Hobsbawm (1987, p. 67), in 1897 the British Prime Minister told the French ambassador to Britain that "if you [the French] were not such persistent protectionists, you would not find us so keen to annex new territories". Needless to say, the British were just as protectionist as the French and the British navy was heavily used to protect trade routes. Similar considerations apply to the expansionary acquisitions of the United States in the late nineteenth and early twentieth centuries, namely Alaska, Hawaii, Samoa, Cuba and the Philippines. At the same time, in response to European protectionism, the United States also turned protectionist in this period.

---

[44] See Hobsbawm (1987).

[45] See Estevadeordal, Frantz and Taylor (2003) for a more detailed discussion.

In summary, from the point of view of the colonizers, Empires were a brilliant solution to the trade-off between size and heterogeneity. Large empire guaranteed large markets, especially necessary when protectionism was on the rise, but at the same time, by not granting citizenship to the inhabitants of the colonies, the problem of having a heterogeneous population with full political rights was reduced.

4.5. Borders in the interwar period

Figure 1 shows all the countries created and eliminated in five years periods from 1870 until today.[46] The dip at the beginning of the figures highlights the unification of Germany. This figure shows that in the interwar period after the Treaty of Versailles, borders remained essentially frozen, despite the fact that many nationalistic aspiration had been left unanswered by the peace treaty. In fact, a common view amongst historians is that the Treaty of Versailles vastly mishandled the border issue. Nevertheless, borders remained virtually unchanged, in a period in which free trade collapsed. No decolonization occurred. Amongst the new country creations, at least one, Egypt (independent in 1922) is merely an issue of classification: it was largely independent from Britain, but its status switched from a protectorate to a semi-independent country. Leaving aside the

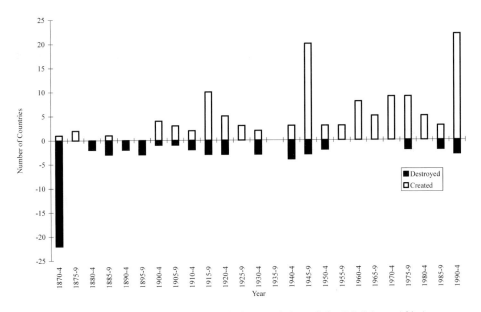

Figure 1. Countries created and destroyed (5-year periods, excludes Sub-Saharan Africa).

---

[46] This figure exclude Sub-Saharan Africa, given the difficulty of identifying borders before the colonization period.

Vatican City, the only other countries created between 1920 and the Second World War were Ireland (1921), Mongolia (1921), Iraq (1932), and Saudi Arabia (1932).

The interwar period was characterized by a collapse of free trade, the emergence of dictatorships, and by a belligerent state of international relationships. The Great Depression completed the gloomy picture and precipitated the rise of protectionism. These are all factors that, according to our analysis, should *not* be associated with the creation of new countries, in fulfillment of nationalistic aspirations. In addition, these elements (lack of democracy, international conflicts, protectionism) would make colonial powers hold on to their empires and repress independent movements. In fact, all the colonial powers were adamant in refusing self-determination of colonies during this period. This combinations of events, protectionism and maintenance of large countries and empire, stands in sharp contrast with what happened in the aftermath of the Second World War.

4.6. Borders in the post–Second World War period

In the fifty years that followed the Second World War, the number of independent countries increased dramatically. There were 74 countries in 1948, 89 in 1950, and 193 in 2001. The world now comprises a large number of relatively small countries: in 1995, 87 of the countries in the world had a population of less than 5 million, 58 had a population of less than 2.5 million, and 35 less than 500 thousands. In the same 50 years, the share of international trade in world GDP increased dramatically. The volume of imports and exports in a sample of about 60 countries has risen by about 40 percent.

We should stress that the increase in international trade in the last half-century, as documented in Figure 2, is not the simple result of an accounting illusion. In fact, if

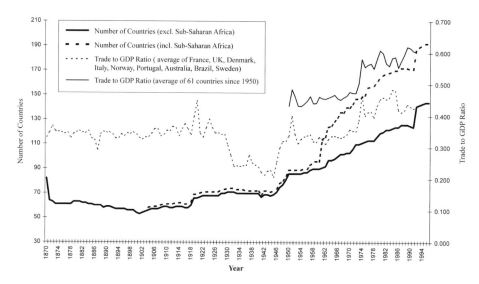

Figure 2. Trade openness and the number of countries.

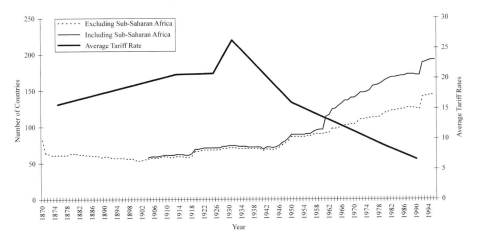

Figure 3. Average tariff rate and the number of countries (unweighted country average of average tariff rate for Austria, Belgium, France, Germany, Sweden, USA).

two countries were to split, their resulting trade to GDP ratios would automatically increase, as former domestic trade is now counted as international trade. But Figure 2 only features the average trade to GDP ratio for a set of countries *whose borders did not change since 1870*. Furthermore, Figure 3 uses average tariffs on foreign trade for a selection of countries with available data, a more direct reflection of trade policy, to display a similar historical pattern. Obviously, such policy measures are not subject to the accounting illusion either.

The correlation between the number of countries and trade liberalization is captured by Figures 4 and 5 which plot the detrended number of independent countries against the detrended trade to GDP ratio, including Sub-Saharan Africa from 1903 onward, and without it from 1870 to 1905.[47] In both cases the correlation is very strong. Since both variables are detrended, this positive correlation is not simply due to the fact that both variables increase over time. In Figure 2, note the sharp drop in the number of countries between 1870 and 1871, due to the unification of Germany. While 1871 is on the "regression line", 1870 is well above it, suggesting that there were "too many" countries before the German unification, relative to the average level of openness.

Not only have the recent decades witnessed an increase in the number of countries, but many regions have demanded and often obtained more autonomy from their central governments. In fact, decentralization is very popular around the world. The case of Québec is especially interesting. The push for independence in Québec was revamped by the implementation of the North American Free Trade Agreement (NAFTA). The freer trade in North America, the easier it would be for a relatively small country, like Québec, to prosper. As we discussed above, at least for Canada, national borders still

---

[47] All these figures are take from Alesina, Spolaore and Wacziarg (2000).

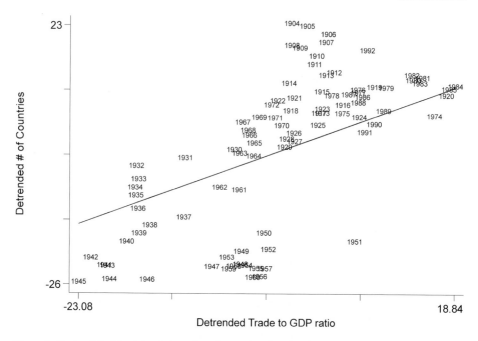

Figure 4. Scatterplot of the detrended number of countries plotted against the detrended trade to GDP ratio
(with Sub-Saharan Africa – 1903–1992).

matter, so that trade among Canadian provinces is much easier than trade between Canadian provinces and U.S. states. As shown by McCallum (1995), two distant Canadian provinces trade much more with each other than U.S. states and Canadian provinces bordering each other, even though distance is a strong determinant of trade flows. This implies that there might be a cost for Québec in terms of trade flows if it were to become independent and such arguments were made by the proponents of the "no" in the self-determination referendum of 1996. As the perceived economic costs of secession fall with greater North American economic integration, the likelihood of Québec gaining independence can be expected to increase. In fact, the development of a true free-trade area in North America might reduce these costs and make Québec separatism more attractive.

4.7. The European Union

Fifteen European countries have created a union which has several supranational institutions, such as the Parliament, a Court system, a Commission and a Council of Ministers and have delegated to them substantial policy prerogatives. We have argued that more economic integration should have lead towards political separatism. How does the European Union "fit" into this picture?

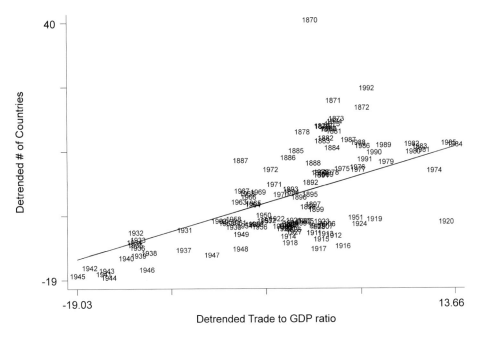

Figure 5. Scatterplot of the detrended number of countries plotted against the detrended trade to GDP ratio (with Sub-Saharan Africa – 1870–1992).

First of all, the European Union is not a state, not even a federation since it does not have the critical determinant of what a state is: the monopoly of coercion over its citizens. Thus, the European Union does not satisfy the Weberian notion of what constitutes a "sovereign state". The newly proposed draft Constitution for Europe states clearly in its article 2 that the European Union is indeed a union of independent countries and not a Federal State. Secondly, as economic integration is progressing at the European level, regional separatism is more and more vocal in several member countries of the Union, such as the U.K., Spain, Belgium, Italy and even France. So much so, that many have argued that Europe will (and, perhaps should) become a collection of regions (Brittany, the Basque Region, Scotland, Catalonia, Wales, Bavaria, etc.) loosely connected within a European confederation of independent regions. In fact, ethnic and cultural minorities feel that they would be economically "viable" in the context of a truly European common market, thus they could "safely" separate from the home country. This argument is often mentioned in the press. For an example pertaining to Scotland, see the *Financial Times*, September 16, 1998: "... the existence of the European Union lowers the cost of independence for small countries by providing them with a free trade area ... and by creating a common currency which will relieve the Scots of the need to create one for themselves".

One way of thinking about the EU is as a supranational union of countries that have merged certain functions needed to guarantee the functioning of a common market and take advantage of economies of scale. Whether or not the attribution of responsibilities and policy prerogatives between the EU and the national government is appropriate or not is an intricate subject which is beyond the scope of this paper.[48]

5. Conclusion

This paper has argued that size matters for economic performance and that country size is endogenous and depends on economic factors such as free trade, public goods provision and preference heterogeneity. We have reviewed and extended a recent literature that has discussed country formation and secession in the context of the theory of economic growth. The econometric and historical evidence is broadly consistent with the implications of these models

Much remains to be done. On the theoretical side, we have shown how scale effects could be derived in a simple neoclassical growth model, without appealing to increasing returns technologies, endogenous R&D or human capital spillovers, but simply by appealing to the existence of a border effect driven by trading frictions. However, whether the scale effects that we observe in the data come from the border effect, technology or spillovers remains to be investigated.

The models that we discussed are based on the assumption that heterogeneity within a country has negative effects on average utility. However, heterogeneity may also bring about some benefits. In fact, the gains from trade in our model do stem from a kind of heterogeneity – the production of different intermediate goods by different regions – and this is why a larger country, for given barriers to trade, brings net economic gains through the trade channel. By "heterogeneity" costs here we mean the specific costs associated with disagreements over the basic characteristics of a government (including policies about official languages, religion, etc.). A richer discussion of the pros and cons of heterogeneity is certainly called for.

On the empirical side, debates are still raging. Even the literature on the effect of trade on economic performance is now subject to debates on the nature and extent of this effect. The literature on the effect of country size is even more contentious. Yet the existence of both of these effects is important to the argument that we proposed about the role of trade openness in the endogenous determination of country size. We have shown that a simultaneous consideration of an economy's openness and of its size led to estimating strong effects of both size and openness on growth in a sample of countries since 1960.

Finally, in a broad historical sweep, we have suggested that the types of trade-offs identified by our framework have been at play at various stages in modern history.

---

[48] For a discussion of this point, see Alesina and Wacziarg (1999).

In a way, current developments provide an ideal setting for observers of country creation. Since the Second World War, increasing globalization has threatened nation-states "from above", while rising regionalism and decentralizing forces have threatened them "from below". The construction of the European Union epitomizes this tension, as a fundamental redrawing of the distribution of political prerogatives is being orchestrated. Powers are being transferred down through decentralization, and up through the European construction. It is likely that if globalization proceeds apace, so will regionalism. If the backlash against globalization succeeds, however, large centralized nation-states could initiate a comeback.

Acknowledgements

We are grateful to the NSF for financial support with a grant through the NBER. We also thank Jessica Seddon Wallack for excellent research assistance. We thank Philippe Aghion, Francisco Alcalá, Michele Boldrin, Antonio Ciccone, Yannis Ioannides and seminar and conference participants at the University of Modena, Harvard University, the European University Institute, the University of Rochester, and New York University for useful comments. All remaining errors are ours.

References

Ades, A., Glaeser, E. (1999). "Evidence on growth, increasing returns and the extent of the market". Quarterly Journal of Economics 114 (3), 1025–1045.

Aghion, P., Howitt, P. (1992). "A model of growth through creative destruction". Econometrica 60, 323–351.

Aghion, P., Howitt, P. (1998). "Market structure and the growth process". Review of Economic Dynamics 1, 276–305.

Aghion, P., Bloom, N., Blundell, R., Griffith, R., Howitt, P. (2002). "Competition and innovation: An inverted U relationship". Working Paper, September. Harvard University.

Alcalá, F., Ciccone, A. (2003). "Trade, the extent of the market and economic growth 1960–1996". Unpublished Manuscript. Universitat Pompeu Fabra.

Alcalá, F., Ciccone, A. (2004). "Trade and productivity". Quarterly Journal of Economics 119 (2), 613–646.

Alesina, A., Baqir, R., Easterly, W. (1999). "Public goods and ethnic divisions". Quarterly Journal of Economics 114 (4), 1243–1284.

Alesina, A., Baqir, R., Hoxby, C. (2004). "Political jurisdictions in heterogeneous communities". Journal of Political Economy 112 (2), 348–396.

Alesina, A., Barro, R., Tenreyro, S. (2002). "Optimal currency areas". In: Gertler, M., Rogoff, K. (Eds.), NBER Macroeconomic Annual, vol. 17. MIT Press, Cambridge, MA, pp. 301–345.

Alesina, A., Devleeschauwer, A., Easterly, W., Kurlat, S., Wacziarg, R. (2003). "Fractionalization". Journal of Economic Growth 8 (2), 155–194.

Alesina, A., La Ferrara, E. (2000). "Participation in heterogeneous communities". Quarterly Journal of Economics 115 (3), 847–904.

Alesina, A., La Ferrara, E. (2002). "Who trusts others?". Journal of Public Economics 85 (August), 207–234.

Alesina, A., Spolaore, E. (1997). "On the number and size of nations". Quarterly Journal of Economics 112 (4), 1027–1056.

Alesina, A., Spolaore, E. (2003). The Size of Nations. MIT Press, Cambridge, MA.

Alesina, A., Spolaore, E., Wacziarg, R. (2000). "Economic integration and political disintegration". American Economic Review 90 (5), 1276–1296.

Alesina, A., Wacziarg, R. (1998). "Openness, country size and the government". Journal of Public Economics 69 (3), 305–321.

Alesina, A., Wacziarg, R. (1999). "Is Europe going too far?". Carnegie–Rochester Conference Series on Public Policy 51 (1), 1–42.

Backus, D., Kehoe, P., Kehoe, T. (1992). "In search of scale effects in trade and growth". Journal of Economic Theory 58 (2), 377–409.

Bairoch, P. (1989). "European trade policy, 1815–1914". In: Mathias, P., Pollard, S. (Eds.), The Cambridge Economic History of Europe, vol. 8. Cambridge University Press, Cambridge, pp. 1–160.

Bardhan, P. (2002). "Decentralization of governance and development". Journal of Economic Perspectives 16 (4), 185–205.

Barro, R.J., Lee, J.-W. (1994). "Data set for a panel of 138 countries", available at http://www.nber.org/data/ .

Barro, R.J., Sala-i-Martin, X. (1995). Economic Growth. McGraw Hill, New York.

Ben-David, D. (1993). "Equalizing exchange: Trade liberalization and income convergence". Quarterly Journal of Economics 108 (3), 653–679.

Bolton, P., Roland, G. (1997). "The breakups of nations: A political economy analysis". Quarterly Journal of Economics (4), 1057–1089.

Braudel, F. (1992). The Perspective of the World: Civilization and Capitalism 15th–18th Century, vol. 3. University of California Press, Berkeley.

Casella, A., Feinstein, J.S. (2002). "Public goods in trade: On the formation of markets and political jurisdictions". International Economic Review 43 (2), 437–462.

Central Intelligence Agency (2002). CIA World Factbook. Brassey's Inc., Dulles, VA.

De Figueiredo, R., Weingast, B. (2002), "Self-enforcing federalism". Working Paper, March. Stanford University.

Dollar, D. (1992). "Outward-oriented developing economies really do grow more rapidly: Evidence from 95 LDCs, 1976–85". Economic Development and Cultural Change 40 (3), 523–544.

Easterly, W., Levine, R. (1997). "Africa's growth tragedy: Policies and ethnic divisions". Quarterly Journal of Economics 111 (4), 1203–1250.

Edwards, S. (1993). "Openness, trade liberalization and growth in developing countries". Journal of Economic Literature 31 (September), 1358–1393.

Edwards, S. (1998). "Openness, productivity and growth: What do we really know?". Economic Journal 108 (447), 383–398.

Estevadeordal, A., Frantz, B., Taylor, A.M. (2003). "The rise and fall of world trade, 1870–1939". Quarterly Journal of Economics 118 (2), 359–407.

Findlay, R. (1996). "Towards a model of territorial expansion and the limits of empires". In: Garfinkel, M., Skaperdas, S. (Eds.), The Political Economy of Conflict and Appropriation. Cambridge University Press, Cambridge, U.K.

Frankel, J.A., Romer, D. (1999). "Does trade cause growth?". American Economic Review 89 (3), 379–399.

Friedman, D. (1977). "A theory of the size and shape of nations". Journal of Political Economy 85 (1), 59–77.

Garner, P. (2001). "The role of rival nation-states in long-run growth". Working Paper. Brown University.

Grossman, G., Helpman, E. (1991). Innovation and Growth in the Global Economy. MIT Press, Cambridge, MA.

Ha, J., Howitt, P. (2004). "Accounting for trends in productivity and R&D: A Schumpeterian critique of semi-endogenous growth theory". Working Paper. Brown University.

Harrison, A., Hanson, G. (1999). "Who gains from trade reforms? Some remaining puzzles". Journal of Development Economics 48, 419–447.

Helliwell, J. (1998). How Much Do National Borders Matter? Brookings Institution Press, Washington, DC.

Herbst, J. (2000). States and Power in Africa. Princeton University Press, Princeton, NJ.

Heston, A., Summers, R., Aten, B. (2002). "Penn World Table, version 6.1". Center for International Comparisons at the University of Pennsylvania (CICUP). October.

Hobsbawm, E. (1987). The Age of Empire. Vintage Books, New York, NY.

Howitt, P. (1999). "Steady endogenous growth with population and R&D inputs growing". Journal of Political Economy 107 (4), 715–730.

Jones, C. (1999). "Growth: With or without scale effects?". American Economic Review Papers and Proceedings 89 (May), 139–144.

Jones, C. (1995a). "R&D-based models of economic growth". Journal of Political Economy 103 (August), 759–784.

Jones, C. (1995b). "Time series tests of endogenous growth models". Quarterly Journal of Economics 110 (2), 495–525.

La Porta, R., Lopez de Silanes, F., Shleifer, A., Vishny, R. (1999). "The quality of government". Journal of Law, Economics and Organization 15 (1), 222–279.

Lucas, R.E. (1988). "On the mechanics of economic development". Journal of Monetary Economics 22, 3–42.

McCallum, J. (1995). "National borders matter: Canada–US regional trade patterns". American Economic Review 85 (3), 615–623.

Merriman, J.W. (1996). A History of Modern Europe: From the Renaissance to the Present. W.W. Norton & Co., New York.

Murphy, K., Shleifer, A., Vishny, R. (1989). "Industrialization and the big push". Journal of Political Economy 87 (5), 1003–1026.

Oates, W.E. (1999). "An essay on fiscal federalism". Journal of Economic Literature 37 (September), 1120–1149.

Obstfeld, M., Rogoff, K. (2000). "The six major puzzles in international finance: Is there a common cause?". In: Bernanke, B.S., Rogoff, K. (Eds.), NBER Macroeconomics Annual, vol. 15. MIT Press, Cambridge MA, pp. 339–390.

Portes, R., Rey, H. (2000). "The determinants of cross-border equity flows". NBER Working Paper 7336, September.

Pritchett, L. (1996). "Measuring outward orientation: Can it be done?". Journal of Development Economics 49 (2), 307–335.

Riker, W.H. (1964). Federalism: Origins, Operation, Significance. Little Brown, Boston.

Rodrik, D., Rodríguez, F. (2000). "Trade policy and economic growth: A skeptics guide to the cross-national evidence". In: Bernanke, B., Rogoff, K. (Eds.), NBER Macroeconomics Annual, vol. 15. MIT Press, Cambridge, MA, pp. 261–325.

Rodrik, D., Subramanian, A., Trebbi, F. (2004). "Institutions rule: The primary of institutions over geography and integration in economic development". Journal of Economic Growth 9 (2), 131–165.

Romer, P. (1986). "Increasing returns and long run growth". Journal of Political Economy 94, 1002–1037.

Romer, P. (1990). "Endogenous technological change". Journal of Political Economy 98 (5), S71–S102.

Rose, A. (2000). "One money, one market: The effect of common currencies on trade". Economic Policy 15 (30).

Sachs, J., Warner, A. (1995). "Economic reform and the process of global integration". Brookings Papers on Economic Activity 1, 1–118.

Smith, A. (1986). An Inquiry into the Nature and Causes of the Wealth of Nations. Penguin Books, Harmondsworth, U.K. (first published 1776).

Spolaore, E. (1995). "Economic integration, political borders and productivity". Prepared for the CEPR–Sapir conference on "Regional Integration and Economic Growth". Tel Aviv University, December.

Spolaore, E. (2002). "Conflict, trade and the size of countries". Working Paper. Brown University.

Spolaore, E. (2005). "The political economy of national borders". In: Weingast, B.R., Wittman, D. (Eds.), The Oxford Handbook of Political Economy. Oxford University Press, Oxford, in preparation.

Spolaore, E., Wacziarg, R. (2005). "Borders and growth". Journal of Economic Growth 10 (4), in press.

Wacziarg, R. (2001). "Measuring the dynamic gains from trade". World Bank Economic Review 15 (3), 393–429.

Wacziarg, R., Welch, K.H. (2003). "Trade liberalization and growth: New evidence". NBER Working Paper 10152, December.

Wilson, C.H. (1967). "Trade, society and the state". In: Rich, E.E., Wilson, C.H. (Eds.), The Cambridge Economic History of Europe from the Decline of the Roman Empire, vol. 4. Cambridge University Press, Cambridge, pp. 487–575.

Young, A. (1998). "Growth without scale effects". Journal of Political Economy 106 (February), 41–63.

Chapter 24

URBANIZATION AND GROWTH

J. VERNON HENDERSON

Brown University

Contents

Abstract	1544
Keywords	1544
1. Facts and empirical evidence	1547
1.1. The size distribution of cities and its evolution	1548
1.1.1. What is a city?	1548
1.1.2. Evolution of the size distribution	1549
1.1.3. Growth in city numbers and sizes	1552
1.1.4. Zipf's Law	1553
1.2. Geographic concentration and urban specialization	1554
1.2.1. Urban specialization	1555
1.2.2. Geographic concentration	1556
1.2.3. Geography	1558
1.3. Urbanization in developing countries	1558
1.3.1. Issues concerning overall urbanization	1559
1.3.2. The form of urbanization: the degree of spatial concentration	1560
2. Cities and growth	1564
2.1. The systems of cities at a point in time	1565
2.1.1. Equilibrium city sizes	1566
2.1.2. Other city types	1569
2.1.3. Replicability and national policy	1571
2.2. Growth in a system of cities	1571
2.2.1. Growth properties: cities	1572
2.2.2. Growth properties: economy	1573
2.3. Extensions	1573
2.3.1. Different types of workers	1573
2.3.2. Metro areas	1574
2.3.3. Stochastic process and Zipf's Law	1576
3. Urbanization and growth	1577
3.1. Two sector approaches, without cities	1577

Handbook of Economic Growth, Volume 1B. Edited by Philippe Aghion and Steven N. Durlauf
DOI: 10.1016/S1574-0684(05)01024-5

    3.2. Urbanization with cities   1579
        3.2.1. Human capital market, migration, savings   1580
        3.2.2. Urban growth and transformation   1581
        3.2.3. Economic growth   1582
    3.3. Extensions and policy issues   1582
        3.3.1. City sizes   1583
        3.3.2. Sequential city formation and governance   1585
4. Some issues for a research agenda   1586
Acknowledgement   1587
References   1587

Abstract

This chapter on urbanization and growth focuses on modeling and empirical evidence that pertain to a number of inter-related questions. Why do cities form in an economy, with so much of economic activity in countries geographically concentrated in cities? Second, how do different types of cities interact with each other in terms of trade and migration? Given the answers to these questions the chapter turns to growth issues. How does a system of cities evolve under economic and population growth; and how does urban growth intersect with, or even define national economic growth? In growth theory, endogenous growth is based on knowledge spillovers and sharing, and evidence suggests that much of that interaction must occur at the level of individual cities. In the early stages of growth, economic development is characterized by urbanization – a spatial transformation of the economy, where the population moves through migration from an agricultural, rural based existence to one where production occurs in cities of endogenous numbers and size. How do we model that transformation process and what are the key aspects of the transformation? In any static, growth, or development–urbanization context, how do governance, institutions, and public policy affect city formation and sizes, which then in turn affect economic efficiency. Cities require enormous public infrastructure investments which affect urban quality of life, in particular health and safety and commuting and congestion costs. Institutions governing land markets, property rights, local government autonomy, and local financing affect the city formation process and city sizes. And national government policies concerning trade, labor policies and national investment in communications and transport infrastructure affect the shape of the urban system. A final set of questions has to do with where cities locate. What is the effect of history, of climate and of natural resource locations, including rivers and natural harbors, on the location of current urban agglomerations?

Keywords

urbanization, system of cities, dual sector models, agglomeration, endogenous growth, rural–urban migration, growth models, spatial distributions

JEL classification: O1, O15, O18, O4, O41, R00, R11

The study of urbanization and growth focuses on five related questions. First, why do cities form and why is economic activity so geographically concentrated in cities? In the USA, only 2% of the land area is covered by the urban built environment. This incredible geographic concentration is the central focus of economic geographers. Economists dating from Marshall (1890) have answered the question by saying urban agglomerations are based on technological externalities – the information spill-over benefits in input and output markets of having economic agents in close spatial proximity, where information decay over space is very rapid. In addition the new economic geography develops the idea that close spatial proximity involves pecuniary externalities – reduces the costs of intermediate and final good trade. Agglomeration benefits are specified typically as applying within industries or sets of inter-related industries; there is considerable debate empirically about their application across industries. That issue, as we will see later, is related to the second set of questions.

How do cities interact with each other, at any instant in time? What are the trade patterns across cities in final and intermediate outputs and how does that correspond to the roles of big and small cities? In what ways are cities specialized by either products or functions, and why? How do these patterns of specialization and diversification relate to city labor force compositions and human capital accumulations?

Given the role of cities at a point in time, the third set of questions asks how urban growth intersects with, or even defines national economic growth? The close connection between urban and national economic growth was recognized by Lucas (1988) and inspired by the development of endogenous growth models. To the extent endogenous growth is based on knowledge spillovers and sharing, given the role of close spatial proximity in spillovers, much of the interaction and sharing must occur at the level of individual cities. Given that, there must also be a close connection between economic development and urbanization. How are the two tied together? In addition the stochastic forces that shock production processes, invention, and technological progress must also play out in an urban form. How does that occur?

The fourth set of questions asks how governance, institutions, and public policy affect urbanization, which then in turn affects economic efficiency and growth. Apart from the long standing analysis of provision and financing of local public goods, there are three issues of interest specific to the urbanization process. First, public infrastructure investments in cities are enormous and the internal structure of cities affects not just the resources devoted to urban living such as commuting and congestion costs, but also affects production efficiency – the extent to which information and knowledge spillovers are fully realized and exploited. Second, institutions governing land markets, property rights, local government autonomy, and local financing including local public debt accumulation affect the city formation process, city sizes, and national economic growth. Finally, national government policies concerning migration, trade policy, national investment in communications and transport infrastructure have profound impacts on the urban system, migration patterns, regional economic development and the like.

The final set of questions has to do with where cities locate and the economic geography of urbanization. In what regions do cities cluster and why are some regions so sparsely populated? What first nature forces of natural resource locations, including rivers and natural harbors, drive the location of economic activity? How do transport costs and technological change in transport costs affect the extent to which coastal versus hinterland regions are inhabited? And what is the role of second nature forces and history on location – how does the accumulation of economic activity based on historical market forces affect the current spatial patterns of economic activity?

This handbook chapter reviews evidence on all these questions and then turns to models that focus on aspects of the middle three questions – how do cities interact with each other; what is the relationship among urbanization, urban growth, national economic growth and economic development; and what is the role of institutions and public policy in shaping urbanization? In terms of the first question on why cities form, there is a splendid handbook paper by Duranton and Puga (2004) reviewing models of the micro-foundations of agglomeration economies and another by Rosenthal and Strange (2004) reviewing empirical evidence on the subject. In terms of the where question, there is little in the way of models that look at the location patterns of individual cities. There are the core–periphery models of economic geography that analyze the allocation of economic activity within a country between a core and periphery region. We will discuss how these models may inform the where question for cities. But they are a topic unto themselves with excellent general handbook coverage in Overman, Redding and Venables (2003) and coverage specific to regional issues in Ottaviano and Thisse (2004), with a review of empirical evidence in Head and Mayer (2004).

The first section reviews data and empirical evidence on aspects of the five questions. The second presents a simple system of cities model, which illustrates the basic organization of the urban sector and the interaction between economic and urban growth. The model serves as a platform to discuss issues of institutions and policy. In the third section, the model in Section 2 is adapted to analyze rural–urban transformation and urbanization as part of economic development; then policy issues for developing countries are analyzed.

1. Facts and empirical evidence

This section reviews basic facts and a body of empirical evidence on systems of cities. We start by looking at evidence based primarily on either the world as a whole or on large developed countries. We look at the evolution of the size distribution of cities, Zipf's Law and related topics. Then we turn to what cities do – evidence on urban specialization and geographic concentration – and where they locate. Finally we turn to evidence that is more specific to the urbanization process in developing countries and issues surrounding that process.

1.1. The size distribution of cities and its evolution

Work by Eaton and Eckstein (1997) on France and Japan and by Dobkins and Ioannides (2001) on the USA, with later work by Black and Henderson (2003) and Ioannides and Overman (2003) on the USA, establish some basic facts about urban systems and their development in France, Japan and the USA over the last century or so. Foremost is that there is a wide relative size distribution of cities in large economies that is stable over time. Big and small cities coexist in equal proportions over long periods of time. Second, within that relative size distribution, individual cities are generally growing in population size over time; and what is considered a big versus small city in absolute size changes over time. Third, while there is entry of new cities and both rapid growth and decline of cities nearer the bottom of the urban hierarchy, at the top city size rankings are remarkably stable over time. Finally, size distributions of cities within countries, at least at the upper tail are well approximated by a Pareto distribution, with Zipf's Law applying in many cases. Establishing these facts raises a variety of issues and different methodological and technical approaches.

1.1.1. What is a city?

The empirical work in Eaton and Eckstein (1997) and subsequent work typically looks at the decade by decade development of urban systems. In doing so, there are critical choices researchers must make when assembling data. First is to define geographically what consists of the generic term "city". The usual definition is the "metro area", where large metro areas like Chicago comprise over 100 municipalities, or local political units. The idea in defining metro areas is to cover the entire local labor market and all contiguous manufacturing, service and residential activities radiating out from the core city, until activity peters out into farm land or very low density development. A second choice concerns how to accommodate changes in geographic definitions over time. One can use whatever contemporaneous definitions the country census/statistical bureau uses; however metro area definitions only start to be applied after World War II. Another approach is to take current metro area definitions and follow the same geographic areas back in time, focusing on nonagricultural activity.

   A third problem concerns how to define "consistently" over time the threshold population size at which an agglomeration becomes a metro area, especially since the economic nature, population density, and spatial development of metro areas have changed so much over the last century. Some authors use an absolute cut-off point (e.g., urban population of 50,000 or more); some use a relative cut-off point (e.g., the minimum size city included in the sample should be 0.15 mean city size); and others look at a set number (e.g., 50 or 100) of the largest cities. The relative cut-off point approach is attractive because it attempts to hold constant the area of the relative size distribution which is examined over time, as illustrated below. In presenting evidence on the topics to follow, whatever choices researchers make can strongly affect specific results. Nevertheless there are a variety of findings that are consistent across studies.

1.1.2. Evolution of the size distribution

In the research, one focus has been to study the evolution of the size distribution of cities, applying techniques utilized by Quah (1993) in examining cross-country growth patterns. Cities in each decade are divided by relative size into, say, 5–6 discrete categories, with fixed relative size cut-off points for each cell (e.g., <0.22 of mean size, 0.22–0.47 of mean size, ... >2.2 mean size). A first-order Markov process is assumed and a transition matrix calculated. In many cases, stationarity of the matrix over decades cannot be rejected, so cell transition probabilities are based on all transitions over time. If M is the transition matrix, i the average rate of entry of new cities in each decade (in a context where in practice there is no exit), Z the (stationary) distribution across cells of entrants (typically concentrated on the lowest cell), and f the steady-state distribution, then

$$f = \left[I - (1 - i)M\right]^{-1} i Z. \tag{1}$$

In the data, relative size distributions are remarkably stable over time and steady-state distributions tend to be close to the most recent distributions. In the studies on the USA, Japan and France, there is no tendency of distributions to collapse and concentrate in one cell, or for all cities to converge to mean size; nor generally is there a tendency for distributions to become bipolar. Distributions are remarkably stable. I illustrate this based on a world cities analysis (although, conceptually, distributions may better apply to countries, within which populations are relatively mobile).

Table 1 gives the size distribution of world metro areas over 100,000 population in 2000. Details on the data are available on-line.[1] Note that much of the world's pop-

Table 1
World city size distribution, 2000

Size range	Count	Mean	Share*
$17{,}000{,}000 \leqslant n_{2000}$	4	20,099,000	4.5
$12{,}000{,}000 \leqslant n_{2000} < 17{,}000{,}000$	7	13,412,714	5.2
$8{,}000{,}000 \leqslant n_{2000} < 12{,}000{,}000$	13	10,446,385	7.5
$4{,}000{,}000 \leqslant n_{2000} < 8{,}000{,}000$	29	5,514,207	8.9
$3{,}000{,}000 \leqslant n_{2000} < 4{,}000{,}000$	41	3,442,461	7.8
$2{,}000{,}000 \leqslant n_{2000} < 3{,}000{,}000$	75	2,429,450	10.1
$1{,}000{,}000 \leqslant n_{2000} < 2{,}000{,}000$	247	1,372,582	18.8
$500{,}000 \leqslant n_{2000} < 1{,}000{,}000$	355	703,095	13.9
$250{,}000 \leqslant n_{2000} < 500{,}000$	646	349,745	12.5
$100{,}000 \leqslant n_{2000} < 250{,}000$	1,240	157,205	10.8
Overall	2,657	658,218	100.0

*A ratio of total population in the group to total population of cities with $\geqslant 100{,}000$.

[1] *http://www.econ.brown.edu/faculty/henderson/worldcities.html.*

ulation in cities over 100,000 are in small–medium size metro areas. 56% are in cities under 2 million, while only 17% are in cities over 8 million. Moreover, all these cities only account for 62% of the world's urban population; the rest live in cities smaller than 100,000. So overall 73% of the world's urban population lives in cities under 2 million in population. While the popular press may focus on megacities, only a small part of the action is there.

Figure 1 plots the relative size distribution of the approximately 1200 metro areas worldwide over 100,000 in 1960 against the relative size distribution of the approximately 1700 metro areas over 200,000 in 2000. Relative sizes are actual sizes divided by the world average size in the corresponding year. The 100,000 versus 200,000 cut-off points for minimum size are relative ones based on a constant minimum to mean size ratio. (Although using an absolute cut-off point in this case has little impact on the figure.) The figure plots the histogram for 20 cells on a log scale. The 1960 versus 2000 distributions for all cities worldwide [Figure 1(a)] and for those in developing and transition economies [Figure 1(b)] almost perfectly overlap. Relative size distributions are stable. Similarly performing transition analysis on world cities for 1960–1970–1980–1990–2000 and calculating the steady state distributions, starting with 5 cells and shares in each of 0.351, 0.299, 0.151, 0.100, 0.0991 in 1960, as we move up the urban hierarchy the steady state shares are 0.324, 0.299, 0.138, 0.122 and 0.117. Again, this indicates rock stability of distributions over time.

An alternative way of expressing this is to calculate spatial Gini's [Krugman (1991b)]. For a spatial Gini rank all cities from smallest to largest on the x-axis and on the y-axis calculate their Lorenz curve – the cumulative share of total sample population. The Gini is the share of the area below the 45° line, between that line and the Lorenz curve. The greater the Gini, the "less equal" the size distribution. The world Gini in 1960 versus 2000 is 0.59 versus 0.56 for developed countries, 0.57 versus 0.56 for less developed countries, and 0.52 versus 0.45 for transition economies as noted in Table 2 columns (1)–(4). Table 2 also lists Gini's for 1960 versus 2000 for 14 countries. Note apart from transition economies (and Nigeria), the lack of change; and note also that transition economies are distinctly "more equal". Transition economies have forestalled the growth of megacities through explicit and implicit (housing availability in cities) migration restrictions, as discussed in Section 3.3.1.

A second finding in examining city size distributions is that, for larger cities, over time there is little change in relative size rankings. In Japan and France, the 39–40 largest cities in 1925 and 1876, respectively, all remain in the top 50 in 1985 and 1990 respectively; and, at the top, absolute rankings are unchanged [Eaton and Eckstein (1997)]. The USA displays more mobility due to substantial entry of new cities. However, while smaller cities do move up and down in rank, the biggest cities tend to remain big over time. So, for example, cities in the top decile of ranking stay in that decile indefinitely, with newer cities joining that decile as the total number of cities expands. Alternatively viewed, based on the Markov transition process, the mean first passage time for a city to move from the top to bottom cell is thousands of years [Black and Henderson (2003)]. In the world cities data, as in the USA data, the probability in the transition matrix of mov-

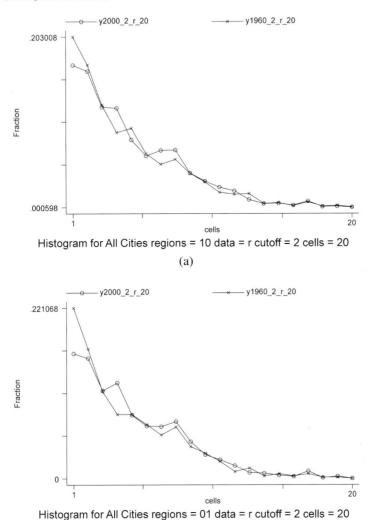

Figure 1. (a) Relative size distribution of cities for all countries. (b) Relative size distribution of cities in developing and transition economies.

ing out of the top cell to the next cell is very small: 0.038 in a decade time frame. Why do big cities stay big? A common answer is physical infrastructure (see Section 3.3.2). Large cities have huge historical capital stocks of streets, buildings, sewers, water mains and parks that are cheaply maintained and almost infinitely lived, that give them a persistent comparative advantage over cities without that built-up stock. A second answer is modeled in Arthur (1990) and Rauch (1993) where, with localized scale externalities in

Table 2
Spatial inequality

	1960		2000		
	Gini	Number of cities	Gini	Number of cities	Rank size coefficient "a"
	(1)	(2)	(3)	(4)	(5)
World	0.59	1197	0.56	1673	n.a.
Developed	0.65	523	0.58	480	n.a.
Soviet bloc	0.52	179	0.45	202	n.a.
Less developed	0.57	495	0.56	991	n.a.
Brazil	0.67	24	0.65	65	−0.87
China	0.47	108	0.43	223	−1.3
India	0.56	95	0.58	138	−1.1
Indonesia	0.52	22	0.61	30	−0.90
Mexico	0.61	28	0.60	55	−1.04
Nigeria	0.31	20	0.60	38	−0.98
France	0.61	31	0.59	27	−0.97
Germany	0.60	44	0.56	31	−0.74
Japan	0.60	100	0.66	82	−1.06
Russia	0.54	79	0.46	91	−1.34
Spain	0.53	27	0.52	20	−0.98
Ukraine	0.44	25	0.40	32	−1.31
UK	0.68	39	0.60	21	−0.83
USA	0.58	167	0.54	197	−1.11

production, large cities with a particular set of industries have a comparative advantage in attracting new firms, relative to cities with a small representation of those industries. Large cities have an established scale, offering high levels of scale externalities, which smaller cities can only achieve quickly if they are able to co-ordinate mass in-migration of firms into their location, something which may be institutionally difficult to do.

1.1.3. Growth in city numbers and sizes

For any steady state size distribution of cities, as urbanization and growth proceed, both the absolute sizes and numbers of cities have grown historically, as a country's urban population expands through rural–urban migration and overall population growth. City sizes in the USA, Japan and France over the past century have grown at average annual rates of 1.2–1.5%, depending on the country and exact time interval, rates which involve city sizes rising 3.3–4.5 fold every century. A small city today which is 250,000 would have been a major center in 1900.

In the world city data set, for comparable sets of countries the numbers of metro areas grew by 62% from 1960–2000 using a relative cut-off point (approximately 100,000 in 1960 versus 170,000 for this sample in 2000). Average sizes grew by about 70%. Decade by decade figures are given in Table 3. Using an absolute cut-off point of 100,000, num-

Table 3
Total numbers of cities and sizes

	1960	1970	1980	1990	2000
Number of cities	969	1,129	1,353	1,547	1,568
Mean size	556,503	640,874	699,642	789,348	943,693
Median size	252,539	275,749	304,414	355,660	423,282
Minimum size	100,082	115,181	126,074	141,896	169,682

bers have about doubled and average sizes grown by 36% over 40 years. However we count cities, it is clear they have grown in population and numbers on an on-going basis over the decades.

The theory section will model city size growth and numbers in developed, or fully urbanized countries in Section 2 and in urbanizing economies in Section 3, as related to technological change induced by knowledge accumulation and demographic changes. There is empirical work relating city size increases to changes in knowledge levels. Glaeser, Scheinkman and Schelifer (1995) in a cross-section city growth framework estimate that controlling for 1960 population, in the USA, cities in 1990 are 7% larger if they had a one-standard deviation higher level of median years of schooling in 1960. Black and Henderson (1999a) place the issue in a panel context for 1940–1990 for the USA controlling for city fixed effects and industrial composition; and they examine the impact of percent college educated (which has enormous time variation). They find a one-standard deviation increase in the percent college educated leads to a 20% increase in city size over a decade.

1.1.4. Zipf's Law

In considering the size distribution of cities, especially in a cross-sectional context, there is a large literature on what is termed Zipf's Law [e.g., Rosen and Resnick (1980), Clark and Stabler (1991), Mills and Hamilton (1994) and Ioannides and Overman (2003)]. City sizes are postulated to follow a Pareto distribution, where if R is rank from smallest r, to largest 1, and n is size

$$R(n) = An^{-a} \qquad (2)$$

given the $\text{Prob}(\tilde{n} > n) = An^{-a}$ and relative rank is $R(n)/r$, or the proportion of cities with size greater than n. Under Zipf's Law $a = 1$, or we have the rank size rule where, for every city, rank times size is a constant, A. Putting (2) in log-linear form, empirical work produces a's that vary across countries, samples and times; but many are "close" to one. This empirical regularity has drawn considerable attention and is often used to characterize spatial inequality, using (2) as a first approximation of the true size distribution. We list sample a coefficients for 2000 for fifteen countries in Table 2, column (5). Note however while people often say that an exponent of 0.74 or 1.34 is "close to" one, such coefficients produce very different city size distributions, than if the coefficient is one.[2] As a declines, or the slope of the rank size line gets flatter, urban concentration is viewed as increasing: for given size changes, rank changes more slowly, or cities are "less equal". In Table 2, the a coefficients and the Gini's are in fact strongly negatively correlated, as one would expect. But we note that typically the log version of Equation (2) is better approximated by a quadratic form than linear one. However one looks at it, Zipf's Law is just an approximation that does well in some circumstances and not so well in others. If one wants to compare measures of urban concentration across countries or over time, rather than compare estimated a's in Equation (2), using Gini's may be more reliable, just as they are for comparisons of income distributions.

If Zipf's Law holds even approximately, why is that? In an interesting development, Gabaix (1999a, 1999b) starts to formalize the underlying stochastic components which might lead to such a relationship, building on Simon (1955). Gabaix shows that if city growth rates obey Gibrat's Law where growth rates are random draws from the same distribution,[3] so growth rates are independent of current size, Zipf's Law emerges as the limiting size distribution (as long as a lower bound on how far cities can deteriorate in size is imposed). Growth is scale invariant, so the final distribution is; and we have a power law with exponent 1. Gabaix sketches an illustrative model, based on on-going natural amenity shocks facing cities of any size, which leads to Zipf's Law for the size distribution of cities. More comprehensive formulations in Duranton (2005) and Rossi-Hansberg and Wright (2004) are discussed in the theory section.

While Gibrat's Law is a neat underlying stochastic process, does it hold up empirically? Black and Henderson (2003) test whether in the relationship, $\ln n_{it} - \ln n_{it-1} = a + \delta t + \alpha \ln n_{it-1} + \varepsilon_{it}$, $\alpha = 0$, as hypothesized under the Law. The Law requires ε_{it} to be i.i.d., so simple OLS suffices. Black and Henderson find $\alpha < 0$ under a variety of circumstance and subsamples, under appropriate statistical criteria, which rejects Gibrat's Law. Ioannides and Overman (2003) examine the issue more thoroughly in a nonparametric fashion, characterizing the mean and variance of the distribution from which growth rates are drawn. The mean and variance of growth rates do seem to vary with city size but bootstrapped confidence intervals are fairly wide generally, allowing for the possibility of (almost) equal means.

1.2. Geographic concentration and urban specialization

Geographic concentration refers to the extent to which an industry k is concentrated at a particular location or, more generally concentrated at a few versus many locations nationally. A common measure of concentration of industry k at location i is $l_{ik} = X_{ik} / \sum_i X_{ik}$, where X_{ik} is location i's employment or output of industry k. Thus l_{ik} is location i's share of, say, national employment in industry k. In contrast

---

[2] I do not report standard errors since OLS estimates of standard errors are biased downwards.

[3] Actually the requirement is that they face the same mean and variance in the drawing.

to geographic concentration, specialization refers to how much of a location's total employment is found in industry k, or $s_{ik} = X_{ik}/\sum_k X_{ik}$. As Overman, Redding and Venables (2003) demonstrate, if we normalize l_{ik} by location i's share of national employment ($s_i \equiv \sum_k X_{ik}/\sum_k \sum_i X_{ik}$) and s_{ik} by industry k's share of national employment ($s_k \equiv \sum_i X_{ik}/\sum_k \sum_i X_{ik}$) we get the same measure – a location quotient, or

$$q_{ik} = X_{ik} \frac{\sum_k \sum_i X_{ik}}{\sum_k X_{ik} \sum_i X_{ik}}. \tag{3}$$

The distribution of q_{ik} across industries k, compared over time for a city would tell us about how city i's specialization patterns are changing over time. And the distribution of q_{ik} across locations i, over time would tell us whether industry k is becoming more or less concentrated over time at different locations. In a practical applications looking at many industries and cities over time or across countries, the issue concerns how to produce *summary* measures to describe either how overall concentration varies across industries or how one city's specialization compares with another's. Another issue concerns how to factor in the different forces that cause specialization or concentration phenomena. The literature uses a variety of approaches. We start by looking at urban specialization.

1.2.1. Urban specialization

Evidence on countries such as Brazil, USA, Korea, and India [Helpman (1998) and Lee (1997)] indicate that cities are relatively specialized. The traditional urban specialization literature going back to Bergsman, Greenston and Healy (1972) uses cluster analysis to group cities into categories based on similarity of production patterns – correlations (or minimum distances) in the shares of different industries in local employment s_{ik}. Cluster analysis is an "art form" in the sense that there is no optimal set of clusters, and it is up to the researcher to define how fine or how broad the clusters should be and there are a variety of clustering algorithms.

Using 1990 data for the USA, Black and Henderson (2003) group 317 metro areas into 55 clusters, "defining" 55 city types based on patterns of specialization for 80 2-digit industries. They define textile, primary metals, machinery, electronics, oil and gas, transport equipment, health services, insurance, entertainment, diversified market center, and so on type cities, where anywhere from 5–33% of local employment is typically found in just one industry. They show that production patterns across the types are statistically different and that average cities and educational levels by type differ significantly across many of the types. Specialization especially among smaller cities tends to be absolute. At a 3-digit level many cities have absolutely zero employment in a variety of categories. So in the 1992 Census of Manufactures for major industries like computers, electronic components, aircraft, instruments, metal working machinery, special machinery, construction machinery, and refrigeration machinery and equipment, respectively, of 317 metro areas 40%, 17%, 42%, 15%, 77%, 15%, 14% and 24% have absolutely zero employment in these industries.

Kim (1995) in looking at the USA examines how patterns of specialization have changed over time, by comparing for pairs (i, j) of locations $\sum_k |s_{ik} - s_{jk}|$ and by estimating spatial Gini's for industry concentration. He finds that states are substantially less specialized in 1987 than in 1860, but that localization, or concentration has increased over time. For Korea, as part of the deconcentration process noted earlier, Henderson, Lee and Lee (2001) find that from 1983 to 1993, city specialization as measured by a normalized Hirschman–Herfindahl index,

$$g_j = \sum_k (s_{jk} - s_j)^2, \tag{4}$$

rises in manufacturing, while a provincial level index declines. Cities become more specialized and provinces less so. Clearly the geographic unit of analysis matters, as do the concepts. City specialization as envisioned in the models presented below is consistent with regional diversity, when large regions are composed of many cities of different types.

Henderson (1997) for the USA and Lee (1997) for Korea show that the g_j index of specialization in manufacturing declines with metro area size. Smaller cities are much more specialized than larger cities in their manufacturing production. More generally, Kolko (1999) demonstrates that larger cities are more service oriented and smaller ones more manufacturing oriented. For six size categories (over 2.5 million, 1–2.5 million, ... <0.25 million, nonmetro counties) Kolko shows that the ratio of manufacturing to business service activity rises from 0.68 to 2.7 as size declines, where manufacturing and business services account for 35% of local private employment. The other 65% of local employment is in "nontraded" activity whose shares do not vary across cities – consumer services, retail, wholesale, construction, and utilities.

1.2.2. Geographic concentration

What about concentration of industry – the extent to which a particular industry is found in a few versus many locations? In an extremely important paper, Ellison and Glaeser (1999a) model the problem using USA data, to determine the extent of clustering of plants within an industry due to either industry-specific natural advantages (e.g., access to raw materials) or spillovers among plants. Plants locate across space so as to maximize profits and profits depend on area specific natural advantage, spillovers, and an i.i.d. drawing from Weibull distribution. The idea is to explain the joint importance of spillovers and natural advantage in geographic concentration.

Geographic concentration for industry j is $G_j = \sum_i (s_{ji} - x_i)^2$, where s_{ji} is the share of industry j in employment in location i, and x_i is location i's share in total national employment (to standardize for location size). Where $0 \leqslant \gamma^{na} \leqslant 1$ represents the importance of natural advantage (where the variance in relative profitability of a location is proportional to γ^{na}) and γ^s represents the fraction of pairs of firms in an industry between which a spillover exists, under their assumptions, Ellison and Glaeser show that

$$E[G_j] = \left(1 - \sum_i x_i^2\right)(\gamma_j + (1 - \gamma_j)H_j), \quad \gamma_j \equiv \gamma_j^{na} + \gamma_j^s - \gamma_j^s \gamma_j^{na}, \qquad (5)$$

where H_j is the standard Hirschman–Herfindahl index of plant industrial concentration in industry j. So $E[G_j]$ adjusts γ_j for variations in location size $(1 - \sum x_i^2)$ and industry concentration H. Using (5) and estimates of G_j, H_j and $(1 - \sum x_i^2)$, the empirical part of their paper calculates γ_j for all 3- or 4-digit manufacturing industries across states and countries. They show for 4-digit industries that $G > (1 - \sum x_i^2)H$ in 446 of 459 industries, where $G \leqslant (1 - \sum x^2)H$ only if $\gamma \leqslant 0$. That is, almost all industries display some degree of spatial concentration due to either natural advantage or spillovers. Second they argue that 25% of industries are highly concentrated ($\gamma > 0.05$) and 43% are not highly concentrated ($\gamma < 0.02$). In a later article, Ellison and Glaeser (1999b) argue that, based on econometric results relating location choices to natural advantage measures, 10–20% of γ in Equation (5) is accounted for by natural advantage. The rest is due to intra-industry spillovers, a rather critical finding in urban analysis indicating the importance of understanding the nature of scale externalities.

In an important working paper, Duranton and Overman (2005), look at geographic concentration using British data. Rather than model the underlying stochastic process of industrial location under specific assumptions to yield a specific index, Duranton and Overman take a nonparametric approach, where they also focus on how to test statistically whether industries are significantly concentrated. They calculate the distribution of all pair-wise distances between plants in an industry. Distributions shifted to the left have a greater concentration of short pair-wise distances and are more spatially concentrated. The authors have the advantage of knowing "exact" plant locations (basically within a city block or so), rather than having to rely on, say, county locations, which in the US can cover vast distances. They develop a framework to test observed industry distributions against the "counterfactual" of what distributions would look like if firms choose locations randomly, given (a) the set of locations in the UK for industrial plants is limited, (b) bilateral distances between all possible points are not independent, and (c) industry sizes or numbers of plants differ. The framework involves repeated sampling for an industry without replacement from the set of national industrial sites with the sample size equal to industry size. Following that procedure, they construct 95% confidence intervals to test if observed distributions depart from randomness.

Compared to Ellison–Glaeser, in practical applications their approach captures a nuanced aspect of spatial clustering. For relatively concentrated industries, the Ellison and Glaeser index is typically dominated by the county with the highest share (given squared shares in the index), telling us the extent to which an industry is concentrated in just one place. The Duranton–Overman approach tells us more generally about spatial clustering over the whole country. So in Ellison and Glaeser, an industry which has a high concentration in one county but is otherwise very dispersed across the 3000 USA counties may look more concentrated than an industry which is concentrated in, say 3–4 nearby counties, with little representation elsewhere. But the latter would be well represented in Duranton and Overman.

1.2.3. Geography

A variety of recent studies have examined the role of geography, primarily natural features, in the spatial configuration of production and growth of cities. Rappaport and Sacks (2003) herald the role of coastline location in the USA, as a factor promoting city growth. In a related study, Beeson, DeJong and Troeskan (2001) look at USA counties from 1840–1990. They show that iron deposits, other mineral deposits, river location, ocean location, river confluence, heating degree days, cooling degree days, mountain location, and precipitation all affect the base 1840 county population significantly. However for 1840–1990 *growth* in county population, only ocean location, mountain location, precipitation, and river confluence matter, controlling for 1840 population. That is, first nature items strongly affected 1840 and hence indirectly 1990 populations; but growth from 1840–1990 is independent of many first nature influences. Ocean location as Sacks' suggests has persistent growth effects.

Both these studies ignore the geography of markets and the role of neighbors in influencing city evolution. Dobkins and Ioannides (2001) show that growth of neighboring cities influences own city growth and cities with neighbors are generally larger than isolated cities. Black and Henderson (2003) put neighbor and geographic effects together. They calculate normalized market potential variables (sum of distance discounted populations of all other counties in each decade, normalized across decades). They find climate and coast affect relative city growth rates; but market potential has big effects as well, although they are nonlinear. Bigger markets provide more customers, but also more competition, so marginal market potential effects diminish as market potential increases. High market potential helps explain why North-East cities in the USA maintain reasonable growth, given for historical reasons, they are in the most densely populated area, despite the hypothesized natural advantages of the West.

1.3. Urbanization in developing countries

Urbanization, or the shift of population from rural to urban environments, is typically a transitory process, albeit one that is socially and culturally traumatic. As a country develops, it moves from labor-intensive agricultural production to labor being increasingly employed in industry and services. The latter are not land-intensive and are located in cities because of agglomeration economies. Thus urbanization moves populations from traditional rural environments with informal political and economic institutions to the relative anonymity and more formal institutions of urban settings. That in itself requires institutional development within a country. It spatially separates families, particularly by generation, as the young migrate to cities and the old stay behind.

Urbanization is a spatial transition process. By upper middle income ranges, countries become "fully" urbanized, in the sense that the percent urbanized levels out at

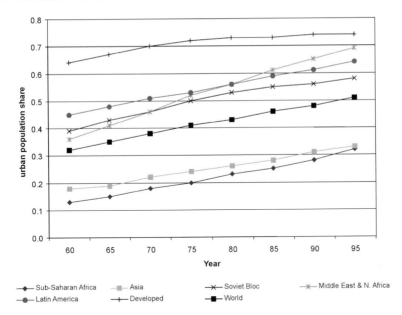

Figure 2. Share of urban population in total population. (Average over countries within groups.)

60–90% of the national population living in cities. The actual percent urbanized with full urbanization varies with geography, the role of modern agriculture in the economy, and national definitions of urban. This idea of a transitory phenomenon is illustrated Figure 2, comparing different regions of the world in 1960 versus 1995. While urbanization increased in all regions of the world over those 35 years, among developed countries there is little change since 1975. By 1995 Soviet bloc and Latin American countries had almost converged to developed country urbanization levels. Only Sub-Saharan African and Asian countries still face substantial urbanization in the future. Although urbanization is transitory, given the total spatial transformation and accompanying institutional and social transformation involved, as a policy issue, urbanization is very important to developing countries. Here we review some basic facts and issues about the process.

1.3.1. Issues concerning overall urbanization

As noted above, urbanization is the consequence of changes in national output composition from rural agriculture to urbanized modern manufacturing and service production. As such, Renaud (1981) makes the basic point that government policies bias, or influence urbanization through their effect on national sectoral composition. So policies affecting the terms of trade between agriculture and modern industry or between traditional small town industries (textiles, food processing) and high tech large city industries affect the rural–urban or small–big city allocation of population. Such policies include tariffs, and price controls and subsidies. The idea that government policies affect urbanization primarily through their effect on sector composition is a key point of empirical studies of urbanization by Fay and Opal (1999) and Davis and Henderson (2003). These studies show that, indeed, urbanization which occurs in the early and middle stages of development is determined largely by changes in national economic sector composition and in technology. Government policies tend to affect urbanization only indirectly through their effect on sector composition.

Urbanization promotes benefits from agglomeration such as localized information and knowledge spillovers and thus efficient urbanization promotes economic growth. Writers such as Gallup, Sachs and Mellinger (1999) go further to suggest that urbanization may "cause" economic growth, rather than just emerge as part of the growth process. The limited evidence so far suggests urbanization does not cause growth per se. Henderson (2003) finds no econometric evidence linking the extent of urbanization to either economic or productivity growth or levels. That is, if a country were to enact policies to encourage urbanization per se, typically that would not improve growth.

Finally on urbanization, there is an informal notion [Mills and Becker (1986) and World Bank (2000)] that the transitory urbanization process follows the same stages as population growth (the "demographic" transition between falling death rates and falling fertility rates) – an S-shaped relationship where urban population growth is slow at low levels of development, then there is a period of rapid acceleration in intermediate stages, followed by a slowing of growth. However the data suggest otherwise at least over the last 35 years. Figure 3 illustrates after parceling out the effect of national population, or country size, based on pooled country data every 5 years from 1965–1995. In Figure 3 the log of national urban population is an increasing concave function of the log of income per capita, indicating the *growth* rate of urban population is a concave increasing function of income levels [Davis and Henderson (2003)].

1.3.2. The form of urbanization: the degree of spatial concentration

In 1965, Williamson (1965) published an innovative paper based on cross-section analysis of 24 countries in which he argued that national economic development is characterized by an initial phase of internal regional divergence, followed by a phase of later convergence. That is, a few regions initially experience accelerated growth relative to other (peripheral) regions, but later the peripheral regions start to catch up. Barro and Sala-i-Martin (1991, 1992) present extensive evidence on this for the USA, Western Europe and Japan, by examining the evolution of inter-regional differences in per capita incomes. While inter-regional out-migration from poorer regions plays a role in catch-up, it may not be critical. For Japan, the authors argue that later convergence of backward regions occurred mostly through improved productivity in backward regions.

The urban version of this divergence–convergence phenomenon looks at urban primacy. Following Ades and Glaeser (1995), conceptually the urban world is collapsed into two regions – the primate city versus the rest of the country, or at least the urban portion thereof. The basic question concerns to what extent urbanization is concentrated, or confined to one (or a few) major metro areas, relative to being spread more evenly

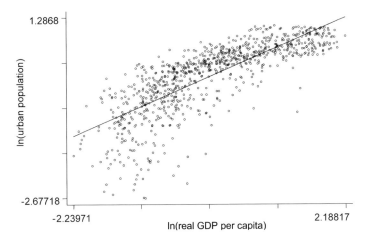

Figure 3. Partial correlation between ln(urban population) and ln(real GDP per capita), controlling for ln(national population), 1965–1995.

across a variety of cities. Primacy is commonly measured by the ratio of the population of the largest metro area to all urban population in the country [Ades and Glaeser (1995), Junius (1999) and Davis and Henderson (2003)]. A more comprehensive measure might use either a spatial Gini or a Hirschman–Herfindahl index (HHI) from the industrial organization literature.

Corresponding to Williamson's hypothesis, these papers find an inverted-U-shape relationship, where relative urban concentration first increases, peaks, and then declines with economic development. Despite different concentration measures and methods, Wheaton and Shishido (1981) examining a HHI using cross-section nonlinear OLS and Davis and Henderson (2003) examining primacy using panel data methods and instrumental variables estimation find that concentration rises, peaks in the $2000–4000 range (1985 PPP dollars), and then declines. As Figure 4 illustrates, without conditioning on other variables affecting primacy, the inverted-U relationship of primacy against income is noisy and only apparent in the raw data in earlier time periods [cf. 1965–1975 in part (a) with 1985–1995 in part (b)].

Lee (1997) explores the relationship between changes in urban concentration and industrial transformation for Korea. The idea is that manufacturing is also first very concentrated in primate cities at early stages of development and then decentralizes to such an extent that at the other end of economic development it is relatively more concentrated in rural areas, as in the USA today, as noted earlier. Seoul's urban primacy peaked around 1970 and while Seoul's *absolute* population has continued to grow, its *share* has declined steadily. At the urban primacy peak in 1970, Seoul had a dominant share of national manufacturing although the other major metro areas, Pusan and Taegu, also had large shares. During the next 10–15 years, manufacturing suburbanized from Seoul to satellite cities in the rest of Kyonggi province (its immediate hinterland), as well as to

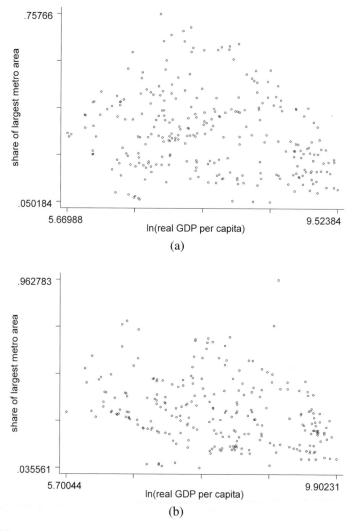

Figure 4. Primacy and economic development. (a) Early period: 1965–1975. (b) Recent period: 1985–1995.

satellite cities surrounding Pusan and Taegu. Such suburbanization of manufacturing has been documented also for Thailand [Lee (1988)], Colombia [Lee (1989)], and Indonesia [Henderson, Kuncoro and Nasution (1996)]. But the key development following the early-1980s in Korea is the spread of manufacturing from the three major metro areas (Seoul, Pusan and Taegu) and their satellites to rural areas and other cities. The share of rural areas and other cities in manufacturing rose from 26% in 1983 to 42% in 1992, in a time period when national manufacturing employment is fairly stagnant and rural areas and other cities actually continue to experience modest absolute population losses. That is, manufacturing deconcentrated both relatively and absolutely to hinterland regions. This deconcentration coincided with economic liberalization, enormous and widespread investment in inter-regional transport and infrastructure investment, and fiscal decentralization [Henderson, Lee and Lee (2001)] and is consistent with core–periphery reversal in the new economic geography literature discussed later.

Given the urban primacy relationships, the immediate issue is the "so-what" question. How is urban concentration important to growth? For example, is there an optimal degree of urban primacy with each level of development, where significant deviations from this level detract from growth? Conceptually there should be an optimal degree of primacy, where optimal primacy involves a trade-off of the benefits of increasing primacy – enhanced local scale economies contributing to productivity growth – against the costs – more resources diverted away from productive and innovative activities to shoring up the quality of life in congested primate cities. In the first econometric examination of this so-what question, Henderson (2003), using panel data and instrumental variables estimation for 1960–1990, finds that there is an optimal degree of primacy at each level of development that declines as development proceeds. Optimal primacy is the level that maximizes national productivity growth. Initial high relative agglomeration is important at low levels of development when countries have low knowledge accumulation, are importing technology, and have limited capital to invest in widespread hinterland development. However the desirability of high relative agglomeration declines with development. Error bands about optimal primacy numbers are quite tight. Second, large deviations from optimal primacy strongly affect productivity growth. An 33% increase or decrease in primacy from a typical best level of 0.3 reduces productivity growth by 3 percentage points over five years, a big effect. There is some tendency internationally to excessive primacy, with the usual suspects such as Argentina, Chile, Peru, Thailand, Mexico and Algeria having extremely high primacy.

Why would countries significantly deviate from desired levels of concentration? There is a considerable literature on how government policies and institutions foster excessive concentration. In Ades and Glaeser (1995), the basic idea is that national policy makers favor the national capital (or other seat of political elites such as São Paulo in Brazil) for reasons of personal gain. For example, direct restraints on trade for hinterland cities such as inability to access capital markets or to get export or import licenses favor firms in the national capital. Policy makers and bureaucrats may gain as shareholders in such firms, or they may gain rents from those seeking licenses or other exemptions to trade restraints [see Henderson and Kuncoro (1996), on Indonesia]. Indirect trade protection for the primate city can also involve under-investment in hinterland transport and communications infrastructure.

Whether as true beliefs or as a justification to cover rent-seeking behavior, policy makers in different countries often articulate a view that large cities are more productive and thus should be the site for government-owned heavy industry (e.g., São Paulo or Beijing–Tianjin historically). Later we will point out that it may be that output per worker in heavy industries is higher in the productive external environment of large metro areas. It just is not high enough to cover the higher opportunity costs of land and labor in those cities, which is one reason why those state-owned heavy industries lose money in such cities.

Favoritism of a primate city creates a nonlevel playing field in competition across cities. The favored city draws in migrants and firms from hinterland areas, creating an extremely congested high cost-of-living metro area. Local city planners can try to resist the migration response to primate city favoritism by, for example, refusing to provide legal housing development for immigrants or to provide basic public services in immigrant neighborhoods. Hence the development of squatter settlements, bustees, kampongs and so on. But still, favored cities tend to draw in enormous populations.

Is there econometric evidence indicating that politics plays a role in increasing sizes of primate cities? Ades and Glaeser (1995) based on cross-section analysis find that, if the primate city in a country is the national capital, it is 45% larger. If the country is a dictatorship, or at the extreme of nondemocracy, the primate city is 40–45% larger. The idea is that representative democracy gives a political voice to the hinterland regions limiting the ability of the capital city to favor itself. Apart from representative democracy, fiscal decentralization helps to level the playing field across cities, by giving political autonomy for hinterland cities to compete with the primate city.

Davis and Henderson (2003) explore these ideas further, examining in a panel context the impact upon primacy of democratization and fiscal decentralization from 1960–1995. Using a panel approach with IV estimation, they find smaller effects than Ades and Glaeser, but still highly significant ones. Examining both democratization and fiscal decentralization together, they find moving from the extreme of least to most democratic form of government reduces primacy by 8% and from the extreme of most to least centralized government reduces primacy by 5%. Primate cities which are national capitals are 20% larger and primate cities in planned economies with migration restrictions are 18% smaller. Finally they find transport infrastructure investment in hinterlands which opens up international markets to hinterland cities reduces primacy, as the core–periphery models of the new economic geography tend to predict. A one-standard deviation increase in either roads per sq. kilometer of national land area or navigable inland waterways per sq. kilometer each reduce primacy by 10%.

2. Cities and growth

To establish the links between cities, growth, urbanization, urban concentration and policy, we look at models in which cities are a defined unit, endogenous in number and size. These are systems of cities models which date to Henderson (1974), with a variety of substantial contributors to further development [Hochman (1977), Kanemoto (1980), Henderson and Ioannides (1981), Abdel-Rahman and Fujita (1990), Helsley and Strange (1990), Duranton and Puga (2000) and Rossi-Hansberg and Wright (2004), to name a few]. Here I outline the model in Black and Henderson (1999a) which is an endogenous growth model of cities, examining the growth-urban connection. The analysis is broken into several parts. The first reviews the traditional static model, focused on city formation and the determination of the sizes, numbers, and industrial composition of cities in an economy at a point in time. A thorough review of static models is in Abdel-Rahman and Anas (2004), so our treatment focuses on what we need to analyze growth, and later urbanization and development. We then turn to the growth part, focusing on steady-state growth and a variety of extensions covering stochastic processes and analysis of functional specialization. Section 3 turns to rural–urban transformation, or urbanization under economic development. That section also discusses issues of city debt finance and land market institutions.

2.1. The systems of cities at a point in time

Consider a large economy composed of two types of cities, where there are many cities of each type and each type is specialized in the production of a specific type of traded good. We will show why (when) there is specialization momentarily; the generalization to many types of goods and cities is straightforward. To simplify the growth story, each firm is composed of a single worker. In a city type 1, in any period, the output of firm i in a type 1 city is

$$X_{1i} = D_1 \left(n_1^{\delta_1} h_1^{\psi_1} \right) h_{1i}^{\phi_1}, \quad 0 < \delta_1 < \frac{1}{2}, \tag{6}$$

where h_{1i} is the human capital of the worker and is his input in the production process. A worker-firm is subject to two local externalities. First is own industry localization economies, the level of which depends on the total number of worker-firms, n_1, in this representative type 1 city. There is a large literature on micro-foundations of localization economies, with an excellent analysis and review in Duranton and Puga (2004). While the concepts are discussed in Marshall (1890), the formal literature dates to Fujita and Ogawa (1982) who model micro-foundations as exogenous information spillovers that enhance productivity but decay with spatial distance between plants. Such spillovers can be made endogenous [Kim (1988)] with the volume of costly "contacts" being a firm choice variable. But the modern literature on micro-foundations as reviewed in Duranton and Puga moves on to try to model *why* contacts matter, rather than just assuming they matter.

In this section spatial decay is all or nothing – no decay within the city's; 100% across cities. As such in (6), n_1 could represent the total volume of local spillover communications, where δ_1 is the elasticity of firm output with respect to n_1. The restriction $\delta_1 < 1/2$ which limits the degree of scale economies ensures a unique solution in an economy composed of many type 1 cities. Without the restriction, all X_1 production crowds into just one city. Note the production process ignores land, collapsing the central business district (CBD) to a point. There is a recent literature building upon Fujita and Ogawa where firm density is endogenous in a spatial CDB with information spillover decay. There market equilibrium density is nonoptimal because firms in making location decisions do not recognize that choices leading to greater densities would enhance information spillovers [Lucas and Rossi-Hansberg (2002) and Rossi-Hansberg

(2004)]. The issue of central city design and zoned density is an important one in the design of cities in developing countries. But it is beyond the scope of this review.

The second externality in (6) derives from h_1, the average level of human capital in the city, which represents local knowledge spillovers. $h_1^{\psi_1}$ could be thought of as the richness of information spillovers $n_1^{\delta_1}$, so that knowledge enhances (multiplies) local information spillovers, or gives better information. Alternatively it could just represent the level of local technology, which increases as average education increases locally.

Given this simple formulation the wage of worker i in city type 1 is

$$W_{1i} = X_{1i}. \tag{7}$$

In an economy of identical individual workers in type 1 cities, individuals will all have the same human capital level (either exogenously in a static context, or endogenously in a growth context). Thus total city output is

$$X_1 = D_1 h_1^{\phi_1 + \psi_1} n_1^{1+\delta_1}. \tag{8}$$

2.1.1. Equilibrium city sizes

Equations (6) and (8) embody the scale benefits of increases in local employment, where output per worker is an increasing function of local own industry scale. Determinant city sizes arise because of scale diseconomies in city living, including per capita infrastructure costs, pollution, accidents, crime, and commuting costs. In Henderson (1974) those are captured in a general cost of housing function, but most urban models consider an explicit internal spatial structure of cities. As noted all production occurs at a point, the CBD. Surrounding the CBD in equilibrium in local land markets is a circle of residents each on a lot of unit size. People commute back and forth at a constant cost per unit (return) distance of τ. That cost can be from working time, or here an out-of-pocket cost paid in units of X_1. Equilibrium in the land market is characterized by a linear rent gradient, declining from the center to zero at the city edge where rents (in agriculture) are normalized to zero. Standard analysis dating to Mohring (1961) gives us expressions for total city commuting and rents, in terms of city population where[4]

$$\text{total commuting costs} = bn_1^{3/2}, \tag{9}$$

$$\text{total land rents} = \frac{1}{2}bn_1^{3/2}, \quad b \equiv \frac{2}{3}\pi^{-1/2}\tau. \tag{10}$$

---

[4] An equilibrium in residential markets requires all residents (living on equalize size lots) to spend the same amount on rent, $R(u)$, plus commuting costs, τu, for any distance u from the CBD. Any consumer then has the same amount left over to invest or spend on all other goods. At the city edge at a radius of u_1, rent plus commuting costs are τu_1 since $R(u_1) = 0$; elsewhere they are $R(u) + \tau u$. Equating those at the city edge with those elsewhere yields the rent gradient $R(u) = \tau(u_1 - u)$. From this, we calculate total rents in the city to be $\int_0^{u_1} 2\pi u R(u)\,du$ (given lot sizes of one so that each "ring" $2\pi u\,du$ contains that many residents) or $\frac{1}{3}\pi\tau u_1^3$. Total commuting costs are $\int_0^{u_1} 2\pi u(\tau u)\,du = \frac{2}{3}\pi\tau u_1^3$. Given a city population of n and lot sizes of one, $n_1 = \pi u_1^2$ or $u_1 = \pi^{-1/2}n^{1/2}$. Substitution gives us Equations (9) and (10).

Equation (9) represents the key resource costs, where marginal commuting costs are increasing in city population. Rents are income to, potentially, a city developer or to rentiers.

How do cities form and how are sizes determined? We start with a specific mechanism and discuss how it generalizes below, and what happens if such a mechanism is not present. There is an unexhausted supply of identical city sites in the economy, each owned by a land developer in a nationally competitive urban land development market. A developer for an occupied city collects local land rents, specifies city population (but there is free migration in equilibrium), and offers any inducements to firms or people to locate in that city, in competition with other cities. Population is freely mobile.

The land developer maximizes

$$\max_{n_1, T_1} profit_1 = \frac{1}{2} b n_1^{3/2} - T_1 n_1,$$

$$\text{subject to} \quad W_1 + T_1 - \frac{3}{2} b n_1^{1/2} = I_1, \tag{11}$$

where T_1 is the per firm subsidy (e.g., in practice, in a model with local public goods, a tax exemption), I_1 is the real income per worker available in equilibrium in national labor markets under free mobility, which a single developer takes as given. In the constraint, I_1 equals wages in (7), plus the subsidy, less per worker rents plus commuting costs paid from (9) and (10). Maximizing with respect to T_1 and n_1 and imposing perfect competition in national land markets so $profit_1 = 0$ ex post, yields

$$T_1 = \frac{1}{2} b n_1^{1/2}, \tag{12}$$

$$n^* = \left(\delta_1 2 b^{-1} D_1 \right)^{2/(1-2\delta_1)} h_1^{2\varepsilon_1}, \tag{13}$$

$$\varepsilon_1 \equiv \frac{\phi_1 + \psi_1}{1 - 2\delta_1}. \tag{14}$$

This solution has a variety of properties heralded in the urban literature. First it reflects the Henry George Theorem [Flatters, Henderson and Mieszkowski (1974), Stiglitz (1977)], where the transfer per worker/firm exactly equals the gap $(\delta_1 W_1)$ between social and private marginal of labor to the city, and that subsidy which prices externalities is exactly financed out of collected land rents at efficient city size. That is, total land rents cover the cost of subsidies needed to price externalities, as well as the costs of local public goods in a model where public goods are added in. Second the efficient size in (13) is the point where real income, I_1, peaks, as an inverted-U-shape function of city size, as we will illustrate later in Figure 5. If $\delta_1 < 1/2$, we can show that I_1 is a single-peaked function of n_1, so n_1^* is the unique efficient size. If $\delta_1 > 1/2$, in essence there will only be one type 1 city in the economy, because net scale economies are unbounded. Given n_1^* is the size where I_1 peaks, n_1^* is a free mobility equilibrium – a worker moving to another city would lower real income in that city and be worse off. Finally city size is increasing in technology improvements: τ declining, δ_1 rising, D_1 rising, or local knowledge accumulation (h_1) rising.

By substituting in the constraint in (11), we can define relationships among real income, wages, and human capital. Substituting in first for T_1 and then n_1 we get

$$I_1 = W_1 - bn^{1/2} = (1 - 2\delta)W_1 = Q_1 h_1^{\varepsilon_1}, \tag{15}$$

where Q_1 is a parameter cluster. Note real income is wages deflated by urban living costs; and that real income rises with human capital.

Institutions and city size.   I have specified the equilibrium in national land markets, given competitive developers. Helsley and Strange (1990) put this in proper context, specifying the city development game, determining how many cities will form and what their sizes (n^*) will be. Henderson and Becker (2001) show that the resulting solutions (with multiple factors of production) are (1) Pareto efficient, (2) the only coalition proof equilibria in the economy, (3) unique under appropriate parameters, and (4) free mobility ones where the developer specified populations are self-enforcing. They also show that, under appropriate conditions, such outcomes arise (1) in an economy with no developers but with city governments, where city governments can exclude residents ("no-growth" restrictions) to maximize the welfare of the representative local voter; and (2) in a growing economy where developers form new cities and old cities are governed by passive local governments. Note for developing countries the key ingredients: either national land markets must be competitive with developers free to form new cities or atomistic settlements can arise freely and local autonomous governments can limit their populations as they grow (as well as provide infrastructure once that is accounted for – see Section 3.3.2).

Absent such institutions, cities only form through "self-organization". In the model here with perfect mobility of resources, the result is potentially enormously oversized cities [Henderson (1974), Henderson and Becker (2001)]. Nash equilibrium city size in atomistic worker migration decisions lies between efficient size, n^*, and a limit size to the right, $n_{\max}$, where city size is so large with such enormous diseconomies that the population is indifferent between being in a rural settlement of size 1 (the size of a community formed by a defecting migrant) and $n_{\max}$. That is, given an inverted-U shape to real income I_1, self organization has cities at the right of the peak n^*, potentially at $n_{\max}$ where $I_1(n = 1) = I_1(n = n_{\max})$. The problem is the familiar one of co-ordination failure.

Consider a large economy with growing population, where, in size, all cities are at or just beyond n^*. Timely formation of the next city to accommodate this population growth requires en mass movement of population from existing cities into a new city of size n^*. Without co-ordination in the form of developers or city governments, no such en mass movement is possible, so people wait to migrate from existing cities to a new city until existing cities have all grown to $n_{\max}$, where it pays individual migrants to exit cities to set up their own tiny "city". At that "bifurcation point" [Krugman (1991a)], in equilibrium these milling migrants coalesce into 1 or more new cities of size greater than or equal to n^*, at which point, again, all then existing cities start to grow again with national population growth until they too hit the bifurcation point $n_{\max}$. This dismal process is what faces countries where local autonomy and national markets are poorly functioning, so that there are no market or institutional mechanisms to co-ordinate en mass movements of people. However the process we have outlined involving population swings across cities and potentially enormously over-populated cities may not be consistent with the data. In Section 3 we will outline a model with immobile capital, where self-organization can involve "commitment" given irreversibility of investment decisions. In that context outcomes, while still inefficient, are not so dismal.

2.1.2. Other city types

In Black and Henderson (1999a), X_1 city type 1 is an input into production of the single final good in the economy X_2 (from which, hence in a growth context human capital is also "produced"). In many models all outputs of specialized city types are final consumption goods. But here we follow Black and Henderson, without loss of generality. X_2 is produced in type 2 cities where the output for worker/firm j is correspondingly,

$$X_{2j} = D_2\left(n_2^{\delta_2} h_2^{\psi_2}\right) h_{2j}^{\theta_2} X_{1j}^{1-\alpha}. \tag{16}$$

As in type 1 cities, per worker output is subject to own industry local scale externalities and to local knowledge spillovers. However now there is an intermediate input X_{1j}, which is the numeraire good, with X_{2j} priced at P in national markets. The analysis of city sizes and formation for type 2 cities proceeds as for city type 1, with corresponding expressions, other than the addition of an expression for P in n_2^* and I_2 and a restriction for an inverted-U shape to I_2 that $\delta_2 < \alpha/2$.

In a static context the model is closed by utilizing the national full employment constraint

$$m_1 n_1 + m_2 n_2 = N, \tag{17}$$

where m_1 and m_2 are the numbers of each type of city and N is national population. The second equation (to solve the 3 unknowns P, m_1 and m_2) equates real incomes as in Equation (15) across cities ($I_1 = I_2$), where individual workers move across cities to equalize real incomes. Finally, there is an equation where national demand equals supply in either the market. That is, the supply, $m_1 X_1$, equals the demand for X_1 as an intermediate input, $m_2 n_2 x_1$, and for producing commuting costs ($m_1(bn_1^{3/2}) + m_2(bn_2^{3/2})$) from Equation (9). In this specific model, the solution yields values of m_1, m_2 and P that are functions of parameters and h_1 and h_2. In a static context of identical workers, one would impose $h = h_1 = h_2$. We will discuss momentarily the solution for h_1 and h_2 and the model in the growth context. Later in Section 3, we will detail solutions for prices and numbers of cities in a simpler but related two sector model. Here given log-linear production functions and a single final consumption good, as Black and Henderson show, X_1/X_2 and m_1/m_2 will be constant over time, independent of h.

In the static context where, labor mobility requires $I_1 = I_2$, in the larger type of city, say type 1, commuting and land rent costs will be higher. Thus, if real incomes are equalized, from (15), $W_1 > W_2$ as a compensating differential for higher living costs. Firms in type 1 cities are willing to pay higher wages because type 1 cities offer them greater scale benefits. Empirical evidence shows as cities move from a small size (say, 50,000) to very large metro areas, the cost-of-living typically doubles [Thomas (1978) and Henderson (2002)], explaining the fact that nominal wages also double.

Another issue discussed at length in Section 1.3 is that policy makers may favor large cities because they view them as "more productive". Indeed for an industry found in smaller towns, it may be that the externalities they face in Equations (6) or (16) may be higher in a larger city. However that does not mean they locate there. Although externalities may be higher, in order for them to locate there, it must be sufficiently relatively higher to afford the higher wage and land rents, compared to a smaller city. If not, their profit maximizing or cost minimizing location is the smaller city.

Specialization. This analysis presumes cities specialize in production. That is an equilibrium outcome under a variety of conditions. In the model described so far, there are no costs of inter-city trade: no costs of shipping X_1 as inputs to X_2 type cities and shipping X_2 back as retail goods in X_1 type cities. All transport costs are internal to the city, given the relative greater importance of commuting costs in modern economies. Given that and given scale economies are internal to the industry, any specialized city (formed by a developer) out-competes any mixed city. The heuristic argument is simple. Consider any mixed city with $\tilde{n}_1$ and $\tilde{n}_2$ workers in industry 1 and 2. Split that city into two specialized cities, one with just $\tilde{n}_1$ people and the other with just $\tilde{n}_2$. Scale economies are undiminished ($\tilde{n}_1^{\delta_1}$ and $\tilde{n}_1^{\delta_2}$ in both cases in industries 1 and 2, respectively) but per worker commuting costs are lower in the specialized cities compared to the old larger mixed cities, so real incomes are higher in each specialized city compared to the old city.

Having own industry, or localization economies is a sufficient but not necessary condition for specialization. Industries can instead all have "urbanization" economies where scale depends on total local employment. However if the degree of urbanization economies differs across industries, then each industry has a different efficient local scale and is better off in a different size specialized city than any mixed city. Mixed cities occur more in situations where each good has localization economies enhanced by separate spillovers from the other industry or sharing of some common public infrastructure [Abdel-Rahman (2000)].

A basic problem in these urban models is the lack of nuance on transport costs. Either transport costs of goods across cities is zero or infinite as for housing, and potentially other nontradables. A recent innovation is to have generalized transport costs (without a specific geography) where the cost of transporting a unit of X_1 to an X_2 city is t_1 and the cost of shipping X_2 back to an X_1 city is t_2, an innovation due to Abdel-Rahman (1996) in a model similar to the one used here (one intermediate and one final good) and then generalized by Xiong (1998) and Anas and Xiong (1999). Now whether there are specialized as opposed to diversified cities depends on the level of t_1 and t_2. At appropriate points as t_1 or t_2 or both rise from zero, X_1 and X_2 will collocate (in developer run cities) in one type of city, while there may be some cities specialized in one of either X_1 or X_2. More generally with a spectrum of, say, final products, we would expect that some products with low enough t's will always be produced in specialized cities, some high enough t's will be in all cities, and some with middle range t's will be produced in some cities (ones with bigger markets) but not others (with smaller markets). No one has yet simulated this more complex outcome.

2.1.3. Replicability and national policy

At the national level in a large economy with many cities, at the limit, there are constant returns to scale, or replicability. If national population doubles, the numbers of cities of each type and national output of each good simply doubles, with individual city sizes, relative prices and real incomes unchanged.[5] With two goods and two factors, basic international trade theorems (Rybczynski, factor price equalization, and Stolper-Samuelson) hold [Hochman (1977), Henderson (1988)]. This gives an urban flavor to national policies [Renaud (1981), Henderson (1988)]. For example trade protection policies favoring industry X_1 produced in relatively large size cities over industry X_2 produced in smaller type cities will alter national output composition towards X_1 production and increase the number of large relative to small cities. National urban concentration will rise. Similarly subsidizing an input such as capital for a high tech product, X_1, again, say, produced in a larger type of city will cause the numbers of that type of city to increase, raising urban concentration.

2.2. Growth in a system of cities

Black and Henderson (1999a) specify a dynastic growth model where dynastic families grow in numbers at rate g over time starting from size 1. If c is per person family consumption, the objective function is $\int_0^\infty \frac{c(t)^{1-\sigma}-1}{1-\sigma} e^{-(\rho-g)t} \, dt$ where ρ ($> g$) is the discount rate. Dynasties can splinter (as long as they share their capital stock on an equal per capita basis) and the problem can be put in an overlapping generations context with equivalent results [Black (2000)], under a Galor and Zeira (1993) "joy of giving" bequest motive.

The only capital in the model is human capital and as such there is no market for it. Intra-family behavior substitutes for a capital market. Specifically families allocate their total stock of human capital (H) and members across cities, where Z proportion of family members go to type 1 cities (taking Zh_1e^{gt} of the H with them) and $(1-Z)$ go to type 2 cities [taking $(1-Z)h_2e^{gt}$ with them]. Additions to the family stock come from the equation of motion where the cost of additions, $P\dot{H}$, equals family income $Ze^{gt}I_1+(1-Z)e^{gt}I_2$, less the value of family consumption of X_2, or Pce^{gt}. Constraints

---

[5] Here with h_1 and h_2 yet to be solved we would need to double the numbers of people with h_1 and h_2, respectively. Below we will see the solution with growth to h_1 and h_2 is national scale invariant.

prohibiting consumption of human capital, nontransferability except to newborns, and nontransferability within families across city types (either directly or indirectly through migration) are nonbinding on equilibrium paths.

Families allocate their populations across types of cities, with low human capital types (say h_1) "lending" some of their share ($h = H/e^{gt}$) to high human capital types (say h_2). High human capital types with higher incomes ($I_2 > I_1$ if $h_2 > h_1$) repay low human capital types so $c_1 = c_2 = c$ (governed by the family matriarch). This in itself is an interesting development story, where rural families diversify migration destinations (including the own rural village) and remittances home are a substantial part of earnings. In Black and Henderson if capital markets operate perfectly for human capital (i.e., we violate the "no slavery" constraint) or capital is physical and capital markets operational, one dynastic family could move entirely to, say, type 1 cities and lend some of their human capital to another dynastic family in type 2 cities. With no capital market, each dynastic family must operate as its own informal capital market and spread itself across cities.

In this context Black and Henderson show that, regardless of scale or timing in the growth process, h_1/h_2 and I_1/I_2 are fixed ratios, dependent on θ_i in Equations (6) and (16). As θ_1/θ_2 (the relative returns to capital) rises, h_1/h_2, I_1/I_2 and also n_1/n_2 rise. Z and m_1/m_2 are all fixed ratios of parameters θ_i, δ_i and α under equilibrium growth. Equilibrium and optimal growth differ because the private returns to education in a city, θ_i, differ from the social returns, $\theta_i + \psi_i$. But local governments cannot intervene successfully to encourage optimal growth. Why? With free migration and "no slavery", if a city invests to increase its citizens' education, a person can take their human capital ("brain drain") and move to another city (be subsidized by another city to immigrate, given that city then need not provide extra education for that worker). This model hazard problem discourages internalization of education externalities.

2.2.1. Growth properties: cities

From Equation (13), equilibrium (and efficient) city size in type 1 cities is a function of the per person human capital level, h_1, in type 1 cities. After solving out the model (for P), the same will be true of type 2 cities. City sizes grow as h_1 and h_2 grow, where, under equilibrium growth given h_1/h_2 is a fixed ratio, $\dot{h}_1/h_1 = \dot{h}_2/h_2$ where a dot represents a time derivative. Then

$$\frac{\dot{n}_2}{n_2} = \frac{\dot{n}_1}{n_1} = 2\varepsilon_1 \frac{\dot{h}}{h}, \qquad (18)$$

where $\dot{n}_i/n_i$ is the growth rate of efficient sizes n_i^*.

For the number of cities, the issue is whether growth in individual sizes absorbs the national population growth, or more cities are needed. Given

$$\frac{\dot{m}_1}{m_1} = \frac{\dot{m}_2}{m_2} = g - \frac{\dot{n}_i}{n_i} = g - 2\varepsilon_1 \frac{\dot{h}}{h}, \qquad (19)$$

the numbers of cities grow if $g > \dot{n}_i/n_i$. Note growth in numbers and sizes of cities is "parallel" by type, so the relative size distribution of cities is constant over time. Parallel growth with a constant relative size distribution of cities as reviewed in Section 1.1 is what is observed in the data. This result generalizes to many types of cities under certain conditions. For example, with the log-linear production technologies we assumed and with many varieties of output consumed under unitary price and income elasticities of log-linear preferences, parallel growth results.

2.2.2. Growth properties: economy

Ruling out explosive or divergent growth, there are two types of growth equilibria. Either the economy converges to a steady-state level, or it experiences endogenous steady-state growth. Convergence to a level occurs if $\varepsilon \equiv \varepsilon_1(1 - (\alpha - 2\delta_2)) + \varepsilon_2(\alpha - 2\delta_2) < 1$, where ε is a weighted average of the individual city type. In that case at the steady-state $\bar{h}$, $\dot{n}_i/n_i = 0$ and $\dot{m}_i/m_i = g$, or only the numbers but not sizes of cities grow just like in exogenous growth [Kanemoto (1980), Henderson and Ioannides (1981)]. If $\varepsilon = 1$ then there is steady-state growth, where $\bar{\gamma}^h = \dot{h}/h = (A - \rho)/\sigma$ (where the transversality condition requires $A > \rho$). In that case $\dot{n}_i/n_i = 2\varepsilon_1(A - \rho)/\sigma$, or cities grow at a constant rate. and their numbers also increase if $g > 2\varepsilon_1(A - \rho)/\sigma$. This "knife-edge" formulation of whether there is endogenous growth or not dependent on the value of ε is not essential. For example in Rossi-Hansberg and Wright (2004) endogenous growth can occur more generally in a context where human capital accumulation involves worker time and the growth rate of human capital is a log-linear function of the fraction of time devoted to human capital accumulation, as opposed to production.

2.3. Extensions

There are three major extensions to the basic systems of cities models. First people may differ in terms of inherent productivity or in terms of endowments. Second, while we have discussed the issue of city specialization versus diversification, we have not developed insights into a more nuanced role of small highly specialized cities versus large diversified metro areas in an economy.

2.3.1. Different types of workers

Turning to the first extension, Henderson (1974) has physical capital as a factor of production owned by capitalists who need not reside in cities. Equilibrium city size reflects a market trade-off between the interests of city workers who have an inverted-U shape to utility as a function of the size of the city they live in and capitalists whose returns to capital rise indefinitely with city size (for the same capital to labor ratio). There is a political economy story, where capitalists collectively in an economy have an incentive to limit the number of cities, thus forcing larger city sizes. Helsley and Strange

(1990) have a matching model between the attributes of entrepreneurs and workers and Henderson and Becker (2001) a related two class model. Again the two class model yields a conflict between the city sizes that maximize the welfare of one versus another group, which is resolved in competitive national land development markets.

In a different approach Abdel-Rahman and Wang (1997), Abdel-Rahman (2000) and later Black (2000) look at high and low skill workers who are used in differing proportions in production of different goods. Black has one traded good produced with just low skill labor and a second traded good produced with high skill workers and inputs of a local nontraded good produced with just low skill workers. High skill workers generate production externalities in the form of knowledge spillovers for all traded goods. In Black, urban specialization with all high skill workers (and some low skill workers) concentrated in one type of city producing the first type of good is efficient; but a separating equilibrium that would sustain this pattern, where low skill workers and low tech production stay in their own type of city (rather than trying to cluster with high tech production) is not always sustainable. Black characterizes conditions under which a separating equilibrium will emerge.

It is important to note that there is a much more developed literature on inequality induced by neighborhood selection, where the characteristics of neighbors affect skill acquisition (e.g. average family background in the classroom affects individual student performance). That leads to segregation of talented or wealthier families by neighborhood [Benabou (1993), Durlauf (1996)] and can help transmit economic status across generations, promoting inter-generational income inequality.

2.3.2. Metro areas

Simple indices of urban diversity indicate that smaller cities are very specialized and larger cities highly diversified. So the question is what is the role of large metro areas in an economy and their relationship to smaller cities. Henderson (1988) and Duranton (2005) have a first nature – second nature world, where every city has a first nature economic base and footloose industries cluster in these different first nature cities. In general the largest centers are those attracting the most footloose production to their first nature center. The Duranton paper is discussed in more detail in Section 2.3.3. However, it seems that today few metro areas have an economic base of first nature activity. Accordingly recent literature has focused on the role of large metro areas as centers of innovation, headquarters, and business services [Kolko (1999)].

The Dixit–Stiglitz model opened up an avenue to look at large metro areas as having a base of diversified intermediate service inputs, which generate scale-diversity benefits for local final goods producers. That initial idea was developed in Abdel-Rahman and Fujita (1990) and has led to a set of papers focused on the general issue of what activities, under what circumstances are out-sourced. Theory and empirical evidence [Holmes (1999) and Ono (2000)] suggest that as local market scale increases, final producers will in-house less of their service functions. The resulting increased out-sourcing encourages competition and diversity in the local business service market, encouraging further out-sourcing.

In terms of incorporating this into the role of metro areas versus smaller cities, Davis (2000) has a two-region model, a coastal internationally exporting region and an interior natural resource rich region. There are specialized manufacturing activities which, for production and final sale, require business service activities, summarized as headquarters functions. Headquarters purchase local Dixit–Stiglitz intermediate services such as R&D, marketing, financing, exporting, and so on. Headquarters' activity is in port cities in the coastal region. The issue is whether manufacturing activities are also in these ports versus in specialized coastal hinterland cities versus in specialized interior cities. If the costs of interaction (shipping manufactured goods to port and transactions costs of headquarters-production facility communication) between headquarters and manufacturing functions are extremely high, then both manufacturing and headquarters activities will be found together in coastal port cities. Otherwise they will be in separate types of cities where manufacturing cities will be in coastal hinterlands if costs of headquarters-manufacturing interaction are high, relative to shipping natural resources to the coast. However if natural resource shipping costs are relatively high, then manufacturing cities will be found in the interior. Duranton and Puga (2001) have a very similar model of functional specialization, without the regional flavor. If there is specialization, then there are headquarter cities where headquarters outsource local services in diversified large metro areas, while production occurs in specialized manufacturing cities.

In a different paper Duranton and Puga (2000) develop an entirely different and stimulating view of large metro areas. In an economy there are m types of workers who have skills each specific to producing one of m products. Specialized cities have one type of worker producing the standardized product for that type of worker subject to localization economies. Diversified cities have some of all types of workers. Existing firms at any instant die at an exogenously given rate; and, in a steady-state, new firms are their replacement. New firms do not know "their type" – what types of workers they match best with and hence what final product they would be best off producing. To find their type they need to experiment by trying the different technologies (and hence trying different kinds of workers). New firms have a choice. They can locate in a diversified city with low localization economies in any one sector. But in a diversified city they can experiment with a new process each period until they find their ideal process. At that point they relocate to a city specialized in that product, with thus high localization economies for that product. Alternatively new firms can experiment by moving from specialized city to specialized city with high localization economies, but face a relocation cost each time. If relocation costs are high, it is best during their experimental period to be in a diversified city. This leads to an urban configuration of experimental diversified metro areas and other cities which are specialized in different standardized manufacturing products.

The Duranton and Puga model captures a key role of large diversified metro areas consistent with the data. They are incubators where new products are born and where new firms learn. Once firms have matured then they typically do relocate to more specialized cities. This also captures the product-life cycle for firms in terms of location patterns. Fujita and Ishii (1994) document the location patterns of Japanese and Korean electronics plants and headquarters. In a spatial hierarchy megacities house headquarters activities (out-sourcing business services) and experimental activity. Smaller Japanese or Korean towns have specialized, more standardized high tech production processes and low tech activity is off-shore.

2.3.3. Stochastic process and Zipf's Law

Gabaix (1999a, 1999b) argues that if, there is a stochastic process where individual city growth rates follow Gibrat's Law – the growth rate in any period is unrelated to initial size – then the size distribution that emerges will follow Zipf's Law. Beyond specifying a stochastic process where shocks to productivity or preferences follow a random walk, to get the result in a model where there is an endogenous number of cities of efficient sizes, as opposed to just fixing the number of cities [Gabaix (1999a) and Duranton (2005)] requires considerable structure, with a variety of such issues being analyzed in Cordoba (2004). We follow Rossi-Hansberg and Wright (2004) who adapt the model we have presented. In their base case there is only human capital; and technology and preferences are log-linear. They have many final output industries and hence types of specialized cities. They group industries and specialized city types into sets. Within each set industries and city types have the *same* technology but each individual industry draws its own permanent shock each instant. In terms of the shock they assume that $D_1(t)$ in the equivalent of Equation (6) follows a finite-order Markov process. Finally and critically to have Gibrat's Law lead to Zipf's Law, they must impose an arbitrary lower bound on the sizes that cities can fall to [Gabaix (1999a)]. These assumptions lead to Zipf's Law holding for each set of industries and they show one can aggregate across sets of industries to get Zipf's Law in aggregate. It goes without saying many of the assumptions imposed to get Zipf's Law are very strong, a key point made in Cordoba (2004).

In a recent paper, Duranton (2005) tries to model "micro-foundations" for the stochastic process affecting city sizes and as a result ends up modeling an important overlooked aspect of city evolution. Duranton has "first nature" (immobile given natural resource location) production and "second nature" (mobile, or footloose) production in m cities, where m is given by the number of immobile natural resource products, each needing their own city. So, in contrast to Rossi-Hansberg and Wright the number of cities is fixed; but given that restriction a lot is accomplished. In the paper there are $(n \gg m)$ products, in a Grossman and Helpman (1991) product quality ladder model. The latest innovation in each product is produced by the monopolist holding the patent and only this top quality is marketed for any product. Investment in innovation to try to move the next step up in the quality ladder in industry k and get the next patent in k, can also lead to the next step up in a different industry – i.e., there can be cross-industry innovation. For footloose industries, to partake of a winning innovation occurring for industry k in city i, requires industry k production to locate in city i where the inno-vator is. Presumably co-location of the inventor and production makes the information needed for the transition to mass production cheaper to exchange (e.g., the workers in the innovative firm take over production). Innovation follows a stochastic process where innovation probabilities depend on R&D expenditures. Industry jumps from city to city according to where the latest innovation is, and city growth also follow a stochastic process. The resulting stochastic process of city growth and decline results in steady state size distributions that are similar to Zipf's Law. Adding in considerations of urban scale economies in the innovation process helps explain the long right tails in actual city size distributions, as they differ from Zipf's Law.

Duranton's formulation has the nice feature that cities have patterns of production specialization which change over time. This seems to fit the data; and Duranton's pa-per in fact models the evolution of industry structure of cities. We know from Black and Henderson (1999b) and Ellison and Glaeser (1999b) that industries move "rapidly" across cities, with city specialization changing over time for cities. Any city is very slow to gain a high share of any particular industry's production (given there are many possible industries to gain a share from) and is very quick to lose a high share (given many competitor cities).

3. Urbanization and growth

The previous section examined a fully urbanized economy where all production occurs in cities. City sizes grow with improvements in technology; but, absent stochastic el-ements, individual cities grow in parallel, with the relative numbers of different types of cities and the relative size distribution of cities time invariant. Here we examine a nonsteady state world in which an economy has an agriculture sector that is shrinking with economic development and an urban sector that is growing. We briefly review tra-ditional dual sector models and the new economic geography models, both of which examine sectoral transformation, but without cities per se and generally without eco-nomic growth. Then we present an endogenous growth model in which there is sectoral change with cities.

3.1. Two sector approaches, without cities

Urbanization involves resources shifting from an agricultural to an urban sector. The dual economy models dating back to Lewis (1954) look at sectoral change but are really static models. They focus on the question of urban " bias", or the effect of government policies on the urban–rural divide, and the efficient rural–urban allocation of population at a point in time. These two sector models have an exogenously given "sophisticated" urban sector and a "backward" rural sector [Rannis and Fei (1961), Harris and Todaro (1970), and others] as now well exposited in textbooks [e.g., Ray (1998)].

In these models, the marginal product of labor in the urban sector is assumed to exceed that in the rural sector. Arbitrage in terms of labor migration is limited by inefficient (and exogenously given) labor allocation rules such as farm workers being paid average rather than marginal product or artificially limited absorption in the urban sector (e.g., formal sector minimum wages). The literature focuses on the effect on migration from the rural to urban sector of policies such as rural–urban terms of trade, migration restrictions, wage subsidies, and the like.

The final and most complex versions of dual sector models are in Kelly and Williamson (1984) and Becker, Mills and Williamson (1992), which are fully dynamic CGE models. They have savings behavior and capital accumulation, population growth, and multiple economic sectors in the urban and rural regions. Labor markets within sector and across regions are allowed to clear. The models analyze the effects of a wider array of policy instruments, including sector specific trade or capital market policies for housing, industry, services and the like. However the starting point is again an exogenously given initial urban–rural productivity gap, sustained initially by migration costs and exogenous skill acquisition. On-going urbanization is the result of exogenous forces – technological change favoring the urban sector or changes in the terms of trade favoring the urban sector.

As models of urbanization, these dual economy ones are a critical step but they suffer obvious defects. First how the dual starting point arises is never modeled. Second, and related to the first, there are no forces for agglomeration that would naturally foster industrial concentration in the urban sector. Finally although the models have two sectors there is really little spatial or regional aspect to the problem. There is a new generation of two-sector models, the core–periphery models, which attempt to address some of these defects. The core–periphery models ask under what conditions in a two-region country, industrialization, or "urbanization" is spread over both regions versus concentrated in just one region.

Compared to the dual economy models, Krugman's (1991a) paper explicitly has scale economies that foster endogenous regional concentration. Second, while there are two regions, no starting point is imposed, where one region is assumed to start off ahead of the other. Industrialization may occur in both regions or in only one region. One region can become "backward" (under certain assumptions), or, if not backward (lower real incomes) at least relatively depopulated [Puga (1999)]. But these are outcomes solved for in the model. Third the models have some notion of space represented as transport costs of goods between regions.

The models are focused on a key developmental issue – the initial development of a core (say, coastal) region and a periphery (say, hinterland) region, as technology improves (transport costs fall) from a situation starting with two identical regions. As such they do relate to the earlier discussion in Section 1.3 of urban concentration in a primate city versus the rest of the urban sector. Some work [Puga (1999), Fujita, Krugman and Venables (1999, chapter 7), Helpman (1998) and Tabuchi (1998)] also analyzes how under certain conditions, with further technological improvements, there can be reversal. Some industrial resources leave the core; and the periphery also industrializes/urbanizes. However core–periphery models have limited implications for urbanization per se, since in many versions including Krugman (1991a) initial paper, the agricultural population is fixed.

Unfortunately, to date core–periphery models have been almost exclusively uni-dimensional in focus, asking what happens to core–periphery development as transport costs between regions decline. They are not focused on other forms of technological advance, let alone endogenous technological development. With a few exceptions such as Fujita and Thisse (2002) and Baldwin (2001), the models are static. But even in these exceptions, there is still the focus on *exogenous* changes in transport technology. Compared to the older dual economy literature, generally core–periphery models have no policy considerations of interest to development economists, such as the impact of wage subsidies, rural–urban terms of trade, capital market imperfections. An exception is that some papers have examined the impact on core–periphery structures of reducing barriers to international trade, such as tariff reduction; and papers are starting to explore issues of capital market imperfections. The core–periphery model is an important in-novation in bringing back the role of transport costs, largely ignored in urban systems work, to the forefront. Excellent summaries of the key elements include Neary (2001), Fujita and Thisse (2000) and Ottaviano and Thisse (2004), with the latter two develop-ing many extensions. Fujita, Krugman and Venables (1999) stands as a basic reference on detailed modeling.

The dual economy and core–periphery models are regional models, with limited ur-ban implications. Urban models are focused on the city formation process, where the urban sector is composed of numerous cities, endogenous in number and size. Efficient urbanization and growth require timely formation of cities. As policy issues the extent of market completeness in the national markets in which cities form, the role of city governments and developers, the role of inter-city competition, and the role of debt fi-nance and taxation are critical. In the next section we analyze an urbanization process in which there are cities. Then we turn to a discussion of some key policy issues.

3.2. Urbanization with cities

Here I present a simple two sector model of urbanization with cities, adapting the model in Section 2 following Henderson and Wang (2005a, 2005b). The urban sector is ex-actly like the X_1 city sector earlier, with production technology given in (6). The other sector is food produced in the agriculture sector, which we make now the numeraire (since there may initially be no urban sector). As a result, for type 1 cities in the urban sector, Equation (7) for wages, Equations (9) and (10) for commuting costs and rents, and Equation (15) for income are all redefined to be multiplied by the price of X_1, p. The city size equation is the same, invariant to relative prices. Critical here is

$$I_1 = W_1(1 - 2\delta_1) = pQ_1 h_1^{\varepsilon_1} \tag{15a}$$

for Q_1 a parameter cluster.

Agriculture. Rural output per worker is $D_a h_a^{\psi_a} h_a^{\theta_a}$ or $D_a h_a^{\varepsilon_a}$, so rural wages and real income are

$$W_a = D_a h_a^{\varepsilon_a}, \quad \varepsilon_a \equiv \psi_a + \theta_a. \tag{20}$$

As such the rural sector is very simple: no commuting costs, no agglomeration economies and no diminishing returns to land. As in the urban sector, productivity is affected by individual human capital accumulation $h_a^{\theta_a}$, and by sector knowledge spillovers $h_a^{\psi_a}$.

Preferences and urbanization. To have sectoral transformation we need to move away from the world of unitary price and income elasticities in Section 2, so growth between sectors is not parallel. Here we assume preferences have the form

$$V = \left(x + a^\gamma\right)^\alpha, \quad \gamma, a < 1, \tag{21}$$

where a is consumption of agricultural products. In Equation (21) agricultural demand is income inelastic, with a demand function

$$a = \gamma^{1/(1-\gamma)} p^{1/(1-\gamma)}. \tag{22}$$

3.2.1. *Human capital market, migration, savings*

The urbanization process as a "transitory" phenomenon is not a steady state process. To simplify, following much of the literature, we introduce an explicit market for human capital, as though human capital investments were not embodied. And we assume an exogenous savings rate s. For the former, now each person in the economy has a human capital level h, which can be used in production or can be loaned out. I now flesh out the equations of the model, that in Section 2 were skimmed over. The capital market equalizes capital returns across sectors, so $r = p\theta_1 D_1 h_1^{\theta_1+\psi_1-1} n_1^{\delta_1} = \theta_a D_a h_a^{\theta_a+\psi_a-1}$. Substituting in for n_1 from (13),

$$p = Q_2 h_a^{\varepsilon_a} h_1^{1-\varepsilon_1} \tag{23}$$

recalling $\varepsilon_a \equiv \psi_a + \theta_a$ and $\varepsilon_1 \equiv (\theta_1 + \psi_1)/(1 - 2\delta_1)$; Q_2 is a parameter cluster.

Free migration requires net urban incomes including capital costs to equal the same for agriculture, or $I_1 + r(h - h_1) = W_a + r(h - h_a)$. Utilizing (15),

$$W_1 - W_a = pbn^{1/2} + r(h_1 - h_a). \tag{24}$$

With free migration equalizing real incomes across sectors, urban wages exceed rural wages by (commuting) cost-of-living differences [the first term on the right-hand side of (24)], and by a factor compensating if human capital requirements in the urban sector exceed those in the rural, as I assume.

If we substitute in (24) for W_1, W_a, p and r and rearrange, we get

$$h_a = h_1 \frac{\theta_a}{\theta_1} \left(\frac{1 - \theta_1 - 2\delta}{1 - \theta_a} \right). \tag{25}$$

A sufficient condition for $h_1 > h > h_a$, or the urban sector to be human capital inten-sive, is that $\theta_1 > \theta_a$, as assumed.

To close the model requires three relationships. First is national full employment of capital and labor so

$$n_a h_a + n_1 m_1 h_1 = hN, \tag{26a}$$

$$n_a + m_1 n_1 = N, \tag{26b}$$

where m_1, as before, is the number of type 1 cities and N is the national population. The third equation equates the demand for food equal to its supply. But that requires a digression on how human capital is produced and the nature of savings. Since we want to be able to start with a purely rural economy, we do not want to have it produced just from X_1 as in Section 2.

We assume human capital production in each sector is made from goods from that sector (where an equal expenditure in any sector results in the same human capital), which is almost like assuming, for a fixed savings rate, a fixed fraction of working time in any sector is needed to produce a unit of human capital. Second, we assume savings at the rate s are from wage income net of rental costs, or from $I_1 - rh_1$, and $W_a - rh_a$, which magnitudes are equalized by migration. Thus in the food market total production $n_a D_a h_a^{\varepsilon_a}$ equals food consumption demand $N(p\gamma)^{1/(1-\gamma)}$ [see (22)] plus agricultural savings, or $n_a D_a h_a^{\varepsilon_a} = N(p\gamma)^{1/(1-\gamma)} + sn_a(W_a - rh_a)$. Substituting in for r, for p from (22), W_a from (20) and for h_a from (25) we get

$$n_a/N = Q_3 h_1^{(\gamma\varepsilon_a - \varepsilon_1)/(1-\gamma)} \tag{27}$$

with Q_3 a parameter cluster. We assume $\gamma\varepsilon_a - \varepsilon_1 < 0$, so the social returns to human capital in the urban sector exceed those in the rural sector discounted by γ. With eco-nomic growth in human capital, the rural sector diminishes. Note in (27) for there to be an urban sector, h_1 must be large enough so $n_a/N < 1$, as we explain below. Of course h_1 is linked to h through (26a) where with substitutions

$$h_1 \left(1 - Q_4 h_1^{(\gamma\varepsilon_a - \varepsilon_1)/(1-\gamma)}\right) = h, \tag{28}$$

where given $\gamma\varepsilon_a - \varepsilon_1 < 0$, $dh_1/dh > 0$, once there is an urban sector. Q_4 is a parameter cluster.

3.2.2. Urban growth and transformation

Once an urban sector exists, city growth is as in Section 2, $\dot{n}_1/n_1 = 2\varepsilon_1 \dot{h}_1/h_1$, so cities grow with human capital accumulation. The growth in number of cities now depends on the rate of urbanization, as well. Combining Equations (26a) and (26b), with dif-ferentiation $\dot{m}_1/m_1 = (N/m_1 n_1)g - \dot{n}_1/n_1 - (n_a/m_1 n_1)\dot{n}_a/n_a$. If we differentiate Equation (27) for $\dot{n}_a/n_a$ and combine this becomes

$$\frac{\dot{m}_1}{m_1} = g - \frac{\dot{n}_1}{n_1} - \frac{n_a}{m_1 n_1} \frac{\gamma\varepsilon_a - \varepsilon_1}{1 - \gamma} \frac{\dot{h}_1}{h_1}. \tag{29}$$

As before, the rate of growth of numbers of cities is increased by national population growth, g, and reduced by growth in individual city sizes. Now it is also enhanced by economic growth which increases relative demand for urban products and draws labor out of agriculture, as captured by the last term in Equation (29).

3.2.3. Economic growth

Given the savings rule, total human capital increases by $\dot{H} = s[m_1 n_1 (I_1 - rh_1) + n_a(W_a - rh_a)]$ each instant so the per person change in capital is $\dot{h}/h = \dot{H}/H - g$. Given $I_1 - rh_1 = W_a - rh_a$, with substitutions we have

$$\frac{\dot{h}}{h} = sQ_5 h_1^{\varepsilon_a - 1}\left(1 - Q_6 h_1^{(\gamma\varepsilon_a - \varepsilon_1)/(1-\gamma)}\right)^{-1} - g, \tag{30}$$

where $Q_6 < Q_4$ for parameter clusters. In terms of growth, if $\varepsilon_a < 1$ *and* urbanization occurs, we have steady state *levels* given $\dot{h}/h$ declines with increases in h_1, and hence h. If $\varepsilon_a = 1$, we approach steady state *growth* once h_1 gets large so $n_a N \to 0$ and the expression in parentheses in Equation (30) approaches 1. However in either case at low levels of development in Equation (27), n_a/N is bounded at 1 where Equation (27) defines a critical h_1 and hence h in Equation (28), say h_c, below which $n_a/N = 1$. To have steady-state levels with urbanization given we start at $n_a/N = 1$ with $\dot{h}/h = \dot{h}_a/h_a = -g + (1 - \theta_a)h_a^{\varepsilon_a - 1}$, requires $h_c < (g/(1 - \theta_a))^{1/(\varepsilon_a - 1)}$, so we pass the critical h at which urbanization starts before hitting the potential steady-state value of h without urbanization. Otherwise the economy can be stuck with no urbanization. Details of this and issues of multiple equilibria are discussed in Henderson and Wang (2005a).

3.3. Extensions and policy issues

There are three general sets of policy issues. First concerns whether in the context of the models in Sections 2 and 3.2, the national composition of cities of different types is efficient. We have already discussed this issue: in many contexts asking whether the national composition of cities is efficient is the same as asking if national output composition is efficient. If there are national policy biases such as trade policies favoring steel products over textile products, with urban specialization, if steel is produced in bigger types of cities than textiles, the numbers of larger cities relative to smaller ones and hence urban concentration will increase. The second set of policy issues concerns whether, in general, city sizes are likely to be efficient and we discuss this in Section 3.3.1.

The second general set of issues deals with factors we have ignored. In particular, the modeling in Sections 2 and 3.2 assumes a nice smooth process where (i) all factors of production are perfectly mobile and malleable, (ii) city borrowing and debt accumulation have no role, (iii) "lumpiness" problems that arise in city formation when economies are small are ignored: while m must be an integer in reality, in the analysis it is treated as any positive number where the number of cities grows at a rate $\dot{m}/m$, rather than by 0, 1 or 2. A model that incorporates these features is outlined in Section 3.3.2, which brings to the forefront a variety of policy issues.

3.3.1. City sizes

A perpetual debate in particular developing countries is whether certain megacities are oversized, squandering national resources that must be allocated to commuting, congestion, and transport in those cities and resulting in low quality of life in the polluted, unsanitary and crowded slums of such cities. In other countries, especially former planned economies, the debate goes the other way: are cities too small? The growth connection is straightforward. Either squandered resources in over-sized cities or too small cities with unexploited scale economies mean lower income levels, potentially lower savings, lower capital accumulation and thus lower growth rates. While calculations are tedious, in the steady state growth in Section 2.2.2 where $\gamma^h = \dot{h}/h = (A - \rho)/\sigma$, A depends on urban parameters (for example, increasing with human capital returns) and will be lowered if city sizes are inefficient.

Using a simple, partial equilibrium diagram, it is possible to illustrate both issues: the megacity "problem" and the planned economy problem. The diagrams point to first-order effects. For the megacity problem, suppose there are a variety of type 1 cities in an economy with free mobility of labor and institutions supporting efficient city formation. In Figure 5(a), the representative city has a size n_1^*, where real income as function of city size peaks at I_1^*, tangent to the perfectly elastic national supply curve of labor to the city, given perfect labor mobility. Suppose one particular type 1 city is favored relative to the rest, where various types of favoritism are discussed in Section 1.3.2. For example it may have special public services compared to other cities financed out of national taxes. Those favors raise the realized utility, or real income that residents in the favored city potentially receive, shifting up the inverted-U real income curve. That upward shift draws migrants into the city expanding its size to n_{mega}. But at n_{mega}, the net income *generated by* the city, ignoring its nationally financed favors, is only net I_m. The gap, $I_1^* - I_m$, times the population represents "squandered resources". Of course, such squandering would in general equilibrium affect prices, lowering the height of the population supply curve and the inverted-U's.

A second issue in city formation concerns poor institutions in national land markets and in local governance which limit the number of cities that can form. Suppose that, in villages which might become cities, local governments by institutional restrictions cannot expand infrastructure (see the next section), cannot rezone and build on urban fringe land, and cannot offer subsidies to incoming firms. And suppose developers cannot assemble large tracts of land for development because property rights are ill-defined. These villages cannot grow into cities; as well, entirely new cities cannot form. If the number of cities is bindingly limited, so there are too few cities, all existing cities under free migration are too big. In Figure 5(a), suppose we reconsider the figure ignoring the representative city curve and assume all cities have inverted-U's like the favored city. Then, in this reinterpretation of the figure, I_F is the potentially attainable real income

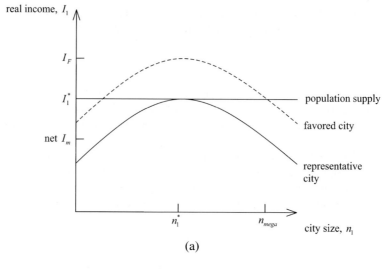

(a)

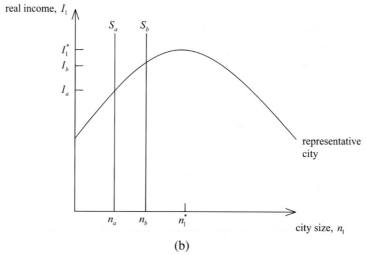

(b)

Figure 5. City sizes. (a) Favored cities. (b) Migration restrictions.

in all cities (ignoring general equilibrium effects) if cities could freely form. Given restricted numbers, rather than operating at I_F (with size n_1^*), cities are overcrowded; and in equilibrium they operate at, say I_1^* (with size n_{mega}), with the same national supply curve of labor as labeled in the figure. The restrictions result in losses related to the gap $I_F - I_1^*$.

The planned economy problem is entirely different. Former "planned" economies like China have formal migration restrictions limiting the visas given for rural people to move to cities and limiting migrants' access to jobs, housing, medical care and schooling in destination cities to reduce the incentive to migrate. Some former planned economies (as well as China) limited migration through housing provision and land development. If the state provides and allocates all housing assignments, migrants cannot move unless housing is provided in the destination. As we saw in Table 2, countries like China and Russia have very low urban concentration compared to other large countries. Figure 5(b) captures the essence of the problem. While the representative city has an inverted-U where real income is maximized at n_1^*, migration restrictions for cities a and b restrict sizes to n_a and n_b and real incomes to I_a and I_b. Au and Henderson (2005) estimate these inverted-U's for different types of cities in China in 1997 and find that 30% of cities are significantly undersized – below the lower 95% confidence interval on their equivalent to n_1^*. The productivity losses from being undersized are enormous: 30–50% or more loss in GDP per capita for many cities.

3.3.2. Sequential city formation and governance

In a working paper, Henderson and Venables (2005) take a new approach to city formation. They assume a context where (1) there is a steady-flow of migrants from rural to urban areas, and (2) urban residence requires a fixed investment in nonmalleable, immobile capital (housing, sewers, water mains, etc.). Cities form sequentially without population swings, so migrants all flow first into city 1 until its equilibrium size is reached (abstracting from any on-going technological change), and then all future migrants all go to a second city until its equilibrium size is reached, and so on. This is a very different process than when all resources are mobile. In the usual models in a small economy, when the second city forms, it takes half the population of the first at that instant, and when the third forms it takes one third of the then population of the first two. Cities grow way past n_1^*, shrink back to n_1^*, and then grow again, shrink, and on so. With fixed capital, such population swings would mean periods of abandoned housing. With sufficiently high required fixed capital investments, all population swings are eliminated in equilibrium. Each new city starts off tiny with no accumulated scale effects and low productivity. It grows steadily absorbing all new rural–urban migrants until its growth interval is complete and it reaches steady state size; then a new city starts off growing from a tiny size.

With sequential city formation without population swings, given discounting of the future, efficient city size requires cities to grow past the equivalent of n_1^* to their steady-state size n_{opt}, at which point real income per worker is declining. Intuitively, growing past n_1^*, with declining but still high real income, postpones the formation of a new city with tiny population, no scale effects and very low incomes. The paper then looks at equilibrium city formation in two contexts.

First is a situation with no "large agents" in national land markets – no developers and no city governments. In a model with perfect mobility of resources as discussed in Section 2, city formation with atomistic agents is a disaster due to coordination failure. A new city can only form when old cities are so big that the income levels they offer have fallen to the point where they equal what a person can earn in a city of size one. Having immobile capital presents a commitment device [Helsley and Strange (1994)], so individual, sequentially rational builders switch from building in an old city to building in a new one at a "reasonable time". Real incomes are still equalized across cities through migration. Given big old cities have high nominal incomes and the tiny new one low nominal income, housing rents adjust in old cities to equalize real incomes. Housing rents in old cities change over the growth cycle of a new city, starting very high and then declining [see also Glaeser and Gyourko (2005)]. In this context, equilibrium city sizes may even be smaller than optimal ones. The deviation from optimum has not to do with coordination failure which is solved despite the absence of "large" agents, but with the present value of externalities created by the marginal migrant in an old versus a new city.

With developers or full empowered local governments, externalities are appropriately internalized and city sizes are n_{opt}. However, apart from financing the housing and infrastructure capital, to induce new migrants to move to a new city with its low real income and scale economies in a timely fashion, governments must subsidize in-migration of worker-firms. To do this they must borrow and, in fact, public debt accumulates over the entire growth interval of a city and only starts to be paid off once it reaches steady-state size. Debt ceilings, or limits for cities which are common in many countries curtail subsidies to in-migrants and postpone new city formation. Debt limited cities are too big. The paper also explores the effects of limits on local tax property tax powers.

4. Some issues for a research agenda

A handbook paper is a place to offer research suggestions, as well as summarize the state of knowledge. While various avenues of research are noted throughout, here I summarize three key suggestions. In all the spatial and urban work, transport costs are either absent or treated as a technology parameter that may exogenously change. In an actual development and growth context, transport costs reflect public infrastructure investment decisions, subject to political influence. Models need to endogenize transport costs, so spatial structures across regions and cities are an outcome of investment decisions. A similar comment involves mobility costs of workers, which are related to both transport and communication infrastructure investments.

A second key research issue involves spatial inequality as it evolves with growth in a context where workers have different ability endowments and choose different human capital levels. In most spatial and urban models, workers are identical, except for their degree of mobility. But with urbanization, it may be that it is higher ability rural folks who urbanize and acquire modern skills, increasing real income gaps between high and low ability people. We have no models that directly address these issues and provide a comprehensive framework to evaluate spatial inequality, or cross-space income differences.

Finally, we do not really have models that address the evolution of city production patterns with on-going technological change. While we have looked at parallel growth and urbanization, we know city functions also change over time. In less developed countries, bigger cities may be focused on manufacturing, but somehow with growth and technological change, big cities tend to specialize more in service functions, purchased by manufacturers and retailers in smaller cities. While we have models of functional specialization, we haven not modeled this evolution in city roles over the development process.

Acknowledgement

I thank Diego Puga for very helpful comments on a preliminary draft of this chapter.

References

Abdel-Rahman, H. (1996). "When do cities specialize in production". Regional Science and Urban Economics 26, 1–22.

Abdel-Rahman, H. (2000). "City systems: General equilibrium approaches". In: Huriot, J.-M., Thisse, J.-F. (Eds.), Economics of Cities: Theoretical Perspectives. Cambridge University Press, Cambridge, pp. 109–137.

Abdel-Rahman, H., Anas, A. (2004). "Theories of systems of cities". In: Henderson, J.V., Thisse, J.-F. (Eds.), Handbook of Regional and Urban Economics, vol. 4, Cities and Geography. North-Holland, Amsterdam, pp. 2293–2340.

Abdel-Rahman, H., Fujita, M. (1990). "Product variety, Marshallian externalities, and city sizes". Journal of Regional Science 30, 165–185.

Abdel-Rahman, H., Wang, P. (1997). "Social welfare and income inequality in a system of cities". Journal of Urban Economics 41, 462–483.

Ades, A.F., Glaeser, E.L. (1995). "Trade and circuses: Explaining urban giants". Quarterly Journal of Economics 110, 195–227.

Anas, A., Xiong, K. (1999). "The formation and growth of specialized cities". Mimeo. State University of New York at Buffalo.

Arthur, B. (1990). "Silicon valley locational clusters: When do increasing returns to scale imply monopoly?". Mathematical Social Sciences 19, 235–251.

Au, C.C., Henderson, J.V. (2005). "How migration restrictions limit agglomeration and productivity in China". Mimeo. Brown University.

Baldwin, R.E. (2001). "Core–periphery model with forward-looking expectations". Regional Science and Urban Economics 31, 21–49.

Barro, R., Sala-i-Martin, X. (1991). "Convergence across states and regions". Brookings Papers on Economic Activity 1, 107–182.

Barro, R., Sala-i-Martin, X. (1992). "Regional growth and migration: A Japan–USA comparison". Journal of Japanese and International Economics 6, 312–346.

Becker, G., Mills, E., Williamson, J.G. (1992). Indian Urbanization and Economic Growth Since 1960. Johns Hopkins Press, Baltimore.

Beeson, P.E., DeJong, D.N., Troeskan, W. (2001). "Population Growth in US Counties, 1840–1990". Regional Science and Urban Economics 31, 669–700.

Benabou, R. (1993). "Workings of a city: Location, education, and production". Quarterly Journal of Economics 108, 619–652.

Bergsman, J., Greenston, P., Healy, R. (1972). "The agglomeration process in urban growth". Urban Studies 9, 263–288.

Black, D. (2000). "Local knowledge spillovers and inequality". Mimeo. University of California, Irvine.

Black, D., Henderson, J.V. (1999a). "A theory of urban growth". Journal of Political Economy 107, 252–284.

Black, D., Henderson, J.V. (1999b). "Spatial evolution of population and industry in the USA". American Economic Association Papers and Proceedings 89 (May), 321–327.

Black, D., Henderson, J.V. (2003). "Urban evolution in the USA". Journal of Economic Geography 3, 343–373.

Clark, J.S., Stabler, J.C. (1991). "Gibrat's Law and the growth of Canadian cities". Urban Studies 28, 635–639.

Cordoba, J.-C. (2004). "On the size distribution of cities". Mimeo. Rice University.

Davis, J. (2000). "Headquarter service and factory urban specialization with transport costs". Mimeo. Brown University.

Davis, J., Henderson, J.V. (2003). "Evidence on the political economy of the urbanization process". Journal of Urban Economics 53, 98–125.

Dobkins, L.H., Ioannides, Y.M. (2001). "Spatial interactions among U.S. cities: 1900–1990". Regional Science and Urban Economics 31, 701–732.

Duranton, G. (2005). "Urban evolutions: The fast, the slow, and the still". Mimeo. University of Toronto.

Duranton, G., Overman, H. (2005). "Testing for localization using micro-geographic data". Review of Economic Studies, submitted for publication.

Duranton, G., Puga, D. (2000). "Nursery cities: Urban diversity process innovation, and the life cycle of products". American Economic Review 91, 1454–1477.

Duranton, G., Puga, D. (2001). "From sectoral to functional urban specialization". LSE Discussion Paper 2971. CEPR.

Duranton, G., Puga, D. (2004). "Microfoundations of urban agglomeration economies". In: Henderson, J.V., Thisse, J.-F. (Eds.), Handbook of Regional and Urban Economics, vol. 4. North-Holland, Amsterdam, pp. 2003–2118.

Durlauf, S.N. (1996). "A theory of persistent income inequality". Journal of Economic Growth 1, 75–93.

Eaton, J., Eckstein, Z. (1997). "Cities and growth: Evidence from France and Japan". Regional Science and Urban Economics 27, 443–474.

Ellison, G., Glaeser, E. (1999a). "The geographic concentration of us manufacturing: A dartboard approach". Journal of Political Economy 105, 889–927.

Ellison, G., Glaeser, E. (1999b). "The geographic concentration of industry: Does natural advantage explain agglomeration?". American Economic Association Papers and Proceedings 89, 311–316.

Fay, M., Opal, C. (1999). "Urbanization without growth: Understanding an African phenomenon". Mimeo. World Bank.

Flatters, F., Henderson, J.V., Mieszkowski, P. (1974). "Public goods, efficiency, and regional fiscal equalization". Journal of Public Economics 3, 99–112.

Fujita, J., Krugman, P., Venables, A.J. (1999). The Spatial Economy: Cities, Regions, and International Trade. MIT Press, Cambridge, MA.

Fujita, M., Ishii, T. (1994). "Global location behavior and organization dynamics of Japanese electronic firms and their impact on regional economies". Paper Presented for Prince Bertil Symposium on the Dynamic Firm, Stockholm.

Fujita, M., Ogawa, H. (1982). "Multiple equilibria and structural transition of non-monocentric configurations". Regional Science and Urban Economics 12, 161–196.

Fujita, M., Thisse, J.-F. (2000). "The formation of economic agglomerations". In: Huriot, J.-M., Thisse, J.-F. (Eds.). Cambridge University Press, New York.

Fujita, M., Thisse, J.-F. (2002). Economics of Agglomeration. Cambridge University Press, New York.

Gabaix, X. (1999a). "Zipf's Law and the growth of cities". American Economic Association and Proceedings 89, 129–132.

Gabaix, X. (1999b). "Zipf's Law for cities: An explanation". Quarterly Journal of Economics 114, 739–767.

Gallup, J.L., Sachs, J.D., Mellinger, A. (1999). "Geography and economic development". International Regional Science Review 22, 179–232.

Galor, O., Zeira, J. (1993). "Income distribution and macro economics". Review of Economic Studies 60, 35–52.

Glaeser, E., Gyourko, J. (2005). "Urban decline and durable housing". Journal of Political Economy 113, 345–375.

Glaeser, E., Scheinkman, J., Schelifer, A. (1995). "Economic growth in a cross-section of cities". Journal of Monetary Economics 36, 117–134.

Grossman, G., Helpman, E. (1991). "Quality ladders in the theory of growth". Review of Economic Studies 58, 43–61.

Harris, J., Todaro, M. (1970). "Migration, unemployment and development: A two sector analysis". American Economic Review 40, 126–142.

Head, K., Mayer, T. (2004). "The empirics of agglomeration and trade". In: Henderson, J.V., Thisse, J.-F. (Eds.), Handbook of Regional and Urban Economics, vol. 4, Cities and Geography. North-Holland, Amsterdam.

Helpman, E. (1998). "The size of regions". In: Pines, D., Sadka, E., Zilcha, I. (Eds.), Topics in Public Economics: Theoretical and Applied Analysis. Cambridge University Press, Cambridge, U.K., pp. 33–54.

Helsley, R., Strange, W. (1990). "Matching and agglomeration economies in a system of cities". Regional Science and Urban Economics 20, 189–212.

Helsley, R., Strange, W. (1994). "City formation with commitment". Regional Science and Urban Economics 24, 373–390.

Henderson, J.V. (1974). "The sizes and types of cities". American Economic Review 61, 640–656.

Henderson, J.V. (1988). Urban Development: Theory, Fact and Illusion. Oxford University Press, London.

Henderson, J.V. (1997). "Medium size cities". Regional Science and Urban Economics 27, 449–470.

Henderson, J.V. (2002). "Urban primacy, external costs, and quality of life". Resource Economics and Energy 24, 95–106.

Henderson, J.V. (2003). "The urbanization process and economic growth: The so-what question". Journal of Economic Growth 8, 47–71.

Henderson, J.V., Becker, R. (2001). "Political economy of city sizes and formation". Journal of Urban Economics 48, 453–484.

Henderson, J.V., Ioannides, Y. (1981). "Aspects of growth in a system of cities". Journal of Urban Economics 10, 117–139.

Henderson, J.V., Kuncoro, A. (1996). "Industrial centralization in Indonesia". World Bank Economic Review 10, 513–540.

Henderson, J.V., Kuncoro, A., Nasution, P. (1996). "Dynamic development in Jabotabek". Indonesian Bulletin of Economic Studies 32, 71–96.

Henderson, J.V., Lee, T., Lee, J.Y. (2001). "Scale externalities in Korea". Journal of Urban Economics 49, 479–504.

Henderson, J.V., Venables, A.J. (2005). "The dynamics of city formation: Finance and governance". Mimeo. LSE.

Henderson, J.V., Wang, H.G. (2005a). "Urbanization and city growth". Journal of Economic Geography 5, 23–42.

Henderson, J.V., Wang, H.G. (2005b). "Urbanization and city growth: The role of institutions". Mimeo. Brown University.

Hochman, O. (1997). "A two factor three sector model of an economy with cities". Mimeo.

Holmes, T. (1999). "Localization of industry and vertical disintegration". Review of Economics and Statistics 81, 314–325.

Ioannides, Y.M., Overman, H.G. (2003). "Zipf's Law for cities: An empirical examination". Regional Science and Urban Economics 33 (1), 127–137.

Junius, K. (1999). "Primacy and economic development: Bell shaped or parallel growth of cities". Journal of Economic Development 24 (1), 1–22.

Kanemoto, Y. (1980). Theories of Urban Externalities. North-Holland, Amsterdam.

Kelly, A.C., Williamson, J.G. (1984). What Drives Third World City Growth? A Dynamic General Equilibrium Approach. Princeton University Press, Princeton, NJ.

Kim, H.S. (1988). "Optimal and equilibrium land use pattern in a city: A non-parametric approach". Ph.D. Thesis. Brown University.

Kim, S. (1995). "Expansion of markets and the geographic distribution of economic activities: The trends in US manufacturing structure, 1860–1987". Quarterly Journal of Economics 95, 881–908.

Kolko, J. (1999). "Can I get some service here? Information technology service industries, and the future of cities". Mimeo. Harvard University.

Krugman, P. (1991a). "Increasing returns and economic geography". Journal of Political Economy 99, 483–499.

Krugman, P. (1991b). Geography and Trade. MIT Press, Cambridge, MA.

Lee, K.S. (1988). "Infrastructure constraints on industrial growth in Thailand". World Bank INURD Working Paper No. 88-2.

Lee, K.S. (1989). The Location of Jobs in a Developing Metropolis. Oxford University Press, London.

Lee, T.C. (1997). "Industry decentralization and regional specialization in Korean manufacturing". Unpublished Ph.D. Thesis. Brown University.

Lewis, W.A. (1954). "Economic development with unlimited supplies of labor". Manchester School of Economic and Social Studies 22, 139–191.

Lucas, R.E. (1988). "On the mechanics of economic development". Journal of Monetary Economics 12, 3–42.

Lucas, R.E., Rossi-Hansberg, E. (2002). "On the internal structure of cities". Econometrica 70 (4), 1445–1476.

Marshall, A. (1890). Principles of Economics. MacMillan, London.

Mills, E., Becker, C. (1986). Studies in Indian Urban Development. Oxford University Press, London.

Mills, E., Hamilton, B. (1994). Urban Economics. Scott–Foresman, Glenview, IL.

Mohring, H. (1961). "Land values and measurement of highway benefits". Journal of Political Economy 49, 236–249.

Neary, J.F. (2001). "Of hype and hyperbolas: Introducing the new economic geography". Journal of Economic Literature 49, 536–561.

Ono, Y. (2000). "Outsourcing business service and the scope of local markets". CES Discussion Paper CES 00-14.

Ottaviano, G., Thisse, J.-F. (2004). "Agglomeration and economic geography". In: Henderson, J.V., Thisse, J.-F. (Eds.), Handbook of Regional and Urban Economics, vol. 4, Cities and Geography. North-Holland, Amsterdam, pp. 2563–2605.

Overman, H., Redding, S., Venables, A.J. (2003). "The economic geography of trade, production and income: A survey of empirics". In: Harrigan, J., Choi, K. (Eds.), Handbook of International Trade. Blackwell, Oxford.

Puga, D. (1999). "The rise and fall of regional inequalities". European Economic Review 43, 303–334.

Quah, D. (1993). "Empirical cross section dynamics and economic growth". European Economic Review 37, 426–434.

Rannis, G., Fei, J. (1961). "A theory of economic development". American Economic Review 51, 533–565.

Rappaport, J., Sacks, D. (2003). "The US as a coastal nation". Journal of Economic Growth 8, 5–46.

Rauch, J.E. (1993). "Does history matter only when it matters a little? The case of city-industry location". Quarterly Journal of Economics 108, 843–867.

Ray, D. (1998). Development Economics. Princeton University Press, Princeton, NJ.

Renaud, B. (1981). National Urbanization Policy in Developing Countries. Oxford University Press, London.

Rosen, K., Resnick, M. (1980). "The size distribution of cities: An examination of the Pareto law and primacy". Journal of Urban Economics 81, 165–186.

Rosenthal, S., Strange, W. (2004). "Evidence on the nature and sources of agglomeration economies". In: Henderson, J.V., Thisse, J.-F. (Eds.), Handbook of Regional and Urban Economics, vol. 4, Cities and Geography. North-Holland, Amsterdam, pp. 2119–2172.

Rossi-Hansberg, E. (2004). "Optimal urban land use and zoning". Review of Economic Dynamics 7, 69–106.
Rossi-Hansberg, E., Wright, E.M. (2004). "Urban structure and growth". Mimeo. Stanford University (May).
Simon, H. (1955). "On a class of skew distribution functions". Biometrika 44, 425–440.
Stiglitz, J. (1977). "The theory of local public goods". In: Feldstein, M.S., Inman, R.P. (Eds.), The Economics of Public Services. MacMillan, London, pp. 273–334.
Tabuchi, T. (1998). "Urban agglomeration and dispersion: A synthesis of Alonso and Krugman". Journal of Urban Economics 44, 333–351.
Thomas, V. (1978). "The measurement of spatial differences in poverty: The case of Peru". World Bank Staff Working Paper No. 273.
Wheaton, W., Shishido, H. (1981). "Urban concentration, agglomeration economies, and the level of economic development". Economic Development and Cultural Change 30, 17–30.
Williamson, J. (1965). "Regional inequality and the process of national development". Economic Development and Cultural Change 13 (June), 3–45.
World Bank (2000). Entering the 21st Century: World Development Report 1999/2000. Oxford University Press, London.
Xiong, K. (1998). "Intercity and intracity externalities in a system of cities: Equilibrium, transient dynamics, and welfare analysis". Unpublished Ph.D. Thesis. State University of New York at Buffalo.

PART VI

GROWTH IN BROADER CONTEXTS

Chapter 25

INEQUALITY, TECHNOLOGY AND THE SOCIAL CONTRACT

ROLAND BÉNABOU

Princeton University,
NBER,
CEPR,
IRP
and
BREAD

Contents

Abstract	1596
Keywords	1596
Introduction	1597
1. Inequality, redistribution and growth	1600
1.1. Production, preferences and policy	1601
1.2. Distributional dynamics and aggregate growth	1603
1.3. Voter preferences, political power and equilibrium policy	1606
2. Sustainable social contracts	1609
2.1. Dynamics and steady states	1609
2.2. Which societies grow faster?	1611
3. Technology and the social contract	1612
3.1. Exogenous technical change and the viability of the welfare state	1613
3.2. Skills, technology and income inequality	1618
3.3. Technological choice and endogenous flexibility	1619
4. Endogenous institutions and endogenous technology	1623
5. Exporting inequality: Spillovers between social contracts	1627
5.1. A shift in one country's technological frontier	1628
5.2. A shift in one country's political institutions	1629
6. Conclusion	1629
Acknowledgements	1630
Appendix: Proofs	1630
References	1635

Handbook of Economic Growth, Volume 1B. Edited by Philippe Aghion and Steven N. Durlauf
© 2005 Elsevier B.V. All rights reserved
DOI: 10.1016/S1574-0684(05)01025-7

Abstract

The distribution of human capital and income lies at the center of a nexus of forces that shape a country's economic, institutional and technological structure. I develop here a unified model to analyze these interactions and their growth consequences. Five main issues are addressed. First, I identify the key factors that make both European-style "welfare state" and US-style "laissez-faire" social contracts sustainable; I also compare the growth rates of these two politico-economic steady states, which are not Pareto-rankable. Second, I examine how technological evolutions affect the set of redistributive institutions that can be durably sustained, showing in particular how skill-biased technical change may cause the welfare state to unravel. Third, I model the endogenous determination of technology or organizational form that results from firms' tailoring the flexibility of their production processes to the distribution of workers' skills. The greater is human capital heterogeneity, the more flexible and wage-disequalizing is the equilibrium technology. Moreover, firms' choices tend to generate excessive flexibility, resulting in suboptimal growth or even self-sustaining technology-inequality traps. Fourth, I examine how institutions also shape the course of technology; thus, a world-wide shift in the technology frontier results in different evolutions of production processes and skill premia across countries with different social contracts. Finally, I ask what joint configurations of technology, inequality and redistributive policy are feasible in the long run, when all three are endogenous. I show in particular how the diffusion of technology leads to the "exporting" of inequality across borders; and how this, in turn, generates spillovers between social contracts that make it more difficult for nations to maintain distinct institutions and social structures.

Keywords

inequality, welfare state, technical change, skill bias, human capital, redistribution, social contract, political economy

JEL classification: D31, O33, J3, H10

Introduction

The distribution of human capital and income lies at the center of a nexus of forces that shape a country's economic, institutional and technological structure. This chapter develops a unified model to analyze these interactions and their implications for growth, emphasizing in particular the mechanisms that allow different socioeconomic structures to perpetuate themselves, and those pushing toward convergence.[1] The analysis centers around five main questions.

1. *Why do countries at similar levels of development choose widely different social contracts?* Redistribution – through taxes and transfers, unemployment and health insurance, education finance and labor market regulation – displays remarkable variations even among countries with similar economic and political fundamentals. I thus ask what makes both European-type welfare states and US-type, more laissez-faire social contracts sustainable in the long run, together with their respective levels of inequality.[2] I then examine the efficiency and growth properties of these two regimes (which cannot be Pareto ranked) and ask what shocks might cause each one to unravel. The model also sheds light on the contrasting historical development paths of North and South America, and on the more recent experience of East Asia versus Latin America.

2. *How does skill-biased technical and organizational change impact the viability of redistributive institutions?* Over the last twenty-five years, most industrialized countries experienced a considerable rise in wage inequality.[3] This trend is generally attributed to three main factors: skill-biased technical change, international trade (which lies outside the scope of this chapter), and institutional change, such as the erosion of the minimum wage and the decline of unions. But minimum wages, labor market legislation and union power are endogenous outcomes, to the same extent as social insurance and education policy; and indeed, they evolved quite differently in Continental Europe or Canada and in the United States.[4] Analyzing redistributive institutions as a whole, I show how skill-biased technical change can cause the welfare state to unravel, and examine more generally how technological evolutions affect the set of social contracts that can be sustained in the long run.

---

[1] The main channels through which inequality and redistributive institutions can in turn affect growth were exposited in Bénabou (1996b).

[2] I shall limit my scope here to politico-economic persistence mechanisms that reflect differences in agents' economic interests and political power [Bénabou (2000), Saint-Paul (2001), Hassler et al. (2003), Alesina, Glaeser and Sacerdote (2001)] rather than social norms [Lindbeck (1995)] or differences in beliefs about the mobility process and the determinants of individual income [Piketty (1995), Bénabou and Tirole (2006), Alesina and Angeletos (2005)].

[3] See, e.g., Autor, Katz and Krueger (1997) or Berman, Bound and Machin (1997).

[4] See, e.g., Freeman (1996), Fortin and Lemieux (1997), Lee (1999) or Acemoglu, Aghion and Violante (2001).

The previous questions aim to explain differences in redistributive policies (together with their growth implications) and the role of technology in their evolution. The next two take the reverse perspective.

3. *What determines the types of technologies and organizational forms used by firms?* Production processes – and in particular their degree of skill bias – are themselves endogenous, adapting over time to the skills of the labor force.[5] I develop here a new and very tractable model of technology choice, based on the idea that firms tailor the *flexibility* of their production processes (substitutability between different labor inputs) to the distribution of human capital in the workforce. The main prediction is that the more heterogeneous are workers' skill levels, the more flexible and wage-disequalizing the equilibrium technology will be. In a homogeneous country like Japan, by contrast, production will involve much tighter complementarity between workers' tasks. Integrating this model with the previous analysis of human capital dynamics, I also show that firms' choices involve externalities that tend to result in excessive flexibility and a suboptimal growth rate, or even in self-sustaining technology-inequality traps.

4. *What types of societies and institutions are most conducive to the emergence of skill-biased technologies and organizational forms?* Through their influence on the distribution of human capital, public policies in the fiscal, labor market and especially educational arenas are important determinants of what innovations can be profitably developed and adopted; the same is true for immigration. One notes, for instance, that skill-biased technical change and reorganization occurred first, and to a greater extent, in the United States compared to Europe – and within the latter, more so in England than on the Continent. Combining the technology and policy components of the model, I show how a world-wide shift in the technological frontier leads to different evolutions of production processes and skill premia across countries with different social contracts.

Two extensive but essentially disconnected literatures have examined the economic determinants and consequences of redistributive policies on the one hand, those of biased technical change on the other.[6] Yet in reality both are endogenous and jointly determined. The ability to conduct a unified analysis of human capital dynamics, technology and institutions is a novel and key feature of the framework developed in this chapter. It makes it possible to address important questions such as the second, fourth and especially fifth ones on the list:

5. *What "societal models" – joint configurations of technology, inequality, and policy – are feasible in the long run? In particular, how does the diffusion of technology affect nations' ability to maintain their own redistributive institutions and social structures?* Analyzing the case of two countries linked by the (endogenous)

---

[5] See, e.g., Kremer and Maskin (1996), Acemoglu (1998), Kiley (1999), Lloyd-Ellis (1999) and Vindigni (2002). Relatedly, Grossman and Maggi (2000) show how the skill distribution matters for international specialization, and Legros and Newman (1996) how the wealth distribution affects the organization of firms.

[6] See the previously cited references, as well as the other ones given throughout the chapter.

diffusion of their domestically developed technologies, I show how inequality tends to be "exported" to the less heterogeneous one. This mechanism, in turn, generates spillovers between the social contracts of different nations, transmitting even purely political shocks and potentially triggering "chain reactions" that can cause major shifts towards a common, and generally inegalitarian, outcome.

The chapter is organized in two main parts, corresponding respectively to the left- and right-hand sides of Figure 1.[7] The first of these two feedback loops centers on political-economy interactions. I thus present in Sections 1 and 2 a model of inequality, growth and redistributive policy in a context of imperfect credit and insurance markets [based on Bénabou (2000)]. I first analyze how macro and distributional dynamics are affected by redistributive policies, then how the latter are themselves determined from the preferences and political power of different social classes. Finally, I identify the conditions under which a single or multiple politico-economic steady states arise.

The second and most novel part of the chapter incorporates the role of technology and its interactions with redistributive institutions. I first consider in Section 3 the impact of exogenous skill-biased technical change on inequality and the political equilibrium. I then study how technology responds to the composition of the labor force, through firms' choices of their degree of flexibility. In Section 4 both sides of Figure 1 are brought together to analyze the long-run determination of institutions, technologies and the distribution of human capital. In Section 5, finally, I show how technology diffusion leads to the "exporting" of inequality and international spillovers between social contracts. Section 6 concludes. All proofs are gathered in the Appendix.

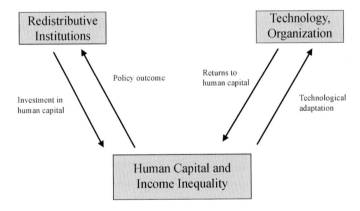

Figure 1. The links between inequality, technology and redistributive institutions.

---

[7] Each arrow on the diagram actually corresponds to a specific equation or proposition in the model. From left to right, these are Equation (11), Proposition 3, Equation (1) or later Equation (28), and Proposition 8.

1. Inequality, redistribution and growth

The model presented in this section [drawing on Bénabou (2000)] can be summarized by *two key relationships* between inequality and redistribution; both arise from imperfections in credit and insurance markets, and are illustrated on Figure 2.

The first locus summarizes the *political mechanism*: in each period, the equilibrium rate of redistribution chosen by voters is a U-shaped function $\tau = T(\Delta)$ of inequality in human capital, measured here as the variance of a log-normal distribution. The downward-sloping part of this curve, which is the crucial one, reflects a very general intuition: while asset market imperfections create a scope for efficient redistributive institutions (to provide social insurance and relax credit constraints), these institutions command much less support in an unequal society than in a relatively homogeneous one. Thus, starting from $\Delta = 0$, where there is unanimous support for the ex-ante efficient degree of redistribution, growing inequality increases the fraction of agents rich enough to lose from, and therefore oppose, all but relatively low levels of τ. The upward-sloping part of the curve, in contrast, is shaped by the standard skewness effect, which eventually dominates: rising numbers of poor will eventually impose more redistribution, well beyond the point where it ceases to be efficient.[8]

The second curve on Figure 2 represents the *accumulation mechanism*: since redistribution relaxes the credit constraints bearing on the poor's human capital investments,

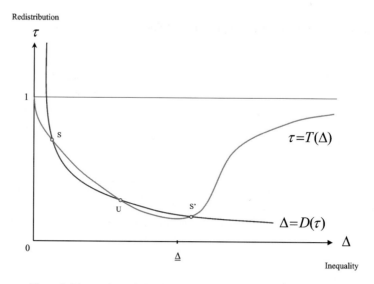

Figure 2. The two key relationships between inequality and redistribution.

---

[8] See, e.g., Alesina and Rodrik (1994) or Persson and Tabellini (1994) for models leading to such a positive slope. The empirical evidence (discussed at the end of this section) for both countries and US states provides little support for the standard view of a positive relationship between inequality and redistribution.

long-run inequality is a declining function $\Delta = T(\tau)$ of the rate of redistribution. When the two curves have several intersections, as illustrated on the figure, these correspond to *multiple politico-economic steady states* that are sustainable under the same fundamentals. One, with low inequality and high redistribution, corresponds to a European-type welfare state; the other, with the reverse configuration, to a US-type, more laissez-faire society.

In this and the next section I will derive the two loci from an explicit dynamic model and identify the configurations of economic and political parameters under which alternative social models can coexist. In later sections I shall investigate how the two curves, and therefore the equilibrium set, are affected by exogenous technical change, then ultimately extend the analysis to the case where technology itself adapts endogenously to the distribution of skills in the population.

1.1. Production, preferences and policy

The economy is populated by overlapping-generations families, $i \in [0, 1]$. In generation t, adult i combines his human capital k_t^i with effort l_t^i to produce output, subject to a productivity shock z_t^i,

$$y_t^i = z_t^i (k_t^i)^\gamma (l_t^i)^\delta. \tag{1}$$

At this point the technology is exogenous and does not explicitly involve interactions among workers. Later on I will introduce a richer production structure, where agents with different skill levels perform complementary tasks and the degree of substitutability between them is optimally chosen by firms. The return to human capital γ and the mean of the productivity shocks z_t^i will then be endogenous functions of the current distribution of human capital. From the point of view of an individual worker-voter, however, this richer structure will retain an earnings function very similar to (1), so all the results obtained with this unconstrained reduced form will remain directly applicable.

Public policy or labor market institutions redistribute income through taxes and transfers, or a wage-equalization scheme, that transform each agent's gross earnings (or marginal revenue product) y_t^i into a disposable income $\hat{y}_t^i$, as specified below. These resources finance both the adult's consumption c_t^i and his investment or educational bequest e_t^i:

$$\hat{y}_t^i = c_t^i + e_t^i, \tag{2}$$

$$k_{t+1}^i = \kappa \xi_{t+1}^i (k_t^i)^\alpha (e_t^i)^\beta, \tag{3}$$

where ξ_{t+1}^i represents the child's unpredictable ability, or simply luck, and $\alpha + \beta\gamma \leqslant 1$. There is thus no loan market for financing individual investments (e.g., children cannot be held responsible for the debts of their parents), and no insurance or securities market where the idiosyncratic risks z_t^i and ξ_{t+1}^i could be diversified away.[9] Both shocks are i.i.d. and log-normal with mean one, and initial endowments are also log-normally distributed across families: thus $\ln z_t^i \sim \mathcal{N}(-v^2/2, v^2)$, $\ln \xi_t^i \sim \mathcal{N}(-w^2/2, w^2)$ and $\ln k_0^i \sim \mathcal{N}(m_0, \Delta_0^2)$.

Agents' preferences over their own consumption, effort, and child's human capital are defined recursively over their lifetime. Once he has learned his productivity z_t^i, agent i chooses his effort and consumption to maximize,

$$\ln V_t^i \equiv \max_{l_t^i, c_t^i} \left\{ (1 - \rho) \left[\ln c_t^i - \left(l_t^i \right)^\eta \right] + \rho \ln E_t \left[k_{t+1}^i \right] \right\}. \tag{4}$$

The disutility of effort is measured by $\eta > 1$, which corresponds to an intertemporal elasticity of labor supply of $1/(\eta - 1)$. The discount factor ρ defines the relative weights of the adult's own felicity and of his bequest motive.[10]

At the beginning of period t, when evaluating and voting over redistributive policies, the agent does not yet know his lifetime productivity z_t^i. The resulting uncertainty over his ex-post utility level V_t^i is reflected in his ex-ante preferences, with a risk-aversion coefficient of a:

$$U_t^i \equiv \ln \left(E_t \left[\left(V_t^i \right)^{1-a} \middle| k_t^i \right]^{1/(1-a)} \right). \tag{5}$$

This recursive specification allows a to parametrize the insurance value of redistributive policies, just as the labor supply elasticity $1/(\eta - 1)$ parametrizes the effort distortions.[11]

The redistributive policies over which agents vote are represented by simple, progressive schemes that map a market income y_t^i (marginal revenue product) into a disposable income $\hat{y}_t^i$, according to

$$\hat{y}_t^i \equiv \left(y_t^i \right)^{1-\tau_t} \left(\tilde{y}_t \right)^{\tau_t}. \tag{6}$$

The break-even level $\tilde{y}_t$ is determined by the balanced-budget constraint, which requires that net transfers sum to zero. Thus, denoting per capita income by y_t, it must be that

$$\int_0^1 \left(y_t^i \right)^{1-\tau_t} \left(\tilde{y}_t \right)^{\tau_t} \, di = y_t. \tag{7}$$

---

[9] The absence of any intertemporal trade is clearly an oversimplified (but quite common) representation of asset market incompleteness, making the model analytically tractable. Zhang (2005) extends a simplified version of the present model (with a zero–one policy variable and no political-economy mechanism) to allow for physical capital and financial bequests. He obtains similar results for the effects of inequality, plus new ones on convergence speeds to the steady-state.

[10] His (relative) risk-aversion with respect to the child's endowment k_{t+1}^i at that stage is normalized to zero, but this plays no role in any of the results. A dynastic specification of preferences [Bénabou (2002)] also leads to similar aggregate and distributional dynamics, but is less simple to work with.

[11] When $a \neq 1$ these recursive preferences are not time-separable [see, e.g., Kreps and Porteus (1979)], as risk-aversion differs from the inverse of the intertemporal elasticity of substitution in consumption, which by (4) remains fixed at one. This last assumption, common to many papers in the literature, helps make the model analytically solvable.

The elasticity τ_t measures the degree of *progressivity*, or equalization, of redistributive institutions.[12] Three types of redistributive mechanisms can be considered here, being close to formally equivalent in this model. The first one, on which the exposition will generally focus, is that of fiscal policy, which equalizes disposable incomes through *taxes and transfers*. A second is *wage or earnings compression* through labor market institutions and policies favorable to workers with relatively low skills: minimum wage laws, union-friendly or right-to-strike regulations, firing costs, public sector pay and employment, etc.[13] The third one is *education finance*, where τ_t now applies only to human capital expenditures e_t^i, as opposed to all of income y_t^i. This may be achieved through a policy of school funding equalization across local communities, the presence of a centrally financed public-education system, or more generally by subsidizing differentially the education of rich and poor students.[14] Under either of the three above interpretations of τ_t, incentive compatibility requires that $\tau_t \leqslant 1$; on the other hand a regressive policy $\tau_t < 0$ cannot be ruled out a priori, and indeed one does observe such policies, typically in countries characterized by high inequality and a powerful ruling class.

1.2. Distributional dynamics and aggregate growth

Taking policy as parametrically given for the moment, I first consider the resulting economic decisions of individual agents, then the economy-wide dynamics of human capital and income.

PROPOSITION 1. *Given a rate of redistribution τ_t, agents in generation t choose a common labor supply and savings rate: $l_t = \chi(1 - \tau_t)^{1/\eta}$ and $e_t^i = s\hat{y}_t^i$, where $\chi^\eta \equiv (\delta/\eta)(1 - \rho + \rho\beta)/(1 - \rho)$ and $s \equiv \rho\beta/(1 - \rho + \rho\beta)$.*

---

[12] When $\tau_t > 0$ the marginal rate rises with pretax income, and agents with average income are made better off: $\bar{y}_t > y_t$. The elasticity of aftertax to pretax income is indeed the "right" measure of equalization: the posttax distribution induced by a fiscal scheme Lorenz-dominates the one induced by another (for all pretax distributions), if and only if the first scheme's elasticity is everywhere smaller [Fellman (1976)].

[13] With the "autarkic" production function (1) the equivalence between the wage-income-equalization and the fiscal-redistribution interpretations of τ_t is immediate. It continues to hold when we move in Section 3.1 to a richer production structure with interacting agents.

[14] See Bénabou (2000) for this version of the model. Some of the formulas change slightly from those presented here for fiscal policy, but without affecting the qualitative nature of any of the results. There are, on the other hand, important quantitative differences between the growth and welfare implications of the two policies; see Bénabou (2002) and Sheshadri and Yuki (2004) for comparative analyzes. Previous models of redistribution centering on education finance include Becker (1964), Loury (1981), Glomm and Ravikumar (1992), Saint-Paul and Verdier (1993), Bénabou (1996b) and Fernandez and Rogerson (1998). On the empirical side, see Krueger (2002) for a comprehensive summary and discussion of the evidence on targeted education and training policy interventions, from preschool to the college level.

The fact that savings are unaffected is due to the imperfect-altruism assumption made regarding preferences.[15] Labor supply, on the other hand, declines in τ_t with an elasticity of $1/\eta$, and this single distortion will suffice to demonstrate how the efficiency costs and benefits of redistributive institutions shape the set of politico-economic equilibria.

Given Proposition 1, and substituting (6) into (3), the law of motion for human wealth is log-linear

$$\ln k^i_{t+1} = \ln \xi^i_{t+1} + \beta(1 - \tau_t) \ln z^i_t + \ln \kappa + \beta \ln s$$
$$+ \left(\alpha + \beta\gamma(1 - \tau_t)\right) \ln k^i_t + \beta\delta(1 - \tau_t) \ln l_t + \beta\tau_t \ln \tilde{y}_t. \tag{8}$$

This linearity reflects the absence of any nonconvexities in the model, making clear that the multiplicity of equilibria will arise solely through the general-equilibrium feedback from the income distribution onto the political determination of τ_t.[16] These simple conditional dynamics also imply that human capital and income always remain lognormally distributed across agents:

$$\ln k^i_t \sim \mathcal{N}\left(m_t, \Delta^2_t\right), \tag{9}$$
$$\ln y^i_t \sim \mathcal{N}\left(\gamma m_t + \delta \ln l_t - v^2/2, \gamma^2 \Delta^2_t + v^2\right), \tag{10}$$

where m_t and Δ^2_t evolve according to two simple linear difference equations obtained by taking means and variances in (8), and given in the Appendix. Since the growth of mean income y_t is of more direct economic interest than that of mean log-income m_t, I present here the equivalent characterization of the economy's dynamic path in terms of two linear difference equations in Δ^2_t and $\ln y_t = m_t + \Delta^2_t/2$.

PROPOSITION 2. *The distributions of human capital and income at time t are given by* (9)–(10), *where* $l_t = \chi(1 - \tau_t)^{1/\eta}$. *The evolution of inequality across generations is governed by*

$$\Delta^2_{t+1} = \left(\alpha + \beta\gamma(1 - \tau_t)\right)^2 \Delta^2_t + \beta^2(1 - \tau_t)^2 v^2 + w^2, \tag{11}$$

and the growth rate of aggregate income by

$$\ln \frac{y_{t+1}}{y_t} = \ln \tilde{\kappa} - (1 - \alpha - \beta\gamma) \ln y_t + \delta(\ln l_{t+1} - \alpha \ln l_t)$$
$$- \mathcal{L}_v(\tau_t)\frac{v^2}{2} - \mathcal{L}_\Delta(\tau_t)\gamma^2\frac{\Delta^2_t}{2}, \tag{12}$$

---

[15] In Bénabou (2002) I develop and calibrate a version of the present model with dynastic preferences, where τ_t does affect the savings rate. On the other hand, agents are then able (and will indeed want) to use additional policy instruments, such as consumption taxes and investment subsidies, to alleviate this distortion.

[16] Or/and a feedback from the distribution onto the technology γ, once it is endogenized later on. By contrast, nearly all models in the literature that feature multiple equilibria rely on investment thresholds [e.g., Galor and Zeira (1993), Banerjee and Newman (1993)], indivisibilities in effort [Piketty (1997)], or nonhomotheticity in preferences [e.g., Moav (2002)]. For a discussion of indivisibilities, see also Mookherjee and Ray (2003).

where $\ln \tilde{\kappa} \equiv \gamma(\ln \kappa + \beta \ln s) - \gamma(1-\gamma)w^2/2$ *is a constant and*

$$\mathfrak{L}_v(\tau) \equiv \beta\gamma(1-\beta\gamma)(1-\tau)^2 \geqslant 0,$$

$$\mathfrak{L}_\Delta(\tau) \equiv \alpha + \beta\gamma(1-\tau)^2 - (\alpha + \beta\gamma(1-\tau))^2 \geqslant 0.$$

Equation (11) shows how inequality in the next generation stems from three sources: the varying abilities of children (w^2), shocks to family income (v^2), and differences in parental human capital (Δ_t^2), which matter both through family income and at-home transmission. Redistribution equalizes the disposable resources available to finance educational investments (but not social backgrounds), thus limiting both cross-sectional inequality and the persistence of family wealth, $\alpha + \beta\gamma(1-\tau_t)$; conversely, it increases *social mobility*.

Equation (12) makes apparent the growth losses from inequality due to credit constraints, and how redistribution's impact on growth involves a trade-off between incentive and investment-allocation effects.[17] The effort distortion corresponds to the term in δ, which declines with parallel increases in τ_t and τ_{t+1}. The reallocation of human capital investments across differentially wealth-constrained agents is captured by the terms in $\mathfrak{L}_v(\tau_t)$ and $\mathfrak{L}_\Delta(\tau_t)$. When $\alpha = 0$ both are equal and proportional to the concavity $\beta\gamma(1-\beta\gamma)$ of the common accumulation technology facing all families: differences in parental human capital and productivity shocks simply combine into variations in disposable income, $(1-\tau_t)^2(\gamma^2\Delta_t^2+v^2)$, which credit constraints then translate into inefficient variations in investment, reducing overall growth proportionately. When $\alpha > 0$, however, disparate family backgrounds k_t^i represent complementary inputs that generate differential returns to investment, thus reducing the desirability of equalizing resources. Thus $\mathfrak{L}_\Delta(\tau)$ now differs from $\mathfrak{L}_v(\tau)$ and it is minimized for $\tau = (1-\alpha-\beta\gamma)/(1-\beta\gamma)$, which decreases with α.

The term in $-\ln y_t$ in the growth equation, finally, reflects the standard convergence effect. It disappears under constant aggregate returns, namely when $\alpha + \beta\gamma = 1$, or when the constant κ in (3) is replaced by a knowledge spillover such as

$$\kappa_t \equiv \left(\int_0^i (k_t^i)^\gamma \, \mathrm{d}i\right)^{(1-\alpha-\beta\gamma)/\gamma}. \tag{13}$$

This last variant yields an *endogenous-growth* version of the model, where all the predictions obtained with a constant κ in (12) now directly transpose from short-run growth and long-run per capita income to *long-term growth rates*.

---

[17] See Bénabou (1996b) for an overview of the literature on the relationship between inequality and growth, which is not the main focus of the present paper. In particular, inequality can also have positive effects on growth when there are nonconvexities in either the investment technology [e.g., Galor and Zeira (1993)] or in preferences [e.g., Galor and Moav (1999)]. For recent contributions to the empirical debate, see Forbes (2000) and Banerjee and Duflo (2000).

Are the potential growth-enhancing effects of redistributive policies in the presence of credit constraints significant, or trivial compared to the standard deadweight losses? While the answer must ultimately come from empirical studies of specific policy programs or experiments, recent quantitative models suggest very important long-run effects, ranging from several percentage points of steady-state GDP to several percentage points of long-run growth, depending on the presence of accumulated factors, such as physical capital or knowledge spillovers, that complement individual human capital. Calibrating to US data a model with neither effort distortions nor complementarities, Fernandez and Rogerson (1998) find that complete school finance equalization raises long-run GDP by 3.2%. In a model with both educational and financial bequests, Sheshadri and Yuki (2004) find that a mix of fiscal and educational redistribution that approximates current US policies raises long-run income by 13.5%, relative to laissez-faire. This more substantial impact primarily reflects the induced adjustment of physical capital, but it remains a level effect due to decreasing returns to the two types of capital together. In a dynastic-utility version of the present model with endogenous growth [Bénabou (2002)], I find that the growth-maximizing value for fiscal redistribution is $\tau_{\text{fisc}} = 21\%$, which corresponds to a share of redistributive transfers in GDP of 6%; in spite of reduced labor supply this raises the long-run growth rate by 0.5 percentage points. Under the alternative policy of progressive education finance, the growth-maximizing equalization rate for school expenditures is $\tau_{\text{educ}} = 62\%$, which raises long-run growth by 2.4 percentage points. In both cases, the efficient policy involves the top 30% of families subsidizing the bottom 70%, whether through the fiscal or the education system.

1.3. Voter preferences, political power and equilibrium policy

I now turn to the determination of policy, which reflects both individual citizens' preferences and the allocation of power in the political system. In each generation, before the productivity shocks z_t^i are realized, agents vote on the rate of redistribution τ_t to which they will be subject; again, this could be through the fiscal system, labor market regulation, or education finance. Applying Propositions 1 and 2 to Equations (4)–(5), an individual i's intertemporal welfare U_t^i can be computed from (5) as a function of the proposed policy τ_t, his endowment k_t^i, and the overall distribution of human capital (m_t, Δ_t), which is the system's state variable.[18] Defining the composite efficiency parameter

$$B \equiv a + \rho(1-a)(1-\beta) \geqslant 0, \tag{14}$$

whose interpretation is given below, the resulting first-order condition for agent i's ideal

---

[18] See the Appendix. Note that due to the model's overlapping-generations structure, voting involves no intertemporal strategic considerations.

tax rate takes the form

$$\frac{\partial U_t^i}{\partial \tau_t} = (1 - \rho + \rho\beta)$$

$$\times \left[\gamma \left(m_t - \ln k_t^i \right) - \frac{\delta}{\eta} \left(\frac{\tau}{1 - \tau} \right) + (1 - \tau)\left(\gamma^2 \Delta_t^2 + B v^2 \right) \right] = 0. \quad (15)$$

The first term inside the brackets, which disappears when summing across agents, reflects the basic redistributive conflict: since τ_t reallocates resources (spent on both consumption and children's education) from rich to poor households, the latter want it to be high, and the former, low. The next two terms represent the *aggregate welfare cost* and *aggregate welfare benefit* of a marginal increase in τ_t. First, there is the deadweight loss due to the distortion in effort: it is proportional to the labor supply elasticity $1/\eta$, and vanishes at $\tau = 0$. Second, the term $(1 - \tau_t)(\gamma^2 \Delta_t^2 + B v^2)$, which is maximized for $\tau_t = 1$, embodies the (marginal) efficiency gains that arise from better insurance and the redistribution of resources towards more severely credit-constrained investments. Indeed it is clear from (14) that the composite parameter B multiplying the variance of adults' income shocks v^2 is monotonically related to both *risk-aversion a* and to the extent of *decreasing returns* in human-capital investment, $1 - \beta$.[19] As to initial income inequality, the term $\gamma^2 \Delta_t^2$ reflects two motives for redistribution.[20] First, relaxing preexisting credit constraints tends to increase overall growth [see the last term in (12)], and therefore also average welfare. Second, with concave (logarithmic) utility functions, average welfare increases whenever individual consumptions (of c_t^i and k_{t+1}^i) are distributed more equally. Equivalently here, this captures the effect of skewness: given m_t, a higher Δ_t^2 implies a higher per capita income $\ln y_t = m_t + \Delta_t^2/2$, making redistribution more attractive for the median voter, and more generally at any given level of k_t^i.

From this analysis it easily follows that agent i's preferred tax rate, obtained as the unique solution $\tau_t^i < 1$ to the quadratic Equation (15), decreases with his endowment k_t^i and increases with the ex-ante benefits from redistribution $B v^2$. Similarly, $|\tau_t^i|$ decreases with $1/\eta$, as a more elastic labor supply magnifies the distortions that result from redistributive policies – whether progressive, $\tau > 0$, or regressive, $\tau < 0$.

I now turn from the preferences of different classes of voters to their political power or influence over the process that determines the actual τ_t. Even in advanced democracies, poor and less educated individuals have a lower propensity to register, turn out to vote and give political contributions, than better-off ones. For voting itself the tendency is relatively moderate, whereas for contributing to campaigns it is drastic. Even for political activities that are time- rather than money-intensive, such as writing to

---

[19] More specifically, under constant returns ($\beta = 1$) the term $(1 - \rho + \rho\beta)B v^2$ reduces to $a(1 - \tau)v^2$, which is the insurance value of a marginal reduction in the lifetime resource risk $(1 - \tau)^2 v^2/2$ faced by agents. Conversely, for risk-neutral agents who care only about their offspring ($a = 0, \rho = 1$) that same term becomes $\beta(1 - \beta)(1 - \tau)v^2$, which is the gain in expected (and aggregate) human capital growth resulting from a marginal decrease in the variability of post-tax resources $(1 - \tau)^2 v^2/2$, given the concavity of the investment technology.

[20] See Bénabou (2000) for the exact decomposition.

Congress, attending meetings, trying to convince others, etc., the propensity to participate rises sharply with income and education. These facts are documented for instance
in Rosenstone and Hansen (1993), while Bartels (2002) provides a striking study of
how they translate into disproportionate political influence. Studying the roll calls of
US senators in three Congresses he finds that their votes are more responsive, by a
factor ranging from 3 to 15, to the views of their constituents located the 75th income
percentile than to those of the 25th; and again more responsive, by a factor of 2–3, to the
views of the 99th percentile than to those of the 75th. In less developed countries there
is also extensive vote-buying, clientelism, intimidation and the like, which are likely to
result in even more bias.

To summarize this political influence of human and financial wealth in a simple manner I shall assume that *the pivotal voter is located at the* $100 \times p^*$th *percentile* of the
distribution, where the critical level p^* can be any number in $[0, 1]$. A perfect democracy corresponds to $p^* = 1/2$, while an imperfect one where participation or influence
rises with social status corresponds to $p^* > 1/2$.[21] Given that k_t^i is here log-normally
distributed, an equivalent but more convenient measure of the political system's departure from the democratic ideal is

$$\lambda \equiv \Phi^{-1}(p^*), \tag{16}$$

where $\Phi(\cdot)$ denotes the c.d.f. of a standard normal. I shall refer to λ as the degree of
wealth bias in the political system, and focus on the empirically relevant case where
$\lambda > 0$.[22] Given the location of the pivotal voter, the policy outcome is simply obtained
by setting $\ln k_t^i - m_t = \lambda \Delta_t$ in the first-order condition $\partial U_t^i / \partial \tau = 0$. This yields the
quadratic equation

$$\frac{1}{1 - \tau_t} = \frac{1}{\lambda} \left[\frac{\gamma^2 \Delta_t^2 + B v^2}{\gamma \Delta_t} - \frac{\tau_t}{\eta \gamma \Delta_t (1 - \tau_t)^2} \right]. \tag{17}$$

When labor supply is inelastic ($1/\eta = 0$), it is immediately apparent that this equilibrium tax rate is U-shaped in Δ_t, and minimized where $\gamma^2 \Delta^2 = B v^2$. This is true more
generally.

PROPOSITION 3. *The rate of redistribution* $\tau_t = T(\Delta_t)$ *chosen in generation t is such
that*

---

[21] Since individual preferences are single-peaked and the preferred policy is monotonic in k_t^i, it is easy to
show that such a critical p^* is a sufficient statistic for any *ordinal* weighing scheme where each agent's
opinion is affected by a weight, or relative probability of voting, ω^i (with $\int_0^1 \omega^j \, dj = 1$), that increases
with his *rank* in the distribution of human capital or income. Alternatively, political influence may depend on
individuals' income *levels*. Thus, with ω^i proportional to $(y^i)^\lambda$ it can be shown that the pivotal voter has rank
$p^* = \Phi(\lambda \Delta)$, so that λ in (16) is simply replaced by $\lambda \Delta$. As intuition suggests, this alternative formulation
only reinforces the key result that efficient redistributions may decline with inequality, since it implies that
the political system tends to becomes more biased towards the wealthy as inequality rises.
[22] Recent papers that aim to endogenously explain the allocation of political power in a country (corresponding here to the parameter λ) include Bourguignon and Verdier (2000), Pineda and Rodriguez (2000),
Acemoglu and Robinson (2000) and Baland and Robinson (2003).

(1) τ_t *increases with the ex-ante efficiency gain from redistribution* Bv^2 *and decreases with the political influence of wealth,* λ;
(2) $|\tau_t|$ *decreases with the elasticity of labor supply* $1/\eta$;
(3) τ_t *is U-shaped with respect to inequality* Δ_t. *It starts at the ex-ante optimal rate* $T(0) > 0$, *declines to a minimum at some* $\underline{\Delta} > 0$, *then rises back towards* $T(\infty) = 1$. *The larger* Bv^2, *the wider the range* $[0, \underline{\Delta})$ *where* $\partial\tau_t/\partial\Delta_t < 0$.

The first two results show that equilibrium policy depends on the costs and benefits of redistribution and on the allocation of political influence in a sensible manner. The third one confirms the key insight that efficient redistributions may *decrease* with inequality; more specifically, it yields the U-shaped function $\tau = T(\Delta)$ shown on Figure 2. The underlying intuition is simple, and very general: (a) when distributional conflict $\gamma\Delta$ is small enough relative to the ex-ante efficiency gains Bv^2, there is widespread support for the redistributive policy, so its equilibrium level is high; (b) as inequality rises, so does the proportion of agents rich enough to be net losers from the policy, who will *block* all but relatively low levels of τ_t; (c) at still higher levels of inequality, the standard skewness effect eventually dominates: there are so many poor that they *impose* high redistribution, even when it is very inefficient.[23]

It is now well recognized that the standard median-voter model's prediction of a positive effect of inequality on redistribution fails to explain the empirical patterns actually observed, both across countries [see, e.g., Perotti (1996), Bénabou (1996a, 2000), Alesina, Glaeser and Sacerdote (2001)] and within them [see Rodriguez (1999) for panel-data tests on US states]. Among developed countries, in particular, the relationship is in fact negative [Pineda and Rodriguez (2000)]. The present framework explains how and when greater inequality will indeed *reduce* redistribution, or even result in *regressive* policies – both in the short run (Proposition 3) and in the long-run, where both are endogenous (Proposition 4). Furthermore, the distinctive *nonmonotonic* relationship predicted by the model turns out to have empirical support: in tests using cross-country data, Figini (1999) finds in a significant U-shaped effect of income inequality on the shares of tax revenues and government expenditures in GDP; De Mello and Tiongson (2003) find a similar pattern for government transfers.

2. Sustainable social contracts

2.1. Dynamics and steady states

The joint evolution of inequality and policy is described by the recursive dynamical system

$$\begin{cases} \tau_t = T(\Delta_t), \\ \Delta_{t+1} = \mathfrak{D}(\Delta_t, \tau_t), \end{cases} \tag{18}$$

---

[23] A similar form of nonmonotonicity (U-shape, or even declining throughout for λ high enough) is obtained with a Pareto distribution by Lee and Roemer (1998).

where $T(\Delta_t)$ is given by Proposition 3 and $\mathfrak{D}(\Delta_t, \tau_t)$ by (11). Under a time-invariant policy, in particular, long-run inequality decreases with redistribution

$$\Delta_\infty^2 = \frac{w^2 + \beta^2(1 - \tau)^2 v^2}{1 - (\alpha + \beta\gamma(1 - \tau))^2} \equiv D^2(\tau). \tag{19}$$

A steady-state equilibrium is an intersection of this downward-sloping locus, $\Delta = D(\tau)$, with the U-shaped curve $\tau = T(\Delta)$, as illustrated in Figure 2. The following key proposition identifies the conditions under which multiple intersections occur.

PROPOSITION 4. *Let* $1 - \alpha < 2\beta\gamma$. *When the normalized efficiency gain B is below some critical value* $\underline{B}$ *there is a unique, stable, steady state. When* $B > \underline{B}$, *on the other hand, there exist* $\underline{\lambda}$ *and* $\bar{\lambda}$ *with* $0 < \underline{\lambda} < \bar{\lambda}$, *such that:*
(1) *For each* λ *in* $[\underline{\lambda}, \bar{\lambda}]$ *there are (at least) two stable steady states.*[24]
(2) *For* $\lambda < \underline{\lambda}$ *or* $\lambda > \bar{\lambda}$ *the steady state is unique.*

These results can shed light on a number of important issues and puzzles raised in the Introduction.

First, they explain how countries with similar economic and political fundamentals can nonetheless sustain very different redistributive institutions, such as a *European-style welfare state* and a *US-style laissez-faire social contract*. Notably, these two societies cannot be Pareto ranked. Recall also that τ_t can be equally interpreted as describing tax-and-transfer policy, labor market regulation, or (with some minor changes) education finance policy. Moreover, it is clear that the model's key mechanism makes these multiple dimensions of policy complementary, so that they will tend to covary positively across countries, as indeed they do empirically. A more egalitarian education system, for instance, tends to reduce income inequality, which in turn increases political support for fiscal redistribution or labor-earnings compression – and vice versa. Summarizing a large collective research project on Sweden, Freeman (1995) emphasizes the presence of such complementarities, describing "*a highly interrelated welfare state and economy in which many parts fit together (be they subsidies, taxes, wage compression etc.)*".

Second, the two conditions required for multiplicity embody *very general intuitions* that are easily understood in the context of Figure 2. To start with, the ex-ante welfare benefits of redistribution must be high enough, relative to the costs.[25] Otherwise the T curve will be upward-sloping except over a very narrow initial range, and consequently have a unique intersection with the D curve; economically speaking, we would be close to the standard, complete-markets case. In addition, the political power of the wealthy must lie in some intermediate range, otherwise the T curve will lie too high or

---

[24] See Bénabou (2000) for additional results on the number of stable steady states ($n \leqslant 4$), including conditions ensuring that $n = 2$.

[25] The claim with respect to the benefits is clear from Proposition 4; with respect to the costs one can show, under additional technical assumptions, that the threshold $\underline{B}$ shifts up as the labor supply elasticity $1/\eta$ rises.

too low relative to the D curve, and again there will be a unique intersection, with high inequality and low redistribution, or vice-versa.

Third, while in the short-run the relationship is nonmonotonic, there emerges in the long-run a *negative* correlation between inequality and redistribution, as indeed one observes between the United States and Europe, or among advanced countries in general [Pineda and Rodriguez (2000)].

Fourth, *history matters* in an important and plausible way: temporary shocks to the distribution of wealth (immigration, educational discrimination, demand shifts) as well as to the political system (slavery, voting rights restrictions) can permanently move society from one equilibrium to the other, or more generally have long-lasting effects on inequality, growth, and institutions. In particular, the model provides a formalization of Engerman and Sokoloff's (1997) thesis about the historical origins of South and North America's very different development paths, which they trace back to the former set of New World colonies having had much higher initial inequality (Δ_0) and a much more concentrated power structure (λ_0) than the latter.[26]

Finally, the model also shows that *different sources of inequality* have different effects on redistributive institutions – which, in particular, sheds doubt on the possibility of empirically estimating a catch-all relationship between inequality and redistribution, or inequality and growth. Indeed, one can show (provided $1/\eta$ is not too large) that the threshold for multiplicity $\underline{B}$ is a decreasing function of the variance ratio v^2/w^2, with $\lim_{v/w \to 0}(\underline{B}) = +\infty$ and $\lim_{v/w \to +\infty}(\underline{B}) = 0$. Quite intuitively, income *uncertainty* interacts with the incompleteness in insurance and credit markets in generating ex-ante efficiency gains from redistribution, as reflected by the term Bv^2 in (17). By contrast, a greater variance w^2 of the endowments that agents receive *prior* to choosing policy increases the distributional conflict between *identifiable losers and gainers* from the policy. Thus, whereas an increase in the variability of sectoral shocks (similar to v^2) will lead to an expansion of the welfare state, a surge in immigration that results in a greater heterogeneity of the population (similar to a rise in w^2) can easily lead to cutbacks, or even a large-scale dismantling. We shall observe similar effects when studying the political implications of skill-biased technical change.

2.2. Which societies grow faster?

As mentioned earlier, the steady states corresponding to different social contracts are not Pareto-rankable: rich enough agents always prefer a more laissez-faire society, while those who are poor enough always want more of a welfare state. One may still ask, however, how these two social models compare in terms of aggregate growth. This question is important first for its policy content, and second to know whether one should expect any empirical relationship between inequality and growth, when account is taken

---

[26] This, in turn, was due to reasons linked to the technologies required for the different goods these colonies were producing – a point I shall come back to in Section 3.1.

of the fact that *both* are endogenous. The answer hinges on the basic trade-off, discussed earlier, between the distortions induced by redistribution and its beneficial effect on credit-constraints (magnified, in the long run, by the fact that it also reduces income inequality $\gamma \Delta_\infty$). This is made clear by the following results, which apply equally in the short and in the long run.[27]

PROPOSITION 5. *Compared to a more laissez-faire alternative τ', a more redistributive social contract $\tau > \tau'$ is associated with lower inequality, and*

(1) *has higher growth when tax distortions are small ($1/\eta \approx 0$) relative to those induced by credit constraints on the accumulation of human capital ($\beta\gamma < 1$);*

(2) *has lower growth when tax distortions are high ($1/\eta > 0$) and the credit-constraint effect is weak ($\beta\gamma \approx 1$).*

The first scenario, of *"growth-enhancing redistributions"*, seems most relevant for developing countries, where capital markets are less well functioning, and for redistribution through public investments in human capital and health. One may contrast here the paths followed by East Asia and Latin America in those respects. The result may also help understand why regression estimates of the effects of social and educational transfers on growth are often significantly positive, or at least rarely significantly negative.

The second, *"Eurosclerosis"* scenario can account for why Europeans consistently choose more social insurance than Americans – at the cost of higher unemployment and slower growth – even though they are not necessarily more risk-averse. The intuition is that, in more homogeneous societies, there is less erosion of the consensus over social insurance mechanisms which, ex-ante, would be valued enough to compensate for lesser growth prospects.[28]

Putting the two cases together, finally, Proposition 5 can also be related to the empirical findings of Barro (2000) that inequality tends to be negatively associated with subsequent growth in poor countries, but positively associated with it in richer ones. To the extent that poor countries are also those where credit markets are least developed, Proposition 5 predicts that inequality-reducing policies will give rise to just such a dichotomy.

3. Technology and the social contract

I shall now extend the model to analyze how technology and redistributive institutions both affect inequality and respond to it, and consequently how they *influence each*

---

[27] See Section 1.2 for the simple correspondence between the stationary and the endogenous-growth versions of the model, where policy affects growth in the short- and the long-run, respectively.

[28] For the specific case of unemployment insurance, Hassler and Rodriguez-Mora (1999) provide a complementary explanation, based on interactions with workers' specialization (or lack thereof) that can result in multiple equilibria.

other – as described on Figure 1. Of particular interest are the following questions. First, how does technical change impact the sustainability of welfare-state and laissez-faire social contracts? Second, what types of societies are likely to be leaders or early adopters in developing or implementing flexible, skill-biased technologies or organizational forms? More generally, how do the skill distribution among workers and the production side of the economy shape each other, through human capital investments and technology choices? Finally, what happens in the long run when technological and institutional factors evolve interdependently – within a country, and possibly even across countries?

3.1. Exogenous technical change and the viability of the welfare state

I first examine here how technical or organizational change that increases the return to human capital affects redistributive institutions. This policy response represents an additional channel through which technological evolutions affect the income distribution, in addition to their direct impact via the wage structure.

Figure 3 illustrates the effects of an increase in γ, the coefficient on human capital in the production and earnings function (1). As will from now on be made explicit in the notation, this affects both of the key curves describing the inequality-redistribution nexus:

(i) The intergenerational-transmission locus $\Delta = D(\tau; \gamma)$ shifts up, and becomes less steep: for any given human capital inequality Δ_t and policy τ there is more inequality in incomes $\gamma \Delta_t$, hence also in investments, and consequently more inequality of human capital (and of course income) in all subsequent periods.[29]

(ii) The policy locus $\tau = T(\gamma \Delta)$ shifts down over $[0, \underline{\Delta})$, and up over $(\underline{\Delta}, +\infty)$: since what matters for the political outcome is *income* inequality $\gamma \Delta$ [see (17)], an increase in γ for given Δ has the same U-shaped effect on redistribution as an increase in Δ for given γ – initially lowering τ, then raising it.

Figure 3 directly yields a local analysis of the more egalitarian, welfare-state equilibrium – and more generally, of any steady state that occurs along the declining portion of the T locus.[30]

---

[29] Recall that a worker's human capital reflects his individual ability, family background, and parental investment in education: $k_t^i = \kappa \xi_t^i (k_{t-1}^i)^\alpha (e_{t-1}^i)^\beta$. The kind of technical change considered here raises the return to all three components of k_t^i equally. In Galor and Tsiddon (1997) by contrast, major innovations raise the relative return to pure ability, whereas subsequent learning-by-doing innovations raise the relative return to inherited human capital. In Galor and Moav (2000) human capital is also sector-specific, and therefore eroded by new technologies, to an extent that decreases with individual ability. In these models technological innovations can thus raise as well as lower intergenerational mobility.

[30] For steady-states that occur on the rising part, local comparative statics are ambiguous. Note, however, that in versions of the model where power inequality rises with income or human wealth inequality – meaning that λ increases with Δ (see footnote 21) – the declining portion of the locus is wider and the increasing portion reduced, making it easier to rule out such equilibria. For instance, if political power ω_i is proportional to $(y_i)^\lambda$ – e.g., "one dollar, one vote" for $\lambda = 1$ – then λ is simply replaced by $\lambda \Delta$ everywhere. As seen from (17), for $1/\eta = 0$ the $T(\gamma \Delta)$ curve is then decreasing throughout.

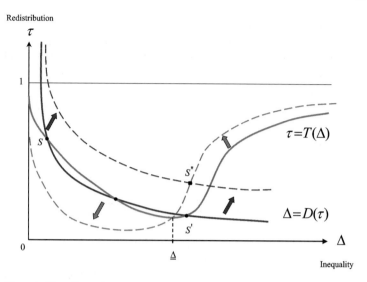

Figure 3. The effects of an increase in the returns to human capital, $\gamma = (\sigma - 1)/\sigma$.

PROPOSITION 6. *Let (Δ, τ, γ) be such that (Δ, τ) is a stable steady state under the technology γ, with $\Delta < \underline{\Delta}(Bv^2; \gamma)$. A marginal increase in γ results in higher long-run human capital and income inequality, as well as in less redistribution.*

The policy response thus amplifies the direct effect of skill-biased technical progress on disposable incomes – and, over time, on the distributions of human capital and earnings. Figure 3 also suggests that it can have, in the long run, much more drastic consequences for redistributive institutions: starting from a situation with multiple steady states, an increase in γ tends to undermine the sustainability of the "Welfare-State" equilibrium. Similarly, we shall see that starting from a configuration with a single "Welfare-State" it can make a second, "Laissez-Faire" equilibrium appear. Such a *global* analysis is potentially quite complicated, however, since in general there may be more than two stable equilibria, and some may also occur in the upward-sloping portion of the $\tau = T(\gamma \Delta)$ locus, where the policy response has a dampening rather than an amplifying effect on inequality. To demonstrate the most interesting insights, I shall therefore impose some simplifying assumptions. First, I restrict voters to a choice between only two policies:

- A generous *"Welfare State"* social contract, corresponding to a relatively high rate of redistribution $\bar{\tau} \in (0, 1)$.
- A more *"Laissez Faire"* social contract, corresponding to a relatively low rate of redistribution $\underline{\tau} \in (0, \bar{\tau})$.

Once again, τ can be interpreted as corresponding to either fiscal redistribution, wage compression through labor market regulation, or education finance progressivity. To further simplify the problem I abstract from labor supply distortions ($1/\eta = 0$) and assume that B is large enough that both potential steady states are always on the downward-sloping part of the $\tau = T(\Delta\gamma)$ curve, which is the one of most interest.[31]

Given an initial distribution of human capital Δ_t, the more redistributive policy $\tau_t = \bar{\tau}$ is adopted over $\tau_t = \underline{\tau}$ if $U_t^i(\bar{\tau}) > U_t^i(\underline{\tau})$ for at least a critical fraction $p^* \equiv \Phi(\lambda)$ of the population. Note from (15) that with $1/\eta = 0$, $\partial U_t^i/\partial\tau_t$ is linear in τ_t, so the preceding inequality evaluated at $\ln k_t^i = m_t + \lambda\Delta_t$ takes the form

$$(\bar{\tau} - \underline{\tau})\left[\gamma\lambda\Delta_t + (1 - \underline{\tau})(\gamma^2\Delta_t^2 + Bv^2)\right] < (\bar{\tau} - \underline{\tau})^2\left(\frac{\gamma^2\Delta_t^2 + Bv^2}{2}\right),$$

or

$$\lambda < \left(1 - \frac{\bar{\tau} + \underline{\tau}}{2}\right)\left(\gamma\Delta_t + \frac{Bv^2}{\gamma\Delta_t}\right). \tag{20}$$

We first see that the *political influence of wealth* must not be too large, compared to the *aggregate welfare gain* from redistribution relative to laissez faire (net of the dead-weight loss, which I am here abstracting from). Second, preexisting income inequality *raises the hurdle* that public policy must overcome, as the ex-ante benefit term Bv^2 is divided by $\gamma\Delta_t$. This effect impedes the adoption of more redistributive institutions ($\tau = \bar{\tau}$) where they had not previously been in place, because of the greater divergence of interests that results over time from a more laissez-faire system ($\tau = \underline{\tau}$). Pushing in the other direction – namely, intensifying the demand for redistribution as inequality rises – are the effects of skewness and initial credit-constraints, reflected in the additive term $\gamma\Delta_t$. As a result of these offsetting forces, the right-hand side of (20) is U-shaped in $\gamma\Delta_t$. To focus on the long-run, let us now replace human capital inequality Δ_t with its asymptotic value under a technology γ and a constant policy τ – namely, by (11),

$$D(\tau, \gamma) \equiv \sqrt{\frac{w^2 + \beta^2(1 - \tau)^2 v^2}{1 - (\alpha + \beta\gamma(1 - \tau))^2}}, \tag{21}$$

which is the long-run inequality in human capital resulting from a constant policy τ and technology γ. Given γ, the policy-inequality pair $(\bar{\tau}, D(\tau, \gamma))$ is thus a politico-economic steady state if

$$\lambda < \left(1 - \frac{\bar{\tau} + \underline{\tau}}{2}\right)\left(\gamma D(\tau, \gamma) + \frac{Bv^2}{\gamma D(\tau, \gamma)}\right) \equiv \bar{\lambda}(\gamma; B). \tag{22}$$

---

[31] The required condition appears in Proposition 7. It is thus not inevitably the case that skill-biased technical progress leads to a retrenchment of redistributive institutions; the model allows for the reverse case, for steady-states that occur on the rising part of the T locus. The case on which I focus, however, appears to be the most relevant for recent trends, and in any case is the more robust, since: (i) when multiple steady states exist, there is always at least one the declining part; (ii) in simple and plausible variants of the model, the T locus is decreasing throughout (see footnote 30).

Conversely, the laissez-faire configuration $(\underline{\tau}, D(\underline{\tau}, \gamma))$ is a politico-economic steady state given γ if

$$\lambda > \left(1 - \frac{\bar{\tau} + \underline{\tau}}{2}\right)\left(\gamma D(\underline{\tau}, \gamma) + \frac{Bv^2}{\gamma D(\underline{\tau}, \gamma)}\right) \equiv \underline{\lambda}(\gamma; B). \tag{23}$$

The two regimes coexist if and only if $\underline{\lambda}(\gamma; B) < \bar{\lambda}(\gamma; B)$, or

$$\frac{\bar{\lambda}(\gamma; B) - \underline{\lambda}(\gamma; B)}{\gamma D(\underline{\tau}, \gamma) - \gamma D(\bar{\tau}, \gamma)} = \left(1 - \frac{\bar{\tau} + \underline{\tau}}{2}\right)\left(\frac{Bv^2}{\gamma^2 D(\bar{\tau}, \gamma) D(\underline{\tau}, \gamma)} - 1\right). \tag{24}$$

We thus obtain here the analogue, for a discrete policy choice, of Proposition 4: multiplicity requires that B be large enough compared to income inequality (and, in general, to $1/\eta$),

$$B > \left(\frac{\gamma^2}{v^2}\right) D(\bar{\tau}, \gamma) D(\underline{\tau}, \gamma) \equiv \underline{B}(\gamma), \tag{25}$$

and that the wealth bias λ be neither too high nor too low, given the technology γ: $\lambda \in [\underline{\lambda}, \bar{\lambda}]$, defined by (22)–(23).[32] Now, furthermore, we shall see that (under appropriate conditions) the *skill bias* γ must also be neither too high nor too low, given λ. This result is illustrated in Figure 4.

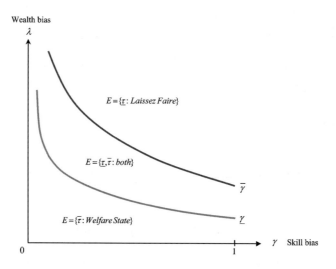

Figure 4. Technology, political influence, and the social contract. E denotes the set of stable steady-states.

---

[32] Note also that as B increases both $\underline{\lambda}$ and $\bar{\lambda}$ rise, but (24) shows that the interval $[\underline{\lambda}, \bar{\lambda}]$ widens. When (25) does not hold, on the other hand, we have $\bar{\lambda} < \underline{\lambda}$. For $\lambda \notin [\bar{\lambda}, \underline{\lambda}]$ there is a unique steady state, but for $\lambda \in [\bar{\lambda}, \underline{\lambda}]$ the economy can instead be shown to cycle between the two regimes, as in Gradstein and Justman (1997). This feature reflects the restriction of policy to a binary choice.

PROPOSITION 7. *Let $1/\eta = 0$ and $Bv^2 > \gamma_{\max} D(\underline{\tau}, \gamma_{\max})$, where $\gamma_{\max} \equiv (1 - \alpha)/\beta$. There exist two skill-bias thresholds $\underline{\gamma}(\lambda; B) < \bar{\gamma}(\lambda; B)$, both decreasing in λ and increasing in B, such that*

    (i) *for $\gamma < \underline{\gamma}(\lambda; B)$, the unique steady state corresponds to the welfare-state outcome $(\bar{\tau}, \bar{D}(\bar{\tau}, \gamma))$;*

    (ii) *for $\gamma \in [\underline{\gamma}(\lambda; B), \bar{\gamma}(\lambda; B)]$, both $(\bar{\tau}, D(\bar{\tau}, \gamma))$ and $(\underline{\tau}, D(\underline{\tau}, \gamma))$ are stable steady states;*

    (iii) *for $\gamma \in [\bar{\gamma}(\lambda; B), \gamma_{\max}]$, the unique steady state is laissez-faire, $(\underline{\tau}, D(\underline{\tau}, \gamma))$.*

These results have a number of important implications.

First, they confirm that *the Welfare State becomes unsustainable* when technology becomes too skill-biased; and, conversely, that multiple social contracts can coexist only when γ is in some intermediate range.[33] We see here again at work the general insight that sources of heterogeneity that are predictable on the basis of initial endowments – a greater variance of abilities w^2, as discussed earlier, or greater skill bias γ, as here – push equilibrium institutions towards less redistribution.

Second, Proposition 7 also reveals interesting interactions between *the production and political "technologies"*. As seen on Figure 4, in a country with relatively little wealth bias the welfare state is – for better of for worse – much more "immune" to skill-biased technical change than in one where λ is high. Similarly, a given change in the political system will have very different effects on redistributive institutions, depending on how skill-biased the technology is. Finally, the "surest way" to set out on a course of persistently high inequality and inefficiently regressive (or insufficiently progressive) institutions is to start out with *both* a production structure that generates high wage inequality, and a political system marked by a high degree of bias. As demonstrated by Engerman and Sokoloff (1997), such were the initial conditions found in the plantation-based and natural-resource based colonies of Central and South America in the 16th and 17th centuries – in contrast to those of North America, where agriculture was not subject to significant increasing returns to scale and initial institutions were much less oligarchic.

Third, our result can also be related to that of Acemoglu, Aghion and Violante (2001), who show that skill-biased technical progress may cause a decline in unionization. While their model is quite different, it shares the two key features emphasized in previous sections. First, relatively rich agents – namely skilled workers – are pivotal, in the sense that it is their willingness to leave or avoid the unionized sector that limits the extent of wage compression. Second, in making this mobility decision – voting with their feet – they trade off redistributive losses (unions redistribute towards unskilled workers, who are a majority in the unionized sector) against ex-ante efficiency benefits:

---

[33] Hassler et al. (2003) also show that the "welfare-state" equilibrium in their model no longer exists above a certain level of skill bias. The mechanism is quite different, however: it is the *anticipation* of a higher skill premium that causes more agents to invest in education – to the point where, ex-post, a majority of them end up with high incomes (the distribution is negatively skewed), and therefore oppose redistribution.

unions provide insurance through wage-sharing and/or a safeguard against the "holdup" by firms of workers' specific human capital investments; even when they play no such role, leaving the unionized sector involves mobility costs. Consequently, when skill-biased technical change makes the interests of the two classes of workers too divergent, redistributive institutions – here, union participation – will decline. Moreover, this can happen inefficiently.[34]

3.2. Skills, technology and income inequality

I now turn to the reverse mechanism and examine how inequality itself *feeds back* onto the nature of technical change, making γ endogenous. Recognizing that individuals do not produce in isolation, I model production interactions with a simple specialization structure where workers perform complementary tasks.[35] Final output is produced by competitive firms, using a continuum of differentiated intermediate inputs

$$y_t = A_t \left(\int_0^\infty z_t(s) x_t(s)^{(\sigma-1)/\sigma} \, ds \right)^{\sigma/(\sigma-1)} , \qquad \sigma \geqslant 1, \tag{26}$$

where $x_t(s)$ denotes the quantity of input s, $z_t(s)$ an i.i.d. sectoral shock, and A_t a TFP parameter. Workers specialize in a single good, which they produce using their human capital and labor. Since they face downward-sloping demand curves each selects a different task, $s(i) = i$, and produces $x_t^i = k_t^i l_t^i$ units, where l_t^i is endogenously chosen. The unit price for his output is thus

$$p_t^i = A_t^{(\sigma-1)/\sigma} z_t^i \left(\frac{k_t^i l_t^i}{y_t} \right)^{-1/\sigma} . \tag{27}$$

The corresponding hourly wages are $\omega_t^i = p_t^i k_t^i$, and the resulting incomes

$$y_t^i = \omega_t^i l_t^i = z_t^i \left(k_t^i l_t^i \right)^{(\sigma-1)/\sigma} A_t^{(\sigma-1)/\sigma} (y_t)^{1/\sigma} \equiv \widetilde{A}_t z_t^i \left(k_t^i \right)^\gamma \left(l_t^i \right)^\delta . \tag{28}$$

This earnings function is exactly the same as in previous sections [see (1)], with

$$\gamma = \delta \equiv \frac{\sigma - 1}{\sigma} , \tag{29}$$

except for the extra TFP factor $\widetilde{A}_t \equiv A_t^{(\sigma-1)/\sigma} (y_t)^{1/\sigma}$, which acts as a shift in the mean of the productivity shocks z_t^i. While $\widetilde{A}_t$ varies endogenously with the economy's state variables (m_t, Δ_t^2), individual workers and voters take it as given in their decisions over

---

[34] Relatedly, note from Figure 4 that a minor change in γ can trigger a significant decline in redistribution from $\bar{\tau}$ to $\underline{\tau}$, and recall from Proposition 5 that the latter can easily lead to lower aggregate growth. The same is clearly true for average welfare, e.g. when $1/\eta = 0$.

[35] Building on those in Bénabou (1996a) and Tamura (1992), themselves based on Romer (1987).

(l_t^i, c_t^i) and their votes over τ_t.[36] Consequently, the entire analysis of earlier sections still applies, with the simple substitution of $\widetilde{A}_t z_t^i$, wherever z_t^i previously appeared. Conditional on γ, distributional dynamics and the political equilibrium thus remain essentially unchanged, and so do the corresponding $\Delta = D(\tau, \gamma)$ and $\tau = T(\gamma \Delta)$ loci.

I now consider firms. Recall that in equilibrium all workers supply the same effort $l_t^i = l_t$ and the distribution of human capital remains log-normal, $\ln k_t^i \sim \mathcal{N}(m_t, \Delta_t^2)$. The output of a representative firm is thus

$$y_t = A_t l_t \left(\int_0^1 \left(k_t^i \right)^{(\sigma-1)/\sigma} di \right)^{\sigma/(\sigma-1)} = A_t l_t e^{-\Delta_t^2/(2\sigma)} \left(\int_0^1 k_t^i \, di \right). \tag{30}$$

Keeping average human capital constant, the loss $e^{-\Delta_t^2/(2\sigma)}$ makes apparent the productivity costs imposed by (excessive) *heterogeneity of the labor force*: poorly educated, insufficiently skilled production and clerical workers drag down the productivity of engineers, managers, scientists, etc. We also see that a production technology with greater substitutability between the tasks performed by different types of workers reduces these costs of skill disparities [Bénabou (1996a), Grossman and Maggi (2000)]. Indeed, this greater *flexibility* allows firms to more easily substitute towards the more productive workers, and correspondingly reduce their dependence on low-skill labor. This may be achieved by internal retooling, reorganization, or by outsourcing certain activities to competitive subcontractors.[37] One can also think of a higher σ as a more discriminating search technology, resulting in more assortative matching between workers – that is, in a more *segregated* production structure [Kremer and Maskin (1996, 2003)].[38]

Naturally, production processes with less complementarity between workers of different skills result in greater inequality of wages and incomes, as they have the effect of *uncoupling* their marginal products,

$$\mathrm{Var}\left[\ln y_t^i \right] = \left(\frac{\sigma_t - 1}{\sigma_t} \right)^2 \Delta_t^2 = \gamma_t^2 \Delta_t^2. \tag{31}$$

3.3. Technological choice and endogenous flexibility

More flexible technologies and production processes require costly investments or reorganizations. Moreover, their benefits to an individual firm are endogenous even in the

---

[36] Note again the role of the overlapping-generations structure with "imperfect" altruism in simplifying the voting problem. Observe also that τ_t can now, as claimed earlier, be interpreted as the extent of *wage income compression*, i.e. the degree of progressivity in the mapping [defined by (6)] from workers' true marginal revenue products y_t^i [given by (28)] to the labor earning they actually receive, $\hat{y}_t^i$.

[37] On organizational change, see for instance Caroli and Van Reenen (1999) and Thesmar and Thoenig (2000).

[38] When labor supply is endogenous, $1/\eta > 0$, a higher σ also induces workers to increase their labor supply, as they face a less elastic demand curve: by Proposition 1, $l_t = \chi(1 - \tau_t)^{1/\eta}$, with now $\gamma = (\sigma - 1)/\sigma$. This effect is independent of any issues of skill heterogeneity or wage inequality, however.

short run (i.e., given the skill composition of the labor force), as they depend on the decisions of other firms, which affect the wage structure.

I therefore now model firms' choices of technology or organizational form, proposing a new and very simple formulation that highlights the roles of heterogeneity and flexibility. In every period, firms have access to a menu of potential technologies with *different elasticities of substitution* $\sigma \in [1, +\infty)$ and associated costs $c(\sigma)$; the latter result in a TFP factor $A(\sigma) = e^{-c(\sigma)}$, with $c' > 0$ and $c'' > 0$.[39] Given the distribution of workers' human capital $\ln k_t^i \sim \mathcal{N}(m, \Delta_t^2)$ and the technology σ_t used by its competitors, each firm chooses its own technology $\hat{\sigma}$ as a best response. This results in a marginal cost of

$$A(\hat{\sigma})^{-1} \left(\int_0^1 (z_t^i)^{\hat{\sigma}} (p_t^i)^{1-\hat{\sigma}} \, di \right)^{1/(1-\hat{\sigma})}. \tag{32}$$

Substituting from (27) for the equilibrium input prices p_t^i and normalizing by the other firms' marginal cost (see the proof of Proposition 8), the firm's relative marginal cost is equal to

$$mc(\hat{\sigma}|\sigma_t) = \left(\frac{A(\sigma_t)}{A(\hat{\sigma})} \right) \left(\int_0^1 (k_t^i)^{(1-\hat{\sigma})/\sigma_t} \, di \right)^{1/(1-\hat{\sigma})}$$
$$\times \left(\int_0^1 (k_t^i)^{(1-\sigma_t)/\sigma_t} \, di \right)^{-1/(1-\sigma_t)},$$

or

$$mc(\hat{\sigma}|\sigma_t) = \exp\left[c(\hat{\sigma}) - c(\sigma_t) + \frac{\Delta_t^2}{2} \left(\frac{\sigma_t - \hat{\sigma}}{\sigma_t^2} \right) \right]. \tag{33}$$

The first-order condition for this convex minimization problem is

$$c'(\hat{\sigma}) = \frac{\Delta_t^2}{2\sigma_t^2}. \tag{34}$$

Intuitively, the marginal benefit of flexibility rises with the variability of skills in the labor force, but decreases with the degree to which other firms choose technologies that allow them to more easily substitute toward better workers, since in doing so they drive up the skill premium.

PROPOSITION 8. *There is a unique symmetric equilibrium in technology choice. The more heterogeneous the workforce, the more flexible and skill-biased the technology used by firms:* $\sigma_t = \sigma^*(\Delta_t)$ *is the solution to* $c'(\sigma^*) = \Delta^2/2(\sigma^*)^2$, *with* $0 < \partial \ln \sigma^* / \partial \ln \Delta < 1$.

---

[39] I thus abstract here from the intertemporal (investment) aspects of innovation that would be part of a more complete (but also more complicated) model of technological change; see, e.g., Acemoglu (1998), Kiley (1999), Lloyd-Ellis (1999) or Aghion (2002).

This result has several interesting implications.

A first one is the *magnification of wage inequality*: the return to human capital $\partial \ln \omega_t^i / \partial \ln k_t^i = (\sigma_t - 1)/\sigma_t$ is higher where the labor force is more heterogeneous, further amplifying wage differentials across educational levels. This simple prediction could be tested empirically across countries and/or time periods.[40]

A second implication is the potential for "*immiserizing technological choices*". Proposition 8 states that σ increases with Δ; conversely, because of credit constraints, human capital heterogeneity itself rises over time with $\gamma = (\sigma - 1)/\sigma$, and in the long run $\Delta = D(\tau, \gamma)$, which is increasing in γ. Could these two mechanisms reinforce each other to the point of resulting in multiple steady states *even under a fixed policy* – whether activist or laissez-faire – and even though, once again, there are no nonconvexities in the model? The idea is that a high degree of skill bias results in very low wages for unskilled workers, severely limiting the extent to which they can invest in human capital (for themselves or their children). This, in turn, leads firms to again choose a very flexible, skill-biased technology in the next period, and so on. Conversely, a less skilled-biased technology and a less dispersed distribution of human wealth could be self-sustaining. To examine this possibility, note first that

$$\frac{\partial \ln \sigma^*}{\partial \ln \Delta} = \left(1 + \frac{1}{2}\frac{c''(\sigma_t)}{c'(\sigma_t)}\right)^{-1} < 1 \tag{35}$$

by Proposition 8, while (21) yields

$$\frac{\partial \ln D(\tau, \gamma)}{\partial \ln \sigma} = \frac{\beta(1-\gamma)(1-\tau)(\alpha + \beta\gamma(1-\tau))}{1 - (\alpha + \beta\gamma(1-\tau))^2}, \tag{36}$$

where, as usual, $\gamma = (\sigma - 1)/\sigma$. If the product of these two derivatives is everywhere less than 1, there is a unique equilibrium. If it exceeds 1 for some value of σ, on the other hand, there may be multiplicity. It is easily verified that $\partial D(\tau, \gamma)/\partial \ln \sigma < 1$ if and only if

$$\left(\alpha + \beta\gamma(1-\tau)\right)\left(\alpha + \beta(1-\tau)\right) < 1. \tag{37}$$

The first term is always less than one (or else inequality explodes; moreover, this can never occur when τ is endogenously chosen), but the second need not be, especially if $\tau < 0$. We can thus conclude that the kind of "*technology-inequality trap*" described above becomes a real possibility under *regressive or insufficiently progressive* policies. In particular, education systems that result in significant resource disparities between students, such as private financing or local (property-tax based) school funding as in the United States, are fertile ground for the joint emergence of highly skill-biased production processes and a persistently skewed skill distribution. Furthermore, as we shall see

---

[40] Kremer and Maskin (1996) present evidence for a related intervening mechanism (similar to $\partial \sigma^*/\partial \Delta > 0$ in this model), although not for how educational returns and wage inequality are ultimately affected. They show that in US states characterized by greater human capital inequality, there is more segregation of workers by skills (the ratio of within- to between-plant skill dispersion is lower).

further, endogenizing τ only increases the likelihood of such outcomes, since the degree of redistribution tends to fall with inequality.

A third point is that even under the less extreme conditions where no such trap exists, firms' decisions involve a *dynamic externality* that tends to result in *excessively skill-biased* or flexible technologies. Indeed, each takes the distribution of skills it faces as given but neglects the effects of its own flexibility on workers' human capital invest-ments, and therefore on subsequent distributions. More specifically, while a marginal change in σ_t has only second-order effects on the current production costs faced by firms, it has three first-order effects on growth.[41] First, a lower σ_t would reduce cur-rent income inequality $\gamma_t \Delta_t$, which is growth enhancing given the presence of credit constraints. This would in turn lower the skill disparities Δ_{t+k} that firms will face in the future, as well as the costs $c(\sigma^*(\Delta_{t+k}))$ they will bear to adapt to this heterogene-ity. Although $\gamma_t = (\sigma_t - 1)/\sigma_t$ also affects in a somewhat complex way the concavity of educational investment (where it interacts with α, β and τ_t), it is easy to identify cases where growth *in every period* would be higher if firms collectively chose less skill-biased technologies.

For instance, let $\alpha = 0$, $\beta = 1$ and $1/\eta = 0$ (inelastic labor supply), and fix any constant policy τ; the interactions of technology choice and policy decisions will be ex-amined in the next section. In the resulting steady state, the degree of flexibility and the dispersion in skills are given by the two equations $\sigma_\infty = \sigma^*(\Delta_\infty)$ and $\Delta_\infty = D(\tau, \gamma_\infty)$, where $\gamma_\infty \equiv (\sigma_\infty - 1)/\sigma_\infty$.[42] The corresponding asymptotic growth rate is computed in the Appendix, and equals

$$g_\infty = \ln \kappa + \ln s - c(\sigma_\infty) - \frac{D(\tau, \gamma_\infty)^2}{2\sigma_\infty}. \tag{38}$$

A marginal reduction in σ from its equilibrium value, if it were permanently imple-mented by all firms, would then increase steady-state growth, since

$$\left. \frac{\partial g_\infty}{\partial \sigma} \right|_{\sigma=\sigma_\infty} = -c'(\sigma_\infty) + \frac{\Delta_\infty^2}{2\sigma_\infty^2} - \frac{1}{2\sigma_\infty} \left(\left. \frac{\partial D^2(\tau, \gamma_\infty)}{\partial \sigma} \right|_{\sigma=\sigma_\infty} \right)$$

$$= -\frac{1}{2\sigma_\infty^3} \left(\frac{\partial D^2(\tau, \gamma_\infty)}{\partial \gamma} \right) < 0. \tag{39}$$

In this expression the first two terms cancel out by the first-order condition (34), while the last one reflects the dynamic externality. The above result holds more generally for any equilibrium path that is either near the steady state, or such that σ_t converges to its long-run value from above (see the Appendix).

---

[41] As explained in footnote 38, when $1/\eta > 0$ a higher σ_t also raises the return to labor supply $\delta_t = (\sigma_t - 1)/\sigma_t$, inducing all agents to work more.

[42] I assume here that (37) holds, so that this steady state is unique (given τ), although this is inessential to the argument.

Inefficient choices of technology or firm organization arise in a number of models where market imperfections create an excessive role for the distribution of financial or human wealth to shape the structure of production, with the result of exacerbating inequality and making it more persistent. In Banerjee and Newman (1993) and Legros and Newman (1996), for instance, the moral-hazard problem affecting entrepreneurship combines with an unequal wealth distribution in forcing too many agents to work for low wages in large firms, rather than setting up their own. In Vindigni (2002) an extreme example of the technology trap studied above occurs, as firms' decisions (choosing the arrival rate of exogenously skill-biased innovations) can permanently confine some dynasties of workers below the fixed income threshold required to invest in human capital.[43] In Grossman (2004), a high variance of human capital in the labor force increases the incentives of the most skilled agents to work in sectors where individual productivity is observable, rather than in those where output is team-determined; because they fail to internalize the spillovers they would have on team productivity, the resulting occupational segregation is inefficiently high.

4. Endogenous institutions and endogenous technology

Combining the main mechanisms analyzed in previous sections yields a model where the distribution of human capital, the technologies used by firms and the policy implemented by the state are all endogenous – as they are in reality. The dynamical system governing the economy's evolution remains recursive:

$$
\begin{cases}
\gamma_t = \Gamma(\Delta_t), \\
\tau_t = T(\Delta_t \gamma_t), \\
\Delta_{t+1} = \mathcal{D}(\Delta_t, \tau_t; \gamma_t),
\end{cases}
\tag{40}
$$

where $\Gamma(\Delta) \equiv (\sigma^*(\Delta) - 1)/\sigma^*(\Delta)$ represents the technology outcome given by Proposition 8, $T(\gamma \Delta)$ the policy outcome given by Proposition 3 and $\mathcal{D}(\Delta, \tau, \gamma)$ the transmission of human capital inequality given in Proposition 2. The resulting aggregate growth rate, $\ln(y_{t+1}/y_t) = g(\tau_t, \Delta_t, \gamma_t)$, follows from Proposition 2. Finally, steady states are solutions to the fixed-point equation

$$
\Delta = \mathcal{D}\big(\Delta, T\big(\Delta; \Gamma(\Delta)\big), \Gamma(\Delta)\big).
\tag{41}
$$

This structure makes clear the presence of important *multiplier effects*: a transitory shock affecting inequality (e.g., more idiosyncratic uncertainty v^2) or the political system (a higher λ) will be amplified through technology decisions, the policy choice, and

---

[43] A more benign form of multiplicity (with greater wage inequality now going together with more, rather than less, total human capital) occurs in Acemoglu (1998). In his model, a relative abundance of skilled workers makes it more profitable for firms to develop skill-biased technologies; this then raises the wage premium, encouraging more workers to become skilled.

the intergenerational transmission mechanism, and may thus have considerable long-term consequences.[44] Most importantly, in accounting for changes in inequality *one can no longer treat technological and institutional factors as separate*, competing explanations: both are jointly determined, and complementary. The model thus shows how, in the words of Freeman (1995), one needs to think of *"the Welfare State as a system"*.

To demonstrate these points I shall assume from here on a piecewise-linear technological frontier. Flexibility is free up to σ_L, then has a marginal cost of $M > 0$, up to a maximum level $\sigma_H > \sigma_L$,

$$c(\sigma) = \begin{cases} 0 & \text{for } \sigma < \sigma_L, \\ M(\sigma - \sigma_L) & \text{for } \sigma \in [\sigma_L, \sigma_H], \\ +\infty & \text{for } \sigma > \sigma_H. \end{cases} \tag{42}$$

I will denote $\gamma_i = (\sigma_i - 1)/\sigma_i$, $i \in \{L, H\}$. The analogue of Proposition 8 in this case is very simple, as the first-order condition in a symmetric equilibrium involves the comparison

$$M \gtreqless \frac{\Delta_t^2}{2\sigma_t^2}. \tag{43}$$

The unique symmetric outcome is thus $\sigma_t = \sigma_L$ when $\Delta_t^2/2M < \sigma_L^2$, and $\sigma_t = \sigma_H$ when $\Delta_t^2/2M > \sigma_H^2$. When $\Delta_t^2/2M \in (\sigma_L^2, \sigma_H^2)$, on the other hand, firms mix between σ_L and σ_H, in proportions such that the resulting factor prices make each one indifferent; this equilibrium will be denoted σ_{LH}.[45] Focusing now on technology-inequality steady states, for any $\tau \leqslant 1$ and $\sigma \geqslant 1$ the *marginal benefit of flexibility* [right-hand side of (43)] equals

$$R(\tau, \sigma) \equiv \frac{D(\tau; (\sigma - 1)/\sigma)^2}{2\sigma^2},$$

where $D(\tau, \gamma)$ is the asymptotic variance under the policy τ and return to skill γ, given by (21). Thus, under any time-invariant policy τ, whether exogenous or endogenous:

- For $M > \max\{R(\tau, \sigma_L), R(\tau, \sigma_H)\}$, the unique technological steady state is σ_L.
- For $M < \min\{R(\tau, \sigma_L), R(\tau, \sigma_H)\}$, it is σ_H.
- If $R(\tau, \sigma_L) > R(\tau, \sigma_H)$, then for $M \in [R(\tau, \sigma_H), R(\tau, \sigma_L)]$ it is the mixed-strategy outcome σ_{LH}.
- If $R(\tau, \sigma_L) < R(\tau, \sigma_H)$, then for $M \in [R(\tau, \sigma_L), R(\tau, \sigma_H)]$ there are three technological steady states: σ_L, σ_H and σ_{LH}; the first two are stable, the third one unstable.

---

[44] The long-run multiplier for any shock to the $\mathcal{D}$ function (e.g., a change in w^2) is

$$\mu \equiv \left(1 - \mathcal{D}_1 - \mathcal{D}_2\left(\frac{\partial T}{\partial \Delta} + \frac{\partial T}{\partial \Gamma}\frac{\partial \Gamma}{\partial \Delta}\right) - \mathcal{D}_3\frac{\partial \Gamma}{\partial \Delta}\right)^{-1}.$$

Similarly, the long-run effects on inequality of a shock to the T function (e.g., a change in λ) it is $\mu\mathcal{D}_2(\partial T/\partial \lambda)$.

[45] It is not necessary to provide here the full characterization of this mixed-strategy equilibrium.

Furthermore, since $R(\tau, \sigma)$ is decreasing in τ, we have the proposition.

PROPOSITION 9. *More skill-biased technologies appear first in, and less skill biased technologies disappear first from, countries that have less redistributive fiscal, educational or labor market institutions. For any $M > 0$:*

(1) *If σ_H is a steady-state equilibrium technology under a constant redistributive policy τ, this remains true under any less progressive policy $\tau' < \tau$.*

(2) *If σ_L is a steady-state equilibrium technology under a constant redistributive policy τ', this remains true under any more progressive policy $\tau > \tau'$.*

These results are illustrated in Figures 5 and 6 for two cases where: (i) $R(\underline{\tau}, \sigma_H) < R(\bar{\tau}, \sigma_L)$, implying that for each M there is a unique technology compatible in the long-run with each policy $\tau \in \{\underline{\tau}, \bar{\tau}\}$;[46] (ii) $R(\underline{\tau}, \sigma_L) < R(\bar{\tau}, \sigma_H)$, implying that for either policy $\tau \in \{\underline{\tau}, \bar{\tau}\}$ there is a range of M's where multiple technologies are sustainable. The message is essentially the same in both cases, showing how a *world-wide shift* in the set of feasible technologies can result in *different evolutions* of both production processes and the skill premium across countries. In particular, the model can help explain why skill-biased technical change and reorganization occurred first, and to a greater extent, in the United States compared to Europe – and within Europe, more so in England than on the Continent.[47]

Indeed, consider two countries, C_1 and C_2, that are initially identical in all respects, including both using the technology σ_L, except that one is in a laissez-faire equilibrium, $\tau = \underline{\tau}$, and the other in a welfare state, $\tau = \bar{\tau}$. Suppose now that the technological frontier gradually flattens (M declines), meaning that flexibility becomes cheaper to achieve. As shown on Figures 5 and 6, the more skill-biased technology σ_H becomes (all or part of) another feasible equilibrium in C_1 before it does in C_2; similarly, σ_L first ceases to be viable (by itself or as part of a mixed equilibrium) in the laissez-faire country, while it is still sustainable in the more redistributive one.

Going further, there are in fact *reciprocal interactions* between the economy's *technology response* and *policy response* to shocks. Proposition 9 and Figures 5 and 6 show

---

[46] For instance, under condition (37), $\partial \ln \Delta_\infty / \partial \ln \sigma < 1$, so $R(\underline{\tau}, \sigma_H) < R(\underline{\tau}, \sigma_L)$ provided σ_H and σ_L are close enough. If $\underline{\tau}$ and $\bar{\tau}$ are also not too different, then $R(\bar{\tau}, \sigma) \lesssim R(\underline{\tau}, \sigma)$ for $\sigma = \sigma_H, \sigma_L$, so the thresholds rank as illustrated on Figure 5.

[47] Acemoglu (2003) proposes a different mechanism, based on imperfectly competitive labor markets, through which the wage-compression policies of continental European countries may have caused technological progress there to be less skill-biased than in the United States. In his model, a binding minimum wage makes low-skill workers' compensation a fixed price, whereas for high-skill workers the binding constraint for the firm is rent sharing (due to search market frictions), which acts as a tax on productivity improvements. As a result, firms in high minimum-wage countries have greater incentives to invest in technologies that are complementary to low-skill labor than high-skill labor. In both Acemoglu's and the present model, the effects of policy on technology are indirect, operating through either the distribution of skills or equilibrium wages. In Krusell and Rios-Rull (1996), by contrast, agents with different vintages of human capital vote directly on whether or not to allow the adoption of new technologies by firms.

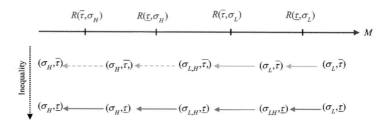

Figure 5. The response of technology and policy to a decline in the cost of flexibility [case (i)]. Under each range of M appears the unique (σ, τ) such that $(\sigma, \Delta = D(\tau; 1-1/\sigma))$ is a stable steady state given τ and M. The subset reached via solid lines corresponds to the stable steady states in (σ, Δ, τ) jointly, when policy is endogenous as well.

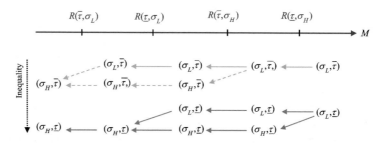

Figure 6. The response of technology and policy to a decline in the cost of flexibility [case (ii)]. Under each range of M appear the values of (σ, τ) such that $(\sigma, \Delta = D(\tau; 1 - 1/\sigma))$ is a stable steady state given τ and M. The subset reached via solid lines corresponds to the stable steady states in (σ, Δ, τ) jointly, when policy is endogenous as well.

that feasible new technologies are not implemented unless institutions are sufficiently inegalitarian. But, conversely, the occurrence of technical change alters these same institutions, as seen in Proposition 7. Indeed, suppose that

$$\underline{\lambda}(\gamma_L; B) < \lambda < \bar{\lambda}(\gamma_L; B), \tag{44}$$

where $\bar{\lambda}$ and $\underline{\lambda}$ were defined in (22) and (23). These inequalities imply that: (i) under the technology σ_L, both social contracts $\underline{\tau}$ and $\bar{\tau}$ are political steady states; (ii) under σ_H, $\bar{\tau}$ is a political steady state, while $\underline{\tau}$ is one if and only if we also have $\lambda < \bar{\lambda}(\gamma_H; B)$.

When this last inequality holds, the set of stable politico-economico-technological steady states (with endogenous τ, Δ and σ) is the same as described on Figures 5 and 6. When $\lambda > \bar{\lambda}(\gamma_H; B)$, however, the more redistributive social contract $\bar{\tau}$ is not *politically* sustainable under the amount of inequality that results, in the long run, from the technology σ_H. Therefore one must remove from the set of steady states on each figure the "branches" corresponding to this outcome; these are indicated by the dashed lines. The remaining solid lines then indicate that *only certain politico-technological configurations* can be observed in the long run: (a) for low values of M, e.g. for $M < R(\bar{\tau}, \sigma_L)$ on the first figure, the only feasible social contract is $\underline{\tau}$, together with the technology σ_H;

(b) on the second figure, for $M \in (R(\bar{\tau}, \sigma_L), R(\underline{\tau}, \sigma_L))$ only the egalitarian social contract and the egalitarian technology, or the inegalitarian social contract and inegalitarian technology, are mutually compatible.

5. Exporting inequality: Spillovers between social contracts

The model also allows us to think about spillovers between national policies or institutions, operating via technological and organizational diffusion. The basic idea is illustrated in Figure 7, which shows how the social contract in Country 2 can, over time, be affected by technological or even purely political shifts in Country 1, propagated along the channels indicated by the solid lines on the diagram.

As seen in the previous section, firms operating in countries with more laissez-faire fiscal, educational or labor market policies have greater incentives to develop and adopt low-complementarity production processes. Suppose now that the cost of imitating, adapting or copying a more flexible technology or organizational form, once it has been developed and implemented elsewhere, is lower than the cost of innovation; in terms of the model, it is $m < M$. This lower marginal cost may for instance reflect, as in Acemoglu (1998), an imperfect international enforcement of property rights over technological or organizational innovations. As we shall see, redistributive institutions in one country will then be significantly affected, perhaps even completely undermined, by technological or political changes occurring in another.[48]

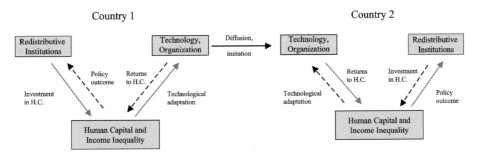

Figure 7. International spillovers between social contracts.

---

[48] As mentioned earlier I abstract here from international trade, which could be yet another channel of transmission. See Grossman and Maggi (2000), Grossman (2004) or Thoenig and Verdier (2003) for papers that study the effects of trade openness on technical and organizational change, although not their political economy implications.

5.1. A shift in one country's technological frontier

I shall focus here on parameter configurations that satisfy the following conditions:

$$\max\{\underline{\lambda}(\gamma_L; B), \bar{\lambda}(\gamma_H; B)\} < \lambda < \bar{\lambda}(\gamma_L; B), \tag{45}$$

$$\max\{R(\underline{\tau}, \sigma_L), R(\underline{\tau}, \sigma_H)\} < M, \tag{46}$$

$$m < R(\bar{\tau}, \sigma_L) < M' < \min\{R(\underline{\tau}, \sigma_L), R(\underline{\tau}, \sigma_H)\}, \tag{47}$$

which imply in particular that $M > M' > m$. As shown as part of Proposition 10, these conditions also ensure that the technology σ_L allows for both social contracts $\underline{\tau}$ and $\bar{\tau}$, and conversely that σ_L is an equilibrium technology under both social contracts (no firm wants to switch to σ_H).

PROPOSITION 10. *Assume that conditions* (45)–(47) *are satisfied, and consider two countries, C_1 and C_2, that both start in steady state, with the same technology σ_L. Suppose now that the cost of flexibility in country C_1 declines from M to M'.*
  (1) *If both C_1 and C_2 were initially in the more egalitarian of the two regimes compatible with σ_L nothing happens, in the sense that $(\bar{\tau}, \gamma_L, D(\bar{\tau}, \gamma_L))$ remains a stable steady state for both countries.*
  (2) *If C_1 was initially in the more inegalitarian regime $(\underline{\tau}, \gamma_L, D(\underline{\tau}, \gamma_L))$, the long run outcome is for* both *countries to switch to the technology σ_H, and for country C_2 to also adopt the more unequal social contract $\underline{\tau}$: the unique steady state for the two countries is now $(\underline{\tau}, \gamma_H, D(\underline{\tau}, \gamma_H))$.*

The intuition is as follows. Even as M declines to M', firms faced with the skill distribution $D(\bar{\tau}, \gamma_L)$ resulting from $\bar{\tau}$ do not find it profitable to switch technology. Given the higher dispersion $D(\underline{\tau}, \gamma_L)$ that prevails under $\underline{\tau}$, however, if country C_1 starts in this regime all firms there will eventually switch to technology σ_H.[49] Next, given the lower cost of flexibility m to which firms in C_2 now have access through imitation, σ_L is no longer viable there even under $\bar{\tau}$. And, in turn, with the higher income inequality that results in the long run from technology σ_H, the only politically sustainable social contract is $\underline{\tau}$.

These results make clear how technological change (a shift in the frontier) has significant effects only when it is *mediated* through specific institutions – namely, which social contract C_1 had adopted; and, conversely, how under such conditions it will then affect institutions in other countries, namely here in C_2.

---

[49] I leave aside the dynamics here, but they are straightforward: since (45) implies that (25) holds for $\gamma = \gamma_L, \gamma_H$, we always operate on the portion of the $T(\gamma\Delta)$ curve where increases in inequality imply decreases in the tax rate.

5.2. A shift in one country's political institutions

I consider now a second scenario, namely the transmission of *a political shock*. Having seen earlier how the mere fact of being in different institutional steady states (say, for historical reasons) can lead to very different technological trajectories, I shall assume here that C_1 and C_2 both start in the egalitarian steady state $(\bar{\tau}, \gamma_L, D(\bar{\tau}, \gamma_L))$, with the same technology σ_L. Let C_1 now experience an increase in the political influence of wealth, from λ to λ'. This may reflect a rising importance of *lobbying and campaign contributions*, an exogenous *decline in unionization*, or a lower *electoral turnout* by the poor. It may even simply represent the political outcome during a particular period in which the electorate stochastically shifted to the right.[50] I shall assume here the following conditions:

$$\bar{\lambda}(\gamma_H; B) < \lambda < \bar{\lambda}(\gamma_L; B) < \lambda', \tag{48}$$

$$m < R(\bar{\tau}, \sigma_L) < M < \min\{R(\underline{\tau}, \sigma_L), R(\underline{\tau}, \sigma_H)\}. \tag{49}$$

PROPOSITION 11. *Assume that conditions (48) and (49) are satisfied. Consider two countries, C_1 and C_2, that both start in the egalitarian steady state, $(\bar{\tau}, \gamma_L, D(\bar{\tau}, \gamma_L))$, with the same technology σ_L. Suppose now that the political influence of wealth in country C_1 rises from λ to λ'. The unique long run outcome is for both countries to switch to the technology σ_H and the more unequal social contract $\underline{\tau}$, thus ending up at the steady state $(\underline{\tau}, \gamma_H, D(\underline{\tau}, \gamma_H))$.*

As a result of the initial political shift, redistribution τ_1 (fiscal, educational, or via labor-market institutions) in country C_1 declines. This leads over time to a rise in human capital inequality Δ_1, to which firms respond by adopting more flexible, wage-disequalizing technologies, switching from σ_L to σ_H and further precipitating the shift from $\bar{\tau}$ to $\underline{\tau}$. Their counterparts in C_2, which would not have developed such technologies by themselves, now find it profitable to copy them from C_1. This results in a rise in income inequality $\gamma_2 \Delta_2$ in C_2 (and, over time, in human–capital inequality Δ_2 itself) that ultimately leads to the unraveling of the Welfare State in that country as well.

6. Conclusion

This chapter offers a new, unified model to analyze the reciprocal interactions between the distribution of human wealth, technology, and redistributive institutions. It identifies in particular certain core mechanisms that allow alternative societal models to persist,

---

[50] Indeed, the political shock need not be permanent, provided the speed at which λ reverts to its previous value is low enough, relative to those of human capital adjustment and technological or organizational evolution.

as well as powerful forces pushing towards uniformization. Key among the former is the interplay of imperfections in asset markets and in the political system that can lead to multiple steady states where inequality and redistribution are negatively correlated. Among the latter is skill-biased technical change, which can potentially lead to the unraveling of the Welfare State. When technological or organizational form is endogenous, moreover, firms respond to greater human capital heterogeneity with more flexible technologies, further exacerbating income inequality. The possibility for firms in different countries to thus choose technologies adapted to the local labor force can also make it easier to sustain multiple social models. The international diffusion of technology, however, implies that the more flexible, skill-biased technologies profitably developed in nations with greater inequality and less redistributive institutions may then be imitated by firms in other countries, thereby triggering a "chain reaction" that moves the whole system towards a common outcome that is more inegalitarian – technologically, economically and politically speaking. Such international spillovers between national social contracts are important concerns in the debate over globalization, and warrant further research.

Acknowledgements

I thank for useful remarks Philippe Aghion, Omer Moav and participants at the CEPR conference on Education and Inequality (Paris, May 2003). I am grateful to the MacArthur Foundation for financial support and to the Institute for Advanced Study for its hospitality over the academic year 2002–2003.

Appendix: Proofs

PROOFS OF PROPOSITIONS 1–5. [See Bénabou (2000)]. I shall only provide here:
  (i) the formula for the break-even income level $\tilde{y}_t$ where $\hat{y}_t^i = y_t^i$,

$$\ln \tilde{y}_t = \gamma m_t + \delta \ln l_t + (2 - \tau_t)\gamma^2 \frac{\Delta_t^2}{2} + (1 - \tau_t)\frac{v^2}{2}; \tag{A.1}$$

  (ii) the laws of motion for (m_t, Δ_t^2) that underlie Proposition 2,

$$m_{t+1} = (\alpha + \beta\gamma)m_t + \beta\delta \ln l_t$$
$$+ \beta\tau_t(2 - \tau_t)\left(\frac{\gamma^2\Delta_t^2 + v^2}{2}\right) + \ln(\kappa s^\beta) - \frac{w^2 + \beta v^2}{2}, \tag{A.2}$$

$$\Delta_{t+1}^2 = (\alpha + \beta\gamma(1 - \tau_t))^2 \Delta_t^2 + \beta^2(1 - \tau_t)^2 v^2 + w^2; \tag{A.3}$$

(iii) the formula for each agent's intertemporal welfare that underlies Proposition 3: under a rate of redistribution τ_t,

$$U_t^i = \bar{u}_t + A(\tau_t)\big(\ln k_t^i - m_t\big) + C(\tau_t)$$
$$- (1 - \rho + \rho\beta)(1 - \tau_t)^2 \left(\frac{\gamma^2 \Delta_t^2 + B v^2}{2}\right), \tag{A.4}$$

where $\bar{u}_t$ is independent of the policy τ_t, $B \equiv a + \rho(1 - a)(1 - \beta)$ was defined in (14) and

$$A(\tau) \equiv \rho\alpha + (1 - \rho + \rho\beta)\gamma(1 - \tau), \tag{A.5}$$
$$C(\tau) \equiv (1 - \rho)\big(\delta \ln l(\tau) - l(\tau)^\eta\big) + \rho\beta\delta \ln l(\tau). \tag{A.6}$$

The first-order condition (15) readily follows. $\qquad\Box$

PROOF OF PROPOSITION 7. Because $D(\tau, \gamma)$ is increasing in γ for all τ the functions $\bar{\lambda}(\gamma; B)$ and $\underline{\lambda}(\gamma; B)$ are both U-shaped in γ, and minimized at the point where $\gamma D(\tau, \gamma) = v\sqrt{B}$, for $\tau = \bar{\tau}, \underline{\tau}$ respectively. Furthermore, the minimum of $\bar{\lambda}(\gamma; B)$ occurs to the right of that of $\underline{\lambda}(\gamma; B)$. Under the assumption that $v\sqrt{B} > \gamma_{\max} D(\underline{\tau}, \gamma_{\max})$ we have $\gamma D(\bar{\tau}, \gamma) < \gamma D(\underline{\tau}, \gamma) < v\sqrt{B}$ for all $\gamma \leqslant \gamma_{\max}$, implying that both $\bar{\lambda}(\gamma; B)$ and $\underline{\lambda}(\gamma; B)$ are decreasing in γ over $[0, \gamma_{\max}]$; they are obviously increasing in B. Inverting these functions with respect to γ yields the claimed properties of $\underline{\gamma}(\lambda; B)$ and $\bar{\gamma}(\lambda; B)$. $\qquad\Box$

PROOF OF PROPOSITION 8. Consider a firm $\hat{\imath} \in [0, 1]$ with technology $\hat{\sigma}$ and associated productivity factor $\widehat{A} \equiv A(\hat{\sigma})$. Its marginal cost is

$$MC(\hat{\sigma}|\sigma_t) \equiv \min_{\{\hat{x}_t^i\}} \left\{ \int_0^1 p_t^i \hat{x}_t^i \, di \,\Big|\, \widehat{A} \left(\int_0^1 z_t^i (\hat{x}_t^i)^{(\hat{\sigma}-1)/\hat{\sigma}} \, ds\right)^{\hat{\sigma}/(\hat{\sigma}-1)} = 1 \right\}. \tag{A.7}$$

The first-order condition for cost-minimization is

$$p_t^i = \hat{\mu}_t \widehat{A} z_t^i (\hat{x}_t^i)^{-1/\hat{\sigma}} \left(\int_0^1 z_t^i (\hat{x}_t^i)^{(\hat{\sigma}-1)/\hat{\sigma}} \, ds\right)^{1/(\hat{\sigma}-1)} = \hat{\mu}_t \widehat{A} z_t^i (\hat{x}_t^i)^{-1/\hat{\sigma}} (\widehat{A})^{-1/\hat{\sigma}}$$

or

$$\hat{x}_t^i = \hat{\mu}_t^{\hat{\sigma}} \widehat{A}^{\hat{\sigma}-1} \left(\frac{p_t^i}{z_t^i}\right)^{-\hat{\sigma}}.$$

Therefore,

$$\hat{\mu}_t = \int_0^1 p_t^i \hat{x}_t^i \, di = \hat{\mu}_t^{\hat{\sigma}} \widehat{A}^{\hat{\sigma}-1} \left(\int_0^1 z_t^i \left(\frac{p_t^i}{z_t^i}\right)^{1-\hat{\sigma}} \, di\right)$$

or

$$\hat{\mu}_t = \widehat{A}^{-1} \left(\int_0^1 (z_t^i)^{\hat{\sigma}} (p_t^i)^{1-\hat{\sigma}} \, di\right)^{1/(1-\hat{\sigma})}, \tag{A.8}$$

which establishes (32). Now, replacing the equilibrium prices from Equation (27) yields

$$\hat{\mu}_t = \widehat{A}^{-1} A_t^{(\sigma_t - 1)/\sigma_t} \left(\frac{y_t}{l_t} \right)^{1/\sigma_t} \left(\int_0^1 z_t^i (k_t^i)^{(\hat{\sigma}-1)/\sigma_t} \, di \right)^{1/(1-\hat{\sigma})}$$

$$= \widehat{A}^{-1} A_t^{(\sigma_t - 1)/\sigma_t} \left(\frac{y_t}{l_t} \right)^{1/\sigma_t} \left(\int_0^1 (k_t^i)^{(\hat{\sigma}-1)/\sigma_t} \, di \right)^{1/(1-\hat{\sigma})},$$

since the z_t^i's and k_t^i's are independent. We now eliminate the terms common to all firms by computing firm $\hat{\imath}$'s relative marginal cost

$$mc(\hat{\sigma} | \sigma_t) \equiv \frac{\hat{\mu}_t}{\mu_t}$$

$$= \left(\frac{A_t}{\widehat{A}} \right) \left(\int_0^1 (k_t^i)^{(\hat{\sigma}-1)/\sigma_t} \, di \right)^{1/(1-\hat{\sigma})} \left(\int_0^1 (k_t^i)^{(\sigma_t-1)/\sigma_t} \, di \right)^{-1/(1-\sigma_t)}.$$

Finally, using the fact that $\ln \int_0^1 (k_t^i)^\chi \, di = \exp[\chi m_t + \chi^2 \Delta_t^2 / 2]$ for all χ, this yields

$$mc(\hat{\sigma} | \sigma_t) = \left(\frac{A(\sigma_t)}{A(\hat{\sigma})} \right) \exp\left[\frac{\Delta_t^2}{2} \left(\frac{1-\hat{\sigma}}{\sigma_t^2} - \frac{1-\sigma_t}{\sigma_t^2} \right) \frac{\Delta_t^2}{2} \right]$$

$$= \left(\frac{A(\sigma_t)}{A(\hat{\sigma})} \right) \exp\left[\frac{\Delta_t^2}{2} \left(\frac{\sigma_t - \hat{\sigma}}{\sigma_t^2} \right) \right]. \tag{A.9}$$

The (necessary and sufficient) first-order condition for firm $\hat{\imath}$ is therefore $c'(\hat{\sigma}) = \Delta_t^2 / 2\sigma_t^2$. Evaluating it at $\hat{\sigma} = \sigma_t$ yields the technology-equilibrium condition $\sigma_t^2 c'(\sigma_t) = \Delta_t^2 / 2$, which by convexity of $c(\cdot)$ has a unique solution $\sigma^*(\Delta_t)$, increasing in Δ_t. Finally, the result that $\partial \ln \sigma^* / \partial \ln \Delta \in (0, 1)$ is established in Equation (35). $\square$

PROOF OF SECTION 3.3'S CLAIMS CONCERNING GROWTH WITH ENDOGENOUS TECHNOLOGY. In the general growth formula (12), $\delta \ln l_t$ is now replaced everywhere [according to (28)] by

$$\ln \widetilde{A}_t + \delta_t \ln l_t = \ln l_t + \ln\left(A_t^{(\sigma_t - 1)/\sigma_t} (y_t)^{1/\sigma_t} \right)$$

$$= \delta_t \ln l_t + \gamma_t \ln A(\sigma_t) + (1 - \gamma_t) \ln y_t.$$

This leads to

$$\gamma_t \ln \frac{y_{t+1}}{y_t} = \gamma_t \left[\ln \kappa + \beta \ln s + \delta_{t+1} \ln l_{t+1} - \alpha \delta_t \ln l_t + \ln A(\sigma_{t+1}) - \alpha \ln A(\sigma_t) \right]$$

$$- \gamma_t (1 - \gamma_t) \frac{w^2}{2} - \beta \gamma_t (1 - \beta \gamma_t)(1 - \tau_t)^2 \frac{v^2}{2}$$

$$- \left[\alpha + \beta \gamma_t (1 - \tau_t)^2 - (\alpha + \beta \gamma_t (1 - \tau_t))^2 \right] \frac{\gamma_t^2 \Delta_t^2}{2}. \tag{A.10}$$

For $\alpha = 0$ and $\beta = 1$, this simplifies to

$$\gamma_t \ln \frac{y_{t+1}}{y_t} = \gamma_t \Big[\ln \kappa + \ln s + \delta_{t+1} \ln l_{t+1} + \ln A(\sigma_{t+1}) \Big]$$

$$- \gamma_t (1 - \gamma_t) \bigg[\frac{w^2}{2} + (1 - \tau_t)^2 \frac{v^2}{2} + (1 - \tau_t)^2 \Big(\frac{\gamma_t^2 \Delta_t^2}{2} \Big) \bigg]$$

$$= \gamma_t \Big[\ln \kappa + \ln s + \ln l_{t+1} + \ln A(\sigma_{t+1}) \Big]$$

$$- \gamma_t (1 - \gamma_t) \bigg[\frac{w^2}{2} + (1 - \tau_t)^2 \frac{v^2}{2} + (1 - \tau_t)^2 \Big(\frac{\gamma_t^2 \Delta_t^2}{2} \Big) \bigg], \qquad \text{(A.11)}$$

or finally, since $\Delta_{t+1}^2 = \gamma^2 (1 - \tau_t)^2 \Delta_t^2 + (1 - \tau_t)^2 v^2 + w^2$,

$$\ln \frac{y_{t+1}}{y_t} = \ln \kappa + \ln s + \delta_{t+1} \ln l_{t+1} + \ln A(\sigma_{t+1}) - (1 - \gamma_t) \frac{\Delta_{t+1}^2}{2}$$

$$= \ln \kappa + \ln s + \ln l_{t+1} - c(\sigma_{t+1}) - \frac{\Delta_{t+1}^2}{2\sigma_t}. \qquad \text{(A.12)}$$

Substituting for Δ_{t+1}^2 from (11), the growth rate between t and $t + 1$ is thus

$$g_t = \ln \kappa + \ln s + \delta_{t+1} \ln l(\tau_{t+1}) - c(\sigma_{t+1}) - \frac{\mathcal{D}(\Delta_t, \tau_t; \gamma_t)^2}{2\sigma_t}.$$

Therefore, with fixed labor supply $(1/\eta = 0)$, if all firms are forced to use technology $\sigma_t - d\sigma$ instead of σ_t in every period the impact on growth will be $d\sigma$ times

$$\frac{\partial g_t}{\partial \sigma} \bigg|_{\sigma = \sigma_t} = -c'(\sigma_{t+1}) + \frac{\Delta_{t+1}^2}{2\sigma_t^2} - \frac{\Gamma'(\sigma_t)}{2\sigma_t} \Big(\frac{\partial \mathcal{D}^2(\Delta_t, \tau_t; \gamma_t)}{\partial \gamma} \Big)$$

$$= -\frac{\Delta_{t+1}^2}{2} \Big(\frac{\sigma_t^2}{\sigma_t^2} - 1 \Big) - \frac{\Gamma'(\sigma_t)}{2\sigma_t} \Big(\frac{\partial \mathcal{D}^2(\Delta_t, \tau_t; \gamma_t)}{\partial \gamma} \Big),$$

where we have used the condition for equilibrium technology choice in Proposition 8. The growth impact is thus positive in all periods provided that either $\sigma_{t+1}^2 \approx \sigma_t^2$ (we start in or near the steady state), or $\sigma_{t+1}^2 \leqslant \sigma_t^2$ (we start with "excessive" heterogeneity with respect to the steady state). $\qquad \square$

PROOF OF PROPOSITION 10. We begin with some preliminaries. Given a technology σ and associated $\gamma = (\sigma - 1)/\sigma$, recall from (22) and (23) that the tax rate $\bar{\tau}$ is a steady-state political equilibrium, which we shall denote as $\bar{\tau} \in \mathcal{P}(\sigma; \lambda)$, if and only if $\lambda \leqslant \bar{\lambda}(\gamma, B)$. Similarly, $\underline{\tau} \in \mathcal{P}(\sigma; \lambda)$ if and only if $\lambda \geqslant \underline{\lambda}(\gamma, B)$.

Conversely, given a tax rate τ we see from (43) that the technology σ_L and associated $\gamma_L = (\sigma_L - 1)/\sigma_L$ is a technological steady state when the slope of the technology frontier is M, which we denote as $\sigma_L \in \mathcal{T}(\tau; M)$, if and only if

$$M \geqslant \frac{\mathcal{D}(\tau; \gamma_L)^2}{2\sigma_L^2} \equiv R(\tau, \sigma_L). \qquad \text{(A.13)}$$

Similarly, the technology σ_H and associated $\gamma_H = (\sigma_H - 1)/\sigma_H$ is a technological steady state, which we denote as $\sigma_H \in \mathcal{T}(\tau; M)$, if and only if

$$M \leq \frac{D(\tau; \gamma_H)^2}{2\sigma_H^2} \equiv R(\tau, \sigma_H). \tag{A.14}$$

A policy-technology combination $(\tau, \sigma) \in \{\bar{\tau}, \underline{\tau}\} \times \{\sigma_L, \sigma_H\}$ is then a full steady state if and only if $\tau \in \mathcal{P}(\sigma; \lambda)$ and $\sigma \in \mathcal{T}(\tau; M)$. Clearly, there are at most four stable steady states (we restrict attention here to cases where the technology equilibrium is in pure strategies). We now proceed through a sequence of three claims, which together establish the proposition.

CLAIM 1. *For a country facing the technological frontier M, the only steady states are* $(\bar{\tau}, \sigma_L)$ *and* $(\underline{\tau}, \sigma_L)$.

Indeed, the first inequality in (45) states that $\sigma_L \in \mathcal{T}(\underline{\tau}; M)$ and this is easily seen to imply that $\sigma_L \in \mathcal{T}(\bar{\tau}; M)$. Conversely, the second inequality states that $\sigma_H \notin \mathcal{T}(\underline{\tau}; M)$ and this is easily seen to imply that $\sigma_L \in \mathcal{T}(\bar{\tau}; M)$. Finally, the fact that $\underline{\lambda}(\gamma_L; B) < \lambda < \bar{\lambda}(\gamma_L; B)$ due to (45) means that $\underline{\tau} \in \mathcal{P}(\sigma_L; \lambda)$ and $\bar{\tau} \in \mathcal{P}(\sigma_L; \lambda)$.

CLAIM 2. *For a country facing the technological frontier M', the only steady states are* $(\bar{\tau}, \sigma_L)$ *and* $(\underline{\tau}, \sigma_H)$.

Indeed, note first from (47) that $R(\bar{\tau}, \sigma_L) < M'$ means that we still have $\sigma_L \in \mathcal{T}(\bar{\tau}; M')$; by contrast, $M' < \min\{R(\underline{\tau}, \sigma_L), R(\underline{\tau}, \sigma_H)\}$ means that $\sigma_H \in \mathcal{T}(\underline{\tau}; M')$ but $\sigma_L \notin \mathcal{T}(\underline{\tau}; M')$. The only possible equilibria are thus $(\bar{\tau}, \sigma_L)$, $(\underline{\tau}, \sigma_H)$ and $(\bar{\tau}, \sigma_H)$. Turning now to (45), the fact that $\lambda < \bar{\lambda}(\gamma_L; B)$ means that $\bar{\tau} \in \mathcal{P}(\sigma_L; \lambda)$; the fact that $\bar{\lambda}(\gamma_H; B) < \lambda$, on the other hand, means that $\underline{\tau} \in \mathcal{P}(\sigma_H; \lambda)$ but $\bar{\tau} \notin \mathcal{P}(\sigma_H; \lambda)$. So only the first two of the three preceding configurations are full equilibria.

CLAIM 3. *For a country facing the technological frontier m, the only steady state is* $(\underline{\tau}, \sigma_H)$.

Observe from (47) that m satisfies all the same inequalities as M', except that $m < R(\bar{\tau}, \sigma_L)$ whereas $R(\bar{\tau}, \sigma_L) < M'$. This means that whereas we had $\sigma_L \in \mathcal{T}(\bar{\tau}; M')$, we now have $\sigma_L \notin \mathcal{T}(\bar{\tau}; M')$. This rules out the equilibrium $(\bar{\tau}, \sigma_L)$, leaving only $(\underline{\tau}, \sigma_H)$. □

PROOF OF PROPOSITION 11.

CLAIM 1. *In the initial parameter configuration, $(\bar{\tau}, \sigma_L)$ is a steady state (and even the only steady state with policy $\bar{\tau}$).*

Indeed, the fact that $\bar{\lambda}(\gamma_H; B) < \lambda < \bar{\lambda}(\gamma_L; B)$ means that $\bar{\tau} \in \mathcal{P}(\sigma_L; \lambda)$, whereas $\bar{\tau} \notin \mathcal{P}(\sigma_H; \lambda)$. The rest of the claim follows from the fact $\sigma_L \in \mathcal{T}(\bar{\tau}; M)$, since $M > R(\bar{\tau}, \sigma_L)$.

CLAIM 2. *After the political shift in C_1, $(\underline{\tau}, \sigma_H)$ is the only steady state for that country.*

First, since $\lambda' > \bar{\lambda}(\gamma_L; B) > \bar{\lambda}(\gamma_H; B)$ we now have $\bar{\tau} \notin \mathcal{P}(\sigma_L; \lambda')$ and $\bar{\tau} \notin \mathcal{P}(\sigma_H; \lambda')$, so there is no steady state with policy $\bar{\tau}$. Moreover, since $M < R(\underline{\tau}, \sigma_L)$ we have $\sigma_L \notin \mathcal{T}(\underline{\tau}; M)$, so the only possible equilibrium is $(\underline{\tau}, \sigma_H)$. It is indeed an equilibrium, as $M < R(\underline{\tau}, \sigma_H)$ means that $\sigma_H \in \mathcal{T}(\underline{\tau}; M)$, while $\bar{\lambda}(\gamma_H; B) < \lambda'$ means that $\underline{\tau} \in \mathcal{P}(\sigma_H; \lambda')$.

CLAIM 3. *After C_1 has switched to the technology σ_H, so that C_2 faces the technology frontier m, the only steady state for C_2 is $(\underline{\tau}, \sigma_H)$.*

First the fact $m < R(\bar{\tau}, \sigma_L) < R(\underline{\tau}, \sigma_L)$ implies that $(\bar{\tau}, \sigma_L)$ is no longer a technological equilibrium, and a fortiori neither is $(\underline{\tau}, \sigma_L)$. Second, the fact $m < \min\{R(\underline{\tau}, \sigma_L), R(\underline{\tau}, \sigma_H)\}$ means that the only technological equilibrium under policy $\underline{\tau}$ is σ_H. Finally, since $\lambda > \bar{\lambda}(\gamma_H; B), \underline{\tau} \in \mathcal{P}(\sigma_H; \lambda)$ whereas $\bar{\tau} \notin \mathcal{P}(\sigma_H; \lambda)$, which concludes the proof. $\qquad\square$

References

Acemoglu, D. (1998). "Why do new technologies complement skills? Directed technical change and inequality". Quarterly Journal of Economics 113 (4), 1055–1090.

Acemoglu, D. (2003). "Cross-country inequality trends". Economic Journal 113, 121–149.

Acemoglu, D., Aghion, P., Violante, G.L. (2001). "Deunionization, technological change and inequality". Carnegie–Rochester Conference Series on Public Policy 55, 229–264.

Acemoglu, D., Robinson, J. (2000). "Why did the West extend the franchise?". Quarterly Journal of Economics 115 (4), 1167–1195.

Aghion, P. (2002). "Schumpeterian growth theory and the dynamics of income inequality". Econometrica 70 (3), 855–882.

Alesina, A., Angeletos, G.M. (2005). "Fairness and redistribution: US vs. Europe". American Economic Review 95 (4), 960–980.

Alesina, A., Glaeser, E., Sacerdote, B. (2001). "Why doesn't the U.S. have a European-type welfare state?". Brookings Papers on Economic Affairs (2), 187–277.

Alesina, A., Rodrik, D. (1994). "Distributive politics and economic growth". Quarterly Journal of Economics 109 (2), 465–490.

Autor, D., Katz, L., Krueger, A. (1997). "Computing inequality: Have computers changed the labor market?". Quarterly Journal of Economics 113 (4), 1169–1214.

Baland, J.M., Robinson, J. (2003). "Land and power". Mimeo. University of California Berkeley.

Banerjee, A., Duflo, E. (2000). "Inequality and growth: What can the data say?". Journal of Economic Growth 8 (3), 267–299.

Banerjee, A., Newman, A. (1993). "Occupational choice and the process of development". Journal of Political Economy, 274–278.

Barro, R. (2000). "Inequality and growth in a panel of countries". Journal of Economic Growth 5, 5–32.

Bartels, L. (2002). "Economic inequality and political representation". Mimeo. Princeton University.

Becker, X. (1964). Human Capital. Columbia University Press, New York.

Bénabou, R. (1996a). "Heterogeneity, stratification, and growth: Macroeconomic implications of community structure and school finance". American Economic Review 86 (3), 584–609.

Bénabou, R. (1996b). "Inequality and growth". In: Bernanke, B.S., Rotemberg, J.J. (Eds.), National Bureau of Economic Research Macro Annual, vol. 11. MIT Press, Cambridge, MA, pp. 11–74.

Bénabou, R. (2000). "Unequal societies: Income distribution and the social contract". American Economic Review 90, 96–129.

Bénabou, R. (2002). "Tax and education policy in a heterogeneous agent economy: What levels of redistribution maximize growth and efficiency?". Econometrica 70, 481–517.

Bénabou, R., Tirole, J. (2006). "Belief in a just world and redistributive politics". Quarterly Journal of Economics, in press.

Berman, E., Bound, J., Machin, S. (1997). "Implications of skill-biased technological change: International evidence". Quarterly Journal of Economics 113 (4), 1245–1280.

Bourguignon, F., Verdier, T. (2000). "Oligarchy, democracy, inequality and growth". Journal of Development Economics 62 (2), 285–314.

Caroli, E., Van Reenen, J. (1999). "Skill biased organizational change? Evidence from a panel of British and French establishments". CEPREMAP Working Paper 9917.

De Mello, L., Tiongson, E. (2003). "Income inequality and redistributive government spending". IMF Working Paper 314.

Engerman, S., Sokoloff, K. (1997). "Factor endowments, institutions, and differential growth paths among new world economies". In: Haber, S. (Ed.), How Latin America Fell Behind: Essays on the Economic Histories of Brazil and Mexico 1800–1914. Stanford University Press, Stanford, pp. 260–304.

Fellman, J. (1976). "The effect of transformations on Lorenz curves". Econometrica 44 (4), 823–824.

Fernandez, R., Rogerson, R. (1998). "Public education and the dynamics of income distribution: A quantitative evaluation of education finance reform". American Economic Review 88 (4), 813–833.

Figini, P. (1999). "Inequality and growth revisited". Trinity College Economic Papers 2/99, September. Dublin.

Forbes, K. (2000). "A reassessment of the relationship between inequality and growth". American Economic Review 90 (4), 869–887.

Fortin, N., Lemieux, T. (1997). "Institutional changes and rising wage inequality: Is there a linkage?". Journal of Economic Perspectives 11 (2), 75–97.

Freeman, R. (1995). "The large welfare state as a system". American Economic Review Papers and Proceedings 85 (2), 16–21.

Freeman, R. (1996). "Labor market institutions and earnings inequality". New England Economic Review (May/June), 169–172.

Galor, O., Moav, O. (1999). "From physical to human capital: Inequality in the process of development". CEPR Discussion Paper 2307, December.

Galor, O., Moav, O. (2000). "Ability biased technological transition, wage inequality, and economic growth". Quarterly Journal of Economics 113 (4), 1055–1090.

Galor, O., Tsiddon, D. (1997). "Technological progress, mobility, and growth". American Economic Review 87 (June), 363–382.

Galor, O., Zeira, J. (1993). "Income distribution and macroeconomics". Review of Economic Studies 60 (1), 35–52.

Glomm, G., Ravikumar, B. (1992). "Public vs. private investment in human capital: Endogenous growth and income inequality". Journal of Political Economy 100, 818–834.

Gradstein, M., Justman, M. (1997). "Democratic choice of an education system: Implications for growth and income distribution". Journal of Economic Growth 2 (2), 169–184.

Grossman, G. (2004). "The distribution of talent and the pattern and consequences of international trade". Journal of Political Economy 112 (1), 209–239.

Grossman, G., Maggi, G. (2000). "Diversity and trade". American Economic Review 90 (5), 1255–1275.

Hassler, J., Rodriguez-Mora, J. (1999). "Employment turnover and the public allocation of unemployment insurance". Journal of Public Economics 73 (1), 55–83.

Hassler, J., Rodriguez-Mora, J., Storesletten, K., Zillibotti, F. (2003). "The survival of the welfare state". American Economic Review 93 (1), 87–112.

Kiley, M. (1999). "The supply of skilled labor and skill-biased technological progress". Economic Journal 109 (October), 708–724.

Kremer, M., Maskin, E. (1996). "Wage inequality and segregation by skill". NBER Working Paper 5718.

Kremer, M., Maskin, E. (2003). "Globalization and inequality". Mimeo. Harvard University.

Kreps, D., Porteus, E. (1979). "Dynamic choice theory and dynamic programming". Econometrica 47 (1), 91–100.

Krueger, A. (2002). "Inequality, too much of a good thing?". Mimeo. April. Princeton University.

Krusell, P., Rios-Rull, J.V. (1996). "Vested interests in a positive theory of stagnation and growth". Review of Economic Studies 63, 301–329.

Lee, D. (1999). "Wage inequality in the united states during the 1980s: Rising dispersion or falling minimum wage?". Quarterly Journal of Economics 114 (3), 977–1023.

Lee, W., Roemer, J. (1998). "Income distribution, redistributive politics, and economic growth". Journal of Economic Growth 3, 217–240.

Legros, P., Newman, A. (1996). "Wealth effects, distribution, and the theory of organization". Journal of Economic Theory 70 (2), 312–341.

Lindbeck, A. (1995). "Welfare-state disincentives with endogenous habits and norms". Scandinavian Journal of Economics 97 (4), 477–494.

Lloyd-Ellis, H. (1999). "Endogenous technological change and inequality". American Economic Review 89 (1), 47–77.

Loury, G. (1981). "Intergenerational transfers and the distribution of earnings". Econometrica 49, 843–867.

Moav, O. (2002). "Income distribution and macroeconomics: The persistence of inequality in a convex technology framework". Economics Letters 75 (2), 147–287.

Mookherjee, D., Ray, D. (2003). "Persistent inequality". Review of Economic Studies 70, 369–393.

Perotti, R. (1996). "Growth, income distribution and democracy: What the data say". Journal of Economic Growth 1 (2), 149–187.

Persson, T., Tabellini, G. (1994). "Is inequality harmful for growth? Theory and evidence". American Economic Review 84 (3), 600–621.

Piketty, T. (1995). "Social mobility and redistributive politics". Quarterly Journal of Economics 110 (3), 351–442.

Piketty, T. (1997). "The dynamics of the wealth distribution and interest rate with credit-rationing". Review of Economic Studies 64 (2), 173–190.

Pineda, J., Rodriguez, F. (2000). "The political economy of human capital accumulation". Mimeo. February. University of Maryland at College Park.

Rodriguez, F. (1999). "Does inequality lead to redistribution? Evidence from the united states". Economics & Politics 11 (2), 171–199.

Romer, P. (1987). "Growth based on increasing returns due to specialization". American Economic Review 77 (May), 56–62.

Rosenstone, S., Hansen, J. (1993). Mobilization, Participation and Democracy in America. MacMillan Publishing Company, New York.

Saint-Paul, G. (2001). "The dynamics of exclusion and fiscal conservatism". Review of Economic Dynamics 4, 275–302.

Saint-Paul, G., Verdier, T. (1993). "Education, democracy and growth". Journal of Development Economics 42 (2), 399–407.

Sheshadri, A., Yuki, K. (2004). "Equity and efficiency effects of redistributive policies". Journal of Monetary Economics 57 (1), 1415–1447.

Tamura, R. (1992). "Efficient equilibrium convergence: Heterogeneity and growth". Journal of Economic Theory 58 (2), 55–76.

Thesmar, D., Thoenig, M. (2000). "Creative destruction and firm organizational choice". Quarterly Journal of Economics 115 (4), 1201–1239.

Thoenig, M., Verdier, T. (2003). "A theory of defensive skill-biased innovation and globalization". American Economic Review 93 (3), 709–728.

Vindigni, A. (2002). "Income distribution and skilled-biased technical change". Mimeo. June. Université de Toulouse.

Zhang, J. (2005). "Income ranking, convergence speeds, and growth effects of inequality with two-dimensional adjustment". Journal of Economic Dynamics and Control 29 (3), 547–566.

Chapter 26

SOCIAL CAPITAL

STEVEN N. DURLAUF

University of Wisconsin

MARCEL FAFCHAMPS

University of Oxford

Contents

Abstract	1640
Keywords	1640
1. Introduction	1641
2. Social capital: Basic concepts	1642
2.1. Defining social capital	1642
2.2. The efficiency of social exchange	1645
2.2.1. Social networks and search	1646
2.2.2. Social capital and trust	1646
2.2.3. Social capital and public goods	1647
2.3. Social capital and development	1648
2.4. Social capital and equity	1650
3. When does social capital matter?	1651
3.1. Sources of inefficiency	1651
3.2. Channels	1652
3.2.1. Information sharing	1653
3.2.2. Group identity and modification of preferences	1654
3.2.3. Coordination and leadership	1656
3.3. Formal theory	1658
4. From theory to empirics: Econometrics and social capital	1660
4.1. Externalities and individual vs. aggregate effects	1661
4.1.1. Fallacy of composition	1661
4.1.2. Free riding	1663
4.2. Model specification	1663
4.2.1. Exchangeability	1663
4.2.2. Instrumental variables	1666
4.2.3. Group effects versus social capital effects	1666

Handbook of Economic Growth, Volume 1B. Edited by Philippe Aghion and Steven N. Durlauf
© 2005 Elsevier B.V. All rights reserved
DOI: 10.1016/S1574-0684(05)01026-9

4.3. Identification	1667
4.3.1. Individual-level data	1667
4.3.2. Aggregate data	1669
4.3.3. Identification with predetermined social capital	1670
4.4. Additional issues	1671
5. Empirical studies of the effects of social capital	1672
5.1. Individual-level studies	1672
5.1.1. Social capital and development	1672
5.1.2. Social capital in OECD societies	1676
5.2. Aggregate studies	1680
6. Empirical studies of the level and determinants of social capital	1685
7. Suggestions for future research	1688
8. Conclusions	1692
Acknowledgements	1693
References	1693

Abstract

This chapter surveys research on social capital. We explore the concepts that motivate the social capital literature, efforts to formally model social capital using economic theory, the econometrics of social capital, and empirical studies of the role of social capital in various socioeconomic outcomes. While our focus is primarily on the place of social capital in economics, we do consider its broader social science context. We argue that while the social capital literature has produced many insights, a number of conceptual and statistical problems exist with the current use of social capital by social scientists. We propose some ways to strengthen the social capital literature.

Keywords

development, growth, identification, inequality, networks, social capital, trust

JEL classification: E26, O10, O40, L14, Z13

...in every community there seems to be some sort of justice, and some type of friendship, also. At any rate, fellow-voyagers and fellow-soldiers are called friends, and so are members of other communities. And the extent of their community is the extent of their friendship, since it is also the extent of the justice found there ...What is just ...is not the same for parents towards children as for one brother towards another, and the same for companions as for fellow-citizens, similarly with the other types of friendship ...what is unjust towards each of these is also different, and become more unjust as it is practiced on closer friends. It is more shocking, e.g., to rob a companion of money than to rob a fellow-citizen, to fail to help a brother than a stranger, and to strike one's father than anyone else. What is just also naturally increases with friendship, since it involves the same people and extends over an equal area.

Aristotle, *Nicomachean Ethics*, Book VIII, 9.61 [Aristotle (1985)].

1. Introduction

Social capital represents one of the most powerful and popular metaphors in current social science research. Broadly understood as referring to the community relations that affect personal interactions, social capital has been used to explain an immense range of phenomena, ranging from voting patterns to health to the economic success of countries. Literally hundreds of papers have appeared throughout the social science literature arguing that social capital matters in understanding individual and group differences and further that successful public policy design needs to account for the effects of policy on social capital formation.

This chapter is designed to survey research on social capital. We will give primary focus to the role of social capital in economic growth and development as suggested by the presence of this chapter in the *Handbook of Economic Growth*. That being said, this survey will discuss social capital in general as there is no part of the social capital literature that may plausibly be treated as orthogonal to the issues that arise in relating social capital to economic growth. Our objectives are threefold. First, we provide an overview of conceptual issues that underlie social capital studies. Second, we identify some general flaws we see in the empirical social capital literature. While we would hardly claim that every social capital study suffers from these problems, we do claim that they are prevalent in the literature. Third, we make a number of recommendations on how to strengthen the social capital literature. In assessing empirical work, we will focus almost exclusively on statistical analysis of social capital. This is not because we regard qualitative studies as unimportant (we will in fact advocate their greater use in the course of our discussion) but because such studies raise very distinct conceptual and interpretative questions from their quantitative counterparts.

Much of our discussion is critical. We argue that empirical social capital studies are often flawed and make claims that are in excess of what is justified by the statistical exercises reported. However, this should not be taken as an indictment of research on social capital per se. In our judgment the role of social factors in individual and group outcomes is of fundamental importance in most of the contexts in which social capital has been studied. Hence we regard the empirical social capital literature as addressing major outstanding issues in many areas of social science. Our intent in this survey is to evaluate what is currently known and to make suggestions on how to improve future research.

The chapter is organized as follows. Section 2 contains a discussion of how economists and other social scientists have attempted to define social capital. The section also reviews some of the contexts in which social capital has been argued to play an important causal role in various sociological outcomes. Section 3 discusses efforts to theorize about social capital; both heuristic and conceptual arguments are discussed as well as formal analyses. Section 4 discusses econometric issues that arise in the efforts to develop empirical evidence of the role of social capital as a determinant of socioeconomic outcomes. Section 5 reviews the empirical literature on social capital; while this literature is far too large to cover comprehensively we believe our survey captures the range of contexts in which social capital effects have been evaluated. Section 6 reviews empirical studies that analyze the determinants of social capital. Section 7 contains some suggestions for improving social capital research. Section 8 concludes.

2. Social capital: Basic concepts

2.1. Defining social capital

Since Loury (1977) introduced it into modern social science research and Coleman's (1988) seminal study placed it at the forefront of research in sociology, the term social capital has spread throughout the social sciences and has spawned a huge literature that runs across disciplines. Despite the immense amount of research on it, however, the definition of social capital has remained elusive. From a historical perspective, one could argue that social capital is not a concept but a *praxis*, a code word used to federate disparate but interrelated research interests and to facilitate the cross-fertilization of ideas across disciplinary boundaries. The success of social capital as a federating concept may result from the fact that no social science has managed to impose a definition of the term that captures what different researchers mean by it within a discipline, let alone across fields.[1]

While conceptual vagueness may have promoted the use of the term among the social sciences, it also has been an impediment to both theoretical and empirical research of

---

[1] Even if a precise definition of social capital were attempted, it is likely to be no less vague than other similar concepts. The term capital, for instance, is used to describe different things – from finance to machinery to infrastructure. Human capital similarly has many different meanings, such as education, nutrition, health, vocational skills, and knowledge. This kind of vagueness, however, is less problematic as long as researchers agree on some basic principles.

phenomena in which social capital may play a role.[2] In order to anchor our discussion of social capital, we need a substantive definition. We begin our search by listing a number of definitions that have been proposed by some of the most influential researchers on social capital. We begin with Coleman (1990) who defines social capital as

> ... social organization constitutes social capital, facilitating the achievement of goals that could not be achieved in its absence or could be achieved only at a higher cost (p. 304).

Putnam, Leonardi and Nanetti (1993) provides a similar characterization,

> ... social capital ... refers to features of social organization, such as trust, norms, and networks that can improve the efficiency of society ... (p. 167).

Both definitions emphasize the beneficial effects social capital is assumed to have on social aggregates. According to these definitions, social capital is a type of positive group externality. Coleman's definition suggests that the externality arises from social organization. Putnam's definition emphasizes specific *informal* forms of social organization such as trust, norms and networks. In his definition of social capital, Fukuyama (1997) argues that only certain shared norms and values should be regarded as social capital:

> Social capital can be defined simply as the existence of a certain set of informal rules or norms shared among members of a group that permits cooperation among them. The sharing of values and norms does not in itself produce social capital, because the values may be the wrong ones ... The norms that produce social capital ... must substantively include virtues like truth-telling, the meeting of obligations, and reciprocity (pp. 378–379).

Other definitions characterize social capital not in terms of outcome but in terms of relations or interdependence between individuals. In later research, Putnam (2000) defines social capital as

> ... connections among individuals – social networks and the norms of reciprocity and trustworthiness that arise from them (p. 19).

Ostrom (2000) writes:

> *Social capital* is the shared knowledge, understandings, norms, rules and expectations about patterns of interactions that groups of individuals bring to a recurrent activity (p. 176).

In a similar vein Bowles and Gintis (2002) state:

> Social capital generally refers to trust, concern for one's associates, a willingness to live by the norms of one's community and to punish those who do not (p. 2).

---

[2] Criticisms of the vagueness and inconsistency of various definitions of social capital may be found in Dasgupta (2000), Durlauf (2000), Manski (2000) and Portes (1998). Arrow (2000) goes so far as to suggest that the term social capital be abandoned.

Finally, one finds in a recent book-length treatment, Lin (2001),

> ...social capital may be defined operationally as *resources embedded in social networks and accessed and used by actors for actions.* Thus, the concept has two important components: (1) it represents resources embedded in social relations rather than individuals, and (2) access and use of such resources reside with actors (pp. 24–25).

From these definitions, we can distinguish three main underlying ideas:
(1) social capital generates positive externalities for members of a group;
(2) these externalities are achieved through shared trust, norms, and values and their consequent effects on expectations and behavior;
(3) shared trust, norms, and values arise from informal forms of organizations based on social networks and associations.

The study of social capital is that of network-based processes that generate beneficial outcomes through norms and trust.

By this definition social capital is always desirable since its presence is equated with beneficial consequences. This formulation is quite unsatisfactory from the perspective of policy evaluation [e.g., Durlauf (1999, 2002b), Portes (1998)]: if one denies the appellation of social capital to contexts where strong social ties lead to immoral or unproductive behaviors, there is nothing nontrivial to say in terms of policy. Presumably it is social structures, not their consequences, which can be influenced by policymakers. Unless we know under what conditions social structures generate beneficial outcomes, we cannot orient policy. We also note that the benefits that social capital generates for one group may disadvantage another, so that the combined effect on society need not be positive. We come back to this issue later.

The three main ideas outlined above often appear intertwined in the mind of their proponents so that one in isolation would probably not be considered social capital. For instance, there are many phenomena that generate positive (or negative) externalities. According to the definitions listed here, they would probably not be considered social capital unless they involve norms or trust. There appears to be more confusion as to whether all three parts of the definition are required for social capital. Norms and trust can be based on formal institutions such as laws and courts without reference to social networks. Yet the literature sometimes has referred to such generalized trust as social capital [e.g., Knack and Keefer (1997)]. It is also unclear whether (1) and (3) alone constitute social capital. In his seminal work on job markets, for instance, Granovetter (1975) discusses how social networks are activated to share job market information, thereby facilitating job search and raising the efficiency of the job matching process. This process does not, by itself, require shared norms or values. Fafchamps and Minten (2002) use the phrase 'social network capital' to describe this phenomenon.

From the perspective of empirical work, a definition of social capital limited to (1) and (2) is problematic. Things like 'norms' and 'shared values' are notoriously difficult to measure. This has led some of the less rigorous work in this area to present evidence of a beneficial group effect as evidence of social capital itself, and consequently to conclude that social capital is good. This kind of circular reasoning is of course not satisfactory since it is ultimately tautological and is not falsifiable.

A definition of social capital suitable for rigorous empirical work must identify observable variables that can be used as proxies for social capital [Portes (2000)]. Norms, trust, and expectations of behavior are very broad ideas that encompass no end of phenomena. Identifying a commonly acceptable set of proxies for social capital has therefore proved a formidable task and many different variables have appeared in empirical papers purportedly to measure it. Another problem has to do with the extent to which the variables used identify well-defined social influences – part (3) of our definition. Adherence to norms can be induced for many reasons, including many that cannot be reasonably construed as social. Consequently, evidence of adherence to norms does not, by itself, constitute evidence of the importance of social networks. To the extent that social networks and associations are part of the definition of social capital, evidence must also be provided that trust and shared norms are achieved via social interaction based on interpersonal networks and associations.

2.2. The efficiency of social exchange

Perhaps a more fruitful approach for our purpose is to proceed by example, that is, to select one specific phenomenon and use it to illustrate how research on social capital can be organized. Much of the commonality in definitions of social capital and in examples given by respective authors is the focus on interpersonal relationships and social networks and their effect on the efficiency of social exchange – whether the provision of a public good, as in Coleman's work, or the better organization of markets, as in Granovetter's. At the heart of the concept of social capital is the idea that positive externalities cannot be achieved without some kind of coordination, i.e., there is coordination failure. Much of the interest in social capital stems from efforts to understand how socially efficient outcomes can occur in environments in which the sorts of conditions necessary for the classical First Welfare Theorem are not fulfilled. Efficiency of social exchange is thus a good vantage point around which to organize our assessment.

One important potential role for social capital concerns its ability to ameliorate potential inefficiencies caused by imperfect information. As Hayek (1945) was among the first to point out, information asymmetries are an inescapable feature of human society. As a result, exchange is hindered either because agents who could benefit from trade cannot find each other, or because, having found each other, they do not trust each other enough to trade. In either case, some mutually beneficial exchange does not take place. Similar principles apply to the provision of public goods. Search and trust are thus two fundamental determinants of the efficiency of social exchange. If we can finds ways of facilitating search and of fostering trust, we can improve social exchange.

There are basically two ways of achieving these dual objectives: via formal institutions (e.g., a stock exchange or a trading fair) or via interpersonal relationships (e.g., word-of-mouth communication of opportunities, repeated interactions which benefit both parties). The literature on social capital focuses principally on the latter. In the following discussion, we illustrate how social networks can raise efficiency. We begin by examining the possible effects of social networks on search. In so doing, we focus only on parts (1) and (3) of our definition of social capital since norms and trust are not central to the circulation of information (although they can play a subsidiary role). We then turn to trust, the externalities it generates, and the way to sustain trust through social networks. Public goods are discussed in the following subsection. The relationship between social capital and economic development is examined next. The last subsection explores the relationship between social capital and equity.

2.2.1. Social networks and search

The role of social capital in search can be illustrated by comparing US equity and labor markets. Given the existence of a stock market, it is very easy for a seller of stock to find a buyer at the market clearing price. This is not the case in labor markets where no equivalent institution circulates accurate and up-to-date information about jobs and workers. In his path-breaking study of the US labor market, Granovetter (1975) brought to light the role played by interpersonal relationships in channeling information about jobs and job applicants. A large proportion of jobs are allocated on the basis of personal recommendation and word-of-mouth. This can be understood as an endogenous, spontaneous adaptation to the absence of a formal clearing house equivalent to the stock market.[3]

As this comparison demonstrates, observing that social capital plays a role in markets does not, by itself, constitute evidence that social capital is necessary and should be nurtured. Depending on the circumstances, the development of formal institutions may be a superior alternative.

2.2.2. Social capital and trust

As argued in Fafchamps (2004), trust may be understood as an optimistic expectation or belief regarding other agents' behavior. The origin of trust may vary.[4] Sometimes, trust arises from repeated interpersonal interaction. Other times, it arises from general knowledge about the population of agents, the incentives they face, and the upbringing they have received [Platteau (1994a, 1994b)]. The former can be called personalized trust and the latter generalized trust. The main difference between the two is that, for each pair of newly matched agents, the former takes time and effort to establish while the latter is instantaneous.

---

[3] This is not to say that efforts have not been made to emulate the stock market model – from employment offices to Internet sites to temporary employment agencies. But to date none of these institutions seems capable of conveying sufficiently precise information about jobs and job applicants, especially regarding worker environment, work ethics, and personal motivation. See Fafchamps (2002) and Kranton (1996) for models of spontaneous market emergence organized around interpersonal relationships.

[4] Sometimes trust is misplaced, but for the sake of brevity, we ignore this possibility here.

In most situations, trusting others enables economic agents to operate more efficiently – e.g. by invoicing for goods they have delivered or by agreeing to stop hos-
tilities. Whenever this is the case, generalized trust yields more efficient outcomes than
personalized trust. The reason is that, for any pair of agents, generalized trust is established faster and more cheaply than personal trust. This observation has long been made
in the anthropological literature on generalized morality. Fostering generalized trust can
thus potentially generate large efficiency gains. How this can be accomplished, however,
is unclear.

Clubs and networks are different concepts having to do with the structure of links
among economic agents. Clubs describe finite, closed groupings. Networks describe
more complex situations in which individual agents are related only to some other
agents, not all. The term 'network' is sometimes used to describe the entire set of links
among a finite collection of agents. Other times, it is used to describe the set of links
around a specific individual. To avoid confusion, we refer to the second concept as a
subjective network.

Among other things, clubs and networks can be used to describe the extent to which
personalized and generalized trust exist in a population. Perfect generalized trust corresponds to the case where all agents belong to a single club (or complete network)
and trust all other members. Situations in which generalized trust exists only among
sub-populations [say, Jewish diamond dealers in New York, cf. Bernstein (1992)] could
be described as small clubs. Situations in which individual agents only trust a limited
number of agents they know individually can be described as a network.

From the above discussion, it is immediately clear that if trust is beneficial for
economic efficiency, the loss from imperfect trust can be visualized as the difference
between the actual trust network and the minimum network that would support all mutually beneficial trades. Following this reasoning, inefficiency is expected to be highest
in societies where the trust network is very sparse [Granovetter (1995)]. Inefficiency
is also large when subgroups who could benefit a lot from trading with each other are
prevented from doing so by mutual isolation. This is true even if many links exist within
each subgroup.

2.2.3. Social capital and public goods

In the preceding subsection we discussed the role of trust in fostering exchange. Trust
is also an essential ingredient in the delivery of public goods. In many cases, the state
can organize the provision of public goods by taxing individuals. Whenever this is true,
trust is not essential. But there are many forms of public goods that cannot be harnessed
through state intervention.

In his work on PTA run schools, for instance, Coleman (1988) shows that parental
involvement in school affairs has a beneficial external effect on student achievement,
probably because it leads children to believe their parents care about their education.
Parental involvement, in turn, requires trust to reduce and solve interpersonal conflicts
and to minimize fears of free-riding. In this example, the externality is a public good

that cannot be harnessed by state intervention. Voluntary participation by parents is essential.

In poor countries, there are many situations in which the state could, theoretically, intervene to provide a public good, but where it is unable to do so because its tax base and its capacity to organize are limited. Collective action can serve as a substitute for the state. However, because collective action cannot rely on the coercive power of the state (e.g. the ability to tax and enforce contracts), it is much harder to set in motion. Two essential ingredients are then required: leadership and trust. A leader is required who is capable of convincing community members that they should voluntarily contribute to the public good. Trust is necessary to resolve conflicts among competing interests and to reduce fears of free-riding. Leaders can also help raise the level of trust in the community.

What the above discussion indicates is that delivering public goods via voluntary organizations depends critically on local trust and leadership. If these ingredients are absent, for instance after a civil war, then state intervention is likely to be much easier. Furthermore, good local leaders are rare. Projects that work well in one place because of strong local involvement need not be replicable elsewhere if local leaders are weak. Pilot projects of public good delivery through local communities may provide wrong signals if their placement is correlated with the presence of good local leaders who managed to attract the pilot project to their community.

2.3. Social capital and development

Much of the interest in social capital stems from the view that the absence of social capital represents one of the major impediments to economic development; Woolcock (1998) provides a wide ranging conceptual analysis of the role of social capital for developing societies and economies; a range of applications of social capital to economic development are collected in Dasgupta and Serageldin (2000) and Grootaert and van Bastelear (2002). In fact, much of the current interest in social capital stems from the now classic book by Putnam, Leonardi and Nanetti (1993) which argues that northern Italy developed faster than southern Italy because the former was better endowed in social capital – measured by membership in groups and clubs. One of the major claims in this literature is that social capital can facilitate the solution of collective action problems.

However, when focusing on advanced societies, the effects of social capital on economic performance are less obvious. For example, Putnam (2000), focusing on the US experience since the 1950s, argues that social capital, defined as membership in formal and informal clubs, has declined monotonically since the 1950s. This is true for all states, all decades, and all measures of social capital. However, he finds no relationship between the speed of the decline of social capital and economic performance across US states or across time periods. Further, the relationship between social capital and socioeconomic outcomes is even harder to characterize when one looks at subperiods. For example, the 1990s were a period of rapid economic growth in the US yet it is also a period of rapid decline in social capital, at least based on the sorts of measures he uses. To be clear, Putnam does attempt to associate higher social capital with better socioeconomic outcomes, our point is that the relationship between the two for the United States is even at first glance relatively complicated.

The differences between the case of Italian regions and that of the United States is suggestive of how one might think about the relationship between development and social capital. One interpretation of these differences is that for the United States, generalized trust has improved over the period studied, so club membership has become less necessary.[5] In contrast, the Italian experience relates to an earlier period in which generalized trust may have been insufficient or incomplete and small clubs helped broaden the range of personalized trust. This raises the general possibility that clubs and networks are important at intermediate levels of development. Their function is to broaden the range and speed of social exchange beyond the confines of inter-personal trust. But once a sufficiently high level of generalized trust has been achieved, clubs and networks are no longer necessary and wither away [North (2001)]. A similar kind of reasoning can be followed for public goods. In undeveloped economies, the state is weak and under-funded. Consequently it cannot organize the delivery of all needed public goods. This is particularly true for local public goods or for public goods that require a modicum of voluntary involvement to limit free-riding (of which corruption is but one manifestation).

Social capital provides an alternative. Clubs formed for noneconomic purposes (e.g., religious worship) have leaders. In the absence of public good provision by the state, these leaders may decide to mobilize club members (e.g., the religious congregation) to provide missing public goods. History is replete with examples of faith-based organizations intervening to build schools and clinics and to provide a variety of public services. Here, sharing a common religious fervor is the basis for trust and the religious hierarchy provides the necessary leaders. Some large secular organizations have adopted similar practices – e.g., political parties yesterday, nongovernmental organizations (NGOs) today.[6]

These issues have immediate implications for empirical work on social capital. The difficulty comes from the fact that first-best outcomes can in principle be achieved without paying attention to clubs and networks. Generalized trust in commercial contracts, for instance, can theoretically be achieved via laws and courts. Because of the possibility that revenues may be collectively raised via taxation, public goods can in principle

---

[5] In this discussion, we stipulate that Putnam's claims about declining US social capital are correct. In fact, this claim has been subjected to important criticism. Skocpol (1996), has argued, for example, that while participation in local groups has declined, participations in larger organizations such as the American Association of Retired Persons has increased, and that what really needs be understood is the nature of voluntary group memberships and the like, rather than the number of memberships per se. See Skocpol (2003) for a detailed elaboration of this idea. One important implication of Skocpol's work for economists is that many of the measures that have been proposed to quantify social capital may be fundamentally flawed.

[6] One classic historical example is the role of the Social Democratic Party in organizing a range of social and cultural activities for its members in Imperial Germany, see Blackbourn (1997, chapter 8).

be organized by the state at lower cost in terms of public mobilization and leadership skills. As North (1973, 1990) has argued, the rise of the Western world is precisely due to the invention of institutions that protect property rights and make the state more effective at delivering public goods. Clubs, networks, and community-based voluntary organizations can improve efficiency in economic exchange and public good delivery. But these are typically second-best solutions. The first-best approach is generally to develop well-functioning legal institutions and state organizations.[7]

Whether or not social capital raises efficiency we therefore argue depends on the level of institutional development. Suppose that laws and courts are insufficient to ensure respect of commercial contracts. This situation can arise anywhere [Bernstein (1996)] but it is probably most severe in poor countries where many transactions are small and buyers and sellers are too poor for court action to yield reparation [Bigsten et al. (2000), Fafchamps and Minten (2002)].[8] In such an environment, market exchange relies on a combination of personalized trust, legal institutions (e.g., to enforce large contracts and to punish thieves), and informal institutions (e.g., reputation sharing within business networks and communities). Whether or not social capital facilitates exchange can then be seen as a test of the strength and reach of formal institutions.

A similar line of reasoning holds for public goods. Public good delivery is best accomplished when the power of the state to tax and mobilize resources is combined with trust and community involvement. The reason is that, without voluntarily accepted discipline, government action is ineffective: taxes do not get paid, rules are not followed, civil servants become corrupt, and free riding reigns. Discipline in turn depends on the perceived legitimacy of government action and the degree of public involvement in the decision-making process. It also depends on identification with the political elites, sense of national urgency, and many other factors which are still poorly understood. The bottom-line, however, is clear: without some form of voluntary acceptance by the public, government efforts to provide public goods are likely to fail. Social capital is thus probably essential for public good delivery. But the forms it may take are likely to vary depending on local conditions, i.e., from generalized trust in government and formal institutions to interpersonal trust mobilized via clubs and networks.

2.4. Social capital and equity

We have argued that trust is essential to both economic exchange and public good delivery. We have also argued that clubs and networks can facilitate search and provide an imperfect substitute to generalized trust: in the absence of generalized trust, it may be necessary to rely on clubs and networks. Unlike generalized trust, however, clubs

---

[7] Bowles and Gintis (2002) elaborate this type of reasoning, although in their view social capital plays a role in overcoming limits to government intervention generated by information constraints and so acts as a complement to government institutions in producing efficient outcomes.

[8] Except through forced labor, as in 19th century England and France. But this is of course now outlawed in most countries.

and networks often have distributional consequences that may be quite inequitable. The reason is that, unlike generalized trust, clubs and networks only offer a partial or uneven coverage of society. If the benefits of social capital principally accrue to network members, those who happen to be included benefit from increased efficiency but those that are excluded do not. As Fafchamps (2002) and Taylor (2000) have shown, the creation of clubs or networks can even penalize nonmembers. This is because members of a club or network find it easier to deal with each other and, as a result, may stop dealing with nonmembers.[9]

Clubs are least conducive to equity when membership is restricted to a specific group (e.g., men or whites) or when new members are not accepted (e.g., established firms only). Even when new members are accepted without restriction, historical events can shape the composition of clubs for decades whenever entry is slow. In this case, equal opportunity need not be realized because old members have enjoyed the benefits of membership for much longer. By extension, clubs are likely to have undesirable consequences on equity whenever (1) club membership is beneficial to members and (2) entry into the club is not instantaneous. Put differently, clubs raise equity concerns whenever they have real economic benefits.

The creation of clubs may thus reinforce polarization in society between the 'in' group and the 'out' group. Investing in social capital by promoting clubs can thus have serious equity repercussions. This is true even if we ignore the fact that certain clubs may collude to explicitly dominate or exclude others (e.g., the Ku Klux Klan). A similar situation arises with networks because better connected individuals profit from their contacts [Fafchamps and Minten (2002)]. Social capital can be used by certain groups to overtake others, generating between-group inequality and political tension. To the extent that between-group inequality itself favors crime and riots and deters investment, promoting social capital by promoting specific groups may, in the long-run, be counterproductive.

3. When does social capital matter?

The conceptual discussion has clarified the definition of social capital and its possible role in the development process. This discussion, however, has not precisely identified the conditions under which social capital matters. To achieve this, we need a general conceptual framework in which there is room for social capital to be beneficial.

3.1. Sources of inefficiency

For social capital to increase Pareto efficiency, the decentralized equilibrium without social capital must not be Pareto efficient in the first place. Social capital can only have

---

[9] Of course, this is not to say that impersonal markets based on generalized trust treat all groups fairly. Statistical discrimination, for instance, naturally arises even in the absence of clubs and networks [e.g., Fafchamps (2003)].

a beneficial effect in a second-best world. Deviations from first-best outcomes arise for a variety of reasons including externalities and free-riding, imperfect information and enforcement, imperfect competition, and the like. For social capital to be beneficial, it must therefore resolve or compensate for one of these sources of inefficiency. Secondly, whatever the source of inefficiency, there are only a limited number of ways by which social capital – or any other mechanism – may improve upon a decentralized equilibrium. First, it may resolve a coordination failure in an economy that has multiple Pareto-ranked equilibria. Second, it may alter individual incentives so as to replace the decentralized equilibrium with a superior one. Third, it may affect the technology of social exchange, for instance by opening new avenues for the circulation of information.

From these two preliminary observations, it is immediately obvious that social capital will never be the only possible solution to inefficiency. There always exist alternative mechanisms to solve coordination failure, improve individual incentives, and upgrade the technology of social exchange – such as contracts, vertical integration, state intervention, or redefinition of property rights. Of course, there are many circumstances in which social capital is a less expensive or simpler institutional solution, but it is important to recognize that it can never be the only one.

These observations have immediate implications regarding empirical investigation. Suppose social capital improves efficiency by solving a coordination failure problem. For this to occur, the economy must have multiple Pareto-ranked equilibria. Social capital provides the leadership or coordination device necessary to select a superior equilibrium among the many possible ones. Suppose further that the researchers have multiple observations of such economies, some with social capital and some without. Since nothing precludes these economies from achieving a high equilibrium without social capital, it is inherently difficult to test its effect. Furthermore, social capital may arise endogenously as an institutional response to an inferior equilibrium. To the extent that social capital does not always succeed in moving the economy to the better equilibrium, one could have the paradoxical situation in which economies with social capital are on average at a lower equilibrium than those without. This is a standard difficulty with multiple equilibria but it is not always adequately recognized in empirical work.

Even when there is a single equilibrium, social capital never is the only possible way of improving efficiency by altering incentives or technology. Identifying the effect of social capital requires that the researcher adequately control for other possible institutional solutions. Here too, self-selection is a concern.

3.2. Channels

The literature has identified a number of channels by which social capital improves efficiency. Most of these channels fall under one or a combination of the following three categories: information sharing, group identity, and explicit coordination.

3.2.1. Information sharing

It is a commonplace that human beings derive satisfaction from interacting with others. Socializing often involves the transfer of information, even if the purpose of socialization is not to transfer this information. The sharing of information is then a by-product of social interaction, a Marshallian externality. To the extent that the shared information is economically useful, socialization generates a positive externality.

Socialization may also be initiated with the intent of acquiring a specific piece of information. In this case, the transfer of information is the purpose of socialization. Because interacting with others is also a consumption good, collecting information through socialization benefits from a kind of 'subsidy' relative to nonsocial forms of information collection (e.g., going to the library).

The literature on social capital contains many applications of this simple idea. Barr (2000), for instance, argues that social networks among Ghanaian entrepreneurs serve to channel information about new technology. Fafchamps and Minten (1999), Granovetter (1975, 1995), Montgomery (1991), Rauch (1996), Rauch and Casella (2003) and many others have emphasized the role of social networks in conveying information about employment and market opportunities. Fafchamps (2004), Greif (1993), Johnson, McMillan and Woodruff (2000), Kandori (1992) and McMillan and Woodruff (2000) have brought to light the role of social networks in circulating information about breach of contract, thereby enabling business groups to penalize and exclude cheaters. Wade (1987, 1988) discusses the role of social capital in reducing incentive problems in teams by circulating information about effort. This point has also been made in the theoretical literature on industrial organizations, where the possibility for members of a team of workers to monitor and penalize each other has been shown to increase efficiency. Social capital may also circulate information about what tasks need to be done and when. Platteau and Seki (2002) provide an illustration of this idea in the case of Japanese fishermen and the coordination of their fishing efforts to minimize cost (e.g., exchange information about fish location) and maximize revenue (e.g., coordinate the landing of fish to maximize prices). The different mechanisms that link networks and economic outcomes may be simultaneously present; Rauch and Trindade (2002), for example, argue that the role of ethnic Chinese networks in bilateral trade between countries reflects both the ability of networks to match buyers and sellers in product characteristic space as well as to facilitate social sanctions.

While the evidence provided is impressive, the literature remains somewhat naïve in its assumption regarding the ease with which accurate information can be exchanged. In practice, three conditions must be satisfied for social capital to raise Pareto efficiency through the sharing of information: (1) imperfect information must be the source of inefficiency; (2) there are disincentives to spread erroneous information; (3) there are no obstacles to Pareto efficiency other than imperfect information. Even if social capital satisfies the first condition, it may not satisfy the other two. It is also important to recognize that the information sharing benefits generated by social capital can always be obtained in another way. For instance, information sharing can be explicitly organized and budgeted within a large organization, whether public or private (enterprise, NGO). To empirically test the effect of social capital, one should control for the possible presence of such organizations.

It is so customary to blame imperfect information for economic inefficiency that other sources of inefficiency, such as imperfect contract enforcement and insufficient protection of property rights, are sometimes disregarded. Fafchamps (2002), for instance, shows how the decentralized enforcement of contracts naturally takes the form of relational contracting, even without exchange of information. In this example, contract enforcement is the channel through which social capital raises efficiency, not information sharing. In his analysis of market institutions in Sub-Saharan Africa, Fafchamps (2004) points out that incentives often exist to distort the conveyed information, either to hurt a competitor or to hide one's own shortcomings. Interviews with entrepreneurs suggest that gossip is never regarded as reliable information. Guaranteeing that accurate information is transferred through social networks requires the existence of punishment mechanisms – such as the loss of reputation – penalizing false reporting. Finally, there often are obstacles to Pareto efficiency other than imperfect information. The most common one is coordination failure. We revisit this issue below.

3.2.2. Group identity and modification of preferences

Under the general heading of group identity and modification of preferences, we put various effects that arise because identification with a group or network affects individual preferences and choices. Economists usually regard individual preferences as exogenously given and relatively stable over time. As psychologists have shown, however, individual preferences can be manipulated through advertising or propaganda. Individual preferences can also fluctuate over time in a systematic, somewhat predictable fashion. Impulses are one particularly relevant example of such phenomenon. Individuals have been shown to violate their own stated preferences in response to an impulse – to eat, to drink, to buy.

This introduces time inconsistency in preferences. Because agents anticipate they may be subject to impulses, they often resort to various 'tricks' that limit their future choices – such as putting money on a savings account that cannot be accessed easily, or carrying a limited amount of cash when shopping. Agents may also voluntarily enter in restrictive social arrangements in order to protect themselves against their own impulses. Alcoholics Anonymous is a good example of such a process. Participation in Rotating Savings and Credit Associations (ROSCAs) can similarly be understood as a way of forcing oneself to save.

The literature on social capital is replete with descriptions of such virtuous processes. Because these descriptions implicitly assume that social capital alters individual preferences, they often seem alien to economists. One such claim often made in the literature is the idea that social capital favors altruism and raises concerns for the common good – the 'touchy-feely' side of social capital. To see how even a minor increase in altruism can raise efficiency, consider a standard prisoner's dilemma (PD) game with standardized payoff matrix

$$
\begin{array}{cc}
 & \begin{array}{cc} \textit{Cooperate} & \textit{Defect} \end{array} \\
\begin{array}{c} \textit{Cooperate} \\ \textit{Defect} \end{array} & \left(\begin{array}{cc} (1,1) & (-a,b) \\ (b,-a) & (0,0) \end{array} \right)
\end{array}
$$

with $a > 0$, $b > 1$. It is standard that $(Defect, Defect)$ is the unique Nash equilibrium. Now suppose that players become altruistic, so that their utility is the weighted sum of their individual payoff Π_i and their opponent's individual payoff Π_j, so that $U_i = (1 - \alpha)\Pi_i + \alpha\Pi_j$ where $\alpha > 0$. In this case, *Defect* is no longer necessarily a best response strategy; $(Cooperate, Cooperate)$ is now a Nash equilibrium if $1 > b(1 - \alpha) - a\alpha$ or equivalently, $\alpha > (b - 1)/(b + a)$. This condition can be satisfied for values of α well below one half, implying that, depending on the values of a and b, even moderate levels of altruism can eliminate the prisoner's dilemma. Similar reasoning can be applied to games with inferior equilibria, such as the assurance game: in these games some altruism can also eliminate Pareto inferior outcomes. The intuition behind this result is obvious: the more players internalize others' payoffs, the more they care about Pareto efficiency. When both players give equal weight to their payoff and others', they only care about aggregate welfare, what we call the common good. In this case, the equilibrium is always Pareto efficient.[10] Altruism provides an efficient solution to free-riding – a principle that most religions seem to have discovered centuries ago.

The relationship between altruism and social capital probably has to do with group identity [Akerlof and Kranton (2000)]. Economic experiments using the dictator game and the trust game indeed suggest that agents exhibit more altruism and play more cooperatively if they have been induced to identify with a group [e.g., Fershtman and Gneezy (2001)].[11] This is true even if members of the group are unknown and even if they are not even seen during the experiment. These results suggest that group identification may trigger agents to adopt more altruistic preferences, thereby yielding more efficient group outcomes. If identification with a group is necessary for preferences to become more altruistic and better aligned with the common good, efforts to foster a sense of community may naturally be seen as an essential component of social capital by many researchers. This probably explains why community building is often construed as a way to foster social capital.

Social capital may also affect preferences in other ways. As argued by Fafchamps (1996) and Platteau (1994a), several mechanisms can be used to enforce contractual obligations: legal and extra-legal penalties, loss of reputation, and guilt. These same mechanisms can enforce contributions to the public good in case individual preferences are not aligned with the common good. By circulating information, social capital

---

[10] Note that the common good equilibrium is Pareto efficient in both the original, selfish preferences Π_i and in the altruistic preferences $U_i = (1 - \alpha)\Pi_i + \alpha\Pi_j$.

[11] In the trust game players play sequentially. Player 1 gives an amount X to player 2. This amount is multiplied by the researcher, usually by 2 or 3. Player 2 then gives an amount Y to player 1. There is no repetition.

can magnify reputational sanctions, a point we have discussed in the previous sub-section. Group identification can also raise guilt for acting against the group's common interest. In our PD game, this is formally equivalent to deducting the subjective cost associated with guilt, call it g, from the payoff b associated with defection. If this feeling is strong enough so that $b - g < 1$, defection is deterred. Since Max Weber, the literature on market development has emphasized the role played by religion in fostering business honesty [Ensminger (1992), Geertz, Geertz and Rosen (1979), Poewe (1989)]. Communist work ethics propaganda can be seen as a similar effort to improve team performance by raising guilt among shirkers. One should not dismiss the power of such propaganda, especially when it is present in conjunction with other incentives including coercion, as evidenced by the Stakhanovite movement in the Soviet Union in the 1930s, see Siegelbaum (1988) for a nuanced discussion.

By favoring identification with a group, social capital may also affect preferences through mimicry. In the literature, this idea appears in many guises, the phrase most commonly used being 'role model'. Coleman's example of PTA-run schools is a good illustration. According to Coleman, children whose parents are involved in running the school adopt a more positive attitude towards study. This change in preferences cannot be understood as altruism: it is in the children's long-term self-interest to study. Nor does it appear to be purely the result of a sharpened sense of guilt for not studying. Rather it is related to a demonstration or role model effect: children change their preferences to mimic that of their parents. By visibly and credibly demonstrating their positive attitude towards school, parents induce a change in attitude among their children.

This kind of phenomenon is related to what economists have called 'herding behavior', that is, the drive to mimic the behavior of others. More research is needed in this area to fully comprehend the phenomenon and its implications for economic efficiency. As has been argued formally in Blume (2002), however, mimicry need not result in superior equilibria: nothing in mimicry itself precludes agents from copying bad behaviors instead of good ones. One famous example is that of a group of high school students who refused to take their graduation exam as a symbol of group identity, even though doing so hurt them all. Other examples of bad mimicry involve hazing, gang rape, crime culture, and the like. Unlike altruism, mimicry is a double-edged sword.

3.2.3. Coordination and leadership

Some of the beneficial effects of social capital on preferences occur by osmosis, without any purposeful action by anyone: people chat around a glass of beer and, quite by chance, a relevant piece of information is exchanged. In many cases, however, the benefits of social capital are only achieved through purposeful action: someone has to want to improve the group's welfare and must do something about it for benefits to materialize. This is particularly true of any benefit that requires coordination in order to be achieved.

This raises a host of difficult issues having to do with the decision making process within groups. It is well beyond the scope of this chapter to discuss these issues in detail. A few remarks are nevertheless in order. First, two essential ingredients seem to play fundamental roles in purposeful group action: leadership, and rules regarding group decision making. At this level of generality, their respective role is unclear. What is inescapable, however, is that neither of them constitutes social capital.

In very informal groupings, leadership is likely to be essential to alter individual preferences and elicit voluntary contributions to the common good. While social capital may assist the action of leaders by facilitating the circulation of information and favoring group identification, the respective roles of leadership quality and social capital are likely to be extremely difficult to disentangle. This has important implications for empirical work: if good leadership is required to achieve the coordination required to benefit from social capital, testing the effect of social capital requires controlling for the quality of leadership.

This observation also has implications for policy. Good leaders may improve efficiency by using the levers of social capital – e.g., by fostering altruistic preferences and concern for the common good; favoring group identification; preaching good behavior and making free-riders feel guilty; encouraging mimicry of good behavior through role models and the manipulation of group symbols and representations (e.g., religion, ideology). This is what practitioners in the field call 'building social capital'.[12] Many NGOs, for instance, are engaged in precisely this kind of work. Sometimes they focus on the identification and training of local leaders, something to which many NGOs refer as an example of 'capacity building' [Barr, Fafchamps and Owens (2004)].

Purposeful coordination can also be obtained through formal rules by which decisions are made and deviance penalized. A simple majority rule combined with fines and jail sentences for free-riders is in many cases sufficient to reach efficiency. As long as free-riding is not so prevalent as to overwhelm policing, punishments directly alter incentives in ways that align individual behavior with the common good. In this case, social capital plays little role – except perhaps in coordinating not to overwhelm the enforcement apparatus. Leadership also becomes less critical since there is no need for a charismatic leader who can affect individual preferences directly. All that is required is a 'bureaucratic' leader who can apply and enforce the rules decided by the group.

A proper investigation of the importance of social capital in economic life therefore requires a careful analysis of the rules by which decisions are reached. It is important not to credit social capital with outcomes due to formal rules. This means distinguishing between the benefits resulting directly from formal organization and the indirect benefits members derive from contact with each other. For instance, the Rotary Club has a decision-making body to coordinate the date and venue of its next dinner. The coordination benefit of meeting on the same day in the same place follows directly from the Club's formal rules. But once at the dinner, there is probably no coordinated mechanism to share information among members.

---

[12] To a number of economists, these forms of policy intervention may seem unusual because they have no effect on material incentives but operate only through mental representations. We revisit these issues in greater detail below.

This same sort of reasoning applies to schools. In addition to the effects of student attitudes discussed by Coleman, PTA-run schools have an organizational structure different from that of other schools. In particular, decisions are taken differently and funding is allocated in a different manner when parents and teachers possess decision making power in schools. As Jimenez and Sawada (1999) have shown in the case of El Salvador, PTA-run schools tend to provide greater remuneration and select better teachers than other schools. These schools also exhibit lower rates of teacher absenteeism. At least part of these differences may plausibly be attributed to differences in funding and internal decision-making rules. Disentangling these effects from those of social capital is likely to be difficult and contentious.

3.3. Formal theory

While the ideas associated with social capital have been linked to many strands of modern microeconomic theory, there has been relatively little formal modeling of social capital per se. One reason for this, we conjecture, is the absence of a generally accepted and coherent definition of social capital, as discussed.

In terms of the efforts to embody social capital in formal economic models, one approach that has been taken is to incorporate social capital in models in the context of repeated prisoner's dilemma games. In environments in which agents change partners, the sustainability of a cooperative equilibrium depends on either the likelihood with which a match today will be repeated in the future and/or the ability of an agent to access information about the past behavior of a new partner [Kandori (1992)]. In this context, social capital is interpreted in terms of the factors that facilitate the existence of a cooperative equilibrium. Routledge and von Amsburg (2003), using a prisoner's dilemma environment of the type we described above, define social capital as present whenever a cooperative equilibrium exists; the key variable that determines whether cooperation can occur is the probability of trade between a pair of agents. Intuitively, if this probability is high, two agents meeting today are likely to meet in the future, so that any loss from cooperation today is compensated by future cooperation in the repeated relationship. Routledge and von Amsberg apply this idea to study how migration across regions or sectors, can, by lowering the likelihood of repeated interactions, lead to a loss of social capital. Annen (2003) defines social capital as an individual's reputation for cooperation in prisoner's dilemma games. In his analysis, this reputation depends on the extent to which information transmission about past behavior is reliable and the complexity of the network in which agents interact. Changes in either reliability or complexity can thus alter levels of social capital. Annen focuses on the question of when increases in network complexity lead to a reduction of network size or an increase in network size accompanied by greater investment in communication capacity.

Other formal theory relevant to social capital includes efforts to model the notions of trust and trustworthiness. Zak and Knack (2001) study a general equilibrium growth model in which agents facing moral hazard problems decide how much to invest in monitoring. The presence and strength of formal and informal sanctions for dishonesty are shown to have powerful implications for growth because of their role in reducing the need to invest in monitoring. Another approach to modeling trust is due to Somanathan and Rubin (2004), who study the evolutionary stability of honest types in a population and provide conditions under which honest players can survive. The notion that some agents are intrinsically more trustworthy than others is employed by Rob and Zemsky (2002) to understand how cooperative versus noncooperative corporate cultures are produced by ex ante differences in the proclivity of agents to cooperate. Huang (2003) extends work of this type to considering how parents might invest in ways to make their children more trustworthy; when the payoff to trustworthy behavior depends on the investments of others, then multiple equilibria in population-level trustworthiness can arise.

Perhaps the most important contribution to formal theory is Dasgupta (2003) which provides a wide ranging discussion of the relationship between social capital and formal modeling. Dasgupta argues that social capital should not be defined in terms of the presence of cooperation or some other outcome; rather that it should be regarded directly as social structure,

> ... social capital is most usefully viewed as a system of interpersonal networks ...
> If the externalities network formation gives to are "confined", social capital is an aspect of "human capital", in the sense economists use the latter term. However, if network externalities are more in the nature of public goods, social capital is a component of what economists call "total factor productivity" (pp. 6–7).

Dasgupta's analysis is important as it indicates how the role of social capital in growth cannot be reduced to the addition of a variable to a linear cross-country growth regression. His analysis is also important in its recognition that theoretical claims about the desirability of the sorts of social structures that have been equated to social capital are to some extent artifices of particular modeling assumptions. For example, he argues that the claim that repetition of a one-shot game necessarily benefits the players of the game is not a generic finding and in fact does not generally hold for payoff structures other than the prisoner's dilemma, going on to argue that work such as Fudenberg and Maskin (1996) shows how social capital can lead to exploitive relationships. As such Dasgupta's analysis makes clear how functional notions of social capital are inconsistent with rigorous theorizing. Other conceptual discussions of social capital and social science include Ostrom and Ahn (2002) and Paldam and Svendsen (2000); the former is particularly interesting to contrast with Dasgupta (2003) as it is written from the perspective of noneconomists and indicates some of the conceptual gaps between economists and other social scientists on this topic.

Dasgupta's equating of social capital with social structure is reflected in a number of theoretical developments to link social capital with network formation. Redondo-Vega (2003) studies the evolution of a social network that links agents both through the determination of playing partners in repeated PDs and through the way in which information about previous play is used. Agents also receive opportunities to form new network links with others. An important substantive feature of the analysis is that various types of uncertainty affect measures of network density, measures which formally capture some of intuitive ideas behind the idea of rich versus poor social capital. Rauch and Watson (2004) model the formation of partnerships between others with whom one has previously worked versus strangers; while the former are less costly to form the latter produce higher expected profits. They show how the resultant social networks can exhibit clusters (densely interconnected subgroups within a population) and bridges (sparse connections between clusters), which have been described by Burt (2000) as salient features of social capital as embodied in networks. This type of work illustrates the great potential for the new economic theory of networks, see Jackson (2003) for an outstanding survey, in providing a rigorous foundation for social capital theories.

4. From theory to empirics: Econometrics and social capital

Having clarified the relationship between social capital and the efficiency of social exchange, we now turn to the statistical analysis of the effects of social capital. We first revisit the points raised in this section, such as the distinction between individual and aggregate efficiency effects. We then ask whether it is possible to uncover social capital effects from the sorts of data available to social scientists. In particular, we discuss the issue of identification, that is, of whether a role for social capital can be uncovered when other types of social effects may be present.

Standard practice in economics and sociology is to run regressions of some outcome of interest against a set of controls and some asserted empirical proxies for social capital. These regressions are often justified by an informal argument that the empirical proxies act as instrumental variables for the unobserved 'true' social capital measure. At one extreme, one finds analyses such as Furstenberg and Hughes (1995) in which the probability that an individual drops out of school is related to variables such as the presence of a father in the household or the educational aspirations of the person's friends. In contrast, studies such as Knack and Keefer (1997) attempt to explain growth differences across entire countries using survey measures of trust.

In this section, we discuss some general econometric issues that arise in social capital studies of this type. We first examine difficulties inherent in the estimation of the benefits from social capital on the basis of individual data. These difficulties are not specific to social capital and are shared by other externalities. But they are often ignored in empirical work.

Second, we discuss the question of model specification. In particular, we review some requirements for treating a given social capital regression as causal. Next, we discuss identification. In this case, we assume that a researcher has the 'correct' model of some outcome of interest and ask whether observational data on the phenomena will allow for the identification of a causal relationship between social capital and the outcome.

The basic econometric issues associated with identifying a role for social capital may be understood in the context of cross-sections. While panel data have certain advantages, notably that they allow for the researcher to control for fixed effects across units, the conditions under which social capital effects may be identified are not qualitatively different.

4.1. Externalities and individual vs. aggregate effects

As we have discussed in Section 2, the literature on social capital is interested in externalities arising from coordination failure. Much of the empirical work on social capital seeks to identify the effect of social capital on an outcome variable of interest, say ω_i. This variable of interest can be measured at the aggregate level – e.g., country growth – or at the individual level – e.g., performance of a pupil on an exam. Empirical work on social capital can thus be divided into individual and aggregate level regressions.

The first difficulty many researchers encounter is that individual returns to social capital often are poor predictors of aggregate externalities. There are two main reasons for this: fallacy of composition and free riding. A fallacy of composition arises whenever social capital pegs individuals against each other. In a situation of competition for a finite resource, the gains made by those with more social capital lead to losses for those without, relative to a situation without social capital. Free riding is the opposite situation in which aggregate social gains are larger than those appropriated by the owners of social capital. We discuss them in turn.

4.1.1. Fallacy of composition

To illustrate fallacy of composition, consider a simple job search example inspired by Granovetter's work. Suppose there are M job openings and N job seekers, all identical, with $N > M$. Suppose that employers and workers do not know each other and are matched at random. Since $N > M$, all positions are filled and each worker has an equal probability M/N of getting a job. Total surplus is the sum of employer and worker surplus. Since all workers are equivalent, total surplus is the same irrespective of which workers get the available jobs.

Next suppose that, because of interpersonal connections, a group of workers C hears about the open positions before other workers. Further suppose that $C < M$. Consequently C workers get a job with probability 1. Other workers get the remaining jobs with probability $(M - C)/(N - C)$ which is smaller than M/N. Total surplus is unchanged since workers are equivalent. Social networks – in this case the existence of a better connected group of workers – have no effect on the efficiency of social exchange. But they have important distributional consequences, which can be measured by regressing the probability of obtaining a job on group membership. Doing so in our example would yield a coefficient of $1 - (M - C)/(N - C)$ on membership in the group even though the net effect of social networks on aggregate welfare is zero. What this example illustrates is that social networks can have private returns even when they have no effect – other than distributional – on the efficiency of social exchange. Observing private returns to social networks should therefore not be construed as evidence of social capital. In our example, social networks actually generate a discriminatory outcome, which is inconsistent with equality of opportunity as conceptualized by Roemer (1998) for example.[13]

The above reasoning can be extended to situations where groups, not individuals, compete with each other. Consider, for instance, high schools competing to place their graduates at Harvard. We assume that the number of admissions in Harvard is fixed and that the university selects the students with the best grades on a standardized test. Suppose that Coleman is right and that, because of the social capital effects of parental involvement in school affairs, students in PTA-run schools obtain better grades. As a result, they are more likely to go to Harvard than students from nonPTA schools. Whether or not this raises social welfare depends on how critical high school education is to university learning.

To illustrate this point, suppose that students learn all they need to know at Harvard. The only purpose of high school education is to screen out less able students. Further assume that the minimum grade required to be admitted at Harvard is higher than the grade necessary to earn one's degree: some applicants do not get in even though, if they did, they would earn their degree. In this case, the role of social capital is again to enable one group – students in PTA schools – preferential access to a rationed resource – admission at Harvard. The effect of social capital is distributional. Regressing the probability of admission in Harvard on social capital would yield a positive coefficient even though, in this example, the effect of social capital on the efficiency of social exchange is zero. Of course, we do not claim that the above example is an accurate depiction of the education system. The only purpose of the example is to illustrate the danger of estimating the beneficial effect of social capital by comparing individual or group outcomes according to whether or not they have social capital. Whenever social capital enables one group to displace another, a statistical comparison of the two groups is bound to overestimate the efficiency gain from social capital.

This example exposes another ambiguity of the concept of social capital. In our review of definitions of social capital, we noted that most authors associate social capital with the idea of beneficial group externalities. In the above – admittedly extreme – example, groups of students in PTA-run schools benefit from the social capital generated by their parents. But society as a whole does not. According to our definition, there is social capital at the level of each group but not at the aggregate level. This contradiction serves to remind us that it is perilous to define a social process as necessarily having beneficial effects.

---

[13] A similar example could be constructed in which it is the effect of social capital on trust that matters. For instance, imagine silk produced in China and consumed in Europe. Chinese silk producers do not trust European consumers so that direct sale is not possible. A group of traders who manages to gain the trust of both producers and consumers can then capture the silk trade.

4.1.2. Free riding

It is also possible that social capital generates beneficial externalities but yields no (or few) individual returns for the holders of social capital. A case in point is when the external effects of social capital are fully captured by outsiders – i.e. individuals or groups who are outside the social networks or do not share the norms and values of the group – who do not incur the cost of generating the externality.

To see this, consider N groups of fishermen tapping the same fishing ground.[14] Without collective action, there is over-fishing. Suppose that fishing groups with better social capital enforce self-restraint – either through shared norms or through relational contracting – while others do not. Gains from self-restraint are shared among all fishermen, irrespective of whether they have social capital or not. Social capital increases aggregate social welfare but fishermen with less social capital have higher profit because they free ride: they benefit from the self-restraint of others without having to incur any cost. Regressing fish catch on social capital would result in a zero or negative coefficient on social capital even though it has a positive social return.

The externality can also be pecuniary. Keeping the fishing example, a similar result obtains if the fishing groups do not share a common fishing ground but sell their fish on the same market: social capital makes collusion to restrict supply possible since all fishermen benefit from higher fish prices.[15] To ascertain the effect of social capital, one needs to compare fishing groups who do not compete with each other by either accessing the same fishing ground or by selling fish on the same market.

What these examples demonstrate is that, in the presence of fallacy of composition or free riding, individual returns from social capital are poor indicators of aggregate returns. If social capital enables certain individuals or groups to capture rents at the expense of others (e.g., jobs in a nonclearing labor market, entry at Harvard when the entry criterion is excessive), individual returns to social capital exceed social returns, and social capital generates unequal outcomes. In contrast, if social capital generates positive externalities not fully appropriated by owners of social capital, individual returns underestimate social returns.

4.2. Model specification

4.2.1. Exchangeability

As we have noted, social capital studies have been applied to a remarkably large number of units of observation, ranging from individual farmers to countries. One natural question is whether these studies in fact use comparable observations. At an abstract

---

[14] This example is inspired by the work of Platteau and Seki (2002) on Japanese fishermen.

[15] An example of this situation is OPEC: not all oil producing countries are members, but they all benefit from higher prices even though only members of the cartel restrict their production.

level, comparability of observations is a requirement for virtually all causal studies. We raise the question in the context of social capital studies for several reasons.

First, social capital studies, particularly those that employ aggregate data, often use relatively crude sets of control variables. As a result, the residuals in the sample will contain forms of heterogeneity that call into question the placement of the observations in a common regression.

Second, social capital studies often fail to account for the reasons why different agents come to have different levels of social capital. As Durlauf (2002c) states,

> ... statistical analysis of social capital typically compare outcomes for individuals or aggregates who have social capital versus those who do not. These studies, in turn, typically do not incorporate a separate theory of the determinants of social capital, although they do often employ instrumental variables to account for the endogeneity of social capital. However, without a theory as to why one observes differences in social capital formation, one cannot have much confidence that unobserved heterogeneity is absent in the samples under study (p. 464).

Notice that this argument is more general than simply arguing that social capital is an endogenous variable. Since the groups in which individuals are organized often are endogenous, there will be various forms of sample selection that need to be accounted for in empirical work.

To see that these are more than abstract concerns, consider the regressions employed in Helliwell and Putnam (2000) to show the effects of social capital on economic growth. These authors regress regional output growth in Italy against initial output and measures of civic community, institutional performance, and citizen satisfaction. They find that these three measures explain persistent differences in regional growth rates and conclude that this supports social capital explanations of economic performance. Among the many questionable assumptions that underlie such a conclusion is the assumption that the regression they employ is using comparable objects as observations. In other words, the analysis assumes that each observation is generated by a common growth process. What must be assumed about the growth process in different regions when one includes Northern and Southern Italian regions in a regression? One answer to this question is that one must assume that given the variables included in the regression, the errors for the observations of different regions cannot be distinguished, at least from the perspective of their distributions. Put differently, one must assume that the regression is such that there is no reason to expect that the error from a particular region has a nonzero expected value, for example. But how can a regression of this crudity make such a breathtaking claim? The historical and social science literatures give any number of reasons why this assumption is false in contexts such as Italian regimes. But if the assumption is false then one cannot defend the interpretation provided by Helliwell and Putnam (2000) for their regression results.

Brock and Durlauf (2001b) argue that a way to formalize the notion of comparability is via the mathematical concept of exchangeability. We introduce this formalism as it provides a way of providing a link between the ways one thinks about data as a social scientist and the sorts of statistical assumptions that underlie regression exercises.

Suppose that for each of I observations, one has associated information F_i. This information may include factors that are quantifiable, such as the savings rate of a country, as well as factors that are not necessarily quantifiable, such as knowledge of a country's culture. Suppose that some outcome ω_i is generated by the linear model

$$\omega_i = \gamma Z_i + \eta_i, \tag{1}$$

where Z_i represents that part of F_i that is controlled for in the regression. Typically, models such as (1) are interpreted as meaning that, except for differences in the value of Z_i, ω_i may be thought of as draws from a common distribution, which in turn means that the η_i's are drawn from a common distribution. Notice, however, that this notion of being drawn from a common distribution should be determined relative to the complete information set available for each observation, i.e. F_i. Hence, interpretation of (1) presupposes that having controlled for the various Z_i's, one has no information that allows one to distinguish the residuals. Formally, the errors η_i are F_i-conditionally exchangeable, which means that

$$\mu(\eta_1 = a_1, \ldots, \eta_K = a_K | F_1 \ldots F_I)$$
$$= \mu(\eta_{\rho(1)} = a_1, \ldots, \eta_{\rho(K)} = a_K | F_1 \ldots F_I), \tag{2}$$

where $\rho(\cdot)$ is an operator that permutes the K indices.

Exchangeability is a useful formalization because it creates a benchmark for the assessment of empirical studies. In fact, many of the standard problems that arise in regression analysis amount to exchangeability violations. For example, when a regressor is omitted from a regression, this will mean that the errors in (1) are no longer exchangeable as the distribution of a given error will depend on the distribution of the included and omitted variables. Similarly, if there is parameter heterogeneity between observations, this will imply that the distribution of a given error depends on which country it is associated with. To take a third example, self-selection can induce exchangeability violations as the errors associated with one observation may be differentiated from other differences in the implications of self-selection for the conditional expectations of the residuals. To be clear, as Brock and Durlauf (2001b) observe, exchangeability is not necessary for causally interpreting regressions. For example, heteroskedasticity in errors is an exchangeability violation, but is compatible with a structural regression interpretation. What we argue here is that good empirical practice requires that one assess whether conditional exchangeability of errors holds for the regression under study. To be more precise, we believe that a good empirical practice is to ask, for a given regression specification whether, given the information a researcher possesses about the individual observations, the researcher can justify the assumption of (2) and if not, determine whether the regression retains the interpretation the researcher wishes to place upon it.

4.2.2. Instrumental variables

As observed above, in many contexts social capital is endogenous social capital. The problem of endogeneity is obvious in many contexts; when one talks about membership in organizations, one must account for the fact that membership is a choice variable. In other cases, the endogeneity problem is more subtle. Measures of trust are often used to characterize social capital. Since trust presumably is related to trustworthiness in actual behavior, such measures will exhibit endogeneity problems as well.

Many researchers have recognized that social capital is endogenous and so have employed instrumental variables to allow for consistent estimation of parameters. Leaving aside issues of self-selection that are not often not appropriately addressed by instrumental variables approaches, the use of instrumental variables in social capital studies can be subjected to criticism. Specifically, in many social capital studies the choice of instrumental variables often appears to rely on ad hoc and untenable exogeneity assumptions.

For example, Narayan and Pritchett (1999), using village level data, argue that measures of village level trust can instrument for measures of group memberships. In their analysis social capital effects are argued to occur when one individual's 'associational life' affects others in his village; measures of associational life include factors such as the number of group memberships. Since associational life may be a consumption good and thereby an increasing function of individual income, Narayan and Pritchett argue that it must be instrumented if one wants to identify how social capital causally affects income. Yet, there is little reason that such a variable is a valid instrument. As pointed out above, if trust is related to trustworthiness, as presumably is the case, then there is no reason why trustworthy behavior is any different than membership in an organization in terms of whether it is a choice variable. And without a theory of what determines trustworthy behavior, there is little hope of identifying credible instrumental variables for it in these types of regressions.

The choice of instrumental variables is often one of the most difficult problems in empirical work. In social capital contexts, the absence of explicit modeling of the process by which groups are formed and social capital created means that an empirical researcher is forced to rely on intuition and guesswork. While this does not condemn all studies using instrumental variables, we do believe that inadequate attention has been paid to justifying instrumental variables in social capital contexts.

4.2.3. Group effects versus social capital effects

A final specification issue in social capital studies concerns the question of distinguishing between social capital and other group effects. There is no shortage of reasons why group memberships influence individuals. For example, in recent models of income inequality, primary emphasis has been given to peer group effects and role model effects as influencing educational outcomes for youths. This creates a relationship between the outcomes for a given youth and the outcomes of others in his community of residence.[16] In many modern growth models, a key assumption is the presence of various types of increasing returns to scale that are produced by externalities. These types of models often take the form of positing that the productivity of a given actor depends on the human and physical capital stocks of others. From the perspective of statistical modeling, the description of individual behavior will require the incorporation of various group-level variables.

From the perspective of empirical work, the problem is simple. If one claims that a social capital effect is present for some behavior on the basis of the statistical significance of a group-level variable, this claim will not be credible unless one is able to argue that the group-level variable is capturing social capital versus some alternative group-level effect. This problem is particularly serious when social capital is endogenous, since aggregate levels of social capital are then determined by other group-level variables, which, in absence of strong prior information, presumably include whatever aggregate variables have been omitted from a regression explaining outcomes.

4.3. Identification

The question of social capital and other group effects leads to the question of identification. In this section, we assume that the model under study is correctly specified and evaluate what model parameters can be recovered from observational data. This work is developed in Durlauf (2002c), a paper which builds on early work by Manski (1993) and later work by Brock and Durlauf (2001a, 2001c) on identifying group effects in data. Our basic framework treats the level of social capital in a community as an endogenous variable that represents the aggregation of individual-specific social capital levels [for example, investments in individual-specific social capital as in Glaeser, Laibson and Sacerdote (2002)]. As such, the determination of how social capital effects individuals is an example of the 'reflection problem' that Manski's seminal (1993) paper characterizes; identification problems arise when one needs to distinguish the effects of the choices of others versus the characteristics of others on an individual. Identification questions when social capital is exogenous are discussed separately.

4.3.1. Individual-level data

We first consider the case where one wishes to understand the effect of social capital on some individual outcome ω_i. For individual-level data, linear versions of social capital models can be expressed as follows. Suppose that each agent i is a member of some group $g(i)$. Each individual chooses an outcome variable that is linearly dependent on some control variables. Assume these variables are of four types: an r-dimension vector of variables that are measured at the individual level, X_i; an s-dimension vector of

---

[16] See Durlauf (2001, 2002a) for discussion of a range of possible group-level influences on individual behavior.

variables (often called contextual effects) that are measured at the group level and are predetermined at the time that choices are made, $Y_{g(i)}$; an individual's expectation of the average choice of others, $E(\omega_{g(i)}|F_{g(i)})$ [called an endogenous effect, cf. Manski (1993)], where this expectation is made conditional on some information set $F_{g(i)}$; and expected social capital in the community, $E(SC_{g(i)}|F_{g(i)})$. The assumption that individual behavior depends on expected rather than actual social capital does not result in any loss of generality. Similarly, our assumption that agents react to the expected behaviors and social capital levels in their group rather than the expected levels among group members other than themselves has no bearing on the analysis, cf. Brock and Durlauf (2001a, 2001c).

We assume that the X_i and $Y_{g(i)}$ vectors are components of the information sets from which expectations are formed; these expectations are further assumed to be rational, so we work with mathematical expectations rather than subjective beliefs. The behavioral outcome is described by

$$\omega_i = k + cX_i + dY_{g(i)} + J_1 E(\omega_{g(i)}|F_{g(i)}) + J_2 E(SC_{g(i)}|F_{g(i)}) + \varepsilon_i. \tag{3}$$

In order to close the model, it is necessary to specify how group level social capital is determined. We assume that group level social capital is the average of individual social capital levels, SC_i. These levels are determined by an individual-level behavioral equation that is analogous to (3),

$$SC_i = \bar{k} + \bar{c}X_i + \bar{d}Y_{g(i)} + \overline{J_1} E(\omega_{g(i)}|F_{g(i)}) + \overline{J_2} E(SC_{g(i)}|F_{g(i)}) + \eta_i. \tag{4}$$

The identification problem amounts to asking whether the parameters in (3) are uniquely determined by the reduced form equations that describe ω_i and SC_i. In order to solve for these reduced form equations, one first applies an expectations operator to both sides of (3) and (4). For the outcome equation,

$$E(\omega_{g(i)}|F_{g(i)}) = k + cX_{g(i)} + dY_{g(i)} + J_1 E(\omega_{g(i)}|F_{g(i)}) + J_2 E(SC_{g(i)}|F_{g(i)})$$

or

$$E(\omega_{g(i)}|F_{g(i)}) = \frac{k + cX_{g(i)} + dY_{g(i)} + J_2 E(SC_{g(i)}|F_{g(i)})}{1 - J_1}, \tag{5}$$

and for the social capital equation

$$E(SC_{g(i)}|F_{g(i)}) = \bar{k} + \bar{c}X_{g(i)} + \bar{d}Y_{g(i)} + \overline{J_1} E(\omega_{g(i)}|F_{g(i)}) + \overline{J_2} E(SC_{g(i)}|F_{g(i)})$$

or

$$E(SC_{g(i)}|F_{g(i)}) = \frac{\bar{k} + \bar{c}X_{g(i)} + \bar{d}Y_{g(i)} + \overline{J_1} E(\omega_{g(i)}|F_{g(i)})}{1 - \overline{J_2}}. \tag{6}$$

In these expressions, $X_{g(i)}$ is the within-group average of X_i and represents the relevant set of variables that relate individual characteristics of group members to the group-level behaviors. Substituting out $E(\omega_{g(i)}|F_{g(i)})$ and $E(SC_{g(i)}|F_{g(i)})$ in (3) and (4) using the expressions in (5) and (6) produces reduced form expressions for ω_i and SC_i. Durlauf

(2002c) verifies the following proposition, which describes necessary conditions for identification.

PROPOSITION 1 (Identification in linear individual-level models with social capital). *Identification of the parameters in Equation* (3) *requires:*

   (i) *The dimension of the linear space spanned by elements of* $(1, X_i, Y_{g(i)})$ *is* $r + s + 1$.
   (ii) *The dimension of the linear space spanned by the elements of* $(1, X_i, X_{g(i)}, Y_{g(i)})$ *is at least* $r + s + 3$.

What this proposition states is that identification depends critically on the relationship between the vector $X_{g(i)}$ that does not appear in the behavioral Equations (3) and (4) and the vectors X_i and $Y_{g(i)}$ that do appear in these equations. Intuitively, the key idea is that identification of Equation (3) fails if $E(\omega_{g(i)}|F_{g(i)})$ and $E(SC_{g(i)}|F_{g(i)})$ are linearly dependent on the other terms in the regression, i.e. $(1, X_i, Y_{g(i)})$. Each of these variables is a linear function of $Y_{g(i)}$ and $X_{g(i)}$. So, if $X_{g(i)}$ is linearly independent of these other regressors, identification may hold.

What does this theorem require in terms of empirical implementation? A key requirement is that there are at least two X_i variables whose within-group averages are not elements of $Y_{g(i)}$. The existence of such variables will of course depend on context. For example, one can imagine situations in which an individual's age affects his behavior, but not the average age of others in his group. The need for such prior information illustrates how field work and qualitative studies can augment formal statistical analyses.

4.3.2. Aggregate data

A number of social capital studies employ data that are aggregated. Typically, these studies explore the average behavior of groupings which define the social environment for the individuals that comprise them. From the perspective of estimation, one can think of such models as taking within group averages of (3) and (4), so that

$$\omega_g = k + dY_g + J_1 E(\omega_g|F_g) + J_2 E(SC_g|F_g) + \varepsilon_g \tag{7}$$

and

$$SC_g = \bar{k} + \bar{d}Y_g + \overline{J_1} E(\omega_g|F_g) + \overline{J_2} E(SC_g|F_g) + \eta_g, \tag{8}$$

where ω_g and SC_g are group level averages.

Necessary conditions for identification in this case are also developed in Durlauf (2002c). To characterize these conditions, let $H_{\omega,g}$ and $H_{SC,g}$ denote the linear spaces spanned by those regressors Y_g with nonzero coefficients in Equations (7) and (8), respectively. Let $H_{SC,g}^c$ denote that part of $H_{SC,g}$ that is orthogonal to $H_{\omega,g}$ (i.e. the linear space formed by the orthogonal complements of any basis of $H_{SC,g}$ after being projected on $H_{\omega,g}$). These spaces are used in the following proposition on identification.

PROPOSITION 2 (Identification of social capital effects with aggregate data).
  (i) *Identification of the parameters in Equation* (7) *requires that the dimension of the linear space* $H^c_{SC,g}$ *is at least* 2.
  (ii) *If J_1 is known to equal* 0, *then identification of the parameters of Equation* (7) *requires that the dimension of the linear space* $H^c_{SC,g}$ *is at least* 1.

Relative to the identification condition for the individual level model, there are some important differences. Specifically, in the aggregate case, one no longer has access to instrumental variables based on the averaging of individual-level variables. In order to achieve identification, it is necessary to have prior knowledge of aggregate variables that affect social capital but do not affect the aggregate outcome under study. Intuitively, in the aggregate data case, one is in essence working with a standard simultaneous equations system, so cross-equation exclusion restrictions must be employed to achieve identification.

To repeat, the import of these various econometrics issues depends on the context under study, the data available to a researcher, etc. The issues raised in this section should be regarded as providing benchmarks in the assessment of empirical studies; their salience will depend on the context that is under study.

4.3.3. Identification with predetermined social capital

When social capital is predetermined, the relevant individual level equation is now

$$\omega_i = k + cX_i + dY_{g(i)} + J_1 E(\omega_{g(i)}|F_{g(i)}) + J_2 SC_{g(i)} + \varepsilon_i \tag{9}$$

which means that social capital enters the equation in a symmetric way to the contextual effects $Y_{g(i)}$. Identification for models of this type has been initially studied in Manski (1993) and subsequently by Brock and Durlauf (2001a, 2001b); an identification problem still exists because of the potential multicollinearity of $E(\omega_{g(i)}|F_{g(i)})$ with the other control variables in (9). Durlauf (2002c) provides the following necessary conditions for identification.

PROPOSITION 3 (Identification of individual level behavioral equation with exogenous social capital). *Identification of the parameters in Equation* (9) *requires*:
  (i) *The dimension of the linear space spanned by elements of* $(1, X_i, Y_{g(i)}, SC_{g(i)})$ *is $r + s + 2$.*
  (ii) *The dimension of the linear space spanned by the elements of* $(1, X_i, X_{g(i)}, Y_{g(i)}, SC_{g(i)})$ *is at least $r + s + 3$.*

However, unlike the endogenous social capital case, it may be possible to identify whether the role of social capital is nonzero even if (9) is not identified. Following an argument of Manski (1993), observe that the reduced form for (9) is

$$\omega_i = \frac{k}{1 - J_1} + cX_i + \frac{J_1 c}{1 - J_1} X_{g(i)} + \frac{d}{1 - J_1} Y_{g(i)} + \frac{J_2}{1 - J_1} SC_{g(i)} + \varepsilon_i. \tag{10}$$

Identification of the compound parameter $J_2/(1 - J_1)$ is sufficient for determining whether there is some social capital effect. Identification of this parameter requires that the social capital variable is not linearly dependent on the other variables in (10); formally [Durlauf (2002c)] verifies:

PROPOSITION 4 (Identification of a social capital effect when social capital is exogenous). *If the dimension of* $(1, X_i, X_{g(i)}, Y_{g(i)}, SC_{g(i)})$ *exceeds that of* $(1, X_i, X_{g(i)}, Y_{g(i)})$ *then the presence of a social capital effect may be identified from* (10).

Proposition 4 may be readily extended to the case of aggregate data; if aggregate social capital is exogenous then it is simply nothing more than an additional regressor in an aggregate outcome regression. On the other hand, if one is working with aggregate data and social capital is exogenous, then it is impossible to identify any of the model parameters. The reason is simple: there are no longer any instrumental variables available from the social capital equation to instrument $E(\omega_{g(i)}|F_{g(i)})$, so no analog to Proposition 3 exists.

4.4. Additional issues

A number of difficulties beyond identification plague empirical work on social capital. As we have emphasized in Section 2, reliance on interpersonal relationships and networks can often be seen as a symptom that formal institutions do not work well.[17] To illustrate how this might impact statistical analysis, suppose we have data on labor markets in different countries and we seek to estimate whether the density of social networks raises the average quality of the match between workers and employers. Suppose for the sake of argument that we have a convincing measure for the average quality of the match. Regressing this measure against the density of social networks is likely to yield incorrect results if the researcher does not control for differences in formal institutions across the countries.

For instance, employment offices may play an active match-making role in some countries. Failing to control for employment offices would underestimate the effect of social capital. In fact, if employment offices channel information more efficiently than interpersonal networks and if these networks arise in response to the absence of employment offices, countries with more networks will have less efficient labor markets.

Studies of the effects of social capital on the delivery of public goods suffer from other problems as well. Earlier in this section we have argued that social capital is difficult to disentangle from other group effects. One such group effect likely to influence

---

[17] This does not imply that networks would never be observed in well-developed markets. Through interpersonal relationships, economic agents may form coalitions to subvert the market equilibrium to their advantage. Think of cartels, for instance. Clubs and networks can similarly be used to bias market outcomes, e.g., to ban nonwhites or women from certain jobs. Political clientelism is another example [Bayart (1989)]. In all these cases, social capital actually reduces aggregate welfare.

empirical work is the role of leadership. Community leaders often play a crucial role in fostering the creation of social capital – e.g., membership drive – that they can harness for a particular goal. Observing a relationship between social capital and the presence of a public good may be due to the presence of a third, unobserved factor: leadership. The distinction between the two effects is important for policy because good community leaders are rare and leadership is much harder to replicate than groups.

5. Empirical studies of the effects of social capital

Following the econometric discussion, the literature on the effects of social capital may be divided into two types: individual and aggregate studies.

5.1. Individual-level studies

Individual-level studies of social capital may be divided into studies that focus on developing societies and studies that focus on OECD societies. This division reflects more than data sets. Studies of social capital in developing societies are associated with somewhat different questions than their OECD (primarily United States-based) counterparts. This division reflects differences in underlying concerns. Development scholars are interested in social capital as a mechanism to ameliorate society-wide problems whereas interest in advanced societies tends to derive from concerns about the persistence of social exclusion and poverty in affluent societies.

A typical social capital study in this literature posits an individual outcome of the form

$$\omega_i = \gamma X_i + \pi Y_{g(i)} + J SC_{g(i)} + \varepsilon_i, \tag{11}$$

where, following previous notation, X_i denotes a set of individual controls, $Y_{g(i)}$ denotes a set of group controls and $SC_{g(i)}$ denotes social capital. As such, Equation (11) corresponds to the case of exogenous social capital discussed in Section 3. Evidence for the relevance of social capital is equated with the statistical significance of the coefficient J. In the various tables we have constructed to summarize various empirical papers, we report dependent variables and social capital measures, as well as findings based on the statistical significance standard.

5.1.1. Social capital and development

Links between social capital and development have been examined in a range of contexts. One reason for this is that the failure of many developing economies to achieve sustained growth has led social scientists to look for previously unexplored factors in the development process. Table 1 lists a number of studies of social capital in developing societies.

As the table indicates, a range of alternative outcomes have been studied. Similarly, a range of social capital measures have been employed. While these studies are quite disparate, there are some commonalities. First, these development studies typically focus on measures describing the social networks in which individuals participate. Fafchamps and Lund (2003), Fafchamps and Minten (2001, 2002), Grootaert (2000), Isham (2002) and Narayan and Pritchett (1999) all give primary focus to the role of memberships in various organization and trading networks as determinants of economic outcomes. The quite different social capital measures used by Lee and Brinton (1996) and Palloni et al. (2001) reflect the different outcomes they are measuring (immigration and placement in elite firms.) Further, the studies in Table 1 give primary focus to participation in organizations that can provide economic benefits in terms of information sharing and the production of collective goods. In this sense, these studies focus on economic benefits to organizations as opposed to more tangible psychological and social benefits.

From the perspective of the discussion of identification in Section 3, several questions arise. First, how does one differentiate social capital effects from the presence of other group effects such as information spillovers, or the presence of common factors such as legal or political institutions? In the papers discussed here, relatively little attention has been paid to this question. Notice that the failure to consider this issue is not necessarily a damning criticism, in the sense that one may have reasons to rule out such effects in advance. However, these studies also typically fail to make good arguments that alternative social determinants of outcomes can be ignored. This strikes us as a more serious indictment in that social capital variables can easily proxy for such factors. Put differently, we have argued that social capital represents a new explanation of individual and aggregate outcomes primarily to the extent that it embodies certain types of informal norms. The empirical literature typically does not contrast this view with alternative perspectives on social interactions.

In our judgment, the more successful studies of social capital and development are those that have focused on specific phenomena that have been placed under the social capital rubric. Unsurprisingly, Fafchamps and Minten (2002) is in our view a good example of this approach. As indicated in the paper's title, the focus of the analysis is less on social capital per se than on the role of social networks in affecting trader profitability. This paper focuses on agricultural traders in Madagascar. These traders are intermediaries between farmers and various markets in the country. Because the goods they sell (staples such as rice, potatoes and beans) are well defined (the basic goods are homogeneous and are distinguishable by observable features such as whether they have been milled or converted to flour, etc.), it is relatively easy to measure the value added associated with a trader's activity. Fafchamps and Minten (2002) find that measures of the size of an individual trader's business network are positively associated with value added and total sales. The paper argues that a relationship between networks and these economic outcomes may be understood in the context of models of imperfect information and monitoring, which provides a clear theoretical motivation for the empirical framework as well as a plausible theoretical interpretation for the various findings.

Table 1

Individual-level studies of social capital in developing countries

Study	Agents	Outcomes	Social capital measures	Findings
Carter and Maluccio (2003)	Households in KwaZulu-Natal, South Africa	Child height for age	Number of associations in community and interaction of family income with community income	Social capital helps ameliorate effects of individual-specific economic shocks
Fafchamps and Minten (2002)	Food traders in Madagascar	Value added and total sales	Number of traders known, number of relatives in agricultural trade, number of potential informal traders	Number of traders known and number of potential informal traders statistically significant
Grootaert (2000)	Rural households in Indonesia	Per capita household expenditure	Number of memberships in associations, diversity of memberships, number of meetings of associations, index of participation in decision making, measure of cash contribution to associations, measure of time contribution to association, measure of orientation towards community	Social capital index statistically significant; number of memberships, internal heterogeneity of associations and level of participation in decisionmaking appear most important
Isham (2002)	Households in rural Tanzania	Adoption of improved fertilizer	Village level measures of ethnic homogeneity for organizations in which households are members, levels of participation of household in organization decisionmaking, and extent to which leaders of village organization have different livelihoods than village members	Social capital measures are generally statistically significant predictors of adoption, but some regional differences exist
Krishna (2001)	Villages in Rajastan, India	Performance with respect to common land development, poverty reduction, and employment	Survey measures of participation in labor-sharing groups, trust, solidarity, and reciprocity	Efficacy of social capital is related to strength of leaders of associations, patron–client relations, etc.
Krishna and Uphoff (1999)	Villages in Rajastan, India	Collective action to restore degraded or vulnerable common lands	Social capital index based on survey answers to questions on level of collective action in village, village governance, village sense of obligation, etc.	Index is a strong predictor of better development outcomes

Table 1
(Continued)

Study	Agents	Outcomes	Social capital measures	Findings
Lee and Brinton (1996)	Graduates of elite colleges in South Korea	Employment opportunities at large firms	Private social capital (family and friendship ties) and institutional social capital (social ties provided by university, e.g. introductions to firms)	Institutional rather than private social capital is important in determining employment opportunities
Maluccio, Haddad and May (2001)	Households in KwaZulu-Natal, South Africa	Per capita total expenditure	Index of individual memberships in groups, reflecting number, gender heterogeneity, and performance, based on survey responses. Community social capital levels computed as aggregates of individual indices	Individual and community social capital measures statistically significantly associated with expenditure in 1998 but not 1993
Narayan and Pritchett (1999)	Households in rural Tanzania	Per capita household expenditure	Social capital indices constructed for both households and villages. Indices based on memberships in groups, characteristics of the groups, and household values and attitudes	Village social capital dominates individual social capital
Palloni et al. (2001)	Sibling pairs in Mexico	Migration to the United States	Previous migration of one sibling	Likelihood of migration is increased if a sibling has already migrated
Pargal, Huq and Gilligan (1999)	Households in Dhaka, Bangladesh	Establishment of voluntary solid waste management (VWSM) systems for neighborhoods	Indices of trust, reciprocity, and sharing for neighborhoods	Reciprocity index is best predictor of likelihood that a neighborhood has VWSM system
Varughese and Ostrom (2001)	Groups of forest users in Nepal	Level of collective activity, monitoring of forest use, enforcement of harvesting constraints, etc.	Homogeneity within group in wealth, caste, ethnicity	No necessary relationship between homogeneity and level of collective action; institutional design is more important

Finally, it should be noted that while the different studies in Table 1 consistently support a role for social capital in facilitating various economic outcomes, two of the studies, Krishna (2001) and Varughese and Ostrom (2001), argue that there are important subtleties in this relationship that need to be accounted for. Krishna (2001) finds that for villages in Rajastan India, the relationship between conventional social capital measures and outcomes such as common land development and poverty reduction is sensitive to a notion of effective governance Krishna calls 'capable agency'. By capable agency, Krishna refers to factors such as strong leadership in organizations, frequent interactions between villagers and clients, etc. His argument is that the density of organizations, a variable often used to measure social capital, will be associated with socially better outcomes only when capable agency is present. Varughese and Ostrom (2001) find, based on a study of groups of forest users in Nepal, that levels of collective action are not well predicted by measures of ethnic, caste, and religious homogeneity within these groups. These sorts of variables are often used to proxy for social capital. Varughese and Ostrom (2001) conclude that institutional design, how decisions are made, etc., can overcome barriers to cooperation that are induced by heterogeneity. Taken together, these studies illustrate that successful group activities depend on more than the presence of social ties per se.

5.1.2. Social capital in OECD societies

Just as social capital has been used to explain a range of outcomes in developing economies, so it has been used to explain a range of US phenomena. Table 2 reports a number of such studies.

In comparing Tables 1 and 2, a number of differences may be identified. First, social capital studies for affluent societies are far more heterogeneous than those which we report for developing economies. One finds studies of social capital for the United States that explore outcomes ranging from mental health [Furstenberg and Hughes (1995)] to dropping out of high school [Teachman, Paasch and Carver (1997)] to criminal activity [Hagan and McCarthy (1995)]. We do not believe this reflects differences in our choices of what studies to report. Rather, interest in social capital in advanced societies has been motivated by different phenomena than in the case of developing economies. In particular, the focus on social capital appears to be motivated by a desire to understand how some individuals avoid self-harming behaviors of various types.

Second, social capital studies for affluent societies focus on somewhat different variables to proxy for social capital than their development counterparts. This may be seen in the frequent examination of parental influences in Table 2. A common assumption in studies for the US is that the parent, child, neighborhood and school relationships are a primary form of social capital. McNeal (1999), for example, explicitly argues that parent/child interactions closely correspond to what Coleman originally meant by social capital.

Another feature that distinguishes the literature on OECD societies is its focus on traditionally sociological concepts in construing social capital. One important notion is intergenerational closure, which holds when parents of a given child know both his friends as well as his friends' parents; both Morgan and Sorenson (1999a) and Sandefur, Meier and Hernandez (1999) treat closure as an important aspect of social capital. This variable arises because, as argued originally in Coleman (1988), control and monitoring of children is sensitive to the ways that a family is embedded in a community.

While OECD social capital studies typically are based on richer data sets than those available for developing countries, these studies often suffer from serious flaws. One problem is that little discipline has been imposed on the empirical proxies used for social capital, which makes many of the empirical claims in this literature incredible. For example, authors such as Furstenberg and Hughes (1995), McNeal (1999) and Sandefur, Meier and Hernandez (1999) treat the number of family moves as a measure of social capital for youths. The idea is that the more a family moves, the weaker the social ties between the youth and his community. This is certainly a plausible claim. However, it does not suffice to make family moves a valid social capital measure. Since moves are endogenous, the variable in essence provides an indictor for those characteristics that determine the moves. Such characteristics can be associated with different youth outcomes for reasons that have nothing to do with social capital. For example, families who make more moves plausibly contain parents who are less interested in their children than those who make fewer, since such parents may be putting less weight on the costs to children of changing neighborhoods. Parents with less interest in their children [which can be formalized by using Loury's (1981) model of intergenerational mobility and allowing for heterogeneity in the rates at which parents discount offspring utility] will presumably invest less in their children, altering their outcomes in ways similar to the purported effects of lower social capital. Our point is not that one explanation or the other is correct, but rather that neither is identified from the data. Put differently, there are good reasons to believe that there are systematic differences in the unexplained components of individual behavior that render standard estimation methods inconsistent; specifically, families asserted to posses high levels of social capital, from the perspective of the estimated model, may be expected to be associated with higher levels of parental interest in children, which means the residuals in the associated regressions no longer have conditional expectations of 0. As such, this discussion is an illustration of an exchangeability violation of the type discussed in Section 3; Furstenberg and Hughes (1995) are especially susceptible to this criticism due to the lack of attention to control variables.

Similarly, little attention is typically given to the identification problem of distinguishing social capital from endogenous or other group effects. This failure derives from the flexibility of the social capital definitions that are employed. Is a psychological propensity to behave similarly to one's peers a form of social capital? The answer to this question is unclear from the literature, since such a propensity could easily count as a type of social norm.

While none of the studies in Table 2 can be said to fully address these general statistical questions, some of the studies are nevertheless clearly valuable contributions. One paper we would identify is Morgan and Sorenson (1999a). This paper is noteworthy for

Table 2
Individual-level studies of social capital: OECD countries

Study	Actors	Outcomes	Social capital measures	Findings
Costa and Kahn (2003b)	Union soldiers in the US Civil War	Performance over course of war in terms of promotions, desertion, etc.	Homogeneity of companies of soldiers with respect to ethnicity, occupation, and age	More homogeneous companies are associated with more promotions and lower rates of desertion
Fernandez, Castilla and Moore (2000)	Phone center employers	Returns to investments	Use of employees social networks in making new hires	Investment in use of employee referrals is shown to be quite profitable
Frank and Yasumoto (1996)	French financial elite; i.e. prominent individuals associated with financial institutions	Business dealings with one another	Reciprocity, trust. Actors are organized into subgroups based on friendship ties. Trust, equated with absence of hostile business actions, such as a hostile takeover, is expected to be higher between members of common subgroup. Reciprocity, defined as supportive actions such as helping a firm fend off a hostile takeover is expected to be higher between subgroups	Basic predictions confirmed
Furstenberg and Hughes (1995)	Children of teenage mothers in US	Graduation from high school, college enrollment, economic status, avoidance of live birth, avoidance of criminal activity, mental health	Within family social capital (presence of father in home, parents' expectations for school performance, etc.), family links to community (religious involvement, help network, neighborhood quality, etc.)	Various outcomes and social capital measures statistically significantly associated, even controlling for some human capital measures
Guiso, Sapienza and Zingales (2004a)	Households in Italy	Financial activities such as use of formal credit, portfolio behavior	Electoral participation and blood donation and province level	Social capital measures for both current location and place of birth predict use of formal credit, and investment in stocks rather than cash. Effects stronger for the poorer and less educated
Hagan, MacMillan and Wheaton (1996)	Teenagers in Toronto	Level of educational attainment, occupational status	Parental involvement with children, family moves across neighborhoods	Both types of social capital statistically significant in predicting outcomes

Table 2
(Continued)

Study	Actors	Outcomes	Social capital measures	Findings
Hagan and McCarthy (1995)	Teenagers in Canada	Various forms of criminal behavior	Social variables such as criminal mentors and criminal social networks	Social variables predict criminality
McNeal (1999)	Teenagers in US	Academic achievement in science, truancy, staying in school	Parental interactions with child and with school	Favorable social capital effects on child outcomes seem only to apply to white students from middle and upper class backgrounds
Morgan and Sorenson (1999a)	Teenagers in US	Test scores in mathematics	Social closure around school, parental involvement in school, parental knowledge of friends	Social closure is negatively associated with test scores, in contradiction to standard predictions of social capital analyses
Parcel and Menaghan (1993)	Children in US	Index of child behavioral problems	Miscellaneous measures of family structure, parents' working conditions, and parents' personal resources, such as sense of self-estimation	Role of family social capital generally confirmed through statistical significance
Sandefur, Meier and Hernandez (1999)	Teenagers in US	Intergenerational closure, parent/child interactions, high school graduation, post-secondary enrollment, enrolling in a four-year college	Family structure, number of times child changed schools, Catholic High school attendance	Various social capital measures are associated with outcomes in ways predicted by theory
Sun (1999)	Teenagers in US	Academic performance measured by test scores	Structural measures (number of school changes, family structure) and process variables (parent child interactions, participation in activities, number of parents known)	Various process variables associated with test scores
Teachman, Paasch and Carver (1997)	Teenagers in US	Dropping out of high school	Family social capital (living arrangements with parents, intensity of interactions with parents), community social capital (attendance in Catholic school, number of changes in school, measures of interactions of parents with schools and friends)	Attending a Catholic school and family structure robustly statistically significant across alternative specifications

its careful attention to different causal mechanisms by which social capital may matter and by the care with which empirical proxies are constructed. We would also note that the paper focuses on a very specific issue, namely why Catholic schools appear to out-perform their public counterparts, where there are good prior reasons to believe social factors matter.[18] Palloni et al. (2001) is in many ways a very different study, yet is also very admirable. This analysis focuses on a very simple notion of social capital, in study-ing the effect on an individual's migration decision of prior migration by a sibling. What commends this study is the immense care taken to deal with questions of unobserved heterogeneity and common factors between siblings unrelated to social capital.

Before leaving this section, we draw attention to Costa and Kahn (2003b), which provides an historical perspective on social capital. In this paper, the behavior of union soldiers in the Civil War is examined, with particular attention to rates of promotion and desertion across different companies of soldiers. Costa and Kahn find that ethnic and occupational homogeneity of companies was conducive to braver conduct by soldiers. While far removed from the types of behaviors that are usually studied using social capital, the behavior of soldiers is in fact an excellent phenomenon to examine, given the well documented role of social factors in battlefield conduct.[19] We believe creative exploration of data sets like this can add a great deal to the understanding of social capital.

5.2. Aggregate studies

At the beginning of Section 3, we outlined the difficulty of estimating the beneficial effects of social capital from individual data. We now turn to empirical studies that rely on aggregate data and examine whether they provide more convincing evidence of social capital. Table 3 reports a number of social capital studies that employ such data. As the table indicates, a large number of aggregate level social capital studies have focused on the relationship between social capital and per capita output growth at a high level of aggregation, such as a country or region. As such, most of the studies of this type are variants on empirical growth regressions that have become a workhorse of modern growth economics.[20] An assessment of the aggregate studies using social

---

[18] Morgan and Sorenson (1999a) has in fact engendered some controversy, see Carbonaro (1999) and Hallinan and Kubitschek (1999). The main thrust of these criticisms concerns the extent to which the so-cial closure measures used by Morgan and Sorenson fully capture the relevant social dynamics. We believe that the rejoinder Morgan and Sorenson (1999b) effectively answers these objections; equally important, these objections do not mitigate the reasons we admire the study. The level at which debate on this paper occurred is far deeper than the great majority of efforts to link social capital concepts to data.

[19] To be clear, social factors can play a negative role in military behavior, such as in violence against civilians. See Aaronson (1999) for discussion of the social dynamics that occurred among US soldiers during the My Lai massacre of Vietnamese civilians.

[20] See Durlauf and Quah (1999) and Temple (1999) for surveys of the methods and findings of the empirical growth literature.

capital is therefore essentially equivalent to an assessment of a set of growth regressions designed to establish that a particular variable is causally related to growth.

Growth regressions of the type found in the studies of Table 3 have been subjected to very serious methodological criticisms; examples include Brock and Durlauf (2001b), Durlauf (2000), Durlauf and Quah (1999) and Temple (2000). As argued in these papers, growth regressions suffer from several fundamental problems that make implausible the types of causal inferences one typically finds in the empirical literature. First, there is the problem of the choice of control variables. Growth theories are open-ended, which means that one growth theory does not have any logical implications for the truth or falsity of another. Hence, there is no natural way, when one wishes to test the importance of a given theory, to identify the appropriate set of theories to incorporate in a correctly specified structural growth model. As Durlauf and Quah (1999) indicate, there are in fact more extant growth theories than there are countries to which they are supposed to apply. As a result, any given growth regression may be subjected to the criticism that relevant control variables have been omitted. While there are some possible ways to deal with this problem, see Fernandez, Ley and Steel (2001), this problem has not been addressed in any social capital and growth studies, as far as we know.

Second, growth regressions typically fail to account properly for parameter heterogeneity across countries. Evidence of such heterogeneity may be found in Desdoigts (1999), Durlauf and Johnson (1995) and Durlauf, Kourtellos and Minkin (2001); theoretical models that imply heterogeneous growth processes for different groups of countries include Azariadis and Drazen (1990) and Howitt and Mayer-Foulkes (2002). Failure to account for parameter heterogeneity calls into question the structural interpretation of a social capital variable as it may be proxying for this form of heterogeneity. One example that is suggestive of this possibility concerns the role of ethnic heterogeneity in growth, a question studied by Easterly and Levine (1997).[21] In this paper, the authors argue that ethnic conflict inhibits public good creation and so acts as an impediment to growth. Ethnic conflict is instrumented with a measure of ethnolinguistic diversity which proves to be strongly negatively associated with growth. Since Sub-Saharan Africa has exceptionally high levels of ethnolinguistic diversity, the authors conclude that this is an important mechanism in understanding Africa's growth problems. Brock and Durlauf (2001a) reexamine this study, allowing for various types of exchangeability violations due to parameter heterogeneity, and find that the relationship between ethnolinguistic diversity and growth appears only for Sub-Saharan Africa; this variable does not help explain growth patterns in the rest of the world. Brock and Durlauf's finding illustrates how growth explanations may well not be constant across countries. And for the African case, it is unclear whether the growth findings are causal or whether ethnolinguistic diversity simply proxies for some other form of 'African exceptionalism'.

---

[21] It should be noted that Easterly and Levine (1997) does not explicitly focus on social capital; however, the mechanisms by which ethnic heterogeneity can affect economic performance are in many cases the same as have been proposed in the social capital literature.

Table 3

Aggregate-level studies of social capital

Study	Units	Outcomes	Social capital measures	Findings
Beugelsdijk and van Schalk (2001)	European regions	Per capita output growth	Trust, group participation	Group participation helps explain growth, but not trust
Easterly and Levine (1997)	Nations	Per capita output growth	Ethnic heterogeneity measured by ethnolinguistic diversity within a country	Per capita growth negatively associated with ethnolinguistic heterogeneity; important in explaining poor performance of Sub-Saharan Africa
Goldin and Katz (1999)	Iowa counties in 1915	High school attendance	Population size of towns, density of religious organizations, percentage of population that is native born	Small towns led expansion of high school attendance. Positive relationship with other possible social capital variables
Guiso, Sapienza and Zingales (2004b)	Nations	Trade and investment across countries	Trust	Inter-country trade and investment positively associated with trust towards country, even after controlling for a range of factors
Helliwell (1996)	Asian nations	Per capita output growth	Participation in associations, trust	Social capital measures contribute little once other factors such as openness are accounted for
Helliwell and Putnam (2000)	Regions in Italy	Per capita output growth	Measure of civic community (index of associations, newspaper readership, and political behavior), institutional performance, citizen satisfaction with government	For the various measures, higher social capital associated with higher growth
Knack and Keefer (1997)	Nations	Per capita output growth	Indices of civic cooperation (measuring questions such as whether it is ever justified to cheat on taxes) and trust (percentage of individuals who say most people can be trusted)	Social capital measures help predict growth

Table 3
(Continued)

Study	Units	Outcomes	Social capital measures	Findings
La Porta et al. (1997)	Nations	Government efficiency (level of corruption, etc.), participation in politics and associations, social efficiency (infrastructure quality, infant mortality, educational level, etc.)	Trust	Trust generally statistically significant
Lochner et al. (2003)	Chicago neighborhoods	Aggregate and disease-specific mortality rates for neighborhoods and gender and ethnic groups within neighborhoods	Measures of trust, reciprocity, group participation	Social capital measures help to predict white mortality; relationship with mortality of blacks is weaker
Paxton (2002)	Nations	Index of liberal democracy	Number and types of international nongovernment organization in country, trust	Democracy and social capital reciprocally related; number of trade unions, sport associations and religious organizations negatively associated with democracy, number of others positively associated
Robison and Siles (1999)	US states	Means and coefficients of variation for household income	Measures of family structure, educational achievement, crime and labor force participation	Higher social capital proxies generally associated with higher means and lower dispersion in household income
Zak and Knack (2001)	Nations	Per capita output growth	Trust	Trust predicts growth even when factors such as property rights are controlled for

Taken as a whole, these arguments imply that the social capital/growth studies do not meet the exchangeability requirements that we discussed in Section 3. While this reflects more general failings of the empirical growth literature [Brock and Durlauf (2001b)], it is also the case that growth studies using social capital have been quite insensitive to efforts in the growth literature to address these problems.

Beyond questions concerning the comparability of observations, there are unresolved issues concerning causal interpretation of growth regressions that apply to the social capital case. This is especially important given the endogeneity of aggregate measures of social capital. We are unaware of any social capital study using aggregate data that addresses causality versus correlation for social capital and growth in a persuasive way. While this is a broad brush with which to tar this empirical literature, we believe it is valid. A related problem is that we are unaware of any compelling instrumental variables for social capital in these regressions. This failure is a corollary of the absence of any strong theories of aggregate social capital determination in the social science literature that would allow one to characterize appropriate instruments.

When one turns from national-level growth studies to other aggregate studies, the plausibility of claims concerning social capital becomes stronger in some cases. Guiso, Sapienza and Zingales (2004b) find evidence that trust helps explains trading and investment patterns between countries. An interesting feature of their analysis is that the correlation between levels of trade and trust cannot be explained by measurable factors such as quality of legal systems. A recent study by Goldin and Katz (1999) is particularly interesting in its focus on the sources for the rise of high school attendance in Iowa in the early part of the twentieth century. By focusing on characteristics of Iowa counties, they are able to avoid some of the clear problems of exchangeability that plague studies using coarser levels of aggregation. But even here, other problems arise: more important, the data available are quite weak in the sense that the variables which suggest the presence of social capital effects could equally well suggest alternative explanations. The specific variables that seem most suggestive of social capital effects are the percentage of native born citizens and the population of towns; high percentages of native born and low population sizes are each associated with higher high school attendance. Clearly, linking these correlations to a causal role for social capital or other type of social influence is speculative. To be fair, Goldin and Katz (1999) point out that there may be alternative explanations, such as the smaller towns having fewer opportunities for those without high school educations.[22]

Overall, we conclude that aggregate social capital studies have not been successful in providing compelling empirical evidence on the effects of social capital. These studies require identifying assumptions that are incredible by conventional social science reasoning. We believe that research efforts should be directed towards micro-level studies

---

[22] At the other extreme, the effort by Robison and Siles (1999) to link aspects of state level income distributions to various social capital proxies fails to make any serious effort to ensure exchangeability; in addition the variables used to measure social capital, such as labor force participation, render the claims made about social capital untenable.

as the problems with country-wide studies seem too intractable to overcome. Data at lower levels of aggregation, such as county data for a homogeneous place like 1915 Iowa, are likely to be more amenable to persuasive analysis, provided the issues of exchangeability and identification can be addressed adequately.

6. Empirical studies of the level and determinants of social capital

Interest in the effects of social capital has spawned a related literature of the level of social capital and how this level is determined. Table 4 lists a range of studies that have explored this issue. It is worth noting that while attention has been given to questions of model specification and identification for models in which social capital is a causal determinant of various outcomes, we are unaware of any formal analysis that have been applied to models of social capital formation. Our conjecture is that the arguments applied to models of social capital effects can be extended in a straightforward fashion to models of social capital determinants, but this remains to be done.

One important question in the literature on the formation of social capital has been whether the extremely prominent claims by Putnam (1995, 2000) that social capital in the US has experienced a major decline are correct, and if so, whether this decline can be attributed to those factors he has described, namely, increased watching of television and the passing of the World War II generation. It appears that many of Putnam's claims have not withstood careful scrutiny. Paxton (1999) shows that there is little evidence of secular declines of trust or overall associational activity in the US. Bianchi and Robinson (1997) find little evidence that patterns of television viewing have much relationship to maternal employment status or other family factors often asserted to lead to lower social capital. Costa and Kahn (2003a), using more disaggregated measures of associational activity, find declines in social capital measures that are qualitatively similar to what Putnam has claimed. However, they find rather different explanations. Their analysis concludes that the decline in social capital produced 'outside the home' such as volunteering is explained to a large extent by the rise in female labor force participation in the last 4 decades. This study also finds that declines in social capital produced 'inside the home' such as frequency of socializing is strongly related to increases in neighborhood heterogeneity. One important implication of this work is that it places claims about a decline in US social capital in a different normative light. If increasing female labor force participation is due to the breakdown of discriminatory barriers against women in labor markets and if increasing neighborhood heterogeneity reflects a breakdown of the levels of social and ethnic segregation in the US, then perhaps declines in social capital are best thought of as an unfortunate but necessary side effect of a movement towards a more just society and so should not be mourned.

One important aspect of this research is the move towards a causal understanding of the processes by which social capital is formed. One interesting example of such work is Brehm and Rahn (1997) who employ General Social Survey data to study the reciprocal interaction of community involvement and trust in others. Their analysis finds a stronger

Table 4

Studies of social capital formation and the level of social capital

Study	Agents	Social capital measures	Potential determinants	Findings
Alesina and La Ferrara (2002)	Adults in US	Trust	Miscellaneous personal and community characteristics	Low social capital measures for individuals are associated with membership in groups that have experienced discrimination (e.g. being African American), lack of economic success, community heterogeneity, experience of personal trauma
Bianchi and Robinson (1997)	Pre-teenagers in California	Time spent on studying and activities other than watching television	Family structure, parental characteristics, mother's labor force status	Study is higher and television watching lower among children of better educated; children of working mothers watch less television than others
Brehm and Rahn (1997)	Adults in US	Civic engagement and civic trust	Reciprocal relationship between engagement and trust, confidence in institutions, life satisfaction, ethnicity, socioeconomic status, and many others	Participation strongly affects trust, each positively associated with socioeconomic status, confidence, negatively associated with being black
Charles and Kline (2002)	Adults in US	Carpooling	Ethnicity of neighbors	Ethnic heterogeneity reduces social capital formation for some pairings, notably whites and blacks and whites and Hispanics
Costa and Kahn (2003a)	Adults in US	Volunteering, socializing, nonchurch memberships	Gender, community characteristics (race and income heterogeneity)	Declines in social capital produced outside the home such as volunteering are strongly related to higher female labor force participation; declining social capital within home such as frequency of socializing is strongly related to higher community heterogeneity
DiPasquale and Glaeser (1999)	Adults in US	Citizenship (voting in local elections, helping solve local problems, knows school head, etc.)	Home ownership	Homeownership helps predict a range of citizenship variables
Fafchamps (2003)	Traders in Benin, Madagascar and Malawi	Trust in trading relationships	Ethnicity and religious similarity, gender, network effects	Ethnicity, religion and gender appear to have little effect on trust. Individuals possessing large numbers of business contacts give and receive more trust

Table 4
(*Continued*)

Study	Agents	Social capital measures	Potential determinants	Findings
Gugerty and Kremer (2002)	Women's groups and school development projects in western Kenya	For women's groups, group size, attendance, financial status and level of interactions with other groups and individuals; For schools, participation in school development projects	Funding of groups and funding of school textbooks	Grants to women's groups appear to have had little effect on the capacities or size of women's groups; grants to governing committees of schools and increases in textbook funding were associated with increased participation of parents in school development; additional effects were found for textbook funding
Hofferth, Boisjoly and Duncan (1999)	Adults in US	Access to time and financial assistance from relatives and friends	Previous provision of time and financial assistance to those same relatives and friends	Time and assistance from friends is predicted by past provision, but not time and assistance by relatives
Miguel, Gertler and Levine (2001)	Districts in Indonesia	Density of community organizations	Rapid industrialization within district	Industrialization, if anything was associated with rising density of organizations. Districts that neighbored districts experiencing rapid industrialization exhibited some declines, possibly due to out-migration
Oliver (1999)	Adults in US	Local civic participation	Community affluence and associated levels of social needs, competition for resources induced by population heterogeneity	Heterogeneous, middle income cities exhibit higher levels of civic participation than heterogeneous, affluent cities
Paxton (1999)	Adults in US	Trust, participation in various associations	Time	No strong evidence of declines in social capital in the US since the 1970s
Rahn and Rudolph (2002)	Adults in US	Trust in local government	Measures of political institutions, political culture, income inequality, ethnic fractionalization, ideological polarization, controls for individual characteristics	Ideological polarization, income inequality, and political culture are more important than political institutions in explaining variation in trust
Sampson, Morenoff and Earls (1999)	Adults in Chicago	Intergenerational closure, reciprocal social exchange, and shared expectations for informal social control	Miscellaneous neighborhood characteristics	Residential stability and relative affluence predict intergenerational social closure and reciprocal exchange, whereas neighborhood disadvantage predicts low expectations of shared child control

causal relationship between community participation to trust than the converse. This finding is indicative of the empirical importance of Dasgupta's (2003) argument that social capital should be modeled as a network.

Other studies have focused on identifying predictors of trust. For the US, Alesina and La Ferrara (2002) find that trust in others is negatively associated with community heterogeneity. Rahn and Rudolph (2002) extend work of this type in an analysis of the determinants of trust in local government. This paper finds that political culture and community heterogeneity play an important role in explaining trust. Interestingly, trust does not appear to be influenced by the form of local government as trust levels are not predicted by whether a community has a mayor or city manager (the latter implying less popular control of local government). These studies are best regarded as reduced form analyses in that issues of causality are not specifically addressed.

An especially important effort to understand the formation of social capital is the Project on Human Development in Chicago Neighborhoods (PHDCN). This is a remarkably detailed data collection project that covers several hundred neighborhoods in Chicago. These data are proving to be very useful in delineating the detailed social structure of neighborhoods. As described in Sampson, Morenoff and Earls (1999, p. 639), the available data include responses to questions such as "About how often do you and people in your neighborhood do favors for each other?" and the likelihood that one's neighbors would intervene if one's child were observed skipping school.

Sampson, Morenoff and Earls (1999) use the PHDCN to study a range of social aspects of neighborhoods. In particular, they distinguish the social capital of a neighborhood as "the resource potential of personal and organizational networks" (p. 635) from the collective efficacy of a neighborhood, "a task-specific construct that relates to the shared expectations and mutual engagement by adults in the active support and social control of children." (p. 635). The purpose of this distinction is to differentiate general notions of neighborhood social resources from the use of these resources. By delineating how neighborhood members help one another, for example through monitoring one another's children, Sampson, Morenoff and Earls (1999) give a rich portrait of how neighborhoods benefit their members, illustrating how help in childrearing or trust among neighbors are important mediating variables in understanding why poor neighborhoods have adverse effects on their members. By uncovering specific mechanisms by which neighborhoods matter, this study moves beyond the common use of social capital variables in which the link between the variable and a behavioral outcome is metaphorical and all too often a black box.

7. Suggestions for future research

As our discussion suggests, we believe that social capital studies have very often been unpersuasive. We make the following suggestions as to how one can improve this literature.

First, empirical analyses need to step back from grandiose approaches to social capital and focus on the more mundane but potentially far more fruitful task of analyzing specific social components to individual behavior. This does not require abandonment of social capital as a general organizing idea or metaphor, but rather means that evidence in favor of social capital should be derived from specific claims about social influences on individuals.

A useful contrast may be made between the Helliwell and Putnam (2000) paper, the study of regional differences in growth rates in Italy that we have criticized earlier, and a recent study by Glaeser et al. (2000) that explores the determinants of trust. Rather than run regressions that make incredible assumptions about the exchangeability of regional growth rates, Glaeser et al. employ well crafted experiments to see how attitudes and background characteristics influence the choice of strategies in various economic experiments. In the context of these experiments, notions such as trust are quite well defined since it amounts to expectations about the play of other agents in the game. This well-defined environment provides much more compelling evidence of how trust influences behavior than can be obtained from ad hoc regressions. The use of experiments to understand social capital is further developed in Carter and Castillo (2003, 2004), who consider how variation in roles by players in economic experiments can allow for differentiation between altruism and trust as determinants of behaviors.

The importance of experimental evidence should not be exaggerated. Economic experiments are not a panacea for the limits of inference with observational data. One problem is generalizability; it is far from clear how behavior in economic experiments maps into behavior in the larger economy and society, although Glaeser et al. make an important advance in this regard by attempting to correlate behavior in experiments with behavior in the "real world" by participants. Further, as discussed by Manski (2002) in an important recent paper, there are identification problems in experiments as it is often difficult to distinguish behavior that is driven by altruistic preferences from behavior driven by selfish preferences but with expectations of trustworthy behavior by others. Nevertheless, Glaeser et al. and Carter and Castillo represent a style of research that is an important advance in the social capital literature.

In addition, moving the discussion of social capital away from generalities to specific mechanisms in the way we suggest will allow one to deal with issues of endogeneity and exchangeability more effectively, since it will facilitate more precise and comprehensive modeling of causal mechanisms than one finds in the social capital literature. While the great majority of social capital studies include numerous control variables, the choice of these variables is rarely determined by careful delineation of the determinants of behavior of the agents under study. In addition, there has been little attention to questions of parameter heterogeneity.

A concrete implication of this discussion is that future research on social capital by the World Bank, for example, should be careful about the use of highly aggregated data. It is difficult to make compelling exchangeability arguments for data sets in which the observations are countries or regions. Ad hoc assumptions concerning the legitimacy of instrumental variables have plagued this literature for good reason: theories of social capital formation are underdeveloped so that it is difficult for researchers to sensibly construct aggregate measures of social capital.

Second, we believe that future data collection exercises must explicitly attempt to gather information on group-level influences, rather than on social capital alone. This should include measures of the quality of leadership. At the core of virtually all micro-economic reasoning is the general idea that decisions are purposeful outcomes based on an individual's preferences over outcomes, constraints on what actions are feasible, and beliefs over the consequences of those actions. The new social economics [cf. Durlauf and Young (2001)], is based upon the recognition that these three components to decisions are deeply influenced by social factors. A data collection exercise designed to explain a given set of outcomes should therefore be based on the development of a typology of what sorts of social factors affect each of the components and the development of plausible empirical analogs to these social factors.[23]

The sorts of detailed data collection we advocate are in fact underway in some cases. In particular, the Project on Human Development in Chicago Neighborhoods and data collection based on the World Bank Social Capital Assessment Tool are exemplary. In each case, the levels of specificity in terms of uncovering how individuals interact in villages, communities and social networks is a great advance over the crude measures often used in social capital studies. The most obvious suggestion in terms of the design of these studies would be the exploration of the extent to which the existing survey questions are adequate in terms of dealing with the specification and identification problems we discuss in Section 3. There is no quick answer to this as it would require integrating some theoretical modeling with the survey design. Nevertheless, the payoffs to such an endeavor could be quite high.

How does our admittedly very general advice differ from the way in which data collection on social capital is typically done? We have already discussed one difference, namely, the effectiveness of data collection is augmented when attention is paid to the uses to which the data will be applied. To repeat, the analysis of potential identification problems should inform data collection and not just define limits to which a data set may be used. Another important difference is that this approach avoids privileging social factors that can be construed as 'social capital' over others. As we have argued, the failure to consider alternative social explanations to social capital is an important source of skepticism with respect to existing studies. More importantly, there is no a priori reason to assume that social capital is a more likely source of important effects than other

---

[23] Sandefur and Laumann (1998) argue in favor of understanding social capital in terms of its benefits, identifying these as provision of information, influence and control in dealing with others, and social solidarity between individuals. These types of benefits represent combinations of the preferences, constraints, and beliefs we advocate employing. An advantage of our approach is that our categories represent empirically meaningful differences in the determinants of individual behavior whereas the Sandefur and Laumann categories are necessarily interdependent and do not correspond to any 'natural kinds' in terms of either individual activity or collective action, at least as far as we can tell. For example, trust will affect information transmission.

social factors. Another difference is that our proposed approach, by separating social factors as concepts from empirical measurement, will avoid conflating the two, as often occurs. Finally, the exercise of modeling individual choice in order to determine what is meant by social factors should provide some guidance as to the appropriate levels at which these factors should be measured. Does an individual's or a society's level of trust matter for individual conduct? The appropriate answer to a question like this should derive from the decision problem at hand. Empirical studies of social capital have largely not addressed this question.

Third, there needs to be greater recognition of the limits to statistical analysis in contexts such as the evaluation of social capital. This is partly a restatement of the first suggestion in that there simply do not exist any available data or methodology that can allow an assessment of the broad claims of the sort one finds in the social capital literature. But beyond this, we believe economists need to be more receptive to the sorts of evidence found in other disciplines beyond the quantitative analyses that are standard in economics. For example, sustained descriptive histories can teach us much about the ways that social structures influence individual conduct even if they are not constructed in the form of claims about F-statistics and the like. At the other extreme, there is a wealth of information in the social psychology literature that addresses in precise ways the inchoate ideas about individual behavior that underlie the social capital literature. This suggestion requires greater openmindedness on the part of economists to nonstatistical sources of information. But the payoffs can be high both in terms of substantive understanding as well as in facilitating quantitative analyses. As the discussion of identification argued, social capital effects can only be revealed if one has prior information on what group effects do not directly influence individuals. This is information that nonstatistical studies may be able to provide.[24]

In fact, it is reasonable to argue that some aspects of the question of how social capital has facilitated socioeconomic or political development should be treated in the same spirit as questions such as what led to the emergence of democracy in ancient Athens versus a martial culture in ancient Sparta or what were the causes of World War I. These are not meaningless questions; but it is necessary to accept limits as to the quantitative precision with which such questions can be answered and what it means to say the question has been answered. Nor is there any reason to believe that persuasive evidence on social capital cannot be marshaled using narrative methods. Ogilvie (2004a, 2004b) does precisely this in her historical investigations of the role of social capital in early modern Germany for understanding questions concerning both economic development and the status of women respectively.

None of this suggests that statistical analysis should play anything other than a primary role in social capital studies; our argument is that the credibility of the social capital literature will be augmented when nonstatistical evidence is better used to motivate assumptions and suggest appropriate ways for formulating hypotheses.

---

[24] Of course, qualitative studies are not immune to the overinterpretation (due to ignoring identification problems) and overclaiming (due to exaggeration of the import of statistical findings taken on their own terms) that we have criticized in quantitative studies. See Tarrow (1996) for criticisms along these lines.

8. Conclusions

In this chapter we have tried to provide an overview of the state of social capital research by both describing the state of the conceptual, theoretical and econometric literatures on social capital and by surveying a number of empirical studies. Our overall assessment of the social capital research is quite mixed. In terms of conceptual and theoretical studies of social capital, there is a considerable amount of ambiguity and confusion as to what social capital means. One conclusion we draw from our survey is that the most successful theoretical work on social capital is that which, following Dasgupta (2003), models social capital as a form of social network structure and uses the presence of that structure to understand how individual outcomes are affected in equilibrium. From the empirical perspective, the role of networks in facilitating exchange is one of the most compelling empirical findings in the social capital literature [cf. Fafchamps (2004)], so a more narrow focus on this type will likely not diminish the importance of social capital as a concept.

With respect to empirical work in general, social capital research has led to the development of a number of interesting data sets as well as the development of a number of provocative hypotheses, much of the empirical literature is at best suggestive and at worst easy to discount. So while one can point to no end of studies in which a variable that is asserted to proxy for social capital has some effect on individuals or groups, it is usually very difficult to treat the finding as establishing a causal role for social capital. We have highlighted a number of studies that we think are particularly strong, but those studies we find persuasive are relatively exceptional. The defects of the empirical social capital literature are unfortunate, since the work on social capital is an active front along which the 'undersocialized conception of man' for which economics has been criticized [Granovetter (1985)] is being addressed.

One recommendation we make in regard to empirical studies is that the social capital literature pay far more attention to formal issues of identification, self-selection and unobserved group characteristics. These issues have been extensively studied in the closely related context of social interactions [cf. Brock and Durlauf (2001c)] and many ideas from that literature may be applied to social capital. In addition, we believe that empirical social capital studies must do a much better job of differentiating between social capital effects and alternative types of group effects. One possibility in developing more persuasive evidence of social capital effects is the broader use of survey data. Such an approach has proven quite successful in recent efforts to understand how individual wellbeing, i.e. happiness, is affected by socioeconomic outcomes.[25]

Attempts to provide social richness to economic analysis will only succeed if the theoretical and empirical work that accompanies this effort is subjected to the same rigorous standards that are required of other analyses in economics. In contrast, the

---

[25] See Blanchflower and Oswald (2004) and Graham and Pettinato (2001) for excellent examples of this type of work.

extravagant claims so often found in this literature [the most prominent example of which is Putnam (2000)] are easy to undermine when these standards are applied and so will not contribute to social science in the long run.[26] Beyond the failure to contribute to the social science enterprise, there is a legitimate concern that studies which make excessive claims and unsupported assertions can have the long run effect of discrediting social capital as an idea. In conclusion, what the social capital literature ultimately needs is more matter and less art.

Acknowledgements

We thank Christian Grootaert for initiating this work and for helpful suggestions. The first author thanks the University of Wisconsin and John D. and Catherine T. MacArthur Foundation. The second author thanks the Economic and Social Research Council (UK) for its support. The work is part of the programme of the ESRC Global Poverty Research Group. Both thank the World Bank for financial support. Ritesh Banerjee, Ethan Cohen-Cole, Artur Minkin, Giacomo Rondina and Chih Ming Tan have provided excellent research assistance. Carol Graham and Jim Magdanz have provided useful comments on an earlier draft.

References

Aaronson, E. (1999). The Social Animal, eighth ed. Worth Publishers, New York.
Akerlof, G., Kranton, R. (2000). "Economics and identity". Quarterly Journal of Economics 115 (3), 715–753.
Alesina, A., La Ferrara, E. (2002). "Who trusts others?". Journal of Public Economics 85, 207–234.
Annen, K. (2003). "Social capital, inclusive networks, and economic performance". Journal of Economic Behavior and Organization 50, 449–463.
Aristotle (1985). "Nicomachean Ethics". Transl. by T. Irwin. Hackett Publishing, Indianapolis.
Arrow, K. (2000). "Observations on social capital". In: Dasgupta, P., Seragilden, I. (Eds.), Social Capital: A Multifaceted Perspective. World Bank, Washington, DC, pp. 3–5.
Azariadis, C., Drazen, A. (1990). "Threshold externalities in economic development". Quarterly Journal of Economics 105, 501–526.
Barr, A. (2000). "Social capital and technical information flows in the Ghanaian manufacturing sector". Oxford Economic Papers 52 (3), 539–559.
Barr, A., Fafchamps, M., Owens, T. (2004). "The resources and governance of non-governmental organizations in Uganda". CSAE Working Paper. Oxford University.
Bayart, J.-F. (1989). L'Etat en Afrique: la politique du ventre. Fayard, Paris.
Bernstein, L. (1992). "Opting out of the legal system: Extralegal contractual relations in the diamond industry". Journal of Legal Studies 21, 115–157.

---

[26] See Durlauf (2002b) for an extended critique of Putnam (2000) which addresses the problem of excessive and unsupported claims, faulting Putnam both for not dealing with some of the identification problems we have described in Section 4 as well as for failing to analyze social capital in a fashion conducive to rigorous policy analysis.

Bernstein, L. (1996). "Merchant law in a merchant court: Rethinking the code's search for immanent business norms". University of Pennsylvania Law Review 144 (5), 1765–1821.

Beugelsdijk, S., van Schalk, T. (2001). "Social capital and regional economic growth". Mimeo. Tilburg University.

Bianchi, S., Robinson, J. (1997). "What did you do today? Children's use of time, family composition, and the acquisition of social capital". Journal of Marriage and the Family 59, 332–344.

Bigsten, A., Collier, P., Dercon, S., Fafchamps, M., Gauthier, B., Gunning, J.W., Isaksson, A., Oduro, A., Oostendorp, R., Patillo, C., Soderbom, M., Teal, F., Zeufack, A. (2000). "Contract flexibility and dispute resolution in African manufacturing". Journal of Development Studies 36 (4), 1–37.

Blackbourn, D. (1997). The Long Nineteenth Century. Oxford University Press, New York.

Blanchflower, D., Oswald, A. (2004). "Well-being over time in Britain and the USA". Journal of Public Economics 88, 1359–1386.

Blume, L. (2002). "Stigma and social control: The dynamics of social norms". Mimeo. Department of Economics, Cornell University.

Bowles, S., Gintis, H. (2002). "Social capital and community governance". Economic Journal 112 (483), 419–436.

Brehm, J., Rahn, W. (1997). "Individual-level evidence for the causes and consequences of social capital". American Journal of Political Science 41 (3), 999–1023.

Brock, W., Durlauf, S. (2001a). "Interactions-based models". In: Heckman, J., Leamer, E. (Eds.), Handbook of Econometrics, vol. 5. North-Holland, Amsterdam, pp. 3297–3380.

Brock, W., Durlauf, S. (2001b). "Growth empirics and reality". World Bank Economic Review 15 (3), 229–272.

Brock, W., Durlauf, S. (2001c). "Discrete choice with social interactions". Review of Economic Studies 68 (2), 235–260.

Burt, R. (2000). "The network structure of social capital". In: Sutton, R., Shaw, B. (Eds.), Research on Organizational Behavior, vol. 22. JAI Press, Greenwich, pp. 345–423.

Carbonaro, W. (1999). "Opening the debate: On closure and schooling outcomes". American Sociological Review 64, 682–686.

Carter, M., Castillo, M. (2003). "An experimental approach to social capital in South Africa". Mimeo. University of Wisconsin.

Carter, M., Castillo, M. (2004). "Morals, markets and mutual insurance: Using economic experiments to study recovery from hurricane Mitch". Mimeo. University of Wisconsin.

Carter, M., Maluccio, J. (2003). "Social capital and coping with economic shock: An analysis of stunting of South African children". World Development 31 (7), 1147–1163.

Charles, K., Kline, P. (2002). "Relational costs and the production of social capital: Evidence from carpooling". NBER Working Paper no. 9041.

Coleman, J. (1988). "Social capital in the creation of human capital". American Journal of Sociology 94, S95–S121.

Coleman, J. (1990). The Foundations of Social Theory. Harvard University Press, Cambridge.

Costa, D., Kahn, M. (2003a). "Understanding the decline in American social capital, 1953–1998". Kyklos 56 (1), 17–46.

Costa, D., Kahn, M. (2003b). "Cowards and heroes: Group loyalty in the American Civil War". Quarterly Journal of Economics 118 (2), 519–548.

Dasgupta, P. (2000). "Economic progress and the idea of social capital". In: Dasgupta, P., Seragilden, I. (Eds.), Social Capital: A Multifaceted Perspective. World Bank, Washington, DC, pp. 325–424.

Dasgupta, P. (2003). "Social capital and economic performance: Analytics". In: Ostrom, E., Ahn, T. (Eds.), Foundations of Social Capital. Edward Elgar, Cheltenham, pp. 309–339.

Dasgupta, P., Serageldin, I. (2000). Social Capital: A Multifaceted Perspective. The World Bank, Washington, DC.

Desdoigts, A. (1999). "Patterns of economic development and the formation of clubs". Journal of Economic Growth 4 (3), 305–330.

DiPasquale, D., Glaeser, E. (1999). "Incentives and social capital: Are homeowners better citizens?". Journal of Urban Economics 45 (2), 354–384.

Durlauf, S. (1999). "The case 'against' social capital". Focus 20, 1–4.

Durlauf, S. (2000). "Econometric analysis and the study of economic growth: A skeptical perspective". In: Backhouse, R., Salanti, A. (Eds.), Macroeconomics and the Real World. Oxford University Press, Oxford, pp. 249–262.

Durlauf, S. (2001). "A framework for the study of individual behavior and social interactions". Sociological Methodology 31, 47–87.

Durlauf, S. (2002a). "The memberships theory of poverty: The role of group affiliations in determining socioeconomic outcomes". In: Danziger, S., Haveman, R. (Eds.), Understanding Poverty in America. Harvard University Press, Cambridge, pp. 417–443.

Durlauf, S. (2002b). "Bowling alone: A review essay". Journal of Economic Behavior and Organization 47 (3), 259–273.

Durlauf, S. (2002c). "On the empirics of social capital". Economic Journal 112 (483), 459–479.

Durlauf, S., Johnson, P. (1995). "Multiple regimes and cross-country growth behavior". Journal of Applied Econometrics 10, 365–384.

Durlauf, S., Kourtellos, A., Minkin, A. (2001). "The local Solow growth model". European Economic Review 45, 928–940.

Durlauf, S., Quah, D. (1999). "The new empirics of economic growth". In: Taylor, J., Woodford, M. (Eds.), Handbook of Macroeconomics. North-Holland, Amsterdam, pp. 235–308.

Durlauf, S., Young, H.P. (2001). "The new social economics". In: Durlauf, S., Young, H.P. (Eds.), Social Dynamics. MIT Press, Cambridge, MA, pp. 1–14.

Easterly, W., Levine, R. (1997). "Africa's growth tragedy: Politics and ethnic divisions". Quarterly Journal of Economics 112, 1203–1250.

Ensminger, J. (1992). Making a Market: The Institutional Transformation of an African Society. Cambridge University Press, New York.

Fafchamps, M. (1996). "The enforcement of commercial contracts in Ghana". World Development 24 (3), 427–448.

Fafchamps, M. (2002). "Spontaneous market emergence". Topics in Theoretical Economics 2 (1). Article 2. Berkeley Electronic Press at http://www.bepress.com.

Fafchamps, M. (2003). "Ethnicity and networks in African trade". Contributions to Economic Analysis and Policy 2 (1). Article 14. Berkeley Electronic Press at http://www.bepress.com.

Fafchamps, M. (2004). Market Institutions in Sub-Saharan Africa. MIT Press, Cambridge, MA.

Fafchamps, M., Lund, S. (2003). "Risk sharing networks in rural Philippines". Journal of Development Economics 71, 261–287.

Fafchamps, M., Minten, B. (1999). "Relationships and traders in Madagascar". Journal of Development Studies 35 (6), 1–35.

Fafchamps, M., Minten, B. (2001). "Social capital and agricultural trade". American Journal of Agricultural Economics 83 (3), 680–685.

Fafchamps, M., Minten, B. (2002). "Returns to social network capital among traders". Oxford Economic Papers 54, 173–206.

Fernandez, C., Ley, E., Steel, M. (2001). "Model uncertainty in cross-country growth regressions". Journal of Applied Econometrics 16 (5), 563–576.

Fernandez, R., Castilla, E., Moore, P. (2000). "Social capital at work: Employment at a phone center". American Journal of Sociology 105, 1288–1356.

Fershtman, C., Gneezy, U. (2001). "Discrimination in a segmented society: An experimental approach". Quarterly Journal of Economics 116 (1), 351–377.

Frank, K., Yasumoto, J. (1996). "Linking action to social structure within a system: Social capital within and between subgroups". American Journal of Sociology 104 (3), 642–686.

Fudenberg, D., Maskin, E. (1996). "The Folk theorem in repeated games with discounting". Econometrica 54, 533–556.

Fukuyama, F. (1997). "Social capital". Tanner Lecture on Human Values.

Furstenberg, F., Hughes, M. (1995). "Social capital and successful development among at-risk youth". Journal of Marriage and the Family 57, 580–592.

Geertz, C., Geertz, H., Rosen, L. (1979). Meaning and Order in Moroccan Society. Cambridge University Press, Cambridge.

Glaeser, E., Laibson, D., Sacerdote, B. (2002). "An economic approach to social capital". Economic Journal 112 (483), 437–458.

Glaeser, E., Laibson, D., Scheinkman, J., Soutter, C. (2000). "Measuring trust". Quarterly Journal of Economics 115, 811–846.

Goldin, C., Katz, L. (1999). "Human capital and social capital: The rise of secondary schooling in America, 1910 to 1940". Journal of Interdisciplinary History 29, 683–723.

Graham, C., Pettinato, S. (2001). Happiness and Hardship: Opportunity and Insecurity in New Market Economies. Brookings Institution Press, Washington, DC.

Granovetter, M. (1975). Getting a Job: A Study of Contacts and Careers. University of Chicago Press, Chicago, second ed. 1995.

Granovetter, M. (1985). "Economic action and social structure: The problem of embeddedness". American Journal of Sociology 91 (3), 481–510.

Granovetter, M. (1995). "The economic sociology of firms and entrepreneurs". In: Portes, A. (Ed.), The Economic Sociology of Immigration: Essays on Networks, Ethnicity, and Entrepreneurship. Russell Sage Foundation, New York, pp. 128–165.

Greif, A. (1993). "Contract enforceability and economic institutions in early trade: The Maghribi traders' coalition". American Economic Review 83 (3), 525–548.

Grootaert, C. (2000). "Social capital, household welfare, and poverty in Indonesia". Mimeo. World Bank.

Grootaert, C., van Bastelear, T. (Eds.) (2002). The Role of Social Capital in Development An Empirical Assessment. Cambridge University Press, Cambridge.

Gugerty, M., Kremer, M. (2002). "The impact of development assistance on social capital: Evidence from Kenya". In: Grootaert, C., van Bastelear, T. (Eds.), The Role of Social Capital in Development: An Empirical Assessment. Cambridge University Press, Cambridge, pp. 213–233.

Guiso, L., Sapienza, P., Zingales, L. (2004a). "The role of social capital in financial development". American Economic Review 94 (3), 526–566.

Guiso, L., Sapienza, P., Zingales, L. (2004b). "Cultural biases in economic exchange". Mimeo. University of Sassari.

Hagan, J., MacMillan, R., Wheaton, B. (1996). "New kid in town: Social capital and the life course effects of family migration on children". American Sociological Review 61, 368–385.

Hagan, J., McCarthy, B. (1995). "Getting into street crime: The structure and process of criminal embeddedness". Social Science Research 24, 63–95.

Hallinan, M., Kubitschek, W. (1999). "Conceptualizing and measuring school social networks: Comment on Morgan and Sorenson". American Sociological Review 64, 687–693.

Hayek, F.A. (1945). "The use of knowledge in society". American Economic Review 35 (4), 519–530.

Helliwell, J. (1996). "Economic growth and social capital in Asia". In: Harris, R. (Ed.), The Asia Pacific Region in the Global Economy: A Canadian Perspective. University of Calgary Press, Calgary, pp. 21–41.

Helliwell, J., Putnam, R. (2000). "Economic growth and social capital in Italy". In: Dasgupta, P., Seragilden, I. (Eds.), Social Capital: A Multifaceted Perspective. World Bank, Washington, DC, pp. 253–266.

Hofferth, S., Boisjoly, J., Duncan, G. (1999). "The development of social capital". Rationality and Society 11 (1), 79–110.

Howitt, P., Mayer-Foulkes, D. (2002). "Technological innovation, implementation, and stagnation: A Schumpeterian theory of convergence clubs". Working Paper no. 9104. National Bureau of Economic Research.

Huang, F. (2003). "Social trust, cooperation, and human capital". Mimeo. Singapore Management University.

Isham, J. (2002). "The effect of social capital on fertilizer adoption: Evidence from rural Tanzania". Journal of African Economics 11 (1), 39–60.

Jackson, M. (2003). "A survey of models of network formation: Stability and efficiency". Mimeo. Division of Humanities and Social Sciences, California Institute of Technology.

Jimenez, E., Sawada, Y. (1999). "Do community-managed schools work? An Evaluation of El Salvador's EDUCO program". World Bank Economic Review 13 (3), 415–441.

Johnson, S., McMillan, J., Woodruff, C. (2000). "Entrepreneurs and the ordering of institutional reform: Poland, Slovakia, Romania, Russia and Ukraine compared". Economics of Transition 8 (1), 1–36.

Kandori, M. (1992). "Social norms and community enforcement". Review of Economic Studies 59, 63–80.

Knack, S., Keefer, P. (1997). "Does social capital have an economic payoff? A cross-country investigation". Quarterly Journal of Economics 112, 1252–1288.

Kranton, R. (1996). "Reciprocal exchange: A self-sustaining system". American Economic Review 86 (4), 830–851.

Krishna, A. (2001). "Moving from the stock of social capital to the flow of benefits: The role of agency". World Development 29, 925–943.

Krishna, A., Uphoff, N. (1999). "Mapping and measuring social capital: A conceptual and empirical study of collective action for conserving and developing watersheds in Rajastan, India". Social Capital Initiative Working Paper no. 13. World Bank.

La Porta, R., Lopez-de-Silanes, F., Shleifer, A., Vishny, R. (1997). "Trust in large organizations". American Economic Review 87, 333–338.

Lee, S., Brinton, M. (1996). "Elite education and social capital: The case of South Korea". Sociology of Education 69, 177–192.

Lin, N. (2001). Social Capital. Cambridge University Press, Cambridge.

Lochner, K., Kawachi, I., Brennan, R., Buka, S. (2003). "Social capital and neighborhood mortality rates in Chicago". Social Science and Medicine 56, 1797–1805.

Loury, G. (1977). "A dynamic theory of racial income differences". In: Wallace, P., LeMund, A. (Eds.), Women, Minorities, and Employment Discrimination. Lexington Books, Lexington, pp. 153–186.

Loury, G. (1981). "Intergenerational transfers and the distribution of earnings". Econometrica 49, 843–867.

Maluccio, J., Haddad, L., May, J. (2001). "Social capital and household welfare in South Africa". Journal of Development Studies 36 (6), 54–81.

Manski, C. (1993). "Identification of endogenous social effects: The reflection problem". Review of Economic Studies 60, 531–542.

Manski, C. (2000). "Economic analysis of social interactions". Journal of Economic Perspectives 14, 114–136.

Manski, C. (2002). "Identification of decision rules in experiments on simple games of proposal and response". European Economic Review 46, 880–891.

McMillan, J., Woodruff, C. (2000). "Private order under dysfunctional public order". Michigan Law Review 98 (8), 2421–2458.

McNeal, R. (1999). "Parental involvement as social capital: Differential effectiveness on science achievement, truancy, and dropping out". Social Forces 78 (1), 117–144.

Miguel, E., Gertler, P., Levine, D. (2001). "Did industrialization destroy social capital in Indonesia?". Mimeo. Department of Economics, University of California at Berkeley.

Montgomery, J. (1991). "Social networks and labor-market outcomes: Toward an economic analysis". American Economic Review 81 (5), 1408–1418.

Morgan, S., Sorenson, A. (1999a). "Parental networks, social closure, and mathematics learning: A test of Coleman's social capital explanation of school effects". American Sociological Review 64, 661–681.

Morgan, S., Sorenson, A. (1999b). "Theory, measurement, and specification issues in models of network effects on learning: Reply to Carbonaro and to Hallinan and Kubitschek". American Sociological Review 64, 693–700.

Narayan, D., Pritchett, L. (1999). "Cents and sociability: Household income and social capital in rural Tanzania". Economic Development and Cultural Change 47 (4), 871–897.

North, D. (1973). The Rise of the Western World. Cambridge University Press, Cambridge.

North, D. (1990). Institutions, Institutional Change, and Economic Performance. Cambridge University Press, Cambridge.

North, D. (2001). "Comments". In: Aoki, M., Hayami, Y. (Eds.), Communities and Markets in Economic Development. Oxford University Press, Oxford, pp. 403–408.

Ogilvie, S. (2004a). "Guilds, efficiency and social capital: Evidence from German proto-industry". Economic History Review 57 (2), 286–333.

Ogilvie, S. (2004b). "How does social capital affect women? Guilds and communities in Early Modern Germany". American Historical Review 109 (2), 325–359.

Oliver, J. (1999). "The effects of metropolitan economic segregation on local civic participation". American Journal of Political Science 43, 186–212.

Ostrom, E. (2000). "Social capital: A fad or fundamental concept?". In: Dasgupta, P., Seragilden, I. (Eds.), Social Capital: A Multifaceted Perspective. World Bank, Washington, DC, pp. 172–214.

Ostrom, E., Ahn, T. (2002). "A social science perspective on social capital: Social capital and collective action". Mimeo. Workshop in Political Theory and Policy Analysis, Indiana University.

Paldam, M., Svendsen, G. (2000). "An essay on social capital: Looking for smoke behind the fire". European Journal of Political Economy 16, 339–366.

Palloni, A., Massey, D., Ceballos, M., Espinosa, K., Spittel, M. (2001). "Social capital and international migration: A test using information on family networks". American Journal of Sociology 106, 1262–1298.

Parcel, T., Menaghan, E. (1993). "Family social capital and children's behavioral outcomes". Social Psychology Quarterly 56 (2), 120–135.

Pargal, S., Huq, M., Gilligan, D. (1999). "Social capital in solid waste management: Evidence from Dhaka, Bangladesh". Social Capital Initiative Working Paper no. 16. World Bank.

Paxton, P. (1999). "Is social capital declining? A multiple indicator assessment". American Journal of Sociology 105, 88–127.

Paxton, P. (2002). "Social capital and democracy: An interdependent relationship". American Sociological Review 67, 254–277.

Platteau, J.-P. (1994a). "Behind the market stage where real societies exist – Part I: The role of public and private order institutions". Journal of Development Studies 30 (3), 533–578.

Platteau, J.-P. (1994b). "Behind the market stage where real societies exist – Part II: The role of moral norms". Journal of Development Studies 30 (3), 753–817.

Platteau, J.-P., Seki, E. (2002). "Community arrangements to overcome market failure: Pooling groups in Japanese Fisheries". In: Aoki, M., Hayami, Y. (Eds.), Communities and Markets in Economic Development. Oxford University Press, Oxford, pp. 344–402.

Poewe, K. (1989). Religion, Kinship, and Economy in Luapula, Zambia. The Edwin Mellen Press, Lewinston.

Portes, A. (1998). "Social capital: Its origins and application in modern sociology". Annual Review of Sociology, 1–14.

Portes, A. (2000). "The two meanings of social capital". Sociological Forum 15 (1), 1–12.

Putnam, R., Leonardi, R., Nanetti, R. (1993). Making Democracy Work: Civic Traditions in Modern Italy. Princeton University Press, Princeton.

Putnam, R. (1995). "Tuning in, tuning out: The strange disappearance of social capital in America". Political Science & Politics 28 (December), 664–683.

Putnam, R. (2000). Bowling Alone. Simon and Schuster, New York.

Rahn, W., Rudolph, T. (2002). "A multilevel model of trust in local government". Mimeo. University of Minnesota.

Rauch, J. (1996). "Trade and search: Social capital, Sogo Shosha, and spillovers". Working Paper no. 5618. National Bureau of Economic Research.

Rauch, J., Casella, A. (2003). "Overcoming informational barriers to international resource allocation: Prices and ties". Economic Journal 113 (484), 21–42.

Rauch, J., Trindade, V. (2002). "Ethnic Chinese networks in international trade". Review of Economics and Statistics 84 (1), 116–130.

Rauch, J., Watson, J. (2004). "Clusters and bridges in networks of entrepreneurs". Mimeo. University of California, San Diego.

Redondo-Vega, F. (2003). "Building social capital in a changing world: A network approach". Mimeo. University of Alicante.

Rob, R., Zemsky, P. (2002). "Social capital, corporate culture, and the incentive intensity". RAND Journal of Economics 33 (2), 243–257.

Robison, L., Siles, M. (1999). "Social capital and house income distributions in the United States: 1980, 1990". Journal of Socio-Economics 28, 43–93.

Roemer, J. (1998). Equality of Opportunity. Harvard University Press, Cambridge.

Routledge, B., von Amsburg, J. (2003). "Social capital and growth". Journal of Monetary Economics 50 (1), 167–194.

Sampson, R., Morenoff, J., Earls, F. (1999). "Beyond social capital: Collective efficacy for children". American Sociological Review 64, 633–660.

Sandefur, G., Meier, A. Hernandez, P. (1999). "Families, social capital, and educational continuation". Mimeo. Department of Sociology, University of Wisconsin, Madison.

Sandefur, R., Laumann, E. (1998). "A paradigm for social capital". Rationality and Society 10 (4), 481–501.

Siegelbaum, L. (1988). Stakhanovism and the Politics of Production in the USSR, 1935–1941. Cambridge University Press, New York.

Skocpol, T. (1996). "Unravelling from above". The American Prospect 7 (25), 20–25.

Skocpol, T. (2003). Diminished Democracy: From Membership to Management in American Civic Life. University of Oklahoma Press, Norman.

Somanathan, E., Rubin, R. (2004). "The evolution of honesty". Journal of Economic Behavior and Organization 54, 1–17.

Sun, Y. (1999). "The contextual effects of community social capital on academic performance". Social Science Research 28 (4), 403–426.

Tarrow, S. (1996). "Making social science work across space and time: A critical reflection on Robert Putnam's making democracy work". American Political Science Review 90 (2), 389–397.

Taylor, C. (2000). "The old-boy network and the young-gun effect". International Economic Review 41 (4), 871–891.

Teachman, J., Paasch, K., Carver, K. (1997). "Social capital and the generation of human capital". Social Forces 75 (4), 1–17.

Temple, J. (1999). "The new growth evidence". Journal of Economic Literature 37, 112–156.

Temple, J. (2000). "Growth regressions and what the textbooks don't tell you". Bulletin of Economic Research 14, 395–426.

Varughese, G., Ostrom, E. (2001). "The contested role of heterogeneity in collective action: Some evidence from community forestry in Nepal". World Development 29, 747–765.

Wade, R. (1987). "The management of common property resources: Finding a cooperative solution". World Bank Research Observer 2 (2), 219–234.

Wade, R. (1988). "The management of irrigation systems, how to evoke trust and avoid prisoners' dilemma". World Development 16 (4), 489–500.

Woolcock, M. (1998). "Social capital and economic development: Toward a synthesis and policy framework". Theory and Society 27, 151–208.

Zak, P., Knack, S. (2001). "Trust and growth". Economic Journal 111, 295–321.

Chapter 27

THE EFFECT OF ECONOMIC GROWTH ON SOCIAL STRUCTURES

FRANÇOIS BOURGUIGNON

The World Bank

Contents

Abstract	1702
Keywords	1702
Introduction	1703
1. Statistical relationships between growth and social structures	1705
2. The effect of economic growth on social structures: Theoretical considerations	1711
2.1. The sectoral shift view	1713
2.2. General equilibrium models of the distributional effects of growth	1715
2.3. Nonlinear savings behavior	1719
2.4. The role of technical progress	1720
2.5. Conclusion	1722
3. The effect of economic growth on social structures: Empirical evidence	1723
3.1. The sectoral shift effect of growth on social structures	1723
3.2. Effect of growth on inequality between socio-economic groups	1726
3.2.1. Sectoral income differentials	1726
3.2.2. Effect of education on earnings	1727
3.2.3. Gender earnings differentials	1730
3.3. Effects of growth on inequality among individuals	1731
3.3.1. Correlation between growth and inequality: rise and fall of the Kuznets curve	1732
3.3.2. Towards structural estimates of the effects of growth on distribution?	1734
3.3.3. Case study analysis	1736
4. Conclusions	1739
4.1. The foremost importance of sectoral shift phenomena	1739
4.2. The role of market integration	1739
4.3. Social costs of transitory adjustment	1740
4.4. Effect of growth on social structures through social institutions	1740
Acknowledgements	1742
References	1742

Handbook of Economic Growth, Volume 1B. Edited by Philippe Aghion and Steven N. Durlauf
© 2005 Elsevier B.V. All rights reserved
DOI: 10.1016/S1574-0684(05)01027-0

Abstract

Changes in social structures occurring during the process of economic growth can be considered *direct* consequences of this process, while other changes are caused by factors such as technological progress, that affect *simultaneously* social structures and growth. This chapter focuses on that part of the circular argument that goes from growth to social structures. It does not consider the effect of social changes on growth. The chapter is thus an attempt to isolate the pure "income effect" in the evolution of social structures and to disentangle the effect of economic growth from the effect of other factors in observed changes in social structures. Section 1 examines the nature of the statistical relationships existing between social indicators and development across countries and/or across periods, in order to illustrate the differences in social structures associated with differences in income. It also discusses the difficulty of obtaining precise estimates of the size of the income effect from this kind of evidence and the need to rely on more structural analyses. Section 2 reviews theoretical models of the effect of economic growth on social structures, with an emphasis on several dimensions of social differentiation and on economic inequality. Section 3 focuses on the empirical evidence in support of this structural view of the consequences of growth for social structures. Section 4 concludes by emphasizing the importance of sectoral shifts, the role of the market in integrating the economy and society, and the social costs of sectoral adjustments. The effect of changes in social structures on social institutions and on social relations is only briefly discussed in the Conclusions.

Keywords

economic development, sectoral structure, income distribution, labor market, wealth accumulation, social indicators, demographics

JEL classification: D300, E100, J200, O110, O410

Introduction

If economic growth actually resembled the 'extended reproduction' envisioned by Marx and implicit in the steady state regimes of many contemporary growth models, one would not expect growth to have major social consequences. All economic magnitudes, including the standards of living of individuals or social groups, would be kept in the same proportion to each other, so that only the scale of the economy would be changing over time.

Of course, economic growth is something more than a mere uniform change of scale of economic magnitudes. For a host of reasons, it is in the very nature of growth to modify economic structures and, because of this, to affect social structures and social relations. For instance, growth may modify the sectoral structure of an economy, leading firms in one sector to close down and firms in other sectors to be created or expand. Growth modifies the structure of prices, thus affecting the standard of living of households in a way that depends on their consumption preferences. In other cases, growth will call on some particular skills, increasing the remuneration of those endowed with those skills and also, possibly, their decision-making power within society. Finally, growth may reduce the availability of public goods like clean air or water, requiring public intervention in order to maintain the adequate supply of environmental goods. In all these cases, it is not only the economic structure – i.e., the relative importance of sectors, labor skills, remuneration of factors, and size of the public sector – that may be modified by growth. It is also the whole social structure – that is, the relative weight of socio-economic groups or the way in which individuals define themselves with respect to the rest of the society – that is affected. As a consequence, social relations that govern how individuals in a society interact with each other through explicit or implicit rules may also be modified by economic growth and may in turn affect the growth process itself.

Rough evidence of such changes is provided by simple comparisons of economic and social structures and institutions across countries which have reached different levels of development. At the risk of caricaturing, it is sufficient to compare poor Sub-Saharan African countries today with some highly developed countries in Europe, North America or in the South Pacific. At one end of the spectrum, one observes largely rural societies dominated by household farms, few wage workers except in the limited urban sector, social protection ensured by an extended family system and a relatively small public sector often controlled by an unstable oligarchy. At the other end, one finds almost exclusively democratic urban societies with salaried employment and private ownership of capital as the main economic organization, with sophisticated redistribution systems run by governments that are 3–4 times larger than these observed in poorer countries.

It is tempting to attribute all of these differences to economic growth and to expect that growth in the poorest countries will progressively make them comparable to developed countries today. Unfortunately, matters are not so simple. In particular, it is clear that differences in economic and social structures and institutions cause differences in the pace and structure of economic growth as much as they are caused by it. But it is also the case that some other factors may be influencing simultaneously both the process of economic growth and social structures and institutions. For example, a longer life expectancy due to technical advances in the field of health is likely to modify social structures through the aging of the population but it is also likely to modify economic behavior and the growth process, for instance because higher saving rates are rendered necessary by the prospect of longer periods of inactivity. In turn, this effect on economic growth rates and on the level of development may affect social structures and institutions by changing the weight of particular sectors in the economy.

The effects of economic growth on social structures are more complex than suggested by the reduced form regressions found in recent literature. The relationships are likely to be nonlinear (as hypothesized, for instance, by Kuznets for income inequality) and to depend on several country characteristics, including policy and institutional variables. This chapter argues that simple statistical methods are unable to identify these forces and these interactions, and that the limited number of observations available is a serious hindrance for this identification. Under these conditions, the only methodological approach able to identify the social consequences of economic growth is of a structural nature. It first requires establishing hypotheses about the channels through which economic growth may affect the social structures under analysis. These hypotheses should then be empirically tested, provided of course that the data necessary to do so are available.

The purpose of this chapter is to examine, among the changes in social structures that may be observed along the growth path of a country or when comparing countries at different levels of development, those that may be considered as *direct* consequences of economic growth. Other changes, thus, have to be considered as autonomous or possibly caused by factors or initial conditions that may have also affected growth but that have only an *indirect* relation to growth. An important example of such autonomous changes would be technological progress.

As noted above, some of these direct social consequences of growth may affect the pace and the structure of future growth and thus feed back into themselves through various channels. For instance, growth may under some circumstances generate more inequality in the distribution of economic resources, and this increased inequality may in turn affect the dynamics of the economy. For analytical expediency, this chapter focuses on that part of the circular relationship that goes from growth to social structures and ignores the other side of the circle. It turns out that the economic mechanisms that lie behind the two parts of the circle are quite different; it would be too ambitious a task to deal with them simultaneously. Readers interested in the effect of social structures and institutions on growth should refer to other chapters in this Handbook.

The social consequences of growth may be of diverse nature. A natural distinction to be made is between the consequences of growth for 'social structures' and the consequences for 'social relations' and 'social institutions'. As suggested by Kuznets (1966, pp. 157–158), *changes in social structures* have to be understood essentially as the differential effects of economic growth on predetermined social groups. For example, urban skilled workers may benefit more from economic growth at some stage than un-skilled workers, rentiers more than farmers, men than women, or young people than older people. Growth may also affect the size of those various groups. Some substantial proportion of people migrate from the countryside to the cities under the pressure of ur-ban growth, or more people may be willing to acquire a secondary or tertiary education. In both cases, social distances between individuals are modified. Changes in *social insti-tutions* may result from changes in these social structures or from autonomous forces. For instance, changing the weight of specific socio-economic groups within society modifies the dominant mode of social relations, and changing the economic distance between individuals may modify the way they interact.

This chapter concentrates on the consequences of growth for social structures rather than for social institutions or relations. Its ambition is to identify the role played by economic growth in observed changes in social structures and to disentangle it from other factors. Casual comparison of social structures in developed and developing coun-tries shows obvious and enormous differences. However, just because these two country groups differ by their mean income level does not imply that observed social differences must be exclusively attributed to economic growth per se. There may be many other rea-sons for these differences. In particular, it is possible that initial or historical conditions are responsible for some specific social evolution and for a particular growth path in a given country. It is also possible that exogenous forces, such as technical progress, have a direct specific impact on social structures, on the one hand, and on the pace and struc-ture of economic growth, on the other. Analyzing the social consequences of growth consists of trying to isolate somehow the pure 'income effect' in the evolution of social structures.

This chapter is organized in three parts. The first part introduces the topic by exam-ining the nature of the statistical relationships existing between several social indicators and development across countries and/or across periods. It illustrates the differences in social structures associated with differences in income, but it also shows the diffi-culty of obtaining precise estimates of the size of the 'income effect' from this kind of evidence and the need to rely on more structural analysis. The second part reviews theoretical models of the effect of economic growth on social structures, with an empha-sis on several dimensions of social differentiation and on economic inequality. Finally, the third part focuses on the empirical evidence in support of this structural view of the consequences of growth for social structures. It leads in particular to re-examining the evidence discussed in the first part under a different angle.

1. Statistical relationships between growth and social structures

One may think of literally thousands of aggregate characteristics of societies showing extremely high degrees of correlation with indicators of economic development, either when comparing different countries at different levels of development or when analyz-ing the evolution of a single country over time. Collecting all existing results of this nature in the economic and noneconomic literature is beyond the scope of this chapter.[1] Moreover, it is not clear how informative these correlations are from the point of view of causality. This section aims at showing that even the most sophisticated statistical techniques for the analysis of the relationship between socio-economic indicators and the level of development are unlikely to permit identifying the desired causality link between them. Given the available evidence, identifying that link requires dealing implicitly or explicitly with structural models, rather than with the reduced form models behind correlation analysis, whatever the degree of technical sophistication of that analysis.

As an example of the correlation approach to the consequences of growth, Table 1 shows the relationship between the level of economic development and a few indicators that very roughly describe changes in societies' economic and social structure generally associated with economic growth. As it will be seen later in this chapter, these indicators describe important channels through which growth and development may modify social structures. They include the size of the government, the level of urbanization, education, health, demographic patterns, labor force participation, gender differences and income inequality. The first three columns of the table report the results of a simple regression of these indicators on GDP per capita expressed in 2000 US dollars after correction for purchasing power parity. The first two columns are based on pure cross-country observations – observed country means for the 1970s and the 1990s – whereas the third one is based on a pooling of all data available across countries and years during the period 1960–2002.[2]

It can be checked there that, with two exceptions, all indicators appear to be significantly and strongly correlated with economic growth. For instance, focusing on the pooled regression, the GDP share of public expenditures is shown to increase by 0.5 percentage point when GDP increases by \$1,000 (thus confirming 'Wagner's law') although this coefficient is not statistically significant for the 1970 cross-section. Likewise, the urbanization rate is shown to increase by 0.3 percent and the literacy rates by 3–4 percentage points in presence of the same increase in income per capita, whereas fertility decreases by 0.15 children; the 1970 cross-section shows slightly different results in all of these cases. As a final example, income inequality and female gender bias appear to be significantly and negatively correlated with growth. In the case of the former, a parabolic regression exhibits the familiar inverted-U shape introduced by Kuznets some 50 years ago[3] – with a nonsignificant result occurring with the 1990 cross-section.

---

[1] For an early comprehensive attempt of this type, see Adelman and Morris (1967) who argue that development is a complex multi-causal process explained by many interactions between social, economic, political and institutional variables and use factor analysis to reduce the large number of explanatory variables into a small number of key categories. Zhang et al. (2004) present a typology of development strategies applying the same technique to Sub-Saharan Africa.

[2] All data are from World Bank's SIMA database [World Bank (2003)].

[3] On the basis of historical data, Kuznets (1955) proposed the hypothesis that income inequality tended to increase in a first stage of economic development and to fall in a second one. See the discussion in Section 2 below.

All these results are interesting. Yet, there are various reasons to think that simple regression on a cross-section of countries or even on a pool of cross-section time-series observations is a very crude approach to identifying the consequences of growth. On the one hand, the existence of a correlation does not say much about the causality link between two variables. Causality may be direct in either one direction, or possibly in both. It may also be indirect and simply reflect the fact that the two variables under scrutiny are both related to a common set of other variables. On the other hand, GDP per capita tends to increase more or less regularly over time so that there may be a confusion between its effect on socio-economic indicators and that of other variables with a comparable time trend.

Alternative econometric specifications permit taking into account some of the preceding points. At the same time, however, they often modify the order of magnitude and the significance of the preceding relationships. In a few instances, they even modify their direction.

The next four columns of Table 1 show estimates of the growth sensitivity of socio-economic indicators obtained with alternative econometric specifications. In all cases, the sample is obtained by pooling country data over various years in the periods 1960–2002. In column (4), a set of year dummy variables is added to the regression. This accounts for the fact that socio-economic indicators might evolve over time under the influence of some common factors independent of national economic growth. In column (5), it is a set of country dummy variables that is introduced so as to control for 'fixed effects' or, in other words, the effect of largely unobserved fixed country characteristics that might affect both the original level of GDP per capita and that of the indicator under scrutiny. The corresponding estimate of growth sensitivities thus abstracts from differences in country means and takes into account only differences in the average time behavior of GDP per capita and socio-economic indicators across countries. Column (6) combines both approaches by abstracting from differences in country means as well as from an exogenous nonlinear time trend common to all countries. Finally the estimates in column (7) are obtained by running the simple regressions of socio-economic indicators on GDP per capita in decadal differences.

Adding a common nonlinear time trend to the original simple model does not modify the growth sensitivity of the socio-economic indicators in a significant way. More substantial changes are obtained when fixed country effects are introduced. As could be expected, growth sensitivity generally falls when cross-country differences are ignored, or more exactly when cross-country differences are attributed to fixed characteristics that include, inter alia, initial development levels. The effect of growth on the urbanization rate, the literacy rate or life expectancy is divided by about 2. The growth sensitivity of the GDP share of public expenditures becomes nonsignificant, the same being true of income inequality, both with the linear and with the parabolic model. The only exception is labor force participation of women, the effect of growth on which tends to increase when controlling for fixed effects. Changes with respect to simple estimates are still bigger when fixed effects are introduced both for countries and years. In some

Table 1
Estimated growth elasticity of selected economic and socio-demographic indicators

Dependent variable	Simple regression on country means		Pooling		Fixed effects		Decadal differences
	1970s	1990s	No other variable	+Nonlinear trend	No other variable	+Nonlinear trend	
	(1)	(2)	(3)	(4)	(5)	(6)	(7)
Public expenditures (% GDP)	**0.47**	**0.63**	**0.50**	**0.58**	**0.07**	**0.25**	**0.27**
T-statistic	(0.86)	(5.19)**	(12.22)**	(15.58)**	(1.74)	(4.12)**	(1.26)
Number of observations	105	131	2546	2546	2546	2546	202
Agricultural/nonagricultural productivity differential	**NA**	**0.01**	**0.01**	**0.01**	**0.005**	**0.01**	**0.09**
T-statistic	NA	(2.38)*	(6.71)**	(6.49)**	(2.92)**	(3.89)**	(2.23)*
Number of observations	NA	91	1323	1323	1323	1323	53
Urbanization rate (Cox)	**0.49**	**0.35**	**0.33**	**0.34**	**0.15**	**0.11**	**0.11**
T-statistic	(5.35)**	(3.23)**	(14.38)**	(15.08)**	(30.33)**	(17.79)**	(5.33)**
Number of observations	118	166	4008	4008	4008	4008	265
Literacy rate among adults (Cox)	**3.57**	**2.79**	**3.67**	**3.21**	**1.74**	**1.06**	**0.58**
T-statistic	(1.6)	(2.53)*	(11.71)**	(10.58)**	(18.48)**	(8.94)**	(1.32)
Number of observations	90	126	3056	3056	3056	3056	200
Average schooling year in total over 25	**0.76**	**0.30**	**0.33**	**0.33**	**0.15**	**0.02**	**0.02**
T-statistic	(8.21)**	(17.60)**	(28.00)**	(27.69)**	(17.86)**	(2.01)*	(1.51)
Number of observations	93	99	575	575	575	575	189
Life expectancy (years)	**2.94**	**1.01**	**0.97**	**0.94**	**0.30**	**0.05**	**0.06**
T-statistic	(11.36)**	(12.00)**	(29.77)**	(28.15)**	(20.17)**	(2.66)**	(1.79)
Number of observations	114	167	2219	2219	2219	2219	260
Fertility (number of children)	**−0.49**	**−0.15**	**−0.15**	**−0.12**	**−0.04**	**0.07**	**0.06**
T-statistic	(7.60)**	(11.49)**	(28.94)**	(25.05)**	(12.23)**	(26.99)**	(8.46)**
Number of observations	119	167	2526	2526	2526	2526	265

Table 1
(Continued)

Dependent variable	Simple regression on country means				Pooling				Fixed effects				Decadal differences	
	1970s (1)		1990s (2)		No other variable (3)		+Nonlinear trend (4)		No other variable (5)		+Nonlinear trend (6)		(7)	
	(y)	(y^2)	(y)	(y^2)	(y)	(y^2)	(y)	(y^2)	(y)	(y^2)	(y)	(y^2)	(y)	(y^2)
Male/female differential in adult literacy (%)	**−1.49**		**−0.94**		**−1.02**		**−0.99**		**−0.56**		**−0.20**		**−0.19**	
T-statistic	(1.88)		(5.80)**		(25.60)**		(23.35)**		(29.60)**		(8.96)**		(3.28)**	
Number of observations	90		126		3056		3056		3056		3056		200	
Male/female differential in life expectancy (year)	**−0.45**		**−0.13**		**−0.12**		**−0.11**		**0.01**		**0.02**		**0.01**	
T-statistic	(8.06)**		(7.81)**		(21.16)**		(17.92)**		(3.51)**		(3.12)**		(0.9)	
Number of observations	114		167		2219		2219		2219		2219		260	
Income inequality (Gini)	**−1.60**		**−0.27**		**−0.51**		**−0.50**		**0.07**		**0.11**		**0.04**	
T-statistic	(4.40)**		(2.69)**		(8.08)**		(7.24)**		(1.41)		(1.14)		(0.31)	
Number of observations	52		54		389		389		389		389		92	
Income inequality (Gini)	**2.37**	**−0.43**	**−0.03**	**−0.01**	**−1.11**	**0.03**	**−1.06**	**0.03**	**−0.16**	**0.01**	**−0.15**	**0.01**	**−0.43**	**0.01**
T-statistic	(1.21)	(2.05)*	(0.06)	(0.43)	(5.31)**	(3.28)**	(4.52)**	(2.64)**	(0.81)	(1.22)	(0.44)	(0.78)	(1.36)	(1.83)
Number of observations	52		54		389		389		389		389		92	
Female labor force participation	**−0.83**		**0.12**		**0.19**		**0.09**		**0.53**		**0.33**		**0.34**	
T-statistic	(2.17)*		(1.23)		(8.42)**		(4.01)**		(52.33)**		(27.55)**		(4.74)**	
Number of observations	113		156		3811		3811		3811		3811		251	
Female labor force participation	**−5.25**	**0.49**	**−0.65**	**0.03**	**−0.20**	**0.02**	**−0.29**	**0.02**	**1.12**	**−0.02**	**0.87**	**−0.01**	**0.86**	**−0.01**
T-statistic	(2.79)**	(2.19)*	(1.35)	(1.51)	(1.58)	(2.77)**	(2.44)*	(2.85)**	(50.98)**	(29.48)**	(31.42)**	(21.32)**	(5.66)**	(4.05)**
Number of observations	113		156		3811		3811		3811		3811		251	

Source: Author's calculation on WDI data.   *Notes*. Robust T-statistics in brackets. Cox transformation of variable x is $x/(1-x)$. Labor force participation in %.

* significant at 5%.
** significant at 1%.

cases – as for instance with fertility and gender life expectancy differential – the sign of growth sensitivity is even reversed.

Of course, such a correction of the original estimates may well be excessive. Adding a time trend is certainly bound to reduce growth sensitivity estimates, especially when estimation abstracts from cross-country differences. The time trend is likely to pick up those changes in the indicators which are independent from country specific economic growth. Yet, results obtained with that method are not always very convincing. In particular, that fertility would significantly increase as a response to growth once independent forces are taken into account, as shown in the last two columns of Table 1, seems to be in contradiction with the intuition of most demographers.[4] The results shown in Table 1 are likely to mask some heterogeneity among countries with respect to the drop in fertility that is not dependent on economic growth.

The estimates reported in the last column of Table 1 confirm the preceding results. Restricting the analysis to correlation in decadal differences overall shows the same order of magnitude for the growth sensitivity of socio-economic indicators, but also makes those sensitivities often nonsignificant.[5] In comparison with simple regressions and correlations, estimates based on differences or on fixed effects thus suggest that the evolution of the few general socio-economic indicators considered in Table 1 probably obeys other forces in addition to economic growth, or that the effect of growth is less simple than implicitly assumed in these statistical models. In particular, it is quite possible that the effects of growth on socio-economic indicators are strongly heterogeneous across countries. Identifying that heterogeneity or the forces other than economic growth that affect the evolution of socio-economic indicators is thus necessary in order to identify the true social consequences of economic growth. But the econometric approach illustrated in this section is unlikely to meet that objective.

Taking into account this heterogeneity across countries and going beyond the simple statistical techniques used to produce the results of Table 1 meets a fundamental constraint: the limited number of observations. Estimating the preceding model country by country on a time series basis would certainly permit to fully account for country specificity. But it would only inform us about the consequences of growth at a particular stage of the development process of a given country. On the other hand, taking into account observed heterogeneity by interacting growth rates or development levels with a host of country characteristics and policy variables and by introducing nonlinearity is also bound to run into too few degrees of freedom. Social consequences of growth take time to show up, so that the informational content of annual time series is not proportional to the length of these series. In Table 1, one can see that there is little difference between

---

[4] See for instance Easterlin (1996, chapter 8) and Lee (2003).

[5] The difference in T-statistics between columns (6) and (7) is mostly due to the fact that the regression in column (7) relies on fewer observations. Note, however, that ignoring possible correlation in the residuals of the regressions behind column (6) for contiguous years may tend to a gross underestimation of the variance of the estimates.

the last two columns even though column (6) relies on full annual series whereas column (7) uses only decadal differences. This means that the information that matters is not year-to-year fluctuation but 'episodes' of growth characterized by uniformly high, moderate or low growth rates. If this is the case, then available data may make it difficult to estimate with satisfactory precision the observed heterogeneity in the consequences of growth.[6]

In summary, the analysis in this section suggests that other forces than economic growth are behind the time evolution of most socio-economic indicators, even though the absolute value of simple correlation coefficients is often very high. It is also possible that the effect of economic growth on these indicators and the social features they describe is too complex to be described by simple regression analysis. In particular, the relationship may be nonlinear – as hypothesized for instance by Kuznets for income inequality – or it may depend on specific country characteristics, including policy and institutional variables. There is no simple statistical method to identify a priori these other forces or these interactions, and limited observations may also be a serious hindrance for this identification.

Under these conditions, it is likely that the only methodological approach able to help identify and understand the consequences of economic growth is of a 'structural' nature. In other words, what is required is to establish hypotheses on the phenomena that guide the overall evolution of the socio-economic indicators under analysis and to test the corresponding model. This is in stark contrast with the reduced form approach so often found in the literature and illustrated by Table 1. Within a structural approach, a theoretical model of the behavior of the socio-economic indicator being studied must first be established on the basis of economic theory. This is what the next section attempts to do for some possible social consequences of growth.

2. The effect of economic growth on social structures: Theoretical considerations

Does economic growth tend to affect people's income and welfare in the same way? Alternatively, does economic growth tend to favor the expansion of some particular socio-economic groups with respect to others? Of course, these two types of changes in social structures are related to each other. It is because economic growth favors urban workers over rural workers that the latter tend to migrate to the cities and the size of the agricultural population declines. Likewise, it may be because, in some circumstances,

---

[6] Another approach to estimating the growth sensitivity of social indicators would be to estimate jointly the difference equation in column (7) and the level equations in columns (1) and (2). Resulting estimates would simply be midway between the original estimates. Working with annual series, it would also be possible to explicitly introduce some lag in the effect of growth on social indicators and to use GMM-based Arellano–Bond or Blundell–Bond 'system' estimates [Arellano and Bond (1991), Blundell and Bond (1998)] instead of the fixed effect model (6). Given the proximity of the estimates in columns (6) and (7), the overall sensitivity is likely to be not very different from the estimates shown in these columns.

growth favors skilled work that parents have an incentive to send their children to school for longer periods and the literacy rate in the labor force tends to rise. In line with the plea for a 'structural approach' to these questions in the preceding section, this section reviews various theoretical models meant to describe the 'distributional' consequences of growth.

It is well known, since the pioneering work by Chenery and Syrquin (1975) on the structural aspects of growth, that growth favors some specific sectors and therefore specific social groups, mostly those who work in them or consume their products. Thus, when growth occurs, changes take place in the weight of these sectors in the economy and in the weight of these groups in the population. However, it is not necessarily the case that those changes also produce permanent modifications in relative incomes. Indirect mechanisms might partially or completely compensate for these direct effects by spreading them to the rest of the society. Competition in the labor market may spread sectoral effects to the whole economy, for instance, or migration may be a natural response to urban-oriented growth leaving urban–rural income differentials unchanged. Evaluating this chain of effects may require fairly elaborate models, however. Evaluating the effect of growth on social structures thus is more or less straightforward depending on what aspect of social structures is being studied. Given the considerable interest it provoked in the literature over the past 30 years or so, this review concentrates on the issue of income inequality, while considering at the same time related dimensions of social differentiation.

The relationship between economic growth and the inequality of the distribution of income and economic resources in general has attracted the interest of economists ever since the classical age of the discipline. More recently, very much interest arose with Kuznets' (1955) observation that, historically, inequality tended to increase in a first stage and then to decrease at a later stage of development. Cross-country analysis undertaken in the early 1970s by Paukert (1973) and Ahluwalia (1976a) seemed to confirm that there was indeed an inverted-U shape relationship between inequality and the level of development, as measured by the GDP per capita.

As can be seen in at the bottom of Table 1, the cross-country data available circa 1970 seemed indeed in full agreement with Kuznets' hypothesis. Data that became available later did not confirm that feature of the 1970 sample, however, whereas estimations based on panel data suggested that, in many countries, the evolution of inequality did not fit Kuznets' patterns. In Table 1, the coefficient of GDP per capita (y) and its square (y^2) show an inverted-U curve in 1970s, a significant U-shaped curve when these data are pooled together with more recent data, and a nonsignificant relationship when controlling for fixed effects.

Interestingly enough, the debate about the Kuznets hypothesis gave rise to a renewal of the theoretical literature on the general effects of growth on inequality. That literature also provides a representation of the channels through which economic growth may affect social structures in general. This literature is briefly reviewed in what follows.

The literature on the effect of growth on inequality emphasizes two fundamental channels: sectoral shifts, on the one hand, and factor markets on the other. Both channels have been represented with different types of modeling and have been subject to continuous scrutiny and analytical elaboration. They remain the cornerstones of any analytical approach to the social consequences of growth.

2.1. The sectoral shift view

The explanation that Kuznets himself gave to the inverted-U curve hypothesis was based on the sectoral shifts away from traditional agriculture that characterizes long-run economic growth. In effect, the model he had in mind was very much along the lines of the classical surplus labor model as formulated in the modern literature by Lewis (1954) and later by Fei and Ranis (1965). There are two sectors in the economy with fixed relative prices and fixed relative incomes. The development process consists of shifting some proportion of the population from one sector to the other. An obvious formalization of this model is as follows. Let y_i be the fixed income level in sector i, and n_i the share of the population in that sector. Let sector 2 be traditional agriculture and suppose that income in that sector is smaller than in the 'modern' sector, labeled 1 – i.e. $y_1 > y_2$. Long-run growth in that model is then essentially described by the increase in the proportion of the population employed in the modern sector, n_1, for fixed income levels y_1 and y_2. Such a process may for instance be explained by some capital accumulation taking place in sector 1 and some labor-market imperfection preventing labor remuneration to equalize in the two sectors.

This simple representation of the process of economic growth has obvious implications for social structures in general. Everything depends on the interpretation given to the two sectors 1 and 2. If sector 2 is indeed identified with traditional agriculture, then the drop in n_2, and the consequent increase in n_1, implies altogether an increase in urbanization and all social transformations that may possibly accompany it, like lower fertility, higher school enrollment, higher crime rate, etc. But the dichotomy between sectors 1 and 2 may also represent manufacturing versus services, formal versus informal or high versus low technology. In each case, growth comes with a more or less rapid modification in the structure of society in a particular dimension.

This framework may be easily extended so as to represent the evolution of income inequality within society. Following Robinson (1976), let income inequality be measured by the variance of the logarithm of income.[7] Thus, denote as V_i the variance in sector i and assume that this variance is constant. Total income inequality in the economy is then given by

$$V = n_1 V_1 + (1 - n_1) V_2 + n_1 (\text{Log } y_1)^2$$
$$+ (1 - n_1)(\text{Log } y_2)^2 - \left[n_1 \text{ Log } y_1 + (1 - n_1) \text{ Log } y_2 \right]^2, \qquad (1)$$

---

[7] Knight (1976) and Fields (1979) use the same framework but different income inequality measures. Anand and Kanbur (1993) present a more general version of this model where the analysis is conducted in terms of the full distribution of income in both sectors and in the whole economy rather than on a specific summary inequality measure.

where use is made of the fact that $n_1 + n_2 = 1$. As before, the development level of the economy is fully described by the proportion of people in sector 1, n_1. If it is assumed that $V_1 > V_2$, then total inequality in (1) is a parabolic function of n_1. Under some plausible conditions on the values of V_1, V_2, y_1 and y_2, total inequality may thus go up and then down as observed by Kuznets on some historical data.

Yet, this result on inequality, and more generally the fact that this model represents the social consequences of growth through a single parameter, n_1, must be taken with very much care. First, as n_1 is bounded, it may well be the case that inequality will be increasing or decreasing monotonically throughout the development process. Depending on the various parameters of the model, the time profile of inequality may be extremely flat or, on the contrary, have a sizable slope. Second, representing growth through a mere sectoral shift of the population may seem overly simplistic and restrictive. Assuming that income in the two sectors of the economy does not change along with growth is equivalent to assuming that markets are imperfectly competitive or that compensating phenomena are at work. Practically, more people in sector 1 could lower the relative price of that sector's output. This might reduce the initial level of inequality between the two groups of workers and may be enough to prevent inequality among individuals to go up in the first stage of the process just described. Likewise, it is restrictive to assume that migration from one sector to the other is distribution-neutral. A change in n_1 is likely to modify both V_1 and V_2. The direction of that change will depend on whether migration concerns the least well-off people in sector 2 or people in the middle of the income scale.

In short, representing economic growth through a simple sectoral shift parameter appears unsatisfactory to account for the effect of growth on social structures, except maybe in very particular cases where inequality across socio-economic groups may indeed be considered as constant. In general, however, the implicit fixed price assumption in the sectoral shift model seems unduly restrictive.

Several authors have proposed extensions of the preceding model for the analysis of the evolution of inequality among individual incomes. In some cases, the conclusion of an inverted-U shape relationship between growth and inequality was reinforced, as in Rauch (1993), for instance, while in other cases, the inverted-U shape conclusion was undermined – see for instance the demand-based models by Bacha and Taylor (1978), de Janvry and Sadoulet (1983) or Bourguignon (1990).

It is not clear that the inverted-U-shaped relationship between inequality and the level of development is an important issue by itself. It may have been important in the debate of the early 1970s on whether development efforts had to concentrate solely on growth as opposed to growth and distribution.[8] What seems more important today is the recognition that at all stages of the development process economic growth has indeed the capacity of modifying social structures, and in particular the hierarchy of relative

---

[8] Chenery et al. (1974) provides a good summary of the various elements of this debate. A detailed account of the recent history of economic thought in this area is offered by Arndt (1987).

incomes among individuals or socio-economic groups, through its natural sectoral bias. The way in which this bias is actually translated into more or less inequality is likely to be country-specific, but this strand of the literature suggests that it is not justified a priori to start from the postulate that economic growth is neutral in the sense that it affects everybody's living standard in the same proportion.

It is interesting that this emphasis on the sectoral bias of growth as the source of social changes is still present in the recent literature on inequality. Indeed, several authors see the appearance of a new branch in the Kuznets curve in the surge of wage and income inequality observed in the US economy in the late 1970s and in the 1980s – see for instance List and Gallet (1999). This evolution is often interpreted as the consequence of technical progress and/or international trade. A new sectoral specialization is appearing and social structures are affected by a progressive transition of the whole labor force towards the most modern sectors of the economy, in a process reminiscent of the industrialization process behind Kuznets' original argument.[9]

2.2. General equilibrium models of the distributional effects of growth

The sectoral shift view of the distributional consequences of growth refers to a 'fix-price' view of economic development where population movements across sectors or socio-economic groups respond to some disequilibrium. This disequilibrium may itself be caused by economic growth, but that relationship and the growth process itself are not explicitly considered. An alternative approach to the distributional effects of economic growth consists of considering changes in factor prices that may take place along the growth path, together with the factor accumulation behavior that is causing growth. Such an analysis is equivalent to linking the micro-economic analysis of distribution with standard macro-economic theories of growth and the functional distribution of national income. Sectoral differences and disequilibria which were prominent in the preceding approach are now ignored because it is now implicitly assumed that factor and good markets are permanently in equilibrium. The theoretical framework thus is that of dynamic general equilibrium rather than that of temporary fix-price partial equilibrium.

Numerous dynamic general equilibrium models have been proposed to analyze the relationship between economic growth and inequality, many of them inspired by the recent revival of the growth literature. No attempt will be made here to give an exhaustive summary of that literature, which in effect tends to concentrate on the way inequality affects economic growth rather than the opposite.[10] Instead, this section looks at the other face of the coin, namely what is to be learned from this literature about the distributional consequences of growth.

Following the pioneering paper by Stiglitz (1969), assume that the income, y_i, of agent i comes on the one hand from labor and on the other hand from the return on

---

[9] For empirical evidence from the US, see Katz and Autor (1999) and Baumol, Blinder and Wolff (2003).

[10] For a survey of this literature, see Aghion, Caroli and Garcia-Peñalosa (1999), Benabou (1996) or Bertola (2000), as well as other chapters in this volume.

his/her wealth, k_i. To simplify, assume that all agents have the same labor productivity and supply one unit of labor. Thus their labor income is uniform and equal to the wage rate w. These assumptions are more general than they look at first sight if k_i incorporates both physical (or financial) and human capital. The uniformity of labor income thus is an assumption that tries to represent the fact that (raw) labor income is in general more equally distributed than physical or human capital. Generalizing the following argument to the case of some exogenous distribution of labor productivities does not raise major difficulty. Denoting the rate of return to capital by r leads to the following definition of individual income

$$y_i = w + rk_i. \tag{2}$$

Expression (2) shows a first way through which growth may affect the distribution of income among individuals. By modifying the relative rewards of labor and capital, growth modifies relative individual incomes. For a given distribution of wealth, the distribution becomes more equal when the relative reward of labor rises.

As growth proceeds through the accumulation of individual wealth, there is a second way by which it may modify the distribution of income and wealth. A simple general assumption is that saving or investment by agent i, S_i, is a linear function of the various sources of income

$$S_i = \alpha r k_i + \beta w - \gamma, \tag{3}$$

where α is the marginal propensity to save out of capital income, β out of labor income and γ stands for the effect on savings of the existence of some minimum consumption level. Assuming in addition a depreciation of capital at rate δ, for all agents i, leads to the following accumulation behavior

$$\dot{k}_i = (\alpha r - \delta)k_i + \beta w - \gamma \tag{4}$$

or in growth rates

$$\frac{\dot{k}_i}{k_i} = (\alpha r - \delta) + \frac{\beta w - \gamma}{k_i}, \tag{5}$$

where the notation "˙" refers to infinitesimal time change.

It may appear that the preceding specification only allows for the representation of the evolution of the distribution of income and assets among individuals and does not permit analyzing social structures as described by the composition and relative income of socio-economic groups. This is not the case, however. It is sufficient to define socio-economic groups by some particular endowments of assets for (1) to describe the evolution of the relative incomes between, for instance, unskilled workers and skilled workers, or between workers and 'capitalists'. In effect, what matters here is the return to the various types of assets that are used to define socio-economic groups. The evolution of these rates of return defines the evolution of between group inequality. Likewise, Equations (4)–(5) implicitly define the dynamics of group composition. For instance, some unskilled workers – with k initially equal to zero – acquire some positive human capital (k) and become skilled workers, whereas some skilled workers may become 'capitalists'. Thus, it should be clear that all that follows applies as well to a description of the effects of growth on inequality among individuals as well among socio-economic groups on social structures.

An obvious implication of the linearity of (4) is that the distribution of wealth and income *does not affect* the aggregate growth path of the economy and therefore the evolution of the factor prices, w and r, that comes with it. Yet, it can be seen in (5) that another implication of that saving function is that *growth generally induces a change in* wealth or income inequality. In the general case, inequality decreases or increases with growth depending on whether savings out of wages, βw, cover the dissaving due to minimum consumption γ, or not.[11] Since the wage rate is expected to increase with growth, inequality may increase with growth in a poor economy but this evolution may reverse itself when the economy has reached a certain level of affluence, in a process that is consistent with the Kuznets hypothesis.

This is an extremely simplified model. At the same time, it incorporates enough flexibility to analyze several interesting issues. To do so, it is helpful to derive from the preceding equation the time behavior of relative incomes. It is easily shown that the evolution of the relative income of two agents i and j is given by

$$\frac{\dot{y}_i}{y_i} - \frac{\dot{y}_j}{y_j} = \left(\frac{1}{y_j} - \frac{1}{y_i}\right)\{w(\dot{r}/r - \dot{w}/w) + w(\alpha r - \delta) - r(\beta w - \gamma)\}. \tag{6}$$

This expression shows that distributional changes along a growth path have various sources. The first term in the curly bracket on the right-hand side corresponds to the changes in factor prices resulting from growth, whereas the last two terms correspond to capital and noncapital sources of savings, respectively. Sources for distributional changes are thus richer than with the sectoral shift approach. As mentioned above, the accumulation component may be compared, to some extent, to population shifts in the sectoral model. Differential accumulation behavior in the present representation of growth is equivalent to individuals moving from one socio-economic group to another. But, of course, it also corresponds to possible changes in 'within-sector' inequality parameters (V_i). The factor price effect corresponds to a change in the income differential across groups, that is the ratio y_1/y_2 in the sectoral shift model.

Expression (6) readily shows what evolution in factor prices and what kind of saving behavior may be responsible for increasing or decreasing income disparities among individuals or socio-economic groups along the growth path. According to the factor price effect, any increase in the reward to capital, relative to labor, increases inequality by lowering the relative income of 'pure' workers. The same is true of a high propensity to save out of capital income. On the contrary, a high propensity to save out of labor

---

[11] Results would not be qualitatively different if it were assumed that savings cannot be negative but are nil if income is below minimum consumption – see Stiglitz (1969) and Bourguignon (1981).

incomes contributes to more equality in the economy, at least after a wage threshold has been passed.

Of course, accumulation behavior and factor price changes cannot be considered as independent of each other. In this respect, it is interesting to consider some particular cases of the preceding general model. A first simple case is when agents save only out of their capital income ($\beta = 0$) and there is no minimum consumption requirement ($\gamma = 0$). It is well known that such a saving behavior can be obtained as the implication of a simple life cycle consumption allocation model.[12] As can be seen in (5), the rate of growth of individual wealth is then the same for all agents with positive initial wealth, which implies that the distribution of wealth remains constant over time, maintaining the features inherited from history. Note that this does not necessarily mean that the distribution of income will remain constant since relative factor prices and factor shares in individual incomes may change along the growth path. Yet, in the standard neo-classical framework with unit elasticity of substitution between capital and labor, it is easily shown that the distribution of relative incomes remains constant over time, precisely because the factor shares of total and individual incomes are constant.[13]

A related particular case, very much emphasized in the recent literature, arises when $\beta = \gamma = 0$, the rate of return to capital is constant and the wage rate grows at the same rate as individual and aggregate wealth. This would correspond to an economy where output is proportional to capital and is divided in constant proportion between labor and capital. The implicit growth model behind this description could be a version of the Harrod model or the 'aK' endogenous growth model proposed by Frankel (1962), extended later by Romer (1986) and others. The implications of these two particular cases are worth to be stressed. They indeed provide an interesting benchmark where *economic growth is essentially distribution neutral*, even after taking into account both the process of wealth accumulation and its effects on good and factor markets. However, it can be seen that this result is not so much due to the assumptions made on the production side of the economy – i.e. constant or declining returns to scale – as to the assumption that savings arise only out of capital income.

Another interesting particular case is the one originally explored by Stiglitz (1969). Assume that $\alpha = \beta$ and that factor prices are determined by the marginal products of an increasing and concave aggregate production function. Then, the aggregate economy behaves as in the well-known Solow model (1956), with the distribution of income

---

[12] In an infinite horizon model it is necessary to assume first that the inter-temporal elasticity of substitution (σ) is constant. If r is the rate of interest and ρ the utility discount rate, this leads to a constant rate of optimal consumption $g = \sigma(r - \rho)$. It is sufficient to assume that noncapital income grows at the same rate g, as will be the case at the steady state in an economy with constant returns to scale, to obtain that savings are proportional to existing wealth – see Bertola (1993).

[13] The unit elasticity of substitution ensures that aggregate shares of capital and labor in total income are constant. As all individuals accumulate capital at the same rate, individual shares of total capital remain constant. Together, this implies that both individual capital and labor incomes grow at the same rate as the whole economy.

following a Kuznets curve if the wage rate is initially low enough. More interestingly, and somewhat paradoxically, it can be shown that the distribution of income and wealth tends asymptotically towards full equality if the steady-state wage/profit rate ratio is large enough.[14] This result is considerably weakened if labor productivity and labor incomes are assumed to be heterogeneous across individuals. The distribution of both wealth and total income may then be shown to converge asymptotically to the distribution of labor productivities.

2.3. Nonlinear savings behavior

The preceding results are all based on the assumption that the wealth accumulation process underlying growth is linear with respect to individual wealth. This assumption is debatable. There are various reasons why savings may be thought to be a nonlinear function of income or wealth, even when saving behavior is strictly assumed to result from inter-temporal optimization. Liquidity constraints and/or credit market imperfections are the most obvious factors that may explain such nonlinearities. For instance, credit rationing may imply that zero is a lower bound for the savings of somebody with zero wealth. Combining this feature and the preceding linear model leads to savings being defined by

$$S_i = \text{Inf}\{0, \alpha r k_i + \beta w - \gamma\}.$$

In effect, this apparently small modification is sufficient to drastically alter the conclusions obtained previously. First, aggregating individual accumulation behavior leads to a change in aggregate wealth that depends on the distribution of wealth. Thus, the distribution of wealth affects the aggregate growth path of the economy, which was not the case before. Second, some of the conclusions obtained previously on the evolution of the distribution of income and wealth do not hold anymore. In particular, the result that the distribution of income tends towards equality in the Solow–Stiglitz model is not anymore granted. Depending on the initial distribution of wealth, inequality may well be nondecreasing throughout the whole growth path of the economy. Analogous conclusions may be obtained with more general nonlinear specifications of the saving function.[15]

---

[14] Namely, $w/r > \gamma/\delta$ at the steady state. The proof of the convergence towards equality is simple. Equation (5) may be rewritten as $\dot{k}_i = [\alpha(r\bar{k} + w) - \delta\bar{k} - \gamma] + [(\alpha r - \delta)(k_i - \bar{k})]$ where $\bar{k}$ is the mean wealth in the economy. At the steady state of the economy, the first square bracket on the right-hand side is nil and the first term in the second square bracket is negative. It follows that individual wealth necessarily converges towards the mean wealth $\bar{k}$. In comparison with the general model, this proof shows that the equal distribution asymptotic result in this particular case is due to: (a) the equal marginal propensity to save out of capital and labor income; (b) decreasing marginal returns to production factors.

[15] Of course, the inegalitarian steady-state result may be obtained for any saving function that is convex with respect to income or wealth. Schlicht (1975) and Bourguignon (1981) offer a general treatment of convex saving functions within a Solow–Stiglitz framework, without analyzing the reasons for convexity. Moav (2002) reaches the same conclusions assuming intertemporally maximizing agents with convex bequest functions.

A way of justifying nonlinear saving functions is to account for the fact that the rate of return to capital in the original (linear) model above may be heterogeneous across agents with different levels of wealth or income. Credit market imperfections associated with the existence of some indivisible investment project with an exogenous rate of return are sufficient to generate such a result. For moral hazard or adverse selection reasons those individuals who have to borrow to undertake this project face a borrowing rate of interest above rates served on conventional savings – and possibly decreasing with the amount borrowed, or equivalently their wealth.

Under the preceding assumptions, the original individual accumulation equation writes then

$$\dot{k}_i = \alpha \big[r(k, k_i)k - \delta \big] k_i + \beta w - \gamma, \tag{7}$$

where $r(\cdot)$ is a function of k_i that has the shape of an inverted U – poor people are credit rationed and only people in some intermediate wealth range are borrowers facing an implicitly higher rate of return on their wealth.

A significant proportion of the recent literature on the effects of the wealth distribution on economic growth is implicitly based on credit market imperfections and an accumulation equation of type (7). This is true in particular of the seminal papers by Galor and Zeira (1993), Banerjee and Newman (1993), Aghion and Bolton (1996) and Piketty (1997). These models also have implications for the distributional consequences of growth. As the rest of the literature, however, they suggest that all types of evolution are possible, from continuously increasing or decreasing inequality to Kuznets-curve-like movements.

2.4. The role of technical progress

The preceding is based on a view of economic growth being essentially driven by factor accumulation. Growth modifies the distribution of income and wealth among individuals or across socio-economic groups essentially because individuals or groups do not accumulate at the same rate and because factor accumulation may cause changes in the remuneration of the productive factors owned by individuals. But, of course, another engine of growth is technical progress, which may itself modify both the relative remunerations of productive factors and factor accumulation behavior.

If technical progress is neutral, affecting the remuneration of all factors in the same way, then nothing has to be changed in the preceding argument. An issue arises when technical progress is 'biased' in the sense that it favors one factor more than others. A case that has received very much attention in the recent literature is that of the 'skill-biased' technical change, which is a shift in technology that increases the demand for skilled labor.[16]

---

[16] See Acemoğlu (2002), Katz and Autor (1999).

From a theoretical point of view, one may analyze the effect of skill-biased technical change on social structures as resulting simply from a change in the return to the human capital component of individual wealth in the preceding framework. The increased demand for skilled labor increases the return to skill and, other things being equal, increases the income differential between skilled and unskilled workers. Of course, an increase in the return to skill is likely to cause an acceleration in the human capital accumulation, reducing progressively the differential between skilled and unskilled workers and, at the same time, shifting workers towards high skill socio-economic groups. The effect of this 'race' between technical change and education or training was first analyzed by Tinbergen (1975). Since then, it received very much attention.[17] In effect, the implications of this race for inequality are a priori ambiguous since it depends on the speed at which the demand for skilled labor increases following some technological innovation and the speed at which skill accumulation responds on the supply side of the labor market. If growth is seen as successive waves of skill-biased technical innovations, it may thus be accompanied by long-run fluctuations in earning differentials across skill groups of workers. These fluctuations may also be influenced by the fact that the bias of technical change may itself be affected by the skill differential and the relative availability of skilled workers, as in Acemoğlu (2002).

The dynamics of the earning differential are not necessarily as simple as the preceding supply-demand argument would imply. For instance, Aghion, Caroli and Garcia-Peñalosa (1999) and Aghion (2002) develop an original model of the diffusion of an innovation in General Purpose Technology where skill-biased technical change contributes to a continuous increase in the skill wage differential, after a preliminary period where the differential remains constant. The skill gap starts increasing when all skilled workers have been absorbed by firms which have adopted the new technology and the gap keeps increasing as long as other firms seek to adopt the new technology too. All firms eventually adopt the new technology and all workers acquire the new skill. In effect, this process combines both a sectoral shift of the type analyzed above and a general equilibrium price effect.

Although most of the effect of skill-biased technical change is expected to take place between skill groups, some authors insist that it may also affect inequality within groups. Any innovation requires adaptation of the first workers who are confronting it, and this adaptation is easier for workers with some specific ability on top of the skill required to perform the new task. The increased remuneration of that specific ability contributes to increasing the degree of inequality among workers, an inequality that may persist over time if the adaptation to the new technology has created a new type of human capital among the workers who were first exposed to the technical innovation [see Violante (1997), Rubinstein and Tsiddon (1998), Aghion, Howitt and Violante (2002)].

---

[17] For recent formalizations of this argument see Eicher (1996), Galor and Tsiddon (1997). See also the survey by Aghion, Caroli and Garcia-Peñalosa (1999).

2.5. Conclusion

To conclude this section on the theoretical mechanisms through which growth affects social structures, it must be emphasized that, as mentioned in the case of technical progress, sectoral shift and general equilibrium mechanisms are not necessarily mutually exclusive. It was already seen above how the individual asset accumulation Equations (4)–(5) could actually represent the shift of individuals across socio-economic groups defined by their factor endowments. More explicitly, however, recent theoretical models built on the imperfect credit market mechanism actually combine the factor market and the sectoral shift approach. An interesting aspect of the model proposed by Banerjee and Newman (1993), for instance, is that the distribution of wealth in the economy practically determines economic agents' kind of occupation and the sector where they operate. People with little wealth are pure wage workers, employed either in the formal or the informal sectors. People with a higher initial level of wealth engage in small businesses and determine the size of the 'informal' sector, whereas richer people are the owners, managers and top employees in the formal sector. The change in the wealth distribution that takes place, together with growth, over time thus has the effect of changing the distribution of occupations in the economy and the relative size of the formal and informal sectors. To some extent, this particular dynamic general equilibrium model provides a kind of formalization of the intersectoral shifts emphasized in the Kuznets tradition of the analysis of the effects of growth on inequality.

Overall, the short preceding review shows that considerable effort has been devoted to identifying and understanding the mechanisms through which growth affects social structures and inequality. As far as social structures are concerned, the analysis points to the evolution of the employment structure of the population away from lowest-productivity sectors and occupations. An obvious social consequence of growth thus is to reduce the share of the population living in traditional agriculture in a first stage, in informal nonagricultural activities in a second stage, in 'low-tech' manufacturing activities in a third stage, etc. At the same time, the accumulation of human capital implies that growth comes with a continuous reduction in the share of the population with no or low education.[18] On the other hand, the economic analysis of growth is largely inconclusive concerning other aspects of social structures and the distribution of wealth or income.

In this respect, three sources of ambiguity must be stressed. First, theory is necessarily silent on aspects of social structures that do not appear as central in economic growth mechanisms. That the population shifts sector and occupation in a well-defined direction is one thing. Whether this movement is uniform across population subgroups defined by gender or ethnicity is another thing – about which economic growth theory

---

[18] The preceding argument is straight economics. But the increase in schooling has also a demographic explanation. The demand for children – and thus family size and human capital levels – changes with economic growth. One tends to observe fewer and better-'quality' children at higher levels of income per capita. For surveys of this literature, see the two volumes of Rosenzweig and Stark (1997) and Rosenzweig (1990).

has little to say. This is essentially because factor endowments put forward by growth theory do not incorporate this dimension of social differentiation. Second, whether the shift of the population from one sector or socio-economic group to another is accompanied by an increase in income differentials among those sectors or groups is unclear. For instance, the share of educated people in the population is increasing with growth, but that evolution is in theory consistent with constant, increasing or decreasing income differentials between educational levels. Third, if economic theory permits us to identify the various channels through which growth may affect inequality among individuals, the sum total of these effects is ambiguous: no change, equalizing or unequalizing evolution throughout the whole growth process, or the inverted-U shape put forward by Kuznets. This conclusion holds whatever the analytical framework being used, whether theoretical models belong to the sectoral shift fix-price or to dynamic general equilibrium modeling tradition.

3. The effect of economic growth on social structures: Empirical evidence

The preceding analysis suggested various channels through which growth is affecting social structures: (a) by shifting individuals from one sector or socio-economic group to another; (b) by modifying income differentials across sectors and socio-economic groups; (c) by modifying income and welfare disparities across individuals. Of course, these three channels are not independent. In particular, it must be clear that sectoral shifts and inequality changes between socio-economic groups have a direct impact on inequality among individuals.

This section briefly reviews the empirical evidence available on these three channels. Both on a cross-country and case study basis, the sectoral shift effect of growth turns out to be the fundamental way through which economic growth affects social structures. Cross-country analysis is less conclusive about the differential effects of growth across socio-economic groups or among individuals. However, this certainly does not mean that growth has no impact on social structures outside the sectoral shift component. Rather, case studies suggest that this effect is more complex and most likely strongly country-specific.

3.1. The sectoral shift effect of growth on social structures

Two rows in Table 1 illustrate the power of growth-related sectoral shift to influence on social structures. Urbanization and all the phenomena that it entails is the first example. The structural explanation behind it is clear. It has to do with the falling share of agriculture – or, better said, of low-productivity traditional agriculture – throughout the growth process. Although only a reduced form model appears in Table 1, coefficients shown there are strongly significant, and it would be relatively easy to devise a structural model focusing more on the mechanisms behind the urbanization process with equally strong statistical significance.

A second sectoral shift effect of growth shown in Table 1 concerns education. Here again, the positive correlation with development levels is very strong. It is true that the coefficient obtained with decadal differences is not statistically significant, but this might have to do with the extremely long lags with which changes in schooling behavior, possibly generated by economic growth, spread to the whole population.[19] It is also true that focusing on literacy rates yields a perspective on education and skills that may seem too narrow. However, it is unlikely that considering the proportion of 'skilled workers' in the labor force – assuming that some uniform definition of skills is available across countries – or the proportion of people with secondary education would yield very different qualitative results.[20] In effect, regressing the average number of years of schooling of individuals in the labor force on GDP per capita in Table 1 yields results qualitatively similar to the regression on literacy rate.

One could undoubtedly multiply regressions showing strong structural effects of economic growth through which changes in social structures are likely to occur. For instance, one could focus on the weight of the manufacturing or the service sector instead of focusing on agriculture, or one could focus on the relative weights of low- and high-tech industries or enterprises. Interestingly, this kind of approach to growth – which was prominent in the 1970s, as a continuation of Kuznets research program on 'modern economic growth' and under the impulsion of Chenery and associates[21] – is presently weakening. There are various reasons for this neglect, in particular for developed countries as will be seen below. Yet, it would be wrong to conclude from this relative lack of interest that sectoral shift phenomena have disappeared from the research agenda when analyzing the social effects of growth. Indeed, the whole recent literature on the skill bias in the sources of growth and, in particular, technical progress or international trade [see, for instance, the survey by Katz and Autor (1999) and Baldwin and Cain (2000)] may be considered as an updated sectoral shift argument in the analysis of growth and its effects.[22]

Changes in female labor force participation may also be considered as a sectoral shift phenomenon. But it may also be considered as deriving from a change in behavior itself caused by economic growth. According to the sectoral shift logic, women would be moving from being 'inactive' or more exactly specialized in low-productivity domestic production to market employment at a higher level of productivity. According to the behavioral interpretation, the role of women would have been changing in a way concomitant with growth but under forces of a different nature. For instance, some authors

---

[19] From this point of view, empirical evidence may seem more pertinent. See Clemens (2004), Lindert (2003) and Krueger and Lindahl (2001).

[20] For a more detailed analysis of the way in which the structure of the population by educational level changes with the level of development, see Thomas, Wang and Fan (2000).

[21] See Chenery et al. (1974) and Chenery and Syrquin (1975). For a more recent statement and a comparison with the contemporaneous growth literature, see also Syrquin (1994).

[22] It is true that much of that literature is concerned with changes in skilled/unskilled wage differential, an issue which we take up in the next subsection, but the basic argument – which goes back to Tinbergen (1975) – is that the evolution of technology which is behind economic growth requires more educated labor.

see an explanation of the increased female labor force participation in most developed countries after World War II as resulting from the excess demand in the labor market that developed during the war and that had to be filled, a phenomenon that produced a durable change in behavior. Others would insist that the drop of fertility, partly due to the diffusion of contraceptive means in the last three decades or so, was the reason behind women's increased labor force participation.[23]

The preceding phenomena may well provide a partial explanation for the fast increase in female labor force participation in the developed world over the last 60 years or so. However, regressions in Table 1 reveal a rather strong association between participation and economic growth that is not due to cross-country differences, whereas both the fertility and the World War II argument would suggest that those cross-country differences should dominate. Pure cross-country regressions in the first columns of Table 1 yield insignificant results or wrongly signed coefficients when participation is specified as a linear function of GDP per capita. On the contrary, strongly significant results are obtained when within-country time behavior of participation and GDP per capita is taken into account. The simple structural argument that increased female labor force participation may correspond to a shift from low- to higher-productivity occupations is not undermined by the data. Interestingly enough, the same difference between cross-country and within-country estimates appears when participation is regressed on a quadratic form of GDP per capita. A U-shaped relationship is obtained when not controlling for country fixed effects, whereas a monotonic relationship holds in the opposite case.[24]

For the sectoral shift effect of growth on social structures to be of relevance, it is necessary that it takes place between sectors or socio-economic groups with sufficient initial important differences in terms of welfare level. This is certainly the case for the shift across skill (or education) levels, between traditional agriculture and the modern sector of the economy in developing countries or between inactivity and market work for women. Things are less clear in the case of sectoral shifts in developed countries when markets function smoothly and tend to equalize returns of human capital across occupations or sectors. Most likely, this is the reason why this dimension is somewhat neglected in the recent growth literature in developed and emerging countries. The attention there tends to concentrate on differences in the evolution of returns to assets and in their accumulation rather than their sectoral allocation.

The previous remark illustrates possible differences across countries that are hidden by the cross-country work that has been referred to. That differences do exist between

---

[23] The first hypothesis is critically reviewed by Goldin (1991). For the second, see for example Birdsall and Chester (1987), Asbell (1995), Goldin and Katz (2002).

[24] On the U-shaped female labor force participation function see Durand (1975) or Goldin (1995). The decreasing part of the curve is explained by the decline in female unskilled employment opportunities due to the contraction of the agricultural sector, whereas the increasing part would be due to rising education. See, for instance, Clark, York and Anker (2003). In Table 1, a parabolic shape is obtained when controlling for fixed effects, but the top of the curve occurs at income levels much above what is observed in the sample. Thus, the U-shape hypothesis is not confirmed.

developed and developing countries in terms of the social consequences of sectoral shifts of population due to growth is obvious. In Table 1, these differences often are accounted for through the Cox transformation on the dependent variable. But other country differences might exist so that one would ideally like to estimate sectoral shift equations using national time series rather than a cross-section of countries. To some extent, this country specificity is what Chenery and his associates were after when they tried to identify 'patterns of development' among developing countries. Unfortunately, due to lack of adequate data, they most often had to rely on calibrated structural models rather than time series structural econometrics. The situation has changed little since then.

3.2. Effect of growth on inequality between socio-economic groups

As mentioned above, the sectoral shift effect of economic growth is important to explain social structures inasmuch as it is accompanied by a persistent differential between socio-economic groups or sectors, in terms of current of permanent income or welfare level. At the same time, it may be envisaged that economic growth contributes to a deepening, or on the contrary, to a weakening of this social differentiation. In effect, those two evolutions are certainly not independent. Sectoral shifts need income differentials to develop and, in turn, they produce changes in these differentials. This subsection focuses on the potential effects of growth on earnings or income differentials across socio-economic groups. Given the dualism with the sectoral shift argument, we adopt the same presentation as in the previous subsection and consider in turn income differentials between sectors – essentially agriculture and the rest of the economy, between skills or educational levels, and between genders.

3.2.1. Sectoral income differentials

The regressions in Table 1 illustrate the fact that sectoral productivity – and presumably income – differentials tend to diminish with economic growth. Thus, growth contributes to harmonize social structures across sectors. The process behind this is clear and has indeed very much to do with the sectoral shift process. As growth proceeds and high-productivity activities arise, people tend to leave low-productivity occupations predominantly located in traditional agriculture. But, this migration process contributes to increasing productivity and income in the sector of origin – and possibly to lower income growth in the sector of destination. The 'dualism' of the economy, emphasized by early development economists, tends to diminish with growth. It eventually vanishes when the economy is more mature and market mechanisms ensure the equalization of productivity and earning rates across sectors.

At early stages of development, the preceding process is undoubtedly a powerful source of changes in social structures. At later stages, the emphasis on the agricultural sector is probably ill-placed. A comparison between informal and formal (nonagricultural) sectors would be more appropriate. If comparable data were available across countries on this formal/informal distinction, they would probably show a similar phenomenon, that is a narrowing of productivities and incomes across sectors as the informal sector loses weight. At some point, however, the issue becomes essentially that of the functioning of the labor market. The difficulty then is to identify whether earning differentials are due to some segmentation of the labor market or correspond to the self-selection of individuals across jobs with different characteristics and productivity levels.[25] Undoubtedly, these differences raise important social issues regarding the social status differential of workers linked to workers' social status. But they are of a nature different from the social transformations taking place at earlier stages of development, and it is not clear whether they may be unambiguously associated with growth.

3.2.2. *Effect of education on earnings*

In a competitive factor market environment, it was argued above that differences in productive asset bundles owned by individuals would be a better indicator of social differentiation than the sector of occupation. Education was thus seen as an important dimension of social differentiation. In this context, the sectoral shift analysis coincides with the change in the distribution of the population, or possibly the labor force, in terms of educational levels. It is now time to examine whether earning differentials across educational groups – often assimilated to skill groups – tend to change in a systematic fashion with economic growth.

There is a huge literature on earning differentials by educational or skill levels and their evolution over time. This is not the place to summarize it.[26] There is considerably less literature on comparing differentials across countries. To our knowledge, the main contributor in this area is Psacharopoulos, who devoted very much effort to the collection of rates of return to education derived from the estimation of Mincerian earning equations based on labor force or household surveys around the world – see in particular Psacharopoulos (1994) and Psacharopoulos and Patrinos (2002). Putting together Psacharopoulos' findings and the lessons from country studies on the evolution of earning differentials leads to some interesting and somewhat paradoxical conclusion. Namely, cross-country comparisons suggest that there is a strong long-run tendency for earning differentials across educational levels to fall, whereas country studies show a very high level of medium-run variability without clear trend.

Table 2 shows mean earning differentials across schooling levels for country groups defined by GDP per capita. These groups cover a total of 98 developed and developing countries for which Mincerian earning equations were available during the period extending from 1970 to 1996, the most recent estimate being used (usually from the late

---

[25] For references, see Ashenfelter and Card (1999). See also Card (1999) which reviews the methodological problems involved in estimating the causal effect of education on earnings.
[26] See Katz and Autor (1999).

Table 2
Earning differentials by educational levels (%)

	Primary vs. no schooling	Secondary vs. primary	Tertiary vs. secondary	Average earning differential by year of schooling
Low-income countries (GDP per capita less than $755)	25.8	19.9	26	10.9
Middle-income countries (to $9265)	27.4	18	19.3	10.7
High-income countries (GDP per capita more than $9265)	NA	12.2	12.4	7.4

Source: Psacharopoulos and Patrinos (2002).

1980s or early 1990s). All individual earners are supposed to be covered by the data, whether they are wage earners or self-employed. The striking fact is that earning differentials tend to decline with the level of average income above primary, whether the differential is taken between secondary and primary, or between tertiary and secondary. The last column of the table shows the average rate of return by year of schooling for the same data sets. They, also, fall with the level of GDP per capita.

This empirical regularity – which nevertheless hides very much variability across countries – is consistent with a simple competitive story of the labor market. As the accumulation of human capital proceeds, the return to skill tends to fall. If cross-country differences are taken to represent the effect of long-run growth, then the idea behind this story is essentially that the demand for skilled labor tends to grow at a slower pace than supply, thus reducing gaps between educational groups. Interestingly enough, however, time series analyses for countries where successive estimates of the Mincerian equation are available tell a different story. Restricting now the analysis to the average rate of return by year of schooling, it can be seen in Figure 1 that practically all evolutions are possible over period extending from 8 to 23 years. Near constancy as in the case of Brazil to steady increase as in the US between 1976 and 1990, a phenomenon extensively studied in the literature, to steady decline as in the case of The Netherlands, to erratic behavior as in Sweden.

There are various reasons behind this paradoxical difference between cross-sectional and time series evidence. First, time variations in returns per year of schooling may have different origins depending on the level of development. They may originate more across primary and secondary in developing countries and more between secondary and tertiary or even within tertiary in developed countries.[27] This is because practically everyone has 8 years of schooling or more in developed countries, whereas most low-income and middle-income countries are far from that goal. Second, there may be

---

[27] This is a natural consequence of the fact that schooling until middle secondary has been compulsory in developed countries for quite a long time.

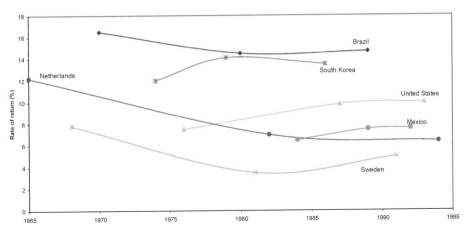

Figure 1. Evolution of rate of return to education (years of schooling). *Source*: Based on Psacharopoulos and Patrinos (2002).

problems of comparability of samples across countries at different levels of development. In particular, most earning equations are estimated on samples of urban workers. This group of workers represents a high percentage of the labor force in high-income countries, much less in others. Third, the period on which time series are observed may not be long enough to be fully consistent with cross-country differences in development levels.

Finally, there are reasons to expect some time specificity in the evolution of the rate of return to schooling and skill differentials in general. As alluded to before, they are related to Tinbergen's (1975) idea of the race between technology and education driving the evolution of skill differentials in earnings. For more or less continuous progress achieved on the educational side, it is sufficient to imagine fluctuations or trends in a definite direction in skill-biased technical progress – or possibly in trade policies – to generate time series behavior of the type shown in Figure 1. Alternatively, one may also think of technical progress and its diffusion in the economy following a continuous – not necessarily linear – trend and the educational response intervening with a different time profile to generate various patterns in the evolution of the rate of return to schooling.[28]

For all preceding reasons, it is not contradictory to infer from existing evidence that, indeed, a narrowing of skill differentials and a fall in the rate of return to education is accompanying growth in the long-run, at least in the early stages of development. At the same time, however, this trend may be hidden for long or short periods by accelerations of skill-biased technical progress, major changes in the international trade environment of a country, and velocity of the supply response to changes in skill differentials.

---

[28] See for instance Aghion (2002). See also the chapter by Jorgenson in this volume.

3.2.3. Gender earnings differentials

The examination of evidence on gender gaps in individual earnings leads to conclusions opposite to the preceding ones. There, one observes a rather clear downward trend in most countries, although information is scarce for developing countries. By contrast, cross-country comparison points to no systematic differences between countries ranked by development level.

There are relatively few cross-country comparisons of male–female earnings differentials in the literature except for developed countries. Terrell (1992) collected estimates on male–female earning differentials from the ILO Yearbook of Labour Statistics. She found very much cross-country variability, and more importantly as much variability within low- and middle-income countries as within high-income countries. For instance the female–male earnings ratio varied from 0.60 to 0.85 in developed countries, and from 0.50 to 0.90 in developing countries. Of course, the problem is that the samples on which these ratios are evaluated, typically salaried urban workers, differ quite substantially across countries. Thus, the comparison may be of little relevance between a country where 80% of both men and women are in that group and countries where only 20% of men and still a lower proportion of women qualify. This is what explains the paucity of cross-country comparisons encompassing the whole world. Better comparisons can be performed using indirect indicators of earnings. For instance, the regression on male–female difference in literacy rates in Table 1 shows a steady decline with the development level both across countries and across 10-year periods. However, literacy or schooling differences constitute only one among many determinants of earnings differences. Not much is known about gender differences in these other dimensions, nor about their impact on earnings differentials.[29]

In contrast to cross-country, time series of female–male earning ratios available in developed countries show an unambiguous increase over the last few decades. In the US, for instance, this ratio increased from 0.56 to 0.72 between the late 1960s and the late 1990s – see Welch (2000). Comparable increases are observed in European countries.[30] Only a few data points are available for middle-income countries but they reflect a parallel evolution. Between the early 1980s and the mid-1990s, the female–male ratio among wage earners increased from 0.74 to 0.80 in Taiwan, from 0.62 to 0.72 in Colombia, and from 0.52 to 0.61 in Brazil.[31]

The problem is to know whether such an evolution should be related to economic growth or not. This requires distinguishing between two sources of change in female–male earnings ratios, one associated with the differential evolution of the characteristics

---

[29] The life expectancy regression in Table 1 also shows an evolution that seems relatively more favorable to women along the growth process in pure cross-section. Yet, the sign of the coefficient is reversed when fixed effects are taken into account and the coefficient is insignificant in decadal differences. More detailed characteristics are analyzed in the World Bank (2001).

[30] For a thorough and exhaustive discussion of these issues, see for instance Gunderson (1989).

[31] The latter figures are taken from Bourguignon, Ferreira and Lustig (2004).

of female and male workers, and the other with changes in the remuneration of these characteristics – i.e. the well-known Oaxaca–Blinder decomposition. In effect, it so happened that the increase in female wage employment concomitant with the previous evolution contributed overall to a lowering of the average skill of employed women in many instances, an effect contributing to a widening rather than a narrowing of the gap. Thus, the observed narrowing must prominently be due to changes in remunerations rather than in the differential characteristics of male and female workers.

The issue then arises of the source of changes in remunerations. Are they related to specific observed characteristics or more diffuse in the whole labor force? In the latter case, it would then be tempting to associate the decline in the female–male ratio to noneconomic phenomena like the evolution of social norms about gender differences, to regulation in the labor markets – minimum wage for instance – or, in some countries, to some kind of affirmative action policies. All these phenomena probably bear some responsibility for the narrowing of the male–female gap, but there also is indirect evidence that it may be due to a change in the remuneration rate of some specific characteristics that distinguish male and female work. This indirect evidence is the positive correlation that has been noted between the female–male earnings ratio and the degree of inequality of male earnings, both in time series – see Blau and Kahn (1997) and Welch (2000) – and in a cross-section of developed countries – see Blau and Kahn (2003). A possible interpretation of that correlation is that changes in male earnings inequality reflect changes in the remuneration rate of earnings determinants, the relative intensity of which happens to differ much between male and female labor. As observed worker characteristics like education or experience do not appear to have played this role, this explanation must rely on unobserved earnings determinants. For instance, Welch (2000) refers to "brains relative to brawn", with the idea that the relative remuneration of brains in the labor market increases with technical progress, and in effect with economic growth, whereas woman labor is typically more intensive in that factor.

Such an interpretation of the narrowing female–male earnings gap in high-income – and possibly some middle-income countries – is attractive. Yet, it remains to be tested more carefully, a challenging task given that this hypothesis is essentially based on unobserved labor characteristics. At this stage, it is thus difficult to conclude whether it is indeed economic growth that so strongly influences this fundamental dimension of social differentiation. At the same time, it is worth stressing that the preceding issues probably arise only beyond some development level where the labor market is sufficiently unified and competitive. The thinness of the modern labor market and the low weight of women in that market may explain why low income countries are not really comparable to others in terms of gender earnings differentials.

3.3. Effects of growth on inequality among individuals

The preceding subsections looked into how growth affects the structure of the population by sector of activity and by socio-economic groups defined by some observed characteristics, and how it affects income differentials between them. It is now time to consider the possible effect of growth on the overall distribution of income among all individuals in the population. Such a perspective goes beyond the preceding points of view in that it adds to the analysis the possible effect of growth on unobserved individual characteristics through changes in disparities within socio-economic groups. The analysis will proceed in three steps. First, the observed statistical relationship between development levels and income inequality is briefly discussed for a sample of countries and periods where comparable data are available. Second, a more structural approach is discussed where additional variables representing in some way the socio-economic group structure of the population are introduced. Finally, semi-structural studies of the evolution of the distribution in selected countries are discussed. Interestingly enough, the conclusions obtained about the effect of growth on inequality vary rather radically from one approach to another.

3.3.1. Correlation between growth and inequality: rise and fall of the Kuznets curve

As illustrated in the bottom of Table 1, the cross-country evidence on the distributional effects of growth is essentially inconclusive. It is true that a cross-section of countries taken in the 1970s suggests a parabolic relationship that seems in agreement with Kuznets' hypothesis. But cross-sections taken at a later date, and presumably with better data, fail to yield statistically significant results. More importantly, when controlling for country fixed effects so as to isolate the average consequences of within-country growth on distribution, no statistically significant effect can be identified either.

The preceding results fit well the existing literature on the distributional consequences of growth and the Kuznets curve. Back in the 1970s and in the early 1980s, several papers provided pure cross-sectional estimates of the distributional consequences of growth that seemed in agreement with Kuznets' hypothesis, with very much emphasis on the estimation of the turning point at which further growth would cause inequality to go down rather than up – see, in particular, Paukert (1973), Ahluwalia (1974, 1976a and 1976b), Lecaillon et al. (1984). This early literature was very much criticized for its lack of econometric rigor and the quality of the data being used – see, in particular, Anand and Kanbur (1991). When better and more complete data became available, it indeed turned out that the parabolic shape of the relationship between income and inequality was a feature of the 1970s. This feature vanished with the data available in subsequent periods, whereas the first attempts at controlling for country fixed effects confirmed that the findings based on the observations of the 1970s were not robust – see Anand and Kanbur (1993), Fields and Jakubson (1994) and Deininger and Squire (1998), probably the most data-comprehensive analysis available although it relies on secondary data sources.

The interest in the Kuznets hypothesis has not completely vanished today and this hypothesis is frequently revisited in the light of new data and estimation techniques. But the cottage industry that developed around trying to confirm or reject this hypothesis is in decline.[32] At this stage, it seems fair to say that a consensus has emerged according to which available data *do not suggest any strong and systematic relationship* between inequality and the level of development of an economy. Even those authors who identified a significant relationship agree that it is weak and explains little of the observed differences in inequality.[33]

As in the preceding sections, it may be worth exploring how time series compare to cross-country differences in terms of the correlation between income inequality and development levels. Indeed, considerable attention has been given lately to the evolution of inequality and to the question of whether there was a systematic tendency for modern growth to generate more inequality, as observed in a few countries during the 1980s. This literature is mostly concerned with developed countries because of data availability, even though time series of distribution data in those countries are not always consistent – see Atkinson and Brandolini (2001). The common conclusion of most existing analyses is that inequality has substantially increased in a number of countries between the mid-1980s and the mid-1990s – 12 out of the 17 countries analyzed by Gottschalk and Smeeding (2000). Yet, this evolution must be contrasted with the fact that inequality had been declining in almost all developed countries throughout the 1960s and the 1970s, so that inequality in many countries today is comparable to what it was 30 years ago. It is also worth stressing that inequality failed to increase in a few countries, most likely thanks to very efficient – and possibly increasingly so – redistribution. Time series in developed countries thus seem to confirm the evidence based on cross-country analysis, namely that there is no significant long-run trend, related to the growth process or not, affecting the degree of within-country inequality.

Although data are still more shaky, the same conclusion seems to hold for middle- and low-income countries. Cornia (2001) and Cornia, Addison and Kiiski (2004) find that, out of 34 developing countries for which they have several observations between the 1950s and the mid-1990s, inequality is higher in the terminal period for 15 of them, equal for 14 and lower for 5. Yet, little is said about the intermediate years. When data are available, a U-shape evolution is observed in a number of cases where inequality is found to be increasing when comparing the terminal and the initial years. Overall,

---

[32] No reference has been made here to the historical literature on the Kuznets curve. It generally points to sizable changes in some particular inequality measures over long periods of time, which sometimes conform with Kuznets' own finding. Yet, the problem is that it relies on very rough measures of inequality – see p. 46.

[33] See for instance the conclusion reached by Barro (2000) and his reference to Papanek and Kyn (1986) for a similar statement. No mention has been made here of the few studies focusing on the effect of the rate of growth, rather than the level of economic development on inequality. Lundberg and Squire (2003) and Banerjee and Duflo (2003) find that faster economic growth tends to be associated with increasing inequality, but here again the effect is extremely small. Note finally that, after raising the same hopes as the Kuznets hypothesis in the 1970s and 1980s, the recent literature on the reverse causation, seems also to converge to the conclusion of no 'systematic' effect of inequality on growth. This was pointed out by Benabou (1996) and has been confirmed since then by contradictory results obtained with different specifications and samples – see Banerjee and Duflo (2003).

clear ascending or descending trends over long periods of time thus are infrequently observed.

Dealing with the effect of growth on social structures, one might prefer to use the concept of poverty, which may have a firmer social connotation than inequality. With this concept, a dimension of social structures is simply the poor–nonpoor difference, that is the proportion of people living in poverty and the distance at which those people find themselves from the poverty line and from the average income of the nonpoor. Of course, if income is taken as the only dimension of welfare, poverty and inequality are rather equivalent concepts when poverty is defined in relative terms, as for instance the proportion of people living with less than 50% of the median income. Poverty, then, becomes a particular inequality measure and much of the preceding argument presumably applies to poverty as well as inequality. Things are different when poverty is defined in absolute terms, as with the widely used international poverty line of $1 a day or any national poverty line representing the minimum budget deemed necessary for survival. Growth then plays a direct role to explain the evolution of poverty. In particular, if the distribution of relative incomes remains constant over time, then changes in poverty essentially reflect uniform income growth in the population. On the contrary, when distribution changes over time, economic growth may play a more complex role depending on its actual effects on distribution.[34] That cross-country analysis fails to find any systematic relationship between distribution and growth suggests indeed that growth has the simpler and more direct impact on poverty that was just mentioned. This is essentially the argument that led Dollar and Kraay (2002) to conclude that 'growth is good for the poor'. However, it will be seen below that this conclusion may hide considerable disparities across countries.

3.3.2. Towards structural estimates of the effects of growth on distribution?

By focusing on the correlation between inequality and development levels, both in cross-section and time series, the preceding section does not do justice to existing work. Most empirical models that may be found in the literature actually comprise additional variables that may explain the evolution of inequality alongside with, or independently from growth. For instance, the regressions in the pioneer paper by Ahluwalia (1976b) had the income share of various quantiles on the left-hand side and a host of variables on the right-hand side, together with GDP per capita and its square. These variables included the GDP share of agriculture, some educational indicators and some fertility indicators. Thus, the effect of the development level of inequality was supposed to come on top of the effects of sectoral shifts, and associated changes in relative factor rewards. In terms of the analysis in this chapter, the implicit objective of such a specification is somewhat unclear. The distribution between socio-economic groups implicitly defined

---

[34] On the identity that relates income distribution, poverty and growth see Fields (2001), Ravallion and Datt (2002) or Bourguignon (2003).

by variables like the GDP share of agriculture or the degree of urbanization and its impact on overall inequality is taken care of precisely by the presence of these variables in the regression. Under these conditions, the purpose of keeping GDP per capita among the regressors could only have been to identify the effect of economic growth on the distribution of income *within* those groups, a rather restrictive objective. Retrospectively, the economic framework behind those regressions thus appears as essentially ad hoc, between the reduced form model implicit in the regressions in Table 1 and a true structural model identifying the channels through which growth may indeed affect the distribution. Unfortunately, this imprecision of the economic framework behind the regressions being estimated is rather common in the empirical literature on inequality and development.

Using structural forms in cross-country regressions is possible, but probably requires gathering the appropriate data. In Bourguignon and Morrisson (1990, 1998), for instance, the objective is to explain cross-country differences in distribution explicitly through a model resembling (2) above but with a larger number of assets. Agent's income is thus taken to be given by

$$y_i = \sum_j a_{ij} w_j F_j,$$

where a_{ij} is the share of factor j owned by agent i, the total endowment of factor j is given by F_j, and w_j is its remuneration rate. Endogenizing the latter within the framework of a small open economy, it is then possible to write the overall distribution of income $\{y\}$ as

$$\{y\} = H\lfloor\{a..\}, F., p, t\rfloor, \tag{8}$$

where the arguments of the function $H(\cdot)$ are the distribution of resources in the population $\{a..\}$, the vector of total endowments $F.$, the vector of international prices faced by the economy p, and the tax rates and tariffs that it imposes t. Then, one may try to proxy for these various arguments by aggregate data available on a comparable basis across countries and use the resulting empirical model to analyze the effects of economic growth on the distribution.

The two papers referenced above stop short of the latter objective, mostly because of the difficulty of identifying all the variables necessary for the analysis and the necessity of using very imperfect proxies, which prevent proceeding with a truly structural analysis. For instance, physical capital per worker is approximated by GDP per capita. This is not unjustified for a given value of other aggregate endowments of productive factors, but this makes it impossible to distinguish the distributional effects of capital accumulation and of total factor productivity. Even so, however, the analysis shed light on the effects of the ownership distribution variables – land, human capital – on the distribution of income at one point of time, as well as on the impact of relative aggregate endowments (land, physical and human capital and raw labor) and policy variables like trade protection. In line with the argument in the previous sections, it also showed the importance of labor market competitive imperfection, and in particular the 'dualism' of the economy as represented by the relative productivities of the agricultural and nonagricultural sectors.

Going beyond these partial results and analyzing the potential effects of growth in the distribution of income within the framework of (8) is still on the agenda. Better data are necessary. As rough as existing empirical applications may be, however, this analysis suggests that the distributional effects of growth are complex and most likely to be strongly differentiated across countries. With the preceding specification and in view of the results obtained, it appears clearly that growth affects the distribution through various channels – changes in relative factor endowments, changes in the distribution of these factors, changes in policies, changes in the functioning of factor markets – and in a way that may depend on the initial value of these various macro-economic characteristics.

3.3.3. Case study analysis

Should one then conclude with Dollar and Kraay (2002) that growth is distributionally neutral and therefore that "growth is good for the poor", whatever the engine behind it? The preceding argument suggests that it would be going too far. What the important literature on the effect of growth on inequality shows is essentially that there is apparently no significant relationship that would be valid across countries and time periods. It certainly does not say that this is true for specific countries during a particular period. Sizable changes have been observed in several countries in the recent past, the causes of which are not always readily apparent but which are not necessarily independent from economic growth and some of its features.[35] In effect, most case studies on the evolution of inequality over time single out characteristics of the growth process or of policies behind it that are responsible for specific distributional changes. The debate that took place recently on whether recent increases in earnings inequality in various developed countries were due to technical progress and the consequent shift of developed economies towards high-tech is a good example of such an approach.

An important stream of case studies on the distributional consequences of growth is found in the historical literature. Following the example of Kuznets himself, numerous economic historians tried to identify the trend in some inequality measure over long periods of time. Findings often conform with the Kuznets curve hypothesis. Yet, a common problem is that very much of that literature relies on very rough measures of inequality often based on a few macro-economic characteristics and ignores important sources of micro-economic heterogeneity. Because of this, it tends to over-emphasize the role of phenomena like urbanization or the shift away from self-employment – that is, sectoral shift phenomena. A survey of findings is offered by Lindert (2000) and Morrisson (2000).

---

[35] See for instance Atkinson and Brandolini (2001) for developed countries and Ravallion and Chen (1997) for developing countries.

Identifying empirically the forces through which economic growth may shape the distribution of income in actual growth experiences is a difficult task because it requires correcting the observed evolution of the distribution for sources of change unrelated or very loosely related to growth. An exercise of this type was undertaken in a series of case studies that explore the microeconomics of income distribution dynamics (MIDD) in a small number of middle-income countries.[36] The following example illustrates the difficulty of empirically isolating the distributional effects of growth and shows at the same time the major potential role that growth plays in distributional issues.

The methodology used in the MIDD study consists in decomposing the observed change in the distribution of earnings or per capita income into three types of effects, which parallel the general argument in this chapter. The first type corresponds to changes in the structure of earnings for given socio-demographic characteristics of individuals, and possibly by labor market segment if the labor market is imperfectly competitive. The second set of effects corresponds to a change in the labor supply of individuals or household members, and possibly their allocation across labor market segments. The final set of effects includes those occurring due to a change in the distribution of socio-demographic characteristics of individuals and households. In terms of the analysis in this chapter, the second and third type of effects would, in some sense, correspond to the shift of people across socio-demographic groups, whereas the first one would correspond to changes in income differentials across these groups, a residual term actually included in the third effect, accounting for changes in the distribution within groups. Each effect is estimated by simply substituting in the initial year the characteristics of the final year in one of the various dimensions just indicated, or vice versa. Thus, the effect of the structure of earnings is obtained by simulating what would be the distribution of income in year 1 if the structure of earnings by socio-demographic characteristics (gender, education, region, etc.) had been the one observed in year 2. The 'fertility effect' is obtained by importing in the initial year the same relationship between family size and parents' characteristics (education, age, race, region, etc.) as the one observed in the terminal year, etc.[37]

This methodology has been applied, among other countries, to Brazil during the period 1976–1996.[38] What is remarkable during that period in Brazil is that neither the mean income – or GDP per capita – of the Brazilian population nor inequality changed much, even though most usual aggregate inequality measures show a moderate decline. From this direct observation, one might then conclude that very slow growth was associated in Brazil with virtually no change in the distribution of earnings or income. This would be erroneous, however. What happened is that other phenomena compensated for the distributional effects of slow growth. The decomposition methodology presented above led to 3 conclusions:

---

[36] Bourguignon, Ferreira and Lustig (2004).

[37] This methodology is explained in detail in chapter 2 of Bourguignon, Ferreira and Lustig (2004). See also Bourguignon, Fournier and Gurgand (2001).

[38] See Ferreira and Paes de Barros (1999, 2004).

(a) Over the period under analysis, family size went down significantly and more so among people with low education and income. Because of this factor, inequality in Brazil should have substantially declined.

(b) The structure of earnings changed moderately against least-skilled and self-employed workers.

(c) It also turned out that the occupational structure of the population was modified. Employment in general, and employment in the formal sector in particular, had gone down, hitting more severely the segments of the population with the lowest education levels and at ages where access to the labor market is the least easy – young and old people. Overall, however, these various changes tended to compensate each other.

Although the methodology described above does not include any formal representation of the labor market and the way it may be affected by growth, it is difficult not to relate points (b) and (c) to the sluggish growth performance of Brazil during the two decades under analysis. Within a dual economy framework, which seems to fit well the Brazilian economy, the general story would thus be as follows. Slow growth was responsible for a weak labor market, which may have caused an increasing skill differential in the earnings of wage workers and self-employed, as well as job losses or worker discouragement among the least skilled. Both phenomena, but mostly the latter, actually contributed to an increase in inequality. The reason why this inequality increase did not actually show up is that it was compensated by falling family sizes which were more pronounced at the bottom of the distribution – and to a lesser extent progress in the education level of the poorest. Slow growth in Brazil might thus have been responsible for increased inequality after all.

This example shows that identifying the actual effects of economic growth on the social structure of a population may require more than simply observing the changes in that structure and the rate of growth during a given time period. Some of the observed change in social structures may indeed be directly imputed to what is happening on the economic growth front, but may also be due to other concomitant phenomena which are independent of growth or very indirectly related to it. With this example in mind, one may then understand perfectly that the phenomena put forward by economic theory to explain how economic growth is likely to affect social structures may be difficult to observe in actual growth episodes. This is because parallel phenomena, not directly related to growth – but not necessarily independent from it either – affect the distribution and introduce some noise in the observation, both in cross-sectional and time series analyses.

The important point here is that the channels identified by theory may well prove empirically relevant when the necessary correction of available data for other nonneutral distributional phenomena has been made. Of course, the difficulty is to know whether these phenomena are themselves growth dependent or not. In the preceding case, did the change in fertility take place in an autonomous way, or was it the result of economic growth per se, or possibly the result of an educational improvement which itself could have been autonomous or the result of growth? It is this kind of structural model that must be confronted with the data, rather than the very reduced-form models behind cross-sectional work or simple comparisons of changes in inequality and income per capita measures. This is a much more difficult exercise, which has barely begun.[39]

4. Conclusions

Some strong conclusions emerge from our review of the literature on the consequences of economic growth for social structures. They may be summarized as follows.

4.1. The foremost importance of sectoral shift phenomena

If we take a historical or a cross-country perspective, it is clear that the major consequences of economic growth for social structures go through sectoral shifts of the population, and possibly, at a later stage, through shifts across more narrowly defined socio-economic groups. The shift from traditional agriculture to modern agriculture or nonagricultural activities in the urban sector is at the heart of the social and cultural history of most industrialized countries. It is still today at the heart of the social evolution in countries that are 'emerging' as well as in those at a much earlier stage of development. The sectoral shift is also present in so-called advanced countries that have started their journey towards the 'post-industrialization' stage where most activity will increasingly be directly or indirectly linked to services of various types rather than manufacturing. Transforming factory workers into administrative employees involves major changes in social structure, just like transforming small farmers into industrial workers.

Other important shifts take place throughout the growth process, the most powerful ones from a social point of view being the drive towards education and a skilled labor force and a fuller integration of women into market activities.

4.2. The role of market integration

It was observed historically that economic development proceeds together with a 'marketization' of societies. Markets develop by covering an increasing share of all transactions. The most significant difference between sectoral shifts observed in industrialized countries on the one hand and in low- or lower-middle-income countries on the other is not only the nature of the sectors involved but also the degree of market integration of society. Sectoral shifts at early stages of economic growth take place within markets that are functioning very imperfectly. Because of this, they have a strong impact on society, radically changing relative income levels and income-related behaviors. At later stages of development, markets function better and sectoral shifts take place in a smoother

---

[39] Steps in that direction have been taken in the recent 'micro–macro' literature. See in particular Browning, Hansen and Heckman (1999), Bourguignon and Pereira da Silva (2003, introduction), Heckman, Lochner and Traber (1998), Townsend and Ueda (2003).

manner. At the limit, some sectors may lose weight in favor of others with only small changes taking place in the structure of earnings and in the social features associated with it. With such a market integration, the real issue is the speed of adjustment to growth, i.e., whether the structure of the demand for productive factors changes faster than the supply of these factors, modifying in one direction or another the structure of remunerations of these factors. Thus, economic growth in a market integrated economy has social consequences different from less integrated economies. In the former case, economic growth may take place in a somewhat 'balanced' way without any marked impact upon social structures and, in particular, on the distribution of well-being within the population. This is what is implicitly assumed in many contemporaneous models.

4.3. Social costs of transitory adjustment

In reality, such balanced growth paths are unlikely to be observed. In presence of any permanent shock in technology or in policy, adjustment lags in either the demand or the supply side of factor markets produce tensions with possibly durable social effects. Case studies of both developing and developed countries reveal the presence of such tensions. Unemployment problems in some European countries or the rise in earnings inequality in the US during the 1980s and 1990s are sometimes seen as symptoms of such tensions. Even though these disequilibria may be expected to be transitory, they may have powerful and long-lived social consequences, potentially able to affect future economic growth. A fortiori, this conclusion holds true when markets mechanisms are working imperfectly.

Some other dimensions of social structures have been examined in this chapter that fit these conclusions or may be direct consequences of them. This is the case in particular of the economic role of women and male–female economic and social differences. Sectoral shifts explain the changing roles of men and women, whereas the move towards market integrated economies may be the cause of increased female labor force participation, as well as of decreasing male–female differences both in the economic and the social spheres.

These are important conclusions. Yet, as indicated at the beginning of this chapter, this is only part of the whole story. Two other parts are missing. The first is the second half of the circle that links economic growth and social structures. By choice, this chapter has focused on the social consequences of growth, but the effect of changes in social structures on the pace and structure of economic growth is equally important – as shown in various chapters of this Handbook. The second missing part has to do with the effect of changes in social structures on social institutions themselves, and on social relations. This is briefly discussed in closing this chapter.

4.4. Effect of growth on social structures through social institutions

In addition to the changes in social structures resulting directly from economic growth, the general way in which individuals relate with each other is also likely to be modified under the effect of growth. For instance, a more affluent population may have more time and interest for collective tasks and for political participation, thus modifying the nature of the public decision-making process. As another example, a higher standard of living may induce a higher risk aversion and therefore a demand for more social insurance. We conclude this chapter by focusing on two examples of how social relations are likely to be modified under the effect of economic growth, with the social structure effect analyzed above often playing an intermediate role in that evolution.

The first example has to do with the size of the public sector. It is the well-known "law of expanding state activities" formulated in 1883, in the midst of a period of rapid industrialization and social change, by Adolf Wagner [Wagner (1883), Cameron (1978)]. Several explanations have been proposed to explain this law, some of them directly linked to growth and some others indirectly, through the channels of increasing education and political participation.[40] Theories of the direct link between economic growth and government size emphasize the income elasticity of the demand for certain types of public goods, such as roads or education, or for the correction of negative public externalities due to growth, such as pollution or congestion. Theories of the indirect link insist on the redistribution role of government and the way in which growth may affect the factors that determine that role. For instance, in the classic Meltzer and Richard (1981) paper, the growth of government is explained by the combination of the expansion of universal suffrage and initial inequality in the distribution of income. Then the drive towards democracy is explained by the effect of economic growth on political participation, either through a direct income effect,[41] or through an indirect one as in the political economy models proposed for instance by Justman and Gradstein (1999) or Acemoğlu and Robinson (2000a, 2000b). A second channel is education brought about by, or coming together with, growth.[42]

It is difficult to test for the relationship between economic growth and government size while taking into account the various channels mentioned above. In a cross-country reduced form framework, however, it is interesting that the relationship is a rather weak one, especially when one controls for fixed county effects – see Table 1.[43]

As a second and not unrelated example, consider the demand for social insurance. As with Wagner's law, there are direct and indirect effects of growth on social insurance and family structures. Direct effects may operate through risk aversion or idiosyncratic risks themselves increasing with the income level, or through richer societies being able to afford the fixed costs of social insurance "technology" (related to monitoring of

[40] These different theories regarding the size of government are reviewed by Lybeck and Henrekson (1988), who focus on empirical tests of these theories, and Mueller (2003).

[41] See, for instance, Frey (1971, 1972), Huntington and Nelson (1976), Gradstein and Justman (1995).

[42] See the sociological literature on political participation, for instance Brady, Verba and Schlozman (1995). See also the formal analysis of the link between democracy, education and growth in Bourguignon and Verdier (2002).

[43] Some authors also postulate an inverted-U curve relationship between government size and income level. See Grossman (1987, 1988) and Peden (1991).

income, contribution collection, management and information systems and other organizational costs of social insurance).[44] An indirect effect of growth on social insurance
is via urbanization and the consequent phasing out of high fertility and extended household arrangements throughout societies. This creates a demand for a substitute to the
insurance provided by the extended family system in poorer societies.

These two examples of the way social institutions may be affected directly or indirectly by economic growth show the power of economic growth and its determinants to
transform the social functioning of societies and not only their economic characteristics.
Of course, these changes in the way individuals relate to each other, the way they make
public decisions and the nature of these decisions come on top of all other effects of
growth. These include changes in consumption behavior caused by increasing income
and technical progress as well as the changes in social structures analyzed throughout
this chapter. More than in the latter cases, however, changes in social institutions are affected by a host of noneconomic phenomena that make it difficult to identify and isolate
the role of economic growth. Economic determinism might be dangerous here. In-depth
case studies combining the whole range of social sciences would seem the appropriate
way of approaching this issue.

Acknowledgements

This paper was finished, with great difficulty, after I joined the World Bank as Chief
Economist in the summer 2003. I am grateful to Philippe Aghion for useful comments.
I thank for their patient and efficient help Jean-Jacques Dethier and Victoria Levin.
Views expressed here are essentially personal and do not engage the World Bank in any
manner.

References

Acemoğlu, D. (2002). "Technical change, inequality and the labor market". Journal of Economic Literature 40
    (1), 7–72.
Acemoğlu, D., Robinson, J.A. (2000a). "Why did the west extend the franchise? Democracy, inequality and
    growth in historical perspective". Quarterly Journal of Economics 115 (4), 1167–1199.
Acemoğlu, D., Robinson, J. (2000b). "A theory of political transitions". MIT Working Paper.
Adelman, I., Morris, C.T. (1967). Society, Politics and Economic Development – A Quantitative Approach.
    Johns Hopkins University Press, Baltimore.
Aghion, P. (2002). "Schumpeterian growth theory and the dynamics of income inequality". Econometrica 70
    (3), 855–882.
Aghion, P., Bolton, P. (1996). "An incomplete contracts approach to financial contracting". In: Brennan, M.J.
    (Ed.), The Theory of Corporate Finance, vol. 1. Elgar, Cheltenham, U.K., pp. 381–402.
Aghion, P., Caroli, E., Garcia-Peñalosa, C. (1999). "Inequality and economic growth: The perspective of the
    new growth theories". Journal of Economic Literature 37 (4), 1615–1660.

---

[44] As in the modeling of financial development in Saint-Paul (1992) or Tressel (2003).

Aghion, P., Howitt, P., Violante, G. (2002). "General purpose technology and wage inequality". Journal of Economic Growth 7 (4), 315–345.

Ahluwalia, M. (1974). "Income inequality: Some dimensions of the problem". Finance and Development 11 (3), 2–8.

Ahluwalia, M. (1976a). "Income distribution and development: Some stylized facts". American Economic Review 66 (2), 128–135.

Ahluwalia, M. (1976b). "Inequality, poverty and development". Journal of Development Economics 3, 307–342.

Anand, S., Kanbur, R. (1991). "Inequality and development: A critique". Journal of Development Economics 41, 19–43.

Anand, S., Kanbur, R. (1993). "The Kuznets process and the inequality-development relationship". Journal of Development Economics 40 (1), 25–52.

Arellano, M., Bond, S. (1991). "Some tests of specification for panel data: Monte Carlo evidence and an application to employment equations". The Review of Economic Studies 58 (2), 277–297.

Arndt, H.W. (1987). Economic Development: The History of an Idea. University of Chicago Press, Chicago and London.

Asbell, B. (1995). The Pill: A Biography of the Drug That Changed the World. Random House, New York.

Ashenfelter, O.C., Card, D. (Eds.) (1999). Handbook of Labor Economics, vol. 3. North-Holland, Amsterdam.

Atkinson, A.B., Brandolini, A. (2001). "Promise and pitfalls in the use of 'secondary' data-sets: Income inequality in OECD countries as a case study". Journal of Economic Literature 39 (3), 771–799.

Bacha, E.L., Taylor, L. (1978). "Brazilian income distribution in the 1960s: 'Facts', model results and the controversy". Journal of Development Studies 14 (April), 271–297.

Baldwin, R.E., Cain, G.G. (2000). "Shifts in relative U.S. wages: The role of trade, technology, and factor endowments". Review of Economics and Statistics 82 (4), 580–595.

Banerjee, A., Duflo, E. (2003). "Inequality and growth: What can the data say?". Journal of Economic Growth 8 (3), 267–299.

Banerjee, A.V., Newman, A. (1993). "Occupational choice and the process of development". Journal of Political Economy 101 (2), 274–298.

Barro, R.J. (2000). "Inequality and growth in a panel of countries". Journal of Economic Growth 5 (1), 5–32.

Baumol, W.J., Blinder, A.S., Wolff, E.N. (2003). Downsizing in America: Reality, Causes, and Consequences. Russell Sage Foundation, New York.

Benabou, R. (1996). "Inequality and growth". NBER Macroeconomics Annual 1996, 11–76.

Bertola, G. (1993). "Factor shares and savings in endogenous growth". American Economic Review 83 (5), 1184–1198.

Bertola, G. (2000). "Macroeconomics of income distribution and growth". In: Atkinson, A.B., Bourguignon, F. (Eds.), Handbook of Income Distribution, vol. 1. North-Holland, Amsterdam.

Birdsall, N., Chester, L.A. (1987). "Contraception and the status of women: What is the link?". Family Planning Perspectives 19 (1), 14–18.

Blau, F., Kahn, L. (1997). "Swimming upstream: Trends in the gender wage differential in the 1980s". Journal of Labor Economics 15 (1), 1–42.

Blau, F., Kahn, L. (2003). "Understanding International Differences in the Gender Pay Gap". In: Garcia, B., Anker, R., Pinnelli, A. (Eds.), Women in the Labour Market in Changing Economies: Demographic Issues. Oxford University Press, Oxford.

Blundell, R., Bond, S. (1998). "Initial conditions and moment restrictions in dynamic panel data models". Journal of Econometrics 87 (1), 115–143.

Bourguignon, F. (1981). "Pareto superiority of unegalitarian equilibria in Stiglitz' model of wealth distribution with convex saving function". Econometrica 49 (6), 1469–1475.

Bourguignon, F. (1990). "Growth and inequality in the dual model of development: The role of demand factors". The Review of Economic Studies 57 (2), 215–228.

Bourguignon, F. (2003). "The growth poverty inequality triangle". Processed. World Bank, Washington, DC.

Bourguignon, F., da Silva, L.P. (Eds.) (2003). The Impact of Economic Policies on Poverty and Income Distribution. Oxford University Press/World Bank, Washington, DC.

Bourguignon, F., Ferreira, F., Lustig, N. (Eds.) (2004). Microeconomics of Income Distribution Dynamics in East Asia and Latin America. Oxford University Press/World Bank, Washington, DC.

Bourguignon, F., Fournier, M., Gurgand, M. (2001). "Fast development with a stable income distribution: Taiwan, 1975–1994". Review of Income and Wealth 47 (2), 139–163.

Bourguignon, F., Morrisson, C. (1990). "Income distribution, development and foreign trade: A cross-sectional analysis". European Economic Review 34, 1113–1132.

Bourguignon, F., Morrisson, C. (1998). "Inequality and development: The role of dualism". Journal of Development Economics 57 (2), 233–257.

Bourguignon, F., Verdier, T. (2002). "Is financial openness bad for education? A political economy perspective on development". European Economic Review 44, 891–902.

Brady, H., Verba, S., Schlozman, K. (1995). "Beyond SES: A resource model of political participation". American Political Science Review 89 (2), 271–294.

Browning, M., Hansen, L.P., Heckman, J.J. (1999). "Micro data and general equilibrium models". In: Taylor, J., Woodford, M. (Eds.), Handbook of Macroeconomics, vol. 1A. North-Holland, Amsterdam, pp. 543–633 (Chapter 8).

Cameron, D. (1978). "The expansion of the public economy: A comparative analysis". American Political Science Review 72 (4), 1243–1261.

Card, D. (1999). "Causal effect of education on earnings". In: Ashenfelter, O., Card, D. (Eds.), Handbook of Labor Economics, vol. 3A. North-Holland, Amsterdam, pp. 1801–1863.

Chenery, H., Ahluwalia, M.S., Bell, C.L.G., Duloy, J.H., Jolly, R. (1974). Redistribution with Growth: Policies to Improve Income Distribution in Developing Countries in the Context of Economic Growth: A Joint Study. Oxford University Press, Oxford. Commissioned by the World Bank's Development Research Center and the Institute of Development Studies, University of Sussex.

Chenery, H.B., Syrquin, M. (1975). Patterns of Development, 1950–1970. Oxford University Press, London (for the World Bank).

Clark, R., York, A., Anker, R. (2003). "Cross-national analysis of women's labour force activity since 1970". In: Garcia, B., Anker, R., Pinnelli, A. (Eds.), Women in the Labour Market in Changing Economies: Demographic Issues. Oxford University Press, Oxford, pp. 13–34.

Clemens, M. (2004). "The long walk to school: International education goals in historical perspective". Working Paper No. 37. Center for Global Development. March.

Cornia, G.A. (2001). "Social funds in stabilization and adjusment programmes: A critique". Development and Change 32 (1), 1–32.

Cornia, G.A., Addison, T., Kiiski, S. (2004). "Income distribution changes and their impact in the post-Second World War period". In: Cornia, G. (Ed.), Inequality, Growth and Poverty in an Era of Liberalization and Globalization. Oxford University Press, Oxford, pp. 26–54.

de Janvry, A., Sadoulet, E. (1983). "Social articulation as a condition for equitable growth". Journal of Development Economics 13 (3), 275–303.

Deininger, K., Squire, L. (1998). "New ways of looking at old issues: Inequality and growth". Journal of Development Economics 57 (2), 259–287.

Dollar, D., Kraay, A. (2002). "Growth is good for the poor". Journal of Economic Growth 7 (3), 195–225.

Durand, J. (1975). The Labor Force in Economic Development: A Comparison of International Census Data, 1946–66. Princeton University Press, Princeton, NJ.

Easterlin, R.A. (1996). Growth Triumphant: The Twentieth Century in Historical Perspective. University of Michigan Press, Ann Arbor, MI.

Eicher, T. (1996). "Interactions between endogenous human capital and technical change". Review of Economic Studies 63 (1), 127–144.

Fei, J.C.H., Ranis, G. (1965). "Innovational intensity and factor bias in the theory of growth". International Economic Review 6 (2), 182–198.

Ferreira, F., de Barros, R.P. (1999). "The slippery slope: Explaining the increase in extreme poverty in urban Brazil, 1976–1996". Revista de Econometria 19 (2), 211–296.

Ferreira, F., de Barros, R.P. (2004). "The slippery slope: Explaining the increase in extreme poverty in urban Brazil". In: Bourguignon, F., Ferreira, F., Lustig, N. (Eds.), Microeconomics of Income Distribution in East Asia and Latin America. Oxford University Press/World Bank, Oxford, pp. 83–124.

Fields, G.S. (1979). "A welfare economic approach to growth and distribution in the dual economy". The Quarterly Journal of Economics 93 (3), 325–353.

Fields, G.S. (2001). Distribution and Development: A New Look at the Developing World. Russell Sage Foundation/MIT Press, Cambridge, MA.

Fields, G.S., Jakubson, G.H. (1994). "New evidence on the Kuznets curve". Mimeo. Cornell University.

Frankel, M. (1962). "The production function in allocation and growth: A synthesis". American Economic Review 52 (5), 995–1022.

Frey, B. (1971). "Why do high income people participate more in politics?". Public Choice 11, 100–105.

Frey, B. (1972). "Political participation and income level". Public Choice 13, 119–122.

Galor, O., Tsiddon, D. (1997). "Technological progress, mobility and economic growth". American Economic Review 87 (3), 363–382.

Galor, O., Zeira, J. (1993). "Income distribution and macroeconomics". The Review of Economic Studies 60 (1), 35–52.

Goldin, C. (1991). "The role of World War II in the rise of women's employment". American Economic Review 81 (4), 741–756.

Goldin, C. (1995). "The U-shaped female labor force function in economic development and economic history". In: Schultz, T.P. (Ed.), Investment in Women's Human Capital and Economic Development. University of Chicago Press, Chicago, pp. 61–90 (Chapter 3).

Goldin, C., Katz, L.F. (2002). "The power of the pill: Oral contraceptives and women's career and marriage decisions". Journal of Political Economy 110 (4), 730–770.

Gottschalk, P., Smeeding, T. (2000). "Empirical evidence on income inequality in industrialized countries". In: Atkinson, A., Bourguignon, F. (Eds.), Handbook of Income Distribution, vol. I. North-Holland, Amsterdam, pp. 261–297.

Gradstein, M., Justman, M. (1995). "A political interpretation of the Kuznets Curve". Manuscript, Ben Gurion University.

Grossman, P.J. (1987). "The optimal size of government". Public Choice 53, 131–147.

Grossman, P.J. (1988). "Government and economic growth: A nonlinear relationship". Public Choice 56, 193–200.

Gunderson, M. (1989). " Male–female wage differentials and policy responses". Journal of Economic Literature 27 (1), 46–72.

Heckman, J.J., Lochner, L., Traber, E. (1998). "Explaining rising wage inequality: Explorations with a dynamic general equilibrium model of labor earnings with heterogeneous agents". Review of Economic Dynamics 1, 1–58.

Huntington, S.P., Nelson, J.M. (1976). No Easy Choise. Political Participation in Developing Countries. Harvard University Press, Cambridge, MA.

Justman, M., Gradstein, M. (1999). "The democratization of political elites and the decline in inequality in modern economic growth". In: Brezis, E.S., Temin, P. (Eds.), Elites, Minorities and Economic Growth. Elsevier, North-Holland, New York, pp. 205–220.

Katz, L.F., Autor, D.H. (1999). "Changes in the wage structure and earnings inequality". In: Ashenfelter, O., Card, D. (Eds.), Handbook of Labor Economics, vol. 3A. North-Holland, Amsterdam, pp. 1463–1555.

Knight, J.B. (1976). "Explaining income distribution in developing countries: A framework and an agenda". Oxford Bulletin of Economics and Statistics 38 (3), 161–177.

Krueger, A., Lindahl, M. (2001). "Education for growth: Why and for whom?". Journal of Economic Literature 39 (4), 1101–1136.

Kuznets, S. (1955). "Economic growth and income inequality". American Economic Review 45 (1), 1–28.

Kuznets, S. (1966). Modern Economic Growth: Rate, Structure and Spread. Yale University Press, New Haven.

Lecaillon, J., Paukert, F., Morrisson, C., Germidis, D. (1984). Income Distribution and Economic Development: An Analytical Survey. International Labour Office, Geneva, Switzerland.

Lee, R. (2003). "The demographic transition: Three centuries of fundamental change". The Journal of Economic Perspectives 17 (4), 167–190.

Lewis, A. (1954). "Development with unlimited supplies of labor". The Manchester School of Economic and Social Studies 22 (2), 139–191.

Lindert, P.H. (2000). "Three centuries of inequality in Britain and America". In: Atkinson, A., Bourguignon, F. (Eds.), Handbook of Income Distribution. North-Holland, Amsterdam, pp. 167–216.

Lindert, P.H. (2003). Growing Public: Social Spending and Economic Growth since the Eighteenth Century. Cambridge University Press, Cambridge.

List, J.A., Gallet, C.A. (1999). "The Kuznets curve: What happens after the inverted-U?". Review of Development Economics 3 (2), 200–206.

Lundberg, M., Squire, L. (2003). "The simultaneous evolution of growth and inequality". Economic Journal 113 (487), 326–344.

Lybeck, J.A., Henrekson, M. (1988). Explaining the Growth of Government. North-Holland, Amsterdam.

Meltzer, A., Richard, S. (1981). "A rational theory of the size of government". Journal of Political Economy 89 (October), 914–927.

Moav, O. (2002). "Income distribution and macroeconomics: The persistence of inequality in a convex technology framework". Economics Letters 75 (2), 187–192.

Morrisson, C. (2000). "Historical perspectives on income distribution: The case of Europe". In: Atkinson, A., Bourguignon, F. (Eds.), Handbook of Income Distribution. North-Holland, Amsterdam, pp. 217–260.

Mueller, D.C. (2003). Public Choice III. Cambridge University Press, Cambridge.

Papanek, G., Kyn, O. (1986). "The effect on income distribution of development, the growth rate and economic strategy". Journal of Development Economics 23 (1), 55–65.

Paukert, F. (1973). "Income distribution at different levels of development: A survey of evidence". International Labor Review 108 (2/3), 97–125.

Peden, E.A. (1991). "Productivity in the United States and its relationship to government activity: An analysis of 57 years, 1929–86". Public Choice 86 (December), 153–173.

Piketty, T. (1997). "The dynamics of the wealth distribution and the interest rate with credit rationing". The Review of Economic Studies 64 (2), 173–189.

Psacharopoulos, G. (1994). "Returns to investment in education: A global update". World Development 22 (9), 1325–1343.

Psacharopoulos, G., Patrinos, H. (2002). "Returns to investment in education: A further update". World Bank Policy Research Working Paper 2881. The World Bank, Washington, DC.

Rauch, J.E. (1993). "Productivity gains from geographic concentration of human capital: Evidence from the cities". Journal of Urban Economics 34 (3), 380–400.

Ravallion, M., Chen, S. (1997). "What can new survey data tell us about recent changes in distribution and poverty?". World Bank Economic Review 11 (2), 357–382.

Ravallion, M., Datt, G. (2002). "Why has economic growth be more pro-poor in some states of India than in others?". Journal of Development Economics 68 (2), 381–400.

Robinson, S. (1976). "A note on the U hypothesis relating inequality and economic development". American Economic Review 66 (3), 437–440.

Romer, P. (1986). "Increasing returns and long-run growth". Journal of Political Economy 94 (5), 1002–1037.

Rosenzweig, M. (1990). "Population growth and human capital investments: Theory and evidence". Journal of Political Economy 98, S12–S70.

Rosenzweig, M., Stark, O. (Eds.) (1997). Handbook of Population and Family Economics, vol. 2. North-Holland, Amsterdam.

Rubinstein, Y., Tsiddon, D. (1998). "Coping with technological progress: The role of ability in making inequality persistent". Processed. Tel Aviv University, Tel Aviv.

Saint-Paul, G. (1992). "Technological choice, financial markets and economic development". European Economic Review 36 (4), 763–781.

Schlicht, E. (1975). "A neoclassical theory of wealth distribution". Jahrbücher für Nationalökonomie und Statistik 189 (1/2), 78–96.

Solow, R.M. (1956). "A contribution to the theory of economic growth". The Quarterly Journal of Economics 70 (1), 65–94.

Stiglitz, J. (1969). "Distribution of income and wealth among individuals". Econometrica 37 (3), 382–397.

Syrquin, M. (1994). "Structural transformation and the new growth theory". In: Pasinetti, L.L., Solow, R.M. (Eds.), Economic Growth and the Structure of Long-Term Development. St. Martin's Press, New York, pp. 3–21.

Terrell, K. (1992). "Female–male earnings differentials and occupational structure". International Labour Review 131 (4/5), 387–404.

Thomas, V., Wang, Y., Fan, X. (2000). "Measuring education inequality: Gini coefficients of education". World Bank Working Paper 2525, December.

Tinbergen, J. (1975). Income Difference: Recent Research. North-Holland, Amsterdam.

Townsend, R.M., Ueda, K. (2003). "Financial deepening, inequality, and growth: A model-based quantitative evaluation". International Monetary Fund Seminar Series 40, March, 1–64.

Tressel, T. (2003). "Dual financial systems and inequalities in economic development". Journal of Economic Growth 8, 223–257.

Violante, G.L. (1997). "Technological process and skill dynamics: A solution to the wage dispersion puzzle". Mimeo. University College London..

Wagner, A. (1883). "Finanzwissenschaft", third ed., Leipzig. Partly reprinted in: Musgrave, R.A., Peacock, A.R. (Eds.), Classics in the Theory of Public Finance. Macmillan, London, 1958, pp. 1–8.

Welch, F. (2000). "Growth in women's relative wages and in inequality among men: One phenomenon or two?". American Economic Review 90 (2), 444–449.

World Bank (2001). Engendering Development. Policy Research Report. Oxford University Press, Oxford (published for the World Bank).

World Bank (2003). "Statistical information management & analysis (SIMA)". Online database.

Zhang, X., Johnson, M., Resnick, D., Robinson, S. (2004). "Cross-country typologies and development strategies to end hunger in Africa". International Food Policy Research Institute DSDG. Discussion Paper No. 8. June.

Chapter 28

ECONOMIC GROWTH AND THE ENVIRONMENT: A REVIEW OF THEORY AND EMPIRICS

WILLIAM A. BROCK

University of Wisconsin, Madison

M. SCOTT TAYLOR

University of Wisconsin, Madison
and
National Bureau of Economics Research, Cambridge, MA

Contents

Abstract	1750
Keywords	1750
1. Introduction	1751
2. Preliminaries	1757
2.1. Scale, composition and technique	1757
3. Stylized facts on sources and sinks	1761
4. Some illustrative theory	1772
4.1. The Green Solow benchmark	1772
4.2. Intensifying abatement: the Stokey alternative	1778
4.3. Composition shifts: the source and sink model	1787
5. Induced innovation and learning by doing	1798
5.1. Induced innovation and the Kindergarten Rule model	1799
5.1.1. Tastes	1800
5.1.2. Technologies	1801
5.1.3. From individual to aggregate production	1801
5.1.4. Endowments	1805
5.1.5. The Kindergarten rule	1805
5.2. Empirical implications	1810
5.3. Balanced growth path predictions	1810
5.4. The Environmental Catch-up Hypothesis	1811
5.5. The ECH and the EKC	1813
5.6. Pollution characteristics	1814
6. Conclusion and suggestions for future research	1816
References	1819

Handbook of Economic Growth, Volume 1B. Edited by Philippe Aghion and Steven N. Durlauf
© 2005 Elsevier B.V. All rights reserved
DOI: 10.1016/S1574-0684(05)01028-2

Abstract

The relationship between economic growth and the environment is, and will always remain, controversial. Some see the emergence of new pollution problems, the lack of success in dealing with global warming and the still rising population in the Third World as proof positive that humans are a short-sighted and rapacious species. Others however see the glass as half full. They note the tremendous progress made in providing urban sanitation, improvements in air quality in major cities and marvel at the continuing improvements in the human condition made possible by technological advance. The first group focuses on the remaining and often serious environmental problems of the day; the second on the long, but sometimes erratic, history of improvement in living standards. These views are not necessarily inconsistent and growth theory offers us the tools needed to explore the link between environmental problems of today and the likelihood of their improvement tomorrow. This review articles discusses and evaluates the theoretical literature linking environmental quality to economic growth. We focus on three questions. These are: (1) what is the relationship between economic growth and the environment? (2) how can we escape the limits to growth imposed by environmental constraints? and (3) where should future research focus its efforts? For the most part, we discuss the link between industrial pollution and growth, but also show how this most recent work is related to earlier contributions on exhaustible resources and growth. While no review can settle the perennial debate over the limits to growth, this review moves the literature forward by identifying important unresolved theoretical questions, reports on the results of recent empirical work, and provides an integrative assessment of where we stand today.

Keywords

sustainable development, pollution, limits to growth, environmental Kuznets curve, natural resources

JEL classification: E0, O13, O4, Q0

1. Introduction

The relationship between economic growth and the environment is, and will always remain, controversial. Some see the emergence of new pollution problems, the lack of success in dealing with global warming and the still rising population in the Third World as proof positive that humans are a short-sighted and rapacious species. Others however see the glass as half full. They note the tremendous progress made in providing urban sanitation, improvements in air quality in major cities and marvel at the continuing improvements in the human condition made possible by technological advance. The first group focuses on the remaining and often serious environmental problems of the day; the second on the long, but sometimes erratic, history of improvement in living standards.

These views are not necessarily inconsistent and growth theory offers us the tools needed to explore the link between environmental problems of today and the likelihood of their improvement tomorrow. It allows us to clarify these conflicting views by use of theory, and when differences still remain, to create useful empirical tests that quantify relative magnitudes.

For many years, the limited natural resource base of the planet was viewed as the source of limits to growth. This was, for example, the focus of the original and subsequent "Limits to Growth" monograph and the efforts by economists refuting its conclusions.[1] Recently however it has become clear that limits to growth may not only arise from nature's finite source of raw minerals, but instead from nature's limited ability to act as a sink for human wastes. It is perhaps natural to think first of the environment as a source of raw materials, oil and valuable minerals. This interpretation of nature's service to mankind led to a large and still growing theoretical literature on the limits to growth created by natural resource scarcity. Empirically it led to studies of the drag limited natural resources may have on growth, and a related examination of long run trends in resource prices.[2]

Nature's other role – its role as a sink for unwanted by-products of economic activity – has typically been given less attention. As a sink, nature dissipates harmful air, water and solid pollutants, is the final resting place for millions of tons of garbage, and is the unfortunate repository for many toxic chemicals. When the environment's ability to dissipate or absorb wastes is exceeded, environmental quality falls and the policy response to this reduction in quality may in turn limit growth. Growth may be limited because reductions in environmental quality call forth more intensive clean up or abatement efforts that lower the return to investment, or more apocalyptically, growth may be limited when humans do such damage to the ecosystem that it deteriorates beyond repair and settles on a new lower, less productive steady state.[3]

---

[1] See Nordhaus (1992) for the latest refutation.

[2] For work on resource price trends see most importantly Barnett and Morse (1963) and Slade (1987).

[3] This branch of the literature relies on case study evidence of irreversible damage created in the past and argues that our now greater technological capabilities may portend even worse outcomes in the future. For

This link between growth and the environment has of course received much more attention recently because of the rapidly expanding empirical literature on the relationship between per capita income and pollution. This literature, known as the Environmental Kuznets Curve (EKC) literature has been enormously influential. So to a certain extent, the tables have now turned: there is far less concern over the ultimate exhaustion of oil or magnesium, and far more concern over air quality, global warming, and the emissions of industrial production.

The economics literature examining the link between growth and the environment is huge; it covers, in principle, much of the theory of natural resource extraction, a significant body of theory in the 1960s and 1970s on resource depletion and growth; a large literature in the 1990s investigating the implications of endogenous growth theories; and a new and still burgeoning literature created in the last decade examining the relationship between pollution and national income levels. Every review has to make difficult choices about exclusion and we make ours on the basis of novelty. There are excellent book length treatments on the depletion of renewable and nonrenewable resources, and several reviews of endogenous growth theory's contributions already exist.[4] This leaves us to focus on the relatively new theoretical literature linking environmental quality to income levels. For the most part, we discuss the link between industrial pollution and growth, but also show how this most recent work is related to earlier contributions on exhaustible resources and growth.

While no review can settle the perennial debate over the limits to growth, this review hopes to play a positive role in moving the literature forward by identifying important unresolved theoretical questions, reporting on the results of recent empirical work, and providing an integrative assessment of where we stand today.[5] To do so, we focus on three questions. These are: (1) what is the relationship between economic growth and the environment? (2) how can we escape the limits to growth imposed by environmental constraints? and (3) where should future research focus its efforts?

To answer these questions we start by introducing definitions and providing a preliminary result linking the environment and growth. We define the scale, composition and technique effects of growth on the environment, and then use these definitions to prove a useful but negative result on the limits to growth. We show that changes in the composition of national output – as occur when the economy specializes in relatively less pollution intensive services or relatively less natural intensive industries – can at

---

a primarily theoretical discussion of irreversibilities and hysteresis caused by nonlinearities see the symposium edited by Dasgupta and Maler (2003). For related nonlinear theory see Dechert (2001). For case study evidence from prehistory see Brander and Taylor (1998).

[4] See the classic book length treatments of renewable and nonrenewable resources by Clark (1990) and Dasgupta and Heal (1979). A good introduction to the relationship between endogenous growth theory and the environment is contained in the review by Smulders (1999).

[5] Whether there are serious limits to growth is an unending controversy that reached its peak with the publication of the Limits to Growth by Meadows et al. (1972). See the subsequent contributions by Solow (1973) followed by Meadows, Meadows and Randers (1991) and then Nordhaus (1992).

best delay the impact of binding environmental constraints. In the long run, emission intensities must fall towards zero if growth is to be sustainable.

In many models this constraint is met through the substitution of clean inputs for dirty ones, in others via increased abatement, and in still others through some combination of technological progress and the other channels. This result is helpful to us because it allows us to distinguish between empirical regularities that are consistent with a short run growth and environment relationship (along a transition path) from those consistent with the long run relationship (along a balanced growth path). It also helps us sort through the literature by focusing on how a given model can generate what we take as our definition of sustainable growth: a balanced growth path with increasing environmental quality and ongoing growth in income per capita.[6]

With our definitions and result in hand we then turn to present some stylized facts on the environment and growth. These facts concern the trend and level of various pollutants, and measures of the cost of pollution control. In many cases, the data underlying the construction of these facts is of limited quality; the time periods are sometimes insufficiently long to draw strong conclusions and the relevant magnitudes imprecise relative to their constructs in theory. Nonetheless, they are the best data we have.

Overall these data tell three stories. The first is that by many measures the environment is improving at least in developed countries. The level of emissions for regulated pollutants is falling, and the quality of air in cities is rising. The U.S. and other advanced industrial countries have seen secular improvements in the quality of their environments over the last 30 years. To a large extent cities are cleaner than in the past, emissions of health-threatening toxics are reduced, and in some cases changes in environmental quality are quite dramatic.

The second feature of the data is that pollution control measures have been both relatively successful and relatively cheap. While there are severe difficulties in measuring the full cost of environmental compliance most methods find costs of at most 1–2% of GDP for the U.S. Comparable figures from OECD countries support this finding.[7]

The last feature of the data is that there is a tendency for the environment to at first worsen at low levels of income but then improve at higher incomes. This is the so-called Environmental Kuznets Curve. We first present raw emission data drawn from the U.S. and then briefly review the empirical literature on the Environmental Kuznets Curve that relies on cross-country comparisons. The raw data from the U.S. are unequivocal,

---

[6] This is different from other definitions. We wanted to avoid stagnation as a sustainable growth path and hence require positive growth; but with positive income growth giving more marketable goods along the balanced growth path it seems only appropriate to require an improving environment as well since this gives us more nonmarket goods.

[7] Aggregate compliance costs were reported in a 1990 EPA study that has apparently never been updated. [See EPA (1990) Environmental Investments: The cost of a clean environment.] The earlier study predicted year 2000 compliance costs of approximately 200 billion dollars (1990 dollars), but recent EPA publications (EPA's 2004 Strategic Plan) distances themselves from this estimate and reiterates just how difficult it is to estimate compliance costs.

while the cross-country empirical results are far less clear but generally supportive of the finding.

Having reviewed the relevant data and set out definitions we turn to a review of the theory. To do so, we develop a series of 4 simple growth and environment models. The models serve as a vehicle to introduce related theoretical work. For the most part we focus on balanced growth path predictions and eschew formal optimization taking as exogenous savings or depletion rates and sometimes investments in abatement. We do so because in many cases, these rates must be constant along any balanced growth path and hence we identify a set of feasible conditions for sustainable growth. Moreover the resulting simplicity of the models allows us to identify key features of fully developed research contributions already present in the literature. In some cases, the choice of abatement or savings matters critically to the point we are making and hence in those cases we provide optimal rules.

The 4 models were developed to highlight the different ways we can meet environmental constraints in the face of ongoing growth in per capita incomes. In the first, which we dub the Green Solow model, emission reductions arise from exogenous technological progress in the abatement process. Although this model is very simple it provides three key results. First, we show that even with the economy's abatement intensity fixed, the dynamics of the Solow model together with those of a standard regeneration function are sufficient to produce the Environmental Kuznets Curve. The transition towards any sustainable growth path has environmental quality at first worsening with economic growth and then improving as we approach the balanced growth path. This is a surprising result. While numerous explanations for the EKC relationship have been put forward, this explanation is simple, novel, and quite general as it relies only on basic properties of growth functions.

Second, the Green Solow model forms a useful benchmark since this model predicts that a more strict pollution policy has no long run effect on growth. In true Solow tradition, different abatement intensities create level differences in income but have no effect on the economy's growth rate along the balanced growth path. This result provides partial justification for the current practice of measuring the costs of pollution control to an economy as the sum of current private and public expenditures with no correction for the reduction in growth created. It also points out the stringent conditions needed for a stricter policy to cause no drag whatsoever on economic growth.

Third, the model clearly shows how technological progress in goods production has a very different environmental impact than does technological progress in abatement. Technological progress in goods production creates a scale effect that raises the emissions growth rate, technological progress in abatement creates a pure technique effect driving emissions downwards. In this first model both rates are exogenous, and as such they provide especially clean examples of scale and technique effects for us to refer to later. And as we show throughout the review, the presence or absence of technological progress in abatement is key to whether we can lower emissions, support ongoing growth, and provide reasonable predictions for the costs of pollution control.

The second model, which we dub the Stokey Alternative, was inspired by Nancy Stokey's (1998) paper on the limits to growth. Here we present a simplified version to highlight the role abatement can play in improving the environment over time. The model we present focuses on balanced growth paths and not the transition paths as emphasized by Stokey, but nevertheless it contains two results worthy of note. The first is simply the observation that once we model abatement as an economic activity that uses scarce resources, increases in the intensity of abatement that are needed to keep pollution in check will have a drag on economic growth. Rising abatement creates a technique effect by lowering emissions per unit output, but also lowers pollution by lowering the growth rate of output.

By rewriting the model along the lines of Copeland and Taylor (1994) so that pollution emissions appear as if they are a factor of production, it is now relatively simple to conduct growth drag exercises for the cost of pollution control in much the same way that others have examined the growth drag of natural resource depletion.[8] By doing so, the model makes clear the limits to growth brought about by environmental policy.

The second feature we focus on is the model's prediction of rising abatement intensity. In models with falling pollution levels, neoclassical assumptions on abatement, and no abatement specific technological progress, the intensity of abatement must rise continuously through time. For example, in Stokey's analysis the share of output allocated to abatement approaches one in the limit. Since this share represents pollution abatement costs relative to the value of aggregate economic activity, models that rely on abatement alone tend to generate counterfactual predictions of ever-rising abatement costs. This is true even though ongoing economic growth is fueled by technological progress, and hence this result reinforces our earlier remarks about the importance of technological progress in abatement.

Our third model links the source and sink roles of nature by assuming energy use both draws down exhaustible resource stocks and creates pollution emissions that lower environmental quality. This "source and sink" formulation allows us to consider how changes in the energy intensity of production help meet environmental constraints. In this model, the intensity of abatement is taken as constant and there is no technological progress in abatement. Instead the economy lowers its emissions to output ratio over time by adopting an ever cleaner mix of production methods. As such the model focuses on the role of composition effects in meeting environmental constraints. We show that the economy is able to grow while reducing pollution because of continuous changes in the composition of its inputs, but this form of "abatement" has costs. Growth is slowed as less and less of the natural resource can be used in production.

This "source and sink" formulation is important in linking the earlier 1970s and 1980s literature focusing on growth and resource exhaustion with the newer 1990s literature focusing on the link between economic growth and environmental quality. We show that the finiteness of natural resources implies a constraint on per capita income growth that

---

[8] See for example Nordhaus (1992).

is worsened with higher population growth rates. This constraint is relaxed if the rate of natural resource use is slower as this implies reproducible factors have less of a burden in keeping growth positive. But sustainability also requires falling emissions, and this constraint is most easily met if the economy makes a rapid transition away from natural resource inputs as this reduces the energy and pollution intensity of output.

Putting the constraints from the source and sink side together, we show there exist parameter values for which the twin goals of positive ongoing growth and falling emission levels are no longer compatible. This is not a doomsday prediction. Together with our previous analysis it suggests that abatement or composition shifts alone are unlikely to be responsible for the stylized facts. Technological progress directly targeted to lowering abatement costs (i.e. induced innovation) must be playing a key role in determining growth and environment outcomes. Therefore, in the remainder of the paper we turn to a model where technological progress in abatement is set in motion by the onset of active regulation and works to generate sustainable growth paths.

To highlight the importance of technological progress in abatement our final model draws on the analysis of Brock and Taylor (2003) by adopting their Kindergarten Rule model. While the previous models were useful vehicles to discuss the literature and describe possibilities, they were necessarily incomplete because they eschew formal optimization. Optimizing behavior is however important in discussions of the magnitude of drag created by pollution policy, and also important in discussions concerning the timing or onset of active regulation. The Kindergarten model provides two contributions to our discussion.

First, it shows how technological progress in abatement can hold compliance costs down in the face of ongoing growth. In contrast to the Solow model, there are ongoing growth drag costs from regulation, but as long as abatement is productive we can generate sustainable growth without skyrocketing compliance costs. By highlighting the important role for progress in abatement, the model points out the need to make endogenous the direction of technological progress as well as its rate.

Second, the model generates a first worsening and then improving environment much like that in Stokey (1998). In contrast however to the methods employed in the empirical EKC literature, we show that the path for income and pollution will differ systematically across countries. This systematic difference leads to the model's Environmental Catch-up Hypothesis relating income and pollution paths to countries initial income levels. Poor countries experience the greatest environmental degradation at their peak, but once regulation begins environmental quality across both Rich and Poor converges. Despite this, at any given income level an initially Poor country has worse environmental quality than an initially Rich country. Moreover, since both Rich and Poor economies start with pristine environments, the qualities of their environments at first diverge and then converge over time. In addition to this cross-country prediction, the model also links specific features of the income and pollution profile to characteristics of individual pollutants such as their permanence in the environment, their toxicity, and their instantaneous disutility. Together these predictions suggest a different empirical methodology than that currently employed, and expand the scope for empirical work in this area considerably.

The final section of our review is a summary of the main lessons we have drawn from the literature, offers suggestions for future research and briefly discusses some of the most important topics that we did not discuss elsewhere in the review.

2. Preliminaries

2.1. Scale, composition and technique

We start with some algebra linking emissions of a given pollutant to a measure of economic activity, its composition and the cleanliness of production techniques. By doing so we illustrate that any growth model that predicts both rising incomes and falling pollution levels has to work on lowering pollution emissions via one of three channels. Consider a given pollutant and let E denote the sum total of this pollutant's emissions arising from production across the economy's n industries.[9] Let a_i denote the pounds of emissions per dollar of output produced in industry i, s_i denote the value share of industry i in national output, and Y national output. Then by definition total emissions E are given by

$$E = \sum_{i=1}^{n} a_i s_i Y, \quad \text{where} \quad \sum_{i=1}^{n} s_i = 1. \tag{1}$$

Since this is a definition we can differentiate both sides with respect to time to find

$$\widehat{E} = \sum_{i=1}^{n} \pi_i [\hat{a}_i + \hat{s}_i] + \widehat{Y}, \quad \text{where} \quad \pi_i = \frac{E_i}{E}, \tag{2}$$

where a "$\;\hat{}\;$" over x indicates $[\mathrm{d}x/\mathrm{d}t]/x$. Changes in aggregate emissions can arise from three sources that we define to be the scale, composition and technique effects.[10]

To start, note that holding constant the cleanliness of production techniques and the composition of final output constant (i.e. holding both $\hat{a}_i = 0$ and $\hat{s}_i = 0$ for all i) emissions rise or fall in proportion to the scale of economic activity as measured by real GDP or Y. This is the scale effect of growth and unless it is offset by other changes, emissions rise lock step with increases in real output.

Alternatively, we can hold both the scale of real output and the techniques of production constant to examine the impact of changes in the composition of output. To do so,

---

[9] The pollutant could instead be produced via consumption. In that case we adopt weights reflecting industry i's share in final demand. This has little impact on our results here, but would have some relevance in an open economy setting.

[10] See Copeland and Taylor (1994) for model based definitions of these effects in a static setting. This terminology was popularized by Grossman and Krueger's (1993) NAFTA study.

in (2) we set $\widehat{Y} = 0$ and $\hat{a}_i = 0$ for all i as this isolates the pure composition effect on pollution emissions,

$$\widehat{E} = \sum_{i=1}^{n} \pi_i \hat{s}_i. \tag{3}$$

Emissions fall via the pure composition effect if an economy moves towards producing a set of goods that are cleaner on average than the set they produced before. To see why this is true, note that the change in value shares across all n industries must sum to zero; i.e. $\sum_{i=1}^{n} ds_i = 0$. Now using this result in (3) we obtain the change in emissions arising from a pure composition effect as

$$\widehat{E} = \sum_{i=1}^{n} \hat{s}_i [\pi_i - s_i]. \tag{4}$$

Given our definitions for $\hat{\pi}_i$ and s_i, $\pi_i - s_i > 0$ if and only if $E_i / p_i y_i > E/Y$. In words, the element $\pi_i - s_i$ is positive if and only if industry i's emissions per dollar of output is greater than the national average. Define a dirty industry as one whose emissions per dollar of output exceed the economy wide average E/Y; define a clean industry as one where emissions per dollar of output are less than the economy average. Then Equation (4) holds that aggregate emissions fall from the pure composition effect whenever the composition of output changes toward a more heavy reliance on clean industries and rises otherwise.

Finally, emissions can fall when the techniques of production become cleaner even though output and its composition remain constant. To isolate this technique effect, we set $\widehat{Y} = 0$ and $\hat{s}_i = 0$ for all i to find that emissions fall if emissions per unit output fall for all activities. In this case we find

$$\widehat{E} = \sum_{i=1}^{n} \pi_i \hat{a}_i \tag{5}$$

and hence if techniques are getting cleaner, emissions per unit of output fall, and overall emissions fall from this pure technique effect.

When the environment is modeled as a sink for human wastes it is often assumed that emissions together with natural regeneration determine environmental quality. When the environment adjusts relatively slowly to changes in the pollution level, natural regeneration can play an important role in determining environmental quality. A typical and very useful specification assumes the environment dissipates pollutants at an exponential rate. Let X denote environmental quality and let the pristine level be given by $X = 0$. Then since the flow of emissions per unit time is E, the evolution of environmental quality is given by

$$\dot{X} = E - \eta X, \quad \text{where } \eta > 0. \tag{6}$$

This formulation is convenient because it is generally assumed that X must be bounded for human life to exist and hence (6) yields a simple negative linear relationship between the steady state flow of pollution E, and environmental quality X. A bound on X then implies a similar bound on steady state emissions, E.[11] Moreover, given the linear relationship any scale, composition or technique effect on emissions is translated directly into impacts on environmental quality, X.

One cost of (6) is that the percentage rate of natural regeneration is independent of the state of the environment. A common modification is to assume the rate of natural regeneration rises as X gets further and further from its pristine level. Letting $\eta = \eta(X)$, we can introduce this possibility by writing the evolution of X as

$$\dot{X} = E - \eta(X)X, \quad \text{where } \eta'(x) > 0, \tag{7}$$

$\eta(X)$ is often assumed to be linear so that $\eta(X)X$ becomes the familiar logistic function for growth in X.

An alternative and equally valid interpretation of (2) is that E is the instantaneous flow of natural resources used in production. Under this interpretation, Equation (1) gives us an economy wide factor demand for this natural resource evaluated at the equilibrium level of use given by E. For example, the demand for oil equals the sum of demand arising from all sectors of the economy. In this interpretation a_i are barrels of oil used per unit of output in industry i, s_i is the value share of industry i in national output, and Y is again national output.

For example, if the flow of resources extracted is falling at some constant rate over time while real output is rising, then we know that some combination of changes in energy efficiency per unit of output (a technique effect) and changes in the output mix to less energy intensive goods (a composition effect) must be carrying the burden of adjustment. Changes in resource use over time can then be linked to the relative strength of scale, composition and technique effects. To complete the translation let the current stock of natural resources S be given by our initial endowment K less any diminution caused by humans, X. If we make this translation in (6), and set regeneration equal to zero we obtain the standard equation governing stock depletion in exhaustible resources

$$\dot{S} = -E. \tag{8}$$

Alternatively, we can make the same translation but leave open the possibility of regeneration. Making the translation in (7) gives us the standard accumulation equation for a renewable resource such as a forest or fishery when growth is stock dependent,

$$\dot{S} = \eta(S)S - E. \tag{9}$$

---

[11] Along a balanced growth path the time rate of change of X must equal that of E. To see this divide both sides of (6) and note that a constant rate of change in X requires the ratio E/X to be constant.

And again if $\eta(S)$ is linear we obtain the familiar logistic growth for a naturally regenerating resource.[12]

Although (1) is a definition it implicitly contains an assumption on how economic growth and the environment interact. Note that the value shares sum to 1 and $a_i(t) \geqslant 0$ for all i and t. Assume that $a_i(t)$ for all i and t. This assumption turns out to be an important, because if some activities are perfectly clean, or approach perfectly clean activities in the limit, then it is possible for composition effects alone to hold pollution in check despite ongoing growth. Conversely, if all economic activities must pollute even a small amount, then environmental quality can only rise in the long run via continuous changes in the techniques of production and these may run into diminishing returns.

It is not helpful here to enter into philosophical discussions over the definition of pollution or the likelihood of today's unwanted outputs becoming tomorrow's valuable inputs. Instead we just note that all production involves the *transformation* of one set of materials into another and that this transformation requires work. All work requires energy and energy is always wasted in work effort. Therefore some unintentional by products of production are always produced and we most often call these by products pollution. Since this is a statement of belief and not a rigorous proof, we note this as an assumption.

ASSUMPTION 1. Pollution is a by-product of all production

$$\text{for all } i, t \geqslant 0, \quad \liminf\{a_i(t)\} > 0. \tag{10}$$

This implies that there exists for each i, a strictly positive $\varepsilon > 0$ such that $a_i(t) > \varepsilon$. With Assumption 1 in hand, it is now possible to show that positive output growth and falling pollution levels require falling emissions per unit of output in the long run. That is, composition effects are at best a transitory method to lower pollution emissions. Let us explain in detail why this conclusion holds. Suppose there is a bound, $B > 0$ such that if $E(t)$ exceeds B, human life cannot exist. Then if $Y(t)$ goes to infinity as t goes to infinity, (10) implies

$$E(t) \leqslant B \quad \Longrightarrow \quad \sum_{i=1}^{n} a_i(t)s_i(t) \leqslant \frac{B}{Y(t)} \quad \text{for all } t \geqslant 0. \tag{11}$$

---

[12] It should be noted however that different assumptions on $\eta(S)$ can lead to drastically different conclusions when they lead to growth functions with what biologists call critical depensation [see Clark (1990) for a formal definition and discussion]. Critical depensation refers to a property of the natural growth function such that at some minimum S, natural growth becomes negative. Natural growth can turn negative because of predator prey interactions across species, or because the species has a minimum viable population. Introducing thresholds and critical depensation into either (9) or (7) can alter results considerably. Unfortunately little is known about the extent of nonconvexities of this type empirically. For theoretical work examining their impact see the symposium edited by Dasgupta and Maler (2003). Scheffer and Carpenter (2003) document some examples of catastrophic regime shifts in ecosystems.

Thus we must have

$$\overset{*}{a_i}(t) := \min\left\{a_i(t)\right\} \leqslant \frac{B}{Y(t)} \to 0 \quad \text{as } t \to \infty. \tag{12}$$

But (12) contradicts Assumption 1. Hence if we are to have bounded emissions with growing $Y(t)$, we must have the cleanest industry emission rate $\overset{*}{a_i}(t)$ going to zero. Therefore, falling pollution levels and rising incomes are only possible if there are continual reductions in emissions per unit output and zero emission technologies are possible, at least in the limit.

3. Stylized facts on sources and sinks

We present three stylized facts drawn from post–World War II historical record.[13] We present data on pollution emissions and environmental control costs and leave the discussion of energy prices to later sections. Since data is typically only available for pollutants that are presently under active regulation we discuss the U.S. record with regard to its six so-called criteria air pollutants, but amend these with international sources where possible. These are: sulfur dioxide, nitrogen oxides, carbon monoxide, lead, large particulates and volatile organic compounds.[14] With the exception of lead, these air pollutants all typically classified as irritants and so we also briefly discuss the U.S. history of regulation of long-lived and potentially harmful chemical products. For the most part we present data on emissions rather than concentrations because data on emissions covers a much longer time period and is unaffected by industry location and zoning regulation. On the other hand, the longest time spans of data (from 1940 onwards) reflect some changes in collection and estimation methods.[15] Nevertheless, this data is the best we have available and where possible we direct the reader to concentration data and related empirical work. In addition we present data on industry pollution abatement costs from Vogan (1996), although these are only available for the 1972–1994 period.

We start by presenting in Figure 1 emissions per dollar of GDP for all pollutants except lead. Lead is excluded since data is only available over a much shorter period. As shown, emissions per unit of output for sulfur, nitrogen oxides, particulates, volatile organic compounds and carbon monoxide all fall over the 1940–1998 period. For ease of

---

[13] As we proceed we also present evidence on energy, minerals and land prices as they become relevant.

[14] The long series of historical data presented in the figures is taken from the EPA's 1998 report National Pollution Emission Trends, available at *http://www.epa.gov/ttn/chief/trends/trends98*.

[15] As methods of estimation improve new categories of emissions are included and some revision occurs as well. For example, prior to 1985 the PM10 data excluded fugitive dust sources and other miscellaneous emissions, so these are eliminated from the time series graphed in Figure 7. As well revision occurs. A close look at the 2001 Trends report shows that emissions reported for our pollutants during the 1970s and 1980s does not exactly match the figures given in the 1998 report. We use the 1998 figures rather than those from 2001 since the 2001 report only contains estimates to 1970, and we import the EPA's graphics directly into our figures because we cannot match them precisely from the raw data.

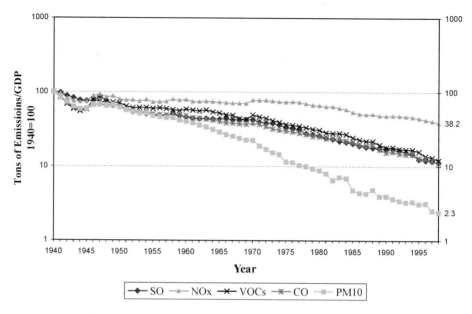

Figure 1. Emission intensities, 1940–1998. Tons of emissions/real GDP.

comparison emission intensities were normalized to 100 in 1940 and the figure adopts a log scale. PM10 fell by approximately 98%, sulfur, volatile organic compounds and carbon monoxide fell by perhaps 88%, and nitrogen oxides fell by perhaps 60%. Somewhat surprisingly, it is also apparent that if we exclude the years of World War II at the start of the data, the rate of reduction for each pollutant appears to be roughly constant over time.

Although there is a tendency to see good news in falling emission intensities, there are good reasons for not doing so. One reason is simply that real economic activity increased by a factor of 8.6 over this period and this masks the fact that emissions of many of these pollutants rose during this period. The second is that this measure – like that for aggregate emissions – has very little if any welfare significance. Since our measure is physical tons of emissions added up over all sources, it necessarily ignores the fact that some tons of emissions create greater marginal damage than others.[16]

Our second stylized fact is presented in Figure 2. In it we plot business expenditures on pollution abatement costs per dollar of GDP over the period 1972–1994. These twenty-two years are the only significant time period where data is available.[17] As

[16] In contrast, a quality-adjusted measure of emissions would add up the various components weighing them by their marginal damage; or a quality-adjusted measure of aggregate concentrations in a metropolitan area would weigh concentrations in each location by the marginal damage of concentrations at point (urban, industrial, suburban, etc.).

[17] In 1999 the PACE survey was run again this time as a pilot project. Using the 1999 survey we find the ratio of PACE to GDP of approximately 1.9% which is very much in line with Figure 2. This 1999 survey

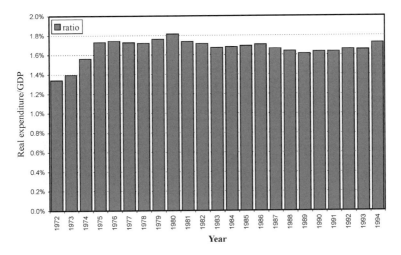

Figure 2. Pollution abatement costs, 1972–1994. PACE/GDP.

shown, pollution abatement costs as a fraction of GDP rise quite rapidly until 1980 and then remain relatively constant. As a fraction of overall output, these costs are relatively small. Generating a similar plot for costs as a fraction of manufacturing value-added produces similar results. Alternatively, if we consider pollution abatement costs specifically directed to the six criteria air pollutants and scale this by real U.S. output, the ratio is then incredibly small – approximately one half of one percent of GDP – and has remained so for over twenty years [see Vogan (1996)].[18]

Data from other countries supports the general conclusion that pollution abatement costs are a small fraction of GDP and show perhaps a slight upward trend. For example, total expenditures by both government and business in France rose from 1.2% of GDP in 1990 to 1.6% in 2000. Over the 1991–1999 period, these same expenditures in Germany rose from 1.4% of GDP to 1.6%. Austria and The Netherlands show somewhat higher expenditures on the order of 2.1% and 1.6% in 1990 rising to 2.6% and 2.0% in 1998. While this data is clearly fragmentary, expenditures in the order of 1–2% of GDP seem to be the norm in OECD countries, with perhaps half of this being spent by private establishments and the remainder by governments.[19]

These figures however reflect to a certain degree the changing composition of output over time and therefore understate the impact higher pollution abatement costs have

---

is different in some respects from earlier ones. For details see the Survey of Pollution Abatement Costs and Expenditures, U.S. Census Bureau 1999 available at *http://www.census.gov/econ/overview/mu1100.html*.

[18] These figures are also similar to those presented in the review of pollution abatement costs in Jaffe, Peterson and Portney (1995).

[19] These data are drawn from the Organization for Economic Cooperation and Development 2003, "Pollution abatement and control expenditures in OECD countries", OECD Secretariat, Paris.

had on some industries. Levinson and Taylor (2003) for example argue that since the composition of U.S. manufacturing has been shifting towards less pollution intensive industries, aggregate measures understate the true costs of pollution regulations. They construct estimates of pollution abatement costs holding the composition of industry output fixed at the 2 and 3 digit industry levels and then compare these estimates with estimates allowing the composition of output to change. In all cases, holding the composition of U.S. output fixed in earlier periods leads to a higher estimate of industry wide abatement cost increases. As a result, the small increases in pollution abatement costs shown in the aggregate data are at least partially due to the U.S. shedding some of its dirtiest industries over time.

Our third and final fact is presented in Figures 3–8. These figures show a general tendency for emissions to at first rise and then fall over time. Since the U.S. exhibited trend growth in real per capita income of approximately 2% per year over this period, the time scale in the figures could just as well be replaced by income per capita. Note that the falling emissions/intensities reported in Figure 1 are necessary but not sufficient for this result. This pattern in the data is visible for all pollutants except nitrogen oxides that may at present be approaching a peak in emissions. Conversely, particulate pollution peaked much earlier than the other pollutants, while lead has a dramatic drop in the mid-1970s. These raw U.S. data support the contention that environmental quality at first deteriorates and then improves with increases in income per capita.

Another interesting aspect of these figures is the breakdown of emissions by end-use category. Apart from some exceptions arising from the miscellaneous category the within-pollutant source of the emissions remains roughly constant in many of the figures. For example, consider SO_2. Aggregate emissions follow an EKC pattern, but the components of fuel combustion and industrial processes do as well. A similar pattern is found in volatile organic compounds, but less so in the case of carbon monoxide which

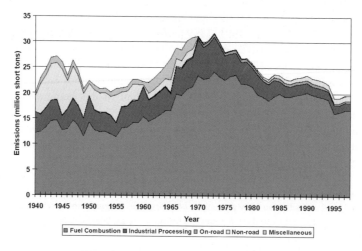

Figure 3. Sulfur dioxide emissions, 1940–1998.

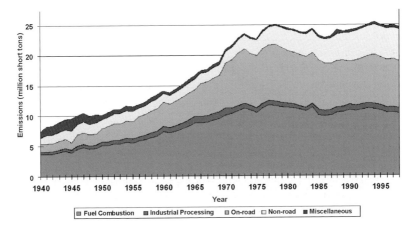

Figure 4. Nitrogen oxide emissions, 1940–1998.

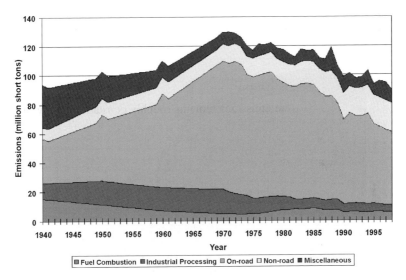

Figure 5. Carbon monoxide emissions, 1940–1998.

presumably is due to the change in automobile use over the period. In total the rough constancy in the within-pollutant sources of emissions suggests that the overall EKC pattern is not driven by strong compositional shifts.

Our finding of an EKC in the raw emission data is consistent with the recent flurry of formal empirical work linking per capita income and pollution levels. This empirical literature was fueled primarily by the work of Grossman and Krueger (1993, 1995) who found that, after controlling for other noneconomic determinants of pollution, measures

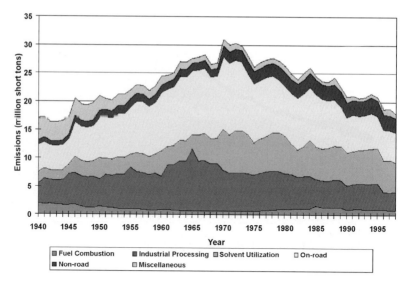

Figure 6. Volatile organic compounds, 1940–1998.

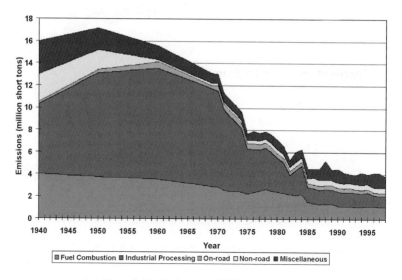

Figure 7. Particular matter PM10, 1940–1998.

of some (but not all) pollution concentrations at first rose and then fell with increases in per capita income.[20] Their work is important in several respects: it brought the empiri-

---

[20] In addition to Grossman and Krueger (1993, 1995), other early contributions are Shafik and Bandyopad-hyay (1994), Selden and Song (1994), Hilton and Levinson (1998), Gale and Mendez (1998).

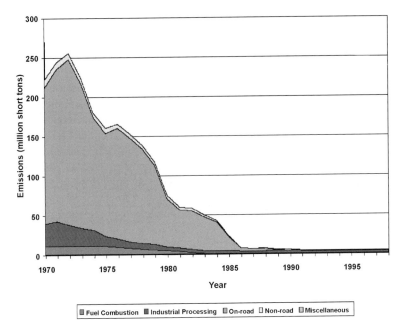

Figure 8. Lead emissions, 1970–1998.

cal study of aggregate pollution levels into the realm of economic analysis; it debunked the commonly held view that environmental quality must necessarily decrease with economic growth; and it provided highly suggestive evidence of a strong policy response to pollution at higher income levels.

Unfortunately, empirical research has progressed very little from this promising start. Subsequent empirical research has focused on either confirming or denying existence of similar relationships across different pollutants.[21] Subsequent research has shown that the inverse-U relationship does not hold for all pollution, and there are indications the relation may not be stable for any one type of pollution.[22] Since the empirical work on the EKC typically employs cross-country variation in income and pollution to identify parameters, it is perhaps not surprising that there are signs of parameter instability. This instability could arise from country specific differences in the mechanism driving the two processes, but very little, if any, work has gone into evaluating the various hypotheses offered for the EKC. This interpretation of the econometric problems is of course consistent with our finding that the raw U.S. data offers a dramatic confirmation

---

[21] See, for example, Selden and Song (1994), Harbaugh, Levinson and Wilson (2002) and the surveys mentioned previously.

[22] Hilton and Levinson (1998) contains some of the most convincing evidence of an EKC. Harbaugh, Levinson and Wilson (2002) examines the sensitivity of the original Grossman and Krueger finding to new data and alternative functional forms.

of Grossman and Krueger's cross-country results. Cross-country differences leading to parameter instability are of course irrelevant in a one-country context.

In its original application, the EKC was interpreted as reflecting the relative strength of scale versus technique effects. However, it is difficult to support this interpretation. To isolate either the scale or technique effect we need to hold constant the composition of output, but this is not typically done in this literature. Therefore, the shape of the EKC may reflect some mixture of scale, composition and technique effects.

Despite these criticisms, the major and lasting contribution of this literature is to suggest a strong environmental policy response to income growth. The EKC studies are generally supportive of the hypothesis that income gains created by ongoing growth lead to policy changes that in turn drive pollution downwards. However, as our discussion in later sections will show, an EKC is compatible with many different underlying mechanisms and is entirely compatible with pollution policy remaining unchanged in the face of ongoing growth.

While most studies do not present evidence that allows us to distinguish between the underlying mechanisms responsible for the EKC, two recent studies offer additional insights. Hilton and Levinson (1998) examine the link between lead emissions and income per capita using a panel of 48 countries over the twenty-year period 1972–1992. This study is important because it finds strong evidence of an inverted-U-shaped relationship between lead emissions and per capita income, and then factors the changes in pollution into two different components. The first is a technique effect that produces an almost monotonic relationship between lead content per gallon of gasoline and income per capita. The second is a scale effect linking greater gasoline use to greater income.[23] This study is the first to provide direct evidence on two distinct processes (scale and technique effects) that together result in an EKC.

To interpret the empirical evidence as reflecting scale and technique effects one needs to rule out other possibilities. Although the authors do not couch their analysis in this context, their analysis implicitly presents the necessary evidence. First, they document a significant negative relationship between the lead content of gasoline and income per capita (post 1983). This relationship shows up quite strongly in just a simple cross-country scatter plot of lead content against income per capita. Since lead content is arguably pollution per unit output, it is difficult to attribute the negative relationship to much other than income driven policy differences.[24]

Second, the authors find a hump-shaped EKC using data from the post-1983 period, but in earlier periods they find a monotonically rising relationship between lead emissions and income. The declining portion of the EKC only appears in the data once the

---

[23] Lurking in the background of this study is a composition effect operating through changes in the fleet of cars. This composition effect is not investigated in the paper, although it may be responsible for the jump in lead per gallon of gasoline use at low income levels shown in Figure 4.

[24] To be precise we should note that since lead content per gallon is an average, and cars differ in their use of leaded versus unleaded gas, the composition of the car fleet is likely to be changing as well. Therefore, the fall in average lead content may reflect an income-induced change in the average age of the fleet (which would lower average lead content) plus a pure technique effect.

negative health effects of lead had become well known. The emergence of the declining portion in the income pollution relationship is very suggestive of a strong policy response to the new information about lead. The fact this only appears late in the sample makes it difficult to attribute the decline in lead to other factors that could be shifting the demand for pollution. For example if the declining portion of the EKC was due to increasing returns to scale in abatement, then it should appear in both the pre- and post-1983 data. If it was due to shifts in the composition of output arising naturally along the development path, why would it only appear in the post-1983 data? While it is possible to think of examples where these other factors are at play, the scope for mistaking a strong policy response for something else is drastically reduced in this study. The natural inference to draw is that the decline only occurs late in the sample because with greater information about lead's health effects, policy tightened and emissions fell.

A second important study is Gale and Mendez (1998). They re-examine one year of sulfur dioxide data drawn from Grossman and Krueger's (1993) study. The study does not offer a theory of pollution determination, but is original in investigating the role factor endowments may play in predicting cross-country differences in pollution levels. They regress pollution concentrations on factor endowment data from a cross-section of countries together with income-based measures designed to capture scale and technique effects. Their results suggest a strong link between capital abundance and pollution concentrations even after controlling for incomes per capita. Their purely cross-sectional analysis cannot, however, differentiate between location-specific attributes and scale effects. Nevertheless, their work is important because the strong link they find between factor endowments and pollution suggests a role for factor composition in determining pollution levels. That is, even after accounting for cross-country differences in income per capita, other national characteristics matter to pollution outcomes.

Combining our three stylized facts on pollution emissions presents us with an important question. How did aggregate emissions and emissions per unit output fall so dramatically in the U.S. without raising pollution abatement costs precipitously?

There are several possible explanations. One possibility is that ongoing changes in the composition of U.S. output have led to a cleaner mix of production that has lowered both aggregate measures of costs and emissions. The downward trend in emissions per unit output shown in Figure 1 prior to the advent of the Clean Air Act suggests some role for composition effects. While changes in the composition of U.S. output are surely part of the story, there are reasons to believe that they cannot be the most important part. Over the 1971–2001 period of active regulation by the EPA, total emissions of the 6 criteria air pollutants (nitrogen dioxide, ozone, sulfur dioxide, particulate matter, carbon monoxide and lead) decreased on average by 25%. Over this same period, gross domestic product rose 161% and pollution abatement costs have risen only slightly.[25] The magnitude of these emission reductions is too large for it to reflect composition changes alone.

---

[25] These figures are from the EPA's Latest Findings on National Air Quality, 2001 Status and Trends, available at *http://www.epa.gov/air/aqtrnd01/* published September 2002.

To get a feel for the magnitudes involved note that if changes in the composition of output over the 1971–2001 period are to carry all the burden of adjustment, then we would set the changes in a_i to zero in (2). Then using the EPA's estimate of an average 25% reduction for E and the 161% increase for Y, we find that the weighted average of industry level changes must add up to -186% change. This is just too large a realignment in the composition of industry to be credible.

It is also apparent from the figures that emissions for most pollutants have been falling since the early 1970s and as we saw earlier there are limits to how far aggregate emissions can fall via composition effects. Our earlier discussion of the static nature of the within-pollutant sources of emissions also argues against strong composition effects. Finally, there is little evidence that international trade is playing a major role in shifting dirty goods industries to other countries but stronger composition effects after the advent of federal policy in early 1970s would be necessary to explain the fall in emissions seen in the figures.[26] For this set of reasons it seems clear that composition effects alone cannot be responsible for the result.

Another possible explanation is that ongoing growth in incomes has generated a strong demand for environmental improvement. In this account, income gains over the post–World War II period produce a change in policy in the early 1970s and usher in the EPA and the start of emission reductions. While this explanation fits with the decline in emission to output ratios and the lowered emissions since the early 1970s, it too cannot be the entire story. As we discuss in Section 4, if rising incomes are to be wholly responsible for the change in pollution policy, agents must being willing to make larger and larger sacrifices in consumption for improving environmental quality. For example, the theory models of Stokey (1998), Aghion and Howitt (1998), Lopez (1994), etc. all require a rapidly declining marginal utility of consumption to generate rising environmental quality and ongoing growth. But as Aghion and Howitt note:

> Thus it appears that unlimited growth can indeed be sustained, but it is not guaranteed by the usual sorts of assumptions that are made in endogenous growth theory. The assumption that the elasticity of marginal utility of consumption be greater than unity seems particularly strong, in as much as it is known to imply odd behavior in the context of various macroeconomics models... (p. 162).

A rapidly declining marginal utility of consumption is required in earlier work because increasingly large investments in abatement are required to hold pollution in check.[27] This implies the share of pollution abatement costs in the value of output approaches one in the limit, which is inconsistent with available evidence.[28]

---

[26] See for example Antweiler, Copeland and Taylor (2001) and Grossman and Krueger (1993).

[27] This restriction also implies a large income elasticity of marginal damage and many question whether the demand for a clean environment can be so income elastic. For example, McConnell (1997) argues that current empirical estimates from contingent valuation and hedonic studies do not support the very strong income effects needed.

[28] See the discussion in Aghion and Howitt (1998, pp. 160–161) and our discussion of abatement in Section 5 of Brock and Taylor (2003).

A final possibility is technological advance. Ongoing technological progress in production *and* abatement could simultaneous drive long run growth and hold pollution abatement costs in check. Technological progress in goods production could be the driving force for growth in final output, while technological progress in abatement allows emissions per unit of output to fall precipitously without raising environmental control costs skyward. In this explanation, income gains from ongoing growth are responsible for the onset of serious regulation in the 1970s, but the advent of regulation then brought forth improvements in abatement methods. As a consequence agents have not been required to make increasingly large sacrifices in consumption for improving environmental quality. As we show in Section 4, this explanation is consistent with the predictions of both our Green Solow and Kindergarten models.

Before we proceed we should note that the stylized facts given thus far exclude a discussion of many other pollutants. By selecting only pollutants for which data is available we may have erred on the side of optimism since the measurement of pollutants is almost always a precursor to their active regulation. One important omission from the above is any discussion of air toxics such as benzene (in gasoline), perchloroethylene (used by dry cleaners), and methyl chloride (a common solvent). These are chemicals are believed to cause severe health effects such as cancer, damage to the immune system, etc. At present the EPA does not maintain an extensive national monitoring system for air toxics, and only limited information is available.[29]

Another omission is any discussion of the set of long-lived chemicals and chemical by-products that have found their way into waterways, soils and the air. These products have very long half-lives and produce serious health and environmental effects. Prominent among these in U.S. history are DDT, PCBs, lead, and most recently CFCs. Official estimates on emissions of these pollutants is difficult to find, but historical accounts and partial data indicate their emissions follow a pattern roughly similar to that of lead shown in Figure 8. As shown by the figure the history of lead is one of strong initial growth in emissions, followed by a rapid phase-out and virtual elimination. In fact, lead continues to be emitted in small amounts, whereas PCB emissions rose from very low production levels in the 1930s to millions of pounds per year of production in the 1970s, to end with a complete ban in 1979. Similarly, DDT was used extensively after World War II but banned in 1972. CFC production in the U.S. rose quickly with the advent of refrigeration and air conditioning, but this set of chemicals now faces a detailed phase-out with CFC-11 and CFC-12 already facing a complete production ban. The salient feature of these accounts is strong early growth followed by quite rapid elimination.

A final failing of these data is that they are on emissions and not concentrations.[30] Concentration data is available for most of these data at least over the last 20–30 years, but the data is well known to be noisy and suffers from other problems related to comparability over time. Nevertheless most aggregate measures of air quality in cities have

---

[29] See U.S. EPA, Toxic Air Pollutants, at *http://www.epa.gov/airtrends/toxic.html*.

[30] Note however that much of the empirical EKC work employs pollution concentration data as does Antweiler, Copeland and Taylor (2001).

been improving over time. For example, data on the number of U.S. residents living in counties that were designated nonattainment because of their failure to achieve federal air quality standards shows that over the 1986 to 1998 period these numbers have been falling quite dramatically for sulfur dioxide, nitrogen oxide, carbon monoxide, lead and PM10. The number of people living in counties who failed the federally mandated ozone air quality has however risen from 75 million in 1986 to 131 million in 1998.[31]

4. Some illustrative theory

4.1. The Green Solow benchmark[32]

Every model relating economic growth to emissions or environmental quality has by construction made implicit assumptions regarding the strength of scale, composition and technique effects. These assumptions are often hidden in choices made over functional form, over the number of goods, the inclusion of finite resources, or in assumptions concerning abatement. Since we have data on the composition of output, its scale, and emissions per unit of output, it is often useful to divide models into categories according to their reliance on scale, technique and composition effects rather than model specifics like the number of goods, types of factors or assumptions over abatement. By dividing up the literature along these lines, we can weigh the relative merits of model's that rely exclusively on composition effects by looking at their strength in the data rather than by asking ourselves far less obvious questions such as are capital and resources good or poor substitutes or does abatement exhibit increasing returns.

The literature linking growth and pollution levels is immense starting with very early work in the 1970s by Forster (1973), Solow (1973), Stiglitz (1974), Brock (1977) and others, and culminating in the more recent work investigating the Environmental Kuznets Curve such as Stokey (1998), Aghion and Howitt (1998), or Jones and Manuelli (2001). Although the earlier and late literatures differ greatly in their assumptions regarding the driving force behind growth, all models of economic growth must produce changes in scale, composition, or techniques that satisfy (1). Models that produce similar aggregate relationships between income and pollution often rely on different mechanisms to drive pollution downward. Because of these differences, they have other observable implications that we can use for evaluation.

To start our enquiry into the various mechanisms authors have employed to generate sustainable growth or an EKC prediction, we develop an augmented Solow model where exogenous technological progress in both goods production and abatement leads

---

[31] For these data see U.S. Environmental Protection Agency, Office of Air Quality Planning and Standards, National Air Quality and Emissions Trend Report, 1998 (EPA, Research Triangle Park, NC, 2000) and earlier trend reports.
[32] For a detailed exposition see Brock and Taylor (2004).

to continual growth with rising environmental quality. This is the simplest model to explore the importance of technological progress in driving down emissions per unit of output.

Consider the standard one sector Solow model with a fixed savings rate s. Output is produced via a CRS and strictly concave production function taking effective labor and capital to produce output, Y. Capital accumulates via savings and depreciates at rate δ. We assume the rate of labor augmenting technological progress is given by g. All this implies

$$Y = F(K, BL),$$
$$\dot{K} = sY - \delta K, \tag{13}$$
$$\dot{L} = nL,$$
$$\dot{B} = gB.$$

To model the impact of pollution we follow Copeland and Taylor (1994) by assuming every unit of economic activity, F, generates Ω units of pollution as a joint product of output. The amount of pollution released into the atmosphere may differ from the amount produced if there is abatement. We assume abatement is a CRS activity and write the amount of pollution abated as an increasing function of the total scale of economic activity, F, and the economy's efforts at abatement, F^A. If abatement at level A, removes the ΩA units of pollution from the total created, we have

$$E = pollution\ created - pollution\ abated$$
$$= \Omega F - \Omega A\left(F, F^A\right)$$
$$= \Omega F\left[1 - A\left(1, \frac{F^A}{F}\right)\right]$$
$$= Fe(\theta), \quad \text{where } e(\theta) \equiv \Omega\left[1 - A(1, \theta)\right] \text{ and } \theta \equiv \frac{F^A}{F}, \tag{14}$$

where the third line follows from the linear homogeneity of A, and the fourth by the definition of θ as the fraction of economic activity dedicated to abatement.

The relationship in (14) requires several comments. The first is simply that (14) is a single output analog of (1) showing that emissions are determined by the scale of economic activity F, and the techniques of production as captured by $e(\theta)$. The second is that the production of output per se and not input use is the determinant of pollution. Since there is only one output, this means the composition effect must be zero. In a subsequent section we alter our formulation to consider pollution created by input use, but note in passing here that making pollution proportional to the employment of capital has no effect on our results. Finally, since F^A is included in F, even the activity of abatement pollutes.

To combine the assumptions on pollution in (14) with our Solow model, it is useful to assume the economy employs a fixed fraction of its inputs – both capital and effective labor – in abatement. This means the fraction of total output allocated to abatement θ

is a fixed much like the familiar fixed saving rate assumption.[33] As a result, output available for consumption or investment Y, becomes $[1 - \theta]F$. In addition we must adopt some assumption concerning natural regeneration. To do so we assume the quality of the environment evolves over time according to (6). Therefore, the evolution of environmental quality is given by

$$\dot{X} = Fe(\theta) - \eta X. \tag{15}$$

Finally, since the Solow model assumes exogenous technological progress, we assume emissions per unit of output fall at the exogenous rate g^A. Putting these assumptions together and transforming our measures of output and capital into intensive units, our amended Solow model becomes:

$$
\begin{aligned}
y &= f(k)[1 - \theta], \\
\dot{k} &= sf(k)[1 - \theta] - [\delta + n + g]k, \\
E &= BLf(k)e(\theta), \\
\dot{X} &= E - \eta X, \\
\dot{\Omega} &= -g^A \Omega,
\end{aligned}
\tag{16}
$$

where k is K/BL and y is Y/BL; i.e. capital and output measured in intensive units. The top line of (16) repeats the basic Solow model where net output is a fraction of total output. Taking θ as given, and assuming the Inada conditions, there is a k^* such that output, capital, and consumption per person all grow at rate g.

Using standard notation, direct calculation reveals that along the balanced growth path we must have $g_y = g_k = g_c = g > 0$. A potentially worsening environment however threatens this happy existence. From (16) it is easy to see that constant growth in environmental quality requires $g_x = g_E$. Since k^* is constant along the balanced growth path, the growth rate of emissions is simply

$$g_E = g + n - g^A \tag{17}$$

which may be positive, negative, or zero. The first two terms in (17) represent the scale effect on pollution since output grows at rate $g + n$. The second term is a technique effect created not by greater abatement efforts, but because emissions per unit output fall via exogenous technological progress at rate g^A.

Therefore our requirements for sustainable growth are very simple in this model,

$$
\begin{aligned}
g &> 0, \\
g^A &> g + n.
\end{aligned}
\tag{18}
$$

---

[33] We treat θ as endogenous when examining transition paths in Section 5. It is possible that no abatement is optimal in some limited circumstances, but in models generating balanced growth this would imply every increasing pollution levels. In models without growth, such as Keeler, Spence and Zeckhauser (1972), a Murky Age or Polluted Age equilibrium result is possible with θ set to zero.

Technological progress in abatement must exceed that in goods production because of population growth; and some technological progress in goods production is necessary to generate per capita income growth.

The Green Solow model, although very simple, demonstrates several important points. The first is that investments to improve the environment may cause only level and not growth effects. This is obviously true here since the growth rate of per capita magnitudes is explicitly linked to the rate of technological progress, but not to θ. By setting the time derivative of capital per effective worker to zero in (16) it is straightforward to show that a tighter environmental policy (higher θ) lowers output, capital and consumption per worker, but has no effect on their long run growth rates.

The implied income and consumption loss from a tighter policy is however quite small. Adopting a Cobb–Douglas formulation for final output with the share of capital equal to α shows that the ratio of consumption per person along the balanced growth paths of the economy adopting weak versus strong abatement is just

$$
\frac{c_w}{c_s} = \left[\frac{1 - \theta_w}{1 - \theta_s} \right]^{1/(1-\alpha)}
\tag{19}
$$

since both economies grow at rate $g + n$. If weak abatement means adopting a share of pollution abatement costs in national output of 0.5%, and strong abatement means 10%, then consumption per person will differ by 16% along the balanced growth path (assuming capital's share in output is 0.35). Therefore, a twenty-fold difference in the intensity of abatement creates only a 16% difference in consumption per person!

The calculation however seems to imply that environmental policy cannot be much of a limit on economic growth. Recall though that for any given choice of abatement intensity, if we are to have ongoing growth, an improving environment, and a constant (relative) cost of environmental policy, then technological progress in abatement must be sufficiently strong. This is clear from (17) which we can interpret and saying that sustainable growth in income per capita is only possible at the rate of technological progress in abatement. If technological progress is slower than that given in (18) then one of two things must happen. Either additional investments in abatement are undertaken to maintain environmental quality, or environmental quality must decline. At this point however we should note that the strict concavity of A implies there are diminishing returns to greater and greater abatement efforts. From (14) we find that $e'(\theta) = -A_2 < 0$, but $e''(\theta) = -A_{22} > 0$. Therefore, in the absence of strong technological progress in abatement, growth in income per capita is only consistent with lower pollution levels if abatement grows over time.[34]

One final observation concerns the transition path of the model. Despite the fact that environmental policy is fixed and there are no composition effects in our one good framework, simulations of the Green Solow model produce a path for income and environmental quality tracing out an Environmental Kuznets Curve. This surprising result

---

[34] A rising intensity of abatement will lower growth rates introducing other problems in meeting the sustainability criteria. We leave this issue for the next section.

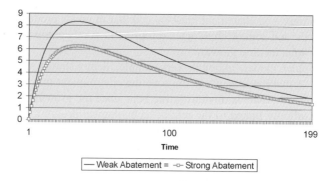

Figure 9. The Green Solow benchmark.

is shown graphically in Figure 9, where we present the trajectories for two economies that are identical in all respects except for their abatement intensity. Each starts from an initially pristine environment and a small initial capital level. Strong abatement refers to a 10% share of output spent on abatement; weak abatement to a 0.5% share. The other parameters were chosen for the purposes of illustration. Per capita income grows at 1% along the balanced growth path, the population grows at 2% and the abatement technology improves at 5%. Note that these parameters ensure that growth is sustainable according to (18). Capital's share is set at 0.35, the savings rate is 10% and depreciation is 2%. Regeneration is set with $\eta = 0.1$ implying a 10% rate for any $X > 0$.

As shown, the environment at first worsens and then improves as the economy converges on its balanced growth path. Note that along the balanced growth path emissions fall and the environment improves at 2% per unit time, which is close to what the simulation delivers in its last periods.

This result follows for three reasons. First, the convergence properties of the Solow model imply that output growth is at first rapid but then slows as k approaches k^*. With a fixed intensity of abatement, pollution emissions grow quickly at first but slower later. Therefore, part of the dynamics is governed by the convergence properties of the neoclassical model.

Second, when we start at a pristine environment the effective rate of natural regeneration is zero. This is true because "nature" is at a biological equilibrium with $X = 0$. When production begins the environment deteriorates. At $X = 0$, the introduction of any emissions overwhelms the rate of regeneration and lowers environmental quality. As X rises, natural regeneration rises. This must be a feature of the regeneration function in order for $X = 0$ to be a stable biological equilibrium.

Third, we have assumed emissions fall along the balanced growth path.

Together the first two facts imply that at the outset of economic growth the rapid pace of growth swamps nature's slow or zero regeneration; but the economic growth rate slows and regeneration rebounds. As we approach the balanced growth path natural regeneration must overwhelm the now less rapid inflows of pollution. The environment improves.

It is important to recognize that this result is more general than our Cobb–Douglas technology and instead relies on quite general properties of production and growth functions. To verify write the dynamic system governing k and X as

$$\dot{k} = sf(k)[1 - \theta] - [\delta + n + g]k,$$

$$\dot{X} = c_0 \exp[-c_1 t] f(k) - \eta X,$$

(20)

where $c_0 > 0$ and $c_1 = g^A - (g + n) > 0$ are positive constants. To show the environment must at first worsen evaluate the accumulation equation for X at $t = 0$. Since the environment is initially pristine, $X(0) = 0$, and the initial capital stock cannot be zero so $k(0) > 0$. Substituting these values into (20) and evaluating shows the environment must at first worsen. X has to be growing at least initially. To examine the rest of the transition path recall that $k(t)$ is increasing in time until it reaches k^* because this is, after all, a Solow model. Using this fact, we can bound the path for X by noting

$$\dot{X} = c_0 \exp[-c_1 t] f(k) - \eta X < c_0 \exp[-c_1 t] f(k^*) - \eta X.$$

(21)

Therefore for any $t > 0$, $X(t)$ must be below the solution to the ordinary differential equation $\dot{X} = c_0 \exp[c_1 t] f(k^*) - \eta X$, $X(0) = 0$. This ordinary differential equation has a closed form solution showing $X(t)$ tends to zero as t goes to infinity. Using the inequality in (21) we can conclude that pollution must fall along its trajectory.[35]

This explanation for the EKC is entirely distinct from those offered in the literature. There are no composition effects, no income induced change in pollution policy, no increasing returns to abatement, no evolution of the political process, and no international trade. The result follows primarily from the mechanics of convergence coupled with the dynamics predicted by a standard natural regeneration function. Moreover, from (14) it is easy to see that emissions per unit of GDP falls *both* during the transition and along the balanced growth path at the constant rate g_A (recall Figure 1 at this point). This is quite surprising because both output and emissions growth varies over time, with the level of emissions tracing out an EKC! Since θ is fixed throughout, the share of pollution abatement costs in value-added is constant. Therefore, although very simple, the Green Solow model matches three important features of the data: declining emissions to GDP ratios, the EKC, and pollution abatement costs that are roughly constant over time.

The Green Solow model bears a family resemblance to several papers examining the growth and pollution link within a neoclassical framework. Forster (1973) examines a neoclassical model with zero population growth and no technological progress in either abatement or production. His main result is that steady state consumption per person and capital per person are lower when society invests in pollution control since these controls lower the net return to capital.

Although Forster's assumptions on abatement and pollution creation are different from ours, we can reproduce his main results in our fixed savings rate setting by adopting his assumptions of $g_A = g = n = 0$. When we do so we find steady state capital

---

[35] With a further assumption on technology we can ensure the EKC must be single humped. Our Cobb–Douglas formulation adopted in the figure is covered by our assumption.

per person and consumption per person both fall with increases in θ while pollution is lowered. Forster's work is important because it was perhaps the first examination of optimal pollution control in a neoclassical setting.

The Green Solow model is also similar to the neoclassical model adopted in Stokey (1998), but differs in that Stokey gives no role to technological progress in abatement. As a result increasing abatement intensity must carry the day in reducing pollution. Stokey also generates the EKC prediction but her result follows from a change in pollution policy along the transition path. Her simulations of the model must reflect the dynamic forces we have identified since the model is neoclassical and the evolution equation for the environment is identical.

More closely related work is Bovenberg and Smulders (1995). In their endogenous growth formulation "pollution augmenting technological progress" holds pollution in check *and* drives long run growth. In their two-sector model, ongoing investments in the knowledge sector raise the productivity of pollution leading to a balanced growth path with a constant level of environmental quality. Again our Green Solow model reproduces the flavor of their results. Setting $n = 0$ to mimic their zero population growth assumption, and assuming $g = g_A$ to mimic the identical rates of technological progress found in both sectors, we find from (22) that emissions are constant along the balanced growth path and output per person grows at rate g.

This similarity should not be all that surprising because Bovenberg and Smulders' "pollution augmenting technological progress" is very similar to our technological progress in abatement. To see why divide both sides of our emissions function in (14) by Ω, and then employ the monotonicity of A in θ to invert the intensive abatement function and solve for $[1 - \theta]$. Use this to write net output $Y = F[1 - \theta]$ available for consumption or investment as

$$Y = G\big(F(K, BL), AE\big), \tag{22}$$

where $A = 1/\Omega$ and G is both CRS and concave. Hence "pollution augmenting technological progress" is equivalent to our technological progress in abatement.

4.2. Intensifying abatement: the Stokey alternative

We now amend our Green Solow model to incorporate a role for an active environmental policy. In the model above reductions in pollution came about solely because of changes in the emission technology and not because society allocated more resources to pollution prevention. In an important paper Nancy Stokey [Stokey (1998)] presented a series of simple growth and pollution models to investigate the links between the limits to growth and industrial pollution. She examined the ability of these models to reproduce the results of empirical work finding an Environmental Kuznets Curve and investigated how an active environmental policy may place limits on growth. An important feature of Stokey's analysis was its dependence on increased abatement and tightening regulations to drive pollution downward.

Her analysis contains two contributions. The first is a simple explanation for the empirical finding of an Environmental Kuznets Curve. Like Lopez (1994) before her, and Copeland and Taylor (2003) after, Stokey shows how an income elastic demand for environmental protection can usher in tighter regulations and eventually falling pollution levels. This assumption on tastes, together with certain assumptions on abatement, succeeds in generating a first worsening and then improving environment as growth proceeds.

Stokey's second contribution was to investigate whether there are limits to growth imposed by regulating industrial pollution. In Section 5 we discuss her analysis within an AK framework; here we focus on her work within the neoclassical model that formed the bulk of her paper. To do so we make the smallest departures possible from the Green Solow model. We again take the savings rate as fixed, but allow the intensity of abatement to vary over time. Since we are primarily interested in feasibility rather than optimality, our fixed savings rate assumption will simplify the analysis with little or no cost. Stokey assumed zero population growth, exogenous technological progress in goods production, a Cobb–Douglas aggregator over capital and labor in final goods production, and adopted an abatement function drawn from Copeland and Taylor (1994). In Stokey's analysis an optimizing representative agent determine savings and abatement decisions.

Although it is not obvious from Stokey (1998), a process of pollution abatement is implicit in her analysis. In Stokey's formulation the planner chooses a consumption path and the techniques of production as indexed by "z". The choice of techniques determines the link between potential output, F, and final output Y available for consumption or investment. The two are related by $Y = Fz$; while aggregate emissions are given by $E = Fz^\beta$ for some $\beta > 1$. To see how this choice of "techniques" is really one over abatement intensity make the change of variables $(1 - \theta) = z$, and then let $e(\theta) = (1 - \theta)^\beta$ for $\beta > 1$. It is now easy to see that the "techniques" chosen by the planner correspond to choices over the abatement intensity θ. The resulting $e(\theta)$ is just a specific form of an emissions function coming from the assumptions of constant returns to abatement and pollution being a joint product of output. Since θ is in principle observable, we conduct our analysis in this unit.

Our amended model assumes zero technological progress in abatement, and to follow Stokey adopts the specific emissions function given above and a Cobb–Douglas aggregator over factors. The model is described by:

$$Y = F[1 - \theta],$$
$$F \equiv K^\alpha (BL)^{1-\alpha},$$
$$\dot{K} = sY - \delta K,$$
$$\dot{L} = nL,$$
$$\dot{B} = gB,$$
$$E = Fe(\theta) \equiv F[1 - \theta]^\beta.$$

(23)

To examine the feasibility of balanced growth with a nondeteriorating environment we start with the last equation in (23) giving emissions and log differentiate to find

$$G_E = \alpha G_k + (1 - \alpha)(g + n) + G_{e(\theta)}, \tag{24}$$

recall G_E must be zero or negative or else the environment deteriorates. In the absence of technological progress in the emissions function, this implies the growth rate of emissions per unit of output $G_{e(\theta)}$ must be negative. To identify what this may imply for growth, we must eliminate G_K. To do so, note balanced growth requires Y/K constant. Divide both sides of the final goods production function by Y^α. Rearrange and log differentiate with respect to time to find

$$G_Y = G_K = g + n + \frac{G_{e(\theta)}}{(1 - \alpha)\beta}, \tag{25}$$

where G_Y is the growth rate of final output. At this point it is worthwhile to note that final output growth is reduced by active abatement since $G_{e(\theta)}$ must be negative.

To determine the evolution of emissions along the balanced growth path substitute (25) into (24) and rearrange slightly to obtain

$$G_E = g + n + \frac{G_{e(\theta)}}{(1 - \alpha)\beta} + \frac{(\beta - 1)G_{e(\theta)}}{\beta}. \tag{26}$$

The first two terms of this expression, $(n + g)$, represent the scale effect of growth. They represent the growth rate of emissions that would arise along the balanced growth path if θ and hence environmental policy, was held constant. This is clear from (23) since if θ is constant $G_{e(\theta)} = 0$.

The final two terms in (26) represent the technique effect created by lowering emissions per unit output along the balanced growth path. This technique effect is itself composed of two parts. The first component is the reduction in the growth rate of final output caused by the diversion of resources to abatement. Since θ is increasing along the balanced growth path, the growth rate of F exceeds that of final output by this amount.[36] Therefore, this component of the technique effect lowers pollution by slowing down the growth rate of final output [recall (25)].

The second component of the technique effect is the reduction in emissions per unit of final output created by abating more intensively. This is the standard component identified in static models. This component of the technique effect need not be as large as previously to lower pollution. To see this solve (26) for the rate at which emissions per unit of output must fall to drive emissions downward. Algebra yields

$$-G_{e(\theta)} > \frac{g + n}{1 + [\alpha/[(1 - \alpha)\beta]]} \tag{27}$$

which is smaller than the minimum rate of $(g + n)$ needed in (17). Not surprisingly because abatement has a negative effect on growth rates, it has less of a role to play in

---

[36] The growth rate of θ and $e(\theta)$ are related by $G_{e(\theta)} = -\beta[\theta/(1 - \theta)]G_\theta$.

lowering emissions per unit of output. Therefore in set-ups where abatement is respon-sible for pollution reduction, the burden is shared across two margins: abatement lowers growth rates and abatement also lowers emissions per unit output.

These two roles for abatement now introduce the possibility that a sustainable growth path may not exist. To see why, note that the reduction in growth created by environ-mental policy is very similar to the growth drag found in models with either fixed land or exhaustible natural resources.[37] In the case with fixed or declining resources the ratio of resource use to effective labor falls along the balanced growth path and this lowers growth rates. The same is true here once we make the right translations. To see this parallel, use the final goods production function and the emissions function to write net output as if pollution were an input into production. Doing so we find

$$Y = F^{1-1/\beta} E^{1/\beta}. \tag{28}$$

Along the balanced growth path E must fall while F grows; therefore the reduction in E works very much like the exhaustion of a resource that lowers growth. It is now apparent that while (27) tells us that the decline in emission intensity must be sufficiently fast to lower emissions; Equation (25) tells us this same magnitude cannot be too large if we are to have positive growth in income per capita. Solving (25) for the implied restriction and combining with (27) yields, after some manipulation,

$$g > -G_{e(\theta)} > \frac{g+n}{\alpha + (1-\alpha)\beta}. \tag{29}$$

The range given by this inequality defines the set of emission intensity reductions that are consistent with declining emissions and positive per capita output growth: i.e. sus-tainable growth. If we recall that $\beta > 1$, then it is straightforward to see that the feasible region is not empty when there is zero population growth. When $n > 0$ the region may not exist. By equating the two sides of (29) we can solve for the relationship between population growth and parameters that must be true for a sustainable growth path to exist. Algebra gives us

$$g \frac{(1-\alpha)(\beta-1)}{\beta} > n \frac{1}{\beta}. \tag{30}$$

The left-hand side of (30) is exactly labor's share in final goods production [use (28) and the definition of F] times the rate of labor augmenting technological progress g. The right-hand side is exactly emissions share in final output, $1/\beta$, times the rate of population growth n. The intuition for this condition is straightforward, and is identical to that we give later in a model where exhaustible energy resources create drag.

The left-hand side of the expression represents the Solow forces of technologi-cal progress raising growth to the extent determined by labor's share and the rate of progress. The right-hand side could be called the Malthusian forces since they capture

---

[37] An excellent review of growth drag is contained in Jones (2002, Chapter 9).

the impact of diminishing returns caused by a falling ratio of emissions to effective labor along the balanced growth path. These forces are stronger the more important are emissions in the production of final output, and stronger the faster is population growth.

If the inequality in (30) goes the other way then we have two choices. Either per capita income growth is negative and emissions fall; or, per capita income growth is positive but emissions rise. In either case we do not have sustainable growth according to our definition.

This observation of course suggests we follow the path of earlier authors and calculate the growth drag due to pollution policy. For example, Nordhaus (1992) adopts a model similar to (28) with emissions E replaced by either land or an exhaustible natural resource and then generates estimates for the drag caused by finite land and natural resources. But without a formal framework in which to estimate the long run growth impact of tighter environmental policy, Nordhaus resorts to estimates of contemporaneous expenditures on abatement to calculate future costs of pollution control.

We can go further here, although our methods are far from ideal. To generate an estimate for the growth drag caused by environmental policy we need estimates of β, α and $G_{e(\theta)}$. We note using (23) that $G_{e(\theta)} = G_{E/Y}\beta/[\beta - 1]$ where $G_{E/Y}$ is the observable growth rate of emissions per unit of final output. For various measures of E it is shown in Figure 1. We take capital's share of production, α to be 0.35. To eliminate the parameter β write emissions per unit of output, using (23) as $E/Y = (1 - \theta)^{\beta-1}$. Since we have data on emissions, final output and pollution abatement costs we could in theory estimate β. Using this estimate we could then calculate the growth drag due to pollution policy. Since our purpose is not to provide definitive answers but rather suggest a methodology, take the log of E/Y and differentiate with respect to time to find

$$\beta = 1 - \frac{G_{E/Y}}{G_\theta}\frac{1-\theta}{\theta}, \tag{31}$$

where G_θ is the growth rate of the pollution abatement cost share, and θ the average pollution abatement cost share over the period in consideration. Now use (31) to eliminate β and now rewrite (25) as

$$G_y = g + n - \frac{G_\theta}{1-\alpha}\frac{\theta}{1-\theta}. \tag{32}$$

The drag due to environmental policy is now directly linked to observable measures: the share of pollution abatement costs in the value of overall economic activity, and the percentage growth rate of this measure. To investigate what a reasonable magnitude of growth drag may be, we report in the table below a series of illustrative calculations. Recall that the share of pollution abatement costs in either manufacturing value-added or GDP is small – on the order of 1 or 2%. In certain industries it can of course be much higher. Take 1970 as the base year and set the pollution abatement costs share in that year at 1%. Then applying growth rates of 2.5 to 7.5% per year in this cost share, we obtain with the help of (32), the following results.

The first column of Table 1 assumes the share of pollution abatement costs in the value of output rises from 1% to a little over 2% in thirty years. The other columns report larger increases for illustrative purposes, although they are far in excess of the historic increases as shown by our data in Figure 2. A striking feature of the table is that the drag due to environmental policy is very small except in extreme cases. When pollution abatement costs rise from 1% to a little over 2% in 30 years, the drag on growth is only 6 hundredths of 1% point. When pollution abatement costs grow by 5% per year, the policy reduces growth by 0.2%. If costs grow by the extremely large 7.5% per year, drag is now $\frac{1}{2}$ of 1% point which is significant. Note that growth in per capita income, $G_Y - n$, over the last 50 years is approximately 2% per year; therefore the last column would predict an ever strengthening environmental policy that raise the share of pollution abatement costs in value-added by 7.5% year would reduce per capita income growth by 25%.

To a certain extent the relatively small effects in Table 1 are not that surprising. If pollution abatement costs as a fraction of value-added are in the order of 1%, it is difficult to see how even relatively large percentage increases in their level would lower growth tremendously. To go slightly further, note from (31) that if $G_{E/Y}$ and G_θ are of the same magnitude, then it is easy to see that β is approximately $1/\theta$.[38] This implies the share of emissions in final production in (28), $1/\beta$ is on the order of 0.01 or 0.02. And if pollution emissions are such an unimportant input into the production of final output, then drag from any reduction in emissions over time must also be small.

Despite the optimistic results in Table 1 concerning growth rates, models that rely on active abatement often contain the prediction that abatement becomes a larger and larger component of economic activity. This is a direct consequence of two facts. The first is that for emissions to fall, emissions per unit of output must shrink continuously with ongoing growth. The second is that with constant returns to abatement, lowering emissions per unit output comes at increasing cost. As a consequence, an implication of an exclusive reliance on abatement is that abatement costs rise along the growth path to eventually take up most of national product. To verify this, return to our simple example

Table 1
The drag of pollution policy on growth (percentages)

	2.5	5.0	7.5
PAC share percentage increase per year	2.5	5.0	7.5
Pollution abatement costs share 1970	1.0	1.0	1.0
Pollution abatement cost share 2000	2.1	4.3	8.8
Average $\theta/[1-\theta]$ across period	1.57	2.72	5.15
Growth drag percentage	0.06	0.2	0.5

[38] This may not be such a bad assumption. In Figure 1 it appears that the growth rate of emissions per unit output for each pollutant may be roughly constant over the last 50 years. The important point is that the two growth rates are of a similar magnitude and not necessarily equal.

and note $G_{e(\theta)}$ is constant along the balanced growth path. Using our specific emission function in (23), we know

$$G_{e(\theta)} = -\beta \frac{\dot{\theta}}{1-\theta}. \tag{33}$$

Solving this differential equation for θ yields

$$\theta(t) = 1 - \left(1 - \left(1 - \theta(0)\right)\right)e^{(G_{e(\theta)}/\beta)t} \tag{34}$$

starting from some $\theta(0)$ near the balanced growth path we see that as time goes to infinity θ goes to one because $G_{e(\theta)} < 0$. Abatement must take up a larger and larger share of national product as time progresses. This is an uncomfortable conclusion in light of the data we have already presented showing a relatively weak increase in abatement over time. In addition the reader may wonder why it is that agents would willingly make such sacrifices in final consumption necessary for such a large abatement program.

At this point it is useful to refer to Stokey (1998) explicitly for an answer since Stokey's analysis shows that consumer's are indeed willing to make the sacrifice needed in net output to lower pollution albeit under certain conditions. Specifically, by adopting a CRRA utility function Stokey shows emissions fall along the balanced growth path if and only if the elasticity of marginal utility with respect to consumption exceeds one. Only if consumers valuation of consumption falls quickly are they willing to take a smaller and smaller slice of (an ever expanding) national income as growth proceeds.

Stokey's analysis also allows for a more theoretically based growth drag calculation. By adopting specific functional forms, Stokey solves for the growth rate of final output and emissions in terms of primitives. By rearranging slightly and recasting these results in terms of our notation we find the growth rate of output per person and overall emissions are just

$$G_y = g - g \frac{\sigma + \gamma - 1}{\sigma + \gamma - 1 + (1 - \alpha)(\beta - 1)\gamma},$$
$$G_E = \frac{1 - \sigma}{\gamma} G_y, \tag{35}$$

where σ is the elasticity of marginal utility in the CRRA utility function, $\gamma \geqslant 1$ is a measure of the convexity of damages from pollution, α is capital's share, g is the exogenous rate of labor augmenting technological progress. There is zero population growth so $n = 0$.[39]

In comparison to our simple example the drag of environmental policy is now directly linked to the primitives of tastes and technology although it reflects similar forces at work. For example, by rearranging we can isolate the percentage reduction in growth

[39] This is found by rearranging (3) on p. 14 of Stokey (1998). To rewrite the equation in our set up we need to note the rate of labor augmenting technological progress would be $g/(1 - \alpha)$ which we write as g in the above.

caused by active pollution policy

$$G_y = g\left[1 - \frac{1 - G_{E/Y}}{1 - G_{E/Y} + (1 - \alpha)(\beta - 1)}\right], \tag{36}$$

the greater is the rate of reduction in emissions per unit output, $G_{E/Y}$, and the larger is emissions share in final output $1/\beta$, the greater will be the drag. This is the same set of forces we found using our simpler framework.

We can of course estimate growth drag in this optimizing framework as well. In order to replicate the Environmental Kuznets Curve Stokey adopts a set of parameters for all the primitives we need. In doing so, the model predicts the EKC found in empirical work, but using these same values for capital's share, the abatement technology, etc. we find that growth drag is an unbelievable 60% of potential growth. Using the parameter specification chosen to mimic the EKC, growth in income per capita in the absence of pollution policy is 4% per year.[40] But using (35) growth is actually approximately 1.6% per year with active pollution policy; therefore, growth in income per person is slowed by 60% from what it would be in the absence of environmental concerns. This is clearly far too high.

If we lower the elasticity of marginal utility to approach the lowest limit consistent with falling pollution (σ approaching 1), and set $\gamma = 1$, then drag hits its minimum. But even in this case, drag is almost 55% of potential growth. The problem with these calculations is Stokey's assumption of $\beta = 3$, which implies a share of pollution emissions in final output of $1/3$ which is clearly far too high. Altering β to values similar to those used in our growth drag calculations suggests a much smaller drag.

For example, from Figure 1 it is apparent that 3 of the U.S. criteria pollutants had an emissions per unit of output in 1998 that were just $1/10$ of their value in 1940. This implies a growth rate of approximately -4% per year from these pollutants. Assuming the share of emissions in final output is 0.02, β is 50, and with a capital share of 0.35 we find the percentage reduction predicted by (36) to be just 0.03. Therefore a 2% growth rate would be reduced to just 1.94% because of the drag of environmental policy.[41]

We would hasten to add however that these calculations are purely for illustration. They demonstrate how the growth drag due to environmental policy may be calculated from primitives on technologies, abatement costs, knowledge of historic growth, and emission levels. We leave it to future research to develop and refine these methods to generate estimates of the growth drag due to environmental policy.[42]

---

[40] This is just the effective rate of labor augmenting technical change which is $g/(1 - \alpha) = 0.024/0.6$ in Stokey's notation.

[41] The problem with this set of parameters is that the output elasticity of emissions in production is far too high at $1/3$. If the regulator used pollution taxes to implement the social optimum, this implies that at all periods of time the share of pollution taxes in value-added would be $1/3$. Setting β much higher generates numbers closer to those we reported in Table 1.

[42] Other methods used to estimate the impact of tighter pollution policy on growth include the use of quite detailed computable general equilibrium models of the U.S. economy, econometric studies, and more ag-

Many other papers rely on an active role for abatement in lowering pollution levels, and therefore must contain predictions for both the drag of environmental policy and the evolution of pollution abatement costs over time. In some work, abatement is specified differently so that it escapes diminishing returns by assumption. For example, early work by Keeler, Spence and Zeckhauser (1972) examines no growth steady states and assumes foregone output is the *only input* into abatement. As a result of this assumption, marginal abatement costs are constant in their formulation. Even with constant marginal abatement costs they find that when abatement is not very productive a "Murky Age" equilibrium arises: abatement is not undertaken and emissions are high in the steady state. Alternatively, when abatement is very productive in reducing emissions, the steady state is given by a Golden Age equilibrium with active abatement and lower emissions.

Other related work appears in Lopez (1994) and Copeland and Taylor (2003). In these contributions an optimizing social planner chooses the optimal level of abatement but factor supplies and technology are taken as parametric in their exclusively static analyses. Both adopt formulations where abatement is a constant returns activity using conventional inputs and examine how once for all growth in either technology or factor endowments affect pollution levels.[43] When growth is fueled by neutral technological progress, Copeland and Taylor show that emissions fall with this source of growth if the elasticity of marginal damage from pollution exceeds one. In a CRRA framework this corresponds to the condition Stokey derived of $\sigma > 1$.

In contrast when growth occurs by primary factor accumulation alone, then Lopez (1994) shows that whether pollution rises or falls now depends on both the elasticity of substitution between factor inputs and the income elasticity of marginal damage. If the elasticity of substitution between primary factors and emissions is large, then emissions fall quite easily. When production is Cobb–Douglas, Lopez's condition is identical to that of Stokey and $\sigma > 1$ generates the result that emissions fall with growth.

Together these contributions demonstrate that an improving environment and rising incomes are surely feasible in a standard neoclassical model where abatement is a constant returns activity. This path is also optimal under certain conditions. But by relying exclusively on changes in the intensity of abatement to lower pollution levels consumers must be willing to make rather large sacrifices for a cleaner environment over time. It is in fact this rather large willingness to sacrifice for a cleaner environment that leads to regulation in the first place.

In Stokey (1998), regulation is at first not present as the shadow value of capital is too high and the shadow value of pollution too low when growth begins for the planner to

---

gregative data exercises like the one we just conducted. The results from these studies are quite different. For example, Jorgenson and Wilcoxen (1990) build a 35 industry model of the U.S. economy to estimate the impact of pollution abatement costs and motor vehicle emission standards on overall output and growth. They find that output growth in the U.S. was reduced by almost 0.2% over the 1973–1985 period by these environmental policies, and in level terms U.S. real GDP is lower by a quite significant 2.6%.

[43] Lopez (1994) does not present an abatement function per se but it is implicit in his use of the revenue function listing primary factors and emissions as productive factors.

allocate any output to abatement. An important input into this decision is that the marginal product of the first unit of abatement is bounded above even at zero abatement.[44] As a result, no abatement is undertaken $\theta = 0$ and pollution rises lock-step with output. Once the environment has deteriorated sufficiently and the now larger capital stock has depressed its shadow value, active abatement begins. There is then a transition period and the economy approaches the balanced growth path described previously.

This explanation for the EKC is very persuasive. It links rising income levels with a lower shadow cost of abatement and a higher opportunity cost of doing nothing. It captures the idea that policy responds positively to real income growth and generates an EKC is a straightforward way. We have already seen however that a further implication of the model is an ever-rising pollution abatement cost share that may be inconsistent with the data. In addition we should note that this explanation predicts a constant emissions to output ratio prior to the regulation phase when emissions are rising. After regulation begins, the emissions to output ratio falls and does so at a constant rate along the balanced growth path [see (35)]. Figure 1 however shows the emission to output ratio was falling long before emissions peaked in Figures 3–8. Therefore, using this data as our guide the model misses entirely the long reduction in emissions per unit output that occurred in the U.S. prior to peak pollution levels being achieved.

These observations suggest, at the very least, that other forces are simultaneously at work and partially responsible for the falling emissions to output ratio and roughly constant control costs in the U.S. historical record. One natural candidate is of course changes in the composition of output towards less energy intensive, and hence less pollution intensive, goods. Much has been made recently about the dematerialization of production and its environmental consequences, and hence we now turn to examine a model relying on just these effects.

4.3. Composition shifts: the source and sink model

There are several ways to escape a worsening environment as economic growth proceeds. One possibility is for technological progress in abatement to lower pollution levels as shown in the Green Solow model; another is intensified abatement as shown by the Stokey Alternative. A third method is to alter the composition of output or inputs towards less pollution intensive activities. In this section we investigate the implication of changing energy use in production. Much of current concern over pollution arises from energy use and hence if the economy as a whole could conserve on energy this would have important implications for environmental quality. But raising energy efficiency per unit of output comes at some cost because energy is a valuable input and constraining its use will lower overall productivity. These losses must be compensated for by increases in capital, effective labor or new technology if growth is not to be slowed. Therefore, solving our pollution problems by altering an economy's input mix

---

[44] We will show this in Section 5.

may introduce significant drag. These growth concerns are of course one of the major reasons why many countries have delayed ratification of the Kyoto protocol; and why many developing countries refuse to sign the agreement.

While many models investigating the growth and pollution relationship rely on compositional changes to lower pollution levels, few make the role of energy explicit in their analyses. For example, Copeland and Taylor (2003) present a "Sources of Growth" explanation for the Environmental Kuznets Curve arguing that if the development process relies heavily on capital accumulation in the earliest stages and human capital formation in later stages, these changes will alter the pollution intensity of production so that the environment should at first worsen and then improve over time. Related empirical work in Antweiler, Copeland and Taylor (2001) finds growth fueled by capital accumulation is necessarily pollution increasing, while growth fueled by neutral technological progress lowers pollution levels. Behind these results is presumably a link between the different types of growth, energy use, and emissions.

Similarly, in Aghion and Howitt (1998)'s analysis of long run growth and environmental outcomes, their clean capital – knowledge – takes on a larger and larger role in growth in the long run and this too creates an eventually improving economy. But since they adopt the same assumptions on abatement as Stokey (1998), even with a changing composition of output large increases in abatement must made to hold pollution down to acceptable levels.

In most of these formulations the link to energy use is at best implicit with the reader having to interpret capital or other productive factors in a broad way to include energy or other natural resources. One of the major accomplishments of the early resource literature was to identify how and where finite resources impinge on the growth process. By ignoring the role of exhaustible resources in generating pollution, we run the risk of making pollution reductions look relatively painless because these analyses will miss the induced drag on economic growth. In this section we make the connection between energy use, growth and environmental outcomes precise by combining earlier models of growth and exhaustible resources with newer models examining the pollution and growth link. By doing so we demonstrate how some of the results of the earlier 1960s and 1970s literature on natural resources and growth have relevance today.

One of the major research questions of the earlier "limits to growth" literature was the extent to which exhaustible natural resources impinged on growth. Seminal contributions by Solow (1974) and Stiglitz (1974) showed that growth with exhaustible resources was indeed possible, although it required a joint restriction on the rate of population growth, technological progress and the share of natural resources in output. There are two well-known results from this literature.

The first, due to Solow (1974), is that a program of constant consumption is feasible even with limited exhaustible resources and a constant population if the share of capital in output exceeds the share of resources in final output. This observation led to a consideration of the optimal rate of savings to maximize the constant consumption profile. The answer was provided by John Hartwick (1977) and embodied in the now-famous Hartwick's rule: invest all the rents from the exhaustible resource in capital and future generations will be as well off as the currently living despite the asymptotic elimination of natural resources.[45]

The second result, due to Stiglitz (1974), is that growth in per capita consumption is possible with positive population growth if the rate of resource augmenting technological progress exceeds the population growth rate. Our formulation will also yield a similar restriction on technological progress to generate positive per capita output growth, but in addition we add the further restriction that environmental quality improves. Therefore, even when growth with exhaustible resources is feasible in terms of generating positive output growth [as required by Stiglitz (1974)], it may be unsustainable because this same plan implies rising pollution levels.

We remain as close as possible to our earlier formulation while introducing a role for natural resources. We make two important changes. First, we introduce energy as an intermediate good. The intermediate good "energy" is produced from an exhaustible natural resource R, capital, and labor via a CRS and strictly concave production technology. Final output (used for investment or consumption) is then produced via capital, labor and the energy intermediate. To keep things simple we assume both production functions are Cobb–Douglas, and to remain consistent with our earlier formulations we assume technological progress is labor augmenting.[46]

Our second change is to assume pollution is produced via energy use, and not the overall scale of final goods production. In doing we sever the strong link we had thus far between pollution and final output by making pollution the product of input use. We retain our earlier assumption that pollution can be abated, but take the fraction of resources devoted to abatement as constant. We have already shown in the Stokey Alternative that increasing abatement creates drag on economic growth; here we show that even with the abatement intensity fixed, a move towards less energy intensive production lowers growth while it reduces the growth rate of emissions.

With these assumptions in hand, the production side of the economy becomes

$$Y = K_y^{b_1}(BL_y)^{n_1} I^{b_2},$$
$$I = K_I^{b_3}(BL_1)^{n_2} R^{b_4}[1 - \theta],$$

(37)

where I is the energy intermediate, θ is the fraction of the energy industry's activities devoted to abating pollution, R denotes the flow of resources used per unit time, and subscripts denote quantities of capital and labor used in final good production Y, and the intermediate good energy I.

Capital and labor has to be allocated efficiently across the two activities – intermediate and final good production. It is straightforward to show that this implies a constant

---

[45] Adopting Hartwick's rule in our source-and-sink model leads to increasing utility over time as the environment improves with resource exhaustion. Proof available upon request.

[46] This implicitly assumes that energy is not an essential input into production; i.e. energy per unit of output is not bounded below.

fraction of the capital stock is employed in intermediate good production and the remainder in final goods. The same is true for labor. This allows us to aggregate and rewrite the production function for final good output as follows

$$Y = K^{a_1}(LB)^{a_2}R^{a_3}[1-\theta]^{b_2} \tag{38}$$

which is necessarily CRS with $a_1 + a_2 + a_3 = 1$.[47]

To complete the model we add equations governing the labor force and technology growth, the relationship between extraction and the resource stock S, plus our abatement assumptions linking emissions to energy use I. These conditions are:

$$\dot{K} = sY - \delta K,$$
$$\dot{L} = nL,$$
$$\dot{B} = gB, \tag{39}$$
$$E = I\Omega e(\theta) = I\Omega[1-\theta]^{\beta},$$
$$\dot{S} = -R,$$

where $e(\theta)$ measures the flow of emissions released per unit of energy used. It is instructive at this point to rewrite the emissions equation to focus on the role of a changing composition of inputs in determining pollution levels. To do so define the variable $\chi = I/Y$ which is the ratio of energy use to final good production, or what is commonly called the energy intensity of GDP. Then rewriting the emissions function we find

$$E = \chi Y e(\theta). \tag{40}$$

A change in emissions can now come from any one of three sources: scale effects via changes in final good output Y; composition effects coming from changes in the energy intensity of final good production χ; and technique effects that lower $e(\theta)$ directly.

We examine balanced growth paths and impose two requirements on the set of paths we investigate. First, as usual we require nondeteriorating environmental quality. Second, we require positive growth in per capita income.[48]

To solve for a balanced growth path note Y/K must be constant along any such path. Using this requirement we can log differentiate (38) with respect to time, impose the

---

[47] Algebra shows $a_1 = b_1 + b_2 b_3$, $a_2 = n_1 + b_2 n_2$ and $a_3 = b_2 b_4$.

[48] To this the reader may choose to add various efficiency conditions. For example, Stiglitz (1974) imposes the arbitrage condition requiring the return on capital equal that of the resource. This additional constraint is the well-known Hotelling (1931) result that the rate of capital gain on the resource in situ must equal the return on capital. This efficiency condition fails here because energy use creates the disutility pollution. We could impose a similar efficiency condition but its form would depend on how pollution entered utility. Alternatively, or in addition, the reader may add a condition requiring the marginal rate of substitution between consumption and pollution equal its marginal product. We leave a discussion of optimality until Section 5.

requirement that Y/K be constant, and find the growth rate of final output[49]

$$G_Y = (g+n) - \frac{a_3}{1-a_1}\big[(g+n) - g_R\big]. \tag{41}$$

The first term is the usual growth rate of output in the Solow model; the second is a negative element capturing the growth drag caused by natural resources. To see why this term appears suppose resources were in unlimited supply; then their services could grow over time at the same rate as effective labor and we would have $g_R = g + n$. In this case, capital, output, resources and effective labor would grow at the rate $g + n$ and there would be no resource drag. In fact, however, the resource base $S(0) > 0$ is finite and exhaustible, and this implies that $g_R < 0$.[50] Any nonpositive g_R is feasible because we can always choose the level of resource use such that the finite stock is eliminated asymptotically. Therefore, the ratio of resources to effective labor in production falls over time and this reduces growth below the Solow level. Indeed as (41) shows, growth in final output could be negative if resource constraints loom too large.[51]

From our earlier equations it is straightforward to show that $a_3 = b_2 b_4$ and hence the existence of finite resources lowers growth by an extent determined by the resource share in final output. To see this note that if the share of final output going to resources approached zero, then a_3 approaches zero, and G_Y in (41) approaches $g + n$ the Solow growth rate.

It is now straightforward to write growth in per capita output as just

$$g_y = g - \frac{a_3}{1-a_1}[g+n-g_R] \tag{42}$$

which shows technological progress has to offset both population growth and the reduction in resources over time in order for per capita income to rise. To make this clear and relate our model here to the Stokey Alternative, suppose the resource in question offered an indestructible flow of services per unit time; i.e. suppose it was Ricardian land. Then $g_R = 0$ and growth in per capita income is positive if and only if

$$a_2 g > a_3 n. \tag{43}$$

The left-hand side of (43) represents the Solow forces of technological progress the strength of which depends on the share of labor in overall production and the rate of labor augmenting technological progress. Aligned against these are the Malthusian forces lowering output per person by applying more and more labor to the fixed stock of land. The rate of population growth and the share of land in production determine the strength

---

[49] It is helpful to recall θ is constant and (38) is CRS.

[50] From our stock equation we have $S(t) = S(0) - \int_0^t R(\tau)\,d\tau$ where $S(t)$ must be nonnegative. This implies that $R(\tau)$ cannot rise over time along a balanced growth path.

[51] Recall however the Solow result [see Solow (1974)] that with zero technological progress and zero population growth, a program of constant consumption can be maintained as long as the share of resources in final output is less than the share of capital. We cannot derive this condition from (41) directly because we have already imposed a constant Y/K, which is inconsistent with this program.

of the Malthusian forces. Note the similarity between (43) and our earlier (30). The condition in (43) arises when $g_R = 0$ and $g_y > 0$; the condition in (30) has $g_E = 0$ and $g_y > 0$. Note the parallel between emissions and resources.

To generate falling pollution we will need a strong compositional shift and hence $g_R < 0$ is our standard case with our first condition for sustainability given by (42). Our second condition is that pollution must fall over time. Log differentiating our emissions function in (39) yields

$$g_E = -g_a + g_\chi + g_y + g_{e(\theta)}. \tag{44}$$

To eliminate the possibility of emissions falling because of technological progress in abatement as in the Green Solow model, we set g_A to zero. To eliminate the possibility of greater abatement efforts holding pollution in check as in the Stokey Alternative, we set $g_{e(\theta)} = 0$. This leaves only changes in the composition of inputs to offset the rising scale effect of ongoing growth.

Straightforward calculations then show that the growth rate of energy per unit of final output is simply given by

$$g_\chi = -[1 - b_3]\left[\frac{b_4}{1 - b_3} - \frac{a_3}{1 - a_1}\right][g + n - g_R] < 0. \tag{45}$$

The sign of (45) depends on the large bracketed term which given our correspondences given in footnote 36, is negative. Not surprisingly, the energy intensity of final output must fall over time.

Putting the growth rate of output and energy intensity together we find emissions will fall if and only if

$$g_E = (g + n)\left[b_3 \frac{a_3}{1 - a_3} + b_4\right][(g + n) - g_R] < 0. \tag{46}$$

Note the first element in (46), $(g + n)$, is exactly the scale effect of output growth in the Green Solow model. And instead of technological progress in abatement appearing to offset the scale effect of growth, we now have emissions per unit of final output falling from the composition effect given by the second negative term. The growth rate of output is lowered by the drag of natural resources and hence as the economy "abates" by altering its input mix this creates drag much as in Stokey (1998).

There is a tension therefore between the desirability of moving away from natural resource use in order to lower pollution emissions and the cost of doing so in terms of growth. This of course is a primary concern of many developing countries and has limited their participation in the Kyoto Protocol to limit global warming. Because of our addition of a fixed natural resource, in some cases, composition effects alone cannot generate positive balanced growth with a nondeteriorating environment.

To investigate we graph G_y from (42) and G_E from (46) in Figure 10. We have graphed these growth rates against the rate of change in effective labor per unit resource, that is against $[(g + n) - g_R]$, since this term plays a key role in both emissions growth and per capita growth. There are several things to note about it. First, suppose resources

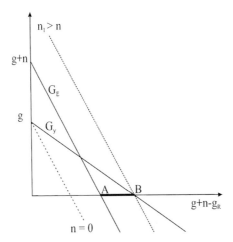

Figure 10. Feasibility: resource drag and per capita growth.

were in unlimited supply; then their services could "grow" over time at the same rate as effective labor $g + n$. Such a wonderful existence corresponds to points along the vertical axis in the figure. In particular we see that with no resource drag, per capita output growth equals g. With a finite resource base the growth rate of resource use must be negative and this means that per capita income growth must be lower as shown by the negatively sloped line labeled G_y starting at g and intersecting the horizontal axis at point B. Movements along this line correspond to changes in the growth rate of resource use g_R.

Similarly, if there were unlimited resources the energy intensity of GDP would remain constant and emissions would rise lock step with output. This unlimited resources scenario corresponds to a point along the vertical axis with the rate of aggregate output growth and emissions of $n + g$. Again, since resource use must decline over time the true growth rate of emissions must be lower as shown by the line labeled G_E that intersects the horizontal axis at A. The growth rate of emissions falls as we move to the right along this line because final output grows more slowly, and final output uses less energy per unit output.

From these observations it is clear that at all points to the left of A, growth in emissions is positive; points to the right of A, growth in emissions is negative. Similarly, all points to the left of B have positive per capita output growth; points to the right have negative growth. Putting these results together we see that ongoing growth in per capita incomes and an improving environment may not be feasible in some cases. In particular, the bold line segment AB represents the feasible region. Taking g and n as exogenous, this region gives us a range of resource exploitation rates, g_R, that are consistent with our twin goals.[52]

---

[52] You can derive the exact extraction level associated with any rate of exploitation by employing the materials balance constraint for resources.

To understand the determinants of the feasible region it proves useful to consider the zero population growth case. If population growth is zero, then the two lines have the same vertical intercept as shown by the dotted $n = 0$ line that is parallel to G_E. Whether positive growth and falling emissions is possible only depends on the relative slopes of G_E versus G_y. Algebra tells us a region such as AB will always exist with zero population growth. The logic is simply that emissions growth falls with both reduced output growth *and* a changing energy intensity of production. Both occur as we increase drag by moving right in the figure. Therefore, once resource drag has lowered per capita output growth to zero at a point like B the scale effect is zero, but emissions growth must be strictly negative because the composition effect is still driving energy intensity downwards. Consequently, a feasible region like AB exists.

When population growth is positive, this logic fails. As we raise the population growth rate the G_E curve shifts to the right and eventually intersects the horizontal axis at B. This in effect raises the scale effect. At this point, positive growth with declining emissions is not possible. The reason is simply that emissions growth is rising in n (a scale effect), whereas growth in output per capita relies falls with n because of resource drag. Once we choose n large enough – as shown by the dashed line labeled $n_1 > n$ – the feasible region disappears.[53]

These results have a decidedly negative flavor to them. An environmental policy that lowers the growth rate of emissions and lowers the energy intensity of final output, also lowers per capita growth to such an extent that an improving environment and real income gains may be unattainable. There are several reasons why we should be cautious in interpreting these negative results. The first is simply that we have ruled out a role for active abatement as in the Stokey Alternative. And we have ruled out technological progress as in the Green Solow model. While adding more avenues of adjustment is always good, active abatement lowers pollution emissions but creates drag just as reducing energy use does. Routine calculations show that if we let all three avenues of adjustment operate, we can write our two balanced growth path requirements as

$$G_y = \underbrace{g}_{\text{Green Solow}} - \underbrace{RD\big[(g+n) - G_R\big]}_{\text{natural resource drag}} + \underbrace{PPD[G_{e(\theta)}]}_{\text{pollution policy drag}} > 0,$$

$$G_E = \underbrace{g + n - g_A}_{\text{Green Solow}} - \underbrace{EI\big[(g+n) - G_R\big]}_{\text{composition effect from changing energy intensity}} \qquad (47)$$

$$+ \underbrace{TE[G_{E(\theta)}]}_{\text{technique effect from active abatement}} < 0,$$

where RD is a positive constant representing resource drag, and PPD a positive constant representing pollution policy drag. Note that in general with both resource exhaustion

---

[53] The issue of feasibility also arises in the Stokey Alternative although we did not focus on it there. Recall Stokey (1998) assumed $n = 0$. Our analysis here suggests that this is not an innocuous assumption.

and abatement rising, there are two sources of drag on per capita income growth. Corresponding to each source of drag is of course a component of emission reduction. In the second equation *EI* is a positive coefficient representing energy intensity changes. This corresponds to a composition effect. In addition *TE* is a positive coefficient representing changes coming from increased abatement; this represents a technique effect.

Putting all this together in terms of our figure, we find that allowing for technological progress in abatement shifts the growth of emissions line G_E inward expanding the feasible region. This should come as no surprise. Adding active abatement shifts both lines down (the economy grows slower as do emissions), having an ambiguous effect on the feasible region. Raising population growth from zero however shrinks the region making it more likely that both requirements cannot be met.

What then are we to make of our stylized facts from the introduction? Emission levels have been falling in many countries while growth in per capita income remained positive. Pollution abatement costs have trended upwards but only slowly, and energy prices – while rising – have not been rising at fast rates.[54] We have already seen that these features are roughly consistent with the Green Solow model, but less so with the Stokey Alternative. Here we find that relying on changes in energy intensity alone can work in lowering emissions but it does so only with strong compositional shifts towards less energy intensive goods. In our formulation these shifts are only consistent with a rising real price of energy over time. To see this note that energy's share in final output is fixed; take final output as the numeraire, and conclude that the real price of energy must rise along the balanced growth path at the rate $-\chi > 0$.

In Figure 11 we plot the real price of three energy sources: oil, natural gas, and coal. For ease of reading all prices are set to 100 in 1957. It is very risky to draw any strong conclusions from this data. The real price of oil has almost doubled since 1957; the price of natural gas is rising quite quickly, while the price of coal has increased the least over the period. Naturally these price increases have created some composition effects as predicted by our source and sink model, but only over certain periods of time. For example, Sue Wing and Eckhaus (2003) examine the history of energy intensity in U.S. production and divide its changes into those accruing from a changing mix of U.S. industries and those accruing from within industry improvements in energy efficiency (which would correspond to a fall in Ω). Their findings suggest that from the late 1950s until the mid-1970s changes in the composition of U.S. industries played a major role in reducing overall energy intensity. But during the 1980s and 1990s the reduction in U.S. aggregate energy intensity has come from improvements in energy efficiency at the industry level. Therefore changes in the composition of output cannot carry the burden of explanation of our data.

Instead these compositional changes must have been helped along by significant technological progress in abatement or energy efficiency (Ω). The evidence for these

---

[54] Note from (37) that the relative price of energy to final good output must rise along the model's balanced growth path because we have already shown that the energy intensity of production, χ, falls over time [see (45)].

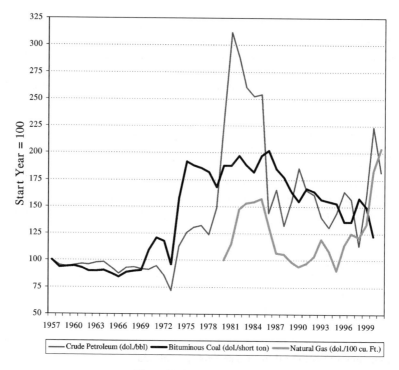

Figure 11. Real energy prices.

changes is very strong. For example in a detailed study of the energy efficiency of consumer durables Newell, Jaffe and Stavins (1999) find strong support for a significant role for autonomous technological progress (over 60% of the change in energy efficiency), and supporting roles for induced innovation created by higher energy prices. Similar evidence is presented by Popp (2002) who examines the impact of higher energy prices on the rate of innovation in key energy technologies. Using a database of U.S. patenting activity over the 1970–1993 period, Popp explains variation in the intensity of energy patenting across technology groups as a function of energy prices, the existing "knowledge stock" in a technology area and other covariates such as federal funding for R&D. There are two main results from the study. The first is that a rise in energy prices shown in Figure 11 created induced innovation and a burst in patenting activity after the oil price shocks.

The second major result is that while prices are a significant determinant of patenting activity, other factors are also very important. For example, the existing stock of knowledge (as measured by an index of previous patenting weighted for impact) in a technology area has a large impact on subsequent patenting. For example, Popp reports that the average change in knowledge stocks over the period raise patenting activity on average by 24%; while the average change in energy prices over the period raise patenting on average by only 2%. Knowledge accumulation and spillovers are very important in determining the pace of future innovation.[55]

Taking these considerations into account would likely expand our feasible region AB. For example, if the emission intensity Ω fell when either energy prices rose (as in the source-and-sink model) or abatement intensified (as in the Stokey Alternative), then composition changes and active abatement could play a smaller role in checking the growth of pollution. This would of course make feasibility more likely.

Adding complications to our existing models would however take us too far afield, and as yet we know of no research that explicitly links energy prices, induced innovation and pollution emissions within a growth framework. Instead we take a small step towards a theory of induced innovation in the next section when we introduce a model with learning by doing in abatement and reconsider our stylized facts. But before doing so, we should note that we have, to a certain extent, stacked the decks against sustainable growth by assuming environmental quality has no effect on production possibilities. We have assumed that reducing the flow of emissions has only a cost in terms of drag and no benefit in terms of heightened productivity in goods production due to higher environmental quality. Several authors have however postulated a direct and positive link between the productivity of final goods output and environmental quality. This link casts doubt on the validity of growth drag exercises like ours. A typical formulation would add to our models a shift term on the final goods production function that is increasing in environmental quality. For example, Bovenberg and Smulders (1995) and Tahvonen and Kuuluvainen (1991) both postulate this type of additional interaction. Once we allow for a direct productivity response to an improved environment it is not clear that emission reductions lower growth. Bovenberg and Smulders, and Tahvenen both give sufficient conditions under which this additional channel dominates.

In general the less important are emissions in the direct production function, the more responsive is natural growth to a reduction in emissions, and the greater is the marginal productivity boost from a cleaner environment, the more likely it is that these secondary effects will dominate. While it is certainly plausible that a deteriorating environment will lower productivity, it is however unclear how important these impacts are empirically. We suspect that for most of industrial production these environmental impacts are small, or at least fairly elastic over the current range of exploitation. Certain industries such as farming or fishing are certain to have larger productivity effects from an improved environment, but these industries are small contributors to GDP in developed countries. It is likely that these induced productivity effects are greatest in poor developing economies and as yet have escaped the notice of serious empirical researchers.

---

[55] Related empirical work by Kaufman (2004) however is less sanguine about the ability of technical change to lower energy intensity in the long run. Kaufman examines the 1929–1999 period and argues that estimates of autonomous energy efficiency increases have been drastically overstated because changes in the composition of inputs and outputs have had led to a significant lowering of energy intensity. Instead he argues that inter fuel substitutions and reductions in household energy purchases are largely responsible for the declining trend in the energy intensity of GDP.

While it is certainly possible for these direct productivity effects to exist, we feel the biggest restriction imposed by our analysis thus far is its failure to link the rising costs of pollution control to innovation targeted at raising the productivity of abatement. Induced changes in technology of this sort are likely to lower energy intensity over time given the price paths shown in Figure 11; and induced innovation in abatement technologies are likely to be forthcoming as abatement costs rise. Both of these induced effects would lower emissions per unit final output by altering Ω. There is of course a large body of empirical research finding just such effects. But clearly these links are important although difficult to model in a growth framework, for as Popp notes:

> The most significant result [sic of the study] is the strong, positive impact energy prices have on new innovations. This finding suggests that environmental taxes and regulations not only reduce pollution by shifting behavior away from polluting activities but also encourage the development of new technologies that make pollution control less costly in the long run ... simply relying on technological change is not enough. There must be some mechanism in place that encourages new innovation (p. 178).

With this quote in mind we now turn to consider the impact of technological progress spurred on by the introduction of regulation.

5. Induced innovation and learning by doing

The series of models we have examined thus far explain the growth and environment history by focusing on technological progress in goods production, increased abatement efforts or changes in the composition of output over time.[56] Missing from this list is a consideration of induced innovation lowering abatement costs. Induced innovation or learning by doing is prominent in both growth theory [since the writings of Arrow (1962)], and in environmental economics more generally. For example, Jaffe, Peterson and Portney (1995) stresses the role of induced technological advance in solving pollution problems and holding down abatement costs. New growth theory generally often adopts formulations that are in essence learning by doing models. In models where knowledge accumulates over time, innovators learn from this stock of knowledge. In models of human capital acquisition the evolution of human capital reflects learning of past generations. And the simplest AK specification can be thought of a model where learning by doing in capital accumulation generates constant returns at the economy wide level.

The possibility of learning by doing offers several new features to the growth and environment relationship. First, if abatement efforts are subject to learning by doing then

---

[56] To this we could add the set of papers invoking political economy arguments. See, for example, Jones and Manuelli (2001) and the related empirical work by Barret and Graddy (2000).

this feature alone may generate the prediction of a first worsening and then improving environment. In a static setting, learning by doing is identical to increasing returns, and Andreoni and Levinson (2001) show how increasing returns to abatement can generate an EKC in a partial equilibrium endowment economy.[57]

Secondly, learning by doing alters the costs of pollution control. If learning by doing effects are unbounded, then growth with falling pollution levels could conceivably come at decreasing cost to society. In a world with bounded learning by doing the implications are less clear, but it seems likely that the drag of pollution policy may be smaller if learning by doing effects are present. An important feature of the static analysis mentioned above is that the authors generate falling pollution levels under quite weak assumptions on preferences. Specifically they do not need to adopt formulations where the demand for environmental protection is very income elastic. This suggests that a parallel dynamic analysis may escape these restrictions as well, because the cost of environmental control is now lower.

Third, if learning by doing arises from economy wide growth in the knowledge stock then learning by doing models offer the possibility of linking technological progress in abatement with that in goods production. As our previous analysis makes clear the relative rates of technological progress in goods production and abatement are key to determining the sustainability of a balanced growth path. This was especially clear in the Green Solow model, but was implicit in the other formulations because the absence of technological progress in abatement required other compensating changes to hold pollution in check. Learning by doing models give us one way to make our assumptions about knowledge spillovers and technological progress consistent across sectors.

Finally, although learning by doing is often modeled as a passive activity and not purposeful investment, learning by doing can be a form of induced innovation. If a worsening environment necessitates the imposition of pollution controls, and abatement is subject to learning by doing, we have effectively followed the advice of Popp in identifying a causal factor behind subsequent improvements in abatement technology.

5.1. Induced innovation and the Kindergarten Rule model

To discuss these issues, we now introduce the Kindergarten Rule model of Brock and Taylor (2003). This model, like those in the static literature, relies on learning by doing in the abatement process to hold pollution in check. Importantly, though since learning by doing is really an assumption about knowledge spillovers, the Kindergarten model adopts a consistent set of assumptions regarding the beneficial impact of knowledge spillovers. It assumes, similar to the AK growth literature that knowledge spillovers in capital accumulation lead to constant returns at the aggregate level. Similarly, knowledge spillovers in abatement eliminate diminishing returns to abatement. As a consequence, we obtain a relatively simple model of growth with pollution controls where

---

[57] Copeland and Taylor (2003) extend their analysis to a two-sector general equilibrium model with industry wide external economies in abatement and replicate their finding for a production economy.

learning by doing reduces abatement costs but does not eliminate the drag of environmental policy entirely.

In order to focus on the *implications* of ongoing technological progress for the environment and growth, Brock and Taylor (2003) adopt the very direct link between factor
accumulation and technological progress employed by Romer (1986), Lucas (1998) and
others. By doing so they generate a simple one-sector model of endogenous growth and
environmental quality. But as is well known, one-sector models of endogenous growth
blur the important distinction between physical capital and knowledge capital and force
us to think of "capital" in very broad terms.[58]

For simplicity they adopt a conventional infinitely lived representative agent, and
assume all pollution is local. There is one aggregate good, labeled Y, which is either
consumed or used for investment or abatement. There are two factors of production:
labor and capital. There is zero population growth and hence $L(t) = L$; recall it is the
rate of population growth relative to the rate of technological progress that is key, so
here one of these rates is set to zero. In contrast to labor, the capital stock accumulates
via investment and depreciates at the constant rate δ.

5.1.1. Tastes

A representative consumer maximizes lifetime utility given by:

$$W = \int_0^\infty U(C, X) e^{-\rho t} \, dt, \tag{48}$$

where C indicates consumption, and X is the pollution stock. Utility is increasing and
quasi-concave in C and $-X$ and hence $X = 0$ corresponds to a pristine environment.
When we treat X as flow, $X = 0$ occurs with zero flow of pollution. When we allow
pollution to accumulate in the biosphere we assume the (damaging) service flow is
proportional to the level of the stock. Taking this factor of proportionality to be one,
then X is the damaging service flow from the stock of pollution given by X.

A useful special case of $U(C, X)$ is the constant elasticity formulation where

$$U(C, X) = \frac{C^{1-\varepsilon}}{1-\varepsilon} - \frac{BX^\gamma}{\gamma} \quad \text{for } \varepsilon \neq 1,$$

$$U(C, X) = \ln C - \frac{BX^\gamma}{\gamma} \quad \text{for } \varepsilon = 1, \tag{49}$$

where $\gamma \geqslant 0$, $\varepsilon \geqslant 0$ and B measures the impact of local pollution on a representative
individual.

---

[58] Extensions of their framework to allow for purposeful innovation and a distinction between these two
forms of capital, along the lines of Grossman and Helpman (1991) or Aghion and Howitt (1998), seem both
feasible and worthwhile.

5.1.2. Technologies

The assumptions on production are standard. Each firm has access to a strictly concave and CRS production function linking labor and capital to output Y. The productivity of labor is augmented by a technology parameter T taken as given by individual agents. Following Romer (1986) and Lucas (1998) we assume the state of technology is proportional to an economy wide measure of activity. In Romer (1986) this aggregate measure is aggregate R&D, in Lucas (1998) it is average human capital levels; in AK specifications it is linked to either the aggregate capital stock or (to eliminate scale effects) average capital per worker. We assume T is proportional to the aggregate capital to labor ratio in the economy, K/L, and by choice of units take the proportionality constant to be one.[59]

5.1.3. From individual to aggregate production

Although we adopt a social planning perspective, it is instructive to review how firm level magnitudes aggregate to economy wide measures since this makes clear the assumptions made regarding the role of knowledge spillovers. We aggregate across firms to obtain the AK aggregate production function as follows:[60]

$$
\begin{aligned}
Y_i &= F(K_i, T L_i), \\
Y &= \sum_i F(K_i, T L_i), \\
Y &= T L F(K/T L, 1), \\
Y &= K F(1, 1) = A K,
\end{aligned}
\tag{50}
$$

where the first line gives firm level production; the second line sums across firms; the third uses linear homogeneity and exploits the fact that efficiency requires all firms adopt the same capital intensity. The last line follows from the definition of T.

Summarizing: diminishing returns at the firm level are undone by technological progress linked to aggregate capital intensity leaving the social marginal product of capital constant.

We now employ similar methods to generate the aggregate abatement technology. To start we note pollution is a joint product of output and we take this relationship to

---

[59] As is well known, one-sector models of endogenous growth blur the important distinction between physical capital and knowledge capital and force us to think of "capital" in very broad terms. Extensions of our framework along the lines of Grossman and Helpman (1991) or Aghion and Howitt (1998) seem both possible and worthwhile. These extensions would however add additional state variables making our examination of transition paths difficult.

[60] Implementing our planning solution by way of pollution taxes and subsidies to investment and abatement should be straightforward. We leave this to future work.

be proportional.[61] By choice of units we take the factor of proportionality to be one. Pollution emitted is equal to pollution created minus pollution abated. Abatement of pollution takes as inputs the flow of pollution, which is proportional to the gross flow of output Y^G, and abatement inputs denoted by Y^A. The abatement production function is standard: it is strictly concave and CRS. Therefore denoting pollution emitted by P, we can write pollution emitted by the ith firm as

$$P_i = Y_i^G - a(Y_i^G, Y_i^A). \tag{51}$$

Now consider a Romeresque approach where individual abatement efforts provide knowledge spillovers useful to others abating in the economy. To do so we again introduce a technology shift parameter Γ, and assume it raises the marginal product of abatement. To be consistent with our earlier treatment of technological progress in production we assume Γ is proportional to the average abatement intensity in the economy, Y^A/Y^G. Then much as before we have the individual to aggregate abatement technology transformation as

$$
\begin{aligned}
P_i &= Y_i^G - a(Y_i^G \Gamma, Y_i^A), \\
P_i &= Y_i^G [1 - \Gamma_a(1, Y_i^A/Y_i^G \Gamma)], \\
\sum_i P_i &= \sum_i Y_i^G [1 - \Gamma a(1, Y_i^A/Y_i^G \Gamma)], \\
P &= Y^G [1 - \Gamma a(1, 1)], \quad a(1, 1) > 1, \\
P &= Y^G [1 - \theta a(1, 1)], \quad \theta \equiv Y^A/Y^G,
\end{aligned}
\tag{52}
$$

where the first line introduces the technology parameter Γ; the second exploits linear homogeneity of the abatement production function; the third aggregates across firms; the fourth recognizes that efficiency requires all firms choose identical abatement intensities, uses the definition of Γ and notes that for abatement to be productive it must be able to clean up after itself. The fifth line defines the intensity of abatement, $\theta \equiv Y^A/Y^G$. Since abatement can only reduce the pollution flow we must have $\theta \leqslant 1/a(1, 1)$.[62]

It is important to note that the aggregate relationship between pollution and abatement given by the last line in (52) is consistent with empirical estimates finding rising marginal abatement costs at the firm level. Each individual firm has abatement costs

---

[61] Nothing is lost if we assume pollution is produced in proportion to the services of capital inputs. The service flow of capital is proportional to the stock of capital, and the stock of capital is proportional to output.

[62] Adding the possibility of investments in restoration would probably strengthen the case for sustainable growth. Abatement of pollution and restoration are however distinct activities. We imagine that a restoration production function would take as an input the current damage to the environment – our stock variable X – and then apply inputs to restore it. This is quite different from abatement which operates to lower the current flow of pollution by use of variable inputs.

given by foregone output used in abatement, and hence partially differentiating the second line of (52) and rearranging we find

$$\frac{\partial Y_i^A}{\partial P_i} = \frac{-1}{\partial a / \partial Y_i^A} < 0, \qquad \frac{\partial^2 Y_i^A}{\partial P_i^2} > 0. \tag{53}$$

Marginal abatement costs are rising at the firm level.

Marginal abatement costs at the society level, are however, constant. To see why totally differentiate (52) allowing Γ and individual abatement to both vary. We find

$$\frac{dY_i^A}{dP_i} = \frac{-1}{\partial a / \partial Y_i^A} - \frac{\partial a / \partial Y_i^G}{\partial a / \partial Y_i^A} \frac{d\Gamma}{dP_i}, \tag{54}$$

Γ is the average abatement intensity in the economy, which given identical firms, is just the abatement intensity for the typical ith firm. Using $\frac{d\Gamma}{dP_i} = [1 / Y_i^G][dY_i^A / dP_i]$ and rearranging (54) we obtain

$$\frac{dY_i^A}{dP_i} = -\frac{Y_i^A}{[[\partial a / \partial Y_i^A] Y_i^A + [\partial a / \partial Y_i^G] \Gamma Y_i^G]}$$

$$= -\frac{Y_i^A}{a(Y_i^A, \Gamma Y_i^G)} = -\frac{1}{a(1,1)} < 0, \tag{55}$$

where the first line follows from rearrangement and the second by CRS in abatement. The result given in (55) is identical to what we find by differentiating the aggregate relationship between pollution and abatement given in the last line of (52).

Summarizing: diminishing returns at the firm level, that lead to rising marginal abatement costs, are undone by technological progress linked to aggregate abatement intensity leaving the social marginal cost of abatement constant.

The formulations of learning by doing that we have adopted are extreme. In general we would expect the productivity in abatement (or production) to adjust gradually in response to a slow moving measure of knowledge capital. In the cases developed here however the productivity boost from an increased knowledge capital occurs instantaneously. So instead of Γ being a complicated function of the abatement intensities adopted in the infinite past history of the economy weighed by their relevance to productivity today, it is simply proportional to the current intensity. This is of course an abstraction, but a useful one since it frees us from keeping track of the evolution of two additional state variables (knowledge capital in abatement and knowledge capital in production), and allow us to capture the main feature of learning by doing models by linking the productivity of abatement to the intensity of this activity at the economy wide level. It also yields simple linear forms for production and abatement that add greatly to the model's tractability. This last features is especially important in a model where the stock of environmental quality has already raised the number of state variables to two.

Putting these pieces together our planner faces the aggregate production relations for output and abatement given by the last lines of (50) and (52) together with the atemporal resource constraint linking gross output, abatement and net production

$$Y = Y^G - Y^A. \tag{56}$$

The Kindergarten model is only one approach to modeling endogenous growth and environment interactions. Closely related approaches in an AK framework are those of Stokey (1998), Smulders (1994) and Smulders and Gradus (1996). These papers all adopt AK models, but end up with different conclusions. Early work in a one-sector framework by Smulders (1994) and Smulders and Gradus (1996) demonstrated how continuing economic growth and constant environmental quality are compatible in an AK model. In contrast, Stokey (1998) demonstrated how continuing growth and constant environmental quality are not possible within an AK set-up. The difference in their results comes from their different assumptions on abatement. To see why this is true, start with (51), ignore knowledge spillovers, and work forward using now familiar steps to find:

$$P_i = Y_i^G \phi(1-\theta), \quad \phi(\theta) \equiv \left[1 - a(1, 1-\theta)\right]. \tag{57}$$

Stokey employs the specific function form for ϕ given by $(1-\theta)^\beta$ for $\beta > 1$, and this implies the CRS abatement production function given by

$$a\left(Y_i^G, Y_i^A\right) = Y_i^G\left[1 - \left(1 - \frac{Y_i^A}{Y_i^G}\right)^\beta\right]. \tag{58}$$

Using (57) it is now easy to show abatement is subject to diminishing returns,

$$\frac{\partial P_i}{\partial Y_i^A} = -\beta(1-\theta)^{\beta-1} < 0, \qquad \frac{\partial^2 P_i}{\partial Y_i^{A2}} > 0$$

which implies marginal abatement costs are rising at the aggregate level. Setting $Y^A = 0$ we find the first unit of abatement lowers pollution by the amount $\beta > 1$, somewhat similar to our formulation where $a(1, 1) > 1$.[63] If we now combine (57) with (50), recall net output is $(1-\theta)$ times gross output, and introduce the variable $z = 1 - \theta$, we find the exact specification employed in Stokey (1998)

$$Y = AKz, \qquad P = AKz^\beta. \tag{59}$$

Stokey's (1998) result that growth is not possible follows from matching an AK aggregate production function with strictly n eoclassical assumptions on abatement adopted from Copeland and Taylor (1994). That is, if we think of the AK model as one of knowledge spillovers then Stokey has assumed these spillovers occur in production but not abatement. By doing so, she eliminates "technological progress" in abatement and this eliminates the possibility of sustainable growth.

---

[63] Since the marginal product of abatement is bounded at zero, Stokey (1998) shows no regulation is undertaken initially and pollution rises lock-step with output.

Comparing our approach to the work of Smulders is more difficult because abatement is not specifically modeled and he considers a variety of formulations. By specializing his framework to the AK paradigm we find

$$Y = \alpha K, \qquad P = \left[\frac{K}{A} \right]^{\gamma}. \qquad (60)$$

The first element is just a standard AK production function. The second relates what Smulders refers to as net or emitted pollution to the capital stock K, and abatement A. If we employ (60) and solve for emissions per unit of gross output we find

$$\frac{P}{Y} = \left[\frac{K}{A} \right]^{\gamma} \Big/ \alpha K. \qquad (61)$$

If the economy allocates a fixed fraction of its output to abatement, K/A is constant, and emissions per unit of gross output fall with the size of the economy. This reflects a strong degree of increasing returns. Moreover, the reader may note from (60) that pollution emitted goes to infinity as abatement goes to zero, which is inconsistent with pollution being a joint product of output. Therefore, Smulders and Gradus (1996) match AK aggregate production with assumptions on abatement ensuring increasing returns; and, in contrast with the Kindergarten specification, assume pollution is not a joint product of output.

5.1.4. Endowments

We treat pollution as a flow that either dissipates instantaneously – such as noise pollution – or a stock that is only eliminated over time by natural regeneration – such as lead emissions or radioactive waste. When X is a stock we have

$$\dot{X} = AK[1 - \theta a] - \eta X, \qquad (62)$$

where η represents the speed of natural regeneration, and where for economy of notation we have denoted $a(1, 1)$ by a. When X is a flow we have

$$X = AK[1 - \theta a].$$

5.1.5. The Kindergarten rule

We focus first on the possibility of balanced and continual growth, leaving to the next section a discussion of transition paths. Before we proceed with the formal analysis it proves instructive to step back slightly to consider the feasibility and optimality of sustainable growth. From our assumptions on abatement it is clear that if θ is set high enough all pollution emissions will be eliminated and we will enter a zero emission world. Therefore as long as $a > 1$ there will exist a $\theta < 1$ that generates zero emission technologies. And if $\theta < 1$ then some output will be left over for consumption and investment which will in turn drive growth in output. It appears then that feasibility is guaranteed by knowledge spillovers in abatement generating a constant marginal product.

The assumption of $a > 1$ is innocuous. Recall that abatement, like all other economic activities, pollutes. One unit of abatement creates one unit of pollution, but cleans up $a > 1$ units of pollution. It is only this surplus between costs and benefits, $1 - 1/a > 0$ that makes abatement useful at all! But even if growth is feasible, abatement is costly and this will cause drag as in our earlier formulations. The remaining questions for sustainability are how large is this drag, how much will it lower the return to capital, and what restrictions on preferences will be needed to generate sustainable growth.

To answer these questions consider the following problem:

$$\text{Maximize} \int_0^\infty U(C, X)e^{-\rho t} \, dt$$

$$\begin{aligned} \text{s.t.} \quad & K(0) = K_0, \qquad X(0) = X_0 \quad \text{and} \quad \theta \leqslant 1/a, \\ & \dot{K} = AK[1 - \theta] - \delta K - C, \\ & \dot{X} = AK[1 - \theta a] - \eta X, \end{aligned} \tag{63}$$

where we adopt $U(C, X)$ from (49). Recall the fraction of gross output allocated to abatement is θ and since the flow of pollution into the environment cannot be negative this will never exceed $1/a$. We can write the Hamilton–Jacobi–Bellman equation as

$$\begin{aligned} \rho W(K, X) = \text{Maximize} \Big\{ H = {} & \frac{C^{1-\varepsilon}}{1-\varepsilon} - \frac{BX^\gamma}{\gamma} \\ & + \lambda_1 \big[AK[1 - \theta] - \delta K - C \big] \\ & + \lambda_2 \big[AK[1 - \theta a] - \eta X \big] \Big\}, \end{aligned} \tag{64}$$

where $\rho W(K, X)$ is the maximized value of the program for the given initial conditions $\{K_0, X_0\}$, and H is the current value Hamiltonian for our problem. The controls for this problem are consumption C, and abatement intensity θ.

Observe the term involving our control variable, θ,

$$\text{Maximize} \big\{ AK\theta[-\lambda_1 - a\lambda_2] \big\} \quad \text{s.t.} \quad 0 \leqslant \theta \leqslant 1/a,$$

where λ_1 is the positive shadow value of capital and λ_2 is the negative shadow cost of pollution. Since the Hamiltonian is linear in θ, the value of the term $S = [-\lambda_1 - a\lambda_2]$ will largely determine the optimal level of abatement. When $S > 0$, the shadow cost of pollution is high relative to that of capital. In this case abatement is relatively cheap and maximal abatement will be undertaken. Conversely when $S < 0$ the shadow value of capital is high relative to that of pollution. In this case abatement is relatively expensive and zero abatement will occur. Finally, when $S = 0$, the shadow values are equated and active, but not necessarily maximal, abatement will occur. Therefore, the value of S determines when and if the economy switches from a zero-to-active-to-maximal abatement regime. We deal with these possibilities in turn.

Regardless of the value of S, the optimal level of consumption will always satisfy

$$\frac{\partial H}{\partial C} = C^{-\varepsilon} - \lambda_1 = 0 \tag{65}$$

although the shadow value of capital and its dynamic path may differ across regimes.

When $S > 0$, maximal abatement occurs and the dynamics are given by

$$
\begin{aligned}
&S > 0, \\
&\theta = \theta^K, \quad \theta^K \equiv 1/a, \\
&\dot{\lambda}_1 = -g\lambda_1, \quad g \equiv A\left[1 - \theta^K\right] - \delta - \rho, \\
&\dot{K} = [g + \rho]K - C(\lambda_1), \quad K(0) = K_0, C(\lambda_1) \equiv \lambda_1^{-1/\varepsilon}, \\
&\dot{\lambda}_2 = \lambda_2[\rho + \eta] + BX^{\gamma - 1}, \\
&\dot{X} = -\eta X, \quad X(0) = X_0.
\end{aligned} \tag{66}
$$

By choosing the intensity of abatement $\theta = \theta_K$ there are no net emissions of pollution and the environment improves at a rate given by natural regeneration. We dub θ_K "the Kindergarten rule" because when economies adopt the Kindergarten rule pollution is cleaned up when it is created.[64]

Alternatively, S may be exactly zero. In this case we have an interior solution for abatement, with the following dynamics:

$$
\begin{aligned}
&S = 0, \\
&\theta \in \left[0, \theta^K\right], \\
&\dot{\lambda}_1 = -g\lambda_1, \\
&\dot{K} = \left[A[1 - \theta] - \delta\right]K - C(\lambda_1), \quad K(0) = K_0, C(\lambda_1) \equiv \lambda_1^{-1/\varepsilon}, \\
&\dot{\lambda}_2 = \lambda_2[\rho + \eta] + BX^{\gamma - 1}, \\
&\dot{X} = AK[1 - a\theta] - \eta X, \quad X(0) = X_0.
\end{aligned} \tag{67}
$$

In this situation pollution is not completely abated, and hence the evolution of environmental quality reflects both the level of active abatement and natural regeneration. And finally, with no abatement at all we must have $S < 0$. Both pollution and output

---

[64] This is one of the most common rules taught in Kindergarten. For a list of common Kindergarten rules see *All I Really Need to Know I Learned in Kindergarten: Uncommon Thoughts on Common Things* by Robert Fulgham. Fulgham argues that the basic values we learned in grade school such as "clean up your own mess" (in effect our Kindergarten rule) and "play fair" are the bedrock of a meaningful life.

rise over time yielding

$$S < 0,$$
$$\theta \in 0,$$
$$\dot{\lambda}_1 = -\lambda_1[A - \delta - \rho] - \lambda_2 A,$$
$$\dot{K} = [A - \delta]K - C(\lambda_1), \quad K(0) = K_0, \, C(\lambda_1) \equiv \lambda_1^{-1/\varepsilon}, \tag{68}$$
$$\dot{\lambda}_2 = \lambda_2[\rho + \eta] + B X^{\gamma-1},$$
$$\dot{X} = AK - \eta X, \quad X(0) = X_0.$$

Consider growth paths with active abatement. Then from (67) and (66) we find the shadow value of capital falls over time at a constant exponential rate,

$$-g \equiv \frac{\dot{\lambda}_1}{\lambda_1} = -\big[A[1 - \theta^k] - \rho - \delta\big] < 0 \tag{69}$$

provided the net marginal product of capital, at the Kindergarten rule level of abatement, $A[1 - \theta_K]$, can cover both depreciation and impatience. We leave for now a detailed discussion of what this requires and assume it is true: $g > 0$. Then it is immediate that consumption rises at the constant rate $g_C = g/\varepsilon > 0$.

From the capital accumulation equations in both (66) and (67) we can now deduce that capital and output must grow at the same rate as consumption if θ is constant over time. To determine whether the intensity of abatement is constant over time, consider the accumulation equation for pollution

$$\dot{X} = AK[1 - \theta a] - \eta X. \tag{70}$$

There are two ways (70) can be consistent with balanced growth. The first possibility is that we have a maximal abatement regime where $S > 0$ holds everywhere along the balanced growth path. In this situation, K grows exponentially over time and θ is set to the Kindergarten rule level. Using (66), this balanced growth path must have

$$\dot{X} = -\eta X \quad \text{and} \quad \theta = \theta^k. \tag{71}$$

In this scenario, the environment improves at the rate η over time and abatement is a constant fraction of output $1 > \theta_K > 0$. As time goes to infinity the economy approaches a pristine level of environmental quality. Therefore the balanced growth path exhibits constant growth in consumption, output, capital and environmental quality. Consumption is a constant fraction of output and we have

$$g_c = g_k = g_y = g/\varepsilon > 0, \qquad g_x = -\eta < 0. \tag{72}$$

A second possibility is that abatement is active but not maximal. Define the deviation of abatement from the Kindergarten rule as $D(\theta) = (\theta_K - \theta)/\theta_K$. Using this definition rewrite (70) to find

$$\frac{\dot{X}}{X} = \frac{AK[D(\theta)]}{X} - \eta. \tag{73}$$

It is apparent that if the deviation of abatement from the Kindergarten rule fell exponentially, then it may be possible for X to fall exponentially while K rises. That is, in obvious notation, a possible balanced growth path would have

$$g_k + g_D = g_x < 0. \tag{74}$$

In this situation abatement is at an interior solution at all times and becomes progressively tighter over time approaching the Kindergarten rule asymptotically. The inflow of pollution from production into the environment is always positive but environmental quality improves nevertheless. This intuitive description suggests that the possibility of this outcome must rely on both the pace of economic growth and the ability of the environment to regenerate. This is indeed the case as Brock and Taylor (2003) show that a necessary condition for us to remain in an $S = 0$ regime is simply

$$\eta(\gamma - 1) > g. \tag{75}$$

This condition reflects two different requirements. The first is simply that γ cannot equal one. If it did then the (instantaneous) marginal disutility of pollution is a constant and λ_2 is a constant as well. This would also imply that consumption be fixed as well. This is inconsistent with growth of any sort.

Assuming γ not equal to one is necessary for balanced growth with an interior solution for abatement. But a second condition must also hold. Natural regeneration, η, must be sufficiently large relative to the growth rate g. If the rate of regeneration is high and growth rates quite low, then the optimal plan is to use nature's regenerative abilities to partially offset the costs of abating because the shadow value of foregone output is high in slow growth situations. Conversely, if regeneration is low and the growth rate g relatively high, then no amount of abatement short of the Kindergarten rule will hold pollution to acceptable levels.

This intuition suggests a natural corollary for the case of flow pollutants. If pollution has only a flow cost it is "as if" the environment is regenerating itself infinitely fast. This intuition suggests that as we let η get large, the results in the stock pollutant case should replicate those for a flow. This intuition is, in fact, correct. Brock and Taylor prove that when $g > 0$ and X is a flow pollutant, then sustainable economic growth with an ever improving environment is possible and optimal. With a flow pollutant, if $\gamma > 1$, then the intensity of abatement approaches the Kindergarten rule level of abatement, θ_K, asymptotically. Alternatively, if $\gamma = 1$, then $\theta = \theta_K$ everywhere along the balanced growth path.

These results are important in showing how the Kindergarten rule generates sustainable growth. Sustainable growth requires two conditions. The first is that $g > 0$. The assumption $g > 0$ requires the marginal product of capital, adjusted for the ongoing costs of abatement, be sufficiently high. A necessary condition is that $A[1 - \theta_K]$ be positive, but this is guaranteed as long as abatement is a productive activity. Given abatement is productive, we still require the adjusted marginal product of capital, $A[1 - \theta_K]$, to offset both impatience and depreciation. If abatement is not very productive, then $1/a$ will be close to one and growth cannot occur. If capital is not very productive or if the level of impatience and depreciation are high then ongoing economic growth cannot occur. These are however very standard requirements for growth under any circumstances; therefore our addition of the further requirement that abatement be productive seems both innocuous and natural in our setting.[65]

The second is that $h = g(1 - 1/\varepsilon) + \rho > 0$. This condition is the standard sufficiency condition for the existence of an optimum path in an AK model with power utility.[66] This condition is of course weaker than that needed in earlier models generating declining pollution levels. For example, ε is just σ in the CRRA specification we used earlier and we have already seen that Stokey (1998), Lopez (1994) and other require $\sigma > 1$ to generate declining emissions. Here the requirement is far weaker and this follows from the fact that consumer's are not required to make larger and larger sacrifices in consumption to fund an every growing abatement program.

5.2. Empirical implications

The Kindergarten model relies heavily on the assumed role of technological progress in staving off diminishing returns to both capital formation and abatement. It is impossible to know a priori whether technological progress can indeed be so successful and hence it is important to distinguish between two types of predictions before proceeding. The first class of predictions are those regarding behavior at or near the balanced growth path. This set has received little attention in the empirical literature on the environment and growth, although balanced growth path predictions and their testing are at the core of empirical research in growth theory proper [see the review by Durlauf and Quah (1999)]. The second set of predictions concern the transition from inactive to active abatement and these are related to the empirical work on the Environmental Kuznets Curve. [See Grossman and Krueger (1993, 1995) and the review by Barbier (1997).]

5.3. Balanced growth path predictions

Using our previous results it is straightforward to show that near the balanced growth path we must have: convergence in the quality of the environment across all countries sharing parameter values but differing in initial conditions; the share of pollution abatement costs in output approaching a positive constant less than one; overall emissions rates falling and environmental quality rising; and emissions per unit output falling

---

[65] In Keeler, Spence and Zeckhauser (1972) a similar condition describes their Golden Age capital stock. In their model with no endogenous growth the Golden Age capital stock is defined by (in our notation) the equality $f'(K)[1 - 1/a] - \delta = \rho$ simulations of the model assume a to be 12 (see p. 22). Chimeli and Braden (2005) assume a similar condition. Both studies assume abatement or clean up is a linear function of effort thereby ignoring the reality of diminishing returns and the necessity of ongoing technological progress.

[66] Denote the growth rate in an AK model with power utility by g^*, then in terms of our parameters we have $g^* = g/\varepsilon$ and the standard condition is $\rho + (\varepsilon - 1)g^*$. This is equivalent to $h > 0$. See Aghion and Howitt [1998, Eq. (5.3)].

as production processes adopt methods that approach zero emission technologies. The model also presents predictions for the intensity of abatement that we discuss subsequently.

Whether the cross-country predictions will be borne out by empirical work is as yet unknown but an examination of U.S. data shows the model's strongest predictions – those regarding falling emissions and improving environmental quality – are not grossly at odds with available U.S. data. The most favorable evidence for the model is the slow movement in pollution abatement costs in the face of dramatically declining pollution levels. The model explains this feature of the data by recourse to specifics of the abatement function that hold abatement costs down much as exogenous technological progress does in the Green Solow model.

The prediction of declining emission intensities along the balanced growth path is consistent with the data shown in Figure 1, but as in Stokey (1998) the model only predicts declining emissions to output ratios after regulation begins.

5.4. The Environmental Catch-up Hypothesis

We have so far focused on balanced growth paths but the large EKC literature concerns itself with what must be transition paths towards some BGP. To examine these predictions and these always exhibited active abatement. It is however natural to ask predictions we present several transition paths in Figure 12. One of these paths is that of a Poor country having small initial capital K^P but a pristine environment. The other is the path of a Rich country starting again with a pristine environment but with a much larger initial capital K^R. Each economy starts with a pristine environment in Stage I and grows. During this stage there is no pollution regulation: the environment deteriorates, X rises, and the capital stock grows until the trajectory hits the Switching Locus labeled SL. Once the economy hits the Switching Locus active regulation begins and the economy enters Stage II.[67]

It is apparent from the figure that the Poor country experiences the greatest environmental degradation at its peak, and at any given capital stock, (i.e. income level) the initially Poor country has worse environmental quality than the Rich. Moreover, since both Rich and Poor economies start with pristine environments, the qualities of their environments at first diverge and then converge. This is the Environmental Catch-up Hypothesis.

Divergence occurs because the opportunity cost of abatement (and consumption) is much higher in capital poor countries. A high shadow price of capital leads to less

---

[67] Brock and Taylor (2003) show the exact position and shape of the locus depend on whether parameters satisfy the fast growth or slow growth scenario. For the most part we will proceed under the assumption that economic growth is fast relative to environmental regeneration; that is (75) fails strongly and we have $\eta(\gamma - 1) > g$. This implies $\theta(t) = \theta_K$ everywhere along the balanced growth path (Figure 12 implicitly assumes this result). For illustrative purposes we will sometimes discuss the parallel flow case [where we can think of η approaching infinity but (75) failing because $\gamma = 1$].

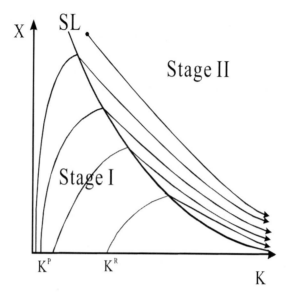

Figure 12. Transition paths.

consumption, more investment and rapid industrialization in the Poor country. Nature's ability to regenerate is overwhelmed. The quality of the environment falls precipitously. In capital rich countries the opportunity cost of capital is lower: consumption is greater and investment less. Industrialization is less rapid and natural regeneration has time to work. The peak level of environmental degradation in the Rich country is therefore much smaller. But once we enter Stage II abatement is undertaken and since abatement is an investment in improving the environment, it is only undertaken when the rate of return on this investment equals (or exceeds) the rate of return on capital. Since economies are identical, except for initial conditions, rates of return are the same across all countries in Stage II. Equalized rates of return require equal percentage reductions in the pollution stock. Therefore absolute differences in environmental quality present at the beginning of Stage II disappear over time.

Note how similar this intuition for the ECH is to that given for the EKC prediction in the Green Solow model. In the Green Solow model initially rapid growth overwhelms nature's ability to dissipate pollution starting from its initial position at a biological equilibrium. Eventually growth slows and the environment's regenerative powers restore its quality slowly over time. Growth is initially rapid in the Solow model because of diminishing returns. In the Kindergarten model, growth is initially rapid because there is no regulation and no drag from pollution policy to lower the marginal product of capital. And once regulation is active, growth slows because regulation lowers the net marginal product of capital. The environment's regenerative powers then restore its quality slowly over time. Both explanations have nature overwhelmed early on and both give prominent roles to a declining marginal product of capital.

The discussions above, and Figure 12, assume the fast-growth–slow-regeneration as-sumptions hold. We chose this case to discuss and illustrate because it illustrates the forces at work very clearly. Since many of the same conclusions hold when growth is relatively slow we only provide a sketch here of some differences. There is again a Switching Locus which divides Stage I from Stage II. The Switching Locus again de-fines a unique X^* that is declining in K^*. The most important difference is that once a trajectory of the system hits this new Switching Locus it remains within it forever. If the economy is below the locus then abatement is inactive and K rises at a rapid rate: X in-creases rapidly until the Switching Locus is reached in finite time. If the initial (K, X) is above the locus, maximal abatement is undertaken but this drives down the shadow cost of pollution very quickly and we again hit the locus, this time, from above.

Once on the locus, countries remain trapped within it thereafter and this implies the economy's choice of abatement remains interior; i.e. the trajectory follows along the Switching Locus maintaining $MAC = MD(K, X)$ throughout. Over time abatement rises and the intensity of abatement approaches the Kindergarten rule in the limit. There-fore, the slow growth case is very similar except that the model now predicts an strong form of convergence. All transition paths remain on the Switching Locus once active abatement begins; therefore policy active countries share the same path for environmen-tal quality and income levels in Stage II.

5.5. The ECH and the EKC

Brock and Taylor prove that economies follow the Stage I–Stage II life cycle pro-ducing an EKC like relationship between income and environmental quality.[68] Their income and growth prediction is however somewhat different from a standard EKC result. They predict that countries differentiated only by initial capital exhibit initial di-vergence in environmental quality followed by eventual convergence.[69] Moreover, as Figure 12 makes clear countries make the transition to active abatement at different in-come and peak pollution levels. This of course throws into question empirical methods seeking to estimate a unique income-pollution path. More constructively it suggests that an important feature of the data may well be a large variance in environmental quality at relatively low-income levels with little variance at high incomes. Empirical work by Carson, Jean and McCubbin (1997) relating air toxics to U.S. state income levels is supportive of this conjecture:

---

[68] The addition of perfect capital markets can affect the pollution and income path greatly. To a certain extent a country is running down its environment initially to accumulate capital. With *perfect* capital markets it is possible to eliminate Stage I entirely in some cases. Given many less developed countries have very limited and imperfect access to capital markets it is difficult to know the empirical importance of this result. It suggests however that access to capital markets may be an excluded country characteristic in EKC style regressions.

[69] It is possible to show X is rising throughout Stage I and this ensures points along the Switching Locus do indeed represent peaks in pollution levels.

Without exception, the high-income states have low per capita emissions while emissions in the lower-income states are highly variable. We believe that this may be the most interesting feature of the data to explore in future work. It suggests that it may be difficult to predict emission levels for countries just starting to enter the phase, where per capita emissions are decreasing with income (pp. 447–448).

In some cases however, (initially) Rich and Poor will make the transition at the same income level but still exhibit our Catch-up Hypothesis. To investigate, we report the switching locus in the fast growth case. It takes on an especially simple form given by

$$MAC = \frac{1}{a} = \frac{B}{[\rho + \gamma \eta]} X^{*\gamma - 1}[hK]^\varepsilon = MD\big(K^*, X^*\big) \qquad (76)$$

which is the downward sloping and convex relationship between pollution and capital depicted in Figure 12. The left-hand side of (76) represents marginal abatement costs. The right-hand side is marginal damage evaluated at $\{K^*, X^*\}$. Marginal damage is increasing in the pollution stock provided γ exceeds one, and since the flow of national (and per capita) income Y is always proportional to K, it is apparent that the income elasticity of marginal damage with respect to flow income is given by ε. Large values of ε correspond to the strong income effects referred to earlier.

Let γ approach one. Then the slope of the Switching Locus approaches infinity and all countries attain their peak pollution levels at the same K^*. But even with a common turning point differences in environmental quality remain. Moreover, these are not simple level differences because countries initially diverge and then converge after crossing K^*. To eliminate our catch-up hypothesis we must assume regeneration is infinitely fast: X is a flow. In this case Brock and Taylor show the Switching Locus is again vertical at a given K^*. More importantly, since pollution is proportional to production before K^*, and policies are identical after K^*: initial conditions no longer matter.

These results tell us that when pollution is strictly a flow, all countries share the same income-pollution path. We have generated an EKC, and empirical methods used to estimate a unique income-pollution path are appropriate. But when pollution does not dissipate instantaneously, initial conditions matter. We have the Environmental Catch-up Hypothesis, and empirical methods must now account for the persistent role of initial conditions.[70] It is easy to see the two hypotheses are mutually exclusive and exhaustive.

5.6. Pollution characteristics

The ECH focuses on cross-country comparisons in pollution levels, but says little about how predictions vary with pollutant characteristics. And while most authors have focused on generating an EKC relationship there has been very little work examining

---

[70] This result may explain why empirical research investigating the EKC has been far more successful with air pollutants like SO_2, than with water pollutants or other long lasting stocks [see the review by Barbier (1997)].

how these predictions vary with pollutant characteristics. This is unfortunate since there is good data in the U.S. and elsewhere that could be fruitfully employed to test within country but across pollutant predictions. This is especially important since many models can generate the EKC result.

To demonstrate the Kindergarten model's across pollutant predictions consider regeneration first and start from a position where $\eta = 0$ (radioactive waste). Brock and Taylor (2003) show that the Switching Locus in Figure 12 shifts outwards as we raise η. The response is to delay action and allow the environment to deteriorate further. Once we raise η sufficiently the economy eventually enters the fast regeneration regime and here we find abatement delayed in another manner – it is introduced slowly by the now gradual implementation of the Kindergarten rule. Faster regeneration then implies that countries either begin abatement at higher income levels or allow their environments to deteriorate more before taking action. Surprisingly, fast regeneration will be associated with lower and not higher environmental quality – at least over some periods of time or ranges of income.[71]

A change in regeneration rates also affects the pace of abatement. If a pollutant has a long life in the environment, then once abatement begins it is clear that natural regeneration can play only a small role. Consequently the optimal plan calls for an initial period of inaction before starting a very aggressive abatement regime: the immediate adoption of the Kindergarten rule. When η is relatively large we are in the fast regeneration regime and abatement is intensified gradually and only approaches the Kindergarten rule level in the limit.

Putting the predictions for the timing and intensity of abatement together, Brock and Taylor find that very long-lived pollutants should be addressed early with their complete elimination compressed in time. It is optimal to delay action on short-lived pollutants and adopt only a gradual program of abatement. This description of optimal behavior is of course consonant with the historical record in several instances where long-lived chemical discharges and gas emissions were eliminated very quickly by legislation, whereas short-lived criteria pollutants have seen active regulation but not elimination over the last 30 years.

Pollutants also differ in their toxicity. The marginal disutility of toxics could exceed those classified as irritants, and damages from toxics may rise more steeply with exposure. The first feature of toxics implies their abatement should come early. This is clear from (76) where increases in B shift the Switching Locus inwards and hasten

---

[71] An especially colorful example of delay in abatement caused by rapid natural regeneration is that of the City of Victoria in British Columbia. Every day, the Victoria Capital Regional District (CRD) dumps approximately 100,000 cubic meters of sewage into the Juan de Fuca Strait. Scientific studies have long argued that since the sewage is pumped through long outfalls into cold, deep, fast moving water there is no need for treatment. The CRD has always used these studies to delay building a treatment facility. Current plans are for secondary treatment to begin in 2020, but until then over 40 square kilometers of shoreline remains closed to shell fishing. Background information can be found at the Sierra Legal Defense fund site *http://www.sierralegal.org/m_archive/1998-9/bk99_02_04.htm*.

abatement. Surprisingly very convex marginal damages (a high γ) call for the gradual and not aggressive elimination of pollution. The logic is that any reduction in the concentration of toxics has a large impact on marginal damage. Therefore, only by lowering emissions slowly can we match a steeply declining value of marginal reductions with a falling opportunity cost of abatement. Therefore, although toxics may have large absolute negative impacts on welfare, this argues for their early, but not necessarily aggressive, abatement.

And finally how does the income elasticity of the demand for environmental quality (ε) affects the onset and pace of regulation? We have already shown that the restriction of $\varepsilon > 1$ is not needed to generate sustainable growth. This parameter does however have a role to play in determining the timing of regulation. To illustrate its role consider the fast growth regime and let the gross marginal product of capital, A, rise. This necessarily raises g and if $\varepsilon > 1$, the Switching Locus shifts in. Abatement is hastened. When $\varepsilon < 1$, abatement is delayed and peak pollution levels shift right.[72] A similar set of results holds for increases in the productivity of abatement although there is an additional conflicting force. Therefore, in contrast to earlier work Brock and Taylor (2003) finds that the income elasticity of marginal damage has an important role to play in determining the income level at which abatement occurs and the resulting pollution level, but virtually no role in determining if the environment will improve nor its rate of improvement.

6. Conclusion and suggestions for future research

The relationship between economic growth and the environment is not well understood: we have only limited understanding of the basic science involved – be it physical or economic – and we have very limited data. In this review we have tried to evaluate ongoing efforts, both theoretical and empirical, to understand this relationship. We started by introducing definitions for the scale, composition and technique effects of growth on pollution, and then constructed three simple theoretical models to highlight the role each can play in generating sustainable growth. Throughout we have tried to link these models to the existing literature and in a very rudimentary way evaluated their predictions using data on pollution emissions, abatement costs and resource prices.

This is a research topic on the periphery of growth theory proper. It placement reflects the lack of a core model to work with and the paucity of data for empirical analyses. This is unfortunate because an understanding of the relationship between economic growth and the environment may be key to long run prosperity; it is certainly of interest to developing country governments searching for a balance between material growth and environmental protection, and it is also of great interest in the developed world given current debates over global warming, its costs, and the costs of its amelioration.

---

[72] Our use of the terms delayed or hastened does not refer to calendar time, but rather to whether actions occur at a higher or lower income level.

Our review has revealed much heterogeneity in terms of approach and methods used in theoretical work. Some heterogeneity is to be expected, but too much dissipates effort. By examining the pollution creation and abatement process in some detail we hoped to direct future efforts more productively. We showed that standard assumptions such as CRS and concavity of the abatement production function lead to tractable formulations where pollution emissions appear in much the same way as other factors. By doing so we were able to show how we can evaluate the costs of environmental policy in a manner similar to that used to evaluate the drag of natural resources on growth. By making this connection precise we provided a bridge between the early resources and growth literature of the 1970s with the recent literature on pollution and income. We also hope to instill in others the need to provide micro foundations for assumptions over the amount of pollution emitted or abated in production, since we have repeatedly shown the importance of these assumptions for a model's ability to generate sustainable growth.

Our theoretical review contains three main messages. The first comes directly from our Green Solow model where we showed how the typical convergence properties of the neoclassical model together with a standard natural regeneration function yield an Environmental Kuznets Curve. This suggests that efforts to explain the EKC via complicated processes of political economy, IRS, freer trade, and differential factor growth, etc. may be unnecessary. At the very least it points out that the interplay of natural and Solow growth dynamics certainly work towards this finding.

Our second message concerns drag. We have shown throughout that efforts to limit pollution and raise environmental quality create a drag on growth rates. This finding was stronger in some cases since rapid population growth could eliminate the possibility of sustainable growth entirely. The drag calculations we provided are for illustration and not meant to substitute for more serious enquiry that must include empirical estimation of key parameters. Nevertheless these calculations are helpful in focusing our efforts on key parameters (the share of emissions in final good production or the rate of change in pollution abatement costs), and demonstrate how difficult it is to generate sustainable growth in a country with significant population growth. The calculations also offer a quick litmus test; if a specification suggests environmental policy reduces growth by 40%, something is surely amiss. It is hoped that drag calculations of the type we have conducted become a more standard feature in the literature.

Finally, we have shown how different assumptions on abatement can produce very different results for sustainability (recall the contradictory results of Smulders and Stokey in the AK model). To a certain extent progress in this literature has been slowed because researchers have too many degrees of freedom in choosing their specification. Some restrictions are imposed by the requirement of a balanced growth path, but this still leaves much leeway to the researcher. We have adopted a consistent specification of pollution creation and abatement based on the common, if not innocuous, assumptions of constant returns, concavity and pollution being a joint product of output. Within these confines we have then argued that technological progress in abatement, distinct from that in final goods, is key to generating sustainable growth at reasonable costs. By identifying this as a key requirement we hope to direct future research efforts towards a theory of induced innovation where both relative prices and pollution regulations determine the pace and direction of improvements in abatement technology.

Our review of empirical work shows that the existing literature has made relatively few contributions to our understanding. The Environmental Kuznets Curve stands out as a key empirical regularity, but continued progress in this area can only come with a more serious consideration of other related data. One contribution of this review has been to show that many of the theoretical models capable of generating an EKC also contain predictions in other directions that are worthy of examination. The simple Green Solow model had strong predictions for the emission intensity of GDP; the Stokey Alternative contained sharp predictions about the time profile of abatement costs; the Source-and-Sink model contained links between energy prices, energy use, and pollution levels; and finally, the Kindergarten model produced a cross-country catch-up hypothesis as well as yielding several within-country but across-pollutant predictions. Further real progress in our understanding can only come from a tighter connection between theory and data.

This review has been limited by its focus. It has been a review of work linking industrial pollution and growth with only small asides to consider natural resource use. In many cases the formal structure of the models resembled those in the renewable resource literature, but we did not provide a review of findings there. As such we have sidestepped the rather thorny issues of property rights protection and the efficiency of environmental policies. We have done so not because we believe that these issues do not merit attention, but rather because adding a useful discussion of these topics would make this review unwieldy. It should be emphasized however that a common feature of the resources we examined was their well-defined property rights. This is true for air quality when the quality is determined by local pollution; and it is true of oil and other energy resources.

There are however an important class of resources where property rights enforcement is lax or where no property rights exist at all. Property rights problems arise in three main areas. These are: local and transnational fisheries; the global atmospheric commons; and lastly, the forest stocks in many developing countries. It is somewhat ironic that these renewable resources are under far more threat than the so-called exhaustible resources such as oil, gas or minerals. The reason for this is inescapable: the diffuse nature of many of these resources has led to a lack of property rights and very little management. Therefore, while our focus on industrial pollution is perhaps defensible in that it determines the air quality and health prospects for hundreds of millions of people across the globe, we should not forget other vexing problems arising from the lack of property rights. And while our data and the existing empirical results suggest that many local pollution problems are well in hand or respond well to increases in incomes brought about by growth, global pollution problems, such as global warming, are far more difficult to solve.[73] Therefore, it may be that the real threat to continued

---

[73] See Schmalensee, Stoker and Judson (1998) and Holtz-Eakin and Selden (1995).

growth arises not from the relatively small drag introduced by existing environmental policies, but from the absence of new policies to stem more serious global problems.

References

Aghion, P., Howitt, P. (1998). Endogenous Growth Theory. MIT Press, Cambridge, MA.

Andreoni, J., Levinson, A. (2001). "The simple analytics of the Environmental Kuznets Curve". Journal of Public Economics 80 (2), 269–286.

Antweiler, A., Copeland, B., Taylor, M.S. (2001). "Is free trade good for the environment". American Economic Review 94 (1), 877–908.

Arrow, K. (1962). "The economic implications of learning by doing". The Review of Economic Studies 29 (3), 155–173.

Barbier, E. (1997). "Environmental Kuznets Curve special issue: Introduction". Environment and Development Economics 2, 369–381.

Barnett, H.J., Morse, C. (1963). Scarcity and Growth: The Economics of Natural Resource Availability. Johns Hopkins University Press, Baltimore.

Barret, S., Graddy, K. (2000). "Freedom, growth, and the environment". Environment and Development Economics 5, 433–456.

Bovenberg, A.L., Smulders, S. (1995). "Environmental quality and pollution augmenting technological change in a two sector endogenous growth model". Journal of Public Economics 57, 369–391.

Brander, J.A., Taylor, M.S. (1998). "The simple economics of Easter Island: A Ricardo–Malthus model of renewable resource use". American Economic Review 88 (1), 119–138.

Brock, W.A. (1977). "A polluted Golden Age". In: Smith, V.L. (Ed.), Economics of Natural and Environmental Resources. Gordon and Breach Science Publishers, London, pp. 441–462.

Brock, W.A., Taylor, M.S. (2003). "The Kindergarten Rule for sustainable growth". NBER Working Paper w9597, April.

Brock, W.A., Taylor, M.S. (2004). "The Green Solow model". NBER Working Paper w10557, June.

Carson, R.T., Jean, Y., McCubbin, D. (1997). "The relationship between air pollution emission and income: U.S. Data". Environment and Development Economics 2 (4), 433–450.

Chimeli, A.B., Braden, J.B. (2005). "Total factor productivity and the environmental Kuznets Curve". Journal of Environmental Economics and Management 49 (2), 366–380.

Clark, C. (1990). Mathematical Bioeconomics. Wiley, New York.

Copeland, B.R., Taylor, M.S. (1994). "North–South trade and the environment". Quarterly Journal of Economics 109, 755–787.

Copeland, B.R., Taylor, M.S. (2003). Trade and the Environment: Theory and Evidence. Princeton University Press, Princeton, NJ.

Dasgupta, P., Heal, G. (1979). Economic Theory and Exhaustible Resources. Cambridge Economic Handbooks. Cambridge University Press, Cambridge.

Dasgupta, P., Maler, K. (2003). "The economics of non-convex ecosystems: Introduction". Environmental and Resource Economics 26 (4), 499–602.

Dechert, W.D. (Ed.) (2001). Growth Theory, Nonlinear Dynamics and Economic Modeling. Edward Elgar, Cheltenham.

Durlauf, S.N., Quah, D.T. (1999). "The new empirics of economic growth". In: Taylor, J.B., Woodford, M. (Eds.), Handbook of Macroeconomics, vol. 1. Elsevier Science, Amsterdam, pp. 235–308 (Chapter 4).

EPA (1990). Environmental Investments: The Cost of a Clean Environment.

Forster, B.A. (1973). "Optimal capital accumulation in a polluted environment". Southern Economic Journal 39, 544–547.

Gale, L., Mendez, J.A. (1998). "A note on the relationship between, trade, growth, and the environment". International Review of Economics and Finance 7 (1), 53–61.

Grossman, G.M., Krueger, A.B. (1993). "Environmental impacts of a North American free trade agreement". In: Garber, P. (Ed.), The US–Mexico Free Trade Agreement. MIT Press, Cambridge, MA, pp. 57–125.

Grossman, G.M., Krueger, A.B. (1995). "Economic growth and the environment". Quarterly Journal of Economics 110 (2), 353–377.

Grossman, G.M., Helpman, E. (1991). Innovation and Growth in the Global Economy. MIT Press, Cambridge, MA.

Harbaugh, W., Levinson, A., Wilson, D.M. (2002). "Reexamining the empirical evidence for an Environmental Kuznets Curve". The Review of Economics and Statistics 84 (3), 541–551.

Hartwick, J.M. (1977). "Intergenerational equity and the investing of rents from exhaustible resources". American Economic Review 67 (5), 972–974.

Hilton, H., Levinson, A. (1998). "Factoring the Environmental Kuznets Curve: Evidence from automotive lead emissions". Journal of Environmental Economics and Management 35, 126–141.

Holtz-Eakin, D., Selden, T. (1995). "Stoking the fires? CO_2 emissions and economic growth". Journal of Public Economics 57, 85–101.

Hotelling, H. (1931). "The Economics of Exhaustible Resources". Journal of Political Economy 39 (April), 137–175.

Jaffe, A.B., Peterson, S.R., Portney, P.R. (1995). "Environmental regulation and the competitiveness of U.S. manufacturing: What does the evidence tell us?". Journal of Economic Literature 33 (1), 132–163.

Jones, C.I. (2002). Introduction to Economic Growth, second ed. W.W. Norton & Company, New York.

Jones, L.E., Manuelli, R.E. (2001). "Endogenous policy choice: The case of pollution and growth". Review of Economic Dynamics 4 (2), 245–517.

Jorgenson, D.W., Wilcoxen, P.W. (1990). "Environmental regulation and U.S. economic growth". RAND Journal of Economics 21, 314–340.

Kaufman, R.F. (2004). "The mechanisms for autonomous energy efficiency increases: A cointegration analysis of US energy/GDP ratio". The Energy Journal 25 (1), 121–144.

Keeler, E., Spence, M., Zeckhauser, R. (1972). "The optimal control of pollution". Journal of Economic Theory 4, 19–34.

Levinson, A., Taylor, M.S. (2003). "Unmasking the pollution haven effect". Paper Presented at the NBER Environmental Economics Meetings, Boston, Summer. Available at http://www.ssc.wisc.edu/~staylor/.

Lopez, R. (1994). "The environment as a factor of production: The effects of economic growth and trade liberalization". Journal of Environmental Economics and Management 27, 163–184.

Lucas, R.E. (1998). "On the mechanics of economic development". Journal of Monetary Economics 22, 3–42.

Meadows, D.H., Meadows, D.L., Randers, J., Behrens, W.W. (1972). The Limits to Growth. Universe Books, New York.

Meadows, D.H., Meadows, D.L., Randers, J. (1991). Beyond the Limits. Earthscan Publications, London.

McConnell, K.E. (1997). "Income and the demand for environmental quality". Environment and Development Economics 2, 383–399.

Newell, R.G., Jaffe, A.B., Stavins, R.N. (1999). "The induced innovation hypothesis and energy saving technological change". Quarterly Journal of Economics 114 (3), 941–975.

Nordhaus, W. (1992). "Lethal model 2: The limits to growth revisited". Brookings Papers on Economic Activity 2, 1–59.

Popp, D. (2002). "Induced innovation and energy prices". American Economic Review 92 (1), 160–180.

Romer, P. (1986). "Increasing returns and long run growth". Journal of Political Economy 94 (October), 1002–1037.

Schmalensee, R., Stoker, T.M., Judson, R.A. (1998). "World carbon dioxide emissions: 1950–2050". The Review of Economics and Statistics 80 (1), 15–27.

Scheffer, M., Carpenter, S.R. (2003). "Catastrophic regime shifts in ecosystems: Linking theory to observation". Trends in Ecology and Evolution 18 (12), 648–656.

Selden, T., Song, D. (1994). "Environmental quality and development: Is there a Kuznets curve for air pollution emissions?". Journal of Environmental Economics and Management 27, 147–162.

Shafik, N., Bandyopadhyay, S. (1994). Economic Growth and Environmental Quality: Time Series and Cross Country Evidence. The World Bank, Washington, DC.

Slade, M.E. (1987). "Trends in Natural Resource commodity prices: An analysis in the time domain". Journal of Environmental Economics and Management 9, 122–137.

Smulders, J. (1994). Growth Market Structure and the Environment: Essays on the Theory of Endogenous Economic Growth. Tilburg University, Tilburg.

Smulders, S. (1999). "Endogenous growth theory and the environment". In: van den Berg, J.C.J.M. (Ed.), Handbook of Environmental and Resource Economics. Edward Elgar, Cheltenham, pp. 610–621.

Smulders, S., Gradus, R. (1996). "Pollution abatement and long-term growth". European Journal of Political Economy 12, 505–532.

Solow, R.M. (1974). "Intergenerational equity and exhaustible resources". Review of Economic Studies 41 (Symposium), 29–46.

Solow, R. (1973). "Is the end of the world at hand". Challenge 2 (March–April), 39–50.

Stiglitz, J. (1974). "Growth with exhaustible natural resources: Efficient and optimal growth paths". In: The Review of Economic Studies, vol. 41. Symposium on the Economics of Exhaustible Resources, pp. 123–137.

Stokey, N. (1998). "Are there limits to growth". International Economic Review 39 (1), 1–31.

Sue Wing, I., Eckhaus, R.S. (2003). "The energy intensity of US production: Sources of long-run change". Paper Presented at the 5th USAEE/IAEE Session of the Allied Social Science Association meeting, January 4, Washington, DC.

Tahvonen, O., Kuuluvainen, J. (1991). "Optimal growth with renewable resources and pollution". European Economic Review 35, 650–661.

Vogan, C.R. (1996). "Pollution abatement and control expenditures: 1972–94". Survey of Current Business (September), 48–67.

AUTHOR INDEX

n indicates citation in a footnote.

Aaronson, E. 1680n
Aaronson, S. 1354n
Abdel-Rahman, H. 1564, 1565, 1570, 1574
Ableidinger, J., *see* Case, A. 518n
Aboud, A., *see* Barrett, C.B. 339, 355
Abowd, J.M. 1331n
Abraham, A. 1306n
Abramovitz, M. 198, 212, 582, 590, 604, 781,
  784, 804, 806
Acemoglu, D. 71n, 99, 102n, 120n, 130, 131,
  135, 136, 138n, 140–143, 150, 150n, 154n,
  193n, 223n, 277, 277n, 278, 302, 326, 349,
  357, 393, 395, 395n, 397n, 398, 402, 410,
  413, 414, 417, 417n, 419, 422–424, 428, 430,
  432, 435, 438, 448, 450, 453, 458, 461, 463,
  464, 500n, 502, 503, 506, 541n, 607, 639n,
  651, 654, 656–658, 662, 710n, 734n, 807n,
  820, 835, 871, 871n, 876, 880, 883, 923, 938,
  943n, 1000, 1005, 1033, 1054, 1055, 1106,
  1283, 1298, 1299n, 1305, 1307, 1307n, 1323,
  1327, 1328, 1339n, 1351, 1361, 1425n,
  1453n, 1472n, 1490n, 1597n, 1598n, 1608n,
  1617, 1620n, 1623n, 1625n, 1627, 1720n,
  1721, 1741
Addison, J.T. 1330, 1330n
Addison, T., *see* Cornia, G.A. 1733
Adelman, I. 1706n
Ades, A.F. 398, 1021, 1422n, 1518, 1560,
  1561, 1563, 1564
Adsera, A. 328
Agell, J. 662
Agénor, P.-R. 648
Aghion, P. xiin, 16n, 28, 69, 70, 71n, 82, 82n,
  86, 89, 90, 92n, 102, 102n, 104, 106n, 107n,
  114, 144, 157, 157n, 223, 256n, 354n, 388,
  398, 499, 501, 510n, 529, 537, 539n, 820,
  822, 872, 874, 879, 887, 899, 938, 986n,
  1018, 1020n, 1069, 1070, 1073, 1087n, 1089,
  1090, 1090n, 1092, 1103, 1106, 1116n, 1296,
  1302, 1303, 1311, 1313, 1314n, 1315, 1332,
  1333, 1347, 1504n, 1517n, 1620n, 1715n,

  1720, 1721, 1721n, 1729n, 1770, 1770n,
  1772, 1788, 1800n, 1801n, 1810n
Aghion, P., *see* Acemoglu, D. 71n, 99, 102n,
  277n, 428, 871, 871n, 943n, 1000, 1327,
  1597n, 1617
Ahluwalia, M.S. 1712, 1732, 1734
Ahluwalia, M.S., *see* Chenery, H.B. 1714n,
  1724n
Ahn, S. 633
Ahn, T., *see* Ostrom, E. 1659
Aiyagari, S.R. 543
Aiyar, C.V., *see* Timberg, T. 479, 480, 483, 525
Aiyar, S. 684
Aizcorbe, A. 749
Aizenman, J. 38, 654, 655
Akerlof, G. 645, 1655
Albrecht, J. 1338n
Alcalá, F. 658, 659, 662, 1096, 1422n, 1516,
  1516n, 1519, 1525, 1526, 1530
Aleem, I. 479, 480, 480n, 483
Alesina, A. 278, 398, 399, 538n, 652, 653,
  655, 656, 662, 1422n, 1502, 1502n, 1503,
  1503n, 1505, 1505n, 1506, 1510, 1510n,
  1511n, 1513, 1514n, 1518n, 1519, 1519n,
  1525n, 1530, 1530n, 1535n, 1538n, 1597n,
  1600n, 1609, 1686, 1688
Allen, F. 871, 876, 881, 882, 884, 886, 909,
  918, 918n, 920
Allen, R.C. 436, 1138n
Altonji, J.G. 700
Alvarez, F. 41n, 1470n
Amable, B. 663
Amir, R. 350
Amsden, A.H. 1001n, 1004n
Anand, S. 1713n, 1732
Anant, T.C.A., *see* Segerstrom, P.S. xiin, 71n,
  114, 127n, 1070n, 1425n
Anas, A. 1570
Anas, A., *see* Abdel-Rahman, H. 1565
Anderson, G. 594, 595, 595n
Anderson, J.E. 985n

Anderson, R.D. 210, 211, 211n
Anderson, S. 521n
Ando, A., *see* Modigliani, F. 1425n
Andorka, R. 201, 202
Andrade, E. 598
Andreoni, J. 1799
Andres, J. 598, 598n
Angeletos, G.-M. 515, 544n
Angeletos, G.-M., *see* Alesina, A. 1597n
Angeletos, M., *see* Aghion, P. 107n, 879
Angrist, J., *see* Acemoglu, D. 502, 710n
Anker, R., *see* Clark, R. 1725n
Annen, K. 1658
Anselin, L. 644
Antrás, P. 131n, 135, 1130
Antweiler, A. 1770n, 1771n, 1788
Aoki, M. 981, 983, 1425n
Aportela, F. 520
Arellano, M. 541n, 630n, 632, 633, 900, 901,
   1048, 1711n
Arestis, P. 905
Aristotle, 1641
Armendariz de Aghion, B., *see* Aghion, P.
   107n
Arndt, H.W. 1714n
Arnold, L.G. 1425n
Arrow, K.J. xiv, 78n, 113, 1070, 1070n, 1643n,
   1798
Arthur, B. 1551
Arthur, W.B. 302
Artzrouni, M., *see* Komlos, J. 223n
Asbell, B. 1725n
Ashenfelter, O.C. 1727n
Ashraf, N. 522
Aslund, A. 989, 999
Aston, T.H. 441
Aten, B., *see* Heston, A. xii, 303n, 491, 562,
   685, 804n, 826, 828, 830, 831, 834, 1412,
   1519
Atje, R. 894
Atkeson, A.A. 1098n, 1204, 1296, 1325,
   1360, 1452n
Atkinson, A.B. 131n, 1733, 1736n
Atkinson, T.R. 1214
Attanasio, O. 1356
Au, C.C. 1585
Auerbach, A.J. 847n
Autor, D.H. 1283n, 1302n, 1597n
Autor, D.H., *see* Katz, L.F. 1281, 1281n, 1282,
   1285, 1715n, 1720n, 1724, 1727n

Azariadis, C. 164n, 256n, 303, 317, 318n, 331,
   333, 373, 398, 588, 597, 607, 653, 999, 1000,
   1021, 1681

Bacha, E.L. 1714
Backus, D.K. 1096, 1425n, 1517
Bagehot, W. 867, 871, 880
Bahadur, C., *see* Sachs, J.D. 298, 300n, 304n
Bahk, B.H. 1204, 1294, 1295n, 1296
Bailey, R.W., *see* Addison, J.T. 1330, 1330n
Baily, M.N. 718, 771n, 779n
Bairoch, P. 185, 192, 193, 282, 282n, 410,
   1373, 1373n, 1377, 1377n, 1532
Baker, E. 316, 349, 368
Baker, G.P. 1322, 1325
Baland, J.-M. 1608n
Baland, J.-M., *see* Anderson, S. 521n
Baldwin, J.R. 786n
Baldwin, R.E. 281n, 1425n, 1486n, 1579, 1724
Baltagi, B. 644
Bandiera, O. 339, 349
Bandyopadhyay, S. 598, 598n
Bandyopadhyay, S., *see* Shafik, N. 1766n
Banerjee, A.V. 92n, 354n, 355n, 356, 398, 399,
   441, 479, 480n, 481, 483, 494, 495, 507–511,
   511n, 513, 515–518, 525, 528, 530, 537,
   539n, 541, 544n, 617, 887, 1604n, 1605n,
   1623, 1720, 1722, 1733n
Banerjee, A.V., *see* Aghion, P. 82n, 107n, 879
Banfield, E.C. 402
Banks, R.B. 939–941
Baqir, R., *see* Alesina, A. 1505n
Barbier, E. 1810, 1814n
Bardham, P. 1425n
Bardhan, P. 364n, 367, 398, 501n, 513, 1505n
Barlevy, G. 33, 34, 45
Barnett, H.J. 1751n
Barr, A. 1653, 1657
Barret, S. 1798n
Barrett, C.B. 326n, 339, 355
Barro, R.J. xi, xin, 16n, 25, 28, 77, 78n, 105,
   120n, 122n, 139n, 195, 196n, 216, 224n,
   283n, 402, 403, 491n, 495, 518, 581, 582n,
   586n, 587, 587n, 589, 591, 592, 540n, 541,
   604, 604n, 605, 606, 618, 625, 630, 638, 647,
   651–660, 662, 685, 694, 695, 821, 826, 827,
   829–831, 834, 835, 837–839, 846, 938, 940,
   944, 945n, 948, 1037, 1046, 1044n, 1046,
   1099n, 1103n, 1445, 1509n, 1519, 1523,
   1560, 1612, 1733n
Barro, R.J., *see* Alesina, A. 1505n
Barro, R.J., *see* Becker, G.S. 1261, 1262

Barro, R.J., *see* Lee, J.-W.   701, 702, 703n, 704
Barro, R.M.   24
Bartel, A.P.   938, 1205, 1301, 1318
Bartels, L.   1608
Barth, J.R.   922
Barzel, Y.   436
Basta, S.S.   490
Basu, A.   283n
Basu, K.   373
Basu, S.   734n, 938, 942, 943, 1296, 1427n
Bates, R.H.   443–445
Batou, J., *see* Bairoch, P.   410
Battalio, R.C., *see* Van Huyck, J.B.   330
Battistin, E., *see* Attanasio, O.   1356
Baumol, W.J.   77n, 582, 586n, 590, 604, 786,
   804, 827, 1117, 1715n
Baxter, M.   1425n
Bayart, J.-F.   1671n
Beath, J.   349
Beaudry, P.   660, 1304
Beck, T.   653, 655, 661, 897, 897n, 900, 902,
   904, 904n, 907n, 912, 913n, 914–920, 922,
   923, 923n
Beck, T., *see* Levine, R.   84, 661, 897, 898,
   898n, 899, 900, 1033
Becker, C., *see* Mills, E.   1560
Becker, G.S.   224n, 227, 228, 229n, 235, 423,
   518, 780n, 852n, 1021, 1261–1264, 1300,
   1378, 1578
Becker, G.S., *see* Barro, R.J.   224n
Becker, R., *see* Henderson, J.V.   1568, 1574
Becker, X.   1603n
Beeson, P.E.   1558
Behrens, W.W., *see* Meadows, D.H.   1752n
Behrman, J.R.   709
Bekaert, G.   653, 661, 907
Bekar, C., *see* Lipsey, R.G.   1295
Bell, B., *see* Nickell, S.   1350
Bell, C.L.G., *see* Chenery, H.B.   1714n, 1724n
Ben Porath, Y.   258n
Ben-David, D.   659, 1091n, 1514
Ben-Zion, U., *see* Razin, A.   224n, 1261, 1264
Bénabou, R.   259n, 538n, 541, 1021, 1574,
   1597n, 1599, 1600, 1602n–1605n, 1606,
   1607n, 1609, 1610n, 1618n, 1619, 1630,
   1715n, 1733n
Bénabou, R., *see* Fukao, K.   1485n
Benassy, J.-P.   120
Bencivenga, V.R.   150n, 875, 877, 878, 895,
   896, 923

Benhabib, J.   81, 398, 495, 538n, 903, 938,
   939, 953, 959, 959n, 1018n, 1263
Bennell, P.   484, 484n, 487
Bentolila, S.   1340
Berdugo, B.   279n
Berdugo, B., *see* Hazan, M.   230, 230n, 236n,
   260–262, 1266
Berg, M.   1160n
Berger, A.N.   897
Bergh, A.E., *see* Lipscomb, A.A.   1069
Berghahn, V.R.   214
Bergsman, J.   1555
Berkowitz, D.   1007, 1008
Berle, A.A.   873
Berman, B.J.   449
Berman, E.   1597n
Bernanke, B.S.   82n, 731, 731n
Bernard, A.   584, 588, 599–602, 604n
Berndt, E.R.   1196n
Bernhardt, D., *see* Lloyd-Ellis, H.   537n
Bernstein, L.   1647, 1650
Berry, T.S.   1218n, 1220n
Berthelemy, J.   653
Bertocchi, G.   193n, 259n, 263, 264, 278n
Bertola, G.   1312, 1336n, 1340, 1342, 1715n,
   1718n
Bertrand, M.   522, 909
Besley, T.F.   429n, 508, 516, 650, 999, 1005
Bessen, J.   145, 1204
Beugelsdijk, S.   658, 1682
Bezuneh, M., *see* Barrett, C.B.   339, 355
Bhargava, A.   655
Bhattacharya, S.   871
Bhide, A.   882, 895
Bianchi, M.   331, 594, 621n
Bianchi, S.   1685, 1686
Bigsten, A.   481, 1650
Bikhchandani, S.   516n
Bils, M.   495, 502, 653, 687n, 698, 706, 833,
   938, 1104n
Binder, M.   581, 592, 627, 645
Binswanger, H.   508
Binswanger, H., *see* Rosenzweig, M.R.   515
Birdsall, N.   974n, 1725n
Bisin, A.   266n
Black, D.   1548, 1550, 1553–1555, 1558, 1564,
   1569, 1571, 1574, 1577
Black, S.W.   884
Blackbourn, D.   1649n
Blackburn, K.   871
Blades, D.   784n

Blanchard, O.   1288, 1340, 1350, 1351
Blanchflower, D.   511n, 1692n
Blattman, C.   656
Blau, F.D.   1266, 1267, 1267n, 1731
Blau, F.D., *see* Bertola, G.   1312, 1340
Blaut, J.M.   1170n
Bleaney, M.   1327
Blinder, A.S., *see* Baumol, W.J.   1715n
Bliss, C.   593
Blomstrom, M.   627, 656, 659
Blonigen, B.   654
Bloom, D.E.   256, 261n, 277n, 335, 400, 621, 652, 654, 655, 657
Bloom, B., *see* Aghion, P.   89, 90, 102n
Bloom, N., *see* Aghion, P.   1504n
Blum, J.   433
Blume, L.   1656
Blundell, R.   76, 86, 89, 633, 1331n, 1355, 1356, 1711n
Blundell, R., *see* Aghion, P.   89, 90, 102n, 1504n
Board of Governors of the Federal Reserve System,   1213n
Bockstette, V.   662
Bodenhorn, H.   923n
Bodie, Z., *see* Merton, R.C.   869, 886, 919
Boisjoly, J., *see* Hofferth, S.   1687
Boldrin, M.   28, 30, 62, 234n, 1088, 1207, 1265
Bolton, P.   1320, 1321, 1504n, 1506, 1510n
Bolton, P., *see* Aghion, P.   92n, 354n, 537, 539n, 887, 1720
Bond, E.   26
Bond, S.   627, 632, 660
Bond, S., *see* Arellano, M.   541n, 632, 900, 1048, 1711n
Bond, S., *see* Blundell, R.   633, 1711n
Boone, J.   89
Boone, P., *see* Aslund, A.   989
Boot, A.W.A.   881–883
Booth, A.   1327
Borghans, J.A.M.   266
Borghans, L.   1303
Borghans, L., *see* Borghans, J.A.M.   266
Borjas, G.J.   142n, 1021, 1035
Boserup, E.   239, 239n, 1069
Bosworth, B.P.   660, 746n, 771n, 972
Bosworth, B.P., *see* Collins, S.M.   996n
Botticini, M.   1155
Bottomley, A.   480n
Boucekkine, R.   259
Bouillon, C.P.   1035

Bound, J., *see* Berman, E.   1597n
Bourguignon, F.   259n, 399, 519, 1441, 1608n, 1714, 1717n, 1719n, 1730n, 1734n, 1735, 1737n, 1739n, 1741n
Bourguignon, F., *see* Levy-Leboyer, M.   188, 214
Boustan, L., *see* Aghion, P.   102n
Bovenberg, A.L.   1778, 1797
Bover, O., *see* Arellano, M.   633, 901
Bowles, S.   212n, 259n, 266n, 303, 1643, 1650n
Bowlus, A.J.   1354, 1356, 1357
Boyce, S., *see* Gertler, P.J.   498
Boyce, W.E.   1099n
Boyd, J.H.   871, 874, 875, 879, 886, 920, 923
Boyd, R.   266n
Boyer, G.   272n
Braden, J.B., *see* Chimeli, A.B.   1810n
Bradstreet Co.,   1200n
Brady, D.S.   1196n
Brady, H.   1741n
Brander, J.A.   1752n
Brandolini, A., *see* Atkinson, A.B.   1733, 1736n
Branstetter, L.G.   938
Braudel, F.   150, 1530n
Braverman, L.   1311
Brehm, J.   1685, 1686
Breiman, L.   619n
Brems, H.   1425n
Brennan, R., *see* Lochner, K.   1683
Brenner, R.   427, 440, 441, 455
Bresnahan, T.F.   1185, 1295, 1322
Breusch, T.   644
Brewer, J.   456
Brezis, E.S.   278n
Brezis, S.L.   1427n, 1453n
Bridgman, B.   1414
Brinton, M., *see* Lee, S.J.   1673, 1675
Britnell, R.H.   1118n
Brock, S., *see* Binder, M.   627
Brock, W.A.   16, 308n, 320, 559n, 560n, 581, 609, 610, 611n, 612–615, 639, 645, 971n, 1664, 1665, 1667, 1668, 1670, 1681, 1684, 1692, 1756, 1770n, 1772, 1772n, 1799, 1800, 1809, 1811n, 1815, 1816
Brock, W.H.   1138n, 1152
Broner, F.   1490n
Brown, G.I.   1141
Browning, M.   235n, 1739n
Bruland, T.   1169

Bruno, M.   655, 1044n, 1048n
Brunton, D.   455
Bryant, L.   1140, 1140n
Brynjolfsson, E.   806n, 807n, 1322n
Brynjolfsson, E., *see* Bresnahan, T.F.   1322
Buchanan, R.A.   1164
Buera, F.   537, 543
Buiter, W.H.   1425n
Buka, S., *see* Lochner, K.   1683
Bulli, S.   596, 597
Bun, M.   634
Bureau of Economic Analysis,   751, 754, 784
Bureau of Labor Statistics,   759n, 784, 806
Burgess, R., *see* Aghion, P.   986n
Burgess, R., *see* Besley, T.F.   650, 999, 1005
Burt, R.   1660
Burton, M.   1139
Byushgens, S.S., *see* Konus, A.   750

Caballero, R.J.   338n, 1204, 1350
Cagetti, M.   542
Cai, F., *see* Lin, J.Y.   980
Cain, G.G.   1266
Cain, G.G., *see* Baldwin, R.E.   1724
Cain, L.   1163n, 1311
Calderón, C.   662
Calderón, C., *see* Loayza, N.V.   978n
Caldwell, J.C.   1265
Caldwell, W.J.   234n
Calomiris, C.   878n
Calvet, L., *see* Angeletos, G.-M.   515, 544n
Calvo, G.   986n
Cameron, D.   1741
Cameron, R.   208n, 453, 909, 910, 910n
Campbell, J.Y.   768n, 806n, 1342
Campos, N.   627
Canning, D., *see* Bloom, D.E.   256, 277n, 335,
    621, 654, 655
Cannon, E.   593, 1103
Canova, F.   618, 619, 622
Canova, F., *see* Bertocchi, G.   193n, 278n
Cantor, N.F.   440
Caplow, T.   1251
Caprio Jr., G.   874, 885, 923n
Caprio Jr., G., *see* Barth, J.R.   922
Carbonaro, W.   1680n
Card, D.   694, 702n, 1285n, 1313, 1330,
    1330n, 1360, 1727n
Card, D., *see* Ashenfelter, O.C.   1727n
Cardosso, F.H.   428
Cardwell, D.S.L.   1128n, 1150

Carlaw, K., *see* Lipsey, R.G.   1295
Carlin, W.   920
Carlino, G.   602
Caroli, E.   1322, 1619n
Caroli, E., *see* Aghion, P.   1715n, 1721, 1721n
Carosso, V.   879
Carpenter, S.R., *see* Scheffer, M.   1760n
Carroll, C.   543
Carson, R.T.   1813
Carter, M.   1674, 1689
Cartwright, F.F.   1169n
Carvalho, I.   519
Carver, K., *see* Teachman, J.   1676, 1679
Case, A.   518n
Case, A., *see* Besley, T.F.   516
Casella, A.   1510n
Casella, A., *see* Rauch, J.E.   1653
Caselli, F.   136n, 140, 277n, 499, 507, 535,
    543, 579, 589, 607, 629, 632, 638, 653, 654,
    656, 683, 690, 711, 711n, 712n, 714, 714n,
    723n, 724, 725, 725n, 728, 733, 734, 734n,
    736n, 953, 1048, 1263, 1302, 1302n, 1304,
    1315n, 1446n
Cashin, P.   586n
Cass, D.   xi, 16, 17, 298, 388
Castilla, E., *see* Fernandez, R.   1678
Castillo, M., *see* Carter, M.   1689
Castro, R., *see* Cohen-Pirani, D.   1301n
Cavalcanti-Ferreira, P., *see* Pessoa, S.   483
Cavalli-Sforza, L.L.   266n
Caves, R.E.   842
Ceballos, M., *see* Palloni, A.   1673, 1675, 1680
Central Intelligence Agency,   1519
Cervellati, M.   259, 1145
Cetorelli, N.   156, 913
Chakraborty, S.   882
Chamberlain, G.   805
Chanda, A.   279n, 727n
Chanda, A., *see* Bockstette, V.   662
Chandler, T.   410
Chandler Jr., A.D.   755n, 806
Chaney, T.   1342
Chang, R.   1425n
Chang, S., *see* Powell, C.   498
Chari, V.V.   1019n
Charkham, J.   885
Charles, K.   1686
Charlesworth, A.   436
Chaudhuri, K.N.   282
Chaudhuri, S., *see* Ravallion, M.   513
Checchi, D.   356

Checkland, S.G.   910n
Chen, D.L., *see* Kremer, M.   224n, 272n
Chen, S.   297n
Chen, S., *see* Ravallion, M.   1736n
Chen, X., *see* Li, R.   490
Chenery, H.B.   1712, 1714n, 1724n
Chesher, A.   618
Chesnais, J.   202, 226n
Chester, L.A., *see* Birdsall, N.   1725n
Chèvre, P., *see* Bairoch, P.   410
Chiappori, P.-A., *see* Bourguignon, F.   519
Chimeli, A.B.   1810n
Chitnis, A.   1134n, 1163n
Cho, D.   660
Choi, S.-Y.   751n, 807n
Chong, A., *see* Calderón, C.   662
Chow, G.C.   751
Christensen, C.M.   807n
Christensen, K., *see* Kohler, H.   269n
Christensen, K., *see* Rodgers, J.L.   269n
Christensen, L.R.   684n, 781n, 787, 805
Christian, M.S.   54n
Christopher, H., *see* Aghion, P.   938
Christopoulos, D.K.   906
Chui, M.   1425n
Chun, H.   1303
Ciccone, A.   145, 145n, 656
Ciccone, A., *see* Alcalá, F.   658, 659, 662,
    1096, 1422n, 1516, 1516n, 1519, 1525, 1526,
    1530
Ciccone, A., *see* Matsuyama, K.   349
Cipolla, C.M.   234, 272, 273
Claessens, S.   653, 661, 874, 913, 914
Clark, C.   719n, 1752n, 1760n
Clark, G.   181, 182n, 183, 183n, 188, 197, 205,
    209, 213, 228, 235, 254, 255, 266, 271, 272,
    718n, 1098n, 1099, 1387
Clark, J.S.   1553
Clark, R.   1725n
Clarke, G.   921n
Clemens, M.A.   282n, 1724n
Clow, A.   1150n
Clow, N.L., *see* Clow, A.   1150n
Coale, A.J.   190, 200n
Coase, R.H.   422, 872n, 1319
Coate, S.T.   513
Coate, S.T., *see* Besley, T.F.   429n
Coatsworth, J.H.   443
Cochrane, E.W.   1144
Cody, M.L.   270n
Coe, D.T.   79n, 842, 852n, 938

Cohen, D.   590, 1354n
Cohen, M.N.   275n
Cohen, W.M.   78n, 89, 136
Cohen-Pirani, D.   1301n
Cole, A.H.   1137n
Cole, H.   544
Cole, H., *see* Ohanian, L.E.   1098n
Colecchia, A.   785n, 786n, 1346
Coleman, J.   1642, 1643, 1647, 1677
Coleman, W.J., *see* Caselli, F.   140, 277n, 607,
    711n, 723n, 724, 725, 725n, 728, 733, 734,
    734n, 736n, 1263
Collard, F., *see* Beaudry, P.   660
Collier, P.   567n, 1017
Collier, P., *see* Bigsten, A.   481, 1650
Collins, S.   996n
Collins, S.M., *see* Bosworth, B.P.   660, 972
Comin, D.   1102n, 1204, 1342
Commission on Macroeconomics, and Health,
    490
Congressional Budget Office,   746n
Conley, T.G.   339, 349, 516, 645
Connolly, M.   260n
Conrad, K.   718n
Constant, E.W.   1153
Cook, D.   640, 660
Cook, J.P., *see* Van Huyck, J.B.   330
Cooley, T.F.   1294
Cooney, E.W.   1168n
Cooper, R.W.   145
Copeland, B.R.   1755, 1757n, 1773, 1779,
    1786, 1788, 1799n, 1804
Copeland, B.R., *see* Antweiler, A.   1770n,
    1771n, 1788
Cordoba, J.-C.   1576
Cornia, G.A.   1733
Corrado, C.   752
Corrado, L.   601n
Corriveau, L.   71n
Costa, D.   1678, 1680, 1685, 1686
Coulombe, S.   656
Cowan, R.   1122n
Cowen, T.   910n
Cowles, A.   1200n
Cozzi, G.   1094, 1308
Crafts, N.F.R.   197, 206, 255
Craig, F.W.S.   215
Cressy, D.   272n
Crisp, O., *see* Cameron, R.   909
Croarken, M.   1158n
Crouch, T.   1153n

Crouzet, F. 1157
Cubberly, E.P. 210, 211
Cull, R. 909
Cumings, B. 405n
Cummings, D., *see* Christensen, L.R. 684n,
  781n, 787, 805
Cummins, J.G. 1189, 1292, 1293, 1295, 1304,
  1305, 1309, 1309n, 1337
Cuñat, A. 1425n, 1463n
Currais, L., *see* Rivera, B. 662
Currie, J. 704, 705n
Curtin, P.D. 417
Cutler, D.M. 1355

Da Rin, M. 340, 343
da Silva, L.P., *see* Bourguignon, F. 1739n
Dagenais, D., *see* Dagenais, M. 642
Dagenais, M. 642
Dahan, M. 224n
Dalgaard, C.-J. 165, 224n
Dalgaard, C.-J., *see* Aiyar, S. 684
Dalgaard, C.-J., *see* Chanda, A. 279n, 727n
Darnton, R. 1137, 1157n
Darwin, C. 268
Dasgupta, A. 479, 480
Dasgupta, P. 373, 537, 1643n, 1648, 1659,
  1688, 1692, 1752n, 1760n
Datt, G., *see* Ravallion, M. 1734n
David, P.A. 301, 806n, 1069n, 1132, 1146n,
  1184, 1187, 1204, 1295
David, P.A., *see* Abramovitz, M. 198, 212, 806
Davids, K. 1137n, 1166
Davidson, R. 643
Davis, D. 1446n
Davis, J. 1560, 1561, 1564, 1575
Davis, R. 453
Davis, S.J., *see* Attanasio, O. 1356
Dawkins, R. 269
Dawson, J.W. 37
de Barros, R.P., *see* Ferreira, F. 1737n
de Figueiredo, R. 1505n
de Gregorio, J. 654, 878
de Hek, P.A. 39, 54n, 61, 61n
de Janvry, A. 1714
de la Croix, D. 224n
de la Croix, D., *see* Boucekkine, R. 259
de la Fuente, A. 694, 875
de la Torre, A., *see* Birdsall, N. 974n
de Mello, L. 1609
de Menil, G. 1008
de Nardi, M., *see* Cagetti, M. 542

de Soto, H. 364
de Vries, J. 150, 185, 193, 453, 454, 1161n
Dean, E.R. 784n
DeAngelo, H. 882
Dear, P. 1135n
Deardorff, A.V. 1453n, 1463n
Deaton, A. 513, 543, 544n
Debreu, G. 19
Dechert, W.D. 350, 1752n
Dehejia, R. 907, 908
Deidda, L. 653
Deininger, K. 538, 1732
DeJong, D.N., *see* Beeson, P.E. 1558
Dellas, H. 54n
DeLong, J.B. 573n, 586n, 590, 604, 643, 656,
  660, 828, 879, 990, 1065n
Demetriades, P.O. 653, 661, 662, 905, 906
Demetriades, P.O., *see* Arestis, P. 905
Demirgüç-Kunt, A. 881, 886, 889, 894n, 907n,
  914, 916–920
Demirgüç-Kunt, A., *see* Beck, T. 655, 661,
  897, 897n, 907n, 914–918, 920, 922, 923,
  923n
Demsetz, H. 422
Den Haan, W.J. 326, 1329n, 1346
Denison, E.F. xi, 684n, 751, 780, 783n, 784,
  803, 803n, 804, 805
Dercon, S. 340, 357, 357n
Dercon, S., *see* Bigsten, A. 1650
Dertouzos, M. 782n
Desdoigts, A. 331, 620, 620n, 1681
Deurenberg, P., *see* Li, R. 490
Devereux, M.B. 124, 126, 126n, 876, 1425n,
  1463n
Devine, W.D. 1190
Devleeschauwer, A., *see* Alesina, A. 278, 653,
  1505
Dewatripont, M. 884, 920, 989n
Dewatripont, M., *see* Aghion, P. 874
Dewatripont, M., *see* Bolton, P. 1320, 1321
Diamond, D.W. 874, 875, 877, 878, 878n
Diamond, J.M. 277, 400, 413, 857, 1095
Diamond, P. 733n
Dickens, R. 1331n, 1356
Dickens, W.T. 1326
Diebold, F. 603
Diewert, W.E. 750, 760n, 783n
Dimaria, C.H. 350
DiNardo, J. 1326
DiNardo, J., *see* Card, D. 1313, 1360

Dinopoulos, E.   93n, 127n, 142, 1094, 1307,
1308n, 1425n
Dinopoulos, E., *see* Segerstrom, P.S.   xiin, 71n,
114, 127n, 1070n, 1425n
DiPasquale, D.   1686
DiPrima, R.C., *see* Boyce, W.E.   1099n
Diwan, I.   130
Dixit, A.K.   113, 116, 398, 429n, 1005, 1007,
1008, 1070, 1082, 1446n
Djankov, S.   99, 425, 426, 506, 509n,
1006–1008, 1395
Djankov, S., *see* Claessens, S.   874
Do, T.   508
Dobb, M.H.   427
Dobbs, B.J.T.   1132
Dobkins, L.H.   1548, 1558
Doepke, M.   227, 227n, 230, 236n, 255, 258,
260, 261, 263, 278, 280, 1262, 1262n, 1265,
1266, 1378
Doepke, M., *see* de la Croix, D.   224n
Dollar, D.   652, 657–659, 661, 1033, 1422n,
1425n, 1514, 1734, 1736
Dollar, D., *see* Collier, P.   1017
Domar, E.   446, 774, 774n, 779
Doménech, R., *see* de la Fuente, A.   694
Doms, M.   270n, 752, 755, 756
Donovan, A.L.   1138, 1138n
Dooley, M.   1319n
Doppelhofer, G.   587, 612–615
Dornbusch, R.   143, 1463n, 1468
Dougherty, C.   787, 805
Doughty, D., *see* Rodgers, J.L.   269n
Douglas, P.H.   781
Dow Jones and Company, Inc.,   1206n
Dowrick, S.   591, 592, 604n, 1409n
Draper, D.   559n, 582
Drazen, A., *see* Azariadis, C.   317, 318n, 331,
588, 597, 607, 653, 999, 1000, 1021, 1681
Dreze, J.   498
Driscoll, J.   644
DuBoff, R.B.   1187n, 1189n, 1191n
Duck, N., *see* Cannon, E.   593
Duffy, J.   257n, 605n, 620, 938
Duflo, E.   482, 495, 502, 516, 519, 521, 522,
694
Duflo, E., *see* Banerjee, A.   398, 617, 1605n,
1733n
Duflo, E., *see* Banerjee, A.V.   481, 483, 507,
511, 525, 528, 530, 541
Dulberger, E.R.   749, 751, 774n
Dulberger, E.R., *see* Berndt, E.R.   1196n

Duloy, J.H., *see* Chenery, H.B.   1714n, 1724n
Dun and Bradstreet, Inc.,   1210n
Duncan, G., *see* Hofferth, S.   1687
Dunn, T.A., *see* Altonji, J.G.   700
Dunne, T., *see* Doms, M.   270n
Durand, J.   1725n
Duranton, G.   1325n, 1547, 1554, 1557, 1564,
1565, 1574–1576
Durham, W.   266n
Durlauf, S.N.   77n, 256, 259n, 318n, 331, 368n,
398, 402, 515, 561n, 579n, 582n, 589, 607,
617–619, 619n, 622, 631, 647, 804n, 942,
1574, 1643n, 1644, 1664, 1667, 1667n,
1668–1671, 1680n, 1681, 1690, 1693n, 1810
Durlauf, S.N., *see* Bernard, A.   584, 588,
599–602
Durlauf, S.N., *see* Bowles, S.   303
Durlauf, S.N., *see* Brock, W.A.   559n, 560n,
581, 609, 610, 611n, 612–615, 639, 645,
971n, 1664, 1665, 1667, 1668, 1670, 1681,
1684, 1692
Dybvig, P.H., *see* Diamond, D.W.   877
Dyck, A.   917, 918n
Dyson, T.   190n

Eamon, W.   1132
Earls, F., *see* Sampson, R.   1687, 1688
Easterlin, R.A.   270n, 1148n, 1262, 1710n
Easterly, W.   278, 303, 314n, 326, 331, 565,
567n, 568n, 573, 605, 615, 625, 636, 645n,
653–659, 684n, 781n, 826n, 829, 833, 870n,
923, 953, 971n, 973n, 996, 1005, 1009,
1018n, 1030n, 1032–1034, 1036n, 1045n,
1050n, 1054, 1055, 1505, 1681, 1681n, 1682
Easterly, W., *see* Alesina, A.   278, 653, 1505,
1505n
Easterly, W., *see* Bruno, M.   655, 1044n, 1048n
Eaton, J.   56, 59n, 79n, 493, 647, 711, 820,
822, 835, 837, 841, 842, 854n, 938, 1470n,
1548, 1550
Echevarria, C.   1263
Eckhaus, R.S., *see* Sue Wing, I.   1795
Eckstein, Z.   227n, 1281, 1281n, 1282, 1282n,
1283, 1283n, 1284, 1285
Eckstein, Z., *see* Botticini, M.   1155
Eckstein, Z., *see* Eaton, J.   1548, 1550
Economics and Statistics Administration,
746n, 778n, 807n
Edgerton, R.B.   402
Edison, H.   907n
Edlund, L.   231

Edmonds, E.   512
Edwards, S.   653, 663, 1514, 1514n
Eeckhout, J.   938
Eggimann, G.   410
Eichengreen, B.   652
Eicher, T.   1721n
Eicker, F.   643
Eisenberg, M.J.   1249
Eisenstein, E.   1122n
Ekelund Jr., R.B.   1162
Elliott, P.   1149
Ellison, G.   516n, 517, 1556, 1557, 1577
Elston, M., *see* Powell, C.   498
Endler, J.A.   265n
Engerman, C.   1118n
Engerman, S.L.   212n, 278, 302, 443, 449, 923, 1005, 1054, 1611, 1617
Engerman, S.L., *see* Fogel, R.W.   1265
Ensminger, J.   1656
EPA,   1753n
Epifani, P.   142n
Ergungor, O.E.   919
Erlich, I.   231n
Ertman, T.   452
Ervin, L., *see* Long, J.   643
Esfahani, H.   655, 662
Espinosa, K., *see* Palloni, A.   1673, 1675, 1680
Esquivel, G., *see* Caselli, F.   136n, 579, 589, 629, 632, 638, 653, 654, 656, 683, 953, 1048, 1446n
Estevadeordal, A.   216, 1532, 1532n
Eswaran, M.   508
Ethier, W.J.   113, 116, 1082
Evans, E.J.   459
Evans, G.   149n, 158, 162, 164n, 165
Evans, P.   77, 599, 603
Evenson, R.E.   78n, 852n

Fafchamps, M.   480, 513, 1644, 1646, 1646n, 1650, 1651, 1651n, 1653–1655, 1673, 1674, 1686, 1692
Fafchamps, M., *see* Barr, A.   1657
Fafchamps, M., *see* Bigsten, A.   1650
Fafchamps, M., *see* Durlauf, S.N.   402
Fairchilds, C.   1118n
Fajnzylber, P., *see* Loayza, N.V.   978n
Faletto, E., *see* Cardosso, F.H.   428
Fama, E.   872n
Fan, J., *see* Claessens, S.   874
Fan, X., *see* Thomas, V.   1724n
Farber, H.S.   1326

Farrell, J.   428n
Farrington, B.   1134
Fatás, A.   36, 37, 45, 47
Fattouh, B., *see* Deidda, L.   653
Fay, M.   1560
Faye, M., *see* Sachs, J.D.   298, 300n, 304n
Fazzari, S.   511n
Feder, B.   1198
Feder, G.   659
Federal Reserve Bank of Dallas,   1258n
Federal Reserve Bank of St. Louis,   1213n
Feenstra, R.C.   711n, 1425n
Fei, J.C.H.   1713
Fei, J.C.H., *see* Rannis, G.   1577
Feinstein, C.H.   197, 255
Feinstein, C.H., *see* Matthews, R.C.   195, 197
Feinstein, J.S., *see* Casella, A.   1510n
Feld, L.   656
Feldman, M.W., *see* Cavalli-Sforza, L.L.   266n
Fellman, J.   1603n
Fernald, J., *see* Basu, S.   1296
Fernandez, C.   587, 587n, 612, 613, 613n, 614, 1681
Fernandez, R.   259n, 262n, 1268, 1603n, 1606, 1678
Fernandez-Villaverde, J.   227, 228, 236n, 255, 255n, 258, 261, 278, 280, 1238n, 1262
Ferreira, F.   1737n
Ferreira, F., *see* Bourguignon, F.   1730n, 1737n
Fershtman, C.   1655
Feynman, R.P.   1009
Feyrer, J.   256n, 332n, 606, 707n
Fiaschi, D.   256n, 598
Field, A.   212n
Fields, G.S.   1713n, 1732, 1734n
Figini, P.   1609
Findlay, R.   217, 281n, 1425n, 1510n
Finegan, T.A., *see* Margo, R.A.   1249
Fink, G.   897
Fischer, S.   654–656, 825n, 1033
Fischer, S., *see* Dornbusch, R.   143, 1463n, 1468
Fisher, A.   719n
Fisher, I.   749
Fisher, O'N.   1425n
Fisman, R.J.   889, 904n, 912n
Fitschen, A., *see* Klitgaard, R.   1036
Flam, H.   1425n
Flamm, K.   751, 807n
Flannery, M.   878n
Flatters, F.   1567

Flinn, C.   1354
Flora, P.   205–207, 209, 211, 215, 226, 255
Flug, K.   1301
Fogel, R.W.   1265
Fogli, A., *see* Fernandez, R.   262n, 1268
Foray, D., *see* Cowan, R.   1122n
Forbes, K.J.   541, 541n, 542, 653, 655, 1605n
Forslid, R., *see* Baldwin, R.   1425n, 1486n
Forster, B.A.   1772, 1777
Fortin, N.M.   1597n
Fortin, N.M., *see* DiNardo, J.   1326
Foster, A.D.   239n, 482, 495–497, 500n, 516, 938
Fournier, M., *see* Bourguignon, F.   1737n
Fox, R.   1138, 1163n
Francois, J.F.   1425n
Francois, P.   157n
Frank, A.G.   428, 1170n
Frank, K.   1678
Frankel, J.A.   99, 639, 640, 659, 663, 975, 1032, 1096, 1422n, 1515, 1525
Frankel, M.   xin, 1103, 1103n, 1718
Frankenberg, E., *see* Thomas, D.   490
Franses, P., *see* Hobijn, B.   599, 601
Frantz, B., *see* Estevadeordal, A.   216, 1532, 1532n
Fraumeni, B.M.   760n
Fraumeni, B.M., *see* Jorgenson, D.W.   760n, 763, 774, 774n, 782n, 783n, 1291
Freeman, R.B.   488n, 496, 1007, 1326n, 1328, 1597n, 1610, 1624
Freeman, R.B., *see* Borjas, G.J.   142n
Freeman, S.   354n
Frenkel, J.   1425n
Freshwater, D., *see* Rupasingha, A.   658
Freudenberger, H.   433
Frey, B.   1741n
Friedman, D.   1510n
Friedman, E.   999
Friedman, J.   620n
Friedman, J., *see* Breiman, L.   619n
Friedman, J., *see* Thomas, D.   490
Friedman, M.   593, 599, 1354
Fudenberg, D.   1659
Fudenberg, D., *see* Ellison, G.   516n
Fujita, J.   1578, 1579
Fujita, M.P.   1021, 1486n, 1565, 1576, 1579
Fujita, M.P., *see* Abdel-Rahman, H.   1564, 1574
Fukao, K.   1485n
Fukuyama, F.   1643

Fullerton, D., *see* King, M.A.   847n
Funke, M.   145n
Furfine, C.H.   885
Furstenberg, F.   1660, 1676–1678
Futia, C.A.   311n, 376

Gabaix, X.   1554, 1576
Gabaix, X., *see* Chaney, T.   1342
Gale, D.   874, 1425n
Gale, D., *see* Allen, F.   876, 881, 882, 884, 886, 918, 918n, 920
Gale, L.   1766n, 1769
Galetovic, A.   871
Gallet, C.A., *see* List, J.A.   1715
Gallup, J.L.   655, 662, 1560
Galor, O.   92n, 176n, 177, 193n, 194n, 212n, 224n, 228–231, 231n, 232, 235n, 236, 236n, 237, 239n, 255n, 256n, 257–259, 259n, 260–264, 266, 267n, 270n, 272n, 274, 275, 278–282, 351, 354n, 398, 441, 537, 583n, 872, 878, 887, 1098n, 1099, 1118n, 1146, 1261, 1264, 1266, 1267, 1302, 1378, 1425n, 1571, 1604n, 1605n, 1613n, 1720, 1721n
Gambera, M., *see* Cetorelli, N.   913
Gancia, G.   130, 143, 144, 1425n
Gancia, G., *see* Epifani, P.   142n
Garby, L., *see* Li, R.   490
Garcia-Peñalosa, C., *see* Aghion, P.   1715n, 1721, 1721n
Garcia-Peñalosa, C., *see* Checchi, D.   356
Garicano, L.   1321
Garner, P.   1513n
Garrard, J.   460
Gates, B.   1193n
Gatti, R., *see* Dollar, D.   661
Gauthier, B., *see* Bigsten, A.   1650
Ge, Y., *see* Anderson, G.   595
Geertz, C.   1656
Geertz, H., *see* Geertz, C.   1656
Gelb, A.   711n
Gelos, R.G.   507, 508
Gennaioli, N., *see* Caselli, F.   507, 535, 543
Germidis, D., *see* Lecaillon, J.   1732
Geroski, P.A.   86, 89, 939n
Gerschenkron, A.   79, 99, 433, 882, 937, 971
Gertler, M.   1490n
Gertler, M., *see* Bernanke, B.S.   82n
Gertler, P.J.   498, 513
Gertler, P.J., *see* Banerjee, A.V.   508, 509
Gertler, P.J., *see* Miguel, E.   1687
Ghatak, M.   537

Ghatak, M., *see* Banerjee, A.V. 508, 509
Ghate, P. 479, 480
Giavazzi, F. 636, 636n, 646
Gilbert, C.L. 985n
Gilligan, D., *see* Pargal, S. 1675
Gillispie, C.C. 1132n, 1139
Gintis, H., *see* Bowles, S. 212n, 259n, 1643, 1650n
Glaeser, E.L. 278–280, 425, 426, 1020n, 1553, 1586, 1667, 1689
Glaeser, E.L., *see* Ades, A.F. 1021, 1422n, 1518, 1560, 1561, 1563, 1564
Glaeser, E.L., *see* Alesina, A. 1597n, 1609
Glaeser, E.L., *see* DiPasquale, D. 1686
Glaeser, E.L., *see* Djankov, S. 1006–1008
Glaeser, E.L., *see* Ellison, G. 517, 1556, 1557, 1577
Glass, A.J. 1425n
Glick, R., *see* Aizenman, J. 654, 655
Glomm, G. 1603n
Glynn, P.W. 311n
Gneezy, U., *see* Fershtman, C. 1655
Goddard, N. 1138n
Goetz, S. 590
Goetz, S., *see* Rupasingha, A. 658
Goldin, C. 198, 212, 214, 233n, 257n, 1205, 1250n, 1266, 1267, 1267n, 1268, 1282, 1309, 1309n, 1310, 1311, 1311n, 1360, 1682, 1684, 1725n
Goldin, C., *see* Katz, L.F. 1205, 1205n
Goldsmith, R.W. 781, 867, 881, 889, 890, 918, 918n
Goldstein, M. 482, 495, 508
Goldstone, J.A. 997, 1171n
Golinski, J. 1138, 1139
Gollin, D. 721, 723n, 731, 833, 949n, 1387
Gollin, D., *see* Evenson, R.E. 852n
Gollop, F.M. 763n
Gollop, F.M., *see* Jorgenson, D.W. 725, 760n, 763, 774, 774n, 782n, 783n, 1291
Goodfriend, M. 222n, 1099
Gordon, R.J. 746n, 751, 752, 783n, 806n, 1185, 1196n, 1292, 1295n, 1298n, 1334n, 1360
Gordon, R.J., *see* Baily, M.N. 779n
Gort, M. 1206
Gort, M., *see* Bahk, B.H. 1204, 1294, 1295n, 1296
Gorton, G. 878n
Gosling, A. 1326

Gottschalk, P. 1286, 1331, 1336, 1342, 1350, 1356, 1733
Gottschalk, P., *see* Dooley, M. 1319n
Gould, E.D. 231, 1336, 1337, 1359
Gourinchas, P.-O. 687n
Graddy, K., *see* Barret, S. 1798n
Gradstein, M. 367n, 1616n, 1741n
Gradstein, M., *see* Justman, M. 1741
Gradus, R., *see* Smulders, S. 1804, 1805
Graham, B.S. 256, 337, 607n, 623, 723n, 727
Graham, C. 1692n
Granato, J. 658
Grandmont, J.-M. 164n
Granger, C.W.J. 603
Granovetter, M. 1644, 1646, 1647, 1653, 1692
Grant, B.R. 265n
Grant, P.R., *see* Grant, B.R. 265n
Grantham-McGregor, S., *see* Powell, C. 498
Graves, M.A.R. 452
Greasley, D. 601
Green, A. 197, 207, 207n, 208–211
Green, D.A., *see* Beaudry, P. 660, 1304
Green, J., *see* Scotchmer, S. 144, 145
Greenbaum, S.J., *see* Boot, A.W.A. 882
Greenspan, A. 746n
Greenston, P., *see* Bergsman, J. 1555
Greenwood, J. 150n, 229n, 262n, 541n, 715, 768, 783n, 871, 876, 880, 881, 888, 1098n, 1106, 1185, 1194, 1204, 1207, 1227n, 1230n, 1231n, 1238n, 1245n, 1252n, 1262n, 1264n, 1291, 1292, 1294–1296, 1301, 1302, 1312, 1312n, 1338, 1425n
Gregory, P.R. 433
Greif, A. 298n, 401, 1117, 1171, 1172, 1653
Grier, K.B. 33, 581n
Griffith, R. 78n
Griffith, R., *see* Acemoglu, D. 102n
Griffith, R., *see* Aghion, P. 89, 90, 102n, 107n, 1504n
Griffith, R., *see* Blundell, R. 76, 86, 89
Griffiths, J. 1128n, 1159n
Griliches, Z. 133n, 782, 782n, 806n, 839n, 847, 938, 1069, 1198, 1205, 1298
Griliches, Z., *see* Jorgenson, D.W. 759, 760n, 782, 783, 783n, 784
Grilli, V. 661
Grimm, B.T. 748, 750, 752
Grimm, B.T., *see* Parker, R.P. 754
Grootaert, C. 1648, 1673, 1674
Gross, N. 433
Grossman, E., *see* Kendrick, J.W. 781n

Grossman, G.M.   xiin, 71n, 78n, 114, 121n,
123, 127n, 128n, 129, 145n, 223, 281n, 388,
499, 501, 822, 937, 938, 1069, 1070, 1073,
1087n, 1089, 1090, 1090n, 1092, 1103, 1106,
1414, 1425n, 1504, 1517n, 1576, 1598n,
1619, 1623, 1627n 1757n, 1765, 1766n, 1769,
1770n, 1800n, 1801n, 1810
Grossman, H.I.   259n, 398, 399, 429n
Grossman, P.J.   1741n
Grossman, S.J.   422, 872, 873, 882, 896
Grove, A.S.   807n
Gruber, J., *see* Gertler, P.J.   513
Guagnini, A., *see* Fox, R.   1163n
Guaresma, J.   654, 661
Guesnerie, R., *see* Azariadis, C.   164n
Gugerty, M.K.   521n, 1687
Guidotti, P., *see* de Gregorio, J.   654
Guiso, L.   896, 896n, 908, 923, 1678, 1682,
1684
Gullickson, W.   774
Gunderson, M.   1730n
Gunning, J.W., *see* Bigsten, A.   1650
Gunning, J.W., *see* Collier, P.   567n
Gurgand, M., *see* Bourguignon, F.   1737n
Gurkaynak, R.S., *see* Bernanke, B.S.   731, 731n
Gurley, J.G.   867, 875
Gurr, T.R., *see* Ross, J.I.   450n
Gutierrez, H.   417
Gylfason, T.   1030n
Gyourko, J., *see* Glaeser, E.L.   1586

Ha, J.   92n, 96n, 1517
Habakkuk, H.J.   133n
Haber, S.H.   442, 443, 885, 887, 888, 908, 909,
923
Haber, S.H., *see* Maurer, N.   885
Habicht, J.-P., *see* Thomas, D.   490
Haddad, L., *see* Maluccio, J.   1675
Haefke, C., *see* Den Haan, W.   1346
Hagan, J.   1676, 1678, 1679
Haggard, S.   994n, 998n
Hahn, J.   633, 634n
Haider, S.   1331n
Haiss, P., *see* Fink, G.   897
Hall, A.R.   618, 1131, 1132n
Hall, B.H.   839n, 847
Hall, R.E.   136n, 277, 277n, 314, 314n, 402,
605, 606, 643, 652, 654, 658, 662, 684, 685,
688, 751n, 782n, 806n, 829, 833, 938, 1005,
1018n, 1032, 1097, 1294, 1296, 1325, 1390n,
1445, 1466n

Hall, S.   584
Hallinan, M.   1680n
Hamermesh, D.S.   131n, 732, 1297n, 1307n
Hamilton, B., *see* Mills, E.   1553
Hamilton, G., *see* Clark, G.   182n, 228, 235,
266, 271
Hammour, M.L., *see* Caballero, R.J.   1204,
1350
Hamoudi, A.   655
Hansen, B.   620
Hansen, G.D.   176n, 236n, 262–264, 264n,
1099, 1238n, 1264, 1374–1376, 1380, 1383,
1386, 1389, 1396
Hansen, H.   1350
Hansen, J., *see* Rosenstone, S.   1608
Hansen, L.P., *see* Browning, M.   235n, 1739n
Hanson, G., *see* Harrison, A.   1515n
Hanushek, E.A.   239n, 656, 700, 702n, 704,
705n, 938, 1018n
Harbaugh, W.   1767n
Harberger, A.C.   560, 616, 768, 774, 969
Harchaoui, T.M., *see* Baldwin, J.R.   786n
Hardin, R.   450n
Harley, C.K., *see* Crafts, N.F.R.   255
Harper, M.J., *see* Dean, E.R.   784n
Harper, M.J., *see* Gullickson, W.   774
Harrigan, J.   718
Harris, C., *see* Aghion, P.   86, 89, 398
Harris, D.   662
Harris, J.R.   725n, 1127n, 1132n, 1156n, 1158,
1577
Harrison, A.   655, 657, 659, 1515n
Harrison, G.W.   985n
Harrison, P.   875
Harrod, R.   779
Hart, O.D.   429, 512
Hart, O.D., *see* Grossman, S.J.   422, 873, 882
Hartwick, J.M.   1788
Harvey, C.R., *see* Bekaert, G.   653, 661, 907
Hasan, I., *see* Berger, A.N.   897
Hassler, J.   239n, 1597n, 1612n, 1617n
Hatta, T.   985n
Hausman, J., *see* Hahn, J.   634n
Hausmann, R.   646, 990, 992, 999, 1000, 1003
Hautvast, J.G., *see* Li, R.   490
Hayashi, F.   768
Hayek, F.A.   1319, 1645
Hazan, M.   230, 230n, 231n, 236n, 259–262,
1266
Head, K.   1547
Heal, G., *see* Dasgupta, P.   1752n

Healy, R., *see* Bergsman, J.   1555
Heathcote, J.   1282n, 1331n, 1355–1357, 1425n
Hecht, J.   752n
Heckman, J.J.   710n, 1318, 1319, 1354–1357, 1360, 1739n
Heckman, J.J., *see* Browning, M.   235n, 1739n
Heckman, J.J., *see* LaLonde, R.J.   1360
Heilbron, J.L.   1151n
Helleiner, G.K.   986n
Helliwell, J.   658, 1504n, 1664, 1682, 1689
Hellmann, T.   981, 982
Hellmann, T., *see* Da Rin, M.   340, 343
Hellwig, M.   883
Hellwig, M., *see* Gale, D.   874
Helpman, E.   124, 128–130, 157, 807n, 937, 1107, 1200, 1207, 1337, 1425n, 1446n, 1483n, 1555, 1578
Helpman, E., *see* Coe, D.T.   79n, 842, 852n, 938
Helpman, E., *see* Flam, H.   1425n
Helpman, E., *see* Grossman, G.M.   71n, 78n, 114, 121n, 127n, 128n, 129, 145n, 223, 281n, 388, 499, 501, 822, 937, 938, 1069, 1070, 1073, 1087n, 1089, 1090, 1090n, 1092, 1103, 1106, 1414, 1425n, 1504, 1517n, 1576, 1800n, 1801n
Helsley, R.   1564, 1568, 1573, 1574, 1586
Henderson, D.   605, 605n, 606, 607
Henderson, J.V.   661, 1556, 1560, 1562–1564, 1566, 1568, 1570, 1571, 1573, 1574, 1579, 1582, 1585
Henderson, J.V., *see* Au, C.C.   1585
Henderson, J.V., *see* Black, D.   1548, 1550, 1553–1555, 1558, 1564, 1569, 1571, 1577
Henderson, J.V., *see* Davis, J.   1560, 1561, 1564
Henderson, J.V., *see* Flatters, F.   1567
Henderson, S.G., *see* Glynn, P.W.   311n
Hendricks, L.   684, 833, 1380n, 1390n
Hendry, D.   612, 640
Henrekson, M., *see* Lybeck, J.A.   1741n
Henry, P.   636, 646, 907n
Herbst, J.I.   432, 1506n
Hercowitz, Z.   768
Hercowitz, Z., *see* Flug, K.   1301
Hercowitz, Z., *see* Greenwood, J.   715, 768, 1106, 1291, 1292, 1294, 1295
Hernandez, D.J.   233
Hernandez, P., *see* Sandefur, G.   1677, 1679
Herrendorf, B.   1395n

Heston, A.   xii, 303n, 491, 562, 685, 804n, 826, 828, 830, 831, 834, 1412, 1519
Heston, A., *see* Kravis, I.B.   803
Heston, A., *see* Summers, R.   582, 685, 720, 804, 1037, 1403–1406
Hibbs, D.A.   277n
Hickman, W.B.   1214
Hicks, J.R.   133n, 398, 440, 877
Hicks, L., *see* Caplow, T.   1251
Higgins, M.   660
Higgins, R.C.   915
Higuchi, Y., *see* Mincer, J.   1317, 1318
Hilaire-Pérez, L.   1133n, 1142n, 1165n
Hill, C.   402, 454, 456
Hill, R.   721
Hills, R.L.   1139n
Hilton, H.   1766n, 1767n, 1768
Hilton, R.   427
Hirschman, A.O.   971, 998
Hirshleifer, D., *see* Bikhchandani, S.   516n
Hirshleifer, J.   398
Hitt, L.M., *see* Bresnahan, T.F.   1322
Hitt, L.M., *see* Brynjolfsson, E.   806n, 1322n
Ho, M.S.   1294n
Ho, M.S., *see* Jorgenson, D.W.   779, 782n
Hobijn, B.   599, 601, 1207, 1215n
Hobjin, B.   1293
Hobsbawm, E.   1532, 1532n
Hochman, O.   1564, 1571
Hodges, J., *see* Draper, D.   582
Hoeffler, A.   629
Hoeffler, A., *see* Bond, S.   632
Hoff, K.   299, 303, 330, 364, 367n, 368, 369, 480n, 999, 1001
Hoff, K., *see* Bowles, S.   303
Hofferth, S.   1687
Hoffmaister, A.W., *see* Coe, D.T.   79n, 852n
Hoffman, P.T.   1387
Holmes, T.J.   1300n, 1310n, 1414, 1574
Holmstrom, B.   872, 878, 895
Holtz-Eakin, D.   632, 1818n
Homer, S.   1213n, 1220n
Honkapohja, S., *see* Evans, G.   149n, 158, 162, 164n, 165
Hoover, K.   611, 612, 643
Hoover's, Inc.,   1210n
Hopenhayn, H.A.   1208
Hopkins, D.R.   1169n
Horn, J.   1128, 1168

Hornstein, A.   1204, 1295, 1295n, 1296,
  1297n, 1307, 1309n, 1332, 1333, 1346, 1347,
  1347n, 1349, 1350, 1393n
Horowitz, D.L.   432
Horrell, S.   230n, 260n
Hoshi, T.   884n, 918n
Hotelling, H.   1790n
Howitt, P.W.   77, 81, 93n, 277n, 500n, 647,
  820, 822, 835, 836n, 837, 839, 841, 843, 939,
  1094, 1453n, 1517, 1681
Howitt, P.W., *see* Aghion, P.   xiin, 16n, 28, 69,
  70, 71n, 82, 86, 89, 90, 102n, 106n, 114, 144,
  157, 157n, 223, 256n, 388, 398, 499, 501,
  510n, 529, 820, 822, 872, 899, 1018, 1020n,
  1069, 1070, 1073, 1087n, 1089, 1090, 1090n,
  1092, 1103, 1106, 1116n, 1296, 1302, 1313,
  1314n, 1315, 1332, 1333, 1347, 1504n,
  1517n, 1721, 1770, 1770n, 1772, 1788,
  1800n, 1801n, 1810n
Howitt, P.W., *see* Ha, J.   92n, 96n, 1517
Hoxby, C.M.   1324n
Hoxby, C.M., *see* Aghion, P.   102n
Hoxby, C.M., *see* Alesina, A.   1505n
Hristoforova, S., *see* Fink, G.   897
Hsieh, C.-T.   493, 494, 687n, 728n, 1019n
Hu, D., *see* Goetz, S.   590
Huang, F.   1659
Hubbard, G., *see* Fazzari, S.   511n
Hubbard, T.N., *see* Baker, G.P.   1322, 1325
Hudson, D.   1142n
Huggett, M.   1295n, 1356
Hughes, K., *see* Rodgers, J.L.   269n
Hughes, M., *see* Furstenberg, F.   1660,
  1676–1678
Hultberg, P.   663
Hulten, C.R.   655, 716n, 759n, 782n, 783n,
  1292
Human Mortality Database,   204
Hummels, D.   835
Humphries, J.   1128
Humphries, J., *see* Horrell, S.   230n, 260n
Hung, V.T.Y., *see* Blackburn, K.   871
Huntington, S.P.   1741n
Huq, M., *see* Pargal, S.   1675
Hurt, J.   209
Hussein, K., *see* Demetriades, P.O.   905, 906
Huybens, E.   886, 923
Hwang, J., *see* Blattman, C.   656
Hyslop, D.   1358

Ichimura, H., *see* Attanasio, O.   1356
Ichino, A., *see* Bertola, G.   1336n, 1342

Imbs, J.   157, 1000n
Impullitti, G., *see* Cozzi, G.   1308
Inglehart, R., *see* Granato, J.   658
Ingram, B.   1302
Inkster, I.   1144
Inoue, A., *see* Diebold, F.   603
International Monetary Fund,   1017
Ioannides, Y.M.   1548, 1553, 1554
Ioannides, Y.M., *see* Dobkins, L.H.   1548, 1558
Ioannides, Y.M., *see* Henderson, J.V.   1564,
  1573
Irwin, D.A.   807n, 1295n
Isaksson, A., *see* Bigsten, A.   481, 1650
Isham, J.   1673, 1674
Ishii, T., *see* Fujita, M.P.   1576
Islam, N.   582n, 586n, 628, 629, 635, 635n,
  683, 786, 804n, 805, 806, 938
Israel, J.I.   454
Iversen, T.   1326
Iyer, L., *see* Do, T.   508
Iyigun, M.F.   259n

Jacklin, C.   878
Jackson, M.   1660
Jacob, M.C.   1137n
Jacoby, H.G.   498, 878
Jaffe, A.B.   1763n, 1798
Jaffe, A.B., *see* Newell, R.G.   1796
Jakubson, G.H., *see* Fields, G.S.   1732
Jalan, J.   339, 1035
Jalan, J., *see* Ravallion, M.   1035
James, H.   1164n
Jamison, D., *see* Bhargava, A.   655
Jayaratne, J.   907, 907n
Jean, Y., *see* Carson, R.T.   1813
Jeanne, O., *see* Gourinchas, P.-O.   687n
Jensen, M.   872n, 873, 874, 882
Jensen, M., *see* Fama, E.   872n
Jensen, R.   1425n
Jeong, H.   543
Jimenez, E.   1658
John, A., *see* Cooper, R.W.   145
Johnson, D.G.   1355, 1385
Johnson, G.E.   703n
Johnson, M., *see* Zhang, X.   1706n
Johnson, P.A.   332n, 597, 598, 606, 620n
Johnson, P.A., *see* Durlauf, S.N.   77n, 256, 331,
  579n, 589, 607, 619, 619n, 622, 942, 1681
Johnson, P.A., *see* Temple, J.W.   658, 659
Johnson, S.   508, 914, 999, 1653

Johnson, S., *see* Acemoglu, D. 193n, 277, 278, 302, 393, 397n, 402, 410, 413, 414, 417, 417n, 419, 453, 464, 506, 639n, 651, 654, 656–658, 662, 923, 1005, 1033, 1054, 1055
Johnson, S., *see* Aslund, A. 989, 999
Johnson, S., *see* Friedman, E. 999
Johnson, W.R., *see* Neal, D.A. 704, 705n
Jolly, R., *see* Chenery, H.B. 1714n, 1724n
Jones, C.I. xin, 92, 93, 98, 117n, 176n, 219, 236n, 256, 261, 563, 626, 822, 838, 841, 843, 857, 1079, 1079n, 1087, 1089, 1091–1093, 1094n, 1095, 1098n, 1099, 1100, 1100n, 1102, 1103n, 1105n, 1120, 1147, 1264, 1305n, 1504n, 1517, 1517n, 1781n
Jones, C.I., *see* Bernard, A. 604n
Jones, C.I., *see* Hall, R.E. 136n, 277, 277n, 314, 314n, 402, 605, 606, 643, 652, 654, 658, 662, 684, 685, 688, 829, 833, 938, 1005, 1018n, 1032, 1097, 1390n, 1445, 1466n
Jones, C.P., *see* Wilson, J.W. 1207n
Jones, E.L. 277, 397, 1171
Jones, L.E. 16n, 19, 20, 23, 23n, 39, 41n, 60, 61, 61n, 586n, 820, 823, 825, 1103n, 1266, 1267, 1772, 1798n
Jones, L.E., *see* Boldrin, M. 234n, 1265
Jones, R., *see* McEvedy, C. 410
Jorgenson, D.W. 682n, 719n, 725, 757n, 759, 759n, 760, 760n, 763, 763n, 769, 771, 774, 774n, 779, 782, 782n, 783, 783n, 784, 785n, 786n, 787, 788n, 805, 870, 1290n, 1291, 1292n, 1294, 1346, 1352n, 1786n
Jorgenson, D.W., *see* Christensen, L.R. 684n, 781n, 787, 805
Jorgenson, D.W., *see* Conrad, K. 718n
Jorgenson, D.W., *see* Dougherty, C. 787, 805
Jorgenson, D.W., *see* Ho, M.S. 1294n
Jovanovic, B. 500n, 525, 715, 1185, 1189, 1204, 1206, 1207, 1210, 1295n, 1296, 1300, 1333, 1335n, 1344
Jovanovic, B., *see* Atje, R. 894
Jovanovic, B., *see* Eeckhout, J. 938
Jovanovic, B., *see* Greenwood, J. 150n, 541n, 783n, 871, 876, 888, 1185, 1207, 1338
Jovanovic, B., *see* Hobijn, B. 1207, 1215n
Judd, K.L. 113, 122n, 145n, 1070n
Judson, R.A. 634
Judson, R.A., *see* Schmalensee, R. 1818n
Juhn, C. 1285, 1286, 1288n
Jung, W.S. 905
Junius, K. 1561

Justman, M. 1741
Justman, M., *see* Gradstein, M. 1616n, 1741n

Kaganovich, M. 20
Kahin, B., *see* Brynjolfsson, E. 807n
Kahn, C., *see* Calomiris, C. 878n
Kahn, L.M., *see* Bertola, G. 1312, 1340
Kahn, L.M., *see* Blau, F.D. 1266, 1267, 1267n, 1731
Kahn, M., *see* Costa, D. 1678, 1680, 1685, 1686
Kalaitzidakis, P. 610
Kalemli-Ozcan, S. 157, 227n
Kambourov, G. 1335n, 1336, 1337
Kanbur, R. 513
Kanbur, R., *see* Anand, S. 1713n, 1732
Kandori, M. 1653, 1658
Kanemoto, Y. 1564, 1573
Kaplan, H.S., *see* Robson, A.J. 276n
Karlan, D.S. 521n
Karlan, D.S., *see* Ashraf, N. 522
Karlan, D.S., *see* Bertrand, M. 522
Karyadi, D., *see* Basta, S.S. 490
Kaserer, C., *see* Wenger, E. 884, 885, 918n
Kashyap, A. 878n
Kashyap, A., *see* Hoshi, T. 884n, 918n
Katsoulacos, Y., *see* Beath, J. 349
Katz, L.F. 777n, 807n, 1205, 1205n, 1281, 1281n, 1282, 1285, 1297–1299, 1715n, 1720n, 1724, 1727n
Katz, L.F., *see* Autor, D.H. 1283n, 1597n
Katz, L.F., *see* Borjas, G.J. 142n
Katz, L.F., *see* Goldin, C. 198, 212, 257n, 1205, 1682, 1684, 1725n
Katz, L.M., *see* Cutler, D.M. 1355
Katz, L.M., *see* Goldin, C. 1282, 1309, 1309n, 1310, 1311, 1311n, 1360
Kauffman, S.A. 1147
Kaufman, R.F. 1797n
Kaufman, R.F., *see* Haggard, S. 998n
Kaufmann, D. 649, 974n
Kaufmann, D., *see* Friedman, E. 999
Kawachi, I., *see* Lochner, K. 1683
Keefer, P. 658, 662
Keefer, P., *see* Knack, S. 402, 403, 506, 649, 658, 1644, 1660, 1682
Keele, K.D. 1169
Keeler, E. 1774n, 1786, 1810n
Keeler, M. 455
Kehoe, P.J., *see* Atkeson, A.A. 1098n, 1204, 1296, 1325, 1360, 1452n

Kehoe, P.J., *see* Backus, D.K.   1096, 1425n, 1517

Kehoe, P.J., *see* Chari, V.V.   1019n

Kehoe, T.J.   350

Kehoe, T.J., *see* Backus, D.K.   1096, 1517

Keirzkowsky, H., *see* Findlay, R.   281n

Keller, W.   79n, 852, 857, 949n

Kelley, A.   657

Kelley, E.M.   1210n, 1212

Kelly, A.C.   1578

Kelly, F.C.   1153n

Kelly, M.   586n, 1359

Kelly, T.   654

Kendrick, J.W.   781, 781n, 784, 1218n

Kennedy, C.   131n

Kenny, C.   1032

Kettlewell, H.B.D.   265n

Keyser, B.W.   1139

Keyssar, A.   448

Khan, B.Z.   1165, 1166

Khan, M., *see* Luintel, K.B.   906n

Kierzkowski, H., *see* Findlay, R.   1425n

Kihlstrom, R.   513

Kiiski, S., *see* Cornia, G.A.   1733

Kiley, M.T.   806n, 1305, 1598n, 1620n

Killick, T.   447

Kim, H.S.   1565

Kim, M., *see* Grossman, H.I.   259n, 398, 399

Kim, S.   1555, 1556

Kim, S., *see* Nadiri, M.I.   938

Kimko, D.D., *see* Hanushek, E.A.   656, 702n, 704, 705n, 938, 1018n

King, I.   1332n

King, M.A.   847n

King, R.G.   314n, 316n, 653, 661, 684, 781n, 870n, 871, 876, 880, 890–893, 895n, 898

Kingdon, G.G., *see* Dreze, J.   498

Kirby, P.   1155

Kirkwood, T.B.L.   275n

Kiviet, J.   634

Kiviet, J., *see* Bun, M.   634

Kiyotaki, N.   350

Klapper, L.F., *see* Berger, A.N.   897

Klasen, S.   661

Klein, M.   907n

Klenow, P.J.   135, 136n, 499, 604–606, 627, 646n, 647, 648, 684, 688, 689, 698, 706, 833, 834, 938, 948, 1018n, 1032, 1390n, 1445, 1466n

Klenow, P.J., *see* Bils, M.   495, 502, 653, 687n, 698, 706, 833, 938, 1104n

Klenow, P.J., *see* Heckman, J.J.   710n

Klenow, P.J., *see* Hsieh, C.-T.   493, 687n, 1019n

Klenow, P.J., *see* Hummels, D.   835

Klenow, P.J., *see* Irwin, D.A.   807n, 1295n

Klepper, S.   591, 642

Kline, P., *see* Charles, K.   1686

Klitgaard, R.   1036

Knack, S.   402, 403, 506, 649, 656, 658, 1644, 1660, 1682

Knack, S., *see* Keefer, P.   658, 662

Knack, S., *see* Zak, P.   658, 1658, 1683

Knight, J.B.   1713n

Knight, J.B., *see* Gelb, A.   711n

Knight, M.   579, 683, 1446n

Knight, M., *see* Loayza, N.V.   1425n

Knowles, K.   1158

Knowles, S.   653, 655

Kocherlakota, N.R.   626, 1355, 1414

Kogel, T.   236n, 262

Koh, W., *see* Baltagi, B.   644

Kohler, H.   269n

Kohler, H., *see* Rodgers, J.L.   269n

Kolko, J.   1556, 1574

Komlos, J.   223n

Kongsamut, P.   1263

König, W.   1165

Konus, A.   750

Koopmans, T.C.   xi, 16, 17, 298, 388

Koren, M.   718n

Kormendi, R.L.   32, 45, 581n, 654–657, 659

Kortum, S.S.   820, 823, 1089, 1105, 1199

Kortum, S.S., *see* Eaton, J.   79n, 493, 647, 711, 820, 822, 835, 837, 841, 842, 854n, 938, 1470n

Kosmin, B.A.   1035

Kotwal, A., *see* Eswaran, M.   508

Kourtellos, A.   618, 621

Kourtellos, A., *see* Durlauf, S.N.   617, 618, 1681

Kraay, A.   1490n

Kraay, A., *see* Dollar, D.   652, 658, 659, 1422n, 1734, 1736

Kraay, A., *see* Driscoll, J.   644

Kraay, A., *see* Kaufmann, D.   649

Kramarz, F., *see* Abowd, J.M.   1331n

Kranakis, E.   1141

Kranton, R.   1646n

Kranton, R., *see* Akerlof, G.   1655

Krasker, W.   649n

Kraus, F., *see* Flora, P. 205–207, 209, 211, 215, 226, 255
Kravis, I.B. 803
Krebs, T. 61, 62n, 876n
Kreiner, C.T., *see* Dalgaard, C.-J. 165, 224n
Kremer, M. 221n, 223, 224n, 239n, 272n, 340, 346, 497, 498, 596, 597, 827, 857, 1021, 1088, 1095, 1098–1100, 1147, 1324, 1598n, 1619, 1621n
Kremer, M., *see* Duflo, E. 482, 495, 516, 521, 522
Kremer, M., *see* Easterly, W. 326, 565, 568n, 625, 655, 656, 659, 829, 996, 1036n
Kremer, M., *see* Gugerty, M.K. 1687
Kremer, M., *see* Miguel, E. 490, 498, 517, 521
Kreps, D. 1602n
Krishna, A. 1674, 1676
Kroft, K. 34, 35
Krolzig, H.-M., *see* Hendry, D. 612, 640
Kronick, D.A. 1134n, 1163
Kroszner, R., *see* Cowen, T. 910n
Krueger, A.B. 491, 540n, 653, 661, 705n, 938, 1018n, 1331n, 1603n, 1724n
Krueger, A.B., *see* Autor, D.H. 1283n, 1597n
Krueger, A.B., *see* Card, D. 702n
Krueger, A.B., *see* Farber, H.S. 1326
Krueger, A.B., *see* Grossman, G.M. 1757n, 1765, 1766n, 1769, 1770n, 1810
Krueger, A.B., *see* Katz, L.F. 777n
Krueger, A.O. 973n
Krueger, D. 1302, 1355–1357
Krugman, P.R. 143n, 157, 328n, 398, 974, 1021, 1340, 1425n, 1453n, 1485, 1485n, 1550, 1568, 1578, 1579
Krugman, P.R., *see* Brezis, E.S. 278n
Krugman, P.R., *see* Brezis, S.L. 1427n, 1453n
Krugman, P.R., *see* Fujita, J. 1578, 1579
Krugman, P.R., *see* Fujita, M.P. 1021, 1486n
Krugman, P.R., *see* Helpman, E. 124, 1446n, 1483n
Kruk, M., *see* Sachs, J.D. 298, 300n, 304n
Krusell, P. 131n, 398, 399, 434, 1196n, 1205, 1298, 1304, 1414, 1625n
Krusell, P., *see* Greenwood, J. 715, 768, 1106, 1291, 1292, 1294, 1295
Krusell, P., *see* Hornstein, A. 1204, 1295, 1295n, 1296, 1297n, 1307, 1332, 1333, 1346, 1347, 1347n, 1349, 1350
Krussel, P. 515, 544n
Kubitschek, W., *see* Hallinan, M. 1680n
Kuczynski, P.-P. 974n

Kuersteiner, G., *see* Hahn, J. 634n
Kugler, M., *see* Neusser, K. 905
Kuhn, T.S. 175n
Kumar, K.B. 917n
Kumar, K.B., *see* Krueger, D. 1302
Kuncoro, A., *see* Henderson, J.V. 1562, 1563
Kupperman, K.O. 420
Kurian, G.T. 212
Kurlat, S., *see* Alesina, A. 278, 653, 1505
Kuuluvainen, J., *see* Tahvonen, O. 1797
Kuznets, S. 217, 434, 719n, 768, 779, 780, 780n, 781, 781n, 782, 782n, 784, 786, 791, 792, 803, 804, 806, 1069, 1201n, 1373, 1704, 1706n, 1712
Kuzynski, R.R. 201
Kwan, F.Y.K. 123
Kydland, F., *see* Backus, D. 1425n
Kyle, A.S. 872
Kyn, O., *see* Papanek, G. 1733n

La Ferrara, E., *see* Alesina, A. 662, 1505n, 1686, 1688
La Porta, R. 84n, 399, 425, 426, 506, 658, 874, 885, 887, 892, 897, 922, 923, 1033, 1505, 1683
La Porta, R., *see* Djankov, S. 99, 425, 426, 506, 509n, 1006–1008, 1395
La Porta, R., *see* Glaeser, E.L. 278–280
Lachman, S.P., *see* Kosmin, B.A. 1035
Lack, D. 231, 269, 269n
Ladron de Guevara, A. 26
Laeven, L. 885
Laeven, L., *see* Caprio Jr., G. 874, 885, 923n
Laeven, L., *see* Claessens, S. 653, 661, 913, 914
Laeven, L., *see* Demirgüç-Kunt, A. 907n
Laffont, J.-J. 509n
Laffont, J.-J., *see* Kihlstrom, R. 513
Lagerlof, N.-P. 234, 236n, 238, 255, 259, 261, 262, 278, 280
Lagerlof, N.-P., *see* Edlund, L. 231
Lai, E.L.-C. 124, 130, 1425n
Lai, E.L.-C., *see* Grossman, G.M. 123
Lai, E.L.-C., *see* Kwan, F.Y.K. 123
Laibson, D. 520
Laibson, D., *see* Glaeser, E.L. 1020n, 1667, 1689
Laitner, J. 1207, 1263
LaLonde, R.J. 1360
Lambsdorff, J.G. 364
Lamo, A. 598, 598n

Lamo, A., *see* Andres, J.   598, 598n
Lamoreaux, N.   879, 888
Landefeld, J.S.   750n
Landes, D.   561
Landes, D.S.   207, 277, 402, 419, 1171
Landes, W.   1249
Lang, L., *see* Claessens, S.   874
Lang, S.   458, 459
Lapham, B.J., *see* Devereux, M.B.   124, 126, 126n, 1425n
Lasota, A.   377
Lau, L.J.   759n, 980
Lau, L.J., *see* Bhargava, A.   655
Laumann, E., *see* Sandefur, R.   1690n
Laurini, M., *see* Andrade, E.   598
Lavezzi, A.M., *see* Fiaschi, D.   256n, 598
Law, S., *see* Demetriades, P.O.   653, 661, 662
Lawrence, D.A., *see* Diewert, W.E.   760n
Layard, R., *see* Nickell, S.   1340, 1341, 1353
Lazear, E.P., *see* Freeman, R.B.   1328
Le Van, C., *see* Dimaria, C.H.   350
Leamer, E.   609, 610, 649
Leamer, E., *see* Klepper, S.   591, 642
Lebergott, S.   1228, 1229, 1246, 1249n, 1258n, 1259n
Leblang, D., *see* Eichengreen, B.   652
Leblang, D., *see* Granato, J.   658
Leblebicioglu, A., *see* Bond, S.   627, 660
Lecaillon, J.   1732
Lederman, D.   833, 834, 839, 846, 849, 854
Lee, D.   1299n, 1597n
Lee, F., *see* Coulombe, S.   656
Lee, J.-W.   701, 702, 703n, 704
Lee, J.-W., *see* Barro, R.J.   105, 195, 216, 283n, 491n, 589, 638, 653, 655–659, 685, 694, 695, 826, 827, 829–831, 834, 846, 948, 1037, 1519
Lee, J.Y., *see* Henderson, J.V.   1556, 1563
Lee, K.S.   586n, 629, 634, 635, 1562
Lee, R.D.   182n, 272n, 1098–1100, 1710n
Lee, S.J.   459, 1673, 1675
Lee, T.C.   1555, 1556, 1561
Lee, T.C., *see* Henderson, J.V.   1556, 1563
Lee, W.   1609n
Lefort, F., *see* Caselli, F.   136n, 579, 589, 629, 632, 638, 653, 654, 656, 683, 953, 1048, 1446n
Legovini, A., *see* Bouillon, C.P.   1035
Legros, P.   1598n, 1623
Leland, H.   39
Lemieux, T., *see* Card, D.   1285n
Lemieux, T., *see* DiNardo, J.   1326

Lemieux, T., *see* Fortin, N.M.   1597n
Leonard, H., *see* Leamer, E.   609
Leonard, J.S., *see* Dickens, W.T.   1326
Leonardi, R., *see* Putnam, R.D.   402, 658, 1643, 1648
Lerner, J.   1165n, 1166, 1199
Lerner, J., *see* Kortum, S.   1199
Lester, R.K., *see* Dertouzos, M.   782n
Lettau, M., *see* Campbell, J.   1342
Levchenko, A.   1428n, 1491n
Levhari, D.   39, 44, 113n, 870
Levin, R.C., *see* Cohen, W.M.   89, 136
Levine, D.K., *see* Boldrin, M.   28, 30, 62, 1088, 1207
Levine, D.K., *see* Kehoe, T.J.   350
Levine, D.K., *see* Miguel, E.   1687
Levine, P., *see* Chui, M.   1425n
Levine, R.   84, 441, 493, 575, 609, 610, 645, 647, 648, 653–657, 659, 661, 877, 886, 893–895, 895n, 896, 896n, 897, 898, 898n, 899–901, 907, 907n, 918n, 919, 1033
Levine, R., *see* Barth, J.R.   922
Levine, R., *see* Beck, T.   653, 655, 661, 897, 897n, 900, 902, 904, 904n, 907n, 912, 915, 918–920, 922, 923, 923n
Levine, R., *see* Boyd, J.H.   923
Levine, R., *see* Caprio Jr., G.   874, 885, 923n
Levine, R., *see* Demirgüç-Kunt, A.   881, 894n, 907n, 918, 920
Levine, R., *see* Easterly, W.   278, 314n, 326, 331, 567n, 605, 615, 645n, 653–659, 684n, 829, 833, 870n, 923, 1005, 1018n, 1032, 1050n, 1054, 1055, 1505, 1681, 1681n, 1682
Levine, R., *see* Edison, H.   907n
Levine, R., *see* King, R.G.   653, 661, 684, 870n, 871, 876, 890–893, 895n, 898
Levine, R., *see* Laeven, L.   885
Levinson, A.   1764
Levinson, A., *see* Andreoni, J.   1799
Levinson, A., *see* Harbaugh, W.   1767n
Levinson, A., *see* Hilton, H.   1766n, 1767n, 1768
Levinthal, D.A., *see* Cohen, W.M.   78n
Levy, F.   1281, 1281n
Levy, F., *see* Autor, D.H.   1302n
Levy, F., *see* Murnane, R.J.   704, 704n
Levy, P.A.   1326n
Levy-Leboyer, M.   188, 214
Lewis, A.   1713
Lewis, H.G., *see* Becker, G.S.   228
Lewis, W.A.   413n, 719n, 1577

Ley, E., *see* Fernandez, C.   587, 587n, 612, 613, 613n, 614, 1681
Li, C.-W.   1095
Li, H.   462, 541, 655, 662
Li, Q.   602
Li, R.   490
Li, S.   1005
Li, W.   26
Li, Z., *see* Lin, J.Y.   980
Licandro, O., *see* Boucekkine, R.   259
Lichbach, M.I.   450n
Lichtenberg, F.R.   656, 1206
Lichtenberg, F.R., *see* Bartel, A.P.   938, 1205, 1301
Ligon, E., *see* Conley, T.G.   645
Lillard, L.A.   1318
Limao, N.   300n, 349n
Lin, I.-F., *see* Case, A.   518n
Lin, J.Y.   978n, 980
Lin, N.   1644
Lindahl, M., *see* Krueger, A.B.   540n, 653, 661, 938, 1018n, 1724n
Lindauer, D.L.   973n, 1009
Lindbeck, A.   779n, 1321, 1330, 1597n
Lindert, P.H.   214, 459, 460, 1724n, 1736
Lindert, P.H., *see* Williamson, J.G.   1205
Lindquist, M.J.   1300, 1301
Lipscomb, A.A.   1069
Lipset, S.M.   1035
Lipsey, R.G.   1295
Lipsey, R.G., *see* Blomstrom, M.   627, 656, 659
Lipton, D.   989
List, J.A.   1715
Liu, M., *see* Lin, J.Y.   978n
Liu, Z.   589, 617, 618
Livi Bacci, M.   185, 1148n
Livingston, F.   266n
Livshits, I., *see* Bridgman, B.   1414
Ljungqvist, L.   354n, 1342, 1344, 1346
Lleras-Muney, A., *see* Dehejia, R.   907, 908
Lloyd-Ellis, H.   537n, 1302, 1598n, 1620n
Lloyd-Ellis, H., *see* Francois, P.   157n
Lloyd-Ellis, H., *see* Kroft, K.   34, 35
Loayza, N.V.   661, 903, 978n, 1425n
Loayza, N.V., *see* Beck, T.   900, 902
Loayza, N.V., *see* Easterly, W.   953
Loayza, N.V., *see* Knight, M.   579, 683, 1446n
Loayza, N.V., *see* Kraay, A.   1490n
Loayza, N.V., *see* Levine, R.   84, 661, 897, 898, 898n, 899, 900, 1033
Lochner, K.   1683

Lochner, L., *see* Heckman, J.J.   1318, 1319, 1354–1357, 1739n
Loewy, M.   602
Loh, W.-Y.   620n
Londregan, J.B.   661
Londregan, J.B., *see* Dixit, A.K.   429n
Long, B.T., *see* Hoxby, C.M.   1324n
Long, J.   643, 1155
Long, S.K.   498
Lonsdale, J., *see* Berman, B.J.   449
Lopez, R.   985n, 1770, 1779, 1786, 1786n, 1810
Lopez-de-Silanes, F., *see* Djankov, S.   99, 425, 426, 506, 509n, 1006–1008, 1395
Lopez-de-Silanes, F., *see* Glaeser, E.L.   278–280
Lopez-de-Silanes, F., *see* La Porta, R.   84n, 399, 425, 426, 506, 658, 874, 885, 887, 892, 897, 922, 923, 1033, 1505, 1683
Lora, E.   976, 977, 978n
Loury, G.C.   354, 537, 1603n, 1642, 1677
Love, I.   916
Love, I., *see* Fisman, R.J.   889, 904n, 912n
Lowood, H.   1143, 1143n
Lucas, R.E.   xin, 101, 176n, 221n, 257n, 314n, 316, 388, 491, 558, 807, 819–821, 825, 843, 849, 867, 1079, 1092, 1098n, 1099, 1103, 1104, 1148, 1504, 1546, 1565, 1800, 1801
Lucas, R.E., *see* Alvarez, F.   1470n
Lucas, R.E., *see* Stokey, N.L.   311n, 320, 376
Lucas Jr., R.E.   23, 24, 30, 62, 329, 768, 1295n, 1336, 1342, 1359, 1378, 1400
Luckhurst, K.W., *see* Hudson, D.   1142n
Lui, F.T., *see* Erlich, I.   231n
Luintel, K.B.   906n
Luintel, K.B., *see* Arestis, P.   905
Lund, S., *see* Fafchamps, M.   513, 1673
Lundberg, M.   1733n
Lundberg, S.   519
Lundblad, C., *see* Bekaert, G.   653, 661, 907
Lundborg, P.   1442n
Lundgren, A.   1151n
Lundström, S.   661
Lustig, N., *see* Bouillon, C.P.   1035
Lustig, N., *see* Bourguignon, F.   1730n, 1737n
Lybeck, J.A.   1741n
Lyons, R.K., *see* Caballero, R.J.   338n

Maasoumi, E.   595
MacArthur, R.H.   231, 269
Macfarlane, A.   1152, 1152n

MacGee, J., *see* Bridgman, B. 1414
Machin, S. 1288, 1326
Machin, S., *see* Berman, E. 1597n
Machin, S., *see* Gosling, A. 1326
MacKinnon, J. 643
MacKinnon, J., *see* Davidson, R. 643
MacLean, B.K. 975, 1001n
MacLeod, C. 1165
MacMillan, R., *see* Hagan, J. 1678
Madalozzo, R., *see* Andrade, E. 598
Maddala, G. 618
Maddison, A. 76, 175, 179–182, 187–189,
 196, 199, 204, 218, 219, 219n, 228n, 256,
 307, 307n, 405, 565, 601, 785n, 786, 803,
 803n, 804, 969, 1091, 1098, 1117n, 1171,
 1373, 1374, 1377n, 1386, 1388, 1398, 1403,
 1405, 1410, 1411
Mafezzoli, M., *see* Cuñat, A. 1425n, 1463n
Magendzo, I., *see* Edwards, S. 653
Maggi, G., *see* Grossman, G.M. 1598n, 1619,
 1627n
Magill, M. 373
Mailath, G., *see* Cole, H. 544
Majluf, N., *see* Myers, S.C. 872n
Majumdar, M. 350
Maksimovic, V., *see* Beck, T. 914, 916, 917
Maksimovic, V., *see* Demirgüç-Kunt, A. 886,
 889, 914, 916, 917, 919
Malaney, P., *see* Bloom, D.E. 655
Maler, K.-G. 779n
Maler, K.-G., *see* Dasgupta, P. 1752n, 1760n
Malkiel, B., *see* Campbell, J.Y. 1342
Mallon, R., *see* Van Arkadie, B. 976n
Mallows, C., *see* Draper, D. 582
Maloney, W.F., *see* Lederman, D. 839, 854
Malthus, T.R. 221, 221n, 1261, 1374
Maluccio, J. 1675
Maluccio, J., *see* Carter, M. 1674
Mamuneas, T. 618
Mamuneas, T., *see* Kalaitzidakis, P. 610
Mankiw, N.G. xii, 77, 477, 502, 578, 586n,
 587n, 598, 604, 605, 618, 629, 637, 642, 647,
 657, 684, 689, 804, 805, 821, 1018n, 1022n,
 1050, 1097, 1445, 1466n
Mankiw, N.G., *see* Barro, R.J. 647
Manova, K., *see* Aghion, P. 107n, 879
Manovskii, I., *see* Kambourov, G. 1335n,
 1336, 1337
Mansfield, E. 942n
Manski, C. 516n, 645, 1643n, 1667, 1668,
 1670, 1689

Mantoux, P. 1168
Manuelli, R.E. 62, 1296, 1333n, 1338
Manuelli, R.E., *see* Jones, L.E. 16n, 19, 20, 23,
 23n, 39, 41n, 60, 61, 61n, 586n, 820, 823,
 825, 1103n, 1266, 1267, 1772, 1798n
Marcet, A., *see* Canova, F. 618, 619
Margo, R.A. 1249
Margo, R.A., *see* Goldin, C. 1311n
Margolis, D.N., *see* Abowd, J.M. 1331n
Marimon, R. 1345
Marin, J.M., *see* de la Fuente, A. 875
Marion, N., *see* Aizenman, J. 38
Marshall, A. 400, 1546, 1565
Martin, G., *see* Macfarlane, A. 1152, 1152n
Martin, P. 36, 156, 1490n
Martin, P., *see* Baldwin, R. 1425n, 1486n
Martin, R., *see* Corrado, L. 601n
Masanjala, W. 612–615
Masanjala, W., *see* Papageorgiou, C. 619
Maskin, E.S., *see* Bessen, J. 145
Maskin, E.S., *see* Dewatripont, M. 884, 920
Maskin, E.S., *see* Fudenberg, D. 1659
Maskin, E.S., *see* Kremer, M. 1324, 1598n,
 1619, 1621n
Maskus, K.E., *see* Yang, G. 130, 1425n
Massey, D., *see* Palloni, A. 1673, 1675, 1680
Masters, W.E. 277n, 653, 654, 658
Mastruzzi, M., *see* Kaufmann, D. 649
Mateos-Planas, X. 715
Matoussi, M.S., *see* Laffont, J.-J. 509n
Matsuyama, K. 120n, 143n, 157, 158, 160n,
 281n, 303, 318n, 328n, 329, 335n, 349, 351,
 354n, 358, 537, 999, 1000, 1425n, 1470n,
 1473n, 1485n, 1487n, 1490n
Matsuyama, K., *see* Ciccone, A. 145, 145n
Matthews, R.C. 195, 197
Maurer, N. 443, 885
Maurer, N., *see* Haber, S.H. 443, 887, 923
Mauro, P. 506, 638, 649, 652, 661
May, J., *see* Maluccio, J. 1675
Mayer, C., *see* Carlin, W. 920
Mayer, D., *see* Howitt, P.W. 500n
Mayer, T., *see* Head, K. 1547
Mayer-Foulkes, D. 77, 77n
Mayer-Foulkes, D., *see* Aghion, P. 82, 106n,
 256n, 510n, 529, 899
Mayer-Foulkes, D., *see* Howitt, P.W. 81, 277n,
 939, 1681
McArthur, J.W. 654, 656
McArthur, J.W., *see* Sachs, J.D. 298, 300n,
 304n

McCall, J.J. 1344
McCallum, J. 1504n, 1536
McCarthy, B., *see* Hagan, J. 1676, 1679
McCarthy, D. 654
McCleary, R., *see* Barro, R.J. 402, 651, 658, 662
McClellan III, J.E. 1135n, 1143, 1144
McClelland, C.E. 211
McCloy, S.T. 1128n
McConnell, K.E. 1770n
McConnell, S. 1313n
McCord, G., *see* Sachs, J.D. 298, 300n, 304n
McCubbin, D., *see* Carson, R.T. 1813
McDaniel, T. 433
McDermott, J. 224n, 1414
McDermott, J., *see* Goodfriend, M. 222n, 1099
McEvedy, C. 410
McFadden, D., *see* Diamond, P. 733n
McGrattan, E.R. 25, 684n, 804n, 1019n, 1325, 1407n
McGrattan, E.R., *see* Chari, V.V. 1019n
McGrattan, E.R., *see* Jones, L.E. 1266, 1267
McGuckin, R. 1206
McKendrick, N. 1131
McKenzie, D. 481, 661
McKinnon, R.I. 867, 909, 910
McKinsey Global Institute, 500, 501
McLanahan, S., *see* Case, A. 518n
McMillan, J. 1653
McMillan, J., *see* Johnson, S. 508, 914, 999, 1653
McMillan, M.S., *see* Masters, W.E. 277n, 653, 654
McNeal, R. 1676, 1677, 1679
McNeil, M. 1134n, 1135n
Meadows, D.H. 1752n
Meadows, D.L., *see* Meadows, D.H. 1752n
Means, G.C., *see* Berle, A.A. 873
Meckling, W.R., *see* Jensen, M. 872n, 873, 874
Medoff, J.L., *see* Freeman, R.B. 1328
Meghir, C. 1331n
Meghir, C., *see* Aghion, P. 102, 104
Meguire, P.G., *see* Kormendi, R.L. 32, 45, 581n, 654–657, 659
Meier, A., *see* Sandefur, G. 1677, 1679
Meier, G.M. 867
Melka, J., *see* Van Ark, B. 786n
Mellinger, A., *see* Gallup, J.L. 655, 662, 1560
Meltzer, A. 1741
Menaghan, E., *see* Parcel, T. 1679
Mendez, J.A., *see* Gale, L. 1766n, 1769

Mendoza, E. 38, 39, 59, 61
Merriman, J.W. 1532
Merton, R.C. 869, 872, 886, 919
Merton, R.K. 1133n
Michelacci, C. 602, 603
Mieszkowski, P., *see* Flatters, F. 1567
Miguel, E. 490, 498, 517, 521, 660, 1687
Miguel, E., *see* Kremer, M. 498
Milanovic, B. 978n
Milesi-Ferretii, G., *see* Grilli, V. 661
Milgrom, P. 1310, 1320
Milgrom, P., *see* Greif, A. 298n
Miller, M.H. 867
Miller, M.H., *see* Grossman, S.J. 896
Miller, R., *see* Doppelhofer, G. 587, 612–615
Miller, W.B., *see* Rodgers, J.L. 269n
Mills, E. 1553, 1560
Mills, E., *see* Becker, G.S. 1578
Mills, L., *see* Carlino, G. 602
Mincer, J. 1266, 1317, 1318
Minier, J. 652
Minkin, A., *see* Durlauf, S.N. 617, 618, 1681
Minten, B., *see* Fafchamps, M. 1644, 1650, 1651, 1653, 1673, 1674
Mira, P., *see* Eckstein, Z. 227n
Mirman, L.J. 377
Mirman, L.J., *see* Amir, R. 350
Mirman, L.J., *see* Brock, W.A. 16, 308n, 320
Mitch, D. 207, 460, 1155
Mitchell, B. 194
Mitchell, M.F. 1310, 1320
Mitchell, M.F., *see* Holmes, T.J. 1300n, 1310n
Mitra, T., *see* Majumdar, M. 350
Moav, O. 224n, 231n, 1604n, 1719n
Moav, O., *see* Galor, O. 176n, 194n, 212n, 228, 230–232, 235n, 236, 236n, 239n, 258, 259, 259n, 260, 261, 263, 264, 266, 272n, 274, 275, 278–280, 1146, 1302, 1605n, 1613n
Moav, O., *see* Gould, E.D. 231, 1336, 1337
Möbius, M. 1321
Modigliani, F. 1425n
Moen, E.R. 1339
Moersch, M., *see* Black, S.W. 884
Moffitt, R., *see* Gottschalk, P. 1286, 1331, 1336, 1342, 1356
Mohring, H. 1566
Mokyr, J. 176n, 183n, 197, 207n, 209, 270n, 277, 304n, 306, 434, 561, 1115, 1119, 1123, 1126, 1127, 1129–1131, 1135, 1147, 1162, 1167, 1167n, 1377n
Molana, H. 1425n

Montesquieu, C.S. 400
Montgomery, J. 1653
Montiel, P., *see* Easterly, W. 953
Moody's Investors Service, 1210n
Mookherjee, D. 259n, 303, 317, 326, 326n, 354n, 537, 537n, 1604n
Moore, G.E. 748n, 750n
Moore, J.H, *see* Hart, O.D. 512
Moore, J.H., *see* Kiyotaki, N. 350
Moore, P., *see* Fernandez, R. 1678
Moore Jr., B. 425
Morales, M.F. 871
Morck, R. 872–874, 883, 884, 884n, 887, 918n
Morduch, J. 340, 357n, 515
Morelli, M., *see* Ghatak, M. 537
Morenoff, J., *see* Sampson, R. 1687, 1688
Morgan, D. 885
Morgan, E.S. 448
Morgan, S. 1677, 1679, 1680n
Morris, A.G., *see* Shan, J.Z. 892
Morris, C.T., *see* Adelman, I. 1706n
Morrisson, C. 213, 214, 1736
Morrisson, C., *see* Bourguignon, F. 1441, 1735
Morrisson, C., *see* Lecaillon, J. 1732
Morse, C., *see* Barnett, H.J. 1751n
Mortensen, D.T. 1331, 1332, 1346, 1349
Morus, I.R. 1150n
Mosse, W.E. 433
Motley, B. 655
Motohashi, K., *see* Jorgenson, D.W. 786n
Moulin, S., *see* Kremer, M. 497
Moulton, B.R. 754n
Mountford, A. 281n, 1425n
Mountford, A., *see* Galor, O. 176n, 193n, 236n, 258, 263, 264, 280–282
Mueller, D.C. 1741n
Mueller, E. 1265
Mukand, S. 1007, 1008, 1008n
Mulani, D., *see* Comin, D. 1342
Mulder, N., *see* van Ark, B. 786n
Mullainathan, S., *see* Bertrand, M. 522
Muller, D.K. 211
Mulligan, C.B. 25, 1103n
Munshi, K. 497, 516, 517n
Munshi, K., *see* Banerjee, A.V. 483, 495, 507, 511n, 517
Murdoch, P. 1139
Murdock, K., *see* Hellmann, T. 981, 982
Murmann, J.P. 1164
Murnane, R.J. 704, 704n
Murnane, R.J., *see* Autor, D.H. 1302n

Murnane, R.J., *see* Levy, F. 1281, 1281n
Murphy, K.M. 145, 340–342, 364, 365, 398, 503, 506n, 653, 711n, 996n, 999, 1001, 1021, 1285, 1288n, 1359, 1504
Murphy, K.M., *see* Becker, G.S. 224n, 235, 1021, 1378
Murphy, K.M., *see* Jensen, M. 874
Murphy, K.M., *see* Juhn, C. 1285, 1286
Murphy, K.M., *see* Katz, L.F. 1297–1299
Murphy, M., *see* Dyson, T. 190n
Murray, C., *see* Bhargava, A. 655
Murshid, K. 479, 480
Musson, A.E. 1128n, 1132
Myaux, J., *see* Munshi, K. 517n
Myers, M.G. 1425n
Myers, S.C. 872n
Myrdal, G. 400

Nadiri, M.I. 938
Nadiri, M.I., *see* Hultberg, P. 663
Nagypal, E., *see* Eckstein, Z. 1281, 1281n, 1282, 1282n, 1283, 1283n, 1284, 1285
Naim, M. 974n
Nakamura, M., *see* Morck, R. 884, 918n
Namunyu, R., *see* Kremer, M. 497
Nanetti, R.Y., *see* Putnam, R.D. 402, 658, 1643, 1648
Narayan, D. 1666, 1673, 1675
Narayan, D., *see* Woolcock, M. 1020n
Nardinelli, C. 1249, 1265
Nasution, P., *see* Henderson, J.V. 1562
Neal, D.A. 704, 705n
Neal, L. 456
Neary, J.F. 1579
Neary, J.P., *see* Anderson, J.E. 985n
Neary, P. 142n
Neher, A.P. 234n
Nelson, J.M., *see* Huntington, S.P. 1741n
Nelson, M. 654
Nelson, R.L. 1206n
Nelson, R.R. 78, 98, 102, 239, 270n, 373, 939, 1122n, 1162n, 1205, 1301, 1304
Nerlove, M. 632
Neumann, G., *see* Ingram, B. 1302
Neumark, D. 1286, 1335
Neusser, K. 905
Newell, R.G. 1796
Newey, W., *see* Holtz-Eakin, D. 632
Newman, A.F. 513
Newman, A.F., *see* Banerjee, A.V. 92n, 354n, 398, 399, 441, 513, 515, 537, 539n, 544n, 887, 1604n, 1623, 1720, 1722

Newman, A.F., *see* Legros, P.   1598n, 1623
Newton, A.P.   420
Ngai, L.R.   1374n, 1402n
Ngyen, S., *see* McGuckin, R.   1206
Nickell, S.   76, 86, 89, 631, 1340, 1341, 1341n, 1350, 1353
Nishimura, K.   308n, 350
Nishimura, K., *see* Dechert, W.D.   350
Nishimura, K., *see* Magill, M.   373
Noh, S.J., *see* Grossman, H.   429n
Nordhaus, W.D.   113, 122, 1065n, 1070, 1751n, 1752n, 1755n, 1782
Norman, V., *see* Dixit, A.K.   1446n
North, D.C.   150, 277, 301, 364, 367, 388, 419, 423, 427, 429n, 443, 453, 457, 463, 1005, 1007, 1054, 1117, 1127, 1649, 1650
Nugent, J., *see* Campos, N.   627
Nunziata, L., *see* Nickell, S.   1341n
Nurkse, R.   297, 719n
Nyarko, Y., *see* Jovanovic, B.   1204, 1295n
Nyarko, Y., *see* Majumdar, M.   350

Ó Gráda, C., *see* Allen, R.C.   1138n
Oates, W.E.   1505n
O'Brien, P.   1161n
Obstfeld, M.   876, 1425n, 1490n, 1504n
Ocampo, J.A.   974n, 998n, 999
Odedokun, M.   653
Odling-Smee, J.C., *see* Matthews, R.C.   195, 197
Oduro, A., *see* Bigsten, A.   1650
OECD Employment Outlook,   1288
Ofek, H.   266
Ogawa, H., *see* Fujita, M.P.   1565
Ogburn, W.F.   1268
Ogilvie, S.   1691
Ohanian, L.E.   1098n
Ohanian, L.E., *see* Krusell, P.   131n, 1196n, 1205, 1298, 1304
Ohlsson, H., *see* Agell, J.   662
Ohm Kyvik, K., *see* Rodgers, J.L.   269n
Oliner, S.D.   754, 771, 774n, 785n, 1291, 1294
Oliner, S.D., *see* Aizcorbe, A.   749
Olivei, G., *see* Klein, M.   907n
Oliver, J.   1687
Olivetti, C., *see* Fernandez, R.   262n, 1268
Olley, G.S.   481
Olshen, R., *see* Breiman, L.   619n
Olson, M.C.   429n, 434, 658
Olson, O., *see* Hibbs, D.A.   277n
Olsson, O.   1120, 1123

Onatski, A., *see* Kremer, M.   596, 597, 827
Oniki, H.   1463n
Ono, Y.   1425n, 1574
Oostendorp, R., *see* Bigsten, A.   1650
Oostendorp, R., *see* Freeman, R.B.   488n
Opal, C., *see* Fay, M.   1560
Oppenheimer, V.K.   1268
Organization for Economic Co-operation and Development,   807n
Ormrod, D.   1161n
O'Rourke, K.H.   217
O'Rourke, K.H., *see* Findlay, R.   217
Ortega, F.   1442n
Ortigueira, S.   1327, 1329
Ortigueira, S., *see* Ladron de Guevara, A.   26
Ospina, S., *see* Huggett, M.   1295n
Ostrom, E.   1643, 1659
Ostrom, E., *see* Varughese, G.   1675, 1676
Oswald, A., *see* Blanchflower, D.   511n, 1692n
Ottaviano, G.I.P.   349, 1547, 1579
Ottaviano, G.I.P., *see* Baldwin, R.E.   281n, 1425n, 1486n
Oulton, N., *see* Basu, S.   1296
Overman, H.G.   1547, 1555
Overman, H.G., *see* Duranton, G.   1557
Overman, H.G., *see* Ioannides, Y.M.   1548, 1553, 1554
Overton, M.   435, 436
Owen, A., *see* Judson, R.A.   634
Owen, P., *see* Knowles, S.   653
Owens, T., *see* Barr, A.   1657
Oxley, L., *see* Greasley, D.   601
Ozler, S., *see* Alesina, A.   652, 655, 656, 662

Paap, R.   594, 595
Paasch, K., *see* Teachman, J.   1676, 1679
Pagan, A., *see* Breusch, T.   644
Pagano, M.   923
Pakes, A., *see* Olley, G.S.   481
Paldam, M.   1659
Palloni, A.   1673, 1675, 1680
Panagariya, A., *see* Lopez, R.   985n
Pandey, P., *see* Hoff, K.   330
Pannabecker, J.R.   1137n
Papageorgiou, C.   619, 620n
Papageorgiou, C., *see* Duffy, J.   257n, 605n, 620, 938
Papageorgiou, C., *see* Masanjala, W.   612–615
Papanek, G.   1733n
Papell, D.H., *see* Ben-David, D.   1091n
Papell, D.H., *see* Li, Q.   602

Papell, D.H., *see* Loewy, M.   602
Parcel, T.   1679
Parente, S.L.   136n, 277, 303, 434, 507, 715,
   820, 821, 827, 831, 835, 836n, 837, 843, 844,
   943n, 948n, 1263, 1375, 1376, 1380, 1390,
   1392, 1392n, 1395, 1395n, 1396, 1404,
   1405n, 1406, 1407, 1413n, 1414
Parente, S.L., *see* Gollin, D.   721, 723n
Pargal, S.   1675
Parker, R.P.   754
Parker, R.P., *see* Landefeld, J.S.   750n
Parry, J.H.   453
Paserman, M., *see* Gould, E.D.   1359
Paterson, D., *see* Cain, L.   1311
Patillo, C., *see* Bigsten, A.   1650
Patrick, H.T.   875
Patrick, H.T., *see* Cameron, R.   909
Patrinos, H.A.   1035
Patrinos, H.A., *see* Psacharopoulos, G.   206n,
   484, 487, 489, 834, 1035n, 1727–1729
Paukert, F.   1712, 1732
Paukert, F., *see* Lecaillon, J.   1732
Paulson, A.   542
Paxson, C., *see* Case, A.   518n
Paxson, C., *see* Deaton, A.   544n
Paxton, P.   1683, 1685, 1687
Pearlman, J., *see* Chui, M.   1425n
Peden, E.A.   1741n
Peek, J.   884n
Pennacchi, G., *see* Gorton, G.   878n
Pennington, D.H., *see* Brunton, D.   455
Pereira, A.S.   255
Peretto, P.F.   93n, 1094
Peretto, P.F., *see* Connolly, M.   260n
Perez, S., *see* Hoover, K.   611, 612, 643
Perez-Sebastian, F., *see* Duffy, J.   257n
Perkins, W.R., *see* Amir, R.   350
Perotti, R.   398, 1609
Perotti, R., *see* Alesina, A.   398
Perri, F., *see* Heathcote, J.   1425n
Perri, F., *see* Krueger, D.   1355–1357
Perron, P.   601
Persson, J.   586n
Persson, T.   398, 399, 538n, 636n, 642, 655,
   1600n
Pesaran, M.H.   584, 601, 634, 644
Pesaran, M.H., *see* Binder, M.   581, 592, 645
Pesaran, M.H., *see* Lee, K.S.   586n, 629, 634,
   635
Pessoa, S.   483
Petersen, B., *see* Fazzari, S.   511n

Petersen, M.A.   889
Peterson, S.R., *see* Jaffe, A.B.   1763n, 1798
Pettinato, S., *see* Graham, C.   1692n
Petzold, C.   747n
Pfenning, W., *see* Flora, P.   205–207, 209, 211,
   215, 226, 255
Pfleiderer, P., *see* Bhattacharya, S.   871
Phelps, E.S.   39, 44, 1070
Phelps, E.S., *see* Nelson, R.R.   78, 98, 102,
   239, 270n, 939, 1205, 1301, 1304
Philippe, M., *see* Baldwin, R.E.   281n
Philippon, T., *see* Chaney, T.   1342
Philipson, T.J., *see* Becker, G.S.   852n
Phillips, P.   635, 644
Philpin, C.H.E., *see* Aston, T.H.   441
Picon, A.   1136n
Pierce, B., *see* Juhn, C.   1285, 1286
Piketty, T.   92n, 354n, 424, 537, 539n, 1283,
   1597n, 1604n, 1720
Piketty, T., *see* Aghion, P.   82n
Pincus, S.   455
Pineda, J.   1608n, 1609, 1611
Ping, W., *see* Bond, E.   26
Piore, M.J.   1324n
Pirenne, H.   398, 440
Pischke, J.-S., *see* Acemoglu, D.   1328
Pissarides, C.A.   398, 1331, 1332n, 1346
Pissarides, C.A., *see* Mortensen, D.T.   1331,
   1332, 1346, 1349
Pistaferri, L., *see* Meghir, C.   1331n
Pistor, K.   1007, 1008
Pistor, K., *see* Berkowitz, D.   1007, 1008
Platteau, J.-P.   370n, 1646, 1653, 1655, 1663n
Plosser, C.I., *see* King, R.G.   880
Poewe, K.   1656
Polanyi, M.   1121, 1123
Polemarchakis, H.M., *see* Galor, O.   1425n
Pollak, R., *see* Lundberg, S.   519
Pollard, S.   910n, 1157n, 1161
Polterovich, V.   1002n
Pomeranz, K.   217, 217n, 280n, 1135, 1171n
Poole, K., *see* Londregan, J.B.   661
Popov, V., *see* Polterovich, V.   1002n
Popp, D.   1796
Porter, M.E.   165
Porter, R.   1127, 1135n, 1136n, 1140
Portes, A.   1643n, 1644, 1645
Portes, R.   1504n
Porteus, E., *see* Kreps, D.   1602n
Portney, P.R., *see* Jaffe, A.B.   1763n, 1798
Postan, M.M.   428n, 440

Postel-Vinay, G., *see* Piketty, T.   92n
Postlewaite, A., *see* Cole, H.   544
Powell, C.   498
Powell, R.   429n
Pratt, J., *see* Krasker, W.   649n
Pregibon, D., *see* Draper, D.   582
Prescott, E.C.   136n, 314n, 316n, 605–607, 684, 1410n
Prescott, E.C., *see* Boyd, J.H.   871
Prescott, E.C., *see* Cooley, T.F.   1294
Prescott, E.C., *see* Hansen, G.D.   176n, 236n, 262–264, 264n, 1099, 1238n, 1264, 1374–1376, 1380, 1383, 1386, 1389, 1396
Prescott, E.C., *see* Hornstein, A.   1393n
Prescott, E.C., *see* Lucas Jr., R.E.   1336, 1342
Prescott, E.C., *see* McGrattan, E.R.   25, 1325, 1407n
Prescott, E.C., *see* Parente, S.L.   136n, 277, 303, 434, 507, 820, 821, 827, 831, 835, 836n, 837, 843, 844, 943n, 948n, 1375, 1376, 1380, 1390, 1392, 1392n, 1395, 1395n, 1396, 1404, 1405n, 1406, 1407
Prescott, E.C., *see* Stokey, N.L.   311n, 320, 376
Preston, I., *see* Blundell, R.   1331n, 1355, 1356
Price, D.J.D.   1151n, 1152
Priestley, J.   1134n
Pritchett, L.   76, 219, 256, 316n, 331, 562, 573, 625, 630, 631, 636, 637, 641, 646, 710, 716, 830, 833, 1018n, 1020n, 1441, 1515n
Pritchett, L., *see* Easterly, W.   326, 565, 568n, 625, 655, 656, 659, 829, 996, 1036n
Pritchett, L., *see* Hausmann, R.   646, 990, 992
Pritchett, L., *see* Lindauer, D.L.   973n, 1009
Pritchett, L., *see* Narayan, D.   1666, 1673, 1675
Prskawetz, A., *see* Kogel, T.   236n, 262
Przeworski, A.   277n
Psacharopoulos, G.   206n, 484–487, 489, 686, 694, 834, 1035n, 1727–1729
Puga, D.   1425n, 1487n, 1578
Puga, D., *see* Duranton, G.   1547, 1564, 1565, 1575
Putnam, R.D.   658, 1643, 1648, 1685, 1693, 1693n
Putnam, R.D., *see* Helliwell, J.   402, 658, 1020n, 1664, 1682, 1689
Putterman, L., *see* Bockstette, V.   662

Qian, J., *see* Allen, F.   909
Qian, M., *see* Allen, F.   909
Qian, N.   497
Qian, Y.   980

Qian, Y., *see* Lau, L.J.   980
Qiu, L.D., *see* Lai, E.L.C.   124
Quadrini, V.   542
Quah, D.T.   77n, 84, 256, 331–333, 354n, 565, 587n, 596, 596n, 597–599, 606, 1069n, 1088n, 1549
Quah, D.T., *see* Durlauf, S.N.   256, 582n, 631, 804n, 1680n, 1681, 1810
Quiggin, J., *see* Dowrick, S.   591

Raboy, D.G., *see* Wiggins, S.N.   1199
Racine, J., *see* Maasoumi, E.   595
Radlet, S.   298
Rahn, W.   1687, 1688
Rahn, W., *see* Brehm, J.   1685, 1686
Rajan, R.G.   882, 883, 885, 887, 910, 912, 912n, 923, 1320n
Rajan, R.G., *see* Diamond, D.W.   878n
Rajan, R.G., *see* Kashyap, A.   878n
Rajan, R.G., *see* Kumar, K.B.   917n
Rajan, R.G., *see* Petersen, M.A.   889
Ram, R.   653
Ramakrishnan, R.T.S.   871
Ramey, G.   33, 34, 45, 150, 659
Ramey, G., *see* Den Haan, W.   1346
Ramey, V., *see* Ramey, G.   33, 34, 45, 150, 659
Ramirez, M., *see* Esfahani, H.   655, 662
Ramsey, F.P.   xiv, 1230, 1251
Ranciere, R., *see* Loayza, N.V.   661, 903
Randall, A.J.   434, 1168
Randers, J., *see* Meadows, D.H.   1752n
Rangel, A., *see* Helpman, E.   1337
Ranis, G., *see* Fei, J.C.H.   1713
Rannis, G.   1577
Rao, P.D.S.   720
Rappaport, J.   1558
Rappaport, N.J., *see* Berndt, E.R.   1196n
Rashad, R.   752n
Rasul, I., *see* Bandiera, O.   339, 349
Rauch, J.E.   502, 1425n, 1551, 1653, 1660, 1714
Ravallion, M.   513, 1035, 1734n, 1736n
Ravallion, M., *see* Chen, S.   297n
Ravallion, M., *see* Coate, S.T.   513
Ravallion, M., *see* Jalan, J.   339, 1035
Ravikumar, B., *see* Glomm, G.   1603n
Ray, D.   330, 354n, 398, 513, 522n, 1577
Ray, D., *see* Adsera, A.   328
Ray, D., *see* Dasgupta, P.   373, 537
Ray, D., *see* Mookherjee, D.   259n, 303, 317, 326, 326n, 354n, 537, 537n, 1604n

Ray, R., *see* Chakraborty, S. 882
Razin, A. 224n, 1261, 1264
Razin, A., *see* Frenkel, J. 1425n
Razo, A., *see* Haber, S.H. 887, 923
Rebelo, S.T. 30, 118n, 820, 823, 1017, 1018n, 1032, 1033, 1103
Rebelo, S.T., *see* Easterly, W. 1033
Rebelo, S.T., *see* King, R.G. 314n, 316n, 781n
Rebelo, S.T., *see* Kongsamut, P. 1263
Rebelo, S.T., *see* Stokey, N. 24
Redding, S. 349n
Redding, S., *see* Aghion, P. 986n
Redding, S., *see* Griffith, R. 78n
Redding, S., *see* Overman, H.G. 1547, 1555
Redondo-Vega, F. 1659
Rees, A. 784
Reffett, K., *see* Mirman, L.J. 377
Reichlin, L. 596
Reid, M.G. 1262, 1263
Reiter, S. 1120
Reitschuler, G., *see* Guaresma, J. 654, 661
Renaud, B. 1559, 1571
Renelt, D., *see* Levine, R. 493, 575, 609, 610, 645, 647, 648, 654–657, 659, 901, 1033
Resnick, D., *see* Zhang, X. 1706n
Resnick, M., *see* Rosen, K. 1553
Restuccia, D. 493, 720, 721, 723n
Rey, H., *see* Martin, P. 156, 1490n
Rey, H., *see* Portes, R. 1504n
Rey, P., *see* Aghion, P. 874
Reynolds, A. 431, 432
Ricardo, D. 1374
Ricci, L., *see* Edison, H. 907n
Rice, E., *see* DeAngelo, H. 882
Richard, J.-F., *see* Berkowitz, D. 1007, 1008
Richard, S., *see* Meltzer, A. 1741
Richards, F.J. 947n
Richardson, P.J., *see* Boyd, R. 266n
Riker, W.H. 1532
Ringer, F. 209, 460
Rioja, F. 903
Ríos-Rull, J.-V. 1263
Ríos-Rull, J.-V., *see* Krusell, P. 131n, 398, 399, 434, 1196n, 1205, 1298, 1304, 1414, 1625n
Ríos-Rull, J.-V., *see* Parente, S.L. 1413n, 1414
Rivera, B. 662
Rivera-Batiz, L.A. 120n, 124, 125, 126n, 820, 822, 1075n, 1425n
Rivkin, S.G., *see* Hanushek, E.A. 702n
Rob, R. 1659
Rob, R., *see* Jovanovic, B. 500n, 715

Robbins, D. 1308
Robert-Nicaud, F., *see* Baldwin, R. 1486n
Roberts, J., *see* Milgrom, P. 1310, 1320
Robertson, D. 634
Robertson, D., *see* Hall, S. 584
Robertson, D., *see* Knowles, K. 1158
Robertson, R., *see* Toya, H. 660
Robin, J.-M., *see* Bowlus, A.J. 1354, 1356, 1357
Robinson, E., *see* Musson, A.E. 1128n, 1132
Robinson, J.A. 422, 867
Robinson, J.A., *see* Acemoglu, D. 193n, 277, 278, 302, 393, 397n, 402, 410, 413, 414, 417, 417n, 419, 432, 435, 448, 450, 453, 458, 461, 463, 464, 506, 639n, 651, 654, 656–658, 662, 923, 1005, 1033, 1054, 1055, 1608n, 1741
Robinson, J.A., *see* Baland, J.M. 1608n
Robinson, J.A., *see* Bianchi, S. 1685, 1686
Robinson, J.A., *see* Duflo, E. 482, 495, 516, 521, 522
Robinson, S. 1713
Robinson, S., *see* Zhang, X. 1706n
Robison, L. 1683, 1684n
Robson, A.J. 266n, 276n
Roche, D. 1136n
Rodgers, J.L. 269n
Rodgers, J.L., *see* Kohler, H. 269n
Rodney, W. 428
Rodríguez, F. 558, 971n, 986, 1050, 1422n, 1609
Rodríguez, F., *see* Pineda, J. 1608n, 1609, 1611
Rodríguez, F., *see* Rodrik, D. 1515, 1516
Rodriguez, M., *see* Diamond, P. 733n
Rodriguez, R. 282n
Rodríguez-Clare, A. 143n, 349, 715, 1001
Rodríguez-Clare, A., *see* Klenow, P.J. 136n, 499, 604–606, 627, 646n, 647, 648, 684, 688, 689, 698, 706, 833, 834, 938, 948, 1018n, 1032, 1390n, 1445, 1466n
Rodriguez-Mora, J.V., *see* Hassler, J. 239n, 1597n, 1612n, 1617n
Rodrik, D. 278, 349, 462, 646, 654, 658, 659, 975, 981–984, 986n, 990, 996n, 997, 999, 1001, 1002, 1004n, 1005, 1006, 1515, 1516
Rodrik, D., *see* Alesina, A. 398, 399, 538n, 655, 1600n
Rodrik, D., *see* Diwan, I. 130
Rodrik, D., *see* Hausmann, R. 646, 990, 992, 999, 1000, 1003
Rodrik, D., *see* Mukand, S. 1007, 1008, 1008n

Rodrik, D., *see* Rodríguez, F. 558, 971n, 986, 1050, 1422n
Rodrik, D., *see* Rodriguez, R. 282n
Roe, M. 873n, 923
Roemer, J. 1662
Roemer, J., *see* Lee, W. 1609n
Rogers, C.A., *see* Martin, P. 36
Rogers, M., *see* Dowrick, S. 604n
Rogerson, R. 1264, 1289, 1352
Rogerson, R., *see* Benhabib, J. 1263
Rogerson, R., *see* Fernandez, R. 259n, 1603n, 1606
Rogerson, R., *see* Gollin, D. 721, 723n
Rogerson, R., *see* Parente, S.L. 1263
Rogoff, K., *see* Gertler, M. 1490n
Rogoff, K., *see* Obstfeld, M. 1504n
Roland, G., *see* Bolton, P. 1504n, 1506, 1510n
Roland, G., *see* Dewatripont, M. 989n
Roland, G., *see* Lau, L.J. 980
Romer, D. 424, 592
Romer, D., *see* Frankel, J.A. 99, 639, 659, 663, 1032, 1096, 1422n, 1515, 1525
Romer, D., *see* Mankiw, N.G. xii, 77, 477, 502, 578, 586n, 587n, 598, 604, 605, 618, 629, 642, 647, 657, 684, 689, 804, 805, 821, 1018n, 1022n, 1097, 1445, 1466n
Romer, P.M. xin, xiin, 93n, 114, 116, 116n, 125n, 147, 155n, 166, 223, 300, 317, 318n, 388, 558, 590, 591, 606n, 659, 660, 804, 805, 820, 822, 823, 833, 838, 857, 943, 1017, 1020n, 1065, 1066, 1070, 1073, 1082, 1088–1090, 1092, 1103, 1103n, 1106, 1107, 1504, 1517n, 1618n, 1718, 1800, 1801
Romer, P.M., *see* Evans, G. 158, 162, 165
Romer, P.M., *see* Rivera-Batiz, L.A. 120n, 124, 125, 126n, 820, 822, 1075n, 1425n
Roodman, D., *see* Easterly, W. 1050n
Root, H. 1162
Rose, A. 1505n
Rosen, H., *see* Holtz-Eakin, D. 632
Rosen, K. 1553
Rosen, L., *see* Geertz, C. 1656
Rosen, S. 1321
Rosenberg, N. 144, 1152, 1160, 1169
Rosengren, E.S., *see* Peek, J. 884n
Rosenstein-Rodan, P.N. 340, 341, 398, 503, 1001
Rosenstone, S. 1608
Rosenthal, J.-L., *see* Piketty, T. 92n
Rosenthal, S. 1547

Rosenzweig, M.R. 239n, 496, 497, 511, 514, 515, 1722n
Rosenzweig, M.R., *see* Behrman, J.R. 709
Rosenzweig, M.R., *see* Binswanger, H. 508
Rosenzweig, M.R., *see* Foster, A.D. 239n, 482, 495–497, 500n, 516, 938
Rosenzweig, M.R., *see* Munshi, K. 497
Ross, J.I. 450n
Rossi, P.E., *see* Jones, L.E. 23, 23n
Rossi-Hansberg, E. 1554, 1564–1566, 1573, 1576
Rossi-Hansberg, E., *see* Garicano, L. 1321
Rossi-Hansberg, E., *see* Lucas, R.E. 1565
Rostow, W.W. 304n, 330, 719n, 971
Rotella, E., *see* Cain, L. 1163n
Roubini, N. 653, 923
Roubini, N., *see* Alesina, A. 652, 655, 656, 662
Rousseau, P.L. 653, 661–663, 903–906, 1200n
Rousseau, P.L., *see* Jovanovic, B. 525, 1185, 1189, 1204, 1206, 1207, 1210, 1296, 1335n, 1344
Routledge, B. 1658
Rowe, D.C., *see* Rodgers, J.L. 269n
Roy, D., *see* Subramanian, A. 984
Roy, S., *see* de Hek, P.A. 39
Rubin, R., *see* Somanathan, E. 1659
Rubinstein, Y. 1721
Rudolph, T., *see* Rahn, W. 1687, 1688
Ruelle, D. 1145n
Ruffin, R.J. 1425n
Ruiz-Arranz, M. 1299n
Rupasingha, A. 658
Russell, R., *see* Henderson, D. 605, 605n, 606, 607
Rustichini, A., *see* Benhabib, J. 398, 538n
Ruttan, V.W. 748n

Sabel, C.F., *see* Piore, M.J. 1324n
Sabot, R.H., *see* Gelb, A. 711n
Sacerdote, B., *see* Alesina, A. 1597n, 1609
Sacerdote, B., *see* Glaeser, E.L. 1020n, 1667
Sachs, J.D. 298, 300n, 304n, 400, 413, 615n, 653–657, 659, 954, 956, 956n, 1050, 1422n, 1515, 1515n
Sachs, J.D., *see* Bloom, D.E. 400, 652, 654, 655, 657
Sachs, J.D., *see* Gallup, J.L. 655, 662, 1560
Sachs, J.D., *see* Hamoudi, A. 655
Sachs, J.D., *see* Lipton, D. 989
Sachs, J.D., *see* Masters, W.E. 654, 658
Sachs, J.D., *see* McArthur, J.W. 654, 656

Sacks, D., *see* Rappaport, J.   1558
Sadik, J., *see* Berdugo, B.   279n
Sadoulet, E., *see* de Janvry, A.   1714
Saenz, L., *see* Lederman, D.   833, 834, 846, 849
Saez, E., *see* Piketty, T.   1283
Saggi, K., *see* Glass, A.J.   1425n
Sahasakul, C., *see* Barro, R.M.   24
Sahay, R., *see* Cashin, P.   586n
Saint-Paul, G.   266, 398, 876, 1321, 1597n, 1603n, 1742n
Saint-Paul, G., *see* Bentolila, S.   1340
Saito, M., *see* Devereux, M.B.   1425n
Sakellaris, P.   54n, 1294
Sakellaris, P., *see* Dellas, H.   54n
Sala-i-Martin, X.   219, 493, 586n, 611, 612, 650n, 653–659, 1032, 1097
Sala-i-Martin, X., *see* Barro, R.J.   xin, 16n, 28, 77, 78n, 120n, 122n, 139n, 196n, 495, 582n, 586n, 587, 587n, 591, 604n, 605, 606, 647, 660, 821, 827, 835, 837–839, 938, 940, 944, 945n, 1046, 1099n, 1103n, 1509n, 1523, 1560
Sala-i-Martin, X., *see* Doppelhofer, G.   587, 612–615
Sala-i-Martin, X., *see* Mulligan, C.B.   1103n
Sala-i-Martin, X., *see* Roubini, N.   653, 923
Samaniego, R.M.   1414
Sampson, R.   1687, 1688
Samuelson, P.A.   131n, 734n, 1446
Samuelson, P.A., *see* Dornbusch, R.   143, 1463n, 1468
Sandberg, L.G.   1155n
Sandefur, G.   1677, 1679
Sandefur, R.   1690n
Sanderson, M.   197, 207, 207n, 208
Santos, M.S., *see* Ladron de Guevara, A.   26
Sapienza, P., *see* Guiso, L.   896, 896n, 908, 923, 1678, 1682, 1684
Sarel, M.   1044n
Sargent, R.-M.   1135
Sargent, T.J., *see* Ljungqvist, L.   1342, 1344, 1346
Sarte, P., *see* Li, W.   26
Sattinger, M.   1338
Satyanath, S., *see* Miguel, E.   660
Sauré, P.   1425n
Savvides, A.   79n
Savvides, A., *see* Mamuneas, T.   618
Saw, P.L.S., *see* Wellisz, S.   984
Sawada, Y., *see* Jimenez, E.   1658
Scharfstein, D.   874

Schattschneider, E.E.   434
Scheffer, M.   1760n
Scheinkman, J., *see* Glaeser, E.L.   1553, 1689
Schelifer, A., *see* Glaeser, E.L.   1553
Scherer, F.   89
Schiantarelli, F., *see* Bond, S.   627, 660
Schiff, E.   1166
Schlicht, E.   1719n
Schlozman, K., *see* Brady, H.   1741n
Schmalensee, R.   1818n
Schmidt, P., *see* Ahn, S.   633
Schmidt, R., *see* Kelley, A.   657
Schmidt-Traub, G., *see* Sachs, J.D.   298, 300n, 304n
Schmitz, J.A.   718
Schmitz, J.A., *see* McGrattan, E.R.   804n, 1019n
Schmitz Jr., J.A.   1392n
Schmitz Jr., J.A., *see* Holmes, T.J.   1414
Schmitz Jr., J.A., *see* McGrattan, E.R.   684n
Schmookler, J.   133n
Schmookler, J., *see* Griliches, Z.   133n
Schmukler, S., *see* Levine, R.   896n
Schoar, A.S.   1206
Schoar, A.S., *see* Bertrand, M.   909
Schofield, R.S.   273
Schofield, R.S., *see* Wrigley, E.A.   182n, 184, 185, 191, 192, 204, 226, 255
Schreyer, P.   746, 756, 784, 785, 785n, 787
Schreyer, P., *see* Colecchia, A.   785n, 786n, 1346
Schultz, T.P.   497, 528n
Schultz, T.P., *see* Rosenzweig, M.R.   496, 497
Schultz, T.W.   239n, 270n
Schumpeter, J.A.   113, 133n, 867, 871
Schwert, G.W.   1206n
Scotchmer, S.   144, 145
Scott, J.C.   434
Scrimshaw, N.S., *see* Basta, S.S.   490
Seers, D., *see* Meier, G.M.   867
Segenti, E., *see* Miguel, E.   660
Segerstrom, P.S.   xiin, 71n, 114, 127n, 937, 1070n, 1089, 1105, 1425n
Segerstrom, P.S., *see* Dinopoulos, E.   127n, 142, 1307, 1308n, 1425n
Segerstrom, P.S., *see* Lundborg, P.   1442n
Seki, E., *see* Platteau, J.-P.   1653, 1663n
Selden, T.   1766n, 1767n
Selden, T., *see* Holtz-Eakin, D.   1818n
Sen, A., *see* Hoff, K.   368, 369
Şener, F.   1425n

Serageldin, I., *see* Dasgupta, P. 1648

Servén, L., *see* Kraay, A. 1490n

Seshadri, A., *see* Greenwood, J. 229n, 262n, 1098n, 1194, 1227n, 1230n, 1231n, 1238n, 1245n, 1252n, 1262n, 1264n, 1312, 1312n

Seshadri, A., *see* Manuelli, R.E. 62

Sevilla, J., *see* Bloom, D.E. 256, 277n, 335, 621, 654, 655

Shaban, R. 508

Shafik, N. 1766n

Shan, J.Z. 892

Shapin, S. 1132n, 1133n

Shapiro, C. 807n

Sharfstein, D., *see* Hoshi, T. 884n, 918n

Sharif, R. 941

Shastry, G.K. 708

Shaw, E.S., *see* Gurley, J.G. 867, 875

Shell, K. 17, 113, 1070

Sheshadri, A. 1603n, 1606

Sheshinski, E. 1070n

Sheshinski, E., *see* Levhari, D. 113n

Shi, S. 1339

Shi, S., *see* Devereux, M.B. 1463n

Shibata, A., *see* Ono, Y. 1425n

Shiller, R.J. 806n

Shiller, R.J., *see* Campbell, J.Y. 768n, 806n

Shin, Y., *see* Pesaran, M.H. 634

Shioji, E. 586n, 650

Shipp, S., *see* Johnson, D.G. 1355

Shishido, H., *see* Wheaton, W. 1561

Shleifer, A. 158n, 873, 873n, 882, 999, 1117

Shleifer, A., *see* Djankov, S. 99, 425, 426, 506, 509n, 1006–1008, 1395

Shleifer, A., *see* Glaeser, E.L. 278–280, 425, 426

Shleifer, A., *see* La Porta, R. 84n, 399, 425, 426, 506, 658, 874, 887, 892, 897, 922, 923, 1033, 1505, 1683

Shleifer, A., *see* Murphy, K.M. 145, 340–342, 364, 365, 398, 503, 506n, 653, 711n, 996n, 999, 1001, 1021, 1504

Sibert, A. 1425n

Sichel, D.E., *see* Aizcorbe, A. 749

Sichel, D.E., *see* Oliner, S.D. 754, 771, 774n, 785n, 1291, 1294

Sicherman, N., *see* Bartel, A. 1301, 1318

Sickles, R., *see* Hultberg, P. 663

Siebert, W.S., *see* Addison, J.T. 1330, 1330n

Siegel, D., *see* Lichtenberg, F.R. 1206

Siegelbaum, L. 1656

Siegler, M.V. 37

Siles, M., *see* Robison, L. 1683, 1684n

Simhon, A., *see* Gould, E.D. 231

Simon, B. 208

Simon, H.A. 301, 1554

Simon, J.L. 1069, 1070, 1148n

Singh, R., *see* Nelson, M. 654

Sirri, E.R. 879, 880

Siu, H., *see* Jones, L.E. 39, 60, 61, 61n

Sjostrom, T., *see* Ghatak, M. 537

Skaperdas, S. 398

Skiba, A.K. 350, 543

Skidmore, M., *see* Toya, H. 660

Skocpol, T. 1649n

Slade, M.E. 1751n

Slemrod, J. 1033

Slok, T., *see* Edison, H. 907n

Smeeding, T.M., *see* Gottschalk, P. 1350, 1733

Smith, A. 179n, 440, 880, 1117, 1157n, 1264, 1504

Smith, A., *see* Krussel, P. 515, 544n

Smith, B.D. 922

Smith, B.D., *see* Bencivenga, V.R. 150n, 875, 877, 878, 895, 896, 923

Smith, B.D., *see* Boyd, J.H. 874, 875, 879, 886, 920, 923

Smith, B.D., *see* Greenwood, J. 880, 881

Smith, G.W., *see* Devereux, M.B. 876

Smith, J.G. 1136n, 1137n, 1141n

Smith, J.G., *see* LaLonde, R.J. 1360

Smith, R., *see* Huybens, E. 886, 923

Smith, R., *see* Lee, K.S. 586n, 629, 634, 635

Smith, R., *see* Pesaran, M.H. 634

Smulders, J. 1804

Smulders, S. 1752n, 1804, 1805

Smulders, S., *see* Bovenberg, A.L. 1778, 1797

Smulders, S., *see* van de Klundert, T. 93n, 1425n

Snelders, H.A.M. 1143n

Snooks, G. 1117n

Snower, D.J., *see* Lindbeck, A. 1321, 1330

Snyder, W., *see* Morrisson, C. 213, 214

Soares, R.R. 231n, 259

Soares, R.R., *see* Becker, G.S. 852n

Soderbom, M., *see* Bigsten, A. 481, 1650

Soekirman, D.S., *see* Basta, S.S. 490

Sokoloff, K.L., *see* Engerman, S.L. 212n, 278, 302, 443, 449, 923, 1005, 1054, 1611, 1617

Sokoloff, K.L., *see* Khan, B.Z. 1165, 1166

Solmon, L., *see* Landes, W. 1249

Solow, R.M.   xi, 17, 113, 223, 298, 307, 388,
    558, 560, 715, 768, 779, 779n, 780n,
    781–783, 783n, 784, 791, 792, 804–806, 821,
    1070, 1074, 1101–1103, 1230, 1251, 1290,
    1332, 1375, 1382, 1421, 1718, 1752n, 1772,
    1788, 1791n
Solow, R.M., *see* Baily, M.N.   718
Solow, R.M., *see* Dertouzos, M.   782n
Somanathan, E.   1659
Song, D., *see* Selden, T.   1766n, 1767n
Song, S., *see* Baltagi, B.   644
Soon, C.   996
Sorensen, B.E., *see* Kalemli-Ozcan, S.   157
Sorenson, A., *see* Morgan, S.   1677, 1679,
    1680n
Soutter, C., *see* Glaeser, E.L.   1689
Spadafora, D.   1136n
Spagat, M., *see* Bertocchi, G.   259n
Sparrow, W.J.   1141
Spence, M.   116, 1070, 1082
Spence, M., *see* Keeler, E.   1774n, 1786, 1810n
Spencer, B.J., *see* Dowrick, S.   1409n
Spiegel, M.M., *see* Benhabib, J.   81, 495, 903,
    938, 939, 953, 959, 959n, 1018n
Spilimbergo, A., *see* Sakellaris, P.   54n
Spittel, M., *see* Palloni, A.   1673, 1675, 1680
Spolaore, E.   1502n, 1506, 1508n, 1509n,
    1513, 1514n, 1518n, 1519, 1525
Spolaore, E., *see* Alesina, A.   1422n, 1502,
    1502n, 1506, 1510, 1510n, 1511n, 1513,
    1519, 1519n, 1525n, 1530, 1530n, 1535n
Spree, R.   214
Squire, L., *see* Deininger, K.   538, 1732
Squire, L., *see* Li, H.   462
Squire, L., *see* Lundberg, M.   1733n
Srinivasan, S., *see* Basu, S.   1296
Srinivasan, T.N., *see* Levhari, D.   39, 44, 870
Stabler, J.C., *see* Clark, J.S.   1553
Stacchetti, E., *see* Jones, L.E.   39, 60, 61, 61n
Stachurski, J.   311n, 332n, 377n
Stachurski, J., *see* Azariadis, C.   333, 398, 597
Stachurski, J., *see* Mirman, L.J.   377
Stachurski, J., *see* Nishimura, K.   308n, 350
Stafford, F.P., *see* Johnson, G.E.   703n
Standard and Poor's Corporation,   1210n
Stangeland, D., *see* Morck, R.   874, 884n
Stark, O., *see* Rosenzweig, M.R.   1722n
Starr, R.M., *see* Bencivenga, V.R.   877, 895,
    896
Starrett, D.   349
Stasavage, D.   456

Stavins, R.N., *see* Newell, R.G.   1796
Steel, M., *see* Fernandez, C.   587, 587n, 612,
    613, 613n, 614, 1681
Stein, J.C.   874
Stein, J.C., *see* Kashyap, A.   878n
Stengos, T., *see* Kalaitzidakis, P.   610
Stengos, T., *see* Liu, Z.   589, 617, 618
Stengos, T., *see* Maasoumi, E.   595
Stengos, T., *see* Mamuneas, T.   618
Stephenson, E.F., *see* Dawson, J.W.   37
Stern, B.J.   1168
Stern, N.   998
Stern, S., *see* Porter, M.E.   165
Stevenson, J.   458
Stewart, L.   1151
Stigler, G.J.   781
Stiglitz, J.E.   143n, 509, 513, 872, 881, 882,
    974n, 1103, 1463n, 1567, 1715, 1717n, 1718,
    1772, 1788, 1789, 1790n
Stiglitz, J.E., *see* Atkinson, A.B.   131n
Stiglitz, J.E., *see* Dixit, A.K.   113, 116, 1070,
    1082
Stiglitz, J.E., *see* Grossman, S.J.   872
Stiglitz, J.E., *see* Hellmann, T.   981, 982
Stiglitz, J.E., *see* Hoff, K.   367n, 480n, 999,
    1001
Stiroh, K.J.   778n, 779
Stiroh, K.J., *see* Jorgenson, D.W.   757n, 759n,
    760, 760n, 763n, 769, 771, 774, 779, 782n,
    785n, 1291
Stock, J., *see* Kremer, M.   596, 597, 827
Stoker, T.M., *see* Schmalensee, R.   1818n
Stokey, N.L.   24, 187n, 217, 311n, 320, 376,
    820–822, 1099, 1425n, 1755, 1756, 1770,
    1772, 1778, 1779, 1784, 1784n, 1786, 1788,
    1792, 1794n, 1804, 1804n, 1810, 1811
Stokey, N.L., *see* Alvarez, F.   41n
Stokey, N.L., *see* Rebelo, S.T.   1033
Stolyarov, D., *see* Laitner, J.   1207
Stone, C., *see* Breiman, L.   619n
Stone, L.   273
Storesletten, K., *see* Hassler, J.   1597n, 1617n
Storesletten, K., *see* Heathcote, J.   1282n,
    1331n, 1355–1357
Strahan, P.E., *see* Jayaratne, J.   907, 907n
Strange, W., *see* Helsley, R.   1564, 1568, 1573,
    1574, 1586
Strange, W., *see* Rosenthal, S.   1547
Strauss, J.   490, 491, 512n, 519
Streufert, P., *see* Ray, D.   354n
Strulik, H., *see* Funke, M.   145n

Stulz, R.M. 873, 918, 923
Subramanian, A. 984
Subramanian, A., *see* Rodrik, D. 278, 654, 658, 659, 990, 1005, 1516
Sue Wing, I. 1795
Sugden, R. 329
Sul, D., *see* Phillips, P. 635, 644
Summerhill, W., *see* North, D.C. 419
Summers, L.H. 978n
Summers, L.H., *see* DeLong, J.B. 643, 656, 660
Summers, L.H., *see* Easterly, W. 326, 565, 568n, 625, 655, 656, 659, 829, 996, 1036n
Summers, L.H., *see* Krueger, A.B. 1331n
Summers, L.H., *see* Shleifer, A. 882
Summers, R. 582, 685, 720, 804, 1037, 1403–1406
Summers, R., *see* Heston, A. xii, 303n, 491, 562, 685, 804n, 826, 828, 830, 831, 834, 1412, 1519
Summers, R., *see* Kravis, I.B. 803
Sun, F., *see* Shan, J.Z. 892
Sun, Y. 1679
Sunde, U., *see* Cervellati, M. 259, 1145
Sussman, N., *see* Berdugo, B. 279n
Sussman, O. 875
Sussman, O., *see* Harrison, P. 875
Svendsen, G., *see* Paldam, M. 1659
Svensson, J. 506
Swagel, P., *see* Alesina, A. 652, 655, 656, 662
Swallow, B.M., *see* Barrett, C.B. 326n
Swan, T.W. 113, 558
Swank, D. 659
Swartz, S. 641
Sylla, R.E. 886
Sylla, R.E., *see* Homer, S. 1213n, 1220n
Sylla, R.E., *see* Rousseau, P.L. 653, 661, 906
Symons, J., *see* Robertson, D. 634
Syropoulos, C., *see* Dinopoulos, E. 1425n
Syrquin, M. 1724n
Syrquin, M., *see* Chenery, H.B. 1712, 1724n

Tabellini, G., *see* Giavazzi, F. 636, 636n, 646
Tabellini, G., *see* Persson, T. 398, 399, 538n, 636n, 642, 655, 1600n
Taber, C., *see* Heckman, J.J. 1318, 1319, 1354–1357
Tabuchi, T. 1578
Tadesse, S. 919
Tahvonen, O. 1797
Takahashi, T., *see* Matsuyama, K. 1487n

Takeyama, L., *see* Johnson, P.A. 620n
Tamura, R.F. 236n, 261, 263, 820, 821, 1099, 1378, 1618n
Tamura, R.F., *see* Becker, G.S. 224n, 235, 1021, 1378
Tan, C.M. 620
Tan, H.W., *see* Lillard, L.A. 1318
Tarr, D.G., *see* Harrison, G.W. 985n
Tarrow, S. 450n, 462, 1691n
Tavares, J. 638, 661
Tawney, R.H. 393, 402
Taylor, A.M. 281n
Taylor, A.M., *see* Estevadeordal, A. 216, 1532, 1532n
Taylor, C. 639n, 1651
Taylor, L., *see* Bacha, E.L. 1714
Taylor, L.L., *see* Hanushek, E.A. 702n
Taylor, M.S. 1425n
Taylor, M.S., *see* Antweiler, A. 1770n, 1771n, 1788
Taylor, M.S., *see* Brander, J.A. 1752n
Taylor, M.S., *see* Brock, W.A. 1756, 1770n, 1772n, 1799, 1800, 1809, 1811n, 1815, 1816
Taylor, M.S., *see* Copeland, B.R. 1755, 1757n, 1773, 1779, 1786, 1788, 1799n, 1804
Taylor, M.S., *see* Levinson, A. 1764
Teachman, J. 1676, 1679
Teal, F., *see* Bigsten, A. 1650
Teixeira, A. 1414
Teixeira, A., *see* Herrendorf, B. 1395n
Temple, J.R.W. 560n, 562n, 580, 590, 591, 611n, 626, 626n, 629–631, 641, 642, 658, 659, 725n, 938, 971n, 997, 1032, 1680n, 1681
Temple, J.R.W., *see* Bond, S. 632
Temple, J.R.W., *see* Graham, B.S. 256, 337, 607n, 623, 723n, 727
Tenreyro, S., *see* Alesina, A. 1505n
Tenreyro, S., *see* Caselli, F. 690
Tenreyro, S., *see* Koren, M. 718n
ter-Weel, B., *see* Borghans, J.A.M. 266
Terrell, K. 1730
Thaicharoen, Y., *see* Acemoglu, D. 464, 662, 1055
Thakor, A., *see* Boot, A.W.A. 881–883
Thakor, A., *see* Ramakrishnan, R.T.S. 871
The Commercial and Financial Chronicle, 1200n, 1206n
The New York Times Co., 1200n
Thesmar, D. 1324, 1619n
Thesmar, D., *see* Bertrand, M. 909
Thisse, J.-F., *see* Fujita, M.P. 1579

Thisse, J.-F., *see* Ottaviano, G.I.P. 349, 1547, 1579

Thoenig, M. 142n, 1627n

Thoenig, M., *see* Thesmar, D. 1324, 1619n

Thomas, D. 490

Thomas, D., *see* Currie, J. 704, 705n

Thomas, D., *see* Strauss, J. 490, 491, 512n, 519

Thomas, R.P., *see* North, D.C. 150, 388, 423, 427, 463, 1005

Thomas, V. 1570, 1724n

Thomis, M.I. 434

Thompson, P., *see* Dinopoulos, E. 93n, 1094

Thorne, S. 1151n

Thoursie, P., *see* Agell, J. 662

Thursby, M., *see* Jensen, R. 1425n

Tilly, C. 462

Tilly, R., *see* Cameron, R. 909

Timberg, T. 479, 480, 483, 525

Timmer, M., *see* van Ark, B. 786n

Tinbergen, J. 781, 781n, 784, 1721, 1724n, 1729

Tiongson, E., *see* de Mello, L. 1609

Tirole, J. 69, 367, 518

Tirole, J., *see* Bénabou, R. 1597n

Tirole, J., *see* Holmstrom, B. 872, 878, 895

Tobin, J. 768

Todaro, M., *see* Harris, J.R. 725n, 1577

Tollison, R.D., *see* Ekelund Jr., R.B. 1162

Tomes, N., *see* Becker, G.S. 1261, 1262, 1264

Topa, G., *see* Conley, T.G. 645

Topel, R., *see* Murphy, K.M. 1288n, 1359

Tornell, A. 398, 464

Townsend, R.M. 423, 513, 542, 543, 874, 1739n

Townsend, R.M., *see* Jeong, H. 543

Townsend, R.M., *see* Paulson, A. 542

Toya, H. 660

Traber, E., *see* Heckman, J.J. 1739n

Trajtenberg, M., *see* Bresnahan, T.F. 1185, 1295

Trajtenberg, M., *see* Helpman, E. 807n, 1200, 1207

Tranter, N.L. 1148

Travis, A. 1152

Treadway, R., *see* Coale, A.J. 190, 200n

Trebbi, F., *see* Rodrik, D. 278, 654, 658, 659, 1005, 1516

Trefler, D. 1466

Tressel, T. 1742n

Trindade, V. 1001

Trindade, V., *see* Rauch, J.E. 1653

Triplett, J.E. 750n, 751, 774, 774n, 799, 806n

Triplett, J.E., *see* Bosworth, B.P. 746n, 771n

Troeskan, W., *see* Beeson, P.E. 1558

Troske, K.R., *see* Doms, M. 270n

Tsiddon, D. 351n

Tsiddon, D., *see* Brezis, E.S. 278n

Tsiddon, D., *see* Brezis, S.L. 1427n, 1453n

Tsiddon, D., *see* Dahan, M. 224n

Tsiddon, D., *see* Galor, O. 239n, 1302, 1613n, 1721n

Tsiddon, D., *see* Rubinstein, Y. 1721

Tsionas, E.G., *see* Christopoulos, D.K. 906

Tufano, P., *see* Sirri, E.R. 879, 880

Tukey, J., *see* Friedman, J. 620n

Tullock, G., *see* Grier, K.B. 33, 581n

Turnovsky, S.J. 56n

U.S. Bureau of the Census, 233, 1227n, 1258n

Udry, C.R. 480, 513, 519

Udry, C.R., *see* Bardhan, P. 398, 513

Udry, C.R., *see* Conley, T.G. 339, 349, 516

Udry, C.R., *see* Goldstein, M. 482, 495, 508

Ueda, K., *see* Townsend, R.M. 542, 543, 1739n

Uglow, J. 1135n, 1137, 1162n

Ulph, D., *see* Beath, J. 349

Unger, R.M. 1007n

United Nations, 784n

United Nations Development Program, 491n

United States Bureau of Economic Analysis, 1188n, 1191n, 1200n, 1201n, 1218n, 1220n

United States Bureau of the Census, Department of Commerce, 1184n, 1193n, 1196n, 1198n, 1218n

University of Chicago Center for Research on Securities Prices, 1200n

Uphoff, N., *see* Krishna, A. 1674

Urrutia, C., *see* Restuccia, D. 493

Uzawa, H. 23

Uzawa, H., *see* Oniki, H. 1463n

Valev, N., *see* Rioja, F. 903

Valls Pereira, P., *see* Andrade, E. 598

Vamvakidis, A. 282n, 986

Van, P.H., *see* Basu, K. 373

van Ark, B. 786n

van Ark, B., *see* Wagner, K. 718n

Van Arkadie, B. 976n

van Bastelear, T., *see* Grootaert, C. 1648

van de Klundert, T. 93n, 1425n

van der Woude, A.M., *see* de Vries, J. 453, 454, 1161n

van Dijk, H., *see* Paap, R.   594, 595
van Elkan, R.   1425n
Van Huyck, J.B.   330
Van Reenen, J., *see* Blundell, R.   76, 86, 89
Van Reenen, J., *see* Caroli, E.   1322, 1619n
Van Reenen, J., *see* Griffith, R.   78n
Van Reenen, J., *see* Hall, B.H.   847
van Schalk, T., *see* Beugelsdijk, S.   658, 1682
Van Zanden, J.L.   1158
Vandenbroucke, G., *see* Greenwood, J.   1227n, 1231n, 1262n
Vandenbussche, J., *see* Aghion, P.   102, 102n, 104
Vanek, J.   1425n
Varangis, P., *see* Gilbert, C.L.   985n
Vargas Llosa, M.   414
Varian, H.R., *see* Shapiro, C.   807n
Varoudakis, A., *see* Berthelemy, J.   653
Varughese, G.   1675, 1676
Veitch, J.M.   394
Velasco, A., *see* Hausmann, R.   1003
Velasco, A., *see* Tornell, A.   398
Véliz, C.   402, 419
Velloso, F., *see* Pessoa, S.   483
Venables, A.J.   1485n
Venables, A.J., *see* Fujita, J.   1578, 1579
Venables, A.J., *see* Fujita, M.P.   1021, 1486n
Venables, A.J., *see* Henderson, J.V.   1585
Venables, A.J., *see* Krugman, P.R.   143n, 398, 1485
Venables, A.J., *see* Limao, N.   300n, 349n
Venables, A.J., *see* Overman, H.G.   1547, 1555
Venables, A.J., *see* Puga, D.   1425n
Venables, A.J., *see* Redding, S.   349n
Ventura, J.   143n, 733, 1430n, 1452n, 1453n, 1464n, 1490n
Ventura, J., *see* Acemoglu, D.   820, 835, 1453n, 1472n
Ventura, J., *see* Broner, F.   1490n
Ventura, J., *see* Kraay, A.   1490n
Verba, S., *see* Brady, H.   1741n
Verdier, T., *see* Ades, A.F.   398
Verdier, T., *see* Bisin, A.   266n
Verdier, T., *see* Bourguignon, F.   259n, 399, 1608n, 1741n
Verdier, T., *see* Saint-Paul, G.   398, 1603n
Verdier, T., *see* Thoenig, M.   142n, 1627n
Vermeersch, C.   498
Vernon, R.   127
Verrecchia, R.E., *see* Diamond, D.W.   874
Vickers, B.   1134

Vickers, J., *see* Aghion, P.   86, 89, 398, 938
Villanueva, D., *see* Knight, M.   579, 683, 1446n
Villanueva, D., *see* Loayza, N.V.   1425n
Vincenti, W.   1153
Vindigni, A.   1598n, 1623
Vines, D., *see* Molana, H.   1425n
Violante, G.L.   1286, 1316, 1333n, 1334, 1335, 1337, 1721
Violante, G.L., *see* Acemoglu, D.   1327, 1597n, 1617
Violante, G.L., *see* Aghion, P.   102n, 1302, 1313, 1314n, 1315, 1333, 1721
Violante, G.L., *see* Cummins, J.G.   1189, 1292, 1293, 1295, 1304, 1305, 1309, 1309n, 1337
Violante, G.L., *see* Heathcote, J.   1282n, 1331n, 1355–1357
Violante, G.L., *see* Hornstein, A.   1332, 1333, 1346, 1347, 1347n, 1349, 1350
Violante, G.L., *see* Krusell, P.   131n, 1196n, 1205, 1298, 1304
Vishny, R.W., *see* La Porta, R.   84n, 399, 425, 426, 506, 658, 874, 887, 897, 922, 923, 1033, 1505, 1683
Vishny, R.W., *see* Murphy, K.M.   145, 340–342, 364, 365, 398, 503, 506n, 653, 711n, 996n, 999, 1001, 1021, 1504
Vishny, R.W., *see* Shleifer, A.   873, 873n, 882, 999, 1117
Vogan, C.R.   1761, 1763
Voigt, S., *see* Feld, L.   656
Vollrath, D., *see* Galor, O.   263, 264, 279
Volpin, P., *see* Pagano, M.   923
von Amsburg, J., *see* Routledge, B.   1658
Voth, H.-J.   197, 255
Voth, J., *see* Antrás, P.   1130
Vroman, S., *see* Albrecht, J.   1338n

Wachtel, P., *see* Rousseau, P.L.   661, 662, 903–905
Wacziarg, R.   575, 630, 636, 637, 646, 647, 659, 1515, 1516, 1516n
Wacziarg, R., *see* Alesina, A.   278, 653, 1422n, 1502, 1503, 1503n, 1505, 1506, 1510n, 1514n, 1518n, 1519, 1519n, 1525n, 1535n, 1538n
Wacziarg, R., *see* Imbs, J.   157, 1000n
Wacziarg, R., *see* Spolaore, E.   1506, 1508n, 1509n, 1513, 1514n, 1518n, 1519, 1525
Wacziarg, R., *see* Tavares, J.   638, 661
Wade, R.   1653
Wagner, A.   1741

Wagner, K.   718n
Walker, S., *see* Powell, C.   498
Wallerstein, I.M.   428
Wang, H.G., *see* Henderson, J.V.   1579, 1582
Wang, J.-Y.   1425n
Wang, M., *see* Blonigen, B.   654
Wang, P., *see* Abdel-Rahman, H.   1574
Wang, Y., *see* Thomas, V.   1724n
Warner, A.M.   636
Warner, A.M., *see* Sachs, J.D.   615n, 653–657,
   659, 954, 956, 956n, 1050, 1422n, 1515,
   1515n
Watson, J., *see* Rauch, J.   1660
Wattenberg, B.J., *see* Caplow, T.   1251
Watts, G.W., *see* Cole, A.H.   1137n
Weatherill, L.   1118n
Weber, M.   401, 419
Weeks, M., *see* Corrado, L.   601n
Weel, B., *see* Borghans, L.   1303
Wei, S.-J.   989n
Weil, D.N.   200n, 708
Weil, D.N., *see* Basu, S.   734n, 938, 942, 943
Weil, D.N., *see* Galor, O.   176n, 177, 228, 229,
   231n, 232, 235n, 236, 237, 255n, 257, 258,
   261–263, 267n, 270n, 272n, 278, 280, 1098n,
   1099, 1118n, 1146, 1261, 1264, 1266, 1267,
   1378
Weil, D.N., *see* Mankiw, N.G.   xii, 77, 477,
   502, 578, 586n, 587n, 598, 604, 605, 618,
   629, 642, 647, 657, 684, 689, 804, 805, 821,
   1018n, 1022n, 1097, 1445, 1466n
Weil, D.N., *see* Shastry, G.K.   708
Weil, P., *see* Basu, S.   1427n
Weinberg, B.A.   1285, 1312, 1316, 1317
Weinberg, B.A., *see* Gould, E.D.   1336, 1337
Weingast, B.R.   429n
Weingast, B.R., *see* de Figueiredo, R.   1505n
Weingast, B.R., *see* Greif, A.   298n
Weingast, B.R., *see* North, D.C.   419, 453, 457
Weinstein, D.E.   884, 918n
Weisdorf, J.L.   259, 261
Weisenfeld, S.L.   266n
Weiss, A., *see* Stiglitz, J.E.   872
Weitzman, M.L.   1066, 1080, 1107
Welch, F.   938, 1730, 1731
Welch, F., *see* Murphy, K.M.   1285
Welch, I., *see* Bikhchandani, S.   516n
Welch, K.H., *see* Wacziarg, R.   636, 646, 659,
   1516
Welling, L., *see* King, I.   1332n
Wellisz, S.   984

Welsch, H.   652
Welsch, R., *see* Swartz, S.   641
Wenger, E.   884, 885, 918n
Werner, A., *see* Gelos, R.G.   507, 508
West, K., *see* Brock, W.   559n, 610, 611n,
   612–615
Western, B., *see* Farber, H.S.   1326
Westphal, L.E., *see* Evenson, R.E.   78n
Wheaton, B., *see* Hagan, J.   1678
Wheaton, W.   1561
Whelan, K.   783n, 1106
Whinston, A.B., *see* Choi, S.-Y.   751n, 807n
White, H.   643
White, H., *see* MacKinnon, J.   643
Whiteley, P.   658
Wiarda, H.J.   419
Wickens, M., *see* Hall, S.   584
Wiggins, S.N.   1199
Wilcoxen, P.W., *see* Jorgenson, D.W.   1786n
Willett, J.B., *see* Murnane, R.J.   704, 704n
Williams, D., *see* Kenny, C.   1032
Williams, E.E.   428
Williams, J.C.   1091n
Williams, J.C., *see* Jones, C.I.   838, 1087
Williamson, J.G.   213, 973, 989, 1033, 1205,
   1560
Williamson, J.G., *see* Becker, G.   1578
Williamson, J.G., *see* Blattman, C.   656
Williamson, J.G., *see* Bloom, D.E.   261n, 655
Williamson, J.G., *see* Clemens, M.A.   282n
Williamson, J.G., *see* Kelly, A.C.   1578
Williamson, J.G., *see* Kuczynski, P.-P.   974n
Williamson, J.G., *see* Lindert, P.H.   214
Williamson, J.G., *see* O'Rourke, K.H.   217
Williamson, O.   422
Williamson, R., *see* Stulz, R.M.   923
Williamson, S.D.   880
Williamson, S.D., *see* Greenwood, J.   1425n
Wilson, C.H.   1161n, 1470n, 1531
Wilson, D.J.   712
Wilson, D.J., *see* Caselli, F.   711, 712n, 714,
   714n
Wilson, D.J., *see* Sakellaris, P.   1294
Wilson, D.M., *see* Harbaugh, W.   1767n
Wilson, E.O., *see* MacArthur, R.H.   231, 269
Wilson, J.W.   1207n
Winter, S., *see* Nelson, R.R.   1122n
Wittman, D.   423
Wodon, Q., *see* Ravallion, M.   1035
Wolf, H., *see* McCarthy, D.   654
Wolfe, T.   747n

Wolfenzon, D., *see* Morck, R. 873, 874, 883, 887

Wolfers, J., *see* Blanchard, O. 1288, 1340

Wolff, E.N., *see* Baumol, W.J. 1715n

Wolpin, K.I., *see* Eckstein, Z. 227n

Wolpin, K.I., *see* Lee, D. 1299n

Wolpin, K.I., *see* Rosenzweig, M.R. 239n, 511, 514

Wolthuis, J. 212

Wong, L.Y. 1338, 1339n, 1350n

Wong, R.B. 1171n

Wood, A. 140

Wood, H.T. 1142n

Woodruff, C., *see* Johnson, S. 508, 914, 999, 1653

Woodruff, C., *see* McKenzie, D. 481

Woodruff, C., *see* McMillan, J. 1653

Woolcock, M. 1020n, 1648

World Bank, 974n, 984, 1017, 1037, 1560, 1706n, 1730n

World Development Indicators, 200, 203

Wright, E.M., *see* Rossi-Hansberg, E. 1554, 1564, 1573, 1576

Wright, R.E. 880n, 881n, 908

Wright, R.E., *see* Benhabib, J. 1263

Wright, R.E., *see* Parente, S.L. 1263

Wright, R.E., *see* Williamson, S.D. 880

Wrigley, E.A. 182n, 184, 185, 191, 192, 201, 204, 226, 255

Wu, S., *see* Maddala, G. 618

Wu, Y., *see* McCarthy, D. 654

Wuketits, F. 1151

Wulf, J., *see* Rajan, R. 1320n

Wurgler, J. 914

Wyckoff, A.W. 756n, 785, 785n, 803

Xie, D. 145n

Xie, D., *see* Kongsamut, P. 1263

Xiong, K. 1570

Xiong, K., *see* Anas, A. 1570

Xu, L.C., *see* Clarke, G. 921n

Xu, L.C., *see* Cull, R. 909

Xu, Y., *see* Campbell, J.Y. 1342

Xu, Z. 906

Yafeh, Y., *see* Weinstein, D.E. 884, 918n

Yan, H., *see* Li, R. 490

Yanagawa, N. 1425n

Yang, D.T., *see* Restuccia, D. 720, 721, 723n

Yang, G. 130, 1425n

Yang, S., *see* Brynjolfsson, E. 806n

Yanikkaya, H. 986

Yasumoto, J., *see* Frank, K. 1678

Yates, P.L. 217

Yeung, B., *see* Morck, R. 872–874, 883, 884n, 887

Yi, K.-M., *see* Kocherlakota, N. 626

Yin, W., *see* Ashraf, N. 522

Yip, C.K., *see* Bond, E. 26

Yip, E., *see* Jorgenson, D.W. 787, 788n, 805

York, A., *see* Clark, R. 1725n

Yorukoglu, M., *see* Greenwood, J. 262n, 1098n, 1194, 1204, 1230n, 1252n, 1296, 1301, 1302, 1312

Yosha, O., *see* Kalemli-Ozcan, S. 157

Young, A.A. 93, 114, 121n, 143n, 145, 145n–147n, 153, 157, 281n, 349, 493, 494, 751, 837, 993, 997n, 1018n, 1094, 1119n, 1412n, 1425n, 1517

Young, H.P., *see* Durlauf, S.N. 1690

Youngson, A.J. 1169

Ypma, G., *see* van Ark, B. 786n

Yu, W., *see* Morck, R. 872

Yuki, K., *see* Sheshadri, A. 1603n, 1606

Yun, K.-Y., *see* Jorgenson, D.W. 759n, 760n

Zachariadis, M. 94n

Zachariadis, M., *see* Savvides, A. 79n

Zaffaroni, P., *see* Michelacci, C. 602, 603

Zagha, R., *see* Williamson, J.G. 989

Zak, P. 658, 1658, 1683

Zamarripa, G., *see* La Porta, R. 885

Zanforlin, L., *see* Calderón, C. 662

Zeckhauser, R., *see* Keeler, E. 1774n, 1786, 1810n

Zeira, J., *see* Galor, O. 92n, 259n, 351, 354n, 398, 441, 537, 872, 878, 887, 1571, 1604n, 1605n, 1720

Zeira, J., *see* Harrison, P. 875

Zejan, M., *see* Blomstrom, M. 627, 656, 659

Zeldes, S. 515

Zelizer, V.A. 1246n

Zemsky, P., *see* Rob, R. 1659

Zervos, S., *see* Levine, R. 653, 655, 661, 886, 893, 894, 895n, 907, 907n

Zeufack, A., *see* Bigsten, A. 1650

Zhang, J. 1602n

Zhang, X. 1706n

Zhao, R., *see* Parente, S.L. 1414

Zhu, X., *see* Restuccia, D. 720, 721, 723n

Ziegler, D., *see* Pollard, S. 910n

Zietz, J. 643

Zilibotti, F.   150n, 160n, 318n
Zilibotti, F., *see* Acemoglu, D.   71n, 99, 102n,
   120n, 130, 131, 136, 138n, 140, 142, 143,
   150, 150n, 154n, 223n, 277n, 326, 357, 398,
   428, 500n, 503, 541n, 607, 734n, 871, 871n,
   876, 880, 883, 943n, 1000, 1425n, 1490n
Zilibotti, F., *see* Aghion, P.   986n
Zilibotti, F., *see* Doepke, M.   230, 260, 261,
   1266
Zilibotti, F., *see* Marimon, R.   1345
Zillibotti, F., *see* Hassler, J.   1597n, 1617n
Zilsel, E.   1138n
Ziman, J.   1147, 1150n

Zingales, L.   883
Zingales, L., *see* Dyck, A.   917, 918n
Zingales, L., *see* Guiso, L.   896, 896n, 908,
   923, 1678, 1682, 1684
Zingales, L., *see* Kumar, K.B.   917n
Zingales, L., *see* Rajan, R.G.   882, 885, 887,
   910, 912, 912n, 923
Zinman, J., *see* Bertrand, M.   522
Zoabi, H., *see* Hazan, M.   231n, 259
Zoido-Lobaton, P., *see* Friedman, E.   999
Zoido-Lobaton, P., *see* Kaufmann, D.   649
Zou, H.-F., *see* Clarke, G.   921n
Zou, H.-F., *see* Li, H.   462, 541, 655, 662

SUBJECT INDEX

1870 Education Act   209
1902 Balfour Act   209
β-convergence   582, 586, 828
σ-convergence   582, 828

abatement   1755, 1773
abatement intensity   1776
absorptive capacity   78
Académie Royale des Sciences   1137, 1143
access costs   1121
accumulation mechanism   1600
accumulation technology   1605
acquiring and processing information   871
acquis communautaire   1008
Adam Smith   1134
adaptation   1000
adaptive efficiency   1127
Adolf Wagner   1741
adoption and imitation R&D   857
adult mortality rate   708
advantage of backwardness   79
adverse selection   1720
age of the leadership   1208
agglomeration effects   326, 1473, 1481, 1483, 1484, 1486, 1487
aggregate demand   503
aggregate production function   475, 1383, 1391
aggregation   543
agriculture   229, 275, 443, 683, 721, 1227
air pollutants   1761
AK model   10, 823, 1017, 1104, 1779
Albrecht von Haller   1140
Alessandro Volta   1151
Alexander Chisholm   1159
alternating current   1195
appropriate incentives   973
appropriate institutions   100
appropriate technology   500, 734
appropriate technology and development   136
arable land   725
arbitrage equation   1080
Archibald Cochrane   1142
Arthur E. Kennelly   1153
Arthur Young   1138

Asian financial crisis   969
assembly lines   1310
assortative matching   1324, 1335
asymmetric information   981
Atlantic trade   217
autarky   1422, 1426, 1436, 1437, 1439, 1441, 1443–1446, 1452, 1456, 1463, 1464, 1466, 1472, 1485–1488
average labor productivity   769, 778, 800

baby boom   1231
baby bust   1231
balanced growth path   1077, 1404, 1775, 1776, 1794
balanced growth rate   824
Balassa–Samuelson effect   1002
banking   343, 867, 868, 878, 881–886, 893, 895, 907, 913, 916, 918–920
bargaining power   497
barriers to international trade   1507, 1508, 1512
barriers to technology adoption   717, 818, 827
barriers to trade   1507–1510, 1512, 1532, 1538
BEA–IBM constant quality price index   751
benefits to backwardness   837
Benjamin Franklin   1140
Benjamin Huntsman   1128
Benjamin Thompson   1141
Berlin Academy   1143
Bertrand competition   345
"best-practice"   981
bifurcation   323
big push   340, 503, 973, 1001
Birmingham Lunar Society   1142
birthweight   709
black market premium   1019
borders   1501, 1502, 1504–1507, 1510, 1511, 1513, 1517, 1518, 1533, 1535
borrowing constraints   82, 358
buffer stock of children   227

Caldwell hypothesis   1265
capital accumulation   233, 890, 895, 901, 1021, 1788

capital consumption   787
capital deepening   777
capital flight   994
capital flows   505, 533
capital income tax   845
capital market imperfections   872
capital markets   234, 477, 509
capital quality   761, 791
capital service flows   761
capital share   xxiv, 686, 696, 1021, 1379, 1382,
      1387, 1388, 1394, 1397, 1399, 1405
capital stock   791, 891, 1024, 1790
capital taxation   21
capital-embodied technical change   1292, 1333,
      1346
capital-embodied technological change   1279
capital–output ratio   484
capital-skill complementarity   257, 1298, 1307,
      1308, 1361
carbon monoxide   1772
carded wool and linen   1130
Carl Linnaeus   1135
Cavendish   1151
central bank independence   974
centralized bargaining   1326, 1329
CES   683
child labor   230, 373, 1228
child labor law   230
chlorine bleaching   1127
choice of plant technologies   1392
city formation   1585
city sizes   1566, 1568, 1583
civil liberties   1006
Claude Berthollet   1128, 1133, 1141
Clean Air Act   1769
Coase Theorem   422
Cobb–Douglas production function   504, 683,
      1379, 1382, 1383, 1391
cognitive ability   1312
Colin MacLaurin   1139
collateral   350
collective action   391, 1663
collective bargaining   1325
college premium   1282, 1286
colonial powers   1054
colonialism   217
Combination Act   1168
commercial capitalism   1171
commitment problem   390
common law   506
common property   422

communications technology   751
comparative advantage   857
competition   7, 423, 1409, 1412
competitive fringe   73
competitive search   1339
complementarity   162, 365, 1598
complementarity in innovation   144
complete convergence   595
composition of capital   682
composition of the capital stock   711
computers   747
conditional convergence   591, 1046
confined exponential diffusion   939
conflict of interest   390
constant elasticity formulation   1800
constant returns to scale   477, 527, 825, 1018,
      1290, 1501, 1504
constant returns to scale technology   1379
consumption   514, 1018, 1186, 1355
contract enforcement   973
convergence   81, 308, 337, 477, 577, 583, 804,
      899, 937, 941, 997, 1400, 1403, 1413,
      1605
convergence clubs   77, 81, 256, 938, 943
convergence hypothesis   561
convex neoclassical model   307
convex technology   15, 314
coordination   328, 330, 1645
coordination failure   503, 1001, 1329, 1645
Copernicus   306
core–periphery models   1578
corporate governance   870, 872, 875, 882–884,
      922, 974
corruption   364, 506, 883, 974
cost of living   1473, 1474
country size   842, 1501–1506, 1509, 1510,
      1513, 1514, 1516, 1518–1522, 1524–1527,
      1530, 1531, 1538
Crawshays   1159
creative destruction   1070, 1332
credit constraints   205, 360, 509, 1600
credit market   303, 351, 477, 509
credit market imperfections   1720
crime   1713
criteria pollutant   1785
Crompton   1159
cross-country growth regression   xxiii, 576, 971
cross-country income distribution   330, 597,
      887, 920, 921
cross-country regressions   506, 900, 919
cross-sectional risk   876

crude birth rates   190, 191, 201
crude marriage rates   191
culture   397, 922, 923, 1115, 1268
currency board   994

d'Alambert   1137
Daniel Defoe   1127
Darwinian methodology   265
Darwinian survival strategies   231
David Hartley   1136
David Mushet   1130
Davies Gilbert   1139
de facto political power   391
de jure political power   391
debt contracts   871, 883
debt sustainability   973
decentralization   1505, 1535, 1539
default   350, 355
demand for human capital   205
demand spillovers   341
democracy   392, 1006, 1409
demographic patterns   177, 190, 1100, 1147,
      1231, 1706
deposit insurance   907, 908
depreciation rate   690
desired consumption   1204, 1217
deskilling   1160
destruction of steam technology   1191
deterministic cycles   158
deunionization   1326, 1328
devaluation   990
development   990, 1017
development accounting   499, 681
development trap   940
dictatorship   392
Diderot   1136, 1137
diffusion   1136
diffusion lags   1194
diffusion of technology   1598
diminishing returns   308, 503, 523, 825, 1021,
      1430–1436, 1439, 1442, 1444–1446, 1453,
      1455, 1456, 1461, 1464, 1466, 1472, 1490
directed technical change   130, 1306, 1312,
      1322
distance to the technological frontier   99
distribution of entries across sectors   1202
distribution of firm sizes   531
distribution of ratings for issues of new corporate
      bonds   1214
distribution of wealth   476
distributional conflict   1609

distributional dynamics   582
divergence   635
diversification   357, 870, 875, 876, 1001
diversified metro areas   1575
double their per capita income   1403
dual economy models   1577
dualism   1726
Dugald Stewart   1134
dynamic efficiency   986
dynastic construct   1380

earnings compression   1603
earnings volatility   1331
economic development   867, 1706
economic geography   1547
economic institutions   389
economic integration   1436, 1438–1441, 1450,
      1453, 1490, 1511–1513, 1536
economic losers   xxi, 434
economies of scale   1503, 1512, 1538
Edgeworth–Pareto substitutes   1252
education   102, 490, 496, 1116, 1155, 1238,
      1706
education finance   1603, 1606
education premium   1300, 1303, 1336, 1354,
      1355
education reforms   230
effective knowledge   1124
efficiency   531, 687, 1399, 1645
efficient institutions   xxi, 422
elasticity of female labor supply   1267
elasticity of substitution   8, 728, 1027, 1297,
      1379
electricity   1184, 1197, 1310
emission intensity of GDP   1818
emissions   1753, 1769
employment rate   1289, 1352
Encyclopedias   1137
Encyclopédie   1137
endogenous fluctuations   157
endogenous growth theory   558, 820, 1017,
      1021, 1079, 1778
endogenous institutions   1623
endogenous skill-bias   132
endogenous supply of skills   1307
endpoints of a GPT era   1194
energy   1755, 1789, 1790
enforcement of contracts   1032
entrepreneurs   523, 998, 1119
entrepreneurship   998
entry, exit and mergers   1186, 1204
environment   1751

Environmental Catch-up Hypothesis   1811
environmental control costs   1761
Environmental Kuznets Curve (EKC)   1752
environmental quality   1751, 1758
epistemic base   1123
equity markets   878, 920, 1650
eras of GPT adoption   1208
Erasmus Darwin   1135, 1140
escape competition effect   88
estimates of aggregate relative efficiency   1394
ethnic differentials   1035
ethnic groups   1034
ethnic heterogeneity   1681
ethnolinguistic fractionalization   954, 1055
European colonialism   396
European mortality   417
Eurosclerosis   1612
event study approaches   xxiii, 636
evolution   231
evolution of inequality   1604
evolution of the size distribution of cities   1549
evolutionary advantage   232
ex-post real interest rates   1220
exchange   881
exchangeability   581, 1663
exhaustible natural resource   1788
exhaustible resource   1755
exogenous technological progress   1774
expanding variety   116
expectational indeterminacy   162
expectational stability   163
experience premium   1285, 1313–1315, 1318, 1319
experimental philosophy   1163
exponential diffusion   939
export-processing zone (EPZ)   984
expropriation   394, 402
extended family system   1742
extended reproduction   1703
extent of the market   1514
external finance   910, 911, 914, 915
external financing constraints   868
externalities   326, 476, 502, 817, 819, 1000, 1020, 1503, 1504, 1644
extractive institutions   1054
extrinsic mortality risk   275

factor accumulation   317, 493, 1786
factor neutral   728
factor price equalization   1446, 1448, 1452, 1453, 1456, 1459, 1461, 1464–1466, 1472, 1476, 1480

factor prices   212
factor shares   729
factor-biased innovation   131
factor-specific productivity   1289
factor-specificity   1360
factory system   306, 1160
family size   1737
farmers   1705
female education   234
female labor force participation   233, 1229
female–male earning ratios   1730
female's age of marriage   191
fertility   174, 177, 182, 183, 191, 226, 373, 1072, 1104, 1115, 1148, 1227, 1233, 1377, 1378, 1381–1383, 1386, 1399, 1400, 1710, 1737, 1794
feudal   440
feudalism   440
finance companies   918
financial contracting   528
financial development   81, 150, 504, 890, 891, 898, 901, 911, 916, 919, 921, 1033, 1220
financial development indicators   890
financial functions   869, 870
financial instruments   869
financial intermediaries   871, 889, 890, 898,
financial liberalization   974
financial markets   890, 918
"financial restraint"   981
financial sector reform   979
financial structure   920
first product or process innovation   1210
first-generation idea-based growth models   1092
fiscal decentralization   1564
fiscal policy   21, 923, 1033
fiscal system   1606
fix-price   1715
fixed costs   299, 340, 527
flexible technologies   1598, 1613, 1619
food-canning   1150
foreign exchange   1020
formal institutions   1005, 1671, 1713
fractionalization   1505
Francis Bacon   1133, 1134
Francis Home   1138
Francis Jeffrey   1134
Francis Upton   1153
free riding   873, 875, 882, 1661
free trade   1034
free trade club   1408, 1409, 1411–1413

frictional inequality   1331, 1333
frictions in the labor market   1280
frontier technology   100
functional form   538
functional specialization   1575
functioning of the financial system   890

gas-lighting   1127
gender differences   1706
gender gap   232, 1266
gender wage gap   1285, 1312
General Electric (GE)   1211
General Motors (GM)   1211
general purpose technologies   1107, 1295,
    1313, 1721
general skills   1337
genetic evolution   260
geography   277, 337, 339, 349, 397, 609, 620,
    922, 923, 1054, 1554
George Campbell   1136
George Cayley   1140
George Melville   1153
George Stephenson   1141
Gibrat's Law   1554
Gini coefficients   536, 920
glass industry   1127
globalization   280, 1426, 1436–1439, 1441–
    1444, 1446, 1448, 1451, 1452, 1454–
    1456, 1463, 1464, 1472–1475, 1480–1482,
    1485–1488, 1490, 1491
Gompertz growth model   947
government failures   505, 998
GPT eras   1185
gradualism   989
Grande Encyclopédie   1136
Great Depression   1262
Great Divergence   174
Green Solow model   1754
growth accounting   314, 1101
growth disasters   322, 567
growth miracles   xxiii, 322, 565, 1389, 1397,
    1403, 1412
growth rates   819
growth slowdown   xxiii, 567, 825
growth strategies   971
guilds   1162
Gustave Adolphe Hirn   1150
Gustave-Gaspard Coriolis   1159

Harberger triangles   1030
health   265, 490, 682, 1706

hedonic model   750, 751
Henry Cort   1139
Henry George Theorem   1567
Hermann Claudius   1153
heterodoxy   1004
heterogeneity   491, 1502, 1505, 1506, 1510–
    1513, 1533, 1538, 1611, 1736
heteroskedasticity   640
"Hicks-neutral"   767
high-quality institutions   1005
high-school movement   1311
Hirschman–Herfindahl index   1556
historical self-reinforcement   317, 355
HIV/AIDS   971
home goods   1252
Hong Kong   984
horizontal innovation   114
horsepower in manufacturing   1187, 1188
hours worked   695
household appliances   1312
household capital   1252
household production   1227
household products   1258
housework   1251
human capital   174, 178, 340, 354, 475, 491,
    682, 786, 806, 818, 872, 878, 938, 949,
    1017, 1067, 1104, 1116, 1148, 1230, 1318,
    1360, 1504, 1517, 1597, 1717
human capital externalities   502, 821, 1518
human capital promoting institutions   278, 280
humoral theory of disease   1124
Humphry Davy   1133, 1141, 1152

idea production function   1107
idea-based growth models   1090
ideas   819, 1065
identity   1654
imitation   73, 100, 127, 857
imitation costs   946
impatience traps   373
imperfect competition   340, 1082
import licenses   1031
import tariffs   1002
import-substituting industrialization (ISI)   984
import-substitution   973, 1034
improvement in the efficiency of the GPT   1195
incidental institutions   xxi, 425
income disparity   304
income tax   1019
incomplete contracts   429, 518

increasing returns   299, 476, 501, 623, 1018, 1066, 1068, 1073, 1086, 1106, 1501, 1504, 1799
indivisibilities   357
indivisible projects   880
induced innovation   1798
Industrial Enlightenment   306, 1134
industrial policies   975
Industrial Revolution   176, 306, 877, 1098, 1115
industrialization   174, 1000, 1227, 1504, 1531
industry-level studies   919
inequality   212, 302, 536, 1597, 1600
infant and child mortality rates   225
infant mortality rates   226
inflation   903, 916, 1027
informal credit   480
informal sector   1026
information asymmetries   871, 878, 885, 922
information technology   746, 755, 756, 765, 771, 797, 798, 1184, 1194, 1279, 1293, 1301, 1303, 1320
informational complementarities   1321
initial conditions   320, 335, 598
initial public offerings (IPOs)   1200
innovation   27, 82, 100, 101, 857, 881, 1000, 1119, 1185, 1210
institutions   6, 7, 69, 277, 301, 364, 388, 506, 579, 867, 923, 973, 997, 1007, 1032, 1054, 1088, 1107, 1115, 1162, 1166, 1516, 1536, 1711
insurance   303, 351, 512, 878
insurance companies   918
intangible capital   1393, 1394
integrated circuits   747
integrated economy   1425, 1426, 1430, 1431, 1433, 1437–1439, 1441, 1443, 1444, 1446–1450, 1453, 1455–1457, 1465, 1472, 1475, 1476, 1482, 1483, 1488
intellectual property rights   128, 1119, 1165
inter-temporal optimization   1719
interest rates   479, 1204
intermediaries   869, 890, 918
internal combustion   1196
internal finance   910
international diffusion of knowledge   821
international externalities   818
international financial codes and standards   974
International Monetary Fund   298
international trade   216, 281, 1425, 1446, 1472, 1473, 1490

internationally harmonized prices   785, 806
Internet   751
interstate commerce clause   1408
intertemporal elasticity of substitution   1032
intertemporal externality   117
intrinsic mortality risk   275
inventions   1119
investment   xxvii, 101, 197, 478, 493, 506, 819, 914, 998, 1018, 1106, 1200, 1397, 1400, 1407

Jacquard loom   1127
Jacques-François Demachy   1137
James Keir   1128, 1136, 1151, 1159
James P. Joule   1139, 1149
James Watt   1136, 1159
Japanese "model"   1007
Jean-Antoine Chaptal   1128
Jean-Victor Poncelet   1159
Jesse Ramsden   1128
job destruction   1332, 1335, 1346
John Coakley Lettsom   1140
John Ericsson   1140
John Farey   1127
John Harrison   1128
John Herschel   1135
John Kay   1159
John Playfair   1163
John Roebuck   1159
John Smeaton   1128, 1157, 1159
John Whitehurst   1137, 1159
joint stock company   879
Jonas W. Aylsworth   1153
Joseph Banks   1140
Joseph Black   1128, 1136, 1139
Joseph J. Lister   1152
Joseph Priestley   1133, 1136
Josiah Wedgwood   1151
just-in-time production   1409

K and r strategies   231
kinship   xx, 364, 367
knowledge   1017, 1071
knowledge externalities   87, 818, 1105, 1566, 1605, 1799
knowledge or technology component   1390
Kuznets hypothesis   1282
Kyoto Protocol   1792

labor augmenting technological progress   1773
labor force participation   233, 1285, 1706
labor inputs   761, 776, 805

labor market   1340, 1353, 1606, 1712
labor mobility   1342
labor productivity   527, 1410, 1411
labor quality   763, 794
labor share   1288, 1347
labor-augmenting technological change   1022
Laggards   1402
Lagrange stability   377
laissez-faire   120, 994, 1597, 1601
land productivity   183
land–labor ratio   183
language   1121
late starters   1376, 1396, 1401
law and finance   887
law and order   1117
leadership   1648, 1657
learning   516, 1360
learning and sunspots   162
learning externalities   821, 999
learning-by-doing   821, 1000, 1295, 1314, 1334
Leblanc soda making   1127
legal system   508, 868, 869, 886, 887, 898, 919,
    922, 923
less developed economies   174
life expectancy   185, 276, 954, 1704
life insurance   897
lifetime earnings   1354
limited enforcement of contracts   1355
limited patent protection   122
limits to growth   1751, 1788
liquidity   355, 872, 875–877, 882, 894, 896, 897
literacy rates   197
loan renegotiations   884
lobbying   1629
local financial development   896, 908
local government   1688
local markets   1473, 1487, 1489
localization economies   1565
logistic diffusion   939
logistic technology diffusion   942, 946
Lombe brothers   1149
Louis Navier   1159
Louis Pasteur   1150
Louis-Jacques Goussier   1137
love of variety   822
Luddite rebellion   1167
Ludwig Prandtl   1153

machine-breaking   1167
macroeconomic policies   986, 1017, 1033
macroeconomic volatility   879, 1045

macroinventions   1129
malnutrition   373
Malthusian models   174, 180, 182, 252, 256,
    855, 1099, 1378, 1781
Manchester Literary and Philosophical Society
    1142
manufacturing   911, 1229
Marc I. Brunel   1159
marginal abatement costs   1786
maritime technology   1118
market capitalization   895, 916
market frictions   349, 867, 869, 873, 999
market integration   1739
market liberalization   993
market power   343, 345
market size   1430, 1432–1436, 1438–1440,
    1444–1446, 1450, 1452, 1453, 1455, 1456,
    1459, 1461, 1464, 1472, 1487–1490, 1501,
    1504, 1505, 1514, 1516, 1518, 1519, 1532
marketization   1739
markets   868, 869, 881, 883, 885, 886, 890, 893,
    918, 919, 973, 994, 1119
marriage age   191
marriage institutions   231
Marshallian dynamics   328, 366
mass production   1311
master–apprentice relationship   1128
matching   340, 346, 1332, 1338, 1346, 1347,
    1361
Matthew Boulton   1162
mechanization   1229
megacities   1550, 1583
memory chips   748
mercantilism   1126, 1162
metallurgical knowledge   1132
Michael Faraday   1156
microinventions   1125
microprocessors   748
microscope   1152
Microsoft Corporation   750, 1212
migration   369, 1712
Mincerian returns to education   484, 700, 1727
minimum wage   1603
misallocation of capital   478
model uncertainty   559, 612, 613
Modern Growth Regime   176
Modified Political Coase Theorem   424
monitoring   870, 875, 1742
moral hazard   981, 1322, 1720
mortality   184
multi-sector growth models   4, 5

multifactor productivity   784
multiple regimes   145, 150, 162, 335, 621, 622, 727, 1021, 1338, 1659

natural experiment   396
natural resources   1751, 1791
natural selection   231
Nelson–Phelps hypothesis   937, 1301
neoclassical models   xx, 15, 307, 475, 494, 853, 1021, 1022, 1374
Neolithic period   275
network externalities   339, 349, 368, 1189
network formation   1659
Nevil Maskelyne   1158
new good externalities   819
Nicolas Appert   1150
nitrogen oxide   1772
non-aggregative growth models   478, 505, 535
nonconvex growth   319, 353
nonrivalry   857, 1065, 1072, 1086
nonrivalry of ideas   1073, 1106
nontraded goods   1473, 1519, 1520
norms   302, 1644
North American Free Trade Agreement   1408
North–North trade   216
North–South trade   216

occupation-specific human-capital   1336
old age insurance   369
old-age security hypothesis   234
on-the-job training   1318
open knowledge   1121
open science   1132
openness to international trade   1032
opportunity cost of capital   510
opportunity cost of children   228
optimal allocation   1080
optimal scale   531, 1310
organization of education   102
organizational capital   1206, 1296, 1325
organizational structure   1321, 1598, 1613
outsourcing   1574
outward-orientation   973
own-account software   754

parental education   700
partial convergence   584
patents   69, 1082, 1105, 1165, 1166, 1186, 1198
Penn World Tables   685, 804
Philippe LeBon   1128
physical capital   682, 818, 895, 901, 1019, 1393, 1394

Pierre Louis Guinand   1127
Pierre-Simon de Laplace   1151
pivotal voter   1608
policy   69, 355, 868, 886, 1017, 1054, 1093, 1769
political factors   xxi, 214, 389, 390, 423, 432, 868, 922, 923, 1599, 1600, 1606, 1609
politico-economic steady states   1599
pollution   1755, 1766, 1816
pollution abatement   1763, 1779
Post-Malthusian Regime   177, 186
poverty   537, 622, 920, 921, 986, 1017, 1021, 1146
pre-demographic transition era   235
precautionary demand for children   227
predation   394
preference for offspring's quality   231
prescriptive knowledge   1122
price liberalization   979
price taking   314
primary electric motors   1187
printing press   1121
prisoner's dilemma   1654
private good   1018
private property   422
private rate of return   845
product cycle   1576
product cycle trade   127
product-market competition   69, 718
production function   528, 768, 1280
productivity   87, 136, 217, 316, 475, 491, 500, 527, 747, 783, 890, 895, 901, 1184, 1186, 1203, 1204, 1227, 1295, 1346
property rights   15, 388, 508, 914, 973, 1032, 1818
propositional knowledge   1121, 1123
protectionism   1515, 1532–1534
prudential regulation   974
public education   194
public enterprises   975, 1001
public goods   1503, 1505, 1510–1512, 1531, 1538, 1648, 1649, 1703

quality of goods   67, 69, 714, 782, 791, 822, 1292
quantity–quality trade-off   231, 1239

R.J. Petri   1152
Ramsey–Cass–Koopmans model   587
Realschulen   1164
redistributive institutions   1597, 1614

redistributive policies   1359

Reform Act of 1884   215

Reform Acts of 1867 and 1884   214

regulations   508, 868, 869, 886, 922, 923, 1787, 1816

relative efficiency   1399

relative price of equipment   1196, 1298, 1308

relative prices   1027, 1713

relative wages of women   225

religion   194, 400, 923

René Réaumur   1124, 1139

rentiers   1705

rents   394

replacement level   191

replication argument   1066

reputation   367, 518

research and development   70, 120, 712, 818, 833, 841, 845, 854, 879

residual inequality   1361

Richard Roberts   1128, 1159

Richard Trevithick   1139, 1159

rise in the factory   1169

risk   157, 227, 355, 368, 513, 870, 876, 922

Robert continuous paper-making   1127

Royal Society   1135

Sadi Carnot   1149

savings   520, 867, 901, 1380, 1704, 1719

scale effects   92, 124, 501, 837, 999, 1088, 1089, 1095, 1096, 1101, 1516–1518, 1530, 1531, 1538, 1752, 1757

schooling   197, 496, 682, 828, 954, 1227, 1713

Schumpeterian effect of product market competition   88

Schumpeterian growth paradigm   69

scientific management   1230

scientific revolution   270, 1131

secession   1506, 1513, 1514, 1536, 1538

Second Industrial Revolution   178, 225, 1229

second-generation reforms   974

sector effects   47, 682, 1289, 1291, 1703, 1713, 1739

semi-endogenous growth theory   96

semiconductors   746, 747, 1291

shock therapy   989

Simon Newcomb   1153

size distribution of cities   1548

size of countries   1502, 1505, 1510, 1512, 1514, 1530

size of the public sector   1703

skills   134, 205, 229, 239, 257, 281, 1204, 1205, 1227, 1240, 1279, 1283, 1297, 1298, 1300, 1303, 1306–1308, 1310, 1311, 1314, 1315, 1321, 1327, 1329, 1334, 1338, 1344, 1349, 1354, 1361, 1597, 1598, 1613, 1616, 1620, 1703, 1705

Smithian growth   1116

social capital   402, 923, 1020, 1641

social contract   1597, 1609

social differentiation   1705

social exchange   1645

social institutions   1705

social insurance   1006, 1600, 1741

social interactions   1673

social learning   516

social mobility   1605

social networks   1644

social policy   986

social preferences   1007

social rate of return   838, 1087

social relations   1703

social safety nets   974

social structure   1659

socialist economic system   1050

Society of Arts   1142

sociopolitical stability   194

Solow model   17, 580

Solow regime   159

Solow residual   494, 681

Solow variables   580

South Asia   307, 971

specialization   299, 349, 823, 881, 1504

spillovers   327

static efficiency   986

Statute of Artificers   1168

steady states   578, 1018

steampower   1129, 1130, 1191

steelmaking   1130, 1132

stock markets   874, 877, 882, 886, 893–895, 912, 1206

stock of capital   198

stock of knowledge   1796

stock prices   1204

Stone–Geary preferences   1032

structural evolution   976, 1263, 1352, 1451, 1452, 1455, 1456, 1461, 1463, 1464, 1466, 1470, 1480

stylized facts   561, 1771

Sub-Saharan Africa   175, 304, 307, 971, 1703

subsistence level   179

sustainability   174, 997, 998, 1753, 1774

symmetry-breaking   362
systems of cities   1547, 1565

targeted anti-poverty programs   974
taxes   869, 979, 1018, 1019, 1380, 1603
Tayloristic   organization   1311,   1321,   1324,
     1330
teacher–pupil ratios   698
technical externalities   300
technical progress   1705, 1720
technique   1120, 1752, 1758
technische Hochschulen   1164
technology   77, 83, 140, 150, 174, 178, 190,
     239, 339, 373, 478, 496, 499, 501, 516,
     577, 818, 867, 871, 876, 937, 941, 1017,
     1022, 1116, 1131, 1144, 1204, 1217, 1227,
     1229, 1256, 1304, 1308, 1337, 1339, 1350,
     1392, 1598, 1627, 1628, 1754, 1756, 1775
terms of trade   835
The Reform Act of 1832   214
theory of aggregate production function   1391
theory of relative efficiencies   1389
theory of TFP   1375, 1390
theory open-endedness   639
thermodynamics   1149
Thomas Alva Edison   1153, 1184, 1250
Thomas Jefferson   1069, 1137
throstles   1129
tightness   1125, 1152
Tobern Bergman   1124
Tobias Mayer   1158
total factor productivity   478, 499, 605, 607,
     684, 767, 835, 940, 1289, 1291, 1375,
     1379, 1380, 1382
trade   842, 974, 1001, 1050, 1106, 1186, 1204,
     1218, 1307, 1504–1506, 1510, 1513, 1514,
     1516, 1518, 1519, 1530, 1538, 1817
transitions   176, 332, 494, 980, 1026, 1073,
     1374, 1375, 1549, 1775
Treaty of Rome   1410

trust   1117, 1643, 1644, 1646
twin-peaks   596

unemployment   696, 1279, 1288, 1328, 1331,
     1340, 1345, 1347
unskilled labor   1229, 1705
urban growth   193, 408, 1546, 1554, 1560,
     1561, 1581, 1706, 1712

vintage capital   1300, 1315, 1332, 1334, 1336,
     1337, 1347, 1361
voluntary organizations   1648

wages   131, 142, 213, 232, 262, 686, 1158,
     1279, 1281, 1327, 1328, 1340–1342, 1347,
     1352, 1629
Wagner's law   1706
Washington Consensus   973, 1033
welfare states   1597, 1601
Western Offshoots   175, 186
Wilbur Wright   1153
William Cruickshank   1151
William Cullen   1138
William Ellis   1137
William Murdoch   1159
William Nicholson   1140, 1152
William Petty   1069
William Rankine   1139, 1150
William Thomson   1150
wind power   1129
women's liberation   1250
World Bank   1730
world technology frontier   836
World War II   1262, 1725
worldwide changes in patent policy   1199
Wright brothers   1153
wrought iron   1129

Zipf's Law   1548

HANDBOOKS IN ECONOMICS

1. HANDBOOK OF MATHEMATICAL ECONOMICS (in 4 volumes)
   Volumes 1, 2 and 3 edited by Kenneth J. Arrow and Michael D. Intriligator
   Volume 4 edited by Werner Hildenbrand and Hugo Sonnenschein

2. HANDBOOK OF ECONOMETRICS (in 6 volumes)
   Volumes 1, 2 and 3 edited by Zvi Griliches and Michael D. Intriligator
   Volume 4 edited by Robert F. Engle and Daniel L. McFadden
   Volume 5 edited by James J. Heckman and Edward Leamer
   Volume 6 is in preparation (editors James J. Heckman and Edward Leamer)

3. HANDBOOK OF INTERNATIONAL ECONOMICS (in 3 volumes)
   Volumes 1 and 2 edited by Ronald W. Jones and Peter B. Kenen
   Volume 3 edited by Gene M. Grossman and Kenneth Rogoff

4. HANDBOOK OF PUBLIC ECONOMICS (in 4 volumes)
   Edited by Alan J. Auerbach and Martin Feldstein

5. HANDBOOK OF LABOR ECONOMICS (in 5 volumes)
   Volumes 1 and 2 edited by Orley C. Ashenfelter and Richard Layard
   Volumes 3A, 3B and 3C edited by Orley C. Ashenfelter and David Card

6. HANDBOOK OF NATURAL RESOURCE AND ENERGY ECONOMICS
   (in 3 volumes). Edited by Allen V. Kneese and James L. Sweeney

7. HANDBOOK OF REGIONAL AND URBAN ECONOMICS (in 4 volumes)
   Volume 1 edited by Peter Nijkamp
   Volume 2 edited by Edwin S. Mills
   Volume 3 edited by Paul C. Cheshire and Edwin S. Mills
   Volume 4 edited by J. Vernon Henderson and Jacques-François Thisse

8. HANDBOOK OF MONETARY ECONOMICS (in 2 volumes)
   Edited by Benjamin Friedman and Frank Hahn

9. HANDBOOK OF DEVELOPMENT ECONOMICS (in 4 volumes)
   Volumes 1 and 2 edited by Hollis B. Chenery and T.N. Srinivasan
   Volumes 3A and 3B edited by Jere Behrman and T.N. Srinivasan

10. HANDBOOK OF INDUSTRIAL ORGANIZATION (in 3 volumes)
    Volumes 1 and 2 edited by Richard Schmalensee and Robert R. Willig
    Volume 3 is in preparation (editors Mark Armstrong and Robert H. Porter)

11. HANDBOOK OF GAME THEORY with Economic Applications (in 3 volumes)
    Edited by Robert J. Aumann and Sergiu Hart

12. HANDBOOK OF DEFENSE ECONOMICS (in 1 volume)
    Edited by Keith Hartley and Todd Sandler

13. HANDBOOK OF COMPUTATIONAL ECONOMICS (in 2 volumes)
    Volume 1 edited by Hans M. Amman, David A. Kendrick and John Rust
    Volume 2 is in preparation (editors Kenneth L. Judd and Leigh Tesfatsion)

14. HANDBOOK OF POPULATION AND FAMILY ECONOMICS (in 2 volumes)
    Edited by Mark R. Rosenzweig and Oded Stark

15. HANDBOOK OF MACROECONOMICS (in 3 volumes)
    Edited by John B. Taylor and Michael Woodford

16. HANDBOOK OF INCOME DISTRIBUTION (in 1 volume)
    Edited by Anthony B. Atkinson and François Bourguignon

17. HANDBOOK OF HEALTH ECONOMICS (in 2 volumes)
    Edited by Anthony J. Culyer and Joseph P. Newhouse

18. HANDBOOK OF AGRICULTURAL ECONOMICS (in 4 volumes)
    Edited by Bruce L. Gardner and Gordon C. Rausser

19. HANDBOOK OF SOCIAL CHOICE AND WELFARE (in 2 volumes)
    Volume 1 edited by Kenneth J. Arrow, Amartya K. Sen and Kotaro Suzumura
    Volume 2 is in preparation (editors Kenneth J. Arrow, Amartya K. Sen and Kotaro Suzumura)

20. HANDBOOK OF ENVIRONMENTAL ECONOMICS (in 3 volumes)
    Edited by Karl-Göran Mäler and Jeffrey R. Vincent

21. HANDBOOK OF THE ECONOMICS OF FINANCE (in 2 volumes)
    Edited by George M. Constantinides, Milton Harris and René M. Stulz

22. HANDBOOK OF ECONOMIC GROWTH (in 2 volumes)
    Edited by Philippe Aghion and Steven N. Durlauf

All published volumes available

FORTHCOMING TITLES

HANDBOOK OF EXPERIMENTAL ECONOMICS RESULTS
Editors Charles Plott and Vernon L. Smith

HANDBOOK OF THE ECONOMICS OF GIVING, ALTRUISM AND
RECIPROCITY
Editors Serge-Christophe Kolm and Jean Mercier Ythier

HANDBOOK ON THE ECONOMICS OF ART AND CULTURE
Editors Victor Ginsburgh and David Throsby

HANDBOOK OF LAW AND ECONOMICS
Editors A. Mitchell Polinsky and Steven Shavell

HANDBOOK OF ECONOMIC FORECASTING
Editors Graham Elliott, Clive W.J. Granger and Allan Timmermann

HANDBOOK OF THE ECONOMICS OF EDUCATION
Editors Eric Hanushek and Finis Welch

HANDBOOK OF ECONOMICS OF TECHNOLOGICAL CHANGE
Editors Bronwyn H. Halland and Nathan Rosenberg